THIRD EDITION

Psychology and Law

Theory, Research, and Application

Curt R. Bartol
Anne M. Bartol
Castleton State College

THOMSON
WADSWORTH

Australia • Canada • Mexico • Singapore • Spain
United Kingdom • United States

THOMSON
WADSWORTH

Psychology Editor: *Michele Sordi*
Assistant Editor: *Jennifer Wilkinson*
Editorial Assistant: *Chelsea Junget*
Marketing Manager: *Chris Caldeira*
Marketing Assistant: *Laurel Anderson*
Advertising Project Manager: *Brian Chaffee*
Project Manager, Editorial Production: *Kirk Bomont*
Print/Media Buyer: *Rebecca Cross*
Permissions Editor: *Sarah Harkrader*
Production Service: *UG / GGS Information Services, Inc.*
Text Designer: *John Edeen*
Cover Designer: *Bill Stanton*
Cover Image: *DigitalVision*
Cover Printer: *Phoenix Color Corp.*
Compositor: *UG / GGS Information Services, Inc*
Printer: *Phoenix Color Corp.*

Printed in the United States of America
1 2 3 4 5 6 7 07 06 05 04 03

For more information about our products, contact us at:
Thomson Learning Academic Resource Center
1-800-423-0563
For permission to use material from this text, contact us by:
Phone: 1-800-730-2214
Fax: 1-800-730-2215
Web: http://www.thomsonrights.com

Library of Congress Control Number: 2003107739

ISBN 0-534-52818-X

THIS BOOK IS PRINTED ON ACID-FREE RECYCLED PAPER

Wadsworth/Thomson Learning
10 Davis Drive
Belmont, CA 94002-3098
USA

Asia
Thomson Learning
5 Shenton Way #01–01
UIC Building
Singapore 068808

Australia/New Zealand
Thomson Learning
102 Dodds Street
Southbank, Victoria 3006
Australia

Canada
Nelson
1120 Birchmount Road
Toronto, Ontario M1K 5G4
Canada

Europe/Middle East/Africa
Thomson Learning
High Holborn House
50/51 Bedford Row
London WC1R 4LR
United Kingdom

Latin America
Thomson Learning
Seneca, 53
Colonia Polanco
11560 Mexico D.F.
Mexico

Spain/Portugal
Paraninfo
Calle/Magallanes, 25
28015 Madrid, Spain

To Kai,

The charmer who has captured our hearts.

Biographical Information

Curt R. Bartol has been a college professor and a consultant to law enforcement since 1972, when he earned his Ph.D. in Personality/Social Psychology from Northern Illinois University. At Castleton State College in Vermont, he designed and taught a wide range of psychology courses, including Criminal Behavior, Forensic Psychology, Profiling, Psychology and Law, Juvenile Delinquency, Biopsychology, Social Psychology, and Abnormal Psychology. In 1996 he was instrumental in creating and launching Castleton's graduate program in Forensic Psychology and served as its Director until 2001. He continues to teach and consult with that program.

As a consultant to law enforcement, he administers screening tests to candidates and promotional exams for municipal and state law enforcement agencies. He is also the Editor of *Criminal Justice and Behavior*, the official journal of the American Association for Correctional Psychologists.

In addition to *Psychology and Law*, he has written *Criminal Behavior*, now in its 6th edition, *Juvenile Delinquency: A Systems Approach*, and *Delinquency and Justice*, 2nd edition, which he co-authored with Anne Bartol. He has published extensively in the field of forensic psychology.

Anne M. Bartol earned a Ph.D. in Criminal Justice from the State University of New York at Albany in 1991. She also holds a Master's Degree in Journalism with a law focus from the University of Wisconsin/Madison and a Master's Degree in Criminal Justice from SUNY/Albany.

She has held faculty positions in criminal justice at State University of New York/Brockport and Castleton State College. Over a 25-year teaching career, she has taught courses including Juvenile Justice, The Press and the Law, Women and Criminal Justice, Introduction to Criminal Justice, Corrections, Criminology, Occupational Crime, Law and Society, and Judicial Process. She served as Book Review Editor of *Criminal Justice and Behavior* and, with Curt Bartol, co-authored *Juvenile Delinquency: A Systems Approach, Delinquency and Justice*, and *Psychology and Law*.

Table of Contents

CHAPTER 12

Juvenile Delinquency and Justice 375

CHAPTER 13

The Psychology of Criminal Behavior 408

Preface

Students in the behavioral sciences are often fascinated by law, but many have had limited exposure to its content. This text is intended as an upper-level introduction to both the legal process and the psychological research that relates to it. Throughout the book, we provide numerous examples of the ways in which psychologists interact with the legal system.

The third edition of this book is long overdue. Although the authors have had good intentions of revising the text every few years, life, other scholarly pursuits, and many reasons to celebrate have intervened. Meanwhile, between editions, the field of psychology and law has developed steadily, not waiting for lagging authors. In the earlier editions of the book, psychology and law was described as a specialty that was growing but was still without moorings. Today, despite the broad diversity of topics subsumed within that specialty, a unifying theme is much more apparent. Professional organizations, scholarly journals, and graduate training programs have all contributed to making psychology and law research-based, while incorporating the valuable contributions of practicing psychologists. This book strongly reflects this dual emphasis.

Like previous editions, the text has three additional purposes. *First*, it helps the student to become skillful at discriminating between knowledge that is well supported and misinformation that is based upon unwarranted assumptions and popular myths. Such skill requires the student to develop a healthy skepticism about unverified statements presumed to be valid simply because they are offered by experts who exude self-confidence. *Second*, the text tries to help the student realize that scientific knowledge is not absolute in the sense of offering established fact or "ultimate truth." Scientific knowledge is tentative, fallible, and developing. Throughout the book, research will be qualified by cautionary phases, such as "research to date," or "thus far the evidence seems to indicate." In many areas, students will be reminded that more research is needed before something can be established with confidence. Unfortunately, this cautionary approach can be problematic when psychologists interact with the legal system because representatives of the law—e.g., police, lawyers and judges, and corrections officials—often hope for more definitive answers. *Third*, the text approaches psychology as fundamentally a scientific enterprise whose primary mission is to create or continually reconstruct testable theory. This process allows psychologists to progress steadily toward understanding human behavior. Although much of what we have learned so far can be applied to the law, we must continue to work toward systematizing and synthesizing valid and significant research findings about law-related behavior into viable, testable theory.

It would be unrealistic to claim that this book will bridge what is still an enormous gap between psychology and law. Law is a practical, tradition-bound endeavor that is strongly influenced by moral, social, and political pressures. Though it can surprise—as when a court announces a landmark, sweeping decision or a legislature passes a law with widespread effect—it is basically a conservative enterprise. Representatives of the law often view the science of psychology with suspicion and skepticism, convinced that psychology must prove its worth in *meaningful* application before it can be accepted and trusted. Psychologists, on the other hand, often view law as cloaked in unsupported assumptions and maddeningly unresponsive to the findings of science. When questions of treatment are at issue, the law and its representatives are sometimes regarded as obstructionists. Many psychologists do not understand, for example, why persons who are mentally disordered should be allowed to refuse medication, or why state prison systems do not fund more rehabilitation programs. Nonetheless, psychology and law continually interact with one another and should seek mutual respect, if not common ground.

This third edition has been extensively updated and, in many ways, overhauled. The organization of the book has not changed dramatically, with the exception of a chapter on the psychology of law enforcement being moved from early in the book to the end (Chapter 14) to reflect a chapter progression from general principles to specific practices. That law enforcement chapter has been substantially revised and includes material on police discretion, profiling, the use of force, fitness for duty evaluations, suicide by cop, and hostage-taking incidents. We have also added a separate chapter on juvenile delinquency and juvenile justice (Chapter 12), which includes material on legal issues relating to juveniles, the role of psychologists consulting with the juvenile justice system, and examples of treatment programs for juvenile offenders. Other significant content-related changes include the following:

- Information on careers in forensic psychology and graduate training in psychology and law (Chapter 1);
- A detailed review of the *Daubert* trilogy, the three cases in which the U.S. Supreme Court attempted to create and clarify a standard for admitting expert testimony (Chapter 1);
- A substantially expanded chapter on assessment and testing, with emphasis on psychological tests used in forensic settings (Chapter 2);
- New material on mental health courts, drug courts, and domestic violence courts (Chapter 3);
- Updated research on risk assessment, competency to stand trial, and competency to consent to treatment (Chapters 4 and 5);
- Legal issues relating to the civil commitment of sex offenders (Chapter 5);
- Approaches to, and trends in, the community treatment of the mentally disordered, including orders for community treatment as alternatives to involuntary civil commitment (Chapter 5);
- Research and commentary on a number of issues relating to the death penalty, including death-qualified juries, risk assessment at capital sentencing, psychological assessments of competency for execution, and the treatment of offenders sentenced to death (Chapters 6 and 10);
- New material on jury nullification and jury decision making (Chapters 6 and 7);
- Updated research and commentary on hypnosis, the polygraph, repressed memory, children's memory, coerced confessions, and false confessions (Chapters 8 and 9);
- Assessment and treatment roles of psychologists consulting with adult and juvenile corrections, including model treatment programs (Chapters 10 and 12);
- Discussion of end-of-life issues, particularly physician-assisted life termination, and expanded treatment of other family law issues such as the effects of divorce, divorce mediation, and custody evaluations (Chapter 11);
- Psychological research relating to the psychopath and to the serious crimes of serial and mass murders, murder and aggravated assault, crimes of intimidation, sexual assault, child abuse, domestic violence, workplace violence, and arson (Chapter 13).

Boxes from the previous editions have been revised and updated or replaced with boxes reflecting contemporary material. For example, in addition to recent U.S. Supreme Court decisions, this edition includes boxes on racial profiling, the events of 9/11, domestic violence courts, hate crimes, common diagnoses, and jury nullification.

As in earlier editions, we have submitted parts of the manuscript to students for their review. Partly in response to their suggestions, we have included more summary statements throughout the book and have included boxed material highlighting current issues. Graduate assistants Naomi Freeman, Amie Gates, and Amy Leeper offered particularly valuable suggestions and efficiently performed research tasks. However, we are indebted to all of our students, past and present, in both psychology and criminal justice, who have kept us energized and have made it possible for both of us to love the classroom.

We are also deeply grateful for the help we received from the reviewers of the manuscript. As evidence of that appreciation, we have enthusiastically incorporated the great majority of their suggestions. They are Jack Chambliss, University of South Carolina, Neil Mulligan, University of North Carolina, Chapel Hill, Will Pelfrey, University of South Carolina, and Paul Skolnick, California State University, Northridge.

Had it not been for the enthusiasm, encouragement, and persistence of Senior Acquisitions Editor Michele Sordi, this edition would have taken much longer to produce. We are indebted to her and to the able professional staff at Wadsworth Publishing. They include Chris Caldeira, Marketing Manager, Jennifer Wilkinson, Assistant Editor, Chelsea Junget, Editorial Assistant, Laurel Anderson, Marketing Assistant, Darin Derstine, Managing Technology Project Manager, Kirk Bomont, Production Project Manager, and Vernon Boes, Art Director. Finally, Gretchen Miller shepherded the manuscript through its final editing process with competence and skill. Thank you all.

Curt R. Bartol
Anne M. Bartol

CHAPTER 1

Introduction

This book is about psychological knowledge as it pertains to law. It is designed to educate interested students about contemporary psychological research and theories that are pertinent to the legal system. It identifies unwarranted assumptions and misinformation about human behavior, but it also recognizes the limitations of psychological knowledge itself. The text's mission is to inform students about the relationship between psychology and law, encourage critical thinking about the two disciplines, communicate trends in psycholegal research, and suggest how the two disciplines might better understand and relate to one another.

The field of psychology and law is very broad, extremely diverse, and still expanding rapidly. Most of the research in psychology and law has been published during the past two decades. Anything dealing with law is within its bailiwick and is fodder for empirical study and practical application. As a result, psychological researchers have examined issues ranging from the capacity of adolescents to consent to medical treatment to the effect of media publicity on juries. Today psychological practitioners or clinicians are consulting with lawyers, working in court clinics, evaluating children for custody decision making, and offering a wide range of testing and counseling services to law enforcement, corrections, and a wide range of social agencies.

Despite this extensive and exciting involvement, the relationship between psychology and law was, for quite awhile, a vessel without moorings. The field evolved slowly over several decades without any one benchmark to clearly signify its formal acceptance. However, in the 1970s, a literature and research explosion occurred in many areas of psychology and law, indicating the field had come of age. In addition, the American Psychology-Law Society was formed, which later merged with Division 41 of the American Psychological Association in 1981. The first psychology and law graduate program began at the University of Nebraska in 1974, and the American Board of Forensic Psychology was launched to certify practitioners as experts in psychology and law in 1978. One of the earliest textbooks in the field, *Social Psychology in Court*, written by Michael Saks and Reid Hastie, was published in 1978.

Although psychology and law continued to develop rapidly over the next decade, its very diversity defied a neat definition of the field. As Melton (1992, p. 382) noted, ". . . it has no explicit perspective whatsoever that guides the choice of topics for research—a deficit that, without remediation, will doom the field to little continuing influence on legal scholarship and policy and that indeed will leave persistent questions about why the field exists at all." Students and professionals in the discipline reported that it was somewhat frustrating to work in an area that was ill-defined and constantly changing (Hafemeister, Ogloff, & Small, 1990). Furthermore, as in any rapidly developing field, there was debate about the direction the field should take. The debate was often between those who believed psychologists should be cautious in communicating information to the law and those who believed psychology should be actively involved in bringing about social change.

Psychology and law clearly is still in a state of flux, but there have been considerable advancements in the field. New paradigms, or models, are being proposed as a means of structuring the field and recognizing some of its frustrations (e.g., Monahan & Walker, 1988; Otto & Heilbrun, 2002; Wexler & Winick,

1991, 1996). These new models, which will be integrated throughout the text, testify to their sponsors' commitment to the continuing development of the field. The book is written in this spirit of confidence that psychology has a great deal to offer to law—and students are invited to share in the excitement.

Nevertheless, many challenges remain. Even the definitions of the two main themes, "psychology" and "law," can be elusive. In this text, psychology is defined broadly as the *science* of behavior and mental processes. But let's be honest: Defining psychology is not easy, largely because of its own enormous diversity. Few—if any—writers have been able to define psychology well enough to be accepted by all psychologists. A statement by Ludy Benjamin (2001, p. 740) is instructive here:

> No doubt many psychologists were drawn to their field because of its diversity of subject matter. Biologists and chemists can find a home in psychology. Physicists can find much interest in contemporary work in perception. Anthropologists, sociologists, economists, and political scientists could be happy in social psychology, cognition, development, and other psychological subfields. Business people, educators, and healers all can find a home. The quantitatively inclined are welcomed, as are the computer scientists. Sports fans too can pursue their love in psychology. Even historians can find work in this field.

Defining law is not any easier. "The question, 'What is law?' haunts legal thought, and probably more scholarship has gone into defining and explaining the concept of law than into any other concept still in use in sociology and jurisprudence" (Vago, 2000, p. 7). Also as Vago noted (2000, p. 3) "Law reflects the intellectual, social, economic, and political climate of its time," and is thus always in a state of change or revision. For the moment, we will adopt a very broad definition of law as a process of producing and applying a body of written rules governing society, recognizing that this definition, like all others, is far from a perfect one. Viewing law as a process, however, encourages us to think of it as continually subject to change and interpretation, a critical feature in the interaction of law and psychology. ▶ [In Chapter 3 we will discuss various classifications of law, which make its study more manageable.]

Contrasting Psychology and Law Approaches

The study of psychology and law itself can be approached from many angles, and divided and subdivided many ways. Haney (1980) has suggested a perceptive approach to the psychology and law relationship, which we adopt and integrate throughout the text. He believes it is useful to distinguish three relationships: (1) psychology in the law; (2) psychology and the law; and (3) psychology of the law.

Psychology in the Law

The "psychology in the law relationship" has been the most common one and may be the source of much of the malaise within the discipline. In this situation, representatives of the legal system use psychologists and their knowledge to influence the outcomes of specific cases, as by having them testify about a defendant's mental condition or consult with attorneys regarding jury selection. The important aspect to remember about this relationship is that representatives of the law take the initiative by calling on psychology when they need it, and sometimes only when it is to their advantage to do so. As Shuman and Sales (1999, p. 8) point out, "Experts may be put on a very short financial leash, which means that they are unlikely to spend the time necessary to master the legal question, critically review all the scientific literature, and educate the attorney. Rather, they typically testify about what they 'know'." Thus, after gaining the psychologist's testimony or acquiring the relevant psychological knowledge, representatives of the legal system dismiss the psychologist and the relationship is terminated.

In this context, psychology is applied within the restrictions of the standard legal process. The law asks specific, narrow questions that psychologists are required to answer within a legal context. Thus the "law side" of the relationship not only controls the scope of the issue, but also translates the meaning of answers provided by the "psychology side." The nature of this relationship limits the impact psychology can have on law and its beliefs about human behavior. "We'll call you when we need you," asserts the legal system, and psychologists conform to that role. It should be emphasized that not all judges and lawyers see the utility of psychology in this limited way. Many see considerable value in psychology beyond the pessimistic view that it is simply a source for gaining an advantage within the courtroom.

It should not be assumed that psychology has no influence within that legal context, however. Quite the contrary. When mentally disordered individuals are involved, for example, studies show a high rate of agreement between the recommendations of psychologists and the final decisions of those who sought their input. The point is that the psychology in the law relationship does not permit psychological knowledge to be communicated to its full potential. The next relationship, psychology and the law, is far more likely to do this.

Psychology and the Law

In this relationship, neither psychology nor law dominates or dictates to the other. Rather, psychology is viewed as a separate discipline analyzing and examining various components of the law from a psychological perspective and developing psychological research and theory. With the execution of well-designed studies and the thoughtful formulation of theory to tie the results of these experiments together, psychology can develop an impressive body of psychological knowledge relevant to the legal system. It can question whether the numerous legal assumptions about human behavior are empirically supported. For example, can decision making by jurors really be unaffected by information they are told to disregard? Are eyewitnesses, so heavily relied upon in the criminal courts, generally accurate in their recollection of events surrounding a crime? Do mentally disordered individuals have the ability to make decisions in their own best interest? What are the limitations of psychological tests used by employers to screen prospective employees? In the psychology *and* law relationship, psychology tries to answer these questions and communicate them to the law. Ideally, then, the relationship is truly interdisciplinary. Even if the legal system chooses not to change its policies and procedures in the direction of the scientific evidence, the body of psychological knowledge remains intact. Eventually, educated members of society concerned about psychological fictions underlying the law may demand the change.

Wexler and Winick (1991; Wexler, 1990b, 1992) argue that psychology and law, particularly mental health law, have not yet become truly interdisciplinary. Mental health law is that subset of the law that deals with individuals who are or are suspected to be mentally disordered (Wexler, 1981). It covers such issues as insanity, the administration of psychoactive medication, and the involuntary civil commitment of the mentally disordered, to name but a few. In the early 1990s, noting that mental health law had developed as a "rights-oriented" approach which had reached a stalemate, Wexler and Winick called for a new paradigm which would recognize law's potential as a therapeutic agent to bring about positive change. Acknowledging that an emphasis on legal rights was vital in the early years of modern mental health law, Wexler (1992, p. 29) suggested that . . . "a nearly exclusive emphasis on this approach is both risky and, after 20 years, sterile." Thus emerged the paradigm of **therapeutic jurisprudence**, which argues that legal decision makers should evaluate the therapeutic as well as the negative psychological and behavioral consequences of the law under consideration. Essentially, the therapeutic jurisprudence perspective urges social scientists and legal scholars to study the therapeutic implications of various legal rules and practices (Winick, 1995b).

Wexler and Winick, as advocates of therapeutic jurisprudence, do not suggest that therapeutic considerations should hold precedence over legal considerations; rather, they ask for a truly interdisciplinary relationship whereby decisions are made only after being fully informed by the findings of psychological research (Winick, Wexler, & Dauer, 1999). We will return to the Wexler and Winick suggestions in later chapters, because they represent some of the most current thought in the continuing struggle to define the relationship between psychology and law.

We make no pretense that legal reform built upon sound psychological principles will occur with ease. Law's practices are built upon a foundation of long traditions and conservative attitudes toward innovations. It does not change unless there is a cogent reason for doing so. More importantly, law is often skeptical about psychology and about the abuse of discretion by its representatives. However, it is precisely this mutually independent psychology and law relationship that holds promise for improvement in both disciplines. An incisive comment by John Conley (2000, p. 827) illustrates the nature of the relationship well: "Just as lawyers-in-training must be taught to appreciate the culture of social science, so social scientists must develop a greater appreciation of the culture and traditions of law. Irrational as some of these traditions may seem, they are ancient and deeply ingrained."

Psychology of the Law

The third relationship, psychology of the law, represents a more abstract approach to law as a determinant of behavior. How does law affect society and how does society affect laws? How successful are laws and the consequences for their violation in controlling and altering human behavior? Why are some laws embraced, some tolerated, and others resisted? What factors surround discretion in the enforcement of laws? The psychology of law poses and grapples with these questions.

A significant contribution in the psychology of the law area is the book *Crimes of Obedience* (Kelman & Hamilton, 1989), which identifies social psychological factors that operate in individuals who commit crimes at the direction of those higher in authority. Another good example is Tyler's (1990) *Why People Obey the Law*, an incisive examination of psychological principles associated with legal behavior. The authors of each of these books try to understand why individuals both defy and conform to the law.

This text includes material relevant to all three relationships, although it will focus on the first two. It is not a "how-to" book, although it often describes how forensic psychologists do their work. It will not train you how to testify in court, prepare a profile of a serial murderer, or decide which of two parents should be given custody of a minor child. However, the book does require the reader's basic understanding of the philosophy and methods of the behavioral sciences, because it will discuss many research studies applicable to the legal process. Despite the rapid growth of research in psychology and law, there is still a great need for well-designed and well-executed studies directed at the many legal assumptions about human behavior. There is an even stronger need for psychological theories that encompass and explain the results of this research.

The next section will focus on the relationship between science and the courts. The U.S. Supreme Court has issued several landmark rulings in an effort to delineate what constitutes "acceptable science" when expert witnesses testify during both criminal and civil trials. The major contribution that expert witnesses can make in a case derives from their ability and scientific knowledge to draw inferences from the facts that a jury—or other fact-finder—would not be able to draw (Goodman-Delahunty, 1997). As noted by Jane Goodman-Delahunty (1997, p. 122): "The introduction of expert testimony in legal proceedings, particularly testimony regarding social and behavioral scientific evidence, has rarely been accomplished without controversy." Since this book is about the current and future relationships between the science of psychology and the law, it will be instructive to cover appellate decisions, particularly those of the Supreme Court, in some detail before proceeding.

Appellate Court Cases and the Methods of Science

Courts often turn to scientific experts for help in understanding complex matters that are beyond the knowledge of the average lay person. However, before admitting such expert testimony into a court proceeding, a judge must be satisfied that an expert has the proper credentials and that the expert's knowledge is sound. Appeals courts then have often been faced with the question, "What is the appropriate standard by which to measure this expert information?"

The *Frye* Test

Until recently, the most frequently cited case on the admissibility of scientific evidence was decided by the U.S. Court of Appeals of the District of Columbia in 1923. In *Frye v. U.S.* (1923), the court was asked to allow polygraph evidence which supported James Alphonzo Frye's contention that he was not guilty of robbery and murder. The 19-year-old Frye had taken and passed a "systolic blood pressure deception test" administered by lawyer-psychologist William Marston. Frye's attorney had asked that Marston be allowed to testify to the results, but the court denied the request. The attorney then asked if Marston could conduct the test in the jury's presence. That request was also denied. The Court of Appeals upheld the decision of the lower court. Quoting from the brief submitted by Frye's lawyer, the appeals court agreed that:

> When the question involved does not lie within the range of common experience or common knowledge, but requires special experience or special knowledge, then the opinions of witnesses skilled in that particular science, art, or trade to which the question relates are admissible in evidence.

However, the court added the following requirement:

> Just when a scientific principle or discovery crosses the line between the experimental and demonstrable stages is difficult to define. Somewhere in this twilight zone the evidential force of the principle must be recognized, and while courts will go a long way in admitting expert testimony deduced from a well-recognized scientific principle or discovery, the thing from which the deduction is made must be *sufficiently established to have gained general acceptance in the particular field in which it belongs* (italics added).
>
> We think the systolic blood pressure deception test has not yet gained such standing and scientific recognition among physiological and psychological authorities as would justify the courts in admitting expert testimony deduced from the discovery, development, and experiments thus far made (*Frye v. U.S.*, 1923, p. 1014).

In short, *Frye* made "general acceptance" of scientific knowledge the standard or test for admitting expert scientific testimony into federal courts. If the knowledge was not recognized and accepted by the scientific community at large, it could not be admitted as scientific evidence. For the greater part of the 20th century, the *Frye* test was widely applied by federal courts, and many state courts accepted the same standard. In 1975, however, Congress adopted the Federal Rules of Evidence (FRE), which included a slightly different standard—specifically, that scientific evidence be relevant and reliable. Even so, various state and federal court decisions continued applying a variety of standards (including the *Frye* standard) and with varying rigor (Shuman & Sales, 1999).

The Daubert Case

In 1993 the U.S. Supreme Court, in what is now considered a far-reaching, landmark case (*Daubert v. Merrell Dow Pharmaceuticals, Inc.*, 1993), significantly modified the *Frye* standard in favor of the test found in the Federal Rules of Evidence. The *Frye* test has not completely disappeared, though, as we will see shortly. Two minor children (Jason Daubert and Eric Schuller) and their parents sued Merrell Dow Pharmaceuticals, Inc., arguing that the children's serious birth defects were caused by their mother's ingestion of Bendectin, a prescription antinausea drug manufactured by the company. Merrell Dow submitted expert evidence that the drug had not been shown to be a risk factor for human birth defects. The plaintiffs (the petitioners), however, obtained the testimony of eight experts who had conducted new studies and re-analyzed previous research. The federal district court and a federal appeals court both rejected the new evidence, ruling that it did not meet the *Frye* standard of "general acceptability." The U.S. Supreme Court, however, unanimously ruled that "general acceptability" was too austere and should no longer be the criterion in federal trials. The Court asserted that:

> The merits of the *Frye* test have been much debated, and scholarship of its proper scope and application is legion. Petitioners' primary attack, however, is not on the content but on continuing authority of the rule. They contend that the *Frye* test was superseded by the adoption of the Federal Rules of Evidence. We agree.

Therefore, in *Daubert*, the Court emphasized that the traditional *Frye* standard should be replaced by the Federal Rules of Evidence (FRE). (◙ See **Box 1-1** for a description of three FREs that are relevant to

BOX 1-1
Federal Rules of Evidence (Effective December 1, 2000)

ARTICLE VII. OPINIONS AND EXPERT TESTIMONY

Rule 701. Opinion Testimony by Lay Witnesses
If the witness is not testifying as an expert, the witness' testimony in the form of opinions or inferences is limited to those opinions or inferences which are (a) rationally based on the perception of the witness, and (b) helpful to a clear understanding of the witness' testimony or the determination of a fact in issue, and (c) not based on scientific, technical, or other specialized knowledge within the scope of Rule 702.

Rule 702. Testimony by Experts
If scientific, technical, or other specialized knowledge will assist the trier of fact to understand the evidence or to determine a fact in issue, a witness qualified as an expert by knowledge, skill, experience, training, or education, may testify thereto in the form of an opinion or otherwise, if (1) the testimony is based upon sufficient facts or data, (2) the testimony is the product of reliable principles and methods, and (3) the witness has applied the principles and methods reliably to the facts of the case.

Rule 703. Bases of Opinion Testimony by Experts
The facts or data in the particular case upon which an expert bases an opinion or inference may be those perceived by or made known to the expert at or before the hearing. If of a type reasonably relied upon by experts in the particular field in forming opinions or inferences upon the subject, the facts or data need not be admissible in evidence in order for the opinion or inference to be admitted. Facts or data that are otherwise inadmissible shall not be disclosed to the jury by proponent of the opinion or inference unless the court determines that their probative value in assisting the jury to evaluate the expert's opinion substantially outweighs their prejudicial effect.

expert testimony by psychologists and other scientists.) A majority of the Court also made it clear that trial judges should screen any and all scientific testimony or evidence admitted to assure that it has three critical elements: (1) *relevancy*; (2) *legal sufficiency*; and (3) *reliability*. All three elements are important in deciding on the acceptability of the scientific evidence presented by the experts.

Relevancy refers to the expectation that the scientific findings must be directly pertinent to the specific case being presented. When the relationships between the scientific evidence and the facts of the case are not adequately demonstrated, the evidence is not admissible. Goodman-Delahunty (1997, p. 130) provides a good example. The defendant was charged with the statutory rape of his daughter. The defense tried to show—through expert testimony—that the defendant did *not* belong in a category that characterized 40% of incest abusers. Presumably, individuals in this group, a large minority of incest abusers, are fixated pedophiles (child molesters). "The defense sought to show that because the defendant did not exhibit the characteristics of a fixated pedophile, he was unlikely to have committed the crimes charged against him. The court pointed out that the defendant was never charged with being a fixated pedophile, and unless the defense could show a link between nonproclivity for pedophilia and nonproclivity for incest abuse, the relevance of the testimony was lacking."

The *Daubert* criterion of *legal sufficiency* refers to the expectation that the expert evidence be probative rather than prejudicial. In other words, the scientific evidence must provide proof or evidence to the issues of the case, rather than misleading, prejudicing, or confusing the jury. If the impact of the evidence is more prejudicial than probative, the court may exclude the expert testimony. For example, "some courts merely preclude the expert from mentioning the term 'rape trauma syndrome' while favoring the more neutral term 'posttraumatic stress disorder,' because the former tends to give the impression that rape had occurred, which is prejudicial" (Goodman-Delahunty, 1997, p. 130). Still, some lawyers have argued that expert testimony is prejudicial by its very nature because an expert may be perceived by jurors to possess some sort of deep knowledge and skill considerably beyond the layperson (Goodman-Delahunty, 1997).

The third criterion articulated by *Daubert* refers to *reliability*. The Court specified four standards that federal trial judges should apply in deciding on the reliability of the scientific evidence presented by the expert witness or witnesses. The four standards are: (1) whether the scientific theory or technique can be and has been tested; (2) the error rate of the particular scientific technique; (3) whether the theory or technique has been subjected to peer review and publication; and (4) general acceptance of the theory or technique within the scientific community. However, an absence or weakness in one of the four standards would not necessarily exclude the evidence.

The first standard refers to whether a scientific theory is formulated in such a way as to be capable of being tested and *falsified* by a researcher, often referred to as "falsifiability." This point is an important one in the world of science but it is also somewhat difficult to understand. For example, in *Daubert*, Chief Justice Rehnquist expressed difficulty in understanding the concept when he noted: "I defer to no one in my confidence in federal judges; but I am at loss to know what is meant when it is said that the scientific status of a theory depends on its 'falsifiability,' and I suspect some of them will be, too." It is important, therefore, that we explain the concept more fully before moving on.

In his classical work, *The Logic of Scientific Discovery*, the famous philosopher of science, Karl Popper (1968) (referred to by the Justices in *Daubert*), asserted that a truly scientific statement not only is capable of being verified or shown to be correct for the time being, but also is capable of being *falsified* or shown to be incorrect. A scientific explanation must have falsifiability, or refutability, or testability (all meaning essentially the same thing). In fact, Popper argued that one crucial criterion of a scientific statement is its constant vulnerability to being refuted by common experience or observation. That is, the terms in any scientific statement or theory must be so precise, clear, and unambiguous that anyone planning to test the statement clearly understands what it is saying and can test it and potentially show the statement to be incorrect. "A theory which is not refutable by any conceivable event is nonscientific," Popper (1962, p. 26) affirms. According to Popper, the prudent scientist must ask, "Is it conceivable to set up conditions where the statements accounting for the observed phenomena could be shown to be incorrect?" If such conceivable conditions cannot be proposed, the statement or theory is not scientific. A truly scientific statement, then, is constantly at risk of being shown incorrect in accounting for observations and experience.

To describe the differences between scientific verifiability and falsifiability, Popper used the scientific statement, "All swans are white." No matter how many times we may observe white swans, our observations do not fully justify the conclusion that *all* swans are white. Verification is forever inconclusive. If, after one million observations (verifications), *one* black swan is seen, the statement "all swans are white" has become incorrect. In a sense, we have learned much more about our statement by this one falsification than by millions of verifications. One falsification has forced a revision of our thinking about swans, rendering the original statement non-universal. Now, we must try to develop a better scientific statement, such as "*Most* swans are white," or "All young swans are white." This characteristic of science is what Popper called the "asymmetry of scientific discovery."

Falsifiability means that every scientific statement remains tentative forever because it is only a human interpretation of the known universe and is consequently always subject to revision. This is the nature of scientific discovery. Scientific knowledge is an open system that is tentative, fallible, and developing. Scientific statements are not *proved*, only supported or not supported. Popper's emphasis on falsification encourages a critical appraisal of popular, expert, or scientific statements. If they are *susceptible* to being

BOX 1-2
Journals Devoted to Psychology and Law

American Journal of Forensic Psychiatry
American Journal of Forensic Psychology
Australian Journal of Forensic Psychology
Behavioral Sciences and the Law
Criminal Behaviour and Mental Health
Criminal Justice and Behavior
International Journal of Law and Psychiatry
Journal of Forensic Psychology Practice
Journal of Forensic Sciences
Journal of Police and Criminal Psychology
Journal of Psychiatry and Law
Journal of the American Academy of Psychiatry and Law
Journal of Threat Assessment
Law and Human Behavior
Law of Psychology Review
Legal and Criminological Psychology
Psychiatry, Psychology and Law
Psychology, Crime & Law
Psychology, Public Policy, and Law

shown wrong, they should be viewed with caution, although not necessarily discarded. If they are convincingly falsified, however, we must look for a better explanation.

The Supreme Court's second reliability standard refers to the question: Is there a known or potential error associated with the scientific evidence? The standard implies that federal courts should determine the acceptable level for an error rate. However, the Court did not define error rate, nor did it provide guidance by indicating what the acceptable level might be. And, precisely how should these considerations be applied to the evidence presented in a case?

The third standard of scientific evidence reliability recommended by the Court in *Daubert* refers to the question: Have the findings been subjected to peer review and publication? In other words, has the evidence been reviewed by other experts (peers) in the field and met with their approval? Most professional and scholarly journals and periodicals in science (including the social and behavioral sciences) require that each manuscript undergo a rigorous evaluation by other experts before being accepted for publication. If the majority of these reviewers believe the manuscript falls short of the scientific requirement of solid methodology, analysis, conclusions, or contributions to the literature, the manuscript is likely to be rejected by the journal editor. Therefore, if research is published, the Court can assume that the evidence has some level of acceptance by the scientific community. (■ **Box 1-2** provides a list of journals devoted to psychology and law.)

The fourth standard refers to the question: Is the technique or methodology at issue generally accepted? Note that this standard is really a reiteration of the *Frye* standard. Therefore, the *Frye* standard did not disappear. Instead, it became one of four factors to be taken into consideration by federal courts in deciding whether scientific evidence is reliable and should be admitted. Once again, however, it is important to emphasize that reliability is only one aspect of the decision making recommended by the Court (■ see **Box 1-3**).

Supreme Court Decisions After *Daubert*

The *Daubert* rule was reaffirmed and extended by the U.S. Supreme Court in *General Elec. Co. v. Joiner* (1997) and *Kumho Tire Co., Ltd. v. Carmichael* (1999). The *Joiner* case centered on identifying the cause of lung cancer diagnosed in Robert Joiner, an electrician who worked for the Water and Light Department of Thomasville, Georgia, for over eighteen years. Although Joiner was a smoker and came from a family with a history of lung cancer, his suit (originally filed in a Georgia state court) alleged that his exposure to electrical transformer chemicals (PCBs, dioxin, and furans) "promoted" his lung cancer. The defendants (General Electric, Westinghouse Electric, and Monsanto) moved the

BOX 1-3
Evaluation of Scientific Evidence

The process of evaluating scientific evidence, as outlined in *Daubert v. Merrell-Dow Pharmaceuticals,* proceeds approximately as follows:

1. The judge determines that the expert has proper credentials.
2. The judge then determines that the evidence is:
   - Relevant (pertinent to the case being presented)
   - Legally sufficient (probative value outweighs prejudicial value)
   - Reliable (scientifically acceptable)
3. The following questions can be asked to determine whether the evidence is reliable:
   - Can and has the theory been tested?
   - What is the error rate?
   - Has the theory or technique been subjected to peer review?
   - Is the theory or technique generally accepted in the scientific community?

case to federal court, requesting a **summary judgment** (a request for prompt and expeditious disposition of a controversy without a trial). Joiner argued against a summary judgment, specifying that there were numerous disputed factual issues that required resolution by a jury. In **depositions** (oral or written testimony of witnesses taken under oath outside the courtroom), Joiner's experts testified that the chemicals can promote cancer and were likely responsible for Joiner's cancer. However, in opposition to Joiner, the trial court granted summary judgment, largely because it concluded that Joiner's experts failed to demonstrate the scientific link between the chemical exposure and his cancer. Joiner appealed to a higher federal court, the Court of Appeals of the Eleventh Circuit, which reversed the lower court's ruling, saying that the lower court had erred in excluding the testimony of Joiner's expert witnesses.

The U.S. Supreme Court, however, unanimously supported the decision of the district court to exclude the expert testimony. Two of Joiner's four experts were not willing to link increases in lung cancer to exposure to PCBs. The other two, who were more willing to do that, had conducted studies that the judge thought were not directly related to the case or that included exposure to other contaminants, in addition to PCBs. Reviewing this proferred evidence, the Supreme Court decided that the district court judge had not abused his discretion by refusing to admit the expert testimony. The *Joiner* case established that decisions made by trial judges will be overruled only if it can be demonstrated that they abused their discretion. As a result of that decision, it is clear that to be admissible, experts must adequately explain their scientific conclusions to trial judges (Blanck & Berven, 1999).

In *Kumho*, the Court considered whether an engineer's expert testimony—concerning the role a defective tire played in causing an auto accident—met the *Daubert* test. The engineer's testimony had been classified as "technical" rather than traditionally "scientific." Basically, the question raised by *Kumho* relates to the admissibility of expert opinion based on *clinical* experience and observation rather than science that is normally conducted under controlled laboratory conditions (Blanck & Berven, 1999). The Court concluded that the admissibility rules articulated by *Daubert* extended to clinical and technical knowledge. Therefore, the *Kumho* conclusion means that federal trial courts should apply the *Daubert* standard to what was traditionally considered "nonscientific" testimony from experts. This would include the clinical testimony of psychologists and other mental health workers. As Otto and Heilbrun (2002) note, it is now clear that clinicians as well as researchers are scientists for the purpose of providing expert testimony. ▶ [The topic of clinicians as scientists will be discussed again in Chapter 3.]

Although *Daubert* and succeeding cases do not require judges to become "amateur scientists," they do expect them to become familiar with strengths and weaknesses of science (Blanck & Berven, 1999). The three cases together—sometimes called the *Daubert* trilogy—now form the basis for the admittance of scientific expert testimony in federal courts. Many states have adopted the *Daubert* standard, but about 17 states continue to use the *Frye* "general acceptance" standard (Kassin et al., 2001).

Ways of Knowledge and the Methods of Science

It is helpful to set the stage for a discussion of psychological research by touching on the philosophy of science. The work of American philosopher Charles Peirce is instructive. Peirce outlined four general ways through which humans develop beliefs and knowledge about their world (Kerlinger, 1973).

First, there is the **method of tenacity**, where people hold firmly to their beliefs about others because they "know" them to be true and correct, simply because they have always believed and known them to be true and correct. These beliefs are tightly embraced, even in the face of contradictory evidence: "I know I'm right, regardless of what others say or the evidence indicates." This form of knowledge is typically acquired from various sources in the social environment, but then the person closes his or her mind to further contradictory information. Confirmatory information is usually allowed into the person's cognitive template, but material that is inconsistent with existing beliefs is not.

The second way of knowing and developing beliefs is the **method of authority**. Here, people believe something because individuals and institutions in authority proclaim it to be so. If the courts over the years have said it is so, it is so. If a well-recognized and respected legal scholar makes an argument in favor of or against a proposition, that scholar's name is cited as authoritative evidence for the proposition's soundness or unsoundness. Education is partly based on this method of knowing, with authority originating from teachers, scholars, experts, and the "great masters" they cite. Elementary school children often quote the authority of their teacher as indisputable evidence in support of an argument; college students often assert, "It says so in the book." Tyler's (1990) research, however, suggests that this expressed allegiance to authority will not necessarily translate to action unless people believe in the legitimacy of the authoritative source.

The **a priori method** is a third way of obtaining knowledge. Evidence is believed correct because "it only stands to reason" and logical deduction. The *a priori* method is the dominant approach to knowledge in the legal process. The legal system is replete with formal rules that govern the admissibility of evidence and are intended to present information in a logical, orderly fashion. The legal system also relies heavily on precedent, or the principles of law that have already been developed in past cases. Primary sources such as court decision, statutes, constitutions, and administrative regulations are consulted by attorneys as they prepare their cases and by judges as they render their decisions. To a lesser extent, law is also derived from secondary sources, such as law reviews, legal treatises, social science journals, books, and other reference works. Basically, however, legal knowledge is derived after consultation with previous authority and a subsequent process of deduction. This method may be tempered, though, by another line of reasoning, which emerged during the 1920s and 1930s as the legal realist movement (Melton, 1987) and which continues to have support today. The legal realist believes that cases should not be resolved exclusively *a priori*, or with reference to what happened in the past; rather, the law should take into consideration social reality. In other words, the law should be responsive to a society's needs and concerns at a particular time.

The fourth way of obtaining knowledge is the **method of science**, which is the testing of a statement or set of statements through observations and systematic research. On the basis of this systematic study, statements about natural events or processes are revised, reconstructed, or discarded. Science is an enterprise under constant change, modification, and expansion rather than an absolute, unalterable fact-laden system. Science teaches us that there are few certainties in the natural world and that we should base our decisions and expectations on "the best of our knowledge" at any particular time in history. The method of science, while certainly not the only approach, is the dominant approach to obtaining knowledge in psychology.

Peirce's four methods of knowing provide a rough framework for determining the source of one's knowledge, and they will be useful guides throughout the remainder of the book. With the possible exception of the method of tenacity, each method has its place in the accumulation of knowledge, as long as we recognize which method we are using to obtain our knowledge and also understand the limitations of each. Authoritative sources and reasoning both are valuable contributors to our beliefs and opinions. The method of science provides us with additional information about the "soundness" of our authoritative and logical knowledge, and it promotes a critical and cautious stylistic way of thinking about our beliefs.

Scientific knowledge, because it is based on systematic observations, hypothesis testing, experiments, and testable statements, places itself permanently at risk of being falsified or shown to be incorrect. In *Daubert*, the Supreme Court stated that scientific knowledge and theories should be subjected to testing for falsification or to peer review and publication. They are constantly updated to account for observations and experiments, and they attempt to make predictions beyond our present experience. Ultimately, scientific knowledge seeks the underlying order of things. The method of science is a testable, self-corrective approach to knowledge that offers one of the most powerful sources available for the understanding of human behavior.

Research Methods and Strategies

People hold many assumptions about human behavior, and the science of psychology tries to test the validity of these assumptions. Many forms of behavior have come under its scrutiny. An experimental or empirical psychologist studies organisms to understand, predict, and control (or, in the case of humans, to help them to control) their behavior, behavior being what organisms do, or how they act. The methods of study vary greatly, from simple, direct observation in natural environments to complex experimental manipulations in laboratory settings. Throughout the book, we will be citing many examples of research using these varied strategies.

The Experimental Method

Many psychologists are convinced that human behavior can best be understood if researchers use the experimental method, which requires careful control and measurement of the phenomena being studied. Often, these research psychologists bring the phenomenon to be studied into the laboratory, where conditions can be manipulated or controlled with precise equipment and procedures, and where many possible extraneous factors can be discarded, minimized, or accounted for.

One early—now classic—experiment in psychology and law was conducted by a group of research psychologists (Davis, Kerr, Atkin, Holt, & Meek, 1975), who wondered how the size of a jury affected its final decision. Traditionally, juries in England, Canada, and the United States comprise twelve persons, who are usually required to arrive at a unanimous decision. In the 1960s, states began to experiment with smaller jury sizes and with majority verdicts, especially in civil cases (Kalven & Zeisel, 1966; Wrightsman, 1977). Today, three-fourths of the states allow various trials with juries of fewer than twelve members, and six-member juries are common in federal civil trials (Abraham, 1998).

Davis and his colleagues (1975) designed an experimental situation that simulated trial conditions, or a "mock trial" as it is called in the research literature. Various six- and twelve-person "juries" listened to a tape recording that contained an abbreviated version of the transcript of an actual trial. Some of the juries were instructed to come to a unanimous decision regarding guilt or innocence; other juries were told they must reach a two-thirds majority decision within the same time period. The twelve- and six-person juries generally arrived at the same decision (the defendant was found not guilty) whether or not they were forced to unanimity. The juries differed in group process, however. Specifically, unanimous juries (both 6 and 12 person) needed a larger number of poll votes and longer deliberation time before reaching a verdict. On the basis of this experiment, the researchers concluded that jury size does not appear to affect the final verdict, but does affect the length of time and the manner of arriving at the final decision. One limitation shared by many studies using simulated juries, however, is their generalizability to the actual jury decision making process. ▶ [We will cover this issue when we discuss additional contemporary research on juries in Chapters 6 and 7.]

Quasi-Experimental Designs

Realistically, many questions cannot be subjected to the experimental control and general confines of the psychological laboratory. Researchers then must use designs that allow them to study subjects outside their direct control and to examine already existing conditions. These are called quasi-experimental experiments. For example, let's say a biopsychologist wants to examine the effect of lowering the legal level of blood alcohol content (BAC) for DUI on fatal traffic accidents. A "pure experimental method" would require a laboratory setting where subjects' blood alcohol level was manipulated and simulated driving scenarios were set up—to the point of permitting a fatal accident! Obviously, this is out of the question. The more realistic method is to work outside the laboratory, by: (1) examining a state law which lowered the BAC levels; (2) finding the number of fatalities that occurred prior to its enactment (pretest); and (3) comparing that to the number of fatalities that occurred after the law was enacted (posttest). The method is not perfect because the researcher cannot control for other factors that might have affected the fatality rates. Thus, the quasi-experimental design is a pragmatic approach to research in an effort to collect the best data under conditions that are less than ideal (Leary, 1991).

Survey Research

Survey research involves obtaining information about people by asking them well-prepared questions, usually in written form. Alternately, interviewers ask the questions and record the answers. Respondents are asked about their attitudes, beliefs, and typical ways of acting in various situations. Survey researchers almost always use sampling techniques, because it would be prohibitively expensive to question everyone in the population being studied. Thus, the researcher obtains a representative segment, a sample, through the process of statistical randomization. Randomization ensures that each person in the relevant population has an equal chance of being selected for an interview.

Survey research is used more extensively by sociologists, political scientists, and economists than by psychologists. However, such research can be very helpful to psychologists trying to determine characteristic beliefs and attitudes of certain populations. For example, psychologists interested in the effects of pre-trial publicity on jury verdicts may survey public opinion following news coverage of a case soon to go to trial. Constantini and King (1980/1981) surveyed Californians about their knowledge and attitudes about three criminal cases. They found that respondents with greater knowledge about each case were more likely to favor the prosecution (Carroll, et al., 1986). In fact, they learned that this pre-trial information was the strongest predictor of their decision making about the case, regardless of other demographic or attitudinal characteristics of the respondents. We cannot assume that the same effects would occur in an actual trial situation, however.

Meta-Analysis

Science is a cumulative process, with new research building on research conducted earlier. But scientific results are often controversial and equivocal, with studies reaching different conclusions on the same dependent variable. For example, what type of therapy is most effective for the treatment of sex offenders? Or, what prevention programs are most effective in reducing delinquency? Or, are men more aggressive than women in their interpersonal relationships? The many studies on these topics often suggest different answers. Meta-analysis can provide a very powerful estimate of what the correct answers are. **Meta-analysis** is a statistical method for summarizing the results of many different studies focusing on a specific question or issue. Meta-analysis is particularly useful at aggregating well-done studies that have small sample sizes so that conclusions can be made on a large segment of the population. A critical aspect of meta-analysis is deciding what studies to include in the procedure, because poorly designed or methodologically weak studies may lead to misleading results. Researchers today are particularly interested in using meta-analysis to evaluate the effectiveness of rehabilitation or treatment programs in juvenile and adult corrections. ▶ [We will discuss the results of this approach in Chapters 10 and 12.]

Legal Research

Students unfamiliar with law and legal research are often hesitant to approach legal materials, feeling deterred by the apparent "mystique" surrounding American law. Actually, locating information pertaining to cases, statutes, and legal topics is a straightforward process. Most libraries have general source materials about Congress, the U.S. Supreme Court, and the American judicial system, including excellent fundamental books on the structure of the courts. Many also have the publication *Words and Phrases*, which gives legal definitions for certain terms and refers the reader to those cases which helped define them. *Black's Law Dictionary*—available in both hard cover and in pocket-sized editions—is an indispensable source for anyone interested in law.

Sizeable libraries list among their holdings *U.S. Reports* or the *Supreme Court Reporter*, both of which contain complete decisions of the U.S. Supreme Court. It is a simple process to locate a case, given its name (e.g., *Miranda v. Arizona*) and a cite (384 U.S. 436). The student has only to go to volume 384 of *U.S. Reports* and the case will be at page 436. The same principle is used to record lower court cases. Decisions of federal appellate courts are found in the *Federal Reporter* (e.g., 465 F.2d 496). The *Federal Supplement* holds federal district court cases. State court decisions are found in state reporters (e.g., 134 Cal. Rptr. 595) and in regional volumes (e.g., 159 S.W 291).

Without the case name, and with only a general subject area to research, the process becomes more involved, but it is still manageable. In this situation, a student makes use of a limited subject index at the back of the case reporter or one of several special indexes, often called case digests.

The *American Digest System*, used in American law libraries, makes use of a "key number" system developed by West Publishing Company. In it, law is divided into seven main classes, each class into subclasses, and each subclass into topics. When a case is received for indexing, each point of law covered in the case is isolated and summarized in a headnote, which is then assigned a topic and a key number. Although the system sounds complex, it is relatively simple once the researcher has located the current digest, which will then refer him or her to appropriate cases on the subject of interest. Law libraries also carry other indexes or digests, including the *Supreme Court Digest*, which lists all cases heard by the U.S. Supreme Court, and a variety of specialized digests, including those of state and regional cases.

In addition to cases, a wide variety of law journals are available to those interested in in-depth discussion of legal issues. Although we highlighted social science journals devoted to psychology and law in Box 1-2, it is important to point out that virtually every law school produces a journal of legal research and commentaries on the law and significant court cases. These journals typically carry the law school's name (e.g., *Yale Law Journal, Stanford Law Review*). Independent publishing companies or professional associations also publish such journals (e.g., *Criminal Law Reporter, ABA Journal*). The search process described above will often lead to these sources. Today, the legal researcher's task also is aided by computerized data search services, including the legal LEXIS and WESTLAW. Additionally, students can easily access statutes, cases, and legal concepts via a multitude of search engines and web sites. Two very helpful sites are www.findlaw.com and www.supct.law. cornell.edu.

Research Terms and Concepts

Validity

Psychological research deals extensively with the question of **validity**, which asks, "Are we measuring what we claim to be measuring? It is different from the question of **reliability**, which asks, "Would we get the same results if we used different examiners or if we measured this next week?" Of the two concepts, validity is the more critical. Think of a yardstick on which the space intervals between the lines are not accurate. The yardstick itself is reliable: different persons using it would obtain the same measurement, and the same measurement would be obtained over different periods of time. Yet the yardstick is not a valid instrument because its individual units of measurement are flawed.

In psychological research, validity is subdivided into many forms, ▶ [which will be discussed in Chapter 2]. For the moment, we should distinguish between **external validity** (also called **ecological validity**) and **internal validity**.

External or ecological validity refers to the degree of generalizability research findings have to other populations and other situations. Usually, the degree of external validity is approximated by conducting further research using different populations, at different times, and in different situations. External validity helps answer the question: "To what extent can we safely conclude that these results remain consistent across time, place, and persons?" (Note that we are not asking whether the methods we used to obtain the results would yield the same results in other situations, which would be inquiring about reliability.) To use a jury research example once again, studies using videotaped reenactments of actual court cases are likely to have more external validity than studies using a written description of a case and asking subjects to deliberate to reach a verdict, simply because they come closer to approximating reality. Recognizing this, psychologist Steven Penrod has prepared a number of such videos for use in jury research. Therefore, although high external validity is difficult to obtain in the psychology and law area, efforts are continually made to try to achieve it. It is important to do this, because the lack of external validity is a major reason for the conflicting and contradictory results commonly reported in the literature. Results in one study often do not generalize to another study conducted under a different set of circumstances but trying to answer the same question. ◙ **Box 1-4** illustrates an approach whose validity and reliability have been questioned.

Internal validity, on the other hand, deals with the level of confidence we can place in the results obtained in a particular study. In other words, how well done was the study? Did it have basic flaws in its design or in its data collection? Did it really address the question the researcher was trying to answer? Usually, the flaw is a confounding variable that makes it very difficult or impossible to conclude what explains the final outcome. A **confounding variable** is an extraneous variable that interferes with or clouds the research findings. For example, if we are interested in determining how well a psychological test predicts differences in performance between men and women in law enforcement, we must be careful that the groups have received the same kind of training. We must also be sure that their performance is evaluated using the same criteria. If we did not control for these training and evaluation variables, it would be foolhardy to assert that any performance differences between the two groups could be attributed to gender. In this example, training and evaluation become confounding variables.

Both external validity and internal validity are important criteria to use in determining the value of psycholegal research, and we will encounter them repeatedly as we review the research throughout the book. We should be aware, however, that the legal system sometimes uses the term "validity" in a different way than psychology uses it. As Schuller and Vidmar (1992) note, when courts ask whether psychological information is valid, what they really want to know is whether it is reliable. Furthermore, as we saw in our discussion of the *Daubert* case, the Court's view of reliability encompasses aspects of both reliability and validity from a psychological perspective. This is particularly so when we consider the four standards suggested to assess reliability. For example, if a theory or technique has been submitted to peer review, its reliability *and* validity presumably have been scrutinized. This is but one illustration of the numerous inconsistencies in vocabulary that challenge the student of psychology and the law.

Research Strategies

Evidence

The psychologist-philosopher Joseph Rychlak (1968) posited that psychologists gather two types of evidence to help them arrive at knowledge and theories about human behavior. Evidence procured

BOX 1-4
Validity and Reliability of an Equivocal Death Analysis

This is a summary of material taken from an article by Norman Poythress, Randy K. Otto, Jack Darkes, and Laura Starr that appeared in the January 1993 issue of *The American Psychologist*. The interested reader is urged to read the original article for a more complete description of the issues involved.

In 1989, a powerful explosion abroad the USS Iowa killed 47 persons. The U.S. Navy promptly began an intensive investigation to determine its cause. Based on its investigation, the Navy concluded that the explosion was caused by one person, Clayton Hartwig, who also died in the tragedy. During the investigation, information about Hartwig's habits, aspirations, life-style, and personality was gathered from his friends, family members, and shipmates. This information was turned over to the National Center for the Analysis of Violent Crime, a division of the Federal Bureau of Investigation (FBI), for a reconstructive psychological investigation. A reconstructive psychological investigation is an attempt to develop a psychological image of what a dead person was like (his or her personality, habits, intentions, dreams, motivations, life-style, and so on) while alive. The FBI prefers to call this process equivocal death analysis (EDA).

The U.S. House of Representatives Armed Services Committee, however, was not convinced that the conclusions reached by the Navy—that Hartwig was responsible—were the right ones and asked the American Psychological Association for help. The House Committee requested that the APA set up a panel of psychologists to provide independent evaluations of the Navy report and the claims advanced by the FBI. The APA panel found that the FBI's behavioral scientist experts had told the House Committee, in absolute terms, that—through the mysteries of the EDA—they had concluded that Hartwig had acted alone and purposely caused the explosion. Most troubling to the APA panel was the absoluteness and conviction with which the FBI had presented its "facts." One of the Special Agents told the Committee that ". . . he could recall only 3 of 45 cases (7%) in which he was unable to arrive at a conclusive opinion" (p. 9).

However, the APA panel could find no known research that has investigated the reliability or validity of the EDA. It is a method that appears largely based on speculation, hunch, bias, and perhaps folklore. In short, it appears to be largely based on the method of tenacity and has little, if any, scientific foundation. One of the Special Agents demonstrated a disturbing disdain for validity and science in general when he stated:

> I certainly appreciate that wonderful academic approach to a practical problem. It is typical of what we find when we see people who have not had the experience investigating either crime scenes, victims, criminals and so forth in active, ongoing investigations . . . [I]n the field of psychology and psychiatry, there are existing raging arguments about the validity of the very techniques that exist. They won't be resolved in this world. So, to ask us to provide the validity is an exercise in futility (p. 9).

by using experimental methods is called **validating evidence**. It is the evidence or knowledge gained through careful, controlled research. A second type of evidence, most often gathered by applied and clinical psychologists, is called **procedural evidence**. This is the information that clinicians suspect to be correct based on their personal observations, assessments, and interpretations. Procedural evidence includes the elements of common sense, logic, and insight, and it results in a sense of conviction that a given hypothesis accounts for some observations and is useful. Clinicians have had considerable experience working with individuals in a clinical setting, and they use this expertise to form theory about human behavior. For example, police officers who have intervened in domestic disturbances have told clinicians it is wise to separate the disputants in a two-person confrontation (e.g., remove them to different rooms for a "cooling off" period). When one party is aggressing against the other, however, very little *validating evidence* supports this practice (Sherman & Berk, 1984; Sherman, 1992). It is considered a temporary measure which does not solve the underlying conflict. Some research suggests that arrest of the offending party is a more effective measure for deterring him from future incidents (Sherman & Berk, 1984), but other research (Dunford, Huizinga, & Elliott, 1990) suggests that arrest is no more effective than separation or the officer's attempt at mediation. On the other hand, there is *procedural evidence* that both separation and arrest are effective if accompanied by additional intervention strategies, such as referring the victim to social services in the community and providing follow-up support. Validating evidence also supports this.

The experiences of those working within the legal system and those who formulate policy, then, may also be considered procedural evidence. In this sense, clinical psychologists and professionals in other applied disciplines share common ground with participants in the legal system. Both gather procedural evidence. This shared method of science explains, in part, why judges and lawyers often prefer the testimony of clinicians to that of experimentalists.

The two types of evidence—procedural and validating—are interdependent in that they both contribute to our knowledge about human behavior. To reject one or the other severely limits the knowledge we can gain. Although it is sometimes difficult to draw a fine line between these two methods, because both may be considered scientific methods, the distinguishing features between them are replicability and control.

Replicability

The method designed to gain validating evidence demands that the findings be replicable, or able to be repeated by others. Replicability requires that the descriptions of the variables studied and the procedures used to study them be precise and objective enough so that what was done is very clear. We sometimes call this "operationalizing." If researchers wish to study the effects of anxiety on test taking, for example, they must be extremely clear about what is meant by both terms (anxiety and test taking), and precisely what procedures and measurements were used to examine the relationship. These clear descriptions serve as checks on both external and internal validity and are required if the study is to be replicated.

Control

Control refers to the researcher's attempts to account for all potentially influential variables on the relationship being investigated. For example, in the test-taking anxiety study, the researcher must be certain that it is anxiety rather than some extraneous influence like intelligence, time of day, age, or even room temperature that has a significant effect on test-taking performance. These extraneous influences are called secondary variables. The researcher must also be careful to identify and measure the independent and dependent variables. The independent variable is the measure whose effect is being studied (in the above example, anxiety). The dependent variable (test performance), we might say, feels the effect. The dependent variable is the variable that is measured to see how it is changed by manipulations of the independent variable.

The independent variable in most scientific investigations is manipulated in a controlled fashion. In our example, the researcher might want to test the effects of three different levels of anxiety on test taking. This manipulation might require some procedure for inducing anxiety (however defined and measured), such as threatening the subjects with varying dire consequences for failing the exam. In one condition, the subjects may be threatened with having to repeat the test in a much longer session, whereas in another they may be threatened with public exposure of grades on the exam. A third condition might involve no threat or consequence (potentially a no-anxiety condition), and individuals in this group would be considered the controls. The first two groups would be the experimental or treatment groups.

Procedural or clinical evidence may also be gathered in a similar manner, but in a majority of instances it is obtained with considerably less precise objective description and control. From a scientific perspective, its value rests principally in the hypotheses it generates. A hypothesis is a speculative explanation of behavior, and it implies prediction. In the domestic conflict situation referred to earlier, the procedural evidence that referral of victims to follow-up services is effective in preventing future incidents generated a hypothesis that was carefully tested through a carefully controlled experiment.

Clinical Judgment vs. Statistical Prediction

The lines between procedural and validating evidence are often not as sharp as we have described them here. This point can best be illustrated by the long-standing debate over the predictive accuracy of clinical judgment—a form of procedural evidence—versus that of statistical or actuarial methods—forms of validating evidence. Clinical judgment is judgment presumably based on professional and training experience. Clinically based predictions of behavior make use of social history, interviews or other personal contacts, and comments and recommendations from others. Information from various psychological tests or inventories may or may not be included. This clinical material is then used to form an impression of what a person is like and how he or she might act in the future.

The actuarial method employs statistics to identify certain parameters about the person's background and behavior that have been found to be related to the behavior being predicted. These parameters might include age, measurable past behavioral patterns, gender, scores on psychological tests, and occupation. Once these parameters have been identified statistically, probabilities are offered, or critical cut-off points are drawn, relative to the person's future behavior. This process is independent of the evaluator's personal bias or clinical intuition. For example, the actuarial method might predict, on the basis of background and past behavior, that an individual being considered for parole represented a 65% statistical probability of committing another criminal offense within two years. If the parole board has established an objective criterion that anyone with a 50% or higher probability will be denied parole, the actuarial method dictates a decision against parole. In ideal form, the actuarial method is highly objective and mechanical in both data collection and application.

The conceptual difference between clinical judgment and the actuarial or statistical method disappears, however, when the data collection and application become mixed. Hare (1985, 1996) and his colleagues (Hart, Kropp, & Hare, 1988; Serin, Peters, & Barbaree, 1990; Hare, McPherson, & Forth, 1988), have developed a "psychopathy checklist" which, among other things, has been found to predict recidivism on parole. A correctional psychologist might administer this test, but ultimately might offer a clinical judgment based upon impressions garnered from interviewing the inmate and experiences with other similarly situated inmates in the past. Therefore, despite the fact that the test was carefully constructed and based on extensive research with accompanying statistical tables outlining accuracy probabilities in predicting recidivism, the psychologist's recommendation may be swayed by clinical hunch.

On the other hand, the opposite could happen. Data collection may be predominantly clinical in nature, but the psychologist might use specific objective criteria in offering a prediction. For example, the psychologist might obtain vague responses to inkblots and other ambiguous stimuli or ask the individual to respond to hypothetical dilemmas ("What would you do if you were on parole and got a chance to leave the country and start life over again?"). However, in making a final recommendation, the psychologist might be swayed by the inmate's performance on Robert Hare's Psychopathy Checklist.

The debate over which method (in pure form) is superior in accuracy of prediction has existed at least since the mid-1920s (Sawyer, 1966). Thirty years later, Paul Meehl (1954, 1965) brought the controversy to the forefront. Meehl incurred the ire of many clinicians when he concluded, after surveying approximately two dozen studies comparing statistical with clinical predictions, that the statistical methods were clearly superior in predictive accuracy. Subsequent reviews (e.g., Mischel, 1968; Goldberg, 1968, 1970) also found that clinical wisdom was faulty when compared to objective methods of arriving at overall prognostic or diagnostic decisions. Yet, studies have shown that people have a remarkable disregard for statistical data when they make judgments about others (e.g., Kahneman & Tversky, 1973; Nisbett et al., 1976), preferring hunches, intuition, and case-specific information over statistical base rates and tables.

Numerous legal questions have been raised about the use of both statistical and clinical decision making. Tonry (1987) who has summarized them concisely, believes the troubling issues are more ethical than legal, however. Courts have given wide berth to official actions based on prediction. "There are virtually no constitutional impediments to the use of prediction and classification devices in the criminal justice system . . . . The absence of controlling statutes and constitutional doctrines means that analyses of the appropriateness and use of predictions and classifications my be phrased in ethical and policy terms" (1987, pp. 382–383). ▶ [We will discuss the actuarial and the clinical methods of prediction in more detail in the next chapter.]

Clinicians and Researchers

The evidence-gathering distinction between clinicians and researchers within psychology parallels differences in their work settings and, to some extent, in their goals. Researchers are generally affiliated with universities as professors and researchers, or with various research institutions and laboratories. Both federal and state agencies and the private sector also make liberal used of experimental psychologists. The Federal Aviation Agency (FAA), for example, employs psychologists to test the effect of illumination on the readability of control panel dials. Corporations which market products to the general public employ them to test the effect of various advertising approaches.

Clinicians also may be affiliated with industry, often to offer consulting services in employee selection or counseling. Most, though, are in private practice or are associated with mental health agencies, court clinics, correctional institutions, law enforcement agencies, and social service agencies. Clinicians who provide services directly to various aspects of the law often call themselves **forensic psychologists**. Although this is a generic term, those who work closely with law enforcement agencies sometimes prefer to be called **police psychologists** and those working in corrections prefer the title **correctional psychologist**. Increasingly, though, the term "forensic psychologist" is used for those psychologists whose professional time is spent providing direct services to the criminal and civil justice systems.

Clinical psychologists have a practical goal: to determine the nature of a problem and to develop an effective way of solving it. For example, the police psychologist may be faced with developing a workable, valid method for the screening and selection of police candidates. The forensic psychologist may evaluate defendants for criminal courts or be asked by a law firm to advise its partners how to select a jury most favorably inclined toward their client. The correctional psychologist may provide psychological treatment for inmates or help in classifying them for both custody and treatment purposes.

Researchers in psychology, who are usually professors at colleges and universities, have a more generalized goal, one common to all sciences: to amass enough knowledge about a phenomenon to be able to understand and predict it, with an accuracy rate substantially above chance. A researcher studying aggression in the laboratory tries to understand it enough to be able to predict when it will occur. Ideally, clinicians use the information obtained by the researchers and add it to their own procedural evidence, as well as attempt to make predictions.

Before 1988, most psychologists in the United States were members of the American Psychological Association (APA), totaling 67,000 members. However, goal differences between researchers and practitioners (clinicians) prompted many of the researchers to form their own organization in 1988, the American Psychological Society (APS). Currently (2003), there are approximately 155,000 members of the APA and 12,000 members of the APS.

Research and the Legal System

Researchers and clinical psychologists both have much to offer the legal system, as long as the information is presented accurately and with appreciation for the complexity inherent in human behavior. The legal system, as we are using the term here, refers to courts, both civil and criminal, law enforcement agencies, adult and juvenile corrections, and a wide array of administrative agencies. Psychology's contributions will encompass not only direct services to this system but also relevant knowledge in such areas as group behavior, the ability to make decisions, personality typologies, stress, the causes and prevention of crime, and the treatment and rehabilitation of criminal behavior. It is important to note that a legal system that operates in an organized, sequential, and coordinated manner does not exist. Like many other "systems," it is plagued with disorganization, conflict, and ambiguity and is neither smooth running nor inevitably characterized by logical processes. On the other hand, the interdependency of its units and its efforts to achieve some degree of organization must be recognized.

Psychological Theory

As we noted earlier in the chapter, one of the frustrations of doing research in psychology and law is its lack of an anchor, which is partly due to the paucity of theories behind which to rally. Often we find a mass of studies in a given area with no unifying theme. Yet the basic goal of psychological research is theory development, not the unsystematic accumulation of facts. As the philosopher of science Thomas Kuhn (1970) observed, scientific history does not support the contention that science is doing research for its own sake without theoretical commitment. Scientific development depends upon at least "some implicit body of intertwined theoretical and methodological belief that permits selection, evaluation, and criticism" (Kuhn, 1970, pp. 16–17).

A theory is "a set of interrelated constructs (concepts), definitions, and propositions that present a systematic view of phenomena by specifying relations among variables, with the purpose of explaining and predicting the phenomena" (Kerlinger, 1973, p. 9). Psychological theory, therefore, purports to explain and predict human behavior. It offers a general explanation that systematically connects many different behaviors or observations. Moreover, "a theory which is not refutable by any conceivable event is nonscientific" (Popper, 1962, p. 36).

Therefore, as a scientific explanation of behavior, a psychological theory must be able to be tested, falsified, and refuted. The terms in any scientific theory must be as precise as possible, with their meaning and usage clear and unambiguous. Vague and imprecise theories are not falsifiable and hence cannot be tested scientifically. The advantage of vague theory, however, is that it can live on, on borrowed time, without running the risk of being tested and found inadequate. Freudian and neo-Freudian theories are good examples, because they cannot be refuted by the methods of science. How can one "disprove" the existence of the unconscious, the basic element of Freudian theory? The proponents of Freudian theory, then, can remain unchallenged by empirical data. Testable theories, on the other hand, draw heavy empirical scrutiny and critical comment; many fall by the wayside, and nearly all experience extensive revision.

As a result, scientifically powerful and heuristic theories which have the capacity to lead us toward explanations and predictions of behavioral phenomena are under constant revision and reconstruction. To the lay person, they appear fragmented and complicated, and they communicate excessive tentativeness and caution. Untestable theories, on the other hand, offer generalizations which appear to provide answers for human dilemmas, but they are more philosophical than scientific in nature.

The position taken in this book is that the avenue toward explanation and prediction is paved with scientific theory, which promotes experiments, evaluation, and criticism. The development of scientific theory represents the greatest challenge to psychologists studying the legal system today.

Psychologists and Psychiatrists

In the pages ahead, we will review briefly how psychologists interact with the legal system and some of the problems connected with the many roles they take. Prior to any discussion of these roles, however, the reader must be made familiar with the differences between psychology and psychiatry, two of the main professions which try to understand human behavior at the level of the individual. Social workers, nurses, and other mental health professionals, of course, should also be included in the list, but the public does not seem to confuse their disciplines as much as it does psychology and psychiatry. Nevertheless, it is important to note that various mental health professionals are often involved in the clinical work we will be discussing throughout the text. Someone with a Master's Degree or Doctoral Degree in Social Work (MSW or DSW), for example, may be found providing assessment or treatment to various forensic populations. Correctional casework, as well as group treatment in both adult and juvenile settings, is often provided by social workers. Substance abuse counselors, who may hold a Master's Degree specifically in that field, are other examples of professionals working in forensic settings. Thus, while we do not discuss these professionals in detail here, students should be aware of their important contributions.

Many psychiatrists, like psychologists, are closely associated with law, although primarily from a *clinical* perspective. These psychiatrists are often referred to as forensic psychiatrists. In some areas, such as issues relating to insanity determinations by the court, psychiatrists are more visible than psychologists. Law-related *research*, however, tends to be conducted much more by psychologists. It should be emphasized that the following presentation is an abbreviated sketch of the two disciplines and their perspectives. Furthermore, the lines between the two professions are becoming increasingly blurred. For example, one of the major distinctions between these two professions has been the license to prescribe psychoactive drugs. Traditionally, psychiatrists—because of their medical training—could do so, while psychologists could not. Now, even that distinction has changed. On March 6, 2002, New Mexico Governor Gary Johnson signed legislation into law authorizing properly trained psychologists to prescribe psychoactive drugs to patients. This legislation made New Mexico the first state in the country to pass such a law. At this writing, four other states in the country have legislation pending on the issue of extending prescription privileges to psychologists: Georgia, Illinois, Hawaii, and Tennessee. Psychologists in Guam gained prescription privileges in 1999.

Clinical psychologists and counseling psychologists, along with psychiatrists, are trained to provide direct services to persons with emotional, cognitive, or behavioral problems. The "problems," of course, may be relatively minor and transitory; in fact, it is estimated that the vast majority of adjustment problems faced by individuals can be solved in relatively short time. In the United States, for example, the national mean length of psychotherapy is between five and six sessions across a broad array of presenting symptoms (Phillips, 1988).

In order to be a practicing psychologist (such as clinical or counseling psychologist) in the United States and Canada, certain educational, training, and licensure requirements must be met. The practice of psychology is protected by state laws and regulations administered by each state's professional licensing board. The Association of State and Provincial Psychology Boards (ASPPB) has published a booklet entitled *Entry Requirements for Professional Practice of Psychology: A Guide for Students and Faculty*. It contains information on the legal requirements for entry into the practice of psychology. The booklet provides a summary of the typical licensing requirements, information on how to meet these requirements, and information relating to the content of the national exam, called the *Examination for Professional Practice in Psychology* (EPPP). The American Psychological Association (APA) recommends that individuals be eligible to sit for licensure upon completion of the following education and training (Williams, 2002):

- A doctoral degree in psychology from an APA-accredited or CPA (Canadian Psychological Association) accredited university.
- The equivalent of two years of organized, sequential, supervised professional experience, one year of which is an APA- or CPA-accredited

> predoctoral internship. It is recommended that professional training, whether at the predoctoral-level practicum, internship, or postdoctoral level, needs to be organized, sequential, and well supervised with ongoing evaluation of competence in a breadth of professional areas.

The APA expects that all internships that meet the requirement be APA- or CPA-accredited by 2010. The requirements for practicing school psychologists are slightly different.

Psychiatrists are medical doctors (MDs) or, in some cases, doctors of osteopathy (DOs) who specialize in the prevention, diagnosis, and treatment of mental, addictive, and emotional disorders. The American Board of Medical Specialties (ABMS) recognizes both a general specialty certification in psychiatry and, as of 1992, the sub-specialty of forensic psychiatry. This certification also paved the way for the American Board of Psychiatry and Neurology (ABPN) to grant broad board certification in forensic psychiatry in 1994 (Sadoff, 2001). Parenthetically, the American Psychological Association recognized forensic *psychology* as a sub-specialty in 2001. The psychiatrist undergoes the rigors of three or four years of medical school followed by a three- or four-year psychiatric residency, with training in the handling of psychiatric patients. The specific requirements of the residency depend on state, institutional, and professional standards, and to some extent on personal preference. To qualify for the certification in forensic psychiatry, sanctioned by the American Board of Psychiatry and Neurology, the physician must have already been certified as a psychiatrist. He or she may apply for certification in forensic psychology after one year of ACGME (Accreditation Council of Graduate Medical Education) approved residency training in forensic psychiatry.

Traditionally, the training adopts the medical model approach to diagnosis and treatment, including strong reliance on drug treatment. This orientation is not surprising, considering the fact that medical school training has been in the basic biological sciences, such as anatomy, biochemistry, physiology, genetics, microbiology, and cell biology.

According to the *medical model*, psychological abnormality is conceptualized as being analogous to physical disease, and like physical disease, it is classified and treated. Thus, we get the term "mental illness." The classifications are published in the psychiatric profession's *Diagnostic and Statistical Manual* (DSM), now in its fourth edition (DSM–IV) (American Psychiatric Association, 1994). The manual is used widely by psychiatrists and by many psychologists as well. DSM classifications are revised periodically, new disorders are added, and old ones are sometimes removed.

Psychiatrists often accept diagnostic categories as disease categories and treat the behaviors (e.g., hearing voices, compulsive hand-washing, excessive fear of open spaces) as symptoms of a mental disease that, like physical disease, requires medication. Others consider these behaviors to be symptoms of a disorder or a problem in adjustment that may or may not require medication. The medication prescribed is typically in the form of psychoactive drugs, which exert a direct effect on the brain. Today, *exclusive* reliance on the medical model seems to be waning, and drugs, if needed, are seen as a supplement to various forms of psychotherapy. Nevertheless, while there is still considerable concern about the over-prescription of psychoactive drugs and their side-effects, many mental health professionals note that properly prescribed, these drugs have potential for relieving suffering and pain. We will return to this issue at several points in the text, because it represents an important and controversial area in the intersection of law and psychology.

Careers in Psychology

There were an estimated 500,000 psychologists worldwide in the early 1990s, twice the number reported in 1980 (Rosenzweig, 1992). Most of the psychologists in the world are practitioners who are concerned with the application of psychology to human problems. In the United States, there were about 90,000 licensed practicing psychologists in 1995 (Robiner & Crew, 2000), and another 10,000 licensed practicing psychologists in Canada (Hunsley, Lee, & Aubry, 1999). In 1992, only 62,000 to 82,000 psychologists throughout the world reported research as their primary or secondary work activity, and most of them (about half) were in the United States and Canada (Rosenzweig, 1992).

Most of the psychologists in the U.S. and Canada have doctorate degrees. The vast majority have Ph.D.s, while others have the Psy.D. (Doctor of Psychology), a degree that concentrates more on the applied aspects than the research aspects of psychology. The median number of years of full-time study from the baccalaureate to the doctorate in the U.S. is 6.9 (Nixon, 1990).

Careers in Forensic Psychology

The practitioner or applied side of psychology has traditionally been subdivided roughly into four specialties: clinical, counseling, school, and industrial/organizational psychology. In August 2001, the Council of Representatives of the American Psychological Association voted to recognize forensic psychology as a fifth specialty. Before that vote, "it was ultimately decided that the petition for specialization should define forensic psychology narrowly, to include the primarily clinical aspects of forensic assessment, treatment, and consultation" (Otto & Heilbrun, 2002, p. 8).

During the past 20 years, the field has expanded dramatically, with training in forensic psychology at the graduate school, predoctoral, internship, and postdoctoral levels (Otto & Heilbrun, 2002) (■ see **Box 1-5** and ▲ **Table 1-1**). In recent years, a discernible expansion has occurred in the number of doctoral programs in clinical and counseling psychology that offer at least one or more courses or internships in forensic psychology. However, relatively few graduate programs offer formal training exclusively in forensic psychology. In other words, very few programs offer a degree specifically called "forensic psychology," although there are clearly

BOX 1-5
Graduate Training in Psychology and Law

In the 1960s, some colleges and universities in the United States began to establish joint programs in law and another academic area. These programs allowed students to pursue a degree in law (J.D., or Doctor of Jurisprudence) while simultaneously completing requirements for a graduate degree in business, education, economics, or psychology, among others. The first Law and Psychology graduate program began at the University of Nebraska in 1974, and persisted for some time as the largest and most diverse program in the field (Melton, 1990). Eight other programs followed: Johns Hopkins Department of Psychology and the University of Maryland Law School (established in 1979), Hahnemann University Department of Mental Health Services and Villanova College of Law (1979), University of Arizona (1981), Stanford University (1982), University of Hawaii (1989), the University of Minnesota (1989), Widener University and the Delaware School of Law (1989), and the Northwestern University Law School and Northwestern Medical School (1990).

The prospective student in a majority of the psychology and law graduate programs must be admitted to both the law school and the department of psychology. **Table 1-1** lists those universities and colleges in the United States and Canada which continue to offer degrees, concentrations, or a research focus in either psychology and law or forensic psychology. The programs sometime offer a variety of combinations of degrees concentrating on psychology and law, forensic psychology, legal psychology, and correctional psychology. At this writing, no colleges or universities offer a doctoral degree program in police psychology.

Programs are continually changing in focus, research interests, and degrees offered, so interested students should consult specific colleges and universities for updated information. Students are also encouraged to go to the web site of Division 41 (Psychology and Law) of the American Psychological Association, at www.psyclaw.org for further information.

TABLE 1-1

Colleges and Universities Offering Graduate Programs in Psychology and Law

University or College	Location	Degree(s) Offered
Alliant International University	CA	Psy.D., Ph.D. Forensic Psychology
Argosy University	DC	M.A. Forensic Psychology
California Professional School of Psychology–Fresno	CA	Psy.D. Forensic Psychology
Castleton State College	VT	M.A. Forensic Psychology
Chicago School of Professional Psychology	IL	M.A. Forensic Psychology
Dalhousie University	Canada	Ph.D. Clinical Psychology*
Drexel University/Villanova University School of Law	PA	J.D./Ph.D. Psychology and Law
Duke University	NC	J.D./M.A. Psychology and Law
Florida International University	FL	Ph.D. Legal Psychology
Florida State University	FL	Ph.D. Social Psychology*
Fordham University	NY	Ph.D. Clinical Psychology*
John Jay College of Criminal Justice	NY	M.A. Forensic Psychology
Marymount University	VA	M.A. Forensic Psychology
Northwestern University	IL	J.D./Ph.D. Psychology and Law
Pacific Graduate School of Psychology/Golden Gate Univ. School of Law	CA	Ph.D./J.D. Psychology and Law
Queen's University	Canada	Ph.D. Forensic Psychology
Sage Graduate School	NY	M.A. Forensic Psychology
St. Louis University	MO	Ph.D. Social Psychology*
Sam Houston University	TX	Ph.D. Forensic Clinical Psychology
Stanford University	CA	Ph.D./J.D., J.D./M.A., Ph.D./M.L.S. Psychology and Law
Tiffin University	OH	M.A. CJ & Forensic Psychology
University of Alabama	AL	Ph.D. Clinical Psychology*
University of Arizona	AZ	J.D./Ph.D. Psychology and Law
University of British Columbia	Canada	Ph.D. Forensic Psychology
University of Denver	CO	M.A. Forensic Psychology
University of Illinois at Chicago	IL	Ph.D. Social, Clinical, Community*
University of Kansas	KS	Ph.D. Social Psychology*
University of Nebraska–Lincoln	NE	J.D./Ph.D. Psychology and Law Ph.D./M.L.S.Psych & Legal Studies
University of Nevada–Reno	NV	Ph.D. Social Psychology*
University of Texas El Paso	TX	M.A. Clinical Psychology*
University of Virginia	VA	Ph.D. Clinical, Community*
Widener University	PA	J.D./Psy.D. Psychology and Law

* Program has a concentration or research focus in legal psychology, psychology and law, or forensic psychology.

more Master's programs that do so than doctorate programs. Although there are few formal doctoral programs in the discipline, the American Board of Professional Psychology has awarded Diplomate status in Forensic Psychology since the mid-1980s. A "diplomate" is a professional designation signifying that a person has been certified as having advanced knowledge, skills, and competence in a particular specialty. Diplomate certification in forensic psychology attests to the fact that an established organization of peers has examined and accepted the psychologist as being at the highest level of excellence in his or her field of forensic practice.

In this text, **forensic psychology** will refer to the professional *application* of psychological knowledge, concepts, and principles to civil and criminal justice systems. It includes such areas as police psychology, the psychology of crime and delinquency (criminal psychology), correctional psychology (including institutional and community corrections), risk assessment for the schools, custody determinations, victim services, and the delivery and evaluation of intervention and treatment programs for juvenile and adult offenders. The key word in our definition of forensic psychology is "application." For a better organization of the extensive material to be covered in this book, the term "psychology and law" will be used to encompass all aspects of psychology as it relates to the law, especially the empirical research investigating the many topics of law. Because the text will be heavily research-based, there will be extensive research citations throughout the chapters. The term "forensic psychology" will be restricted to the application of psychological research to the legal arena, such as psychological assessment, criminal profiling, implementation of treatment programs for juvenile and adult offenders, jury selection, expert testimony, legislative and governmental policy, and other clinical and consultation services.

Many national and state certification boards have emerged during the past ten years, such as the American Board of Psychological Specialties (ABPS), which is affiliated with the American College and Board of Forensic Examiners. Criteria used by the various boards and organizations to grant credentials or titles vary widely (Otto & Heilbrun, 2002). Note that certification usually requires knowledge and competence in both the applied and research components of the discipline, but certification is largely for those psychologists who provide services to the courts.

In 1991, the American Academy of Forensic Psychology and the American Psychology-Law Society published the *Specialty Guidelines for Forensic Psychologists* (SGFP) (Otto & Heilbrun, 2002). "The primary goal of the SGFP is to improve the quality of forensic psychological services by providing guidance to psychologists delivering services to courts, members of the bar, litigants, and persons housed in forensic, delinquency, or correctional facilities" (Otto & Heilbrun, 2002, p. 7). ■ **Box 1-6** provides a list of psychology-law related organizations.

Psychologists with training in clinical psychology are the most active in the legal system, and they likely constitute the greater part of persons who identify themselves as forensic psychologists. The clinical psychologist generally has a Ph.D.—an academic degree requiring intensive study of research methods, psychological theory, assessment, and psychotherapeutic methods. In addition to academic training, the clinical psychologist typically experiences nine or twelve months of supervised internship in a clinical setting, where the theories and methods acquired in graduate training can be applied to human behavior problems or mental disorders. The counseling psychologist has received much the same training as the clinical psychologist, including the internship. In the past, the major distinction between the two was their

BOX 1-6
Selective Professional Organizations Related to Psychology and Law

American Academy of Forensic Psychology
American Academy of Forensic Sciences
American Association of Correctional Psychology
American College of Forensic Examiners
American College of Forensic Psychology
American Psychology–Law Society (Division 41 APA)
The Society for Police and Criminal Psychology

BOX 1-7
Divisions 18 and 41 of the American Psychological Association

Division 18—Psychologists in Public Service—is concerned with the needs of the public in areas such as psychological practice, research, training, and policy development. The Division consists of five sections representing a variety of settings: (1) community and state hospital psychologists; (2) psychologists working in criminal justice settings (such as corrections); (3) psychologists working in police and public safety settings; (4) program evaluation; and (5) veterans affairs (VA) psychologists. The Division and its sections provide a forum for members to discuss common professional interests, to advocate for the mental health needs of the public, and to promote the use of evaluation and research in public research programs. Members receive the newsletter *Public Service Psychology* three times a year.

Division 41—American Psychology-Law Society—addresses the contributions of psychology to the law and legal institutions, the education of psychologists in legal matters and of law personnel in psychological matters, and the application of psychology to the civil and criminal legal systems. The division holds a biennial spring meeting that includes paper and plenary sessions. Members receive the *American Psychology-Law Society* newsletter three times a year, along with the bimonthly journal *Law and Human Behavior*.

Students—both undergraduate and graduate—may become student members of both divisions, as well as the American Psychological Association (APA). For further information, contact division@apa.org or go to the web site www.apa.org.

focus. The counseling psychologist evaluated and treated adjustment problems, such as those relating to education, job, and personal relationships. The clinical psychologist evaluated and treated the more serious behavior problems. This distinction is rapidly becoming blurred, however, and there is now considerable overlap in their respective focus.

The industrial/organizational psychologist is routinely involved in personnel selection, human factors in machine and equipment design, executive development, consumer research, organizational working conditions, and retirement counseling. The training for this specialty usually involves a heavy emphasis on research design, statistics, knowledge of the research literature as it relates to organizations, and a one-year internship within a relevant organization.

School psychology is a specialty involved in the diagnosis and reduction of social, emotional, and cognitive problems of school-aged children. These psychologists work not only with children with problems but also with parents, teachers, and school administrators. Many such psychologists do not have the Ph.D. or other doctorate degree, but many states provide certification and licensing for school psychologists who have the requisite masters and internship within a school setting.

Psychology and the Courts

Any of the specialties described thus far may include some contact with the judicial system. As we have noted, the forensic psychologist or forensic psychiatrist is most likely to be associated with direct, day-to-day interaction with the courts. Nevertheless, the science of psychology as a whole has much to offer the judicial system. It is worthwhile at this point to comment upon what it can offer as well as on its limitations, or what it cannot.

Psychology cannot provide absolute truths or easy answers. Instead, it has many partial, often tentative answers embedded in probabilities. Research psychology is largely nomothetic as opposed to idiographic in scope. The **idiographic approach** emphasizes the intensive study of one individual. The

nomothetic approach focuses on the search for general principles, relationships, and patterns by combining data from many individuals. Therefore, research psychologists are generally cautious in responding to questioners who demand simple, certain answers or solutions to complex issues pertaining to individual cases. Moreover, the principles and theories proposed by psychology are confirmed only through the collection of consistent and supporting data, a process that not only is long and rigorous, but is also punctuated by debate and differing interpretations of the data. "History suggests that the road to a firm research consensus is extraordinarily arduous" (Kuhn, 1970, p. 15). Psychological theories or "truths" are arrived at primarily through experiments that employ methods emphasizing prediction, measurement, and controlled comparisons.

Courts, like psychology, are concerned with predicting, explaining, and controlling human behavior, but much of the relevant and extensive research available in psychology today is unknown to them, as well as to the legal system as a whole. Daniel Yarmey (1979, p. 10) noted that what Munsterberg, the first forensic psychologist, wrote in 1908 continued to hold toward the end of the 20th century. Munsterberg claimed:

> The court would rather listen for whole days to the "science" of handwriting experts than allow a witness to be examined with regard to his memory and his power of perception . . . with methods . . . of experimental psychology. It is so much easier to be satisfied with sharp demarcation lines . . . ; the man is sane or insane, and if he's sane, he speaks the truth or he lies. The psychologists would upset this satisfaction completely.

Courts look for simple facts that are directly and specifically applicable to the case at hand. To some extent, the psychologist can provide some of these facts. For example, she or he can testify that a defendant achieved a certain score on a psychological test, that the psychologist has treated a defendant for a mental disorder, or that a child displayed distrust or fear of an adult. Many facts that the psychologist can testify to are facts about research findings to date. Because of the complexity of human behavior and the nature of the scientific enterprise, however, these are necessarily tentative. Thus, when courts ask whether an offender will be violent, the psychologist can only provide probabilities, if even that. Even more difficult is the issue of ultimate opinion testimony, which courts often seek from those who are recognized experts in their field. They might ask, for example, which parent should be given custody of a child, or whether a defendant was sane at the time of a crime. For many psychologists, these are legal decisions they should not be making. ▶ [This issue will be discussed more fully in Chapter 3.]

The judicial process demands certainty, or at least the appearance of it, in the courtroom. Because scientific hypotheses and generalizations lack this conclusive certainty, they are held suspect by professional participants in the legal system. Authoritative experts who offer certainty are much preferred over empirical psychology and its cautious approach. As we will note in later ▶ chapters, psychiatrists and clinical psychologists who are willing to make absolute statements and to offer strong opinions and conclusions often are the parties invited to consult in both criminal and civil cases. Many mental health practitioners too often have testified in line with the court's wishes, without emphasizing that caution and tentativeness are required in light of the inconclusiveness of present knowledge.

The Adversarial Model

Research psychology, directed by theory, arrives at "truth" and scientific knowledge through the accumulation of data derived from experiments that emphasize precision, measurement, and control of an array of variables that potentially may contaminate outcomes. Law, on the other hand, uses the adversarial process, which assumes that the best way to arrive at truth is to have proponents of each side of an issue present evidence most favorable to their position. The contenders confront one another in the courtroom, where truth is tested and refined through the "fight" theory of justice (Frank, 1949). It is assumed that justice will prevail once each side has had the opportunity to present its version of the evidence to a neutral decision maker—the judge or the jury. It is assumed, also, that "objective" truth about human behavior cannot be acquired from only one version. Instead, different versions of the truth are sought which, when put together, allow for judgment within an acceptable margin of error.

The adversarial model presents problems for forensic and research psychologists. Not only does it concentrate only on one case at a time, but it also encourages lawyers to dabble in and out of the data pool and pick and choose the segment of psychological information they wish to present in support of their position. The lawyer may select only part of an experiment and present the material out of context. Even in cross-examination, the opposing lawyer may be unaware of the real context or of contradictory findings. This procedure allows distortion and misrepresentation of research findings, since the lawyer's main concern is to provide the decision maker with evidence that will be favorable to the lawyer's client. Therefore, by using legal skill—but without having to appreciate the goals of science—lawyers can apply almost any psychological data in the service of their position. The adversarial model relies not necessarily on truth, but on persuasion (Haney, 1980). Adversary proceedings have the advantage of avoiding the dangers of unilateral dogmatism, but we cannot forget that the essential purpose of each advocate is to outwit the opponent and win the case (Marshall, 1972).

Most psychologists agree that the most desirable role for the psychologist who is called on to be an expert witness is to be an "impartial educator" (McCloskey, Egeth, & McKenna, 1986). Many experienced psychologists, however, contend that this role is extremely difficult if not impossible to maintain. For one thing, there are pressures from the attorney who hired the psychologist. For another, even when the psychologist is court-appointed and is acceptable to both sides (as might happen during pre-trial proceedings), the presiding judge presses him or her to provide dogmatic, "yes" or "no" answers.

To some extent, a more representative view of the research can be presented to the courts during the appellate process, when the interested parties file briefs outlining in detail the evidence supporting their position. ▶ [As we will note and discuss in Chapter 3,] the American Psychological Association has been very active in this brief-writing process. The process makes it more likely that a deciding court will have all available information at its disposal.

Psychologists and Criminal Justice

The criminal justice system is a bureaucracy comprising interacting parts or subsystems—law enforcement, the courts, and corrections (Cole, 1992). It comprises all the institutions, agencies, and processes that deal with violations of the criminal law, and it is by far the most heavily studied component of the legal system. We have already discussed the work of psychologists in courts, including criminal courts. In this section, we focus on police and correctional psychology.

Police Psychologists

Consider the following scenarios:

- Police officers and their significant others are attending a workshop on the stress that is unique to relationships between police and their partners. Participants role-play situations they encounter in their personal lives. A consulting psychologist leads the subsequent discussion.
- A staff psychologist in a metropolitan police department is summoned to talk with a person threatening suicide. Later in the day, the psychologist provides therapy for a police captain becoming increasingly disenchanted with his job and home life.
- A police chief decides not to hire a police officer candidate, partly on the basis of the results of psychological tests that pointed to potential behavioral problems.
- A juvenile charged with burglary is participating in a "family conference," led by a community psychologist. Also present during the conference are the juvenile's parents, the victims of the crime, and a police officer who specializes in work with juveniles.
- A SWAT team called to a hostage situation is accompanied by a police psychologist. During the situation, officers ask the psychologist if she thinks the suspect will really hurt a hostage. In other words, can the suspect be

talked down, or should officers storm the building to rescue the person held captive?

The above examples underscore the need for the services and skills of psychologists in law enforcement. Police are the first line participants in the criminal justice system. Some approaches to psychology and law neglect law enforcement, yet these officers are the agents who interrogate witnesses and suspects, gather a large portion of the evidence in criminal cases, and use their discretionary powers in making arrests and handling potentially dangerous situations. Moreover, police officers are more likely to be eyewitnesses to a crime and even to influence society about the concept of justice. Psychology would be remiss if it failed to study the psychology of law enforcement with the goal of improving the quality of these first line participants in the legal process.

Police psychology is the research and application of psychological principles and clinical skills to law enforcement and public safety (Bartol, 1996). However, the term "police psychology" is imprecise because it implies that the focus is strictly on the police, to the exclusion of other law enforcement agencies, such as deputy sheriffs, fish and wildlife officers, airport security, marshals, and many other types of federal agents. The term "law enforcement" is more encompassing. Still, even that term has its critics, who argue that police do more than enforce the law; they insure public safety through crime prevention and provide a variety of other services. Thus, for our purposes, we will retain the term police psychology as an all encompassing one that includes all agencies and organizations dealing with law enforcement and public safety.

As police agencies have become more professional, police supervisors more educated, and the public more critical and concerned, there has been a substantial increase in the need for forensic and research psychologists to become more involved in pre-employment psychological assessment, fitness-for-duty evaluations (FFDEs), special unit evaluations, discretionary decision making, hostage team negotiations, and deadly force evaluations. Special unit evaluations include the selection and training of special weapons and tactical teams (SWAT), tactical response teams (TRT), and hostage negotiation teams (HNT). Forensic psychologists are also asked to do investigative-type activities, such as criminal profiling, psychological autopsies, hand-writing analysis, and eyewitness hypnosis.

In a survey of 152 police psychologists (Bartol, 1996), 89% of the respondents said they had Ph.D. degrees, followed by Ed.D. degrees (4.5%), master's degrees (3.6%), and Psy.D. degrees (2.7%). Most of the Ph.D.s obtained their degrees in clinical psychology (60.7%), counseling (17%), or industrial/organizational psychology (8%). Twenty-five percent of the respondents were women. Participants in the nationwide survey were also asked to indicate the type of services they provided to police during a typical month, as well as the amount of time they usually spent in each activity. Respondents said that pre-employment screening and assessment consumed the largest percentage (34.3%) of their time. A significant amount of time was also spent in providing services to officers and their families (28.7%), followed by fitness-for-duty evaluations (6.8%), training of personnel (6.9%), and administrative work (3.9%).

Correctional Psychologists

The correctional system is divided into two main components: institutional and community-based corrections. The former is what most people envision when they think of corrections: a tightly controlled living situation behind walls. ▶ [As we will describe in Chapter 10,] however, there is great variation in the physical features of correctional institutions. Community-based corrections refers to the supervision of offenders in the community. It encompasses probation and parole, together with their many variants. Persons on probation and parole, for example, may be living in their own homes or in half-way houses, and may or may not be electronically monitored.

Correctional psychologists work closely with inmates, probationers, and parolees, administering a wide variety of psychological assessment techniques (intellectual, personality, aptitude, vocational, and educational), interpreting results, and preparing comprehensive reports. They are also involved in the development, organization, and administration of individual and group therapy and other rehabilitative programs for treatment of a variety of behavioral problems. Correctional psychologists also offer counseling services to staff, particularly correctional officers who are in most direct contact with inmates.

Research psychologists often study the psychological effects of correctional systems on prisoner behavior. Topics include the general effect of imprisonment on special populations of offenders, such as the mentally disordered or the elderly; the effects of crowding; the effects of isolation; and the outcome of various rehabilitative programs. Interestingly, psychologists in this setting are often criticized for aligning themselves with prison administrators or failing to acknowledge the detrimental effects of incarceration (Roberts & Jackson, 1991).

Psychologists have been active in many facets of the correctional system for more years than in the courts or in law enforcement settings, but their track record of successful change, particularly in the institution, has not been remarkable. This is partly due to the nature of the beast: the correctional system teams with overworked, underpaid, and sometimes undertrained personnel. Its institutions are often outmoded and overcrowded; the working and living settings are depressing and hardly conducive to optimism and promise. Psychologists working in these settings are often confronted with ethical dilemmas which challenge their commitment to rehabilitation.

In this text, we will not portray the relationship between psychology and corrections only with negativism, however. There is ample evidence to support the positive impact of psychology on the correctional system. Despite earlier pessimistic reports about the outcome of treatment programs, for example, some forms of psychological intervention are documented to be effective (Gendreau & Ross, 1991). Psychologist Hans Toch and his colleague Kenneth Adams (Toch & Adams, 1989a, 1989b, 2002), for example, have demonstrated that psychologists working in the correctional system can help prisoners cope with their environment and take concrete steps toward positive change. We will discuss these and other psychological approaches to rehabilitation in ▶ Chapter 12.

Psychology and Criminal Behavior

The causes of crime are multiple. A good grasp of criminal behavior requires combined research from all relevant academic disciplines, including psychology, sociology, psychiatry, anthropology, history, philosophy, biology, and economics. Depending upon one's perspective, crime might be due to economic conditions, violence in the media, deteriorating neighborhoods, inequality and discrimination, family dysfunction, chemical imbalances, or the materialistic values promoted by society, among many other factors. From a psychological perspective, criminal behaviors are acquired by daily living experiences, in accordance with the principles of learning. Each person perceives, codes, processes, and stores these experiences in memory in a unique way. The psychology of crime, therefore, is primarily concerned with how criminal behavior is acquired, evoked, maintained, and modified. However, it is important to remember that human behavior is complex. The caution often seen in psychology's approach to law is especially apparent when we focus on the understanding of criminal behavior.

In addition to understanding the causes of crime, psychologists also suggest and evaluate prevention and treatment strategies directed at reducing criminal behavior in both adults and juveniles. For example, what forms of treatment are effective for which juvenile offenders? What is the likelihood that "shaming" a white-collar offender by heavily publicizing his crime will be effective in deterring him from committing additional crimes? What psychological factors are at work in domestic violence situations or in child sexual assault? Cognitive-social approaches to crime will be emphasized in this book, not only because they offer a contemporary psychological viewpoint, but also because these approaches recognize the many complexities and variables involved in any human behavior.

Summary and Conclusions

This chapter has introduced readers to the plan and goals of the book and to psychology as the science of mental processes and behavior. We have seen that, with caution and with appreciation for the complexity of human behavior, the various segments of the legal system can benefit substantially from psychological knowledge. The book will consider separately psychology's potential contributions to each sector—law enforcement, the civil and criminal courts, criminal behavior, and corrections, both institutional and community based.

The legal system is an assortment of components built primarily on the moral, social, and political perspectives of society. It is highly pragmatic, conservative, and traditional in outlook and process. This is because law cannot respond to every fad or zeitgeist on the horizon; to do so would create the uncomfortable risk of losing its cultural, traditional, and moral bearings. Responsive innovation and excessive creativity would promote legal fluidity, which would raise havoc with the consistency, structure, and orderliness currently existing in the system. Therefore, lawyers and judges are taught to be intellectually conservative, but able to weave legal tapestry based on previous decisions. Occasionally, courts will break radically new ground, either by over-turning long-standing precedent or by interpreting constitutions or statutes in creative ways that reflect the spirit of the times. The landmark cases of *Brown v. Board of Education* (1954) and *Roe v. Wade* (1973) are cases in point. The law generally views the science of psychology with suspicion and skepticism, occasionally utilizing segments of scientific or empirical findings only if advantageous. Therefore, it is unrealistic to expect that the scientific contributions of psychology, as outlined in this text, will be embraced eagerly. What we can hope for is a slow, gradual acceptance of some of the information psychology uncovers, reports, and consistently supports through well-designed research study.

The three possible relationships between psychology and law were outlined. The psychology *in* law relationship, the one most typical today, probably will have limited influence advancing and integrating psycholegal research into the system. Here, law dictates to psychology what it wants and when it wants it, and law proceeds to interpret the material as it wishes. Psychology *and* law, which presumes an equal partnership between the two disciplines, is best suited to the advancement of psychological knowledge in relation to the judicial system.

Psychology and the law arrive at "truth" in decidedly different ways. Truth for psychology is gained through the scientific methods of hypothesis testing, sound methodological construction, quantification, systematic observation, and an attempt at objective interpretation of the data. "Truth" is, of course, an ideal which is seldom reached.

Law, by contrast, relies on the adversarial process to discover "truth." The ambiguity of the law encourages participants to present their best case in a combative fashion. If the law were clear and concise, the adversarial process would be severely undermined. Lawyers selectively choose precedent and current folklore or science to build their case and present their clients in the most favorable light. The chapter outlines the method of science—including its concepts, definitions, and strategies—and how it is used within both the courts and the social sciences. The *Daubert* case provides a convenient linchpin for describing both perspectives. The text will be highly research-based and will follow the many winding pathways of law that the social science research literature takes.

Science rarely provides firm conclusions. Rather, it offers building blocks, limited in scope, toward knowledge. The reader will soon discover in this book that the social sciences offer only segmented, partial answers to complicated, but intriguing puzzles of human conduct. With patience and a very high tolerance for ambiguity, psychology has become an increasingly valuable source of knowledge for the law.

Key Terms

A priori method
Adversarial model
Confounding variable
Correctional psychologist
Deposition
Ecological validity
External validity
Forensic psychologist
Forensic psychology
Idiographic approach
Internal validity
Meta-analysis
Method of authority
Method of science
Method of tenacity
Nomothetic approach
Police psychologist
Procedural evidence
Reliability
Summary judgment
Therapeutic jurisprudence
Validating evidence
Validity

Questions for Review

1. Define and contrast the three relationships between psychology and the law.
2. State the *Daubert* standard for admitting expert testimony in federal courts.
3. How did the U.S. Supreme Court clarify the *Daubert* standard in *General Electric Company v. Joiner* and in *Kumho Tire v. Carmichael*?
4. What four standards for deciding reliability were outlined in *Daubert*?
5. Define and provide one illustration of each of the following: the experimental method, quasi-experimental designs, survey research, meta-analysis, and legal research.
6. Distinguish between internal and external validity and provide an illustration of each.
7. Distinguish between procedural and validating evidence and provide an illustration of each.
8. Define forensic psychology, and discuss the ways in which the field has expanded over the past 20 years.
9. In addition to forensic psychology, give examples of other specialized areas of applied psychology.
10. Give examples of tasks performed by psychologists consulting (a) with courts, (b) with police, and (c) in corrections.

CHAPTER 2

Psychological Assessment, Testing, and the Law

Psychological assessment and psychological testing have become indispensable to the legal system, and as a consequence the number of commercially available assessment measures and tests for forensic applications has increased dramatically in recent years (Otto & Heilbrun, 2002). The two terms, *assessment* and *testing*, are not synonymous. **Psychological assessment**, which also may be called psychological evaluation, refers to all the techniques used to measure and evaluate an individual's past, present, or future psychological status. It usually includes interviews, observations, reviews of case files and records, and various measuring procedures that may or may not include psychological tests. **Psychological testing**, a narrower term, refers specifically to the use of psychological measuring devices. Thus, to use an illustration that encompasses both concepts, a child custody assessment or evaluation might include: (1) mental status and bio-historical interviews of the adults and minor child(ren); (2) psychological testing of the child(ren) and possibly the adults as well; (3) observations of the interaction among the adults and the minor child(ren); and (4) assessment of significant others (Weissman, 1991). As Matarazzo (1990, p. 1000) states: "Psychological assessment . . . is engaged in by a clinician and a patient in a one-to-one relationship and has statutorily defined or implied responsibilities."

Overview of Assessment and Testing

The primary goal of psychological assessment is to reduce the complexity of human behavior to a manageable set of variables so that past and present behavior can be appraised and some parameters of future behavior can be predicted. It is important that this reduction process be undertaken under standardized conditions so that scores and observations of one individual are comparable to other individuals. Psychological tests are usually only one component of the assessment process. They come in different formats and have specified goals. Several tests at a time, usually called "test batteries," are often administered to an individual. Some tests are designed to measure intelligence (the so-called IQ tests), while others try to gauge aptitudes, interest patterns, mental competency, developmental patterns, neuropsychological functioning, malingering, or personality.

In criminal law, specifically relating to criminal courts, assessment and testing are important in at least *five* areas. *First*, they play a major role in the arrest and pre-trial process, when a psychologist may evaluate a defendant's competency to waive legal rights, plead guilty, or stand trial. *Second*, when a defendant raises an insanity defense or a diminished capacity defense, the evaluation of his or her mental state at the time of the crime is crucial. *Third*, assessment and testing are used to help courts determine a defendant's dangerousness to self or others for the purposes of making bail decisions. *Fourth*, the victim of the crime may undergo assessment and testing as evidence that a crime did indeed occur, such as in the case of children. *Fifth*, assessment and testing may provide invaluable information in the sentencing phase of a criminal trial, particularly when the judge is interested in knowing about an offender's amenability to rehabilitation. In sex offense cases, for example, where limited sex offender programs are available, a judge might order the offender to be examined to see whether he would be a good candidate for such a program.

Assessment and testing also have a place outside of the court process, however. Both police and correctional psychologists make extensive use of these techniques. Some criminal justice agencies rely on the psychologist to help make screening, selection, and promotional decisions. Law enforcement candidates and already-employed personnel are often given psychological tests designed to depict their intellectual and emotional functioning. So far, metropolitan police departments have been at the forefront in studying and adopting such procedures, but there is a growing nationwide trend toward using psychological assessment in smaller and rural departments. The psychological assessment of correctional officers is less common, although there is little doubt that it should be considered if corrections are to employ competent, adaptable personnel.

Assessment and testing of jail and prison inmates are also very common. Ideally, the psychological evaluation of offenders should provide valuable insights into the development and treatment of criminal behavior and some understanding of the psychological effects of short-term and long-term imprisonment. It should also help in determining and evaluating rehabilitative strategies and assessing the risk the inmate presents to other inmates and correctional staff. ▶ [As we will see in Chapter 10], the assessment and classification of offender populations has a history of mixed success (Gearing, 1979) but has made considerable progress over the past two decades.

In civil cases, psychological assessment and testing have long been used to determine whether individuals are able to care for themselves or are in need of psychological treatment. Courts today must make judgments about the need for confinement in a mental institution or for treatment services within the community. To make appropriate decisions, they turn to psychologists and psychiatrists for guidance. Heilbrun (1992) points out that psychologists are increasingly asked to assess competencies to consent to medical treatment or research and to enter into a contractual relationship. They are participating in the disability determination process and the process of determining compensation for mental injuries. In family law, in addition to psychological assessment in child custody decisions situations, psychologists are consulted in abuse and neglect determinations, juvenile delinquency dispositions, and end-of-life issues.

Increasingly, assessment and testing procedures are used to determine parental suitability for child custody, to appraise a person's ability and capacity to make wills, or to determine eligibility for federal and state benefits on the basis of mental or emotional incapacity. Work-related personal injury litigation, where plaintiffs seek compensation for an injury allegedly suffered on the job due to negligence on the part of an employer, is a rapidly growing area where assessment plays an integral part. Forensic assessment is also crucial in determining the extent of emotional injury evaluations. Claims of emotional injury in the form of pain and suffering, mental suffering, or emotional harm are often raised in personal injury, harassment, discrimination, disability, and malpractice cases (Boccaccini & Brodsky, 1999).

Personal injury suits need not be job related, of course. For example, let's assume that a fictitious character, Jack Ziggle, is an expert skier. At Killer Mountain, however, he loses control, allegedly because of exposed rocks on the trail, crashes into a tree, and incurs substantial brain damage. Jack sues Killer Mountain, Inc., arguing that it was negligent in carrying out its responsibility to keep the ski trail free of hazards. If the judge or jury agree, the extent of his injuries will be taken into account in assessing the damages—or amount of money—the corporation will have to pay. In cases such as this, the psychological assessment of brain injury and nervous system functioning—a field called forensic neuropsychology—has become almost indispensable (Doerr & Carlin, 1991). The forensic neuropsychologist, retained by the Ziggle family, examines Jack to evaluate the extent of his neurological disability and its long range effects on job opportunities and overall adjustment to society. The corporation, of course, will likely search for another neuropsychologist who will find less disability.

Neurological disabilities are not as straightforward as physical loss, such as the loss of a limb or the complete loss of an organ of sensation. Insurance companies have manuals already listing the usual compensation for the loss of a limb or eye. Neurological impairments, however, are far from clear-cut, and the assessment procedures are often expensive and time consuming. Part of the problem is that disability evaluators and insurance agents have little or no training in the recognition of neurological disorders (Glass, 1991). Another problem is that the psychological and cognitive changes are so subtle that they are sometimes difficult to detect.

In other examples, psychological assessment and testing are frequently used throughout the educational system, not only to measure intelligence and aptitude, but also to diagnose learning disabilities. They also appear in the screening and selection of personnel in business and industry and the military, along with the aforementioned criminal justice system.

This partial list of the various uses of psychological assessment illustrates its pervasiveness. We do not really know the amount or type of testing that goes on nationwide, particularly in forensic settings (Heilbrun, 1992). ■ **Box 2-1** shows the assessment instruments most commonly used by clinical psychologists in the United States [from Camara, Nathan, & Puente, 2000]. We must recognize, though, that there are numerous problems associated with assessment and testing in all of the areas discussed above, as will become clear in the pages ahead.

Generally, psychology's relationship with law vis-à-vis assessment is one of psychology *in* the law. Judges, lawyers, law enforcement and correctional administrators use and interpret the information they have requested of the examiner. The relationship is one maintained for the most part by clinical psychologists and psychiatrists, seldom by research psychologists. In some settings, however, examiners have such a long-standing, mutually respecting relationship with those who seek their services that the relationship could more accurately be termed psychology *and* the law.

Over the years, psychological assessment and testing techniques have generated a spectrum of social concerns and considerable legal scrutiny in both civil and criminal cases. In the civil arena, questions of unfair employment practices, discrimination, and invasion of privacy have been at the forefront. In criminal cases, the issue of self-incrimination has been extremely troubling. Self-incrimination refers to acts or declarations, either as testimony at trial or prior to trial, by which a person implicates him- or herself in a crime.

One purpose of this chapter is to acquaint readers with the many concerns society has, or should have, about assessment methods, particularly psychological tests. Another is to address misunderstanding about the strengths and weaknesses of tests and related procedures. Many of the psychological

BOX 2-1
The Top 11

Following are the psychological tests most frequently used by clinical psychologists who regularly perform psychological assessments in forensic settings:

1. Wechsler Adult Intelligence Scale—Revised WAIS–R
2. Minnesota Multiphasic Personality Inventory–2
3. Wechsler Intelligence Scale for Children—Revised (WISC-R-III)
4. Rorschach Inkblot Test
5. Bender Visual Motor Gestalt
6. Thematic Apperception Test (TAT)
7. Wide Range Achievement Test—Revised and III
8. House-Tree-Person (H–T–P) Projective Technique
9. Wechsler Memory Scale—Revised
10. Millon Clinical Multiaxial Inventory
11. Beck Depression Inventory

Source: Camara, Nathan, & Puente (2000).

assessment and testing instruments have been carefully developed, are backed by considerable research, and have reasonable validity. Many others, however, even those that are commercially sold, lack the reliability, validity, and research support that they should have. In this chapter, we will review some of the basic concepts and applications of psychological measures, with particular attention directed at recently developed forensic measures.

However, the chapter is not intended to provide comprehensive information about specific assessment methods. It is merely a review, description, and evaluation of testing as it relates to the law and forensic issues. Still, some of the more provocative issues surrounding the use of assessment within the legal system will be addressed. ▶ [Additional assessment procedures and psychological tests will be covered in subsequent chapters.]

Forensic Classifications of Assessment and Testing

The chapter will be organized around three general classifications of assessment and testing instruments and techniques, proposed by Kirk Heilbrun, Randy Otto, and Richard Rogers (Heilbrun, Rogers, Otto, 2000; Otto & Heilbrun, 2002). The three categories are: (1) clinical measures and assessment techniques; (2) forensically relevant instruments (FRIs); and (3) forensic assessment instruments (FAIs). The three categories reflect the degree of direct relevance the various tests and techniques have to specific legal issues. For example, the first category, clinical measures and assessment techniques, were developed for the assessment, diagnosis, or treatment planning of clinical, school, or other populations. While important, they were not developed *specifically* in response to legal questions or forensic concerns. They have been developed to assess such things as learning disabilities, emotional or mental disorders, personality traits, aptitude, academic achievement, occupational success, and psychopathology. Consequently, when instruments in this category are used in the forensic arena, it is important that the examiner be particularly skillful and trained in applying the results of the instrument to the legal questions at hand. Far too often, however, psychologists seem to administer tests indiscriminately without a clear idea of how the information gathered will address the substantive issues related to the law (Brodzinsky, 1993).

In the second category, *forensically relevant instruments*, Otto and Heilbrun place those measures and techniques that were designed for research and the identification of certain behavioral, emotional or mental characteristics, but may have considerable direct applicability and relevance to the forensic setting as well. Examples include instruments and techniques to assess malingering or lying, violence risk assessment, and psychopathy.

The third category, *forensic assessment instruments*, "are measures that are directly relevant to a specific legal standard and reflect and focus on specific capacities, abilities, or knowledge that are embodied by the law" (Otto & Heilbrun, 2002, p. 9). Examples include those measures designed to evaluate a criminal defendant's competence to stand trial or an older person's ability to manage legal, financial, and health care matters. The most common forensic assessments in criminal trials are those for competence to stand trial (CST). At least 25,000 criminal defendants are referred annually for CST assessments, probably representing the largest category of psychological assessments in criminal courts (Otto et al., 1998). Competence to stand trial refers to the defendant's current ability to understand legal proceedings and to assist his or her lawyer in planning and conducting a defense. Criminal responsibility, by contrast, refers to the defendant's mental state at the time of the alleged offense.

We will discuss, in a very broad way, instruments and techniques in each of the three categories—general clinical, forensically relevant, and forensic tests and assessments—throughout the remainder of the chapter ◙ **Box 2-2** provides examples of tests that fall into each of these three categories. The specific applicability and relevance of each of the measures to legal topics will be covered more thoroughly in later chapters. ▶ [For example, measures of competency and criminal responsibility will be discussed in Chapter 4, risk assessment measures in Chapter 5, and measures of psychopathy will be discussed in Chapter 10.] Before proceeding, however, it is important that the basic concepts of testing and psychological measurement be presented.

BOX 2-2
Assessment Measures and Techniques—Some Examples

Clinical Measures
- MMPI-2
- Millon (MCMI)
- Rorschach
- Wechsler Adult Intelligence Scale (WAIS)
- Wechsler Intelligence Scale for Children (WISC and WISC-R)
- Thematic Apperception Test (TAT)
- Personality Assessment Instrument (PAI)

Forensically Relevant Measures
- Psychopathy Checklist Series (PCL, PCL-R)
- Rey Visual Memory Test
- Risk Assessment Measures (e.g., HCR-20; VRAG)

Forensic Assessment Measures
- Competency Assessment Measures (e.g., CAI, GCCT, MacCAT)
- Criminal Responsibility (insanity) Measures (e.g., R-CRAS)
- Assessments of Competency to Waive Rights
- Bricklin Perceptual Scales (child custody)

Basic Concepts of Psychological Testing

Psychological tests have many limitations and flaws. If used properly, however, they can be important tools for evaluating intellectual functioning, measuring personality, and describing emotional or psychological status. Testing is a process of reducing the complexity of human behavior to a manageable set of variables so that past and present behavior can be described and future behavior can be predicted. It is a complex enterprise, and procedures vary widely according to the population being tested and the preferred methods of the examiner. Testing basically involves the quantification of a sample of behavior obtained under standardized conditions, with the level of quantification and the degree of standardization varying from test to test. Some tests require a well-trained examiner and must be administered under such highly controlled conditions that they are similar to scientific experiments. Other tests are less standardized and may be given by an untrained examiner, sometimes to large groups.

The four most important concepts to understand in psychological testing—and psychological assessment in general—are reliability, validity, normative distribution, and standard error of measurement. Any testing instrument should be judged according to each of those concepts, whether they are clinical measures, forensically relevant measures, or forensic assessment measures.

Reliability

Reliability refers to the consistency of measurement: a test is reliable if it yields the same results over and over again. A test's reliability may be measured in one of three ways. If different parts of the same test yield the same results, this is **internal consistency**. If the same test yields the same results when administered to the same person at two different times, this is **test-retest reliability**. If the test produces the same results when scored or interpreted by different clinicians or examiners, it is high in **inter-judge reliability**. A highly reliable test will meet all three criteria, but in reality, psychological tests rarely produce identical results again and again. A mathematical index, known as a **correlation coefficient**, is computed to determine the degree to which a test comes close to producing the same results.

A correlation coefficient is mathematical shorthand for describing the relationship one variable has to another. A correlation coefficient tells us two important things about a relationship: (1) the magnitude

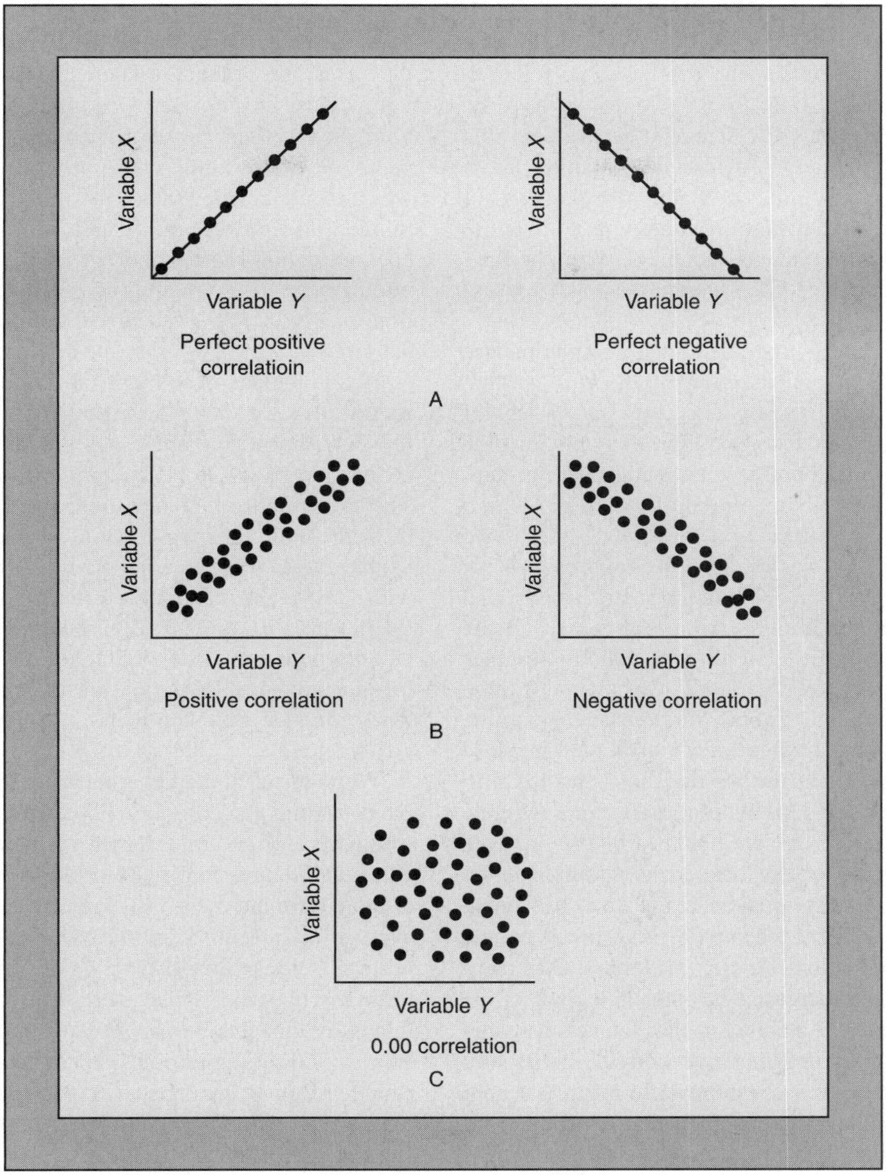

Figure 2-1

Scatter diagram showing (A) perfect positive and perfect negative correlations, (B) positive and negative correlations, and (C) a 0.00 correlation.

of the relationship; and (2) the direction of that relationship. ⊠ (See **Figure 2-1.**) The magnitude is expressed by a number (coefficient) ranging from .00 to 1.00, with 1.00 being a perfect correlation and .00 representing no relationship at all. You have probably had the experience of taking the Scholastic Aptitude Test (SAT), required for admission to many colleges and universities. If the correlation coefficient between the SAT and a student's subsequent grade point average (GPA) were 1.00, then we could predict with 100% accuracy a person's GPA on the basis of his score on the SAT. A zero correlation, on the other hand, would mean there was no relationship; that is, a person's SAT score would have no power in predicting GPA. It would be like guessing a student's GPA without knowing anything about that student. Reliability coefficients in the field of testing range somewhere between these two extremes. The correlation coefficient between the SAT score and subsequent GPA is believed to be approximately .50.

The correlation coefficient also communicates something about the direction of the relationship. Direction informs us what happens to one variable if the other variable changes. For example, as the number of capital punishments increase, what happens to the violent crime rate in the country? Direction is expressed either by a positive (+) sign or a negative (−) sign. For instance, we might see a correlation coefficient of −.70 in a research article, and another of +.50. If one variable changes and the other changes in the same direction (both variables increase or decrease together), we have a positive relationship. As long as both variables change in the same direction, regardless of whether they increase or decrease together, the relationship is positive. In a negative relationship, by contrast, as one variable changes the other variable changes *in the opposite direction*. In the violent crime rate example given above, many observers—believing that the death penalty has a general deterrent effect—would expect a negative correlation. That is, as the number of capital punishments increase, the rate of violent crime should decrease. Actually, social science research does not support this negative correlation (Bohm, 1999). A positive relationship would mean that both the number of capital punishments and the rate of violent crime would go up, or both would go down—also not strongly supported by research. As we will see in ▶ Chapter 10, though, some studies have documented a "brutalizing effect," in that violent crime increases following an execution (Bohm, 1999).

When two variables *are* highly correlated, a common mistake is to assume that one *causes* the other. It is important to realize that *correlation does not imply causation*. A correlation coefficient only tells the degree to which two variables vary together. For example, if a researcher finds a high correlation between high socioeconomic class and intelligence (as measured by a standardized intelligence test), the researcher cannot assume that high socioeconomic class *causes* one to be intelligent, or that intelligence causes higher levels of socioeconomic status. Socioeconomic class *may* be the cause, but we cannot conclude that solely on the basis of a correlation. Moreover, other variables related to socioeconomic class may also have an influence on intelligence. These would include quality of education, nutrition, and exposure to cultural enrichment activities.

Psychological examiners prefer to use psychological tests that have the highest test-retest reliability correlation possible. A test-retest reliability correlation of .90, for example, is usually regarded as solid evidence that subsequent administrations to the same individual would yield very similar results. Within legal contexts, it is not advisable to use a test with a test-retest reliability coefficient of less than .80 (Heilbrun, 1992). Generally, the lower the reliability, the poorer the validity. If the test is also high in inter-judge reliability and in internal consistency, the test has been well developed and solidly constructed.

When the attribute being measured is itself unstable over time, the correlation coefficient will be low. Compare, for example, measurements of intelligence and depression. Intelligence is expected to be a stable attribute over time. If Lucretia scores above average in December and below average in March, we can suspect that something is wrong with the testing instrument. If we were trying to measure a relatively unstable personality attribute like depression, however, we would expect to find different scores from one testing session to another. The fluctuations in scores would reflect mood changes or significant life events that may have occurred between testing dates. Therefore, we would expect a relatively high correlation coefficient in the first example and a lower coefficient in the second, because of the differing nature of personal attributes being measured.

Validity

The reliability of a test merely assures us that we have established a consistently accurate procedure of measurement. Before a test can be meaningful and useful, however, it must also have validity, which tells us whether it measures what it is supposed to measure. For example, if a psychological test is designed to predict how well applicants will perform in law enforcement, we must have evidence that the test in fact does predict this. If not, the test is meaningless, even though it may have very high reliability. Court decisions have barred the use of intelligence tests for the classroom placement of youngsters in school systems in Texas, California, and other states because they lacked demonstrated validity (Matarazzo, 1990; Elliott, 1987). Although we discussed validity briefly in ◀Chapter 1, we will study it in more detail here because it is the most important measure of testing. Like reliability, validity is usually expressed statistically through the computation of a correlation coefficient.

Among the more important forms or types of validity are concurrent and predictive, together called criterion-related validity. **Concurrent validity** is usually determined by comparing one test with another, already established one. For example, suppose we wished to determine whether a test we designed to predict success in law enforcement had concurrent validity. We would administer a test with an established track record of criterion-related validity and also administer our newly constructed test to a group of experienced police officers, and we would compare each person's scores on both tests. If the scores are similar, as determined by a high correlation coefficient (say, .80), we can conclude that our test has a high level of concurrent validity. Concurrent validity also may be established by determining whether our psychological instrument can obtain the same results as other, non-test criteria. For example, can the test results differentiate between poor and satisfactory police officers as rated by their supervisors? In this situation, we would correlate test results with on-the-job ratings provided by the supervisors. If the resulting coefficient is high, our test has good concurrent validity for distinguishing "good" police officers from "poor" officers.

Predictive validity is the degree to which a test predicts a person's subsequent performance on the dimensions and tasks the test is supposed to measure. If a test claims to be able to predict which candidates develop into good or outstanding police officers, its predictive validity should be high, discriminating those who *eventually* perform well from those who do not. If there is empirical evidence that the instrument does have predictive validity, a test is a powerful device for the screening and selection of candidates prior to entry into law enforcement. Obviously, a device that could do this would save both the candidate and the agency valuable time as well as potential difficulty and embarrassment. For example, suppose we have a very high incidence of stress-related disorders within a particular group of police departments. The stress disorders are not only interfering with job performance, but also are resulting in a high turnover rate. In an effort to identify both the stressors and the individuals most prone to stress, the psychologist administers a battery of psychological tests before the officers are hired. He or she then follows them over a number of years, collecting supervisory reports, the officers' own self-reports on stress, and any other information pertaining to stress measures. The psychologist then correlates the pre-employment measures with reported and observed stress levels, paying particular attention to those officers who leave or who perform poorly on the job. If all goes well, the psychologist should be able to identify those tests that predict poor reactions (or good reactions) to stress, and use those tests in future screening of police officers for those departments. This same procedure can be applied to business and industry, identifying those who remain with the company and work out well and those who do not.

We should be careful to add a note of caution with respect to the above illustration, however. The best way to deal with stress among employees may not be to screen out ahead of time those who are most susceptible to it. Rather, the best way may be to improve working conditions, thus minimizing the opportunity for stress to appear. An important thing to remember about predictive validity, therefore, is that it predicts adaptability to the status quo, or to the situation as it exists. The ideal situation may be quite different.

While psychometric (tests and measurement) experts have tried to perfect methods to establish criterion-related validity, representatives of the legal system are often more interested in the issue of **content validity**. "Content-related validity involves essentially the systematic examination of the test content to determine whether it covers a representative sample of the behavior domain to be measured" (Anastasi, 1988, p. 140). In law enforcement, for example, it is recommended that the test content be related to what the officer will encounter on the job, thereby supposedly tapping pertinent skills found in traffic investigation or judgment and reasoning needed to handle domestic disturbances. In pre-trial situations, some defendants are administered tests to determine whether they are competent to stand trial. Some of the recommended tests ask the defendant to explain the judge's role and the role of the attorney.

When emphasis is placed on content validity in this way, the behaviors considered important must be fully described in advance, rather than defined after the test has been prepared. Further, as in the law enforcement context, successful behaviors specific to the various demands of the job must be identified and delineated. Often, this content-validation approach eliminates the use of standard psychological tests and replaces them with made-to-order tests for law enforcement that may be high in content validity but untested as far as reliability and criterion-related validity are concerned. In the competency area, psychologist Thomas Grisso (1986, 1988, 1998) has made impressive strides in developing assessment instruments that are high in reliability, content validity, and criterion-related validity. There are obvious advantages to strengthening content validity, but care must be taken not to sacrifice the other criteria of a test's strengths.

Very often, too, "face validity" is confused with content validity. **Face validity** refers not to what the test actually measures, but to what it superficially *appears* to measure (Anastasi, 1988). If a test "looks valid," or if it appears to measure what should be measured, it has face validity. In reality, there may be no empirical support for these assumptions. Face validity does have some value, because examinees believe the exam is at least pertinent to the job for which they are applying. In addition, Randy Otto et al. (1998) emphasize the importance of face validity for application in the legal context, because any measuring instrument should look pertinent and relevant to the legal questions at hand. However, unless other types of validity are also ensured, a test has little overall worth in measuring what it is supposed to measure.

We should also realize that empirical verification of the reliability and validity of a particular test or assessment instrument may not be enough to convince a court of the soundness of the evidence it provides. For instance, when racial or gender discrimination is involved, a court may be inclined to disregard evidence obtained through the use of even well-validated tests (Heilbrun, 1992). In legal terms, its prejudicial value may outweigh its probative (or evidentiary) value. Thus, the overall extended impact of the discrimination will outweigh the accuracy of the test itself. For example, in employment situations, even if the selection procedure is validated, it may screen out all or most members of a minority group. A judgment may have to be made to allow these otherwise-qualified minorities the opportunity to demonstrate outstanding performance. Also, for any kind of testing or assessment, there is always the danger that the instrument will provide an inaccurate or misleading representation of an individual, or groups of individuals. Finally, psychological tests should not be used by themselves to make decisions. The material they provide should be used in conjunction with other information.

Normative Distribution

A test score by itself tells us little unless we know how other people have scored. Interpretation of results therefore requires that **normative distribution**—sometimes called norms—be developed before a test is put into general use. This is done by giving the test to a representative sample of the population for which that test is designed. The sample is called a standardization or normative group. The statistical position at which an individual scores within this normative group may be expressed in various ways, such as percentile rank or standard score. Knowledge about the standardization group is important because it enables the evaluator to determine if the results are generalizable to the individual or groups of individuals being tested.

Standard Error of Measurement

Joseph Matarazzo (1990), in his Presidential Address to the American Psychological Association, warned that psychologists are increasingly being challenged on the concept of the standard error of measurement of their assessment tools when testifying in the courtroom. When potentially high damage awards are at stake in injury litigation, courts are keenly interested in how much error there is in a test score. Recall in our discussion of the *Daubert* case in ◀ Chapter 1 that the U.S. Supreme Court included error rate as one of the standards for evaluating expert testimony.

The **standard error of measurement** (SEM), also called the standard error of a score, is an index of how much variation we can expect in a test score each time a person takes that same test. Let's assume that the SEM of a particular intelligence test is 5. If Lloyd receives a score of 110 on the test, the SEM informs us that we can expect Lloyd's score to vary between 105 and 115, 68% of the time, or two out of every three times he takes the test.

Clinical Measures and Assessment Techniques

When mental processes such as thinking, learning, perceiving, problem solving, and remembering are measured and evaluated, cognitive assessment is occurring. Ideally, this is accomplished by some combination of interviewing, behavioral observation, and testing. Many cognitive "assessments," however, are more accurately called cognitive "testing," since they consist only of the use of an intelligence or IQ test.

Cognitive Tests and Techniques

One of the first reliable and reasonably valid cognitive ability tests was developed by the French psychologist Alfred Binet. In 1904, Binet and psychiatrist Theodore Simon were asked by the Paris school system to design a test that could identify mentally defective children, who could then be taught effectively at a different pace than normal children. The resulting scale, consisting of thirty problems arranged in ascending order of difficulty, was called the Binet-Simon Scale. The test, which was revised shortly thereafter to establish satisfactory validity, attracted worldwide attention and was adopted and translated into many languages. In 1914, German psychologist William Stern suggested that Binet scores be expressed as a ratio of tested age (mental age score) over chronological age (actual age), multiplied by 100. A ten-year-old with a mental age of 15 would have an IQ of 150 ($15/10 \times 100$), for example. Thus was born the intelligence quotient, known today as the IQ.

In America, L. M. Terman, a psychologist at Stanford University, revised and adapted the test to suit an American population. This revision, first published in 1916, became known as the Stanford-Binet Intelligence Scale. It became the first published intelligence test to provide specific administration and scoring procedures, and the first American test to use the concept of IQ (Laurent, Swerdik, & Rayburn, 1992). An entirely new version of the Stanford-Binet (5th edition) (SB5) was published in 2003. The scale consists of 15 "subtests" that cover five major cognitive areas: general knowledge, fluid reasoning, quantitative reasoning, visual-spatial processing, and working memory. The scale is appropriate to use with children, ages 2 to 17, although the administration manual also includes norms for adults (18 to 85+). It has colorful and child-friendly artwork and manipulatives. The fourth and fifth editions, considered the favorite measure of ability by school psychologists because of their appeal to children, provide multiple IQ scores (called standard age scores or S.A.S.'s) instead of the single IQ score.

For many years, the Stanford-Binet was the most frequently used instrument to measure intelligence until clinical psychologist David Wechsler developed another group of cognitive ability tests (known as the Wechsler scales), beginning in 1939. Both the Stanford-Binet and the Wechsler series of scales have been updated and revised periodically, with the most recent versions having more culturally pluralistic norms. That is, the norms are based on a more representative sample of the general population, a feature that is very important in the eyes of the court. The Wechsler Adult Intelligence Scale (WAIS) was mostly revised in 1997 and is called the WAIS–III to signify "third edition." The WAIS–III measures cognitive functioning in adults with a chronological age between 16 and 89. The Wechsler Intelligence Scale for Children (WISC), first published in 1949, most recently revised in 1991 (WISC–III) is designed for children ages six through seventeen. The Wechsler Preschool and Primary Scale of Intelligence (WPPSI), first developed in the 1960s, and most recently revised in 2002 (WPSSI–III), is designed for children ages two-and-a-half to seven years, three months.

The Wechsler scales tap both the verbal and behavioral components believed to be required in intellectual functioning. For example, the WAIS–R consists of eleven subtests, each of which is assumed to measure a particular ingredient of intelligence. Six of the subtests relate to verbal intelligence, while five are designed to tap behavioral or performance intelligence. Together, the eleven subtests provide a Full Scale IQ. The examiner is thus able to determine the Verbal IQ, the Performance IQ, and the Full Scale IQ. Both the Stanford-Binet 4th edition and the Wechsler series treat intelligence as comprising a number of different abilities, rather than as one general ability or IQ score.

The Stanford-Binet and the Wechsler scales are individual cognitive ability tests, designed to be administered to one examinee at a time by a highly trained and certified examiner. Trained examiners are needed both because the standard of administration is complex and because behavioral observations add substantially to the assessment. Administration time varies, but the tests are usually completed within one hour to 90 minutes, depending on the age and skills of the examinee. Scoring, interpretation, and report writing usually take an additional two to four hours, but newly developed software scoring programs can often cut scoring time substantially. Individual intelligence scales, accordingly, require considerable time and expense, features that have helped stimulate the less expensive, more efficient group cognitive ability tests.

Group tests generally are paper-and-pencil instruments devised for administration to groups of people of various sizes. The convenience and economy of group tests have led to their use in schools and employment offices, in the selection and promotion of law enforcement personnel, and in many other mass-testing situations. One of the most popular group intelligence tests today is the Wonderlic Personnel Test, a 12-minute, easy-to-administer paper-and-pencil test that correlates highly with the WAIS. The Wonderlic was developed by E. F. "Al" Wonderlic in 1937 as part of his doctoral dissertation while at Northwestern University. Overall, the 50-item instrument appears to be an efficient method of assessing global intellectual capacity for both research and applied settings (Dodrill & Warner, 1988; Hawkins et al., 1990). It is used extensively as a quick measure of intelligence by personnel and human resource departments in many organizations and agencies. Approximately 130 million persons have taken the Wonderlic since it was first published. Administration, scoring, and interpretation usually do not require a highly trained examiner, and considerably less interpretation and scoring time are needed compared to individually-administered intelligence tests.

Other examples of group tests of intelligence include the Wide Range Intelligence Test (WRIT) published in 2000. The WRIT is designed to measure verbal (crystallized) intelligence, visual (fluid) intelligence, and general intelligence in ages four to 85 in about 30 minutes. The Slosson Intelligence Test-Revised (SIT-R), published in 1990 and updated with 1997 norms, is presumably free of significant demographic, racial, or gender biases in item content. It is appropriate to use with ages four to adult and takes about 10 to 20 minutes to administer. There are many more of these kinds of group intelligence scales.

While group tests provide a cognitive ability score generally comparable to individual tests (concurrent validity), they do not yield the rich behavioral observation and interpretation so characteristic of individually-administered tests. Also, because of minimal face-to-face contact, the examiner has much less opportunity to establish rapport, obtain cooperation, and maintain the interest of subjects, factors that may affect performance. Therefore, although group tests have undeniable advantages, their shortcomings cannot be overlooked. For thorough assessment, individual tests are more desirable, but because of their economy and practicality, group tests are administered more frequently. Most cognitive ability tests are designed to yield an average standard score of 100 and a standard deviation of about 15. A standard deviation is a statistical index that tells us how spread out the scores are

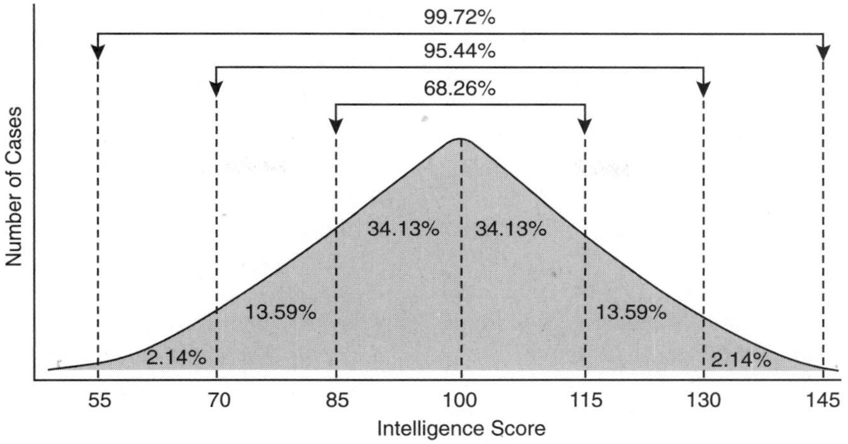

Figure 2-2

■ Distribution of intelligence scores in a normal curve.

around the average or mean score. An average of 100 and a standard deviation of 15 is based on the assumption that the population follows a normal distribution, where a majority of the examinees score somewhere around the middle and only a few score at the ends or poles of the distribution (see **Figure 2-2**). About 68% of the population falls between the IQ scores of 85 and 115. Approximately 95% scores between 70 and 130, and 99.72% between 55 and 145. A person who achieves an IQ score of 130 has scored higher than approximately 98% of the entire population.

As was noted earlier, some states have discontinued the use of cognitive ability testing in their school systems. In the legal context, results of cognitive ability tests are a critical component in the assessment of disabilities. Furthermore, they often appear in family law and criminal law contexts. A juvenile, for example, may be given a cognitive ability test and the results used to argue against his or her being transferred to an adult criminal court. Cognitive ability scores also appear in reports of pre-trial competency and sanity evaluations, presentence investigation reports submitted to sentencing judges, and prison records. Finally, cognitive ability tests are destined to take on a critical role in the death penalty context, because the Supreme Court has ruled that offenders who are mentally retarded may not be put to death (*Atkins v. Virginia*, 2002).

Cognitive Testing in Forensic Settings

This section describes which psychological measures are most preferred by psychologists when conducting forensic evaluations. Please keep in mind that most psychologists use a variety of techniques, measures, and procedures *in combination* when they do forensic evaluations. They may fall into any one of the three categories proposed by Otto and Heilbrun (2002). Furthermore, some psychologists prefer to rely on the interview and observations rather than formal measures for their evaluation of a child, a parent, victim, or defendant. This section merely tries to identify those psychological measures that will be most often discussed throughout the course of the book.

Randy Borum and Thomas Grisso (1995) surveyed experienced forensic psychologists and forensic psychiatrists regarding their use of psychological testing in evaluations for competence to stand trial. Competence to stand trial issues (abbreviated CST) refer to the defendant's mental state at the time of the trial or other judicial proceedings. A majority of the forensic clinicians (78% of the psychologists, and 57% of the psychiatrists) said they usually use the Wechlser Adult Intelligence Scale (WAIS) for evaluations of competence. Psychologists also reported that their second favorite cognitive measure for CST assessments was the Wechlser Memory Scale—Revised (WMS-R), followed by the Wide Range Achievement Test (WRAT), the Shipley-Hartford Institute for Living Scale, the Ammons Quick Test, and the Stanford-Binet.

Marc and Melissa Ackerman (1997) surveyed experienced mental health examiners concerning what psychological tests they used for child custody evaluations for adults (usually for parents) and children. When examiners tested adults, they strongly preferred the WAIS (48%), followed by the WRAT–R or third edition (10%), and the Shipley-Hartford (6%). And when they tested children, the examiners usually selected the Wechsler Intelligence Scale for Children (WISC) or the Stanford-Binet (S-B).

Marcus Boccaccini and Stan Brodsky (1999) surveyed psychologists who completed forensic assessments of emotional injuries. The cognitive instrument most heavily used by the experienced forensic psychologists was the Wechsler Adult Intelligence Scale (WAIS), with 50% of the respondents saying they used the test on a regular basis for such evaluations. Karen Budd and her colleagues (2002) examined the psychological evaluations done on children exposed to abuse or neglect (child protection cases) requested by an urban juvenile court system. They found that "cognitive measures" were conducted in 95% of the cases, while achievement tests were also conducted in 75% of the cases.

Personality Assessment

The term "personality" means different things to different psychologists, but common themes run through their definitions. The definitions of most psychologists focus on some relatively enduring psychological attributes of a person which can generally differentiate that particular person from others.

For example, almost all psychologists agree that some individuals are more anxious and tense than others across a variety of situations. In police work, it is commonly known that some officers respond to stress and life-threatening situations with greater levels of anxiety and agitation than others. They may also take longer to return to their usual day-to-day anxiety levels. Moreover, they consistently react this way under stressful conditions. The personality variable in this instance is anxiety, more commonly called nervousness. For our purposes, personality will be defined as "the combination of all of the relatively enduring dimensions of individual differences on which [the person] can be measured" (Byrne, 1974, p. 26). Personality measurement may be divided into two broad approaches: *projective* and *objective*. These two techniques are distinguished principally by the clarity of stimuli used to obtain responses from subjects.

Projective Measures

Projective measures are designed with the assumption that personality attributes are best revealed when a person responds to ambiguous stimuli. Since projective techniques were developed by psychodynamically-oriented theorists interested in delving into the hidden depths of personality, projective tests generally try to measure unconscious dispositions. Since there is no established meaning to the stimuli, these theorists propose that the responses of subjects reveal significant features about their personalities. Some of these personality features—perhaps even most of them—may be unknown to the respondent. Since psychodynamic theorists consider ambiguous stimulus material "the yellow-brick road to the unconscious," much of the material gained from projective tests is assumed to represent unconscious or subconscious components of the personality.

Some projective (ambiguous) test materials are very abstract, such as inkblots; others are more concrete, such as those depicting pictures of social situations. The most commonly used instrument representing the first category is the Rorschach, while the second category is represented best by the Thematic Apperception Test (TAT).

The Rorschach Developed several decades ago by the Swiss psychiatrist Herman Rorschach, this test is administered by a trained examiner who presents the examinee with a series of ten bilaterally symmetrical inkblots and asks the person to describe what each inkblot resembles or suggests. The response characteristics are used by the clinician as "signs" that reflect the individual's underlying personality dynamics. If you see a killer cyborg in an inkblot, for example, this is supposed to reveal something significant about your personality. Scoring and interpretation are complex tasks requiring different phases of administration and different levels of interpretation. Projective-trained clinicians rate the subject on areas like anxiety, hostility, neurosis, organic brain damage, and psychosis.

The Thematic Apperception Test At about the time the Rorschach was introduced, the American psychologist Henry Murray developed the Thematic Apperception Test (TAT), which consists of 29 pictures on separate cards and one blank card. The cards are presented one at a time, and the individual is instructed to make up a story suggested by each picture, complete with plot and characters. The respondent tells what the situation is, what has led up to the situation, what the characters are feeling and thinking, and what the outcome will be.

The Rorschach and the TAT both have been heavily criticized for their lack of objectivity in scoring and established validity. For example, Anne Anastasi (1988) strongly questions the validity of projective tests and suggests that they may be as much a projection of the examiner's biases, perceptions, and theoretical orientations as they are of the examinee's personality attributes. Their usefulness in the police, forensic, and correctional context is highly debatable, particularly where substantial criterion-related validation is required, as when predicting which candidates will perform well in law enforcement, or whether a defendant is dangerous. Extensive reviews of the research literature have failed to yield many encouraging signs for the empirical value or validity of projective tests (Grove & Barden, 1999; Lilienfeld, Wood, & Gard, 2001), and there is substantial evidence that other psychological instruments provide far more meaningful information for the assessment and prediction of human behavior. In fact, there is considerable evidence to suggest that the Rorschach is potentially highly inaccurate for diagnosis and prediction of behavior in general. After their extensive and thoughtful review of the research literature on projective techniques, Scott Lilienfeld and his colleagues asserted: ". . . we recommend that forensic and clinical psychologists either refrain from administering the Rorschach, TAT, and human figures drawings, or at least limit their interpretations to the very small number of indexes derived from these techniques that are empirically supported" (Lilienfeld et al, 2001, p. 56).

Moreover, the validity and research support for the Rorschach are so questionable that critics believe the instrument fails to meet even the basic requirements set forth by *Daubert* (Grove & Barden, 1999). Yet, the Rorschach has seldom been questioned in court proceedings, being excluded, for example, in only one case of the 7,934 cases using Rorschach testimony (Weiner, Exner, & Sciara, 1996). This infrequency of challenge regarding the Rorschach prompted Grove and Barden (1999, p. 229) to conclude "that very few attorneys conduct rigorous *Daubert* (or even *Frye*) hearings to exclude unreliable, junk science testimony." Not all psychologists, of course, are convinced that the Rorschach is without reliability and validity, and a significant number of clinicians firmly believe in its usefulness in a wide variety of contexts (see Weiner, 2001). In fact, the Rorschach controversy as it relates to the admissibility of expert testimony is the subject of feisty debate in the law and psychology literature.

Objective Personality Inventories

The other personality measure frequently used in clinical practice is the objective test. Basically, a test is objective to the extent that scorers can apply a scoring key and agree about the result. When all steps avoid bias on the part of the examiner who administers, scores, and interprets the tests, objectivity is assured (Mischel & Mischel, 1977).

The vast majority of objective personality inventories have a "self-report" format, meaning that the subjects are expected to respond "true" or "false" to brief statements or descriptions referring to their behavior or attitudes. Because the instruments require self-report responses, they are usually called "inventories" rather than "tests." As we described previously, the most widely-used self-report measure associated with the law is the Minnesota Multiphasic Personality Inventory (MMPI), an inventory also given in a wide variety of employment situations.

The Minnesota Multiphasic Personality Inventory (MMPI) The original MMPI (first published in 1942 and no longer in print) was an extensive (550 to 566 questions) paper-and-pencil inventory that required respondents to answer true or false to questions about themselves. The items sampled a wide range of behaviors, beliefs, and feelings, some of them very personal in nature. For example, questions were asked about religious preference and sexual, sleep, and other physiological habits. Items on the original MMPI were also dated, in that they use outmoded idiomatic expressions and references to literary material and recreational activities which are unfamiliar to most people. Moreover, sexist wording was common throughout.

Many psychologists were unhappy with the original MMPI for other reasons as well. The population used to establish the MMPI norms was highly selective, and did not represent adults from different regional areas, cultural settings, and ethnic and racial groups. Therefore, its applicability to ethnic and racial minorities was highly suspect. For years, however, professionals were reluctant to abandon the original MMPI because of the vast amount of irreplaceable data accumulated on it over years of research.

In 1989, after nearly seven years of research and development, the MMPI–2 was published with national norms that were much more representative of the current population of the United States. In addition, item content was changed to modernize wording and eliminate invasions of privacy, sexist questions, and ambiguity. The format, administration, scoring, and interpretation of the MMPI–2 were intended to be similar to the original MMPI, enabling clinicians to use the instrument in basically the same manner as its predecessor. ◙ **Box 2-3** summarizes differences between the two versions.

Criticism of the original MMPI's content was clearly warranted. Criticism of its validity, however,

BOX 2-3
MMPI–1 and MMPI–2—Key Differences

The original MMPI (the Minnesota Multiphasic Personality Inventory) was developed during the late 1930s and early 1940s at the University of Minnesota Hospitals. Its creators were Starke R. Hathaway, a clinical psychologist, and J. Charnley McKinley, a neuropsychiatrist. Hathaway and McKinley developed the scale primarily as a diagnostic tool that would aid in the classification of psychiatric patients. To construct the scale, they identified a criterion group of patients at the University Hospitals who had been assigned a variety of psychiatric diagnoses. A control (or normative) group comprised friends and relatives visiting non-psychiatric hospital patients, as well as some high school students and administrators.

The MMPI–2 was published in 1989 after seven years of research and development. Many features of the MMPI–2 are highly similar to the original MMPI, but MMPI–2 differs in two important ways.

- The content is different. Designers of MMPI–2 eliminated outmoded words or idiomatic expressions. They improved the grammar, punctuation, and general readability of the scale. New questions are less intrusive. Questions about religious beliefs, sexual behavior, and scatological habits are gone.
- The normative sample is more representative of the general population in the United States. The sample for the first MMPI was white, around 35, married, not generally educated beyond high school, and living in rural areas. The new sample represents all walks of life and a better distribution of ethnic or minority groups (81 percent white, 12 percent African-American, 3 percent Hispanic, 3 percent Native-American, and 1 percent Asian-American).

A special version of the MMPI for adolescents (MMPI-A) was released in August 1992.

seems unjustified and demonstrates lack of knowledge about the instrument's design and intention. Because we may see the same type of attack on the MMPI–2, it is important to address this issue. There is widespread misunderstanding of the original design and purpose of the MMPI, which has led to faulty application, particularly in the criminal justice system. Maloney and Ward (1976) and Dahlstrom (1972) pointed out that clinicians and researchers often confuse two types of assessment: that designed to identify abnormality and that designed to identify personality traits. The MMPI was designed to differentiate "abnormal" persons (as defined by society during the late 1930s and early 1940s) from "normal" persons. It was not intended to be a personality measure which would provide information about personality traits. This misunderstanding has meant that many experiments examining the MMPI's effectiveness to predict strong job candidates based on personality features have been poorly designed. In essence, the test is to be used to screen out inappropriate candidates, not screen in appropriate ones.

The MMPI has drawn the greatest amount of research attention of all psychological inventories. The typical evaluation study relates to the use of the MMPI in law enforcement, because the inventory is widely used in police selection. Much of this research has assumed, however, that the MMPI has the power to appraise both questionable emotional status and *normal* personality traits. Psychopathological detection and personality description demand different methods of assessment. Inventories that try to do both things seem destined for confusion and criticism; the MMPI is not such an inventory. It was intended primarily to detect abnormal behavior. The reader should keep this point in mind when reviewing studies that try to evaluate the MMPI's ability to depict police personalities, or even to distinguish "good" police officers from "bad" ones merely on the basis of these MMPI scores.

Other Objective Personality Measures The Millon Clinical Multiaxial Inventory (MCMI) (Millon, 1994) has limited utility when used with nonpsychiatric samples or for broad assessment questions. It is designed to be used by psychologists and other mental health professions for evaluation of emotional, behavioral, or interpersonal difficulties. Based on Millon's theory of personality, the MCMI–III measures 14 personality patterns that coordinate with DSM–IV Axis II disorders, and 10 clinical syndrome scales related to DSM–IV Axis I disorders. It also contains a validity index to help detect careless, confused, or random responding. The MCMI–III is brief and easy to administer, and it takes only 25 minutes for examinees to complete.

The Personality Assessment Inventory (PAI) (Morey, 1991) is a self-administered, objective inventory of adult personality that provides information on "critical clinical variables." The PAI contains 344 statements to which respondents are asked to rate the degree each statement pertains to them on a 4-point scale (1 = very true, 2 = mainly true, 3 = slightly true, 4 = false). Responses to statements determine scores on four validity scales, eleven clinical scales, five treatment scales, and two interpersonal scales. Research suggests that the PAI may be useful in predicting potential for violence, suicide, aggression, and substance abuse. There is also some evidence (concurrent validity) that the Antisocial Features (ANT) scale of the PAI may measure psychopathy (Edens, Hart, Johnson, Johnson, & Olver, 2000).

Personality Traits: Specific or General?

One of the ongoing controversies in psychology centers on whether personality characteristics are specific to certain situations or generalized across time and place. Is Brutus a timid person, or is he timid only under some conditions? This issue of specificity versus generality is especially relevant to psychological testing, because most testing procedures are predicated on the assumption that the attributes being measured are highly consistent. ▶ [We will also see that this issue is very important in criminal profiling, to be discussed in Chapter 14.]

Personality traits, which are more appropriately thought of as personality predispositions, can be understood only if both the person and the situation are considered. The expressions of a person's traits hinge on a given psychological situation (Mischel & Mischel, 1977; Bowers, 1973; Mischel, 1973). It is a generally held tenet in psychology that behavior results from a complex interaction between these personality predispositions and the situation. Therefore, the degree of consistency in our personality depends to some extent on the situations in which we find ourselves.

There are two crucial aspects to address in determining the consistency of personality traits, *cross-situational* (or trans-situational) consistency, referred to above, and *temporal consistency*, or consistency over time. The latter asks, if a person behaves a certain way now, will he or she behave essentially the same way a month, a year, or even ten years from now, in similar situations?

Consistency over time has never really been in dispute (Mischel & Mischel, 1977). Few psychologists seriously doubt that our lives have temporal consistency and coherence. Most people see themselves and others as relatively stable individuals who exhibit similar behavior over time—at least in dealing with, or responding to, similar situations.

Cross-situational consistency is more involved. Some research suggests our actions are often highly specific to the particular situation and may in fact be unique to that situation. For example, a highly competent and efficient judge may be relaxed and witty in the courtroom on a day-to-day basis, but her demeanor may change dramatically when she sentences an offender to prison. In light of the seriousness of that situation, she may become tense and humorless, though still competent and efficient. However, research focusing on traits has also reported much consistency across situations (Bem & Allen, 1974). In general, evidence indicates that people both discriminate and generalize their behavior as they interact with situations. Some people are consistent in some areas of behavior, but not in others; some are consistent only on some traits. It is quite clear, though, that none of us are consistent on all traits (Mischel & Mischel, 1977).

This intricate and highly individualistic interaction of personality and situation creates problems for psychologists interested in personality assessment. Traditionally, personality research and theory building emphasized the person to the exclusion of the situation. Traditional personality assessment theory (called trait psychology or psychodynamics) assumed that stable personality traits or personality structures were the center of the individual's universe; once these attributes were delineated, accurate prediction of that person's behavior was almost guaranteed. Thus, to say someone had an aggressive personality was to infer a corresponding list of behaviors, most of them negative. We are now realizing, though, that the situation and the meaning of that situation for the person are critical variables. Therefore, rather than relying on a global conclusion that a police candidate has an "aggressive personality," an agency would do well to try to determine how the candidate handles himself or herself in various situations. It is unwarranted to attach negative connotations to a personality label, which in fact tells us very little. Moreover, aggressive behaviors are sometimes necessary in some instances, while inappropriate in others.

The above discussion emphasizes that accurate assessment and prediction require not only an evaluation of the person (as advocated by trait and psychodynamic perspectives), but also an evaluation of the psychosocial environment within which the behaviors we are trying to predict occur. Failure to consider the context of the behavior is destined to result in drawing unwarranted conclusions.

Personality Inventories in Forensic Settings

Borum and Grisso (1995) in their survey of experienced forensic psychologists and psychiatrists found that the overwhelming choice of a personality measure for competence to stand trial evaluations was the Minnesota Multiphasic Personality Inventory (MMPI/MMPI–2). The instrument was used on a regular basis by 94% of the psychologists and 80% of the psychiatrists. The second most common personality measure of both groups for CST determinations was the Millon Clinical Multiaxial Inventory (MCMI) (32%), followed by the Personality Assessment Inventory (PAI) (6%).

The Ackerman and Ackerman (1997) survey of experienced clinicians who do child custody evaluations on a regular basis found that personality inventories most commonly used were the MMPI–2 (92%), followed by the Rorschach Inkblot Method (48%), the Millon Clinical Multiaxial Inventory (MCMI) (34%), and the Thematic Apperception Test (TAT) (29%). When testing children, the examiners preferred the Children's Apperception Test (CAT) or the TAT (37%), followed by the Sentence

Completion (29%), draw a House-Tree-Person (19%), and the Roberts Apperceptions Test (10%). The sum of the percentages exceeds 100 because examiners often use a number of different tests for any evaluation, sometimes called a test battery. Boccaccini and Brodsky (1999) estimate that forensic psychologists use four or five different measures per evaluation.

The Boccaccini and Brodsky (1999) survey of experienced forensic psychologists who completed assessments of emotional injuries in civil suits found that the personality inventories most commonly used were the Minnesota Multiphasic Personality Inventory (94%), the Millon Clinical Multiaxial Inventory (39%), the Rorschach (28%), the Beck Depression Inventory (18%), the Trauma Symptom Inventory (15%), and the Personality Assessment Inventory (14%). It should be noted that in the Boccaccini-Brodsky survey, psychologists were especially drawn to the Trauma Symptom Survey Inventory because of its convincing normative data, validity scales, and research support.

Budd et al. (2002), in their survey of psychological evaluations of children exposed to abuse or neglect in child protection cases, discovered that projective personality measures were used in over 90% of the cases. Objective personality inventories were used in only 19% of the cases.

In summary, the objective personality inventories or methods most frequently used by forensic psychologists involved in conducting evaluations for various legal cases are the MMPI–2, the MCMI, and the PAI. The projective measures most relied on are the Rorschach Inkblots and the TAT.

Forensically Relevant Instruments and Assessment Techniques

Instruments in this category, as explained previously, are not designed specifically to assess performance on specific legal standards. Rather, they focus on clinical constructs that are often pertinent to evaluating persons in the legal system (Otto & Heilbrun, 2002). An outstanding example is the measurement of psychopathy, which has been spearheaded by Robert Hare and his colleagues.

The Psychopathy Checklist Series

Currently, the best measuring instruments for adult *criminal* psychopathy are the Psychopathy Checklist-Revised (PCL-R; Hare, 1991), the shorter 12-item form called the Psychopathy Checklist: Screening Version (PCL:SV), and the P-Scan: Research Version. The newest version is the Psychopathy Checklist: Youth Version (PCL:YV; Forth, Kossen, & Hare, in press), not yet commercially published at this writing. All four measures are conceptually similar and require considerable training to administer professionally.

The PCL-R is the most heavily researched and has been used extensively in recent years. It is estimated that the PCL-R is used in about 60,000 to 80,000 evaluations each year (Otto & Heilbrun, 2002). So far, the research has strongly supported the reliability and validity of the PCL-R for distinguishing *criminal* psychopaths from the general population or nonpsychopaths (Hare, 1996, 1998b; Hare, Forth, & Strachan, 1992). The PCL-R is a 20-item clinical rating scale based on information obtained through a semi-structured interview and personal files (usually prison files) on the individual. It usually takes several hours to administer. Scores are assessed on a 3-point scale (0, 1, 2), depending on the degree to which the individual matches the description of the psychopathic traits. Total scores can range from 0 to 40. Cutoff scores of 30 on the PCL-R have been found to be useful diagnostic indicators of psychopathy, although some clinicians have used scores ranging from 25 to 33 (Simourd & Hoge, 2000). It is important to note that the PCL-R is considered primarily a *dimensional* measure of criminal psychopathy rather than a categorical measure in which a person is classified either a psychopath or nonpsychopath. In other words, the more psychopathic features a person displays, the more likely a person falls into the psychopathy end of the continuum. The P-Scan is a quick screening instrument that requires less training and serves as a very rough screen for possible psychopathic features. The P-Scan still needs much more research before it can be used as a valid measure in active practice.

The PCL:SV is a 12-item scale, derived from the PCL-R, that has two primary purposes: (1) to screen for psychopathy in forensic settings; and

(2) to assess and diagnose psychopathy outside of forensic settings (Hart, Cox, & Hare, 1995). Scores of 18 or higher on the PCL:SV are suggestive of psychopathy, and scores of 13–17 "potential" psychopathy (Hart, Cox, & Hare, 1995). The PCL:SV has been shown to predict post-release violence among forensic psychiatric patients (Hill, Rogers, & Bickford, 1996; Monahan et al., 2001; Strand, Belfrage, Fransson, & Levander, 1999). The instrument takes about one to one hour and a half to administer. Unlike the PCL-R, the PCL:SV can be completed without access to criminal record information. Therefore, the assessment tool is suitable for use in civil psychiatric evaluations and personnel selection, such as law enforcement, correctional work, or military recruiting (Hart, Cox, & Hare, 1995).

The PCL:YV, designed for assessing young offenders, is a modified version of the PCL-R. It is recommended for use with adolescents 13 years or older, and is modified to account for the limited life experiences of adolescents. Basically, the instrument attempts to assess psychopathy across the youth's lifespan, with an emphasis on school adjustment and peer and family relations. The PCL:YV is scored in a fashion similar to the PCL-R. Recent research (Gretton et al., 2001, Långström & Grann, 2000) suggests that, similar to the PCL-R, a cut-off score between 26 and 30 may qualify for a psychopathic classification.

Malingering Measures

The courts often ask mental health professionals to provide their expert testimony or opinion regarding the possibility of malingering. Malingering "is the intentional production of false or grossly exaggerated physical or psychological symptoms" (American Psychiatric Association, 1994, p. 683). The motivation behind malingering is often to obtain financial compensation or benefits, to avoid work, or to evade criminal prosecution. Two major assessment tools specifically designed to measure malingering have been developed.

Structured Interview of Reported Symptoms (SIRS) (Rogers, Gillis, Dickens, & Bagby, 1991; Rogers, 1997) has been developed to assess malingering and feigning (faking) of psychiatric symptoms for adults (ages 18 or older). The SIRS takes about 45 minutes to administer. Although the scales include questions that mental health professionals would generally ask in cases where suspicions of malingering are present, the highly structured interview format and the objectivity of the scoring system make the instrument highly useful for forensic assessments (Melton et al., 1997). Moreover, the scales are geared to minimize the risk that a respondent will be inappropriately identified as malingering (Melton et al., 1997). Most of the extant research has shown that scores on the SIRS have generally been effective in identifying those persons not telling the truth (malingerers) from those telling the truth (Melton et al., 1997). Overall, the reliability of the scales is good, and the construct validity is reasonable.

Another malingering instrument often mentioned in the professional literature is the Rey Visual Memory Test (Rey, 1964). The Rey is a simple 15-item (3 columns × 5 rows) visual memory test developed to detect faking or exaggeration of memory complaints. The test, developed by the French neurologist Andreé Rey, is considered useful for discriminating between individuals who are either motivated to perform well or to malinger, with those motivated recalling more items than malingerers. Other instruments for detecting malingering include certain scales of the MMPI–2 and the Malingering Scale (MgS) (Schretlen, 1986). The MgS is a 90-item, pencil-and-paper test that takes about 20 minutes to complete. Some items of the scale were drawn from existing intelligence tests, while others were rationally derived (Schretlen, Wilkins, Van Gorp, & Bobholz, 1992). Research has suggested that the MgS, when combined with other instruments found to be effective in detecting malingering, may be valuable. Outside of the very encouraging potential of the SIRS, however, very few *single* instruments have been particularly promising in the detection of malingering. ▶ [We will discuss malingering and the use of the polygraph in more detail in Chapter 9.]

Risk Assessment Measures

Risk assessment measures focus on predictions of violence. The Historical/Clinical/Risk Management Scale (HCR–20: Assessing Risk for Violence

(Version 2), developed by Christopher Webster and his colleagues (Webster, Harris, Rice, Cormier, & Quinsey, 1994), is a scale which purports to identify the presence or absence of violence risk factors in adults. As is apparent from the title of the scale, the HCR–20 bases its predictive power on three major areas: (1) past or historical (H) factors; (2) clinical or current (C) factors; and (3) risk management (R) factors. The scale contains ten historical items, five clinical items, and five risk management factors, for a total of twenty items. Historical or H factors include "previous violence," "age at first violent incident," and "early adjustment at home." Other H items include relationship instability, employment problems, substance use problems, and major mental illness. Clinical or "C" items include lack of insight, negative attitudes (antisocial, hostile, angry), and "active symptoms of major mental illness" (Webster et al., 1997b, p. 263). Risk or "R" factors are related to the future circumstances of the individuals being evaluated, such as whether the person is likely to have adequate housing, meals, daily activities, and finances. Research indicates that individuals without these basics are at higher risk for violence than those who have these needs managed and taken care of. Researchers of the HCR–20 found that the historical (H) items are the strongest for predicting future violent actions (Webster et al., 1997b), and C items are second strongest (Borum, 1996). The HCR–20 is still in its infancy and will need much more research before it receives widespread acceptance as a reliable and valid risk-assessment instrument, but the research thus far is very promising.

Dynamic and Static Risk Factors One of the key factors emerging from risk assessment research is the concept of **dynamic risk factors** (Andrews & Bonta, 1998; Andrews, Bonta, & Hoge, 1990). Dynamic risk factors are the ones that *change* over time and situation. For example, attitudes, values, and beliefs have considerable potential for change, in contrast to the more **static risk factors**, such as gender, birth order, ethnic background, and biological parents. The historical or background factors outlined by the HCR–20 are static in nature because they are factors that cannot be changed ("age at first violent act"). Changing attitudes, beliefs, and values is an important mission in corrections, in contrast to simply identifying which static predictors are associated with recidivism, or re-offending. Consequently, the clinical factors of the HCR–20 may be more valuable in predicting violence because they can be changed through rehabilitation or treatment strategies. Cognitive changes can result in a corresponding increase or decrease in recidivism risk (Hanson & Harris, 2000). Preliminary research on violent offenders, for example, finds that dynamic risk factors seem to predict recidivism as well as or better than static, historical variables (Gendreau, Little, & Goggin, 1996; Zamble & Quinsey, 1997).

Dynamic risk factors can be subdivided into *stable* dynamic factors and *acute* dynamic factors (Hanson & Harris, 2000). Stable dynamic factors, although they are changeable, usually change slowly, sometimes very slowly. Consequently, they may take months or even years to change. Acute dynamic factors, on the other hand, change rapidly (days, hours, or even minutes), and include such things as mood swings, emotional arousal, alcohol or drug intoxication. Hanson and Harris (2000) discovered that acute dynamic factors, such as anger and subjective distress, are better predictors of recidivism for sex offenders than are the more stable dynamic factors.

The VRAG A second important risk assessment tool is the Violence Risk Appraisal Guide (VRAG) developed by Grant Harris, Marnie Rice, and Vernon Quinsey (Harris, Rice, & Quinsey, 1993). The VRAG is based on data from 618 men with prior histories of significant violence who were initially confined at the Oak Ridge Division of the Penetanguishene Mental Health Centre in Ontario, Canada. Oak Ridge is a maximum security facility providing assessment and treatment for persons referred from the courts, correctional services, and other provincial psychiatric hospitals in Canada. Twelve variables believed to predict future violence make up the VRAG. The variables include separation from parents by age sixteen or younger, schizophrenia, elementary school maladjustment, alcohol abuse history, and symptoms of psychopathy (PCL-R). Researchers discovered that the VRAG's best predictor of violent recidivism was the score on the PCL-R, and that the scale overall is a useful instrument for predicting criminal violence among men who had already been apprehended for violent crime (Rice, 1997).

Forensic Neuropsychology

Neuropsychology deals with studying and assessing the functioning and dysfunctioning of the human nervous system, particularly the cerebral cortex (the brain). In general, forensic neuropsychology is concerned with the diagnosis and consequence of brain damage within a legal context. Forensic neuropsychology has developed almost exclusively within the realm of civil law, and, until recently, was largely neglected in the criminal law area (Martell, 1992). This situation is slowly changing, particularly in the context of criminal defendants raising defenses based on dysfunctions of the brain. The predominant application of forensic neuropsychology to date, however, has been in civil cases involving disability determination, worker's compensation, and personal injury cases (Martell, 1992).

The forensic neuropsychologist tries to answer three basic questions: (1) Is there brain damage? (2) What was the cause of this brain damage? And (3), what effects will this brain damage or dysfunction have on the behavioral, affective (emotional), and cognitive life of this individual? In the criminal context an additional question is, what effect did the brain damage have on the individual's behavior? Specifically, did it preclude or diminish the defendant's ability to form the necessary mental intent needed to commit the crime?

Neuropsychological assessment techniques vary widely. They may include an evaluation of general intelligence, language, memory, attention, thought processes, perceptual-motor functioning, and/or emotional status. Two of the most widely-used test batteries for the detection of neuropsychological problems are the Halstead-Reitan and the Luria-Nebraska Neuropsychological Battery. In a survey of neuropsychologists, however (Guilmette and Faust, 1987), only 30% of the respondents said they used the Halstead-Reitan regularly, while 20% said they use the Luria-Nebraska regularly. A few (4%) indicated they use a variant of the Luria-Nebraska (called the Luria-Christensen) with regularity. A later survey (Butler, Retzlaff, & Vanderploeg, 1991) found that the use of the Halstead-Reitan remained the same, but the use of the Luria-Nebraska Neuropsychological Battery had declined to 8%. Most neuropsychologists apparently prefer to use various combinations of tests, depending on the individual being tested and the legal questions asked. In most cases, however, mental health professionals prefer the WAIS–R, which seems to be the most widely used general psychological test in neuropsychological assessments. Overall, no single test is adequate for the detection or diagnosis of all suspected brain damage, primarily because of the enormous complexity of the brain (Martell, 1992).

Brain injury can result from a variety of causes, including blows to the head (trauma), changes in oxygen supply (anoxia and hypoxia), drugs and alcohol, and neurotoxins. Head trauma, of course, may result from a wide assortment of causes, ranging from traffic accidents to a brawl in a bar. Anoxia and hypoxia refer to a lack of oxygen, a condition that can cause irreparable damage to particular areas of the central nervous system in a relatively short period of time. Very often, the forensic questions in this area focus on neurological problems of an infant (such as cerebral palsy) as a result of possible professional incompetence during childbirth or during immediate aftercare.

Toxic injury to the brain can result from accidental or incidental exposure to elements in the outdoor environment, food or drink, medication, or features of the workplace (Leestma, 1991). Acute or chronic exposure to toxins may produce changes in the structure and function of the central or peripheral nervous systems, resulting in a wide spectrum of disabling symptoms (Peper, 1999). In the United States, it is estimated that between 8 and 20 million individuals are exposed to neurotoxins each year (Hartman, 1995; Peper, 1999). Certain carpet fibers, for example, have been suspected to emit neurotoxins. Toxic injury can also result through willful consumption of substances with toxic properties or as a result of willful criminal intent. Consumption of inappropriately prescribed drugs may result in nervous system damage, as may consumption of some illegal drugs or very heavy ingestion of alcohol.

There have been numerous illustrations of the harmful effects of toxic substances used indiscriminately, often by major corporations (Mokhiber, 1988). The "corporate roster of wrongdoing" ranges from well-known illustrations like Agent Orange and Love Canal to less publicized cases. The public, though, is rapidly becoming aware of the grave consequences of exposure to toxic materials. As a result, civil suits in this area have proliferated. However, establishing a causal relationship between toxins and actual damage is fraught with difficulties. A popular film, *A Civil Action* (Touchstone Pictures, released 1998), based on Jonathan Harr's book by the same name and recounting cancer-producing water pollution in Woburn, Massachusetts, depicted the many obstacles faced by plaintiffs in bringing these suits. Another noteworthy example is the film *Erin Brokovich* (Universal Studios, released 2000), also based on a true account.

One of the major tasks for neuropsychologists making forensic assessments associated with any of the above areas is to separate pre-existing brain dysfunctions from dysfunctions resulting from a current injury. Conditions that existed prior to the trauma in question are sometimes subtle, complicated, difficult to identify—even by those who know the individual well—and are more common than supposed (Tucker & Neppe, 1991). Another important task is to ensure that the examinee is not malingering (faking) or exaggerating. The ability of neuropsychologists to detect deception is currently a highly controversial area, with heated arguments on both sides concerning the validity of certain methods as well as the interpretation of various studies (Martell, 1992). A third important objective is to make certain that indicators of neurological impairment gathered from neuropsychological assessment are not the result of other factors in an otherwise healthy individual. For example, the apparent impairment may simply be the result of advancing age.

As noted above, neuropsychology is increasingly appearing as an assessment strategy in criminal cases, such as in evaluating the defendant's competency to stand trial or determining whether an insanity defense could be supported. The language "mental disease or defect" which appears in the law related to insanity is broadly interpreted to include not only psychological causes but neurological or physiological ones as well. ▶ [In Chapter 4, we will be addressing these issues in more detail.] Traditionally, the term "functional" has been reserved for suspected psychological causes in mental disorders (such as reactive depression), and the term "organic" has been reserved for suspected or known neurophysiological causes of mental disorders due to trauma or disease. But clinicians today are finding it increasingly difficult to determine whether certain mental disorders, such as schizophrenia, are due primarily to functional or organic causes. Neuropsychology, therefore, can help in determining what effect known brain damage may have on the capacities and behavior of a defendant.

It should be stressed that the field of neuropsychology is developing very rapidly. Current knowledge of the immediate and long-term consequences of brain injury, especially if the injury seems minor or moderate, is limited. Nevertheless, forensic neuropsychologists are indispensable to the process of attempting to determine both direct and indirect physical effects of such injuries.

Assessment Instruments Used in Forensic Settings

According to Otto and Heilbrun (2002), the first instruments specifically designed for use in forensic settings were in the area of competency to stand trial. The very first was created in 1965 by a psychiatrist, Ames Robey. The instrument was more a checklist of criteria for competency to stand trial rather than a psychological assessment tool or test. The checklist had no scoring criteria or norms, and lacked any measure of reliability and validity (Heilbrun, Rogers, & Otto, 2000). Paul Lipsitt, trained as a psychologist and a lawyer, collaborated with others to develop the first generation of forensic assessments (Borum & Otto, 2000). Lipsitt and colleagues (Lipsitt, Lelos, & McGarry, 1971) designed two measures for evaluating competence to stand trial: the Competence Screening Test (CST); and the Competence Assessment Instrument (CAI). Another test developed around this time was the Georgia Court Competency Test. None of these instruments became widely used, nor did they stimulate much research (Borum & Otto, 2000).

Researchers then began to develop instruments for assessing other "competencies," such as competencies to waive a variety of legal rights. Thomas Grisso published a book describing Miranda (*Miranda v. Arizona*, 1966) waiver assessment instruments in 1981. Instruments for use in child custody assessments soon followed. These were the Bricklin Perceptual Scales (Bricklin, 1984) and The Custody Quotient (Gordon & Peek, 1989). The few forensic assessment instruments published prior to 1990 typically suffered from one or more shortcomings. These included a lack of: (a) complete test manuals, describing test development, test use, and test characteristics; (b) adequate data regarding instrument reliability, validity, and psychometric properties; (c) appropriate norms; and (d) commercial publications, making it difficult to obtain and use the instruments (Heilbrun et al., 2000; Poythress et al., 1999).

More forensic assessment instruments and forensically relevant instruments have been published in the past 10 years than in the preceding 40. Heilbrun et al. (2000) identified 33 assessment techniques that had been developed and promulgated for use in forensic evaluations during the 1990s; whereas a total of 10 such instruments were developed prior to 1990.

In the Ackerman–Ackerman survey (1997) of tests used in child custody evaluations, over a third of the psychologists who tested children preferred the Bricklin Perceptual Scales, and they used them on a regular basis in their testing procedure. When adults in child custody cases were tested, the Ackerman–Schoendorf Scales for Parent Evaluation of Custody was the most popular forensic instrument utilized, and it was used on a very regular basis (about 90% of the time) by those psychologists.

Criminal Responsibility Measures

When criminal defendants plead not guilty by reason of insanity, psychologists and psychiatrists usually are asked to conduct criminal responsibility evaluations (loosely called insanity evaluations). Borum and Grisso (1995) discovered that forensic measures are not used very often in these evaluations. Forty-six percent of the psychologists said they never used them in criminal responsibility assessments, and another 20% reported they rarely used them. In their survey, Borum and Grisso found that the only forensic instrument commonly used was the Rogers Criminal Responsibility Assessment Scales (R–CRAS), preferred by 41% of the forensic psychologists and 10% of the forensic psychiatrists.

The R–CRAS is an instrument that allows the examiner to quantify the mental impairment at the time of the crime, to relate the impairment to the appropriate legal standard, and to render an expert opinion with respect to that legal standard. Part I establishes the degree of impairment on psychological variables significant to the determination of insanity. Part II aids in rendering an accurate opinion on criminal responsibility with the American Law Institute standard of insanity, and it also includes the experimental decision models for guilty-but-mentally ill. The scale represents the first serious attempt by a psychologist to develop an instrument that provides empirical assistance for decisions involving legal insanity (Melton et al., 1997). The R–CRAS consists of 25 individual scales which can be subsumed into six summary "psycholegal criteria." The six psycholegal criteria can then be inserted into a decision tree which ultimately produces a recommendation—sane, insane, or no opinion. ▶ [We will discuss evaluations of criminal responsibility in more detail in Chapter 4.]

Competence to Stand Trial Measures

The legal standard for "competence to stand trial" has not changed since the U.S. Supreme Court clarified it in 1960 in *Dusky v. United States*. "The test will be whether [the defendant] has sufficient present ability to consult with his lawyer with a reasonable degree of rational understanding, and whether he has a rational as well as a factual understanding of the proceedings against him" (*Dusky v. U.S.*, 362 U.S. 402). Several instruments have been designed for evaluation of a defendant's competence to participate in legal proceedings, including the Competence Screening Test (CST) (Lipsitt, Lelos, & McGarry, 1971), Georgia Court Competency Test (GCCT) (Wildman et al., 1980), Competency Assessment Instrument (CAI) (Laboratory of Community Psychiatry, 1974), and the Fitness to Stand Trial Interview (Menzies, Webster, Rosech, Jensen, & Eaves, 1984).

The Competence Screening Test (CST) is a 22-item sentence-completion test. Examples of some of the items include "When I go to court the lawyer will . . . " "When they say a man is innocent until proven guilty, I . . . " "What concerns Fred most about his lawyer . . . " (Melton et al., 1997, p. 139). Each item is scored 0, 1, or 2, with 2 indicating a high level of legal comprehension and 0 representing a low level. A total score below 20 suggests some degree of incompetence and a candidate for further examination. The administration and scoring of the CST is standardized. However, both the reliability and validity of the CST are highly questionable, and it should be used only by trained clinicians with great caution and primarily as a rough screening device (Melton et al., 1997).

The Competency Assessment Instrument is a semi-structured interview that is scored with 5 point ratings, with 1 indicating "total incapacity" and 5 representing "no incapacity." The administration and scoring of this instrument is not standardized and the norms are inadequate. The scale does seem to have high face validity which helps in cementing its acceptance into the legal system. Although the CAI may be useful as an interviewing tool, "use of the CAI scales to reach conclusions about competency is inadvisable" (Melton et al., 1997, p. 141).

A promising instrument for competency evaluations developed in recent years has been the MacArthur Competence Assessment Tool—Criminal Adjudication (MacCAT–CA) (Poythress et al., 1989). It is a 22-item instrument designed to evaluate a defendant's capacity (ages 18 years and older) to *proceed to adjudication* in general. In other words, the assessment tool is broader in scope than the other instruments mentioned in this section. For instance, it is designed to measure a defendant's ability to plead guilty as well as his or her competence to stand trial. It is not designed to measure the abilities of a defendant with a low intelligence level (e.g., an IQ below 60). The MacCAT–CA, which takes about 30 minutes to administer and is considered "user-friendly," was field tested on a sample of 107 criminal defendants in a jail and forensic hospital in Virginia (Hoge, Bonnie, Poythress, & Monahan, 1997). The MacCAT–CA has separate assessment procedures for measuring three competence-related abilities:

1. Understanding—capacity for factual understanding of the legal system and the adjudication process)
2. Reasoning—ability to distinguish more relevant from less relevant factual information and ability to reason about the two legal options: Pleading guilty or not guilty
3. Appreciation—capacity to understand his or her own legal situation and circumstances.

Research suggests the MacCAT–CA has good interrater reliability, strong internal consistency, and solid construct validity (Melton et al., 1997; Otto et al., 1998). Still, a considerable amount of research and development is needed if the instrument is to gain widespread acceptability. ▶ [Like criminal responsibility evaluations, evaluations of competency to stand trial will be discussed again in Chapter 4.]

Child Custody Evaluations

Ackerman–Schoendorf Scales of Parent Evaluation of Custody (ASPECT) (Ackerman & Schoendorf, 1992) is not a test *per se* but a "system" developed to provide a practical, standardized, and defensible approach for use in child custody evaluations. It combines the results of psychological testing, interviews, and observations of each parent and child, and produces a Parent Custody Index which guides custody decisions. The Index presumably informs the examiner as to which parent is more effective, and how much more effective that parent is over the other. In addition, the Index differentiates situations in which one parent should obtain full custody from those in which joint custody is more appropriate. Although the ASPECT seems to provide an extensive and varied overview of parents and their perceptions of their child's activities, the instrument lacks sufficient normative, reliability, or validity support (Heinze & Grisso, 1996). For example, the normative sample that was used consisted of highly motivated, cooperative, and bright parents (Heinze & Grisso, 1996).

Bricklin Perceptual Scales (BPS) (Bricklin, 1984) is a clinician-administered custody assessment that measures a child's (ages 6 and up) perceptions of both of his or her parents in four areas: (1) competency; (2) consistency; (3) warmth and empathy; and (4) other admirable character traits. The BPS consists of 64 cards, each about the size of a business envelope. Thirty-two of the cards relate to the mother and 32 to the father. The questions about the cards alternate in their focus on father or mother, and require the child to indicate how well the item describes the parent. On one side of every card, there is an 8-inch long thick black line. The line is broken down into 60 incremental spaces, indicating a response of "not so well" at one end and "very well" at the other. The child sees only the lines, while the examiner sees the test questions and the scoring grids. In response to a question, the child punches a hole somewhere along the line with a stylus-pen, indicating how he perceives each parent. The parent receiving the higher score for each item receives points for that item. The parent achieving the greater number of choices on items overall is assumed to be the "parent of choice," at least in the eyes of the child (Heinze & Grisso, 1996).

The BPS has many psychometric problems and has been criticized extensively. For one thing, the reliability is questionable, with some parents "winning" as the parent of choice in one testing session but "losing" that designation at a later testing, especially if the scores were fairly close during the initial testing (Heinze & Grisso, 1996). In reference to this crucial shortcoming, Heinze and Grisso (1996, p. 299) assert, "This illustrates the importance of taking the standard error of measurement into account when interpreting the result for the test. Bricklin, however, does not report what the standard error of measurement is."

The validity of the BPS is virtually nonexistent, and the scale seems to be biased toward mothers (Heinze & Grisso, 1996). In addition, the scale is potentially weak in generalizability, especially because it does not appear to take into consideration the age and developmental capacities of the child. The language, for example, may be too complex for the younger child. Overall, the test manual is incomplete and fails to provide some of the most basic information about the psychometric properties of the test (Otto & Heilbrun, 2002). Krauss and Sales (2000, p. 868) conclude ". . . there is no evidence that the use of the BPS improves the judgment of clinicians or the quality of child custody decisions." Bricklin also developed an instrument designed to measure children's perceptions of the nature and quality of their relationships with their parents, called the Perception of Relations Test (PORT) (Bricklin, 1994). ▶ [Again, we will return to a discussion of these instruments later in the book, specifically in Chapter 11.]

MacArthur Research Network on Mental Health and Law

A group that has been very actively involved in the development of forensic instruments is the Research Network on Mental Health and Law. Created by the John D. and Catherine T. MacArthur Foundation with a grant to the University of Virginia in 1988, it seeks to accomplish two comprehensive goals. First, it strives to develop new knowledge about the relationships between mental health and the law. Second, it aims to apply that understanding to the development of improved tools and criteria for evaluating individuals and making decisions that affect their lives. The first goal will be discussed throughout subsequent ▶ chapters of the book as pertinent topics arise. The second goal will be our focus in this section, because it relates specifically to instruments designed for forensic settings.

The Research Network comprises experts and researchers from the fields of psychology, sociology, psychiatry, law, and mental health administration and policy. The project has produced a number of reliable and valid tools for assessing and evaluating a range of mental health issues as they relate to the law. Three *major* empirical investigations have been undertaken by the Network: (1) the *Violence Risk Assessment Study*; (2) the *Competence Study*; and (3) the *Coercion Study*. Each of these studies includes the development of forensic instruments. The Network also sponsors investigations into several other areas, such as work disability and the law (Bonnie & Monahan, 1997), and violence risk communication (Slovic, Monahan, & MacGregor, 2000).

The *MacArthur Violence Risk Assessment Study* was the largest of the three major empirical investigations undertaken by the Network. The project was designed to determine whether former mental patients are more violent than other members of the community. If so, how could they be evaluated reliably and accurately? One of the primary goals of the Violent Risk Assessment Study was to develop a clinical tool that could improve both the accuracy and the efficiency of the violence risk assessments that mental health professionals are usually asked to conduct (Monahan et al., 2001). The Risk Assessment Study did find that the prevalence of violence among people discharged from a psychiatric hospital and who had symptoms of substance abuse was significantly higher than the prevalence of violence among other people, an observation to be discussed more fully in ▶ Chapter 4. The MacArthur group then developed the **Iterative Classification Tree (ICT)** method to provide mental health professionals with a technique for estimating the probability of violence of individuals with behavioral or mental disorders. The ICT is really not a testing instrument *per se*; it is more a yes/no flow chart that predicts which psychiatric patients are at high risk for committing violence. The ICT model, which is still very much in development, combines the predictions of several risk assessment models and clinical judgments. It will be covered in more detail later in this chapter.

The *MacArthur Coercion Study* was designed to provide information to policy makers, clinicians, patients, and family members about the appropriate role of coercion—if any—in the provision of mental health services. The project initially tried to answer, "What is it, precisely, that makes patients feel that they have been coerced into a mental hospital?" An empirically-validated measure of perceived coercion—called the Perceived Coercion Scale (Gardner et al., 1993)—was developed as a result of the extensive research conducted in the project.

The *MacArthur Competence Study* comprises three closely related projects: (1) the adjudicative competence project; (2) the juvenile competence study; and (3) the treatment competence project. The adjudicative competence part of the study was designed to develop measures to evaluate the ability of criminal defendants to understand the nature and object of the legal proceedings they are facing, to consult with counsel, and/or to assist in preparing their defense. Research results of this project helped generate the MacArthur Competence Assessment Tool—Criminal Adjudication (MacCAT–CA) (Hoge et al., 1997). In 1997, because the MacCAT–CA cannot be used in a straightforward fashion to assess juvenile competence, the adjudicative competence project was extended to the study of youth's capacities as trial defendants. Eventually, data collection (called the *MacArthur Juvenile Competence Study*) and further development will result in an assessment tool for evaluating juvenile competence.

The treatment competence project was designed to provide information about the decision-making capacities of people who are hospitalized with mental illness. For example, the study examined to what extent people with mental or behavioral disorders can make decisions concerning their own treatment or care. Four legally-relevant abilities were addressed by the project: (1) to state a choice; (2) to understand relevant information; (3) to appreciate the nature of one's own situation; and (4) to reason with information. During the final stages of the Treatment Competence Study, the Network developed and tested an easy-to-use instrument for assessing patients' decision-making abilities called the MacArthur Competence Assessment Tool—Treatment (MacCAT–T) (Grisso & Appelbaum, 1998a). The test measures the ability to consent to treatment and the competence to *refuse* treatment. It prompts the mental health professional to ask questions that assess a patient's understanding, appreciation, and reasoning regarding treatment and intervention decisions. Another instrument, the MacArthur Competence Assessment Tool for Clinical Research (MacCAT–CR) (Appelbaum & Grisso, 2001), is an offshoot of the MacCAT–T. The MacCAT–CR, which can be administered in 20 minutes or less, is designed to assess potential subject's capacities to consent to participate in clinical research. ▶ [These instruments will be discussed again in Chapter 5.]

Prediction of Human Behavior

As was noted at the beginning of this chapter, the primary goal of psychological assessment is to reduce the complexity of human behavior to a manageable set of variables so that past and present behavior can be appraised and some parameters of future behavior can be predicted. The assessment techniques covered in the first half of this chapter—interviews, observations, tests, surveys, decision trees—all involve some attempt to predict human behavior. It is important now that we focus more attention on this effort. Can behavior be predicted?

Norval Morris and Marc Miller (1985) identify three kinds of predictions: (1) anamnestic; (2) actuarial; and (3) clinical. **Anamnestic prediction** is based on how a *particular* person acted in the past in similar situations. For instance, every summer Saturday afternoon when it is sunny John takes his dog for a long walk, after having mowed his lawn. The neighbors can *usually* predict John's dog-walking behavior when these conditions are met (summer, sunny, Saturday, lawn mowed).

The second, **actuarial prediction**, is based on how *groups* of individuals with similar characteristics have acted in the past. The fundamental statistic employed in actuarial prediction is the *base rate*, which is defined as the statistical prevalence of a particular behavior in a given group over a set period of time, usually one year. Insurance companies have compiled extensive statistics on who has traffic accidents. These statistics may show, for example, that 20-year-old males who have mediocre academic records and drive a Trans-Am have a very high probability of being involved in a traffic accident within a two-year period. In fact, the base rate for this group may be 40%. If Skip falls into this group, he will pay much higher insurance rates than a 20-year-old woman with an outstanding academic record and a 9-year-old station wagon. The thing to remember is that actuarial prediction is based on *statistics* compiled on *certain groups* of people.

The third, **clinical** or **experience prediction** is based on experience dealing with a certain clientele. A mental health worker may assert: "Based on my experience in dealing with Charles and others like him, I predict that he will assault someone again within a year." Of the three types of prediction, clinical prediction is the most intuitive and subjective. While clinical experience may be an invaluable source of ideas and useful in acquiring certain skills, it is also fraught with an extensive range of biases and inaccuracies (Grove & Meehl, 1996). A wide range of professionals make clinical predictions, including correctional counselors and case managers, social workers, and probation/parole officers. Therefore, we will use "practitioner" as an all encompassing term that will include not only psychologists and psychiatrists, but all human service professionals who make predictions of human behavior.

Interestingly, the courts have generally responded most favorably to clinical predictions, usually because of the legal preference for human judgment over mathematical or statistical probabilities. Requests for clinical prediction are common. Courts ask practitioners to predict a wide range of behaviors. For example, will a high school student who wrote a threatening note likely harm his fellow students? Will a sex offender re-offend? Can an adolescent function as an independent adult? Will an offender benefit from a rehabilitation program? Will a defendant be able to participate in the trial process? Will one parent be better able than the other to meet the needs of a child? Although the assessment of whether an individual is a risk to others has garnered the most research attention, it is important to keep in mind that the work of clinicians involves prediction or assessment of a wide variety of behaviors.

In requesting these predictions, courts assume that practitioners are more accurate in their judgments of human behavior than are lay persons or those without training. This presumed accuracy and expertise in understanding and predicting others is based upon the special qualifications professionals have acquired through training, experience, and the development of rules and strategies for interpreting human data.

The available research (e.g., Cooper & Werner, 1990; Dawes, Faust, & Meehl, 1989; Faust & Ziskin, 1988; Grove & Meehl, 1996), however, has consistently failed to support the legal assumption of a direct relationship between training (or experience) and accuracy in *clinical prediction*. Actuarial predictions are almost always more accurate than clinical ones (Grove & Meehl, 1996). Even highly trained and experienced practitioners are often no more accurate in their predictions of a variety of human behaviors than nonclinicians or less trained and inexperienced practitioners (Ziskin & Faust, 1988). Howard Garb (1989) summarized the research on clinical experience and accuracy of judgment and concluded that there is *no* relationship. It did not matter whether the clinician had 20 years of experience or one—accuracy was about the same in both cases. Garb did find, however, that *training* and *education* did improve prediction.

Research has also consistently revealed that the accuracy of actuarial prediction is higher than either anamnestic or clinical prediction. Robyn Dawes, David Faust, and Paul Meehl (1989) reviewed nearly 100 comparative studies in the social sciences. They conclude: "In virtually every one of these studies, the actuarial method has equalled or surpassed the clinical method, sometimes slightly and sometimes substantially" (p. 1669).

Actuarial methods also seem to be superior in criminal justice decision making. Actuarial methods have consistently outperformed correctional case workers on predictions of recidivism, for example. "[T]he best predictors of parole violation are the age of first conviction, number of past convictions, and number of prison violations; the subsequent 'knowledge' gained in a parole interview simply *decreases* accuracy in predicting who will remain outside of jail" (Dawes, 1989, p. 464).

The Actuarial vs. Clinical Prediction Debate

Many practitioners, however, have some concerns about simply relying on statistical or actuarial methods for predicting human behavior. Implicit in the concerns of the practitioners is that the prediction of human behavior requires, ultimately, the human ingredients of integration, experience, cognitive processing, and judgment of a wide range of input data. Essentially, it takes humans to predict and understand the complexity of humans. Humans are able to take into account the unique, the unexpected, and the mysterious workings of other human minds. The presumption is that computers and statistical tables based on mathematical probabilities cannot possibly take into consideration individual differences to the same degree.

The debate over the respective merits of actuarial and clinical prediction has waxed and waned over the past four decades, although the actuarial prediction models usually win out. For example, at the end of the 1990s, Litwack and Schlesinger (1999, p. 208) commented, "there has been a refreshing absence from the literature of the polemical and unjustified attacks on clinical assessments that characterized many earlier writings." At the same time, however, the debate was re-ignited when Quinsey, Harris, Rice, and Cormier (1998) published *Violent Offenders*, a book in which they argued forcefully against clinical predictions of dangerousness. Many commentators still now urge recognition of the strengths and weaknesses of both approaches and suggest that predictions ideally should be based on a combination of the two. Actuarial prediction continues to be favored, and some continue to call for only actuarial (e.g., Grove & Meehl, 1996; Quinsey et al., 1998). However, increasingly more commentators are recognizing the supplementary value of clinical experience (e.g., Cunningham & Reidy, 1998). Conversely, those who have favored clinical predictions are recognizing the importance of integrating actuarial data to reduce error in their predictions (e.g., Litwack & Schlesinger, 1999).

Thomas Litwack (2001), in a summary of the prediction debate, has good words to say about violence prediction instruments such as the VRAG but urges caution in rushing to its use at the expense of clinical variables. He sees such instruments, rather, as ways of enhancing or assisting dangerousness assessment tasks, and he observes that even actuarial instruments require, in their scoring, some aspect of clinical judgment.

Hart (1998) and his colleagues (e.g., Webster, Douglas, Eaves, & Hart, 1997a), would like to substitute "structured clinical judgment" for either a traditional clinical method or an actuarial approach. Structured clinical judgment presumably combines the best of the knowledge obtained from professional practice and empirical knowledge; it offers decision-making *guidelines* to clinicians for use in assessing risks in a variety of contexts. Guidelines have been developed to assess risks of spousal violence (Kropp et al., 1995), violence in mentally disordered populations (Webster et al., 1997a), and sexual violence (Boer et al., 1997). Borum (1996) has published an extremely helpful article on guidelines, and Litwack and Schlesinger (1999) cite numerous sources for these guidelines. They also offer a four-point summary of what a "reasonably competent assessment of dangerousness" entails. Briefly:

1. The clinician should obtain details of a person's history of violence and response to treatment for violence.
2. Clinicians should be alert to their own tendencies to avoid, deny, or wishfully minimize violence; the patient should be asked direct

questions about history of and inclinations toward violent behavior.

3. The clinician should consider the circumstances the person may be facing in the future.
4. When in doubt, the clinician should consult with other clinicians.

Litwack and Schlesinger also propose recommendations for avoiding common errors made by clinicians in assessing the potential for harm. They stress obtaining complete information, considering the context of situations in which the person is likely to be in the future, and considering base rate information if these rates are available. They also urge clinicians not to underestimate the potential for violence in female patients who have a history of violence. Although women as a group are far less violent than men, women who have displayed violent behavior in the past are at risk of displaying it again, depending upon the situational contexts.

One solution to the debate may be to develop and refine decision or classification tree models where a variety of statistical and clinical factors can be incorporated into a single model of prediction. A decision or classification tree is a structured sequence of yes or no questions that eventually lead to a decision or classification of a case.

Recall that the *MacArthur Violence Risk Assessment Study* (discussed earlier in chapter) generated the iterative classification tree (ICT). It shows considerable promise in integrating the strengths of multiple approaches. In addition, practitioners should find the classification model easier to use compared to complicated mathematical formulas and equations. This positive feature is especially attractive with the development of computer software designed to make the task that much easier. One of the current limitations of a classification tree model is that—while it is highly powerful in discerning cases that fall into the extreme categories—it is less capable of discriminating cases falling into the middle ranges. For example, in situations requiring a prediction of which psychiatric patients would be violent upon release from a mental institution, the ICT model was very good at distinguishing very high risk patients from very low risk patients (Steadman et al., 2000). However, the drawback was the lack of adequate prediction for those patients falling between the extremes.

Why Clinical Predictions Miss the Mark

Despite recognition that clinical insights are valuable, we must emphasize that actuarial prediction has demonstrated its superiority. Poythress (1992, p. 142) concludes: "In virtually every area of behavior that researchers have pitted clinical prediction against statistical prediction, clinical prediction has been shown to be inferior." The fact remains that when the same input data or predictor variables are given to an individual using statistical tables or formulae and to a clinician, and when each is asked to make specific predictions, the clinician continually fails to achieve a higher "hit" ratio than the person using the statistical procedure. Why is this so?

The process psychologists and other practitioners use in arriving at predictions is not well understood, but available research suggests that they use far less data and are much more simple in their data combinations than even they believe (Wiggins, 1973; Jones, 1977; Dawes, Faust, & Meehl, 1989). In addition, practitioners have considerable difficulty in identifying relevant from nonrelevant information and are at loss in determining how much weight to give the information in making their judgment (Dawes, Faust, & Meehl, 1989). Statistical techniques, on the other hand, such as multiple regression and discriminant analysis, identify predictive variables and eliminate nonpredictive ones, and weight the predictive variables in accordance with the informational contribution to the conclusion.

Further, the interpersonal skills and prejudices of the practitioners may be as much a limitation of data collection as the instruments employed (e.g., Truax & Mitchell, 1971; Mischel, 1981; Dawes, Faust, & Meehl, 1989). Practitioners use these limited data to estimate a person's status with respect to given hypotheses and then use their favorite theoretical model as a basis for prediction. In most instances, the practitioners base their inferences on perceived "regularities" that have been observed in the past between predictor variables and the criterion variables, and this process tends to be an art more than a science. That is, practitioners rely too heavily on intuition and the "unusual case," and this violates the statistical rules of prediction in systematic and fundamental ways (Kahneman & Tversky, 1973).

The well-cited and classic critique of the clinical field of assessment and prediction is a monograph by Walter Mischel, *Personality and Assessment* (1968), which raised incisive questions about the tendency of practitioners to use a small number of behavioral signs to categorize people into fixed slots. Mischel demonstrates that the assessor's favorite theoretical biases enter very clearly into appraisals of other people's functioning. These status determinations in turn are used to predict specific behaviors (such as dangerousness) and to make important decisions about others' lives. Mischel's justified concern was that even highly trained and experienced practitioners infer, generalize, and predict too much from too little information, and they do so in a way that is disconcertingly similar to the personal judgment of nonpractitioners. In addition, the "expert" judgments of practitioners—like everyone else's judgments—are subject to strong biases that often produce serious distortions and oversimplifications in their conclusions about behavior. It should be noted, though, that statistical data also may suffer from a paucity of predictor variables.

Practitioners also have a strong tendency to attribute causality to a person's personality rather than to the circumstances in which the person acts. This well-ingrained clinical proclivity for underestimating the importance of situational determinants and overestimating the importance of the actor's personality was noted as long ago as 1943 (Ichheiser, p. 151). Called **fundamental attribution error**, it is also a common tendency found in people when they are attributing a cause to another person's behavior. Specifically, fundamental attribution error refers to a powerful tendency to explain another person's behavior in terms of dispositional or personality (internal) factors rather than situational or environmental (external) factors. For example, when correctional counselors were asked to explain why inmates had committed crimes that put them in prison, the counselors attributed the causes almost exclusively to dispositional factors or personality factors (such as "meanness" or "laziness") rather than environmental factors, such as upbringing, socioeconomic status, living conditions, or social environment (Saulnier & Perlman, 1981).

There also appears to be a curious need for humans, including practitioners, to favor subjectively vivid but unreliable data over more complete empirical but pallid information, regardless of one's theoretical leaning (Mischel, 1979; Kahneman & Tversky, 1973; Nisbett & Borgida, 1975). Therefore, a person's own account of his or her feelings is considered more revealing than actually observed behaviors. This preference for subjective information over objective data is reflected in the continuing popularity of inkblots and other projective instruments for use in clinical practice, in spite of extensive data showing them to be unreliable and fundamentally invalid (Anastasi, 1988). Researchers cautioning their clinical colleagues about these instruments are often ignored or are told that public pressure forces practitioners to address stressful but complex problems and provide at least a semblance of a solution. Alternatively, those who caution are told they simply do not understand the complexity of human behavior and the value of projective instruments. Recall that earlier in the chapter we made reference to the ongoing debate over the value of the Rorschach and its admissibility under *Daubert* standards.

Research also consistently reveals that people, including professionals, tend to shun statistical or scientific data in favor of interview impressions or face-to-face information (Gottfredson & Gottfredson, 1988; Fong, Lurigio, & Stalans, 1990). On this point, Grove and Meehl (1996, p. 320) issue the following warning: "All policymakers should know that a practitioner who claims not to need any statistical or experimental studies but relies solely on clinical experience as adequate justification, by that very claim is shown to be a nonscientifically minded person whose professional judgments are not to be trusted."

The practitioner may have limited access to a small, non-representative sample of behavior during an artificial, stressful interview or testing session. It is true that the best source of information about our past, present, and future behavior appears to be ourselves (Mischel, 1968; Kenrick & Stringfield, 1980; Bem, 1967, 1972; Monson & Snyder, 1977). We have more data at our disposal, along with direct access to the publicly unobservable affective and cognitive elements that affect and instigate that behavior.

However, it may take several sessions before a practitioner can come to access this information from us. A secondary source of information is someone who knows us well and has had the opportunity to observe us in a variety of situations (Kenrick & Stringfield, 1980). These individuals, often family members or close friends, can corroborate the information we provide. The practitioner does not necessarily consult these secondary sources, however.

The expectations of the referral source also potentially influence the accuracy of clinical judgment. For example, referrals from the court may communicate to the assessor, explicitly or implicitly, some desired direction or conclusion. It is possible that a sizeable number of practitioners slant their assessments to some extent to meet the expectations of the court. If the court expects a practitioner to recommend counseling for an offender, this expectation may be communicated to the evaluator in some manner and may influence the report delivered.

Finally, practitioners may be inaccurate in their clinical predictions because they rarely receive feedback about their judgments. They make predictions but often do not learn the outcome. One of the principles of learning is to receive information about one's performance, an opportunity rarely provided to practitioners.

The foregoing discussion should not be construed as asserting that accurate assessment and predictions about human behavior are impossible. It does warn about the severe limits on the range and level of clinical prediction that can be expected in light of our present knowledge about human behavior. Furthermore, the research also shows that statistical training, designed to promote a deeper understanding of statistical concepts, can provide a set of valuable inferential tools to improve decision making and predictions substantially (Fong, Lurigio, & Stalans, 1990). In addition, Thomas Litwack and Louis Schlesinger (1987) argue that the research on predictions of violence and dangerousness of previously violent people have not really given practitioners a chance to "show their stuff." These scholars contend that practitioners *can* predict reasonably accurate outcomes under some circumstances. ". . . [T]he issue is not simply whether mental health professionals can predict violence, but, rather, what types of predictive statements can they offer, with what type of certainty, with what types of patients, under what types of circumstances" (p. 233).

Therefore, the accurate assessment and clinical prediction of human behavior appears to require careful study of the interaction of the behavior of interest and the psychosocial environment in which it occurs. The best source for this analysis is the person, but other good sources are those who have had the opportunity to observe the person extensively. Accurate assessment and prediction also require, of course, a good understanding of the contaminative influence of personal biases and hunches, along with a heavy reliance on statistical and empirical data developed on the criterion behavior. The advancement of our understanding of human behavior depends upon the empirical study of the interactions of persons and their psychosocial environment.

Testing in Employment

In the *Civil Rights Act of 1964*, Congress addressed the broad spectrum of discriminatory practice in its many forms. Specifically relating to employment, under Title VII of the *Civil Rights Act*, as amended in 1972, it is unfair employment practice if an employer discriminates against an individual or class of individuals on the basis of race, color, gender, religion, or national origin. The law makes it clear that employees and prospective employees are protected against discrimination related to hiring and promotion. As a result, psychological tests which lack adequate validation data or which base classification and cut-off scores on norms developed from a culturally advantaged population are particularly susceptible to lawsuits. When the *Civil Rights Act* was first passed, many psychological tests, especially of the cognitive ability (IQ) variety, came under heavy social and legal attack.

Along with the *Civil Rights Act*, Congress created the Equal Employment Opportunity Commission (EEOC), a federal administrative agency which issues guidelines to employers and generally oversees employment practices to assure that they are in compliance with the law. Among the EEOC's guidelines is the need to demonstrate the job-relatedness of employment tests. The guidelines pertain to any test used to select, transfer, promote, train, refer, and retain employees. It should be noted that state statutes may address the testing issue as well.

If an employer wishes to use a test to screen out or screen in applicants for a position, that test must have been "validated," or shown to be predictive of relevant job behavior. For example, an employer may promote an employee to a position after she or he has scored higher than others on a skills test, which has been demonstrated to predict success at that position. If the company limits a training program to individuals who have "passed" an unvalidated test, however, it is subject to being sued and must be ready to demonstrate that the test predicts success in the training program. It is important to note that the EEOC guidelines do not reject the use of properly validated tests designed to help place people into positions requiring certain skills. They do discourage the use of tests that discriminate against individuals without evidence that the tests are predictive of success in the position.

The U.S. Supreme Court and Employment Discrimination

Since the passage of the *Civil Rights Act of 1964*, the U.S. Supreme Court has heard many cases involving job discrimination issues. In a landmark case that directly addressed psychological assessment, *Griggs v. Duke Power Co.* (1971), the Court interpreted Title VII to forbid employment practices which might seem neutral on their face, but which resulted in a "disparate impact." Therefore, even if an employer did not have an intention to discriminate, if it could be demonstrated that the employer's hiring or promotion practices had a disproportionate impact on members of a protected group, the law was violated. Once disparate impact was demonstrated, the employer would then have to prove that there was a legitimate business need to continue with the practice. In the great majority of cases, no such need could be asserted.

In *Griggs*, 14 African-American employees at a steam station owned by Duke Power Company challenged the legality of general ability exams used to hire and promote. Prior to Title VII, the company had openly discriminated against blacks, assigning them only to the labor detail, where the highest-paid laborer earned less than the lowest-paid white worker in other departments. Faced with Title VII and the EEOC guidelines, the company allowed blacks to transfer if they had a high school diploma (and only 12% of blacks in the state did at that time) or if they could pass two psychological ability and aptitude tests: the Wonderlic Personnel Test and the Bennet Mechanical Comprehension Test. None of these criteria had been shown to measure the ability to learn to perform a particular job. New employees, furthermore, were required to score satisfactorily on two additional aptitude tests.

The petitioners in the *Griggs* case contended that the tests made a disproportionate number of blacks ineligible for a better job. Lower courts rejected their claims because there was no proof that the company intended to discriminate. The U.S. Supreme Court, however, ruled that the intent was irrelevant. Even if a practice seems fair on its face, if discrimination is the effect, intent is not needed.

"(G)ood intent or the absence of discriminatory intent does not redeem employment procedures or testing mechanisms that operate as 'built-in headwinds' for minority groups and are unrelated to measuring job capability. . . . Congress directed the thrust of the (Civil Rights) Act to the consequences of employment practices, not simply to motivation. More than that, Congress has placed on the employer the burden of showing that any given requirement must have a manifest relationship to the employment in question."

The case was a landmark one for two major reasons: (1) It allowed employees to support claims of discrimination by showing disparate impact, an easier task than showing intent to discriminate; and (2) it required the employer to prove that a test which had a disparate impact nonetheless predicted job performance and was thus a legitimate business practice. The burden of proof, then, fell heavily on the employer's shoulders.

The *Griggs* case was cited frequently in *Albermarle v. Moody* (1975), where again a class action suit on behalf of African-American employees was initiated. Albermarle, a company that transformed wood into various paper products, had been administering the Wonderlic Personnel Test and the Revised Beta Exam to prospective employees for skilled-labor jobs. When the *Griggs* decision was announced, Albemarle hired an industrial psychologist to study the job relatedness of its testing program. Although the psychologist performed a concurrent validation between the tests and present employee performance, the U.S. Supreme Court was not satisfied that this met the guidelines established by the EEOC.

Noting that the EEOC's guidelines were based on those of the American Psychological Association, the Court found the psychologist's validation study defective. Among the problems, the Court noted that the study had failed to specify the particular skills needed for the jobs. The test also was not predictive of performance on all of the jobs. Furthermore, the psychologist's procedure relied on subjective and vague supervisory ratings. With its *Albemarle* decision, the Court made it clear that it would not take an employer's word for it that a test had been validated. Furthermore, the Court seemed

to be looking for evidence of construct validity as well as concurrent validity. The very process of validation would be scrutinized.

A new Supreme Court in the 1980s dealt with employment discrimination in a very different manner. Between 1986 and 1991, the Rehnquist Court issued nine rulings that had the collective effect of making it more difficult for employees to win discrimination suits against their employers. The most highly publicized of the decisions, *Ward's Cove Packing Company et al. v. Atonio* (1989) prompted Congress to take action within the *Civil Rights Act of 1991*, an Amendment to the *Civil Rights Act of 1964*. The 1991 law, among other things, clarifies provisions regarding disparate impact actions.

Although the *Ward's Cove* case ◉ (see **Box 2-4**) did not involve psychological assessment, it is

BOX 2-4
Fishy Employment Practices?

Ward's Cove Packing Company had for many years employed Filipinos and Alaskan natives in its seasonal salmon canning operations. The cannery jobs, as the Supreme Court noted in its 1989 decision, were intense, requiring workers to eviscerate fish, pull eggs, clean fish, and operate at a rate of approximately four cans per second. There were also skilled and unskilled non-cannery positions available. These included machinists, engineers, quality control persons, record keepers, kitchen help, deckhands, carpenters, and carpenter's helpers. Filipinos and Alaskan natives, who made up close to half the salmon canning industry, were almost invariably placed in the cannery positions, which paid less. Thus, nearly all cannery workers were non-white. Furthermore, they were housed in separate dorms and ate in separate mess halls, practices which in the words of the dissenters, resembled a "plantation economy" and amounted to overt and institutionalized discrimination.

In his own separate dissent, Justice John Paul Stevens highlighted other problems as well. The more desirable non-cannery jobs were seldom advertised, and there was no pro-

motion to them from the cannery ranks. The intensity of the work precluded on-the-job-training that might help a cannery worker move up in the ranks. Even without additional training, however, cannery workers had demonstrated that they were qualified for advancement. In a footnote, Justice Stevens noted that some cannery workers had a college background and that some later became professionals. Included in the group were an architect, an Air Force officer, and a graduate student in public administration.

As noted in the text, the Court majority placed a heavy burden on the workers to prove that the practices of the company had a disparate impact, meaning that—although the company did not intend to discriminate—the practices they employed had a discriminatory effect. In their concluding paragraph, the dissenters wrote, "Sadly, this [decision] comes as no surprise. One wonders whether the majority still believes that race discrimination—or, more accurately, race discrimination against nonwhites—is a problem in our society, or even remembers that it ever was" (490 U.S. 662).

worthy of note because the decision had an impact on any employment practice that is allegedly discriminatory. The case was a massive blow to employees bringing a disparate impact suit for a number of reasons. Most critical, however, was a major shift in the burden of proof, back to the employees. By a 5–4 vote, the Court ruled that plaintiffs had to identify each objective and subjective employment practice that had the alleged disparate impact and prove that it did. Once the disparate impact was demonstrated, the burden would be shifted to the employer to produce evidence of need to continue the practice. Then, once again, the burden would be shifted back to the plaintiffs, who would have to disprove the employer's claim that the practice was based on legitimate neutral business considerations.

If the employees could not disprove the employer's claim, they would have still one more option. They could persuade the court that an alternative employment practice could also meet the employer's legitimate business needs. The Court was not encouraging about the likelihood of a plaintiff being able to do that, however. The alternative had to be equally effective, and cost could be taken into consideration. "(T)he judiciary should proceed with care before mandating that an employer must adopt a plaintiff's alternative selection or hiring practice . . . " (490 U.S. at 661).

The Court majority did not believe requiring the employees to do all of this would be unduly burdensome. The four dissenters in the case disagreed ◙ (see **Box 2-4**), noting that the additional requirements placed on employees were not in keeping with the spirit of the *Civil Rights Act of 1964*.

Congress agreed with the dissenters. In its 1991 Amendment to the *Civil Rights Act*, Congress made the following points clear: First, once the plaintiff has demonstrated disparate impact, the burden is on the employer to prove the practice is job related and necessary. The plaintiff does not then have to disprove the employer's claim. Second, if the plaintiff demonstrates that an alternative business practice is available and the employer refuses to accept it, the law is violated. Finally, employees are still required to prove that each challenged practice has a disparate impact. However, "if the complaining party can demonstrate to the court that the elements of [an employer's] decision-making process are not capable of separation for analysis, the decision making process may be analyzed as one employment practice."

It is important to keep in mind that the above discussion refers to "disparate impact" rather than "intentional discrimination." The latter, not surprisingly, is extremely difficult to prove. In employment discrimination cases relating to psychological assessment, where predictive validation is a critical issue, a disparate impact claim is more likely to be at issue. Employees could produce statistical data that an unvalidated psychological test effectively prevented them from being promoted. However, intentional discrimination will come into play if the employer adjusts the scores, establishes different cutoff scores, or otherwise alters the scores—practices also prohibited by the *Civil Rights Act of 1991*.

The Americans with Disabilities Act of 1990

In 1990, Congress passed what has become known as the *Americans with Disabilities Act* (ADA), which became fully effective two years later, in July of 1992. The ADA is the most far-reaching Public Law since the Civil Rights Act of 1964, affecting all levels of state and local governments, about 5 million private businesses, and some 43 million Americans defined by the law as physically or mentally disabled. The ADA prohibits employers from discriminating against disabled persons who can perform the essential functions of the jobs they hold or desire to hold. The ADA does not spell out clearly who qualifies as disabled, although it specifically excludes from that category persons with sexual disorders, compulsive gamblers, kleptomaniacs (persons with a compulsive need to steal), pyromaniacs (those with a compulsive need to set fires), homosexuals, and persons with disorders resulting from current illegal use of drugs. The specific exclusion of homosexuals seems odd—why even mention this group? However, Congress apparently wished to recognize that homosexuality is not a mental or sexual disorder. In the years since the passage of the ADA, the courts—including the U.S. Supreme Court—have addressed some of its unanswered questions. Most recently, the Court has issued a number of rulings limiting the reach of the law. In a recent case, for example, the Court ruled that the disability covered by the law had to be one which restricted activities that are of central importance to most people's lives; thus, a person's carpal tunnel syndrome was not considered such a disability (*Toyota v. Williams*, 2002). Additionally, a company may refuse to hire a person with a disability for a job that could exacerbate the problem (*Chevron v. Echazabal*, 2002).

The ADA prohibits questions or questionnaires pertaining to past medical history or that otherwise elicit information about disabilities, unless an applicant has been given a conditional job offer. This raises a problem with respect to many psychological tests. Some items on the MMPI and the MMPI–2, for example, ask about medical history or center around medical or health problems. Does this mean that the MMPI–2 cannot be used, or does it mean that it can be used only after a candidate has reached the final screening stage? Employers and psychologists are reluctant to use any test in this manner because of the lack of precision in test scores and concerns about litigation (Camara & Merenda, 2000). Some psychologists continue to use the MMPI–2 at earlier stages of the application process, but they delete from the test those items that delve into medical history. The ADA further prohibits using qualification standards, employment tests, or other selection criteria that screen out individuals or a class of individuals with disabilities unless the standard, test, or other selection criteria is shown to be job-related and is consistent with business or occupational necessity. It could be argued, for example, that the ability to run is critical to work as a prison corrections officer, and that a person confined to a wheelchair could be screened out of such a position on that basis. On the other hand, the person should not be screened out of working as a counselor or a classification specialist in that prison.

According to the ADA, test procedures and materials must also be administered in such a manner that the test results accurately reflect the applicant's or employee's skills, aptitude, or other relevant abilities that are necessary for the job. This suggests that hiring agencies will be expected to adapt testing procedures if they impede performance of persons with a disability. For example, we might begin to see more braille versions of self-administered paper/pencil tests.

The ramifications of the ADA for psychological testing and assessment are enormous and will draw considerable legal attention in the years to come. It is also the kind of legislation that encourages serious conflicts and battle lines to be drawn between mental health professionals and lawyers. For example, a key question at this point is whether the diagnostic labels placed on many mental disorders qualify as disabilities. If they do, we can expect to see increasing challenges to the validity of these labels and the instruments and methods used to produce them.

Soroka v. Dayton Hudson Corporation

Soroka v. Dayton Hudson Corporation (1991) is important because it represents the first case in which, on the basis if an individual's right to privacy, the use of psychological inventories by an employer in the private sector was challenged (Camara & Merenda, 2000). Target Stores (owned and operated by Dayton Hudson Corporation) administered a battery of psychological inventories to candidates for security officer positions. The battery, called Psychscreen, was a combination of the MMPI (the first and now-retired version) and the California Psychological Inventory (CPI). In the fall of 1989, Sibi Soroka filed a suit in the Alameda County Court in California, arguing, among other things, that the MMPI questions probing religious attitudes, political views, and sexual orientation were invasive, offensive, and not job-related. Later that year and early the following year, Soroka was joined by three other plaintiffs. Their motion for a preliminary injunction to prohibit Target's continued use of Psychscreen was denied by the trial court. Furthermore, the trial court ruled that Target's use of Psychscreen was not unreasonable and that the store had a legitimate reason for screening emotional stability for security positions.

However, the California Court of Appeals reversed the order, and ultimately found that the invasive nature of the inventories violated both the constitutional right to privacy and statutory prohibitions against improper inquiries into a person's sexual orientation and religious beliefs. The California Supreme Court agreed to review the Appellate Court's ruling, but before the review could take place, the parties chose instead to settle out of court.

In the settlement, Target promised to stop using the inventories. Although the agreement settled the dispute, "aspects of the Appellate Court's ruling, which were especially critical of the use of tests containing items judged to be invasive of privacy, continue to have a 'chilling effect' on employers and test publishers. Employers are increasingly reluctant to use personality inventories in personnel decisions given the potential for litigation and reasoning behind the Appellate Court's decisions" (Camara & Merenda, 2000, p. 1167).

Testing in Education

Testing affects most of us in some way, but it is most pervasive in the American educational system. More than 250 million commercial standardized tests designed to measure ability and perception, achievement, emotional stability, and social competencies, as well as interest patterns, are administered annually in our schools. For years, the use of these educational and psychological tests went unchallenged. Prompted by various interest groups, courts in the 1960s began to scrutinize the cultural and social validity of a wide range of testing practices in both the educational setting and in the employment policies of various private companies and public agencies.

One landmark case, *Hobson v. Hansen* (1967), questioned the propriety of using standardized tests to place a disproportionate number of minority children into the lower academic tracks and middle-class white children into higher ones. In *Hobson*, the federal appellate court condemned the practice of rigid, poorly conceived group classifications on the basis of group tests lacking sensitivity to minorities. The court found that the skills measured by the test instruments were not innately intellectual but rather were acquired through cultural experience gained in home, community, and school. Once labeled, the child would carry this label throughout his or her school years, perpetuating the classification and leaving little opportunity to alter it.

Bersoff (1979, p. 50) writes, "With one blow . . . [the] decision in Hobson severely wounded two sacred cows, ability grouping and standardized testing." Perhaps the gravest blow came from the court's insistence that educational grouping must be based on tests that measure innate ability. However, the quest for culturally fair tests or tests that measure innate ability has not been successful. Behavior is a result of the ongoing interaction between cultural-social experience and neurophysiological predisposition and capacity. One component cannot be isolated and measured independently of the other. Therefore, this jurisprudential demand could not be met, and psychological testing within the nation's school systems faced the possibility of elimination.

Amid the controversy, psychologists tried to educate the public and the courts about what psychological tests can do. They argued that standardized tests are useful to some extent in predicting future learning ability. The correlation coefficients of validity between test scores and academic performance are modest, but they are significant and generalizable. Moreover, achievement tests generally demonstrate good content validity and do measure how well students have acquired the skills taught in the school system. Nevertheless, psychologists were hard pressed to justify tests if they were used to discriminate against minority students.

Another landmark case, *Larry P. v. Riles* (1972), questioned the use of individual cognitive ability tests and the existence of special classes for the academically or intellectually handicapped. In 1971, the parents of African-American children attending San Francisco schools filed a class action suit charging discrimination in the educational placement of their children. Children scoring 75 or lower on a cognitive ability test were placed in special educable mentally retarded (EMR) classes. The parents presented affidavits from African-American psychologists who had retested the children and found them to score above the 75 cutoff point. The African-American examiners, while administering the same tests as the previous white examiners, tried to establish rapport during the testing and reworded test items in a way which was consistent with the children's social and cultural background. Of course, altering the testing procedure contaminates the internal validity of the test results, rendering the scores questionable for comparison purposes. Yet, the point made by the African-American examiners cannot be ignored.

The court decided that the defendants (the San Francisco School System and the California Department of Education) could meet the challenge initiated by the suit by showing "a minimally reasonable relationship between the practice of classification and the goal of placement" (Bersoff, 1979, p. 72). The problem now becomes: What constitutes a "reasonable relationship"? What correlation coefficient would satisfy the court's expectations? As noted by Donald Bersoff, validity correlations that psychologists find acceptable (often around .30- to .40-lower than the reliability coefficients they find acceptable) may not satisfy the expectations of the courts. In *Merriken v. Cressman* (1973, p. 920), for instance, it was ruled that "when a program talks about labeling someone as a particular type and such a label could remain with him for the remainder of his life, the margin of error must be almost nil. . . . " "Nil" implies an unusually high correlation, probably ranging between .90 and a perfect correlation of 1.00. Few if any psychological tests demonstrate any type of validity of this magnitude.

Riles (*Larry P. v. Riles*, 1972), which was ultimately resolved by the California Supreme Court, became a long and difficult case because of the numerous important issues raised about the potentially discriminatory classifications in testing and about labeling within the educational system. The case, which produced two federal decisions, took over seven years to settle. The first decision, known as *Riles I* (1972), was concerned only with the propriety of a preliminary injunction to suspend classification on the basis of existing methods of testing the children. *Riles II* (1979) was far more wide ranging, because the court found that the cognitive ability tests used for classification were culturally biased in favor of white children and therefore discriminatory. The court required that the tests used for classification purposes be shown to have clear validity and be appropriate for use with minority children. As Bersoff (1981, p. 1048) explained, "tests would have to be correlated with relevant criterion measures; that is, IQ scores of African-American children would have to be correlated with classroom performance." He adds that, given the stringent criteria outlined by the court, "it is unlikely that any of the currently used cognitive ability tests are valid, which casts doubt on the continued utility of traditional evaluations using psychology's storehouse of standardized ability tests." Even recent re-standardizations of the Wechsler and Stanford–Binet Scales using a representative population of African-American children have failed to satisfy the court's standard of validity.

Psychologists have argued that the conclusions reached in *Riles II* reflect considerable misunderstanding and ignorance of psychological testing and psychometric theory (Bersoff, 1981). The case of *PASE v. Hannon* (1980), however, was more unsettling. There, the court ruled that the cognitive ability tests used by the school system in question did not discriminate against African-American children. That conclusion was reached in a highly subjective and unscientific manner, however. The judge cited each question on the Wechsler and Stanford–Binet Scales and then cited every acceptable response to each item. He decided for himself on the basis of this "analysis" which items were culturally biased. In his judgment, only eight items on the WISC/WISC–R and one item on the Stanford–Binet met his "criterion" for non-bias.

The ultimate resolution of the status of psychological testing and its utility in educational placement appears far down the road. The confusion is at least partly due to lack of knowledge about testing and psychometric theory, which pervades the judicial system and to some extent psychology itself. Psychologists must realize, however, that questions of acceptable social policy also pervade this area. In the opinion of many observers, a psychological test which correlates strongly with academic performance but has a discriminatory impact on a minority group of students has no place in our educational system.

Many of the legal problems encountered in testing could be eliminated, or at least reduced, if test designers and users understood and systematically described the behaviors they were measuring, the tasks to which those behaviors were demonstrably related, the conditions for the instrument's proper use, and the known distortions and potential risks involved (Schwitzgebel & Schwitzgebel, 1980). Before concluding that a test measures "intelligence," one should know (a) the precise behavioral definition of the intelligence to be tapped by that test; (b) the specific behaviors included; (c) what tasks or performance the behaviors are related to; and (d) the inherent dangers and possibility of the test having a discriminatory impact. This would presuppose knowledge about a test's reliability and validity, the methods used to establish its norms, and the standardization procedures. In addition, there must be a continual realization that a test samples a very small segment of behavior under restrictive and artificial conditions. It is unfortunate that a large portion of existing published tests would fail to meet many of these guidelines.

This does not mean that all tests, including cognitive ability tests, are meaningless and useless. We must know what a test can and cannot do, and we must apply it to appropriate populations with a very cautious and scientific attitude. With this approach, we can use valid psychological tests to our advantage and that of the population we are assessing. Shortcuts entail a myriad of potential social damages to consumers in the same manner that a hastily marketed drug may harbor potential physiological damage.

One last area needs attention. Judicial concern about the discriminatory potentials of testing in the educational and employment fields has focused almost exclusively upon ability or intellectual testing, both group and individual. Personality testing has yet to be challenged seriously, although its susceptibility to challenge is extremely high. Personality testing is plagued by vagueness and excessive levels of subjective interpretation backed by little empirical support. Construct validation would be helpful because this form of testing appears to be a good candidate for considerable legal attention in the near future.

The Individuals with Disabilities Education Act

The *Individuals with Disabilities Education Act* (IDEA) was originally enacted by Congress on November 19, 1975. At that time, it was known as the *Education of All Handicapped Children Act*. Congress passed this legislation in response to two federal court decisions (*Pennsylvania Association of Retarded Citizens (PARC) v. Pennsylvania* (1972) and *Mills v. Washington, DC Board of Education* (1972)) which ruled that public education must be extended to include children with disabilities. The *Individuals with Disabilities Education Act Amendments of 1997* (called IDEA 97) were signed into law by President Clinton on June 4, 1997. The final IDEA '97 Regulations were released on March 12, 1999. The Amendments strengthened academic expectations and accountability for the nation's 5.8 million children with disabilities and focused the student's educational planning process by promoting meaningful access to the mainstream education curriculum.

The IDEA is fundamentally a funding statute. It is implemented through allocations of federal funds to those states that agree to abide by its essential requirements (Melton et al., 1997). The term "handicapped children" includes mental retardation, autism, serious emotional disturbance, a variety of physical disabilities, and learning disabilities (including perceptual handicaps, brain injury, minimal brain dysfunction, dyslexia, and development aphasia). ADHD has not been listed as a separate condition of eligibility but, under certain conditions, it *could* render a child eligible under the "other health impaired" section of IDEA 97. The IDEA 97 allows handicapped students ages 3 to 21 (or even older if state rules allow) to qualify.

The IDEA 97 advised that in assessing children with disabilities, school districts may use a variety of assessment techniques to determine the extent to which these children can be involved and can progress through the general curriculum. The techniques may include criterion-related tests, standard achievement tests, diagnostic tests, other tests, and any combination of the above. The Act emphasizes, however, that no single procedure or test can be the sole criterion for determining appropriate educational programs for the child (Melton et al., 1997). The IDEA regulations mandate that the measuring instruments and other evaluation materials must be valid or validated for the specific purpose for which they are used. Furthermore, the examiners and evaluators must be trained to administer the instruments used. For example, because IQ tests are often criticized as not being culturally fair, the IDEA specifies that IQ tests may *not* form the only basis for evaluation.

The IDEA creates a several stage process for evaluating children. Once identified, each child must be evaluated by a multidisciplinary team whose primary objective is to develop an individual education plan, called the IEP. The IEP should be a written document that defines the program and services, including the goals and objectives, and any equipment or accommodations that the educational agency will provide, as well as the student's placement. According to Melton et al. (1997), examiners should consider five traits or skills in evaluating handicapped persons under the provisions of the IDEA: (1) intelligence; (2) language and communication skills; (3) perceptual abilities, including visual, auditory, motor, and attention factors; (4) academic achievement; and (5) behavioral and emotional deficits and problems. The IDEA and its Amendments create a major forensic opportunity for clinicians who are trained in education and developmental psychology (Melton, et al. 1997). A similar opportunity may exist for psychologists in the implementation of the *No Child Left Behind Act of 2001*, which is intended to improve the performance of the nation's elementary and secondary schools while at the same time ensuring that no child is trapped in a failing school.

Summary and Conclusions

The goal of psychological testing and assessment is to reduce the complexity of human mental processes and behavior to a manageable set of variables so that the current and sometimes past status of individuals can be appraised and their future behavior predicted. As such, psychological tests and inventories can be invaluable tools to the psychologist consulting with courts, law enforcement, correctional system, and business and industry. Forensic psychologists administer, score, and interpret thousands of tests every year, and these psychological measures take up a significant portion of their professional time. An understanding of the basic principles of reliability, validity, standard error of measurement, and normative distribution is crucial if one is to evaluate any testing program. Too many agencies have initiated testing programs without any evidence that the instruments they are using are valid or reliable. For this reason, and because we will encounter these instruments throughout the book, it is important that the principles, procedures, concepts, and nature of psychological testing be described in an early chapter.

The first part of the chapter was organized around three general classifications of assessment and testing instruments and techniques: (1) clinical measures and assessment techniques; (2) forensically relevant instruments (FRIs); and (3) forensic assessment instruments (FAIs). The three categories reflect the degree of direct relevance the various instruments have to specific legal issues and topics. The number of commercially available psychological instruments that have clear forensic applications has increased dramatically over the past dozen or so years (Otto & Heilbrun, 2002). The more heavily utilized psychological instruments within these three categories were briefly described in the chapter. Various screening devices are available, with varying limitations and strengths. Unfortunately, many of the commercially available instruments have undergone only preliminary research and development and often do not follow the guidelines established in the *Standards for Educational and Psychological Testing* sponsored by the American Educational Research Association, the American Psychological Association, and the National Council on Measurement in Education (1999). Randy Otto and Kirk Heilbrun (2002, p. 10) admonish that "This situation must be addressed immediately, or forensic psychology will risk its reputation in the courtroom, particularly as legal decision makers become knowledgeable about the science of assessment."

A considerable amount of headway into the validation of testing in forensic settings has been made by the MacArthur Research Network on Mental Health and Law, and this group of scientists should continue to make significant strides in forensic testing and assessment far into the foreseeable future. Still, a considerable amount of research and development remains critical if forensic psychology is to maintain and improve its standing in the legal community. In addition, psychologists must continue to be trained in the testing principles and concepts outlined in the chapter if forensic psychology is to move forward.

Later in the chapter, we covered the broad issue of prediction of human behavior, which is at the core of much psychological assessment. The debate over the relative merits of actuarial (or statistical) prediction and clinical prediction was covered in detail. The weight of the research evidence clearly leans toward statistical prediction as the better forecaster of human behavior. Nevertheless, some combination of both may be in order in situations requiring human judgment. Research on "decision trees," such as that developed by the MacArthur Research Network, shows promise in this regard. The chapter ended with a discussion of testing in employment and education. With its passage of major legislation, Congress has attempted to address disparities and discrimination in each of these areas.

Key Terms

Actuarial prediction	Inter-judge reliability
Anamnestic prediction	Internal consistency
Clinical prediction	Iterative classification tree
Concurrent validity	Normative distribution
Content validity	Predictive validity
Correlation coefficient	Psychological assessment
Dynamic risk factor	Psychological testing
Experience prediction	Standard error of measurement
Face validity	Static risk factor
Fundamental attribution error	Test-retest reliability

Questions for Review

1. Distinguish between psychological testing and psychological assessment.
2. What are the three general classifications of assessment and testing described in the chapter? Provide an illustration of each.
3. Explain the three ways of measuring the reliability of a psychological test.
4. Distinguish between concurrent, predictive, content, and face validity.
5. Define and provide three examples of cognitive tests and three examples of projective tests.
6. What are the major differences between the MMPI and the MMPI–2? What are the strengths and weaknesses of the MMPI–2?
7. List and describe briefly four measures for assessing psychopathy.
8. What are risk assessment measures? Distinguish between dynamic and static factors in the assessment of risk.
9. Discuss the role of forensic neuropsychologists and provide examples of tasks they might perform in both criminal and civil law.
10. Give at least two examples of assessment instruments that might be used in each of the following situations: evaluations of competency to stand trial; evaluations of criminal responsibility; child custody evaluations.
11. What are the respective strengths and weaknesses of actuarial and clinical prediction?
12. Based on material covered in this chapter, what advice would you give to an employer wishing to administer psychological tests in hiring and promotion?

CHAPTER 3

Psychology and the Courts: An Overview

A random survey of 100 adult Americans would very likely find that each has viewed a courtroom scene at some point in adulthood. Before electronic media were allowed in courtrooms, the scene was more likely to be a fictional one, depicted in movies or television programs. Today, technology has allowed us to observe at least some "real" court proceedings from a distance. Even so, we are most likely to see unrepresentative, sensational trials, or those portions of a trial and its aftermath which attract intense public interest, such as the testimony of a key witness or the sentencing of an individual convicted of a heinous crime. Civil trials, compared with criminal trials, get little attention. Furthermore, with rare exceptions, the electronic media do not cover pre-trial proceedings, which can be extensive and result in the resolution of most cases. Research demonstrates that about 90% of criminal cases are settled between a defendant's first court appearance and the trial stage (Neubauer, 2002). About 75% of civil cases that reach the courts are settled without going to trial (Abadinsky, 1995).

Although the media have exposed virtually everyone to courtroom proceedings, far fewer adult Americans have actually been in a courtroom, either as observers or as participants. Nevertheless, the numbers may be still impressive. Many adults have been called to jury duty, in some states quite frequently. In one survey, just over 40% of citizens indicated they had had some experience with their state court system over the past five years (Benesh & Howell, 2001). It is not clear whether this experience included a courtroom appearance, however.

Despite growing familiarity with the courtroom, we are generally less knowledgeable about the structure of courts or the legal questions and standards that judges, lawyers, and jurors must address. Even basic legal distinctions, such as that between criminal and civil law, are foreign to many citizens. This chapter, therefore, introduces the reader to the court system and different categories of law, and discusses the judicial process in both criminal and civil cases. We will cover fundamental concepts and focus on matters relating to courts that are most relevant to psychology. Additionally, we will highlight issues that create special challenges to those trying to "span the boundaries" between psychology and law, which in some ways are such disparate disciplines. Chief among these is the role of the expert witness and the dilemmas that sometime arise for psychologists when they accept this role.

Organization of the Courts

The court system in the United States is a *dual system*, consisting of federal and state courts, which are inter-related yet independent of one another. They may exist in the same geographical location. Federal courts deal with matters arising out of the U.S. Constitution and a wide variety of federal criminal and civil laws, including administrative laws. Additionally, they hear cases involving disputes between citizens of different states, although their power to do this has been shared with state courts in order to lessen the burden on federal courts (Abraham, 1998). Finally, federal courts may settle disputes between a state and another country or its citizens.

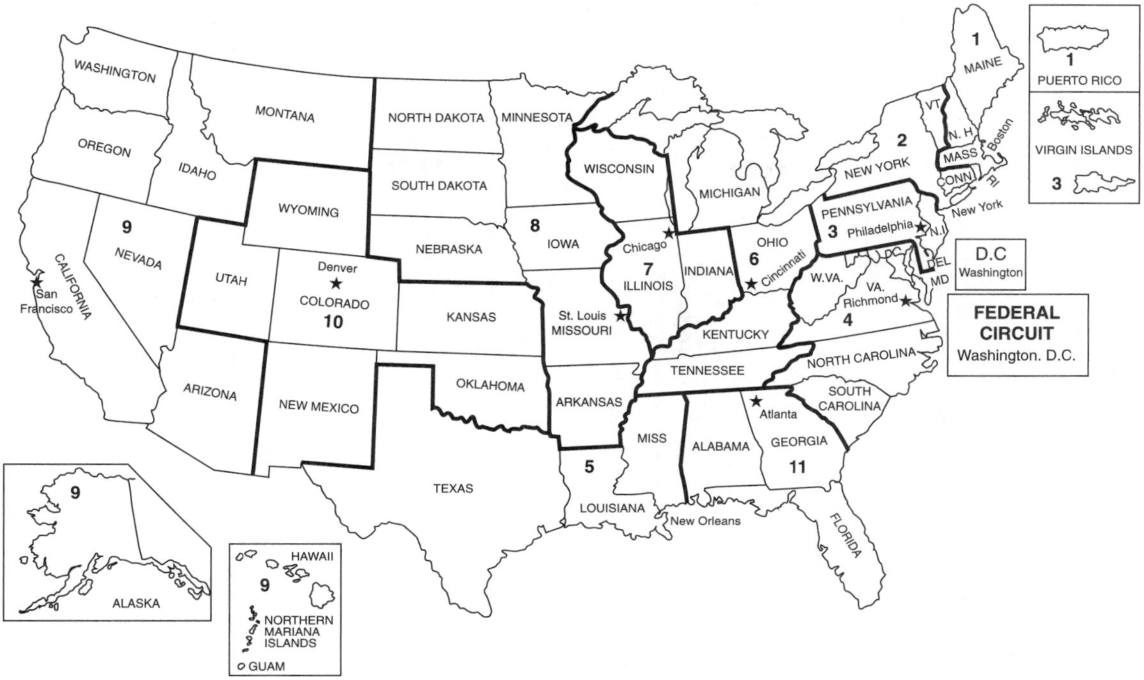

Figure 3-1

The thirteen federal judicial circuits. (Eleven are numbered, plus the D.C. and Federal Judicial Circuits.) *Source:* Administrative Office of the United States Courts, September 1977.

The federal court system has its origin in the Constitution. Article III Section I establishes one Supreme Court and "such inferior Courts as the Congress may from time to time ordain and establish." The very first law passed by the Congress of the United States was the *Judiciary Act of 1789*, which began to create the federal judiciary. Over the years, Congress has tinkered with a variety of courts, adding and deleting them as the country grew and the geography of the nation changed. Today, the federal court system comprises appellate and trial courts. The **appellate courts** consist of one Supreme Court and, at an intermediate level, 13 Courts of Appeal for the various circuits. The **trial courts** in the federal system are the 95 U.S. District Courts. Attached to these District Courts are magistrate judge's courts, where much of the preliminary work on criminal and civil cases is done. Additionally, the federal system includes a variety of **specialized courts**, such as bankruptcy courts, patent courts, and special district courts. **Figure 3-1** provides a view of the judicial circuits.

State courts deal with matters arising under the laws of the 50 states. Structurally, they parallel the structure of federal courts, in that there are both trial and appellate courts. However, there are wide variations in the numbers and levels of courts within each state. Particularly in heavily populated states, a bewildering array of courts can exist. All states have a court of last resort, but some have no intermediate appellate court. In those cases, decisions at the trial court level are appealed directly to the state's court of last resort. The great majority of states today also have a wide variety of specialized courts (e.g., traffic, small claims, and family courts), and, as will be seen shortly, many states are experimenting with other specialized courts like drug, mental health, and domestic violence courts. **Figure 3-2**

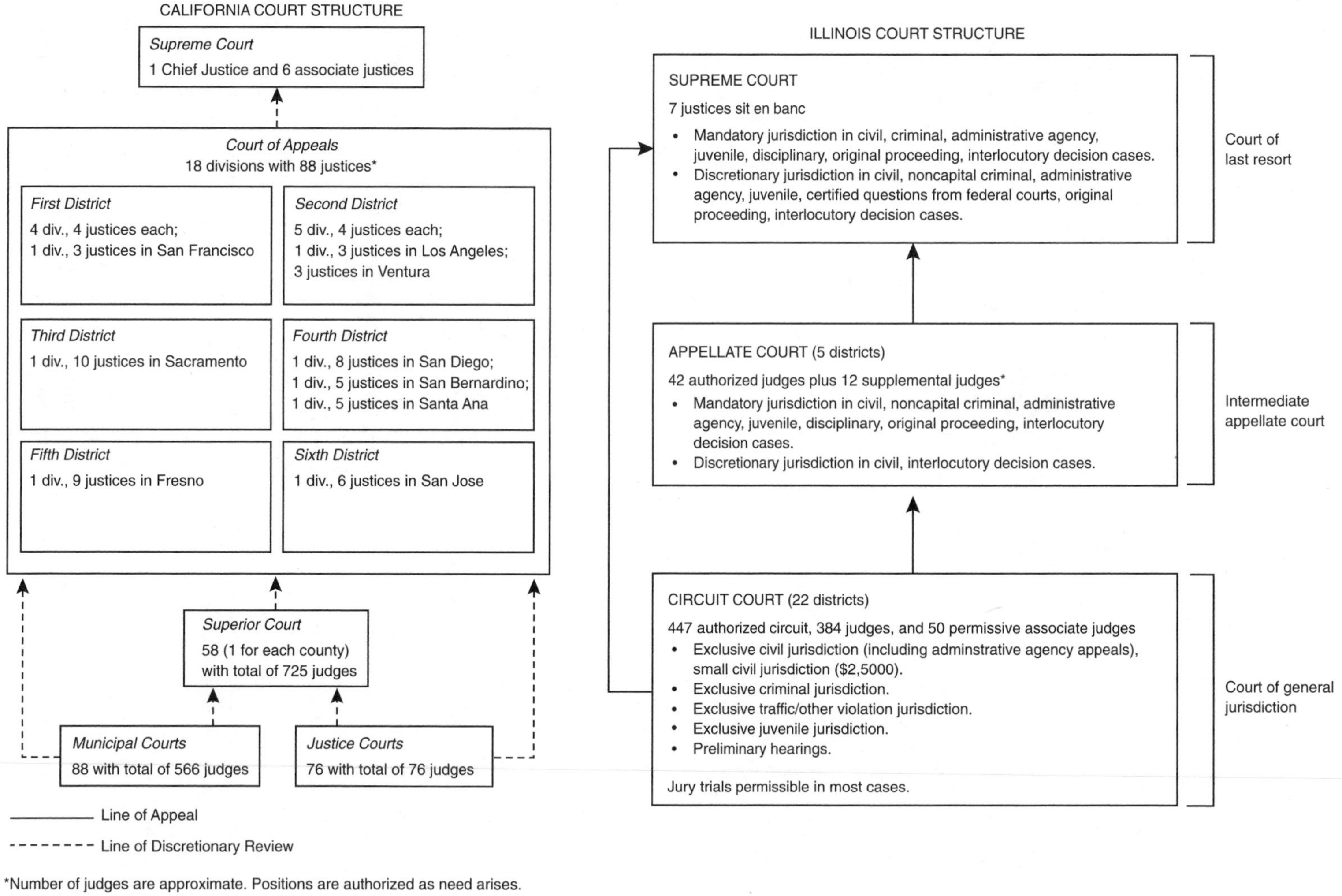
CALIFORNIA COURT STRUCTURE
Supreme Court
1 Chief Justice and 6 associate justices
Court of Appeals
18 divisions with 88 justices*
First District
4 div., 4 justices each;
1 div., 3 justices in San Francisco
Second District
5 div., 4 justices each;
1 div., 3 justices in Los Angeles;
3 justices in Ventura
Third District
1 div., 10 justices in Sacramento
Fourth District
1 div., 8 justices in San Diego;
1 div., 5 justices in San Bernardino;
1 div., 5 justices in Santa Ana
Fifth District
1 div., 9 justices in Fresno
Sixth District
1 div., 6 justices in San Jose
Superior Court
58 (1 for each county)
with total of 725 judges
Municipal Courts
88 with total of 566 judges
Justice Courts
76 with total of 76 judges
Line of Appeal
Line of Discretionary Review
ILLINOIS COURT STRUCTURE
SUPREME COURT
7 justices sit en banc
• Mandatory jurisdiction in civil, criminal, administrative agency, juvenile, disciplinary, original proceeding, interlocutory decision cases.
• Discretionary jurisdiction in civil, noncapital criminal, administrative agency, juvenile, certified questions from federal courts, original proceeding, interlocutory decision cases.
Court of last resort
APPELLATE COURT (5 districts)
42 authorized judges plus 12 supplemental judges*
• Mandatory jurisdiction in civil, noncapital criminal, administrative agency, juvenile, disciplinary, original proceeding, interlocutory decision cases.
• Discretionary jurisdiction in civil, interlocutory decision cases.
Intermediate appellate court
CIRCUIT COURT (22 districts)
447 authorized circuit, 384 judges, and 50 permissive associate judges
• Exclusive civil jurisdiction (including adminstrative agency appeals), small civil jurisdiction ($2,5000).
• Exclusive criminal jurisdiction.
• Exclusive traffic/other violation jurisdiction.
• Exclusive juvenile jurisdiction.
• Preliminary hearings.
Jury trials permissible in most cases.
Court of general jurisdiction
*Number of judges are approximate. Positions are authorized as need arises.

Figure 3-2

Court structure in California and Illinois.

contrasts the court structure in two states (Illinois and California).

The term **jurisdiction** is used to refer to the authority given to a particular court in resolving a dispute. Jurisdiction is best understood as "the geographic area, subject matter, or persons over which a court can exercise authority" (Abadinsky, 1995, p. 144). Occasionally, two or more courts may have the authority to hear a case, called **concurrent jurisdiction**. For example, a particular law violation may have the potential of involving both federal and state courts. An employer who refuses to promote a handicapped employee may be violating both federal and state statutes. In this situation, the person filing suit (the plaintiff) may have the choice of filing in the federal or state court. Likewise, in the criminal context, one incident can represent an alleged violation of both federal and state law. The Oklahoma City Bombing case, in which defendants were tried for crimes related to the bombing of the Alfred E. Murrah Federal Building in 1995, provides a good illustration of this. Timothy McVeigh and Terry Nichols violated both federal and state laws. McVeigh was tried and sentenced to death in federal court. Also in federal court, Nichols pleaded guilty to conspiracy and bombing charges to avoid a death sentence. State prosecutors in Oklahoma then announced that they would try Nichols on state murder charges, presumably in order to obtain the death sentence that he had managed to avoid in federal court.

Trial courts, compared with appellate courts, are divided into courts of **general jurisdiction** and **limited jurisdiction**. Trial courts of general jurisdiction have broad authority to deal with a wide range of issues. Felony trials as well as major trials in civil cases are held in these courts. Courts of limited jurisdiction, by contrast, are the entry-level courts. They typically cannot conduct felony trials, although judges in those courts can hold preliminary hearings, issue search warrants, and conduct a variety of pre-trial proceedings. In state court systems, courts of limited jurisdiction are referred to as lower courts, municipal courts, or inferior courts. Magistrate Judges' Courts, attached to U.S. District Courts, are the courts of limited jurisdiction in the federal system.

We will now look a bit more closely at the work of federal and state courts.

Federal Courts

The subject-matter jurisdiction of federal courts is set forth in Article III Section II of the U.S. Constitution. Clearly, the federal court had high demands imposed on their time right from the outset.

> The judicial Power shall extend to all Cases, in Law and Equity, arising under this Constitution, the Laws of the United States, and Treaties made, or which shall be made, under their Authority;—to all Cases affecting Ambassadors, other public Ministers and Consuls;—to all Cases of admiralty and maritime jurisdiction;—to Controversies to which the United States shall be a Party;—to Controversies between two or more States;—between a State and Citizens of another State;—between Citizens of different States;—between Citizens of the same State claiming Lands under Grants of different States, and between a State, or the Citizens thereof, and foreign States, Citizens or Subjects.

Congress over the years has passed a wide array of laws increasing the work of federal courts. Laws relating to the protection of the environment, employment discrimination, health regulation, crime control, safety in the workplace, and broadcasting are but a few examples. Although Congress has also created administrative agencies, such as the Nuclear Regulatory Commission (NRC), the FCC (Federal Communications Commission), and OSHA (Occupational Safety and Health Administration) to enforce these laws, the federal courts have the ultimate power to resolve disputes arising out of agency decisions. Consequently, the work of federal courts today is both varied and overwhelming. In the period 1960–1983, cases filed in federal district courts more than tripled, from roughly 80,000 to 280,000 (Posner, 1985). Discussing the work of U.S. district and bankruptcy courts, Abraham (1998, p. 174) commented that "the average caseload has grown by more than 4% every year since World War II, doubling every fifteen to twenty years, lead [*sic*] by the civil realm." As we will see below, Congress in recent years also has passed laws in an effort to ease the burden on federal courts.

The 95 U.S. District Courts carry most of the workload in the federal system. At least one district court is situated in each state; California, Texas, and New York each have four such courts. U.S. District Courts also are located in Puerto Rico, the Northern

Mariana Islands, Guam, the District of Columbia, and the Virgin Islands. Congress also has created special district courts, which are three-judge courts to be convened only when necessary. These special district courts are to be distinguished from the specialized courts referred to above. Comprising two district judges and one appeals court judge, the special courts rule on issues relating to the *Voting Rights Act of 1965* and the *Civil Rights Act of 1964*, as well as their respective amendments. They also deal with apportionment cases (Abraham, 1998).

At the next level from the trial courts are the intermediate appellate courts. The United States is divided into thirteen geographically defined jurisdictions or circuits, each with a U.S. Court of Appeals. These federal appellate courts comprise between five and twenty-eight judges, who meet both in panels of three and, in major cases, as a whole (*en banc*). The primary purpose of the Court of Appeals is to review decisions made by the federal district courts within its jurisdiction. Courts of Appeals also review cases heard by specialized courts, such as tax courts, and the various federal administrative agencies. Therefore, defendants or litigants who have lost their cases in a district court or before an agency such as the Federal Communications Commission (FCC) may have their cases reviewed by the Court of Appeals in their circuit.

It is important to note that appellate courts do not conduct trials because their function is to rule on matters of law, not fact. They ask, "Was the law applied properly by the trial court?" rather than, "Was there sufficient time for the defendant to arrive at the murder scene after leaving his office?" To illustrate further, consider the following hypothetical situation. Moe is arrested and charged with kidnapping the child of a prominent political figure. When his case comes to trial in a U.S. District Court, he chooses not to testify, exercising his Fifth Amendment right not to incriminate himself. The prosecutor, in closing arguments to the jury, suggests that Moe must be guilty because of his failure to testify, and the presiding judge does not admonish the jury to disregard the comment. Moe is convicted. Moe's lawyer appeals the conviction on the basis that the prosecutor's comment prejudiced the jury and deprived her client of his Sixth Amendment right to a fair trial. The appeals court, then, is asked to determine whether the law (in this case, involving instructions to the jury) was properly applied. The federal appeals court determines that the law was not properly applied, overturns the conviction, and sends the case back for a new trial.

While the intermediate appellate courts in the federal system must rule on all cases properly presented to them for review, the highest court in the land, the U.S. Supreme Court, has much more discretion. The Supreme Court consists of nine Justices appointed for life by the President, with the advice and consent of the U.S. Senate. One of the nine is designated Chief Justice by the President, and the Court is usually referred to collectively by the name of that individual—for example, the Rehnquist Court. The Supreme Court begins to meet on the first Monday of October each year and usually continues in session until June.

Although what the Court may hear is defined by the Constitution and Congress, the Justices are given nearly complete control of their docket by refusing to hear and review cases as they choose. The cases the Justices select are usually those believed to address important, unanswered questions, and they often involve an interpretation of the U.S. Constitution. A petitioner or appellant requests review by filing documents summarizing the facts of the case, the decision of the lower court, and setting forth argument as to why the Court should hear the case. If four of the nine Supreme Court Justices agree to hear the case, they issue a **writ of certiorari**, calling for the record below to be sent up for review. (A "writ" is a written judicial order; in this case, the lower court is ordered to produce the documents needed to review the proceedings.) In addition, the U.S. Supreme Court, like other federal appellate courts, may receive ***habeas corpus* petitions** on behalf of individuals who believe they are illegally confined, such as in a mental institution or prison. (*Habeas corpus* is Latin for "you have the body.") In 1996, federal courts were asked to review over 68,000 *habeas corpus* petitions.

Although the appellate process may be quite slow, in matters where time is of the essence or where political interests are at stake, it may occur very quickly. The Presidential election of 2000, in which the U.S. Supreme Court intervened and essentially selected George W. Bush as President of the U.S. (*Bush v. Gore*, 2000), is one noteworthy example. Other less-highly publicized cases in recent history have included cases in which U.S. citizens wished to bring medication into the country, death penalty cases, or cases involving press freedoms.

About 5,000 appeals are filed with the U.S. Supreme Court each year, but a vast majority are denied because the subject matter is either not proper or is not of sufficient importance to warrant full Court review. Additionally, there is simply not enough time for the Justices to hear all of the cases that come to their attention. The denials of *certiorari* may or may not include a brief statement explaining why the decision of the lower appellate court must stand. On the average, the Court agrees to hear about 150 to 200 cases each year.

Partly in an attempt to reduce the workload of the federal courts, Congress in recent years has limited the types of cases that can be heard. For example, Congress placed severe limitations on federal court supervision of state prisons when it passed the *Prison Litigation Reform Act* (PLRA) which went into effect in 1996. One provision of that law requires that inmates in state prisons must exhaust all administrative remedies available to them before going to federal courts. In a recent interpretation of the PLRA, the Court ruled that even inmates claiming brutality or excessive force by correctional officials must go through prison grievance proceedings before going to the federal courts (*Porter v. Nussle*, 2002). In the *Antiterrorism and Effective Death Penalty Act of 1996*, Congress also placed strict limits on the filing of *habeas corpus* petitions by inmates in the federal courts. For example, it created a one-year deadline for the filing of these petitions, made it difficult if not impossible to file if a claim was adjudicated on the merits in state courts, and placed limits on successive petitions. As a result of this law, the federal courts are expected to play a much more limited role in death penalty cases.

State Courts

As noted earlier and illustrated in ☒ **Figure 3-2**, state courts follow roughly the same pyramidal structure as the federal courts, usually with one highest appellate court, or court of last resort. Some states choose to call their highest court something other than "Supreme Court," however. Massachusetts's court of last resort, for example, is the Supreme Judicial Court, and New York's highest court is the New York Court of Appeals. In Texas, in addition to the Texas Supreme Court, there is a special court of last resort for criminal cases, the Court of Criminal Appeals. The process and administration of these state courts vary widely from state to state, as do the state laws under which they operate.

State courts have a general, unlimited power to decide almost every type of case, subject only to the limitations of state law. Therefore, state courts, primarily the trial courts, are the place where most of the legal business of American society begins and ends, although it has been asserted that the rate of growth in federal courts is surpassing that in most state courts (Posner, 1985; Abraham, 1998). By the late 1980s, over one million cases were heard yearly by trial courts in the U.S. (Flanagan & Maguire, 1991). The higher or appellate state courts, like federal appellate courts, are created to deal with questions of law that arose in the lower court, often during the trial process.

Public Confidence in Courts

In recent years, a great deal has been written about the lack of confidence the public has in its court system (Flanagan & Longmire, 1996). Psychologist Thomas Tyler (1990) maintains that process is more important than outcome when it comes to measuring satisfaction. That is, if people who use the courts perceive that they have been treated fairly, they will be favorably disposed to the judiciary, even though they may not have won their case. Empirical research lends support to this hypothesis (e.g., Tyler, 1990; Benesh & Howell, 2001). However, studies comparing confidence in courts among users and non-users have arrived at differing conclusions. In an early, nationwide study of confidence in local and state courts (National Center for State Courts, 1978) researchers found that persons who had been to court had less confidence in them than people who had not. A re-analysis of that data found no significant differences, however (Kritzer & Voelker, 1998). Benesh and Howell (2001) polled 1,208 Louisiana citizens and found that 515 had had "some experience with" the state court system during the last five years. Results indicated that the public's perceptions of timeliness, courtesy, and equal treatment all affected confidence in the courts. However, opinions of those who had experience with courts (such as defendants, plaintiffs, witnesses, and jurors) were polarized. Those who had more at stake (e.g., defendants) were less confident in the courts than those who had a substantial measure of control in the outcome (e.g., jurors). Benesh and Howell conclude that future studies attempting to measure public confidence in courts must differentiate among types of citizen involvement.

Other studies have attempted to disentangle race, ethnic, gender, age, and income variables as they relate to confidence in the courts. Not surprisingly, groups that historically have felt the doors of the law closed to them, or have experienced discriminatory treatment by agents of the law, are less trustful of the courts. Brooks and Jeon-Slaughter (2001) found that Black middle-income respondents had less confidence in most courts than lower-income Blacks, but more confidence in the U.S. Supreme Court. These findings are similar to those of other researchers who have found that middle- and upper-income Blacks are more critical of legal institutions in general (e.g., Weitzer & Tuch, 1999; Wortley, Hagan, & Macmillan, 1997). By comparison, de la Garza and DeSipio (2001) found that Latinos had approximately the same level of confidence in courts as non-Hispanic whites, a fact they attributed in part to the generally moderate or conservative political ideology of the Latino population. Additionally, Latinos in their sample were less likely to have experienced the discrimination experienced by other populations. Despite the positive findings, however, a significant minority of Latinos were extremely critical of courts (and of police).

Many commentators have suggested that public confidence in the courts will be restored if courts, as well as other legal institutions, foster therapeutic outcomes (e.g., Casey & Rottman, 2000; Wexler & Winick, 1996). This is in keeping with the concept of **therapeutic jurisprudence** mentioned in ◀ Chapter 1 and defined by David Wexler (1990b, p. 4) as "the study of the use of the law to achieve therapeutic outcomes." Therapeutic jurisprudence has since gained many adherents and will be referenced at several points throughout the book. In the context of this chapter, we ask, "How can courts—which are essentially adversarial in nature—achieve therapeutic objectives?" Doing this would require the cooperation of judges and attorneys as well as a commitment to explore systematically the problems within a given community. Casey and Rottman (2000) have summarized a wide array of court policies, practices, rules, and actions to which principles of therapeutic jurisprudence can be applied ▲ (see **Table 3-1**). They also provide examples of therapeutically-oriented courts, including community-focused, mental health, drug, family, and domestic violence courts. As Casey and Rottman (2000, p. 454) note, however, "(t)he application of therapeutic jurisprudence principles is time consuming, interdisciplinary, and inexact—unattractive features to many judges and court systems . . . Thus the application of therapeutic jurisprudence will not be a 'quick fix' for courts; rather, it will require thoughtful discourse and experimentation."

TABLE 3-1

Features of Courts Oriented Toward Therapeutic Jurisprudence*

- Behavioral contracting
- Specialized dockets
- Ethic of care
- Encourage individual autonomy
- Court appearances scheduled to review defendant's progress
- One-on-one contact between litigants and judges
- Contacts between courts and community services
- Safety, access, convenience
- Courtesy, responsiveness, respect
- Timely disposition of cases
- Public education
- Judicial independence and accountability
- Flexibility
- Application of social science theory and research
- Wide variety of diagnostic tools are available

*Adapted from Casey and Rothman (2000).

Specialized Courts: Drug and Mental Health Courts

Toward the end of the 20th century, a trend toward the creation of specialized courts intended for therapeutic purposes became apparent. Most of these courts focused on drug and mental health problems.

Drug Courts The progenitor of treatment-oriented courts was the drug court, pioneered in Miami, Florida in 1989. A decade later, approximately 500 drug courts operated nationwide (Goldkamp & Irons-Guynn, 2000). Although these courts differ in clientele and in procedure, they typically deal with defendants whose substance abuse is believed to be at the root of their offending. By all accounts, this covers a high percentage of individuals. For example, it is estimated that about 22% of state prisoners and 61% of federal prisoners are drug offenders (Byrne, 1994). About two-thirds of federal prisoners were held for drug offenses in 1998, although the great majority (85%) were incarcerated for trafficking, while only 5% had been convicted of possession (Mumola, 1999). About 70% of all inmates in local facilities had committed a drug offense or used drugs regularly (Wilson, 2000). Arrest data also indicate that about two thirds of arrested males and more than half of all arrested females are under the influence of at least one illicit drug at the time of arrest (Drug Use Forecasting, 1995).

When a drug court exists in a particular location, certain defendants are identified shortly after arrest as good candidates for the court. Typically, these are defendants accused of nonviolent offenses who have been long-time users or addicts. They are then offered treatment in the community as an alternative to continued prosecution. The judge overseeing the drug court typically takes a case-management approach, requiring mandatory drug testing and monitoring the treatment process. Drug court defendants also are asked to make restitution to their victims when appropriate. Research on the success of drug courts has produced mixed results, with some studies suggesting a high level of effectiveness (e.g., Belenko, 1998; Goldkamp & Weiland, 1993) and others showing few if any differences between defendants who go through drug courts and those who go through regular criminal courts. In an effort to reconcile the mixed results, Miethe, Lu, and Reese (2000) suggest that a "shaming" component may provide an explanation for lack of positive results. Their study, involving 301 defendants processed in a drug court in Las Vegas and a control sample of equivalent size and charges, found that drug court defendants had significantly higher recidivism rates, measured by rearrests for drug offenses. After considering a variety of possible explanations, the researchers concluded—based on field observations—that drug court defendants were publicly stigmatized by the presiding judge, who frequently berated them and issued tongue lashings. The approach taken in this court, Miethe et al. observed, was quite the opposite of a reintegrative one. Advocates of therapeutic jurisprudence would certainly maintain that stigmatizing individuals does not foster therapeutic outcomes.

Mental Health Courts More recently, some communities have initiated mental health courts, closely akin to the drug court model. In fact, it is increasingly apparent that the co-occurrence of substance abuse and mental disorder is common in sizeable numbers of criminal defendants. A recent monograph focusing on four mental health courts (Goldkamp & Irons-Guynn, 2000) summarizes the common features of these courts. Typically, mental health courts are:

- Voluntary, requiring the consent of the defendant;
- Available only to individuals with demonstrable mental illness that was likely to contribute to their criminal activity;
- Concerned for public safety;
- Desirous of preventing the jailing of the mentally disordered; and
- Likely to exclude offenders with histories of violence.

Like drug courts, mental health courts differ in a variety of procedures, including the point at which individuals qualify for these services. Nevertheless, drug courts appear to possess more common features and to be established in accordance with a common model. By contrast, considerable difference was observed in the four mental health courts reviewed by Goldkamp and Irons-Guynn. One—the first in the nation mental health court in Broward County, Florida—was designed to divert mentally disordered defendants charged with misdemeanors from the criminal justice process. The other three courts accepted individuals only after conviction, most typically through a guilty plea. Other differences included how criminal charges were resolved, how noncompliant participants were handled, and the type of individual accepted. One court, for example, accepted low-level felony offenders with records of prior conviction in addition to their prior diagnoses of a mental disorder. The others did not accept felony defendants.

Mental health courts must grapple with special problems associated with their voluntary nature, confidentiality, and timeliness (Goldkamp & Irons-Guynn, 2000). Critics have asked, for example, whether a mentally disordered individually truly can comprehend the options offered to him by the mental health court, particularly when the treatment is contingent upon a guilty plea. Acceptance to the court requires the need for obtaining personal information that may well be irrelevant to the criminal charge. Finally, while courts may desire early intervention and efficient processing, the mental health professional needs time to conduct a thorough assessment. "To put it simply, it is hard to rush such an assessment and still have it be accurate and complete" (Goldkamp & Irons-Guynn, 2000, p. 3).

To function efficiently, and presumably to be effective, mental health courts require the cooperation of the judicial system and mental health professionals. Psychologists, psychiatrists, and clinical social workers are typically involved in the screening and the treatment of mental health court clients. However, it is typically the court that decides whether the individual being treated is cooperating and making adequate progress. Critics have noted that lack of available treatment resources could be problematic, and that a judges' subjective decision making on an individual's mental health is unwarranted (Hasselbrack, 2001).

To date, little research is available on the "effectiveness" of mental health courts. Moreover, although there are similarities among the existing courts, there is yet no common, identifiable model—in contrast to the common model adopted by many drug courts across the United States (Steadman, Davidson, & Brown, 2001). Mental health courts help address the problem of mentally disordered individuals in jails, a problem which has become increasingly intractable since the 1960s and 1970s, when the population of public mental institutions was drastically reduced. ▶ [The deinstitutionalization movement will be discussed in Chapter 5.] Some research indicates as much as 16% of the population of jails and prisons, or over a quarter million individuals, may be in need of mental health services (Ditton, 1999). ▶ [The problem is particularly salient in jails, for a variety of reasons, which will be discussed in detail in Chapter 10.] According to a recent government report (Bureau of Justice Statistics, 2001), a quarter of jail inmates in the U.S. said they had received treatment for a major emotional problem. Proponents of mental health courts argue that jails, in particular, cannot provide essential mental health services. Under court supervision, however, many of the individuals in jail could be treated in the community.

To date, it is unclear whether mental health courts significantly have helped prevent recidivism among their clients or have even provided them with needed services. As Steadman et al. (2001, p. 458) write, "In contrast to drug courts, existing mental health courts appear strapped for resources to follow through on their service linkages, to ensure that appropriate services are actually available and provided, and to supervise participation in the services mandated." Nevertheless, mental health courts represent a significant attempt to address problems that tend to be exacerbated by confinement. It remains to be seen whether better planning, funding, and evaluation research will lead to more optimistic conclusions. On the other hand, drug courts also are not exempt from fiscal concerns. As this is being written, some states are reconsidering their ability to fund these courts in light of looming or actual budget deficits.

Another type of specialized court that has begun to attract research attention is the domestic violence court ◙ (see **Box 3-1**). Faced with increasing concern about crimes of violence within the home, some jurisdictions have established courts focused primarily on finding solutions to the underlying problems within the family group. The courts supervise the provision of support services for victims of violence as well as counseling and treatment for offenders, unless contra-indicated. ▶ [Family violence will be discussed again in Chapter 11.]

BOX 3-1
Domestic Violence Courts

Extensive research on domestic violence over the past quarter century strongly indicates that:

- Without some form of intervention, domestic violence accelerates, sometimes ending in the death of the victim.
- Arrest is important, but arrest alone will not significantly reduce the incidence of domestic violence in a household.
- When courts refer abusers to counseling programs, the rate of compliance (no-shows) is quite high, sometimes over one-third of all of those referred.

In an effort to address the problem of domestic violence ▶ [which will be discussed again in Chapter 11], many communities have established specialized courts whose exclusive jurisdiction is domestic violence incidents. Like the mental health courts discussed in this chapter, they vary widely in model and in approach. Following are key features of one representative court, New York State's Domestic Violence Court.

- Both misdemeanor and felony domestic violence crimes are included.
- Victim safety is paramount; an on-site victim advocate provides victims with information, social services, housing, and counseling as needed.
- Offenders are monitored intensively to ensure their compliance with orders of protection.
- Offenders are referred to court-mandated programs as relevant.
- A judge supervises a case from arraignment through its final disposition, including probationary period when applicable.
- On-going evaluation research is performed to examine the performance of the various intervention programs associated with the courts.

Source: Fact Sheet, New York State Division of Criminal Justice Services, March 2000.

Classifications of Law

As we noted in ◀ Chapter 1, few scholars are able to propose a definition of law that will satisfy everyone else. There is less disagreement when scholars discuss classifications or types of law. Law is classified both by its *content* and by its *origin*.

Content Classifications

The traditional content classifications are two-category distinctions between civil and criminal law, or between substantive and procedural law, to be discussed below. Increasingly, scholars prefer to use terms that specify content even more clearly, such as education law, mental health law, environmental law, family law, medical law, and public health law.

Civil and Criminal Law The distinction between civil and criminal law rests primarily on the disputive versus punitive emphasis of a case. In **civil law**, two or more parties (litigants) approach the legal system seeking resolution of a dispute. The **plaintiff**, the person bringing the case, is hoping for some remedy from the law. Although the remedy may include fines or punitive damages, the concept of punishment is not the main purpose of civil law. It is designed to settle disputes, or to "make whole" the person or persons who suffered harm. This is accomplished through such means as monetary awards or **injunctions** (court orders to one party to cease some activity, such as venturing on property). **Criminal law**, on the other hand, involves an alleged violation of rules deemed so important that the breaking of these rules incurs society's formal punishment, which must be imposed by the criminal courts. An important component of criminal law is the need to have the rules stated clearly by Congress, when it comes to federal crimes, and state legislatures, when it comes to state crimes. To be a crime, an action or failure to act must be prohibited or mandated in the statutes, and the maximum punishment for violation of that rule must be specified. This does not mean that the person found guilty of violating the law *will* receive that maximum punishment; rather, it is considered fair that we be warned of the possible punishment before committing a crime.

Although it may not seem difficult to discern criminal from civil law, the lines between the two are sometimes blurred. In most states, for example, if a juvenile is charged with violating the criminal law, he or she will most likely be brought to a juvenile or family court, which is considered a civil rather than a criminal setting. Likewise, a mentally disordered individual charged with a criminal offense may be committed to a mental institution through civil proceedings, rather than led through the criminal courts. This is most likely to occur for minor crimes or because the person has been found incompetent to stand trial and the charges are dismissed. Disputes between private persons or organizations, such as breaches of contract, libel suits, or divorce actions, are clearly cases at civil law. The government may also be a part of a civil suit, either as plaintiff or defendant. However, when the government fines a corporation for dumping hazardous waste, the fine may be either a civil or a criminal penalty. When Michael Milken, Dennis Levine, Ivan Boesky, and their coterie of associates broke rules of the Securities and Exchange Commission (SEC) against insider trading, they were committing both criminal and civil offenses, and all received prison terms (Stewart, 1991). Similarly, the massive cases of Enron Corporation, Anderson Accounting Firm, and WorldCom in 2002 included violations of both criminal and civil laws. Anderson was convicted of obstruction of justice, and Enron was faced with both criminal and civil investigations into its corporate practices.

Cases at civil law are often more complex and difficult than those at criminal law, and the legal territory is more likely to be uncharted. The notorious Agent Orange case, for example, in which approximately 16,000 Vietnam Veteran families sued Dow Chemical and six other chemical companies for exposing them to the toxic effects of a defoliant made of dioxin, took nearly 20 years to settle in the federal courts. Other high profile cases included the tobacco litigation proceedings of the 1990s and the asbestos suits that have reached the courts over the past 40 years. Because most cases are civil rather than criminal, the backlog of civil disputes is very high, and the process of achieving settlement is tedious. This is particularly a problem in the federal courts (Abraham, 1998). Additionally, there is no guarantee that the judgment in a civil case will be enforced. This fact has led to a nationwide movement toward alternative dispute resolution (ADR), where parties attempt to arrive at a solution for their dispute with the help of a trained mediator rather than proceeding with the court process (Schneider, 1999; Wohlmuth, 1990). ▶ [ADR and other mediation approaches are discussed again in Chapter 11.]

A case at criminal law is brought by or in the name of some legally constituted government authority at the federal, state, or local level. In taking a criminal case to court, the proper government authority (called the prosecution) accuses a defendant (or defendants) of a specific violation of law as defined by statute. Like civil cases, criminal cases are backlogged, but the courts are expected to handle them as expeditiously as possible to assure that the defendant is not deprived of his or her due process rights ◙ (see **Box 3-2**). The U.S. Constitution and statutes of the federal government and all states guarantee criminal defendants a speedy trial. Nevertheless, it is a rare individual who can successfully make the case that he or she was deprived of that right. In the leading Supreme Court case on this matter, *Barker v. Wingo* (1972), the Court called the right to a speedy trial a "vague concept" and noted that it was "impossible to determine with precision when the right has been denied" (p. 522). Barker had experienced a highly unusual five-year delay before he was tried. During this time, prosecutors were attempting to convict his co-defendant, who would then testify against Barker. It took six trials for the co-defendant to be convicted. Other events, such as the illness of the chief investigator, contributed to continuances and more delay. Nevertheless, the Court ruled that the delay was not prejudicial and that Barker had not been deprived of his right to a speedy trial.

BOX 3-2
Due Process

The concept of "due process" of law is critically important in all legal arenas, both criminal and civil. The term appears in both the 5th and 14th Amendments of the U.S. Constitution. Due process refers to the rights (substantive due process) and the procedures (procedural due process) to which individuals are entitled when confronted by the awesome power of the government. For example, if the state plans a circumferential highway that will traverse your land, the state must hear your objections and must compensate you if the highway is built. If the state seeks to place you in a mental institution against your will, you are entitled to a judicial hearing, among other safeguards. If the state seeks to convict someone of a crime, many due process guarantees are implicated.

Following is a list of the due process guarantees associated with a criminal charge:

- Notice of charges
- Right to counsel during custodial interrogation
- Right to counsel (if facing at least one day incarcerated)
- Right to jury trial (if facing at least six months incarcerated)
- Opportunity to respond to charges
- Opportunity to confront and cross-examine witnesses and accusers
- Freedom from self-incrimination
- Opportunity to present one's own witnesses
- Decision based upon evidence produced at trial
- Transcript of trial proceedings
- Appellate review procedure

Speedy trial laws do seem to keep the process moving, however, serving as an incentive to avoid unnecessary delay. In a multistate study of felony case disposition, Ostrom and Kauder (1999) found that 66% of the cases were resolved within six months and 88% within a year. The median number of days from arrest to disposition was 126. There was considerable discrepancy between the fastest and slowest courts, however, with the fastest courts resolving 98% of their cases within a year and the slowest only 63% of their cases in the same time frame.

Substantive and Procedural Law Another way of classifying law by content, besides whether it is civil or criminal, is to divide it into substantive and procedural categories. **Substantive law** defines the rights and responsibilities of members of a given society as well as the prohibitions of socially sanctioned behavior. For example, the Bill of Rights in the U.S. Constitution specifies fundamental rights of citizens, such as the right to freedom of speech and the right to be free from unreasonable search and seizure. In landlord–tenant laws, certain duties of both parties are described. Other examples of substantive law include state and federal statutes that define and prohibit fraud, embezzlement, murder, rape, assault, arson, burglary, and other crimes against personal safety and property.

Procedural law outlines the rules for the administration, enforcement, and modification of substantive law in the mediation of disputes. In a sense, procedural law exists for the sake of substantive law. It is intended to give defendants in a criminal case and litigants in a civil case the feeling that they are being fairly dealt with, and that all are given a reasonable chance to present their side of an issue before an impartial tribunal (James, 1965). State laws that tell how to initiate a civil suit or that specify the documents to be filed and the hearings to be held in child custody disputes illustrate procedural law. Other examples are the rules of evidence in criminal courts, such as the type of testimony that may be offered by an expert witness.

Classifying by Origin

Another common method of classifying law is by looking for its sources, such as constitutions, court decisions (case law), statutes, rules of administrative agencies, and treaties. With the exception of treaties, the sources of law exist at both the federal and state (including municipal) levels.

Constitutional law is that contained in the U.S. Constitution and the constitutions of individual states. It provides the guidelines for the organization of national, state, and local government, and places limits on the exercise of government power (e.g., through a Bill of Rights). Thus, in a psychology-related U.S. Supreme Court decision, the Court announced that it was cruel and unusual punishment, in violation of the 8th and 14th Amendments of the Constitution, to execute an individual who is mentally retarded (*Atkins v. Virginia*, 2002).

The law that emerges from court decisions is sometimes referred to as **case law** or "judge-made" law. It has developed from **common law** (local customs formed into general principles) and through precedents set in previous court decisions. Case law may involve the interpretation of a statute. If the legislature of a given state passes a law including a provision that psychiatrists are to conduct evaluations of a defendant's competency to stand trial, for example, a court may be asked to interpret whether the legislature intended "psychiatrist" as a generic term that could also cover psychologists.

The rules and principles outlined in the courts' written decisions become precedent under the doctrine ***stare decisis*** (stand by past decisions) and are perpetuated, unless a later court chips away at or overturns them. *Stare decisis* is more a matter of policy than a rigid requirement to be mechanically followed in subsequent cases dealing with similar legal questions. Thus, while lower courts are expected to follow the precedence set by higher courts, a higher court need not follow strictly the doctrine established by an earlier higher court. They generally do, however, because doing so contributes to efficiency, equality, and the development of the law (Abraham, 1998).

Statutory law refers to written rules drafted and approved by a federal, state, or local law-making body. Thus, local ordinances such as parking regulations are included in this category. Statutes are what most people mean when they refer to "law." They outline what factors entitle a person to initiate a civil suit, for example, or what crimes will be considered felonies or misdemeanors. Congress or state legislatures pass numerous statutes directly relating to psychology. For example, a state legislature may mandate that all law enforcement officers must pass a psychological test before they are hired or that "sexual psychopaths," once released from prison, may be civilly committed to mental institutions. Congress's periodic passing of comprehensive crime control legislation that includes provisions relating to bail reform, insanity, or correctional treatment is another illustration.

Administrative law is created and enforced by representatives of the numerous administrative and regulatory agencies of national, state, or local governments. Examples of such agencies at the federal level are the Nuclear Regulatory Commission (NRC), the Food and Drug Administration (FDA), the Securities and Exchange Commission (SEC), the Federal Communications Commission (FCC), and the ubiquitous Internal Revenue Service (IRS). These and other agencies have been delegated broad rule-making, investigative, enforcement, and adjudicative powers by Congress. Additionally, every state assigns agencies to create, administer, and enforce laws such as those pertaining to zoning, public education, and public utilities. Examples of state agencies that relate to psychology are Departments of Mental Health and the various professional licensing boards that oversee the quality of services provided by psychologists, lawyers, physicians, and other professionals.

The above overview of court structure and fundamental concepts relating to law should offer students a foundation for dealing with material throughout the book. In the next section, we will look at the judicial process in more depth, including how the psychologist might participate at various stages.

The Judicial Process

The judicial or court process in both criminal and civil cases can be divided into four major stages: (1) pre-trial; (2) trial; (3) disposition; and (4) appeals.

Illustrations of what contemporary psychologists can contribute at each of these stages abound. Because of psychology's intense interest in the judicial process and the many issues that arise as a result, these stages will be discussed in detail, together with some illustrative research studies. Unless otherwise specified, the discussion in this chapter relates to both civil and criminal cases.

Pre-Trial Stage

The pre-trial process in a *criminal* case begins when a crime is reported and investigated and evidence begins to accrue. Very early, police may contact a court officer (magistrate or judge) to obtain a warrant to search or to arrest a suspect. The judicial system becomes more involved when police clear a case by arresting a suspect and turning him or her over for prosecution. When a suspect is arrested and held in jail, an initial appearance before a court officer must occur, usually within 24 hours, to assure that there is legal ground to hold the individual. For major federal crimes and for some state violations, **grand juries** directed by the prosecutor weigh evidence, sometimes call witnesses, and decide whether there is sufficient evidence to go forth with prosecution. The **indictment** is the grand jury's formal accusation against the individual. Essentially, the grand jury is agreeing with the prosecutor's assertions. In the absence of a grand jury, the prosecutor takes an accused person directly before a trial court judge for a **preliminary hearing**, called a probable cause hearing in many jurisdictions. The judge in this court, typically a lower court, hears evidence from the prosecutor and decides whether there is sufficient evidence to proceed with prosecution. Preliminary hearings are adversarial, allowing the defendant an opportunity to cross-examine any witnesses the prosecutor may call, as well as present evidence to refute a finding of probable cause. However, preliminary hearings can be and are commonly waived. Such a waiver is an acknowledgement that the state has sufficient evidence against the defendant. The defendant may be planning to plead guilty, may want to save the time that would be spent on the hearing, or want to avoid the publicity that could ensue.

The next step is to formally charge the defendant in an open court, a proceeding called the **arraignment**. In some jurisdictions, arraignments occur before preliminary hearings. At the arraignment, the presiding judge asks defendants if they understand the charges, informs them of their right to counsel, and asks them to enter pleas. At this point, it is not unusual for persons charged with minor offenses and even many felonies to plead guilty and receive an immediate fine or sentence. Two other possible pleas are *nolo contendere* and not guilty by reason of insanity (NGRI), which is actually a not guilty plea accompanied by notice that insanity will be used as a defense. The *nolo contendere* plea indicates that the defendant will not contest the charges but will also not admit guilt. For purposes of the criminal law, both the guilty and the nolo pleas have the same result—a conviction is entered into the record.

A plea of guilty is a waiver of the fundamental constitutional right against self-incrimination—the right to remain silent. Pleading guilty also waives Sixth Amendment Constitutional rights, such as the right to a public trial by a jury of one's peers, the right to confront and cross-examine witnesses, and the right to present witnesses in one's own behalf. In some cases, guilty pleas can be withdrawn. Additionally, a plea of not guilty at the arraignment can be subsequently changed to guilty at later stages of the process, even up to the moment before a jury renders a verdict.

If the defendant pleads not guilty, the judge must decide on conditions of release (amount of bail, release on recognizance, release to the custody of a third party). Judges also can deny bail (**preventive detention**) on the basis that an individual is a high risk for flight or is dangerous to society. This bail decision is made after consideration of the nature and circumstances of the offense, the background of the accused, and recommendations from the prosecutor or other relevant individuals. If a bail amount is set and cannot be posted, or if the individual is denied bail, he or she is placed in or returned to jail.

The not-guilty plea sets the trial process in motion. The next step is one or more pre-trial hearings, during which lawyers for each side present arguments, and during which witnesses, arresting officers, and other parties may present evidence. Numerous decisions may be made during these pre-trial hearings. They include whether evidence is admissible;

whether a trial should be moved because of extensive pre-trial publicity; whether a youth should be transferred to juvenile court; whether a defendant is competent to stand trial; and the aforementioned issue of whether bail should be denied because of the alleged dangerousness of a defendant. The juvenile transfer, competency, and dangerousness issues represent three pre-trial situations in which practicing psychologists are very often involved.

During the pre-trial hearings, and between these and the trial, extensive negotiating and plea bargaining often take place, with the result that criminal cases rarely get to the trial stage. In some jurisdictions, as many as 90% of the defendants charged with crimes plead guilty at arraignment or change to guilty pleas before trial date (Neubauer, 2002).

The pre-trial process in *civil* cases has parallels to the above. When one citizen sues another, there are no grand jury indictments or formal charges, however. Instead, a complaint outlining the alleged wrong and the desired remedy is filed by the plaintiff; the defendant receives a summons; and the defendant has a time limit in which to respond. As in criminal cases, there may be extensive negotiation between parties before they see the inside of a courtroom. Additionally, there are pre-trial conferences with the judge in an attempt to facilitate a settlement. In some jurisdictions, litigants are encouraged or even required to try to settle with the help of a mediator. Unlike criminal cases, speedy trials are not an issue, and years may elapse before a case comes to trial. It has been estimated that 75% of all civil cases are settled between the time a complaint is filed and the trial date (Abadinsky, 1995).

The **discovery process** is an important component of the pre-trial process in both criminal and civil cases. This requires each side to make available information at its disposal to the other side in the preparation of its case. A prosecutor in a criminal case, for example, is obliged to make known exculpatory evidence to the defense. Rubin (Hurricane) Carter, the world middleweight boxing champion who spent 18 years in prison for a crime he did not commit, was freed partly because the prosecutor had failed to tell the defense that another person had confessed to the crime. More recently, the discovery process made headlines in the case of Oklahoma City bomber Timothy McVeigh, who was executed in 2001. McVeigh's original execution date was delayed when it came to light that FBI agents across the country still had in their possession numerous documents that had never been turned over to defense attorneys. Although the documents did not suggest that McVeigh was not responsible for the crime, they did relate to the gathering of evidence in the case. The execution was delayed until defense attorneys had obtained the documents and had time to review them.

As part of the discovery process, **depositions** may be required. These are proceedings during which potential witnesses, including expert witnesses, are questioned by attorneys for the opposing side, under oath and in the presence of a court reporter, although typically away from the courtroom. Some psychologists have commented that the grilling they receive during a deposition can be more extensive than courtroom cross-examination. Furthermore, because most cases are settled before trial, clinicians are more likely to be called to testify in depositions and in pre-trial hearings than in trials. Although the deposition may take place in an informal setting, it is part of the court record, and information obtained may well reappear at the trial. For this reason, Hess (1999) recommends strongly that psychologists not waive their right to review the transcription of the deposition, in the event that clerical errors might appear.

Role of Psychologists In the pre-trial stage, psychologists often consult with key players in the judicial process, particularly lawyers. The emergence of mental health courts discussed above has created new opportunities for clinicians to assist in the early identification of defendants who are mentally disordered and could benefit from community treatment rather than incarceration. An array of other court-ordered or independent evaluations may be conducted at the pre-trial stage as well. Examples are evaluations of a person's competency to stand trial or competency to plead guilty, evaluations of mental state at the time of the offense, or neurological evaluations (as might be required in a civil suit resulting from an automobile accident).

Psychologists who specialize in trial consultation find no shortage of tasks to perform at the pre-trial stage. Lawyers planning their trial strategies may begin alerting potential expert witnesses that they will likely be called to testify on a wide range of psychologically relevant issues. It is at the pre-trial stage, also, that lawyers may be concerned about the potentially damaging effects of pre-trial publicity. Thus, trial consultants are asked to conduct surveys of the community and collect evidence of negative publicity, which would support a motion for a change of venue. Lawyers also may enlist the help of social and behavioral scientists in finding the type of juror who would be most sympathetic to their side. This **"scientific jury selection"** process may include community surveys, focus groups, or even mock trials. Trial consultants also help attorneys prepare witnesses and determine effective strategies for presenting evidence and persuading jurors (Myers & Arena, 2001). ▶ [We will discuss many of these examples of psychological involvement in more detail in the chapters ahead.]

Trial Stage

In both criminal and civil cases, trials follow a similar pattern of stages, beginning with jury selection, unless the verdict will be rendered only by a judge (called a **bench trial** or a **court trial**). Prospective jurors typically fill out questionnaires and answer screening questions to determine their eligibility to serve as jurors. Once assigned to a particular trial, however, the final decision as to whether they will indeed serve on that jury rests with the lawyers and the presiding judge who conduct a formal ***voir dire*** process. This questioning of the jurors to uncover possible bias occurs in open court unless there is reason to ask some questions out of the hearing of the press and public. The main purpose of the *voir dire* is to seat an impartial jury, although it is well recognized that it serves a variety of other functions as well. For example, the *voir dire* provides an opportunity for lawyers to relate to jurors.

During the *voir dire*, attorneys for both sides as well as the judge ask questions of the potential jurors. Attorneys then "challenge" persons they believe should not be on the jury. In most jurisdictions, attorneys are allowed a limited number of **peremptory challenges**, in which the attorney need not provide a reason. Thus, a defense attorney might have a "gut feeling" based on many years of experience that juror X would be unlikely to sympathize with her client. Attorneys may not exercise peremptory challenges on the basis of race or gender, however. If there is suspicion that this is occurring (e.g., that a lawyer is excluding all African-Americans or all women or all men from the jury), the presiding judge must assure that the peremptories are not exercised in a discriminatory fashion (*Batson v. Kentucky*, 1986; *J.E.B. v. Alabama*, 1994; *Purkett v. Elem*, 1995). Most challenges, however, are **challenges for cause**. In a challenge for cause, an attorney has concluded that the potential juror would be unlikely to render an unbiased verdict. The individual may be related to a police officer, for example, and the victim in the case is a police officer; or the potential juror may exhibit prejudice against the group of which the defendant is a member. While peremptory challenges are limited in number (as defined in state and federal statutes), challenges for cause are unlimited.

The jury selection process, ▶ [which will be discussed again in Chapter 6], is followed by opening arguments, the presentation of evidence and the presentation and cross-examination of witnesses for both sides, summations of cases, the judge's instructions to the jury, jury deliberation, and verdict. A few important differences between criminal and civil cases should be noted, however. There is no Constitutional right to a lawyer in civil cases, for example, whereas lawyers are guaranteed to indigent defendants facing the possibility of at least one day incarceration in criminal cases (*Gideon v. Wainwright*, 1963; *Argersinger v. Hamlin*, 1972; *Alabama v. Shelton*, 2002). Defendants in civil cases do not have the right to remain silent, as they do in criminal cases. The right to cross-examine witnesses is also more limited in civil cases, whereas it is a fundamental right in criminal trials. The standard of proof also differs. In criminal cases, each element of the crime must be proved **beyond a reasonable doubt**, whereas judges and juries in civil cases must be convinced by a **preponderance of the evidence** or, in some situations, by **clear and convincing evidence**. Juvenile delinquency proceedings, however, while considered civil in nature, do provide juveniles with the Constitutional guarantees provided adults in criminal courts, although juveniles are not Constitutionally guaranteed a trial by jury. ▶ [These

BOX 3-3
The Burden of Proof

Black's Law Dictionary defines burden of proof as "the obligation of a party to establish by evidence a requisite degree of belief concerning a fact in the mind of the trier of fact or the court."

The three standards of proof discussed in the text are defined and illustrated on the continuum below.

Preponderance of the evidence (1)
Evidence which is of greater weight or more convincing than the evidence offered in opposition. Evidence that the fact sought to be proved is more probable than not.

Clear and convincing proof (2)
Proof which results in reasonable certainty of the truth. More proof than preponderance of evidence, but less than beyond a reasonable doubt.

Beyond a reasonable doubt (3)
Fully satisfied, entirely convinced, satisfied to a moral certainty. (Reasonable doubt is doubt based on reason and arising from evidence or lack of evidence. It is doubt which a reasonable person might entertain; it is not fanciful doubt, not imagined doubt, and not doubt that a juror might conjure up to avoid performing an unpleasant task or duty. Reasonable doubt is such a doubt as would cause prudent men to hesitate before acting in matters of importance to themselves.)

1 2 3

Which—if any—of the following statements reflects the standard of proof necessary for a criminal conviction?

"I think he did it."

"I'm not sure, but it's more likely that he did it than that he didn't."

"I'm pretty sure he did it."

"I'm absolutely positive that he did it—well, maybe there's a pretty good chance that he didn't do it."

---

rights and differences will be discussed in more detail in Chapter 12.] ◙ **Box 3-3** and **Box 3-4** provide definitions of the three above standards of proof.

Role of Psychologists The role of psychologists during the trial stage has received extensive attention. During *voir dire*, the social scientist again may serve as a trial consultant, helping the attorney make decisions as to whether a particular proposed juror is acceptable. In this capacity, the psychologist is essentially a member of the trial team. The consultant may suggest *voir dire* questions to lawyers and make inferences about prospective jurors based on their responses or even on their nonverbal behavior (Strier, 1999). According to Strier (1999), the majority of trial consultants are psychologists by training. ▶ [We will discuss this topic again in Chapter 6.]

Psychologists also are active during the trial stage as expert witnesses. They may testify on matters like criminal responsibility, eyewitness testimony, or the emotional state of a litigant, such as one claiming post-traumatic stress disorder (PTSD). Clinical psychologists report on their evaluations of the individual; research psychologists may be asked to testify about the empirical evidence relating to the disorder. It is not unusual to hear this role disparaged, as in the comment "If you look hard enough, you'll find a shrink willing to testify to anything." We will be discussing this perception and the resultant battle of experts later in the chapter. It is important to note, however, that both clinical and research psychologists have numerous contributions to make relative to the trial stage.

Research psychologists, for example, have valuable information to convey to courts relative to the issue of pre-trial publicity, particularly with respect to criminal cases. The Sixth Amendment of the U.S. Constitution guarantees criminal defendants

BOX 3-4
Beyond a Reasonable Doubt

The Federal Judicial Center (1987) recommends that judges provide the following instructions to jurors regarding their need to find proof beyond a reasonable doubt in a criminal case:

> As I have said many times, the government has the burden of proving the defendant guilty beyond a reasonable doubt. Some of you may have served as jurors in civil cases, where you were told that it is only necessary to prove that a fact is more likely true than not true. In criminal cases, the government's proof must be more powerful than that. It must be beyond a reasonable doubt.
>
> Proof beyond a reasonable doubt is proof that leaves you firmly convinced of the defendant's guilt. There are very few things in this world that we know with absolute certainty, and in criminal cases the law does not require proof that overcomes every possible doubt. If, based on your consideration of the evidence, you are firmly convinced that the defendant is guilty of the crime charged, you must find him guilty. If on the other hand, you think there is a real possibility that he is not guilty, you must give him the benefit of the doubt and find him not guilty.

the right to a speedy, albeit not perfect, trial by an impartial jury of their peers. However, the First Amendment guarantees the press the right to be unhampered by the government in gathering and reporting news. In a line of U.S. Supreme Court decisions (e.g., *Sheppard v. Maxwell*, 1966; *Nebraska Press Association v. Stuart*, 1976; *Richmond Newspapers, Inc. v. Virginia*, 1980), the Court has attempted to balance these two Constitutional rights. Research psychologists have conducted numerous experiments on the effect of negative publicity on juror decision making. Psychological research also has uncovered extensive information about attitude formation and jury behavior, human perception and memory, and the credibility of child witnesses. These and other trial-related topics will be discussed in separate chapters on the psychology of the jury and the psychology of evidence.

Disposition Stage

The third major stage of the judicial process is most relevant to criminal cases, since it is the stage at which a judge or jury impose a sentence or other penalty upon a convicted offender. In the civil process, when a verdict favors the plaintiff, a **judgment** is handed down, specifying the remedy to be borne by the defendant. The standard civil case does not involve the psychologist once this has occurred. Nevertheless, in deciding upon a remedy, judges and juries certainly consider testimony relating to the psychological harm a plaintiff may have suffered. It should be noted, also, that the juvenile process—which is civil—also may involve a "sentence," which is called a **disposition** in juvenile courts. Clinical information is often used in this context.

In criminal cases, it is at the disposition stage that a decision is made whether to incarcerate the individual and for how long and, in death penalty cases, whether to impose the ultimate penalty or an alternative life sentence or life without possibility of parole. Sentencing includes a hearing at which the victim may speak about the effects of the crime and may even take the opportunity to address the offender directly. Judges also may provide the offender with an opportunity to make a statement, including a statement to the victim. This **right of allocution** at sentencing is not a Constitutional right for either the victim or the offender, although some states have provided victims with the right through statutes. In addition to the victim and offender, other individuals on both sides may address the court during the sentencing hearing.

Role of Psychologists Psychologists enter the disposition stage particularly in the criminal process. They may be consulted by the probation officer preparing a **pre-sentence report**, which is a document submitted to the judge intended to provide helpful sentencing information. The report is submitted after the probation officer has conducted a **pre-sentence investigation** (PSI). It typically contains background data on the offender, including prior record, as well as a review of the facts of the case and a summary of victim reactions. The judge also may request, or grant an attorney's request for, a psychological evaluation of the offender's amenability to rehabilitation. For example, a judge may sentence an offender convicted of lewd and lascivious behavior to probation with the condition that he participate in a community-based sex offender treatment program, after having heard from psychologists that the offender would be a good candidate for such a program. The PSI also may include the probation officer's sentencing recommendation. Judges seem to agree with the recommendation in 70–90% of the cases (Clear & Cole, 2000), but it is not clear whether the probation officer actually influenced the judge's decision. As Clear and Cole (2000, p. 182) note, "it is hard to know whether judges are following the officers' advice or whether the officers' experience has given them the ability to anticipate the sentences that the judges would have chosen anyway."

The competency inquiry that may occur early in the judicial process also can reoccur at sentencing. Thus, psychologists may evaluate a recently convicted offender if there is question that he or she does not have sufficient ability to understand the proceedings. Additionally, in the death penalty context, psychological input is often critical. Before the offender can receive the death sentence, the jury weighs aggravating and mitigating circumstances associated with the crime and the offender. Mitigating circumstances—factors that lessen the offender's culpability—are often substantiated by psychologists or other mental health practitioners. A history of abuse as a child, a neurological deficit, and mild cognitive deficiencies are illustrations of mitigating circumstances. Mental retardation, however, may be more than a mitigating circumstance. If significant mental retardation is documented, it is enough to spare an offender the death penalty.

States with the death penalty typically require some prediction of "future dangerousness" of the offender, a standard generally thought to require the input of an examining clinician. Many psychologists have been reluctant to participate in the prediction of dangerousness, particularly when it involves death penalty cases. ▶ [This topic will be discussed in more detail in Chapter 6.]

Appellate Stage

During the appeals process, it will be recalled, a higher court reviews the findings of a lower or trial court on matters of law. This stage involves the filing of the trial transcript and numerous documents on both sides, as well as documents that do not necessarily advocate for one side but are intended to help the appellate court arrive at a decision. The losing party in the trial court files an intention to appeal, which puts the winning party on notice that the case has not ended. The party approaching the appellate court becomes the appellant or petitioner, and the other party becomes the respondent. In criminal cases, the petitioner may appeal the verdict or the sentence, based on any number of decisions made by the judge before and during the trial. The petitioner also may argue that his or her Constitutional rights were violated, as when denied the Sixth Amendment right to adequate assistance of counsel. In civil cases, the losing party may appeal the jury award or may appeal on the basis of errors that allegedly occurred during the trial. It is important to note, though, that in both criminal and civil cases, the attorney during the trial should have objected for the record, providing the trial court with an opportunity to correct the error as soon as it occurred. Even if errors did occur, however, appellate courts decide "whether or not the error(s) was serious enough to justify a new trial or if it was a 'harmless error' not affecting the outcome of the trial" (Abadinsky, 1995, p. 304).

In any given state, the court of last resort—the highest appellate court in the state—has discretion as to whether to hear a case, as long as there has been opportunity for the appeal to be heard in a lower level appellate court (intermediate appeals). If there is no intermediate court, the court of last resort must hear the appeal providing that it has been properly filed and states a legitimate basis for appeal. An offender would not get very far if he were to appeal his four-year sentence on the basis that prisons are, per se, cruel and unusual. On the other hand, if he received a 30-year-sentence for a burglary in which no property was taken, and this was his first criminal conviction, he could argue that this sentence was disproportionate to his crime and would have a good basis for an appeal. In criminal cases, offenders have a Constitutional right to at least one appeal. Persons unable to afford their own lawyer have a right to legal representation during this first appeal.

Role of Psychologists Psychology may enter the appellate process in two primary ways. First, the very basis of the appeal may be a clinician's own involvement in the pre-trial or trial process. For example, a father appealing a custody decision may argue that the one psychologist who interviewed his child did not have the proper credentials as outlined in the statutes. Alternately, a person convicted of rape might appeal his conviction, arguing that expert testimony by a psychologist on rape trauma syndrome should not have been introduced. A second way in which psychology enters the appellate process is through the filing of ***amicus curiae*** (friend of the court) briefs. An *amicus* brief is a document filed by interested parties other than those directly involved in the case (the appellant and the respondent). They file the brief either because they have specialized information that could be helpful to the appeals court in arriving at its decision or because they could be affected by the outcome of the case.

***Amicus* Briefs** Bersoff and Ogden (1991, p. 950) summarize five purposes of the *amicus* brief: (1) to supply information not readily available to the parties in the case; (2) to develop arguments that one party has been able to present only in summary form; (3) to make arguments that one party has been unable to make because of lack of resources; (4) to fill a void by making arguments that one party prefers not to make; and (5) to address the broad social implications of a decision. Considering psychology's interest in discipline-relevant public policy, it is not surprising that the filing of *amicus* briefs on behalf of the profession is both vigorous and controversial.

The American Psychological Association (APA) has aggressively pursued its responsibility to inform the courts about relevant research evidence. As of 1990, the APA had filed 28 *amicus curiae* briefs in U.S. Supreme Court cases and approximately the same number in lower federal and state courts (Bersoff & Ogden, 1991). Between 1990 and 2002, an additional ten briefs were filed with the Supreme Court ▲ (see **Table 3-2**) and approximately twice that number in federal circuit courts of appeal and state courts. Psychologists also sometimes join other concerned social scientists in filing *amicus* briefs. The most well known and widely cited is the brief in the landmark desegregation case *Brown v. Board of Education of Topeka* (1954). A more recent example

TABLE 3-2

Selected *Amicus Curiae* Briefs Filed with the U.S. Supreme Court by the American Psychological Association Since 1990

Case Name	Topic
Sell v. U.S. (2003)	forcible medication of incompetent defendants
Atkins v. Virginia (2002)	death penalty and mental retardation
Boy Scouts of America v. Dale (2000)	homosexuality
Olmstead v. L.C. (1999)	ADA and community treatment of mentally disabled
Jaffee v. Redmond (1996)	psychotherapist-patient privilege
Romer v. Evans (1996)	homosexuality
Harris v. Forklift Systems, Inc. (1993)	sexual harassment
National Kidney Patients Assoc. v. Sullivan (1993) (brief in support of cert. petition)	Medicare
Planned Parenthood v. Casey (1992)	abortion rights
Maryland v. Craig (1990)	child abuse/witnesses
Ohio v. Akron Center (1990)	abortion rights
Washington v. Harper (1990)	inmate right to refuse treatment

BOX 3-5
Highlights of APA Brief in *Boy Scouts of America v. Dale*

Facts of the case: Dale, an assistant scout master, was expelled from the organization after publicly declaring his homosexuality. He sued under a New Jersey State law aimed at reducing prejudice and discrimination against homosexuals. There was no indication or suggestion that Dale was guilty of any child abuse. The Boy Scouts argued that its policy of exclusion was consistent with its mission to promote mental, spiritual, and moral health. They said they had a 1st Amendment right to freedom of association and should not be forced to accept homosexuals. The APA filed its brief in support of a ruling by the New Jersey Supreme Court that Dale should be reinstated and was entitled to damages.

By a vote of 5–4, the U.S. Supreme Court reversed the New Jersey Supreme Court, ruling that the Boy Scout's exclusionary policy was consistent with its 1st Amendment rights.

Following are key points outlined in the APA brief, based on a review of empirical and clinical literature and substantiated in the brief with reference to that literature.

- Exclusion on the basis of sexual orientation is not different in nature than exclusion on the basis of race, gender, or religion.
- Scientific research and clinical experience indicate that sexual orientation is not "voluntary" for most people.
- It is not yet clear what factors lead to a particular sexual orientation: genetic, other biological traits, or early childhood experiences all may contribute.
- Once established, sexual orientation is highly resistant to attempts to change it.
- The psychiatric, psychological, and social work professions do not consider homosexual orientation to be a disorder.
- Empirical studies demonstrate that gay people contribute to society similar to heterosexual people.
- Like married people, gay couples form deep emotional attachments and commitments that endure for decades.
- Gay men are not more likely than heterosexual men to sexually abuse children. Many men who sexually abuse boys are not themselves homosexual. Rather, they are attracted, entirely or predominately, to children.
- Gay men and lesbians are as good parents as their heterosexual counterparts; their children do not differ appreciably from children raised by heterosexuals.
- Children of gay and lesbian parents do not differ in gender identity, gender role, or sexual orientation from children of heterosexual parents.
- Anti-discrimination laws can reduce prejudice; exclusionary policies interfere with this and serve instead to reinforce individual hostility against the excluded minority.

is the brief filed by the Committee of Concerned Social Scientists in *State v. Michaels* (1993), a New Jersey case, which involved the accuracy of child testimony in sexual assault cases. The APA's briefs have "embraced a wide variety of constitutional and civil rights issues about which psychology has significant and pertinent information" (Bersoff & Ogden, 1991, p. 950). The cases have included such issues as the forced medication of inmates; the effects of employment discrimination; civil commitment; gay, lesbian, and bisexual parenting; sexual harassment; the death penalty; and the insanity defense. ■ (See **Box 3-5** for excerpts from a brief filed by the APA covering research on homosexuality and discrimination.)

Michael Saks (1993) distinguishes between two categories of *amicus* briefs: those filed when the group of psychologists has a specific interest in an issue (e.g., the licensing of professions) and those filed because the group possesses research knowledge that should be helpful to the court. As Saks notes, the second type of brief "assumes its traditional role as a true friend of the court" (p. 243). These briefs, he adds, should not be written to advance either party, but simply to provide the court with relevant scientific knowledge.

Despite the fact that associations representing psychologists and other scientists routinely file *amicus* briefs, psychologists are not of a mind on the wisdom of taking a stand on issues of public policy. Additionally, the conclusions drawn in briefs are not always supported by individual psychologists. In the 1990s, there was vigorous debate over the APA's *amicus curiae* brief in *Price-Waterhouse v. Hopkins* (1989), a case in which a woman had successfully sued her employer for sex discrimination. Social psychologist Susan Fiske had testified in trial court about the psychological effects of stereotyping. Price-Waterhouse appealed the judgement, and the case ultimately reached the U.S. Supreme Court. The APA brief in the case reviewed the research literature on stereotyping, but some psychologists later objected that the brief did not adequately represent the research literature (Barrett & Morris, 1993) and essentially misled the Court. The psychologists who prepared the brief—and who included Fiske—retorted that their work was, indeed, representative of the research (Fiske, Bersoff, Borgida, Deaux, & Heilman, 1993). Furthermore, they suggested that their critics did not have the requisite expertise to criticize the brief. "The consensus of those who are expert in the substantive area of gender stereotyping, in which neither Barret nor Morris has a track record, places their perspective as deviant" (Fiske et al. 1993, p. 55). Ironically, as psychologist Michael Saks (1993) concluded, the Court showed no indication of having been influenced by either the APA brief or Dr. Fiske's testimony.

It is not clear to what extent appellate courts are influenced by *amicus curiae* briefs, but social science researchers are encouraged to continue filing them. James Acker (1990), reporting the results of an analysis of briefs filed in 200 criminal cases over a 25-year period, found *amicus curiae* briefs prepared by social scientists were more the exception than the norm. Although Acker was not referring only to psychological briefs, his results are relevant. In his sample of cases, "the vast majority of social science authorities cited in the Court's decisions had been located through the Justices' own efforts, rather than through prior discussion in the briefs or otherwise" (p. 40). When briefs did cite research evidence, they had been prepared by lawyers, government officials, or interested groups other than those possessing expertise in the social sciences. Only a handful had been prepared on behalf of scientifically competent organizations. However, according to Acker (1990, p. 40), this handful "demonstrate dramatically that such organizations can make an important contribution to the transmission of social science information to the Justices. . . ." Acker concluded that Supreme Court Justices can go astray in their interpretation of research results if not guided by competent social scientists.

In a separate analysis of death penalty cases, however, Acker (1991) discovered that social scientists were more likely to be directly involved. They had filed briefs in 34% of the cases (compared to 13% of criminal cases overall). Nonetheless, their research was cited significantly more often in footnotes than in the text of the Court's opinions, reflecting that the Court considered them less important. The research also was cited by dissenters significantly more often than by the Justices in the majority. Politically liberal Justices used social science data more than politically conservative Justices. Acker concluded that, at least for that sample of cases, social science evidence had little impact on the final decision.

Thomas Grisso and Michael Saks (1991) warn psychologists against being discouraged when judicial decisions either ignore social science evidence or do not comport with it. They assert that the U.S. Supreme Court's expertise in Constitutional analysis, and the numerous other sources of information available to the Justices must be considered. Grisso and Saks also argue that the Court has not directly *rejected* social science evidence, but rather has often based its decisions on other grounds. They emphasize that it is important for psychology to continue informing the Court about the findings of research in order "to provide a safeguard against judicial use of erroneous presumptions about human behavior. With this as a criterion for judging success, psychology has reason to take heart" (Grisso & Saks, 1991, p. 208). Saks (1993), however, further cautions psychologists to be conscious of the melding of advocacy and educational roles. In other words, on some issues they may be very tempted to advocate for one side or the other. Their role, however, should be one of providing objective data to assist the courts in arriving at a decision. In the brief-writing process, he notes, "conflict between the duties of conscientious advocates and conscientious psychologists is likely" (p. 238).

The Psychologist as an Expert Witness

Few areas of psychology and law have attracted more attention than the use of psychologists as expert witnesses in courtroom settings. As noted earlier in the chapter, psychologists and other mental health professionals (especially psychiatrists) may be called to testify in pre-trial proceedings, during the trial itself, or at the sentencing stage of criminal cases. When their testimony relates to their evaluations of defendants, victims, plaintiffs, or witnesses, it is considered *clinically based.* Alternately, they may be called to testify because of their *research expertise* on a specific issue, such as the reliability and validity of the polygraph, the effect of divorce on children, or the limitations of eyewitness identification. However, we must be careful not to make too sharp a demarcation between clinical and research skills. When clinicians testify in court proceedings, their testimony is often based on scientific knowledge. As Rotgers and Barrett (1996, p. 468)

BOX 3-6
Jenkins v. U.S.

In the early 1960s, the American Psychiatric Association strongly resisted the move by psychologists to qualify as mental health experts in U.S. courts. In its *amicus curiae* brief in *Jenkins v. U.S.* (1962), the American Psychiatric Association emphasized the extensive medical training of psychiatrists, which made them uniquely qualified to offer diagnoses of mental illness. By contrast, the psychiatrists told the court, psychologists may be highly trained, but they are competent in a very specialized area, which does not include mental illness. They also suggested that the role of the psychologist was to be a helpmate to the psychiatrist.

The American Psychological Association, in its brief, emphasized that psychology is an established science. The brief delineated the ethical responsibilities and the intraprofessional standards that psychologists are expected to embrace. Like the brief of the psychiatrists, the APA brief expanded upon the years of training that culminate in the Ph.D., in particular the Ph.D. held by clinical psychologists.

Following are excerpts from each of the briefs.

American Psychiatric Association

Psychiatrists traditionally have been called upon by our Courts to give expert medical testimony concerning mental illnesses, the productivity thereof and their effects.

The question of whether a person not trained in medicine, not a Doctor of Medicine and not a doctor trained as a specialist in the diagnosis, treatment and care of the mentally ill, can qualify as a medical expert and give expert medical opinions concerning the diagnosis of specific mental diseases and the medical effects thereof is of grave concern to psychiatrists and their Association.

The clinical psychologist, like teachers, ministers, lawyers, social workers and vocational counselors, all utilize their skills as aids only to the psychiatrist in his medical diagnosis, care and treatment of the mentally ill . . . .

The American Psychiatric Association recognizes the clinical psychologist as a highly trained person in a special field of psychological examination. He can provide important relevant data, such as the result from M.A. and I.Q. tests, to the psychiatrist who has the final responsibility for medical diagnosis. But the psychologist, not being a qualified Doctor of Medicine with special training in the mental health field, cannot qualify as a medical expert in the diagnosis, treatment and care of the mentally ill.

have remarked, "The practice of clinical psychology can be conceived of as the art of applying scientific knowledge of human behavior to the analysis of the behavior and psychological states of individuals." Thus, because clinical psychology has adopted the "mantle of science" (p. 468), clinical psychologists should expect to be required to adhere to the same scientific standards of data gathering as other scientific experts (Rotgers & Barrett, 1996).

Expert Certification

In order for an individual to qualify as an expert, courts require that he or she possess specialized knowledge which is "beyond the ken" of the average lay person and which will assist the trier of fact (judge or jury) in understanding technical evidence. In the tobacco litigation cases of the 1990s, for example, medical researchers interpreted complex scientific data to help the courts understand the effects of carcinogens on both smokers and those exposed to second-hand smoke. Obviously, individuals who testify as expert witnesses must first establish their credentials, including the requisite advanced degree, licensing or certification if relevant, and research or practical experience in areas about which they are testifying. Until the mid-20th century, courts were divided over whether psychologists were competent to testify on mental health issues, so the typical expert on issues such as insanity, competency to stand trial, dangerousness, or amenability to treatment was a psychiatrist. In *Jenkins v. United States* (1962), however, the U.S. Supreme Court acknowledged that psychologists as well as psychiatrists could qualify as expert witnesses. In each case, it is left to the discretion of the trial judge to accept or reject an individual's qualifications as an expert, subject to review by appellate courts ■ (see **Box 3-6**). In

BOX 3-6
Jenkins v. U.S. (continued)

American Psychological Association

From a scholarly discipline and science developed mainly in university centers, the result of psychological effort has become recognized as capable of application in many fields of activity . . . .

The foundation stone, however, of all developments of the field continues to be a rigid adherence to the principles of science, to a belief in the value of empirical evidence and verification, and to the development of appropriate theory. These are some of the processes which differentiate the sciences from other approaches to the understanding of human behavior . . . .

It is submitted that psychology in its present state of development is clearly an established science and . . . psychologists are clearly engaged in the practice of an established profession. It would obviously be foolish to assert that any psychologist is testimonially competent to express an expert professional opinion upon all questions relating to the science of psychology. In fact, the Association would oppose any such rule as being contrary to the professional standards to which it and its membership adhere. It is submitted, however, that a psychologist is clearly competent under well-established rules of evidence, to testify as an expert upon matters within the scope of his professional experience . . . .

In the diagnosis of mental disease and mental defect, including the formulation of professional opinions as to causal relationships between mental disease or defect and overt behavior, a principal tool of the clinical psychologist is found in psychological tests . . . .

Infallibility is not claimed for any psychological test, and no professional psychologist would assert that he could reach a valid diagnosis upon the basis of test results alone. However, the use of test results, in conjunction with a review of a person's history and evaluative interviews, can be extremely useful to the clinical psychologist in reaching informed opinions as to the nature and existence of mental disease or defect in a given subject and as to the causal relationship or lack thereof between such mental disease or defect and the subject's overt behavior.

the 1990s, several appeals court cases involved the expert testimony of neuropsychologists and whether they were qualified to testify on the causes of head injuries (e.g., *Huntoon v. TCI Cablevision*, 1998; *Landers v. Chrysler Corporation*, 1997).

Many judges, though, prefer expert testimony from psychiatrists rather than psychologists or other mental health professionals. Despite the clear message in *Jenkins v. U.S.* that psychologists can qualify as expert witnesses in clinical as well as research matters, there has been a continuing preference for psychiatrists. This is probably reflective of the law's "comfort with a medical model" (Melton et al., 1997, p. 23). The preference is especially apparent when clinical information involving interviews and diagnoses is sought (Redding & Reppucci, 1999; Yuille, 1989). Redding, Floyd, and Hawk (2001) sent mail questionnaires to trial court judges, prosecutors, and defense attorneys in Virginia to gather their opinions on expert testimony in a hypothetical insanity case. They found widespread preference for both evaluations and testimony of psychiatrists rather than of psychologists, although doctoral-level psychologists were preferred to all other mental health professionals.

Legal Standards

The trial court judge also decides whether the evidence is relevant to the case at hand. It is important to note, also, that if the proferred testimony has potential for unfair prejudice that would outweigh its value to the trier of fact, it may be disallowed. In a trial with strong overtones of racial bias, for example, testimony on theories of the heritability of intelligence might be considered inflammatory and prejudicial (Rotgers & Barrett, 1996), thereby outweighing its potentially probative value. ◙ (◀ See **Box 1-3** for a review of standards by which to evaluate scientific testimony.)

Until the *Daubert* case discussed in ◀ Chapter 1, once an expert's qualifications were established, an additional standard had to be met. Even if the expert's credentials were flawless, the knowledge about which the expert testified had to be gathered using scientific techniques that have gained general acceptance in the field (*Frye v. U.S.*, 1923). Although this was a federal standard applied in federal courts, many state courts adopted it as well. The standard is well illustrated by referring to literature on domestic violence. In the 1980s and 1990s, many trial courts were asked to admit testimony from psychologists who had done research and had extensive clinical experience with battered women. Psychologist Lenore Walker is widely credited with having "discovered" Battered Woman Syndrome, a collection of thoughts, feelings, and behaviors believed to be held in common by women experiencing domestic abuse (Walker, 1979, 1984, 1989). Nonetheless, courts were reluctant to accept the presence of this syndrome. In the words of one, "the battered woman syndrome is not sufficiently developed, as a matter of commonly accepted scientific knowledge, to warrant testimony under the guise of expertise" (*State v. Thomas*, 1981, p. 137). Today, the trend is to recognize the syndrome and allow expert testimony in the area (Hess & Brinson, 1999; Schuller & Vidmar, 1992). A variety of other syndromes have emerged, however, and each in turn has been challenged to meet the test of acceptance in the field. In fact, psychologists themselves have argued that research evidence in some areas is transferred to the courtroom prematurely, before it has gained general acceptance by the research community. This criticism has been leveled not only at "syndrome" research (Hess, 1999; Otto & Heilbrun, 2002), but also at specific tools used in psychological assessment (Ogloff & Cronshaw, 2001; Otto & Heilbrun, 2002), and issues relating to child custody determinations (Bolocofsky, 1989). Critics have gone as far as to call some experts "junk scientists" (Cornfeld, 1993; Huber, 1991), suggesting that they mislead judges and jurors with the evidence they present.

As noted in ◀ Chapter 1, general acceptance is still a consideration, but it is no longer a *necessary precondition* to the admissibility of scientific evidence. *Daubert* was designed to clarify for federal judges apparent discrepancies in the *Frye* standard and the Federal Rules of Evidence. Although state courts are free to adopt their own rules of evidence, in practice they tend to use federal rules as a model. Under *Daubert*, the judge plays the role of gatekeeper who must decide whether the evidence is relevant and reliable ◙ (**Box 1-3**). Consequently, general acceptance becomes one factor among several for the presiding judge to take under consideration.

Recall that courts often express a strong preference for clinical over statistical data, despite arguments from social scientists that the latter are superior and at least should be considered. The judges and lawyers surveyed by Redding et al. (2001) were "relatively disinterested in statistical or actuarial data" (p. 592), a finding which is disconcerting to social and behavioral scientists. In another survey of 850 judges in nine states (Redding & Reppucci, 1999), a similar aversion to research evidence was found. However, their reactions were modulated by their socio-political views. The judges, along with a comparison group of law students, were presented with hypothetical death penalty cases and provided with evidence on the deterrent effect. Both groups of respondents gave significantly more weight to evidence that supported their death-penalty views than to the evidence that was contrary to their views. Interestingly, a background in science or social science did not help to modulate the bias. (It should be noted that the bulk of social science evidence does not support a deterrent effect for the death penalty [Bohm, 1999]).

In the later Redding et al. (2001) study, Virginia respondents showed some interest in the theoretical and speculative information that experts might provide. The level of interest differed according to their respective roles, with defense lawyers being most interested and prosecutors being least interested. Judges were more similar to prosecutors than to defense lawyers in this regard. Theoretical explanations are presumably useful to defense lawyers in that they might help exculpate the defendant or at least help mitigate the defendant's responsibility. For example, in the case of a battered woman who killed her abuser, the theory that the woman perceived herself as constantly in danger of being killed and unable to leave the abusive situation might help the jury understand her actions. It is important to note that the response rates in this study were fairly low, with only 41% of the judges, 38% of the prosecutors, and 27% of the defense attorneys returning their questionnaires.

Once decisions to certify the expert and admit her or his testimony have been made, the hurdles for the expert witness have not been removed. As many commentators have remarked, testifying in court is not an exercise for the faint of heart. Even if the expert has successfully vaulted the court's credentials and testimony barriers, he or she faces the possibility of being subjected to grueling cross-examination or pitted against another expert with conflicting views. Some experts also face concerns about issues revolving around confidentiality and "ultimate opinion" testimony. We will discuss each of these hurdles below, beginning with the problem of confidentiality.

The Confidentiality Issue

The obligation to maintain confidentiality in the patient-therapist relationship is fundamental. If you entrust the most intimate details of your life, such as your fears or bizarre behaviors, to a clinician, you expect that these will not be repeated outside the clinical setting. Nevertheless, the law places limits on that confidentiality. In many states, clinicians have a duty to warn (and sometimes to protect) third parties who may be in danger from a patient who has threatened their lives. This is referred to as the "*Tarasoff*" requirement, named after a court ruling. ▶ [We will discuss the duty to warn in more detail in Chapter 5.] In all states, practitioners also are required by law to report evidence of child abuse (and in some cases, elderly or other abuse) encountered in their practice to appropriate parties, which may include law enforcement or social service agencies. Court-requested evaluations, which require practitioners to forward written reports to a range of judicial actors, also are not confidential. In these situations, the clinician's client is the court, not the individual being examined. However, psychologists are ethically bound, and in some situations legally bound, to warn the individual of the potential uses of their reports. "If the person [being assessed] is not the client, the psychologist owes no duty of confidentiality to that person; but, because of the requirement of informed consent, must make the fact known to the person being assessed that the information to be obtained is not confidential" (Ogloff, 1999, p. 411).

Generally, when a clinician is called to testify as a witness in a legal proceeding, confidentiality is not protected (Knapp & VandeCreek, 1997). Additionally, if a client sues a therapist, the therapist may rely on confidential information to defend him- or herself (Ogloff, 1999). Nevertheless, all courts recognize some form of patient-therapist privilege under common law as well as state statutes. In a recent U.S. Supreme Court pronouncement on this issue, the Court issued a strong endorsement of confidentiality in federal courts (*Jaffe v. Redmond*, 1996). Police officer Redmond shot and killed an allegedly-armed suspect whom she believed was about to kill another individual. The suspect's family sued, maintaining that he was not armed and that Officer Redmond had used excessive force, a civil rights violation. When the plaintiffs learned that Redmond had attended counseling sessions after the shooting, they subpoenaed her social worker. The social worker provided information about the date and length of meetings, along with brief summary notes, but she refused to answer specific questions about treatment, citing a therapist-patient privilege. The judge refused to recognize the privilege and informed the jury that they were entitled to presume that the testimony would have been damaging to Redmond's case. The jury found for the plaintiffs, but the U.S. Seventh Circuit Court of Appeals set aside the verdict.

In its 7–3 decision, the U.S. Supreme Court affirmed the Appeals Court's decision. The Justices not only recognized the importance of the psychotherapist-patient privileged communication, but also placed licensed social workers under this protective cloak. The Court noted that social workers are licensed to conduct psychotherapy in all 50 states and that they may be the only available source of therapy for many patients. The Court did not consider the privilege absolute, although the Justices did not specify when it would not apply. It is likely, however, that restrictions of the psychotherapist-patient privilege in federal courts would mirror those in states. For example, as noted above, the privilege does not generally apply when courts order examinations or when patients voluntarily introduce their mental health into evidence.

Many legal questions about the privilege remain unanswered, and psychologists continue to struggle with the ethical issues as well. Perlin (1991) has discussed cogently the many problems that he attributes to the power imbalance between the psychologist and the individual he or she is assessing or treating. Under the *Specialty Guidelines for Forensic Psychologists* (Committee on Ethical Guidelines for Forensic Psychologists, 1991), clinicians must inform the individual of the nature and purpose of an evaluation, as well as who will be receiving a report. They also have an obligation to ensure that the individual is informed of his or her legal rights. Nonetheless, even if notified of the limits of confidentiality, the individual in reality has little choice in submitting to the evaluation if he or she has not requested it. Perlin also recognizes that the individual may suffer harm as a result of the psychologist's participation in the evaluation process.

Ultimate Issue or Ultimate Opinion Testimony

In most jurisdictions, *lay* witnesses can testify only to events that they have actually seen or heard firsthand. Their opinions and inferences are generally not admissible (Schwitzgebel & Schwitzgebel, 1980). *Expert* witnesses, on the other hand, testify to facts they have observed directly, to tests they may have conducted, and to the research evidence in their field. Moreover, the opinions and inferences of experts are not only admissible, but are also often sought by the courts. Recall that one of the main roles of experts is to assist triers of fact in matters about which they would not otherwise be knowledgeable.

Currently, there is considerable debate among mental health professionals about the wisdom of offering an opinion on the "**ultimate issue**." The ultimate issue is the final question that must be decided by the court. For example, should the expert provide an opinion about whether the defendant was indeed insane (and therefore not responsible) at the time of his crime? Should the expert recommend which parent should be awarded custody? Should the expert opine that a defendant is competent to be executed? Should the expert recommend that a juvenile's case be transferred to criminal court? It is quite clear that courts frequently request and hope for such opinions (Melton et al., 1997; Slobogin, 1989). Redding, Floyd, and Hawk (2001) found that judges and prosecutors, in particular, wanted the expert to provide an opinion on the ultimate issue of whether a defendant was insane at the time of the offense. Defense attorneys were less likely to support this. The researchers noted that the desire among judges and prosecutors to have this opinion was interesting in light of Virginia's statutory prohibition on such ultimate-issue testimony.

Slobogin (1989) has summarized the arguments for and against allowing testimony on the ultimate legal issue before the courts. While acknowledging that judges, lawyers, and juries all want this testimony, he cautions that courts be extremely wary of its use, allowing it only if rigorously tested through the adversarial process. Ultimate issues, he notes, are moral judgements. Although experts are surely capable of making such judgements, this is not their field of expertise. Those who oppose ultimate issue testimony fear the undue influence of the expert on the fact finder. Michael Saks (1990) has remarked that mental health experts too often see themselves as "temporary monarchs" in the courtroom. "This danger is exacerbated," Slobogin remarks, "if the willingness of the expert to provide an ultimate conclusion and the eagerness of the fact finder to hear it minimize efforts to examine the basis of the conclusion; the opinion on the ultimate issue may come to assume disproportionate weight relative to the underlying facts in the mind or minds of the fact finder[s] because the facts are not developed, or are not properly emphasized" (p. 261).

However, research to date has not supported the undue influence of the expert at the trial stage, even on the ultimate question. A review of contemporary jury research, for example, indicates that, though jurors are not immune to an expert's opinion, their decisions are not unduly dictated by it (Nietzel, McCarthy, & Kern, 1999). While influenced to some extent by the testimony, "the effect is modest and leaves opportunity for both foes and fans of ultimate opinion testimony to find support for their positions" (Nietzel et al., 1999, p. 41). It should be noted, however, that the influence of the expert in *pre-trial* proceedings, such as when the judge is making a decision as to whether a defendant is competent to stand trial, is significant (Melton et al., 1997).

Smith (1991) identifies three possible sources of error in ultimate issue testimony, and notes that these are common occurrences in expert testimony. First, the expert may misunderstand the law and thus reach the wrong conclusion. This is typified when many mental health experts testify about a person's criminal responsibility at the time of the offense or competence to stand trial, two legal constructs to be discussed in the next ▶ chapter. Second, the expert may apply hidden value judgements rather than scientific principles, such as might occur if a psychologist testified that a mother was not a fit parent on the basis of an assumption that she is unfit because she works nights or does not belong to an organized religion. Finally, the expert may arrive at the wrong conclusion in order to produce a desired result. A psychologist might conclude that an individual should be institutionalized, even though he does not meet the criteria for institutionalization. Those who favor testimony on the ultimate issue, however, (e.g., Rogers & Ewing, 1989) argue that judges often depend on it, and that such testimony can be carefully controlled, particularly by means of effective cross-examination.

Reflecting the lack of consensus on this matter, the American Psychological Association has not taken a stand on whether ultimate issue testimony should be provided. The 1994 *Guidelines for Child Custody Evaluations in Divorce Proceedings*, for example, specifically refer to the lack of consensus. Guideline 14 notes that psychologists "are obligated to be aware of the arguments on both sides of this issue and to be able to explain the logic of their own practice." The Guideline further states that, if they choose to make a custody recommendation, the recommendation should be derived from sound psychological data and based on the best interests of the child. Furthermore, they should guard against "relying on their own biases or unsupported beliefs in rendering opinions in particular cases." Likewise, the broader *Specialty Guidelines for Forensic Psychologists* (Committee, 1991) neither encourage nor discourage ultimate issue testimony. They note only that "professional observations, inferences, and conclusions must be distinguished from legal facts, opinions, and conclusions."

Surviving the Witness Stand

"The courtroom is a place best reserved for those who are brave, adventuresome and nimble-witted." This comment (Schwitzgebel & Schwitzgebel, 1980, p. 241) summarizes well the perils inherent in cross-examination and the discomfort almost guaranteed the expert witness. The professional literature contains ample advice for psychologists daring enough to approach the witness stand. Poythress (1979), for example, suggests that good preparation for the psychologist intending to be an expert witness should include thorough experiential learning in mock trial situations, observations of experienced expert witnesses, and specific course work or field placements in forensic settings. Others have addressed both stylistic and substantive effectiveness both on the witness stand and during a wide range of meetings and proceedings that are part of the trial preparation process (e.g., Heilbrun, 2001; Heilbrun, Marczyk, & DeMatteo, 2002; Hess, 1999). Many recommend that psychologists read Ziskin and Faust's three-volume *Coping with Psychiatric and Psychological Testimony* (1994). This resource is on many an attorney's reading list. "Their express purpose is to embarrass mental health professionals out of the courtroom" (Hess, 1999, p. 551). Hess also notes that attorneys in court may insult the experts or the field, and that the expert must be able to monitor her or his emotional reactions.

Courtroom testimony, as suggested by the foregoing, can be a punishing experience even when the expert witness is fully prepared. This is especially true in the behavioral sciences, where complexity compounded by incomplete information is rampant. The underlying reason for cross-examinations, of course, is to " . . . reverse the substance or impact of a witness's testimony" (Brodsky, 1991, p. 1).

Conflicting testimony by two psychologists or two psychiatrists, or by one of each, confuses the courts and the public, and it can undermine the credibility of both professions (Yarmey, 1979). However, differences of opinion between and within professions should not necessarily be interpreted as error or misinformation. The "collision of experts" is partly due to the complexity and ambiguity of the issues about which they are commenting. Problems and inconsistencies may also be due to differences in training and philosophies. In some cases, however, the confusion arises when medical and psychological testimony is so replete with professional jargon and with esoteric, empirically-unsupported speculation that the testimony is nearly, if not completely, useless to the court. This type of confusion, therefore, can be avoided if the experts communicate competently and clearly. In other cases, problems stem from inadequate preparation or poor communication between the expert witness and the lawyer who has called that witness to testify.

Because psychologists represent the science of behavior, they would be well advised to be highly familiar with the behavioral research literature directly related to the legal issue upon which they will testify. They should also be prepared to substantiate the reliability and validity of any assessment instruments and procedures used in arriving at their conclusions. Writing about "survival on the witness stand," Stan Brodsky (1977) notes that this preparation is essential. When experts are able to defend their specific theories, methods, and conclusions, their testimony becomes much more credible. In a later book, Brodsky (1999) continued to advise prospective and experienced expert witnesses about the labyrinths of testifying. Another guide is that authored by Abbott and Batt (1999) which, in the process of summarizing jury research, provides valuable practical advice to trial consultants.

Virtually all writers who give advice to the expert witness emphasize the importance of establishing a communicative relationship with the attorney early in the legal process. "Some attorneys stereotypically view psychologists as soft thinkers, lacking in discipline, while psychologists often regard attorneys as narrowly focused, rigid, and inflexible. These stereotypes result from a failure to understand the other's professional needs at the outset of the consultation" (Singer & Nievod, 1987, p. 530). Singer and Nievod also urge psychologists not to be persuaded to enter the courtroom without advance notice and sufficient preparation time. This occurs with surprising frequency and typifies the relationship psychology in the law described in ◀Chapter 1. Finally, they (1987) warn that a psychologist's work products, such as interview notes, correspondence, and tape recordings relating to the case will be made available to attorneys for both sides under the rules of discovery. "Only wisdom and personal preference can dictate how extensively to maintain case records. There is no one way. If the psychologist takes few notes, an opposing attorney may attempt to characterize these notes as skimpy, careless, or the work of a cursory effort" (Singer & Nievod, 1987, p. 530).

Additional advice for experts is provided by a Canadian judge (Sauders, 2001, pp. 117–118). Sauders reminds experts to "never forget the power and nuance of words." He notes that vague or neutral words like injury or complaint are less likely to be recalled by jurors than "more vivid adjectives or evocative verbs." Experts, he also notes, are not there to advocate but to persuade. "We, the triers of fact, need to understand. As psychologists, you should strive to facilitate our grasp of what it is you do."

Summary and Conclusions

This chapter had two main purposes. The first was to provide an overview of court structure and the judicial process, and to introduce various categories of law. It is important that the reader become familiar with court-related concepts, terms, and processes in order to understand the material that is to follow in later chapters. The second purpose of the chapter was to give readers an overview of the various ways in which psychologists and other mental health professionals interact with the courts and the issues that arise as a result of that interaction.

Among the many changes on the court landscape in recent years has been the emergence of specialized courts. Drug courts, mental health courts, and domestic violence courts, all discussed in the chapter, are good examples of this trend. They also reflect the concept of therapeutic jurisprudence, which sees the potential of law as a therapeutic agent. Drug courts—if they operate properly—represent a willingness on the part of the criminal justice system to recognize the drug problem as a health issue, at least as much as it is a crime issue. Some defendants charged with drug or drug-involved offenses are referred to these specialized courts, where they are offered treatment services in the community and where their progress is closely monitored by the court. Drug courts seem to be a promising strategy both for combating crime and for providing meaningful rehabilitation to some offenders. Nevertheless, research on their effectiveness is mixed. Mental health courts, intended to keep mentally disordered offenders out of jails and prisons whenever possible, are rapidly emerging, though the mental-health court model is less universal than the drug court model. Mental health courts are also typically not well funded in comparison to drug courts. Although some research on the efficacy of mental health courts was covered in the chapter, it is premature to draw conclusions at this point.

The chapter ended with a review of three issues that pose ethical questions for psychologists and on which consensus is often lacking. First, although psychologists are obliged to maintain therapist-patient confidentiality, this confidentiality cannot always be guaranteed when the psychologist is interacting with the court. We saw in the chapter a variety of situations in which confidentiality may be abrogated. A second issue of concern to some psychologists is "ultimate issue" opinion testimony. Judges very often ask psychologists to offer an opinion on what is actually a legal question; for example, is this defendant competent to stand trial? Lively debate has occurred over the past 20 years, with little consensus. Those in favor of "ultimate issue" testimony note that such testimony is what judges want; if not provided, judges' decisions on mental health issues may be misguided. Those against such testimony insist the legal decision should be left to the court, and that even recommending a ruling represents undue influence of the psychologist or other mental health professional. Finally, a third issue involved the very logistics of surviving the witness stand—something that can be daunting to psychologists called to testify. A number of seasoned professionals have published books, articles, and monographs aimed at helping psychologists traverse this formidable territory.

Many of the topics covered here will be reintroduced in the chapters ahead. Directly or indirectly, interactions between courts and psychologists underlie all forensic practice. This is obvious when psychologists serve as trial consultants or perform court-ordered evaluations. Additionally, however—and perhaps not so obviously—the work of forensic psychologists is informed and guided by past court decisions—case law—and virtually all of their professional activities are potentially subject to court oversight. As noted in ◀ Chapter 1, this is still essentially a relationship best characterized as psychology in the law.

Key Terms

Administrative law
Amicus curiae
Appellate court
Arraignment
Bench trial
Beyond a reasonable doubt
Case law
Challenges for cause
Civil law
Clear and convincing evidence
Common law
Concurrent jurisdiction
Constitutional law
Court trial
Criminal law
Deposition
Discovery process
Disposition
General jurisdiction
Grand jury
Habeas corpus petition
Indictment
Injunction
Judgement
Jurisdiction
Limited jurisdiction
Plaintiff
Peremptory challenge
Preliminary hearing
Preponderance of the evidence
Pre-sentence investigation
Pre-sentence report
Preventive detention
Procedural law
Right of allocution
Scientific jury selection
Specialized court
Stare decisis
Statutory law
Substantive law
Therapeutic jurisprudence
Trial court
Ultimate issue
Voir dire
Writ of *certiorari*

Questions for Review

1. Compare and contrast the structure and the functions of federal and state courts.
2. Give an example of any one specialized court and discuss its purposes and operations.
3. Explain the difference between classifying law by content and classifying law by origin.
4. What are some differences between the criminal process and the civil process at each of the following stages: pre-trial, trial, disposition, appeals?
5. Give examples of the tasks performed by forensic psychologists at each of the above four stages.
6. Review the *Daubert* trilogy and the standards for evaluating expert testimony introduced in Chapter 2 and discussed again in this chapter.
7. Give examples of limits on the confidentiality between psychologists and their clients.
8. What is "ultimate issue" testimony? Why are psychologists divided on the matter of whether they should provide it? What are the arguments for and against providing such testimony in court?
9. What advice would you give to the psychologist preparing to testify as an expert in a criminal or civil case for the first time?

CHAPTER 4

Mental Health Law: Competencies and Criminal Responsibility

It should be clear from the previous ◀ chapter that mental health professionals provide a wide range of services to both criminal and civil courts. Among the most crucial of these services is the assessment of defendants who are facing criminal proceedings. Psychologists, psychiatrists, and other mental health professionals are often asked to assess a variety of competencies or abilities relevant to a defendant's participation in the criminal process. After making this assessment, which is followed by a written report, the clinician may be asked to testify in a court proceeding. Some evaluations relate to mental states of victims or witnesses, rather than defendants. A forensic psychologist might assess the ability of a child victim to recollect the crime accurately, for example, or the psychological trauma experienced by a rape victim. Most assessments for the criminal courts are of defendants, however, and they will be the primary focus of this chapter.

The work of forensic psychologists is by no means limited to assessments. If a defendant is determined incompetent to participate in criminal proceedings, he or she may then be treated by psychologists or other mental health professionals. Likewise, if a defendant is found not guilty by reason of insanity or determined to be guilty but mentally ill, treatment also should be provided. As will be seen in this chapter, treatment issues have received far less research attention than assessment issues.

From the moment of arrest, a criminal suspect has a good deal to lose. Arrest itself is a restriction on a person's freedom; while under arrest, the suspect is subjected to questioning by police, who must inform him or her of the right to remain silent and to have a lawyer present before the interrogation process begins (*Miranda v. Arizona*, 1966). The great majority of suspects, both adults and juveniles, waive these rights and speak with police without an attorney present (Neubauer, 2002). Once the suspect is formally charged in court, he or she becomes a **defendant**. Both as a suspect and as a defendant, the individual charged with a crime must make a variety of decisions, all requiring cognitive ability.

Legal Competencies and Mental Capacities: Definitions

Grisso (1986, p. 3) has summarized the competencies or capacities that a criminal suspect or defendant must possess. They include the capacity: (1) to waive rights to silence and counsel "knowingly, intelligently, and voluntarily," prior to questioning by law enforcement officers; (2) to plead guilty; (3) to dismiss counsel, or to conduct one's own defense without benefit of counsel; (4) to stand trial (i.e., to function in the role of defendant in the trial process); (5) to possess the requisite cognition, affect, and volition for criminal responsibility (i.e., the insanity defense); (6) to serve a sentence; (7) to be executed (i.e., to undergo capital punishment). In addition to the above, Melton, Petrila, Poythress, and Slobogin (1997) mention the competencies to consent to a search or seizure, to confess, to refuse an insanity defense, to testify, and to be sentenced. Although these latter competencies fall within Grisso's list, they help define even more clearly the role of the criminal defendant.

Competencies arise in the civil context as well. Civil courts, for example, may be concerned about the competence of mentally disordered individuals to refuse medication, the competence of adolescents to make medical decisions, or the competence of the terminally ill to hasten their deaths. These issues will be discussed in chapters ahead. Here, we focus specifically on mental states of adult criminal defendants, both as they relate to various competencies and as they relate to the issue of criminal responsibility. Although we will refer primarily to psychologists and to psychological research, it is recognized that forensic psychiatrists are equally, sometimes more involved, in this process. As noted in ◀ Chapter 3, perhaps reflecting a preference for a "medical model" with respect to mental disorder, courts tend to favor psychiatric over psychological evaluations. Research on competencies and criminal responsibility, however, is conducted primarily by forensic or clinical psychologists.

When courts, both criminal and civil, inquire into an individual's "competency," the courts often look for specific functional abilities. In the 1980s and 1990s, many psychologists tried to identify these abilities in order to render psychological reports and testimony more useful to the courts (e.g., Grisso, 1986, 1988, 1997; Bonnie, 1992). Appelbaum and Grisso (1988; Grisso & Appelbaum, 1991) developed and tested specific instruments for measuring functional abilities in a variety of legal contexts. They identified four sets of cognitive abilities most often incorporated into legal standards. "These are the abilities to communicate a choice, to understand relevant information, to appreciate the situation and its consequences, and to rationally manipulate relevant information" (Grisso & Appelbaum, 1991, p. 378). This emphasis on abilities rather than on mental disorder per se is significant. As will become apparent throughout this and the following chapter, a diagnosis of mental disorder alone is not enough to demonstrate that a person is legally incompetent. Additionally, in some contexts and before some courts a formal diagnosis is not needed or even desired.

Although psychologists may be asked to assess any one of the abilities identified by Grisso (1986), competency to stand trial and insanity evaluations have traditionally received the most research attention and consequently are highlighted here. In later chapters, other "capacity" related topics are covered. For example, a number of commentators have expressed concern about the ability of mentally disordered suspects to waive their Constitutional rights, including the right to remain silent and the right to a lawyer before custodial interrogation (e.g., Decker, 1996; Perlin, 1996). Another area of intense interest is the assessment of juveniles (Grisso, 1998; Grisso & Schwartz, 2000; Heilbrun, Marczyk, & DeMatteo, 2002). Forensic and clinical psychologists have been performing increasingly more evaluations of juveniles whose juvenile court cases are being considered for transfer to criminal courts (or vice-versa). Questions about whether juveniles are competent to waive their rights to remain silent or to consent to treatment are also being raised. ▶ [These issues will be discussed in Chapter 12.] Competency to consent to treatment and to refuse treatment are still other areas that will be discussed both in this chapter ▶ [and in Chapter 5.] Finally, another "competency" topic that has raised numerous ethical questions is an offender's competency to be executed. In 1986, the U.S. Supreme Court ruled it unconstitutional to execute someone who is so mentally disordered that he or she cannot understand what is happening (*Ford v. Wainwright*). ▶ [That topic will be discussed in Chapter 10.]

Competency to stand trial and **insanity**, the main topics of the present chapter, refer to a defendant's mental capacities at *two different* points in time. Specifically, competency to stand trial (CST) is concerned with the individual's capacity *at the time of the trial* preparation and the trial itself to understand the charges and legal proceedings, and to be able to communicate with his or her attorney. Competency to stand trial is restricted to the present and the foreseeable future—that is, for as long as the trial is expected to last. Furthermore, an evaluation or re-evaluation of the defendant's competency may be conducted at any point during the trial. Typically, though, these evaluations are done early in the criminal process. Insanity, on the other hand, is the legal term for lack of criminal responsibility *at the time of the crime*, as the result of a mental disorder.

A defendant may be sane, or criminally responsible at the time of the crime, but found incompetent at the trial stage. An example is the careless and negligent driver who kills a pedestrian, is charged with vehicular manslaughter, and is so emotionally distraught as a result of the tragedy that he cannot help his attorney in the preparation of a defense. Conversely, a defendant may have lacked criminal responsibility at the time of the crime, but may still be competent at the time of legal proceedings. Indeed, a criminal trial of an individual claiming insanity as a defense cannot be conducted if the defendant is not competent.

It must be emphasized that both terms—insanity and competency to stand trial—are *legal*, not psychological concepts. The court, not the mental health practitioner or clinician, determines who was insane or who is incompetent. In reality, however, judges rely very heavily on the opinion of the examining clinician when it is provided (Melton et al., 1997). A judge's finding that an individual is incompetent to stand trial (IST) means that the defendant is so cognitively or emotionally impaired that it is unfair to continue the criminal process. At this point, court proceedings are held in abeyance until the defendant becomes competent; alternately, the case is dismissed, usually without prejudice (meaning that the prosecutor has the option of re-opening the case at a later date if the defendant regains competency and the statute of limitations has not expired). A judge or jury's verdict that a defendant was not guilty by reason of insanity means that the individual may not be punished. However, he or she may be (and usually is) institutionalized for treatment of the mental disorder.

The terms "competency to stand trial" and "insanity" often confound the public. A long line of research shows psychiatrists and clinical psychologists, lawyers, judges, and legislators also have misconstrued the concepts (Simon & Aaronson, 1988; Melton, 1987; Melton et al., 1997). We will examine each one separately, discuss how it is used in the criminal process, and point out problems associated with this use. An alternative verdict to not guilty by reason of insanity, "Guilty but Mentally Ill," adopted in some states in response to frustrations with the insanity defense, will also be discussed.

Competency to Stand Trial

The U.S. Supreme Court has ruled that defendants are competent to stand trial if they have "sufficient present ability to consult with [their] lawyer with a reasonable degree of rational understanding . . . and a rational as well as a factual understanding of the proceedings . . . " (*Dusky v. U.S.*, 1960, p. 402). Competency requires not only that defendants *understand* what is happening, but also that they be *able to assist* their lawyers in the preparation of their defenses. This is sometimes referred to as the *Dusky* "two-pronged standard." In other words, competency to stand trial is the ability to play the role of defendant (Grisso, 1986; Szasz, 1960). This role is relevant not only at the trial itself, but also in a variety of pre-trial formal and informal proceedings, including plea negotiations, preliminary hearings, and evidence suppression hearings.

Legal Standards

We must emphasize again that a diagnosis of a mental disorder per se does not render an individual incompetent to stand trial. Mental illness or disorder does not equal incompetency. For example, a person with a depressive disorder may be perfectly capable of understanding the proceedings and helping her attorney. On the other hand, another person with the same depressive disorder could be so severely debilitated that he withdraws from the situation and refuses to communicate. As Grisso (1986, p. 95) remarks, "Although psychological symptoms by themselves are not synonymous with legal incompetency, they are certainly relevant for pretrial competency determinations." So, whereas the *lack* of a diagnosis does not serve as a bar to incompetency (Cruise & Rogers, 1998), clinical diagnosis does appear to be a significant contributor to the competency recommendations made by evaluators (Cochrane, Grisso, & Frederick, 2001).

Symptoms associated with a diagnosis of a mental disorder may also interfere with a person's *competency to plead guilty*. Recall that the vast majority of criminal cases that reach the courts are settled by way of a plea bargain. Pleading guilty, in light of its consequences, may require sharper functional ability than going through trial (Halleck, 1980). In pleading guilty, a person waives a number of Constitutional rights, including the Fifth Amendment right not to incriminate oneself and the Sixth Amendment right to a fair trial, along with its accompaniments (e.g., impartial jury of peers; right to confront and cross-examine witnesses). Before accepting a guilty plea, a judge must address the defendant and inquire into the voluntariness of the plea. The judge also must assure that the defendant understands the consequences of waiving his or her Constitutional rights. Not surprisingly, judges vary in how carefully and deliberately they perform this task. In the late 1980s, scholars argued that the failure to monitor guilty pleas more carefully was one of the factors contributing to the influx of mentally disordered persons in jails and prisons (Steadman, McCarty, & Morrissey, 1989).

Nevertheless, the U.S. Supreme Court ruled in *Godinez v. Moran* (1993) that competency to plead guilty does not require a higher or different standard than competency to stand trial. Moran, the defendant in the case, had waived his right to a lawyer and pled guilty to a crime which carried a possible death sentence. The Court reaffirmed the two-pronged *Dusky* standard—(1) ability to consult with one's lawyer; and (2) rational and factual understanding of the proceedings—and applied it to the competency of criminal defendants regardless of the context. For example, the Court majority saw no distinction between (a) deciding to waive a lawyer and plead guilty and (b) participating actively in one's defense or actively assisting one's lawyer. As we noted above, though, the decision to plead guilty, which is often made under stressful conditions, involves the waiver of several Constitutional rights. The decision making process involved is very complex. The *Godinez* decision has been criticized by legal and psychological commentators, as well as by some lower courts (Perlin, 1996; Roesch et al., 1999). One team of researchers (Cruise & Rogers, 1998) called the *Godinez* ruling a "procrustean solution," indicating that the Court forced conformity by arbitrary, even ruthless means. (In Greek mythology, Procrustes was a giant who stretched or shortened captives to fit one of his iron beds!)

Psychologists are most likely to be asked to evaluate a defendant for competency very early in the criminal process, although rarely before custodial interrogation. Typically, at the defendant's arraignment or shortly thereafter, a motion is made by either the defense lawyer or the prosecutor to inquire into the defendant's competency. The presiding judge also has the authority to raise the competency issue. The judge and both attorneys are all "officers of the court" and thus are expected to preserve the integrity of the judicial process. Numerous factors can trigger a competency inquiry. The arresting police officer may have noticed bizarre behavior, for example, or the person may have attempted to commit suicide while detained in jail pending arraignment. Research has found that competency evaluations are also precipitated by previous psychiatric hospitalizations as well as psychologically irrelevant factors, including political motives, a defense lawyer's wish to "buy time," and homelessness (Nicholson & Kugler, 1991). Most requests for competency evaluation are neither denied by the judge nor challenged by the opposing attorney (Roesch & Golding, 1987; Roesch, Zapf, Golding, & Skeem, 1999).

As noted above, severe mental disturbance is not sufficient to produce a finding of incompetence to stand trial. As Roesch et al. (1999, p. 329) posit, "it must be further demonstrated that such severe disturbance in *this* defendant, facing *these* charges, *in light of existing* evidence, anticipating the substantial effort of a *particular* attorney with a *relationship of known characteristics*, results in the defendant being unable to rationally assist the attorney or to comprehend the nature of the proceedings and their likely outcome." Increasingly more clinicians are promoting this "context-specific" approach to competency evaluations. It requires the clinician's extensive knowledge of the facts of the case and what decisions might be awaiting the defendant. A defendant charged with a first-time nonviolent felony, may be competent to plead guilty after an attorney has negotiated a plea that will result in probation and restitution. The same defendant, charged with a violent felony carrying a maximum sentence of 20 years imprisonment, may not be competent to assist his attorney during a protracted trial, however. Revising the scenario once again, the same defendant carrying a possible penalty of death or a life sentence, may not be competent to plead guilty because he may not understand the ramifications of a life in prison sentence. Empirical research has demonstrated this variability in competency across areas of functioning (e.g., Grisso, Appelbaum, Mulvey, & Fletcher, 1995; Skeem et al., 1998).

Incidence of Competency to Stand Trial Evaluations

Estimates of the number of defendants evaluated for competency to stand trial in the United States range from 50,000 (Skeem et al., 1998) to 60,000 (Bonnie & Grisso, 2000). The great majority, typically in the vicinity of 80%, are found competent (Cochrane et al., 2001). It is believed that between 3% and 8% of all felony defendants are assessed for competency (Hoge et al., 1997; Roesch et al., 1999; Winick, 1995a). Surveys of public defenders suggest that there are competency to stand trial concerns for 10–15% of all criminal defendants, including those charged with felonies and misdemeanors (Melton et al., 1997). The competency inquiry has been called "the most significant mental health inquiry pursued in the system of criminal law" (Stone, 1975, p. 200). In a line of decisions (e.g., *Dusky v. U.S.*, 1960; *Pate v. Robinson*, 1966; *Drope v. Missouri*, 1975), the U.S. Supreme Court has made it clear that the conviction of an incompetent defendant violates due process of law. If state legislatures wish, they may allocate to the defendant the burden of proving incompetency by a preponderance of the evidence (*Medina v. California*, 1992). In most states, as well as in federal law, this is the case. However, due process is violated if the defendant is required to prove incompetency by clear and convincing evidence (*Cooper v. Oklahoma*, 1996). ◄ (See **Box 3-3** for a review of these burdens of proof.)

An Example: *Cooper v. Oklahoma*

The facts in *Cooper v. Oklahoma* illustrate many of the concepts we have been discussing. Byron Keith Cooper was charged with the brutal killing of an 86-year-old man in the course of a burglary. The issue of his competency to stand trial was raised five different times, three times during the pre-trial proceedings, once the day his trial was about to begin, and once again at his sentencing. When the question of his competency was first raised by his defense counsel, a judge ordered that Cooper be examined by a psychologist. Based on the psychologist's recommendation, the judge then ruled him incompetent to stand trial (IST) and sent him to a mental hospital, where he stayed for three months. At a second competency hearing, a new judge found him competent to stand trial, despite conflicting opinions from two psychologists. A week before the trial, a defense attorney again raised the competency issue, but the judge refused to reverse his earlier decision.

The first day of Cooper's trial, his bizarre behavior prompted the court to inquire again into his competency. A psychologist concluded that he was probably incompetent, but might be rendered competent if treated aggressively. The court nonetheless found him competent, although this trial judge voiced considerable uncertainty. As quoted in the Supreme Court's decision, the judge stated:

> "My shirtsleeve opinion of Mr. Cooper is that he's not normal. Now, to say he's not competent is something else. But you know, all things considered, I suppose it's possible for a client to be in such a predicament that he can't help his defense and still not be incompetent. I suppose that's a possibility, too. I think it's going to take smarter people than me to make a decision here. I'm going to say that I don't believe he has carried the burden by clear and convincing evidence of his incompetency and I'm going to say we're going to go to trial" (p.1374).

During his competency hearing, Cooper talked to himself and to an imaginary spirit he claimed was giving him counsel. On the witness stand, he claimed that the lead defense attorney was trying to kill him. During his trial, he wore prison overalls because the civilian clothes he had been offered were "burning" him. He did not communicate with his defense counsel; through much of the trial he crouched in the fetal position and talked to himself. He was convicted of first degree murder, and the jury recommended the death penalty.

Cooper's competence was again at issue at the sentencing hearing, when his defense lawyer moved for a mistrial or a reexamination of his client's competence. The judge denied the request and sentenced Cooper to death as the jury recommended. The Oklahoma Court of Criminal Appeals upheld the conviction, referring to the inexactness and uncertainty of competency proceedings and the fact that a "truly incompetent criminal defendant can prove incompetency with relative ease."

In its unanimous opinion, the U.S. Supreme Court noted that Cooper was "more likely than not" incompetent. The Court rejected the likelihood that Cooper might have been malingering. "We presume . . . that it is unusual for even the most artful malingerer to feign incompetence successfully for a period of time while under professional care." The Justices noted that an erroneous determination of competency, which was a high risk when the burden of proof was so heavy, threatened the very fairness of the trial itself. They also added that the great majority of states pose no such heavy burden—clear and convincing evidence—on the defendant to prove competency.

Cooper's situation was atypical insofar as the burden of proof is concerned because only a handful of states at that time required defendants to prove their incompetency by clear and convincing evidence. However, the case illustrates the uncertainties about competency (as evidenced by the comments of the judge and the Court of Criminal Appeals); the duty of the presiding judge to make the ultimate decision; the role of the evaluating clinicians; and the state's determination to render an incompetent defendant competent and take him to trial.

The Competency Evaluation Process

Until the late 1980s, the typical competency evaluation was conducted while the defendant was hospitalized in a mental institution for anywhere from 15–90 days (Nicholson & Kugler, 1991). Researchers found that judges and lawyers often distrusted outpatient evaluations, believing they could not adequately assess a defendant's competency (Melton et al., 1985). Beginning in the 1990s, competency evaluations were increasingly conducted in outpatient facilities or in jails or courthouses (Roesch et al., 1999). This can be attributed to a variety of factors including lower cost, increase in arrest rates, the lack of space in institutions, and the development of competency assessment instruments such as those discussed in ◀ Chapter 2.

Although competency to stand trial and insanity are often interrelated (Golding & Roesch, 1987), they require separate assessments and determinations. Consequently, we will discuss the assessment of competency in this part of the chapter and the assessment of sanity later on. Traditionally, psychiatrists and psychologists failed to focus on the limited issue of a defendant's competency to stand trial (Grisso, 1988; Saks, 1990). Instead, they traveled into irrelevant conceptual terrain in their competency reports as well as in their courtroom testimony. Some examiners concentrated on a defendant's dangerousness, for example (Grisso, 1988; Menzies, 1989), or on the defendant's state of mind at the time of the offense, which is critical to the insanity issue but not the competency issue. Some statutes and courts continue to nurture this misinterpretation by requiring or allowing a dual-purpose evaluation of both the defendant's competency to stand trial and mental state at the time of the offense (MSO). One study found that 47% of competency evaluations also addressed questions of sanity (Warren, Fitch, Dietz, & Rosenfeld, 1991). Roesch, Zapf, Golding, and Skeem (1999) are very critical of this common practice, recommending instead that separate interviews with distinct reports be prepared. "A trier of fact is required to separate these issues, but it is cognitively almost impossible to do so when the reports are combined" (Roesch et al., 1999, p. 343).

There is a wide variety of professional literature advising clinical psychologists and other examiners how to conduct competency evaluations for the courts (e.g., Golding et al., 1999; Grisso, 1986, 1988; Heilbrun et al., 2002; Melton et al., 1997). Additionally, *Ethical Principles of Psychologists* (Committee, 1991) include a short section on forensic assessments in general (Section 7.02) which cautions that reports and recommendations must be based on information and techniques sufficient to provide appropriate substantiation of the findings. Clinical misconceptions about competency evaluations have apparently lessened with the availability of published guidelines and instruments for assessing both competency and insanity (Golding et al., 1999). Nevertheless, as Cruise and Rogers (1998, p. 44) state, "There is no clear consensus on a standard of practice for competency evaluations."

In recent years, some states have begun to require certification or credentialing of mental health professionals who conduct competency evaluations as well as criminal responsibility (CR or MSO) evaluations. At least nine states require some type of certification (Farkas, DeLeon, & Newman, 1997; Otto & Heilbrun, 2002). However, statutes rarely prescribe the method of evaluation, though some states (e.g., Florida and Utah) have specific requirements. In most states, how competency is assessed depends upon the examiner's training and theoretical orientation. Some examiners prefer only the clinical interview, while others choose the interview in combination with projective or objective testing instruments. Still others use a wide-ranging assessment procedure that includes psychological tests, interview information, observation, and extensive background and social history.

An important principle related to the competency evaluation is the warning that must be given to the defendant. In the case of a court-ordered evaluation, the defendant should be told of the purpose of the examination as well as how its results will be used. Confidentiality is not guaranteed, because the court, not the defendant, is the client of the examining clinician. Nevertheless, material gathered in the course of the competency evaluation may not be used in the guilt phase of the case or at sentencing without a *Miranda*-type warning (*Estelle v. Smith*, 1981). Smith was evaluated for competency by a psychiatrist who later testified at the sentencing phase of his case. Based on the clinical information obtained during the pre-trial evaluation, the psychiatrist testified that Smith was a danger to society and consequently a good candidate for capital punishment. The Supreme Court ruled that, since the examining clinician had not informed Smith of his right to remain silent, the information could not be used against him. The *Estelle* case has virtually put a stop to the use of incriminating information derived in pre-trial evaluations for sentencing purposes.

As discussed in ◀ Chapter 2, a robust debate has occurred in the literature over the use and misuse of psychological tests in forensic practice. Heilbrun (1992) and Otto and Heilbrun (2002) note that there has been little data on how such tests are used. In an attempt to rectify this situation, Borum and Grisso (1995) surveyed forensic psychiatrists and psychologists on their use of psychological tests while evaluating competency to stand trial (CST) and criminal responsibility (CR). Testing was considered more important for the CR evaluations than the CST evaluations, however. Psychologists were slightly more likely than psychiatrists to rate testing as essential or recommended in CR examinations (68% of the psychologists, 61% of the psychiatrists); for the CST examinations, 51% of the psychologists and 45% of the psychiatrists rated testing as essential or recommended. Nevertheless, the great majority of both clinical groups *did* use psychological tests and inventories, the most common for psychiatrists being intellectual and cognitive instruments and for psychologists being objective personality inventories. As will be noted shortly, special instruments developed specifically for competency and criminal responsibility evaluations, generically known as FAIs (forensic assessment instruments), were *not* widely used.

Borum and Grisso (1995) note that their research suggests the need for additional data and commentary on acceptable standards of practice for forensic evaluations. "Together, these findings do not support a standard that requires testing in every criminal forensic case performed by a psychologist. . . . On the other hand, test use . . . appears to be sufficiently frequent to be the norm rather than the exception. This would suggest, perhaps, that in CST and CR evaluations, psychologists ought to be held accountable to explain why they have *not* used psychological testing in those cases in which they do not" (Borum & Grisso, 1995, p. 471).

Forensic Assessment Instruments

As discussed in ◀ Chapter 2, researchers over the last quarter century have developed a variety of instruments specifically designed for use in forensic settings. Known collectively as forensic assessment instruments (FAIs), they are intended to aid clinicians conducting a wide variety of evaluations, including those for competency and criminal responsibility. In a recent commentary on the state of forensic psychology, Otto and Heilbrun (2002) note that the past 10 years have seen the development of more such tests than in the previous

40 years. They add, however, that far too many of these tests have been published and marketed after very limited research and precursory development. The knowledge that examiners are using numerous nonvalidated and inadequate assessment techniques and instruments is sobering. Otto and Heilbrun (2002, p. 10) warn that "This situation must be addressed immediately, or forensic psychology will risk its reputation in the courtroom, particularly as legal decision makers become more knowledgeable about the science of assessment."

Presumably, the information collected by forensic assessment instruments should have a content particularly relevant to addressing the legal questions posed by the courts (Grisso, 1986). In the following section, we will briefly describe those instruments relevant to assessing competency. Later in this chapter, forensic instruments relating to criminal responsibility will be covered. In later chapters, instruments relating to the waiving of certain Constitutional rights (e.g., "Miranda" rights), assessment of parenting skills, and risk assessment of sex offenders and other offenders will be discussed.

The Competency Screening Test Included in the competency assessment instruments are screening instruments which are intended to provide a "quick assessment" of a defendant's competency to stand trial. Approximately four of every five defendants evaluated for competency to stand trial are ultimately found competent (Grisso, 1986; Nicholson & Kugler, 1991). This evidence, together with concerns that defendants often are hospitalized needlessly during the evaluation process, led to the development of screening instruments for the quick identification of those who are "obviously competent." As noted in ◀ Chapter 2, the earliest work in this area was a brief checklist (Robey, 1965), which was soon superseded by guidelines proposed by McGarry and his colleagues (Laboratory of Community Psychiatry, 1974). The researchers developed two instruments specifically designed to direct clinicians toward relevant defendant behaviors. One instrument, the Competency Screening Test (CST), produces a summational score of competency to stand trial. The defendant is asked to complete 22 sentences (Example: "When I go to court the lawyer will . . . ") and each response is scored 0, 1, or 2. A total score below 20 usually raises questions about the defendant's competency. The instrument's major advantage is its ability to screen out *quickly* the clearly competent defendants so that a more comprehensive examination can be directed at those defendants whose competency is questionable.

The CST has been found to have a high false-positive rate, however (53.3%). That is, "it tends to identify many individuals as incompetent who are later determined to be competent in hospital evaluations" (Roesch, Zapf, Golding, & Skeem, 1999, p. 338). Additionally, compared with other available tests it is a weak measure of a defendant's ability to communicate with counsel and to have a rational understanding of the legal process (Cruise & Rogers, 1998).

Competency Assessment Instrument The second instrument developed by the McGarry group, the Competency Assessment Instrument (CAI), is not a *screening* test. It is designed to assess all possible legal grounds for a finding of incompetence, although it has been extensively criticized for assuming that the functions associated with competency are covered (Cruise & Rogers, 1998). In a recent analysis of a variety of tests, the CAI was found to perform very weakly (Cruise & Rogers, 1998). That is, the instrument's reliability and correspondence with the *Dusky* standard have not been demonstrated enough to make it a valid instrument for competency assessment (Rogers et al., 2001).

Interdisciplinary Fitness Interview Golding, Roesch, and Schreiber (1984) developed the Interdisciplinary Fitness Interview (IFI), a structured interview "designed to assess both the legal and psychopathological aspects of competency" (Roesch & Golding, 1987, p. 386). A key feature of the IFI is its interdisciplinary nature; it encourages joint interviewing by a clinician and a lawyer. More recently, Golding (1993) revised the instrument to reflect experience, research, and on-going changes in the law. It now attempts to assess competency across various contexts, including competency to waive the assistance of counsel and to choose between different trial strategies. Interestingly, despite this recent revision, Rogers et al. (2001, p. 506) indicate that the IFI "has not generated any further research since its original publication." One reason for this may be the impracticality of the IFI. Few lawyers are likely to be able and willing to sit down with a clinician and administer the instrument. Melton et al. (1997, p. 142) also see this as a major drawback, despite their belief that the IFI is "a time-efficient interview format that produces rich observations with high reliability." However, "most attorneys have neither the time nor the inclination to observe, much less participate in, competency-to-stand-trial evaluations" (p. 142).

Georgia Court Competency Test Also appearing on the scene are the Georgia Court Competency Test (GCCT) and its revision (GCCT–MSH). These are quick measures of competency with good internal consistency and, to some extent, inter-rater reliability. Although impressive reliability scores are associated with the total GCCT score, the jury is still out on the reliability and validity of the scales used to evaluate the *Dusky* standard (Rogers et al., 2001). The GCCT has performed better than the CST or the CAI on assessing factual understanding and rational understanding, as well as on the ability to communicate with counsel (Cruise & Rogers, 1998). Additionally, the latest versions of the GCCT include a promising screen for malingering or feigning incompetence (Gothard, Rogers, & Sewell, 1995). According to Rogers et al. (2001), the most recent version can typically be administered in 15–20 minutes and will serve well enough as a CST screening instrument, if supplemented by additional inquiries about the defendant's relationship with counsel.

The MacArthur Measures The newest competency evaluation instrument is the MacArthur Structured Assessment of the Competencies of Criminal Defendants (MacSAC–CD). It attempts to assess both adjudicative competence and decisional competence, which together comprise the theory of legal competence espoused by Richard Bonnie. Bonnie (1992) has suggested that competency to stand trial involves two primary concepts: (1) ability to understand the proceedings (adjudicative competency); and (2) ability to make decisions in one's own best interest (decisional competency). Ability to understand the proceedings includes understanding the role of various people in the process, understanding and appreciating one's own rights, being able to communicate information to counsel, and ability to appreciate the significance of one's own situation. Decisional competency, on the other hand, includes the ability to engage in reasoning, consider the consequences of several different options (for example, waiving rights), make judgments with input from counsel, and allow lawyers to use certain strategies. Research thus far suggests that the MacSAC–CD, though lengthy and cumbersome to administer and score, is superior to other assessment instruments and shows promise for overcoming criticisms of other competency measures (Cruise & Rogers, 1998; Hoge et al., 1997). Nicholson (1999, p. 150) believed that it "represents a major contribution to the asessment of adjudicative competence." He added that it may be especially helpful in assessing restoration to competence.

A briefer interview based on the MacSAC–CD, called the MacSAC–CA, has since been developed (Otto et al., 1998). Rogers et al. (2001) report that this new version has good internal reliability for its three scales measuring understanding, reasoning, and appreciation, though inter-item correlations are substantial. However, they raise questions about the interview's inter-rater reliability, suggesting that more data on this issue are desirable. Moreover, Rogers has argued elsewhere (Rogers, 2001) that the MacCAT–CA is not the best match with the two-pronged *Dusky* standard. Nevertheless, he acknowledges that the brief interview can be very useful in assessing the defendant's rational understanding of the proceedings.

Other Competency Measures Rogers and his colleagues are in the process of developing, revising, and assessing their own competency assessment instrument, the ECST (now ECST–R) (Rogers & Grandjean, 2000; Rogers et al., 2001). To some extent, Rogers' sharp criticism of other competency measures should be placed within that context. They have suggested that "clinicians may see the real contribution of the ECST–R in evaluating rational abilities as they relate to the defense counsel and legal proceedings" (Rogers et al., 2001, p. 516).

Competency assessment instruments for use with specialized populations, such as juveniles and the developmentally disabled, have also been developed. Not surprisingly, there appears to be a negative correlation between competency and age, with incompetency more likely to be found in younger defendants (Cooper, 1997; Cowden & McKee, 1995). Although elderly defendants also may be incompetent to stand trial, research has not focused on this age group because they comprise a small proportion of the total population of criminal defendants. ▶ [The competency of juveniles will be discussed in greater detail in Chapter 12]. The Competence Assessment for Standing Trial for Defendants with Mental Retardation (CAST–MR) has been developed by Everington (1990) to assess the competency of defendants who are developmentally disabled.

Despite the robust research and promising findings, the competency assessment instruments do not seem to be widely used, although their use may be increasing. In the Borum and Grisso (1995) study cited earlier, for instance, 40% of psychologists used forensic instruments almost always or frequently, but an almost equal percentage (36%) never used them. Only 13% of *psychiatrists* used them almost always or frequently, while 58% never used them. Nevertheless, Borum and Grisso found it encouraging that "almost half of the experts at least have these instruments in their repertoire" (1995, p. 472).

When forensic instruments are used, they likely supplement traditional clinical methods, particularly the clinical interview (Roesch & Golding, 1987). Borum and Grisso's research indicates that they also supplement, rather than replace, other psychological tests and inventories. More recently, Roesch et al. (1999, p. 327) remind their readers that "the issues surrounding a competency determination are highly complex. An evaluator needs not only a high level of clinical knowledge and skills but also considerable knowledge of the legal system." Nevertheless, they note that competency *screening* instruments have their place with defendants for whom incompetence is clearly not an issue. They save money and time and eliminate unnecessary detention.

Those who favor the instruments also note that the traditional clinical interview or unspecialized tests do not garner support in the empirical literature. At least, "competency measures offer a standardization of competency assessments that is likely to reduce variability due to information and possibly criterion variance" (Cruise & Rogers, 1998, p. 48). Even so, judges who are more familiar with standard psychological tests and inventories like the MMPI–2, the WAIS, and the Rorschach are more likely to favor reports that include a reference to these instruments.

Regardless of the specific procedures used, psychologists conducting competency evaluations should keep three points in mind. First, they must have a thorough understanding of the referral: Who raised the competency issue and why? What specific questions, if any, did the referring agent pose? Were there questions about the intellectual or neurological functioning of the defendant? Second, any tests used should be those for which reliability and validity data have been empirically established and should include at least one instrument specifically designed to assess competency. As Otto and Heilbrun (2002) have pointed out, the proliferation of tests available to forensic practitioners has led to the widespread use of questionable instruments. Judges and lawyers, they add, are becoming quite savvy about clinical tools and will be more likely to challenge clinicians on the reliability and validity of their methods. Third, the examiner must be able to develop a connection between the data collected and the referral questions and to communicate the relationship clearly to the court. The report should be concise, make reference to specific behaviors, and be cautious in setting forth interpretations and conclusions. The clinician should remember that the decision as to whether a defendant is competent to stand trial is to be made by the presiding judge. Despite this, as we discussed in ◀ Chapter 3, many clinicians are not loathe to express an opinion on the ultimate legal issue when asked to do so by the court.

When an evaluation has been completed, the examiner transmits to the court, and often to attorneys, a report that, as noted above, frequently includes a recommendation as to the defendant's competency. The great majority of competency decisions are made on the basis of one clinician's assessment (Melton et al., 1997) and without direct testimony from that clinician. Furthermore, judges rarely disagree with the clinician's recommendation, particularly if the clinician believes the defendant is incompetent. After reviewing a number of studies on this matter, Melton and his colleagues (1997, p. 129) note that "whomever examining mental health professionals characterize as incompetent is likely ultimately to be found incompetent."

The Incompetent Defendant

Most defendants evaluated for competency to stand trial are found competent. In a widely cited study of the minority found IST, Steadman (1979, p. 30) described them as a socially marginal group "with much less than average education and few useful job skills. Most have few community ties, either through employment or family. An unusually high proportion have never married." Nicholson and Kugler (1991), who analyzed 30 studies on competency to stand trial which had been conducted over a 20-year period, reported that the strongest correlates of incompetency were not demographic but rather clinical in nature. Demographic data include factors such as age, gender, employment, and marital status. Clinical data include information about psychological functions. Specifically, in Nicholson and Kugler's summary, defendants found IST: (1) performed poorly on tests specifically designed to assess legally relevant functional abilities; (2) were diagnosed psychotic; and (3) had psychiatric symptoms indicating severe psychopathology.

The relationship between competency status and crime charged appears erratic and varies widely across jurisdictions. Some research has found that defendants ruled IST were most often charged with violent crimes, or at least felony offenses (e.g., Steadman, 1979; Roesch & Golding, 1980; Williams & Miller, 1981). Nicholson and Kugler's examination of 30 studies, however, indicated that the type of offense "likely bears a stronger relation to the decision to refer [for a competency evaluation] than it does to the decision about competency itself" (p. 366). That is, more than half of the competency evaluees in their meta-analysis had been charged with violent crimes, but less than a third of those ultimately found incompetent were in that category. Warren et al. (1997), in a three-state study, found that defendants charged with serious crimes (e.g., homicide and sex offenses) were twice as likely as other defendants to be found competent. Rosenfeld and Ritchie (1998) found a similar relationship between offense severity and the competency determination: persons charged with less serious offenses had significantly higher rates of incompetence. Thus, the recent research and the meta-analysis suggest that defendants with serious charges are less likely to be incompetent, while early research suggests the opposite. Cochrane et al. (2001) seem to shed some light on these seeming inconsistencies in their examination of federal defendants.

The Power of Diagnosis Cochrane et al. reviewed the files of 1,710 criminal defendants who had been referred by federal courts nationwide for forensic evaluations. Competency evaluations were available for 1,424 defendants, and 19% were recommended to be incompetent. The researchers found considerable variance according to the crime charged. The highest percentages of incompetence (all above the 19% mean) were for illegal immigration, threats, murder, and assault. Robbery, drug crimes, weapons violations, and kidnap/hostage offenses were all below the mean, with the last having no incompetent recommendations. When Cochrane et al. controlled for diagnoses, however, there were no statistically significant relationships between any of the charges and incompetence findings. The researchers found that psychoses, organic disorders, and mental retardation were frequent diagnoses in incompetent defendants. They concluded "the main variable that affects psycholegal opinions is the diagnostic presentation of the defendant" (p. 581).

The fact that diagnoses seem to carry so much weight is troubling to many psychologists. Forensic psychologists are usually advised not to include diagnoses in competency reports (Grisso, 1986), and many prefer not to offer psychopathological diagnoses in sanity reports either (Golding & Roesch, 1987). The same reluctance can be seem among forensic psychiatrists in the midst of increasing demands from the legal system to render formal diagnoses (American Psychiatric Association Task Force, 1992). Yet, representatives of the legal system routinely expect diagnoses in clinical reports, and clinicians routinely supply them, even in evaluations of competency to stand trial. In sanity evaluations, diagnoses are the norm. Even though a verdict of insanity is a "moral judgement" (Slobogin, 1989), its foundation is some mental disorder. Specifying the disorder, then, becomes a critical issue to many if not most courts.

Some critics have argued that imposing a diagnosis on a defendant distracts the fact finder from the duty to view both competency to stand trial and insanity as legal, not psychiatric or psychological constructs (Melton, 1987; Golding & Roesch, 1987). Other critics maintain that diagnoses are inherently subjective and unreliable (Ziskin & Faust, 1988). Early research examining the ability of highly trained and experienced clinicians to diagnose or even characterize persons consistently failed to demonstrate even minimal inter-judge reliability (e.g., Spitzer & Fleiss, 1974; Goldberg & Werts, 1966; Golden, 1964; Soskin, 1959; Meehl, 1957). However, more recent research on the DSM–III–R and DSM–IV–R indicates that the reliability of diagnosis has improved significantly (American Psychiatric Association Task Force, 1992; American Psychiatric Association, 2000; Durand & Barlow, 2000).

In light of strong indications that diagnostic presentation is the key factor in incompetency determination, it is not surprising that the competency issue is also raised in the case of defendants charged with misdemeanors. It is widely believed that this is often done as a way of assuring that mentally disordered defendants charged with minor crimes are provided with inpatient treatment. Typically, misdemeanor offenses would result in guilty pleas and a community sentence, such as probation. Prior to the court proceedings, the defendant may be detained in jail, but is unlikely to be receiving appropriate mental health treatment in that facility. Therefore, the presiding judge and the two attorneys may decide informally that a competency evaluation is one way of placing the mentally disordered individual in a treatment setting. The defendant may also be ruled incompetent to stand trial for the same reason—to provide mental health treatment. As will be noted in the following chapter, there are many obstacles to institutionalizing individuals against their will in civil proceedings. Consequently, the criminal proceedings offer an alternative possibility. Still another alternative is offered by the mental health courts discussed in ◀ Chapter 3, which serve to deflect mentally disordered individuals from the typical criminal court process. As more mental health courts emerge, we should be seeing fewer cases referred for competency evaluations as well as fewer individuals being found incompetent to stand trial.

Until 1972, a defendant found IST could face lifetime confinement in a mental institution. It was not uncommon for the defendant to be committed for an indefinite period of time, supposedly until rendered "competent." Early studies reported that about 50% of those found incompetent under these procedures spent the rest of their lives confined in an institution (Hess & Thomas, 1963; McGarry, 1971). It was also estimated that these IST defendants comprised at least 40% of the population in mental institutions (Steadman & Cocozza, 1974).

In the 1972 case *Jackson v. Indiana*, the U.S. Supreme court ruled that persons found IST may be involuntarily confined only for the reasonable period of time necessary to determine whether there is a substantial probability of their becoming competent to stand trial in the foreseeable future. If the defendant was not likely to gain competency in the foreseeable future, civil commitment proceedings must be initiated or the defendant must be released. ▶ [Civil commitment, the subject of Chapter 5, carries due process protections that make it more difficult to place a person in a mental institution against his or her will.] In the *Jackson* case the Court left it to the states to determine what are reasonable amounts of time to strive for competency and how to evaluate the likelihood that competency would be achieved. Indefinite confinement is out of the question, though. States vary in the limitations they have placed on the confinement period. Some have specified time limits, while others base the length of treatment on the maximum sentence the defendant could have received if convicted.

As a result of the *Jackson* case, persons found incompetent to stand trial who have little likelihood of being restored to competency now have their cases dismissed without prejudice, which gives the prosecutor the option of reinstituting charges in the event that the person regains competency. Alternately, such persons may be committed to mental institutions or ordered to participate in outpatient care through civil commitment proceedings.

Drug Treatment in Competency Issues

Most defendants deemed IST eventually are ruled competent and either plead guilty or go to trial. The state, and often the defendant, has a strong interest in going forth with the proceedings. The government's interest is particularly strong in a serious case, of course, such as was demonstrated in *Cooper v. Oklahoma* (1996), discussed earlier in the chapter. While some IST defendants are treated in the community, most are institutionalized for a brief period of time to render them competent. Whether in-patient or out-patient, medication is the most common type of treatment provided to incompetent defendants (Roesch et al., 1999). In some jurisdictions, the treatment phase includes education on the legal system and the consequences of the various decisions made by criminal defendants.

When medication is the option, it is usually in the form of "psychoactive drugs," which "exert their primary effect on the brain, thus altering mood or behavior" (Julien, 1992, p. xii). There is some question whether an incompetent defendant has the right to refuse such medication because state courts and lower federal courts have split on the issue. The trend seems to be in support of the government's strong interest in taking the defendant to trial (e.g., *U.S. v. Charters*, 1988; *Tran van Khiem v. U.S.*, 1992). However, defendants who are considered non-dangerous (e.g., *U.S. v. Brandon*, 1988) have fared better than those who were deemed dangerous to themselves (e.g., *U.S. v. Morgan*, 1999). Courts supportive of a defendant's right to refuse medication have expressed concern over the side effects of the drugs and the degree to which they would impede the defendant's ability to assist in the preparation of a defense. Typically, these courts also require the government to prove that no less intrusive non-drug alternative is available.

The uncertainty over whether incompetent defendants can be medicated against their will to render them competent may well be resolved in the near future. At this writing, the U.S. Supreme Court has just heard arguments in *Sell v. U.S.* (2003), a case in which a defendant was forcibly medicated. Sell, a dentist who was diagnosed with a delusional disorder, was charged and eventually convicted of multiple counts of health care fraud. The trial judge allowed the medication after ruling that Sell would not be competent to stand trial without it, and the U.S. Court of Appeals for the 8th Circuit upheld the judge's order. Note that Sell was not charged with a violent crime, and he was not considered dangerous to himself or others. In his appeal, he argued that forcing him to take psychoactive drugs against his will violated his Constitutional rights under the 1st, 5th, and 6th Amendments. If the U.S. Supreme Court upholds forcible medication for a *non-dangerous* defendant charged with a non-violent offense, we can assume that it would also uphold forcible medication for a *dangerous* defendant. On the other hand, if the Court should rule in Sell's favor, the question of whether a dangerous defendant may be medicated could be left unanswered, unless the Court decides to answer that question as well.

It should be noted, though, that the Court has refused to hear similar appeals in the cases of incompetent defendants charged with violent crimes, including the defendant charged with killing two Capitol police officers in 1998 ◙ (see **Box 4-1**). That case illustrates the dilemma faced by courts when incompetent defendants refuse medication. However, the Court has affirmed the right of a defendant pleading *not guilty by reason of insanity* to be free of psychoactive drugs during his trial (*Riggins v. Nevada, 1992*) ◙ (see **Box 4-2**).

It is clear that medication is the common form of treatment afforded incompetent defendants. Wexler and Winick (1991, p. 314) have remarked that "treatment is probably rarely tailored to the specific abilities needed to be competent to stand trial. It probably has as a goal the treatment of the patient's psychopathology, rather than the short-term goal of restoration to trial competency, or more appropriately to competency to perform the specific trial-related tasks the defendant has been found unable to do." Wexler and Winick recommend a treatment plan "detailing the kinds of treatment attempted and proposed and the anticipated outcome" (1991, p. 315). In keeping with their paradigm of "therapeutic jurisprudence" discussed in ◀ Chapter 1, they would allow incompetent defendants substantial choice in the type of treatment they receive to achieve a restoration of competency.

BOX 4-1
The Rusty Weston Case

In July 1998, a man walked into the Capitol building in Washington, D.C., and shot to death two Capitol police officers. He also shot two other individuals who survived. Rusty Weston, a 42-year-old with a history of paranoid schizophrenia, was arrested at the scene. According to court records, Weston had been suffering from serious mental disorder for nearly two decades and had often refused to take medication.

He had allegedly traveled to Washington, D.C., from his home in Montana to save the world from cannibalism. He reported to several individuals that he went to the Capitol to retrieve a satellite system that could reverse time and fight disease. The Capitol police officers, he said, were impeding his mission. After psychiatrists testified about his mental condition, Weston was declared incompetent to stand trial. Psychiatrists at the competency hearing indicated, though, that psychoactive medication might be able to restore him to competency.

Defense attorneys assigned to Weston's case refused to allow him to take the medication, however. They argued that it would be unethical to make him better because he faced a possible death sentence if he went to trial and were convicted. Prosecutors argued that without the medication Weston might never become competent to stand trial. In September 1999, a year following the shooting, a federal district court judge ordered that medication be forcibly administered. Weston's attorneys appealed that order, and the Court of Appeals for the D.C. Circuit reversed it. A three-judge panel ruled that the district judge must more carefully review the legal issues, including whether medication would alter Weston's demeanor and deprive him of a right to a fair trial. After a 4-day hearing, the district court again allowed the medication, in March 2001. In July 2001, three years after the incident, the Appeals Court upheld the order. "The government's interest in administering antipsychotic drugs to make Weston competent for trial overrides his liberty interest," the three-judge panel wrote. Nevertheless, the court noted that heightened scrutiny is required before forcing medication under these conditions.

In the interim—until the ruling by the Appeals Court—Weston went un-medicated. Detained at Butner, a federal psychiatric facility in North Carolina, he was kept in seclusion because his behavior was hostile and erratic, and staff members were concerned that he would harm himself as well as others. He apparently had not harmed anyone at the facility, however. A psychiatrist at Butner testified that he was essentially being "warehoused" in his psychotic state. One of his defense lawyers maintained publicly that he was better un-medicated, because in his paranoid state he could not realize what he had done. However, defense attorneys also indicated that they would not oppose medication if the prosecutor would agree not to seek the death penalty. They appealed the medication order to the U.S. Supreme Court, but the Supreme Court denied *certiorari*.

At this writing, Weston is being treated with antipsychotic medication in an attempt to render him competent to stand trial. If his case eventually does go to trial, he will likely plead not guilty by reason of insanity.

"The disposition of incompetent defendants is perhaps the most problematic area of the competency procedures" (Roesch, Zapf, Golding, & Skeem, 1999, p. 333). A survey of 128 forensic facilities confirms the suspicion that incompetent defendants do not receive treatment specifically geared to their needs (Siegel & Elwork, 1990). Over half the facilities surveyed did not treat incompetent

BOX 4-2
Synthetic "Sanity" at Trial: *Riggins v. Nevada*

Riggins, a defendant charged with murder, was being held in pre-trial detention when he complained of hearing voices and having difficulty sleeping. He was prescribed the antipsychotic drug Mellaril along with the anticonvulsant drug Dilantin, both of which he had taken in the past. The drugs had the effect of stabilizing his behavior, and he was found competent to stand trial.

Riggins then raised an insanity defense. He asked the court to suspend the Mellaril during his trial because it infringed upon his freedom and would impede his ability to help his lawyer. Moreover, he argued that the jury should observe him in his natural, unmedicated state, as he had been in at the time of the crime. The district court judge refused his request without explaining why. Riggins was tried while on medication, convicted, and sentenced to death.

The U.S. Supreme Court ruled, in a 7–2 decision, that the trial judge had been too quick to reject Riggins's request and that the judge should have conducted a hearing before allowing the medication. Forcible administration of medication into a non-consenting person's body is a deprivation of due process, guaranteed by the 14th Amendment. Furthermore, it also implicates the 6th Amendment right to a fair trial, because medication might alter one's normal demeanor and interfere with the ability to help one's lawyer. Despite this, the Justices said the interests of the government in bringing a case to trial and the interests of the individual should be balanced. The government could justify the forced medication by establishing that it could not obtain an adjudication of guilt or innocence by using a less intrusive alternative. The defendant, however, was entitled to a hearing on the issue.

defendants any differently than the general mentally disordered population. As a result of their discovery, Siegel and Elwork developed a standardized treatment approach specifically designed to restore defendants to competency. It included both traditional mental health therapy and exercises geared to criminal defendants. The researchers used videotapes, problem-solving group sessions, and various techniques to teach defendants courtroom procedures and how to interact with lawyers and other participants (Elwork, 1992). The approach highlights the need for mental health experts to integrate both legal and psychological considerations into their practices (Elwork, 1992).

Insanity

To paraphrase a key federal case, if a person chooses to do evil through the exercise of his or her free will, that person must bear criminal responsibility (*U.S. v. Brawner*, 1972). Conversely, if free will is absent, the person is not responsible. The criminal law requires that *mens rea* (guilty mind) be demonstrated before an individual can be convicted of a crime. Although there are exceptions to this requirement for certain offenses (called **strict liability offenses**), most crimes require a showing of "evil intent." The public is acquainted with this principle in law primarily through the insanity defense, because extensive publicity often accompanies a claim that a person who clearly committed an illegal act was not responsible because of a mental disorder that robbed him or her of free will.

Criminal defendants may also use other, less-publicized affirmative defenses to argue that they should not be held criminally responsible. These include, but are not limited to, self-defense, consent, and necessity. None of these defenses to criminal conduct is as controversial as the insanity defense, however. Moreover, the defendants are not claiming an absence of free will. The defendant who has killed an attacker in **self-defense**, for example, was acting consciously to save her or his own life. The defendant accused of sexual assault who uses **consent** as a defense is claiming that his alleged victim willingly engaged in sexual activity, with no evil intent on his part. The animal rights activist who breaks down the doors of a research laboratory, releases experimental animals, then raises a **necessity defense** is saying that she had to commit the crimes in order to prevent the greater evil of allowing animals to suffer.

Public attention to the insanity defense typically peaks in the wake of a shocking, highly publicized crime. In 1982, John Hinckley was acquitted of the attempted assassination of then-President Ronald Reagan and the attempted murder of his press secretary, James Brady. That Hinckley fired the weapon was not in dispute. The federal jury, however, found him not guilty by reason of insanity, a verdict that outraged and confused the public, yet was consistent with federal insanity statutes in effect at that time. The acquittal prompted the U.S. Congress to change these statutes, thereby making it more difficult for defendants pleading not guilty by reason of insanity. We will discuss these revised statutes shortly. For the moment, it is important to note that, over 20 years later, Hinckley remains institutionalized in a mental hospital, although he has been allowed to take supervised day trips to the homes of friends and relatives.

More recently, the case of Andrea Yates attracted wide public attention. Yates is the Texas woman who drowned her five young children in a bathtub in 2001. She had a history of mental disorders, including diagnoses of postpartum psychosis. Even prosecutors acknowledged her illness. Nevertheless, applying the test for insanity used in Texas, jurors convicted her, apparently concluding that she knew the difference between right and wrong despite her mental illness. Jurors did not sentence her to death, however, because they did not believe she was a continuing danger to society, a required finding for imposing the death penalty in Texas. She was sentenced to life in prison without possibility of parole. Because jurors decided she was not dangerous, they did not have to answer the accompanying question of whether her mental disorder was a mitigating factor sufficient to spare her the death sentence.

Insanity Standards

Just as mental disorder does not equal incompetence to stand trial, neither does mental disorder equal insanity. It is possible for a person to be diagnosed with a disorder and still be criminally responsible. In a hypothetical example, James, charged with tax evasion, is known to have an obsessive-compulsive disorder ▲ (see **Table 4–1**), displayed in his need to open and close doors, file drawers, kitchen cabinets and the like repeatedly to be sure they are shut. The reality of his disorder does not absolve him of responsibility for tax evasion. Some serious mental disorders, however, such as paranoid schizophrenia ▲ (see **Table 4–1**), are widely believed to rob their victims of rational thought. Even so, we cannot assume that a paranoid schizophrenic who burglarizes a home will be found NGRI. Again using the Andrea Yates case as illustration, there was virtually no disagreement that she suffered from serious mental disorder, including postpartum psychosis ▲ (**Table 4–1**). Yet jurors were able to conclude that she was still capable of knowing the difference between right and wrong.

In order to help judges and juries decide whether someone accused of a crime was indeed insane, a variety of tests have been established. These tests vary widely among the states, but they usually center around one of three general models: the **M'Naghten Rule** and the **Durham Rule** (named after court cases), and the **ALI Rule** (proposed by the American Law Institute in its Model Penal Code). A modified form of this last test, called the **Brawner Rule**, was in use in federal courts when John Hinckley was acquitted. Today, the federal courts abide by a substantially "tougher" variant of the ALI Rule. A minority of states also recognize an **irresistible impulse test**. The modal insanity defense criteria today involve the ALI formulation or restricted versions of the traditional M'Naghten test, minus a volitional prong (Golding et al., 1999). Each of these will be discussed shortly. ◙ (See **Box 4-3** for a summary of the tests in state and federal courts.)

Interestingly, despite these elaborate attempts at establishing insanity standards, when cases involving an insanity defense get to a jury, jurors do not necessarily apply them. Norman Finkel and his colleagues (Finkel, 1988, 1991; Finkel et al., 1985)

TABLE 4-1

Common—and Not So Common—Diagnoses

Following are partial descriptions of some of the disorders mentioned throughout the text. For more detailed information, readers should consult the DSM–IV.

Attention Deficit/Hyperactivity Disorder (ADHD)
Six or more of a group of symptoms of inattention that have persisted for at least 6 months to a degree that is maladaptive and inconsistent with developmental level, or six or more of a group of symptoms of hyperactivity–impulsivity that have persisted as above. Examples of symptoms of inattention include forgetfulness in daily activities, difficulty organizing tasks and activities, and careless mistakes in schoolwork and daily tasks, among many others. Examples of symptoms of hyperactivity–impulsivity include frequent fidgeting, difficulty playing quietly, or frequently interrupting others, among other symptoms.

Antisocial Personality Disorder
A pervasive pattern of disregard for and violation of the rights of others occurring since age 15 years (although children under 18 should not be given this diagnosis). Diagnosis requires the presence of three or more of a list of seven symptoms. Examples are impulsivity or failure to plan ahead, lack of remorse, and consistent irresponsibility. (Note: This diagnostic category is now virtually identical to the "psychopath" described in the text.)

Conduct Disorder
A repetitive and persistent pattern of behavior in which the basic rights of others or major age-appropriate societal norms or rules are violated. This diagnostic category is reserved for children under 18.

Dissociative Identity Disorder (formerly Multiple Personality Disorder)
Two or more distinct identities or personality states recurrently take control of a person's behavior. There is inability to recall important personal information, not attributed to ordinary forgetfulness.

Obsessive–Compulsive Disorder
The individual has recurrent obsessions or compulsions that are time consuming or cause the person marked distress or significant impairment. Disturbances due to physiological effects of drugs or medication or to another medical condition are not included. Repeated thoughts about contamination, horrific impulses, counting, hand washing are examples.

Posttraumatic Stress Disorder (PTSD)
To qualify for this diagnosis, the person must have been exposed to a traumatic event that involved threat of serious harm or death to self or others *and* must have responded to that event with intense fear, helplessness, or horror. The traumatic event is then persistently re-experienced in a range of possible ways (e.g., recurrent distressing dreams). The individual avoids stimuli associated with the trauma, and there are persistent symptoms of increased arousal. Examples of these latter symptoms are difficulty falling or staying asleep, outbursts of anger, and exaggerated startle response.

Schizophrenia
Two or more of the following, each present for a significant portion of time during a one-month period: delusions, hallucinations, disorganized speech, grossly disorganized or catatonic behavior, negative symptoms (e,g, affective flattening).

Schizophrenia, Paranoid Type
A type of schizophrenia in which the following criteria are met: (a) preoccupation with one or more delusions or frequent auditory hallucinations; (b) none of the following is prominent: disorganized speech, disorganized or catatonic behavior, or flat or inappropriate affect.

Source: American Psychiatric Association, Diagnostic and statistical manual of mental disorders, 4th ed. (DSM–IV), 1994.

found that mock jurors who were given no instructions could not be distinguished from jurors who were given variants of the standard insanity instructions mentioned above. Ogloff (1991) reached similar conclusions. Golding et al. (1999, p. 383) suggest that the "admittedly vague and nonspecific linguistic terms of insanity standards" are at fault. The negative attitudes toward insanity discussed earlier also may be the culprits, however, particularly in light of the fact that juries are less likely than judges to find a defendant NGRI (Callahan et al., 1991). Jurors appear to rely on their own cognitive constructs and attitudes toward insanity rather than on the legal instructions provided them by the courts. As Finkel (2000, p. 607) concludes, "The empirical evidence leaves little doubt that jurors' constructs of sane and insane, and the law's, are significantly different. Moreover, the evidence leaves little doubt that the law's repeated attempts, via changing legal tests, to get jurors to relinquish their constructs for the law's constructs have failed."

The M'Naghten Rule: The Right and Wrong Test

The most frequently used test for insanity today is some variant of the M'Naghten Rule, which originated in mid-nineteenth century Britain. The rule itself was derived from the "wild beast" test established by English courts in 1724 (Marshall, 1968). According to this test, individuals were not responsible for their actions if they "could not distinguish good from evil more than a wild beast" (Leifer, 1964, p. 825). In 1760, the words "right from wrong" were substituted for "good from evil" (Sobeloff, 1958).

Shortly thereafter, English courts began to use a different test, one focusing on a defendant's "irresistible impulse." On the basis of new psychiatric insights derived from the writings of psychiatrist Isaac Ray, "mental unsoundness" moved to the forefront, and persons who demonstrated it were deemed not responsible, even when they had attempted to assassinate the Queen of England. An individual was not responsible "if some controlling disease was . . . the acting power within him which he could not resist" (*Regina v. Oxford*, 1840, p. 950). This was the test in use when the case of Daniel M'Naghten reached the courts in 1843.

Daniel M'Naghten believed he was being persecuted by the Tories, England's right-wing political party. He identified his major persecutor as Queen Victoria's Prime Minister, Robert Peel. Traveling to London for the sole purpose of assassinating Peel, M'Naghten fired a shot into the Prime Minister's carriage. His plan might have succeeded had Peel been in the carriage (he was actually riding with the Queen); Peel's secretary, Edward Drummond, died from the bullet intended for his employer.

There was no question that M'Naghten had committed the act, but the issue raised at his trial was his mental state at the time of the homicide. After hearing testimony about his mental unsoundness from medical experts, the prosecutor decided not to press for a guilty verdict. The presiding judge halted the trial and directed the jury to find M'Naghten insane (Finkel, 1988). In other words, because M'Naghten was apparently "mentally ill," it was assumed that he was not responsible for his actions, since he could not resist his impulses to commit deviant acts.

Faced with public outcry and the anger of the Queen, the British House of Lords asked common court judges to examine the insanity issue. "In effect, the judges had to account for a perceived miscarriage of justice" (Simon & Aaronson, 1988, p. 13). This led to the development of a new standard, or actually a re-affirmation of the sixteenth-century right-from-wrong test. Common court judges began applying this test and often noted that, had M'-Naghten been tried under that standard, he would not have been absolved of responsibility. Thus, it is this test, and ironically not the test under which M'Naghten was actually acquitted, which is the basis of the present rule in his name. The irresistible impulse test was rejected by English courts approximately twenty years later (Simon & Aaronson, 1988), but it has survived in a handful of states today.

The M'Naghten rule was adopted as the standard in U.S. courts and came to be commonly referred to as the "right/wrong test." It is generally recognized to state that a defendant is not responsible if he or she committed an unlawful act "while labouring under such a defect of reason, from disease of the mind, as not to know the nature and quality of the act he was doing; or, if he did know it, that he did not know he was doing what was wrong" (Brooks, 1974, p. 135). The M'Naghten Rule emphasizes the *cognitive elements* of (1) being aware of what one was doing at the time of an illegal act, and (2) knowing or realizing right from wrong in the moral sense. The test recognizes no *degree* of incapacity. The apparent simplicity of the rule may be a key to understanding why it continues to be popular, even though there has been extensive debate on the

BOX 4-3
Tests for Insanity in State and Federal Courts

M'Naghten (or some variant)

Did the defendant know what he or she was doing? If yes, did the defendant know the difference between right and wrong?

(Arizona, California, Florida, Kansas, Louisiana, Minnesota, Mississippi, Nebraska, New Jersey, North Carolina, Oklahoma, Pennsylvania, South Carolina, South Dakota, Washington)

Durham (modified)

Was the defendant's action the "product" of a mental illness?

(New Hampshire)

Irresistible Impulse

As a result of mental disease, was the defendant driven to commit an act by forces outside of his or her control?

(Colorado, Georgia, Iowa, New Mexico, Virginia)

ALI/Substantial Capacity (or some modification)

As a result of mental disease or defect, did defendant lack substantial capacity to appreciate the criminality of the conduct (knowledge prong) or to conform the conduct to the requirement of the law (volitional prong)?

Federal courts and some states have eliminated the volitional prong. Alabama, Arkansas, Connecticut, Hawaii, Illinois, Indiana, Kentucky, Maine, Maryland, Massachusetts, Michigan, Missouri, New York, North Dakota, Oregon, Rhode Island, Tennessee, Utah, Vermont, West Virginia, Wisconsin, Wyoming.

No standard: Idaho, Kansas, Montana, Nevada, Utah.

Source: National Center for State Courts.

meaning of the word "know" (Finkel, 1988; Simon & Aaronson, 1988).

For a time, the rule was accepted as the principal standard of criminal responsibility in virtually every American jurisdiction (Saks & Hastie, 1978). However, it was also attacked by several schools of psychiatric and psychological thought, because it was too narrow and not in keeping with current theory and practice. Psychiatrists, who were then the main examiners in matters of criminal responsibility relating to mental states, said it was impossible to convey to the judge and jury the full range of information they obtained from assessing the defendant's responsibility if responsibility was framed solely in terms of cognitive impairment.

The Durham Rule: The Product Test

In 1954, apparently motivated by widespread discontent with the restrictiveness and moral tone of the M'Naghten Rule, U.S. Court of Appeals Judge David Bazelon drafted what was to become the Durham Rule (*Durham v. U.S.*, 1954), sometimes called the "product rule" or "product test." Although Judge Bazelon's opinion is most often associated with this rule, it had for over a century been in operation in New Hampshire, where it was originally framed by a judge who was a friend of Isaac Ray (Finkel, 1988). In fact, the rule has close similarity to the rule under which Daniel M'Naghten was acquitted.

The Durham Rule states that "an accused is not criminally responsible if his unlawful act was the product of a mental disease or mental defect" (Brooks, 1974, p. 176). The rule, therefore, focuses more on mental disorder itself than on the cognitive element of "knowing" the rightness or wrongness of a specific action. The Durham Rule was later clarified in *Carter v. U.S.* (1957), which held that mental illness must not merely have entered into the production of the act, it must have played a necessary role.

Judge Bazelon hoped that the new rule would give psychiatrists the latitude to talk freely about the defendant, whereas before they had to testify within the stricter confines of M'Naghten. By bringing the rule for criminal responsibility up to date with psychiatric theory, it was assumed that the ascription of criminal responsibility would be more "scientific."

The Durham Rule applied in federal courts and was adopted by some states. Its broad scope became its major shortcoming and eventually its downfall, however. Since definitions of mental illness are often vague and subjective, the rule, according to many jurists, gave wide discretionary power to psychiatry. During the time that Durham was in effect, some critics asserted that psychiatrists defined mental illness so broadly that it could be applied to most offenders. Anyone who committed an antisocial act could be viewed as mentally ill: the forbidden act was a product of the disorder. Applied in this way, the Durham Rule could be and was used to exculpate large numbers of offenders who had previously been held responsible.

The rule also created havoc among legal scholars, clinicians, and social and behavioral scientists who tried to define "mental disease" or "defect" and to determine what acts were "products" of such conditions. Expert testimony, not surprisingly, reflected this confusion. Ironically, the Durham Rule was supposed to insure that juries would be able to make more informed decisions about criminal responsibility. Yet psychiatrists were often pressed to offer their opinions on the ultimate issue of insanity. Furthermore, their testimony became so technical and abstruse that the juries were left with little choice but to go along with the experts. When experts disagreed, jurors had great difficulty distinguishing between the merits of their testimony. As Finkel (1988, p. 37) quipped, ". . . the psychiatrist was freer to jargonize." Eventually, the Durham Rule became so unmanageable that it was discarded by most of the jurisdictions that had adopted it, including the federal courts. Some states replaced it with the ALI Rule, while others returned to some variant of the M'Naghten.

The ALI and Brawner Rules

In 1972, in *U.S. v. Brawner*, Judge Bazelon, again writing for U.S. Court of Appeals, D.C. Circuit, ended 18 years of unhappy experimentation with the Durham Rule in federal courts. The court replaced it with a slight modification of the 1962 draft of the Model Penal Code Rule formulated by the American Law Institute (hereafter referred to as the ALI Rule). According to the ALI Rule (Section 4.01):

> (1) A person is not responsible for criminal conduct if at the time of such conduct as a result of mental disease or defect he lacks substantial capacity either to appreciate the criminality (wrongfulness) of his conduct or to conform his conduct to the requirements of the law.
>
> (2) . . . the terms "mental disease or defect" do not include an abnormality manifested only by repeated criminal or otherwise anti-social conduct.

While adopting this ALI Rule, the D.C. Court of Appeals modified it slightly by specifying the "mental disease" or "defect" must be a condition which *substantially* (a) affects mental or emotional processes or (b) impairs behavioral controls. Note that both the ALI Rule and the Brawner Rule permit exculpation based on either cognitive or control incapacity. The control incapacity component resembles the irresistible impulse test which is based upon the defendant's alleged inability to control behavior, whatever might have been his or her cognitive capacity.

Significantly, *U.S. v. Brawner* legitimized what has come to be called the *caveat* paragraph of the ALI Rule. This paragraph, as quoted above, excludes abnormality manifested only by repeated criminal or antisocial conduct. This provision was intended to disallow insanity for psychopaths and sociopaths who persistently violate social mores and often the law. Under the ALI Rule, psychopaths and sociopaths cannot claim that their abnormal condition is a mental disease or defect.

The two rules discussed here are so similar that they are often combined and discussed as the ALI–Brawner Rule. It was the standard in federal courts when John Hinckley was tried and found not guilty by reason of insanity. Hinckley, who was enamored of actor Jodie Foster, lived with the strong delusions that killing the President of the United

States would impress her and bind her to him forever. Hinckley was acquitted because the jury concluded that he lacked substantial capacity to conform his conduct to the requirements of the law. Put another way, his mental illness impaired his behavioral controls.

Today, every state that accepts the insanity defense has adopted some variant of one of the above rules. "Right/wrong" tests appear to predominate, but they are closely followed by versions of the ALI–Brawner rules, which consider an individual's capacity to appreciate the criminality of his or her conduct or to conform the conduct to the requirements of the law. The "product test" is used only in New Hampshire, while the irresistible impulse test has survived in a handful of states. This is not the end of the insanity issue, however, because as we note below, other legal changes have occurred that have had a substantial impact on defendants who plead not guilty by reason of insanity.

Insanity Defense Reform Act of 1984

The Hinckley case—which ironically had many similarities to the case of Daniel M'Naghten—is widely believed to be the precipitating factor of changes in federal legislation. The acquittal provided fuel for extensive debate among members of the public, politicians, and professional groups. Amid public clamor to abolish the defense, the U.S. Congress passed the *Insanity Defense Reform Act of 1984*, which kept the defense in federal law but modified it in important ways. Essentially, Congress made it more difficult for persons pleading not guilty by reason of insanity in federal courts to be acquitted.

Among the major changes were: (1) a shift in the burden of proof; (2) elimination of the volitional (or control incapacity) prong of the insanity standard; (3) alteration of the verdict form; and (4) a limitation on the role of the expert. Each of these major changes is explained below.

Under the new law, federal defendants claiming insanity have to prove that, "as a result of a severe mental disease or defect, [they were] unable to appreciate the nature and quality or the wrongfulness of [their] acts." Prior to this change, once the defendant introduced evidence in support of insanity, the burden was on the prosecution to prove beyond a reasonable doubt that the defendant was sane. This was a critical factor in the Hinckley acquittal, because the jury had heard considerable testimony as to Hinckley's aberrant mental state; proving him sane beyond a reasonable doubt was a formidable undertaking. Now, as a result of the 1984 law, the defendant bears the burden of proving insanity by clear and convincing evidence. Had this law been in effect during the Hinckley trial, Hinckley would have had to convince the jury that he was not sane at the time of the crime.

Congress's elimination of the volitional prong means a defendant cannot claim an inability to conform his or conduct to the requirements of the law. A defendant who appreciates that an act is wrong, therefore, but is unable to control himself by virtue of a mental disorder, would not be absolved of criminal responsibility. Critics of this change have noted that defendants with some so-called compulsive mental disorders such as pyromania and kleptomania would not qualify for insanity acquittal (Simon & Aaronson, 1988). Obsessive–compulsive disorders, such as a person being obsessed with repeated images of hurting a child and feeling compelled to do so, are other examples.

The verdict form, or the way the verdict is expressed, has also changed. Rather than being judged not guilty by reason of insanity, insanity acquittees are judged not guilty *only* by reason of insanity. This is a seemingly minor but symbolically significant change that implies resistance to absolving the defendant: the defendant would be guilty if not for the mental state.

Finally, expert witnesses are no longer allowed to give an opinion as to whether the defendant had the required mental state at the time of the criminal act. They are allowed to describe the defendant's behavior and draw a conclusion as to the alleged mental disorder, but they are not allowed to give an opinion on the ultimate legal issue. This pleases those who do not favor ultimate opinion testimony in any context, a topic we discussed in ◀ Chapters 3 and 4.

Insanity Defense: Related Changes

The 1984 federal law prompted many states to join other states that had already begun to place various restrictions on the insanity defense. Five states—Idaho, Montana, Utah, Nevada, and Kansas—have abolished the defense. Golding et al. (1999) maintain that courts that allow restrictions and outright abolition have sidestepped the question of "ultimate justice," by leaving it to the legislature to adopt these strategies, however unwise they might be. Additionally, abolishing the insanity defense is likely to produce unanticipated outcomes. In a follow-up study of the effect of insanity abolition in Montana, Steadman et al. (1993) found that the number of defendants found incompetent to stand trial (IST) increased proportionally. In other words, it appeared that defendants who formerly would have pled NGRI now made successful incompetency claims. Interestingly, they were more likely to have their cases dismissed and less likely to be hospitalized than comparable defendants during the years when the NGRI defense was available. Commenting on these findings, Borum and Fulero (1999, p. 388) assert, " . . . it is at least questionable whether or not abolition of the insanity defense results in enhancing public safety or in confining for longer periods of time the class of offenders who meet the insanity defense test."

Even without an affirmative insanity defense in the law, states must still allow defendants to introduce evidence of mental disorder. Such evidence may disprove or negate the intent requirement sufficiently to reduce the charge or even to produce complete acquittal. Borum and Fulero (1999) note that abolishing the insanity defense may actually give more life to a defense of diminished capacity, in which the defendant argues that he or she could not form the specific intent required to be held *fully* responsible. Note that diminished capacity is a partial, not complete, defense to criminal conduct.

Shifting the Burden of Proof Following the *Insanity Defense Reform Act of 1984*, many states followed the federal government's lead and began to require defendants to bear the burden of proving their own insanity. Prior to this legislation, state prosecutors were required to prove, usually beyond a reasonable doubt, both that the defendant had committed the crime and was not insane. Today, virtually every state, like the federal government, places the burden of proof on defendants: that is, they must convince the judge or jury either by clear and convincing evidence or by the lesser standard of preponderance of the evidence that they were insane at the time of the crime. Steadman et al. (1993), in a study of Georgia and New York, found that the rate of NGRI pleas declined after the passage of statutes shifting the burden to the defendant by a preponderance of the evidence. Furthermore, for those defendants who pursued an insanity defense, severe psychiatric diagnoses (e.g., schizophrenia or other psychosis) "almost became a prerequisite for success" (p. 44).

Guilty But Mentally Ill In response to disenchantment with the insanity defense, some states have adopted the verdict form, Guilty But Mentally Ill (GBMI). Michigan was the first to adopt this in 1975, following a controversial state Supreme Court decision, *People v. McQuillan* (1974). The Michigan court had ruled that it was unconstitutional to automatically institutionalize defendants found NGRI. The court ruled that a hearing on an individual's present mental state must be held before he or she could be hospitalized. At the time, state institutions held nearly 270 persons who had been found NGRI and subsequently had been hospitalized without hearings (Simon & Aaronson, 1988). Sixty-four of these persons were released after hearings in which they were found "presently sane." One promptly murdered his wife and another committed two rapes (Simon & Aaronson, 1988, p. 188). Public sentiment against the insanity defense, therefore, prompted the passage of a statute designed to restrict it.

At this writing, 12 other states have followed Michigan's lead. In all but two of these states, the GBMI option is intended as an alternative to, not a substitute for, the verdict NGRI. (In Utah and Nevada, the defense has been abolished.) A verdict of GBMI allows jurors a "middle-ground" in the case of allegedly insane defendants, a way of reconciling their belief that a defendant "did it" with their belief that he or she "needs help." Therefore, although states differ in the standards and procedures associated with the GBMI verdict, what all have in common is an apparent wish to reduce the number of insanity acquittals and hold the defendants blameworthy, but still recognize the presence of a mental disorder. Thus, the statutes usually include a provision for psychiatric treatment—although they do not *guarantee* that this treatment will be provided nor typically include additional appropriations for such treatment (Bumby, 1993). Additionally, defendants found GBMI can still be sentenced to death (Borum & Fulero, 1999), although they cannot be executed if, at the time of their planned death, they are so mentally ill that they cannot appreciate what is happening to them (*Ford v. Wainwright*, 1986).

Research on GBMI laws has found that they may not have accomplished their intended purposes of reducing the number of NGRI pleas or acquittals or providing treatment in correctional facilities. In some jurisdictions, the number of successful insanity defenses appeared to have gone down, initially, but subsequent analyses questioned whether this was due to the new verdict form or to other insanity defense reforms (Borum & Fulero, 1999), such as the shift in the burden of proof.

A common finding in studies examining the effect of GBMI reform is the lack of special treatment provided to GBMI offenders, despite the intent of the statutes. In most states, a GBMI verdict is rendered if a defendant's mental disorder substantially impaired his or her ability to conform conduct to the requirements of the law. This substantial impairment would suggest a need for significant treatment, if not hospitalization. Steadman et al. (1993) compared treatment rates in three states and found considerable variation. In Georgia, only 3 of 150 GBMI offenders were hospitalized. In Pennsylvania, where GBMI offenders tend to have the most severe disabilities, three quarters of these offenders did receive treatment. In Illinois, none of the 44 GBMI offenders received treatment. Leblanc–Allman (1998), writing in a law journal, found reason to question the care of 161 GBMI individuals in South Carolina. Once imprisoned, GBMI offenders are rarely distinguished from other mentally disordered offenders in the prison population. Many, if not most, correctional facilities are not equipped to care for these offenders, beyond offering them the standard psychological services included in the Constitutional requirement of adequate health care (*Estelle v. Gamble*, 1976). And, as we will see in ▶ Chapter 10, the quality of health care, both physical and mental, in the nation's jails and prisons leaves very much to be desired.

Numerous commentators have argued that GBMI offenders should have been found NGRI, institutionalized, treated, and—when and if their conditions improved—gradually released into the community under supervision (e.g., Golding et al., 1999). As it now stands, they may be released after serving their prison sentence having received a minimum of mental health care. Although GBMI statutes have remained on the books in a minority of states, they rarely receive positive reviews in the legal literature. The GBMI verdict form has been referred to as "deceptively reformist" (Cohen, 1998, p. 1–7) and as an idea whose time should not have come (Slobogin, 1985). As Cohen (2000) also notes, nearly all scholarly writing has questioned the wisdom and efficacy of the statutes that allow the alternate verdict form.

Frequency of Insanity Defense and Acquittals

Despite the publicity that accompanies major cases, it is a rare defendant who invokes the insanity defense, and when raised it is usually not successful. It is estimated that the defense is raised in less than 1% of all felony cases (Callahan et al., 1991; Golding, Skeem, Roesch, & Zapf, 1999; Simon & Aaronson, 1988). Furthermore, and again contrary to public perceptions, the cases in which the defense is raised are not necessarily the most serious. In an eight-state study, only 14.3% of defendants pleading not guilty by reason of insanity had been charged with murder, for example (Silver, Cirincione, & Steadman, 1994). Interestingly, the insanity defense is also raised in misdemeanor cases as a way to get treatment for mentally disordered individuals. Recall that we discussed this briefly with reference to the request for an evaluation of a defendant's competency to stand trial.

It is extremely difficult to obtain nationwide data on insanity acquittals, because states vary widely in the availability of these statistics. When data are available, the rates vary dramatically among jurisdictions. For example, McGinley and Pasewark (1989) report that in Colorado, 44% of defendants pleading not guilty by reason of insanity (NGRI) were successful, while rates in Michigan, Maine, Minnesota, and Wyoming were 7%, 4%, 3%, and

2%, respectively. In an eight-state study involving nearly 9,000 defendants who pleaded NGRI, Callahan et al. (1991) found an acquittal rate of 25%. Other multi-state surveys have found similar acquittal rates of 20–25% (Cirincione, Steadman, & McGreevy, 1995; Pasewark & McGinley, 1986). In the largest nationwide data collection thus far available, Cirincione and Jacobs (1999) were able to obtain data from 36 jurisdictions (35 states and one Pennsylvania county) over the period 1974–1995. They identified a total of 16,379 acquittals, or a mean of 33.4 insanity acquittals per state per year. These figures mean little without information about the rate of acquittals per insanity defense raised—a figure which the researchers attempted to obtain, without success, although they did report the rate of acquittals per 100,000 population. Interestingly, only 15 of the 36 jurisdictions surveyed could differentiate between felony and misdemeanor acquittals. When they did, misdemeanor acquittals typically accounted for less than 10% of the total, although in one state (Oregon) 21.7% of the acquittals were for misdemeanors.

Impact of Criminal Charges and Diagnosis

Prior research on the criminal charge and the sanity decision suggests that they may be related. (Recall that this was discussed with respect to competency as well.) Warren et al. (1997) found high insanity rates among defendants charged with violent crimes against others, while defendants charged with sex offenses were five times more likely to be found *sane*. Nevertheless, as in the competency context, diagnosis appears to be a critical factor.

Cochrane, Grisso, and Frederick (2001) analyzed nationwide data on 1,710 defendants referred for evaluation by federal courts. The researchers noted that, although the crimes might differ from state crimes (e.g., including more drug-related offenses or bank crimes), there is "no strong reason to believe those charged with similar crimes in the federal system are fundamentally distinct from state offenders" (p. 571). Of the 710 available evaluations for criminal responsibility, 13% were found insane by the court. There was wide variability based on the type of offense, however. The highest rates of insanity (36% and 31%) were for defendants charged with threats and assaults, respectively. Defendants charged with murder had a 15% insanity rate, while some offenses were associated with what the researchers called "surprisingly low" (p. 575) rates. Defendants charged with robbery, white-collar offenses, drug crimes, sex crimes, illegal immigration, or kidnapping belonged in this low category, with the last three offenses resulting in no insanity findings.

Cochrane et al. (2001) examined clinical diagnoses to determine whether there was a mediating effect on the crime charged. Not surprisingly, defendants with diagnoses of psychotic disorders had the highest rates of insanity, followed by affective disorders, and mental retardation. Personality disorders ▲ (see **Table 4-1**) were negatively correlated with findings of insanity. Relationship between charges and the insanity findings (as well as the competence findings) was clearly mediated by the diagnosis. "The current results . . . support our hypothesis that the main variable that affects psycholegal opinions is the diagnostic presentation of the defendant" (Cochrane et al., 2001, p. 581).

Insanity cases often do not go to trial. In an investigation of 316 successful insanity defenses, Rogers, Cavanaugh, et al. (1984) learned that 80% were uncontested by the prosecutor and disposed of informally without trial. The insanity acquittees were then sent to state hospitals. Although nationwide data are not available, NGRI verdicts not infrequently follow stipulation of both prosecutor and defense attorney, based on a forensic examiner's report, and sometimes accompanied by pre-trial courtroom testimony (Golding et al., 1999). A clinician examines the defendant, concludes that an insanity defense could be supported, and both sides accept the clinician's conclusion. Some clinicians are careful not to provide an "ultimate opinion" on whether the defendant was indeed insane, seeing this as a legal determination. As Simon and Aaronson note (1988, p. 9) " . . . in most instances where the insanity defense is successfully invoked, the available evidence of the defendant's abnormal state points so overwhelmingly to a conclusion of insanity that the prosecutor agrees not to formally contest the defense. Instead, prosecutors usually enter into a formal or tacit agreement for an acquittal by reason of insanity. Almost always, this decision is based on a report of the federal or state's psychiatrists that the defendant meets the criteria for insanity." The judge then enters the verdict. Acquittals, particularly felony acquittals, are typically followed by institutionalization, usually for as long as and sometimes longer than imprisonment of defendants convicted on equivalent charges (Borum & Fulero, 1999).

Juries and the Insanity Defense

When insanity cases do go to trial, judges appear to be more sympathetic to the insanity defense than juries. In Callahan et al.'s (1991) eight-state study, only 7% of the acquittals were handed down by juries. Not surprisingly, therefore, Boehnert (1989) found that 96% of defendants found NGRI had opted for a bench (judge) trial rather than a jury trial. Social scientists have continually found that jurors' negative attitudes toward the insanity defense, mental health experts, and/or individuals with severe mental illness have significant effects on their verdicts in insanity cases (e.g., Bailis, Darley, Waxman, & Robinson, 1995; Cutler, Moran, & Narby, 1992; Perlin, 1994; Robinson and Darley, 1995). Commentators recommend that potential jurors be questioned carefully about these attitudes during the *voir dire* process. Judges should be attuned to bias against the insanity defense and should discourage the impaneling of jurors who are predisposed against it (Golding et al., 1999; Perlin, 1994).

Like the general public, jurors also have misconceptions about legal outcomes for persons found not guilty by reason of insanity (NGRI) (Silver, Cirincione, & Steadman, 1994). In the federal government and the great majority of states, a successful insanity defense is no bargain. As we noted above, persons acquitted on this basis are then subject to institutionalization through a civil proceeding. In *Jones v. U.S.* (1983), the U.S. Supreme Court allowed this involuntary civil commitment upon a showing, by a preponderance of the evidence, that an insanity acquittee was mentally ill and dangerous to self or others. The Court noted that Jones's dangerousness and present mental state, rather than his underlying crime, should be the determining factor in when he should be released. (Jones was convicted of stealing a coat.) ◙ (See **Box 4-4** for a review of Supreme Court cases relating to competency and insanity.)

Juror misconceptions about the legal outcomes of an NGRI verdict were at issue in one U.S. Supreme Court case. In *Shannon v. U.S.* (1994), the petitioner argued that jurors should be instructed about the consequences of an insanity acquittal to aid them in their deliberations. Shannon, a convicted felon in possession of a weapon, shot himself in the chest in the presence of a police officer. He survived his suicide attempt, was then indicted for unlawful possession of a firearm, and was tried by a jury. His lawyer asked the U.S. District Court judge to inform the jury that Shannon would be involuntarily committed if he were found not guilty by reason of insanity, in accordance with the *Insanity Defense Reform Act of 1984*. The lawyer feared that jurors would believe Shannon would be released into society and would pose a danger to the community if they found him NGRI. Assuming this, the jury might be tempted to return a guilty verdict. The district judge refused to give the jury this instruction, saying that jurors should focus on the facts of the case rather than the possible outcome of their verdict. Shannon was convicted.

The Supreme Court, with two dissenting opinions, affirmed Shannon's conviction, noting that federal judges were not obliged to instruct juries of the consequences of an NGRI verdict. Rather, juries were to render their verdicts without regard to the consequences or the punishment. Furthermore, the Court said, contemporary jurors are already aware of the outcome of a verdict of NGRI. The Court did not completely foreclose the possibility of such an instruction, however. If the jury heard an improper statement, such as one suggesting that the defendant would go free if found NGRI, it would be necessary for the judge to intervene to counter the misstatement.

The majority ruling in *Shannon v. U.S.* seemed to be going against a trend. Up to that point, many courts and legal commentators favored requiring or at least authorizing judges to instruct juries on the legal consequences of an insanity acquittal (Silver et al., 1994). The dissenting opinion, written by Justice John Paul Stevens, noted that the American Bar Association and an increasing number of states endorse use of that instruction. "As long as significant numbers of potential jurors believe that an insanity acquittee will be released at once, the instruction serves a critical purpose. Yet even if, as the Court seems prepared to assume, all jurors are already knowledgeable about the issue, surely telling them what they already know can do no harm."

BOX 4-4
Competency, Insanity, and the Supreme Court—Cases and Principles

Competency Cases and Principles

Dusky v. U.S. (1960)—Court establishes the two-pronged standard for determining competency to stand trial.

Pate v. Robinson (1966) and *Drope v. Missouri* (1975)—Due process requires a hearing on the issue of competency when there is a bona fide doubt as to the individual's competency.

Jackson v. Indiana (1972)—Indefinite confinement of persons found incompetent is not allowed. Without progress in effort to restore competence, individuals must be released or committed under civil commitment laws.

Estelle v. Smith (1981)—The Fifth Amendment privilege against self-incrimination extends to the pre-trial clinical examination.

Godinez v. Moran (1993)—The two-pronged *Dusky* standard applies to competency to plead guilty as well as competence to stand trial.

Medina v. California (1992)—States may require defendants to prove their incompetence by a preponderance of the evidence.

Cooper v. Oklahoma (1996)—Defendants may not be required to prove their incompetence by clear and convincing evidence; that standard is too high.

U.S. v. Weston (2001)—By denying *certiorari*, the Court allowed the forcible medication of defendants found incompetent to stand trial if the state's interest in bringing them to trial is strong.

Sell. v. U.S. (pending)—Does a non-dangerous, incompetent defendant have a right to refuse antipsychotic medication intended to restore him to competency?

Insanity Cases and Principles

Jones v. U.S. (1983)—Persons found NGRI may be civilly committed but only upon a finding that they are mentally ill and dangerous to self or others.

Ake v. Oklahoma (1985)—Indigent defendants are entitled to the assistance of a psychologist or psychiatrist for independent pre-trial evaluation for the purpose of preparing an insanity defense.

Foucha v. Louisiana (1992)—Persons found NGRI can be civilly committed only for as long as they are *both* mentally ill *and* dangerous.

Riggins v. Nevada (1992)—Defendants pleading NGRI have a right not to be medicated during trial.

Shannon v. U.S. (1994)—Judges do not have to inform jurors of the consequence of an NGRI verdict.

Researchers have begun to explore the effect of informing jurors about the consequences of an NGRI acquittal, and they have found interesting differences between pre- and post-deliberation. In a Canadian mock jury study, Whittemore and Ogloff (1995) found that describing the detention and treatment that acquitted but mentally-disordered defendants could get had no significant effect on the verdicts of individual jurors. Furthermore, only 21% of the jurors who had received these instructions could correctly recall the information. In a more recent mock juror study, though, Wheatman and Shaffer (2001) compared the verdicts of informed jurors *before and after group deliberation*. Undergraduate psychology students saw a videotape based on an actual murder trial in which there was a basis for finding the defendant legally insane. (The videotape had previously been used in research conducted by Cutler, Moran, and Narby [1992].) To increase motivation of the participants, the researchers challenged them to reproduce the actual verdict rendered by the real jurors in the case. Half of the participants were informed, orally, of the treatment an acquitted defendant would receive, while the other half received no such instruction. The mock jurors then rendered verdicts individually before deliberating in six-person juries. After group deliberation, the jurors were asked for a group verdict and also asked what decision they personally favored.

Wheatman and Shaffer learned that jurors who received the dispositional instructions were significantly more likely to favor an NGRI verdict than were jurors who received no such instructions, but only after deliberation. Additionally, the researchers found "leniency" and "harshness" shifts as a result of deliberation. That is, individual jurors who received the instruction became more inclined to find the defendant NGRI after the deliberation, while those who did not receive instructions became more inclined to convict the defendant after deliberation. No juror rendered an outright not guilty verdict. The group verdicts mirrored the above findings, with 60% of the instructed juries rendering a verdict of NGRI. All of the juries who received no instructions found the defendant guilty after deliberation.

The study highlights the crucial roles of both jury instructions and jury deliberation in insanity cases. Wheatman and Shaffer suspected that the insanity defense is unpopular with the public primarily because of fears that successful defendants will go free without being treated. Indeed, the researchers' content analyses of the jury deliberations supported this suspicion. Uninstructed jurors, fearing that a mentally-disordered defendant might be released, are inclined to "play on each others' fears about the release of a defendant found NGRI—to the point of judging him or her unquestionably *sane* so as to justify a conviction" (Wheatman & Shaffer, 2001, p. 182).

Thus, despite the Court's ruling in the *Shannon* case that NGRI defendants are not *entitled* to a jury instruction on consequences, such instructions are advisable. Even so, informing jurors of the consequences of an NGRI verdict is no guarantee of acquittal. Recall that 40% of the juries convicted the defendant, despite being told that he would be detained and treated if found NGRI. Some cases may be so heinous, and/or some juries may be so punitive, that acquittals are unlikely even in the face of strong evidence of serious mental disorder. Such might have been the situation in the Andrea Yates case. Jurors in that case were not informed that she would be hospitalized if found NGRI. Even if they had been, it might have made no difference in their verdict. The drowning of the children may have been so heinous to the jury that even knowing she would not go free might not have led to her acquittal.

NGRI and Its Outcomes

Once committed, persons found NGRI and institutionalized are entitled to periodic review of their status. However, the state may require them to prove that they are no longer mentally ill and dangerous. Depending upon the jurisdiction, the standard of proof may be preponderance of the evidence or clear and convincing evidence. Thus, because it is not a simple task to meet the standard, persons who are found NGRI are often held for longer periods of time than they would have been imprisoned (Golding et al., 1999). In general, they are *not* held for significantly *shorter* periods of time than persons who unsuccessfully pled not guilty by reason of insanity or persons who were convicted without using that defense (Silver, 1995).

In *Foucha v. Louisiana* (1992), however, a divided Supreme Court (5–4) struck down a Louisiana law that allowed continued confinement of insanity acquittees based on dangerousness alone. Foucha had been charged with aggravated burglary and illegal discharge of a firearm. The trial court found him NGRI, and he was then committed to a forensic facility where he remained for nearly four years. A committee recommended that he be conditionally discharged, since there was no evidence of mental illness. The trial judge appointed a different committee, which noted that, although Foucha's mental illness was in remission, it could not certify that he would not be a danger to himself or others if released. The court ordered him returned to the facility. The Louisiana Supreme Court affirmed, noting, among other things, that Foucha had not met his burden of proving that he was not dangerous.

The U.S. Supreme Court did not agree. In a 5–4 decision, the court ruled that insanity acquittees can be held only if they are *both* mentally ill *and* dangerous to themselves or others. Foucha did not meet the test of mental illness. The state sought his continued confinement on the basis of his antisocial personality ◙ (see **Box 4–1**), which had apparently been exhibited in several altercations within the facility. Clinicians testified, however, that there were no signs of psychosis or neurosis. The Supreme Court ruled that once a person is no longer mentally ill he or she must be released from custody. The Court also noted that because the state had absolved Foucha of criminal responsibility, continued confinement would be an unacceptable punishment. With reference to the state's claim that Foucha was dangerous, the Court noted that such preventive detention has been allowed in other cases without proof of criminal guilt (e.g., *U.S. v. Salerno* [1987] where the Court allowed the denial of bail on the basis of dangerousness). However, if this is to be done, careful adversary proceedings to demonstrate dangerousness are needed, and this had not happened in Foucha's case. In fact, the Court indicated that the facts of the case would not support a finding of dangerousness to the degree that would be needed for continued confinement. Had Foucha been mentally ill, the situation would have been different. Finally, the Court noted that the state had the option of filing criminal charges in response to Foucha's assaultive behavior.

However, two more recent Supreme Court decisions (*Kansas v. Hendricks*, 1997; *Kansas v. Crane*, 2002) suggest that in at least one context, that involving sexual predators, the Court is much more willing to give authorities leeway in making decisions that involve mental disorders and dangerousness. Several commentators have noted that, if the *Foucha* case were decided today, the continued confinement would be allowed. As Golding et al. (1999, p. 396) note, "... the trend of the Court is clearly in the direction of loose boundaries with respect to the criteria for mental illness (*Hendricks*) and the criteria for dangerousness in the post-conviction/NGRI context." ▶ [*Kansas v. Hendricks* and *Kansas v. Crane* will be discussed in detail in Chapter 5.] Nevertheless, Foucha's crime was quite different. Although he displayed assaultive behavior within the institution, he had initially been charged with property and public order offenses. Both Hendricks and Crane were charged with sexual offenses, though of different levels of seriousness. Hendricks was convicted of heinous sexual crimes against children. The critical issue may not be so much the Court's view of dangerousness, but the Court's view of sex offenders.

We cannot expect, nor would it be desirable, that insanity acquittees spend a lifetime in mental institutions. Mental disorders can be treated and individuals once haunted by them can lead productive lives. As observed in the *Foucha* case, however, mental illness also can go into remission. Furthermore, many insanity acquittees have "significant lifelong psychopathological difficulties" that can be controlled only to a certain extent and that can produce variable dangerousness (Golding et al., 1999, p. 397). In the 1990s, we began to see an effort in some states to monitor insanity acquittees in the community via a system of "conditional release." Acquittees are discharged, but they remain under supervision of mental health professionals in the community who have been specifically trained for this purpose. To date, although a variety of such programs exist across the United States, they have been subjected to little systematic evaluation (Golding et al., 1999). Conditional discharges are a variant of involuntary outpatient treatment, which will be discussed in ▶ Chapter 5.

Clinical Assessment of Sanity

The role of the psychiatrist or psychologist in an insanity case is essentially to *postdict*. That is, the examiner is asked to assess a person's mental state at the time of the crime. The clinician must determine whether and what sort of disturbances existed at the behavioral, volitional, and cognitive level and clarify how those disturbances relate to the criminal act (Golding et al., 1999).

Insanity evaluations are widely regarded as much more complex than the competency evaluations discussed earlier in this chapter. It is exceedingly difficult to determine what another human being was thinking or feeling at the time of a crime, an event that may have happened weeks, months, or even years previously. Nevertheless, clinicians have made considerable strides in identifying methods for conducting evaluations that will be of use to the courts (Heilbrun et al., 2002; Melton et al., 1997). Furthermore, the APA's *Guidelines for Forensic*

Examiners, discussed earlier in the chapter, also offer some direction.

It is now well recognized that the traditional clinical interview alone is limited in its application to the insanity construct. When Gary Melton and his colleagues (1987) first argued that mental health professionals should function more as investigative reporters than as traditional clinicians, their proposal sounded quite radical. During the 1990s, other forensic clinicians indicated their agreement, recommending that evaluators of mental state at the time of offense (MSO) garner information from third-party sources and crime scene data as well as from the defendant (e.g., Golding, 1992; Golding et al., 1999). David Shapiro (1999, p. 1) states that, "beginning with a clinical interview, the forensic clinician will generate certain hypotheses which will be refined and, in some instances, discarded, as the evaluation proceeds." Shapiro adds that police reports, hospital records, statements of witnesses, psychological tests, and employment records all provide sources of information for the clinician conducting the evaluation. These sources should not be contacted without the examinee's consent, unless the evaluation has been ordered by the court (Shapiro, 1999).

According to Golding et al. (1999), such wide-ranging inquiry is necessary to document the consistency of the information. "This 'consistency' examination is relevant to issues of malingering and aids in supporting or challenging various psychological interpretations of the defendant's MSO" (Golding et al., p. 388). They add that clinicians should, whenever possible, make reference to the scientific data in support of their inferences. Otherwise, they should declare how they arrived at these inferences and be ready to have them scrutinized.

The Slobogin MSE A number of prominent forensic clinicians have developed screening instruments, structured interview protocols, or scales to guide sanity evaluations, which are also called MSO (mental state at the time of offense) or CR (criminal responsibility) evaluations (e.g., Slobogin, Melton, & Showalter, 1984; Shapiro, 1999). Slobogin, Melton, and Showalter (1984) proposed the Mental State at the Time of the Offense Screening Evaluation, called the Slobogin MSE. The test was constructed to help clinicians decide whether an insanity defense or other mental status defense (e.g., diminished capacity) might be supported. The clinician gathers historical information about the individual's psychiatric disorders, information related to the offense, and information regarding mental status at the time of the examination. If these screening data indicate that the defendant might have been insane, he or she is referred for a more comprehensive examination. David Shapiro (1999) offers his colleagues a detailed forensic evaluation outline that includes such headings as the following: documents reviewed and people interviewed; confidentiality waiver; statement of facts; patient's version of offense; behavior in jail; jail psychiatric records; mental status examination; social, criminal, psychiatric, and neurological histories; and reviews of a variety of records, including school, occupational, and medical.

The R–CRAS The dominant forensic assessment instrument related to insanity, however, is the one developed by Richard Rogers and his associates, the Rogers Criminal Responsibility Assessment Scales (R–CRAS) (Rogers, 1984; Rogers & Cavanaugh, 1981). The R–CRAS "was developed as a systematic model for quantifying key symptomatology and applying standardized decision models in the assessment of criminal responsibility" (Rogers & Sewell, 1999, p. 184). Essentially, defendants are rated on a number of characteristics, including psychopathology, reliability of their report of the crime, organicity, cognitive control, and behavioral control. The scales have produced impressive reliability coefficients, specifically along the lines of high agreement between clinicians and courts on the final decision (sanity or insanity). Nicholson (1999) found, however, that the high agreement reported in the literature is likely to be inflated. The scales have been validated primarily with the ALI insanity standard, though Rogers and Sewell (1999) have demonstrated high construct validity addressing components of the M'Naghten and GBMI standards as well. Additionally, they find support for the ability of the R–CRAS to detect malingering. However, the R–CRAS emphasizes quantitative data rather than the qualitative investigation favored by Golding (1992), Melton et al. (1997), and Shapiro (1999). Nevertheless, Rogers argues that this quantitative approach is warranted and that the R–CRAS has been extensively validated through a series of empirical studies (Rogers & Sewell, 1999; Rogers & Shuman, 1999). Nicholson (1999), however, urged caution with respect to the validity analyses. "Perhaps the major limitation of research on the R–CRAS is that of criterion contamination" (Nicholson, 1999, p. 153). Nevertheless, he observed that the R–CRAS, compared with the MSE, is the more thoroughly researched. He adds that it is "the only measure for which an examiner can point to even minimal data regarding inter-rater reliability and construct validity" (p. 155).

Both the MSE and the R–CRAS are currently popular instruments for use in sanity evaluations (or MSO or CR evaluations). Each has its strengths, and it is up to the forensic examiner to decide whether to use one and, if so, which to use. One distinction of the R–CRAS is its association with an ultimate opinion on the sanity issue. Indeed, "Rogers endorsed such testimony and developed the R–CRAS to facilitate a conclusory opinion" (Nicholson, 1999, p. 155). For this reason, the instrument tends not to be favored by clinicians who oppose ultimate issue testimony. Nevertheless, Nicholson recommended that the conclusory statements be avoided if the examiner so wishes. "(T)he examiner who adopts this approach needs to be cognizant that some of the individual items on the R–CRAS incorporate elements of the ultimate legal issue and should therefore be omitted from the examiner's summary description" (Nicholson, 1999, p. 156).

Some scholars have noted that competency assessment instruments are on more solid ground than instruments to assess criminal responsibility (e.g., Grisso, 1996; Nicholson, 1999). Grisso (1996) points to the complexity of the task for assessing criminal responsibility and rapid changes in insanity statutes, making it difficult to identify the standard in various jurisdictions. The legal standard for determining competency is much more straightforward and has remained virtually unchanged since the Supreme Court articulated it in *Dusky v. U.S.* (1960). Nicholson (1999) has remarked on an interesting distinction in research funding. Research on competency instruments has been supported by government grants or private foundations. In contrast, the research on criminal responsibility assessment has been conducted primarily by the developers of the instruments, who are less likely than independent researchers to note the limitations of their instruments. A similar problem can be identified in the area of family law, specifically with respect to child custody evaluations. ▶ [This will be discussed again in Chapter 11.]

Conclusions Although clinicians are offered numerous suggestions for conducting MSO/CR evaluations, the process that *actually* occurs is shrouded in mystery. There is a paucity of research on the techniques used by clinicians (Rogers & Sewell, 1999). Additionally, few systematic studies exist of how and why they reach their decisions and arrive at their recommendations (Grisso, 1986; Homant & Kennedy, 1987). One exception is the previously mentioned study by Borum and Grisso (1995), who have obtained information on the extent of usage of both standard and specialized psychological tests in forensic contexts. In the insanity context, 68% of the psychologists (and 61% of the psychiatrists) reported them as essential or recommended. When specific tests were mentioned, objective personality inventories (usually the MMPI or MMPI–2) were the most frequently endorsed, with intelligence tests the second most frequently used.

Forensic assessment instruments were not frequently used in conducting evaluations for criminal responsibility. Slightly over two-thirds of the psychologists either never used them (46%) or rarely used them (20%). Psychiatrists were even less likely to use forensic instruments: 91% never or rarely used them. Nevertheless, as noted earlier, Borum and Grisso (1995) concluded that FAIs were gaining in acceptance and were less likely to be viewed skeptically than a decade ago. "Future research might document this trend more closely and determine whether there are conceptual or practical advantages that might account for any trends that are demonstrated" (Borum & Grisso, 1995, p. 472.)

In sum, it appears from the available evidence that clinicians still rely heavily on traditional tests that have not been validated for use in the insanity context. As Otto and Heilbrun (2002) have pointed out, a wide range of standard clinical measures have been carefully developed and well validated for clinical practice in general. However, they do not help the forensic practitioner, because they do not squarely face the issues before the courts.

Legal Issues Involving the Forensic Evaluation

The clinician conducting the sanity evaluation, like the competency evaluation, also must be aware of the legal issues involved. Despite the fact that defendants are constitutionally entitled to a psychologist or psychiatrist to prepare their insanity defense (*Ake v. Oklahoma*, 1985), evaluations are often ordered by the court. If so, the forensic examiner's report is shared with prosecutors as well as defense lawyers. The issue of who has access to the clinician's report varies from state to state. In some states, the prosecutor is entitled to the report only if the defendant wishes to introduce it into evidence in support of an insanity defense. In other states, defendants raising issues of competency to stand trial or insanity are understood to have waived the therapist-client privilege insofar as the forensic examiner's reports are concerned. The clinician, then, "warns" the defendant of the limits of confidentiality, specifically letting the defendant know who will have access to the psychological report, and usually requires that the defendant sign a form consenting to the evaluation.

Informed consent may be particularly tricky in the evaluation of persons with mental disorders. Informed consent "refers to a person's agreement to allow something to happen that is based on a full disclosure of facts needed to make the decision intelligently and with knowledge of the risks and alternatives involved" (Heilbrun, Marczyk, & DeMatteo, 2002, pp. 231–232). Thus, not only must defendants be told of the purpose of the evaluation, they also must be competent to consent and must consent voluntarily (Melton et al., 1997). Clinicians who have doubts about an individual's ability to provide informed consent are ethically bound to discuss this with the defendant's attorney as well as the presiding judge.

The need to warn defendants of the possible use of the report is well established, and clinicians do not generally resist it. There is some disagreement on another topic, however, specifically, that of "ultimate issue" testimony discussed in ◀ Chapter 3. Although insanity is a legal determination, to be made by the court, clinicians are often asked for their opinion. A clinician may be asked by the presiding judge, "In your opinion, can an insanity defense be supported?" Or, even more directly, "Was this defendant insane?" In some jurisdictions, examiners are so accustomed to being asked such questions that they automatically include the answer in their written report, in a final recommendation. Under the *Insanity Defense Reform Act of 1984*, experts are not allowed to give ultimate issue testimony in federal courts.

The debate over the wisdom of offering ultimate issue testimony continues without signs of abatement (see, e.g., Rogers & Ewing, 1989, and Shapiro, 1999, in favor; Bonnie, 1992, Heilbrun et al., 2002, and Melton et al., 1997, against). Recognizing the lack of consensus, the APA Guidelines take no stand on the issue; rather, they recommend that clinicians be aware of the arguments on both sides and be ready to explain why they choose to provide or not to provide ultimate issue testimony.

David Shapiro (1999) believes clinicians should offer ultimate issue testimony. He argues that—if responsible clinicians refuse to express these opinions—courts will rely on less scrupulous examiners. He finds that, in his experience, most judges want a clinician's opinion on whether an insanity defense is supportable. "What, unfortunately, happens is that courts will turn to less well-trained, less competent, less ethical individuals who will be glad to give an opinion on any topic without adequate empirical verification" (Shapiro, 1999, p. 27). Shapiro also maintains that a careful and comprehensive forensic evaluation, when its results are conveyed, will describe the defendant's behavior and mental state so well that it is only a very small step to add that the findings constituted the legal criteria for an insanity determination.

Special Conditions and Unique Defenses

Thus far, we have focused exclusively on the insanity defense in our discussion of criminal trials and forensic evaluations. However, a number of other defenses based on mental, neurological, and physiological conditions have been raised in both criminal and civil courts, with varying degrees of success. Among these conditions are Post-Traumatic Stress Disorder, Postpartum Depression and Postpartum Psychosis, the XYY abnormality, amnesia, Battered Woman Syndrome, Holocaust Survivor's Syndrome, sexual addiction, and Multiple Personality Disorder. The most recent entries are False Memory Syndrome and Urban Survival Syndrome (Slobogin, 1999b). Defendants also have raised defenses based on exposure to environmental contaminants, maintaining that the chemicals in those contaminants precipitated their violent behavior. In criminal cases, defendants may claim to have been affected by these conditions in an effort to absolve themselves completely of criminal responsibility—usually through an insanity defense—or to support a claim of **diminished capacity** or **diminished responsibility**. The conditions may also be raised at criminal sentencing, when the judge or jury hears evidence offered in mitigation (to lessen the gravity of the offense).

Syndromes and other special mental conditions may also be relevant if they are found in *victims* of crime. Both Rape Trauma Syndrome and Child Sexual Abuse Accommodation Syndrome—variants of PTSD—can support the prosecutor's evidence that a criminal act occurred. Likewise, evidence of these mental conditions in victims may be introduced in civil cases. In recent years, for example, rape victims and victims of child sexual assault have increasingly initiated civil suits against their aggressors. In such cases, evidence of the above-mentioned syndromes, if admitted into court, can be very relevant.

It is important to acknowledge at the outset the continuing controversy in both law and psychology with respect to these special conditions. They are neither widely accepted nor widely successful, although some have been received better than others by the courts. Slobogin (1999b) notes that testimony on Battered Woman Syndrome, for example, is now accepted in most courts. In fact, he adds, 10 states require by statute that such testimony be admitted in the trials of battered women who assaulted or killed their abusers. Likewise, almost all courts now accept evidence of Vietnam Stress Syndrome. The material in this section outlines the scientific and clinical knowledge of the causes, effects, and legal acceptance of some of these conditions, for illustrative purposes. The reader should be forewarned, however, that the jury is still out with respect to research findings on syndromes and other special conditions.

Post-Traumatic Stress Disorder (PTSD)

According to the Diagnostic and Statistical Manual (DSM–IV, 1994, p. 424), Post-Traumatic Stress Disorder is "the development of characteristic symptoms following exposure to an extreme traumatic stressor involving direct personal experience of an event that involves actual or threatened death or serious injury, or other threat to one's physical integrity; or witnessing an event that involves death, injury, or a threat to the physical integrity of another person; or learning about unexpected or violent death, serious harm, or threat of death or injury experienced by a family member or other close associate." The precipitating event would be markedly distressing to almost anyone. For the person experiencing PTSD it "must involve intense fear, helplessness, or horror (or in children, the response must involve disorganized or agitated behavior)." PTSD is an umbrella term that has been applied to war veterans, survivors of the Holocaust, survivors of the World Trade Center and Pentagon attacks on September 11, 2001, and victims of rape, child abuse, spousal abuse, and sexual harassment, among others. Thus Vietman Stress Syndrome, Battered Woman's Syndrome, Rape Trauma Syndrome, and Child Sexual Abuse Accommodation Syndrome are all variants of PTSD. PTSD may be either acute (duration of symptoms less than 3 months), chronic (when symptoms last longer than 3 months), or with delayed onset (when at least 6 months have passed between the traumatic event and the onset of the symptoms).

The traumatic event that precipitates PTSD may be experienced alone, such as a rape or attempted rape, or it may be experienced in the company of others, such as a flood, hurricane, plane crash, or war. The event is so psychologically distressing that the person takes a very long time to recover, and sometimes never recovers completely. Interestingly, symptoms seem to be more severe and longer in duration if the trauma is perceived by the victim as human made (rape, child abuse, combat) rather than a natural catastrophe (earthquake, flood, hurricane, forest fire) (American Psychiatric Association, 1994). Studies report that between 1 and 2% of all Americans suffer from PTSD (Sutker, Uddo-Crane, & Allain, 1991). This statistic is not surprising considering the many war veterans, victims of crime, and refugees—many of whom have experienced brutal political torture—who are included in the U.S. population. It has been estimated, for example, that about 31% of Vietnam combat veterans experience formally diagnosable symptoms of PTSD at some point during their lifetimes (Kulka et al., 1990, 1991).

In psychological parlance, a **syndrome** is a collection of thoughts, feelings, and behaviors thought to be held in common by individuals experiencing a given situation. Characteristic symptoms of Vietnam veterans, for example, include flashbacks of events, recurrent nightmares, a diminished responsiveness to the external world, feelings of alienation or detachment, over-alertness, headaches, and difficulty falling asleep or concentrating. Rape victims may experience flashbacks of the event, nightmares, depression, fear and anxiety, sexual dysfunction, and hyper-vigilance. Battered women are said to experience feelings of learned helplessness, the development of survival rather than escape skills (e.g., appeasing the batterer rather than planning to leave), traditional beliefs about marriage (e.g., that the husband is the head of the family), low self-esteem, and feelings of depression.

There has been a long-standing debate about the validity and accompanying symptoms of Post-Traumatic Stress Disorder. Methods for objective assessment of PTSD lack solid validity, and the diagnosis depends almost exclusively on self-report. Therefore, there is considerable opportunity for faking the disorder, especially if the individual rehearses and practices the symptoms (Bartol, 2002). This is not to diminish the very real psychological distress experienced by individuals who have experienced traumatic events. Moreover, there is little doubt that highly traumatic events can produce psychological problems in many individuals. The prevalence of these psychological problems along with their assessment is less clear. Thus, many observers question whether PTSD should be used as an excusing condition for crime. As Appelbaum et al. (1993, p. 230) note, the problem of PTSD in the courts is "particularly acute with something as new, as 'unverifiable,' as potentially useful, and as politically charged as PTSD."

As noted earlier in this section, the presence of PTSD in the *victim* has also been introduced into evidence to support the contention that a crime did indeed occur or, at the sentencing stage, to support a harsher sentence. In rape cases, for example, the defendant may contend that the sexual activity was consensual. The prosecution may try to counter this **consent defense** by introducing evidence that the victim suffers from Rape Trauma Syndrome, which is sometimes regarded a type of PTSD (Frazier & Borgida, 1992). A victim who consented to sexual activity is highly unlikely to experience symptoms of PTSD. In a different context, at sentencing, the judge may hear directly from the victim or may have information from a pre-sentence investigation, detailing the psychological trauma she has experienced. **Pre-sentence investigations** (PSIs) are reports, typically prepared by probation officers, that provide information to judges that is presumed to help them in making a sentencing decision.

Interestingly, Slobogin (1999b, p.107) finds that, of all of the categories of Post-Traumatic Stress Disorder, "only the ex-soldiers never experience problems with admissibility." He attributes this to the fact that the veterans are using the disorder to support insanity defenses, while the other syndromes are used to bolster the credibility of witnesses. In the case of Battered Women's Syndrome, where evidence is typically introduced to support a claim of self-defense, Slobogin notes that this is a "stretch of traditional self-defense doctrine," and thereby less likely to be accepted by the courts. Nevertheless, as mentioned above, most states do accept this evidence, although this is still no guarantee that the woman will be acquitted. ▶ [We will discuss Battered Women's Syndrome again in Chapter 11.]

In sum, the general term Post-Traumatic Stress Disorder covers a wide range of traumatic situations. Mental health professionals, in their clinical practices, have consistently encountered symptoms—often debilitating in nature—that individuals experience as a result of these traumas. Researchers, however, have been able to document many of the identified syndromes with only varying success. As a result, some psychologists and legal scholars and some courts prefer to keep "syndrome evidence" out of the courts completely. Slobogin (1999b, p. 119) takes a different approach and remarks as follows: "A criminal justice system that routinely prevented criminal defendants from offering plausible stories based on theories that are accepted by the relevant professionals could well fall into disrepute. If so, once again an obsession with scientific validity would ill-serve the ultimate goals of the system."

Multiple Personality Disorder

Multiple personality disorder (MPD)—also called **dissociative identity disorder**—is sometimes referred to as the "UFO of psychiatry" (Ondrovik & Hamilton, 1991). There is considerable debate among practitioners and scholars as to whether it actually exists. In most instances, MPD may possibly be iatrogenic—that is, unintentionally caused by clinicians or practitioners themselves (Comer, 1992). In other words, clinicians who firmly believe in, and are perceptually sensitive to, MPD look for and interpret a variety of behaviors as symptoms of MPD. The patient then comes to believe—very sincerely—that he or she is afflicted with this disorder.

The essential feature of MPD is "the existence within the person of two or more distinct personalities or personality states that recurrently take control of behavior" (DSM–IV, 1994, p. 484). Each personality may have a distinct personal history, self-image, and identity. Periodically, at least two personalities take full control of the individual. The change from one to the other is often very sudden and is generally triggered by stress or some relevant environmental stimuli. Hypnosis often produces this shift and is the primary tool used in the diagnosis of MPD (Bartol, 2002; Slovenko, 1989). In fact, research suggests that persons with MPD are so susceptible to hypnosis that self-hypnosis may be the primary etiological factor in MPD (Rosenhan & Seligman, 1984). That is, MPDs may enter a self-induced hypnotic trance as they assume their different personalities.

Although MPD became officially recognized by the American Psychiatric Association in 1980, its existence is still debated by the psychological and psychiatric communities. Nevertheless, between 1980 and 1989 the number of cases diagnosed in the United States rose significantly, from 200 to at least 6,000 (Slovenko, 1989). According to those who support its existence, the disorder generally begins in childhood, usually before age nine, and is generally found in persons who have been abused (often sexually) or have suffered another form of severe emotional trauma in childhood. It appears, then, that MPD may be a way of coping with past traumatic experiences. Approximately 75 to 90% of those said to have MPD are female (American Psychiatric Association, 1987).

MPD is very much doubted by the legal community. "As much as this disorder is debated and doubted in clinical circles, the legal world sees the disorder as sensational" (Radwin, 1991, p. 355). On occasion, though, MPD has been used successfully as an excusing condition for criminal responsibility (*State v. Milligan*, 1978; *State v. Rodrigues*, 1984). Both of these cases involved defendants charged with rape. In general, though, MPD has not been a successful defense (Slobogin, 1989, 1999b). One noteworthy case in which MPD failed was the case of Kenneth Bianchi, the notorious Hillside Strangler who murdered at least a dozen women over a one-year period (1977–78) in Los Angeles. Bianchi claimed, under hypnosis, that an alternate personality named "Steve" had actually committed the crimes. A team of experts led by psychiatrist Martin Orne (Orne, Dinges, & Orne, 1984) was able to refute Bianchi's claim of MPD through careful examination of his past and skillful analysis of his behavior under hypnosis. Though Bianchi apparently knew the "textbook version" of MPD, probably from his extensive reading in psychology, he did not know all the subtle clinical features of the disorder recognized by the experts. The team concluded that Bianchi was a psychopath rather than a multiple personality disorder. Bianchi then pled guilty in order to avoid the death penalty.

In sum, although the DSM–IV recognizes MPD—or dissociative identity disorder—many researchers, clinicians, and courts are extremely skeptical of both its existence and its use to absolve defendants of criminal responsibility. Many believe that MPD is nothing more than very good acting or a well-rehearsed collection of roles we all assume from time to time, depending on the situation we find ourselves in.

Amnesia

Amnesia refers to complete or partial memory loss of an incident, series of incidents, or some segment of life's experiences. Amnesia is not simply forgetting a name, a date, an incident, but is reserved for *severely* impaired ability to remember old material or to acquire and retain new material. If the memory loss involves past or old material, the disorder is called **retrograde amnesia** (retro means backward). If the memory loss is largely confined to the acquisition and retention of new material, it is called **anterograde amnesia** (antero means forward). Beyond these two major divisions, there are several subclassifications based on the person's behavior characteristics, the specific brain mechanism involved, and the suspected etiology.

The courts have not been receptive to amnesia as a viable element in either the insanity defense or as a condition that promotes incompetency to stand trial (Rubinsky & Brandt, 1986). This "hard line" approach is partly due to the suspicion that the defendant may be feigning amnesia. It is relatively easy to claim a blackout of reprehensible behavior. Social psychologists have identified a strong tendency to attribute positive things that happen to us to our ability and personality, and to attribute negative things to something outside ourselves or events beyond our control. This phenomenon is called **self-serving bias**. Thus, some people blame alcohol for the reprehensible things they do at a party or the abuse they inflict on their spouse. They can further avoid blame by claiming a lack of memory for the incident. However, the courts have not been sympathetic to defendants who rely on strategies supported by a self-serving bias. For example, in cases involving amnesia brought about by alcohol intoxication (limited amnesia), the courts continue to hold the person blameworthy, since he or she should have known the risks involved in drinking alcohol. In some situations, however, alcohol can support a defense of diminished capacity.

Attempts to use amnesia as the foundation of an insanity defense have met with strong resistance from the courts. For example, one court held that "insanity is the incapacity to discriminate between right and wrong while amnesia is simply the inability to remember" (Rubinsky & Brandt, 1986, p. 30). Thus, amnesia per se fails to qualify as a mental disorder that robs a person of the ability to differentiate between right and wrong. Similarly, amnesia is rarely accepted as a support for incompetency to stand trial. Paull (1993) points out that there have been cases in at least 20 states and 5 federal circuit courts where the court has held that amnesia per se does not render a defendant incompetent.

Amnesia due to acute alcohol intoxication is the most commonly invoked excusing condition in criminal cases (Rubinsky & Brandt, 1986). Interestingly, 30 to 65% of persons convicted of homicide claim they cannot remember the crime (Schacter, 1986b). Most of these offenders said they were heavily intoxicated at the time. People who have committed other violent crimes make similar claims. There is some intriguing evidence that memories developed during acute alcohol intoxication appear to be state-dependent (Rubinsky & Brandt, 1986). That is, memories of what happened under acute intoxication can often only be retrieved if the person returns to a similar intoxicated state.

A major problem for the forensic psychologist or psychiatrist and for the courts is distinguishing genuine amnesia from simulated amnesia. This is particularly true with reference to limited amnesia, in which the individual cannot remember episodes from the recent pass. Nevertheless, recent research has made gains in detecting genuine amnesia. Psychologist Richard Frederick (Frederick, 2000; Frederick & Denney, 1998), for example, notes that complaints of amnesia can be evaluated with recognition tests that are tailored to the information the person claims not to know. He believes such tests are more suitable to detecting amnesia than indirect assessment by the malingering tests, such as were discussed in ◀ Chapter 2.

Summary and Conclusions

Criminal defendants face many decisions in their journey through the criminal justice process. Deciding whether to waive the rights guaranteed to them under the Constitution—particularly the right to remain silent and the right to an attorney—is a critical and potentially life-threatening choice to make. A waiver of one's right to a lawyer early in the criminal process, for example, may be reflected in the sentencing decision. A key role of the criminal defense attorney, if her client is convicted, is to negotiate a sentencing package that will be fair and represent the client's interests. Very few citizens, including criminal defendants, probably think of this when and if they reflect on the right to a lawyer in criminal proceedings.

Criminal defendants routinely waive their rights to attorneys at various critical stages of the judicial process. Waivers of rights must be knowing, voluntary, and intelligent. For the typical criminal defendant, a truly voluntary waiver does not create problems; for the defendant who is mentally disordered, however, the "voluntariness" of the waiver should be carefully scrutinized. The question of whether a mentally-disordered defendant is truly capable of waiving his or her Constitutional rights, therefore, is a critical one for the justice system to answer. Although psychologists and other mental health practitioners may be consulted, it is typically long after the right has been waived, particularly with respect to adult defendants. An individual convicted of a crime, for example, might argue on appeal that he was not competent to waive his right to a lawyer during custodial interrogation by police, even though he "voluntarily" signed a waiver. The psychologist brought in at this stage of the process may, in retrospect, provide helpful information to the courts, but he or she is unlikely to have significant impact. In the juvenile context, by contrast, the competency to waive one's Constitutional rights is a critical issue, particularly as it relates to the cognitive capacity of juveniles.

This chapter has focused on two areas where psychology plays a key role in the processing of mentally disordered defendants: their competency to stand trial and their criminal responsibility at the time of the offense. We reviewed the research as well as the law relating to each of these important constructs. We noted, also, that the competency inquiry can arise in a variety of other contexts, including plea bargaining and pleading guilty, participating in a range of pre-trial proceedings, and being sentenced. Psychologists have long been involved in assessing competency to stand trial and in treating incompetent defendants. The *Dusky* standard for determining competency has remained entrenched in the law since it was first outlined by the Supreme Court in 1960, and it has been extended to other competency issues, including the competency to plead guilty and/or waive one's right to a lawyer. Requiring that a defendant have "sufficient present ability" to understand the proceedings and to help her or his attorney in preparing a defense gives very little guidance to psychologists conducting competency evaluations, however. A variety of forensic assessments instruments specifically geared toward the competency construct have been developed.

Likewise, psychologists have performed "sanity evaluations" and testified in court as to whether an insanity defense could be supported. We reviewed the tests for insanity throughout the United States, research on juror attitudes toward the insanity defense, and current research on the alternative verdict, Guilty But Mentally Ill. Over the past 20 years, since the attempted assassination of President Ronald Reagan, the great majority of states have followed the federal government's lead and have overhauled their insanity statutes. The changes have almost invariably made it more difficult for defendants pleading not guilty by reason of insanity.

We reviewed treatment approaches to both the incompetent defendant and the defendant found not guilty by reason of insanity. Traditionally, treatment has included psychoactive drugs, sometimes to the exclusion of other forms of therapy. Contemporary treatment programs for incompetent defendants are more likely to include education about the legal process, although generally speaking treatment for incompetent, mentally-disordered defendants is indistinguishable from treatment for other mentally-disordered individuals. The defendant found NGRI may be institutionalized only until he or she is no longer mentally ill and dangerous. In many jurisdictions, persons found NGRI bear the burden of proving that they are no longer mentally ill and dangerous, by at least a preponderance of the evidence.

We reviewed a variety of special conditions and unique defenses that have made their way into clinical work and the courts in recent years. Chief among these is Post-Traumatic Stress Disorder, a broad term that covers a variety of more specific "syndromes." Although admitted into evidence guardedly by many courts, these syndromes are often well recognized by mental health practitioners and have also been recognized in the DSM–IV. Researchers have had difficulty validating the syndromes, however, leading to skepticism that they should be admitted into evidence. Nevertheless, some commentators, like Slobogin, argue that criminal defendants in particular should be allowed to introduce syndrome testimony if the clinical community finds support for these disorders.

However, other than the above "special defenses," there have been few changes on the competency and insanity landscape in very recent years. Research suggests that jurors are even less favorably disposed to the insanity defense than in the past, but the alternative GBMI verdict does not appear to be the solution. Mental institutions ill disposed toward keeping NGRI individuals indefinitely release them conditionally, to the supervision of special community programs. While it is possible that the mental health courts described in ◀ Chapter 3 may help deflect some of the mentally disordered from the criminal justice process, the identification and treatment of this group of offenders (and alleged offenders) remains a major challenge to the courts and the criminal justice system in general.

The mentally-disordered defendant has presented intractable problems for the criminal justice system, with the pre-trial and trial issues discussed in this chapter only being the tip of the iceberg. Once mentally disordered defendants enter jails and prisons as sentenced offenders, the problems they face are multiplied, as we will see in some of the chapters ahead.

Key Terms

ALI rule
Anterograde amnesia
Brawner rule
Competency to stand trial
Consent defense
Defendant
Diminished capacity
Diminished responsibility
Dissociative identity disorder
Durham rule
Insanity
Irresistible impulse test
M'Naghten rule
Multiple personality disorder
Necessity defense
Pre-sentence investigation
Retrograde amnesia
Self-defense
Self-serving bias
Strict liability offenses
Syndrome

Questions for Review

1. List the various competencies that might be assessed by psychologists in criminal and civil contexts.
2. Explain the legal difference between incompetence to stand trial and insanity.
3. What is the two-pronged standard for assessing competency to stand trial?
4. Compare and contrast the various instruments used to assess competency to stand trial.
5. Describe the individual most likely to be found incompetent to stand trial, citing such factors as demographic characteristics, crime charged, and clinical diagnosis.
6. Discuss what occurs once an individual is found incompetent to stand trial.
7. List and explain briefly any four tests for insanity used in state courts.
8. What changes were made relative to insanity in federal courts after the Hinckley case? What is the present test for insanity in federal courts?
9. Contrast a verdict of not guilty by reason of insanity (NGRI) and a verdict of guilty but mentally ill (GBMI) in terms of outcome for the defendant.
10. What have we learned from the research on juries and the insanity defense in each of the following areas: (a) attitudes toward the defense; (b) misconceptions about legal outcomes; and (c) application of insanity tests?
11. In what ways are mental responsibility evaluations more complex than evaluations of competency to stand trial?
12. List 5–8 special conditions that are used in some cases as defenses to criminal conduct. Discuss any two in detail.

CHAPTER 5

Mental Health Law: Civil Commitment

We face important decisions about the treatment of mentally disordered individuals who are presumed to be unable to care for themselves independently. The media often give attention to the plight of homeless, many of whom are thought to be mentally disordered. Urban dwellers encounter them on the streets, and virtually every small city and rural community has its familiar resident citizen who displays harmless but bizarre behavior. Unfortunately, the public too often fears these individuals and considers them a threat, not only to themselves, but also to the safety of the community. In reality, the mentally disordered as a group are not violent. Additionally, whenever possible, disabled individuals—including the mentally disabled—are entitled to remain within the community if they wish, and if resources can be provided for them, within reason (*Americans with Disabilities Act*, 1990; *Olmstead v. L.C.*, 1999).

Some mentally disordered individuals, especially those who have a history of violence, do commit violent acts, however. This fact brings into sharp focus the role of the mental health clinician. Psychologists are called upon, not only to offer treatment to the mentally disordered, but also to assess the extent to which they might be at risk for committing violent acts in the community. As we will see in this chapter, this risk assessment enterprise has improved substantially over the past decade.

In the first two-thirds of the 20th century, until approximately the late 1960s, mentally disordered individuals who could not be cared for by their families or friends were very routinely committed to mental institutions, where it was not unusual for them to remain throughout their lives. The appalling conditions under which they were sometimes kept have been amply documented elsewhere, both in court cases and in scholarly literature (Rothman, 1971, 1980). With increasing recognition by the courts of individual rights, involuntary commitment became known as a deprivation of the liberty guaranteed by the Constitution (Wexler, 1990a). As such, commitment of persons to mental institutions against their wills could be accomplished only with careful attention to procedural safeguards, including court hearings and legal representation. Furthermore, involuntary commitment required a showing that the person was dangerous to self or others, or gravely disabled, and that no other alternative to institutionalization was available. Finally, statutes began to require periodic administrative review of the need for continued institutionalization.

These civil commitment laws, which fall into the category "mental health law," exist in all states and the District of Columbia. They identify the standards and procedures to be followed prior to and during commitment. They usually require both evidence of mental disorder or defect *and* some prediction that there will be negative consequences, such as harm to society or to the individual, if the person is not confined. Additionally, they generally require that less restrictive alternatives to hospitalization be considered, particularly when a person is not deemed dangerous. Before placing an individual in a mental institution against his or her will, for example, the judge or hearing officer should consider whether a group home or other carefully supervised community care arrangement would be better than institutional confinement. In increasingly more states, there is also the option of outpatient commitment, which is a means of requiring the individual to participate in treatment in the community. As we shall see, particularly in the case of involuntary hospitalization, there is very often a gap between the law on the books and the law as it operates, or between *de facto* and *de jure* civil commitment proceedings (Turkheimer & Parry, 1992).

Voluntary and Involuntary Commitment

Until quite recently, the literature on civil commitment made a sharp demarcation between voluntary and involuntary commitment, with the latter indicating that the patient had been institutionalized against his or her will. An estimated 25–30% of all patients in public mental institutions were believed to have been committed involuntarily (Monahan & Shah, 1989; Wexler, 1990a). As Carroll (1991) noted, however, the remaining 70% were not necessarily truly voluntary commitments, because an unknown number occurred under the threat of formal commitment proceedings. Complicating this picture is the fact that some presumably *in*voluntary commitments are, actually, voluntary. That is, the involuntary commitment process was used in order to assure that treatment would be expedited (Farabee, Shen, & Sanchez, 2002). Thus, rather than study the artificial distinction between voluntary and involuntary commitments, researchers have begun to focus on the concept of **perceived coercion** in those who are civilly committed. Later in the chapter we will discuss the research conducted on coercion under the auspices of the MacArthur Foundation (e.g., Gardner et al., 1993; Lidz et al., 1995), as well as scales designed to measure perceived coercion.

To complicate the civil commitment issue even more, questions have been raised as to whether the mentally disordered are even competent to make the decision to commit themselves as the result of a 1990 U.S. Supreme Court decision (*Zinermon v. Burch*). In early December 1981, Burch had been found wandering along a Florida highway, bloodied, bruised, and disoriented. He was taken to a private mental health care facility designated by the state to receive patients suffering from mental illness. There he signed forms consenting to admission and treatment on a short-term basis. Staff at the facility diagnosed his condition as paranoid schizophrenia and gave him psychotropic medication. After three days, it was determined that Burch needed long-term treatment, so he was referred to a state mental hospital. Once again, he signed forms requesting admission and authorizing treatment. Still another form authorizing treatment was signed two weeks later. There was ample evidence in the record that he was disoriented, confused, and bizarre in both action and appearance during each form-signing episode. Burch remained in the institution for five more months, until May 1982, during which time no hearing was held regarding either his hospitalization or his treatment. Following his release, he complained that he had been admitted inappropriately and did not recall signing voluntary forms.

The U.S. Supreme Court ruled, in a split 5–4 decision, that Burch had a substantive right to be competent before consenting to voluntary hospitalization and a consequent procedural right to a hearing to determine whether this competency existed. In other words, before being allowed to commit himself to a mental institution, he should have been given a hearing to determine whether he was able to make that decision. According to Bruce Winick (1991b), the Burch case may have widespread, negative implications. If states interpret the Supreme Court's decision as requiring hearings in all voluntary commitments, the voluntary process would become nearly indistinguishable from the involuntary. "Not only would this impose high costs, but it also would undermine much of the presumed value of voluntary admission" (Winick 1991b, p. 94). Furthermore, he argues that a broad reading of the *Zinermon v. Burch* case would, by extension, require a demeaning inquiry into the competency of mentally disordered individuals whenever they make significant decisions.

It remains to be seen whether the case will indeed have a significant effect on voluntary commitments. By far the most research attention and commentary relates to involuntary commitment, though as noted above researchers now prefer to focus on the coercive aspect of commitment, keeping in mind that some voluntary admissions are coerced and some involuntary admissions are not. In Burch's case, there was no evidence of coercion, but there was considerable evidence that he was incompetent to make the decision to commit himself. Despite the trend in the research to consider coercion a critical variable, statutes thus far continue to refer to voluntary and involuntary commitment.

Thus, every state and the District of Columbia allow involuntary civil commitment, which is presumably in the best interest of the patient and, in some cases, for society's protection. Candidates for involuntary civil commitment, however, are disproportionately poor or indigent, uneducated, and unemployed or employed in low status occupations. They do not seem to be disproportionately male or female, although some research suggests that the interaction between age and gender is significant. That is, older women and younger men are more likely to be institutionalized than older men and younger women (Hiday, 1988). Ethnic and racial minorities do not seem to be disproportionately at risk for civil commitment, once economic status, age, and gender are controlled.

The typical stay in a public mental institution following involuntary civil commitment is less than a month, but a substantial number of these short-term individuals are continually at risk of re-commitment (Parry et al., 1991). Virginia Hiday (1988), reviewing the empirical research on civil commitment, observes that the more flagrant and widespread abuses of the past no longer occur. Nonetheless, many questions continue to be raised about conditions of confinement and the treatment that is received in mental institutions, including the rights of patients to refuse medications and the efficacy of various treatment approaches. Additionally, in light of increasing use of outpatient commitment, research on the efficacy of this approach is beginning to appear (e.g., Dennis & Monahan, 1996; Swanson et al., 1999, 2001). Following a historical review of the rationales for involuntary civil commitment, we will address each of these issues separately.

Historical Overview

In the United States, commitment of persons to mental institutions against their will and for long periods can be traced to the historical periods representing the so-called cult of the asylum (Rothman, 1971) and cult of curability (Deutsch, 1949) during the 19th century. Prior to this time, bizarre-acting persons were kept in their own homes or turned into the streets, where many joined the ranks of vagrants and eventually were held in workhouses or jails. In some cases, bizarre "treatments" were attempted. Julien (1992, p. 217) notes that persons displaying what would now be called schizophrenic behavior were treated by such methods as "twirling them on a stool until they lost consciousness or dropping them through a trap door into an icy lake."

In the 19th century, however, institutional confinement began to emerge as a first resort (Dershowitz, 1974, p. 803). It was now assumed that the supposedly safe, protective, and non-stressful environment of the asylum offered the best treatment that society could offer to "lunatics." In reality, of course, institutional confinement was anything but non-stressful. Critics such as Rothman (1980) have argued, also, that institutionalization was more a matter of convenience than genuine concern for the well-being of the mentally disordered. The commitments to institutions required no formalized showing of mental disorder, inability to care for one's self, or dangerousness to self or to others, although the certification of one or two medical doctors was generally required. Consider, for example, New York State's insanity statute, enacted in 1842, barely six years after the state legislature authorized the building of the Utica asylum. "All lunatics, not only the dangerous ones, were to be confined; and they were to be confined immediately upon the occurrence of the disease" (Dershowitz, 1974, p. 808). The statute not only allowed authorities to incarcerate the insane accused of committing deviant acts, but also urged them to "seek out the quiet insane as well so that they might be cured of their disease" (Dershowitz, 1974, p. 808). Medical superintendents claimed 90 to 100% cure rates for "insanity" (Deutsch, 1949; Dershowitz, 1974), without supporting evidence. These claims prompted courts to commit involuntarily numerous persons considered mentally disordered, even if only marginally so. We should note that the term "insanity" is used here in its clinical sense, not in the legal sense discussed in the previous chapter. That is, insanity here refers to mental disorder, not to lack of criminal responsibility at the time of a crime as a result of mental disorder. The power of the state to place individuals in mental institutions against their will, even if they had committed no criminal acts, was derived from the doctrine of *parens patriae*, to which we now turn our attention.

Parens Patriae

Parens patriae (literally, "parent of the country") is the doctrine in law which establishes the right of the state to substitute its presumably benevolent decision making for that of individuals who are said to be unable to make their own decisions. It thus authorizes the state to make and enforce decisions believed to be in the best interest of those individuals who cannot or will not protect themselves, even when they are causing no direct harm to others. It is important to note that the doctrine of *parens patriae* is the basis of other laws as well as those relating to involuntary civil commitments. In juvenile justice, for example, *parens patriae* is cited to justify a state treating juveniles differently from adults for their own protection. Statutes that allow the preventive detention of juveniles charged with even minor crimes are derived from the *parens patriae* doctrine (*Schall v. Martin*, 1984).

Although the state's intercession under the *parens patriae* doctrine is presumed to be in the best interest of the individual, it is essentially coercive (Carroll, 1991), a fact which led to the creation of laws designed to protect individuals against abuse of government power. The question of the person's competency is at the basis of *parens patriae* power (Winick, 1991a). "Only the assumed incompetency of mental patients, not their illness, can justify the law's treating the mentally ill differently from others" (Winick, 1991a, p. 43). Winick argues that the more coercive the state's intervention, such as in over-riding a patient's request to refuse medication, the more rigorously should the state be obliged to demonstrate the individual's incompetency.

To appreciate the crucial place of the *parens patriae* doctrine in mental health law, it helps to consider its ambiguous history, which dates back to ancient Roman law, where it was applied when the head of the family was believed incompetent and in danger of wasting his estate. The state was then vested with the power to declare the person *non compos mentis* and commit him and the estate to the care of curators or tutors designated by the *praetor*. *Parens patriae* was a doctrine applied selectively to persons who had valuable property holdings and other wealth, rather than to the general population.

The concept was adopted from Roman law in the eleventh century by the Anglo Saxon King Aethelred II and developed and expanded during the early years of Edward I's reign (1272–1307) (Kittrie, 1971). The doctrine was first codified in 1324 during the reign of Edward II in the statute *Prerogativa Regis*. It gave the king the power to protect the lands and profits of "idiots" and "lunatics" until their mental restoration (Cogan, 1970).

Scholars have debated whether *parens patriae* has been used throughout its history as a humanistic concept (Cogan, 1970) or as primarily a state fiscal policy to protect wealth and property (Halpern, 1974). Cogan (1970) notes that even under *Prerogativa Regis*, care was taken to limit the King's rights to the lands. For example, the King had guardianship of "natural fools," a term which referred to those mentally incapacitated from birth. He had only unprofitable care of "lunatics," those who lost their "wit" sometime after birth. Cogan (1970, p. 157) surmises that the distinction was made to prevent "enemies of the King from being declared lunatics and having the profits of their lands added to the King's treasury."

Some courts, though, have seen it differently and have noted that it was not only the King who could profit. In *State ex rel Hawks v. Lazaro* (1974), for example, *parens patriae* was called a state fiscal policy "conceived in avarice and executed without charity." Moreover, "while well-meaning people frequently attempted to operate under it [*parens patriae*] for the benefit of their fellowmen, it has often been used as a justification for greedy actions on the part of relatives or for the removal of unwanted or troublesome persons." In the juvenile justice context, the doctrine also has been controversial. While strongly supported by courts in some cases (e.g., *Parham v. J.R.*, 1979; *Schall v. Martin*, 1984), it has been rejected in favor of due process rights in others (e.g., *Kent v. U.S.*, 1966; *In re Gault*, 1967).

One of the earliest American court cases illustrating the full implementation of *parens patriae* power was the 1845 decision of the Massachusetts Supreme Judicial Court, *In re Oakes*. Josiah Oakes, a 67-year-old widower and wharf builder from Cambridge, was committed by his family to McLean Asylum because he was laboring under a "hallucination of mind." His wife had died after a lengthy illness. According to the court record, upon the death of his wife, Oakes seemed unperturbed and did not demonstrate the emotions that could be expected from a person in his right mind. Moreover, he had begun to "manifest a change in character" about six years earlier when a young woman of "bad character" entered his life. His conduct at his wife's funeral showed a "perversion of mind," according to the record. It was also noted that his persistence in his intention to marry the young woman and his refusal to believe the evidence of her bad character were indicative of this perversion.

There was no record of a hearing during the initial commitment process, and Oakes petitioned the court for release, claiming that his family had committed him illegally. In January 1845, the Massachusetts court sat for two days to deliberate the case. Chief Justice C. J. Shaw, considered an "enlightened liberal" (Zilboorg, 1944), delivered the opinion, which kept Oakes confined and set considerable legal precedent.

Deutsch (1949, p. 422) referred to the Oakes case as "one of the most important decisions affecting the civil insane in the history of American jurisprudence." It outlined for the first time the justification and limitations implicit in common law concerning restraint of the insane. Not only did it support the institutionalization of persons considered dangerous to themselves or others, but also asserted the power of the state to detain individuals for remedial treatment against their will. Kittrie (1971, p. 66) comments that the *Oakes* case represents the "cornerstone of the fullfledged modern therapeutic state."

Police Power

Parens patriae remained embedded in law until the 1960s. At that point, concern over the potential for abuse associated with extensive reliance on *parens patriae* as a basis for civil commitment led to the adoption of more restrictive laws. Sometimes called libertarian civil commitment statutes, they sought to limit the *parens patriae* authority of the state. The laws reflected the belief that involuntary civil commitment could be justified only on the basis of dangerousness, reflecting the police power of the state.

"**Police power**" refers to the obligation and responsibility of the state to protect the public from harm to persons or to property. It encompasses the state's power to make laws and regulations for the protection of public health, safety, welfare, and morals (Comment, 1972, p. 158). Thus, while *parens patriae* relates to protection of the individual and infers remedial, therapeutic, and care-giving responsibilities, police power relates to protection of society. While *parens patriae* focuses on the individual's ability to make appropriate decisions concerning his or her welfare, police power revolves around the individual's dangerousness or potential threat to others. Commitment based on a *parens-patriae* rationale requires a demonstrated inability to care for oneself; commitment based on a police-power rationale requires predictability of dangerousness.

The distinction between *parens patriae* and police power becomes nebulous in situations where a person's actions are considered dangerous only to that person and not to society as a whole. Additionally, there are situations in which even danger to oneself is arguable. A mentally-disordered person who attempts and constantly threatens suicide is clearly dangerous to himself, and there is very little debate on this issue (Slovic & Monahan, 1995). Both *parens patriae* and police power rationales would justify his commitment. A mentally-disordered person who lives under a railroad trestle, forages through trash cans for food, and refuses to accept shelter for the impending winter season presents different problems, however. Not everyone agrees that a seeming inability to care for oneself in this way qualifies as dangerous to oneself (Poletiek, 2002; Lidz, Mulvey, Appelbaum, & Cleveland, 1989). Under the *parens patriae* doctrine, this person could be forcefully institutionalized; under police power, he could not. In order to get around this dilemma, some states adopted grave disability statutes, which recognized their responsibility to care for those who cannot care for themselves. Although these statutes appear to be more *parens patriae* in philosophy, even they often require evidence that the person is presently dangerous to him or herself. Thus, to commit the trestle resident against his will, the state would have to demonstrate his dangerousness to himself, by at least clear and convincing evidence (*Addington v. Texas*, 1979).

The Emergence of Due Process

The last quarter of the 20th century saw dramatic changes in mental health law and the treatment of the mentally disordered. Due process has become of paramount consideration in involuntary civil commitment. The U.S. Supreme Court has made it clear that commitment to a mental institution "is a deprivation of liberty which the State cannot accomplish without due process of law" (e.g., *O'Connor v. Donaldson*, 1975, p. 580). Loss of liberty and privacy are clearly entailed in such a commitment. Also at stake may be dignity, one's job, living arrangements, and social relationships. The social stigma that accompanies presumed incompetence and emotional weakness is another factor to take into consideration.

In 1966, a federal court ruled that persons could not be involuntarily committed unless other less drastic alternatives were considered (*Lake v. Cameron*). In 1972, another federal court, ruling in a Wisconsin case, emphasized that due process must be carefully protected in civil commitment proceedings. The court mandated a range of procedures including notice, the opportunity to be heard, and the right to counsel (*Lessard v. Schmidt*). Following the *Lessard* decision, Wisconsin adopted a new mental health statute with procedural safeguards for involuntary commitment proceedings. What happened thereafter was significant. Faced with more restrictive criteria, the state apparently began to take the criminal commitment route. Since it could no longer easily hospitalize individuals who acted in a bizarre but non-dangerous manner, police arrested them on minor charges. They were then found incompetent to stand trial and sent for in-patient psychiatric care for up to 60 days. In the one-year period after the more restrictive civil commitment law went into effect, the number of persons found incompetent to stand trial increased by 42% (Dickey, 1980). Once their commitment time had expired, the criminal charges were dropped (Dickey, 1980).

During the 1970s, other states began to make similar changes in their statutory schemes. By 1978, all but two had afforded greater protections for those faced with civil commitment (Turkheimer & Parry, 1992). Research on the implementation of these statutes, however, indicated that the Wisconsin experience was not uncommon. In Iowa, for example, the legislature passed a new statute designed to limit the number of persons potentially subject to civil commitment (Bezanson, 1975). The law mandated that, prior to involuntary civil commitment, courts must find by clear and convincing evidence that individuals are (1) mentally ill; (2) incapable of making a decision regarding treatment; (3) amenable to treatment; and (4) likely to be dangerous to selves or to others (Stier & Stoebe, 1979). The statute also advocated that defense attorneys challenge the credentials of medical experts, question their diagnoses, offer rebutting expert testimony, and submit factual evidence refuting expert opinions (Stier & Stoebe, 1979). Despite the establishment of these more stringent requirements, an extensive study of the implementation of the new Iowa law found virtually no change in commitment proceedings from the pre-1975 practice of automatic involuntary commitment based on a recommendation by a physician or psychiatrist (Stier & Stoebe, 1979).

In most states, involuntary civil commitment can encompass both emergency detention and long-term commitment. Recall that in *Zinermon v. Burch* (1990), discussed above, Burch had "voluntarily" committed himself for both short-term care and, following that, a longer time period. A typical statute provides for an initial 72-hour evaluation period, a 14-day period of emergency, intensive treatment, and long-term confinement up to 180 days. Although statutes do not always refer specifically to re-commitment hearings, researchers are finding that they are common and that there are significant differences in both the patients involved and the procedures associated with these re-commitments (Parry et al., 1991). ◙ (**Box 5-1** compares key features of civil commitment policies in three states.)

Emergency detention is intended to protect individuals from imminent serious harm to themselves or to prevent injury to others. This short-term confinement presumably provides a "cooling off" period, rarely lasting more than 15 days, during which the person recovers from immediate psychological

BOX 5-1
Civil Commitment in Three States

Laws relating to the involuntary commitment of individuals vary widely across the United States, but there are some common elements. All states allow both temporary and extended commitment and all provide legal representation. The possibility of commitment to outpatient treatment is also common. Below are selected features of the statutes in Texas, South Carolina, and Oregon pertaining to *inpatient* commitment.

Texas

- Temporary commitment is allowed with clear and convincing evidence of mental illness and likelihood of causing harm to self or serious harm to others. This commitment is also allowed if the mentally ill person is suffering severe distress or deterioration and is unable to make rational and informed decisions.
- Extended commitment requires the same evidence as above. In addition, the condition is expected to continue for more than 90 days and the person has already received treatment for at least 60 consecutive days during the last year.
- Temporary commitment hearings do not involve a jury unless the proposed patient requests one; extended commitment hearings *require* a jury unless the person waives one.

Oregon

- Persons may be committed upon clear and convincing evidence that they are mentally ill and a danger to themselves *or* are unable to meet their basic personal needs. Additionally, they may be committed if they have been diagnosed with a major mental disorder (e.g., chronic schizophrenia) for which they have been previously hospitalized and are now showing signs of significant deterioration.
- Judge appoints one examiner, but a second may be appointed on request. Proceedings are open and involve testimony from a wide range of individuals.

South Carolina

- Commitment requires clear and convincing evidence of mental illness *and* a lack of sufficient insight or capacity to make responsible decisions with respect to treatment *or* a likelihood of serious harm to self or others.
- The court appoints two examiners, one of whom must be a licensed physician. If the examiners do not agree on the need for commitment, the court must appoint a psychiatrist as a third examiner. The three are instructed to render a majority opinion. In addition, the proposed patient may request an independent evaluator.

agitation or during which arrangements are made for permanent disposition of the case. Treatment in the form of stabilizing drugs is typically administered. Before the 1970s, the only recourse available to patients to challenge this short-term detention was a ***habeas corpus* petition** to the federal courts. *Habeas corpus* is a petition arguing that one is being detained illegally, in violation of the U.S. Constitution. The statutory changes in the 1970s, however, drastically curtailed the length of time a patient could be held without a hearing, usually 48 hours. In the *Lessard* case, for example, the judge declared 48 hours the maximum time, stating that "such an emergency measure can be justified only for the length of time necessary to arrange for a hearing before a neutral judge at which probable cause for the detention must be established." The fact that a court hearing is held within a short period of time reduces the need for *habeas corpus* petitions.

Long-term confinement, which once could mean a lifetime in an institution, has also been curtailed in most states. Typically, a six-month commitment period occurs, after which a court or an administrative board must review the patient's status. In 1975, the U.S. Supreme Court in *O'Connor v. Donaldson* put states on notice that indefinite confinement of non-dangerous persons, without treatment, was constitutionally unacceptable. If the individual is receiving treatment and is making progress toward recovery, however, extended commitment can occur. Patients may have the burden of proving that they are eligible for release after the long-term period has expired; moreover, as noted above, recommitments are not uncommon.

In 1979, the U.S. Supreme Court ruled in *Addington v. Texas* that a person's extended (as opposed to emergency) committability must be proven in an adversarial hearing at least by clear and convincing evidence; a mere preponderance of the evidence was not enough. The Court did not, however, articulate what the standard or criteria of committability must be (Wexler, 1981). Instead, the Court deferred to clinicians. "Whether the individual is mentally ill and dangerous to either himself or others and is in need of confined therapy turns on the meaning of facts which must be interpreted by expert psychiatrists and psychologists" (at 429).

In the same year, the Court took a very different stance toward the commitment of children. In *Parham v. J.R.* (1979), the Court rejected the argument that children should have the benefit of an adversarial hearing before being committed to mental institutions by their parents or caretakers, including state child welfare officials. All that was needed, the majority said, was "some kind of inquiry" by a neutral fact finder soon after the commitment. The neutral fact finder could, the Court said, be a staff physician. The three Justices who dissented in the case argued that parental decisions to institutionalize their children may be unrelated to the child's mental condition, and that "even well-meaning parents lack the expertise necessary to evaluate the relative advantages and disadvantages of inpatient as opposed to outpatient psychiatric treatment" (442 U.S. at 632). The dissenters also cited a study which concluded that more than half of Georgia's institutionalized children did not need to be so confined. With respect to the "neutral fact finder," the dissenters noted:

> Even under the best of circumstances psychiatric diagnosis and therapy decisions are fraught with uncertainties . . . . These uncertainties are aggravated when . . . the psychiatrist interviews the child during a period of abnormal stress in connection with the commitment, and without adequate time or opportunity to become acquainted with the patient. These uncertainties may be further aggravated when economic and social class separate doctor and child, thereby frustrating the accurate diagnosis of pathology.

The uneasiness expressed by the dissenters in the *Parham* case is reflective of a theme running through many statutes and court cases relating to civil commitment. The fallibility of diagnoses and questions about the effectiveness of various treatment approaches continue to haunt the civil commitment process today. On the other hand, it is important to recognize that restrictive criteria, even for emergency confinement, can create serious problems for the criminal justice system. Both empirical research and government statistics document increases in the number of mentally disordered persons held in local jails (Ditton, 1999; Steadman, McCarty, & Morrissey, 1989; Steadman & Veysey, 1997; Teplin & Pruett, 1992), a problem exacerbated by the chaos and crowded conditions that plague many of those facilities. Researchers in some jurisdictions have found support for a **criminalization thesis**, which argues that otherwise non-criminal individuals are charged with minor crimes such as disorderly conduct or unlawful trespassing in order to justify detaining them in jail, arguably for their own protection (Bonowitz & Bonowitz, 1981; Teplin, 2000; Teplin & Pruett, 1992). Other researchers have found little support for such a phenomenon, however, and believe that the increases in the mentally disordered population in jail is attributed to numerous social factors which cannot be linked directly with restrictive commitment statutes (Arvanites, 1988; Hiday, 1988). Whether a criminalization phenomenon is actually occurring in a particular jurisdiction seems to depend upon policies among law enforcement officers and the availability of community services for the mentally disordered. As noted in ◀ Chapter 3, one of the primary aims of mental health courts is to address this pressing problem.

Commitment Standards

Most states today allow involuntary civil commitment if a person is both mentally ill and a danger to self or others and require that these be proven, at least by clear and convincing evidence. Additionally, approximately 30 states allow involuntary commitment if a person is gravely disabled and unable to care for his or her own needs (Turkheimer & Parry, 1992) ◙ (see ◀ **Box 5-1**). Research indicates that grave disability, rather than dangerousness, appears to be the most frequent basis for civil commitment (Turkheimer & Parry, 1992; Wexler, 1990a). Surprisingly, the gravely disabled are not generally elderly, but consist mostly of disturbed young persons within the 21–35 age range (Wexler, 1990a, p. 173).

The Dangerousness Standard

Although dangerousness is not always precisely defined, some states have led the way in crafting clear criteria. North Carolina law, for example, defines dangerousness to others as follows:

> . . . within the recent past, the individual has inflicted or attempted to inflict or threatened to inflict serious bodily harm on another, or has acted in such a way as to create a substantial risk of serious bodily harm to another, or has engaged in extreme destruction of property; and that there is a reasonable probability that this conduct will be repeated (N.C.G.S. 122C-3 (11)b).

Traditionally, researchers have demonstrated high numbers of "false positives," or overpredictions of dangerousness. Predicting dangerousness—or assessing risk—in civilly-committed populations has been equally daunting. Years ago, Alan Stone (1975, p. 33) remarked that "neither objective actuarial tables nor psychiatric intuition, diagnosis, and psychological testing can claim predictive success when dealing with the traditional population of mental hospitals." Referring to the three standards of proof in legal decision making—preponderance of the evidence, clear and convincing evidence, and beyond a reasonable doubt—Stone asserted that mental health professionals had failed to prove their ability to predict violence by even the lowest criterion, preponderance of the evidence (Monahan & Wexler, 1978). Others agreed. Cocozza and Steadman (1976), for example, concluded that "any attempt to commit an individual solely on the basis of dangerousness would be futile if psychiatric testimony were subjected to any of these three standards of proof" (p. 1101). They added that the research has demonstrated "clear and convincing evidence of the inability of psychiatrists or anyone else to predict dangerousness accurately" (p. 1109).

The past decade has seen notable improvement in the area of predicting violent behavior. Today, the term "risk assessment" is preferred to "prediction of dangerousness" in the research literature. Risk assessment is facilitated with the help of such instruments as the PCL, the PCL–R, and the PCL–SV, which were described in ◀ Chapter 2. Shortly, we will be discussing a major research project focusing on this important topic.

Even with improved prediction, the requirement that dangerousness be proved by clear and convincing evidence, and in some states beyond a reasonable doubt, can be daunting. It has had the effect of limiting the number of individuals hospitalized, particularly for long-term confinements. This has raised the question of whether the public is being protected from potentially harmful individuals as well as whether the individuals themselves are getting the help they need. Additionally, because statutes limit the amount of time people can be held without continuing evidence of dangerousness, mental health practitioners have argued that patients are not institutionalized long enough to provide them with significant treatment (Hiday, 1988). Outpatient commitment

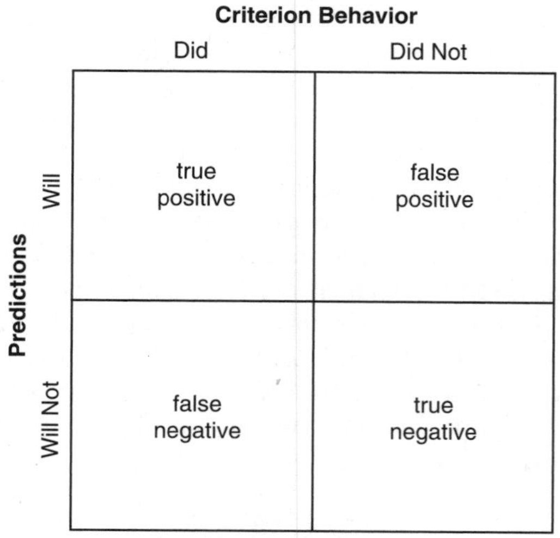

Figure 5-1

Four possible outcomes of predictions.

orders also often include a dangerousness standard (Swartz, Swanson, et al., 1999) as do less formal community supervision or monitoring orders (Dennis & Monahan, 1996).

Researchers have expended considerable energy in their attempts to study dangerousness among the civilly committed. Hiday (1990) followed up over a 6-month-period 727 individuals brought into civil commitment proceedings in North Carolina for mental illness and dangerousness. Psychiatrists had evaluated 2/3 of them as dangerous. In her follow-up study, Hiday used arrest records, patient ward charts, psychiatric evaluations for readmission, civil commitment affidavits for recommitment, and community mental-health-center patient records. Dangerousness was defined by objective criteria, such as actual injury to others and threats of physical injury.

Hiday found no reports of violent acts or threats for 3/4 of the 727 individuals. If we contrast the 1/4 for whom violent acts or threats were reported (182 individuals) with the 2/3 figure predicted by psychiatrists (484) we see the large number of false positives in the sample. Hiday suggests that the low level of violence during the 6-month follow-up indicates that the civil commitment process works because persons received the help they presumably needed either in the hospital or the community. She is careful to note, though, that research from other jurisdictions is needed to see whether these results can be replicated. Another six-month follow-up study (Belcher, 1989) found involvement in criminal activity among a sample of 132 discharged patients but did not indicate the nature of the crimes. Belcher did find, however, that the discharged patients who were homeless were significantly more likely to commit crime, but again it is unclear whether the crimes were violent, property, or public order.

A large body of research has explored the interaction among homelessness, mental disorder, and criminal activity from the perspective of criminal as opposed to civil commitments. The findings suggest that mentally disordered individuals are engaging increasingly more in such activity, but to date the crimes seem to be non-violent, petty, and victimless. Some research, however, (e.g., Martell, 1991) suggests that the subgroup of seriously mentally-disordered persons who are homeless are more at risk for committing violent crimes.

Methodological Problems in Violence Prediction Research

The state of the research on violence prediction leads much to be desired. In a summary article, John Monahan (1996) noticed that research efforts had been hampered by a number of methodological and definitional problems. More precisely, Monahan argued that the empirical research on the risk assessment of violence for the mentally disordered was plagued by four basic methodological problems. The first problem was *impoverished predictor variables*, referring to the factors used to forecast whether violence will occur. A **predictor variable** is a term that is analogous to the term "independent variable" in experimental research. In social science research, a predictor variable generally refers to some measurable factor (an antecedent) that aids in forecasting an outcome or a behavior. Monahan pointed out that there are numerous antecedents to violence—including social, psychological, and biological ones—but much of risk assessment research had focused on only a very narrow range of "cues" or predictor variables (often only one). In addition to the multiple demographic, biological, or social predictor variables to consider in predictions of violence, environmental or situational factors have also traditionally been neglected.

A second problem associated with the methodology of risk assessment was the **criterion variable** (a variable predicted by a predictor variable; in this case, violent behavior), because studies define violence in a multitude of different ways. Violence often means different things to different researchers. In addition, a large portion of violent behavior may go undetected. For example, many previously hospitalized mental patients that demonstrate violent behavior in the community may be simply re-hospitalized rather than formally arrested. If the criterion variable is defined as "official arrest for violent behavior," then the re-hospitalized patients are likely to be overlooked since there was no official intervention by a law enforcement agency.

A third problem relates to the *research designs* used to test risk assessments. One of the major design problems, according to Monahan, is the selection of the sample. For example, some studies restrict their sample to males within the hospital setting, whereas others sample males in a decidedly different context, such as the community. Other studies sample only those subjects who have a history of violent actions, whereas others use a mixed pool of subjects consisting of both already-violent individuals and potentially-violent individuals. Thus, the ecological validity of many of the studies (i.e., the generalizability of results to other situations) is likely to be limited.

Finally, a fourth problem is that research efforts are *rarely synchronized and rarely replicated.* For example, Monahan notes that psychiatrists tend to favor one set of predictor variables, psychologists a second set, and sociologists a third. However, violence is a highly complex behavior that will require the coordinated efforts across many disciplines. Thus, future research in risk assessment should be collaborative, enabling researchers to pool large sources of data and perform elaborate and meaningful statistical analyses.

MacArthur Violence Risk Assessment Study

The MacArthur Violence Risk Assessment Study represents a major ongoing effort to address the methodological problems summarized above. The study (Monahan, Steadman, Silver, et al., 2001; Steadman, Mulvey, Monahan, et al., 1998) has focused on acute civil psychiatric patients at three different sites. Of a total of 12,873 patients admitted in the study period, 1,136 volunteers were ultimately included in the research. Participants were white, African-American, and Hispanic persons 18–40 years old. Extensive data on demographic and historical factors were collected and diagnoses were recorded. Researchers confirmed the medical record diagnoses in 86% of the cases, and the remainder were eventually agreed upon with the help of a consulting psychiatrist.

During hospitalization, the subjects were measured on 134 wide-ranging risk factors. These included factors such as frequency of abuse as a child, frequency of parents fighting with each other, persecutory delusions, violent fantasies, suicide attempts, drug use, number of people in social network, number of negative and positive persons in social network, and homelessness. The patients were then followed after discharge from the institution. Community interviews with the discharged patients were conducted every 10 weeks for a one-year period. Collateral informants, nominated by the patient, were also interviewed. Steadman et al. (1998) reported that 50% of the patients completed all five follow-up interviews, and 84% completed at least one. During the interviews, patients and informants were asked whether and how often the patient had engaged in any of eight categories of aggressive behavior over the past 10 weeks. The categories were based on the Conflict Tactics Scale (Straus & Gelles, 1990), and its expansion (Lidz, Mulvey, & Gardner, 1993).

A key premise of the study was the superiority of actuarial over clinical assessments of risk. The MacArthur researchers hypothesized that the risk factors measured while the patients were in the institution would help predict their level of violence once discharged. Thus, the study had two core goals: "to do the best 'science' on violence risk assessment possible and to produce a violence risk assessment 'tool' that clinicians in today's world of managed mental health services could actually use" (Monahan et al., 2001, p. 9). Without such assistance, Monahan and his colleagues stated, the ability of clinicians to predict violence was "modest at best" (p. 13).

The tool that was ultimately produced over a 10-year period was the *Multiple ICT (Iterative Classification Tree)* described earlier, in ◀ Chapter 2. It places people in 12 different risk groups, 6 low risk, 4 high risk, and 2 average risk. For purposes of developing the tool, 939 of the patients were analyzed (those who completed at least one of the first two follow-up interviews administered 10 and 20 weeks after discharge). Almost half of the 939 were in the low risk group, with the other half of the subjects almost evenly divided between high (27.4%) and average (23.4%) risk.

Of primary importance was the finding that no single risk factor, standing alone, was a significant predictor of violence. Furthermore, no single risk factor had to be present for the individual to demonstrate violent behavior. "Our data are most consistent with the view that the propensity for violence is the result of the accumulation of risk factors, no one of which is either necessary or sufficient for a person to behave aggressively toward others. People will be violent by virtue of the presence of different sets of risk factors. There is no single path in a person's life that leads to an act of violence" (Monahan et al., 2001, p. 142).

Using data from the MacArthur study, Skeem and Mulvey (2001) did try to investigate the strength of one particular variable, however. Specifically, they were curious about the relationship between psychopathy and violence, with psychopathy assessed with the PCL:SV. The PCL and PCL–R were normed on criminal samples, and most of the research has been performed on prisoners, including sex offenders and mentally disordered offenders. Skeem and Mulvey wanted to extend the inquiry to civil psychiatric samples, using the PCL:SV developed by Hart, Cox, and Hare (1995) for psychopathy in noncriminal settings. Prior archival research (Douglas et al., 1999) had found the PCL:SV to be a moderate predictor of violence among civilly committed populations. The Skeem and Mulvey study used interviewers who had completed a full day of training conducted by Stephen Hart and Robert Hare. The PCL:SV was then completed based on interviews with patients and reviews of official records. Only 8% of the study participants were classified as psychopathic (with 22% as "potentially psychopathic"). Despite the low base rate, the researchers found the PCL:SV to be a relatively strong predictor of violence, although the predictive power decreased when researchers controlled for covariates such as recent violence, criminal history, substance abuse, and other personality disorders. Even after statistically controlling for these, however, the PCL:SV improved the prediction of violence. Finally, the predictive power was based principally on the Antisocial Behavior factor in the two-factor model of psychopathy (Skeem & Mulvey, 2001). It should be noted, also, that the violence predicted was serious; "the PCL:SV performed no better than chance in predicting acts of aggression that did not result in injury" (Skeem & Mulvey, 2001, p. 371). Skeem and Mulvey, like the MacArthur researchers as a group, note that no single measure of violence risk should be used to the exclusion of other considerations. Nevertheless, they see the PCL:SV as a promising tool for use by professionals working with civilly committed populations.

Grave Disability

The dangerousness standard, while deserving continued research, cannot overshadow the problems posed by the "grave disability standard." Under grave disability, individuals are judged according to whether they are able to care for themselves and meet their basic needs. This type of standard is increasingly used for involuntary commitment in states.

Turkheimer and Parry (1992) posit that, while studies of prediction of dangerousness abound in the literature, studies of the prediction of the inability to care for oneself have not been undertaken. Wexler and Winick (1991), however, suggested that this may not be crucial, because grave disability statutes generally require proof of actual inability to care for oneself, not presumed or predicted inability. In other words, if a person is committed under a grave disability statute, the law is not predicting that he or she will not be able to care for self; evidence of this inability is available. The law in operation might be quite different from the law on the books. Warren (1977) studied the cases of 100 persons committed to mental institutions in California under both grave disability and dangerousness standards. Although the grave disability statute required a demonstration that the individual was unable to care for him or herself, Warren learned that individuals were committed without such demonstration. Instead, they were committed on the basis of medical conclusions that took into account refusal to take medicine, a prior hospitalization record, a tendency to deny mental illness to the psychiatrist and not to cooperate with mental health personnel, and the amount of rejection expressed by the patient's family. Many of the criteria used to arrive at grave disability were also used as a basis for dangerousness. In almost all the cases, there was a notable failure by the court and the medical expert to try to ascertain the imminence and seriousness of danger to others. Warren (1977) also noted that in a majority of cases, the initial finding of dangerousness to others was replaced by grave disablement for *continued* commitment. Turkheimer and Parry (1992) report that this is a common finding in the research on civil commitment proceedings. In other words, recommitment hearings involve significantly less stringent requirements than initial hearings.

Some research suggests that grave disability is being used more and more as a standard for commitment, and most particularly re-commitment. Pokorny, Shull, and Nicholson (1999), studying commitments and extended commitments of 490 patients, found that dangerousness followed by disability were the critical variables accounting for *initial admission*. For the re-commitment or *extended commitment* process, however, the patient's degree of disability played a more important role than dangerousness. The decision to continue the commitment was also influenced by the age and gender of the patient, and by education and veteran status. Specifically, older males were most likely to be re-committed, while persons with higher education and/or veteran status were least likely. The researchers noted that veterans were eligible for follow-up treatment at a Veterans Administration facility, which could have explained the significance of this factor.

Other aspects of grave disability commitments may be more troublesome than the prediction of behavior. Least restrictive alternatives (alternatives that are less restrictive than hospitalization), for example, seem especially warranted for individuals who are not committed under a dangerousness standard, yet this element of civil commitment is often ignored. Wexler (1990a) also notes that grave disability statutes sometimes allow commitment for a longer period of time than dangerousness statutes.

Research reveals that about one-quarter of the estimated 1.2 million civil commitments each year are involuntary commitments (Monahan & Shah, 1989), but we must always keep in mind the limitations of the voluntary/involuntary dichotomy. Although there are no national data on the standard by which patients are involuntarily committed, researchers have examined this in specific jurisdictions. Thus, Monahan, Ruggerio, and Friedlander (1982) found that 70% of patients civilly committed in California were evaluated as dangerous to themselves, 29% as dangerous to others, and 43% as gravely disabled. One-third of these individuals met two or more of the standards during their commitment evaluation. In another California study, Segal et al. (1988) reported that 60% of the patients involuntarily committed were assessed as dangerous to themselves, 49% as dangerous to others, and 32% as gravely disabled. Again, many of the commitments satisfied at least two of the dangerousness or gravely disabled standards.

In recent years, several commentators have noticed a trend toward more flexible standards for involuntary civil commitment, providing states with more power over the lives of the mentally disordered (Litwack & Schlesinger, 1999; Morse, 1998; McAllister, 1998). This power is particularly evident in the case of sex offenders (Janus & Meehl, 1997). The U.S. Supreme Court's own pronouncements on this issue, in *Kansas v. Hendricks* (1997) and *Kansas v. Crane* (2002), will be discussed later in the chapter. Even in cases that did not involve criminal activity, courts seem to have given leeway to those who seek the commitment, although seeking a less restrictive alternative is still necessary. In a recent case, *Olmstead v. L.C.* (1999), the Supreme Court ruled 6–3 that institutionalized individuals with mental disabilities had a qualified right under the *Americans with Disabilities Act* to a community placement rather than an institutional setting. They should be allowed to be in the community as long as they wished to be and treatment professionals indicated that community placement was appropriate. The case involved two women who were both mentally retarded and diagnosed with mental disorders. They had voluntarily committed themselves to a psychiatric facility but later sought to be released and treated in a community setting. Their request was supported by their treatment providers. The State of Georgia maintained that it did not have the financial resources to accomplish this. The Court majority ruled that unjustified segregation of people with mental disabilities was discriminatory treatment in violation of the law. A state's financial and program resources could be taken into consideration in deciding whether community care was an option, but the state would have to prove to the satisfaction of a court that it would be unreasonable to provide community treatment. The Court also encouraged states to develop and provide a range of community treatment options, although it did not go so far as to say that the right to be treated in the community was a constitutional right.

When treatment providers believe institutionalization is warranted, particularly to protect the community from harm, however, the courts typically accept their judgement over the wishes of the individual to be free. In *U.S. v. Sahhar* (1990), for example, a federal court of appeals ruled that an extended civil commitment could be based on any activity that evinces a genuine possibility of future harm to persons or property. Courts also have ruled that commitment need not be based on *recent overt* acts or threats of violence or on *imminent* dangerousness (Litwack & Schlesinger, 1999).

Civil Commitment Proceedings

Although the law requires an adversarial hearing for civil commitment, hearings are often informal and hinge around opinions of medical or psychiatric practitioners, who may or may not be cross-examined. Family members, social workers, employers, or friends may also testify, but it is not uncommon for a judge to make a decision based solely on clinical testimony or written reports. In some jurisdictions, the affected person does not attend the hearing, under the rationale that his or her condition will be aggravated by the proceedings. In the Iowa study mentioned earlier, however (Stier & Stoebe, 1979), the researchers learned that adversary proceedings with the individual present did not upset the person. In general, despite conventional wisdom among some mental health practitioners that hearings are counter-therapeutic, there is no documentation to that effect. In fact, researchers are now beginning to explore the positive therapeutic effect of a civil commitment hearing (Ensminger & Liguori, 1990).

Despite the due process safeguards introduced to the civil commitment process in the 1970s, statutory requirements for involuntary civil commitments continue to be circumvented by judges, lawyers, and mental health professionals alike, much as they were in the Wisconsin and Iowa studies cited earlier in the chapter. Although research in some jurisdictions suggests that the civil commitment process operates smoothly and with careful attention to due process, the experiences of observers and a fair body of data indicate that this is not the norm (Appelbaum, 1992).

In a review of the literature on civil commitment proceedings, Turkheimer and Parry (1992) identified a litany of problems. Among them were the following:

- attorneys were poorly prepared and often did not perform adversarial roles;
- judges deferred to mental health recommendations or discouraged attorneys from questioning these witnesses;
- least restrictive alternatives to hospitalization were not considered;
- examinations were perfunctory or non-existent; and
- respondents were not advised of their rights, including rights to be represented by counsel.

In a similar review, Hiday (1988) took a more positive stance, concluding that the more flagrant abuses of the civil commitment process no longer occur systematically as they did before reform of civil commitment law. "While statutory definitions of dangerousness are not always explicit and often are vague, they do limit the number of candidates who are involuntarily hospitalized. And while the nonadversary nature and sometimes laxity of legal procedures may convey a sense of injustice, they do review petitioner allegations and hospital practice" (p. 37). She warns, however, that there are signs "the pendulum may be swinging away from protection of individual rights back to the old paternalism" (p. 37).

Parry and his colleagues (1991) found significant differences in procedures between initial or first-time commitments and re-commitments, and concluded that the law was circumvented particularly in the latter. For example, there was no adversarial questioning in 19% of the re-commitments, compared to 4% of initial commitments. Attorneys did not confer with their clients in 80% of the re-commitment hearings, compared to 40% in initial hearings. On average, the re-commitment hearings averaged 8 minutes in length; the initial commitment hearings 14 minutes. Earlier studies have reported commitment hearings lasting an average of 1.9 minutes (Cohen, 1966) to 18.4 minutes (Hiday, 1977). Recall that Pokorny et al. (1999) found that the re-commitment decision was strongly influenced by the degree of the patient's disability. Evidence of disability is undoubtedly easier to obtain when the patient has been under close observation as a result of the initial commitment; therefore, it is not surprising that these second hearings were less adversarial than the first hearings.

What explains this apparent lack of diligence in protecting the legal rights of persons facing involuntary commitment? Some scholars point to the twin failures of deinstitutionalization and community treatment. **Deinstitutionalization** refers to having patients cared for and treated outside the confines of traditional large institutions. The social policy of deinstitutionalization is now widely regarded as having displaced the mentally disordered from mental hospitals to urban "psychiatric ghettos," shelters for the homeless, and (depending on the strength of the criminalization thesis) to jails. According to Turkheimer and Parry (1992, p. 649) "the desultory performance of participants in civil commitment hearings may be related to the absence of less restrictive treatment alternatives . . . ." They note that attorneys representing civil commitment candidates may be afraid their clients will not get the help they need if they are not civilly committed. Furthermore, they may not want to appear socially irresponsible in arguing for the release of persons they believe unable to function on their own. As one attorney whose practice involves the frequent representation of civil commitment candidates has remarked, "There isn't much satisfaction walking out the door arm in arm with your free, but crazy, client."

Proposed Legal Models for Proceedings

Clearly, the adversarial model for civil commitment hearings has not been without its critics. Clinicians have pointed out that involuntary civil commitment hearings pit them against their patients, requiring them to testify against them in a formal proceeding. Additionally, the presumption that patients should not be committed, or should be released from temporary commitment, fails to recognize that numerous clients would benefit by the commitment. Yet there is a legitimate concern that some clinicians may fear the civil suits that could arise out of a "false negative" recommendation, specifically by falsely predicting that the individual will not be a danger and thereby does not need commitment. Clinicians are also more likely than the legal professionals to see a need for commitment when the individual seems to be unable to care for him or herself in the community (Poletiek, 2002). Although clinical recommendations are obviously needed, commitment decisions based exclusively on these recommendations—and most particularly on the recommendation of one clinician—are unwarranted. Proponents of the adversarial model argue that overcommitment is a far greater danger than undercommitment.

Some lawyers have preferred to adopt a "best interest" model of legal representation for clients with mental disabilities. Concerned that abiding by a client's expressed interest will ultimately lead to harm, these lawyers help clients get the help they would want if only they knew what was in their best interest. The "best interest" representation approach, not surprisingly, has been supported by clinicians that believe that this type of "paternalism" has an appropriate place in civil commitment hearings.

Janet Abisch (1995) has proposed a third legal model—a mediational model—that recognizes the therapeutic effects and avoids the anti-therapeutic effects of both the adversarial and best-interest model. In Abisch's scheme, specially-trained "mediational lawyers" would represent mentally disabled clients. In contrast to mediators in other civil contexts, they would not be neutral: the interests of their clients would be foremost. However, "Rather than merely advocating, at face value, the client's decision or deciding for themselves what the client's decision should be, mediational lawyers would work with the client, putting themselves in the client's position in order to learn as much as possible about the situation" (Abisch, 1995, p. 135).

Abisch summarizes the undesirable aspects of both adversarial and best-interest models. Adversarial proceedings are stressful to the mentally disabled, and thereby anti-therapeutic. They strain the relationship between legal and mental health professionals. They promote in the client a distrust of the mental health system, which may be generalized to future contacts with mental health agents. On the other hand, best-interest proceedings give too much deference to experts. They encourage lawyers to be guided by their own biases, play God, and to waive their client's rights. They also provide less incentive to solicit additional expert opinions, probe facts, and seek out alternative dispositions for their clients.

Procedural Justice in Proceedings

Psychologist Tom Tyler (1992) asserts that, regardless of the model used, it is essential that civil commitment hearings deliver **procedural justice**. Like all other court hearings, the civil commitment hearing should have the appearance of fairness, providing the individuals with dignity, a voice, and the potential for engendering trust in the system. Tyler hypothesizes that procedural justice in civil commitment hearings will lead to better treatment outcomes, regardless of the outcome of the hearing itself. Expanding upon Tyler's suggestion, Sydeman et al. (1997) warn that the interpersonal dynamics of those involved in the hearings must be studied. The behavior of judges, lawyers, and clinicians, for example, will likely have to change before procedural justice can be accomplished. Additionally, individuals who are the subjects of these proceedings may be either too suspicious of the motives of the state, too resistive to hospitalization, or too acutely disordered to process the information from the commitment hearing.

Some recent studies have suggested that respondents in civil commitment proceedings *can* discern aspects of procedural fairness, however. Greer, O'Regan, and Traverso (1996) interviewed psychiatric patients immediately following their commitment hearings and learned that these patients perceived most of the professionals, including their own lawyers, as disinterested. Their lawyers were thought to be trustworthy and respectful, however, while the judges, state attorneys, and testifying psychiatrists were believed to be lacking in respect for the respondent and not to be trusted.

Cascardi, Poythress, and Hall (2000) presented mock videotaped commitment hearings to 40 adult patients who had been committed involuntarily to a state civil psychiatric hospital in Florida. The participants were recruited for the study within 30 days of their admission. They viewed a positive procedural justice hearing, in which the respondent's participation was encouraged and his dignity was enhanced. All professionals involved treated the respondent with respect, were attentive, and took great care to explain the proceedings. The psychiatric patients in the study also viewed a negative procedural justice hearing, in which the same cast of characters acted quite differently. In this video, the professionals were distracted, impatient, and disinterested, and the respondent was not given the opportunity to participate meaningfully in the proceedings. The patients in the study viewed both the positive and the negative videos, with the order of presentation counterbalanced. Following the viewing of each video, the patients were asked to rate the behavior of the participants in the hearing and were given questionnaires designed to measure their perceptions of procedural justice. After they had viewed both videos and all other measures had been completed, they were asked about their attitudes toward medication and also asked to rate their own commitment hearing.

Results indicated clearly that the patients did indeed perceive differences between the positive and negative hearings, particularly when they viewed the positive hearing first. Interestingly, viewing the positive hearing first also resulted in a slightly less negative view of the negative hearing. In other words, there was a carry-over effect for the order of presentation of the videos. In actual civil commitment cases, this would suggest that a respondent's first experience with commitment proceedings has a carry-over effect to subsequent proceedings. Cascardi et al. were careful to note that patients in their study had obtained some treatment since admission, which might make them more sensitive to procedural justice signals. Additionally, the research did not address the practical effect of the perceptions. Are respondents who perceive that they were treated fairly more likely to cooperate with treatment than those who perceive that they were not? Although this may seem to be a logical conclusion, this is yet untested. Cascardi et al. mention a number of short-term and long-term outcomes that could potentially occur if patients perceive themselves as having been treated fairly, including enhanced feelings of self-worth, participation in unit activities, compliance with medication, compliance with aftercare, and reduction in recommitment. "It remains for further research to establish which of, and to what degree, these clinical outcomes may be impacted by procedural justice enhancements" (Cascardi et al., 2000, p. 740).

The MacArthur Coercion Study

If an individual perceives that he or she has been treated fairly, it is unlikely that he or she will feel pressured or forced to accept treatment. Does empirical research support this assumption? Recent research, again under the auspices of the MacArthur Foundation, allows us to address this question.

In the 1990s, the MacArthur Research Network conducted a series of studies designed to provide information on the appropriate role of coercion in mental health treatment (Monahan, Lidz, Hoge, et al., 1999). They note that there has been a longstanding debate between clinicians and family members on the one hand, and patients and their advocates on the other, pitting the need for treatment against the desire for autonomy and freedom. MacArthur researchers wished to study the extent to which perceived coercion actually exists; ultimately, they hoped to find a link between perceived coercion and treatment outcomes. Studies in the 1990s gathered information from patients themselves (e.g., Hoge et al., 1997); compared the perceptions of patients, families, and staff (e.g., Hoge et al., 1993; Lidz et al., 1995); and empirically tested a "Perceived Coercion Scale," which was added to the risk assessment battery discussed earlier in this chapter (Gardner et al., 1993).

The following four key findings from the above studies are stated in the Executive Summary (2001):

- Legal status (voluntary vs. involuntary admission) is only a "blunt index" of coercion, since a significant minority of voluntary patients believe they were forced to admit themselves, and a significant minority of involuntary patients believe they freely chose to be hospitalized.
- Patients' accounts of events prior to their hospitalization were as plausible as the accounts of their families and clinicians. However, some patients' views of the need for hospitalization changed over time, with about half of those who initially denied a need for hospitalization acknowledging the need in retrospect.
- The *kind* of pressure applied to the individual is significant. Patients perceive less coercion if pressure is positive (e.g., persuasion) rather than negative (e.g., threats).
- The *amount* of coercion perceived by the patient is strongly related to his or her perception of procedural justice. If patients believed that others treated them with genuine concern and respect, they were less likely to feel coerced. This was true for both voluntary and involuntary patients. On the whole, patients perceived less procedural justice in their admission process than the families or clinicians reported.

As noted by the MacArthur researchers, " 'Coercion' as a field of research in mental health law has come of age" (Executive Summary, p. 3). Continuing research in this area will now focus on the prevalence and determinants of coercion in a wide range of contexts, including both institutional and community treatment. Researchers also have extended coercion studies to criminal justice settings (see, e.g., Farabee, 2002b). A topic of critical importance for future research will be not only defining coercion but also studying its effect on treatment outcomes.

Duty to Warn and/or Protect

Another factor relevant to civil commitment and not yet discussed in this chapter is the concern that a therapist's client may pose a danger to identifiable individuals in the community. In some jurisdictions, mental health practitioners can be held liable for not warning potential victims of violence at the hands of their patients (Gutheil & Appelbaum, 2000). Appelbaum (1992) finds that the advent of these legal rules has left mental health practitioners in a quandary and may even prompt the overuse of the civil commitment process. The leading case on this issue is *Tarasoff v. Regents of the University of California* (1974, 1976). The California Supreme Court first held that, in certain circumstances, when a therapist determines that a patient is a serious danger to another, the therapist has a **duty to warn** the intended victim that he or she may be in danger. Two years later, the court redefined the clinician's duty as a **duty to protect**. The difference is an important one, because protection need not require notification to the intended victim, but it does require active steps on the part of the clinician. For example, depending on the situation, the clinician might warn the potential victim or others who might be able to warn the victim, notify law enforcement, or pursue hospitalization or other intervention (Borum & Reddy, 2001). Despite the change in wording, the element of warning someone remained (Gutheil, 2001).

Subsequent decisions from other jurisdictions differed widely in the interpretation of *Tarasoff*. Some courts extended its reach, some restricted it, and others declined to follow it altogether (Perlin, 1991). The decade of the 1980s was one in which the doctrine was widely applied, while the 1990s saw an interesting trend of rejecting or severely limiting the doctrine in many states (Felthous, 2001). By 2001, legislatures of 22 states had codified the therapist's duty to protect and outlined the discharge of that duty (Walcott, Cerundolo, & Beck, 2001). Most of these statutes trigger a duty to protect only if there is a clearly identifiable potential victim or if there is a very serious threat to public safety as a result of the patient's potential violence. The statutes also protect therapists from liability if they have taken reasonable steps to protect. Court decisions and statutes also vary widely in whether they require that clinicians warn identifiable third parties or control the potentially violent behavior of their patients, such as by hospitalization (Felthous & Kachigian, 2001). Obviously, it is critical that clinicians be aware of how the law is applied in the states in which they practice. ◙ **Box 5-2** provides examples of cases from various jurisdictions in which clinicians allegedly failed to warn or protect individuals in danger from their clients.

In spite of these different legal standards within jurisdictions, many practitioners have interpreted the "spirit" of *Tarasoff* as a national standard of practice. That is, it is the professional responsibility of the clinician to take reasonable steps to protect a "reasonably identifiable victim" (and in some jurisdictions the duty is expanded to include even non-identifiable victims) from serious threats from their clients. Litwack and Schlesinger (1999, p. 195) conclude that one component of the duty to protect is "the duty to conduct a professionally adequate risk assessment when such an assessment is called for." In a different vein, Wexler and Winick (1991) have suggested that in some situations the duty to protect might be turned into a therapeutic tool with potential beneficial effects. If the clinician warns the person allegedly in danger, this might result in joint therapy that contributes significantly to a patient's treatment. Perlin (1991) maintains that mental health practitioners have learned to live with *Tarasoff* and have found sensitive solutions for dealing with the requirements of that case.

According to Appelbaum (1992), however, *Tarasoff*-like requirements offer a strong incentive to practitioners to seek to commit patients who present some risk of violence, even though they are not likely to benefit from hospitalization or do not meet commitment criteria. It is widely believed that these laws have had the unanticipated effect of encouraging practitioners to overpredict dangerous behavior (Turkheimer & Parry, 1992), although there is little direct empirical evidence to support this.

Tarasoff-like requirements also pose some ethical problems for clinicians. Gutheil (2001) notes that a duty to warn is especially problematic. "The question of warning a potential victim of possible harm at the hands of one's patient poses fundamental moral questions about the relationship between the clinician, the patient, and the larger society" (2001, p. 352). The breach of confidentiality is of particular concern. Additionally, however, warning a potential victim might also create havoc in that person's life and would often serve only to increase anxiety. Gutheil recounts an anecdote that did not involve one of his own patients. After being warned by a clinician, a potential victim called police, who could do nothing because the patient had not acted. He then considered and rejected a variety of options including hiring bodyguards, leaving town, and purchasing a handgun. The warning, Gutheil concluded, served only to increase the anxiety of the potential victim.

Appelbaum (1992) also suggests that many practitioners sincerely believe that deeply held values of the mental health profession to provide treatment cannot give way to the goals of the justice system, which are to resolve disputes, impose punishment, protect public safety, and maintain procedural fairness. While recognizing that these are legitimate and important goals, Appelbaum adds that "Conspicuous by its absence in this list . . . is any reference to affording treatment—at a minimum,

BOX 5-2
Select Duty-to-Warn Cases in State Courts and Lower Federal Courts

***Currie v. United States* (1987)**
4th Circuit Court of Appeals
Brief facts: A veteran suffering from Post-Traumatic Stress Disorder threatened to blow up IBM. His therapists at the Veterans Administration (VA) urged him to commit himself; he agreed but did not follow through. VA doctors warned IBM, police, and a variety of other officials. The veteran shot and killed an IBM worker.

Question: Does a psychotherapist have a duty to commit in addition to a duty to warn?

Answer: No. Imposing a duty to commit would violate patient-therapist confidentiality and would also threaten the liberty interest of the patient.

***Estate of Davis v. Yong-Oh Lhim* (1987)**
Michigan Supreme Court
Brief facts: A man discharged from a mental institution shot and killed his mother. The hospital record included no evidence of a threat of violence, with the exception of a brief oral comment made by the man during emergency admission two years earlier.

Question: Can a therapist be sued for "negligent discharge" from a mental hospital for failing to predict violence and failing to warn a potential victim?

Answer: No. The court held that government-employed mental health professionals were immune from tort liability in this situation. The court did not decide whether there was a duty to warn in the state.

***Hedlund v. Superior Court of Orange County* (1983)**
California Supreme Court
Brief facts: A man and woman were being seen in treatment. The man threatened to harm the woman, and the therapist—in accordance with *Tarasoff*—warned her. The man then ran the woman and her son off the road and shot her.

Question: Did the therapist also have the duty to warn of danger to a "foreseeable bystander"—in this case, the son?

Answer: Yes. The court held that the therapist owed a duty to both the woman and the son, because the injury to the son was foreseeable and children are not usually far from their parents.

***Menendez v. State of California* (1992)**
Supreme Court of California
Brief facts: The Menendez brothers, accused of killing their parents, had made statements to psychotherapists. They argued that this was privileged communication, but an appeals court found that considerable material was not privileged under the "dangerous patient exception" (relating to *Tarasoff* duty to warn).

Question: Does patient-therapist confidentiality lose its privileged status once the patient makes a credible threat and once a patient-therapist relationship is terminated?

Answer: No. Some communication does lose its privilege, but only that in which the patient makes actual threats. The court declined to extend *Tarasoff* requirements broadly.

***Williamson v. Liptzin* (2000)**
North Carolina Court of Appeals
Brief facts: A student was treated at a university health center. At the end of the school year, he was sent home with a supply of medication and advised to get follow-up care. Eight months later he shot and killed several people. He was later found NGRI, sued the psychiatrist, and won.

Question: Should the law of proximate causation be extended in this situation to allow liability in this case?

Answer: Pending.

***Peck v. Addison County* (1984)**
Vermont Supreme Court
Brief facts: A patient had, on several occasions, warned his therapist that he planned to set fire to his neighbor's barn. Apparently because there was no threat of violence against an individual, the therapist did not notify the neighbor. Additionally, until that time there was no duty to warn in the state.

Question: Does the duty to warn extend to the duty to warn of threats to property?

Answer: Yes. The court established a duty to warn and held that it extended to serious threats to property.

hospitalization—to persons afflicted with severe mental illness" (Appelbaum, 1992, p. 66).

He argues that neither the justice system nor the mental health system is truly committed to the goals of civil commitment. He envisions, therefore, the creation of a third, independent system whose mission it would be to oversee the commitment process and which would assume all of the responsibilities now assigned to the mental health and justice systems. Some of its features would include clinicians extensively trained not only in evaluation but also in the law; hearing officers with specialized training in clinical and legal aspects of mental disorder; and vigorous advocates for each side. The primary loyalty of all, however, would be the implementation of the civil commitment statute.

Families and Civil Commitment

In the 1960s, psychiatrist Thomas Szasz (1960, 1968) argued forcefully that "mental illness" was a myth perpetuated and supported by his own profession. Although he did not deny the presence of psychological disorder in some individuals, he resisted labeling it as a disease. This disease model enabled the medical profession to control the assessment, care, and disposition of those whom it chose to label "mentally ill." Persons whose behavior or thinking processes were considered deviant could too readily be deprived of their civil liberties through involuntary hospitalization and the coercive techniques that accompanied this restriction on freedom. Drug therapy, electroconvulsive therapy, and psychosurgery—common approaches to treatment at that time—were unwarranted intrusions in the lives of many individuals who had had the misfortune of being placed in mental institutions. Szasz also suggested that psychiatry itself had developed as a tool for ridding people of troublesome family members.

Early studies examining the civil commitment process did indeed find evidence of rejection of the patient by family members. The unavailability or unwillingness of family members to take responsibility for disordered individuals was an implicit criterion for commitment. Warren (1977) found that the family, directly or indirectly, was the source of almost half of the commitments in her sample of California commitments. Stone (1975, p. 46), similar to Szasz, referred to the convenience function, the practice of warehousing one or more family members considered bothersome. He noted that this function had "seldom been explicitly acknowledged, rather it has been hidden behind a promise of technical treatment, although at some points during the past century it has been the only goal actually achieved" (p. 46). Stone added that this convenience function was a "typical instance of the clandestine decision making role of mental health practitioners which allows society to do what it does not want to admit to doing, i.e., confining unwanted persons cheaply."

The restrictive civil commitment statutes that began to emerge in the 1970s placed limitations on warehousing, especially with reference to large public institutions. According to some observers, the "warehousing" function has all but disappeared (Hiday, 1988). Interestingly, many observers are now noting that in some states, community-care homes have taken over the convenience function. On a more positive front, however, later research began to indicate that family members do believe they are acting in the best interest of their loved one when seeking institutionalization and perceive procedural justice in the commitment process (Hoge et al., 1993; Lidz et al., 1995). Moreover, families are increasingly serving as caregivers for the mentally disordered who remain in the community, and they should be given more support by the mental health system (Petrila, 1992). Just as significantly, families and friends have been found to provide needed social support for involuntary civil committees after their release back into the community (Hiday & Scheid-Cook, 1987). It is unfair to families of civil committees, therefore, to portray them as operating in collusion with coercive agents of government and against the interest of their mentally-disordered relatives.

Another consideration, however, is the possibly dysfunctional interaction between the person facing civil commitment and his or her family. Literature on mental disorder is increasingly urging therapists to take the family system into consideration and recognize that positive change is less likely to occur when the individual is isolated from her or his social system. Some persons faced with civil commitment may come from dysfunctional families. As Ensminger and Liguori (1990, p. 259) have noted, "the patient may just be the individual manifesting the most bizarre behavior of a maladaptation of the whole family unit." In a similar fashion, Wexler (1990a) notes that grave disability laws that require evidence of inability to care for oneself can be used by therapists to help a possibly dysfunctional family. The family members must "do something," create challenges for the individual, and urge the individual to take steps toward improving his or her life. "The very process of gathering evidence of a person's committability under a libertarian law may operate therapeutically to render commitment unnecessary!" (p. 184).

Up to this point, we have given little attention to two topics that are crucial to the broad issue of civil commitment. First, what alternatives to institutionalization are possible and what is the likelihood that these alternatives will be effective? Second, what is the role of the psychologist or other mental health practitioner in the treatment process? Put another way, what types of treatment are available to the mentally disordered, both in institutions and under care in community settings? Closely associated with these topics is the mentally-disordered individual's ability to consent to treatment, along with his or her right to receive it and refuse it.

Outpatient Treatment Orders

An undetermined number of individuals who go through civil commitment proceedings are not institutionalized, but rather are "committed" to outpatient treatment, which represents a less restrictive alternative to institutionalization. Such involuntary outpatient treatment also may be ordered as a transitional move for persons discharged from an institution. Rather than given outright release, the individual is assigned to a supervisory status whereby behavior can be monitored and community treatment can be provided. Psychotherapy offered in a community setting or on an outpatient basis has been found to be far more effective than that provided in a hospital or institutional setting (see, generally, Ennis & Litwak, 1974, p. 718, note 80).

As noted earlier in the chapter, dangerousness is one of the factors scrutinized in deciding whether to issue an outpatient order (Swartz et al., 1999). In deciding upon outpatient treatment, some degree of dangerousness to self (and sometimes others) may be present, but presumably not to the extent that institutionalization is warranted. The individual under involuntary outpatient treatment is often ordered to take medication and to attend counseling or therapy sessions, both delivered at a local mental health center or other outpatient clinic (Lickey & Gordon, 1991). Depending upon the location, crisis stabilization units may also be available, in the event that the person suffers a brief relapse and needs temporary crisis care. The outpatient order may or may not include an alternate living arrangement for the person, such as placement in a halfway house or group home.

Studies demonstrate that persons treated in the community recover faster, have fewer relapses, deteriorate less from dependency fostered by hospitalization, maintain employment better, and cost the state about half as much money as similar patients treated in hospitals. As noted earlier, however, the concentrated effort in the 1970s to shift from an institutional to a community model has not been totally successful, often because community resources were not made available. Furthermore, to achieve maximum effectiveness, outpatient programs should be longer in duration, spanning years rather than months (Durham & La Fond, 1990).

Researchers have begun to give considerable attention to this alternative to involuntary institutionalization. Hiday and Scheid-Cook (1987, 1989) contend that outpatient treatment orders are particularly appropriate for the chronic mentally ill who would otherwise be caught in the "revolving door" of hospitalization, release, and rehospitalization. Hiday and Scheid-Cook did an extensive 6-month follow-up study of 1,266 adults who had gone through civil commitment hearings in North Carolina. Persons committed to outpatient treatment, compared to those who had been institutionalized and then released, were more likely to be working, to have maintained contact with community mental health centers, and to have more social contacts at the end of a 6-month follow-up period. Swanson et al. (1999, 2001) studied individuals with both arrest and hospitalization histories who had serious mental disorders but were assigned to involuntary outpatient treatment. One in five were arrested over a 1-year period. However, extended outpatient commitments significantly reduced the probability of arrest. Patients on extended commitments had only a 12% probability of arrest, while those on brief commitments had close to a 50% probability. The lengthy commitment was considered important because it was more likely to improve medication compliance and reduce the incidence of substance abuse. Both substance abuse and lack of compliance with medication have been identified in other research as factors that limit the effectiveness of involuntary outpatient treatment and are associated with offending by persons with serious mental disorders (Bonta, Law, & Hanson, 1998; Borum et al., 1997, 1998).

Numerous researchers and commentators have called for greater use of outpatient treatment orders. Over a decade ago, Turkheimer and Parry (1992) contended that states should not only be required to investigate such less restrictive alternatives, but also to demonstrate their absence. Doing so, they argued, would highlight the lack of effective community treatment outside the hospitalization setting, making it more difficult to ignore this problem. To some extent this call has been heeded, since outpatient treatment orders are enabled by statute in at least 38 states and the District of Columbia (Swanson et al., 2001; Torrey & Kaplan, 1995). Recall, also, that the Supreme Court ruled in *Olmstead v. L.C.* (1999) that the disabled have a right to community treatment, if such treatment is not therapeutically contra-indicated and can reasonably be provided. As a result of that case, it is likely that the remaining states will fall into line.

Development of more community treatment options will not be enough to solve the problems of mentally-disordered individuals, however. Although outpatient treatment appears to be a better alternative than the traditional inpatient treatment offered in institutions, there are clearly problems associated with it. "In some states that have experimented with outpatient commitment, treatment has been imposed on unwilling patients in a more authoritarian and paternalistic manner than is allowed for hospital treatment" (Lickey & Gordon, 1991, p. 376).

A widely-voiced criticism of outpatient treatment is its reliance on pharmacotherapy (Davis, 1976) which is often lauded by the psychiatric profession as the most effective way to deal with many mental disorders. Drugs are available for persons diagnosed with schizophrenia, anxiety, depression, panic disorders, phobias, and obsessive compulsive disorders, to name but a few (Julien, 1992; Lickey & Gordon, 1991). Although institutionalized patients also routinely receive drug therapy, they ironically have more right to refuse it than those in the community, whose freedom may be contingent upon their willingness to "take their meds."

The development of "depot" forms of psychoactive drugs (**depot drugs**), in which the drug is suspended in a medium that the body absorbs slowly, has been considered a great breakthrough by community psychiatrists (Ayd, 1975). When given by injection, the drugs may continue to exert their effect for several weeks and, with technological advances, for months or potentially even years. Depot drugs are especially useful for patients who resist taking medication on a regular basis. Ayd (1975, p. 491) noted that injectable, long-acting drugs were "a most important step forward" because they "remove responsibility for taking medicine from patients unable to assume it."

Supporters of the medical model approach to treatment argue that, when used judiciously and for specified disorders, psychoactive drugs are remarkably successful and side effects can be minimized. Most importantly, they argue, the drugs relieve suffering. According to the medical model, "psychiatric illnesses are similar in important respects to illnesses treated in general medicine. Both types of illness are thought to result from physiological malfunction that leads to the patient's distress and disability" (Lickey & Gordon, 1991, p. 353). Durham and La Fond (1990), after reviewing research studies on the efficacy of various treatment modes, conclude that administering drugs to the mentally disordered as a group is better than doing nothing at all. They note that it is has not been established, however, that drug treatment is effective for patients involuntarily hospitalized.

The other side of the coin is that the various forms of drug treatment for mental disorders have serious limitations (Groves & Schlesinger, 1979). In most cases they merely alleviate some of the symptoms, and drug withdrawal can result in relapses without significant changes in the disordered behavior.

Continuous treatment with drugs can also produce numerous serious side effects (Groves & Schlesinger, 1979). Brooks (1987) describes a range of physical, emotional, cognitive, and social side effects associated with psychoactive medication. The worst is tardive dyskinesia, an irreversible condition for which there is no known cure. Tardive dyskinesia "is a physical disablement manifested by grotesque movements of the face, tongue, mouth, and limbs" (p. 250). It appears to be particularly a risk for long-term chronic patients on psychoactive drugs. Nevertheless, it is clear from the literature that "some drugs are powerfully effective in relieving the symptoms of psychotic disorders" (Harris & Rice, 1994, p. 23).

Moreover, even proponents of drug therapy warn that it should be accompanied by psychotherapy to teach cognitive and social skills and help individuals cope with problems of living (Lickey & Gordon, 1991). As Harris and Rice (1994, p. 23) note, "drug treatment cannot represent a complete solution to the difficulties experienced by persons diagnosed with mental disorders." The extent to which additional help is offered is unknown, but trends in community mental health treatment suggest that a broad approach is being taken (Roesch, 1995; Wettstein, 1998). In fact, community psychology tends to shy away from a focus exclusively on the individual and individual deficits; rather, it tries to capitalize on a person's strengths and to identify factors within the environment that have an impact on behavior, including disordered behavior. The model of community psychology is one that advocates social change (Roesch, 1995). For in the absence of such interventions, drug treatment may well foster a life-long dependency on medication without addressing other root causes of mental disorder.

Fortunately, community treatment for the mentally disordered has progressed far beyond exclusive reliance on psychoactive drugs. Additionally, more sophisticated drugs have limited the previously inevitable negative side effects. Heilbrun and Griffin (1999), reviewing a range of institutional and community treatment for forensic populations, have distinguished among *traditional, contemporary*, and *targeted* services. Although they do not include the involuntary civilly committed who are the topic of the present chapter in this assessment, the distinctions among the types of treatment apply to them as well. Medication, case management, and group and individual therapy belong to the traditional category. Contemporary treatment, by contrast, includes psychoeducational, skills-based services and behavioral interventions "that have become increasingly well regarded during the last 10 years in the United States" (Heilbrun & Griffin, 1999, p. 243). Targeted services are those designed to address specific functional deficits relevant to legal standards. In the case of a person committed for outpatient treatment, a targeted service might be anger management if he has been assessed at moderate risk for violence.

It is clear that some communities are making considerable positive strides in providing effective community treatment for the mentally disordered. Much of the literature to date focuses on forensic populations, such as individuals found NGRI or offenders on probation or parole (see Heilbrun & Griffin, 1999, and Harris & Rice, 1994, for reviews). Because they have been charged with crimes or convicted of crimes, their presumed threat to the community is greater than the threat posed by the non-criminal mentally-disordered individual. Nonetheless, research attention has also been directed at the latter group, particularly within the subfield of community psychology.

Institutional Treatment

Historical accounts of treatment in mental institutions are replete with illustrations of neglect or inhumane practices. The egregious living conditions in many of these institutions have been liberally documented (e.g., Rothman, 1971, 1980). It is generally acknowledged, also, that the dominant philosophy in mental institutions was based upon warehousing rather than treating the mentally disordered. Physical interventions, however, were not uncommon. During the eugenics movement of the 1920s and 1930s, for example, mentally disordered and defective individuals were often sterilized, a practice upheld by the U.S. Supreme Court (*Buck v. Bell*, 1927). Another not uncommon physical intervention was the involuntary frontal lobotomy, used to "cure" a range of mental disorders, from sexual deviance to psychosis (Groves & Schlesinger, 1979).

As more experience with this surgical procedure was gained, it became apparent that early reports of success were exaggerated and misleading. In many patients, the extensive destruction of the frontal lobes did not result in improvement, and in some patients with psychosis the condition was made worse (Freeman & Watts, 1942). Many disturbing side effects were noted several months after surgery, often involving substantial changes in personality and moods (Groves & Schlesinger, 1979). Studies also demonstrated that adequately matched lobectomized patients and non-operated-upon control patients showed no differences in improvement when rate of discharge from mental hospitals was used as a criterion of improvement (Robin & McDonald, 1975).

The gross psychosurgical techniques reported in the earlier years of psychiatry then gave way to the more refined methods of stereotaxic surgery, where minute electrodes could be placed into various parts of the brain with precision. Electrical current or chemicals could then be directed at different "centers" of the brain responsible for a wide assortment of behaviors. This form of surgery was hailed as being able to control a wide variety of thought processes, behaviors, and feelings (Mark & Ervin, 1970). However, many claims were overstated (Valenstein, 1973), and stereotaxic surgery, widely regarded as a radical and unacceptable effort at thought control, did not survive in the U.S.

Similar to community treatment, medication has long been the dominant treatment approach in most mental institutions and for a great majority of patients (Durham & La Fond, 1990). When possible, this traditional treatment was accompanied by family therapy. In recent years, however, other treatment approaches have been taken, including cognitive restructuring, biofeedback, substance abuse treatment, and retraining in attention and memory for neurologically-impaired individuals (Heilbrun & Griffin, 1999). Julien (1992) notes that in 1955, over half a million persons in the United States were residing in state mental hospitals. By 1983, that figure had been reduced by about half, even though admissions to state hospitals doubled. This shift reflects the quick turnover made possible by the uses of psychoactive drugs which enabled hospital staffs to stabilize the mentally disordered and send them back into the community in relatively short time.

Many commentators have been extremely pessimistic about the likelihood of achieving long lasting, positive change as a result of institutional treatment, particularly when individuals are committed involuntarily. As we noted, however, perceived coercion is emerging as a more significant variable than legal status. Durham and La Fond (1990, p. 135) write that although "thousands of research studies" have examined treatment efficacy, "The scientific worth of the empirical evidence in this area is seriously flawed because it does not meet the standard criteria for empirical evidence." They also add, "Virtually no well designed studies have evaluated whether or not psychotherapy is effective in treating mentally ill patients confined against their will to public psychiatric hospitals for treatment" (p. 148). Durham and La Fond (1990) add that even if psychotherapy were found effective, it is an impractical undertaking given the limited staff, time, and other resources available to mental institutions.

However, others are more sanguine about the quality of treatment available in such settings, and suggest that even involuntary confinement can lead to voluntary treatment, which has the highest likelihood of a successful outcome. Conventional wisdom has long held that patients cannot be "coerced" to change; that effective treatment is possible only if the individual wishes to be treated. In the last quarter of the 20th century, however, some research began to challenge this assumption, with studies in some areas (e.g., substance abuse) indicating that clients who were coerced to participate did as well or better than those who voluntarily received treatment (Farabee, 2002b). But this research has not been unequivocal, leading contemporary researchers to try to sort out seemingly discrepant findings. How "coercion" is defined appears to be critical. We cannot assume that a patient admitted "involuntarily" or one that has been mandated to receive treatment is actually perceiving coercion. Further, although individuals may not perceive that they had a choice in being committed or ordered to undergo treatment, they may still perceive that they need such treatment (Farabee, Shen, & Sanchez, 2002). This is why continuing research on the effects of coercion is so critical.

Right to Receive and Right to Refuse Treatment

Involuntary confinement of the mentally disordered has raised important questions about their legal rights to receive and to refuse treatment. "Treatment generally refers to a process of a diagnosis, intervention, and prognosis designed to relieve pain or suffering or to effect a cure" (Cohen, 1998, p. 6-4). Thus, the right to receive treatment represents an affirmative obligation on the part of the state to "do something" designed to improve the individual's mental condition. It does not oblige the state to "cure," since the treatment provided may not be effective. Additionally, the legal right to receive treatment does not require the state of the art treatment available for that particular illness (Cohen, 1998). As a federal court noted in *Rouse v. Cameron* (1966), all that is needed is a bona fide effort to provide patients with an individualized treatment program that includes periodic evaluation. The legal right to refuse treatment recognizes that involuntary medication violates the patient's autonomy and bodily integrity. Under the common law doctrine of informed consent, which has since been recognized in numerous state statutes and integrated into constitutional law (*Cruzan v. Director*, 1990), a competent person has the right to refuse medication and life-sustaining artificial nutrition and hydration. ▶ [That issue will be discussed again in Chapter 11.] The Supreme Court has recognized, though, that there may be a governmental interest that supersedes the right to refuse medication. For example, in *Washington v. Harper* (1990), the Court allowed the forced medication of an inmate on the premise that it was needed to control his dangerous behavior. *Competency* to refuse treatment is a critical component, however. Are mentally-disordered individuals competent to make decisions about treatment regimens deemed to be in their best interest? We will discuss both the right to receive and the right to refuse treatment separately.

Right to Receive Treatment

It can be argued that if the state hospitalizes the mentally disordered against their will, there should be a concomitant requirement to provide treatment. If the treatment that would produce an "adjusted" and "happy" person does not exist or is denied that person, confinement should not continue. On the other hand, if the individual is "dangerous" to self or others and/or gravely disabled, it could be argued that, even in the absence of treatment, continued confinement is justified. In the case of individuals dangerous to themselves but not to others, less restrictive alternative placements should have been investigated and found to be inappropriate.

A key case on the issue of right to treatment is a 1971 federal case, *Wyatt v. Stickney*. An Alabama statute permitted commitment to state institutions "for safekeeping." The court ruled that patients committed involuntarily to a state mental hospital had a constitutional right to a humane physical and psychological environment with adequate professional and nonprofessional staff, and to "receive such individual treatment as will give each of them a realistic opportunity to be cured or to improve his or her mental condition" (*Wyatt v. Stickney*, 1971, pp. 784–785). The court continued, " . . . [to] deprive any citizen of his or her liberty upon the altruistic theory that the confinement is for humane therapeutic reasons and then fail to provide adequate treatment violates the very fundamentals of due process." The court's decision was upheld by an appellate court, in *Wyatt v. Aderholt* (1974).

In the landmark U.S. Supreme Court case *O'Connor v. Donaldson* (1975), the Court retreated on the issue of a *Constitutional* right to treatment, however. Instead, it emphasized that non-dangerous patients in a mental institution had a right to liberty if they were not receiving treatment. In this case, Donaldson had been diagnosed with paranoid schizophrenia and confined to a mental institution for care, maintenance, and treatment upon the recommendations of two nonpsychiatrist physicians and with the approval of his father. He had remained there for fifteen years, despite frequent requests to be released. At no time was he considered a danger to himself or to others.

Donaldson apparently had received nothing but custodial care throughout those fifteen years. The Superintendent of the institution described his treatment as "milieu therapy," but "Witnesses from the hospital staff conceded that, in the context of this

BOX 5-3
Civil Commitment—Key Supreme Court Cases

O'Connor v. Donaldson (1975)—Indefinite confinement of non-dangerous persons, without treatment, violates the Constitution.

Parham v. J.R. (1979)—In civil commitment situations, children are not entitled to the same due process rights as adults.

Addington v. Texas (1979)—The state must demonstrate the need for involuntary civil commitment by at least clear and convincing evidence.

Vitek v. Jones (1980)—Inmates are entitled to a hearing before being transferred to a civil mental institution against their will.

Zinermon v. Burch (1990)—The person who consents to hospitalization must be legally competent to give that consent.

Kansas v. Hendricks (1997)—Dangerous sexual predators may be civilly committed against their will upon the expiration of their prison sentence.

Olmstead v. L.C. (1999)—The mentally disabled have a presumptive right to be treated within the community.

Kansas v. Crane (2002)—Before committing sexual predators, some inability to control their dangerous behavior must be demonstrated.

case, "milieu therapy" was a euphemism for confinement in the 'milieu' of a mental hospital" (*O'Connor v. Donaldson*, 1975, p. 563).

The Supreme Court opinion emphasized that a finding of "mental illness" alone cannot justify involuntary custodial confinement of non-dangerous individuals, nor can "mere public intolerance or animosity" constitutionally justify the deprivation of physical liberty. The Court ruled that, in light of the fact that no treatment was available to Donaldson, he should be released.

In a frequently-cited concurring opinion, the Burger Court highlighted the uncertainties of psychiatric diagnosis and treatment. "Despite many recent advances in medical knowledge, it remains a stubborn fact that there are many forms of mental illness which are not understood, some of which are untreatable in the sense that no effective therapy has yet been discovered for them, and the rates of cure are generally low."

Nearly 30 years later, the efficacy of any one treatment approach has yet to be empirically demonstrated. This may be particularly so with patients who resist being treated, but even this assumption may not be warranted. Recall that the MacArthur coercion study found that half of the patients who initially felt pressured to be institutionalized agreed in retrospect that they were in need of treatment. In similar fashion, research by Farabee, Shen, & Sanchez (2002) suggests that perceived coercion and perceived need for treatment are separate constructs. When the mentally disordered are committed involuntarily or are pressured to seek "voluntary" admission, even with the best intentions or "protective" concerns, control and freedom have been removed from them. It is for this reason that Carroll (1991) favors intervening in such a way that they "perceive" they are making their own decision. Recent research also suggests that the perception may truly be the reality, however. Individuals who are mentally disordered have not necessarily lost decision making ability. In fact, many if not most may be perfectly capable of making treatment decisions. For further elucidation of this point, we turn again to the MacArthur Research Network.

MacArthur Competence Study

In a series of studies (Appelbaum & Grisso, 1995; Grisso, Appelbaum, Mulvey, & Fletcher, 1995; Grisso & Appelbaum, 1995), researchers assessed and compared decision-making competence in three groups: patients hospitalized with mental illness (schizophrenia and depression), patients hospitalized with medical illness, and non-patients recruited from the community. Although the mentally ill showed more decision-making deficits than the other two groups, they were still capable of performing adequately on measures of decision making ability. Only schizophrenic patients with severe psychiatric symptoms performed poorly; the majority of schizophrenic patients nevertheless performed adequately. Patients with depression demonstrated intermediate levels of decision making. The researchers also discovered that, for the schizophrenics, decision making improved after a two-week period of treatment, with decreased symptoms. This led to a recommendation that patients be reassessed periodically for decision making ability.

In the process of conducting the above research, Appelbaum and Grisso and their associates developed and tested the MacArthur Competence Assessment Tool–Treatment (MacCAT–T) discussed briefly in ◀Chapter 2. Recall that the interview format allows clinicians to test decision-making competence in four legally-relevant areas: abilities to state a choice, to understand relevant information, to appreciate the nature of one's own situation, and to reason with information. The great majority of patients in the research performed adequately on at least one of the four measures, and even across all four measures the results were impressive. "Nearly one half of the schizoprhenia group and 76% of the depression group performed in the 'adequate' range . . . and a significant portion performed at or above the mean for persons without mental illness" (Grisso & Appelbaum, 1995, p. 171).

In a precursor of the MacArthur research, Grisso and Appelbaum (1991) had explored the ability of mentally-disordered patients to understand the implications of consenting to and refusing treatment. They compared 51 patients hospitalized in a state mental hospital with control groups of 26 hospitalized in a university medical hospital and 25 outpatients. The psychiatric patients had been diagnosed with major depression (N = 26) or schizophrenia or schizoaffective disorder (N = 25). The medical patients had ischemic heart disease (N = 26) or were non-ill persons being seen at a primary care clinic (N = 25).

Grisso and Appelbaum learned that the schizophrenic patients as a group demonstrated significantly poorer understanding than the other three groups. Nonetheless, they exhibited a wide range of comprehension, indicating that some clearly understood better than others. The risk of poorer understanding was greater in those with severe symptoms and those who had experienced their first hospitalization at adolescence or early adulthood. The depressed patients as a group did not display significantly poorer understanding. Those older at first mental hospital admission and those with more severe depressive symptoms were at greater risk, however.

Also prior to the MacArthur Competence Study, a number of commentators argued that mentally-disordered persons should be consulted on the issue of their own treatment, including permitting or withholding it (e.g., Wexler & Winick, 1991). According to Winick (1991a), we must not assume that patients in mental institutions are incompetent to make any and all decisions, including those relating to their treatment. "Patient choice in favor of treatment appears to be an important determinant of treatment success. Treatment imposed over objections does not work as well" (p. 68). Winick also points out that even "normal" people occasionally lose contact with reality and lack ability to think straight and perform social tasks. Conversely, the mentally disordered function normally some of the time, even in the midst of a psychotic episode. Therefore, we should not assume it is unrealistic to allow them to have some say in their own treatment regimens. The MacArthur Competence Study thus far serves to validate that claim.

Right to Refuse Treatment

The issue of an individual's right to refuse treatment arises most often in the context of intrusive mental health treatments such as psychoactive medications and electroconvulsive therapy (Winick, 1991a). Psychoactive drugs, it will be recalled, are defined as "those drugs that exert their primary effect on the brain, thus altering mood or behavior, or that are used in the treatment of mental disorders" (Julien, 1992, p. xii). As noted earlier in the chapter, they can produce unfortunate side effects, although their success at alleviating symptoms in some severe disorders cannot be denied. Electroconvulsive therapy (ECT) is a treatment usually reserved for severe, chronic depression. It involves the application of electrical impulses through the brain to produce seizures (Durand & Barlow, 2000). Although it has produced some favorable results, scientists do not fully understand how it works (Kendall & Hammen, 1995; Durand & Barlow, 2000). Furthermore, some ECT patients suffer from short-term memory loss and others from notable cognitive defects, and even cardiac complications (Kendall & Hammen, 1995). The great majority of the case law on the right to refuse treatment involves psychoactive drugs, however.

U.S. Supreme Court decisions dealing directly with the right to refuse antipsychotic medication have come from the criminal arena. Prisoners have a liberty interest in being free from the involuntary administration of antipsychotic drugs (*Washington v. Harper*, 1990), but even so such drugs may be administered if the state demonstrates in an administrative proceeding that the inmate is dangerous to self or others. Although the Harper case may appear to support strongly the right to refuse treatment, the fact that the Court did not require judicial oversight of the decision to administer drugs suggests otherwise. As noted earlier, the Court did support the right of a defendant pleading not guilty by reason of insanity to refuse antipsychotic drugs during his trial (*Riggins v. Nevada*, 1992) and it is now considering whether a defendant found incompetent to stand trial has such a right. In still another case, *Perry v. Louisiana* (1990), the Court did not reach the issue of whether a prisoner waiting to be executed had the right to refuse a strong, anti-psychotic medication which would render him competent to go to his death. However, in February 2003, the U.S. Court of Appeals for the 5th Circuit allowed the involuntary medication of death row inmates to render them competent for execution.

Lower courts have supported the right of patients in mental institutions to refuse drug treatment (e.g., *Rogers v. Okin*, 1980; *Rennie v. Klein*, 1983). This refusal can be overridden if patients are dangerous to themselves or others, in an emergency situation, and when patients are mentally incapable of making a rational treatment decision. As noted above, recent research suggests that decision-making ability in this area is far more adequate than had previously been assumed (Grisso & Appelbaum, 1995). Thus far, the right to refuse has been "a right to object and to have one's treatment decision reviewed" (Brooks, 1987, p. 259). When patients in civil mental institutions do challenge the decision to forcibly medicate them, courts rarely rule in their favor (Brooks, 1987; Deland & Borenstein, 1990; Hoge et al., 1990). It should be noted, though, that only a small percentage—7% in one study (Hoge et al., 1990)—do refuse.

Schwartz, Vingiano, and Perez (1990) studied 25 patients in an inpatient psychiatric unit who were being administered involuntary medication. At discharge, 17 of the 25 (whom the researchers called "retrospective compliers") reported that the decision to medicate them against their will had been the correct one. There were seven "retrospective noncompliers," who still disagreed with the decision to medicate. One patient did not respond. When the patients about to be discharged were asked why they had refused medication, only five cited concerns about side effects. Schwartz et al. concluded that resistance to medication was not based on "principled objections" such as concern about autonomy, but rather on "psychotic perceptions, denial and negativism, struggles with staff or family, and other transient, situational factors" (pp. 196, 197).

A comparison of the noncompliers with the compliers indicated that the former had had more past hospitalizations and poorer work histories. They were considered still ill at discharge and "continued to display grandiosity, suspiciousness, paranoia, hostility, conceptual disorganization, unusual thought content, and mannerisms and posturing" (p. 197).

The right of persons committed through *outpatient orders* to refuse treatment is still being debated in the courts. "Aggressive community treatment," as it is called, has become the norm in many jurisdictions. Some research suggests that such mandated treatment is more effective than institutionalization if offered over a one-year period, and if treatment is intensive (Swartz, Swanson, & Wagner, 1999). Other research finds few differences (Steadman, Gounis, & Dennis, 2001), but suggests that the community approach has the advantage of being the least restrictive alternative. Courts, however, are not of one mind as to whether individuals should have a right to refuse such treatment, particularly drug treatment, and the matter is far from settled (Monahan, Steadman, et al., 2001).

Those concerned about giving patients a right to refuse treatment argue that this places patients in the classic situation of "rotting with their rights on"

(Appelbaum & Gutheil, 1979). Instead of being helped by medication, their condition deteriorates progressively while their civil liberties are intact. They note also that courts that support a right to refuse treatment do not take into consideration the realities of many mental disorders, which are characterized by denial and ambivalence. According to Schwartz et al. (1990), autonomy as perceived by the legal system is drastically different from autonomy as perceived by the medical clinician. Mentally-disordered individuals by definition cannot be considered autonomous while plagued by a "disease." One possible solution is for individuals to prepare advance directives for mental health care, similar to those used for other medical care. Via these documents, individuals aware that they are facing a psychological crisis prepare a legal document outlining the types of medication they will and will not accept. All states allow these directives. Monahan, Steadman, et al. (2001) suggest that, although surveys in the mid-1990s indicated that these were not widely used, continued promotion of this option is warranted. They note that, because mental illness is episodic, individuals preparing these directives when they are stable are likely to be aware of what they might face when the severe symptoms re-occur.

The MacArthur Competency to Consent research indicates that decision-making capability is not evenly distributed among individuals with mental disorders. Clearly, questions can be raised about the competency of schizophrenic patients with severe symptoms to make rational decisions about their own treatment. Simply because a mentally disordered person cannot make a rational decision about medication, we should not assume that decisions to medicate should be made without oversight, however. Although psychoactive drug treatment today has made life more tolerable for many people, there are special concerns associated with administering it to individuals who are in an institution or whose freedom in the community is contingent upon taking medication. Public mental institutions, primarily because their residents tend to come from disadvantaged and powerless groups in society, are especially susceptible to taking the path of least resistance in treating patients (Brooks, 1987). Psychoactive medication, which makes patients easier to control, is just such a path. In community settings, the mentally disordered who experience adverse side effects find themselves in a no-win situation, because by refusing to take the drugs they risk re-institutionalization. Cycles of taking and refusing to take drugs are not uncommon.

There is some indication that legal challenges to drug treatment have had a positive effect in some jurisdictions (Brooks, 1987). Specifically, hospitals and community mental health centers have been alerted to the need to monitor carefully the side effects, make decisions on a case by case basis, and avoid policies which encourage blanket administration of psychoactive drugs to all patients. Although this is a step in the right direction, it must be accompanied by continual skepticism about the use of medication as a panacea.

Special Issue: Civil Commitment of Sex Offenders

In the last quarter of the 20th century, the dangerousness of sex offenders has come to the fore. Sex offender statistics are, indeed, sobering. In the mid-1990s, for example, 234,000 offenders convicted of rape or sexual assault were under correctional supervision, about 40% of these incarcerated (Bureau of Justice Statistics, 2001). Concerns that these individuals may re-offend once released has prompted legislation in a variety of areas, including sex offender registration laws. In 2003, the U.S. Supreme Court upheld the sex offender registration laws of two states—Alaska and Connecticut—that were widely considered very restrictive. For example, Alaska's statute allows the public posting of sex offenders' names on the Internet (*Doe v. Alaska,* 2003). More relevant to this chapter, numerous states have passed versions of "sexual predator" legislation that apply in the civil context. The typical statute of this nature allows the civil commitment of convicted sex offenders after they have served their criminal sentence, if they are deemed to be a threat to public safety because of their predicted sexual offending. Like the other civil commitment statutes discussed above, these laws require proof of present mental illness (which may be broadly defined) as well as dangerousness, and they provide for adversarial court proceedings. However, while such involuntary commitments are not automatic, "the operative rule in sex offender commitments seems to be that if at least one expert says that the respondent is dangerous, then a finding to that effect will be made by the court" (Janus & Meehl, 1997).

Forerunners of sexual predator statutes, known as "sexual psychopath" statutes, were widely adopted in the United States from the 1930s to the 1960s, and some remain in existence today. The statutes were applied primarily to mentally disordered sex offenders who were pedophiles or sexual sadists. They were passed on the premise that effective institutional treatment was available for these offenders, particularly for pedophiles. On the surface, then, the statues were rehabilitative in orientation. In the 1960s and 1970s, disenchantment with rehabilitation set in (e.g., Martinson, 1974), and civil libertarians successfully challenged these laws, arguing that they were punitive and did not accomplish their intended purposes. The literature since the 1990s has seen a trend in the direction of "reaffirming rehabilitation" (e.g., Cullen & Applegate, 1998; Farabee, 2002b), although social policy continues to be punitive in its orientation. Nevertheless, clinicians have persisted in their elusive quest for efficacious methods of sex offender treatment (e.g., Burdon & Gallagher, 2002; also see Marshall, 1999, and Rice & Harris, 1997, for reviews of this literature).

In the 1980s and 1990s, public attitudes toward sex offenders prompted legislators in many states to repeal their sexual psychopath laws in favor of statutes that are more clearly protective of public safety as well as punitive in orientation (Simon, 1998). The concept of "mental disorder or mental illness" is vague in many of these statutes. They also typically allow antisocial personality disorder to be sufficient evidence of mental disorder, which was not the case under sexual psychopath statutes (Rice & Harris, 1997). This is an important distinction, because antisocial personality disorder is strongly related to the commission of violent acts (Rice & Harris, 1997).

Over the past 20 years, researchers also have developed risk-assessment instruments for specific use with sex offenders (e.g., Quinsey, Rice, & Harris, 1995; Prentky, Knight, & Lee, 1997a). Modern sexual predator statutes do acknowledge that treatment might still be available, but they do not all guarantee such treatment. The legal right to treatment is predicated upon a disease or medical model; if a disease exists, there is a legal duty to treat. As Cohen (1998, p. 6-4) notes, "not every ailment will be recognized as a disease for the purpose of a legal right to treatment." He adds that terms such as "sexual psychopathy," "sexual predator," and "sexually dangerous" are not clinically recognized within the disease model adopted in law. They may, however, enter into the disease model adopted by clinicians.

Leroy Hendricks serves as a good illustration of the type of offender sexual predator statutes were meant to incapacitate. Hendricks was a pedophile and rapist whose history of sexual offenses against children dated back to 1955. He had served both jail and prison sentences and had been treated in a state mental hospital. In 1984, he was convicted of taking "indecent liberties" with two 10-year-old boys. When he was scheduled for release after serving almost 10 years of his sentence, the State of Kansas committed him to a state mental institution against his will under its *Sexually Violent Predator Act* (SVPA) which required a finding of "mental abnormality" or personality disorder, rather than mental illness. Hendricks himself stated during his commitment proceeding that he was not cured, could not control his sexual urges, and that only his death would guarantee that he would stop victimizing children. The Kansas Supreme Court invalidated the SVPA (thus overturning Hendricks' commitment) because "mental abnormality" does not satisfy the "mental illness" finding necessary for involuntary civil commitment.

In 1997, in *Kansas v. Hendricks*, the U.S. Supreme Court upheld the statute, ruling that the statute's requirement that mental abnormality or personality disorder be demonstrated was sufficient to satisfy due process requirements. Additionally, the Court noted that the abnormality or disorder specified in the statute was one that would make it difficult, if not impossible, for the person to control his dangerous behavior. Opponents of the statute had argued that the statute did not include a legal definition of mental illness endorsed by mental health professionals, but even the Justices dissenting in the case found no problem with the terms used in the statute.

The Court, however, refused to set a standard for the involuntary civil commitment of sexual predators, leaving this up to legislators. The 5–4 majority also noted that the Kansas statute called for a yearly review of the commitment to assure that it was justified. Considering the cursory nature of many re-commitment hearings, this may be an illusory protection.

The Court split on another issue, however. Hendricks had argued—among other things—that his commitment also violated the Constitutional prohibition against double jeopardy, since his commitment hearing essentially amounted to a second criminal proceeding for the same offense, resulting in additional punishment. The Supreme Court majority rejected this argument, distinguishing civil from criminal proceedings and ruling that the state's civil commitment was not punitive in nature. Furthermore, and most surprisingly to many observers, the Court noted that the SVPA was not punitive *even if it failed to offer treatment*, and whether or not treatment was available. In the case of a sexual predator such as Hendricks, the state's overriding interest was safety, and treatment was an ancillary concern.

Dissenting Justices, however, were dismayed at this latter interpretation of the law. While acknowledging that Hendricks was a dangerous pedophile, they noted that he had received hardly any treatment during his years in prison. Additionally, the law under which he was civilly committed also guaranteed no adequate treatment. The dissenters did not say that dangerous persons could not be civilly committed if no treatment was available; rather, specifically because mental health professionals *do* have effective treatment for pedophiles, Hendricks should have access to that treatment if civilly committed. Justice Breyer, writing for the dissent, noted that these and other features of the SVPA "convince me that it was not simply an effort to commit Hendricks civilly, but rather an effort to inflict further punishment on him." Hendricks, it should be noted, was considered dangerous and unable to control his behavior.

Hendricks also had committed his crimes before the Act when into effect. The dissenters found this a violation of the ***ex post facto* clause** of the Constitution, which prohibits the punishment of individuals if the law under which they are punished was not in effect at the time they committed their crime. Since the Court majority concluded that Hendricks was not being punished, they did not see this as an *ex post facto* violation.

Five years later, the Court in *Kansas v. Crane* (2002) revisited the statute and clarified its previous ruling, specifically by ruling that *some* evidence of a mental illness, abnormality, or personality disorder was sufficient for commitment along with *some* inability to control behavior. Michael Crane had convictions for lewd and lascivious behavior and aggravated sexual battery, committed on the same day. He had first exposed himself to an attendant in a tanning salon, then had entered a video store, again exposed himself, then grabbed the clerk and demanded that she perform oral sex on him. Presumably because criminal penalties would not have been severe enough, the state sought to commit him to a civil mental institution under the SVPA. Psychologists testified that he suffered from exhibitionism and antisocial personality disorder, the two in combination qualifying him for commitment. Crane apparently had committed other such incidents, with increasing frequency and intensity. The district court judge ordered the commitment, but the Kansas Supreme Court reversed the decision. It ruled that the *Hendricks* case of 1997 requires a finding that the defendant cannot control his dangerous behavior. The trial court had not made such a finding.

A majority of the U.S. Supreme Court disagreed with the Kansas Supreme Court, but nevertheless found Crane's commitment unacceptable (although it remanded the case for further proceedings consistent with its ruling). First, the Court said that there need be no demonstration of *total or complete lack of control*. Citing *amicus* briefs from the clinical community, it noted that such an absolutist approach was unworkable. Such a stringent standard would result in very few commitments, because most severely ill people retain some ability to control their behavior. However, the Court said, *some* determination of lack of control must be made. " . . . (I)nability to control behavior will not be demonstrable with mathematical precision. It is enough to say that there must be proof of serious difficulty in controlling behavior." The Justices were concerned that, without this determination, the Kansas statute might be used to civilly confine against their will dangerous persons for whom criminal proceedings were more appropriate. Civil commitment, they noted, should not become a mechanism for retribution or general deterrence. Interestingly, the Court left open the question of whether an individual with an emotional or cognitive impairment, but not a volitional one, would be eligible for civil commitment under this statute.

In the dissenting opinion, Justices Scalia and Thomas disagreed that the statute required *any* showing of inability to control one's behavior, and they maintained that the Court majority had "gutted" the ruling in *Hendricks*. According to these Justices, the very existence of a mental abnormality that causes a likelihood of repeated sexual violence establishes the control problem. A separate determination of some lack of control need not be made.

Kansas v. Hendricks has been praised (e.g., McAllister, 1998) and condemned (e.g., Morse, 1998) in the psychological and legal literature. Steven J. Morse (1998, p. 251) believes that the case goes too far protecting the public and "imperils cherished notions of liberty, dignity, autonomy, and justice." McAllister (1998), however, argues that the deference to mental health professionals that is indicated in the opinion is appropriate. Mental health professionals, who have expertise in this area, still lack consensus on what level of mental illness warrants commitment; how can courts be expected to do so? Nevertheless, he notes that mental health experts have an ethical obligation to communicate to the courts any professional consensus on issues that may be relevant.

Still other critics of the case have been concerned about the lack of provision for treatment found in the Kansas law as well as many of its counterparts in other states. As noted by the dissenters, treatment for some sex offenders, particularly pedophiles, is widely available if not universally successful. If individuals are civilly committed, they should at the very least be provided with treatment. Although the literature is mixed with respect to the effectiveness of sex offender treatment, "overall, treated sex offenders fare better than untreated offenders" (Burdon & Gallagher, 2002, p. 98).

Some commentators also argue that the standards of commitment applied by courts in the case of sexual predators is much too low. Janus and Meehl (1997) discover that, in reviewing the civil commitment of sex offenders under sexual predator statutes, appellate courts have indicated that the standard of commitment used by the lower courts is high. That is, sex offenders are not committed unless they are likely or even highly likely to engage in harmful behavior. Janus and Meehl (1997) believe this standard should be scrutinized. "There is good evidence that probability standards actually in use by the courts fall well below the standards that the appellate courts claim are in use" (p. 40). Janus and Meehl examined the civil commitments of 75 sex offenders in Minnesota between 1990 and 1995 and concluded that the most favorable interpretation did not approximate a 75% standard; in fact, there was reason to believe it did not even reach 50%. Janus and Meehl also noted that, when appellate courts overturned civil commitment decisions in these cases (and they rarely did), it was never on the basis of a court using an unacceptable standard of commitment. While cognizant of the public safety concerns that have prompted sexual predator legislation, Janus and Meehl argue that, in the interests of fairness, courts should quantify their standards of commitment and make use of statistics to estimate the probability of recidivism.

The civil commitment of sexual predators is a red hot area in law and is unlikely to be satisfactorily resolved in the near future. Civil libertarians are concerned that statutes like that adopted in Kansas will capture too wide a range of offenders under the civil commitment net, although the more recent *Crane* case has placed some limitations on the practice. Nevertheless, it is unlikely to be a major burden for the state of Kansas to show "some lack of control" on the part of sex offenders it wishes to commit under its SVPA. Critics of the law, and others like it, also point out there is no guarantee that treatment will be provided, even if clinicians offer promising approaches. On the other hand, the public is understandably concerned about the sexual predator who has served his maximum prison sentence and whom the criminal justice system can no longer contain. And, although the clinical literature is hopeful with respect to pedophiles, it is less hopeful with respect to other categories of sex offenders. Alternative solutions to this vexing problem—short of solutions that are inhumane and unconstitutional—have yet to be proposed.

Inmate Transfers

Involuntary civil commitment may also occur in the case of prison inmates who may not be sexual predators or subject to statutes such as that described in the *Hendricks* and *Crane* cases. Correctional statistics indicate that the rate of serious mental disorder among the incarcerated is three times higher than in the general population (National Commission, 1999). An unknown number of inmates are transferred from prisons to mental hospitals for treatment purposes. Typically, these transfers occur when the mental health services within the prison setting cannot accommodate the inmate's treatment needs. Prisons are constitutionally obliged to provide adequate health care, including mental health care, to inmates (*Estelle v. Gamble*, 1976). In many states and in federal prisons, specific facilities within the prison system are designated for mental health treatment; transfer to one of these facilities does not require a hearing, although prisons are advised to provide one if the inmate protests (Palmer & Palmer, 1999). Transfers to a civil mental health facility are of a different sort, however. Although they do not require the involuntary civil proceedings discussed above or earlier in the chapter, an inmate may challenge the transfer in an administrative hearing within the prison setting (*Vitek v. Jones*, 1980).

In the *Vitek* case, the U.S. Supreme Court recognized that a significant deprivation of liberty accompanied the transfer to a mental treatment facility, including one operated specifically for inmate populations. "The stigmatizing consequence of a transfer to a mental hospital for involuntary psychiatric treatment, coupled with the subjection of the prisoner to mandatory behavior modification as a treatment for mental illness, constitute the kind of deprivation of liberty that requires procedural protections" (*Vitek v. Jones*, 445 U.S. at 489-490). Before such a transfer, an inmate is entitled to the following: (1) written notice that a transfer is being considered; (2) a hearing before an independent decision maker; (3) a conditional opportunity to present witnesses and to cross-examine witnesses called by the state; (4) written statements as to the evidence relied upon in making the decision to transfer; and (5) qualified and independent assistance furnished by the State (but this does not necessarily mean the assistance of a *lawyer*). The Court in the *Vitek* case also gave inmates the right to timely and effective notice of all of these foregoing rights. It is important to note that this pre-transfer hearing requirement does not apply to transfers to other prisons or to purely medical facilities, nor to transfers to a treatment facility for evaluation purposes, nor to transfers to a psychiatric unit within the same prison or within another prison. It also does not apply to emergency transfers, which typically allow the mental facility to keep the inmate for 30, 60, or even 90 days, depending upon the jurisdiction.

However, in order to keep the inmate beyond the time allowed under emergency commitment, the usual civil commitment hearing must be held. As legal scholar and practitioner Fred Cohen has noted, however, "when a hearing is subsequently held, it is consistently in front of the same local court and it is a court likely to have grown, shall we say, increasingly friendly to the state's position" (Cohen, 1998, pp. 17-7–17-8).

Nevertheless, Cohen observes that in reality few inmates challenge these transfers to mental facilities. " . . . (W)hile the Court's protective decision ought not to be denigrated, it simply does not strike at a presently significant problem. In my experience, there are far more problems involved (1) in gaining timely admission to a hospital-type facility than in protecting resisting inmates; (2) in retaining the inmate-patient for a sufficient time for treatment to take hold; and (3) in identifying the manipulators who pursue the secondary gains available in being hospitalized" (Cohen, 1998, p. 17-7). Thus, while inmate transfers to civil mental institutions are relevant to the subject matter of this chapter, they rarely attract either legal or research attention.

Summary and Conclusions

A historical overview of involuntary civil commitment in the United States suggests that the most outrageous abuses of the past have disappeared. No longer is it common for patients to be placed in public mental institutions without regard to their constitutional rights or to be kept there indefinitely under unsanitary, physically deteriorating conditions. Moreover, libertarian statutes requiring that candidates for civil commitment be proven dangerous to others or to themselves have replaced statutes based on a *parens patriae* approach, which required only that medical doctors certify mental illness. Gravely disabled statutes, which appear to be the predominant grounds for committing persons today, are more likely to be based on a *parens patriae* philosophy. Even these laws, however, require some showing that the person is both mentally disordered and a threat to his or her own safety.

Reviews of the civil commitment literature indicate, however, that the spirit of the more restrictive commitment statutes may be violated. Civil commitment proceedings in many jurisdictions are perfunctory and non-adversarial and continue to give deference to mental health practitioners. Predictions of dangerousness, or assessments of risk, are particularly troublesome. Empirical research demonstrates that the mentally disordered are rarely as dangerous as they are predicted to be (Hiday, 1988). Fortunately, the MacArthur Violence Risk Assessment study has now provided clinicians with a tool that should enable them to better assess the probability of violent behavior once an individual is discharged to the community.

Cursory commitment proceedings will probably continue to be the norm, however. As Paul Appelbaum (1992) has suggested, neither the law nor the mental health system seem truly committed to a rights-oriented civil commitment process. Lawyers often believe commitment is in the best interest of their client, and mental health practitioners believe the law does not recognize the treatment needs of the mentally disordered. Furthermore, the lack of community alternatives facilitates decisions to hospitalize, even for a shortened period of time. Outpatient orders of commitment, which enable monitoring and treatment of the discharged individual, are effective only if the community resources are available. Nonetheless, the past two decades have seen increasingly more attention paid to providing community treatment alternatives for the mentally disordered.

A key controversial issue facing psychologists and other clinicians since the 1970s has been the duty to warn or protect persons who might be at risk of violence from a patient. Some version of this duty is now found in the statutes or case law of most jurisdictions. Although the duty has become a fact of life, and is even embraced by some clinicians for its therapeutic implications, other clinicians are concerned about its ethical implications.

There appears to be a shift in many jurisdictions in the dominant way of treating the mentally disordered in both public mental institutions and the community. The traditional medication approach, with or without family therapy, is no longer the model of choice. Progressive treatment programs are multi-faceted, including cognitive re-structuring, skills training, and provision of direct services to address the individual's strengths and deficits. Nevertheless, such progressive approaches are not available in many communities and to a wide range of individuals. In these situations, medication alone becomes the fall-back position.

The law has assumed, and continues to assume, that many mentally-disordered persons are not competent to make decisions in their own best interest. The MacArthur Treatment Competence study suggests that this is a gross generalization, yet both hospitalization and unwanted medication may be foisted upon the mentally disordered. Furthermore, whereas courts are increasingly sympathetic to the rights of competent individuals to refuse treatment, the mentally disordered—particularly those who are institutionalized—tend to be omitted from this category. Additionally, the issue of questionable competency has even extended to voluntary civil commitment, as we saw in the Supreme Court's *Zinermon* decision.

The psychology of free will suggests that the perception that one has control over one's destiny is critical to the recovery process for those who are mentally disordered. The therapeutic jurisprudence model of mental health law recognizes this by encouraging mental health practitioners to strive to make the mentally disordered partners in their own treatment. Individuals who perceive that they are being treated fairly are also more likely to consent to treatment regimens. Thus, achieving procedural justice in the admission process is a laudable goal.

Coercion also has become a critical construct in mental health research. The MacArthur Coercion Studies demonstrate that legal status has little correlation with a person's perception of coercion in the admission process. Research also suggests that even perceptions of coercion at admission can co-exist with perceived need for treatment. Whether effective treatment can still be accomplished, even with perceived coercion, remains to be determined, however.

In a cogent analysis of mental health law, John Petrila (1992) implored us to consider the possible relationships between the need for mental health services and social problems such as the lack of employment opportunities and adequate housing. Ronald Roesch (1995) issued a similar call in his Presidential Address before the American Psychology–Law Society. Roesch exhorted his fellow psychologists not to rely exclusively on a model that focuses on individual deficits, individual needs, and individual treatment. Rather, he asked them to adopt a more activist stance, taking a cue from community psychology, which recognizes the complex interaction of individuals and their settings. Virginia Hiday (1988) made a similar point when she argued that libertarian civil commitment statutes cannot be blamed for the increase in mentally disordered individuals on the streets. Neither drug treatment nor psychotherapy should replace needed social changes which would preclude the onset of mental disorder altogether in a significant number of individuals.

As indicated in the chapter, recent scholarship in both legal and clinical literature indicates a resurgence of interest in the civil commitment area, including commitment hearings, outpatient hospitalization, and risk assessment. Whereas the due process reform of the 1960s was clearly needed, a strict adversarial model—and zealous advocacy of the wishes of mentally disabled clients—may not ultimately be in their best interest. That remains to be seen, however, for research addressing coercion, procedural justice, and other models of civil commitment hearings has yet to make the link to treatment outcomes.

Key Terms

Criminalization thesis
Criterion variable
Deinstitutionalization
Depot drugs
Duty to warn/protect
Ex post facto clause
Habeas corpus petition
Parens patriae
Perceived coercion
Police power
Predictor variable
Procedural justice

Questions for Review

1. Contrast involuntary civil commitment before and after the deinstitutionalization movement of the 1960s.
2. Why has the distinction between "voluntary" and "involuntary" civil commitment begun to erode? Which concept or variable are researchers now studying in more depth?
3. What factors are typically taken into account in determining whether an individual should be civilly committed against his or her will? Contrast the two main categories of commitment standards.
4. Explain the doctrine of *parens patriae* and provide one illustration of its use.
5. Summarize the problems encountered by researchers attempting to predict violence.
6. Why is the term "risk assessment" preferable to "violence prediction?"
7. Summarize the goals, methodology, and findings of the Violence Risk Assessment Study.
8. Discuss the significance of *Zinermon v. Burch* and *Olmstead v. L.C.* as they relate to mental health law.
9. What problems have been identified relative to civil commitment proceedings? What solutions have been proposed?
10. What were the goals and findings of (a) the MacArthur Coercion Study and (b) the MacArthur Competence Study?
11. State the controversy regarding clinicians' duty to warn and/or protect, and discuss ways in which this duty varies across the United States.
12. What are outpatient treatment orders? Describe their strengths and limitations.
13. Under what conditions have government officials been allowed by courts to override an individual's right to refuse treatment?
14. What are sexual predator statutes, and how do they relate to civil commitment? State the key elements of the controversy regarding these statutes.

CHAPTER 6

The Psychology of the Jury: Procedural Considerations

"There is nothing else quite like them in our society: A group of strangers brought together and required to sit in silence and listen to different versions of a story in which they have no personal interest, and who are locked inside a room where they must stay while they try to sort out what they believe to be the truth from all they have heard" (Guinther, 1988, p. xiii.) The jury is one of the most powerful components in the American system of justice, with authority to take away freedoms and autonomy from those accused of crime, bestow them, or settle disputes and impose financial liability. It is one of the few channels through which ordinary citizens can impose on society their own standards or biases concerning what is morally or socially right and wrong behavior. Although judges have the power to set aside a jury's guilty verdict or to reduce the monetary awards it imposes, only rarely will they do so. Thus, the jury's responsibility is sobering, and there is good evidence that citizens take their role in the judicial process seriously and try to make the best decision in the case before them. Estimates of the number of jury trials conducted in the United States every year range from over 150,000 (Devine et al., 2001; Landsman, 1999) to 300,000 (Abraham, 1998).

Overview of Jury Procedures

The Sixth Amendment of the U.S. Constitution guarantees the right to a jury trial in criminal cases whenever the potential penalty for the offense is greater than six months' imprisonment or a $500 fine. The Sixth Amendment also guarantees that the accused shall have the right to a speedy public trial by an impartial jury of the jurisdiction where the alleged crime was committed ◙ (see **Box 6-1**). The Sixth Amendment right to a jury covers adults as well as juveniles tried in criminal courts. Youths prosecuted as juvenile offenders in juvenile or family courts have no Constitutional right to a jury trial (*McKeiver v. Pennsylvania*, 1971), although some states allow juries in select cases. The Seventh Amendment guarantees a jury in all *civil* cases where the damages are believed to be above a certain amount, usually $500. Through the Fourteenth Amendment, individual states also must honor the guarantee of a trial by jury in criminal cases. In civil cases, states have more leeway. Some grant no jury trials in civil cases at all, while others do in just a handful (Abraham, 1998). In both criminal and civil cases, defendants may waive the right to a trial by jury and take their chances with a judge, who serves both as a fact finder and determiner of the issues of law. A trial by a judge rather than jury is called a bench trial.

Despite the constitutional guarantees for all defendants, participants in the judicial process are under social, political, and economic pressure to settle a case before it gets to the trial stage. Trials, especially by jury, are time consuming, expensive, and unpredictable, and their unpredictability often prompts even the most experienced attorneys to avoid them if possible. Thus, each case is submitted to a filtering process, replete with discretionary maneuvers which may include plea bargaining, dismissal of charges by the prosecutor or the court, or a mutually agreeable settlement by the parties in a civil suit. In jurisdictions where courts are especially

BOX 6-1
The Sixth and Seventh Amendments

In all criminal prosecutions, the accused shall enjoy the right to a speedy and public trial, by an impartial jury of the State and district wherein the crime shall have been committed, which district shall have been previously ascertained by law, and to be informed of the nature and cause of the accusation; to have the compulsory process for obtaining witnesses in his favor, and to have the Assistance of Counsel for his defence.

In suits at common law, where the value in controversy shall exceed twenty dollars, the right of trial by jury shall be preserved, and no fact tried by a jury, shall be otherwise reexamined in any court of the United States, than according to the rules of the common law.

overburdened, participants are encouraged to pursue alternative dispute resolution, or mediation, before approaching the court. The vast majority of criminal cases are disposed of through plea bargaining or plea negotiation, a procedure in which the defendant pleads guilty to a lesser charge, usually in exchange for a lighter sentence (Alschuler, 1979; Cole, 1992; Neubauer, 2002). Most civil cases today also are settled or dismissed before they take the tedious journey through the entire judicial process. An estimated 75% of all civil cases are settled between the time a complaint is filed and the trial date (Abadinsky, 1995).

When cases do proceed to the trial stage, juries are used in about half of the criminal and civil cases in federal district courts and in fewer than 10% of cases in state trial courts (Vago, 2000). Although approximately three million people are called to jury duty annually, only 60% of these will actually serve on a jury (Vago, 2000). In general, criminal cases are the major consumers of jury trials, perhaps because there is a strong tradition in favor of being judged by a jury of one's peers when one is prosecuted for a criminal offense. On the other hand, the use of juries in civil cases is often discouraged because the litigation revolves around issues that are believed too complicated for the average person to comprehend (e.g., engineering patents, complex scientific data, or trade secrets). In addition, jury instructions in civil cases are notoriously vague and ambiguous, often because the civil law itself is purposefully vague and ambiguous (Greene & Bornstein, 2000). According to Forsterlee, Horowitz, and Bourgeous (1993, p. 14), "in general, jurors in civil trials are required to interconnect and recall more evidentiary elements, combine these elements in different ways, and render more decisions than their criminal jury counterparts." Parenthetically, Britain has eliminated the jury system completely from civil trials because of the usual complexity involved, except in cases involving libel or police misconduct (Vago, 2000).

Therefore, with the exception of personal injury cases, civil cases are usually tried before a judge, if tried at all. More often than not, civil cases are settled before the trial stage. Clearly there are exceptions, with civil cases going to trial and with jurors as the triers of fact. Interestingly, when juries are involved, "in a nonnegligible number of cases [they] render distinctively harsh antidefendant judgments and set dramatically large awards. Virtually all of these extreme verdicts are substantially reduced or reversed by appellate courts" (Hastie, Schkade, & Payne, 1998, p. 288). Perhaps because of the enormous complexity and ambiguity inherent in civil cases, very little research attention has been directed at how jurors interpret, comprehend, and apply instructions in those cases. Almost all the available research on jury instructions has been directed at criminal cases, primarily because the rules and procedures are more precise and substantially less ambiguous. One notable exception is research by Hastie, Schkade, and Payne (1998) which will be covered below. For the most part, however, most of the discussion in this and the following chapter will focus primarily on juries participating in criminal cases.

Jury Research

Social science research on the jury has moved through a number of discernible stages, beginning in the late 1970s when jury research concentrated on the effects of jury size and on whether the jury decision must be unanimous or majority rule (Devine et al., 2001). In the 1980s and 1990s, jury research focused on the characteristics of jurors, jury selection, and the effects of various court procedures on jury decision making. Almost all of the foregoing research was conducted with mock jurors and is referred to as jury simulation research. At the turn of the 21st century, the next phase has yet to be identified. Devine and his associates (2001) believe, however, that research with actual juries may be the new zeitgeist. One example of this shift in emphasis, they say, is the Capital Jury Project, which is a massive field study of jury decision making in capital trials (death penalty or life without parole) involving researchers in 15 states. The data are being gathered through interviews with four randomly selected jurors from each capital trial. ▶ [The Capital Jury Project will be discussed again in Chapter 7.] Another example provided by Devine et al. is the Arizona Jury Reform study, which examines the impact of a jury reform measure allowing jurors to discuss the evidence among themselves while the trial is still in progress, a practice not usually permitted. The results of these projects may well change the thinking about jury procedures and process in the near future.

Social science researchers have examined a wide range of jury topics over the years. Much of the research has tried to find answers to the following questions:

- Do jurors render verdicts based upon evidence presented in the courtroom, irrespective of the characteristics of the attorneys, the litigants, witnesses, or the jurors themselves, or do these extra-evidentiary factors play a significant role in the decision making process?
- Are jury decisions based on whim, sympathy, or prejudice, or on rational, logical foundations?
- Are there procedures or variables that help predict verdicts prior to the trial?
- Can jurors be significantly influenced by events prior to the trial, as by extensive pre-trial publicity?
- How do members of the jury influence one another, both during the trial itself and during the deliberation process?

Answers to these questions are elusive, partly because empirical investigations of jury behavior are hampered by legal restrictions in gaining access to jurors and to the jury process. Deliberations are shrouded in secrecy, and the courts have traditionally resisted any infringement upon the jurors' privacy. Therefore, as noted above, psychologists and other social and behavioral scientists have resorted to simulation research, where some segment of the jury selection or trial process is acted out in a way that approximates the real process, or where subjects read or listen to portions of trial transcripts or tapes. Findings from simulation research must be interpreted in a very guarded manner, however, as will be explained in ▶ Chapter 7.

Experimentation through simulation is only one way psychology can help us understand jury behavior. Psychological theories and information on group decision making, attitude change, attraction, and persuasion—although not directly related to legal matters—can shed light on events that transpire in the courtroom as well as in the privacy of the jury deliberation chamber. Applying psychological concepts in this manner is a good example of the psychology *and* law relationship. This chapter will first give attention to procedural and structural features of the jury and discuss what psychological research has uncovered about both. Then we will focus on juror comprehension of complex instructions. In the following chapter, also covering the psychology of the jury, the decision-making process itself will be discussed. ▶ [Additional jury-related research will be discussed in Chapter 9, specifically as it relates to the effects of prejudicial pre-trial publicity.]

Jury Selection

The U.S. Constitution says very little about the composition of juries other than that they must be impartial and drawn from the local geographical district where the alleged wrong occurred. In interpreting the Constitution, however, the Supreme Court has issued a number of rulings relative to size and composition. Additionally, state and federal laws stipulate specific procedures that must be followed and practices that must be avoided in order to assure that proper juries are constituted (Levine, 2002). These laws outline three guiding principles that govern the procedures for jury selection: (1) all adult citizens are expected to serve on juries if called, unless they are exempted by statute or excused; (2) the jury pool must represent a cross-section of the community; and (3) biased jurors who might decide cases unfairly or with prejudice must be excluded.

The *Venire* and *Voir Dire*

Jury composition is influenced at two stages of selection, *venire* and *voir dire*. In the first stage, a pool of prospective jurors, called the *venire* (from the Latin to come), is drawn from an eligible population presumed to be representative of a local geographical area. Courts have consistently ruled that jury pools must represent a cross section of the community or general population. However, "neither by law nor by the terms of the Constitution does a jury need to be a *microcosm* (italics added) of the larger community. Systematic exclusion is forbidden, but proportional representation is not required" (Abraham, 1998, p. 122).

Historically, juries were not representative of the community, and many citizens were excluded from jury service. Many communities used a "key man" system, whereby outstanding or model citizens submitted names of individuals whom they believed would be good jurors. Obviously the key man system, and other non-random approaches, prevented many citizens from being considered for jury duty. Women, ethnic and racial minority groups, and the economically disadvantaged were often systematically excluded from jury consideration. In 1968, Congress enacted the *Jury Selection and Service Act*, which it broadened in 1975. Under that law, federal grand juries and trial juries must be chosen at random from voter registration lists or lists of actual voters in the district or division where the court convenes. Following Congress's passing of the law, states followed suit in order to achieve juries that are more representative of the community.

Usually, prospective jurors are drawn from voting lists or driver's license lists representing that local geographical area. Theoretically, anyone of voting age can be expected to be called for jury duty unless he or she is on active duty with the military or has served for more than a year in prison and has not been pardoned for the offense (Abraham, 1998). Even when the selection process affords random representation, however, it has traditionally not been difficult to be excused from jury duty. In some states, certain occupations are automatically excluded (e.g., attorneys or physicians). In most states, members of some occupational groups (e.g., teachers, police officers, firefighters) can get excused quite easily at their request. Other persons are excused from jury pools after presenting affidavits from their supervisors attesting to their indispensability or from physicians attesting to their health problems.

Persons on the *venire* remain as potential jurors for a given period, and those individuals are eligible to be called to serve on a specific case. (In the case of grand juries, persons are called to serve for a finite period of time and will review all cases brought to them by the prosecutor during that time period.) Potential members of trial juries then move on to the next stage of jury selection, the *voir dire* (translated loosely as to speak the truth). The *voir dire* is actually the first stage of a trial. It is a presumptively open proceeding that allows the judge and attorneys to question the prospective jurors and possibly disqualify them from jury duty. During *voir dire*, attorneys can apply their own hypotheses about people in an attempt to generate the jury that could be most sympathetic to their client. It is at this juncture that "common-sense psychology" as espoused by attorneys as well as findings from the research are likely to be applied.

Challenges in Jury Selection

The prosecution and the defense (in civil cases, the plaintiff and the defendant) each has two options for challenging the impanelment of a prospective juror: **peremptory challenges** and **challenges for cause**. The peremptory option lets a lawyer request the removal of a prospective juror without giving reason. For example, the prosecuting attorney may consider a potential juror too analytical or too distractible. The defense attorney may simply have a hunch—based on many years' experience—that a person may not be sympathetic to her client. "The essential nature of the peremptory challenge is that it is one exercised without a reason stated, without inquiry and without the court's control. . . . The peremptory permits rejection for a real or imagined practicality that is less easily designated or demonstrable" (*Swain v. Alabama*, 1965, p. 220). The Supreme Court has placed some limitations on the exercise of peremptory challenges, however.

Attorneys are not allowed to use their peremptory challenges to exclude all members of a cognizable group. A **cognizable group** is one that has a definite composition. Moreover, a common thread or basic similarity in attitude *or* ideas *or* experience runs through the group. If the group is excluded from the jury process, its interests cannot be adequately represented (*Black's Law Dictionary*). Thus far, the Supreme Court has ruled that race and gender both define cognizable groups. In *Batson v. Kentucky* (1986) the Court ruled that *prosecutors* may not remove all blacks from juries because they believe they would be sympathetic to a black defendant; in *Georgia v. McCollum* (1992) the Court ruled that *defense lawyers* also could not exercise peremptories on the basis of race. In 1994, in a civil case involving paternity, the Court disallowed peremptories based on gender (*J.E.B. v. Ala.*). Essentially, if the exclusion of a potential juror who belongs to a cognizable group appears to be unacceptable on its face, the presiding judge must be convinced that there is a neutral (as opposed to race- or gender-based) explanation for the challenge (see **Box 6-2** for a discussion of *J.E.B. v. Ala.*).

BOX 6-2
Equal Opportunity in the Jury Box (*J.E.B. v. Alabama*)

J.E.B. was sued for paternity and child support by the state of Alabama, on behalf of T.B., the mother of a minor child. A panel of 36 potential jurors was assembled, and three were removed for cause. Of the remaining 33, 10 were men and 23 were women. During the jury selection process, both lawyers used all but one of their peremptory challenges to remove jurors who were all of one sex. The state's lawyer used nine of ten challenges to remove men; J.E.B.'s lawyer used all but one challenge to remove women. The resulting 12-person jury comprised all women. J.E.B.'s lawyer objected, citing *Batson v. Kentucky*, which prohibits peremptory strikes solely on the basis of race. He argued that the equal protection clause of the 14th Amendment similarly forbids gender-based strikes. The court rejected his claim and empaneled the all-women jury, which then found J.E.B. to be the father of the child. He was then directed to pay child support.

The U.S. Supreme Court found fault with the jury empanelment, holding that gender, like race could not be the basis of peremptory strikes. "Intentional discrimination on the basis of gender by state actors violates the Equal Protection Clause, particularly where, as here, the discrimination serves to ratify and perpetuate invidious, archaic, and overbroad stereotypes about the relative abilities of men and women." After reviewing the history of discrimination against women—who were traditionally not allowed to serve on juries—the court chastised the state for endorsing the same type of discrimination against men. "Respondent . . . urges this Court to condone the same stereotypes that justified the wholesale exclusion of women from juries and the ballotbox." The Constitution "prohibits discrimination in jury selection on the basis of gender, or on the assumption that an individual will be biased in a particular case for no reason other than the fact that the person happens to be a woman or happens to be a man."

The number of peremptory challenges allowed an attorney is restricted by statute or by the presiding judge, who sets the rule in a pre-trial conference. In some jurisdictions, peremptories are not allowed at all, and in some the defense in a criminal trial may be allowed more peremptory challenges than the prosecution. In federal criminal trials, where the final jury size is 12, the prosecution has six peremptories and the defense has 10. In capital offenses, each side is usually allowed 20 challenges. On the other hand, in a federal civil trial where the jury size is six, each side has three peremptories. Trial judges may allow more peremptory challenges if they believe the situation warrants it. For example, when pre-trial publicity is acute and extensive, judges may provide more leeway for the attorneys to play their hunches. The defense in a criminal trial is often allowed extra peremptories because it is recognized that defendants are at risk of losing their freedom in light of the awesome power of government.

A challenge for cause can be exercised whenever it can be demonstrated that a would-be juror does not satisfy the statutory requirements for jury service (e.g., residence, occupational requirements) and has not already been eliminated from the *venire*. More commonly, a challenge for cause is exercised when it can be shown that the prospective juror is so biased or prejudiced that he or she is not likely to render an impartial verdict based only on the law and on evidence presented at the trial. The presumed bias may be either for or against the defendant. Challenges for cause based on bias may be subdivided into those claiming a specific bias and those claiming nonspecific bias (Bermant & Shapard, 1981). A nonspecific bias refers to expected bias due to the fact that a prospective juror is a member of some group or class similar to that of the plaintiff or defendant. If a writer is suing her publisher, for example, the publisher's attorney may want to exclude another writer from the jury. A specific bias refers to situations where the prospective juror has a blood relationship to one of the parties, ties through marriage, or linked economic interests to the case. Specific bias is also demonstrated when a potential juror indicates prejudice against a group to which the defendant belongs. Finally, if a potential juror has already formed an opinion about a case, he or she can be removed for cause. An extremely controversial aspect of jury selection is found in death penalty cases where courts have ruled that jurors must be "death qualified." Social science research indicates that such jurors too often may not be unbiased or representative of the general population. We will discuss this in more detail shortly.

The idealized purpose of *voir dire* is to eliminate potential jurors whose biases may interfere with a fair consideration of the evidence presented at the trial. Bermant and Shapard (1981) refer to this as the "probative purpose" of *voir dire*, probative in that the lawyer or the judge are suggesting that the uncovering of bias "proves" that the defendant will not get a fair trial. However, lawyers often use *voir dire* to gather information and to indoctrinate or ingratiate themselves with jurors (Blunk & Sales, 1977). This strategy to influence the jury is referred to as the "didactic purpose." There is some evidence that a large proportion of the time spend in *voir dire* by lawyers is used to persuade the jury panel to be sympathetic to the lawyer or to the lawyer's clients (Balch, Griffiths, Hall, & Winfree, 1976).

Research on *Voir Dire* Practices

In 1977, the Federal Judicial Center gathered information about then-current *voir dire* practices and opinions of federal district judges (Bermant, 1977). Completed questionnaires from 365 active federal judges and 55 senior judges were used in the analysis. Approximately 70% of the judges said they conducted the *voir dire* examinations themselves in both civil and criminal trials, although they would accept additional questions suggested by counsel. Between one and two percent said they conducted the *voir dire* completely by themselves, rarely seeking or accepting additional counsel from attorneys. Bermant (1977) concluded from this and earlier data that federal judges are increasingly taking over the *voir dire*, leaving little room for lawyer participation.

About three-fourths of the judges stated that ensuring an impartial jury was the primary purpose of the examination. Eighty percent of the judges felt that there was considerable variation among lawyers in conducting the *voir dire*. These data contrast with the opinions of judges about the skills of lawyers during trials. Judges have stated in previous surveys that in about three-fourths of the cases they have heard, the lawyers were about equal in skill (Kalven & Zeisel, 1966; Partridge & Bermant, 1978). This difference is difficult to reconcile with existing data, but it does suggest that although judges believe lawyers vary widely in *voir dire* skills, these skills do not significantly affect the overall quality of advocacy during the trial process.

Another area of interest concerning *voir dire* centers on methods of juror challenge. There are two major methods or strategies by which one may challenge the suitability of a prospective juror (Bermant & Shapard, 1981). One is the **struck jury method**, whereby the judge rules on all challenges for cause before the parties claim any peremptories. In a second method, called **sequential**, the lawyers exercise all of their challenges without knowing the characteristics of the next juror to be interviewed. In this method, overexercise of challenges may result in a challenged juror being replaced by someone even more objectionable. Preliminary research using mathematical models has shown that the struck jury method may be superior in eliminating bias to the sequential method (Bermant & Shapard, 1981), but much more research is needed before firm conclusions can be offered.

Impact of Lawyers on Jurors

The iconoclastic Clarence Darrow swayed juries and stirred the imagination of budding attorneys with his courtroom antics and his rousing summations. His modern television counterparts keep viewers and television jurors alike entertained with legal cunning and acerbic wit. But one need only tune in to Court TV or to local news coverage of a criminal trial to understand that these legal models are not representative of attorneys in American courtrooms. In fact, if the well-respected Kalven-Zeisel project (1966) accurately captures courtroom dynamics, the total impact lawyers have on the trial process is minimal.

Judges surveyed by Kalven and Zeisel concluded that prosecution and defense lawyers were equivalent in skills and in impact in slightly over three-quarters of the 3,567 criminal cases they heard. Even when there was superior performance by one or the other lawyer, however, the jury's decision did not necessarily reflect it. In general, the nature of the case and the evidence presented, not the advocacy skills or the personality of the lawyers, accounted for the final verdict.

Nevertheless, it would be unwise to overlook the immense power held by attorneys in the courtroom, particularly when the evidence is ambiguous or of poor quality. Within broad limits, attorneys are able to direct and redirect testimony, making it appear credible or questionable. Furthermore, when two opposing lawyers are hopelessly ill-matched in ability and/or personal charm, the effect of the stronger attorney on the jury is likely to be considerable. Even though lawyers have this kind of impact within only a narrow range of cases, this small percentage of cases still affects thousands of defendants.

During the trial process, it is the jury or the judge whom the attorneys must persuade. "Hard sells" and strong persuasive appeals are likely to prove counterproductive. Not only does this approach damage the credibility of the communicator, but it also may precipitate psychological **reactance** (Brehm, 1966). When individuals sense or perceive that their freedom of choice is being threatened or forced, they often become aroused and motivated to restore their freedom. Under these conditions, people often resort to making decisions opposite those desired by the communicator. Therefore, a lawyer who implies that jurors have no choice other than to absolve his or her client may soon learn that the jurors do indeed have an alternative. Although the media report anecdotal accounts of individual lawyers influencing jury decision making, research to support this happening on a widespread basis is not available.

Trials, however, are often avenues of last resort, particularly in civil cases. They occur when the respective attorneys have met an impasse in negotiations and the parties cannot agree on a settlement. Even in criminal cases, a trial may be seen as an avenue of last resort, rather than a right guaranteed by the Constitution. Because the judicial system is so dependent upon the plea bargaining process to siphon cases from the court dockets, trial is seen as the least desirable option. In fact, even a defendant who is not guilty of the crime charged may prefer, or be persuaded, to plead guilty and avoid the expense and uncertainty of a trial.

There is little doubt, therefore, that most of what attorneys do on behalf of their clients in both criminal and civil cases is bargain and negotiate. Their ability to persuade is more likely to be tested in the pre-trial arena than during the trial itself. Part of this pre-trial arena includes the attorney's own client, who may be persuaded to accept a settlement or plead guilty to a lesser charge.

Scientific Jury Selection

The possibility that individual juror personality, group status, or demographic characteristics might affect final verdicts has led some attorneys to experiment with new techniques for the *voir dire*. Lawyers have always used their assumptions about human nature to help them select juries, of course. For example, if one's client is a self-made businessperson with politically conservative views who is now charged with tax fraud, one does not want left-leaning political activists on the jury. Nonetheless, the empirical evidence indicates that lawyers who rely on conventional stereotypes are poor at identifying biased jurors (Ellsworth & Reifman, 2000). In fact, "Jury researchers have searched in vain for individual differences—race, gender, class, attitudes, or personality—that reliably predict a person's verdict and have almost always come up empty handed" (Ellsworth & Reifman, 2000, p. 795).

Traditional hunches and guesses about potential jurors are sometimes supplemented by the time-consuming and elaborate procedures of social scientists in the employ of attorneys. This process, alternately called scientific jury selection (Saks & Hastie, 1978) or systematic jury selection (Kairys, Schulman, & Harring, 1975), was launched in the early 1970s. In one of the earliest examples, the defense in the Harrisburg Seven conspiracy trial hired a group of psychologists and other social scientists to help them choose jurors who would be most sympathetic to their clients.

The defense reasoning was understandable. The defendants were antiwar activists who were accused of sabotaging a government installation. The conservative community in which the trial was being held, coupled with the money the state was funnelling into the prosecution, made acquittal unlikely. The social scientists gathered background and demographic information on each potential juror, as well as measures of attitudes, interest patterns, and possible personality characteristics. All of the information was obtained indirectly, since the researchers could not contact members of the *venire* or the jury itself. After the trial, in which the defendants were acquitted, the defense publicly credited its victory in large part to the extensive help of the social scientists (Schulman, et al., 1973). Psychologists were involved in the selection process of other juries during this time as well. In 1972, a group of five psychologists helped defense attorneys select a jury in the trial of Angela Davis, another political activist charged with murder, kidnapping, and conspiracy. She was acquitted. In yet another example, Joan Little, a jail inmate who killed a guard who had sexually assaulted her and was threatening to do so again, was also helped by a scientific jury selection process.

Since then, a growing number of social scientists have been refining and expanding scientific jury selection techniques, and they have participated in highly publicized trials as well as lesser-known ones ◙ (see **Box 6-3**). Along with the attitude and behavioral scales, elaborate statistical procedures and mathematical probability formulae are being applied, presumably to provide attorneys with an educated guess about whether a given individual will be the juror they want for their client. How helpful are these methods? Opinions and findings vary (Suggs & Sales, 1978). Some critics call scientific jury selection little more than "social science jury stacking" (Penrod & Cutler, 1987). Early studies indicated that scientific jury selection was slightly superior to random selection (Padawer-Singer, Singer, & Singer, 1974) or even to the traditional selection methods used by attorneys (Zeisel & Diamond, 1978). These early studies did not consider the quality of legal representation, however. A defendant able to afford a jury or trial consultant would be likely to also afford a private defense team exclusively devoted to the case. While public defenders and private attorneys charging lower fees may be extremely capable, they cannot focus on one case alone.

Once a jury is seated, some behavioral scientists continue to help attorneys by offering opinions regarding the nonverbal behavior of witnesses or jurors during the trial. Additionally, they may offer direct guidance to the attorneys on such matters as how to gain approval or sympathy from jurors, how to phrase questions effectively, or even how to dress. As we noted in ◀ Chapter 3, such trial

BOX 6-3
High-Profile Cases Using Scientific Jury Selection

Joan Little Trial—1975
Little, a young Black woman, was tried for killing a white guard while she was serving time in a local jail after being convicted of breaking and entering, larceny, and receiving stolen property. The guard had allegedly raped her, the only woman being held in the jail. She was acquitted.

John Mitchell and Maurice Stans—1972
Mitchell and Stans were accused of obstructing justice during the Watergate political scandal that eventually ended in the resignation of President Richard Nixon. Both were acquitted.

Harrisburg Seven—1978
The defendants were antiwar activists charged with conspiring to destroy draft records, kidnap presidential advisor Henry Kissinger, and blow up heating tunnels in Washington, D.C. Two of the seven were convicted on minor charges, but the jury deadlocked on conspiracy charges. The government dropped charges rather than asking for a new trial.

Angela Davis—1972
Davis was a militant black activist who was tried on murder, kidnapping, and conspiracy charges connected with an attempt to free George Jackson, another politically active militant, from jail. At the end of a highly publicized and politicized trial, she was acquitted.

Ford Pinto Case—1980
Ford Motor Company was charged with manslaughter in the deaths of persons who were killed when the gas tanks in their Ford automobiles exploded upon impact. Prosecutors maintained that the company knew of the defects and attempted to hide the risks from the public. Key company executives sat at the defense table during the trial. The company was acquitted.

***People v. Buckey* (McMartin Preschool Case)—1990**
Seven teachers at a California day-care center were charged with a wide variety of sex offenses against children in their care. Charges against five were dropped, but two—Peggy McMartin Buckey and her son, Raymond Buckey—were tried. She was acquitted. A mistrial was declared in Raymond Buckey's case, but he was subsequently acquitted.

Rodney King Case—1991
Four white Los Angeles Police officers were charged with aggravated assault in the beating of King, an African-American suspect. They were acquitted in state court but later tried in federal court for violation of King's civil rights, where two of the four were convicted.

O.J. Simpson Case—1994
Simpson, a football superstar, was accused of the murder of his estranged wife, Nicole Brown Simpson, and her friend Ronald Goldman. Simpson was acquitted.

Although most of the above cases ended in not guilty verdicts, we cannot assume that scientific jury selection made the difference.

consulting is becoming more widespread. It is also a lucrative business (Myers & Arena, 2001; Strier, 1999). With trial consultants charging between $75 and $300 an hour, it is unlikely that they will be available to either public defenders or local prosecutors.

In addition to the disparity in who can afford such help, another concern about trial consulting relates to the lack of oversight. Strier (1999) notes that both profit and nonprofit trial consulting can now be found online, but whether online or not, it is largely unregulated. "There are no state licensing requirements, nor is there any binding or meaningful code of professional ethics" (Strier, 1999, p. 96).

Myers and Arena (2001), acknowledging the legitimacy of these concerns, nevertheless are supportive of trial consultation. Psychologists, they believe, can help to restore the balance in the presently unbalanced scales of justice. They note the need for better standards in training and methodology if the field is to advance. Ethical issues that are unique to trial consultation and may not have been encountered by psychologists in more traditional practices also need to be addressed.

Overall, however, when it comes to the jury selection process, we must remember that few juror characteristics have been found to predict with any consistency the outcome of the trial (Ellsworth & Reifman, 2000; Neubauer, 2002; Shaffer & Wheatman, 2000). The persuasiveness and nature of the evidence outweigh strongly any personality or specific characteristics of individual jurors. On the other hand, when the evidence is ambiguous or poorly presented, the characteristics of the jurors might carry greater weight in the decision making process, although it appears that group dynamics and social pressures, rather than individual differences, play the more significant role.

The weight that jurors give to evidence is not surprising if we remember that most people are not familiar with the judicial process and, in fact, are awed by it. Thus jurors tend to be more strongly influenced by the judicial context than by their own personality and attitudes. Within the judicial context, "jurors adopt a role of 'fairness' and 'objectivity' which may be as extreme as they ever have had or will have in their lives" (Saks & Hastie, 1978, p. 70). The jury box and the courtroom itself may exert powerful situational pressures that mitigate the individual differences of the jurors. An exception may be the death penalty context, however, to which we now turn our attention.

Death Sentencing

Jury research on the death penalty has proliferated since the 1970s. During that decade, the U.S. Supreme Court first declared the death penalty, as it was then being applied, cruel and unusual punishment in violation of the Eighth Amendment (*Furman v. Georgia*, 1972). Four years later, the Court approved the death penalty if state statutes were crafted to prevent arbitrary imposition (*Gregg v. Georgia*, 1976). Most death penalty states have responded to the Court's requirements by providing for a bifurcated trial process: the guilt phase and the penalty phase. A jury first must decide whether the defendant is guilty beyond a reasonable doubt. Then, in a separate proceeding, the same jury deliberates whether the death penalty should be imposed. The crucial role of the jury was highlighted in a recent U.S. Supreme Court decision (*Ring v. Arizona*, 2002) in which the Court ruled that jurors, not judges, must make a finding of the aggravating factors that will lead to a death sentence. The decision was a significant victory for opponents of the death penalty because it placed in question the death sentences of numerous death row inmates who had been sentenced to death by judges rather than juries.

The process of imposing the death penalty takes one of two approaches (Costanzo & Costanzo, 1992). In the vast majority of states, jurors are instructed to consider and weigh aggravating and mitigating circumstances. An example of an aggravating circumstance is a particularly heinous method of carrying out the crime, such as evidence that the victim was slowly tortured. Mitigating factors might include age, a childhood marred by extensive physical abuse, or evidence of a mental disability which had not been sufficient to acquit the defendant. Recall, however, that the Supreme Court also has ruled that mental retardation will spare the defendant the death penalty (*Atkins v. Virginia*, 2002).

Another approach in death sentencing asks the jury to address specific questions. Texas, for example, requires that jurors ask: (1) whether the individual acted deliberately and with expectation that death would result; (2) whether there is a probability that the defendant will be a continual danger to society; and (3) whether the individual reacted in an unreasonable manner to the actions of the victim (in other words, whether the attack was unprovoked). However, while allowing states to ask these specific questions of jurors, the U.S. Supreme Court has ruled that jurors also must take into consideration mitigating circumstances (*Penry v. Lynaugh*, 1989). That is, before imposing the death sentence on an offender, jurors must indicate that they have been aware of and have considered factors that might lessen the offender's culpability.

The issue of future dangerousness pervades death penalty sentencing. Note that continual danger to society was one of the components addressed in the specific questions listed above. Additionally, in 21 states statutes specify future dangerousness as an aggravating factor (McPherson, 1996). Federal courts also consider this information at capital sentencing. Psychologists and other clinicians, therefore, are frequently asked to assess the probability that a person convicted of a capital crime will harm again and to communicate this information to the sentencing jury. Some psychologists are concerned, however, that the predictions offered to the judicial system in this context are too infrequently based on empirical data (Grisso & Appelbaum, 1992; Hart, Webster, & Menzies, 1993).

Risk Assessment at Capital Sentencing

As discussed throughout the book, risk assessments—particularly those that are actuarial or statistically based—are becoming increasingly sophisticated. Predictions of dangerousness based primarily or exclusively on clinical observations are very suspect, however. Nonetheless, the U.S. Supreme Court has thus far not recognized this distinction in death penalty cases. To the contrary, the Court has repeatedly upheld death sentences of offenders when predictions of dangerousness were based on clinical or experiential data (e.g., *Barefoot v. Estelle*, 1983; *Estelle v. Smith*, 1981). Moreover, the Supreme Court and many state courts have assumed that jurors are perfectly capable of distinguishing between clinical and other expert testimony and have assumed, also, that they give less weight to the clinical (Krauss & Sales, 2001).

Psychological research has found the opposite, however. Jurors have a preference for expert testimony based on clinical data (Melton et al., 1997; Smith et al., 1996), leading us to conclude that clinical testimony may have an unfair advantage over actuarial. Most recently, Krauss and Sales (2001) demonstrated this effect with mock jurors in a capital sentencing situation. Participants were provided with materials based on an actual case and were asked their assessment of dangerousness at three different time periods: (1) immediately after they had read the case materials; (2) after seeing a video of expert testimony based on either actuarial or clinical data; and (3) after seeing videos in which experts were cross examined or disagreed with each other's opinions of dangerousness. Krauss and Sales found strong juror bias in favor of the clinical evidence compared with the actuarial evidence. Jurors considered the clinical expert more influential and persuasive, even though they believed the level of science was equivalent for the two experts and that they were equally credible.

In summary, psychological research continues to document both the deficiencies of clinical prediction and the juror preference for such testimony. Although we discuss this in the death penalty context here, it is problematic in numerous other contexts. Krauss and Sales offer several suggestions for tackling this issue. They recommend that better methods of instructing jurors should be adopted, with judges informing jurors of the natural, but misguided, preference for clinical data. They also suggest that future research explore alternative ways in which actuarial research might be presented so that it is weighed appropriately by jurors. Finally, "(f)uture empirical research will be especially important in determining how adversary procedures could eliminate or minimize the unfair advantage that accrues to clinical opinion expert testimony" (Krauss & Sales, 2001, p. 305).

Even actuarial data must be used carefully in the death penalty context, however. Cunningham and Reidy (1998, 1999) suggest that the base rate—the fundamental group statistic in risk assessment—often does not justify a prediction of dangerousness in capital offenders. Citing a number of studies (e.g., Brown et al., 1996; Menzies, Webster, McMain, Staley, & Scaglione, 1994; Marquart & Sorensen, 1988, 1989) Cunningham and Reidy note that murderers, including those sentenced to death, have low base rates of prison violence and violent recidivism on parole. In offering predictions of dangerousness in convicted murderers, clinicians also should take into account the effects of aging and the ability of the prison system to contain potentially violent behavior by assigning offenders to varying levels of custody. Essentially, predictions of dangerousness at capital sentencing should be undertaken with extreme caution.

It should be noted that Cunningham and Reidy have elsewhere addressed numerous other issues relating to the mental health expert's role at capital sentencing (Cunningham & Reidy, 2001), in addition to the assessment of risk. For example, they have discussed personality testing, the special problems associated with full disclosure to the offender and informed consent, as well as a variety of ethical vulnerabilities. ▶ [We will return to these additional considerations in Chapter 10.]

The Death Qualification Process

During the *voir dire* in a capital case, prosecutors poll jurors on their attitudes toward the death penalty. Prior to the late 1960s, prosecutors were allowed to automatically remove potential jurors who opposed capital punishment. In the landmark case *Witherspoon v. Illinois* (1968), however, the Supreme Court placed some limitations on this practice. It ruled that prospective jurors could be eliminated only if they made it unmistakably clear that, because of their philosophical opposition to the death penalty, they could not do one or both of two things. First, they could not make an impartial decision as to a defendant's guilt (guilt nullifiers). Second, they could not sentence a convicted offender to death (penalty nullifiers). Later, the Court broadened the pool of potential "excludables" by allowing trial judges the discretion to exclude a juror if the judge believed the juror's views would prevent or substantially impair the performance of the juror's duties (*Wainwright v. Witt*, 1985). In other words, even if a prospective juror says he or she is against the death penalty but could still find a defendant guilty in a capital case, a judge may believe otherwise and the prospective juror could be excluded. It is estimated that this **death qualification** process excludes between 10 and 17% of eligible jurors (Fitzgerald & Ellsworth, 1984).

The nature of the death penalty suggests that any research in this area is extremely critical. As the Supreme Court has noted in numerous decisions, ". . . execution is the most irremediable and unfathomable of penalties; . . . death is different" (*Ford v. Wainwright*, 1986, p. 411). In addition to the nature of the penalty itself, however, we must consider the way in which the death penalty—as a social policy—has been applied. Social science research has uncovered disturbing information in this regard (Bohm, 1999). Many studies reveal, for example, that the death penalty is sought and imposed in arbitrary and discriminatory fashion. Arbitrariness refers to random, irregular, or capricious application of the death penalty, rather than regard for legal factors. Discrimination refers to a disproportionate application of the death penalty to certain groups.

There is ample evidence of arbitrariness in the application of the death penalty. Researchers have found widespread regional variations, even when statutes allow it. For example, the South has led the nation in its use of execution. Additionally, however, even within a given southern state, some offenders are more likely to be sentenced to death if they committed their crime in a certain region. Bohm (1999) notes that offenders in Florida were more than four times more likely to be sentenced to death if they were tried in the panhandle area than in the northern or southern regions of the state. Yet, other regions of the state had between 4.5 and nearly 9 times more homicides than the panhandle area. Arbitrariness has also been demonstrated when prosecutors seek the death penalty in a given case because of extra-legal factors (such as the fact that they are running for re-election or a promise made to the victim's family).

Evidence of discrimination on the basis of race is also evident. Social science research has continually documented that racial minorities, particularly African Americans, are significantly more likely than Whites to be charged with capital crimes and sentenced to death (Acker, Bohm, & Lanier, 1998; Bohm, 1999; GAO, 1990). Additionally, the race of the *victim* plays an important role. When the victim is white and the perpetrator is black, juries are significantly more likely to impose the death penalty than any other racial victim-offender combination. Put another way, given equally grave facts of a case, the black defendant with a white victim is significantly more likely to get the death penalty than the white defendant with a black victim, the white defendant with a white victim, or the black defendant with a black victim (Baldus & Woodworth, 1998).

In addition to race discrimination, some scholars argue that there is gender discrimination, with women being disproportionately spared the death sentence. Although it is estimated that women are responsible for about 4–6 percent of death-penalty eligible crimes, they receive only about 2 percent of all death sentences. Additionally, women on death row are significantly more likely than men to have their sentences commuted to life or life without parole (Bohm, 1999; Streib, 1993).

In addition to the arbitrariness and discrimination found in much of the social science research, other concerns have been highlighted. Social psychologists have conducted studies in two broad areas relating to the death penalty: (1) juror comprehension of instructions, and (2) the effects of the death qualification process on the outcome of the case. Since juror comprehension issues will be covered in the jury dynamics section of this chapter, we turn our attention now to the death qualification process.

A number of studies have compared death qualified jurors to "excludables" and suggest that capital defendants may be at a disadvantage because of the death qualification process (Bohm, 1991, 1999; Haney, 1984; Heilbrun, 1987). It is questionable, for example, whether death qualified jurors are representative of the general population. Fitzgerald and Ellsworth (1984) found that the death qualification process significantly excludes more blacks than whites, more females than males, more lower income people (below $15,000) than higher income people, and more Democrats than Republicans. Death qualified jurors also have been found to favor the prosecution and be conviction prone (Cowan, Thompson, & Ellsworth, 1984; Thompson, Cowan, Ellsworth, & Harrington, 1984), and to be less receptive to mitigating circumstances than excludables (Luginbuhl & Middendorf, 1988). It should be noted, though, that at least one study challenges this evidence. Elliott and Robinson (1991) found that death penalty attitudes did not significantly affect verdicts.

Personality characteristics such as authoritarianism (Middendorf & Luginbuhl, 1981; Moran & Comfort, 1986) and a "just world" orientation (Lerner, 1980; Rubin & Peplau, 1975) also have been associated more with death qualified jurors than exludables. Finally, death qualified jurors are apparently less trustful of psychological and psychiatric testimony (Williams & McShane, 1991) and less likely to consider mental disorder as a mitigating factor (Ellsworth, Bukaty, Cowan, & Thompson, 1984; Williams & McShane, 1991). Haney (1984) has demonstrated that the *voir dire* process itself biases the jury against the defendant, because jurors are asked to imagine the penalty phase long before the defendant has been convicted.

In *Lockhart v. McCree* (1986), the Supreme Court diminished the importance of much of the previously described research evidence, producing extensive criticism among social scientists. McCree had buttressed his claim that he had not received a fair trial with briefs citing research findings that death qualification systematically produces conviction-prone juries. The Court, though, found that evidence unpersuasive, suggesting that McCree would have to show that the jury in his own case was biased. The Court took much the same approach in another death penalty decision the following year (*McCleskey v. Kemp*, 1987), when it rejected the argument that the death penalty as applied in Georgia was administered in a racially-biased manner. Like McCree, McCleskey had ample research data to support his claim; but like McCree, McCleskey was told he would have to prove discrimination in his own case.

In light of those decisions and the likelihood that both the death penalty itself and the death qualification process will not soon disappear, some researchers propose alternative methods of evaluating prospective jurors in death penalty cases. Cox and Tanford (1989), for example, offer QUEST (Qualification by Example Selection Test). QUEST is a questionnaire approach, presumably more private, standardized, and objective than the traditional *voir dire* process. The juror being questioned is also less likely to be influenced by the answers of other prospective jurors or the tones of voice of lawyers.

Cox and Tanford believe that some jurors who may be initially disqualified (excludables) may be prompted to reconsider their position and, consequently, be allowed to serve. Such jurors, they argue, would ultimately be more representative and less biased than the death qualified jurors obtained under the present *voir dire* system.

In the Cox and Tanford study, college students serving as subjects were first asked a "Witherspoon question" embedded in a general attitudinal questionnaire; they also were administered a variety of tests including Rotter's Internal/External Scale, a tolerance for ambiguity scale, and a crime-control/due-process scale. In a second session, the students were administered QUEST, which gives concrete descriptions of increasingly vivid, brutal crimes, and were again queried on death penalty attitudes. By means of this process, Cox and Tanford uncovered "rehabilitated excludables." These were students who, after the session with QUEST, were willing to reconsider their original opinions against the death penalty. The rehabilitated group were also less punitive, more tolerant of ambiguity, and less crime-control oriented than the original death qualified group. Cox and Tanford concluded that QUEST may be a more accurate method of eliciting death penalty attitudes than the *voir dire* questioning and may result in a more equitable process. They acknowledge, however, that more extensive research is needed on the effects of QUEST and whether it generalizes to an older adult population. Furthermore, the new system would require a radical change in the traditional process, something not easily accomplished in law.

Despite setbacks in the effective integration of death penalty jury research with the law, continuing work in this area is critical. Costanzo and Costanzo (1992) offered an excellent research agenda for the future, replete with hypotheses in four areas: (1) the effects of guiding juror discretion; (2) comparisons of juries that vote for life with those that vote for death; (3) the relationship between guilt and penalty phases; and (4) models of decision making in the penalty phase. According to Costanzo and Costanzo (1992, p. 188), however, jury simulation studies in the death penalty context, particularly with respect to the penalty phase, are unlikely to be fruitful: "... it is difficult to recreate the social psychological conditions of an actual penalty phase: the responsibility of the decision, the drama of the courtroom proceedings, the length of time actual proceedings require, and the dynamics already present in a group that has experienced both guilt and penalty proceedings as well as the guilt phase deliberation."

Jury Size and Decision Rule

Whether by historical accident or some unknown logic, the traditional jury in Great Britain, the United States, and Canada has consisted of twelve persons who must come to an unanimous decision. Winick (1979) suggests that the English dislike of the decimal system and an affinity for the number twelve (e.g., twelve pennies in a shilling) account for the system, which originated in 14th century England (Saks, 1977). In 1966, England began to require that only ten out of twelve jurors had to agree on a verdict (Saks, 1977), and soon after that, lawyers in the United States also began to challenge the traditional system. As a result, decision rule, which refers to the proportion of the total number of jurors required to reach a verdict, is no longer always unanimous, since some jurisdictions now allow agreement among fewer individuals (majority or quorum rule). Nor is the twelve-person jury now a universal phenomenon. Approximately 80% of states today allow jury verdicts by 75% of jurors in civil cases; 20% also allow these split verdicts in non-capital criminal cases (Abraham, 1998). Three-fourths of the states also allow some trials with fewer than 12 members on the jury (Abraham, 1998). The U.S. Supreme Court has spoken on each of these trends.

Jury Size

In two landmark decisions, *Williams v. Florida* (1970), which dealt with state criminal trials, and *Colgrove v. Battin* (1973), dealing with federal civil trials, the Court claimed that reduction in jury size would not alter trial results significantly. A six-person jury does not violate a person's constitutional right as laid down by the Sixth Amendment, the Court said in *Williams*, since that amendment mandates a jury "only of sufficient size to promote group deliberation, to insulate members from outside intimidation, and to provide a representative cross-section of the community" (*Williams v. Florida*, 1970, p. 100).

Although the Justices cited social and behavioral research to support their assertions, immediate responses decrying the logic of the two decisions erupted from some social and behavioral science representatives, who were concerned about the Court's misguided and inappropriate use of empirical data (e.g., Saks, 1974, 1977; Walbert, 1971; Zeisel, 1971, 1974). One statement in *Colgrove* was especially troublesome. The Court said that "four very recent studies have provided convincing empirical evidence of the correctness of the Williams conclusion that 'there is no discernible difference between the results reached by the two different sized juries'" (*Colgrove v. Battin*, 1973, fn. 15, p. 11). Most of the "experiments" cited by the Court were not experiments or empirical evidence at all, but the common-sense observations and opinions of individuals with experience in the judicial system. The experiments which the Justices relied upon were permeated with critical methodological flaws to the point of producing poor—or at best unconvincing—scientific evidence. Saks (1974) commented that some of the studies reported in *Colgrove* actually reported data opposite to the interpretation made by the Court.

In *Ballew v. Georgia* (1978), the Supreme Court once again broached the jury size issue, this time drawing a line at the minimum number of jurors to be allowed. Georgia statutes permitted a five-person jury to decide a criminal case, and the petitioner, tried on an obscenity charge, claimed that this five-person-jury law deprived him of due process rights. Since the Court had thus far avoided establishing a constitutional minimum, the Justices apparently decided that a more enlightened ruling was necessary to prevent possible erosion of the jury system.

Arguing that a minimum jury size must be established, the opinion written by Justice Blackmun cited social and psychological research supporting the position that anything below six members violated the Sixth and Fourteenth Amendments. This time, the Court used the available research accurately and carefully, and the Justices somewhat improved their reputation in the eyes of the research community. In *Burch v. Louisiana* (1979), however, the Court made it clear that a six-member jury must render a unanimous verdict.

Research on Jury Size Common sense and information gleaned from the few empirical studies of jury size tell us that there are advantages and disadvantages to both small and large juries. Small groups allow more active participation from all members because people are usually less inhibited in expressing their opinion in a small-group discussion. However, it has also been shown that small groups, to avoid upsetting the group balance, sometimes inhibit expressions of disagreement among participants (Bales & Borgatta, 1955; Slater, 1958). Still, the mere opportunity to speak is greater in a small group.

Larger groups have a number of advantages that are important to note if jury size is being considered. Large groups tend to provide the greater variety of skills and knowledge that may be necessary to arrive at a decision in a complex issue. Larger juries, compared to smaller ones, take significantly longer to deliberate, and are more likely to hang (Saks & Marti, 1997). Large juries appear to remember testimony given during the trial, although small juries have been shown to be better at recalling the arguments presented (Saks, 1977). Also, as jury size increases, a more representative cross section of the community is obtained, thereby assuring minorities a better opportunity to be represented (Zeisel, 1974). A small number of studies have examined the effects of jury size on liability verdicts and damage awards in the context of civil trials (Devine et al., 2001). However, the evidence so far is not conclusive enough to advance the argument as to which jury size is superior.

Larger juries also increase the probabilities of two kinds of minorities being represented: (1) racial, subcultural, or other demographic groups; and (2) opinion minorities. This second type of minority, which refers to those persons within a decision-making group who resist or go against the majority, has significant implications with regard to jury size. We will give this topic greater attention by referring to the research of Robert Roper (1980).

Roper tested a number of hypotheses, but only two directly concern us here. One predicted that juries with viable minorities, defined as at least two members not in agreement with the majority, will "hang" (fail to reach a verdict) more often than juries without viable minorities. Social psychological research initiated by Solomon Asch (1952) found that in group situations, one minority member with even one ally greatly increases his or her resistance

BOX 6-4
Solomon Asch's Classic Conformity Study

A series of ingenious experiments on conformity was carried out by Solomon E. Asch (1951, 1952) many years ago. The experiments are still cited as cogent evidence of the effects of group pressures on conformity, and are relevant to understanding the processes of jury decision making. In the most famous experiment, a group of six subjects (college students) was shown a line of a certain length and asked to say which of three other lines matched it (see illustration). However, all but one of the subjects in the group had been secretly instructed beforehand to select one of the "wrong" lines on each trial or in a certain percentage of the trials. In other words, five of the six subjects were actually part of the experiment, usually called "confederates" in social psychology experiments. The na¨ve subject was placed so that he heard the answers of most of the group before he had to announce his own decision. Asch found that under this form of social pressure a large percentage (75%) of the subjects went along with the group rather than accept the unmistakable evidence of their own eyes. In almost disbelief, Asch wrote: "That we have found the tendency to conformity in our society so strong that reasonably intelligent and well-meaning young people are willing to call white black is a matter of concern. It raises questions about our ways of education and about the values that guide our conduct" (1955, p. 34).

In one variation of his experiment, however, Asch (1956) instructed one of the confederates to give the correct answer and thus dissent from the majority. The effect of this one dissenting opinion on the na¨ve subjects was remarkable: The conformity dropped to one-fourth the level shown by subjects faced with a unanimous majority. Surprisingly, this reduction was greatest when the dissenting confederate views were even more extreme (and wrong) from the majority (Baron & Byrne, 2000). These findings suggest that in jury deliberations, one ally for a single dissenter will make all the difference in the world for him or her to "stick to their guns" and refuse to buckle to group pressure.

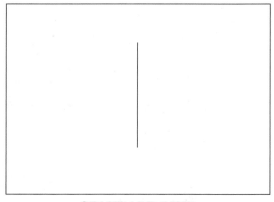

STANDARD LINE

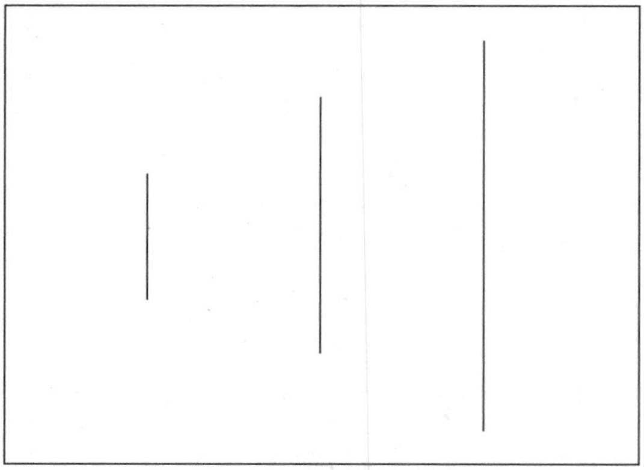

COMPARISON LINES

to persuasion by the majority. On the other hand, one minority member lacking an ally is substantially less likely to resist the majority of three or more ◙ (see **Box 6-4**).

The second relevant hypothesis tested by Roper predicts that larger juries will hang significantly more often than smaller ones. This hypothesis is built upon the observation that viable minorities have a great probability of occurring in larger juries, an observation for which Roper found convincing support in analyzing his own data.

Roper used a simulation design with a strong attempt at establishing ecological validity. A total of 110 mock juries, ranging from six to twelve members, were selected from jury lists of Fayette County, Kentucky. A videotape of a criminal trial was presented in a courtroom, and the juries were then permitted to deliberate for an unlimited amount of time to reach a verdict. The decision could take one of three forms: a guilty verdict, not guilty verdict, or hung jury. Juries that initially reported they were deadlocked were sent back twice to try to reach a decision. If they returned a third time without a verdict, a "mistrial" as the result of a hung jury was declared.

As predicted, juries with viable minorities were more likely to end up hung than juries with nonviable minorities. In addition, the larger the jury, the more likely it was that a viable minority would emerge—hence the more likely that the jury would be hung. The conclusions from the Roper study indicate that viable minorities are more successful at resisting conformity pressures exerted by the majority. Furthermore, larger juries over the long haul will result in significantly fewer convictions, a point which presents an interesting dilemma.

Juries always have the possibility of making either a Type I or Type II decision error. A Type I error is made when an innocent person is convicted; a Type II error when a guilty person is released. Roper's results suggest that, if the judicial system and society wish to avoid making Type I errors, they should endorse twelve-member juries. On the other hand, if Type II errors are to be avoided, six-member juries should be instituted. The dilemma, of course, is deciding which of the two we want least: the occasional conviction of innocent persons or the occasional release of the guilty.

The Dynamite Charge

One additional aspect concerning the viable minority issue needs to be mentioned. When jurors reach a deadlock and are close to mistrial, the judge in some jurisdictions (it is prohibited in some state and federal courts) has the option to use the dynamite charge—also known as the shotgun instruction, the third degree instruction, the nitroglycerin charge, or the hammer instruction (Kassin, Smith, & Tulloch, 1990). The dynamite charge refers to situations where judges, confronted with the possibility of a hung jury, implore the jury to ". . . reexamine their own views and to seriously consider each other's arguments with a disposition to be convinced" (Kassin et al., 1990, p. 538). In other words, the judge attempts to "blast" the decisional log jam into a verdict. The charge may be used in either criminal or civil trials. In *Lowenfield v. Phelps* (1988), the U.S. Supreme Court held that the dynamite charge is not necessarily coercive and reaffirmed its use on a routine basis.

The unfortunate psychological side effects of the dynamite charge, however, are that the minority will feel pressure from the judge to change their vote, and the majority will feel free to exert even more social pressure on the minority. Kassin et al. (1990), in an exploratory study, found that the dynamite charge causes mock jurors in the minority to feel coerced by the majority to change their votes. Another serious drawback, as noted by the researchers, is that jurors may be uncertain of their right to declare a hung jury; the dynamite charge may lead them mistakingly to believe they cannot do this. The dynamite charge issue has not been examined to any great extent by psychologists, and much research needs to be done before we can assess its effect on various cases, jury compositions, and jury sizes.

Conclusions on Jury Size

Arguments about jury size are often tempered by the observation that a majority of criminal cases handled by the courts are clear-cut, where any number of individuals would probably reach the same verdict, whether it be guilty or not guilty. The sensational cases we encounter in the media, where juries deliberate for long periods, represent only a small percentage of all trials ushered through the courts.

However, the research evidence does strongly suggest that 12-person juries, compared to smaller ones, are more likely to: (1) recall more trial testimony; (2) contain members of minority groups; and (3) spend a longer (and perhaps more thoughtful) time in deliberation (Saks & Marti, 1997). Perhaps, the Court erred in allowing smaller trial juries. Saks and Marti (1997, p. 465) emphasize that "In holding that juries smaller than 12 are constitutional, the Supreme Court set aside 600 years of common law tradition and two centuries of constitutional history, including the reversal of its own precedents." Saks and Marti also note that the discernible harmful effects of shrunken juries have prompted some states to move the jury back to its original size of 12.

Decision Rule

An issue closely related to that of jury size is the proportion of jurors needed to agree on a verdict before it may be rendered. In other words, is it constitutionally permissible to allow a less than unanimous decision to convict defendants or to resolve civil matters? It surprises many people to learn that unanimity is not always required.

Currently, 45 states require unanimity in felony criminal verdicts (Louisiana, Montana, Oregon, Oklahoma, and Texas do not), and 27 states require it in misdemeanor verdicts. All states require unanimity in capital cases. Conversely, only 18 states require unanimity in civil verdicts. The size of the majority differs from jurisdiction to jurisdiction. For example, Montana requires two-thirds majority in criminal verdicts, whereas Oregon requires five-sixths majority.

Two key U.S. Supreme Court cases, *Johnson v. Louisiana* (1972) and *Apodaca, Cooper and Madden v. Oregon* (1972) are relevant to this issue. In both cases the Court allowed nonunanimous verdicts, especially in light of the fact that such majority or quorum verdicts would presumably result in fewer hung juries. However, as noted earlier, in *Burch v. Louisiana* (1979) the court noted that a six-member jury must render a unanimous verdict.

Research on Decision Rule Eleven empirical studies have investigated the impact of allowing juries to reach a verdict without total consensus, most of them being done during the late 1970s and early 1980s (Devine et al., 2001). The research finds that juries not required to be unanimous tend to take less time to reach a verdict, take fewer polls (votes), and hang less often (Devine et al., 2001). Several studies have suggested that **quorum juries** (those which do not require a unanimous vote to convict) demonstrate better recall of the arguments and display more communication among members (Saks, 1977). However, it has also been found that quorum juries often stop deliberating the moment they reach the requisite majority (Kalven & Zeisel, 1966; Saks, 1977, 1997), thus providing less opportunity for a minority member or dissenter to argue a position or even be heard at all. Therefore, unanimous juries probably have the advantage of allowing greater minority participation. Moreover, since the first vote of quorum juries generally predicts the final verdict (Saks, 1977), it appears that it is primarily in situations where unanimity is required that the minority can effectively alter the course set by the majority. On the other hand, unanimous juries also are more likely to block verdicts or to result in hung deliberation. In their classic work *The American Jury*, Kalven and Zeisel (1966) cited data that, in jurisdictions requiring unanimous verdicts, 5.6% of juries were hung. This figure compared to 3.1% in jurisdictions that required quorum verdicts.

The available research does not allow us to conclude whether the quorum or the unanimous jury is more advantageous. Regardless of which jury type is chosen, we lose some of the desirable features of the unchosen. It appears, however, that concerns that quorum juries may deprive a defendant of due process are unjustified from the social science perspective. Although unanimous juries, when convicting, seem more certain of a defendant's guilt, they apparently do not render verdicts significantly different from those rendered by quorum juries (Saks, 1977).

Jury Instructions

During a trial, jurors are expected to remain passive, in the sense of having no direct involvement in the proceedings, but they are also expected to be attentive. They must listen to testimony and arguments, pay attention to demonstrations, scrutinize exhibits, and form their impressions. Traditionally, the information had to be acquired and retained through hearing and auditory memory, because jurors were prohibited from taking notes. Note-taking is becoming much more common, however, particularly in complex cases. Judges allow—but do not require—jurors to take notes in increasingly more trials. Regardless of how it gathers its data, "The jury is expected to absorb information and spew out a decision, much like an empty sponge can be filled with liquid and squeezed to obtain what it has absorbed" (Diamond, 1993, p. 425).

After the *voir dire*, and the jury has been selected, the trial follows three main phases: the opening statements, the presentation of evidence and cross-examination of witnesses, and the closing arguments. In criminal trials, the prosecution usually has both the first and the last word. Lawyers often use the opening statement phase to "connect" with the jury, and summarize the position each side plans to take.

The role of the presiding judge is to enforce rules of procedure in the courtroom by controlling the manner in which evidence is presented, by ruling on objections, and by choosing between the procedural arguments of attorneys as to the proper process to be followed. It is also the judge's prerogative to control the courtroom by threatening and imposing contempt citations for disturbances or other interference with courtroom procedure.

Types of Instructions

At various points before, during, and after the trial, the presiding judge will give instructions to the jury. These are usually classified according to the nature of their content and when they are given. **Substantive law instructions** relate to aspects of the specific case at hand. For example, if a defendant is charged with embezzlement, the judge instructs the jury on the elements of that crime and on what must be proved by the prosecution beyond a reasonable doubt. The judge would also explain the concept of reasonable doubt ◀ [recall **Box 3-4**]. In essence, substantive law instructions include information about the law as it applies to the particular case. **Procedural instructions** are those that enlighten jurors about the various rules that apply across a wide variety of cases. For example, the judge explains the roles of judge and jury during the course of the trial or informs jurors whether their decision must be unanimous. The procedural instructions also usually include comments about the jurors' conduct during the trial, their responsibility to avoid representatives of the media, their need for impartiality, and their duty not to discuss the case with other jurors or other persons during recess. They may also include whether the jurors can take notes during the trial. **Preliminary instructions** are given to jurors at the beginning of the trial. They are usually—but not invariably—procedural in nature. For example, the judge will routinely warn non-sequestered jurors in high-profile cases not to expose themselves to media accounts of the case and not to discuss the case with others or among themselves until it is time for deliberation. Dann (1993) offers a radical proposal that this common admonition not to discuss the case among themselves be changed because it is unrealistic, and some jurors will do so anyway. Allowing jurors to engage in focused discussion by telling them what they can and cannot discuss might be more in the interest of justice.

Throughout the trial, the judge also gives a number of warnings to the jury not to consider some kinds of information in arriving at a verdict. For example, if inadmissible evidence is inadvertently or deliberately brought up in court, jurors are told simply to disregard it. In other situations, they are told the information they heard may be used in their deliberations, but only for limited purposes.

J. Alexander Tanford (1990) suggests placing instructions into two main categories: (1) charging instructions; and (2) admonitions. "Charging instructions explain the jury's role, describe relevant procedural and substantive law, and provide suggestions on how to organize deliberations and evaluate evidence" (Tanford, 1990, p. 72). In short, they summarize the juror's duties: listen, assess the credibility of witnesses, weigh the evidence, abide by the law, and render a decision. Note that the charging instructions may be substantive, procedural, and/or preliminary. Also, they may occur at any point during the trial and sentencing.

"Admonitions are given spontaneously in an effort to prevent jurors from misusing potentially prejudicial information" (Tanford, 1990, p. 95). In the legal literature, admonitions are often called **curative instructions** because they are presumed to correct or "cure" potential errors in the trial process. There are two basic types: (1) admonitions that jurors must completely disregard information deemed by the court as being prejudicial; and (2) admonitions that jurors limit their use of certain kinds of evidence. A judge may tell the jury to disregard a witness's comment that a civil defendant has offered to settle the case, or tell a jury to disregard improper remarks made by attorneys during the trial. These are examples of curative instructions of the "disregard type." The classic illustration occurred during the trial of Charles Manson, charged with the highly publicized Tate-LaBianco murders in California in 1969. Manson walked into the courtroom and held up a banner newspaper headline for the jurors to see. The headline was highly inflammatory because it proclaimed that then President Richard M. Nixon had declared that Manson was guilty. The jury was told to disregard the incident. The judge was careful, however, to poll jurors individually in an effort to determine whether they were unduly influenced by the headline.

Limited use evidence "refers to evidence that is introduced for certain purposes but not for others. For example, in certain cases, evidence that a defendant has prior convictions may be used to determine the credibility of statements made by the defendant, . . . but may not be used to show that the defendant has committed an act . . . " (Lieberman & Sales, 1997, p. 600). Not surprisingly, this type of instruction is extremely difficult for jurors to comprehend, as we will see shortly.

In many jurisdictions, judges have adopted pattern instructions rather than instructing jurors in their own words. **Pattern instructions**, often provided by the Federal Judicial Center, are standard or uniform instructions that can be applied across different jurisdictions. Use of these instructions obviously simplifies the role of the judge. Furthermore, the content of the instructions is less likely to be challenged on appeal. On the other hand, pattern instructions, typically drafted by lawyers in an effort to be legally precise, are often very complex and incomprehensible to jurors (Lieberman & Sales, 1997; Tanford, 1990).

Research on Jury Instructions

Does the average juror really understand the requirements and safeguards associated with charging instructions and admonitions? Furthermore, even if the average juror does understand, does he or she do what is legally expected? Finally, what level of comprehension is acceptable? As Elwork, Alfini, and Sales (1987) have asked, What percentage of jurors must understand the instructions in order to ensure a just and fair result? These are questions social science researchers have attempted to answer. Their research is comprehensively summarized in a review by Lieberman and Sales (1997). For clarity, we will adopt Tanford's (1990) two main categories to review the research.

Charging Instructions With great regularity, research has found that jurors—even highly educated individuals—find jury instructions technical, full of ambiguity, and downright confusing (Elwork, Sales, & Alfini, 1977; Lieberman & Sales, 1997, 2000; Ellsworth & Reifman, 2000). This incomprehensibility has a negative effect on juror deliberation, leading jurors to discuss inappropriate topics, neglect important ones, and allow one or two jurors to control the deliberation process (Elwork, Sales, & Alfini, 1977, 1982). The lack of clarity of jury instructions also presents a serious threat to the fairness of jury trials. Although most of this comprehension research has been done with criminal juries, civil juries also demonstrate considerable difficulty in comprehension. Hastie, Schkade, and Payne (1998), for example, found that the overall level of performance for jurors asked to define legal terms that were relevant to their decisions (and that had been defined by the judge) was very low. The median score was 5% correct, and 30% of the participants received a score of 0% correct. The researchers, though, did find individual background factors that predicted better comprehension. For example, jurors who were younger, better educated, and had higher income demonstrated better comprehension.

Even pattern instructions, in their effort at legal precision, have apparently become so full of jargon and qualifying clauses that they are fundamentally incomprehensible to the average citizen. Sometimes it is even difficult to find the verb. "Legalese" by itself is not the only problem, however. A number of grammatical constructions and discourse features (e.g., poor organization within paragraphs, needless redundancy) also contribute to a misunderstanding of the text (Levi, 1990). Efforts have been made to rewrite instructions with attention to psycholinguistic principles with some success (Charrow & Charrow, 1979; Diamond & Levi, 1996; Elwork, Alfini, & Sales, 1977; Kramer & Koening, 1990; Luginbuhl, 1992). However, even improved clarity of the instructions did not improve comprehension to a high level of satisfaction.

Some commentators conclude that the benefits of rewriting and simplifying may be overstated (Lieberman & Sales, 1997; Tanford, 1990). The abstract nature of the law creates its own problems. Legal concepts are often hard to understand—even for law students—because they are so abstract and so removed from any specific context or example. Accordingly, the judge should provide a context for them, refer to the actual evidence, and use numerous examples when providing instructions. As Tanford (1990, p. 102) asserts: "Rewriting some instructions may be a pointless task because it is the law itself that is incomprehensible."

Admonitions: Instructions to Disregard Totally

When jurors are told to do something—like disregard what they may consider critical or enlightening evidence—they are apt to do something just the opposite. As we noted earlier, this is a process social psychologists call reactance (Brehm, 1966). Moreover, telling jurors to disregard or to segment the evidence is likely to highlight the material in their minds even more. "The empirical research clearly demonstrates that instructions to disregard are ineffective in reducing the harm caused by inadmissible evidence and improper arguments" (Tanford, 1990, p. 95). In fact, instructions to disregard may make matters worse (Wolf & Montgomery, 1977). This cognitive process is referred to in the legal literature as the **backfire effect** (Cox & Tanford, 1989). "The backfire effect occurs when jurors pay greater attention to information after it has been ruled inadmissible than if the judge had said nothing at all about the evidence and allowed jurors to consider it" (Lieberman & Arndt, 2000, p. 689). The research indicates, Lieberman and Arndt (2000) conclude, that admonitions to disregard may not only be highly ineffective in many situations, but may serve to draw jurors' attention to inadmissible evidence and essentially increase their reliance on that evidence for making their decision. Pickel (1995) found that the backfire effect occurred when jurors were instructed to ignore inadmissible evidence that indicated the defendant had a prior criminal record. However, the backfire effect did not occur when the jurors were told to disregard inadmissible "hearsay" evidence. Pickel attributed this inconsistency to the jurors' notion of what they (the jury) believe is just and fair, despite what the law says. In other words, they considered it unfair to consider hearsay evidence from a third party, but perfectly justifiable to consider incriminating evidence that had slipped into the trial.

Inadmissible evidence of prior conviction appears to be especially damaging to criminal defendants and most particularly when other evidence of guilt is weak (Lieberman & Sales, 1997). Furthermore, at least one study has found a racial aspect, with white mock jurors more likely to consider prior criminal history when the defendant was black than when the defendant was white (Johnson, Whitestone, Jackson, & Gatto, 1995).

Yet, despite evidence to the contrary, the courts continue to think that admonitions are effective (Tanford, 1990) and "fully protect[s] the defendant's rights" (*People v. Brock*, 1988). The assumption that warnings to disregard are effective, or at least partially effective, on the thinking process and prejudice of the jury is termed, in the legal literature, the **cured-error doctrine**.

It has been suggested that, in actual cases, the group deliberation process will provide checks on the jury. In the event that the group is considering information that they were admonished to ignore, individual jurors can put pressure on the others not to consider that information. We have little evidence that this phenomenon exists, though. Representative is a study by Rose and Ogloff (2001) in which group decision making did not improve juror application of instructions. Additionally, studies that examine the after-the-fact deliberation of actual jurors, usually carried out by polling or interviewing them, support the results of experimental studies. ▶ [We will discuss jury decision making in more detail in Chapter 7.]

Finally, despite the fact that social science research does not support the effectiveness of admonitions to disregard, this does not mean that judges should not issue them. In fact, failure to admonish is grounds for appeal, and a lawyer's failure to object if a request for an admonition is not forthcoming may be grounds for an appeal based on inadequate assistance of counsel. Thus, even though a judge may be very well aware that jurors are likely not to disregard, the judge must make an attempt to cure the error.

Limiting Instructions The courts also continue to believe, too, that limiting instructions satisfy the cured-error doctrine. ". . . (M)ost courts hold 'unquestionably' that limiting instructions should be given, and once given, 'cure' any error" (Tanford, 1990, p. 98). Empirical studies have continually shown that limiting instructions are largely ineffective concerning prior criminal convictions (Wissler & Saks, 1985), evidentiary factors (Greene & Loftus, 1985; Tanford & Penrod, 1982, 1984), inadmissible evidence (Sue, Smith, & Caldwell, 1973), and prior convictions of perjury (Tanford & Cox, 1987, 1988).

Roselle Wissler and Michael Saks (1985) wanted to see whether limiting instructions neutralized the effects of prior criminal convictions on jury verdicts. The subjects, 160 adult men and women from the metropolitan Boston area, were asked to read a two-page case summary and answer some questions on a hypothetical case. Wissler and Saks found that these mock jurors were strongly influenced by the prior criminal history of the hypothetical defendant, especially if the charged crime was similar to a prior conviction. The jurors were far more likely to convict an individual if he had a criminal history than if not, even after being told they could not incorporate that knowledge into their decision. In fact, subjects were willing to admit that the prior conviction evidence made a big difference in their decision and was the primary reason they found him guilty—in spite of being told not to use that information for that purpose. They said it didn't make any difference what kind of warning they received; a prior record predisposed them to think "guilty."

The Wissler and Saks study used volunteers who were found in laundromats, supermarkets, airports, bus terminals, and homes. Had these individuals actually been serving on a real jury, they may have taken their responsibility to disregard prior record more seriously. Even in a more controlled mock-juror setting, the results might have been very different. Nonetheless, the Wissler and Saks research does follow the same trend as other research on disregarding instructions.

Sarah Tanford and Michele Cox (1987) found that prior perjury convictions in a civil trial increased the likelihood that the jury would find against the defendant, whereas evidence of honesty had little impact. They also found that limiting instructions did not remove the detrimental effect of character evidence of dishonesty on jury verdicts. "In summary, research demonstrates that impeachment evidence can be detrimental to a defendant in terms of verdicts, and limiting instructions do not remove this effect" (Tanford & Cox, 1988, p. 480).

The Effects of Joined Trials

When two or more defendants are criminally charged in the same incident, prosecutors may decide to put them on trial together. (Defense attorneys, however, may file severance motions arguing that this is not in the best interest of their clients.) A majority of the courts, including the U.S. Supreme Court, approve of joined trials because they are efficient and economical, and these courts maintain that limiting instructions prevent prejudice to defendants (Tanford, 1990). However, jurors' ratings of defendant's guilt are higher when crimes are joined than when the offenses are tried separately (Horowitz, Bordens, & Feldman, 1980; Tanford & Penrod, 1982, 1984; Greene & Loftus, 1985). Edith Greene and Elizabeth Loftus (1985) conducted two experiments where mock jurors (college students) read evidence from actual criminal cases and decided on the guilt of the defendant. One defendant was charged with either murder or rape, and another defendant was charged with both. Greene and Loftus hypothesized that there would be a spillover effect, where the evidence of the defendant's being charged with both offenses seems to spill over onto, and distort, the evidence presented on any single charge. Thus, this spillover contaminates the trial process and increases the likelihood of a conviction.

In experiment 1, subjects were more likely to convict the defendant accused of both offenses than the defendant charged with only one, thus confirming the spillover effect. The subjects also found the defendant accused of multiple offenses to be more dangerous, less likable, and less believable. Experiment 2 examined the effects of limiting instructions on joined criminal trials. The results were similar to those of experiment 1—that a defendant is judged more harshly if he or she is on trial for multiple offenses. It was clear, also, that limiting instructions had virtually no effect in neutralizing that bias. Defendants charged with multiple offenses were treated more harshly than those defendants charged with only one offense, even when told to disregard that information in delivering a verdict.

Improving Jury Competence

Researchers have proposed methods for improving jury comprehension of instructions. For example, there is evidence that providing jurors with written copies of the instructions, particularly when this is accompanied by oral instructions form the judge, improves comprehensibility (Kramer & Koening, 1990; Praeger, Deckelbaum, & Cutler, 1989). Heuer and Penrod (1989) did not find this improvement, although they did find that jurors receiving written instructions were more satisfied with the legal process. There is some concern that written instructions might increase deliberation time, a factor which speaks to the efficiency of the jury process. Thus far, there is no indication that providing written instructions has this effect (Lieberman & Sales, 1997).

Many experts believe that providing charging instructions about the law at the very end of the trial is a poor procedure for enhancing juror understanding of what is expected of them. Thus, the timing of the instructions is important. Elwork, Sales, and Alfini (1977) and Kassin and Wrightsman (1979) report evidence that jurors are far more likely to understand their charge and all its ramifications if instructions are communicated to them at the beginning of the trial as well as at the end. Although other researchers have not found these effects, Lieberman and Sales (1997) remark that there does not appear to be a detriment to presenting these instructions both pre- and post-trial. The possible improvement in both comprehension and juror satisfaction may lead to a reduction in juror bias, they argue.

Robbennolt et al. (1999) reviewed research on two other approaches to improve juror competence: allowing jurors to ask questions and to take notes. The opportunity to ask questions, if offered, has thus far been limited to misdemeanor trials and to trials in civil cases. Typically, a juror will submit a question in writing to the presiding judge. The judge then asks the question if he or she considers it appropriate. Note taking—as we discussed earlier—has been allowed in both misdemeanor and felony criminal cases as well as in civil trials. In most jurisdictions, the decision as to whether to allow jurors to submit questions and to take notes is left to the trial judge, but some state statutes prohibit note taking by jurors.

Robbennolt et al. (1999) note that the research on both questioning and note taking provides little support for their advantages, but it also provides no clear evidence of harm. Field experiments conducted by Heuer and Penrod (1988, 1989, 1994) on note taking, for example, indicate that it serves as a minor memory aid but does not increase satisfaction with the trial or the verdict. However, claims that allowing jurors to take notes will distort the record, distract other jurors, or consume too much time are unwarranted. Note takers also do not have undue influence over non note-takers, nor do their notes favor one side or the other.

Some research studies do suggest an advantage to note taking, however (e.g., Rosenhan, Eisner, & Robinson, 1994; Horowitz & ForsterLee, 2001). In a mock civil trial experiment conducted in Australia (Horowitz & ForsterLee, 2001), jurors viewed a videotape based on a complex, toxic tort trial, in which four plaintiffs were differentially worthy of civil awards based on their respective injuries. Jurors were assigned randomly to two note-taking conditions (one with access to a trial transcript and one without such access) and two non note-taking conditions (one with access to transcript and one without). The researchers found that jurors who took notes were most competent—defined as being able to differentiate among the plaintiffs in awarding damages. Interestingly, access to the trial transcript did not significantly improve competence. Furthermore, non note-takers who had access to the transcripts were not significantly more competent than non note-takers without access. While some research has indicated that access to transcripts improves juror competence (Bourgeois et al., 1993), Horowitz and ForsterLee speculated that the complexity of the trial portrayed in their research diminished this effect—essentially the complex trial produced a complex transcript. Jurors may have been dissuaded from wading through it. However, both note takers and jurors with access to transcripts were more satisfied with the deliberation process than their comparison groups, suggesting that making transcripts available to jurors may have a positive effect.

Permitting jurors to ask questions appears to promote understanding of the evidence and issues, but it does not help get at truth, increase satisfaction with the trial, or alert counsel to issues that need further development (Robbennolt et al., 1999). On the other hand, there is no evidence that jurors ask improper questions, lose their neutrality, or interfere with the trial strategies of attorneys.

Jury Nullification

Jury nullification is the power of a criminal trial jury to disregard the evidence or judicial instructions because they believe the law is wrong, nonsensical, or misapplied to a particular case. Norman Finkel (2000) refers to jury nullification, in its departure from jury instructions and black-letter law (written law), as a dramatic exemplar of **commonsense justice**. Jurors in nullifying the law, he says, are asserting in effect "to hell with both the law and rule of law" (Finkel, 2000, p. 597). Commonsense justice is what ordinary people think is just and fair. Essentially, "it is what ordinary people think the law ought to be" (Finkel, 1995, p. 2). Jury nullification has both a rather noble and a questionable history. In colonial times, jurors often refused to convict individuals who had been charged with violations of British laws, including John Peter Zenger, who had been charged with seditious libel. Zenger printed material that had not been authorized by the British mayor. On the other hand, jurors have also refused to convict members of the Ku Klux Klan charged in the lynching deaths of black citizens (Scheflin, 1972). Today, it is assumed that nullification most often occurs in cases that involve divisive social issues such as drug possession, euthanasia, and domestic violence (as when a battered woman kills her abuser) (Dilworth, 1997).

After the not-guilty verdict in the infamous O.J. Simpson case, numerous commentators speculated that the jury in that case had practiced nullification. The fact that the jury deliberated for such a short period of time (less than an hour) over a highly complex case provided fuel for those speculations. The argument was made that jurors could not possibly have attended to all they were instructed to do in that short amount of time, and that they deliberately disregarded the evidence as well as the instructions of the presiding judge. Commentators also noted that the jury may have wanted to send a message to police that racism or misconduct would not be tolerated. Other commentators reject the notion of nullification in this case. They argue that the prosecution simply did not prove every element of the crime beyond a reasonable doubt, that jurors were processing this fact as the trial unfolded, and that they had no difficulty arriving at this conclusion once they reached the jury room. Short of obtaining revelations from jurors in the case, we will never know whether nullification was indeed practiced in the Simpson case—but the trial and the resulting verdict clearly brought the issue of nullification to public consciousness.

In most instances, jurors do not realize they can nullify the law and acquit the defendant regardless of the facts. However, in a small minority of states, the law allows the trial judge to inform the jurors that they do have that power. In federal courts, judges are specifically told not to so inform juries (*U.S. v. Dougherty*, 1972). Four studies have examined the impact of informing the jurors that they have the right to disregard the evidence and nullify the law (Devine et al., 2001). The basic finding of these studies reveals that reminding jurors of their power to nullify the law makes them more likely to use it. But jury nullification power is a hotly debated issue, and many claim that jurors should not have the inherent power to throw out the laws of society in any given case, nor should they be reminded of this power, especially when evidence

BOX 6-5
Should Jurors Be Told. . . .?

Defense lawyers in criminal cases sometimes ask judges to instruct jurors that they may set aside the requirements of the law and vote in accordance with their own conscience and sense of justice. In the federal courts and many states, judges are not allowed to tell jurors that they have this power. Following are some of the arguments for and against telling jurors.

Yes. Tell Them.

- In cases where jurors believe strongly that acquittal is warranted, but where they believe that they cannot acquit, this will save them from unnecessary emotional distress.
- The jury is supposed to be the conscience of the community; how can they serve this role if they do not know that they can exercise their conscience?
- If they are not told, and they later find out, they will be bitter about the judicial system.
- It's unlikely that they will nullify; through the group deliberation process, the juror or jurors who favor nullification will likely be persuaded to abide strictly by the law.
- Nullification has a noble history; it has been an important check on government power and abuse.

No. Don't Tell Them.

- Telling jurors invites chaos in the jury room. It seems to negate many if not most other jury instructions.
- The rules of evidence and the established procedures in the courts must be observed.
- Nullification invites abuse. History is replete with illustrations of defendants who have been acquitted by sympathetic juries despite overwhelming proof of guilt.
- Informing jurors of this right suggests that the law endorses it, when the law clearly does not. If it happens, it happens. We don't have to put the idea in their minds.
- Mercy is important. However, the place for mercy is at sentencing, not during the adjudication of guilt or innocence.

of the defendant's guilt is strong. However, as pointed out by Devine et al. (2001), the impact of reminding jurors that they have nullification power is complicated. What they will do with this information depends on many factors, including the nature of the evidence, the source of the reminder, the nature of the crime, the status of the defendants, and the composition of the jury ■ (see **Box 6-5** for a review of arguments for and against informing jurors).

Jury nullification, despite its controversial nature, is a rare phenomenon because most jurors try to follow the letter of the law (and obey the instructions) as closely as possible, even if they disagree with it. Finkel cogently argues that jury nullification is nowhere near as frequent as many critics of the jury allege, and when it does happen, it is usually because of the failure of the jury instructions rather than the failure of the jurors themselves. That is, jury members misunderstand their charge and the instructions provided by the judge, and they then proceed with their commonsense notion of justice.

Death Penalty Cases

The inability of jurors to comprehend instructions relating to capital sentencing is well established (e.g., Diamond & Levi, 1996; Haney & Lynch, 1994; Luginbuhl, 1992; Lynch & Haney, 2000; Wiener et al., 1995). During the sentencing phase of a capital case, jurors must decide whether the person who was convicted should be put to death or given an alternative sentence, such as life or life without parole. The role

BOX 6-6
Jurors Must Decide Death (*Ring v. Arizona*)

In November 1994, a Wells Fargo armored van, along with its driver, was removed from the scene of a department store where it had stopped to pick up money. Police later found the van, the driver dead from a single gunshot wound, and more than $562,000 in cash and $271,000 in checks missing. After a three-month investigation, Timothy Ring—an FBI informant, bail bondsman, and gunsmith—and James Greenham were arrested.

Ring's case was the first to go to trial. The jury had the option of finding him not guilty or convicting him on alternative charges of premeditated murder and felony murder. The jury deadlocked on premeditated murder, but convicted him of felony murder. (A defendant can be convicted of felony murder even if he did not himself pull the trigger, and the jury apparently could not conclude beyond a reasonable doubt that he had.) Under Arizona law, Ring could not be sentenced to death until further findings were made by a judge. Specifically, the judge would have to find at least one aggravating factor. At Ring's sentencing hearing, the judge heard testimony from Greenham—who had by then pleaded guilty to murder and armed robbery. Greenham testified that Ring had been fully involved in the planning of the robbery and, furthermore, that Ring had shot the armed guard. The judge then concluded that Ring had been a major participant in the robbery and had shot the driver of the armored car. These two facts were sufficient for the imposition of the death penalty. The Arizona Supreme Court affirmed the death sentence.

The U.S. Supreme Court—in a decision that surprised many observers—ruled in Ring's favor. Aggravating factors must be found by juries, not by judges, the Court said. The Justices noted that the jury had found Ring guilty only of felony murder, for which the maximum punishment was life imprisonment. Arizona's sentencing scheme, which did not call for juries to be involved in death penalty sentencing, was found constitutionally wanting. The 6th Amendment requires that a jury of one's peers be involved in the decision to put a defendant to death.

of the jury in capital cases has become even more critical as the result of the Supreme Court's recent decision, *Ring v. Arizona* (2002) ■ (see **Box 6-6**). As noted earlier in the chapter, a crucial part of the deliberation involves a consideration of aggravating and mitigating factors. Aggravating factors, raised by the prosecution, must be proved to the jury beyond a reasonable doubt; mitigating factors, raised by the defense, may be proved only to the juror's satisfaction. Additionally, juries are free to find their own mitigating and aggravating factors. They also do not have to be unanimous in their belief that a given factor or factors are mitigating.

Wiener et al. (1995) learned that jurors having low comprehension of death penalty instructions were more likely to impose death rather than a life sentence. Luginbuhl (1992) compared juror comprehension on standard death penalty instructions and instructions which were rewritten to reflect sound linguistic principles. In death penalty cases, it is of course especially important that jurors understand the legal questions they are to address. A study of juror comprehension of instructions in North Carolina (Luginbuhl, 1992) comports with previous research suggesting that even highly conscientious jury members often miss the point in jury deliberations.

Luginbuhl showed a 20-minute videotape of a judge reading instructions (pattern instructions) to 18 groups of subjects (with an average of six subjects in each group). Nine groups heard old instructions previously used in North Carolina courts and nine heard new instructions designed to improve comprehension. The legal rules under the two sets of instructions were the same; only the instructions themselves were different. The new instructions emphasized that mitigating circumstances need be found only by a preponderance of the evidence and that the jury need not be unanimous in finding mitigating circumstances. They also emphasized that mitigating circumstances must be considered together with aggravating circumstances in the final decision.

The subjects were then given an 8-item questionnaire designed to measure their understanding of the decision rules. For example, the jurors were asked:

> Is the burden of proof for mitigating circumstances
> (a) a reasonable doubt or
> (b) simply to the jury's satisfaction?
> (Correct answer *b*)
>
> Does the finding of aggravating circumstances require
> (a) unanimity or
> (b) simply the agreement of one juror?
> (Correct answer *a*)

There was no difference between the two groups on the three questions measuring their understanding of aggravating circumstances, but the "new instruction" groups were significantly better at understanding instructions regarding mitigation. Even so, only 53% of the new instruction group answered all eight questions correctly. Luginbuhl found no differences on demographic variables of race, gender, jury service, attitude toward the death penalty, age, or educational level. He did find a high educational level among his subject pool, however (only 14 of the 115 had no education beyond high school and 53 were college graduates), leading him to wonder how less well-educated groups would have fared. Luginbuhl also notes that defendants convicted under the old rules are beginning to appeal their death sentences, arguing that their sentencing juries might not have understood that mitigating circumstances need not be found unanimously. His research would provide support for this argument.

Diamond and Levi (1996) have established that death penalty instructions themselves seem biased toward a verdict of death. After rewriting instructions in Illinois, they were able to increase comprehension substantially. Considering the significance of a death sentence, attempts to improve juror comprehension of these instructions would seem paramount. This is even more critical now that we know that jurors *must* be involved in death sentencing (*Ring v. Arizona*, 2002).

Summary and Conclusions

Wallace Loh (1979, p. 166) observes that the relationship between psychology and law is marked by recurrent cycles. "Initially, optimistic views regarding the contribution of psychology to law are presented. These are met with skeptical rejoinders from the academic legal community that dampen further interest. A period of silence and inaction follows. The lessons are soon forgotten and a new cycle of optimism-skepticism-silence is repeated."

The early social science research on the jury, conducted during the late 1960s and throughout the 1970s, promoted additional legal skepticism which resulted in a period of silence from the legal profession. Certainly, a large segment of the jury research conducted during that time lacked ecological validity and needed substantial improvement in methodology. In the 1980s, jury research focused on the characteristics of jurors, jury selection, and the effects of various court procedures on jury decision making. In the 1990s and into the new century, most of the psychological research has been directed at how well jurors remember, understand, and apply the judge's instructions. Beginning in this period, the quality of jury research has improved substantially, and serious concerns about internal and ecological validity have been carefully and skillfully addressed. Psychologists and other social scientists have become much more knowledgeable about the legal system and more sophisticated in their methodology. As a result, their contributions are more deserving of attention because they are based on understanding of the processes involved and the role of participants. Furthermore, a good deal of the research in the jury area has now been replicated and clear trends are in evidence.

The major finding that has consistently emerged from this research is that jurors do not remember, understand, or apply the judge's instructions correctly. At first, researchers thought that the average citizen may be limited in understanding the law, but it soon became apparent that the instructions themselves were at fault. Jury instructions are typically written in language that is arcane, convoluted, and inaccessible to citizens, even well-educated ones, unless they happen to be lawyers (Ellsworth & Reifman, 2000). Research has advanced our understanding of the types of instructions that produce comprehension difficulties and the cause of those difficulties (Lieberman & Sales, 2000). In addition, the research has identified remedies that can improve juror comprehension of these instructions, but the courts have been reluctant to incorporate these remedies into their procedures. For example, Ellsworth and Reifman (2000) report that J. Alexander Tanford (1991) published a review of the responses he received from state courts, legislatures, and rule-making commissions to the empirical work on two remedies: (1) pre-instructing the jury on the law; and (2) providing jurors with written copies of instructions. "He found that by far the most common response on the part of all three potential change agents was do nothing . . . ." (Ellsworth & Reifman, 2000, p. 788). When they *did* recommend reforms, the legislatures and commissioners endorsed those recommended by social scientists. The courts, however, recommended the opposite. Tanford (1991, p. 167) concluded, "social science that is at odds with 'common knowledge' is likely to be ignored." However, in reference to the empirical research on jury instructions, law professor John Conley (2000, pp. 829–830) also cautions, "Collectively, they paint a picture of enormous complexity, a reminder that the more one learns, the more one appreciates how much one does not know. . . . As a lawyer, I am reminded of a piece of advice I often give to students and law firm associates: Nine out of 10 times, the best thing to do is nothing at all."

The social science research also finds that admonitions to disregard or use testimony in a limited way are largely ineffective, and may even make matters worse. Depending upon how they are given, these admonitions may provoke jurors into doing the opposite of what they are told. Social psychologists have long observed that people do not like to have their perceived freedom infringed upon. In order to re-establish it, they do just the opposite of what is demanded, a tendency known as reactance. In light of this awareness, it may be wise for judges to appeal to reason and to explain, preferably as part of the charging instructions, *why* some testimony should be disregarded. Reactance is less likely to occur if jurors are told at the beginning of the trial that they may be asked to put some information out of their minds—and why this is necessary. The same information could be repeated in the judge's final charge to the jury.

The issue of the "dynamite charge," where jurors are urged to reevaluate evidence against their own position, is more difficult to address. As we have seen, the dynamite charge is particularly problematic in the case of the lone hold-out. In any case, the psychological pressure placed on dissenters to bend to the wishes of the majority would seem to militate against a fair verdict. At the very least, judges issuing a dynamite charge should make it clear that jurors still have the freedom not to reach a consensus. Research on death qualified juries and on instructions relating to the imposition of the death sentence also deserves the attention of the legal system. It seems quite clear that jurors who are considered qualified to sit in a capital case differ in attitudes and demographic characteristics from non-death-qualified individuals. Additionally, there is indication that instructions regarding the weighing of aggravating and mitigating circumstances in capital cases are not well understood. Although it is premature to draw conclusions about these instructions without further research, studies to date suggest that this issue should be watched very carefully.

The research on jury selection and prediction of juror behavior continues to be equivocal. It remains unclear whether it is the individual differences of jurors (personality, attitudes, values, and beliefs) that make the difference in the final verdict, or whether it is the quality of the evidence and the social pressures of the deliberation process that override those individual differences. It is probably some combination of both, representing an interaction that continually changes within a wide range of factors, such as the quality of the evidence, juror backgrounds and education, the nature of the case and its seriousness, and the degree of understanding the law. Phoebe Ellsworth and Alan Reifman (2000, p. 795) sense that psychologists have temporarily left the area of individual differences for greener pastures (another cycle), as characterized by their remark "Rather than concentrating on weeding unqualified jurors, social scientists have concentrated on ways to modify their task." We will tackle this topic more fully in the next chapter.

Key Terms

Backfire effect	Peremptory challenges
Challenges for cause	Preliminary instructions
Cognizable group	Procedural instructions
Commonsense justice	Quorum juries
Curative instructions	Reactance
Cured-error doctrine	Sequential method
Death qualification	Struck jury method
Jury nullification	Substantive law instructions
Pattern instructions	

Questions for Review

1. Describe the process of selecting jurors to serve on criminal and civil cases.
2. Distinguish between peremptory challenges and challenges for cause, and provide examples of how these challenges are used to strike potential jurors.
3. What is scientific jury selection? Discuss its pros and cons.
4. Researchers have found significant differences between death qualified jurors and non-death-qualified jurors (excludables) on a number of factors. List these differences.
5. Describe the role of jurors in a death penalty case, once they have found a defendant guilty.
6. What is the minimum number of jurors allowed in a jury trial? What decision rule is required if that minimum number is used?
7. Summarize the relative advantages and disadvantages of large and small juries.
8. Summarize the advantages and disadvantages of non-unanimous (or quorum) juries.
9. What have researchers concluded about jury comprehension of each of the following: (a) charging instructions; (b) pattern instructions; (c) instructions to disregard; (d) limiting instructions; and (e) death penalty instructions?
10. Define jury nullification and summarize the arguments for and against informing jurors that they have this power.

CHAPTER 7

The Psychology of the Jury: Jury Decision Making

At the end of the trial, jury members are ushered to special quarters, where they are expected to deliberate in complete privacy until they reach a verdict, or until they believe they are hopelessly deadlocked. No outside participants or information that might contaminate the deliberation are permitted in the jury room. An officer of the court—usually a sheriff's deputy or a U.S. Marshall—guards the door and, if necessary, delivers messages to and from the jury. In high profile cases (e.g., O.J. Simpson case), juries may be sequestered for the length of the trial as well as the deliberation process. The purpose of sequestration is to protect the jury from the media and possible influences of their friends and family. Moreover, in such cases, jurors who are not sequestered could be contacted and even threatened by contacts of the defendant or the victim in a criminal case.

Overview

When a jury begins its deliberation, one of its first decisions is to select one person, called the foreperson or chairperson, to lead subsequent discussions and oversee the votes. Research reveals that the jury chairperson is usually male, middle-aged, of high status in the community, from a managerial or professional occupation, and experienced with regard to jury service (Devine et al., 2001; Strodtbeck, James, & Hawkins, 1957; Strodtbeck & Mann, 1956).

Interestingly, the place where a person chooses to sit at a rectangular table in the deliberation room seems to influence the possibility that he or she will be chosen as chairperson. That is, individuals who sit at the end of the typically rectangular table have a substantially higher probability of being picked than those who locate themselves along the sides (Strodtbeck & Hook, 1961). Of course, it is also expected that high status males would be most likely to seat themselves at the head of the table as a matter of habit. Also, the person who speaks first in the group and/or the first juror to mention the need to elect a chairperson is also more likely than others to be chosen to lead the group (Devine et al., 2001).

It appears that the influence of the jury chairperson on the group's decision making may be significant. He or she usually participates in the deliberation process far more than the other jurors, accounting for 25 to 35% of the speaking time (Devine et al., 2001). The chairperson also controls the polling. Although juries are largely left to determine their own procedures concerning voting on guilt or innocence (called polling), the chairperson often determines or influences the regularity of the voting, the timing, the format, and the sequence. The polling conducted during jury deliberations is not to be confused with "polling the jury."

Polling the jury is a practice whereby jurors are asked individually by the judge, after the verdict is read in the courtroom, whether they assented, and still assent, to the verdict. The procedure may be requested by either the defense or the prosecution at the time the verdict is announced. If the court finds that verdict was not unanimous, when unanimity is required, the jury may be directed to go back into chambers for further deliberation. A jury with no apparent possibility of reaching consensus may also be discharged, ending as a hung jury, and the case may have to be retried.

Once settled in the deliberation chamber, jurors may only request clarification of legal questions from the judge or ask to look at items of evidence. In some cases, they have received permission to visit or revisit the scene of a crime or accident. If jurors have not returned a verdict by the end of their first day of deliberation, non-sequestered jurors may be given accommodations in a hotel and taken back to the deliberation chamber the following day. Judges may also send the jurors home at the end of a day of deliberations, after admonishing them not to discuss the case with anyone. Recalling the principle of reactance discussed in the previous ◀ chapter, we should note the importance of explaining carefully why this non-communication is necessary.

The empirical evidence indicates that most juries in criminal trials do not involve themselves in lengthy deliberations. Kalven and Zeisel (1966), in their well-cited study, found that, for trials lasting one or two days, 55% of the juries took one hour or less to reach a verdict, and 74% of the juries completed their deliberation in less than two hours. Most juries take a vote soon after settling into their deliberation chamber. The University of Chicago Jury Project (Kalven & Zeisel, 1966; ◙ see **Box 7-1**) found that in 30% of the cases jurors reached a unanimous decision after only one vote. In 90% of the cases, the majority on the first ballot won out, regardless of who sat on the jury or who constituted the majority and minority. Lengthier deliberations appear not so much to change a predominant opinion as to bring about consensus. These findings have been more recently replicated by Sandys and Dillehay (1995) and MacCoun and Kerr (1988). Devine et al. (2001) cite extensive data that indicate that—in a 12-person jury—if seven or fewer jurors

BOX 7-1
The Chicago Jury Project

The University of Chicago Jury Project, a classic study in jury behavior, officially began in September 1952 and continued for seven years. It was led by lawyer-academician Harry Kalven, Jr., who worked closely with Professors Hans Zeisel and Fred Strodtbeck, among other scholars. The project's broad goal was to further research in the law and the behavioral sciences by focusing upon the jury system, commercial arbitration, and income-tax law. Numerous articles and several books resulted from the data collected. Among the best known books are: *The American Jury*, by Kalven and Zeisel (1966); *Delay in the Court*, by Zeisel, Kalven, and Buchholz (1959); and *The Jury and the Defense of Insanity*, by Rita James Simon (1967).

At one point the project's methodology resulted in a national scandal, complete with a Senate subcommittee investigation. Researchers had tape-recorded jury deliberations in five civil cases in a federal district court in Wichita, Kansas, without knowledge of the jurors but with the consent of the trial judge and lawyers for each side. This infringement upon the traditional privacy of the jury resulted in public outcry, censure by the U.S. Attorney General, hearings before a Senate subcommittee, the enactment of laws in over 30 jurisdictions prohibiting the taping of jury deliberations, and widespread editorial commentary and news coverage. During the Senate subcommittee meeting, attempts were made to link Kalven and the Dean of Chicago Law School, Edward Levi, to subversive or communist causes. Kalven and Levi defended the methodology of "eavesdropping" on the jury by arguing that the only way to improve the jury system was to collect data on the actual processes which occur within the secrecy of jury deliberation.

The data collected during the taping of the Wichita juries were never used. Data collected through other means (e.g., interviews and surveys of jurors and judges) resulted in one of the most extensive jury studies ever completed by social scientists.

favor conviction at the beginning of deliberation, the jury will probably acquit. In other words, the threshold for acquittal seems to be five. Put another way, if five (or more) jurors are against conviction at the beginning of the deliberation, the chances are slim for an eventual conviction. On the other hand, if 10 or more jurors believe the defendant is guilty in the beginning of deliberation, the jury will probably convict. That is, if two jurors or less believe the defendant is not guilty, the chances are slim for eventual acquittal. And "with 8 or 9 jurors initially favoring conviction, the final verdict is basically a toss-up" (p. 692).

James (1959) examined the specific content of jury deliberations involving mock juries and found that about 50% of the discussion was devoted to personal experiences and opinions. Another 25% was devoted to discussions of procedural issues, 15% to actual testimony, and 8% to the instructions provided by the judge. Another study found that the more highly educated they were, the more jurors emphasized procedure and instruction. Jurors with only a grade-school education were more likely to focus on opinions, testimony, and personal experiences (Gerbasi, Zuckerman, & Reis, 1977).

As part of the extensive Chicago Jury Project, researchers sent questionnaires to judges throughout the country who had presided over a total of 3,567 criminal cases. The judges were asked to record general information about each case, the verdict of the jury, and what they would have decided in the absence of the jury. If they disagreed with the jury, they were asked why the jury probably decided as it did.

Judges agreed with juries in 75.4% of the cases, both believing that 13.4% of the defendants should be acquitted and that 62% of the defendants should be convicted. Although the judges disagreed with juries in about 25% of the cases, most of this disagreement occurred when a defendant had been acquitted. In fact, judges agreed with jurors in fewer than half of the acquittals. Hence, juries appear to be more lenient than judges (a phenomenon called **leniency bias**). This suggests that a defendant has a slightly better chance of being acquitted if he or she elects a jury trial rather than a bench trial. Judges indicated the jurors were influenced by "sentiments" about law and about defendants, extralegal factors that did not enter into the judges' own decisions. While the leniency bias has been continually supported by research on criminal trials, the opposite may occur for defendants in civil trials, where judges seemed to be more lenient toward the defendant (MacCoun & Kerr, 1988).

Some studies report on interviews with jurors in actual capital cases in an attempt to discover what transpired during their decision making in the penalty phase of the trial. Recall that death penalty cases routinely involve a bifurcated or two stage process. In the first stage, jurors determine whether the defendant is guilty of the crime charged. In the second stage, they determine whether to impose the death sentence. Geimer and Amsterdam (1988) interviewed at least three jurors from each of ten capital trials in Florida. They learned that jurors had a presumption of death. That is, they wrongly believed they should impose the death sentence unless convinced otherwise. Under the law, they should have waited to be convinced to impose death. Costanzo and Costanzo (1992), interviewing jurors in one capital case, learned that the jurors did not weigh aggravating and mitigating circumstances and did not agree with attorneys on which evidence was critical to imposing death. Instead, they made their decisions based on values and normative standards, asking themselves such questions as, "Does this person deserve to die?" Not surprisingly, sitting on a death penalty case appears to be quite stressful for jurors. In a study of the effects on jurors of imposing death, Kaplan (1985) found that four of 16 jurors in capital cases appeared to suffer from post-traumatic stress disorder (PTSD) and that most of the others exhibited some symptoms of it (Costanza & Costanza, 1992).

Nearly all psychological investigations of the jury have been conducted under simulated or mock jury conditions. Most often, the jurors have been college students who volunteered to participate as part of a course requirement or for some other compensation. Although it would be helpful to carry out such research in the natural setting (called field settings), ethical considerations, costs, and legal obstacles to obtaining permission to do so all preclude this. However, in recent years, simulation studies on the jury have become far more sophisticated and realistic about jury procedures and process (Bornstein,

1999; Liberman & Sales, 1997). We will return to this topic at the end of the chapter.

Very few psychological investigations of the jury process were conducted prior to 1969 (Weiten & Diamond, 1979), but since then simulation projects have increased dramatically. Although there are critical methodological flaws in many of the studies, the reader should become familiar with some of the frequently cited work to understand what has been attempted.

Anyone reviewing jury simulation literature is confronted with a bewildering array of experiments, using a wide range of methods to investigate an assortment of jury variables. We will attempt to put some order in the disarray by presenting the studies and their findings by topic area and by trying to tie them together through a few theoretical themes. The failure to relate the data to some systematic theory enabling an organized summary of the results is one of the major problems of jury research. The topic areas covered in this section are those that social scientists (usually social psychologists) have isolated. The following presentation by no means covers the constellation of possible variables that can be studied, nor does it describe all of the experiments in the areas discussed. The intent is to provide the reader with highlights and trends of the data, to appreciate the problems faced by investigators, and to suggest future research directions.

The Effects of Defendant and Victim

Physical Attractiveness

According to research in social psychology, most people believe that good-looking people, compared to physically unattractive people, possess socially desirable traits and lead more successful and fulfilling lives (Dion, Berscheid, & Walster, 1972). Moreover, transgressions or violations of the social code are more highly tolerated when they are committed by a physically attractive person (Dion, 1972; Efran, 1974). This may account in part for why convicted felons are appraised as being "uglier" than most people (Cavior & Howard, 1973). "Attractiveness," of course, is a subjective criterion that may be associated with background variables like health care, nutrition, and economic status. Moreover, as society becomes increasingly aware of the broad range of criminal activity perpetrated by the economically advantaged, the connection between crime and attractiveness should become irrelevant.

When Michael Efran (1974) asked college student subjects if they felt physical appearance should play a role in jury decisions, 93% said it should not. Efran then simulated a jury situation, drew different subjects from that same college student population, and asked them to evaluate the guilt or innocence of hypothetical students accused of cheating. The subjects also were asked to mete out punishment. Subjects were shown photographs of the "defendants." The physically attractive defendants were believed less guilty and deserving of less punishment than unattractive defendants accused of the same offense.

Several qualifiers must be attached to the Efran results. First, female subjects always evaluated male defendants and male subjects female defendants. This pairing of opposite gender probably accentuated a possible attractiveness variable. Second, the significant results occurred because male subjects responded favorably to female defendants. Female "jurors" were not as strongly influenced by the male attractiveness. Third, a juror's decision was not made after group discussion (deliberation), but individually and without any influence from others. We do not know whether group influence would have mitigated a possible attractiveness factor. Finally, the results may have been different if the subjects had been faced with a violation of the criminal code rather than a violation of the academic code.

A study by Sigall and Ostrove (1975) suggests that a defendant's physical attractiveness does not always lead to leniency by individual jurors; sometimes the nature of the crime overrides. Subjects (60 male and 60 female undergraduates) were presented trial information about a female defendant accused of either burglary or a swindling scheme. Attractiveness was manipulated by showing the "jurors" photographs of the defendant. There was also a neutral defendant condition, with no photographs shown. The burglary was a breaking and entering and grand larceny of $2,200 in cash and merchandise. In the swindle, the defendant allegedly induced a middle-aged man to invest $2,200 in a nonexistent corporation.

The experimenters not only manipulated the attractiveness of the defendant, but also created a condition under which the defendant used that attractiveness to perpetrate her crime.

Attractive defendants in the swindle scheme received longer sentences than unattractive defendants for the same offense. On the other hand, attractive defendants in the burglary situation received substantially less severe punishment for the same offense. The results suggest, therefore, that good looking criminals may be treated better, as long as they have not capitalized on their looks to commit their crime.

Physical attractiveness also emerged as a significant factor in a study using a simulated civil case involving personal damage suits. Stephan and Tully (1977) reported that mock jurors were inclined to award larger amounts of money for damages when the plaintiffs were attractive. Also of interest was the finding that male mock jurors awarded the male plaintiff the largest amount of money and the female plaintiff the smallest amount. There was no difference in the awards given by female jurors on the basis of gender. In general, gender of defendants has not been found to influence mock jurors in criminal cases (Weiten & Diamond, 1979). Other demographic variables like socioeconomic status or race have been marginally important or not significant at all (Weiten & Diamond, 1979).

It should be noted, however, that research examining the effect of gender, socioeconomic status, and race on actual sentencing decisions suggests that these variables do indeed influence the outcome. Although this research falls out of the realm of psychological research, the reader should be aware of its existence. It has long been recognized that the criminal justice system is more punitive toward defendants of low socioeconomic status, not only at sentencing but at earlier stages of the process as well (Reiman, 1995; Walker, Spohn, & DeLone, 2000). With respect to gender, sentencing outcomes appear evenhanded, but a variety of factors do affect the sentencing decision. Married women, for example, have been found to receive shorter sentences than unmarried women or married men. An unmarried woman with dependent children, on the other hand, receives no favorable treatment (Daly & Tonry, 1997). Female drug offenders without child care responsibilities seem to receive more lenient sentences than male drug offenders without child care responsibilities (Spohn, 1999). Race discrimination continues to haunt criminal justice outcomes and decisions, and this is particularly evident when race and economic status intersect (Walker, Spohn, & DeLone, 2000). Obviously, the above does not do justice to the increasingly complex criminal justice research on actual outcomes. It is surprising, however, that socioeconomic, race, and gender variables do not enter strongly into the social-psychological jury simulation research.

In a Canadian study, Victoria Esses and Christopher Webster (1988) found that physical attractiveness may affect the decision to place offenders into a special classification, called the Dangerous Offender Category, as spelled out in the Canadian Criminal Code. Specifically, physically unattractive sexual offenders were seen by special judicial boards and decision makers as more dangerous than average-looking or attractive sexual offenders. The judicial decision makers believed that the unattractive offenders were less likely to restrain themselves in the future. In the United States, Stewart (1980) reported that the less physically attractive the defendant, the more severe the sentences given by actual trial judges.

In summary, research results thus far suggest that physical attractiveness could be of considerable significance in the courtroom, especially in criminal cases. However, in light of group dynamics and the effects of evidence itself, we must remain extremely skeptical in making inferences about the total impact in a majority of cases. In other words, physical attractiveness is unlikely to be a major determinant of jury verdicts, especially when the strength of the evidence favors one side or the other.

Social Attractiveness

Many of the investigations focusing on social attractiveness have weighted that variable heavily by manipulating several characteristics of a person at the same time. For example, marital status, work history, age, and occupational status have all been used to contribute to overall "social attractiveness." Therefore, it is difficult to know whether any one characteristic outweighed the others, or how combinations of them may have affected the total picture. Mock jurors are usually given descriptions of defendants that include several positive or several negative attributes. The crime is always identical, regardless of the defendant's description. The object of the experiment is to discover whether the socially unattractive defendant will be judged more harshly than the socially attractive one.

One of the earliest such empirical projects was a two-part study designed by Landy and Aronson (1969) examining both victim and defendant social attractiveness. In the first experiment, the hypothetical victim of a drunken driving accident with death resulting was presented as either of high or low social status, and there was no manipulation of the defendant's attractiveness. Jurors were harsher when defendants had killed the high-status victim. In the second experiment, the two levels of victim status were maintained, but the researchers introduced three levels of defendant status (high, neutral, low). Here, high and neutral status defendants were given less harsh sentences than those of low status, even though the offense was identical.

The Landy and Aronson experiments have been criticized on several fronts. The researchers have been accused of stacking the deck by making the victims or the defendants overly attractive and of examining too many variables. Age, past criminal record, occupational status, previous personal tragedies, and friendliness were all included as variables, thus making it difficult to determine precisely which variable or combination of variables affected sentencing. Davis, Bray, and Holt (1977) claimed that neither experiment, by itself, showed an effect for victim attractiveness; it was only after pooling scores across the two studies that an effect emerged. Davis and his colleagues argued that this method is of dubious validity, since the studies differed in samples and procedures.

The Landy and Aronson study stimulated a rash of additional research, because the suggestion that a relationship exists between social attractiveness and decision making by juries was too provocative to ignore. Many of the subsequent studies have provided at least partial support for the hypothesis that defendants who are perceived as socially positive and as responsible members of society receive more lenient treatment than persons seen in a less positive light (Berg & Vidmar, 1975; Kaplan & Kemmerick, 1974; Reynolds & Sanders, 1973; Nemeth & Sosis, 1973; Friend & Vinson, 1974; Izzett & Fishman, 1976; Izzett & Leginski, 1974; Dowdle, Gillen, & Miller, 1974; Kulka & Kessler, 1978; Solomon & Schopler, 1978). One study found that low defendants of low socioeconomic status (e.g., blue-collar) were more likely to receive the death sentence (Judson et al., 1969). However, some research demonstrates that, under some conditions, defendants of high socioeconomic status are apt to be treated more severely than defendants of lower status (Blanck, 1985; Bray et al., 1978). In another study involving a medical malpractice suit, the lower-status defendant (i.e., a medical resident) was convicted less often when remorse was displayed, compared to a higher-status defendant (i.e., a medical director) (Niedermeier et al., 1999). Consequently, the defendant status variable is far more complex than originally supposed, and much of the research has shifted to other areas in recent years.

Attitudinal Attractiveness

Is it any surprise that people tend to like better those persons who agree with them than those who disagree? People who have many of the same attitudes as we do are viewed more positively than people whose attitudes are largely dissimilar. The proportion of similar attitudes expressed by the other person is critical, however (Byrne & Nelson, 1965). If a person only agrees with us on 12 out of 24 topics, he or she is not liked as much as another who agrees with us on four out of six topics (Byrne, 1971). If jurors perceive a defendant (or any litigant) as having many of the same beliefs and attitudes they do, might they be more inclined to view the defendant or litigant favorably and to be more lenient in judging the person's behavior? Like physical and social attractiveness, attitudinal attractiveness has been subjected to empirical study under simulated conditions in an attempt to answer this question.

Griffitt and Jackson (1973) tested the attitude-similarity hypothesis in a criminal case and found that the more similar the defendant's attitudes were to the mock jury's attitudes, the less inclined they were to find him guilty. When they did find him guilty, jurors recommended that the attitudinally similar defendant be given a more lenient sentence.

Mitchell and Byrne (1973) also report some support for the attitude-similarity hypothesis. Their study looked at the relationship between juror-defendant attitude similarity and authoritarianism and how that relationship affected ratings of guilt and sentences. The results suggested that the personality of the juror may play an important role. Only jurors high in authoritarianism were significantly influenced by attitude similarity; they were more likely to consider a dissimilar defendant guilty than one who was like themselves. Furthermore, they recommended more severe sentences for defendants who were dissimilar to themselves. Jurors low on authoritarianism, however, were not influenced by attitude similarity.

As a whole, studies like these indicate that defendants or litigants who are physically and socially attractive, or who are attitudinally similar to mock jurors, will probably receive some degree of leniency or favoritism. If these results were generalizable to actual courtroom situations, it would mean that attorneys could engender sympathy for their clients by emphasizing these attractiveness or attitudinal variables to the jury. On the other hand, in a criminal case an opposite effect might be produced by varying levels of the *victim's* attractiveness. However, we cannot say with assurance that the results can be applied so readily.

An experiment by Izzett and Leginski (1974) suggests that group deliberation reduces the tendency of individuals to give severe sentences to unattractive defendants, but that the effect of the group process on the sentencing of attractive defendants is negligible. Kaplan and Miller (1978) suggest that group deliberations tend to mitigate individual juror biases. On the other hand, Rumsey and Castore (1974) (cited by Davis, Bray, & Holt, 1977) found that mock jurors were lenient toward an attractive defendant both before and after group discussion. At this point, we can only state that attractiveness appears to play a significant role in influencing the judgments of individuals, but the effects of group deliberation remain equivocal.

Many of the studies on the relationship between attitudinal attractiveness and jury decision making have been conducted by social psychologists testing Byrne's (1971) reinforcement theory of attraction, which predicts that the perception of similarity is rewarding and the perception of dissimilarity is nonrewarding, or even punishing. Byrne argues that similarity leads to liking because it gives people independent evidence for the correctness of their own interpretation of social reality. While this theory has support (Clore & Byrne, 1974; Lott & Lott, 1974), it does not explain why jurors would respond favorably to physically or socially attractive defendants, who may not be similar to the jurors themselves.

Other Defendant Characteristics

Criminal History One defendant characteristic that jury research has continually found to be strongly related to jury verdict is criminal history. Prior convictions or arrests of a defendant, unrelated to the crime at hand, are generally regarded as inadmissible evidence during the trial. However, when jurors somehow learn that the defendant does have a history of one or more felony convictions, there is a strong tendency of the jury to find the defendant guilty (Borgida & Park, 1988; Devine et al., 2001). This tendency happens even when jurors are told to disregard the prior criminal record through limiting instructions by the presiding judge (Lieberman & Sales, 1997). In addition, admissible knowledge of a prior criminal history during the sentencing phase of capital cases prompts juries to impose the death penalty (Baldus et al., 1983; Barnett, 1985). In short, knowledge of a prior criminal history appears to be one of the strongest influences of juror decision making, and, in line with commonsense justice, it should come as no surprise.

Defendant Behavior in the Courtroom How the behavior of a defendant in the courtroom affects jury verdicts has received astonishingly little research. Jurors scrutinize the defendant throughout the trial, and they usually notice everything from the defendant's attire to his or her slightest facial expressions. The most comprehensive study done to date on the influence of defendant behavior on jury decision making was conducted by law professor Scott Sundby (1998). Sundby collected data from the California segment of the 14-state Capital Jury Project, which randomly interviews jurors who have served in capital cases. The Capital Jury Project ◙ (see **Box 7-2**) is a nationwide study which is

BOX 7-2
The Capital Jury Project

In 1990, in a project funded by the National Science Foundation, researchers nationwide began interviewing jurors in a number of states who had served on capital cases. Law professors, criminologists, psychologists, law students, graduate students, and other social scientists have participated in this important work. Thus far, approximately 1,115 jurors in 14 different states have been interviewed. The sampling goal of the project was to reach at least four jurors randomly selected from a randomly-selected sample of cases, including cases that ended in a death sentence and cases that ended in a sentence of life imprisonment.

The interviews were extensive, taking from three to four hours for each juror. Jurors were asked about the quality of the evidence, the demeanor of the defendant, the performance of lawyers and judge, the legal instructions, and the process of jury deliberations, among other things. Researchers collected demographic information about each juror (e.g., age, gender, race, religion) and also about each juror's attitudes toward the death penalty and other criminal justice issues.

The project was initiated to investigate whether and to what extent the death penalty is imposed in arbitrary fashion, particularly with respect to race. (It was launched shortly after the U.S. Supreme Court announced its closely-decided and controversial decision *McCleskey v. Kemp*—see text.) The study has uncovered a wealth of information about death sentencing in general, however. As noted in the chapter, for example, some researchers have learned that the demeanor of the defendant—both during trial and during the sentencing proceeding—has an effect on the jury's final decision. Capital jurors also have considerable difficulty understanding the legal instructions provided to them by judges, and they are apparently strongly influenced by their own race, religion, and attitude toward the death penalty.

Since 1993, a number of articles have been published based on the Capital Jury research. Like the Kalven/Zeisel jury project, the Capital Jury Project will likely be cited in scholarly literature for many years to come.

designed to examine the factors that influence the decision of capital jurors on whether to impose the death penalty (Bowers, 1995).

The Sundby project was primarily interested in how remorsefulness (or a lack of it) influences juror decisions concerning death or life-without-parole sentences. In capital cases, defendants often do not display remorse. Observers have noted that they sit passively at their sentencing hearing, staring into space, seemingly not caring whether they live or die. Jurors, however, look for signs of remorsefulness or responsibility to help in their decision making. The Sundby study wanted to confirm these observations.

In the study, jurors placed a great deal of weight on sincere expressions of sorrow, especially in deciding whether to recommend death or life without parole. Nearly 70% of the jurors who voted for the death penalty during the penalty stage said that the lack of remorse by the defendant was the major reason for their death vote. Jurors scrutinized the defendant throughout the course of the trial, and they were quick to recall details about the defendant's demeanor, ranging from his attire to facial expression (Sundby, 1998). During the *early* stages of the trial process, some jurors were surprised at how "normal" the defendants appeared. Some jurors said they looked too nice to commit murder, seemed harmless, or did not look like an evil person. These early impressions, however, soon changed. The adjectives used by most capital jurors in describing the defendant during the later stages of the trial were commonly, "emotionally flat," "arrogant," "cocky," and "nonchalant." Throughout the trial, jurors constantly searched for any indicators of remorse or, at least, some signs of taking responsibility for their actions. This is problematic, though, because defendants during a trial are innocent until proven guilty. They should not be expected to demonstrate remorse. Such a display at sentencing is a different matter. Jurors, however, did not seem to make this distinction. The more accumulated evidence the jury could find that indicated the defendant's acceptance of responsibility for the killing, the more likely they would return a life sentence rather than death. Why? "The reasons are simple: an acknowledgment of responsibility by the defendant tends to soften any appearance that he is dangerously manipulative while also diminishing the jury's tendency to dismiss mitigation evidence as merely another hollow attempt by the defendant to place the blame somewhere else" (Sundby, 1998, p. 1575).

Although all the defendants gave virtually no apparent signs of remorsefulness, another factor that separated defendants who received the death penalty from those who received life was the degree of arrogance and cockiness they demonstrated throughout the trial and penalty phases. For example, jurors were angered by those defendants who laughed during the proceedings, especially during testimony about the victim, and those who openly engaged in flirtatious behavior. Juries who perceived an "arrogant, don't-care, defendant" were far more likely to settle on the death sentence.

In conclusion, once capital juries reach the penalty phase, rarely do defendants persuade juries that they are truly sorry to the point that the jury will vote for a life sentence. Ironically, it appears that juries may be receptive to this persuasion. Furthermore, they do not seem to require total remorse. "Although jurors are certainly more inclined to impose a death verdict on a remorseless figure who sits emotionless throughout the trial, they do not demand full atonement before giving a life sentence. Jurors seem willing to settle for signs that the defendant at least acknowledges some responsibility for the killing—signs that dampen the jurors' concerns over the defendant's dangerousness and make them more receptive to mitigation evidence as to why the defendant does not deserve to be sentenced to death" (Sundby, 1998, p. 1598).

Juror Characteristics and Decision Making

In recent years, very little research has been directed at the personality, demographic, and cognitive processes of jurors. Most of the research concentrating on how juror dispositional variables relate to verdicts or to the comprehension and application of jury instructions was conducted from the late 1960s to the early 1980s. Since the mid-1980s, this type of research has become nearly dormant. Part of the dormancy is due to what may be a premature conclusion that individual backgrounds, personality traits, attitudes, and intelligence are not helpful in predicting what a person will do in a jury situation. There has been a discernible shift in jury research to move from jury *personality* to the jury *situation*. Specifically, jury researchers have concentrated on the situation as the overriding determining factor in jury decision making, rather than the disposition, traits, and attitudes of the juror. For example, Ellsworth and Reifman (2000, p. 795) write: "it is no accident that social psychologists who study juries have attributed deficiencies in jury performance to deficiencies in the situation." Consequently, as we noted in the previous chapter, a vast amount of research over the past two decades has examined jury instructions, jury procedures, the group process, and the flow of information as the major influence of decision making, to the neglect of individual factors. But social science research moves in cycles, exploring one area, moving to another, and then eventually returning to the original area. Currently, dispositional factors are being neglected, but social science may well return to them again. In this section, we will briefly cover some of the more intriguing personality, dispositional, and attitudinal areas that continue to show promise in understanding how juries work.

The Story Model

During the trial a considerable amount of evidence is presented in a disjointed, question-and-answer format, sometimes over a period of several days, weeks, or—in exceptional cases—even months. In order to make a rational judgment about this extensive information, jurors try to comprehend and organize it into some meaningful whole.

Nancy Pennington and Reid Hastie (1986, 1992) developed a heuristic theory of how jurors organize and make sense of the vast array of evidence that is presented during the trial process and how they ultimately decide on guilt or innocence or, in civil cases, on the defendant's degree of responsibility. This popular and well-supported theory is referred to as the **story model**. Pennington and Hastie propose that jurors construct stories in the course of the trial and during the deliberation process that mediate and determine their decisions. In other words, jurors develop their own personal story of "what happened," and this conceptual structure allows them to incorporate the bits and pieces of the trial evidence into it. Overall, they try to arrive at an acceptable and plausible scenario for a crime or a civil situation. As Norman Finkel (1995, p. 63) remarked, "jurors do not so much find reality as *construct* it."

The story model hypothesizes that jurors may develop several plausible but competing stories during the course of a trial, and then they try to base their decision on the story which is acceptable and best fits the evidence. Pennington and Hastie (1992) theorize that three fundamental principles determine the acceptability of the story: (1) coverage; (2) uniqueness; and (3) coherence. Coverage refers to the extent to which the story accounts for the evidence presented during the trial. The greater the story's coverage, the more plausible the story and the more confident the juror is about the story. Uniqueness refers to the extent that one story stands out from the other competing stories. If there are several stories and none is distinctive from the others, then uncertainty will result and no one story is apt to emerge. Under these conditions, the juror will be indecisive.

The third principle of story acceptability, coherence, is more complicated, and is determined by the interaction of three factors: (1) completeness; (2) consistency; and (3) plausibility. Completeness refers to the extent to which a story covers all the bases and contains the highlights of the evidence. Consistency refers to the internal structure of the story. More specifically, a consistent story contains few, if any, internal contradictions. In this sense, the juror wonders "Does the story follow sequentially and make sense?" While consistency refers to internal aspects of the story, plausibility refers to the degree to which the story fits with the juror's version of the world—real or imagined. In other words, plausibility has to do with the relationship between the story and the juror's general knowledge of the world. These three factors combine to yield the coherence of a story.

Some researchers have proposed that jurors are more likely to construct one dominant story early in the trial rather than multiple stories as proposed by the story model. Throughout the trial, jurors try to fit the various pieces of evidence into that one, dominant story (Carlson & Russo, 2001). Carlson and Russo (2001) argue that jurors try to formulate only one coherent account of the crime that is consistent with their prior beliefs, the lawyer's opening statements, and the judge's early instructions. This perspective is slightly different form the Pennington-Hastie story model in that it emphasizes only *one* story is developed early in the trial and is largely built on the strength of the pre-existing beliefs and biases. As the trial progresses, the typical juror will accept or reject new evidence based on how it conforms to their already developed cognitive framework. Material that does not fit is rejected, and material that fits is accepted. Carlson and Russo refer to this process as **predecisional distortion**.

The hypothesis that jurors may have strong preexisting cognitive structures that may significantly slant their story making is also supported by the research of Olsen-Fulero and Fulero (1997), who have studied jury decision making in rape cases. "Overall . . . our work and recent work of others have supported the notion that jurors come to the rape judgment situation with preconceptions and attitudes that lead them to entertain particular stories about what may happen, that the stories are used to process the facts presented in the case, and that these stories are then used to arrive at a legal decision or verdict" (Olson-Fulero & Fulero, 1997, p. 418).

Vicki Smith (1991, 1993) has also found that prospective jurors have a pre-existing conceptual prototype of certain crimes and offenders. Prospective jurors in one of her studies (1991) generally conceived of a kidnapping as being characterized by ransom demands, the victim being a child, the victim being taken away, and the motive being money. Moreover, jurors tended to persist with these conceptions or stereotypes, in spite of jury instructions or points of law. In fact, her research has found that mock jurors actually have little correct information about the law. They do not enter the jury box "empty headed" waiting for their charge. Rather, they have a preconceived notion of the crime scenario and the type of person who would commit such a crime. These personal stories of the crime and their prototypes of crime categories can influence their perceptions of the trial evidence and their verdict decisions. Additionally, Norman Finkel (1988) finds that many jurors have well-established commonsense preconceptions of insanity and that these preconceptions strongly influence insanity verdicts.

Smith and Studebaker (1996) discovered that people's prior knowledge of crime categories plays a much broader role than previously known. For instance, they found that jurors' tendency to use their prior knowledge of crime categories extends not only to the verdict-selection process but also to the fact finding phase. What jurors know—or think they know—about rape, burglary, or embezzlement, for example, affects how they will attend to the evidence presented. Furthermore, similar to jurors, *witnesses* appear to rely heavily on their offender stereotypes. That is, witnesses may fill the gaps in their memories with their preconceived notions of offenders, and this slants their testimony significantly.

If the trial evidence matches this cognitive schema and the defendant follows the preconceived prototype, the juror is most likely to make a verdict decision along the lines of the developed story, regardless of the instructions or legal definitions. Smith found that the schema of laypersons concerning various types of crime were contrary to the way the categories are organized under the law. Smith (1991, p. 870) concludes: "These findings are consistent with research in other areas of social psychology demonstrating the potential dangers of prior knowledge of theories for accurate judgment and decision making."

However, to what extent does the strength of the evidence impact the story-making process? After all, one of Kalven and Zeisel's (1966) major conclusions from their well-respected work on the jury was that the weight of the evidence was the primary determinant of most jury verdicts. Wouldn't it be reasonable to expect, for example, that scientific evidence, such as DNA and fingerprints, will override pre-trial biases and story making during the trial?

Strength of the Evidence

"Strength of the evidence (SOE) is a global term referring to the quantity and quality of evidence presented by the plaintiff/prosecution during a trial" (Devine et al., 2001). Social science research, both in the laboratory and in the field, has demonstrated a strong and consistent relationship between the strength of the evidence and jury verdicts (Devine et al., 2001). However, quantifying the strength of the evidence in any particular trial is a difficult task for any researcher. Furthermore, the instructions concerning the standard of proof provided by the judge in any particular trial may be unclear to jurors and misunderstood by them. Definitions of the standards of proof are not uniform across all jurisdictions, and the U.S. Supreme Court has not mandated that trial courts follow any particular definition (Horowitz & Kirkpatrick, 1996). ◄ Recall that standards of proof were covered in ◙ **Boxes 3-3** and **3-4**.

The effect of evidentiary strength on jurors is clear-cut when the evidence is very strong or very weak. When the evidence against the defendant is strong, the overwhelming tendency is to convict; when the evidence is weak, the overwhelming tendency is to acquit, regardless of the imagined scenario. However, in those cases where the evidence is ambiguous or complicated, the various aspects of the story model are most apt to come into play. Kalven and Zeisel (1966) also concluded that, when the evidence is unclear or does not favor one side, jurors would be liberated from the constraints of the evidence and become most susceptible to the influence of their own thoughts and beliefs.

Hindsight Bias

Another cognitive process that potentially might contaminate jury decision making is **hindsight bias**, which refers to biased judgments of past events after the outcome is known. It is ". . . a projection of new knowledge into the past accompanied by a denial that the outcome information has influenced judgment" (Hawkins & Hastie, 1990, p. 311). Thus, when people learn of an outcome, they typically claim they "knew all along" what it would be. Said another way, "The hindsight bias is the tendency for people with outcome knowledge to believe falsely that they would have predicted the reported outcome of an event" (Hawkins & Hastie, 1990, p. 311). This bias potentially affects how jurors select, process, and integrate evidence for decision making.

Researchers have found evidence of hindsight bias, particularly in medical malpractice or product liability suits. In these types of cases, jurors are supposed to base their judgments on the defendant's behavior prior to the occurrence of the harm or damage. However, knowing that the defendant has curtailed his medical practice following the incident, jurors will find it extremely difficult not to blame him for the harm to the plaintiff. As another example, suppose police officers are charged with excessive force at arrest. The arrest, however, convinces an informant to come forward and help other officers solve a separate murder case. Knowledge that this occurred results in a tendency to excuse the original officers, particularly if the evidence against the officers is not strong. Again, evidentiary strength is likely to override other factors, including hindsight bias.

Casper, Benedict, and Perry (1989), in an effort to determine the power of hindsight bias in jury verdicts, used simulated case materials (on videotape) and mock jurors drawn from college students and adults called for jury service. The researchers reasoned that in many legal disputes jurors are told a "story" that a particular outcome occurred, but they are instructed to ignore the outcome when deciding the important legal issues before them. The videotape showed two attorneys who gave the same general story, but shaded and interpreted the story in different ways for the mock jurors. The central story was that two police officers received a tip from an informant that a man involved in a crime was at a particular address, an apartment building. The informant provided a general, vague description of the man. The officers proceeded to the address and knocked on the first door they saw. The door was answered by a man who followed the description given by the informant. When he refused to allow them in, the officers forced their way in, knocking him to the floor, causing a cut on his forehead. The officers proceeded to search the apartment, causing $600 in damages to the apartment. The scenario clearly illustrated an illegal search.

The researchers set up three possible outcomes to the story. One third of the mock jurors were told that the police search turned up evidence of illegal conduct, one third were told the police found no evidence of illegality, and another third received no outcome information. The jurors were instructed by the mock judge to decide whether the police were liable for any compensatory and punitive damages. The judge's instructions indicated that their decisions should be based on the lawfulness of the police search. The data indicated that the outcome knowledge (hindsight bias) had a significant effect on juror decisions. That is, jurors who had been told that something incriminating had been found during the illegal search of the apartment were less likely to award the plaintiff with compensatory or punitive damages than jurors in the other two conditions.

Similar results were obtained in an experiment by Robbennolt and Sobus (1997). They described scenarios in which a police officer searched a vehicle that matched a drug courier profile; the occupants of the car were removed forcibly and injured. A hindsight bias effect was found in conditions in which drugs were found. Robbennolt and Sobus, however, were also exploring the possible moderating effect of counter-factual thinking, in which people compare real outcomes with imagined alternative outcomes. These researchers found evidence of an interaction between counterfactual thinking and hindsight bias in some, but not all situations. Hindsight bias, then, appears to be a complicated but important cognitive process in juror decision making for cases where an outcome is already known. Together with counterfactual thinking, it may prove to be a highly critical variable in the jury decision making process.

Just World Hypothesis

Psychologists have observed that many people believe the world is a just place, where one gets what one deserves and deserves what one gets (Lerner, 1970, 1980; Montada & Lerner, 1998). This simplistic belief may help to explain why juries sometimes make the decisions they do. In a just world, fate and a person's merit are closely aligned, "good" people are rewarded, and "bad" people are punished. Believers in a just world perceive a connection between what people do, are, or believe in and what happens to them.

According to the **just world hypothesis**, for the sake of cognitive consistency, many people cannot believe in a world governed by a schedule of random reinforcements or events. The suffering of innocent or respectable people—those who have done nothing to bring about their own grief—would be too unacceptable and unjust (Lerner & Simmons, 1966). Actually, research suggests that innocent victims threaten the belief in a just world, because they provide evidence that people may not receive what they deserve (Hafer, 2000). Thus, when tragedy strikes, believers in a just world tend to blame the victims, concluding that these victims must have deserved their fate in some way. For example, some people believe that rape victims are to blame for their rape (Bell, Kuriloff, & Lottes, 1994), and although men tend to be more prone to this myth, a significant number of women (even when they have been victims themselves) also believe in the rape myth (Carmody & Washington, 2001; Jenkins & Dambrot, 1987). In addition, battered wives are often seen as responsible for their abusive husbands' behavior (Summers & Feldman, 1984). An important qualification, however, is that just-worlders tend to attribute causality or blame to the victim only as a last resort, preferring to blame another person or an obvious cause whenever possible. Conversely, there is also a strong propensity to attribute good fortune and luck, like winning a lottery, to having done something good or positive (Rubin & Peplau, 1973).

Researchers examining the hypothesis have found that belief in a just world is positively related to belief in a higher being and religiosity (Staub, 1978; Zuckerman & Gerbasi, 1977); authoritarianism (Rubin & Peplau, 1973); political conservatism and adherence to traditional values (Lerner, 1977; Staub, 1978); trust (Rubin & Peplau, 1975); the "work ethic," where it is assumed that hard work brings just rewards (Zuckerman & Gerbasi, 1977); and a tendency to admire and respect political leaders and powerful institutions (Rubin & Peplau, 1975). Believers in a just world are also presumed to be hostile and unsympathetic toward victims of social injustice, especially when their suffering cannot be easily alleviated (Lerner, 1970; Lerner & Simmons, 1966). Interestingly, this belief is far more prevalent in societies where there are extremes of wealth and poverty (Dalbert & Yamauchi, 1994; Furnham, 1993). Moreover, a just world orientation encourages an adherence to the rules and laws that are intended to guide conduct and control the nature of a society as a whole (rather than a benevolent attitude toward individuals and their specific welfare).

Just-worlders use two dimensions to decide whether others deserve their fates—actions and attributes (Lerner, 1980). To just-worlders, acts displaying cruelty, unfriendliness, stinginess, hostility, or antisocial behavior *deserve* a range of negative consequences. However, attributes like physical attractiveness, intelligence, taste in dress, social status, or social power and influence also affect the impressions and judgments of just-worlders (as well as many other people).

Attractiveness, whether physical or social, is assumed by many people to be deserved. That is, attractive people have earned their attractiveness by being good, positive persons. It follows the same logic as that proposed by Dion, Berscheid, and Walster (1972), that "what is beautiful or socially desirable must be good." Therefore, we would expect jurors who are just-worlders to consider attractive defendants as being basically good and deserving of lenient treatment.

The just world hypothesis has been examined in relation to victims of criminal actions or accidents. Jones and Aronson (1973) investigated several hypotheses, including the prediction that a socially attractive victim of a crime is perceived as more at fault than a less socially attractive victim. Mock jurors were 234 college undergraduates who read a brief case account of either an actual rape or an attempted rape, involving victims presumed to differ in social "respectability" or social attractiveness—a married woman, an unmarried woman who had never had sex, and a divorced woman. The researchers had distributed a pretest questionnaire which indicated that married women and unmarried women who had not had sex were more highly regarded and respectable in society than divorced women. Subjects were presented with descriptions of the crime, the defendant, and the victim, and they were asked how many years the defendant should be imprisoned and how much the victim was at fault.

The first hypothesis predicted that more fault would be attributed to a respectable victim than to a less respectable one. This is in accordance with the just world belief that something tragic does not happen to persons with good character; somehow, they must have done something to bring their fate upon themselves. A second hypothesis predicted that a defendant who injured a respectable person would be punished more severely. As a third hypothesis, Jones and Aronson predicted that an actual rape would be more severely punished than an attempted rape.

The results were generally in the direction of the predictions. Regardless of their own gender, subjects did feel that the women of "high respectability" were more at fault for the rape than the divorced woman. In assigning punishment to the defendant, the subjects gave more severe sentences when an actual rape had occurred. The second hypothesis was only partially confirmed, however. Although more severe sentences were meted out when the victim of an actual rape was married, the jurors drew no distinction between the other two groups; similar punishments were given in both cases. For attempted rape, however, the offender received approximately the same sentence whether the victim was married or unmarried, and received substantially less punishment if the victim had been divorced. Interestingly, the severe punishment for the actual rape of a married compared to an unmarried woman may reflect a perspective that the woman's spouse was injured as well. Thus, though the married woman was considered at fault, the jurors may have been trying to compensate her husband by being especially punitive to the offender.

In general, the results of the Jones-Aronson study lend support to a just world hypothesis concerning the misfortunes of victims. Jurors persisted in attributing fault to women of high respectability who, because the world is just, somehow must have done something to bring the attack upon themselves. This attribution of fault did not affect the severity of punishment given the defendant, however.

There are many unanswered questions regarding the results of the above study, and had Jones and Aronson administered a just world scale to their jurors the results might have proved more intriguing. They are striking enough, however, to make a just world interpretation worth pursuing. In light of changing social mores, results of that study would likely be different today, when society is more sensitive to the issue of rape, regardless of the marital status of the victim.

More research is needed to explore the just world phenomenon in depth. Adrian Furnham (1993) finds that research on the just world hypothesis has progressed through three stages: (1) an experimental, primarily laboratory-based test phase, in which the concept was validated; (2) a correlational phase in which the self-report measures of the concept were developed; and (3) a conceptual research phase which has begun to challenge the notion that the concept is as simple as originally supposed. In the years to come, research is very likely to find that the just world hypothesis, while helping to explain some jury behavior, is probably more complicated and limited in scope than first thought.

Authoritarianism

Authoritarianism is the term used to describe an ideology or an attitude system holding that one should unquestionably accept authority from recognized powerful people and institutions. Since authoritarianism is present in people in varying degrees, it is possible to speak of high or low authoritarians. The former conform strictly to conventional social norms and exhibit black-or-white thinking, rigid prejudice toward those who are different or do not embrace their point of view, and hostility toward those who deviate from established social norms. On jury panels, high authoritarians are hypothesized to be intolerant and to have a tendency to condemn, reject, and punish those who violated conventional wisdom and laws. Therefore, we would expect high authoritarians to convict frequently and to render severe punishment for deviants. On the other hand, it is hypothesized that authoritarians would be more accepting and lenient toward those individuals whom they perceive as sharing their own values.

Low authoritarians demonstrate opposite attitudes. Authority is not inherently respected, but must earn respect. Low authoritarians do not place great value on conventional norms, and they have more tolerance for those who deviate. Sometimes called egalitarians, people low in authoritarianism are believed to be more objective in making jury decisions.

A number of jury simulation studies have examined the authoritarianism continuum and have contrasted persons at both poles. As expected, the research has reported that high authoritarian jurors are more inclined to perceive guilt and give more severe punishments when the defendant is described as attitudinally dissimilar from themselves or as having a negative character (Berg & Vidmar, 1975; Mitchell & Byrne, 1973; Boehm, 1968). It has also been reported that authoritarians are more in favor of the death penalty than egalitarians are (Jurow, 1971) and are especially punitive toward low status defendants (Berg & Vidmar, 1975). Authoritarians are also more prone to make hasty judgments on the basis of subjective or irrelevant characteristics of defendants than their less authoritarian peers (Olsen-Fulero & Fulero, 1997). Narby, Cutler, and Moran (1993), in their meta-analysis of extant research, found that high authoritarians are more likely to convict and impose harsh punishment than low authoritarians. This tendency was especially notable for those individuals who are high in legal authoritarianism. Legal authoritarianism is similar to traditional authoritarianism, except that it reveals attitudes toward the legal system. Specifically, people who are considered high on legal authoritarianism tend to disregard the civil liberties and rights of the accused person, such as the presumption of innocence and various constitutional procedural safeguards (Narby et al., 1993). It will be recalled that authoritarianism was one of the characteristics distinguishing death qualified jurors from non-death qualified jurors, as we noted in ◀ Chapter 6. Olsen-Fulero and Fulero (1997, p. 415) conclude that high authoritarians "not only process information differently in a legal context but also that they are prone to rapid, personological, inferential, and probably emotionally-based decisions that tend to be less accurate than [those of] their more egalitarian peers."

Authoritarians seem to be more strongly influenced by the judge (Bandewehr & Novotny, 1976), but they are also more likely to ignore a judge when told to disregard damaging but inadmissible testimony about a defendant's character. Egalitarians (low authoritarians), presumably because they are open minded, recall more evidence about the crime (Berg & Vidmar, 1975). High authoritarians have also been found to be "source-oriented" and persons low on authoritarianism to be "message-oriented." That is, authoritarians pay comparatively little attention to arguments and testimony and base their responses more readily on the attributes of the sources (Johnson & Steiner, 1967).

Might group interaction limit the impact of an authoritarian personality? Several researchers have addressed this question. Boehm (1968) contended that authoritarians reach their verdicts early in a trial and resist changing their verdict in the face of new information. Egalitarians, on the other hand, presumably resist making early judgments until they are given all the information about a case. Other social psychological research, however, has found that authoritarians are more susceptible to influence than egalitarians are (e.g., Kirscht & Dillehay, 1967; Bray & Noble, 1978).

In an attempt to obtain further information on the effects of group interaction on authoritarians, Bray and Noble (1978) conducted a simulation study in which 44 six-person juries listened to a 30-minute audio-recording of a murder trial based on an actual case. After hearing the tape, subjects entered into group discussion to simulate the jury deliberation process. A verdict could be returned only if five of the six jurors agreed on a decision within 45 minutes; failure to do so resulted in a hung jury.

Prior to the experiment, the subjects were administered psychological scales to determine their level of authoritarianism. In addition, measures of the individual juror's judgments about guilt were made prior to and after the deliberation. The experimenters were interested in both individual juror decisions and in the six-member group jury verdict.

The results revealed that authoritarian jurors and juries reached guilty verdicts more often and imposed more severe punishments than egalitarian ones did. The latter finding is consistent with other studies (e.g, Berg & Vidmar, 1975; Jurow, 1971; Mitchell & Byrne, 1973) and has some potential implications for trials involving capital punishment, as discussed earlier. Authoritarians were more likely than egalitarians to say they would convict when death was a potential penalty.

The data also showed that pre-deliberation to post-deliberation verdict-shifts existed for both authoritarians and egalitarians, although authoritarians exhibited significantly more such shifts. This finding lends credence to the possibility that authoritarians are influenced substantially by group interaction. The direction of the shifts differed: Authoritarians gave more severe sentences after group deliberations, while egalitarians demonstrated a trend toward more lenience. These shifts reflected the choice initially favored by the jurors and provide support for the group-polarization effect to be discussed below.

Although we must be cautious about making generalizations from simulation to actual jury decision making, it does appear that authoritarianism is an influential factor in the jury process. Ellison and Buckhout (1981) concluded that authoritarianism is common and very likely plays a significant role in the judgments made by juries. According to these researchers, scores on the authoritarian scale have been the best predictors of conviction they have encountered. Also, like Bray and Noble, Ellison and Buckhout found that authoritarians are consistently in favor of the death penalty. Devine et al. (2001), in their extensive review of the research, concluded that mock juries containing a high proportion of high authoritarian jurors have tended to convict more often and impose longer sentences than mock juries with a low proportion of such people. Although the authoritarian-convict/punish relationship was the most robust of all the personality variables they reviewed, Devine and his colleagues wonder if the relationship would hold for actual juries.

This leads to an important issue, one that comes in the realm of the psychology and law relationship discussed in ◀ Chapter 1. Some researchers have suggested that authoritarians are undesirable as jurors and should be eliminated in the *voir dire*. But American law is a social and political enterprise developed from the moral fabric of society. If authoritarianism is a common ingredient of American culture and presumably of American juries, and if a democratic system is based on the attitudes of its citizens, shouldn't authoritarians be impaneled representatively? If attorneys are to reject prospective jurors on the basis of personality type, the rejections should be made via established judicial procedures of peremptory and for-cause challenges. A policy decision that would preclude authoritarians (or just-worlders or "neurotics") from being seated on a jury would be ill advised.

In recent years, researchers have preferred the term dogmatism, but the features described are nearly identical to those that characterize authoritarians in earlier research. Individuals high in dogmatism are described as close-minded people who are intolerant of ambiguity, tend to make extreme judgments, and demonstrate unquestioning respect for authority. Dogmatic persons strive to avoid inconsistency in their beliefs and rigid value systems, and they react to inconsistent information by ignoring it (Davis, 1998). However, dogmatic jurors will try very hard to follow orders and instructions given to them by the judge. They often do as they are told, without much thought about the many ramifications of their actions. Research has shown that highly dogmatic jurors are more likely to convict and are more punitive in their judgments compared to their non-dogmatic peers (Shaffer & Wheatman, 2000). Dogmatic jurors, and authoritarian jurors, apparently differ on one important characteristic, though. Dogmatic jurors are capable of putting aside their personal bias and will follow the law to a tee, as long as the law is comprehensible (Lieberman & Sales, 1997).

Group Processes

Deliberation Style

"Deliberation style refers to the manner in which juries approach their task of reaching a verdict, particularly the initial stages" (Devine et al., 2001). One style, referred to by Hastie, Penrod, and Pennington (1983) as **verdict-driven**, is where the ultimate goal of the jury is to reach a verdict as quickly as possible. The verdict-driven jury will often take a vote soon after electing a foreperson and quickly focus their discussions on key facts that are essential to reaching a final outcome. Another style is called **evidence-driven**. In the evidence-driven approach, jurors will delay the vote until after considerable discussion focusing on evaluations of the evidence in the case. Rather than focusing on the verdict, the evidence-driven group will concentrate on developing a logical story from the evidence. Hastie et al. (1983) found that mock jurors using the evidence-driven style tended to deliberate longer, consider the evidence more carefully, and report greater satisfaction with the experience compared to mock jurors using the verdict-driven approach. However, Hastie and his colleagues could not identify how the different styles affected the final verdict.

Although deliberation style appears to be important in understanding the process of how jurors reach decisions, research on the topic has been very sparse, with fewer than a half-dozen studies conducted thus far. How much of an influence the deliberation style has on the final verdict still remains unknown. It appears, though, that juries tend to pursue the verdict-driven approach. The legal system, however, prefers the evidence-driven approach, at least in principle. Devine et al. (2001, p. 701) conclude from their extensive review of the jury literature: "Clearly, the evidence-driven style is closer to the normative ideal desired by the courts; in contrast, many juries adopt the verdict-driven style that seems most likely to lead to the rapid delineation of factions and steadily increasing normative pressure."

Polarization

James Stoner (1961) discovered that when people got together in a group they were more daring or "risky" in their decision making than when they made decisions as individuals. This phenomenon, eventually called the risky-shift effect, stimulated the interest of numerous investigators who generated a collection of studies to test it. As so often happens in psychological research, however, what appeared to be simple was discovered to be highly complex. "Risky shift" was a misnomer that did not portray accurately the effects of groups on individual decisions (Myers & Lamm, 1976). Subsequent research illustrated that group deliberation may produce cautious decisions as well as more risky ones, depending upon the context, and thus was born the group-polarization hypothesis.

The hypothesis states: "The average postgroup response will tend to be more extreme in the same direction as the average of the pregroup responses" (Myers & Lamm, 1976, p. 603). That rather complicated maxim simply means that group interaction tends to draw the average individual pregroup decision more clearly in the direction in which it was already leaning. Hence, if individual members of a group were leaning toward a not-guilty verdict, the group interaction would increase their commitment toward a not-guilty verdict even more. If, on the other hand, individual members tended to believe a defendant guilty, group discussion should encourage a stronger commitment toward a guilty verdict. In civil cases, the individual jurors' beliefs that a plaintiff deserved a substantial award for damages might be reinforced in group discussion, and the ultimate group decision would award even higher damages. Thus, polarization refers to the shift toward the already preferred pole.

Myers and Kaplan (1976) presented subjects with case materials that clearly made defendants in eight hypothetical traffic felony cases appear either guilty or not guilty. If the subjects found the defendant guilty, they were also expected to recommend punishment. The guilty/not-guilty judgments were made on a scale ranging from 0 (definitely not guilty) to 20 (definitely guilty), and the punishment recommendation was given on a scale ranging from 1 (minimum punishment for the infraction) to 7 (maximum punishment).

Myers and Kaplan found that group deliberations polarized the initial response tendencies associated with a case. Mock jurors who leaned toward guilty verdicts and punishment became harsher following deliberations. Those with lenient initial judgments became more lenient after deliberations. When jury deliberations were not allowed, however, judgments did not change from the first to the final rating.

A number of other experiments using simulated jury conditions have demonstrated the shift from prediscussion tendency to postdiscussion certainty (Bray & Kerr, 1979; Kerr, Nerenz, & Herrick, 1979; Bray, et al., 1978; Kaplan, 1977). It appears that group discussion, at least under simulated conditions and with college students as mock jurors, does in fact polarize already existing opinions or beliefs.

Leniency Bias

As mentioned earlier in the chapter, Harry Kalven and Hans Zeisel (1966) in their classic *The American Jury* reported that in criminal trials where the judge disagreed with the jury's decisions, the jury was almost always more lenient toward the defendant than the judge. Overall, jury trials resulted in twice as many acquittals as might have occurred if the cases had been tried only by the judge. This phenomenon, seen primarily in criminal trials, has been called the **leniency bias**. The bias also refers to the frequent observation in mock criminal jury trials that people are prone to vote guilty on their own but are more likely to vote innocent when in group deliberation. The group deliberation process, for some unknown reason, seems to induce criminal jurors to be more lenient.

Leniency bias appears to be especially prevalent in jury deliberations in which there is no clear, predominant preference for conviction or acquittal at the beginning (MacCoun & Kerr, 1988). It is also most likely to occur in situations requiring a dichotomous verdict (guilty or not guilty). Where other alternatives are possible—e.g., guilty but mentally ill—leniency bias has not been demonstrated.

Effects of Expert Testimony

As we have discussed in earlier chapters, expert testimony refers to the courtroom opinion of some individual who possesses special skill or knowledge in some science, profession, or business that is not possessed by the average person. Many studies have examined the effects of expert testimony on mock juries, including the presence or absence of expert testimony, the style and content of the presentation, and the degree to which the expert's testimony is challenged (Devine et al., 2001). The research results thus far are mixed, but much of it suggests that the overall impact of expert testimony on jury decision making is perhaps minimal (Devine et al., 2001). There are situations, of course, in which expert testimony does wield some power on juror decision making, such as when it is tailored to the specific facts of the case at hand, or when it provides novel, useful information to the jury. However, in situations where the expert comes with an array of credentials and degrees, is receiving high payment to testify, and/or has a frequent history of testifying, he or she is perceived by jurors as a "hired gun" (Cooper & Neuhaus, 2000). Experts perceived as hired guns rarely are effective in persuading jurors. If anything, they tend to engender animosity and irritation in the jurors and encourage jurors to rely on their pre-existing opinions and beliefs.

Law Professor Scott Sundby (1997) attempted to identify some empirical answers to how juries react to expert testimony (psychologists and psychiatrists) in capital cases. The study utilized data from the Capital Jury Project discussed earlier in the chapter ■ (see **Box 7-2**). One hundred and fifty-two jurors were interviewed concerning their reactions to expert testimony during the penalty phase. These jurors had served on 36 cases in which the defendant was convicted of first-degree murder and the jury was then asked to return a sentence of death.

Sundby reports that professional expert witnesses were generally viewed negatively by jurors, especially those experts called by the defense. Many expert witnesses were seen simply as not being credible. "The professional expert witness generally was seen as an unreliable storyteller, one likely to spin a tale for her own gain rather than for the enlightenment of the jury. And, with only their own experience and beliefs with which to judge the story's veracity, jurors tended to discredit defense experts' testimony as being at odds with their worldview. The lay witness, in contrast, was far more likely to be perceived as a storyteller without a hidden agenda and, consequently, juries were far more receptive to the story she had to tell" (Sundby, 1997, p. 1136). To be effective, Sundby cautions, the expert's testimony must be integrated with persuasive lay testimony.

Jury Simulation: Critiques and Conclusions

Jury simulation studies that attempt to understand both individual and group decision making are being conducted at a steady pace, but doubts about their external or *ecological validity* persist. Can an experimental situation, using volunteer college students as mock jurors, even approximate a real-life encounter? Studying the jury process is a formidable task. Even if researchers were allowed to observe or manipulate actual jury proceedings, there would be such an annoying myriad of independent variables that experimental control and precise measurement would be nearly impossible. More importantly, of course, such experimentation would border on the ethical, social, and legal issue of what is "just." As a result, many researchers remain favorably disposed to simulation studies using mock jurors and the quality of these studies is improving (Bornstein, 1999; Diamond, 1997; Lieberman & Sales, 2000).

In 1979, Neil Vidmar bluntly summarized the problems with jury simulation research at that time. "It is argued that much jury simulation research, especially that involving investigation of the effects of defendant character on juror-jury decisions, can be fairly described as marked by (a) legal naivete, (b) sloppy scholarship, and (c) overgeneralization combined with inappropriate value judgments" (Vidmar, 1979, p. 96).

Vidmar's first criticism referred to the lack of legal sophistication and knowledge displayed by research psychologists relative to the judicial system. Thus, their experimental designs were flawed by the inclusion of unrealistic scenarios or instructions. Many studies have required subjects to determine the number of years an offender should receive (sentencing), when in actual practice, except for capital cases, juries are rarely involved in sentencing. Some researchers confused criminal and civil trials, as by presenting subjects with criminal trial materials and asking them both to determine guilt or innocence and award damages. More subtle gaffes occurred when researchers were not familiar with statutes, or with what are legally acceptable jury instructions. Sometimes, courtroom procedures have been presented out of sequence, or researchers have failed to provide subjects with clear definitions of the standards of proof for determining guilt—though those standards are not that clear, even when "real" judges explain them.

Researchers also commonly ask subjects to determine degrees of guilt (as on scales from one to ten) rather than simply return a guilty or not-guilty verdict. In defense of this practice, we must note that simple guilty or not-guilty verdicts are difficult to analyze statistically. They result in a "dichotomous" variable—one that has only two possibilities. For ease of analysis and sensitivity to differences, researchers prefer a continuous variable denoted by different degrees, since such a variable allows a more sophisticated computer analysis. In recent years, however, researchers have largely overcome errors in methodology related to ignorance of law and procedure.

As an example of sloppy scholarship, Vidmar noted a frequent, unwarranted practice on the part of researchers to cite inaccurately the findings of Kalven and Zeisel's *The American Jury* and to align their own results with those of that classic study. In essence, Vidmar argues, many investigators are not justified in claiming similarity between their study and the Kalven-Zeisel project, because their results simply do not correspond. The Kalven-Zeisel project was based on actual jury deliberations, compared to a vast majority of studies that are based on mock juries. Some researchers are just as lax with respect to other studies, inaccurately citing results or misunderstanding the theoretical positions of other scholars. This builds pyramids of inaccuracy and misinformation into the research literature.

Vidmar's third criticism pertained to grandiose assertions by researchers that their studies will help solve the problems of the judicial system. "Researchers have tended to puff up the potential importance of their findings without taking into consideration all the other factors that might offset them in a real world trial" (Vidmar, 1979, p. 100).

Several other problems undermine the quality of the simulation research and limit its applicability to the judicial system. An often repeated criticism questions the use of college students as mock jurors. Students at research universities where the studies are generally conducted tend to be from the middle class, well educated, intelligent, young, and liberal in ideology—hardly representative of the population at large from which juries are typically drawn. It can also be argued that the lack of experiential learning by college students is a deficit. In any case, the student subjects are not representative of the population. With increases in continuing education programs and the fact that a greater proportion of the public is college educated, this problem may be attenuated.

Still another problem with jury simulation research pertains to the presentation of materials. In over half of the studies on jury decision making, subjects have been presented with written case materials that are often extremely brief and simplistic summaries of usually hypothetical cases (Bray & Kerr, 1979). In about a third of the experiments, audio presentation has been used, and it too was of short duration (30 to 90 minutes). These time limits and modes of presentation in no way reflect the intricacies of courtroom trials. True jurors receive trial information in uneven, sometimes lengthy time-intervals, through all the sense modalities. By and large, the information is received by hearing or through auditory channels. Jurors rarely read case materials while trials are in progress.

Another fundamental problem is that most jury simulation research has focused on individual juror decisions rather than on collective jury decisions. Those projects that have included group discussion or group-derived verdicts have had unreasonable time restrictions (e.g., a verdict must be reached within 30 minutes) and have used an exceedingly small number of "jurors." They have rarely been asked to return a final group verdict; rather, individual verdicts after group discussion have been sought (Weiten & Diamond, 1979).

Nevertheless, some researchers believe that studying individual jurors is a valid approach. Citing the Kalven and Zeisel data, they argue that the first ballot in deliberation is a strong prediction of the final outcome, even without group discussion. But, although the first vote often does predict the eventual verdict, some group interaction has occurred prior to that vote. The interaction may pertain to evidence or to opinions about a wide range of issues. By preventing at least some group interaction, some researchers have altered significantly the conditions they are trying to simulate. In sum, we have no basis for assuming that group decision making parallels individual decision making.

Conclusions on Simulation Research

The problems discussed above are some of the major flaws making generalizations from laboratory to courtroom risky. While the foregoing may make one wonder if any of the research on jury simulation is of value, it is important to remember that one of the hallmarks of science is to be skeptical of interpretations and to seek alternative explanations and approaches. The behavioral sciences move in a spiral fashion, becoming sounder both in theory and in method as the pioneer approaches are critiqued and improved. We must also keep in mind that a great majority of the jury simulation studies have occurred only since 1970.

Some researchers argue that the simulated jury approach still offers the best alternative to research testing real juries, which is seldom tolerated by the judicial system. Of course, it is possible to study the product of the jury—the verdict—and to obtain demographic and personality characteristics of the jurors, as well as their personal accounts, after their decision has been rendered. The major problem with this product is that the nearly endless list of possible contributors is difficult to disentangle. It is much more advantageous to investigate before and during the decision making process.

After an extensive review of the literature on jury simulation, Brian Bornstein (1999) concludes that—even though the methodology is unrealistic—this is not cause for concern. The decision making processes that are being studied can still be generalized to the decision making of real juries. Furthermore, researchers have not obtained differences between different mock juror samples (e.g., students versus non-student adults) or between different trial media (written summaries versus tapes of actual trials). Shari Diamond (1997) is also sanguine about jury simulation research, but for another reason. She notes that the new generation of jury simulation studies includes many more ecologically valid features than the simulations of old.

Although empirical psychology is self-corrective in the long run, a premature conclusion by researchers that they have discovered the psychological secrets of the jury process through simulation study may do more harm than good. In the landmark death penalty case, *Lockhart v. McCree* (1986), discussed in ◀Chapter 6, the U.S. Supreme Court dealt a heavy blow to research studies using simulated juries. Social science researchers do not need another case like *Lockhart*. Yet Diamond (1997) believes researchers can recover from this, and that courts are willing to be persuaded that simulation studies have relevance. Theories and hypotheses developed within the confines of the artificial atmosphere of the psychological laboratory must be tested against the actual natural event before some tentative conclusions can be advanced. This may require archival and case-by-case analysis of actual trials as well as research with actual jurors. Diamond is advocating these approaches as a second stage in jury research.

Summary and Conclusions

In the summary of the previous chapter, we referred to Wallace Loh's (1979) observation that the relationship between psychology and law is marked by recurrent cycles. Part of this is due to changing interests of psychologists studying the legal system. As a group, research psychologists like to be pioneers, exploring new areas and, perhaps, settling none. Mundane replication and synchronized research efforts tend to draw one away from the excitement of being on the cutting edge of knowledge.

Thus, during the 1970s, jury research in social psychology focused on the physical, attitudinal, and social characteristics of defendants and plaintiffs, and how these features influence jury decision making. During that time, the just world hypothesis generated a good deal of research, as we have noted. There were also attempts to develop "models" of jury decision making, which led to scientific jury selection. Jury size and decision rule, discussed in the previous chapter, were explored but left abruptly for other areas of discovery.

In the 1980s and 1990s, research took a more cognitive approach, focusing first on the effects of curative instructions and admonitions on decision making. Lately, the story model and its offshoots have surfaced as having great promise. Hindsight and similar cognitive biases should continue to draw more attention in the years ahead. Finkel's "commonsense justice" will likely play a major role in the jury decision making research in the years ahead. In fact, the entire research area of cognitive constructs and schemata, beliefs and attitudes, appears to be the direction taken not only by jury research, but by research in psychology and law in general. The beginning of the new millennium has also witnessed a significant increase in research interest on the civil jury and the use of actual jurors in place of mock ones.

In an extensive literature review (206 published studies), Dennis Devine and his colleagues (2001) have identified *four* major themes that have emerged during the last 45 years of jury decision-making research. *First*, jurors frequently do not make decisions in the manner intended by the courts, regardless of how they are instructed. "Instead, decisions are based on past experience in the form of scripts, schemas, stereotypes, and other cognitive mechanism as well as personal beliefs and values about what is right, wrong, and fair" (Devine et al., 2001, p. 699). The exposure of jurors to pre-trial publicity and inadmissible evidence (e.g., prior felony convictions) strongly influence their decision making in most instances. Pre-trial publicity and its effects will be discussed again in ▶ Chapter 8.

Second, juror dispositional characteristics, such as personality, background, and other personal biases, may have significant influences on the jury deliberation and verdict. "Indeed, this review indicates that bias associated with trial participants may be substantial in some instances, particularly bias stemming from jury-defendant demographic similarity, jury personality composition with regard to authoritarianism/dogmatism, and jury attitudes toward accused individuals and verdict options" (Devine et al., 2001, p. 700). As noted in this chapter, some researchers have been quick to disregard the potential influences of individual differences in jury decision making, concluding instead that the power of situational variables (e.g., clarity of jury instructions) overrides dispositional factors (e.g., authoritarianism) or defendant characteristics (e.g., attitudinal similarity). However, the research evidence suggests that, in some cases, situational variables probably play major roles, whereas in others, individual differences seem to dominate.

Third, dispositional characteristics have significantly less influence on jury verdicts when the evidence is cogent and clearly favors one side over the other, a conclusion also reached by Kalven and Zeisel (1966). "However, when the evidence did not clearly favor one side, they (Kalven and Zeisel) hypothesized that jurors would be liberated from the constraints of the evidence and thus more susceptible to influence from extraneous (biasing) factors" (Devine et al., 2001, p. 700). In cases where the strength of the evidence (SOE) is strong or weak, bias factors (e.g., pre-trial publicity) have significantly less influence on jury decision making than when the SOE is moderate.

Fourth, the deliberation processes do make major differences in jury outcomes in some situations. Although the research evidence has continually indicated that, in the vast majority of the cases, the majority on the first ballot usually wins out, the deliberation process has a major influence in overturning the first-ballot vote in at least 10% of the cases. One of the most influential factors in overcoming the initial ballot is the deliberation style taken by jurors while in chambers. While the evidence-driven style is closer to the normative ideal desired by the courts, many juries adopt the verdict-driven style that usually leads to the quick outcome.

The chapter ended with a discussion of jury simulation research, the predominant method used by social scientists studying jury processes. During the 1970s and 1980s, many social psychologists focused on the flaws associated with this technique. Early studies have been roundly criticized for their lack of validity, particularly as they dealt with inadequate sampling of mock jurors and unrealistic trial simulations and scenarios. Later research has been considerably more methodologically sophisticated, and jury simulation has earned a greater respect. The jury simulation research still lacks a firm theoretical foundation, however, and more realistic research designs are still needed. Nevertheless, there is indication that courts may be ready to learn from the lessons of jury simulation studies if researchers are able to advance cogent arguments for their validity.

Key Terms

Evidence-driven deliberation style
Hindsight bias
Just world hypothesis
Leniency bias
Polling the jury
Predecisional distortion
Story model
Verdict-driven deliberation style

Questions for Review

1. Most of the research reviewed in this chapter was conducted with simulation juries. Describe the shortcomings of jury simulation research. How have proponents responded to these criticisms?
2. What are the effects of the following variables on jury verdicts in criminal and/or civil cases: (a) physical attractiveness; (b) social attractiveness; and (c) attitudinal attractiveness.
3. What is the Capital Jury Project? List findings from that project that are described throughout this chapter.
4. What was the Chicago Jury Project and why was it controversial? List findings from the project that are discussed in the chapter.
5. Explain how each of the following might affect jury decision making: the story model; strength of the evidence; hindsight bias; a just-world orientation on the part of the juror; authoritarianism.
6. Discuss the phenomenon of polarization as it relates to jury decision making.
7. What four major themes have emerged from the jury decision making research, according to Devine and his colleagues (2001)?

CHAPTER 8

The Psychology of Evidence: Eyewitness Testimony

It is estimated that over 77,000 suspects per year in the United States become defendants largely on the basis of being identified by one or more eyewitnesses (Wells, et al., 1998). The testimony of a witness can be the most influential parcel of evidence delivered in the courtroom, particularly if the witness claims to have personally seen the legally relevant event, object, or person. The impact of eyewitness testimony is especially great if other kinds of evidence (e.g., weapon or fingerprints) are sparse or unavailable. Elizabeth Loftus (1979), a leading expert in eyewitness testimony, believes that jurors have often been known to accept eyewitness testimony at face value, even when it is heavily contradicted by other evidence. People are apt to believe someone who was at the scene of an incident, despite what experts may assert about the evidence. Even judges, attorneys, and law enforcement officials tend to accept the observations of witnesses, though they are more likely than lay persons to be aware of witness fallibility.

In the mind of prosecutors, eyewitness evidence often has greater legal status than other kinds of evidence. Experienced trial attorneys have long known that visual identification is one of the most cogent forms of evidence that can be presented to jurors and judges. They also fully realize that the quality of eyewitness testimony often determines the outcome of a case, no matter how logically tight and persuasive the arguments presented to the jury are. In her excellent review of eyewitness research, Elizabeth Loftus (1979, p. 19) summarizes the impact of witnesses on the court when she states: "All the evidence points rather strikingly to the conclusion that there is almost nothing more convincing than a live human being who takes the stand, points a finger at the defendant, and says 'that's the one!'." A discredited eyewitness seems to have less impact on jurors than a creditable one, however (Kennedy & Haggard, 1992). In other words, if a defense attorney can create doubt that the witness really saw what he or she claims, the jury is less accepting of the testimony.

The power of eyewitness testimony can be partially explained by the legal profession's traditional reliance on common-sense generalizations about human behavior. Paul Meehl (1971) refers to this legal proclivity as "fireside induction," which is "those commonsense empirical generalizations about human behavior which we accept on the culture's authority, plus introspection, plus anecdotal evidence from ordinary life. Roughly, the phrase 'fireside induction' designates . . . what everybody (except perhaps the skeptical social scientist) believes about human conduct, about how it is described, explained, predicted, and controlled" (Meehl, 1971, p. 66). Thus, "everybody knows" that an eyewitness's account is the best piece of evidence that can be found to assure justice in the courtroom. This is especially true if the person who recalls and identifies the legally relevant information does so with conviction and confidence. Hence, fireside-induction logic holds that the more confident the witness appears, the more accurate is the recall of the event. As we shall see, however, the scientific evidence does not necessarily support this.

Eyewitness testimony is also powerful because of a belief in the ultimate accuracy of observation and human memory. Throughout its long history, law has had to be highly dependent upon what people saw and what people said they saw. Recreations of crime scenes were almost exclusively dependent upon human memory, which was considered to be occasionally fooled, sometimes purposely distorted, but basically accurate. Today, sophisticated technology that can re-create crime scenarios and provide forensic evidence to the smallest detail is being increasingly made available to the courts, but belief in the accuracy of human perception and memory persists.

How reliable is such eyewitness testimony? Most forensic psychologists will answer, "It depends." Eyewitness testimony may be highly reliable under some conditions and extremely unreliable in other settings. However, the psychological research on perception and memory over the past 100 years underscores the discouraging fact that in most cases eyewitness testimony is at least partially unreliable and highly susceptible to numerous influences. For example, the introduction of forensic testing procedures in the United States has resulted in the exoneration of many previously convicted persons. Of the first 40 cases in which DNA evidence was used to overturn the convictions, 36 (or 90%) involved eyewitness identification evidence in which one or more eyewitnesses falsely identified the person (Wells, et al., 1998). Over a third of the wrongful convictions were the result of whites mis-identifying blacks (Dwyer, Neufeld, & Scheck, 2000).

In this chapter, we shall examine psychological research and theory and discover how closely the findings approximate the numerous fireside inductions inherent in the law's reliance upon eyewitness testimony. The general purpose of applied eyewitness-testimony research "is to generate scientific knowledge that will maximize the chances that a guilty defendant will be justly convicted while minimizing the chances that an innocent defendant will be mistakenly convicted" (Wells, 1978, p. 1546). At this point, though research is ongoing, there is enough evidence to urge caution in accepting too readily the accuracy of eyewitnesses.

Problems we encountered in ◀ Chapter 7 pertaining to jury research will not reappear here. Simulation studies, for example, have been quite well accepted in eyewitness research. They are better able to approximate real life witnessing than real life jury decision making. In addition, eyewitness research has the benefit of methodologically sound data about human perception and memory which have been developed by psychologists for nearly a century. These traditional works offer a solid foundation for the study of eyewitness observation. The contributions psychology can make in this area are substantial, and they warrant the careful attention of participants in the judicial system. It is important to note that the research in this chapter refers to the testimony of lay witnesses, to be distinguished from expert witnesses. Lay witnesses testify to personal knowledge of the facts, with opinions and inferences kept to a minimum. As we noted in ◀ Chapter 3, expert witnesses, because of their specialized knowledge, may testify to facts, draw inferences, and render opinions.

Human Perception and Memory

When a person recalls and identifies events, objects, and persons, two fundamental but exceedingly complicated mental processes are at work: perception and memory. In the first, sensory inputs (what one sees, hears, smells, touches, tastes) are transformed and organized into a meaningful experience for the individual. In the second process, the transformed inputs are stored in the brain, ready to be called up when needed. Let us examine each operation in more detail.

Perception

Perceptions are reports of what a person sees or senses at any particular moment. Note that seeing is only a part of the process of perceiving; in fact, what one perceives is not always what one sees. The eye does not relate to the brain like a camera operates on film. The eye communicates by electrochemical "blips" along neural pathways to other neuron cells and eventually to processors in various sections of the brain, specifically in the cerebral cortex. Once these blips (neural impulses) reach the cortex, they may be further coded, reorganized and interpreted, or they may be left undeveloped. Neurophysiological researchers have not yet discovered exactly what happens in the human brain when it receives incoming information, although there are many theories. It is clear, however, that the perception of stimuli and the person's reaction to them depend upon past experiences, especially with similar stimuli. If you were once the beneficiary of a very painful hornet sting, you perceive those insects in a far different way than a friend who has never had such an experience. You do not merely "see" the insect. Perception, then, is an interpretive process, and it appears that our senses are not only physical organs, but social ones as well (Buckhout, 1974).

There is ample evidence in the research literature that people are not consciously aware of the processes that determine their perceptions or the perceptual content of their senses. Yet, these nonconscious processes are extremely important in the representation of events or objects and therefore are crucial determinants of what occurs on the witness stand. Researchers also know that the end products of these perceptual processes are often incomplete, inaccurate, and highly selective. Much external information is either not attended to, lost in the filtering and selection of information, or misinterpreted. Past experience or learning, expectations, and preferences all determine how this partial or incomplete information will be synthesized. Yarmey (1979) reminds us that we should also not forget that many individuals have sensory deficiencies, like visual defects of depth perception, color blindness, failures in adaptation to darkness, and lack of visual acuity. Even before the stimulus information is synthesized at the higher levels of perceptual interpretation, these individual defects may contaminate the information. Human sensory mechanisms are far from perfect, and this basic frailty should not be overlooked in the search for potential errors in eyewitness testimony.

Memory

Memory, the second fundamental process with which we are concerned, is usually studied in three stages: acquisition, retention, and retrieval. Acquisition, also called the encoding or input stage, is intimately involved with the perceptual process, and a clear demarcation between the two is difficult to make. The point at which perception registers in the various areas of the cortex and is initially stored is the point of acquisition. Retention (also called the storage stage) is when information becomes "resident in the memory" (Loftus, 1979). In the retrieval stage, the brain searches for the pertinent information, retrieves it, and communicates it. Any one of these three processes may not function properly, and the result, then, is a failure to remember.

Eyewitness research has continually found that memory is highly malleable and easily subject to change and distortion (Yuille, 1980). Apparently, humans continually alter and reconstruct their memory of past experiences in the light of present experiences, rather than store past events permanently and unchangingly in memory (Leippe, 1980; Yuille, 1980). That is, people rebuild past experiences to fit better their understanding of events. Memory, especially for complex or unusual events, involves the integration of perceptual information with preexisting experiences, as well as with other subjective relevant information that may be introduced later. In this sense, memory is very much a reconstructive, integrative process that develops with the flow of new experiences and thoughts. This perspective is called the **reconstructive theory of memory**.

As is true for the perceptual processes, people are unaware of their memory processes. They are aware of the products or content of memory, but there is every reason to believe they are not aware of the transformations that have occurred during acquisition, retention, and retrieval. While eyewitnesses may remember an event or person, they are *not* conscious of the complex neurological encoding, decoding, organizing, storing, interpreting, and associating that preceded the final memory of that event or person. Moreover, there are ample opportunities for witnesses to encounter additional information after the event and then integrate it unknowingly into their original memories. Therefore, even the most well-intentioned eyewitnesses may err and unconsciously distort their recall and identification. In part, this explains the radically different accounts of the same event that are provided by witnesses who are "absolutely positive" about what they saw ◼ (see **Box 8-1**).

Wells (1995) finds it curious that police usually exercise great caution in their approach to *physical*

BOX 8-1
Eyewitnesses to Crime Often Inaccurate

During a three-week period in October 2002, residents of Maryland, Virginia, and Washington, D. C., were terrorized by sniper attacks that killed at least ten persons and wounded three. Hundreds of detectives, police officers, and federal agents investigating the slayings finally thought they got a break when two witnesses said they saw a white man shoot Linda Franklin, the sniper's ninth victim in the area, in the parking lot of a Virginia shopping center.

However, the fallibility of eyewitnesses quickly emerged. The individuals who said they saw the shootings had such conflicting reports that the police couldn't produce a composite sketch. As one reporter concluded: "It was another murder that showed most poignantly the malleability of eyewitness memory" (Begley, 2002, p. B1).

Eyewitnesses to the earlier sniper shootings in the area asserted with considerable confidence that they had seen a white van with a ladder rack on top leaving the scene. This prompted police to stop and search hundreds of white vans on Interstate 95 in the Virginia and Maryland areas for nearly two weeks. When arrests were made, police learned that the two suspected snipers had not worked out of a white van, but rather out of the trunk of a 1990 blue Chevrolet Caprice sedan. A hole cut in the car's trunk apparently allowed them to fire from the concealment of the car's interior, leaving no witnesses. In fact, police authorities had stopped the Caprice and recorded its New Jersey license plate number at least 10 times, but had no reason to link it to the sniper attacks because they were searching for the white van (Kugler, 2002). On one of those occasions, on October 8, Baltimore Police found the two suspects—who are black—asleep in the blue Caprice about a half-hour's drive from the scene of a shooting a day earlier, in Bowie, Maryland. The police ran a check on the car, found nothing amiss, and allowed them to go. "Like the talking heads on TV, they had convinced themselves that the snipers must be white men driving a white truck" (Wingert et al., 2002, p. 35).

The pair allegedly continued to shoot others until they began to write revealing letters to the police and made phone calls which provided important clues that eventually led to their arrest. It should be mentioned that an eyewitness did report seeing a Caprice driving slowly with its lights off near the scene of one of the shootings on October 8. "But in the dark, the witness remembered the car's color as burgundy, not blue, and the lead was lost in the chatter over white vehicles" (Wingert, et al., 2002, p. 35).

We should note that eyewitnesses to the sniper attacks very probably did see white vans near the scenes of the shootings. In fact, many people living on the East Coast soon realized that white vans are everywhere. However, once one witness singled out a white van, others became sensitized to the presence of similar vehicles. Likewise, once witnesses identified the shooter as a white individual, police looked for white suspects.

evidence at a crime scene, being very careful not to touch or move objects for fear of contaminating the physical evidence, but fail to take precautions in the collection of eyewitness evidence. Police routinely call in special forensic teams to gather and protect the physical evidence. These same police do not seem to accept the premise that eyewitness evidence, like a person's memory of the events, can be contaminated by careless interviewing and misleading commentary. Procedures that are uninformed about the damaging effects that can occur when dealing with fragile memory are misguided, especially in cases in which investigators try to build a solid case based on eyewitness testimony.

Many studies conducted by Elizabeth Loftus (Loftus, 1991; Loftus & Ketchem, 1991) and other psychological scientists show that when people see an event and are later exposed to new and misleading information about the incident, their recollections often become distorted. This phenomenon is known as the **misinformation effect**. For example, a police officer investigating a crime scene may have received some mention of a tattoo from one of the witnesses. He may then ask another witness, "What color was the person's tattoo?" If that witness did not even notice a tattoo at the time, he is apt to include that important bit of information into his subsequent statements. We return to the misinformation effect later in the chapter under the "Witness Testimony: Retention Factors" section.

Repressed Memory

In the 1980s and 1990s, one of the most controversial topics in psychology and law was the validity of repressed memory. **Repressed memory** refers to the psychological process of unconsciously keeping something out of awareness for extended periods of time because of the unpleasant emotions associated with it. Adults who were allegedly the victims of abuse—most typically sexual abuse—assert in civil suits or criminal trials that they had initially forgotten the traumatic experiences but eventually remembered them, usually with the help or guidance of therapists and often under hypnosis. For instance, adults may suddenly remember many years later that their parents were members of a Satanic cult who had fed them "hamburgers" made from human flesh. Under the repeated urging of their psychotherapist, some come to remember that they were sexually abused by their parents during early childhood. These claims must be assessed guardedly. As Lilienfeld and Loftus (1998, p. 471) point out, "The question of whether traumatic memories can be repressed for long periods of time (i.e., years or decades) and then suddenly recovered in intact form is perhaps the most controversial issue in clinical psychology today." Particularly controversial is the assumption by some clinicians that there is a very "strong form of repression, one in which memories of traumatizing events get submerged in the unconscious and are later exhumed in their pristine or veridical form" (Ornstein, Ceci, & Loftus, 1998, p. 997).

In an effort to clear up some of the controversy and heated debate on repressed memories and childhood abuse, the American Psychological Association appointed a "working group" of researchers and clinicians to delve into the issue and try to achieve consensus about the phenomenon. The group, known as *American Psychological Association Working Group on Investigation of Memories of Child Abuse* (1998), discovered that psychologists differ markedly on a wide range of issues concerning repressed memories. At the core of the disagreement was the nature of human memory itself. There was very little consensus about how memory works, or even whether events can be stored in their pristine form like a videotape, waiting to be released at a later date. Many researchers often have trouble accepting the latter view, while many clinicians are more prone to accept it. Some clinicians believe that the memory processing of children is different from that of adults and that childhood trauma may lead to problems in memory storage and retrieval. These clinicians believe that dissociation is a likely explanation for memory that was forgotten and later recalled. Dissociation means that a memory is not actually lost, but rather it is unavailable for retrieval for some time. Some clinicians are convinced that severe forms of child sexual abuse are especially conducive to negative disturbances of memory such as dissociation, also known as delayed memory. Many clinicians that work with trauma victims think that dissociation is an individual's way of protecting herself from the discomfort and anxiety of the memory. Many researchers, on the other hand, contend that there is little or no empirical support for such a theory.

The Working Group members (1998, p. 933) did reach agreement on the following points, however:

- Controversies regarding adult recollections should not be allowed to obscure the fact that child sexual abuse is a complex and pervasive problem in America that has historically gone unacknowledged.
- Most people who are sexually abused as children remember all or part of what happened to them.

- It is possible for memories of abuse that have been forgotten for a long time to be remembered.
- It is also possible to construct convincing false memories for events that never occurred.
- There are gaps in our knowledge about the processes that lead to accurate and inaccurate recollections of childhood abuse.

As mentioned above, a significant number of clinicians and psychotherapists, based on their professional experience, argue that a highly traumatic and terrifying event can indeed be "repressed" from memory, where it resides until exhumed by psychological methods of recovery. Particularly controversial is the use of hypnosis as a method for recovering this recollection. Some scientists have expressed strong concerns about using hypnosis in this fashion (Burgess & Kirsch, 1999; Karlin & Orne, 1997). There is considerable scientific evidence, for example, that hypnosis does not improve accuracy of memory, although it does increase the hypnotized person's confidence in his recall (Lilienfeld & Loftus, 1998; Lynn, Lock, Myers, & Payne, 1997). And one of the major dangers of hypnosis is that it can implant false memories and misinformation in subjects, especially those who are highly suggestible and vulnerable. Others (e.g., Scheflin et al., 1999) are more willing to accept the value of hypnosis under carefully controlled conditions that allow spontaneous recall of past traumatic events. ▶ [Hypnosis will be discussed again in Chapter 9.] The limited amount of scientific evidence on the power of drugs to elicit accurate and truthful memory also demonstrates that "truth serums" are ineffective (Piper, 1993). It appears, for example, that the use of barbiturates, such as sodium amytal or sodium pentathol, merely provides information that is a mixture of truth, distortion, and fantasy. ▶ [This issue is discussed in more detail in ◙ **Box 9-1**.]

Research by Loftus and her colleagues (e.g., Lilienfeld & Loftus, 1998; Loftus, 1979; Loftus & Ketcham, 1996) has consistently challenged the validity of repressed memory and its recovery with an impressive array of well-executed research. After many years of research on forgotten memory, a dominant conclusion seems to be that some past memory *can* be recovered, but the recovered memory is not necessarily accurate. Rather, forgotten or partially remembered events become reconstructed and embellished as the person gains additional information during daily living experiences. Imagination and fantasy play a part in this reconstruction, sometimes to the point of letting the person exaggerate aspects of initial events or perceptions. Memories do not simply get lost but often become distorted—and we reconstruct things as best we can from all the bits and pieces in our memories. People are sometimes surprised when they return as adults to a childhood home, for example. The "large, almost majestic" house is actually a small, unpretentious structure, with very few of the stately features they "remembered." Additionally, the "recall" of events that never actually occurred at all is possible (Coleman, Stevens, & Reeder, 2001). Mental health professionals who work with patients with allegedly repressed memories must be highly attuned to the concerns illustrated by contemporary research on the issue. Serious cases of this distortion process (where the patient becomes convinced and obsessed with the false recollections) are sometimes referred to as "false memory syndrome." On the other hand, we must also be cautious in labeling recollections of abuse as "false memory." Recall the consensus of the APA working group (1998) that it is possible for memories of abuse that have been forgotten for a long time to be remembered.

When cases involving recovered memory testimony reach the courts, the presiding judge must decide whether the evidence meets the criteria for admissibility, as discussed in ◀ Chapters 1 and 3. Under *Daubert v. Merrell Dow Pharmaceuticals, Inc.* (1993), the judge must decide whether the evidence relating to the accuracy of the recovered memory is "relevant and reliable." As noted in ◀ Chapter 1, a later case (*Kumho Tire Co., Ltd., v. Carmichael*, 1999) gave judges considerably more latitude in accepting scientific evidence. Some researchers have suggested that, in light of the *Kumho* case, judges may begin to admit more evidence in cases involving alleged child sexual abuse (Shuman & Sales, 1999). Furthermore, many jurisdictions have adopted delayed discovery rules, which allow the introduction of recovered memory evidence years after the alleged event occurred (Brown et al., 1999; Woodall, 1999). The state of Washington was the first to waive the statute of limitations for "recovered memories."

System and Estimator Variables

Before proceeding further, it is crucial that we describe two key concepts that underlie the research focusing on eyewitness testimony and identification: **system variables** and **estimator variables** (Wells, 1993). System variables refer to those things that can be controlled by people in the criminal justice system when gathering information from eyewitnesses. In other words, they are preventable errors. The number of people in the lineup and how closely they resemble the suspect are things the police can control. How carefully the police collect the information from eyewitnesses is another event they can control. With knowledge and training, errors due to system variable procedures can be reduced. Estimator variables, on the other hand, are sources of eyewitness error or accuracy that are beyond the control of the criminal justice system. For example, stress levels experienced by the witness at the time of the crime, or the length of time the witness observed the perpetrator, are beyond the control of the system. The event has already occurred and is essentially "water under the bridge." Estimator variables represent the basic nature and processes of human perception and memory.

Both variables can be studied under laboratory conditions in order to discover how they affect eyewitness testimony and identification under "real world" conditions. Wells and his colleagues (2000) report that there have been over 1,000 publications on eyewitness issues in psychology since 1979, and a large proportion of them have focused on system variables. While estimator variables are very important in understanding human cognitive processes, system variables reflect the unreliability of eyewitness reports produced by ignorance and faulty procedures undertaken by agents of the criminal justice system, as well as investigators or lawyers gathering evidence in both civil and criminal cases. As such, research on system variables has enormous direct application in improving the gathering of evidence for the courtroom. Janet Reno, U.S. Attorney General under the Clinton Administration, recognized the importance of system-variable research when she assembled a panel of eyewitness researchers, law enforcement officers, and lawyers to produce a guide, subsequently titled *Eyewitness Evidence: A Guide for Law Enforcement* (Technical Working Group for Eyewitness Evidence, 1999). It is most commonly referred to as the NIJ Guide.

In the recent eyewitness literature, the "NIJ Guide" is distinguished from the "Lineups White Paper," which was produced by a committee appointed by the American Psychology-Law Society. This paper recommends guidelines for assembling and conducting lineups and photospreads for eyewitness identification (Wells et al., 1998). The lineups white paper will be discussed more fully later in the chapter.

In the following sections, we will discuss characteristics of the situation, the witness, and the defendant which are believed to be influential in determining the accuracy of eyewitness testimony. Although this classification does not totally represent the interaction that occurs among the variables in determining eyewitness accuracy, it does promote a more organized presentation. Much of the following information comes from research findings in laboratory or experimental settings. Critics of such research often contend that laboratory or simulation conditions do not mimic a "real" situation where there is enormous pressure on the typical eyewitness to identify the offender. Nevertheless, simulation in this context is not as problematical as jury simulation, discussed in ◀ Chapter 7. Wells (1993, p. 555) argues that "there is little or no evidence that the typical eyewitness experiment presents a distortion of what would be expected in actual cases in which the eyewitnesses experience real rather than simulated experiments." Research in simulated conditions identifies and highlights some of the important principles and processes that underlie eyewitness testimony, and it can generalize to real life situations. Experiments offer some hints in understanding the human perception and memory (estimator variables) and hints on how to develop better procedures for gathering eyewitness information (system variables).

Situational Factors of Eyewitness Testimony

Temporal Factors

Courts are most interested in learning details about events that are generally fast moving, unusual, chaotic, and threatening to the observers. In most instances, the legally relevant incident produces a "stimulus overload," where too many things are happening too quickly and under less than ideal conditions for careful scrutiny. Thus far the study of situational factors—which all qualify as estimator variables—has been a relatively neglected area, but the research to date agrees with many commonsense observations about the effects of these factors.

Not surprisingly, the less time a witness has to observe something, the less complete the perception and recall will be. Obviously, studying a topic for a long time will mean a better exam grade, provided that the student was concentrating. There is abundant literature in the field of cognitive psychology and memory to demonstrate that the longer a subject is exposed to material, the more accurate the recall (e.g., Loftus, 1972; Loftus & Loftus, 1976; Klatzky, 1975). Thus, some researchers have found that the longer subjects had to inspect slides of faces, the more accurate they later were at recognizing a given face from photographs (Laughery, Alexander, & Lane, 1971). In addition, Laughery and his colleagues found that the smaller the number of photographs the subjects had to search through, the more likely the subjects were to be accurate. The researchers suggested that law enforcement agencies might keep this in mind when having witnesses look through photo lineups for criminal identification. Fewer photos might result in more accurate recognition. If police do not have a suspect in mind, however, it may not be practical to limit the number of photos.

Closely related to the duration of eyewitness exposure time is frequency of exposure. The more often a witness observes an event or person, the more accurate his or her description or recognition should be. Although there is substantial support for this in the experimental literature, dating as far back as Hermann Ebbinghaus's work in 1885, frequency of exposure has not been examined in studies of eyewitness testimony. Loftus (1979) suggests that perhaps the relationship is such a commonsensical one that it has failed to draw the attention of eyewitness researchers. Additionally, in "real" crime scenes, witnesses are not likely to have seen the perpetrator more than once.

Another temporal factor that is likely to influence witness accuracy is the rate at which things happen. Fast-moving events are more difficult to process, and thus to remember, than slow-moving events, because of the limited processing capacity of human beings and their selective attention mechanisms. Therefore, incidents surrounded by complex activity tend to confuse, even when witnesses have a reasonably long opportunity to observe the occurrence.

It has repeatedly been found that witnesses frequently overestimate the time a criminal incident takes (Buckhout, 1974, 1977; Marshall, 1966; Johnson & Scott, 1976). The entertainment media often depict this by presenting a crime sequence or other traumatic event in slow motion. While Ellison and Buckhout (1981) suggest that some witnesses may consciously lengthen time estimates to strengthen the validity of their descriptions, there is abundant laboratory evidence to indicate that humans generally think unpleasant events last longer than they really do (Loftus, 1979). It appears also that if people feel especially anxious or threatened during an incident, they tend to overestimate its duration even more (Sarason & Stoops, 1978). Therefore, in obtaining evidence from witnesses, it is important to try to determine how long and how often the person observed the incident and how much activity was present. It is important also to realize that the witness very probably is overestimating the event's duration.

Detail Significance

Weapon Focus Not all details of a scene are equally remembered, because certain novel, complex, ambiguous, or arousing features draw more attention than others. Blood, masks, weapons, and aggressive actions are more likely to be noticed than clothing, hair style, height, facial features, or other background stimuli in a crime scene. A gun pointed at a person is likely to be studied more intently than other features impinging on the person at that moment. People are quite certain about whether a gun or a knife was threatening them, but they are perhaps less certain of an assailant's clothes or facial characteristics. This phenomenon is known as weapon focus or weapon effect. Specifically, **weapon focus** refers to the concentration of some victim's or witness's attention on a threatening weapon while paying less attention to other details and events of a crime. In short, it refers to a tunneling of attention.

The primary theoretical underpinning for weapon focus is James Easterbrook's (1959) observation that under high arousal people tend to narrow their attention to the cues that are most threatening or relevant, and correspondingly reduce their attention to other cues in the immediate environment.Therefore, highly anxious or tense individuals will not scan their environments as broadly as less anxious individuals. Easterbrook's classic theory is known as cue utilization theory. It is well known to psychologists, as illustrated in a poll conducted by Yarmey and Jones (1983). In that poll, 90% of the psychologists subscribed to the view that a victim is more likely to focus on a gun, whereas lay people and jurors believed that victims would also get a good look at the offender's face.

The tendency to focus on some details to the exclusion of others is well illustrated by a study in which unsuspecting students sat in an anteroom waiting to participate in an experiment conducted by Johnson and Scott (1976). A no-weapon condition and a weapon condition were used. Subjects in the no-weapon condition overheard a conversation from the experimental room concerning equipment problems, after which an individual entered the waiting room, holding a pen in greasy hands. The individual, who was part of the experiment (a confederate), made a brief comment and then exited quickly. In the weapon condition, subjects overheard an angry confrontation, accompanied by sounds of bottles breaking and chairs crashing. The confederate bolted into the waiting room, holding a bloodied letter opener in blood-stained hands. As in the no-weapon condition, the confederate muttered something and then left.

Subjects were interviewed about the scenario either immediately or one week later. Nearly every subject in the weapon condition described a weapon, while very few of the no-weapon subjects could describe the pen. More importantly, the presence of a weapon (weapon focus compounded by emotional arousal) reduced the ability of the subjects to identify the confederate from a set of 50 photographs. Apparently, the witnesses focused their attention primarily on the weapon rather than on facial features. However, it should be emphasized that in both the weapon and no-weapon conditions, the confederate was only in the presence of the witnesses for about four seconds. A longer exposure time might have dissipated weapon focus.

There are other problems with the experiment as well. The two conditions (weapon or no-weapon) differed in a number of significant ways, preventing a firm conclusion as to what contributed to what. For example, one condition had an argument take place, accompanied by bottles breaking and chairs crashing, whereas the other condition did not. Also, the weapon condition had two highly arousing stimuli—a weapon and a bloody hand. The no-weapon condition had none. Even the statements uttered by the confederate in each condition were different. Furthermore, the subjects were uninvolved (passive observers) in the scenario.

Loftus and her colleagues (1987) tried to correct these shortcomings by setting up conditions where the sole differing condition was the presence of the weapon. College students viewed a series of slides in which a customer goes through the cafeteria line of a fast food restaurant. In one condition the customer pointed a gun at the cashier and she gave him money. In a second condition, the customer handed the cashier a check and she gave him money. The researchers then had the students identify the customer from a 12-person photo lineup. Students in the weapon condition were significantly less accurate than students in the check condition. There was an 8.5% probability of identifying the right customer by chance. Weapon-condition subjects correctly identified the customer only about 15% of the time compared to the check-condition subjects who were accurate 35% of the time. Weapon-condition students were also less accurate when asked details about the customer.

But how realistic is this situation? College students are sitting in the comfort of their environments, passively watching slides in a situation which they know is a psychological experiment. And where is the stress or highly arousing event? At a minimum, Easterbrook's cue utilization theory, premised on high anxiety, should have been tested.

Tooley, Brigham, Maas, and Bothwell (1987) had college students observe slides of various individuals either holding a weapon or some other object in their hands. Subjects were randomly assigned to view the slides while experiencing white noise in the form of a constant, irritating hissing sound or threat of electric shock (high arousal) or without such conditions (low arousal). The researchers hypothesized that, of the two groups, high arousal subjects would be better at recognizing the faces of people without a weapon from those with a weapon. High arousal subjects would be better at recognizing faces than low arousal because they would focus on the most interesting or attention getting stimuli. In the no weapon condition, the prominent stimulus was the face. Recall that Easterbrook's cue utilization theory predicts a focusing on prominent cues under high arousal. If the hypothesis is correct, highly aroused subjects would focus on the weapon to the exclusion of other cues—such as the face—and in the no weapon condition they would focus on the face more. The researchers did find the weapon effect. Subjects as a group were better at identifying the faces of individuals not holding a weapon than the face of those who were. However, when arousal was factored in, aroused subjects did better overall at recognizing faces than low arousal subjects. They were not better (or worse) at distinguishing the faces of those individuals holding a weapon from those holding a non-weapon, however. Thus, this experiment did not support cue utilization theory.

In a more realistic experiment, Maass and Kohnken (1989) tried to reexamine the arousal component of weapon focus by threatening college students participating in an experiment with a needle injection. Maass and Kohnken noted that none of the previous research actually threatened the subjects directly with a weapon. While it would be clearly unethical to approach subjects with a gun or knife, the researchers saw no such objections to approaching volunteers with a syringe. Almost everyone is at least somewhat fearful of an injection, usually stemming from childhood visits to the doctor's office. One-half of the subjects were approached by an experimenter holding a pen and the other half were approached by an experimenter holding a syringe. Furthermore, one-half of the subjects expected to have an injection, whereas the remaining half did not. Thus, there were four conditions in this experiment: (1) approached by experimenter with syringe with expectation to receive injection; (2) approached by experimenter with a pen with expectation to receive injection; (3) approached by experimenter with syringe with no expectation to receive any injection; and (4) approached by experimenter with pen with no expectation to receive any injection. The major dependent variables were based on two different forms of memory, recognition and recall. In the recognition task, subjects were required to identify the face of the experimenter from a seven-person photo lineup (although the experimenter was not actually in the lineup). In the recall task, subjects were required to answer specific questions about the experimenter's face as well as the hand which carried the pen or syringe.

The results showed that the syringe (the weapon) did arouse the subjects, but the threat of an injection by itself did not. Furthermore, subjects exposed to the syringe, with or without expectations of receiving an injection, were more likely to make false identifications in the recognition tasks than the other groups. In addition, the results of the recall tasks demonstrated that the syringe groups were more accurate in recalling details about the hand area of the experimenter (i.e., length, color, and diameter of the syringe) than the non-syringe groups. However, there were no clear trends in who could accurately recall facial cues. The researchers asserted: "At this point, one can only conclude—that contrary to what many jurors and judges believe—the presence of a weapon is in and of itself distracting as well as arousing" (p. 406).

The studies by Maass and Kohnken (1989), Tooley, et al. (1987), and Loftus, et al. (1987) do highlight an important distinction with respect to weapon focus: the attention-getting properties of a weapon and its arousal effect. A weapon is usually novel or attention-getting in and of itself, independent of the arousal inducing properties it has when one is threatened with it. Passive observers watching slides normally do not experience much arousal but the evidence does suggest the weapon distracts the audience temporarily from other environmental cues. Kramer, Buckout, and Eugenio (1990) tested this weapon-distraction hypothesis by showing a series of slides to college students while controlling for arousal. The results supported the viewpoint that a salient weapon, regardless of arousal level, acts as a powerful distractor of attention.

In sum, weapon focus has received strong empirical support. After conducting a meta-analysis on 19 studies investigating the phenomenon, Steblay

(1992, p. 421) concluded: "The weapon focus effect has been found to be relatively robust across variations in stimulus presentation, experimental scenario, and experimenter and subject variables. . . . The weapon focus does reliably occur, particularly in crimes of short duration in which a threatening weapon is visible." Kerri Pickel (1999) contends that the weapon focus occurs because the weapon is unusual to witnesses, and any unusual object could feasibly draw the attention of an eyewitness, at least temporarily. Under these conditions, Pickel points out, fewer attentional resources are available to process other visual details. Therefore, a witness who is very familiar with guns will not experience weapon focus to the same degree as a witness who is unfamiliar with them.

Although the weapon focus effect is probably maximized under conditions in which there is *both* an unusual object *and* high arousal, when a lethal weapon is directed at anyone, arousal (fear) would be a natural (and expected) response from the victim as well as other witnesses. In line with Easterbrook's hypothesis, high arousal most likely accelerates a narrowing of focus and is most likely the major ingredient of weapon focus in crime scenes.

Significance (or What's Happening?) Another aspect which may influence eyewitness accuracy is that persons in the midst of a crime do not always perceive that something significant is happening. People have often been present during the commission of a crime and have failed to realize it. Baron and Byrne (1981) cite the tragic sniper incident on the University of Texas campus in 1966 as an example. Disgruntled student and veteran Charles Whitman managed to gain access to the top of the 307-foot-tall University tower with an arsenal of weapons and began firing at students below. Some heard the shots, noticed bodies falling, and immediately ran for cover. A surprising number of people simply continued along their way without perceiving the seriousness of the situation. Some individuals who survived later said they interpreted the event as a fraternity stunt and did not take it seriously.

Social psychologists (e.g., Darley & Latane, 1968) have studied the phenomenon of "bystander apathy," where people sometimes fail to come to the aid of a victim of an accident or assailant. The researchers have found that in a significant number of cases the observers simply did not interpret the event as serious. (It is possible, of course, that the bystanders told the researchers this to save face.) Therefore, it would seem prudent for law enforcement officers to learn how far the crime had progressed before a witness realized the incident was significant enough to warrant attention. Some witnesses may conclude that a crime is taking place only near the end of the sequence and may embellish the beginning so as not to appear too foolish.

Perceiving the seriousness of an event is as important as perceiving its significance. Leippe, Wells, and Ostrom (1978) staged a theft in front of a group of students waiting to participate in an experiment. The item stolen in one condition was an expensive piece of electronic equipment (high seriousness); in another it was a pack of cigarettes (low seriousness). In both conditions one of the waiting subjects (actually a confederate) grabbed the item, dropped it to assure that everyone present noticed the theft, and quickly left the room. There was no doubt that all the waiting subjects recognized that a theft had happened and knew the relative value of the stolen item.

After the theft, subjects were told individually that it had been planned as part of the experiment, and they were shown six photographs and asked to identify the thief. In the high-seriousness condition, 56% of the subjects made an accurate identification, whereas in the low-seriousness condition only 19% made accurate identification. These results suggest that the perceived seriousness of a crime may be a powerful determinant of accurate offender-identification.

The researchers in the above experiment suggested two possible hypotheses for the increased accuracy as a result of crime seriousness. First, perceived seriousness may prompt witnesses to make full use of selective attention and acquisition processes during the event. Second, the perceived seriousness may have motivated the witnesses to rehearse the event in their memory, which would have improved the retrieval of the information at a later time.

Violence Level of Event Crimes differ in the amount of emotional arousal they generate in both victim and witnesses, probably ranging along a continuum of arousal or generation of stress. Generally speaking, increases in violence produce a corresponding increase in arousal, probably to a peak point where further increases in extreme, terrifying violence no longer increase arousal because the observer chooses not to watch any longer. It has been suggested that the recall and recognition abilities of witnesses (and victims) reflect a negative relationship to that violence-arousal continuum (Clifford & Scott, 1978). That is, the higher the violence level of the crime, and hence the higher the emotional reaction to the incident, the lower the accuracy and completeness of the testimony of witnesses and victims. Clifford and his colleagues have been the leading proponents of the high violence-low accuracy hypothesis; it is worthwhile reviewing two of their experiments designed to test it.

Clifford and Scott (1978) found that persons who watched violent events on videotape were significantly less able to recall the incidents than those who watched non-violent versions. In the non-violent scenario, two police officers searched for a suspect, found him, and entered into a verbal exchange with the man. The exchange culminated in some "weak restraining movements" by one of the officers. In the violent episode, the same situation escalated into a physical confrontation, with one of the officers delivering blows to the suspect.

In addition to the finding that witnesses demonstrated poorer recall of the violent incident, the study also discovered that female subjects were significantly less accurate than male subjects in their recall of the violent film. There were no significant gender differences in recall of the non-violent version.

In another investigation of the effects of violence on eyewitness accuracy, Clifford and Hollin (1981) learned that accuracy depends not only on the level of violence observed, but also on the number of perpetrators. Violent incidents were less well remembered as the number of perpetrators increased, while non-violent incidents yielded no such difference. The results suggest that, in violent events involving more than one offender, the accuracy of eyewitness testimony can be expected to be poorer than in violent events having only one perpetrator. In fact, the Clifford-Hollin data revealed that almost three-fourths of the witnesses observing the violent scenes were incorrect in their identification of the key perpetrator. Apparently, no significant gender differences emerged, since the researchers made no reference to this effect in their report. It seems, therefore, that the influence of violence on the recognition and recall ability of males and females remains equivocal. This is one area in obvious need of further investigation.

The results from the Clifford studies imply that the legal system must be especially careful in its reliance on the testimony of eyewitnesses to a violent episode, especially in cases where violence is high and there are several perpetrators. At the very least, the data certainly counsel against any fireside induction that violence leads to accuracy in testimony.

Interestingly, the violence level of the crime also seems to influence *jurors* strongly. Saul Kassin and David Garfield (1991) found that videotapes depicting a high level of blood and gore of a crime scene had a significant impact on mock jurors. Jurors exposed to a videotape showing an actual crime scene were more inclined to decide in favor of the prosecution and to set lower standards of proof for themselves in making that decision.

Witness Factors: Perceptual and Acquisition Influences

Witness Arousal and Stress

Most criminal incidents precipitate some continuum of stress and emotional arousal in both victims and other witnesses. However, the effects of this emotional arousal on eyewitness testimony have baffled the legal system for many years (Katz & Reid, 1977). Some jurists believe that stress increases the accuracy of witness observation and subsequent testimony. Others think stressful incidents generate so much nervousness that they promote unreliability in witnesses.

An example of the first position is a very old but often cited appellate court opinion quoted by Wall (1965). Two men were accused of torturing and killing a husband and wife, based on the oral dying declaration of the husband. In affirming the conviction and commenting about the victim's ability to identify the accused, the court stated that "every peculiarity of each of the murders . . . must have been literally burned into the memory" of both the husband and his wife (*Commonwealth v. Roddy*, 1898). In another case (*State v. Lanegan*, 1951), a man and his wife had been awakened by an intruder pointing a firearm in their faces and demanding money. The court found these to be "circumstances calculated to impress [the defendant's appearance] upon their minds." In still another example (*U.S. ex rel. Gonzalez v. Zelker*, 1973), the U.S. Court of Appeals defended the validity of a robbery victim's identification by asserting that "the robbery unquestionably made a deep impression on Mrs. D'Amora, who was obviously terrified by Gonzalez when he pointed the gun at her and announced the holdup." However, as Katz and Reid (1977) have observed, the court demonstrated its confusion about the effects of stress by also stating that the same victim should be excused for her inaccurate initial description since "she was understandably nervous at the time of the robbery."

Few court decisions have dealt with the effects of stress on eyewitness or victim accuracy, and any decisions handed down have left the issue vague, confused, and largely unresolved (Katz & Reid, 1977). If a position could be teased out of legal precedent up to this point, it would be the fireside induction that stress or fear increases witness and victim testimonial accuracy.

According to psychological research, does arousal strengthen or weaken memory? Not surprisingly, empirical investigations have found that it sometimes facilitates perception and memory and sometimes hinders these processes. Early researchers hypothesized that the relationship between arousal and performance can be best represented by an inverted U-shaped function: very low or very high levels of arousal reduce perceptions and inhibit memory, while moderate levels facilitate them.

This hypothesized relationship is known as the **Yerkes-Dodson Law**, first proposed in 1908. The relationship depends not only on the existing level of arousal, but also on the difficulty or complexity of the task. If the task is relatively simple, high arousal will improve the performance. If the task is complex, high levels of arousal will decrease performance and moderate levels will improve it. The relationship is also hypothesized for memory and perception. That is, intermediate levels of stress improve memory and perception.

The eyewitness's task in recalling events or persons is an extremely complex one, requiring perceptual and memory components. We can expect, therefore, that the high arousal which is presumably typical of witnesses' reactions to violent crimes causes a spectrum of inaccuracies and incomplete information in testimony. The reader will recall the experiment by Leippe and colleagues (1978) in which either a package of cigarettes or electronic equipment was stolen. The equipment theft produced more accurate descriptions of the perpetrator, very likely because it generated more arousal than the cigarette theft. Moreover, the arousal generated would be moderate, rather than high—and therefore just right to improve performance or identification of the offender. On the other hand, the experiment conducted by Johnson and Scott (1976), which involved a weapon condition (bloody letter opener) and a no-weapon condition (greasy pen), apparently produced such high levels of arousal in the weapon condition that it interfered with accurate recall and recognition of the perpetrator. The Yerkes-Dodson Law suggests that persons who are extremely frightened or emotionally upset during an incident are not the most dependable witnesses to that incident.

More recent research, though, puts into serious question the simple relationship portrayed by the Yerkes-Dodson Law. Based on his extensive review of the literature of the issue, Sven-Åke Christianson (1992) challenges any simple relationship between emotion and memory. It does appear that emotional events are remembered differently than ordinary events, but the nature of the relationship is extremely complicated and depends on a wide range of interacting factors. In some situations, high levels of emotion may even improve certain aspects of memory. In summary, Christianson (1992, p. 303) concludes: "The implication of these interactions is that the Yerkes-Dodson (1908) law does not constitute an appropriate description of the relationship between emotional stress and memory performance."

Expectancies and Stereotypes

A powerful determinant of what a person perceives is what he or she *expects* to perceive in any given situation. Every deer hunting season has its tale of the hunter who mistakenly shoots another hunter, a cow, or a horse in the belief that they are game. Hunters who shoot at these non-game targets typically have high expectations of seeing a deer at any moment. In addition, the hunt traditionally is at its best at dawn and early dusk, because these are times when wildlife is most active in its movement toward feeding areas. These are also times when visibility, particularly at long distances, is poor. A moving shape in the wild may be embellished with antlers by the tense and expectant hunter intent on finding prey.

Many sightings of unidentified flying objects (UFOs), Loch Ness monsters, Bigfoot, "Champ," and other unusual creatures may be explained by expectations of the observers. Psychologists have found that eyes do indeed play tricks. Expectancies shaped by previous experiences and learning (including tales and legends) form cognitive templates to which unusual experiences are compared. Any out-of-the-ordinary sight may he interpreted in such a way that it will fit these cognitive templates. Thus, unusual ripples in a lake at dusk can easily become a highly publicized, unexplained creature.

Incidents of crime, particularly violent ones, are highly unusual events to most persons and are especially susceptible to distortions consistent with expectancies. If we have learned that robbers often carry .38 revolvers, we may see a .38 in our assailant's hand, when it is actually a hammer. In a tragic incident in the late 1990s, police in New York City shot and killed a Haitian immigrant who pulled his wallet from his pocket, presumably to show his green card. Police, who were hunting a suspect, said they thought it was a gun. While there is abundant collateral research clearly and convincingly demonstrating that expectancies influence descriptive accuracy, none has tested the expectancy hypothesis in relation to eyewitness testimony in a simulated crime setting. The substantial body of research already available on related issues, though, would lead us to agree with Loftus (1979, p. 48) that "one thing is clear and accepted by all: expectations have an enormous impact on what a person claims to have seen."

Stereotypes—which are a form of expectancy—are cognitive shorthand devices that allow us to simplify and organize the vast array of social stimuli present in a complex society. We all use them to some extent, and as long as they do not promote social injustices, they tend to be effective and harmless psychological adaptations that help manage our implicit personality theories about others. However, stereotypes can distort our perceptions and subsequent identifications of others. There is evidence that some people may in fact incorporate their stereotype of "criminal" in their identification of suspects. Shoemaker, South, and Lowe (1973) asked subjects to select from a set of 12 facial photographs the person most likely and least likely to have engaged in murder, robbery, or treason. None of the persons in the photos had actually engaged in these behaviors. Subjects tended to categorize the photos into criminal/noncriminal stereotypes, and they also tended to stereotype which faces belonged to what type of behavior. The researchers discovered that males were more likely than females to use facial stereotypes in judging guilt or innocence. The study suggests that many people have stereotypes about how criminals are supposed to look. These stereotypes could influence an eyewitness's selection of a perpetrator, especially if that witness observed the incident under intense stress or other less-than-ideal viewing conditions.

Arthur Lurigio and John Carroll (1985) found that experienced probation officers (POs) have well-developed, rich stereotypes (schemata) of how certain offenders look, the nature of their interpersonal relationships, their prior criminal history, the reasons for their criminal activity, and their prognosis for rehabilitation. For example, experienced POs stereotype a burglar as typically a male in his early 30s, married, any race, intelligent, with an extensive burglary record, and unlikely to change because they are very set in their lifestyle. Welfare fraud, according to the POs, is typically committed by a black woman in her 20s who is unmarried but involved with a male who controls her life. She is easily manipulated and feels forced to commit fraud through concern for her children or her man. The prognosis for these offenders is guarded to good, depending on whether she can break from the relationship.

Lurigio and Carroll found that experienced POs (more than 3 years experience) had richer but fewer schemata than less experienced POs (less than 3 years). The caseloads of the POs were large. Thus, the more experienced ones seem to use these well-developed schemata as a form of cognitive economy so that decisions regarding counseling and referrals and frequency of probationer reporting could be made quickly and confidently. The inexperienced POs had more—but more ambiguous—schemata that were not developed sufficiently to enable them to make quick, efficient decisions about the many probationers on their caseloads. Experienced POs seem to have weeded out many useless stereotypes and enriched the few they retained. There is also some evidence to suggest that experienced police officers use schemata of certain environmental cues to identify suspicious activity (Ryan & Taylor, 1988). Classification committees in prisons are also said to use stereotypes in assigning inmates to various security levels (Clear & Cole, 2000; Johnson, 1996). Although these stereotypes afford cognitive efficiency to their users, their accuracy and validity remain largely untested. Furthermore, they promote the ecological fallacy and produce decisions that are inequitable and simply in error for those individuals who do not fit the cognitive mold.

Witness Memory: Retention Factors

Witnesses, of course, generally must recall events weeks, months, or even years after they occur. Yet cognitive psychology has firmly established that people are less accurate and complete in their accounts of events after a long interval has elapsed between the event and the recall than after a short interval. Part of this inaccuracy stems from the higher probability that new information will be received and processed by the person during the longer interval, a process known as the misinformation effect, which we alluded to earlier in the chapter.

Elizabeth Loftus has designed numerous experiments demonstrating that post-event experiences, such as exposure to additional information, can substantially affect a person's memory of the original event. She showed, for example, that the simple mention of an existing object in an interview significantly increased the probability that the object would be recalled by the witness later on (Loftus, 1975). For example, asking an eyewitness to a traffic accident, "How fast was the car going when it ran the stop sign?" will enhance the recall of the stop sign, even if the witness failed to notice it in the first place. Similarly, casually mentioning an object that did not actually exist in an accident scene increases the likelihood that a witness will later report having seen that nonexistent object (Loftus, Miller, & Burns, 1978).

Loftus (1975, 1977) also found that witnesses compromised their memory when they learned of new information that conflicted with an initial observation. For example, if a witness thought he noticed a red car passing in the wrong lane and the investigating officer mentioned a green car, the witness would be likely to recall an off-colored green or blue-green car in a later report. If a witness thought a vehicle was traveling at 85 mph, and the investigating officer mentioned the speed of 65 mph, the witness would later report the speed to be somewhere between 65 and 85 mph, probably closer to 65. The witness might be aware of the compromise, but it might also be an unconscious phenomenon attributable to perceptual and memory processes occurring outside awareness.

The above studies imply that police officers or attorneys can manipulate a witness's memory by feeding relevant information. However, there is evidence that this is more difficult to do with important or even noticeable factors than with less important details (Loftus, 1979). Furthermore, data also suggest that misleading information provided to witnesses sometime after the event and just before a recall test will have greater impact than misleading information given immediately after the incident (Loftus, Miller, & Burns, 1978). On the other hand, interviewers wishing to maintain a consistent description of the initial incident would be wise to obtain the information immediately after the incident and then reiterate the material before and as close as possible to the time of courtroom testimony.

Witness Confidence: Retrieval Factors

Research on cases in which people were mistakenly convicted by juries has revealed that eyewitness misidentification accounts for more cases than all other causes of wrongful conviction combined (Wells & Bradfield, 1999; Wells et al., 1998). The problem of mistaken identification is made worse when eyewitnesses are wrong yet highly confident of their testimony (Wells & Bradfield, 1999). Persons given to fireside inductions about eyewitness testimony believe that the more confident witnesses are about what they saw, the more accurate their observation and memory. As a result, testimony presented assertively and positively is generally treated with deference by the courts; it is believed to be accurate and truthful (Deffenbacher, 1980). For example, in *Neil v. Biggers* (1972), the U.S. Supreme Court ruled that eyewitness confidence is a valid criterion upon which to judge the trustworthiness of eyewitness testimony.

Studies indicate that the confidence-accuracy relationship assumed by many judges, attorneys, and jurors is far more complicated than they suppose. Yarmey (1979) concludes from his research on the identification of faces, that the confidence-accuracy relationship in that area is exceedingly weak or virtually nonexistent. Leippe (1980) asserts that recognition accuracy has little to do with witness confidence, primarily because people are usually unaware of the inaccurate mental operations that lead to their conclusions. According to Leippe, the conditions under which witnesses observe an incident may affect recognition accuracy but not confidence. Thus, witnesses may be just as confident of what they see under poor observing conditions as they are of what they see under excellent observing conditions. Wells, Lindsay, and Ferguson (1979) found that the confidence of witnesses, whether measured by the witnesses themselves or through jurors' estimates, was unrelated to accuracy in identifying a thief from a six-person picture gallery. In other studies (Lindsay, Wells, & Rumpel, 1981; Clifford & Hollin, 1981; Clifford & Scott, 1978) the confidence-accuracy relationship was also found wanting.

Kenneth Deffenbacher (1980) proposed that the relationship between accuracy and confidence depends upon the conditions under which the eyewitness observes the offender and the incident. Deffenbacher hypothesized that the more optimal the conditions, the stronger the positive relationship between accuracy and confidence. He called this observation the **optimality hypothesis**. Examples of optimal conditions include ample opportunity to see the suspect, high familiarity with the suspect, and low to moderate anxiety in the witness. It is not clear from the available research how many of these conditions must be present to maximize the confidence-accuracy relationship. On the other hand, the confidence-accuracy relationship is in the opposite direction under low optimal conditions. For example, under relatively poor conditions, an eyewitness may be very confident that he or she has correctly identified a suspect, but may be incorrect in the identification.

In sum, any belief that accuracy can be assumed merely on the basis of the confidence expressed by eyewitnesses is untenable, given the present state of psychological knowledge. It is difficult to change these beliefs, however. Fox and Walters (1986) and Penrod and Cutler (1995) have found that jurors continue to use eyewitness confidence as a guide in making their decisions even after being warned several times by an expert that confidence does not necessarily translate into accuracy. Loftus (1986) describes her own trials and tribulations in having the courts accept her expert testimony on eyewitness reliability. Furthermore, she found higher courts unsympathetic, noting that they routinely uphold convictions of defendants when the trial judge refused to permit expert testimony that the defense had tried to offer. In recent years, though, some state supreme courts (e.g., Arizona and California) are beginning to allow expert testimony in the eyewitness area. Furthermore, while many psychologists themselves initially expressed doubts that eyewitness research was sufficiently developed to communicate it to the courts, this is no longer the case.

Gary Wells and Amy Bradfield (Wells & Bradfield, 1998, 1999) have focused on the creation of false confidence by external influences, such as giving feedback to eyewitnesses after they make their identification. "Telling eyewitnesses who have made false identification that they identified the actual suspect or the same person that other witnesses identified leads to robust inflation in the witnesses' confidence in their identification" (Wells & Bradfield, 1999, p. 138). This increased confidence in eyewitnesses' identification generated by external influences is referred to as the **postidentification-feedback effect**.

Wells and his colleagues find that this postidentification-feedback does more than inflate the confidence level of the witnesses; it also distorts eyewitnesses' memory of how confident they were at the time of the initial identification prior to the feedback. In other words, the witnesses may believe that they were highly certain of their identification before feedback, even though they may have wondered at the time. In addition, this confirming feedback distorts the eyewitnesses' recollection of their witnessing conditions, such as how well they were able to see the perpetrator. Most witnesses are convinced that the feedback did not influence their judgments. Wells and Bradfield (1998, p. 360) provide a clear example of these processes from the case *Missouri v. Hutching*, 1996, p. 202):

> "Eyewitness to a crime viewing a lineup: 'Oh, my God . . . I don't know . . . It's one of those two . . . but I don't know . . . Oh, man . . . the guy a little bit taller than number two . . . It's one of those two, but I don't know.'
>
> Eyewitness 30 min later, still viewing the lineup and having difficulty making a decision: 'I don't know . . . number two?'
>
> Officer administering the lineup: 'Okay.'
>
> Months later . . . at trial: 'You were positive it was number two? It wasn't a maybe?'
>
> Answer from eyewitness: 'There was no maybe about it . . . I was absolutely positive.'"

Interestingly, Wells and Bradfield (1999) found it is possible to "inoculate" eyewitnesses against the postidentification-feedback effect by asking them to think about the process prior to the feedback manipulation. For example, the eyewitnesses were instructed to think privately about several variables, such as how certain they were, how good their view was, how long they took to make an identification, prior to the feedback. Wells and Bradfield (1999, p. 142) found that: Eyewitnesses who were instructed to think about these variables prior to the feedback manipulation were largely unaffected by the manipulation, whereas eyewitnesses who were not instructed to think about these variables were strongly affected by the manipulation."

Effects of Drugs and Alcohol on Witness Testimony

Much of the research on eyewitness testimony deals with subjects who are not under the influence of alcohol or other drugs. Police officers interviewing witnesses at the scene report, though, that witnesses are often under the influence of some substance, usually alcohol. One of the few studies in this area was conducted by Yuille and Tollestrup (1990), who explored the effects of alcohol on the memory of male student volunteers who witnessed a staged theft. Three groups were used: an alcohol, a placebo, and a control group. The alcohol group consumed three drinks composed of a mixture of fruit juice (5%) and alcohol (95%). The placebo group was led to believe they had ingested alcohol, but actually consumed only three drinks of fruit juice with a thin layer of alcohol on the surface so that it tasted and smelled like alcohol. The control group did not consume any drinks. Half of the subjects were interviewed immediately after the crime, and all subjects were interviewed one week after the crime. All the subjects were also shown a photo-spread consisting of the thief and seven similar foils (subjects who looked much like the thief) after the second interview.

Alcohol blood levels in the alcohol group averaged .10 (a level that many jurisdictions consider legally intoxicated). The results suggested that even mild intoxication significantly affected eyewitness memory. Members of the control group recalled 20% more information than those in the alcohol group immediately after the crime, suggesting that the alcohol group had stored significantly less information. Even after one week, the control group continued to recall more information about the scene than did the alcohol group. However, the accuracy of the information was similar for both groups, and the alcohol did not interfere with the ability of the witnesses to identify correctly a picture of the culprit one week later.

The evidence indicates that alcohol reduces recall by interfering with the original perception and coding of the event. The finding of Yuille and Tollestrup is consistent with previous research on memory and alcohol that suggests that alcohol has a greater effect on the immediate storage of information than on its retrieval (Hastroudi, et al. 1984).

Some researchers have discovered that if we learn material under certain special conditions, our retrieval of that material will be successful under the same conditions (Bower, 1981). That is, the things we learn in one state—be it happiness, sadness, or intoxication—are sometimes easier to recall when we are again in the same state. This phenomenon is called **state-dependent learning** or **memory**. For example, what is learned when intoxicated is recalled slightly better when again intoxicated. The same applies to being under the influence of other drugs such as marijuana, amphetamines, or narcotics. Theoretically, a conversation a person had in that state may not be remembered when the person is sober or drug free. One way to remember some of the conversation may be to become intoxicated to the same level again. It is possible, then, that witnesses may recall the details of accidents better when they are brought back to the same physiological or mood state they were experiencing at the time of the accidents. Exhilaration, depression, fatigue, and anxiety are examples of other states that might influence one's memory.

Trivial Persuasion

Research suggests that jurors are more persuaded by testimony that is full of trivial details than by testimony that contains less detail (Bell & Loftus, 1988, 1989). Brad Bell and Elizabeth Loftus (1988) had subjects read a summary of a court case where a man was accused of murdering a store clerk during a robbery. Two eyewitnesses, one for the prosecution and one for the defense, described the shooting. The eyewitness for the prosecution was positive that the defendant shot the clerk, whereas the eyewitness for the defense was positive that the defendant had not, suggesting they were matched in level of confidence. The study involved a 2×2 design. In one summary, the prosecution witness described the crime scene in considerable detail (defendant requested tissues, pain reliever, and soda prior to robbery, and the witness even knew brand names); whereas in another summary given to a different group of subjects the witness did not provide much detail (defendant requested some store items). Two other groups of mock jurors read similar summaries (high detail, low detail) presented by the defense witness.

The results suggested that detail was significant in the prosecution-witness condition but not so significant for the defense-witness condition. Mock jurors who read highly detailed testimony by the prosecution witness were more likely to find the defendant guilty than those who read low detailed testimony. Interestingly, the added detail—when presented by the defense witness—did not influence the decision. In another study, however, Bell and Loftus (1989) discovered that mock jurors perceived eyewitnesses who provided more detail as more credible and as having better memory and attention, regardless of which side they represented. In summary, the available evidence suggests that witnesses whose testimony is replete with detail, even if it is not directly relevant to the case, may play a powerful role in encouraging jurors to believe the testimony. Bell and Loftus coin this "trivial persuasion."

Children as Witnesses

Lawyers, judges, and sometimes police have long believed that the information acquired through the interrogation and testimony of children is permeated with far more distortion and inaccuracy than that acquired from young and middle-aged adults (Cohen & Harnick, 1980; Marin et al., 1979; Yarmey & Kent, 1980; Yarmey, 1979). This perception extends to the general public and prospective jurors as well (Ross, Dunning, Toglia, & Ceci, 1990). Survey research suggests that prospective jurors, criminal attorneys, and even psychologists tend to perceive young children as highly susceptible to suggestion and not very accurate in their testimony (Leippe & Romanczyk, 1989; Luus, Wells, & Turtle, 1995; Yarmey & Jones, 1983). According to one survey, defense and prosecuting attorneys view eyewitnesses aged five to nine as having poorer memories and being more suggestible than adults (Leippe, Brigham, Cousins, & Romanczyk, 1989). Defense attorneys were even stronger in this belief than prosecutors, a fact that is not surprising since children are usually testifying for the prosecution. In a recent survey by Saul Kassin et al. (2001), 94% of the experts in forensic psychology or eyewitness testimony believed that young children are more vulnerable than adults to suggestion and other social influences.

The age at which children may testify as credible and competent eyewitnesses in criminal and civil proceedings has long been controversial. Many jurisdictions stipulate that 14 is the minimum age for delivering competent testimony, with exceptions being made only after a judicial inquiry into the child's mental and emotional capacity. Other jurisdictions regularly allow ten-year-olds to qualify as competent witnesses. Many states, however, require that the competency of the child witness under 12 (or even 14) be evaluated prior to allowing the child to testify. These "competency determinations" focus on whether the child knows the difference between telling the truth and lying, appreciates the obligation to tell the truth, and "whether the child is able to observe, remember, and communicate what happened and answer simple questions about the event" (Bulkley, 1989, p. 211). Moreover, judges are encouraged to give cautionary instructions to juries when children testify ■ (see **Box 8-2**).

In recent years, numerous changes have been made to make it easier and less traumatic for a child eyewitness to testify. For example, over half the states have adopted Rule 601 of the Federal Rules of Evidence (Bulkley, 1989), which establishes a rebuttable presumption of competency for children. In other words, children, like adults, are presumed to be competent to testify. Under Rule 601, the normal developmental differences in memory or narration abilities between children and adults are no longer critical in determining a child's competency. Simply because a child cannot narrate an event, he or she is not precluded from testifying. However, a minimum credibility standard must still be met. Child testimony can be rejected "if a reasonable juror could believe that 'the witness is so bereft of his powers of observation, recordation, recollection, and recount as to be so untrustworthy as a witness as to make his testimony lack relevance' " (Bulkley, 1989, p. 212).

In Great Britain, prior to the British Criminal Justice Act of 1988, the uncorroborated evidence of any witness under the age of 14 was not to be taken seriously, even if that witness was under oath (MacKay, 1990). In Scandinavian countries, there is currently no age limit for a child to give testimony, as long as it is clear the child has sufficient understanding and ability to express him or herself (Andenaes, 1990). In Germany, there is also no formal age for competency as a witness, as long as "the child has reached a mental and cognitive stage to make evidential perceptions, to understand questions, and to give a comprehensible report of facts" (Frehsee, 1990, p. 32).

Psychological research on all facets of children's eyewitness testimony has exploded within the past two decades. Part of the impetus for this dramatic increase is awareness that children are highly vulnerable and often the victims of crime—especially

BOX 8-2
Cautionary Instructions

The Federal Judicial Center recommends that trial judges read the following statement to the jury after hearing testimony from a child.

> You have heard the testimony of ____ , and you may be wondering whether his young age should make any difference. What you must determine, as with any witness, is whether that testimony is believable. Did he understand the questions? Does he have a good memory? Is he telling the truth?
>
> Because young children may not fully understand what is happening here, it is up to you to decide whether ____ understood the seriousness of his appearance as a witness at this criminal trial. In addition, young children may be influenced by the way that questions are asked. It is up to you to decide whether ____ understood the questions asked of him. Keep this in mind when you consider ____'s testimony.

Commentary: This instruction is somewhat shorter than the standard child's testimony instruction. The committee believes that it is sufficient to call to the jury's attention the basic difficulties with the testimony of a child, specifically stressing the kinds of issues which may arise in connection with such testimony.

sexual abuse. This increased awareness also prompted a number of reforms during the 1980s to make the legal system more sensitive to child victims (Bulkley, 1989). "Numerous state legislatures and local jurisdictions have adopted innovative approaches to reduce trauma to children and improve prosecutions" (Bulkley, 1989, p. 210).

Children's Memory and Testimony

A fairly consistent collection of data emerging from research by psycholegal developmental psychologists on eyewitness testimony indicates that children generally recall less detail about an event than adults do (Goodman & Hahn, 1987). However, they are also less likely than adults to make errors about what they did see (Goodman & Reed, 1986).

One of the earliest systematic studies on children's testimony was a project by Marin and her colleagues (Marin et al., 1979), which documented that, under certain circumstances, young children can be as accurate in eyewitness accounts as adults. However, the nature of the questioning and the type of memory retrieval required in order to answer are critical variables. Marin's subjects were divided into four groups: kindergartners and first graders, third and fourth graders, seventh and eighth graders, and college students. When recall memory was requested by open-ended questions ("What happened?"), older subjects were able to report more material than younger ones. The younger the subject, the less detail he or she provided in describing an incident. Nevertheless, the younger subjects were *accurate* in the incomplete information they reported. When Marin's task demanded recognition memory (identifying photographs or answering yes and no to a series of questions), younger subjects were just as accurate as the older groups. Furthermore, they were no more easily misled by leading questions than the older subjects.

However, very young children (e.g., three years of age) seem to provide less accurate information than older children across a variety of testimony tasks (free recall, answers to objective and suggestive questions, and eyewitness identifications) (Goodman & Hahn, 1987). Gail Goodman and Rebecca Reed (1986) conducted a study where children three and six years of age and adults interacted (for five minutes) with a man they did not know. Four or five days later, the subjects were asked questions about the incident and tried to identify the man from a photo lineup. Compared to the six-year-olds and the adults, the three-year-olds answered fewer questions correctly, recalled much less about what happened, and were able to identify the man less frequently. The six-year-olds did not differ from the adults in answering questions correctly, or in identifying the man, but they did recall less about the event, a finding which is consistent with the Marin research discussed earlier. In addition to a list of objective (non-leading) questions, the researchers also used a list of suggestive questions designed to imply incorrect information to the subjects. Both the three-year-olds and the six-year-olds were more influenced by these suggestive questions than the adults, indicating that young children may be more suggestible when questioned by an adult. The results do indicate, however, that if six-year-old children are questioned in a nonsuggestive manner and provided with an unbiased lineup, they are at least as accurate as adult witnesses.

Reality Monitoring

Another area of research is concerned with reality monitoring, which refers to a child's ability to distinguish actual from imagined events (Dunning, 1989). Research to date suggests that children older than age eight can usually distinguish between what is fantasy and what is "real" (Dunning, 1989). Research also shows that children as young as four and six years of age can reliably distinguish between fantasy and reality (Ceci & Bruck, 1993; Harris, Brown, Marriott, Whittall, & Harmer, 1991). However, when these same-aged children were told to imagine a pretend character was sitting in a box, the children began to act as though the pretend character was real soon after being told. Twenty-five percent of the children were soon convinced that the imaginary creature could become real, and many had difficulty "giving up" the creature in their minds after the experiment. This study confirms the fact that the boundaries of fantasy and reality for four- and six-year-olds are fragile and quickly can become blurred for them. In summary, the extant research suggests that below the age of eight the distinction between fantasy and the real world begin to blur for the average child (Foley & Johnson, 1985), and accuracy in testimony can be expected to decrease.

Children's Suggestibility and Their Testimony

Another central issue in psycholegal child research is the question of how credible jurors perceive a child witness to be, independent of how accurate the children actually are. The low conviction rate in child sexual abuse cases, for example, has been attributed to juror skepticism about the child's testimony in many cases (*Harvard Law Review*, 1985; Leippe & Romanczyk, 1989).

The highly publicized McMartin trial, which ended with the acquittal of day care workers in California on charges of widespread sexual abuse, may be illustrative. It is widely believed that the children's account of their victimization strained the credulity of jurors in that case. A growing body of research indicates, however, that under certain conditions the public and prospective jurors may perceive the testimony of children as being more credible than the testimony of adults (Ross et al., 1990; Goodman, Bottoms, Hersocvici, & Shaver, 1989). Other researchers have found just the opposite (Goodman et al., 1987; Leippe & Romanczyk, 1987). The mixed findings in the area prompted David Ross and his colleagues (Ross, et al., 1990, p. 18) to posit: " . . . we are led to conclude that witness age has no uniform influence on juror perceptions of credibility. Sometimes jurors view the child as less credible than an adult offering the same testimony; at other times they view the child as more credible."

Ross et al. (1990) offer two possible reasons for these contradictory findings. First, stereotypes may influence social judgment. That is, the public in general may believe that children are usually not confident when confronted with authority, are highly suggestible, and easily confused. The more the child's behavior fits the stereotype (confused, suggestible, compliant), the more convinced the juror is that the child's testimony is suspect. The process is known as assimilation. Juror judgments will assimilate (to incorporate into one's thinking and decision making) their favored stereotype about children's statements. However, if the child witness defies the stereotype, such as being confident, forceful, and consistent, the juror perceives the seemingly atypical child witness as more credible. When stereotypes are violated, there is a tendency for human beings to perceive the individual as more dissimilar to the stereotype than he or she really is, a phenomenon known as perceptual adaptation or contrast effects. Because the child witness in the Ross et al. study violated the stereotype, jurors tended to perceive the child as unusually credible. A similar finding was reported by Leippe and Romanczyk (1989, p. 127) who concluded from their series of studies: "It seems that adults' negative preconceptions about children's memory will not dispose them to reject a child's memory message if the message's quality is sufficiently 'mature' to belie the stereotype." Nigro et al. (1989) also report that when a child witness spoke confidently and without hesitation (called in the research literature "powerful speech") jurors viewed him or her as more credible than an adult. Leippe, Manion, and Romanczyk (1992) report that the more consistent and confident the child witness appears to be, the more believable they are. These findings suggest that a confident child who does not become confused—and acts mature or adult-like—on the witness stand may become a highly credible witness in the eyes of the jury. This conclusion must be tempered a bit, however, by research reported by Gary Wells and his colleagues (Wells, Turtle, & Luus, 1989). Wells et al. argue that people on a jury rarely have heard or seen an actual child eyewitness testify. That is, their stereotypes are not built on actual experiences with child testimony, but are imagined stereotypes and biases, which almost invariably are very negative. When they hear and see an actual child witness, their cherished negative stereotypes and biases may be violated even by the average child witness. The actual event may rarely correspond to the imagined stereotype, setting up a process of contrast effects rather than assimilation.

The second explanation offered by the Ross group for discrepant findings on perceptions of the credibility of children is also interesting. Ross et al. (1990) suggest that there is a difference between trials that require children to remember and those that require them to be honest. For example, if the trial demands accurate recall of a complex crime scene, the jury is inclined to find a child witness less credible than an adult witness. Most adults believe children are less cognitively competent to put together or reconstruct a complex scenario that happened in the "adult world." Therefore, jurors, as a group, are less inclined to believe a child's testimony if it requires the cognitive ability to be precise, to remember, and to understand all the subtle nuances of what happened. On the other hand, jurors are more inclined to find a child witness credible if the trial demands honesty, such as reporting whether they are encouraged to go to school or whether they were asked to deliver drugs. Jurors apparently believe that adults often have ulterior motives for their testimony, whereas children are more straightforward and less likely to lie about things or fabricate events.

There are other important considerations about children's testimony, such as what happens to the child when under direct examination compared to cross examination. Research by Gary Wells and his associates (Wells, Turtle, & Luus, 1989) sheds some light on this issue. The researchers exposed eight-year-old and twelve-year-old children and college students to a staged criminal event (a videotaped abduction of a child from a playground). One day later the children and college students were subjected to direct questioning and cross examination about the event. All age groups were equally accurate about the event during direct examination, but under cross examination, the eight-year-olds were much less accurate than the twelve-year-olds or the college group. The authors attributed this finding to the eight-year-old group's greater susceptibility to misleading information. For example, during cross examination, questions were asked like, "You claimed before that the playground was fairly crowded, is that correct?" (when no such claim had been made), or "In which hand was the man carrying his wallet?" (a wallet was never visible in the scene). Eight-year-olds were more influenced by these misleading questions than the older witnesses. Ceci, Ross, and Toglia (1987) using three- and twelve-year-olds found similar results. To summarize, the susceptibility of young children to suggestion and misleading information appears to be influenced by the nature of the task and the context in which it occurs. Additionally, however, it should be noted that adults also can be influenced by misleading questions, as we discussed earlier in the chapter. Very young age appears to affect the likelihood that this will occur, but advanced age is no guarantee that it will not.

In a careful review of the research literature on the suggestibility of child witnesses, Stephen Ceci and Maggie Bruck (1993) were able to come up with three far-reaching conclusions on the subject. *First*, there appear to be significant age differences in suggestibility, with pre-school aged children being more vulnerable to suggestion than either school-aged children or adults. "In approximately 83% (15 out of 18) of the developmental studies that have compared preschoolers with older children or adults, preschoolers were the most suggestible group. Furthermore, although some experts argue that the suggestibility of children is diminished or nonexistent when the incident in question is personally experienced by the child or is important, the research evidence to date clearly indicates that children can be led to make false or inaccurate statements about very crucial, personally experienced, important events (Ceci & Bruck, 1993). For example, Goodman and Aman (1990) found that three- and five-year-old children frequently gave false answers to questions referring to sexual abuse, such as "Did he touch your private parts?" or to misleading abuse-related questions such as "How many times did he spank you?" Thirty-two percent of the three-year-olds and 24% of the five-year-olds gave inaccurate answers to questions similar to the first question, and 24% of three-year-olds and 3% of five-year-olds gave inaccurate answers to the second type of questions. Similar results were reported by Saywitz, Goodman, Nicholas, and Moan (1991) for five- and seven-year-olds when they were asked misleading abuse-related questions. Thirteen percent of five-year-olds and 7% of the seven-year-olds gave inaccurate reports in response to these questions.

Repeated, suggestive questioning may especially be prone to elicit a distorted, inaccurate answer. Amina Memon and Rita Vartoukian (1996), for example, found that repetition and the nature of the questions asked can have significant implications for accuracy of the children's testimony. Specifically, five- and seven-years-olds in their study witnessed a staged event and then were individually interviewed with closed and open form questions, some of which were repeated in the interview. The children were told beforehand that some of the questions may be repeated. A closed question format generally requires a short "yes" or "no" or multiple-choice answer from the respondent, whereas the open question format generally asks "tell me what you can about what you saw." The researchers found that open questions that were repeated a number of times had little contaminating effect on the accuracy of the children reporting what they saw. On the other hand, those children who were repeatedly asked closed-end questions were less accurate in reporting what they witnessed. One explanation for this difference is that the children may have believed that repetition of the closed-end questions indicated they had answered incorrectly. Repetition of the open-ended questions was interpreted as a request for more information.

A *second* major finding of the Ceci and Bruck review was that children sometimes lie when the motivation for doing so is there. Young children will lie if it is in their best interest or they have been induced to do so. "In this sense, they are probably no different from adults" (Ceci & Bruck, 1993, p. 433). For example, Bette Bottoms et al. (2002) found that threats from loved, trusted adults can be powerful barriers to children's disclosures in forensic contexts. This finding is especially relevant in situations where sexual abusers often exert powerful pressures on child victims not to tell others.

A *third* major finding by Ceci and Bruck is that young children—even preschoolers—are capable of accurately recalling events that are forensically important and relevant. "That their reports are more vulnerable to distortion than those of older individuals, and that they can be induced to lie in response to certain motives, is not meant to imply that they are incapable of providing accurate testimony" (Ceci & Bruck, 1993, p. 433). Most of the research has indicated that young children are able to recall the majority of information they see, even though they may not recall as much detail as older children.

According to Ceci and Bruck, in order to determine the credibility of children's testimony, it is important to examine the conditions prevalent at the time the initial statement was collected from the child. They believe it is especially important to know how many times the child was questioned, who the interviewers were, the kinds of questions that were asked, and the consistency of the child's report over a period of time. In concluding their extensive review of the research, Ceci and Bruck assert (1993, p. 433):

> If the child's disclosure was made in a nonthreatening, nonsuggestible atmosphere, if the disclosure was not made after repeated interviews, if the adults who had access to the child prior to his or her testimony are not motivated to distort the child's recollections through relentless and potent suggestions and outright coaching, and if the child's original report remains highly consistent over a period of time, then the young child would be judged to be capable of providing much that is forensically relevant.

Communication Modality

Another important factor associated with the credibility of child witnesses is communication modality, or the medium through which the child's testimony is presented (Ross, Dunning, Toglia, & Ceci, 1989). Courts are increasingly allowing alternate forms of testimony other than on the witness stand, particularly in civil cases. In criminal cases this is less likely to occur. The Sixth Amendment gives criminal defendants the right to confront their accusers and to cross-examine any witnesses against them. In cases involving child victims, this can be extremely traumatic to the child. The U.S. Supreme Court has allowed some accommodation, but has been reluctant to give blanket approval to alternate forms of testimony. In *Coy v. Iowa* (1988), the Court ruled that a defendant had been denied his right to confrontation because the two 13-year-old girls whom he had allegedly sexually assaulted were allowed to testify behind a screen placed between them and the defendant. In *Maryland v. Craig* (1990), however, the Court allowed closed-circuit television testimony (CCTV) in a case involving a child victim of a sexual assault who was deemed too traumatized to testify in the courtroom. Nonetheless, the Court was closely divided and the issue remains a controversial one (Orcutt et al., 2001). State courts that have allowed the use of closed circuit testimony, however, have generally limited it to cases of child sexual abuse (Davies, 1999).

Some research suggests that CCTV actually results in bias *in favor of the defense* (Ross et al.,

1994; Swim, Borgida, & McCoy, 1993) as well as bias *against the child* who testifies in this way (Orcutt et al., 2001). Other studies have found no significant difference in conviction rates between open court testimony and CCTV (Davies & Noon, 1991; Goodman et al., 1998; Murray, 1995).

Researchers also are beginning to study whether testimony in written form (such as transcripts or a deposition), in auditory format (an audiotape), or visual format (a videotape) make a difference with respect to perceived credibility. Some preliminary data from Ross et al. (1989) suggest that, regardless of witnesses' age, they are seen as more credible when their testimony is videotaped than when it is written. However, modality did not influence juror final ratings of guilt or innocence. In fact, the research at this point is not at all conclusive about how witness age influences ratings of guilt or innocence (Leippe & Romanczyk, 1987; Goodman, Golding, Helgeson, Haith, & Michelli, 1987). All we can tentatively say at this time is that witness age does not appear to influence directly how mock jurors feel about the guilt or innocence of a defendant.

Orcutt et al. (2001) began to pursue a new line of inquiry involving CCTV. Specifically, they wondered whether CCTV affected the ability of jurors to detect deception in children's accounts of victimization. The researchers noted that they wanted to test the assumption that children are more likely to be deceptive in CCTV than in open court, and that jurors are unable to detect that deception. In a complex experimental study, children ages 7–9 played games with a male confederate, in which the confederate either placed stickers on the child's clothing (not-guilty condition) or on exposed body parts (guilty condition). Three weeks later the children testified either in open court or via CCTV. Children in a "deception condition" were instructed to say that the stickers were placed on the exposed body parts when they were actually placed on their clothing.

The researchers found no support for the premise that jurors could not detect deception in CCTV, nor was CCTV testimony associated with bias toward the prosecution. Jurors were significantly more likely to convict the defendant in the guilty condition than in the deception or not guilty conditions, regardless of the modality in which the testimony was presented. Interestingly, however, the jurors evinced negative biases concerning child witnesses who did not testify in an open courtroom setting, and they were less likely to convict the defendants in those cases. Orcutt et al. (2001, p. 370) concluded that "the use of protective measures may not always be in the best interests of justice or the truth-telling child."

Despite the important findings of this study, Orcutt and her colleagues were careful to note the many caveats associated with experimental research on the issue of child testimony. Although some degree of arousal was accomplished, it obviously could not approximate the arousal experienced as the result of an actual trial. The children in the deception condition also did not believe that the "defendant" was in real trouble, and they were encouraged to be actors on the witness stand. Additionally, 19 children "opted out" of the study, refusing to testify. The researchers noted that these could have been the most anxious of the children, or those who would have benefited the most from CCTV. "Thus, the possible enhancing effects of testifying via CCTV may be muted in this study because of selection bias" (Orcutt et al., 2001, p. 369). Despite the above caveats, the key finding that the testifying condition did not affect jurors' ability to detect deception remained robust. "Because children in the deception condition who testified in open court received the same experimental manipulation as those who testified via CCTV, the potential confound of differences in anxiety level is not applicable when examining this comparison" (Orcutt et al., 2001, p. 368).

Stress, Memory, and Suggestibility

We should be wary about making generalizations to real-life incidents, particularly violent incidents, however, when it comes to child testimony. None of the simulated experiments with children involved terrifying depictions of violence, or the stress of being a victim. In an effort to increase the ecological validity of research on witness studies, several research projects have tested the effects of stress on the memory of children. Gail Goodman and her associates (Goodman, Hepps, & Reed, 1986; Goodman, Aman, & Hirschman, 1987) reasoned that venipuncture (blood drawing), inoculations, and going to the dentist are usually very frightening and stressful to children. Therefore, in some ways these situations resemble victimization. In one project, Goodman, Hepps, and Reed (1986) studied children who were faced with a medically necessary venipuncture procedure to determine if their attention would become narrowly focused in a manner hypothesized by Easterbrook (1959). This experimental group was compared with a control group of children matched for age, sex, race, and time in the venipuncture room (but who were not undergoing venipuncture). The results did not support Easterbrook's hypothesis that high levels of stress interferes with a victim's memory of peripheral aspects of a scene. There were no significant differences between the two groups in free recall (amount of information correctly recalled), or the proportion of correct answers to objective questions about the room in which they were sitting. Nor were there differences in responding to suggestive questions or photo identifications of people. In brief, the results did not support the hypothesis that stress interferes with a young victim's memory.

Because the above sample was too small to make sophisticated analyses or far-reaching conclusions, Goodman and colleagues (Goodman, Aman, & Hirschman, 1987) conducted a larger study. Here, they went to an immunization clinic for more subjects (3-, 4-, 5-, and 6-year-olds) and followed a similar experimental procedure, but apparently without a control group. Children had been prescheduled for an inoculation either as part of their normal medical care or as a requirement to attend school. Since some researchers have hypothesized that memory for arousal-producing events increases over time, the Goodman group asked the children to recall the event, and asked objective and subjective questions several days after the inoculation. The children also were asked a set of legal questions typically asked of children during child competence examinations (e.g., "Do you know the difference between the truth and a lie?" and "What happens if you tell a lie?").

Results showed no significant age differences in the children's ability to recall features of the event, nor did their ability decrease (or increase) over time. Age differences did appear in response to objective and suggestive questions, however. Older children (5- and 6-year-olds) were better at answering objective questions after a delay of several days, and they showed greater resistance to the misleading information contained within the suggestive questions. All age groups were more accurate on recalling the "central information" (e.g., physical characteristics of the person who gave the shot, or the actions that took place) than peripheral information (e.g., features of the room). Overall, the projects reported by Goodman suggest that stress had no consistent effect on recall and recognition memory of young children.

Peters (1987) took advantage of a child's visit to the dentist as a naturally stressful event. Subjects consisted of 71 children, ranging in ages from 3 to 8, who visited one of seven male dentists. The children were seen either within hours after their visit or after a period of several weeks. They were all given face and voice recognition tests of both the dentist and the dental assistant or hygienist who saw them. They were also given a recognition test to see if they could remember peripheral details of the visit. Children in the dental condition were as accurate as controls on a battery of subsequent memory tests. Peters admits that the stress level induced by a visit to the dentist is highly unlikely to approximate what children would experience as a witness of a violent crime or a victim of assault or abuse. However, it would be unethical to create in an experimental situation a level of stress comparable to crime-based conditions. Like the Goodman research, the Peters' study suggests that moderate levels of stress have little direct effect on recall or recognition memory.

Older Witnesses

A vast majority of the psycholegal research examining the relationship between age and testimony has focused on the eyewitnesseses testimony of children. Research focusing on the elderly and how the public perceives them as eyewitnesses has so far been underdeveloped. Interestingly, the available research suggests that there are similarities between older witnesses (ages 65–90) and very young witnesses on the matter of accuracy. Advanced age appears to have little impact on the accuracy of recognition memory (Yarmey & Kent, 1980). Older subjects do appear to be less adept at free verbal recall of an incident than younger adults, a finding also reported for children (Brimacombe et al., 1997). Yarmey and Kent also noted, however, that older witnesses were more cautious and less confident in their responses than younger subjects.

Similarities concerning the public's perceptions of child and elderly witnesses have been reported. Yarmey (1984) finds that elderly witnesses are commonly stereotyped as intellectually inferior and unable to recall events compared to younger witnesses. Ross et al. (1989) report that college students found an 8-year-old and a 74-year-old less credible than a 21-year-old with respect to accuracy of memory. Brimacombe et al. (1997) report a similar result, although this study found seniors were perceived as more honest by jurors than younger adults. The young and old witnesses were also perceived as more suggestible. The elderly witness was seen as the most honest of all the witnesses, however. Unfortunately, the memory accuracy and perceptions of the elderly witness have been seriously neglected areas of psycholegal study so far.

Identifying Characteristics of the Offender

The Face

Are witnesses who have observed a face once, perhaps only for a brief moment and often under conditions of stress or poor visibility, able to remember the face well enough to recognize it correctly sometime later? Since courts, particularly criminal courts, rely so heavily on such eyewitness recognition, it is important to consider whether this reliance is justified. In fact, an accumulation of studies demonstrates that the accurate recognition of a relatively unfamiliar face is an extremely complex and error-ridden task. Research by Memon et al. (1988) suggests that witnesses are more accurate if they have a full-face view of a person than a side view. The average person trying to identify a face seen once and for a short time will be accurate about 70% of the time (Goldstein, 1977; Wells & Turtle, 1986). Rarely do studies report more than an 85% accuracy rate. Furthermore, it is highly likely that the research overestimates the accuracy rate. Subjects used in the research are college students whose age and general health may make them better witnesses than the general population (Yarmey, 1984). Additionally, they lack the stress levels characteristic of eyewitnesses to a "real" crime. Nonetheless, we should recall the stress-related research with children that indicates that moderate stress did not significantly influence recollection.

Psychological experiments examining face recognition usually follow a two-step paradigm. Subjects are first shown live people, films, photographs, or face illustrations and are then given either a recognition or recall task to test their memory of the faces. Although the number of faces to study, the length of time allowed, and the time interval between study and test vary from experiment to experiment, the results have been surprisingly consistent.

In one of the earliest such experimental projects on face recognition, Howells (1938) discovered that faces were more difficult to recognize when the lower sections of the face area (middle of the nose down) were covered than when the upper sections were covered. In contradiction to this pioneering study, however, later experiments reported with consistency that the upper portions of the face are decidedly better recognition cues than lower portions (Yarmey, 1979). It is unclear which upper facial features are most important, though.

Research also indicates that the relative importance of facial cues depends upon the particular face being evaluated. For reasons unknown, some faces are easier to discern and elicit more accurate identifications than others. Highly unique faces are better recognized than plain or average faces (Going & Read, 1974; Cohen & Carr, 1975). Faces high and low in attractiveness also are easier to recognize than faces judged to be of medium attractiveness (Shepherd & Ellis, 1973). Distinct faces are easier to recognize than are typical faces (Chiroro & Valentine, 1995; MacLin & Malpass, 2001). There is some evidence to suggest that most people concentrate more on the right side than on the left when looking at a human face (Gilbert & Bakan, 1973; Liggett, 1974). Additionally, the longer a person has to view a face the greater his or her accuracy at recognizing that face at a later time (MacLin, MacLin, & Malpass, 2001).

Unconscious Transference

Some witnesses have mistakenly identified as offenders persons they have seen at some other time and place. This phenomenon, which Glanville Williams (1963) called **unconscious transference**, occurs when a person seen in one situation is confused with or recalled as a person seen in another situation. A witness may have had limited exposure to a face (e.g., on a subway) and, upon seeing the face at a later time, conclude that it is the offender's. Loftus (1979) theorizes that unconscious transference is another feature of the integrative, malleable nature of human memory, where earlier input becomes tangled with later input. It should be recalled that some aspects of perceptual and memory processes are unconscious, and the mixtures produced by them often range widely on a continuum of transformation and potential distortion.

The phenomenon of unconscious transference illustrates that it is highly possible that a store clerk, who is witness to a robbery, might incorrectly identify as the perpetrator an occasional customer who may have some of the features of the actual culprit. However, for unconscious transference to take place, the previous encounters with the innocent face must have been brief. Continual, relatively prolonged encounters, even with nameless faces, would be unlikely to result in incorrect identification.

Unconscious transference may also come into play when witnesses are asked to glance through a series of "mug shots." The unconscious perceptual and memorial processes may prime the witness to identify a suspect seen later on the basis of mug shot exposure rather than on the basis of observation at the scene of a crime (Laughery, Alexander, & Lane, 1971; Laughery, et al., 1974).

Two surveys (Kassin et al., 1989; Kassin et al., 2001) indicate that 81% to 84.5% of psychologists believe that the evidence in support of unconscious transference is reliable enough to be presented in testimony in court. Unconscious transference has also been at the center of several Supreme Court cases, such as *Stovall v. Denno* (1967) and *United States v. Wade* (1967). According to Ross, Ceci, Dunning, and Toglia (1994), however, surprisingly little research has been conducted on unconscious transference, and what has been conducted provides only weak support for the phenomenon. A well-executed mug-shot study by Dysart, Lindsay, Hammond, and Dupuis (2001), for example, could not find evidence for unconscious transference in the false identification data. Furthermore, David Ross and his colleagues have completed several experiments which suggest that the word "unconscious" may not be an appropriate term for the effect. Unconscious transference has usually been conceptualized as an eyewitness misidentifying a familiar but innocent person, but having *no* conscious recollection of the previous encounter with the innocent person. Ross et al. (1994) discovered that witnesses may *consciously* remember having encountered another person as well as the suspect, and are aware they are two different individuals who look alike. However, Ross et al. argue that witnesses may *confuse* the two memories at the time of retrieval when asked to identify the suspect. Consequently, mistaken identity, although unintentional, may reflect a conscious—but confused—process rather than an unconscious one.

Face Recognition

The pioneering Howells study (1938) suggested that subjects who were most accurate in the recognition test for faces were the least accurate in verbally recalling details of the faces. This hints that visual recognition of faces and their verbal recall may be two separate processes. Later studies supported the Howells data (Goldstein & Chance, 1970; Chance & Goldstein, 1976; Malpass, Lavigueur, & Weldon, 1973). This indicates that accuracy of facial recognition is more dependent upon visual encoding than upon verbal processes of memory (Yarmey, 1979). These data suggest that, as a group, witnesses are more accurate at recognition than recall. Law enforcement officials who ask witnesses to describe the offender are tapping a very different and perhaps less accurate perceptual process than when they ask them to pick out an offender from a lineup or series of mug shots. The first task calls for recall memory, the second demands recognition memory. A great wealth of information should not be expected if witnesses are asked to describe the perpetrator. It is a better tactic to pose questions jarring recognition memory, such as "Did he have a beard, a mustache, or was he clean-shaven?" This is especially true if young children or the elderly are witnesses.

As we discussed in ◀ Chapter 7, recall demands a different kind of retrieval operation, requiring a reproduction of the initially seen object or event. Recognition is an operation which simply requires a subject to note whether he or she has seen an object before. An illustration from a typical campus nemesis—testing—will make the point. Multiple choice exams often tap recognition memory, while essay exams usually involve recall memory. Students who resist essay tests sometimes claim that they require too much memorization. The resistance is partly due to the fact that memorization is a more demanding task than recognition. Students find themselves resorting to cue words or acronyms to jog their memory. By doing this, students are altering their task to a process more in line with the easier recognition operation. It will come as no surprise that a long series of experiments in cognitive psychology have confirmed the observation that people find recognition tasks far easier than recall tasks (Klatzky, 1975).

Own-Race Bias (ORB)

There is now considerable evidence that people are much better at discriminating between faces of their own race or ethnic group than they are the faces of other races or ethnic groups. This well-established phenomenon is most commonly called **own-race bias**, abbreviated ORB, but some researchers also refer to it as the "own-race effect" or "cross-race effect." This phenomenon is not restricted to the United States, but is global. Both laboratory and field research across a wide band of cultures and countries have replicated ORB, clearly confirming the effect is a reliable and robust finding (Meissner & Brigham, 2001; Sporer, 2001). Unfortunately, the majority of errors are false alarms (the erroneous identification of an individual who is not the perpetrator, and they appear to be increasing in our society (Meissner & Brigham, 2001). As we will note shortly, however, racial attitudes or prejudice do not appear to account for this phenomenon.

Initially, the research focused on black or white subjects, but it has recently expanded to other racial or ethnic groups. In one of the first laboratory studies to discover ORB, Roy Malpass and Jerome Kravitz (1969) asked 20 black students and 20 white students to examine 20 slides of black and white faces for about two seconds each. The subjects were asked to identify the faces they had initially seen from 80 slides (60 new faces, 20 old ones). The researchers discovered that white observers were more accurate with white faces than with black faces. Black observers, on the other hand, gave equally correct responses for both white and black faces.

These results were later replicated by Cross, Cross, and Daly (1971), who found that whites were more accurate in recognizing faces of their own race (45% correct) than black faces (27% correct). Once again, black subjects were about as accurate with white faces (40% correct) as they were with those of their own race (39% correct). In later research, blacks did exhibit some ORB, however. Chance, Goldstein, & McBride (1975) reported that while whites recognize white faces best, they are even worse at recognizing Asian faces than black faces. Blacks, on the other hand, were more accurate in recognizing black faces, second best with white faces, and least accurate with Asian faces. A similar pattern appears to exist for children (Yarmey, 1979; Feinman & Entwisle, 1976). White and black children are more adept at recognizing faces of their own race. There is also some evidence that recognition accuracy increases with age (Goldstein & Chance, 1964).

Stephanie Platz and Harmon Hosch (1988) asked 86 convenience store clerks to identify three customers who had visited their stores two hours earlier. The three customers were all confederates (assistants to the experiment): One was an African American, another was Mexican American, and the third was a white American. The clerks were superior at identifying customers of their own racial or ethnic group and did not do so well at identifying customers of different racial or ethnic groups. A meta-analysis study by Bothwell, Deffenbacher, and Brigham (1987) also confirmed that both white and black subjects are superior at identifying faces of their own race or ethnic group.

Recent studies and meta-analysis have failed to find a relationship between racial attitudes or prejudice and memory for other-race faces (Meissner & Brigham, 2001), although Wells and Olson (2001) admonish that it may be premature to completely discount prejudice as a possible "moderating variable" in the effect. A **moderating variable** is one that influences—sometimes very subtly—the strength and direction of the relationship between two other variables. For example, although racial prejudice does not seem to be directly associated with ORB by itself, it may a play a mediating role when racial attitudes and interracial contact are examined collectively (Meissner & Brigham, 2001).

Reasons for ORB

There are several possible explanations for ORB. One of the more popular, called the **differential experience hypothesis**, argues that individuals will naturally have greater familiarity or experience with members of their own race and will thus be better able to discern differences among its members. People are typically raised in social environments that require them to recognize own-race faces, beginning at a very early age. The experience presumed to be a significant factor in recognition must be distinguished from mere exposure, however. Growing up in an integrated neighborhood does not necessarily allow one to discern other-race facial characteristics accurately. Rather, it is the frequency of meaningful and positive contacts with other races that engenders perceptual skill in accurate facial discrimination (MacLin & Malpass, 2001). For example, having close friends of other races is more likely to promote facial discernment than having frequent but superficial exposure. Intriguingly, serious white fans of the National Basketball Association demonstrate superior recognition for black faces compared to those whites who do not follow basketball (Li, Dunning, & Malpass, 1998). Since most of the NBA basketball players are black, this finding provides some support for the differential experience hypothesis.

Additional support for the differential experience hypothesis is provided in studies showing that training in face familiarization dissipates the other-race effect (e.g., Elliott, Wills, & Goldstein, 1973; Lavrakas, Burl, & Mayzner, 1976). In the Elliot project, white observers' recognition of unfamiliar Asian faces significantly improved as a result of training in a learning task (paired associates) which increased their attention to identifying features of Asian faces. In another experiment (Ellis, Deregowski, & Shepherd, 1975), white observers from Scotland were found to concentrate more on such features as hair color and texture and color of eyes when looking at white faces. Black observers from Rhodesia, looking at black faces, attended more to facial outline, hair style, eye size, whites of eyes, eyebrows, ears, and chin. These results suggest at least two possible explanations for differences in race identification. People may develop specific strategies based on certain distinguishing cues of the human face to identify same-race members. Or, in light of the Ellis data, blacks may process a greater number of useful facial cues than whites when discriminating own-race members. It is, of course, entirely feasible that blacks use both strategies in facial recognition.

If the strategies used by individuals in identifying same-race members can be delineated, it is possible that the discernment of eyewitnesses may be improved prior to any identification procedure of other-race suspects. However, how crucial initial observations of suspects are and whether they might be improved by employing after-the-fact strategies remains an unanswered question.

A second hypothesis (in contrast to the differential experience hypothesis) pertains only to white *observers*, who seem to be the least able to identify other races. According to this hypothesis, there are differences between the races in the degree of homogeneity of facial features. White faces have more variability in hair, skin, and eye color than black faces and are therefore more discernible to all races. In a series of experiments designed to test this hypothesis, Goldstein and Chance (1976, 1978, 1979) found, however, that white subjects did not perceive Asian faces to be more homogeneous or alike than white faces. This outcome suggests that the explanation of the other-race effect lies not so much in the facial characteristics of the person being observed as it does in the observer.

In sum, the literature is consistent in concluding that people have difficulty recognizing unfamiliar persons of other races. This other-race effect is obviously a critical aspect in the identification of suspects by eyewitnesses. The most valid explanation for the phenomenon at this point appears to be the differential experience hypothesis, which implies that substantial, meaningful interactions with members of a different race may promote strategies for facial discrimination.

Pre-Trial Identification Methods

Legal Considerations

The identification of suspects by victims and other witnesses begins as soon after the offense as possible. Police usually obtain verbal descriptions of the perpetrators from witnesses or show photographs to obtain a preliminary identification. In some instances, the police will have witnesses scan photos of individuals with previous records, either to identify the specific offender or to obtain an approximation of the offender's appearance. Some police agencies routinely ask witnesses to examine a group of photographs (photoboards or mug-shots) fairly well matched to the physical characteristics described, including the person the police suspect to be the guilty party. The validity of these photo identification techniques has been addressed by the nation's highest court in a number of cases.

On February 27, 1964, two men entered a Chicago savings and loan association office. One man pointed a revolver at a teller and demanded that she place money into a sack. Soon afterward, the FBI apprehended two suspects, after tracing a motor vehicle described by one of the bank employees. The FBI then obtained group photographs from relatives of the suspects, which included the suspects, and showed them to five bank employees. All five witnesses identified one of the suspects (Simmons); three identified the other.

After its route through the lower courts, the case was heard by the U.S. Supreme Court as *Simmons v. United States* (1968). Simmons asserted "that his pretrial identification by means of photographs was in the circumstances so unnecessarily suggestive and conducive to misidentification as to deny him due process of law" (*Simmons v. U.S.*, p. 381). The Court, however, felt otherwise. The Justices ruled that the photograph procedure used by the FBI was appropriate under the circumstances, and they elaborated: "convictions based on eyewitness identification at trial following a pretrial identification by photograph will be set aside on that ground only if the photographic identification procedure was so impermissibly suggestive as to give rise to a very substantial likelihood of irreparable misidentification" (p. 384). An example of an "impermissibly suggestive" procedure would be where a black suspect is shown to eyewitnesses among five white persons, or where a perpetrator described as short is shown among tall foils (known innocent persons).

Just prior to *Simmons*, the Supreme Court heard three cases dealing with pre-trial identification abuses (*U.S. v. Wade*, 1967; *Gilbert v. California*, 1967; *Stovall v. Denno*, 1967). In *Wade*, the Court recognized the many problems inherent in pre-trial identification, especially lineups. The Justices ruled that the line-up was a critical stage in prosecution, and therefore, suspects had a Sixth Amendment right to have counsel present to assure an unbiased procedure. In a later case (*Kirby v. Illinois*, 1972), however, the Court distinguished between line-ups that occurred before formal proceedings had been initiated (pre-indictment) and those that occurred after that point (post-indictment). Only the latter—post-indictment line-ups—represented a critical stage and therefore required the assistance of counsel. In *Gilbert*, the Court found the defendant was denied due process of law when he was identified in a large auditorium by 100 witnesses to several different robberies that he had allegedly committed. The Court was concerned about the possible effect of group suggestion on the identification of the defendant.

In *Stovall*, the defendant was brought to the hospital room of the victim, who had been stabbed eleven times. It was one day after major surgery to save the victim's life. The black defendant was handcuffed to one of the five escorting white police officers, who were also accompanied by two staff members of the District Attorney's office. This motley contingent descended upon the hospital room for a "one-man show-up" to request victim identification. The badly injured victim identified Stovall as the offender.

The Supreme Court ruled that, under the unusual circumstances and because of the possible death of the sole witness, the procedure was necessarily suggestive and hence not improper. "The practice of showing suspects singly to persons for the purpose of identification, and not as part of a lineup, has been widely condemned. However, a claimed violation of due process of law in the conduct of a confrontation depends on the totality of the circumstances surrounding it, and the record in the present case reveals that the showing of Stovall to Mrs. Behrent in an immediate hospital confrontation was imperative" (Justice Brennan commenting, p. 292).

In all three of the above cases, the Court acknowledged the inherent dangers of bias in pre-trial identifications and concluded that "counsel is required at all confrontations to promote fairness" (p. 298). The cases specified some of the conditions under which certain identification procedures were permissible and recognized that pre-trial identification is extremely critical in the proceedings against defendants. Nevertheless, the later distinction made between pre- and post-indictment lineups is an important one to keep in mind. For the defendant, the prospect of misidentification is equally threatening, regardless of when the lineup occurs. For the law, only the later lineup is treated as a critical stage.

Lineups and Photospreads

Pre-trial identification methods are especially susceptible to a wide spectrum of biases and error, running from very blatant practices to more subtle innuendo. A police investigator suggesting to the witness that he look closely at "the third one from the right" is subtle innuendo when compared to other practices. Beginning in the 1970s, led by Gary Wells and others, psychologists have been examining more closely the psychology of the lineup and its ramifications for the criminal justice system.

Wells (1993, p. 556) writes, "The function of a lineup is to learn something from the eyewitness's recognition memory that the eyewitness was not able to articulate in verbal recall." Notice that the words recognition and recall are important components of the definition.

Since the witness will look for a suspect in the lineup or photoboard who fits the description given the police, the physical makeup of the members of the lineup is a crucial factor. Frequently, before appearing in lineups, suspects will change their appearance in order to mislead eyewitnesses, a tactic that is often successful (Cutler, Penrod, & Martens, 1987). Individuals being viewed should have as many of the relevant characteristics remembered by the witness as possible. Age, physical stature, race, hair style, and manner of dress—especially if described by the witness—should be approximately the same for all members of the lineup. If the witness remembered the offender as a six-foot-tall individual with blond, wavy hair and a moustache, the lineup is obviously biased if only one person in six follows that description. No matter how many foils are standing in the line, the test is effectively limited to the number of participants who resemble the suspect. We refer to this condition as **composition bias**.

Composition bias has been analyzed in a number of studies, but two which appear especially relevant are those of Wells, Leippe, and Ostrom (1979) and Doob and Kirshenbaum (1973). Using the previous work of Doob and Kirshenbaum, Gary Wells and his colleagues developed a concept they call the **functional size** of a lineup. This refers to the number of lineup members who resemble the suspect in physically relevant features, together with the suspect (similar suspects plus one). By contrast, **nominal size** refers to the actual number of members within the lineup, which may include some very dissimilar foils.

In a typical lineup of six persons, the functional size decreases as the physically dissimilar members of a lineup increase. For a lineup to be considered fair, its functional size should approximate the nominal size. If by employing various measures and statistical tests it is determined that all the members of a six-member lineup have equal probability of being selected on the basis of crucial characteristics, the functional size is six. If only three resemble the suspect, the functional size is four and the nominal size is six.

Obtaining theoretical and statistical indices about composition bias is an interesting academic exercise for researchers, but we also must consider the reality or "ecological validity" of this approach. **Ecological validity** refers to degree of practical or useful application of a theory or idea to the "real world." In other words, how much real-world applicability does a particular finding have? Law enforcement officials and prosecuting attorneys remind us that there are problems in including lineup members who closely resemble the suspect. First, it is often difficult to find persons (outside of members of the police department) who are willing to participate and who resemble the suspect in salient features. A volunteer might be identified as the guilty party! This is particularly a problem for medium-sized city or small-town police departments, where the subject pool is already limited. Second, law enforcement officials worry about the possibility that a high level of similarity between lineup (or photoboard) members may confuse the witnesses and distract from the accurate identification of the primary suspect.

Another problem involves how similar the foils should be to one another. In other words, do we try to match sex, race, height, weight, and age, and stop there, or do we match hair color, hair style, hair length, eye color, nose, eye shape and so forth? If all features matched, correct identification would become impossible as all lineup members would basically look alike, almost like clones (Luus & Wells, 1991). This **match-to-suspect** strategy does not provide clues as to when to stop matching physical characteristics of the foils to the culprit. This strategy seems to recommend theoretically that we continue—if possible—until we obtain clonelike foils. It does not provide us with a magical cutoff point.

Wells (Luus & Wells, 1991; Wells, 1993) suggests a **match-to-description** strategy (or culprit-description), where the selection of distracters is based on the witness's own *description* of the perpetrator. More specifically, Wells argues that the common features shared by the foils should be based primarily on the eyewitness's free recall of the culprit (prelineup description). It is important to realize that foils or distractors in the lineup should be allowed to vary in characteristics not mentioned by the eyewitness. Lineups constructed on the basis of resemblance to the suspect (rather than witness descriptions) are fraught with potential error. That is, when lineup members resemble each other in several physical appearances not described by the eyewitness, the eyewitness may become confused and potentially "identify" the wrong person. More often than not, eyewitness descriptions of the offender are general, incomplete, and focus on one or two physical attributes, such as the hair. Consequently, variation in the physical appearance of lineup members aids in the process of accurate recognition, a process Wells (1993) refers to as propitious (helpful or beneficial) heterogeneity (differences).

The term "free recall" that we associate with the match-to-description strategy is critical here. It refers to the immediate description provided by the eyewitness without directed prompting (leading questions) or comparison stimuli (such as photos). This distinction is important because recall memory is different from recognition memory. The match-to-description strategy utilizes both the free recall description by the eyewitness and the recognition of the culprit in the lineup or photo display. However, this match-to-description strategy could produce lineups where the foils differ dramatically in physical characteristics, while being matched on a few salient characteristics recalled by the witness. The judicial system may have some difficulty with seemingly dissimilar lineups.

Furthermore, recent experiments conducted by Tunnicliff and Clark (2000) suggest that endorsement of either of the above two strategies—match-to-description or match-to-suspect—may be premature. In their experiments, experienced police officers and college students both constructed lineups. Neither the match to description nor the match to suspect approach showed a difference in either correct or false identification. Furthermore, contrary to earlier research, they identified some advantages for the suspect-matched lineups.

A more subtle form of composition bias enters in with respect to who constructs the lineup. As we have learned, people have trouble discriminating the faces of other races, presumably because they do not attend properly to discerning features. If the suspect is black, the lineup constructor is white, and the witnesses are white, we have a situation with much potential bias. This possibility is suggested by John Brigham (1980), who bases his observations on accompanying research. Brigham notes that witness accuracy should be the greatest when the constructor and the lineup members are of the same race and the witness of a different race. Actually, though, witness accuracy should be the greatest when *all*—constructor, lineup members, witness—are of the same race.

Another area of pre-trial identification that must be closely examined is **commitment bias**. When a witness has initially identified a face, even an incorrect one, he or she will be more likely to choose the face again. This phenomenon is an offshoot of the foot-in-the-door technique long studied by social psychologists (Vander Zanden, 1977). It has been demonstrated in several simulated experiments on eyewitness testimony (Brown et al., 1977; Dysart et al., 2001; Gorenstein & Ellsworth, 1980).

Commitment bias is most operative in conditions where witnesses want to please police investigators and also presume that the police have good evidence against someone in the identification proceedings. Because of commitment bias, a witness who initially identifies a suspect, but with some doubts, is more likely to identify the suspect in subsequent exposures with greater conviction. Each subsequent identification promotes greater confidence because of the public and private commitment that "he is the one."

Thus, a witness may begin the identification sequence by saying, "I think maybe he is the one."

The police officer inquires, "Are you sure?"

The witness replies, "Yes, I'm pretty sure."

The police officer inquires further, "Pretty sure?"

The witness affirms, "Yes, I'm sure."

Between the time of this identification procedure and the trial, the witness replays the scene in his or her mind, thereby strengthening the commitment. This is done repeatedly as the trial date approaches. When the prosecuting attorney asks this key witness during the trial, "Are you sure this is the man?" the answer becomes, "Yes, I'm absolutely positive."

John Brigham and Donna Cairns (1988) discovered that commitment bias occurs even in the absence of strong external pressure. They had subjects view a videotape of a staged assault, following which some subjects (the experimental group) attempted to identify the assailant from a set of 18 mug shots. They were told that the assailant may or may not be present in the photos. In order to facilitate a commitment bias, the researchers did not include the suspect in the photographs. Another group of subjects who also viewed the videotape simply rated the photos for attractiveness, without being asked to identify an offender. In this situation, there should be no commitment bias. Two days later, all subjects were asked to identify the assailant from a six-person photo lineup that did contain the assailant. If the experimental subject had made a choice from the earlier mug shots (not all had), the researchers placed that shot into the photo lineup for that subject. Brigham and Cairns found that the experimental subjects demonstrated a strong commitment to their earlier misidentification (or non-identification). That is, they held to their previous inaccurate identification when viewing the photo lineup task that contained the real suspect. Experimental subjects who had not identified the attacker in the mug shots usually did not choose anyone from the subsequent lineup.

Research has revealed a number of additional aspects about lineups that are important system variables. In reference to the structure of lineups, single-suspect lineups appear to be superior to all-suspect lineups (Wells, 1993). A **single-suspect lineup** is where there is one suspect and the other lineup members are known innocents serving as distractors, foils, or fillers. An **all-suspect lineup**, on the other hand, is one where there are no distractors or foils who are known to be innocent. All members in the lineup observed by the witness are potential suspects. Wells (1993) points out that a false identification is much higher in the all-suspect lineup than in the single-suspect lineup. This is because there is no opportunity for the all-suspect approach to reveal eyewitness error, whereas the single-suspect lineup has a known-error category. In other words, the foils or distractors represent obvious errors in the single-suspect lineup but, because there are no known foils or distractors in the all-suspect lineup, errors in that situation are not identifiable. Wells further estimates that approximately one fourth of all lineups used by law enforcement in the United States are all-suspect lineups.

Another type of lineup is the **sequential lineup**, where the eyewitness is presented with one lineup member at a time in sequence. Usually, the eyewitness must decide for each person whether that person is the offender prior to being allowed to see the next person (Wells et al., 2000). Research suggests that simultaneous and sequential procedures result in similar correct identification rates when the offender is *present* in the lineup, indicating that one procedure does not have an advantage over the other under these conditions. However, sequential lineups do significantly reduce the rate of mistaken identifications in conditions where the lineup does *not* contain the suspect (Wells et al., 2000).

Still another, and very controversial identification procedure is the **show-up**. "A show-up is an identification procedure in which police present a single suspect to the eyewitness(es) to see if the eyewitness(es) will identify that person as the perpetrator" (Wells, 2001, p. 795). Unlike the lineup, there are no distracters or foils in a show-up procedure. A show-up is legal in the United States as long as it occurs soon after the offense (within hours) or under circumstances that would make a lineup impracticable or impossible, such as the hospital scene described earlier in the *Stovall* case. Research clearly demonstrates that show-ups are inferior to lineups in relation to the chances of a mistaken identification (Wells, 2001). However, it is not because the show-up makes witnesses more willing to identify someone. Rather, it is because, in a lineup, the error of mistakenly identifying a suspect is spread out among the foils and distracters. In the show-up situation, there is only one choice, right or wrong. Despite the limitations of the show-up, the procedure does present a practical dilemma, "pitting the suggestiveness of the procedure against the need to free innocent persons quickly and the need for public safety" (Wells, 2001, p. 796).

Eyewitnesses are also susceptible to **relative judgment error**, a process "in which the eyewitness chooses the lineup member who most resembles the culprit *relative to the other members of the lineup*" (Wells, 1993, p. 560). This may occur even if the suspect is not actually in the lineup. In other words, the eyewitness selects the person who, out of all the members in the lineup, most closely "looks" like (but does not match exactly) the suspect they observed. One way to control for eyewitness bias is to set up a blank lineup. A blank lineup consists of nothing but foils and contains no suspects. If the eyewitness identifies someone from the blank lineup then the police know that the eyewitness is highly susceptible to identification error.

There are many other sources of bias inherent in pre-trial identification procedures, but those delineated here have received the most attention from psychologists in recent years. One relatively unstudied source is police bias. This refers both to the use of police officers as foils and to the questioning techniques used by the police investigator. The use of officers as foils in a lineup is a practice fraught with potential bias. Certain nonverbal cues, like frequent glances in the direction of the suspect, could easily contaminate an independent judgment by the witness. Leading questions directed toward the witness and the quality of the questioning directed at lineup members by the police investigator can also produce biased results from witnesses who are sensitive to cues from the police. This is one of the reasons why suspects have the right to a lawyer—at least during post-indictment lineups. Defense lawyers should be able to protect their clients from these police tactics. In order for this right to be truly meaningful, however, it should be extended to all lineups, not just those that occur after the formal initiation of proceedings.

The *Lineups White Paper* and the NIJ Guide

The *Lineups White Paper*, alluded to earlier in the chapter, is a document solicited by the executive committee of the American Psychology-Law Society (AP-LS) to recommend improvements to lineups and photospreads, based on research findings about which there is broad agreement by scientists (Wells, 2001). The research in the area of eyewitness identification has become so extensive that the AP-LS decided it was time to make some meaningful recommendations to policy makers and police officials. The document made four far-reaching recommendations for valid procedures in conducting lineups or photospreads (see Wells et al., 1998). *First*, the panel recommended that the person conducting the lineup or photospread should not be aware of which member of the lineup or photospread is the suspect, a basic scientific procedure known as a blind or double-blind testing. The eyewitness should also be informed that the person administering the lineup does not know which person is the suspect in the case. *Second*, eyewitnesses should be told explicitly that the suspect may not be in the lineup or photospread; therefore, they should not feel pressured to identify a perpetrator. This is to prevent the witness from looking for clues or identification information from the administering officer. *Third*, the suspect should not stand out in the lineup or photospread as being different from the distractors, based on the eyewitness's previous description. *Fourth*, a clear statement should be taken from the eyewitness at the time of identification, prior to any feedback from the police that would inform the witness whether he or she had chosen the "right" suspect. This last recommendation is based on the observation that witnesses are often susceptible to inadvertent or intentional communication about the suspect during or immediately after the lineup occurs.

Wells (2001) notes that a prepublication draft of the *Lineups White Paper* was read by then-U.S. Attorney General Janet Reno, who proceeded to assemble a panel of experts to write a guide (the NIJ Guide) especially designed for law enforcement, entitled *Eyewitness Evidence: A Guide for Law Enforcement*. Although the *Lineups White Paper* was prominent in the deliberations of the Reno-NIJ Panel, it was one of many sources of information. In the preface of the 44-page NIJ Guide, Reno (1999b, p. iii) writes: "In developing its eyewitness evidence procedures, every jurisdiction should give careful consideration to the recommendations in this *Guide* and to its own unique local conditions and logistical circumstances." The NIJ Guide provides very useful, detailed recommendations for specific procedures to be followed by all those involved in eyewitness identifications.

Summary and Conclusions

Evidence obtained through traditional procedures of eyewitness questioning and testimony is replete with potential inaccuracies and misconceptions, regardless of the avowed certainty of the witness. Human perception and memory are like unexplored labyrinths where original input becomes altered, partially lost, and transformed into an arrangement that fits our expectancies, experiences, and sometimes the disguised needs of others. Situational, witness, and offender factors intermingle to produce an output which may barely resemble the incident as it "actually" occurred. Eyewitness research often contradicts common sense.

On the other hand, eyewitness information has been, is, and will continue to be a principal source of evidence in both criminal and civil case law. The expanding research evidence does suggest, however, that the judicial system should carefully examine some of its assumptions about eyewitnesses and perhaps even entertain some small but critical changes in procedures. The "commonsense" view that a confident victim is most likely accurate is not supported in the research. Additionally, despite some concerns about child testimony, a rapidly growing body of research evidence supports its accuracy, particularly on direct examination and when not influenced by leading questions. While the research indicates that children generally recall less detail about an event than adults, what they do remember is reliable. The age of the child, however, is an important variable. For example, children under three years of age provide less accurate information than older children. Also, the accuracy of recall seems to show a drop if the child is under age eight. Surprisingly, moderate levels of stress and excitement do not seem to affect children's accuracy any more adversely than it does adults.

Gary Wells (1978) divides eyewitness research into examinations of two sets of variables—estimator variables and system variables. Estimator variables are those situational, witness, and offender cues present at the scene of a crime or incident, such as, violence level, speed of events, the age of the witness, and the race of the perpetrator. No matter what strategy or procedure the law employs, it is unlikely to have major impact on this set of variables. Research on them, as presented in this chapter, can be used to estimate, post hoc, the likely accuracy of a witness. It can also be used to alter beliefs and attitudes about eyewitness testimony. It is likely to have little influence on legal strategy and procedure, however.

In contrast, system variables are under the direct control of the legal system and do lend themselves to changes in strategy and procedure. Examples of system variables include lineup procedures and guidelines, witness interview techniques, and to some extent the length of time between the initial event and subsequent testimony. Research data on system variables do apply to methods presently employed in the judicial system.

J. Alexander Tanford (1991) offers a helpful summary of conditions under which legal decision-makers, including courts, are most likely to heed and not heed social science research. Summarizing the evidence to date, Tanford notes (p. 156) that research will most likely be heeded if it is of high quality, understandable to lawyers, accessible, has "penetrated the culture of the educated elite," and has been available for at least five years. It will also most likely be heeded if it will legitimate decisions reached on pragmatic grounds, and if it has been used by other lawmakers. Social science evidence is *less* likely to be used if it is heavily statistical; contradicts faith or common sense; fails to support the policy predilections of lawmakers; would lead to major political disruption; demonstrates that something is ineffective without providing a better alternative; or reflects values incompatible with principles of law. With the exception of contradicting common sense, the eyewitness research discussed in this chapter seems to have more of the features included in Tanford's first group than in his second.

Key Terms

All-suspect lineup
Commitment bias
Composition bias
Differential experience hypothesis
Ecological validity
Estimator variables
Functional size
Match-to-description
Match-to-suspect
Misinformation effect
Nominal size
Optimality hypothesis
Own-race bias
Postidentification-feedback effect
Reconstructive theory of memory
Relative judgement error
Repressed memory
Sequential lineup
Show-up
Single-suspect lineup
State-dependent learning
System variables
Unconscious transference
Weapon focus
Yerkes-Dodson Law

Questions for Review

1. In what ways is research on eyewitness testimony on a better methodological footing than research on jury decision making?
2. Define the two fundamental processes, perception and memory, including memory's three stages.
3. On which points did the APA Working Group on Memories of Child Sexual Abuse (1998) reach agreement? Is either "side" of the repressed-memory debate favored by these conclusions? Explain your answer.
4. Briefly explain the significance of each of the following to eyewitness testimony: temporal factors (duration, frequency, speed), weapon focus, significance, and violence level.
5. How do (a) stress, (b) expectancies, and (c) stereotypes affect eyewitness accuracy?
6. Eyewitnesses who are highly confident in their testimony are not necessarily the most accurate. Explain, citing relevant research.
7. How does postidentification-feedback affect the accuracy of eyewitness testimony?
8. List six–eight findings from the research on children's testimony.
9. How might unconscious transference and ORB affect eyewitness testimony?
10. Based on psychological research, what recommendations have been made to law enforcement officials with respect to the construction and supervision of lineups?

CHAPTER 9

Psychology of Evidence and Related Issues

Now that the shortcomings and unreliability of some of the information obtained from eyewitnesses have been covered, it is time to give some attention to the information provided by accused persons themselves. The Fifth Amendment of the U.S. Constitution gives criminal suspects and defendants the right not to incriminate themselves, and courts have repeatedly reminded us that individuals may not be forced to confess, testify against themselves, or otherwise to provide evidence that may be damaging to their cases. However, these warnings have not been interpreted to mean that defendants may not plead guilty or testify at their trials if they choose to do so. Neither do the court rulings mean that law enforcement officers cannot interrogate suspects and interview witnesses to gather evidence. At issue, rather, are the warnings given to suspects, the methods of questioning, the conditions under which interrogations are conducted, and the validity of any waivers of rights.

We will begin this chapter with an overall look at psychological information that may be of use to the law in the process of gathering evidence, specifically when law enforcement agents interrogate suspects or interview other persons believed to have knowledge about a crime. We will evaluate some of the myths about nonverbal behavior and discuss various methods designed to detect lying, such as voice detection methods. We will discuss extensively the polygraph and its legal status, and we will do the same for hypnosis. We will briefly review facial composites sometimes used in identifying suspects. Later in the chapter we will redirect attention to the jury in an attempt to decide whether and to what extent jurors can be influenced by pre-trial publicity and cameras in the courtroom.

Criminal Interrogation: Psychology of Confessions

The primary purpose of criminal interrogation is to obtain a confession from a suspect or to gain information that will lead to a conviction. Furthermore, a defendant's own confession is probably the most probative and damaging evidence that can be admitted against him or her, and clearly has a profound impact on jurors. Nevertheless, most convictions are obtained—not from an individual's confession—but from the weight of other evidence gathered by police.

Prior to the 1950s, courts accepted arguments that some methods employing physical restraints, prolonged physical discomfort, beatings, and a wide variety of physical abuses were, not surprisingly, coercive and not to be tolerated. Gradually, courts also began to acknowledge the existence of more subtle forms of "psychological" coercion. Today, a confession is considered coerced if it "was elicited by brute force; prolonged isolation; deprivation of food or sleep; threats of harm or punishment; promises of immunity or leniency; or, barring exceptional circumstances, without notifying the suspect of his or her constitutional rights" (Kassin, 1997, p. 221). Some legal history on the topic will help elucidate the limits and restrictions of criminal interrogations as they exist today.

Legal History of Coerced Confessions

The U.S. Supreme Court lacks a clear consensus about which interrogation methods result in inadmissible confessions, especially now that intense forms of psychological pressures can be skillfully directed at suspects during interrogation. The Court found little problem in identifying coercion in *Brown v. Mississippi* (1936) in which brute physical force was used to force a confession from a suspect. Extracting a confession by using a whip clearly violated the Constitution. In *Ashcraft v. Tennessee* (1944), the defendant was not beaten, but the interrogation lasted for over 36 straight hours. The Supreme Court found it relatively easy to conclude that psychologically-coerced confessions, such as that demonstrated in Ashcraft's case, are not voluntary and therefore are not admissible evidence. Psychological coercion was again frowned on in a later case, *Spano v. New York* (1959). And in the landmark case, *Escobedo v. Illinois* (1964), the Court ruled that the petitioner's confession should not have been admissible in the state court because it was rendered only after Escobedo had repeatedly asked for and been denied counsel. The Court also found that the interrogation methods used by the police had so emotionally upset Escobedo that his capacity for rational judgment was impaired. As a result, his confession did not follow a valid waiver of his Constitutional rights. The best way to prevent potential injustice of this sort, the Justices said, was to allow subjects to be interrogated in the presence of their attorneys. Therefore, the Court held that once a police-interviewing process shifts from an investigatory to an accusatory focus, or once its purpose is to elicit a confession, the individual must be permitted to have counsel present.

Two years later, in *Miranda v. Arizona* (1966), the Court commented extensively on the pressure tactics of interrogation and made several references to the powerful effects of psychological coercion inherent in that process. "We stress that the modern practice of in-custody interrogation is psychologically rather than physically oriented. As we have stated before . . . 'this Court has recognized that coercion can be mental as well as physical, and that the blood of the accused is not the only hallmark of an unconstitutional inquisition' " (p. 448).

The Court felt it was paramount that the accused be notified of the right to remain silent, as well as the consequences that what they say can be used again them if they choose not to. Furthermore, suspects must be told of their right to have an attorney pres-ent with them during the interrogation process. If they cannot afford an attorney, one will be appointed for them. The presence of an attorney, combined with a clear warning, would enable an accused, under compelling circumstances, to tell his or her story without fear, and in a way that eliminates "the evils in the interrogation process." The Court did not require that counsel be present—only that suspects be informed of that right prior to in-custody questioning. It is also important to realize that a suspect does not *have* to be informed *at the moment of arrest*. The operative point in time is *before custodial interrogation*.

A line of U.S. Supreme Court and lower court decisions after *Miranda* have interpreted and applied this phrase, specifying more clearly the situations under which the warnings are and are not required. For example, a person is not in custody during a routine traffic stop (*Berkemer v. McCarty*, 1984). Nor are warnings required prior to the videotaping of a sobriety test (*Pennsylvania v. Muniz*, 1990). The Court also has announced a "public safety exception" to the warning requirement. In *New York v. Quarles* (1984), a police officer quickly asked an in-custody suspect, "Where's the gun?" before warning him of the right to remain silent. The Court allowed this because the suspect had been apprehended in a grocery store and had apparently hidden the weapon, which was a threat to public safety. In one ruling favorable to suspects, the Court ruled that the "equivalent" of custodial interrogation also required the *Miranda* warnings. In that case (*Brewer v. Williams*, 1977), police were transporting a murder suspect to the police station. The victim was a 10-year-old girl who disappeared the day before Christmas. The suspect, Robert Williams, was known to be religious. Police officers began to tell him how unfortunate it was that the murdered child would not be found and would not receive a Christian burial. He then told them where he had hidden the body. The U.S. Supreme Court ruled that while police were not directly interrogating him about the crime, they were performing the equivalent of an interrogation, because their comments were directed at getting him to confess. On that basis, the confession was inadmissible. In a later case (*Rhode Island v. Innis*, 1980), however, the Court allowed a conversation between police officers that had the same effect of prompting the suspect to confess. In that case, the comments were not directed specifically at the suspect.

The interrogation process is a powerful and commonly practiced method of securing evidence and obtaining confessions, even though it would be a mistake to assume that cases against suspects are won only that way. Furthermore, in spite of the Supreme Court's concern about psychological tactics, police classroom instruction and texts continue to advocate them. For example, Inbau and Reid (1967, pp. 213–214) commented,

> interrogations . . . must be conducted under conditions of privacy and for a reasonable period of time; and they frequently require the use of psychological tactics and techniques that could well be classified as "unethical," if we are to evaluate them in terms of ordinary, everyday social behavior. . . . We are opposed . . . to the use of force, threats, or promises of leniency—all of which might well induce an innocent person to confess; but we do approve of *such psychological tactics and techniques as trickery and deceit that are not only helpful but frequently necessary in order to secure incriminating information from the guilty, or investigative leads from otherwise uncooperative witnesses or informants* [italics added].

How can these methods be advocated and used, even after *Miranda*? The answer may lie in a number of decisions by the Burger and Rehnquist Courts that have significantly reduced the scope of that decision. We have already referred to some of these above, pertaining to the issue of defining what consists of custodial interrogation. Other examples abound. In *Harris v. New York* (1971), the Burger Court ruled that statements made by a defendant without *Miranda* warnings could be used if the defendant took the stand in his or her own defense, giving evidence contradicting what he or she had already told police. In *Michigan v. Tucker* (1974), the Court allowed prosecutors to use a statement from an unwarned suspect to locate a witness against that suspect. Still later, the Court refused to extend the requirements of the *Miranda* warning to grand jury witnesses, even though they could become potential defendants (*U.S. v. Manduiano*, 1975). And the Court would not accept the argument that a juvenile's request to see his probation officer required police to stop questioning him (*Fare v. Michael C.*, 1979). ▶ [That case will be discussed again in Chapter 12.]

The Rehnquist Court has likewise continued to narrow the scope of *Miranda* in a number of important cases. In *Duckworth v. Eagan* (1989), the Court by a five-to-four decision, allowed a *Miranda* warning that the dissenters said was ambiguous at best. Police told a suspect, "we have no way of giving you a lawyer, but one will be appointed for you, if you wish, if and when you go to court." The Justices in the majority held that this rendering of the *Miranda* warning did not make the confession inadmissible. More specifically, the Court ruled that the warnings must be considered in the "totality of the circumstances" under which they are given. In *Arizona v. Fulminante* (1991), the Supreme Court found evidence of a coerced confession, but nevertheless allowed a defendant's confession to be used against him. In *Davis v. U.S.* (1994), the Court decided that police do not need to stop questioning a suspect who makes an ambiguous statement about wanting an attorney. Considering the many pro-law enforcement decisions emerging since the original *Miranda* ruling, many observers predicted it was a matter of time before the Court announced the warnings were no longer required. In 2000, the Court did quite the opposite. In *Dickerson v. U.S.*, by a vote of 7 to 2, the Justices said the warnings have become established law, and they affirmed the need for informing suspects of their rights when faced with custodial interrogation.

Interrogative Tactics

Psychological strategies are routinely used in custodial interrogation. Belief in the effectiveness of these strategies is based on procedural evidence and personal experience rather than any validating evidence gained through systematic research. Still, most police officials swear by their usefulness in solving crimes and they employ the strategies, even when defense lawyers are present. Experienced interrogators usually try to make certain that the rights outlined in *Miranda* are read and understood by the subject. If the accused does not request an attorney—and research indicates that most do not—the interrogation can proceed. If an accused requests an attorney, he or she is not subject to further interrogation or questioning until counsel has been made available. Additionally, once the questioning has begun, if the individual requests a lawyer at any time, questioning must stop. In order to be admissible in a criminal proceeding, a confession resulting from interrogation must be made intelligently, knowingly, and voluntarily. Proof of this is usually obtained by having the subject sign a brief, clearly written document attesting to that fact. However, a written document may not be enough because the courts often rely on the "totality of the circumstances" under which the confession was acquired. "Totality of the circumstances" in this context means that the court, in deciding whether the confession was valid, considers the duration and conditions of the detention, the manifest attitude of the police toward the suspect, his or her physical and mental state, and the nature of the pressure used to induce the confession (Abney, 1986).

A wide variety of interrogation manuals is available to law enforcement, but the most well-known source materials on interrogation are Inbau, Reid, and Buckley's *Criminal Interrogation and Confessions* (1986); Macdonald and Michaud's *The Confession: Interrogation and Criminal Profiles for Police Officers* (1987); O'Hara and O'Hara's *Fundamentals of Criminal Investigation* (1981); Gordon and Fleisher's *Effective Interviewing and Interrogation Techniques* (2002); and Aubry and Caputo's *Criminal Interrogation* (1980). The Inbau, Reid, and Buckley book is currently the most popular.

Interrogation as discussed here will be limited to those situations involving criminal suspects. It is a procedure conducted to obtain either an admission of guilt, or clarification and elaboration of certain facts under psychologically coercive conditions. Precisely what constitutes too much coercion is often unclear to police officials, and as suggested in the cases we have reviewed, even courts often do not agree. Some legal scholars (e.g., Abney, 1986, p. 123) have concluded that the police may " . . . properly increase psychological stress and uncertainty by some artifices, tricks, and deceptions." John Hess (1997, p. 36) writes about the approach taken by a seasoned detective when he arrived at that part of the *Miranda* warning that informs the suspect of the right to an attorney. " . . . (H)e would pause, smile, and then interject the observation that of all the criminals waiting on death row, not one of them had gotten there without the benefit of an attorney." However, it is difficult to determine from case law at which point psychological pressure like the above becomes unlawful.

Interviewing, in contrast to interrogation, is designed to obtain clarification and elaboration of relevant facts from witnesses, potential witnesses, victims, or informants. It involves different principles and approaches, which will not be discussed here. The reader should realize, though, that an individual may be interviewed prior to becoming a suspect. In that case, only information obtained from him after he becomes a suspect and has been warned of his rights can be legally used ◘ (**Boxes 9-1** and **9-2** illustrate concerns about two unusual methods of obtaining information.)

Experienced police interrogators use a wide variety of methods and techniques, usually tailored to their personality and style. However, three general psychological principles are emphasized in most interrogation techniques. The *first* pertains to psychological control; the interrogator communicates to the subject that he or she has total control over both the subject and the interrogative situation. The *second* principle involves the use of methods designed to induce tension or guilt in the subject, with the assumption that this will break down the subject's defenses. The *third* principle is that the interrogator must appear confident and in command throughout the interrogation process.

Setting Most outlined procedures for interrogations specify the most conducive setting. In general, a setting which ensures isolation from the psychological security and support of friends or familiar surroundings is advocated. The value of a special interrogation room which deprives the suspect of psychological advantages usually gained from familiar places is strongly emphasized. The setting should be private enough to guarantee no interruptions or distractions that would interfere with the flow of

BOX 9-1 What Is Truth Serum?

The term "truth serum" apparently originated in 1922. It was used by Robert House, a physician who—at the request of police—administered a barbiturate to suspects being interrogated in the Dallas County (Texas) jail. House found that suspects, after taking the drug, became much more communicative, sharing their thoughts and secrets without hesitation. He published several articles on the drug in the years 1921–1929, and the term "truth serum" soon became widespread and popular. Consequently, common misconception quickly emerged across the nation that "truth serum" (especially the barbiturates) will *make* a person tell the truth and will illuminate hidden recesses of the mind. There continues to be lingering belief that various kinds of truth serums can be effective agents in police work or intelligence gathering. For example, during the spring of 2002, former CIA and FBI director William Webster said that the United States should consider administering "truth drugs" to uncooperative al-Qaeda and Taliban captives at Guantanamo Bay, Cuba.

"Truth serum" refers to a collection of barbiturates often used as sedatives, hypnotics (i.e., drugs that induce sleep), or anesthesia. Thiopental sodium, also called sodium pentothal, is the drug most often associated with the term "truth serum." Thiopental sodium is a yellow powder that can be dissolved in water and is usually administered through injection. To date, there is no scientific evidence that the drug suppresses a person's *total* control over what he or she says, *forces* one to behave against his or her better judgment, or *compels* one to provide truthful or reliable information.

Two other drugs that have also been closely associated with truth serum are sodium amytal and scopolamine. Sodium amytal (trademark for amobarbital) is an odorless, white, crystalline powder with a bitter taste that is used as a sedative and hypnotic. The drug was once used for the short-term treatment of insomnia, but now it is sometimes prescribed as a sedative to relieve anxiety, including anxiety before surgery.

Scopolamine is often mentioned as an effective drug for mind control that can be easily slipped into any drink. Scopolamine does inhibit the secretion of saliva and sweat, decrease gastrointestinal secretion and motility, cause drowsiness, dilate the pupils, increase heart rate, and depress motor function. It is used for prevention of nausea and vomiting associated with motion sickness and recovery from anesthesia and surgery. Medically, the drug is administered in such a way as to be absorbed into the bloodstream by applying it to the skin behind the ear.

Scopolamine, it is believed, has been used fairly extensively in police interrogations as an aid for gaining confessions. However, there is no scientific evidence that it was—or is—directly effective. The *threat* of scopolamine during interrogation *may* be successful in obtaining "truthful" confessions from suspects, however. It is *not* a mind-control drug nor does it encourage truth telling. While it is possible that suggestibility and the lowered guard of a person while in the narcotic state might be an advantage in interrogation, there has yet to be a single controlled clinical or experimental study demonstrating that the information produced by drugged individuals is reliable or "truthful" (Piper, 1993).

---

information or contaminate the control and tension-induction methods. This requires a room that is sparsely decorated, with no pictures or other items to encourage a breakdown in concentration or divided attention.

Conduct The three psychological principles of control, tension-induction, and confidence are clearly evident in the conduct the interrogator is recommended to adopt. The interrogator should stand while the subject sits, a method intended to communicate control. A subject's request to smoke should be refused, not only to communicate control but also to preclude the tension-reduction gained from smoking behavior. On the other hand, a cigarette may be *offered* as a gesture of compassion if a suspect seems inclined to confess. When the suspect is answering questions, it is suggested that the interrogator "violate" his or her personal space by standing close so as to induce discomfort and tension.

Psychological control is also communicated through the calm, patient, and systematic approach exhibited by the interrogator throughout the interrogation process. Virtually all manuals and classroom instructors tell the interrogators that time is on their side and that extreme patience, combined with persistence and repetition, will eventually "break" most guilty subjects. Psychological control is also gained when the interrogator is fully informed of all the known facts about the case and all the possible motives. Inconsistencies and distortions are, of course, more likely to be detected by the carefully prepared, informed interrogator.

While control and tension-inducing procedures are being initiated, interrogators are instructed to simultaneously communicate sympathy for and understanding of the subject's predicament. Most manuals recommend that interrogators use only language that can be understood by the subject and that is permeated with the communication, "We are only seeking the truth." Almost all manuals dictate that the subject should be treated with respect, regardless of the nature of his or her alleged offense. It is also advocated that paper and pencil should be kept out of sight because note taking tends to inhibit "free" exchange. Today, many interrogations are audio or videotaped.

The presence of weapons on the interrogator is discouraged, because these objects not only inhibit communication but also may instigate hostility on the part of the subject. If the suspect is not "interrogation-wise"—that is, if the subject has not been questioned in the past—it is suggested that the interrogator sympathize by saying that others in similar situations might have done the same thing. In some instances, manuals suggest that it might be effective to reduce the subject's guilt feelings temporarily by minimizing the moral seriousness of the offense.

Questioning Certain general rules are offered to get the subject to talk about himself or herself. The interrogator is advised to open by asking background questions and general, non-threatening questions that the subject can answer without having to deceive. Most instruction urges the interrogator to observe the mannerisms and behaviors of the subject while he or she is responding. Does the subject appear calm or nervous, intelligent and educated, arrogant, humble? These observations can provide information about what specific strategies to employ, although it is not wise to make conclusive judgments based on such nonverbal behavior, as we shall see later in the chapter.

Question content and form are given considerable attention in interrogation training. Questions should be directed at gaining specific information about details of an incident rather than at seeking a global confession. The interrogator should focus upon chipping away at the subject's resistance, since few persons are eager to incriminate themselves and since immediate confessions will not likely be forthcoming. It is also emphasized that questions be worded in relatively innocuous terms, so that they do not connote a specific offense like "rape," "kill," "shoot," or "molest."

Manuals warn interrogators against becoming personally involved to the point where they might get upset, angry, or otherwise demonstrate lack of control over the process. A subject will welcome the impression that the interrogator has lost confidence in the direction of the conversation. Patience, control, and confidence on the part of the interrogator are essential.

Beyond these general points, specific strategies for dealing with certain types of offenders or kinds of offenses may be outlined. Inbau and Reid (1967) offer a dichotomy based upon the emotionality of offenders. They posit that emotional offenders typically commit crimes against persons, and because they often have strong feelings of remorse are particularly responsive to the "sympathetic" approach. Non-emotional offenders are more likely to commit crimes for financial gain, are highly resistive to being detected and convicted, and are more responsive to commonsense reasoning.

Inbau and Reid also make a division based on whether or not the suspect's guilt is quite certain or questionable. They suggest that, when police are highly confident that they have the right suspect in custody, the interrogator should make this known to

BOX 9-2
Brain Fingerprinting

Obviously, a person who has committed a crime has the details of that crime stored in his or her memory. Is it possible to develop a method whereby the memory of that crime can be retrieved, even over the resistance of the offender? Dr. Lawrence A. Farwell (Farwell & Donchin, 1991; Farwell & Smith, 2001) claims he has developed a procedure that reveals the information stored in the brain with extremely high accuracy. Farwell, who calls his technology "brain fingerprinting," maintains that it can detect memories stored even if the subject doesn't want to recall them.

Farwell's method focuses on a specific brain wave, called a P300, which activates when a person recognizes a familiar object or scene. The subject wears a headband of electrodes and faces a computer screen, which flashes various images, such as weapons, faces, or objects known only to the offender. When there is something familiar about an image, the stimulus triggers the specific electric brain wave which lasts anywhere from 300 milliseconds to 800 milliseconds. The method has impressed intelligence agencies to the point where the CIA has funded some of the research.

The method has also received some recognition in a court case heard in Iowa in 2000 (*State v. Harrington*). Harrington had served 22 years for a murder he claims he didn't commit. In a post-conviction hearing, Harrington's attorney sought a new trial based on newly discovered information. During that proceeding, Farwell testified that his brain fingerprinting method showed that Harrington, who was age 17 at the time of his crime, did not recognize details that would have been known to the murderer and did recognize those consistent with his alibi (Feder, 2001). According to Farwell, Harrington's brain responses showed no memory of the crime scene but did show memories of attending a rock concert with friends that same night. In a 20-page ruling, Judge Tim O'Grady of Pottawattamie County District Court became the first judge to consider brainwave technology as admissible evidence (Feder, 2001).

While the *Daubert* standard for admission of scientific evidence is not required in Iowa state courts, the Pottawattamie County District Court Judge nonetheless used the *Daubert* elements in deciding to admit the testimony. He ruled that brain fingerprinting met all four of the U.S. Supreme Court's criteria. He found that the science had been tested, was peer reviewed and published, deemed to be accurate, and well-accepted in the scientific community. Nonetheless, Judge O'Grady denied Harrington's motion for a new trial, stating that the new evidence (mostly based on several other pieces of evidence besides Farwell's testimony) was unlikely to change the result of the trial.

Despite the ruling, the scientific community has *not* accepted the validity of Farwell's brain fingerprinting technology at this point. Nor has there been any independent research to replicate his claims of accuracy. Until more systematic research is done on the topic, we should remain skeptical about claims of the technique's accuracy. Moreover, if the technology is found through careful scientific study to be reliable, there is no guarantee that this intrusive creation will be used wisely and judiciously. Similar to other evidence-gathering techniques—like hypnosis and the polygraph—courts are more likely to allow brain fingerprinting in criminal cases only if the defendant—not the prosecution—seeks to introduce this evidence.

the suspect from the outset. However, the interrogator is warned not to ask questions which require the suspect to deny guilt repetitively, since repetitive denials render the subject less likely to admit guilt later. The interrogator is told to ask direct questions of the "why" variety, rather than to ask "whether" the person committed the crime.

Cues Interrogators should be alert to a number of physiological indicators of anxiety and stress. This is especially recommended in the case of emotional offenders who are strongly suspected. Sweating, blushing, dry mouth, shaking hands, elbows close to the body, are all nonverbal cues of tension that should be brought to the subject's attention.

The interrogator is further instructed to be alert to deception indicators, such as the subject's avoidance of eye contact, frequent hand to face contact, or even frequent trips to the bathroom. Signs of deception are also claimed to be inherent in the way the subject says things. For example, the interrogator is told to be suspicious of statements that are prefaced by "I swear to God I'm telling the truth" or "I'll swear on a stack of bibles." Suspicion is also drawn to the "spotless record, religious man" routine: "I've never done anything illegal in my life," or "I'm a deeply religious, church-going person." The interrogator is advised to be especially suspicious of the "not that I remember" comment, because it is often used by lying subjects. Therefore, it is implied that deception cues help to establish the guilt or innocence of the interrogation suspect. There is a danger in being too quick to adopt these suggestions, as we will discuss shortly in the section on deception.

Role Playing The sympathetic approach frequently advocated combines tension-induction strategies with humanistic gestures. A pat on the shoulder, a grip on the hand, a proferred cigarette or soft drink or sandwich—all are intended as symbolic gestures of understanding and compassion. Experienced interrogators claim that this is an effective strategy to use with younger subjects or first-time offenders. Some police agencies use the unfriendly-friendly role play routine. Here, an interrogator plays the role of the gruff, insensitive cop who threatens and cajoles the subject. Then, a friendly, sensitive, compassionate officer arrives on the scene, advises his or her colleague to "take it easy," and speaks gently to the subject. The effectiveness of this method is believed to stem primarily from the accent placed on the friendly officer, which ultimately improves the sympathetic approach. Interestingly, in the *Miranda* decision, Chief Justice Warren spoke strongly against the use of this technique, asserting that it was a form of unlawful psychological coercion, but the Court did not outrightly ban it. State courts have been routinely supportive of the tactic when used in moderation (Abney, 1986).

Other Strategies There is no dearth of suggested alternative strategies in the interrogation literature. Have the suspect tell his or her story a number of times, in backward sequence. Then, have the suspect explain the discrepancies that are likely to surface. Or propose a hypothetical situation: "It doesn't look as if you were involved in this crime, but if you had been, what would you have done? What techniques would you have used?" This presumably forces a suspect to propose a modus operandi that may give the interrogator clues to the crime under investigation. Another suggestion is directed at investigations of white-collar crimes. Interrogators are advised to enter the interrogating room armed with official looking papers and to proceed to examine them periodically, sometimes frowning or shaking their heads. This procedure assumes that white-collar offenders are impressed with the power of documents and are apt to become anxious in the face of possible evidence.

If the subject's guilt is uncertain, interrogators must decide whether to treat him or her as guilty or innocent, or to assume a neutral role without implying either. Most experienced interrogators believe it is most effective to take a neutral position until some clearer determination of guilt or innocence can be made. The final determination of guilt, of course, can only be made by judges or juries or by the defendant's own plea in court.

It is often recommended that investigators discover early in the process whether subjects are lying by asking questions to which answers are already known. Alternatively, the interrogator may present fabricated data about the case and notice how the subject deals with it. Any tactic that catches the subject in a lie not only will provide valuable information about the subject's integrity but also will give the interrogator the upper hand, once the subject realizes he or she has been caught fabricating.

Although we have outlined some of the commonly used methods of interrogation, the reader should realize that there are numerous other approaches which various agencies claim are highly effective. All, however, have the three basic ingredients of psychological control, tension-induction, and confidence and persistence on the part of the interrogator.

To what extent psychological manipulation and trickery should he allowed remains problematical. Police officers claim that any further limitations on interrogation procedures would hinder seriously any attempt to solve crimes. Richard Leo (1996) observes that while police agencies have usually complied with the letter of the law, as outlined by *Miranda*, most have not complied with the spirit of the law. That is, police interrogators have become particularly skillful in using deceit, trickery, and psychological pressures in obtaining confessions since *Miranda*. In this vein, Leo (1996, p. 260) asks the incisive question: "Why do suspects usually waive their rights and so often provide incriminating admissions and confessions to police when it so clearly violates their self-interest?" The answer, he says, "lies in the nature of contemporary interrogation strategies, which are based on the manipulation and betrayal of trust" (p. 260).

Leo arrived at his conclusions concerning police deception after directly observing 122 interrogations involving 45 detectives, viewing an additional 30 videotaped custodial interrogations, and attending a half-dozen interrogation training courses. "Although interrogation is fundamentally an information-gathering activity, it closely resembles the process, sequence, and structure of a confidence game," he writes (1996, p. 265). Since *Miranda*, police interrogators have refined their skills in human manipulation and deception, and have become confidence men par excellence. And the courts have continually allowed such manipulation and deception.

In analyzing the specific ploys employed by police interrogators, Kassin and McNall (1991) identify two broad approaches: *maximization* and *minimization*. In maximization, the interrogator uses "scare tactics" to intimidate a suspect into a confession, whereas in minimization the interrogator employs a "soft sell" approach in an attempt "to lull the suspect into a false sense of security by offering sympathy, tolerance, face-saving excuses, and moral justification; by blaming the victim or an accomplice; and by underplaying the seriousness or magnitude of the charges" (Kassin, 1997, p. 223).

The Psychology of False Confessions

Suspects sometime confess to crimes they did not commit. This may be done to protect another person, to become famous, to get things over with if one feels he will not be believed, or for a variety of other reasons. What may be surprising is that some suspects confess to a crime they did not commit because they come to believe they actually *did* commit it.

Kassin and Wrightsman (1985) reviewed the literature on various cases and historical anecdotes and were able to identify three types of false confessions: (1) voluntary; (2) coerced-compliant; and (3) coerced-internalized. The first, a voluntary false confession, is a self-incriminating statement made without external pressure from law enforcement. As an historical example, Kassin (1997) points out that when the Charles Lindbergh baby was kidnapped over 70 years ago, at least 200 people falsely confessed to the crime. One of the major explanations offered over the years for this phenomenon is that some people—living a dire life of no importance—have a need for fame, recognition, or perhaps even self-punishment. A false confession made to protect the real perpetrator would be another example in this voluntary category.

The other two types of false confessions involve pressure from law enforcement officers. Social science research suggests strongly that skillful manipulation, deception, and the confidence game under stressful conditions may lead to false confessions. Gudjonsson (1992) has called this "interrogative suggestibility." Under these circumstances, even an innocent person may come to believe the information provided by police and may also come to believe he or she is guilty of the crime.

Saul Kassin (1997) goes to the social psychology literature to lay the groundwork for a way to classify these two types of coerced false confessions. The social psychological concepts he draws upon are compliance and internalization, originally coined by

Kelman (1958). Compliance is a form of conformity in which we change our *public* behavior—but not our *private* beliefs—to social pressure or threat from another person. Internalization, on the other hand, refers to changes in our private thoughts or beliefs because we sincerely believe in something.

Coerced-compliant false confessions "occur when a suspect confesses in order to escape or avoid an aversive interrogation or to gain a promised reward" (Kassin, 1997, p. 225). This type of false confession is most likely to occur after prolonged and intense interrogation pressures, where sleep deprivation may be a chief ingredient. The suspect finally relents to avoid further discomfort, knowing full-well that he is innocent. A promise of a reduction of penalty is enough in some cases to "give up." And, as Kassin (1997) posits, the pages of legal history are filled with examples of coerced-compliant confessions. Such confessions may be more likely to be made by suspects with prior records, since police will be more suspicious of them and less likely to believe in their innocence.

"Coerced-internalized confessions are those in which an innocent person—anxious, tired, confused, and subjected to highly suggestive methods of interrogation—actually comes to believe that he or she has committed the crime" (Kassin, 1997, p. 226). This may seem preposterous—after all, how could anyone mistakenly believe he or she is responsible for a criminal act? In a series of experiments, Kassin has demonstrated that this is clearly possible. In one study, Kassin and Kiechel (1996) had students participate in what were ostensibly reaction time experiments, one experiment involving a fast-paced task and the other a slow-paced task. Before the experiments, each participant was instructed not to press the "ALT" key on the computer keyboard, no matter what. Doing so, they were told, would cause the program to crash and the data to be lost. (It should be noted that—due to its location on the keyboard—the ALT key does not lend itself to being accidentally pressed.) After 60 seconds into the actual experiment, the computer was intentionally programmed to crash, an event designed to be followed by a highly distressed experimenter accusing the participants of having pressed the forbidden key. All the participants, keep in mind, were truly innocent, and all initially denied the charge. Overall, though, 69% of the 75 participants eventually signed a confession, admitting that they had, in fact, pressed the forbidden key. Furthermore, 28% of the participants seemed to internalize the guilt, and 9% even made up (confabulated) details to support their false beliefs. Additionally, participants in the fast-paced reaction-time experiment were significantly more suggestible than participants in the slow-paced condition. Apparently, subjects working at a faster pace felt they were less able to monitor their performance, and consequently were more likely to believe they could have inadvertently pressed the "ALT" key. The experiment provides cogent support, Kassin and Kiechel conclude, that the presentation of false incriminating evidence can induce people to believe that they are to blame for something they did not do.

Kassin (1997) admonishes that it can be difficult at times to distinguish among the coerced types. Furthermore, some innocent suspects may experience temporary or momentary periods of confusion and self-doubt about the facts, but in the long run do not develop lasting false memories of guilt. Additionally, McCann (1998b) points out that a coerced false confession can be generated in situations where law enforcement is not *directly* involved. Specifically, a pressure to confess may also emanate from family members, friends, gang members, church officials, and other sources besides police authorities. Gudjonsson (1992) estimates, for example, that as many as 25% of young juvenile offenders in detention facilities may have taken the rap to protect an older offender. What's more, in some situations, pressure to confess may originate from some combination of *both* police (custodial) and non-police (non-custodial) sources.

It also should be recognized that there are certainly individual differences in susceptibility to coercive pressure. According to Gudjonsson (1984, 1992), some individuals are unknowingly but particularly susceptible to such influences. Accordingly, he developed a test by which suggestibility is measured, the Gudjonsson Suggestibility Scale (GSS). According to researchers who have used and evaluated the scale (e.g., Kassin, 1997; McCann, 1998a; Merckelbach et al., 1998), persons who receive high scores on the scale are at serious risk of making false confessions, particularly when deceptive information is provided to them by police.

Deception and Lying

Deception is behavior that is intended to conceal, misrepresent, or distort truth or information for the purpose of misleading others. Deception is obviously prevalent in criminal justice, especially in situations where the stakes are high. Parole officers believe that their parole interviews with parolees are fraught with deceptive tactics (Porter, Woodworth, & Birt, 2000). Correctional personnel believe that inmates often try to deceive concerning their level of rehabilitation, degree of remorse, and plans for life in the community. Police officers are constantly suspicious about the truthfulness of suspects and witnesses, and they themselves use deception during custodial interrogation. Jurors and judges are wary of the statements made by a wide collection of people testifying in the courtroom, in both criminal and civil matters.

Attempts at detecting deception extend to areas other than those discussed above. For example, employers try to determine the veracity of prospective employees about their past experience, work behavior, and credentials. In intelligence and security settings, various deception detection techniques are used to identify individuals who might be engaged in damaging or threatening behavior, such as espionage or terrorist activities.

In light of all the situations in which truthfulness is a critical variable, we must ask whether people really are able to detect deception in others. In particular, are professional "lie detectors"—like polygraphers, police officers, and parole officers—good at detecting deception? And if so, are they able to do it consistently?

Research on Deception

The quick answer to the above questions is that very, very few people, professionals or laypersons, are able to detect deception (or honesty) with much accuracy or consistency. Nevertheless, people (especially professionals) firmly believe they can. While our society is replete with folklore concerning how to discern whether someone is lying, the empirical research over the past 30 years cogently demonstrates that the human ability to identify liars from truth tellers is abysmally poor (Bauchner, Brandt, & Miller, 1977; Littlepage & Pineault, 1978; Knapp, 1978; Ekman & Friesen, 1974). Ekman and O'Sullivan (1991) conclude from their review of the research literature that the average accuracy in detecting deceit has rarely been above 60% (with chance being 50%), and, in some studies, the average accuracy is worse than chance. For example, Kraut and Poe (1980) discovered that custom officials were no more accurate at detecting deceit than laypersons. DePaulo and Pfeifer (1986) found no differences in accuracy between federal law enforcement officers, regardless of experience, and college students. Kohnken (1987) reports that police officers were no better than chance at detecting lying or honesty in college students. Furthermore, he found no relationship between confidence in one's ability to detect deception and the actual ability to do so. Porter, Woodworth, and Birt (2000) found that the ability of Canadian federal parole officers to detect deception was less than chance. Similar to previous research, neither level of job experience nor confidence in deception detection ability were related to accuracy rates. Paul Ekman and Maureen O'Sullivan (1991), in an often-cited and well-designed study, compared laypersons and a wide assortment of "professional liar catchers" on the ability to detect deception. Their ambitious project included members of the U.S. Secret Service, Central Intelligence Agency, Federal Bureau of Investigation, National Security Agency, Drug Enforcement Agency, California law enforcement, judges, psychiatrists, college students, and working adults. Only *one* group was able to detect deception beyond chance: agents of the U.S. Secret Service. The 34 Secret Agents were not impressive in their ability to identify deception (64% in overall accuracy), but none of them performed below average, and some (29%) achieved accuracy scores of 80% or more. Another important finding was that the accurate "lie catchers" reported using nonverbal cues (especially subtle facial expressions) as well as verbal clues to identify deceit. In other words, the accurate "lie catchers" used multiple clues rather than relying on any particular single indicator. In another study (Ekman, O'Sullivan, Friesen, & Scherer, 1991), it was found that, when verbal and facial cues are combined, deceptive and honest subjects could be discerned about 86% of the time. The Ekman-O'Sullivan study did not find any differences in the ability of males or females to detect deception, but it did find that older observers were generally less accurate than younger ones.

The Frank and Ekman (1997) study also examined some other aspects of deception detection. Because much of the previous research had looked at low-stake, laboratory-produced lies, Frank and Ekman focused on high-stake, "real-world" deception—that is, lies that occur in situations where the stakes are high and emotions are intense, as would be encountered in police investigations and courtrooms. The researchers found some support that the strong emotions generated in high-stake situations tend to "leak" good clues for deception detection, and that these clues are apparent across other high-stake situations. For example, Frank and Ekman discovered, under high-stake situations, *strong negative* emotions in the facial expressions of 90% of the liars; rarely did they find similar negative emotions in the facial expressions of truth tellers. In low-stake situations, such as would be found in everyday, low-emotional lying, the observer needs to rely more on "thinking" clues, such as words, factual descriptions, pauses, long speech latencies, and speech errors to detect deception. Low-stake lying appears to be more situation specific and probably lends itself to more inaccuracy by observers. Thus, we might posit that a police officer trained in detecting deception is more likely to uncover it during an interrogation than during an interview.

This leads us to another finding from the Frank and Ekman (1997) study. Although there are individual differences in ability to detect deception, some people can be trained to identify deceivers at a better-than-chance level. Studies have demonstrated modest but statistically significant improvements in accuracy after such training, usually in the range of 5% to 10%. Valid, empirically-based training might even improve the accuracy. In the Frank-Ekman research, those persons who were able to detect deception without much training seemed to improve the most with research-based training. Likewise, Porter et al. (2000) discovered that parole officers improved their scores at detecting deception after two days of such training. Kassin and Fong (1999), however, found that *traditional* police training on deception (the Reid Technique of analyzing verbal and nonverbal behavior) actually *decreased* the officers' ability to detect deception. It is possible that the training that many law enforcement officers and detectives receive may contribute to their inaccuracy and perhaps even provide unwarranted confidence in their ability. The research has been consistent in pointing out that the more confident the officer, the worse his or her accuracy (Ekman & O'Sullivan, 1991; Kassin & Fong, 1999; Porter et al., 2000). Jurors and judges are equally poor at detecting deception in children, either through closed circuit television or seeing the child in person (Orcutt et al., 2001).

Nonverbal Behavior

Interrogation procedures in particular often have referents to nonverbal signs of deceit and guilt, as we have seen in the preceding section. Inbau and Reid, for example, assert (1967, p. 34): "When a subject fails to look the interrogator straight in the eye, or when he exhibits a restlessness by leg swinging, foot-wiggling, hand-wringing, finger-tapping, the picking of fingernails, or the fumbling with objects such as a tie clasp or pencil, it is well for the interrogator to get the idea across that he is aware of such reactions and that he views them as manifestations of lying." Other nonverbal behaviors believed to be indicative of guilt or lying include pulsation of the carotid artery in the neck, excessive activity of the Adam's apple, dryness of the mouth, and wiggling of the ears!

Over the past three decades many empirical studies have probed the relationship between nonverbal behavior and deception. Nonverbal cues like facial expressions, body posture, and movements of the legs and feet and arms have drawn the greatest attention. One general observation emerging from early scientific inquiry took researchers aback: Individuals who wish to deceive are also aware of the common folklore, and consequently they try to control the so-called indicators of lying. For example, people who are trying to deceive do not have more frequent eye shifts than truthful communicators (Mehrabian, 1971). Deceitful communicators also may smile more often than truthful communicators (Mehrabian & Williams, 1969), have longer eye contact (Mehrabian, 1971), or in some conditions maintain a more placid expression (McClintock & Hunt, 1975).

The above features all indicate an attempt, or even an over-attempt, to control the normal channels of nonverbal communications. Channels normally used in communicating emotions and feelings, such as facial expressions and eye contact, are held in tight check by the deceiving communicator. Thus, empirical study has found that deceit is not so much communicated through shifty eyes, decreased eye contact, or "evasive" facial expression, but rather through channels that typically are not used in expressing oneself. These more covert nonverbal modalities are called leaky channels by researchers (Ekman & Friesen, 1969, 1974), because they "leak" information not intended by the communicator.

The placid expression, longer eye contact, and tendency to smile are therefore often examples of leaky channels. In further attempts to control communication, deceitful individuals may speak at a slower rate, speak fewer words, but produce more speech errors (Rosenfeld, 1966; Kasl & Mahl, 1965). Their posture often is rigid and stiff (Mehrabian, 1971), and they display very little head nodding (Rosenfeld, 1966). Hand gestures are kept to an unusually low level (Ekman, Friesen, & Scherer, 1976), but there is considerable movement and shifting with feet and legs (Ekman & Friesen, 1969). There is also evidence that deceitful speakers make exceedingly few factual statements, but many sweeping statements (Knapp, Hart, & Dennis, 1974).

Cultural Differences A wide variety of communicative cues may accompany deception, but the fact is that they also may not—or they may accompany truth. One important variable that must be taken into account is cultural or ethnic difference. Researchers have only begun to explore these variables.

It appears that when people from various ethnic groups employ nonverbal behavior that is typical for their group, the behavior may be interpreted as suspicious by other groups. Gaze aversion is a good example of this. In some cultures—particularly some Eastern cultures—direct eye contact is discouraged, and gaze aversion is the norm (Sporer, 2001). In many American Indian cultures, particularly Navajo and Apache, looking into the face of authority figures is considered disrespectful. In European and other Western cultures, it is considered an indicator of deception. Furthermore, *avoidance* of eye contact is often considered a sign of evasion, coldness, fearfulness, shyness, or indifference in Western cultures. Looking someone directly in the eye, on the other hand, is associated with intimacy and sincerity. However, the individual who looks another in the eye too intently, without at any time shifting his or her gaze, may be regarded with suspicion (e.g., as insincere or too eager to assert power over another).

Vrij (2000; Vrij & Windel, 1991; Vrij & Semin, 1996) has conducted a series of studies that compare blacks and whites on certain nonverbal cues. He found that blacks often displayed nonverbal behaviors, such as gaze aversion and frequent smiling that could be misinterpreted by whites as signs of lying. Police interrogation manuals routinely advise interrogators to be suspicious of these characteristics. Yet, they are normal behaviors. They can also be explained by the fact that blacks often have good reason to be suspicious and fearful of police. Gaze aversion and frequent smiling, perhaps as indication of nervousness, could be a reflection of this fear.

Although research on cultural differences in nonverbal behavior is too new to draw many conclusions, it serves to remind us of the pitfalls of making unwarranted assumptions. Research on detection in general warns us that we cannot uncover lying strictly on the basis of nonverbal cues. It is especially foolhardy to accept the prevailing folklore in the area. If anything, the cues associated with deception may be better behavioral indicators of stress and anxiety than they are signs of lying.

Expectancy-Violation Model

Some researchers have taken a different approach to the study of detection deception. Rather than looking only for cues in the person speaking, they also look for cues in the observer or questioner. This approach relies heavily on the observer's perception. It also attempts to explain why certain nonverbal cues raise suspicion that the person being questioned is not telling the truth.

Charles Bond and his colleagues (Bond, Omar, Pitre, Lashley, Skaggs, & Kirk, 1992) have proposed an **expectancy-violation model** to account for what leads people to suspect lying in others. According to this model, people accept at face value nonverbal behaviors that are usual and expected under certain conditions. However, if these nonverbal behaviors are unusual or unexpected, perceivers begin to suspect deception. Specifically, "Perceivers infer deception from nonverbal norm violations when they have reason to question the actor's veracity and when innocent explanations for the unexpected behavior seem less credible" (Bond et al., 1992, p. 969). The expectancy-violation models asserts that deception may be inferred from any nonverbal behavior that violates the norm—in other words, any "weird" behavior is suspect. For example, if high levels of eye contact are expected, and the person avoids eye contact, this norm deviation may be interpreted as highlighting deception. Furthermore, the more frequently a person displays nonverbal behavior that violates the norm, the more dishonest or deceptive the person will appear. In light of the cultural differences discussed above, however, it is important for the observer to understand what is "normal." Nevertheless, the expectancy-violation model shows great promise in the deception literature and will generate more exciting research in the years to come.

Detecting Deception in Court Proceedings

Witness credibility is a highly critical feature of courtroom trials. Jurors and judges not only consider the material presented in the courtroom but also evaluate its veracity. Regardless of the completeness or consistency of the testimony, if the decision makers perceive the source as less than honest, the value of the testimony is severely undermined. Veracity in the courtroom is largely based on the manner in which the testimony is presented. More fundamentally, veracity is primarily determined by the conventional wisdom linked to certain nonverbal cues.

Gerald Miller and his colleagues (1981) conducted several experiments to replicate some previous findings reported in the deception-detection literature. At the same time, they tried to recreate critical aspects of the courtroom in an effort to improve **ecological validity**. The Miller studies were designed to examine the following three major questions (Miller et al., 1981, p. 149):

1. In general, how accurate are jurors in detecting deception?
2. What effects do variations in the mode of presentation of a trial (live, televised, audio only, transcript only, and, in the televised case, color vs. black and white) have on jurors' abilities to detect deception?
3. What sources of information facilitate a juror's ability to distinguish between deceitful and truthful testimony?

The basic experimental design of the Miller studies was modeled after Ekman and Friesen (1974). In that project, motivated subjects were told to lie or to tell the truth about a stressful or nonstressful film they had just seen. The subjects' descriptions of the film were videotaped. Observer-subjects then viewed these videotapes and were asked to decide which narrators were telling the truth and which were lying. Results indicated that observer-subjects were not much better than chance at depicting who was lying and who was not.

Two of the Miller studies deserve our close attention. In the first (Study I), a similar procedure to the one described above was used. However, the videotaped subjects were not only asked to lie or to be truthful about the stimuli they had seen, they were also questioned about the facts of the events they had viewed. Therefore, both emotional and factual content were included in the design, allowing the experimenters to measure accuracy in depicting lying in both emotional and factual testimony. In addition to videotapes, audiotapes and transcripts of the interview were also made to determine the influence of verbal cues compared to visual cues in detection of deception. Furthermore, the individuals interviewed were videotaped in both color and black and white, with sound. Lastly, to determine what bodily, nonverbal cues might best communicate deception, camera shots included either (1) head only, (2) body only, or (3) head and body.

Nineteen male and four female criminal justice undergraduates (seniors) served as the taped interviewees. To insure a reasonably high level of motivation, all the subjects—who were planning careers in law enforcement—were told that the School of Criminal Justice would receive information concerning their cooperation and performance in the experiment.

The observer-subjects who judged the videotapes were 719 undergraduate students enrolled in introductory communication classes and 193 adult residents from the local community. The primary dependent variable was the observer-subject's accuracy in identifying interviewee veracity. Each observer-subject was expected to make 16 accuracy judgments, eight based upon identifying the veracity of statements by means of emotional content and eight by means of factual content.

The results revealed that people are no more accurate than chance in identifying deception. The results also indicated that judgments of witness veracity were not influenced by the use of color as opposed to black and white videotape. More surprisingly, the data suggest modification of Ekman and Friesen's (1969) leaky channel theory. It appears from the Miller study that nonfacial cues are the most reliable cues to deception when lying involves the deceiver's emotional response to events or situations. However, facial cues seem to provide the best information for making judgments about factual veracity. Hence, the leaky channel theory may hold for emotional deception but not for factual deception. It must be remembered, however, that regardless of the source or message content, people tend not to be accurate decipherers of deception in general.

Results from the transcript-only condition, the audio-only condition, and the visual-only condition also cast serious doubts on the assumption that detecting deception is enhanced by the presence of nonverbal behavioral cues. Observer-subjects in the transcript-only condition were as accurate as subjects in the audio-only condition when detecting deception dealing with factual information. Furthermore, audio-only and transcript-only subjects were more accurate than visual-only subjects, suggesting that nonverbal behavioral cues are less dependable sources for determining factual veracity than oral or verbal ones. Relative to detecting deception in expressing emotion, there were no significant differences in accuracy in visual, audio, or transcription sources.

Study II paralleled Study I in design except for four changes. First, in order to more closely approximate actual courtroom procedures, the interviewed subject in Study II was seen or heard live by the observer-subjects, Second, an attempt was made to control for possible sex differences in deceptive behavior by having equal numbers of male and female interviewees. Third, the researchers tried to have the interviewees more ego-involved in their deception by offering monetary prizes. Fourth, while in Study I interviewees acted under both deceptive and truthful conditions, in Study II they were assigned to only one condition.

Observer-subjects either saw, heard, or read interviews, made a judgment as to whether the sources were lying, and specified the amount and type of information used in making their judgment. Those observer-subjects assigned to the live condition watched the interview through a one-way mirror or listened to it.

Again, as in Study I, the results indicated that people are poor judges of the veracity of testimony and can detect deception no more often than chance. Moreover, it does not seem to make any difference in the type and amount of information they receive; they still make poor judgments about veracity. Further, it makes little difference whether the information is live or videotaped. Although much still needs to be resolved, it does seem that the average juror is unable to distinguish between deceptive and truthful testimony. And it does not seem to matter whether the deception is based on factual issues or feelings or emotions about stressful or exciting events.

Voice Detection

Some law enforcement agencies use voice characteristics in an effort to identify suspects or to detect deception. In the identification procedure, it is assumed that each individual has a unique, personal style of speaking due to anatomical, structural differences in the speech mechanisms and the manner in which tongue, lips, and teeth are used. "Voiceprints" are oscillographic representations of spoken sounds that identify these unique elements of vocalization.

Both the scientific community and the courts have guardedly accepted voiceprints as an adequate means of identification under certain conditions.

Courts in several criminal cases have allowed voiceprints as evidence (*U.S. v. Franks*, 1975; *U.S. v. Baller*, 1975; *Commonwealth v. Lykus*, 1975; *State v. Andretta*, 1972), but the courts have attached limitations. For example, courts have ruled that voiceprints could be used only as collaborative evidence, or without contradictory expert testimony or evidence, or to justify an arrest warrant (Schwitzgebel & Schwitzgebel, 1980).

The value of voiceprints as discriminators between deception and truth has yet to be accepted by science or law, however. Proponents argue that a deceptive speaker's voice changes under stress and that these stress-related changes are reflected through minute vibrations or microtremors. The physiological changes are recorded and analyzed by instruments specifically designed for this purpose. While the voice does tend to have a higher pitch under stressful conditions, there is very little evidence that this characteristic is a convincing indicator of deception.

A number of commercial firms have marketed various pieces of hardware claimed to detect stress, and ultimately lying, from live or recorded segments of speech. The level of sophistication and complexity in instrumentation differ widely from one piece of equipment to another. The most extensively marketed and researched instrument is the PSE. In its marketing literature, the manufacturer claims that the PSE is 95 to 99% accurate in discriminating liars from truth tellers. This claim has yet to be substantiated in the published scientific literature, and the manufacturer fails to support it with any cites of replicable research (Hollien, 1980; Yarmey, 1979). Research projects testing the PSE have consistently found that it does no better than chance at identifying deception through voice-stress analysis (Hollien, 1980; Podlesny & Raskin, 1977; Kubis, 1973; Yarmey, 1979). In fact, none of the voice analyzers to date have been able to distinguish deception from truthfulness in the scientific laboratory.

The basis of the PSE's discriminatory power supposedly rests on its sensitivity to slight tremblings (microtremors) that occur in the voice mechanism, apparently in the small laryngeal muscles. However, available research demonstrates that while microtremors do exist in the large muscles, especially in the extremities, they do not appear to exist in the small muscles of the larynx (Hollien, 1980; Bachrach, 1979). Miron (1980) has suggested that the microtremors detected by the PSE might be located in the network of the large, slow-acting muscles that support the laryngeal mechanisms. Considering the extremely high level of sensitivity required to measure even known microtremors in the large muscles using sophisticated laboratory equipment, it seems that the PSE may be based on some voice-stress principle other than microtremors.

In summary, there is little scientific evidence to support the reliability and validity of instruments that attempt to detect deception by means of voice analysis. In light of our present knowledge, reliance on this equipment is risky at best.

The Polygraph

Often called the "lie detector," the polygraph does not really detect lies or deception, but only the bodily responses that accompany emotions and stress. Presumably, when one tries to deceive, there are telltale bodily or physiological reactions that can be measured with sophisticated equipment and detected by a skillful examiner. A trained examiner is often referred to as a polygrapher.

Variants of the modern polygraph have been used in the psychological laboratory for nearly a century, and much cruder versions of its components existed as far back as 300 B.C. (Trovillo, 1939). The Bedouins of Arabia, for example, required the authors of conflicting statements to lick a hot iron; the one whose tongue was not burned was considered truthful (Smith, 1967). The ancient Chinese required people to put rice powder in their mouths and then spit it out (Smith, 1967). If the powder was dry, the individual was lying. The common principle underlying these and other similar methods used throughout history is that the tense, nervous person (the one who is lying) has less saliva (dry mouth and tongue), and thus is more likely to have their tongue burned, spit drier rice powder, or even less able to swallow the "trial slice" of bread, as practiced centuries ago in England.

The Italian physician and anthropologist Cesare Lombroso is credited as the first to use an *instrument* to detect lies in 1881 (Barland, 1988). The device was designed to measure changes in blood volume in the arm which were recorded on chart or graph. However, since the device had the capacity to record only blood volume, it would be more correct to call this early instrument a *mono*graph (one measure) rather than a *poly*graph (many measures). Various other devices and refinements were largely developed in Europe (see Barland, 1988), but the idea of lie detection caught on rapidly in the United States. In 1917 the lawyer-psychologist, William M. Marston developed a form of lie detection technology that gained widespread use in criminal investigation. As a laboratory assistant in psychology at Radcliffe College, Marston discovered a significant positive correlation between systolic blood pressure and lying. The polygraph technique developed as a result of this finding was referred to in *U.S. v Frye*—in fact Marston was the expert witness called to the stand in that case.

Barland and Raskin (1973), however, credit the development of the modern polygraph equipment and technique more to John Larson and Leonarde Keeler (Barland & Raskin, 1973). In 1920, Larson was asked by the chief of police in Berkeley, California to develop a "lie detector" to solve a case under investigation. This detector, according to Barland (1988, p. 75), became "the first true polygraph used for lie-detection purposes." A number of well-publicized successes by Larson and one of his students, Keeler, catapulted the instrument into the limelight. Eventually Keeler began to teach a two-week course for police and military examiners, which soon developed into a six-week course (Barland, 1988; Keeler, 1984). The increasing demand for polygraph examiners resulted in the formation of at least 30 polygraph schools across the United States (Barland, 1988).

Today, a variety of private and government-sponsored polygraphy schools are in operation, almost all of which are accredited by the American Polygraphy Association. The most prestigious and intensive is the one-semester-long school operated by the Department of Defense. The Department of Defense Polygraphy Institute (DoDPI) trains all polygraphers employed by federal agencies with the exception of the CIA, as well as polygraphers employed by many local and state agencies. The DoDPI also includes a research arm, staffed primarily by doctoral-level psychologists (Iacono & Patrick, 1999). Other polygraphy schools vary widely in training and rarely include a research component. The typical polygraph examiner in the United States today does not have graduate psychological or research training, and not all polygraph examiners are licensed, nor are they graduates of accredited schools. Additionally, the profession has "almost no input or oversight from psychology" (Iacono & Patrick, 1999, p. 467).

During its early beginnings, the polygraph was largely confined to criminal investigations and the equipment was almost exclusively *field* polygraphs, which were portable instruments seemingly inferior to more elaborate *laboratory* polygraphs. Laboratory polygraphs are far more sophisticated and sensitive, and can record simultaneously a great number of physiological indices. The field polygraph generally includes measures of respiration, skin conductance or electrodermal response (EDR), blood volume/blood pressure, and heart rate. Despite their simplicity in instrumentation and design, however, with proper calibration and maintenance, standard field polygraphs can measure with reasonable accuracy gross physiological activity.

Most of us are familiar with photographs of examiners administering a field or laboratory polygraph, with the examinee strapped with electrodes and a stylus recording calibrations on a chart. Today, though, many polygraphs have shifted to computerization—called computerized polygraph systems (CPS)—to replace the conventional chart or graph method. Physiological data are stored digitally and are plotted with a printer. Software allows the computer to provide a probability statement as to the likelihood that a person was truthful when responding (Iacono & Patrick, 1999). The polygrapher's opinion, then, can be shaped considerably by the software package that is used. As Iacono and Patrick (1999, p. 441) have noted, "Because this software is sold commercially, the nature of the algorithms and data used to justify the probability statements is propriety. Little is known about their validity."

Although the polygraph is used in numerous contexts, its major areas are in personnel selection or screening by government agencies and in criminal investigations. In 1988, Congress severely limited the extent to which *private* employers can use the polygraph, with the passage of the *Employment Polygraph Protection Act.* This law has, in effect, ended pre-employment screening by private employers as well as the periodic testing of employees to verify their good behavior (Iacono & Patrick, 1999). There are no such restrictions on local, state, and federal government agencies, however, unless state legislatures have deemed otherwise. U.S. governmental counterintelligence polygraph tests, for example, far outnumber those of most other organizations or agencies (Krapohl, 2002). And polygraph screening of police applicants has either remained the same or increased. Meesig and Horvath (1995) report that approximately 99% of the large police agencies and 95% of the small police departments require the polygraph as an integral part of their pre-employment screening procedures. The use of the polygraph is fast becoming a global phenomenon, with prominent use in North America, Israel, and China. Nations of the former Soviet Union, and Eastern Europe are beginning to use the instrument with increasing frequency.

The primary purpose of the pre-employment polygraph test is to verify information provided by the job applicant. Governmental agencies are especially interested in the honesty of applicants in answering questions pertaining to past work history, drug and alcohol use, propensity toward theft, and credentials or qualifications. The examiners are usually licensed or certified after being trained at a school of polygraphy, but most do not have graduate psychological or research training. Although admissions to polygraph schools differ widely, the typical requirement is a bachelor's degree, a personal interview, and a polygraph test (Iacono & Patrick, 1987).

Polygraph Techniques

All polygraph examinations begin with a pre-test interview (Mitchell, 2002; Raskin & Honts, 2002). Usually, the pre-test interview involves gathering biographical information, and verbal or written consent from the examinee. The polygrapher also discusses with the examinee the topics to be covered, and the nature of the polygraph.

The polygraph examination typically consists of four separate phases: (1) data collection; (2) pretest interview; (3) test administration; and (4) posttest interview (Abrams, 1989). In the data-collection stage, the examiner gathers all the relevant information concerning the area under investigation as well as known information about the subject. The pretest interview is intended to establish some rapport with the subject and to explain some of the questions and procedures that will be used during the examination. Often during the pretest interview, questions to be asked on the examination are devised with the cooperation of the subject, so that nothing will be surprising and ambiguities may be cleared up prior to the exam.

One critical phase in all polygraph testing is to establish a "mind set" in the examinee. Specifically, the examiner attempts to convince the examinee that the polygraph is a very powerful detector of lies, and if you do lie, you are surely going to get caught. Truthfulness to all questions is emphasized, and various tactics are sometimes employed by examiners to reach this mind set. For example, to convince the examinee of the power of the instrument, the examiner may ask the examinee to pick a playing card from a deck. However, unknown to the examinee, the cards in the deck are all the same (e.g., jack of clubs). The examinee is then asked not to reveal the card and to say "no" to each question asked by the examiner. Next, the examiner asks the examinee a series of questions about the card picked (e.g., Was it a nine of clubs? Was it the king of spades? Was it the jack of clubs?) while the examiner watches the computer monitor or the moving recording pens on the charts. The examiner then guesses the precise card, impressing the examinee about the mysterious accuracy of the instrument. This mind set may be one of the most important aspects of polygraph testing because it not only promotes honesty but also, on occasion, encourages confessions.

Several polygraph techniques or approaches are used by polygraphers to determine deception or truthfulness during the examination. The test is used in a wide variety of contexts, including criminal investigations, counterintelligence and national security screening, civil litigation and post-conviction assessments. The last category includes situations where the polygraph is used with sex offenders to detect deception in an effort to control recidivism. For example, in 1998, a survey revealed that

35 states were using polygraph testing for monitoring convicted sex offenders (Consigli, 2002).

Until the late 1980s, the **relevant–irrelevant (R–I) technique** was the method of choice for a majority of examiners in pre-employment and employee screening situations (Minor, 1989). Because the law now restricts screening by private employers, it is now chiefly used by government employers. The original R–I method was the one developed by William Marston in 1917; recall that it was the technique considered by the court in *U.S. v. Frye*. It consisted of a list of relevant and irrelevant questions. The underlying assumption of the R–I method is that detected physiological reactions are produced by "fear" of being identified as a dishonest person (Raskin & Honts, 2002). Consistently strong physiological reactions to relevant questions over irrelevant ones were regarded as evidence of deception. However, polygraphers discovered that both truthful and deceptive persons can often show strong reactions to the relevant questions, masking any true differences between honest and dishonest subjects (Iacono & Patrick, 1987). Some current polygraphers still rely on a variant of the R–I method, sometimes referred to as the *relevant–relevant* (*R–R*) procedure. In this method, irrelevant questions are fewer and are used as a rest period or baseline. "This test can more accurately be characterized as a polygraph assisted interview where the development of questions is guided both by a polygrapher's impressions of the examinee's truthfulness as well as the comparative reactions to the various relevant items. . . . If the subject shows persistently strong reactions to one or more content areas in relation to the rest, the examiner concludes that the subject lied or was particularly sensitive about these issues for some hidden reason" (Iacono & Patrick, 1999, p. 447). The examiner then probes these issues. As Iacono and Patrick note, examinees that are adept at explaining away what might have provoked their responses are likely to avoid incrimination.

The two most widely used methods today are the control-of-question test and the guilty knowledge test. The **control-of-question test (CQT)** is, by far, the procedure most preferred by professional polygraphers in the United States and Canada, and also the most controversial in its utility and accuracy (Abrams, 1989; Ben-Shakhar, 2002; Raskin & Honts, 2002). There are many variants of the CQT, including the Reid CQT, the Backster zone comparison test, the Utah probable-lie test, and the Utah directed-lie test. The CQT, which usually requires at least two hours to administer, uses a variety of questioning techniques based on three types of questions: (1) irrelevant or neutral questions; (2) relevant questions; and (3) control questions. Irrelevant questions are those posed about neutral topics, like date of birth, name, age, height, and birthplace. They usually occur at the beginning and end of an examination, but they may be interspersed between other questions to bring the subject down to a normal physiological baseline following questions that generate stress.

The relevant question probes whether the subject committed the crime or behavior in question. For example, "On August 26, at approximately 9:00 p.m., did you break down the door at Mr. Brown's residence?" It is recommended that emotion laden words not be used, since the respondent may respond more to the word than to the question itself.

The control question is as important in determining deception or truthfulness as the relevant question. It is based upon either an assumed or a known lie. An assumed lie is denial of a behavior that most people have very likely committed. For example, "Did you ever steal anything when you were between the ages of five and fifteen?" "Did you ever take advantage of a friend?" "Have you ever lied to a person in a position of authority?"

If the physiological responses associated with relevant questions are higher that those for control questions, the person is assumed to be guilty or untruthful. If, on the other hand, physiological reactions are more pronounced for the control questions than the relevant ones, the examiner assumes innocence, or truthfulness on the relevant issue. One of the main problems with the CQT is the difficulty involved in constructing control questions that will elicit stronger physiological responses in the innocent than relevant questions about the crime (Bull, 1988).

The **guilty-knowledge test (GKT)**—also called the *concealed information test*—has been strongly endorsed by the psychologist and polygraph expert David Lykken (1998) as the most powerful procedure for determining deception or truthfulness.

Although the method is rarely used by professional polygraphers in North America, it is used extensively in Israel and Japan (MacLaren, 2001). Interestingly, while the CQT is the most frequently used method for investigative interrogation in the United States, the GKT is probably the method most endorsed by researchers (Ben-Shakhar, 2002; Ben-Shakhar, Bar-Hillel, & Lieblich, 1986; Kleiner, 2002). The empirical evidence does support the GKT over the CQT in many instances. Furthermore, in a survey conducted by Iacono and Lykken (1997), approximately three-fourths of the scientists polled believed the GKT was based on scientifically sound theory. We will cover the research on the GKT and other measures later in the chapter.

When using the GKT, the examiner uses detailed, publicly unknown knowledge about a crime to construct questions that can be answered only by someone who was present at the scene. Therefore, the GKT does not attempt to uncover "lying," but whether a suspect possesses "guilty knowledge" that only the offender would know about the crime. The answers are offered to the subject in a multiple-choice format. For example, in a case where a robber dropped his hat, Lykken (1988, p. 121) provides an example of GKT as follows:

1. 'The robber in this case dropped something while escaping. If you are that robber, you will know what he dropped. Was it: a weapon? a face mask? a sack of money? his hat? his car keys?'
2. 'Where did he drop his hat? Was it: in the bank? on the bank steps? on the sidewalk? in the parking lot? in an alley?'
3. 'What color was the hat? Was it: brown? red? black? green? blue?'

Since the GKT assumes that the guilty subject will recognize the significant alternative, consistent physiological reactivity to this "correct" answer would indicate deception, regardless of the verbal content of the subject's answers. And since the questions are derived from information presumably not reported in the press and not generally known by the public, innocent subjects rarely give peak physiological reactions to "correct" items. One of the strong points of the GKT is its ability to detect innocent examinees with high accuracy (Ben-Shakhar & Elaad, 2002). For example, research suggests that the GKT is successful in identifying about 84% of the guilty examinees and 94% of innocent examinees (Ben-Shakhar & Furedy, 1990).

The sensitivity of the GKT depends in part on whether the examiner can generate enough items pertaining to the crime scene which a suspect is likely to remember (Lykken, 1988; Ben-Shakhar & Elaad, 2002). Raskin (1988) asserts that the GKT is rarely used in applied criminal cases because its practical utility is severely limited. For example, in a majority of criminal cases, very little inside, salient detail about the crime is known, and when details of the crime are known, they are often made available to suspects by investigators, the media, and defense attorneys. Unfortunately, most training programs for polygraphers do not include the GKT (Bull, 1988).

Countermeasures

Countermeasures are anything that an examinee might do to "fool" the polygraph and the examiner. Studies demonstrate that it may be possible to *train* "guilty" examinees to avoid detection (Ben-Shakhar, 2002; Krapohi, 2002). However, Honts and Amato (2002) report that the prospects for scientific advancement on the effects of countermeasures are not very promising at this point. This is partly due to the fact that research on countermeasures is difficult to conduct unless one has access to considerable resources and governmental financial support. Since the beginning of the 1990s, however, detection of deception research in the United States has been centered at the Department of Defense Polygraph Institute (DoDPI) (Honts & Amato, 2002). Currently, the DoDPI has a policy that all countermeasures research on the polygraph will be classified and not open to the scientific community. With this restriction in mind, this section will consider what the *available* research tells us about countermeasures to the polygraph.

Many types of countermeasures are possible, but the majority falls into the categories of physical, mental, hypnosis, biofeedback, or drugs. The most common physical countermeasures are either pain or muscle tension. For example, biting one's lip or tongue or jabbing oneself with a fingernail may induce enough pain to promote a physiological response that masks the actual response to control questions. Research suggests that even pressing one's toes to the floor is another physical method that may distort polygraph measures based on the CQT, and that using a combination of physical methods, such as biting one's tongue and pressing toes to the floor, may be even more effective than any single physical technique (Gudjonsson, 1988).

Mental countermeasures include any deliberate attempt by an examinee to change his or her thought patterns during the polygraph test in order to distort the results. Examples would include counting backwards from 10, thinking of a sexually arousing scene, or thinking of a very peaceful scene (such as sailing on a very peaceful lake on a sunny afternoon). Any thought that either minimizes the emotional impact of relevant questions or increases physiological arousal across all questions qualifies as a mental countermeasure. While physical countermeasures are often detectible by experienced examiners, mental countermeasures are far more difficult to detect (Ben-Shakhar, 2002). Research suggests that mental countermeasures may be as effective in deceiving the polygraph as physical ones under both the GKT and CQT if the examinee receives *training* in mental countermeasure techniques (Ben-Shakhar & Dolev, 1996; Honts, Devitt, Winbush, & Kircher, 1996). However, research also indicates that spontaneous countermeasures where the examinee tries to influence the outcome of the polygraph without forethought, planning or training, are largely ineffective (Honts & Amato, 2002).

There is very little evidence that drugs—sometimes referred to as "general state countermeasures" because they influence the entire neurophysiological systems—can be used as an effective countermeasure to polygraph testing (Honts, 1987; Honts & Amato, 2002). There is some unreplicated evidence (Waid, Orne, Cook, & Orne, 1981) that a moderate dose of the tranquilizer meprobamate may have helped college students defeat a concealed information procedure (Honts & Perry, 1992), but more research needs to be done before this finding can be substantiated. A study by Iacono, Cerri, Patrick, and Flemming (1992) raises serious doubt about the effectiveness of tranquilizers. They found that meprobamate and diazepam were not effective countermeasures.

Although alcohol does not seem to improve one's chances of "fooling" the polygraph either (Honts & Perry, 1992), Bradley and Ainsworth (1984) report that an individual mildly intoxicated while committing a crime may escape detection during a subsequent polygraph test. Hypnosis has also been tried as a countermeasure. The primary strategy in the use of hypnosis as a countermeasure is to induce a form of amnesia for the behavior in question. However, there is no evidence to date that hypnosis is an effective countermeasure (Gudjonsson, 1988).

While individuals are not likely to beat the polygraph using their own resources, training in physical and mental countermeasures may be effective. Charles Honts and his research group (Honts, Hodes, & Raskin, 1985; Honts, Raskin, & Kircher, 1987) report that a significant proportion of highly motivated laboratory subjects can be trained to "beat" polygraph tests. The possibility of effective countermeasures is especially pertinent when the polygraph is used for espionage purposes. Spies and intelligence agents are probably well-trained in the use of countermeasures for defeating polygraph tests.

Legal Status of the Polygraph

Despite the wide use of the polygraph by government agencies, courts have traditionally not allowed polygraph results as evidence in criminal cases. Charles Daniels (2002, p. 327) writes: "There is no category of evidence in the history of American law that has been subjected to stricter scrutiny by the courts, to greater resistance against admission and to such widespread reluctance to accept scientific developments in the courtroom than has been the case with polygraph evidence."

The precedent of inadmissibility of polygraph evidence was established by *U.S. v. Frye* in 1923. An appellate court in Washington, DC, ruled that information acquired from polygraphic examination was unacceptable because the general scientific community did not endorse it. Since then, many courts have continued to outrightly reject the results of the polygraph whether they have been submitted by the defense or the prosecution as evidence of guilt or innocence (Schwitzgebel & Schwitzgebel, 1980). This "per se" (or outright) exclusion of the polygraph is not universal, however.

Over the years, many scholars argued that the *Frye* test was not only unclear in its terminology but also excessively conservative and restrictive in what type of evidence could be admitted (Monahan & Walker, 1990). In fact, a U.S. Court of Military Appeals decision (*U.S. v. Gipson*, 1987) advocated that *Frye* be replaced by the Federal Rules of Evidence, a decision that was soon mimicked and extended by the U.S. Court of Appeals for the Eleventh Circuit (*U.S. v. Piccinonna*, 1998; Honts & Perry, 1992). The Federal Rules of Evidence introduced more liberal standards in allowing scientific evidence, and were adopted in some jurisdictions as an alternative to *Frye* (Honts & Perry, 1992). The Rules encouraged the "relevancy approach" which treats new, relevant scientific evidence in the same way as the courts treat all other types of evidence. That is, if the evidence is relevant to the issue at hand and is reliable, it may be admitted.

As noted in ◀ Chapters 1 and 4, the *Frye* test has now been replaced in federal courts by the *Daubert* standard, which provides much more leeway for the introduction of scientific evidence. The *Frye* standard of general acceptance can still be used, but it is not the exclusive consideration. Under *Daubert*, judges, as gatekeepers, decide on a case by case basis whether proffered scientific evidence is reliable and relevant to the case at hand. However, in light of *Daubert*, some federal courts have determined that the *per se* exclusion rule no longer applies to polygraphic evidence (e.g., *U.S. v. Cordoba*, 1999), while others have reaffirmed it (*U.S. v. Sanchez*, 1997).

A recent U.S. Supreme Court decision has dealt a blow to the admission of polygraph evidence, although the decision may be interpreted very narrowly. In *U.S. v. Scheffer* (1998), a military case, the Court ruled that the exclusion of *exculpatory* polygraph evidence did not violate the defendant's right to a fair trial in a court-martial proceeding. Furthermore, the Court noted in a footnote that nothing in *Daubert* foreclosed *per se* exclusion of certain types of expert or scientific evidence.

Airman Edward Scheffer had volunteered to work as an informant on drug investigations for the Air Force Office of Special Investigations (OSI). His undercover work required him to submit to both drug testing and polygraph examinations from time to time. After an absence without leave, he was arrested in a routine traffic stop. A urinalysis revealed the presence of methamphetamine, and Scheffer was tried by general court martial on a number of charges. Scheffer maintained that he had innocently ingested the drug, and a polygraph substantiated this. He was denied the opportunity to introduce the polygraph evidence, under Military Rule of Evidence 707, which bars such evidence. The United States Court of Appeals for the Armed Forces, by a 3–2 vote, ruled that this exculpatory *per se* exclusion violated his Sixth Amendment right to present a defense.

The U.S. Supreme Court did not agree. In ruling against Scheffer, the Court stressed the government's legitimate interest in barring unreliable evidence as well as in preserving the jury's function in making credibility determinations. The core of the Court's opinion—written by Justice Clarence Thomas—was the lack of consensus within the scientific community that polygraph evidence was reliable. The scientific community, the Court noted, "remains extremely polarized about the reliability of polygraph techniques."

In a dissenting opinion, Justice John Paul Stevens, citing *Daubert* and *General Electric v. Joiner*, noted that district judges in civilian federal courts now have broad discretion to evaluate the admissibility of scientific evidence and indicated that military judges should be given the same authority. He also cited research that exculpatory polygraph evidence was more valid than inculpatory, because the polygraph is more likely to find innocent people guilty than vice versa. (Exculpatory evidence is evidence that tends to clear one of fault or guilt; inculpatory evidence tends to establish fault or guilt.) Therefore, the results of an exculpatory polygraph should carry more weight with a jury. The majority opinion, Justice Stevens wrote, "rests on a serious undervaluation of the importance of the citizen's constitutional right to present a defense to criminal charge and an unrealistic appraisal of the importance of the governmental interests that undergrid Rule 707."

The *Scheffer* decision provides support to courts wishing to bar the introduction of polygraph evidence, although it may be interpreted very narrowly as a military case with little precedential value to civilian courts. Nevertheless, civilians wishing to introduce the evidence may fare no better. In fact, even the dissent expressed reservations about endorsing polygraph information in civilian cases. Although Justice Stevens championed the Sixth Amendment right to obtain witnesses in one's favor, he noted that disputes about examiner qualifications, equipment, and testing procedures seldom arise with tests conducted by the military. " . . . (M)ilitary practices are more favorable to a rule of admissibility than is the less structured use of lie detectors in the civilian sector of our society. That is so because the military carefully regulates the administration of polygraph tests."

Even with reservations about the validity of the polygraph, the argument for admitting *exculpatory* evidence, submitting it to an adversarial process, and allowing juries to evaluate it is persuasive. Furthermore, increasing sophistication of the instrument and training of the examiners may lead more courts to accept the evidence if the defendant consents or if the defendant requests it. The relevancy standard announced in *Daubert* gives judges considerable leeway to allow the introduction of scientific information, and supporters of the polygraph argue that it is highly accurate (e.g., Raskin et al., 1997). However, the overwhelmingly dominant trend of the post-*Daubert* decisions has been to exclude polygraph evidence, partly due to this wide leeway given the courts (Daniels, 2002). According to Daniels (2002, p. 330), one of the most common reasons for exclusion is the use of federal Rule 403 and its state court equivalents, "which allow a trial judge to disregard other rules of admissibility and exclude evidence that is relatively weak or may cause confusion, consume too much time, or cause unnecessary prejudice to a party."

About half the states do allow judges to admit polygraphic evidence in criminal cases, either in support of the defendant (exculpatory evidence) or through stipulation (Iacono & Patrick, 1999). In the latter, both prosecuting and defense attorneys agree to have the defendant take a polygraph; if the defendant "passes," the prosecutor drops the charges. On the other hand, if the defendant "fails," the prosecutor has the option of introducing the test results during the trial.

Research on the Polygraph

Many researchers continue to be very wary of the polygraph and opposed to the introduction of polygrahic evidence. Iacono and Lykken (1997) conducted a survey of two groups of scientists with the expertise to evaluate the polygraph: Fellows of the American Psychological Association and members of the Society for Psychophysiological Research. The researchers focused on the controlled-question test (CQT), which is the type of polygraph test most frequently brought before the courts, but they also polled the scientists on other polygraphic methods. Neither group considered the CQT scientifically sound or suitable scientific evidence. By contrast, they did view the Guilty Knowledge Test (GKT) more favorably, with 77% of the respondents seeing the method as based on sound scientific principles and theory. Iacono and Lykken note that the scientists were not skeptical about techniques to detect deception. They simply were unconvinced, based on the available research, of the accuracy of the most common tests being used. Approximately one fourth of the sample did advocate admitting CQT evidence into the court, however. This included evidence of both passed and failed tests, although a lower percentage of the APA Fellows (20%) advocated admitting failed CQTs as evidence.

Historically, professional field polygraphers have claimed extraordinary accuracy rates: 92% (Bersh, 1969), 99% (Arther, 1965; MacNitt, 1942; MacLaughlin, 1953), and 100% (Kubis, 1950). The professional polygraph literature also reported with regularity that the trained polygrapher erred not more than 2% of the time, and often less than 1% (Barland & Raskin, 1973). Most psychophysiologists and research psychologists found these statistics hard to believe. In addition to occasional arithmetical errors, none of the published reports gave any details of the methods and procedures used, nor of criteria used to decide accuracy rates. David Lykken (1974) was so disbelieving of the many claims of the early professional polygraphers that he asserted (1974, p. 738): "Claims of 95%, 98%, and even, 100% validity are so implausible, they should be taken seriously only if accompanied by unusually clear, well-replicated empirical evidence. Such evidence is wholly lacking." Today, the research conducted under laboratory or controlled conditions indicates that the correct classification of truthful and deceptive examinees ranges between 70 and 80% (Krapohl, 2002). However, the accuracy can be increased slightly through careful and intensive training of the examiner. Furthermore, in lab studies computerized polygraph systems, in contrast to human evaluations, are slightly more accurate for detecting both innocent and deceptive subjects (Kircher & Raskin, 2002). Unfortunately, polygraphic research conducted under realistic or field conditions is rare.

The accuracy of the polygraph in detecting who is telling the truth and who is deceptive is a highly complicated issue. A number of factors—such as the specific technique used, the nature of the population tested, the issues to be resolved, the context of the examination, whether one is trying to detect truth or deception, the training of the examiner, what cues the examiner considers besides the polygraphic data, or even whether one is examining the victim or the suspect—all must be carefully considered before any tentative conclusions can be advanced. Base rates among those who are tested must also be taken into consideration. Broadly, base rate refers to the frequency of an occurrence. In reference to human behavior, a base rate refers generally to the proportion of the population that has engaged in a particular behavior during their lifetimes. Therefore, the validity of the polygraph depends greatly on the degree to which it adds to the information already known (the base rate) about a relevant population. For example, in a pre-employment screening situation, let's assume that the employer (a police department) wants to reject all prospective employees (police officer candidates) who have used illegal drugs on a regular basis during their lifetimes. Two different base rates have to be considered here. One is the percentage of the population who have used illegal drugs on a regular basis. And the second base rate issue has to do with the percentage of people who lie about it. Police candidates normally have very low base rates for illegal drug use. Let's say for illustrative purposes that only 2% of the applicants for police positions have used illegal drugs on a regular basis during their lifetimes (base rate = 2%). Let's assume further that 50% of these applicants will lie about this use when asked (second base rate = 50%). In this example, the polygraph would have to identify the 1% who lie in order to be highly effective. Otherwise, an examiner who only knew the base rates would be 98% accurate simply by proclaiming everyone is clean, regardless of their polygraph results! The examiner would be 99% accurate if he proclaimed everyone clean except those individuals who admitted it during the interview. When base rates are this extreme it is very difficult for the polygraph to add anything new to what is already known about the relevant population. However, some misguided or unscrupulous individuals could claim that the polygraph is 99% accurate in identifying people who have not used illegal drugs. These individuals are simply describing the base rates, independent of the polygraph data. On the other hand, if 50% of the relevant population used illegal drugs on a regular basis, and all of them lied about it, then the polygraph would have to do better than 50% to be considered effective and adding new information to base rate.

The experience and training of the examiner are also important. Most studies have failed to sample adequately from the total examiner population (Barland, 1988). They often used one or two polygraphers without mentioning the nature of their training or qualifications or procedures. There is, of course, a broad range of examiner training, test techniques, and the type of nonpolygraphic data included in the examiner's decision. None of these variables have been properly studied. As Blinkhorn (1988, p. 37) observes, "Any examination technique which involves live interaction between two people is potentially undermined by unwitting communication . . . Yet the lie detector is treated as if it were simply a matter of the attachment of laboratory instruments, and the polygraph examiner himself is seen as a detector of signals rather than as engaged in a complex and highly loaded social relationship with the examinee." A reading of the research data suggests that original examiners do better when they take account of their observations of the behavior and demeanor of the subjects than when they score the charts blindly. Polygraph practitioners often admit that it is the whole process of examination that has validity, not strictly the charts (Abrams, 1989). In a field study involving the Royal Canadian Mounted Police, Patrick and Iacono (1991) discovered that examiners were influenced by extra-polygraphic data, such as the facts of the case, the behavior of the suspect, or a confession, despite the fact that they typically were warned to ignore such cues. Interestingly, the extra-polygrahic data made their conclusion more accurate. The examiners also were apparently aware that psychophysiological assessment may be biased against the innocent. They were distrustful of polygraph scores that did not suggest truthfulness and gave examinees the benefit of the doubt, preferring to err in favor of the examinee.

One major drawback of a vast majority of the available research on the polygraph testing is that they have not established **ecological validity**. That is, most of the studies have been simulations, usually measuring the physiological responses in subjects who have been told to lie under laboratory conditions. Specifically, the studies typically make use of college students or community volunteers who are asked to enact a mock crime, then are submitted to a polygraph examination. As Lykken (1988) observed, most volunteer subjects regard experiments that involve polygraph examinations as kind of an interesting game. They are usually motivated to produce a truthful outcome simply by cash or other material reward. They really have no reason to fear the results because they will not be suspected, punished, or defamed if the test shows them "guilty" or dishonest.

By contrast, field studies assess the scientific merit of the polygraph administered in actual cases, including criminal cases. A major problem with these studies, however, is establishing "ground truth" (Iacono & Patrick, 1999). Specifically, how do we know whether the person being tested is actually guilty or innocent? As Iacono and Patrick note, researchers have used a variety of methods, including court outcomes, confessions, or independent panels of legal experts, to review case facts.

Relying strictly on the court outcomes is certainly unsatisfactory, since some people are wrongly convicted of crime and, for expediency, some people plead guilty to crimes they did not commit. Furthermore, because defendants must be proved guilty beyond a reasonable doubt, guilty subjects sometimes escape conviction. Relying on confessions is likewise unsatisfactory for a variety of reasons. Confessions may not be truthfully given, as we discussed earlier in the chapter. In addition, a confession elicited after someone failed a polygraph cannot be used to verify the polygraph because it is not independent of test outcome (Iacono & Patrick, 1999). Dohm and Iacono (1993) investigated the use of panels to establish "ground truth." Ground truth, in the social and behavioral sciences, refers to data that are uncontaminated by extraneous influences or factors. It is the "true data." Their panels comprised lay persons, attorneys, and police officers who were asked to review case files and select the guilty party. The panels correctly identified the guilty individual less than 25% of the time. The conclusion: None of these predominant methods used by researchers to establish ground proof is foolproof.

Research on the CQT The specific technique used, of course, must also be a consideration in any discussion of accuracy rates. The CQT is currently the most extensively studied. Fourteen laboratory studies examining this procedure found that, on average, 88.6% of those persons who were guilty were correctly identified, while 82.6% of those who were innocent were correctly identified (Carroll, 1988). These results are based on chance detection rates (base rates) of 50%. However, these experiments demonstrate only a marginal resemblance to actual field lie detection contexts (Carroll, 1988). For those experiments that closely resemble what actually takes place in the field, a slightly different picture emerges. In several studies reviewed by Douglas Carroll (1988), the average success rate of identifying the guilty was 85.4% compared to an average success rate of 76.9% for detecting the innocent. Thus, CQT seems better at detecting the guilty than detecting the innocent, a situation that carries potentially serious ethical, social, and economic ramifications for those individuals falsely accused or suspected.

Ben-Shakhar and Furedy (1990) find fault with the CQT because the procedure depends heavily on subjective impressions of the examiner for its administration and scoring. Thus, objective data are difficult to find in field studies. Furthermore, Ben-Shakhar and Furedy affirm that the fundamental assumptions of the CQT are not only unsupported by scientific research, but the technique in not based on any testable theory.

William Iacono and Christopher Patrick (1987) conducted an **analogue field study** of the CQT. An analogue field study is where the volunteers are genuinely concerned about the outcome of their performance, and a clear criterion identifying who is guilty or innocent is available (Ekman, 1985). The Iacono-Patrick study involved 48 incarcerated criminals, half of whom committed a mock theft. Experienced polygraphers, using CQT procedures, were not told which inmates committed the theft (a blind experimental procedure) and were unaware of the base rate for guilt. Motivation to deceive was established by informing the inmates that consequences for the entire group were dependent on each person's performance. If no more than 10 of the 48 volunteers failed the polygraph test, each inmate would receive \$20 (a handsome sum by prison standards). Otherwise, no one would receive the bonus of \$20. An additional motivator, of course, was the social pressures revolving around an "intact reputation" within prison walls. Polygraphers, using only the physiological data recorded on the charts, were able to classify correctly 87% of the guilty subjects but only 56% of the innocent subjects.

After reviewing the additional research on the CQT, Iacono and Patrick (1999) concluded that this little more than chance accuracy with innocent persons is typical of the CQT. Innocent persons are in considerable danger of being misclassified when this technique is used. On the other hand, the CQT can be easily defeated by a knowledgeable guilty individual who has learned to augment responses to control questions.

Research on the RIT/RCT The RIT (relevant-irrelevant test) or the RCT (relevant control test) screening test, in spite of its wide utilization in industry and pre-employment screening in the past, has yet to be studied with acceptable scientific methodology (Iacono & Patrick, 1987; Lykken, 1988; Raskin & Honts, 2002). Iacono and Patrick (1987) report that, if anything, the extant literature suggests that the RIT (or RCT) is transparent and biased against the innocent, raising some important issues about the damage it may be doing to applicants. Innocent or truthful examinees, who are nervous or upset about being tested, are extremely difficult to distinguish from guilty persons by examiners using this method. Raskin and Honts (2002, p. 5) firmly conclude from their review of the research literature on it, that "The RIT suffers from fundamental flaws in internal, face, and criterion validity, along with lack of standardization of pre-test interview, question sequencing, and procedures for evaluating the test outcome . . . and should not be used."

Research on the GKT Since the GKT is not used widely by professional polygraphers, particularly in the United States and Canada, it is not surprising that there are very few field studies examining its validity. Laboratory studies and researchers, however, have been highly supportive of its validity (Ben-Shakhar & Furedy, 1990; Iacono & Patrick, 1999; Lykken, 1988; Ben-Shakhar & Elaad, 2002). In summarizing mock-crime studies conducted between 1959 and 1984, for example, Iacono (1984) reported that the GKT was 100% accurate in identifying innocent subjects in five of the seven studies reviewed. Four of the studies reported a correct classification rate of at least 88% for guilty subjects. Lykken (1988) reviewed eight laboratory studies in support of his claim for the accuracy of the GKT method. Overall, 97% of the 152 innocent subjects passed the test, and 88% of the 161 guilty subjects failed the test, for a total accuracy rate of 93%. MacLaren (2001) conducted a comprehensive meta-analysis of all the published research examining the accuracy of the GKT and estimated that the technique is accurate somewhere between 76 and 83% of the time.

At this writing, there are only two published reports dealing with the accuracy of GKT *outside* the laboratory (MacLaren, 2001). In one of the studies, Eitan Elaad (1990) examined 98 actual GKT criminal polygraph records (50 innocent and 48 guilty) taken from police investigations of the Israel Police Scientific Interrogation Unit. The guilt or innocence of the examinees had been verified by the confession of the person who had committed the crime under investigation. Ninety-eight percent of the innocent but only 42% of the guilty subjects were correctly classified. Elaad, Ginton, and Jungman (1992), in an additional sample of 40 confession-verified cases, found basically the same results. These results, together with the results from laboratory studies, strongly suggest that the strength of the GKT may be its power to protect innocent suspects from being falsely classified as guilty, and truthful job applicants from being eliminated from further consideration in the screening process.

Many professional polygraphers believe that the polygraph may be more accurate with criminal suspects than with victims (Barland, 1988). Many polygraphers also believe that people who have committed property crimes (theft, burglary) are more difficult to detect than those who have committed crimes against persons, such as assault, robbery, or rape, primarily because the emotional baggage is usually higher for the latter than for the former (Horvath, 1977).

The polygraph is also believed to be more accurate when a suspect denies having physically committed a specific, illegal act (Barland, 1988, p. 83). It is probably less accurate when the suspect admits the act but denies criminal intent, as in claiming it was an accident. What the person was thinking at the time is more difficult to determine than what he or she actually did. If a criminal act is more mental than physical, such as a conspiratorial conversion that occurred months earlier, difficulties are magnified (Barland, 1988).

Summary The few well-executed studies dealing with the accuracy of the polygraph show some commonality: lie detection based on the polygraph is wrong about one third of the time overall (Lykken, 1988). The CQT is effective at identifying the guilty but biased against the innocent or truthful subject. The GKT is good at identifying the innocent, but has practical problems and is not too good at classifying the guilty or deceptive person. An innocent defendant seeking to introduce exculpatory polygraph evidence will likely obtain it through the GKT. The R–I technique does not seem to be effective at all. In reference to the R–I method, Honts and Perry (1992, p. 359) conclude: "Almost all of the scientists involved in detection of deception research reject the notion that the relevant-irrelevant test could be a useful discriminator of truth and deception. When used with naive subjects, the CQT and GKT are likely to produce results that are better than chance, sometimes significantly better than chance."

No matter what method is used, however, it appears that countermeasures have limited capacity to defeat the polygraph. Nevertheless, the overall effectiveness of a polygraph may lie more in its success at persuading individuals to admit the truth because they believe the test is infallible than in the test's actual power to discriminate truth from deception (Lloyd-Bostock, 1989).

Forensic Hypnosis

Hypnosis has long been used as entertainment, as a method of psychotherapy, as a procedure in several branches of medicine, and as a means of enhancing the memory of eyewitnesses and victims in the criminal justice system. For well over a century, it has been widely believed that hypnosis can exhume long-forgotten or buried memories. This belief has frequently been bolstered by anecdotal or clinical claims describing cases where previously inaccessible memories have been brought to light by the mysterious hypnotic trance. Enhancement or revival of memory through hypnosis is known as **hypnotic hypermnesia**. Enhancement or recovery of memory through non-hypnotic methods—free association, fantasy, recall techniques—is called **nonhypnotic hypermnesia**. It was the increased utilization of hypnosis in the courtroom during the 1960s that engendered considerable controversy and precipitated a wealth of research addressing the validity and application of hypnotic hypermnesia in forensic settings (Pettinati, 1988).

The ability to be hypnotized is believed to be an enduring and stable attribute, which peaks during the life cycle in late childhood and declines gradually thereafter (Spiegel & Spiegel, 1987). The ability follows a normal distribution curve similar to intelligence, with most people falling somewhere in the middle of hypnotizability. About 10% of the general population cannot be hypnotized, and 5 to 10% are highly suggestible (Hilgard, 1965). Almost everyone (90%) can experience at least some effects of hypnosis. Among the factors that are important in inducing hypnosis are: (1) the level of trust the subject places on the hypnotist; (2) the subject's motivation and desire to cooperate; (3) the kind of preconceived notions the subject has about hypnosis; and (4) the context and reasons for the hypnosis (e.g., entertainment or critical information gathering). Trust, motivation, a strong belief in its powers, and a serious context (such as a criminal investigation), inspire most people to become hypnotized. Apparently, what distinguishes truly being hypnotized from simple behavioral compliance is the person's ability to experience suggested alterations in perception, memory, and mood (Orne, Whitehouse, Dinges, & Orne, 1988).

Relaxation and concentration are usually the primary goals of hypnosis. Subjects are sitting or lying down, and the hypnotist continually emphasizes quietness, calmness, and drowsiness while remaining concentrated on a target (a candle, a button, a swinging object, or virtually any object that promotes sustained attention). The subject, asked to concentrate only on the target and the hypnotist's voice, is encouraged to drift to sleep, all the while hearing what the hypnotist is saying. The hypnotist generally will suggest different behaviors, moods or thoughts to the subject, and with each behavior or alteration, the subject falls into a deeper trance, or at least becomes increasingly convinced that hypnotism is in effect. Subjects are encouraged to involve themselves in various imaginative scenes, a process that adds to the positive aspects of hypnosis. In fact, "(T)he subject's willingness to accept fantasy as reality during the hypnotic experience, together with the often dramatic vividness of recollections in hypnosis, may inspire great confidence that the recalled material is true to fact" (Orne et al., 1988, p. 25). This characteristic of hypnosis can be very troubling in forensic investigations concerned with recollections of witnesses or victims, as we shall see.

Despite its long history, hypnosis is still at a relatively new level of scientific development, and its application far exceeds our scientific knowledge about the phenomenon. We still do not know precisely what hypnosis is. We have little knowledge of why one person is readily susceptible and why another is not. We do know that hypnosis has no significant physiological effect on bodily functioning other than those that occur in physical relaxation. We know also that hypnosis is not the same as sleep or the same state as that found during sleepwalking. But we know little more than this.

While hypnosis lacks scientific elucidation, there are two major theoretical perspectives directed at explaining the mechanisms behind its effects. The most widely accepted perspective, generally referred to as the **hypnotic trance theory**, assumes that hypnosis represents a special state of consciousness that promotes a high level of responsiveness to suggestions and changes in bodily feelings. Under this special state of consciousness (some argue that it taps the unconscious), the subject may be able to regress to childhood and vividly remember or act out events that have been repressed, or at least put on the "back burner" of memory. While in the trance, subjects may be instructed to feel little or no pain, or to perform acts that they are unable to do when not hypnotized. Individuals can be instructed to sense, feel, smell, see, or hear things not normally possible outside of hypnosis; even memory can be enhanced and drastically improved in some situations. Generally speaking, the deeper the "hypnotic trance" the more intense, detailed, and vivid a scene becomes to the subject. The chief spokesperson for this position has been Ernest Hilgard (1965).

The second position advanced to explain hypnosis is the **cognitive behavioral viewpoint**, which maintains that subjects are not in a special state of consciousness when they appear hypnotized. Rather, hypnosis is a product of certain attitudes, motivations, and expectancies toward the "hypnotic state"—not a mysterious alteration of consciousness. Specifically, people who have a positive attitude toward hypnosis are motivated to be hypnotized, and expect to be hypnotized. They play the role suggested to them by the hypnotist; when the hypnotist suggests to them that they feel relaxed, they will try and probably will feel relaxed.

Theodore X. Barber, the chief advocate of cognitive-behavioral perspective (Barber, Spanos, & Chaves, 1974) has postulated that the good hypnotic subject is one who not only has the proper mixture of attitude, motivation, and expectancy, but also has the ability to think and imagine with the hypnotist. The good hypnotic subject is like the person who watches a motion picture and feels the emotions and experiences of the persons on the screen. Intense and vivid experiences are suggested by the communication; Barber argues that hypnosis is, in most respects, a highly similar experience.

Martin Orne (1970; Orne, Dinges, & Orne, 1984) has hypothesized a similar viewpoint to the cognitive-behavioral theory, suggesting that role playing accounts for much of the so-called hypnotic phenomenon. That is, subjects act the way they think a truly hypnotized individual would act. Orne believes that, "(A) prerequisite for hypnosis is the willingness to adopt the role of the 'hypnotic subject,' with its implicit social contract for uncritical acceptance of appropriate suggestions administered by the hypnotist" (Orne et al., 1988, p. 23). The "hypnotic subject" is willing to relinquish his or her sense of reality temporarily, hold any critical thinking in abeyance, and concentrate on what the hypnotist says. Orne has found in his research that the material described under so-called hypnotic trances is often inaccurate and embellished with many intervening events that occur between the initial incident and the hypnotic session. It appears that hypnotic subjects may be as susceptible to distortions, suggestions, and leading questions as the eyewitnesses described in ◀ Chapter 8. Particularly if the interrogator is a police officer convinced of the powers of hypnosis, he or she is apt to inadvertently suggest events or details that were not present at the crime scene. The hypnotized witness or victim, eager to please the interrogator, can easily imagine a scene decorated with subjective fantasies and thoughts in line with the suggestions of the questioner. Under these conditions, the hypnotized subject may begin to be convinced of the accuracy and power of hypnosis to the same degree as the hypnotist. Furthermore, the subject also may become convinced of the accuracy of his or her account of the imagined scene.

When hypnosis is used as a tool to aid the recall of events that may be either several hours or several years old, the fundamental assumption is that human perception and memory function like a videotape. All the events and details are stored accurately and simply must be recalled or brought to consciousness. We have seen, however, that this assumption is faulty. Human perception and memory are flawed and permeated with inaccuracies and distortions. The frailties of perception and memory, combined with the highly suggestive medium under which hypnosis is conducted, provide a situation where critical inaccuracies have a high probability of occurring.

Research on Forensic Hypnosis

What does the research tell us about the reliability and validity of hypnosis in forensic settings? So far, the studies on forensic hypnosis have focused on three areas: (1) accuracy of recall; (2) posthypnotic confidence of the victim or witness; and (3) suggestibility of the victim or witness during hypnosis.

Accuracy of Recall One way hypnosis is used by forensic investigators is to help individuals remember the details of events that happened in the past—a week, a month, or even years previously. In some instances, the investigation may require digging deep into the past for details of events that happened at an early age. In short, the hypnotized individual is asked to relive an experience from childhood. When hypnosis is used in this way, the procedure is known as **hypnotic age regression**. For example, in some instances, victims or witnesses of a crime may become so emotionally or physically traumatized by the event that they have great difficulty remembering it or even identifying who was involved. This is especially the case if the criminal event happened a long time ago, such as we might find in cases involving sexual abuse during childhood. The hope is that, with the aid of hypnosis, a victim or witness can "regress" back to those early events and reconstruct them in some higher order of accuracy than contained in nonhypnotic memories. However, the research does not seem to support the view that hypnosis enhances memory for events that happened during our childhoods. "On the basis of available data from properly controlled experiments and studies in which the researchers had access to biographical records, there is no support for the view that hypnotic age regression improves accurate recollection of childhood memories" (Orne et al., 1988, p. 36). In fact, there is reason to believe that memories acquired through hypnotic age regression are often far less accurate than nonhypnotic memories.

The available research concerning the ability of hypnosis to enhance memory of *recent* events also has not been very promising. Although some studies have indicated that hypnosis may improve short-term memory, the effect is generally unreliable and subject to considerable error (Kebbell & Wagstaff, 1998; Scoboria, Mazzoni, Kirsch, & Milling, 2002).

Confidence Hypnosis has the uncanny ability to instill a high degree of confidence in our recall of the things we remember under its spell. A highly hypnotizable subject might conclude, "I never realized that's the way it happened. I must have repressed it. It was so vivid when I was hypnotized. After experiencing it under hypnosis, I am convinced now that's the way it happened." However, the research is quite consistent in showing that a high degree of confidence in the veracity of hypnotic material is often a poor fit with the actual facts when independent evidence is available (Sanders & Simmons, 1983; Sheehan, 1988; Sheehan & Tilden, 1983, 1984). Unfortunately, this increased false confidence may permanently distort eyewitness testimony (Pettinati, 1988), or "cement" the subject's memory of the event to the extent that he or she believes it more credible than ordinary memory (Spiegel & Spiegel, 1987). Moreover, the inclination to confabulate and to make up missing information seems to be greater under hypnosis (Orne et al., 1988; Stalnaker & Riddle, 1932). In effect, hypnosis does increase the amount of information and peripheral details recalled, but much of it is incorrect or made up. Consequently, the information gathered from hypnosis is often a subtle mixture of both fact and fantasy (Perry, Laurence, D'eon, & Tallant, 1988).

Suggestibility Memory under hypnosis is highly malleable, especially in highly hypnotizable subjects (Haber & Haber, 2000; Laurence & Perry, 1983). Consequently, leading or suggestive questions or inadvertent responses to environmental cues can have a dramatic effect on posthypnotic recall. Essentially, hypnosis seems to sensitize many subjects to subtle cues that are communicated—often inadvertently—by the hypnotist and others involved in the investigation. In fact, some studies have discovered that hypnotized persons may be more susceptible to leading questions than non-hypnotized persons (Kebbell & Wagstaff, 1998). Although much more research needs to be done, current data indicate that there is a very high risk that counterfactual or inaccurate information will be incorporated into memory during the hypnotic process, especially among highly hypnotizable persons.

Hypnosis also fails to increase recognition accuracy beyond nonhypnotic performance (Sanders & Simmons, 1983; Wagstaff, 1982). Therefore, attempts to improve the recognition of suspects by witnesses and victims through hypnosis are unlikely to improve identifications beyond what could be accomplished by standard investigative procedures.

As we stated in ◀ Chapter 8, research over the past decade has begun to challenge some of these earlier assumptions about the power of hypnosis to promote suggestibility (e.g., Brown, Scheflin, & Hammon, 1998). Scheflin et al. (1999) note that in the Laurence and Perry (1983) study, only a minority of the highly hypnotizable subjects continued to report pseudo-memories after seven days. And, McCann and Sheehan (1988) conducted an experiment which suggested that implanting false memories with hypnosis was far less facile than had been presumed. Proponents of the use of hypnosis to refresh memory also maintain that the artificial, laboratory settings of experiments on hypnosis cannot replicate the emotions and motivations of real victims and witnesses. Hypnosis, with thoughtful safeguards, may be a critically important aid to refreshing memory in persons who have been traumatized and suffer from amnesia (Scheflin et al., 1999).

Legal Status of Hypnosis

Should evidence which has been obtained with the aid of hypnosis be admitted into courts? Obviously, those who oppose the reliability and validity of this evidence respond vehemently in the negative. Thus far, courts in most jurisdictions have agreed with them, but with many exceptions, and legal developments in this area bear close watching.

The first court case which opened the door to hypnotically refreshed recollection was *Harding v. State*, a 1968 Maryland case. The "open admissibility" standard set in that case has been adopted in only two or three states, however (Scheflin et al., 1999). Courts in the majority of states (over two-thirds) have adopted an opposite standard—"*per se* exclusion"—choosing to disallow evidence obtained during or after a hypnotic session. This is similar to the *per se* exclusion rule discussed above in reference to polygraph evidence.

However, this rule was modified in one important way by the U.S. Supreme Court in *Rock v. Arkansas* (1986) ◙ (**Box 9-3**). In that case, the Court ruled that a *per se* exclusion of a criminal defendant's statement, taken under hypnosis, violated the defendant's Sixth Amendment right to a fair trial. Nevertheless, jurisdictions are still free to apply the *per se* exclusion rule to hypnotically-obtained evidence from victims or witnesses. This prohibition on evidence obtained under hypnosis typically applies to the post-hypnotic identification of criminal suspects. In other words, if a victim were to identify her or his aggressor after being hypnotized, the identification would be suppressed in a jurisdiction which uses the *per se* exclusion standard (McConkey & Sheehan, 1995).

A number of commentators have questioned whether the *per se* exclusion rule can survive in light of the Supreme Court's ruling in *Daubert*. The flexibility encouraged in that case would suggest that a rigid rule excluding any particular scientific testimony might be suspect. On the other hand, the Supreme Court's decision in *U.S. v. Scheffer* (1998) allowed the categorical rejection of polygraph evidence in military courts. Moreover, in a footnote, the Court's majority indicated that nothing in *Daubert* precluded the *per se* exclusion of certain scientific evidence.

A less common rule followed in some states allows hypnotically-obtained evidence after a pre-trial review to determine its acceptability. Known as the "totality of circumstances" rule, and favored by proponents of hypnosis, this approach essentially allows judges to rule on the merits of the hypnotic sessions. A good example of this rule as it applies to hypnosis can be found in the federal court case *Borawick v. Shay* (1995), in which Joan Borawick brought a tort action suit alleging that her aunt and uncle sexually abused her when she visited them during summers at their home in her early childhood. (A tort is a civil wrong.) Borawick had no memory of the alleged abuse for more than 20 years until she was hypnotized during a "regression

BOX 9-3
Hypnotically Refreshed Testimony (*Rock v. Arkansas*)

Vacua Lorene Rock was charged with shooting her husband. In order to refresh her memory as to the precise details of the incident, she twice underwent hypnosis by a trained neuropsychologist. The hypnosis prompted her to remember details indicating that she had not had her finger on the trigger. Rather, when her husband grabbed her arm during a scuffle, the gun she was holding had misfired. Investigation of the gun corroborated that it was indeed defective. The trial judge, however, limited her testimony to the memory that she recalled without help of hypnosis, and Rock was convicted of manslaughter. The Arkansas Supreme Court upheld her conviction, ruling that hypnotically refreshed testimony was inadmissible due to its unreliability. The U.S. Supreme Court, however, saw the matter differently. The Justices refused to support a per se exclusion of hypnosis when defendants seek to introduce it on their own behalf. Following are excerpts from the opinion:

> "Hypnosis by trained physicians or psychologists has been recognized as a valid therapeutic technique since 1958, although there is no generally accepted theory to explain the phenomenon, or even a consensus on a single definition of hypnosis. . . . The use of hypnosis in criminal investigations, however, is controversial, and the current medical and legal view of its appropriate role is unsettled. . . . The popular belief that hypnosis guarantees the accuracy of recall is as yet without established foundation and, in fact, hypnosis often has no effect at all on memory. . . . The most common response to hypnosis, however, appears to be an increase in both correct and incorrect recollections (p. 59).
>
> We are not now prepared to endorse *without qualifications* [italics added] the use of hypnosis as an investigative tool; scientific understanding of the phenomenon and of the means to control the effects of hypnosis is still in its infancy. . . . [However, w]holesale inadmissibility of a defendant's testimony is an arbitrary restriction on the right to testify in the absence of clear evidence by the State repudiating the validity of all post-hypnosis recollections" (p. 61).

therapy" session. Her lawyer argued that the evidence of sexual abuse was obtained during a therapeutic session rather than during an investigative hypnosis whose purpose would be to refresh a victim's memory of a crime. Consequently, evidence from the therapeutic hypnosis should be allowed because it is more "scientific" and less subject to contaminating influences. Both the federal district court and the Second Circuit Court of Appeals, applying the *Daubert* standard for admissibility, ruled that the hypnotic evidence was *inadmissible*, but for different reasons.

The lower court concluded that hypnosis is appropriate for the recovery of memory, provided it met certain standards. These standards were: (1) the hypnotist must be appropriately qualified; (2) the hypnotist avoids adding new information to memory; (3) the hypnotist must keep a permanent record of the procedure used; and (4) there must be other evidence to corroborate the hypnotically enhanced testimony. However, the hypnotist in Borawick's case failed to meet even the first standard, so the court ruled that the hypnotically enhanced memory of the events was inadmissible. The appeals court agreed with the ruling of the district court, but it thought that the standards set up by the district court were unnecessarily rigid and restrictive. Future decisions on the issue of hypnotically enhanced memory should be made on a case by case basis by considering all the evidence at hand—in other words, it took a "totality of the circumstances approach." The totality of circumstances standard looks at all the circumstances of a particular case, rather than any one single factor. In this case, the appeals court asserted "after consideration of all the relevant circumstances, the trial court should weigh the factors in favor and against the reliability of the hypnosis procedure in the exercise of its discretion whether to admit the post-hypnotic testimony" (p. 968). The appeals court further noted that the research literature has yet to conclusively demonstrate the reliability or the validity of hypnosis in retrieving repressed memories of traumatic events. The totality-of-the-circumstances rule has been adopted in federal courts as well as in approximately one-third of the states.

The debate over the admissibility of evidence obtained during hypnosis intensified throughout the 1990s. Opponents (e.g., Orne, Whitehouse, Orne, Dinges, 1996; Karlin & Orne, 1997) continue to maintain that lack of validity haunts such evidence and that nonprofessional uses and documented abuses are too egregious to open the door to this testimony. They fear, also, that "disguised hypnosis" in the form of relaxation techniques or guided imagery is becoming all too common during police interrogations. Supporters of hypnosis performed by competent and experienced professionals, following strict guidelines, argue that the *per se* exclusion rule is an unfair restriction on forensic practice and on the rights of victims and witnesses to testify.

The research evidence is quite conclusive on the unreliability of hypnosis as a memory-restoring technique in forensic settings, however. According to Orne and his colleagues, current empirical studies " . . . compel the conclusion that hypnotically induced memories should never be permitted to form the basis for testimony by witnesses or victims in a court of law" (Orne et al., 1988, p. 51). While "never" seems a bit strong, the statement does underscore the extreme caution that is necessary when applying hypnosis in any forensic setting to gain information—whether in the courtroom or through the investigative process. Employing hypnosis to provide leads, especially those that can be corroborated by independent sources, is reasonable, however. Additionally, hypnosis can serve as an information facilitator for individuals who are fearful or embarrassed to report, or motivated by guilt to repress (Orne, et al., 1988). But overall, information gathered through standard forensic investigative techniques are substantially more fruitful than material acquired through the risky business of hypnosis.

Facial Composites in Criminal Identification

Composites are considered indispensable aids to criminal investigation by most police agencies. Composites are reconstructions of faces through memory, and they are built either with the help of an artist's sketching skills or by using the various commercial kits available to law enforcement, such as the American Identikit and the British Photofit. The latter include an assortment of photographed or drawn facial features, which witnesses move about like pieces of a jigsaw puzzle to reconstruct a face. The Identikit, for example, consists of photographic features printed on transparencies. The transparencies can be superimposed by a witness with the help of an individual trained in the procedure until they make up a composite of a face. The Photofit, on the other hand, consists of photographic features printed on cards which can be inserted into a specially designed facial frame to produce a composite.

In recent years, kits have been replaced by computer-based systems where features are stored on discs and the face is put together on a video display unit (Davies, van der Willik, & Morrison, 2000). Presumably, computer-based systems can greatly expand the number and variety of facial features and have an extensive capacity for various manipulations of those features. Examples of the more commonly utilized computer-based production systems for facial composites include the E-Fit (Electronic Facial Identification Technique), the CD–Fit, and Mac–A–Mug Pro systems. Mac–a–Mug Pro is currently the most popular and has the capacity to generate nearly 100 times the number of faces that a mechanical system can produce (Davies et al., 2000). The bottom line, however, ultimately rests with which system (computer-based, mechanical, or artist sketch) can consistently produce the most accurate facial composite for identification.

Many law enforcement agencies claim that face-memory reconstructions by artists based on eyewitness verbal descriptions are superior to other composite reproductions, computer-based or mechanical, but few hard data to support these claims are available. As we learned in the previous ◀ chapter, accurate memory for faces is already difficult to achieve. Composites require one person to transform perception to memory and then to verbal description, at which point another person continues the process, involving another set of perceptions, and finally, motor reproduction by the artist or systems operator. Also, police often make many errors when interviewing witnesses, including asking too many short-answer or leading questions and interrupting frequently (Koehn & Fisher, 1997). Perhaps more critical is how the face is perceived and processed by the human brain. Most people rely on the right hemisphere of the brain to perceive spatial relationships and the immediate recognition of objects. The right hemisphere "sees" a face as a whole, and does not require analyzing each separate piece that makes up the whole. In other words, this part of the human brain perceives faces "holistically" rather than "seeing" a face piece by piece in many separate parts, such as the nose, chin, eyes, ears, and mouth. Consequently, it is "unnatural" for a person to be asked to describe a face sequentially and piecemeal so that a composite of the exact or highly similar face can be produced. Obviously, the likelihood of misrepresentation and inaccuracy throughout this transformation process is very high.

Harmon (1973) asked an artist with experience in drawing police composites to describe verbally a facial image he had seen to another artist with similar police sketching experience. Subjects who knew the verbally described person were able to identify the drawing in only 50% of the cases. On the other hand, when an artist sketched faces from photographs, the subjects correctly identified the drawing 93% of the time. These data suggest that artist sketches based upon *verbal descriptions*—a common way of obtaining composites—are subject to considerable error.

In the usual reconstruction procedure, both the artist and the witness make repetitive attempts at getting facial features "just right." It would appear, therefore, that repeated inaccurate constructions of the feature in question could bias the witness's memory to the point where the witness could not discriminate between the reproductions created by the artist and his or her memory of the offender's face (Yarmey, 1979). Related to this point, we can also assume individual differences in the ability to describe facial features, in that some people have a knack for transforming visual perception and memory into descriptions displaying verbal precision while others lack this ability. In addition, it is likely that certain facial features draw more attention and accuracy than others, which would suggest that people are more accurate with specific facial features than with others.

Most law enforcement agencies, especially those in small cities and towns, rely on commercial composite kits to reconstruct faces from witness accounts, since skillful, experienced artists are not always readily available. The designers of composite kits assume that the world's faces can be reduced to a manageable set of commonalities. All chins, for example, can be reduced to types which approximate all imaginable configurations. The Identikit contains photographic features of 130 hairlines, 102 eyes, 37 noses, 40 mouths, and 52 chins. The Photofit contains photographic features of 89 noses, 99 eyes, 105 mouths, and 74 chins. Theoretically, therefore, the assumption is that all facial parts can be classified into categories. Consequently, their combinations should be able to produce the vast majority of human faces. Most kit designers recognize that the facial reproductions will not be exact, but only close approximations.

All of the kits require witnesses to select individual features from groups of alternatives. Some of the kits use line drawings of the possible features, while others use photographed features from actual faces. Davis, Ellis, and Shepherd (1978) have reported data that the photographic approach is superior to systems using line drawings. There appears to be more information in photographs than in line transcriptions, no matter how much detail is provided in the drawings.

Research by Kenneth Laughery and his colleagues (Laughery & Fowler, 1978; Laughery, Durval, & Fowler, 1977) has reported evidence indicating that composite kits using line drawings are inferior to photographs or even artist sketches. It appears, however, that neither photographed nor line-drawing composite kits nor artist sketches can compare with the information and accuracy provided by actual photographs of the suspects. Law enforcement agencies that use composite facial kits are advised to treat composites, and especially line drawings, with extreme caution in identification of suspects by witnesses.

The research on computer-based production of facial composites is equally pessimistic. Koehn and Fisher (1997) report that the Mac–A–Mug Pro system is not at all useful in realistic forensic settings where the witness must construct composites from memory. A similar finding was reported by Kovera, Penrod, Pappas, and Thill (1997). Kovera and her colleagues had college freshmen prepare from memory composites of other students and faculty from their former high schools. Then the students instructed an experienced Mac–a–Mug Pro system operator on what features to access and edit. Composites were considered completed when the students were completely satisfied with the results. Other students, however, who had attended the same high school could not recognize the composites of either students or faculty members when mixed with composites of strangers. Specifically, only three of the 167 composites were recognizable. The researchers concluded that their study raises doubts about the likelihood that computer-generated composites prepared under forensic settings can produce accurate portrayals of a perpetrator, even if the perpetrator is known by the witness.

Davies et al. (2000) compared the computer-generated composite system, E-Fit, with the mechanical system, Photofit. The computer-generated system showed consistent superiority only when a familiar face was constructed in the presence of photographs, but when participants worked from memory (the more realistic scenario), the computer system proved no better than the mechanical system. Until a system is developed that encourages more "natural" *total* face recognition rather than piecemeal selection of faces, as commonly practice by law enforcement today, the best approach remains the artist sketch or open-ended verbal description by the witness.

A very different approach for identification is used when the skeletal remains are found, and the victim remains unidentified after traditional means of identification fail. The method, two or *three dimensional reconstruction technique*, uses the skull to reproduce the facial structure so that the victim can be more easily identified (see Taylor, 1999, for more information on this topic).

Extraevidentiary Factors

Throughout the course of a trial, jurors must attend to testimony, exhibits, arguments, and the instructions of the judge, and they should resist influence from sources outside the courtroom, or in some cases within the courtroom as well. Jurors are warned not to allow prior information about a case or their personal sentiments enter into their decision making. They must decide cases solely on the evidence before them and on relevant law, as explained by the presiding judge. Realistically, as we learned in the jury ◀ chapters, we know that a variety of factors can have an effect on jurors, including their own biases and values, the opinions of persons they respect, and community sentiments.

Although jury decision making was introduced in ◀ Chapter 8, the subject will not be closed until we consider two influences on jury deliberation that have received extensive attention from the courts, the social science community, and media scholars. They are the alleged influence of extensive pre-trial publicity upon subsequent jury decisions as well as the influence of electronic coverage of jury trials (called the cameras-in-the courtroom issue). The topics are introduced here because of their relevance to the psychology of evidence. Pre-trial publicity allegedly bombards jurors with so much evidence before the actual trial that they are presumably rendered unable to make a fair decision. Cameras in the courtroom may interfere with the presentation of evidence to the jurors in two ways. First, cameras may distract jurors from focusing on the task at hand. Second, they may inhibit witnesses or encourage trial participants to "play to" the cameras, thereby affecting the quality of the testimony, the questions asked, the arguments presented, or the instructions given. Of the two topics, the effect of pre-trial publicity is by far the most researched and the one of greater concern.

Pre-Trial Publicity

Pre-trial publicity raises two major research questions: (1) To what extent does extensive media coverage contaminate jury decision making? (2) Can courts neutralize the influence of the media on prospective and sitting jurors? The judiciary, social science research, and even some members of the press have struggled with these questions, attempting to reach a reasonable balance of the interests of the press and public to cover and be informed on newsworthy events and the interests of criminal defendants. Most recently, the interests of civil litigants have also been addressed.

When especially flagrant, inflammatory pre-trial publicity has been involved, appellate courts have sometimes overturned a conviction (e.g., *Irvin v. Dowd*, 1961; *Sheppard v. Maxwell*, 1966). In the *Dowd* case (1961), after pervasive and highly inflammatory publicity following the murders of six members of a family (the defendant at one point was called a "mad dog" by the press), two-thirds of the jurors said during the *voir dire* that they believed the defendant was guilty. All said they would nevertheless be fair and would consider the evidence impartially. About this, the Supreme Court said, "No doubt each juror was sincere when he said he would be fair and impartial to petitioner, but the psychological impact requiring such a declaration before one's fellows is often its father. Where so many, so many times, admitted prejudice, such a statement of impartiality can be given little weight."

When President John F. Kennedy was assassinated in 1963, it was widely believed that Lee Harvey Oswald—arrested and charged with the crime—would not have received a fair trial anywhere in the United States had he lived, due to the highly prejudicial publicity. (Oswald was shot to death while in police custody less than 48 hours after the assassination.)

Today, many news reporters are professional and more aware of the rights of criminal defendants. Nevertheless, it is their role to provide information about the workings of government—including law enforcement officials and the courts—with minimal, if any, self-censorship. Still common in even highly respected media are extensive stories about a suspect or defendant's background, interviews with persons who knew him, reports of evidence taken during investigations, and even testimony during pre-trial suppression hearings. In the infamous case of the Washington-area snipers in October 2002, some media called for the execution of the two suspects even before the men were formally charged with the murders.

Defense attorneys argue that it is impossible for their clients to be judged by an impartial jury if execution is such a salient media topic or if potential jurors have been exposed to a glut of information prior to the trial. This is particularly so, they say, if the media coverage damns the defendant, is sensational, or includes information that may later be inadmissible during the trial. If, for example, police conducted an illegal search of a suspect's home and found a weapon, that weapon would likely be ruled inadmissible under the law's **exclusionary rule.**

If the press reports that the weapon was found and potential jurors are alerted to that, the defendant's right to a fair trial may be compromised. Likewise, a confession made to police without a knowing and intelligent waiver of one's right against self-incrimination will also likely be excluded under the exclusionary rule. This was a key issue in the 2002 case of John Walker Lindh, the "American Taliban," who allegedly waived his rights and confessed to criminal activities while in detention. His lawyers later argued that he did not give a valid waiver and that his confession should be suppressed. Meanwhile, however, the report of his confession was widely circulated in the media. Lindh eventually pleaded guilty in a Virginia federal district court in July 2002, at least partly because his attorneys had received notice that his confession would *not* be suppressed. Had the confession been suppressed, however, and had the Lindh case gone to trial, we might have serious questions about the effect of the media publicity on his right to a fair trial, as the research to be reviewed shortly will indicate.

The U.S. Supreme Court has carefully guarded the First Amendment right of the press not to be restrained in its reporting of newsworthy events. The landmark case on this issue, *Nebraska Press Association v. Stuart*, was decided in 1976. The unanimous decision essentially stopped some of the practices that many criminal court judges were adopting in the wake of the high-profile, sensational cases of the 1960s. Specifically, many judges began to enjoin the press from printing specific material about a case. Sometimes these restrictive orders (also known as "gag orders") were very general, restricting reporters from informing the public about a wide range of newsworthy information.

The Nebraska case involved the murder of a family in a rural area. Judge Stuart, at the request of both prosecuting and defense attorneys, had forbade print and broadcast journalists from publishing information about the defendant's prior record, an alleged confession, statements made to other persons, and certain aspects of medical testimony revealed in a preliminary hearing. The U.S. Supreme Court unanimously ruled that such prior restraint was an intolerable infringement upon the First Amendment rights of the press, although the Justices were sympathetic to the trial judge's concerns. They noted that he could reasonably have concluded, based on human experience, the publicity might impair the defendant's right to a fair trial. Nevertheless, "His conclusion as to the impact of such publicity on prospective jurors was of necessity speculative, dealing as he was with factors unknown and unknowable" (*Nebraska Press Association v. Stuart*, 1976, p. 563).

Rather than place a prior restraint on the press in high-publicity cases, judges concerned about safeguarding the defendant's right to a fair trial should seek out and employ alternatives, the Court said. Included among these alternatives was extensive *voir dire* questioning to determine whether the jurors had been influenced; admonishing jurors not to be influenced by publicity; changing the location of the trial; sequestering the jury; and postponing the trial. Only when these alternatives are carefully considered and are demonstrated not to work in a particular case can a trial judge tell the news media what they may or may not publish. Because of this very heavy presumption against restricting the press, attempts at these forms of restrictive orders have virtually stopped. However, judges can, and do, issue restrictive orders against other participants in a criminal case, such as attorneys or witnesses.

Research on Effects of Pre-Trial Publicity

In the years since the *Nebraska Press* decision, social scientists have conducted numerous research projects in an attempt to study the impact of pre-trial publicity on jury verdicts. Researchers also have studied the effectiveness of the various alternatives suggested by the Supreme Court. Was the Supreme Court correct in its apparent assumption that publicity would contaminate jury deliberation? If so, what type of publicity might be the most damaging? Would admonitions or careful *voir dire* questioning extinguish negative effects of the publicity? At first, the results were not always clear cut, primarily because a wide variety of methodologies and variables were studied and it was difficult to draw general conclusions. There was research on mock juries and members of the community who were potential jurors in cases; real and simulated cases; publicity offered by the print media, the broadcast media, and both; juror judgments rendered at various points in time (e.g., pre-trial, pre-deliberation, and post-deliberation); high-profile murder cases and less sensational cases involving property crimes.

A decade after the Nebraska case, researchers had not arrived at a consensus about the effects of pre-trial publicity. On the one hand, literature reviews indicated that negative effects on juror verdicts were not sufficiently documented (Carroll et al., 1986); on the other hand, different reviews argued that the adverse effects were, indeed, demonstrated (Fulero, 1987). Particularly problematic, according to Fulero, was emotion-laden publicity, publication of confessions later retracted, and media revelation that the defendant had a prior conviction, especially conviction of a violent offense.

In the 1990s, a spate of research projects began to document that pre-trial publicity was problematic (Fulero, 2002). For example, Gary Moran and Brian Cutler (1991), in a two-part study, examined the effects of pre-trial publicity on jury eligible (*venire*) persons in the context of two criminal trials. In one study, 604 potential jurors were surveyed after one year of news coverage of the investigation, arrest and indictment of defendants accused of distributing large quantities of marijuana. The second study dealt with the murder of a police officer involved in a drug sting. Moran and Cutler found that pre-trial publicity prejudiced prospective jurors against the defendants in both cases, including those jurors who claimed that they were impartial in their judgments.

Also in the 1990s, with the help of meta-analysis, seemingly inconsistent findings from the earlier research were clarified. For example, a meta-analytic review of the pre-trial publicity research (Steblay et al., 1999) lends strong support to the view that media accounts do prejudice jurors. Steblay and her colleagues uncovered 23 research studies published between 1971 and 1996, along with five unpublished studies. Altogether, the meta-analysis provided 44 tests of the hypothesis that pre-trial publicity (PTP) had significant effects on subjects' judgments of guilt or innocence. Subjects exposed to negative PTP were significantly more likely to judge defendants guilty compared to those exposed to less or no negative PTP. Steblay et al. found that the greatest effects were with "realistic" samples. That is, participants of the study were community members who were potential jurors, rather than exclusively college students. Other variables that produced the greatest effects were pre-trial verdict assignments, real as opposed to fabricated pre-trial publicity, and murder or sex abuse cases. One study had found that negative publicity in a *drug* case had a significant effect on the jury decision, however. Interestingly, PTP had a greater effect the more time had lapsed between the media exposure and the judgment. Also, the trial itself seems to attenuate the effects on negative publicity, but the deliberation process seems to increase them. Steblay et al. found that the post-trial pre-deliberation stage was the point at which the publicity had the least effect (compared with pre-trial and post-deliberation stages). The greatest effect was at the pre-trial stage, where the presumption of innocence should be expected.

There is also some evidence to suggest that the pre-trial publicity does not have to be directly related to the case. **General pre-trial publicity**—information that is prominently in the news but is unrelated to the particular case being tried—may strongly influence jury decision making also (Greene, 1990). For example, a defendant may be charged with a hate crime, and the media may run a series of stories on the extent and effect of hate crime in society. There is some indication that these parallel stories negatively influence prospective jurors.

The Steblay et al. meta-analysis (1999) included only five tests of general publicity, with an overall small, though still statistically significant effect. One simulation study included in the meta-analysis (Polvi et al., 1997) uncovered a high effect when a television documentary on sexual abuse was aired while a similar case was being judged. The meta-analysis indicated that the effect of general publicity on jurors is the greatest at the pre-trial stage, becomes less powerful post-trial but before deliberation, and is still problematic after deliberation. The researchers noted that this last figure should be taken cautiously because only four studies included jury verdicts and not all relevant data were reported. Although general publicity had some effect, specific publicity, particularly that involving multiple points of negative information, had the greatest effect.

Pre-Trial Publicity in Civil Cases

Research on the effects of pre-trial publicity has focused almost exclusively on criminal cases, and usually on the effects of the publicity on the defendant. Recent literature has begun to report on civil cases as well, however (e.g., Bornstein, Whisenhunt, Nemeth, & Dunaway, 2002; Vidmar, 2002). As Bornstein et al. noted, increasing media attention on civil litigation, such as the widely covered tobacco industry cases, suggests that this is an area of fruitful inquiry. Furthermore, because the standard of proof is lower in a civil case (preponderance of the evidence rather than beyond a reasonable doubt), "extraneous factors such as PTP might have a greater impact than in criminal cases" (Bornstein et al., 2002, p. 4).

Bornstein and his colleagues assigned participants to one of three conditions, all based on the reading of a case summary about a woman suing a chemical manufacturing company after contracting ovarian cancer, allegedly due to contaminated water from chemicals stored at a nearby dump. In the first condition, the summary contained basic information about the case. In the second, it contained negative information derived from media accounts about the plaintiff. In the third condition, the summary contained negative information about the defendant. Participants who read the negative information about the defendant were more likely to find the defendant liable than participants in the other two conditions. Additionally, there was some negative effect against the plaintiff when the PTP was negative, though the effect was not as robust as in the defendant-negative PTP.

Judicial Remedies

In the *Nebraska Press* case the U.S. Supreme Court had great confidence that the variety of remedies it suggested to combat the presumed effects of pre-trial publicity would be effective. Lower courts, no longer able to place restrictive orders on the press, have adopted these and other alternatives. Thus, they question prospective jurors carefully during the *voir dire* process (the most commonly used remedy); grant motions for a continuance or a change of venue; impose restrictive or "gag orders" on attorneys or witnesses; or admonish the jury to disregard the information obtained from the media. They may also tell jurors not to read or listen to media accounts during the trial.

Several scholars have commented on the judiciary's seemingly widespread faith in these remedies (Kramer, Kerr, & Carroll, 1990; Hans, 1990; Carroll et al., 1986). It is also believed that jury deliberation itself will neutralize the effects of pre-trial publicity, because jurors will point out to each other the inappropriateness of considering the publicity and consequently correct for external influences (Kramer et al., 1990). The available empirical evidence does not support faith in jury deliberation, however. In addition, most of the alternatives suggested by the U.S. Supreme Court in the *Nebraska Press* case have been tested and found wanting.

In a well-designed study, Geoffrey Kramer, Norbert Kerr, and John Carroll (1990) examined the effects of jury deliberation and two judicial remedies: admonitions and trial continuance. Subjects viewed videotapes that included clips of television and newspaper stories relating to the upcoming mock trial. In these videos, two types of pre-trial publicity were dramatized: (1) factual publicity (which contained factual, incriminating information about the defendant, such as the fact that he had a substantial prior criminal record); and (2) emotional publicity (which contained no explicitly incriminating evidence, but did contain material likely to arouse negative emotions). The emotional publicity content, for example, portrayed a 7-year-old girl who had been struck and seriously injured in a hit-and-run accident that occurred shortly after a robbery in which the defendant was a suspect. The description of the hit-and-run vehicle was highly similar to the one used in the robbery. The young girl was personalized and humanized in a video by describing her health and family problems.

The researchers found that admonitions from the judge to ignore all publicity had virtually no effect on jury verdicts, and that jury deliberation actually strengthened the pre-existing bias promoted by the pre-trial publicity. Furthermore, during the deliberation, jurors who had received admonitions were no more likely to point out during deliberation that the information could not be considered than jurors who had not received the warnings. The results did suggest, though, that a 12-day continuance helped reduce bias created by *factually* biasing publicity. The continuance did not have much effect on reducing the *emotionally* biasing publicity, however. Kramer and his colleagues speculated that jurors might forget factual material but be more apt to remember the emotionally tinged material. The study implies that continuance could be useful in reducing bias due to pre-trial publicity that is factual in content, but not so effective when strong emotional content is involved.

Admonitions also did not fare well in the Bornstein et al. (2002) research on civil cases discussed above. In a second experiment, the researchers provided participants with case summaries that were both neutral (control group) and biased against the defendant. However, a judicial admonition not to be swayed by prejudicial publicity was given to one group after they read the materials and to another group both before and after. Only participants given the instructions both before and after rendered verdicts sympathetic to the defendant. Bornstein et al. noted that these findings are consistent with other admonitions-based research, which suggests that admonitions are not demonstrably effective unless they are given prior to the trial. The timing of the admonitions appears to be a crucial factor. The Bornstein et al. study is notable because it extends the concern about PTP to civil cases and implies that plaintiffs as well as defendants can be disadvantaged by negative publicity.

There is reason, also, to question the effectiveness of *voir dire* process in detecting juror bias. First, the process itself is often carried out in a cursory fashion. Individual questioning of jurors, although not a rare occurrence, is not the norm. Judges and lawyers tend to pose questions to the whole group or to smaller subgroups of potential jurors. One exploratory study suggests that, when attornies conduct extensive *voir dire,* bias is more likely to be uncovered (Johnson & Haney, 1994).

Hedy Dexter, Brian Cutler, and Gary Moran (1992) examined the extent to which *voir dire* serves as a remedy for publicity-induced prejudice. Half the subjects (undergraduates) read newspaper articles containing information prejudicial to the defendant in a murder case. A week later, the subjects were subjected to either a minimal or extended *voir dire* by a judge and two attorneys in an actual courtroom. Minimal *voir dire* was based on the standard *voir dire* examination used by the Federal courts. It consists of 10 rather superficial questions that are asked by the judge. The extended *voir dire* involved a one hour information session describing the legal reasons why the news coverage should be ignored. Then they watched a two-hour videotape of the murder trial. Immediately after seeing the tape, the subjects were asked to give their verdicts on the guilt or innocence of the defendant. The results demonstrated that pre-trial publicity increased perceptions of the defendant's guilt. Furthermore, an extended *voir dire* did little to dislodge this prejudicial perception.

As we found in ◀ Chapter 6, dealing with jury instructions, the curative doctrine and other legal remedies to neutralize the prejudicial influence of extraevidentiary material are generally not supported by the research literature. Social scientists therefore continue to try to identify strategies and procedures that might reduce, mitigate, or even eliminate extraevidentiary influences on the cognitive processes of jurors.

Another problem with *voir dire* is that jurors are not likely to reveal their own prejudices, or even information that would suggest bias, particularly in an open court setting. Seltzer, Venuti, and Lopes (1991) interviewed jurors after observing their *voir dire* questioning. They learned that one-fourth had not disclosed their own victimization or that of a family member, even though they had been asked to do so. Researchers also have documented that potential jurors may not even be aware of their biases (Ogloff & Vidmar, 1994). Some research indicates that a sequestered *voir dire* proceeding, of individual jurors in judge's chamber, is more likely to uncover bias, whether or not it is attributable to negative publicity. Sequestered questioning is neither efficient nor legally adivisable, though. The U.S. Supreme Court has already ruled that the questioning of jurors in criminal cases is the first step of the trial and should be undertaken in open court (*Press-Enterprise v. Superior Court of California*, 1984), absent an overriding reason. In order to close the *voir dire* to the press and public, judges must overcome the presumption that it be open.

In a summary article reviewing the research on various remedies, Studebaker and Penrod (1997) conclude that neither extensive *voir dire*, continuance, instructions to the jury to disregard publicity, trial evidence itself, nor the jury deliberation process itself significantly reduce prejudice. Only a change in the location of the trial attenuated the influence of prejudicial publicity. The lesson for judges in a high-publicity case, therefore, is to anticipate the possible prejudicial effects on juries and consider carefully the wisdom of moving the trial to another location. Another possibility is to import a jury from another geographical area (Fulero, 2002). The trial of Timothy McVeigh, convicted and subsequently put to death for the Oklahoma City bombing, was held in Denver after the federal judge determined that publicity would likely deprive McVeigh of an unbiased jury in Oklahoma City. McVeigh's case was an atypical, celebrity case, however. Changes of venue because of extensive publicity are very rare occurrences. Both the Supreme Court and lower courts have made it clear that prejudice cannot be presumed from pervasive and adverse publicity. A recent example of this is the case of Zacarias Moussaoui, the alleged "10th hijacker" on September 11, 2001. Serving as his own lawyer, Moussaoui argued that his trial should be moved from Virginia to a more neutral location. Noting that judges in other terrorism cases have routinely rejected motions for changes of venues, the prosecutor argued that an extensive *voir dire* and a diverse population of potential jurors were adequate guarantees that an impartial jury could be seated. Prosecutors generally oppose a change of venue because of the inconvenience and the expense. Nevertheless, the defendant is entitled to a fair and impartial trial, regardless of the cost (Stuckey, Roberson, & Wallace, 2001).

Solomon Fulero (2002) also has summarized what we know from the literature on pre-trial publicity, including the impact on jury verdicts and the effectiveness of remedies to eliminate bias. Based on research findings, which he cites extensively, Fulero (2002, pp. 127–129) concludes that seven major conclusions can be drawn. They are presented here in paraphrased form, and readers are encouraged to review Fulero's article.

1. Both jury simulation and actual case studies demonstrate that pre-trial publicity has damaging effects on potential jurors. Those exposed to it are more likely to render guilty verdicts in criminal cases.
2. Neither *voir dire* nor admonitions ameliorate the deleterious effects of pre-trial publicity.
3. Even though jurors say they can set aside preconceptions and render an impartial verdict, they are still more likely to vote guilty if exposed to PTP.
4. Continuances are ineffective, particularly with emotion-laden publicity. Fresh publicity brings back the recall. Jury deliberations also do not ameliorate the negative effects.
5. Research has uncovered why or how the pretrial publicity effect happens. For example, jurors remember the publicity and link it to the evidence, and they attribute and make inferences about the defendant's character, among other things.
6. To determine the actual existence and extent of prejudice, surveys of the jury pool must be done. Examination of the actual publicity is necessary, but it is not sufficient.
7. Two effective remedies, once prejudice has been uncovered, are "imported" jurors or a change of venue. In other words, once contamination is uncovered in a given community, the effective remedy is to bring in jurors from another geographical area or to move the trial itself.

Despite the sobering conclusions reached from the above research, reversals of convictions on the basis of prejudicial publicity are not likely to become the norm. We know now that even responsible reporting by the media can result in prejudice to criminal defendants, and to some extent to plaintiffs in civil cases as well. Furthermore, some general publicity on related issues can affect the prosecution's case. It could be asserted that lawyers and judges are slow to integrate this knowledge into practice and into legal decisions. However, it may be logistically impossible to change venue or to import juries in all cases where prejudice is demonstrated. Moreover, cyber technology has vastly increased the reach of publicity in criminal as well as major civil cases. In a society where factual publicity, emotion-laden publicity, and unsubstantiated allegations and rumors are but a click away, controlling their effects is a daunting, perhaps impossible task.

Electronic Coverage of Trials

It is now firmly established in law that the print media have a constitutional right of access to criminal trials, including pre-trial proceedings. Interestingly, the Supreme Court of one state, California, has extended this right of access to civil cases as well (*NBC Subsidiary (KNBC-TV), Inc. v. Superior Court*, 1999). In a highly publicized dispute between the actor Clint Eastwood and a former lover, Sondra Locke, the trial judge had ordered that all proceedings held outside the presence of the jury would be closed to the press and public. In closed session, he then dealt with a number of motions raised by attorneys. The California Supreme Court found both a constitutional and a statutory presumption of openness for civil trials.

Open proceedings are not presumed for broadcast media, however. Broadcast cameras are an increasingly typical part of the furnishings in most courtrooms today, being allowed to some extent, in all but two states. However, the broadcast media do not enjoy the same constitutional right of access that their print counterparts enjoy. Judges can and do bar broadcast coverage on a case to case basis. Broadcast cameras are not allowed at all in most federal courts, although the U.S. Judicial Conference (the policy-making arm of federal courts) has opened the way for individual courts of appeal to allow electronic coverage in the respective circuits (Neubauer, 2002). Opponents of electronic coverage believe that it diminishes the dignity of the courtroom, inviting lawyers and judges to "play" to the cameras. They also express concerns about the effect of cameras on witnesses, including victims of crime. In short, they assume that broadcast equipment and/or the knowledge that the trial goes out to public will adversely affect the judicial process, that participants' conduct will be unnatural, and that the trial will not be fair. Furthermore, such coverage provides a distorted picture of actual court process, since most viewers will only encounter portions of the trial, typically the most sensational parts.

Supporters of electronic coverage champion its educative potential. They say that citizens will become more informed of the judicial process. Some supporters also point out the disparity in recognizing the right of the print media to attend court proceedings but not the right of the broadcast media to record them.

When broadcast technology was in its infancy, many of the arguments raised by opponents were persuasive. In fact, the U.S. Supreme Court ruled, in a 5–4 decision, that broadcasting was a punishment in itself, turning the courtroom into a "stadium setting" (*Estes v. Texas*, 1965). The Justices in the majority believed that the heightened public clamor resulting from radio and television coverage would inevitably result in prejudice. Nearly twenty years later, a different Supreme Court again addressed the question of cameras in the courtroom, in *Chandler v. Florida* (1981), and this Court did an about-face. Noting the sophistication of broadcast technology today, the Justices remarked that there was no inherent prejudicial effect due to the presence of electronic equipment. Nevertheless, they expressed concern about the possible psychological impact of broadcast coverage upon trial participants, particularly the defendant.

Eugene Borgida, Kenneth DeBono, and Lee Buckman (1990) examined some of the key psychological issues associated with electronic media coverage in courtroom trials. Subjects were undergraduate students who served as either witnesses or jurors in three types of mock trials. The investigators did find that electronic equipment has some *perceived* psychological effects on the witnesses in increasing their nervousness. In other words, the student witnesses did feel somewhat uncomfortable about being recorded. However, this witness nervousness did not adversely affect the jurors' perceptions of the quality of the witness testimony, nor did it impede the recall of facts, the flow of information, or the communication in the courtroom.

Nevertheless, questions remain. Will the knowledge that the trial is being broadcast encourage lawyers to "play" to cameras more than they now play to the presence of print reporters? How will cameras affect the decision making process of judges? Both questions reached salience during the trial of O. J. Simpson, charged in the deaths of

Nicole Brown Simpson and Ronald Goldman. It is widely believed that lawyers, the judge, and some witnesses were unacceptably influenced by their newfound media celebrity status. Observers have noted that judges have been reluctant, since that case, to allow electronic coverage (Neubauer, 2002). It can be argued that the legal actors will do a better job in the face of such intense scrutiny, but there is no evidence to that effect as yet.

Most state guidelines allow the presiding judge to prevent the media from televising the jury or broadcasting the testimony of certain victims or witnesses to protect their anonymity to some extent. This does not guarantee that the other witnesses and participants are unaffected. Following the *Chandler* decision and with the increasing dominance of electronic journalism over print, it is very likely that judicial proceedings will be televised with more frequency. Psychological researchers must look for creative research designs to study this growing phenomenon.

Summary and Conclusions

We have continued our concentration on evidence brought before the courts by discussing in this chapter the psychological research related to specific types of evidence gathering. Interrogation, the custodial questioning of criminal suspects or unwilling informants in an effort to persuade them to confess or to gain more information about a crime, is a process fraught with psychological implications and legal mine fields. Although students of psychology and law must be aware of what courts have allowed in relation to custodial interrogation, they must also know what methods are effective in eliciting information and what methods are still used by criminal investigators in interrogatory procedure. The psychology of coerced confessions and its many dangers have become a very important topic in recent years, with Saul Kassin leading the research in the area. Information gathering in nonaggressive situations—such as interviewing witnesses of crimes or taking depositions in criminal and civil cases—was not covered in this chapter. Nonetheless, the psychological principles reviewed here, particularly those relating to nonverbal communication, can be extended to interviewing as well as interrogation.

Another crucial talent for criminal investigators to possess is the ability to detect deceptive responses. Here, law enforcement is sometimes aided by mechanical devices, such as the polygraph, but often investigators look for nonverbal indicators that an individual is being less than truthful. As we have seen, there is no sure way to detect deception. Nonverbal behaviors can be misleading, especially if the investigator has swallowed the prevalent myths about shifty eyes, fumbling behavior, or restlessness. Additionally, cultural differences in communication styles suggest that it is extremely unwise to assume that certain behaviors point to deception.

Sophisticated suspects may well have mastered the "dead giveaways" about which interviewers are often advised—e.g., failure to maintain eye contact, toe-tapping, frequent swallowing. If investigators are determined to use nonverbal indicators, they should pay more attention to the so-called leaky channels, those not typically used in communication. Even so, nonverbal indicators are by no means conclusive evidence of deception.

We warned about the use of the polygraph, hypnosis, and facial composites in gathering evidence. Facial composites, though they may give investigators clues as to the general description of a perpetrator, have the danger of imprinting the wrong face into a witness's memory. Further, computer-generated models have fared no better in helping identify perpetrators, and, in some cases, have done worse than a well-trained sketch artist.

The polygraph has been submitted to considerable empirical research during the past three decades. This research has shown with consistency that even the best trained polygrapher is wrong about one-third of the time in identifying deception, a fact that contributes to the judiciary's reluctance to admit polygraph evidence into the courts, particularly criminal courts. Judges are somewhat less reluctant to admit *exculpatory* polygraph evidence, however.

The three major polygraphy methods vary in their accuracy rates. The CQT seems best at identifying the guilty but is inaccurate in identifying the innocent or truthful person. The GKT, on the other hand, seems to have a good track record at discerning the innocent, but is less than adequate when it comes to identifying the guilty or deceptive person. The R–I method appears inadequate for distinguishing either group. Furthermore, various countermeasures can be used to defeat the polygraph. These data suggest that considerable caution should be exercised when developing conclusions concerning the deceptiveness or truthfulness of a person based on polygraphic measures. The power of the polygraph seems to lie in myth and folklore. If subjects believe in the powers of the polygraph to detect lying, they will be more willing to tell the truth when being examined.

Forensic hypnosis has drawn considerable research interest, but thus far the data have not been promising. To date, the research is quite conclusive that hypnosis is an unreliable technique to use in forensic settings. Human memory appears incomplete, fragile, reconstructive, and highly malleable. The hypnotic state seems to increase and promote these memory shortcomings. Thus, extreme caution is urged when applying hypnosis in the forensic setting in gathering information, whether in the courtroom or through the investigative process. Hypnosis may provide promising leads during an investigation but reliable evidence does not appear to be its forte. Courts have been resistant to allowing hypnotically-refreshed testimony into trials, although it has been noted that a "*per se*" exclusion rule may not survive in light of *Daubert* standards. That is, judges will be expected to review the proferred evidence on a case by case basis to determine its relevance to the case at hand.

The chapter ended with some consideration of the effects of extraevidentiary factors on courtroom participants. Prejudicial publicity has received a good share of attention from researchers conducting simulation studies. We now know that even balanced and responsible reporting can predispose jurors against defendants in both criminal and civil cases. Inflammatory, emotion-laden publicity, which is now widely available from non-traditional news sources, is even more damaging. Furthermore, it is impossible to control other sources of influence on a juror, such as his or her value system, comments from respected persons, community rumors, or even his or her attraction to the prosecutor. The effects of increasing broadcast coverage of criminal trials, and their extension to many other judicial proceedings, is an area demanding research attention.

Key Terms

- Analogue field study
- Cognitive behavioral viewpoint
- Control-of-question test
- Ecological validity
- Exclusionary rule
- General pre-trial publicity
- Guilty-knowledge test
- Hypnotic age regression
- Hypnotic hypermnesia
- Hypnotic trance theory
- Nonhypnotic hypermnesia
- Relevant-irrelevant technique

Questions for Review

1. Under the Constitution—as interpreted by the U.S. Supreme Court—at which point must a criminal suspect be informed of the right to remain silent?
2. Give examples of psychological tactics or techniques used by police to elicit information during the interrogation process.
3. What are the three types of false confessions?
4. Based on research on deception, are *any* verbal or nonverbal cues good indicators of deception? Explain your answer.
5. How do cultural differences between individuals affect the ability to detect deception? Give examples.
6. What is the physiological basis of the modern polygraph? In other words, how does the polygraph "work"?
7. Identify the four phases of the typical polygraph examination.
8. Compare and contrast the relevant-irrelevant technique, the control-of-question test, and the guilty knowledge test, referring to how they are used as well as research on their effectiveness.
9. Summarize the research on hypnosis and each of the following: (a) accuracy of recall; (b) post-hypnotic confidence; (c) suggestibility of witnesses.
10. What legal rule was established in *Rock v. Arkansas*? How might that rule be affected after the *Daubert* case?
11. What conclusions have been reached about the effect of prejudicial pre-trial publicity on jury verdicts?

CHAPTER 10

Correctional Psychology

By the end of the 20th century, about 1 in 32 adults in the United States were under some form of correctional supervision (Bureau of Justice Statistics, 2002a). Correctional supervision includes incarceration in prisons and jails as well as a wide range of alternatives that fall under the rubric "community-based corrections." In addition to the traditional community options of probation and parole, a range of intermediate sanctions are available for persons who have been convicted of crime. Examples are house arrest, electronic monitoring, day reporting, half-way houses, boot camps, and intensive supervision. Although most individuals are serving sentences in the community on probation or parole, incarceration is at a record high level. Since 1980, the incarceration rate in the U.S. has more than tripled. By mid-2001, over 2 million persons were held in jails and prisons, with the greatest population increase occurring in the federal prison system (Bureau of Justice Statistics, 2002a). (**Figure 10-1** illustrates the distribution of offenders under correctional supervision).

Numerous scholars in criminal justice are concerned about the excessive use of incarceration in the United States, particularly when it is applied disproportionately to the poor and to racial or ethnic groups (e.g., Irwin & Austin, 2001; Reiman, 1995; Walker, Spohn, & DeLone, 2000). The crimes for which offenders are incarcerated include, but are not limited to, the most heinous. By the year 2000, 51% of all offenders incarcerated in state prisons were serving time for violent offenses, 20% for drug offenses, 15% for public-order offenses, and 14% for property offenses, such as burglary or larceny (Bureau of Justice Statistics, 2002a). Women, compared with men, are even less likely to be incarcerated for violent offenses, yet since 1990 the number of female prisoners has increased 108% (compared with a male increase of 77%) (Bureau of Justice Statistics, 2001).

Despite the rising incarceration rate, imprisonment does not seem to deter or rehabilitate a substantial number of offenders. A recent government study (Bureau of Justice Statistics, 2002b) tracked former inmates for three years following their release from prisons in 15 states. The former prisoners represented two-thirds of all inmates released from prisons in 1994. A discouragingly high percentage was re-arrested during the three-year period. The highest re-arrest rates were found among motor vehicle thieves (78.8%), those who had been imprisoned for possessing or selling stolen property (77.4%), larcenists (74.6%), burglars (74%), and those in prison for possessing, using, or selling illegal weapons (70.2%). Rapists and those who had

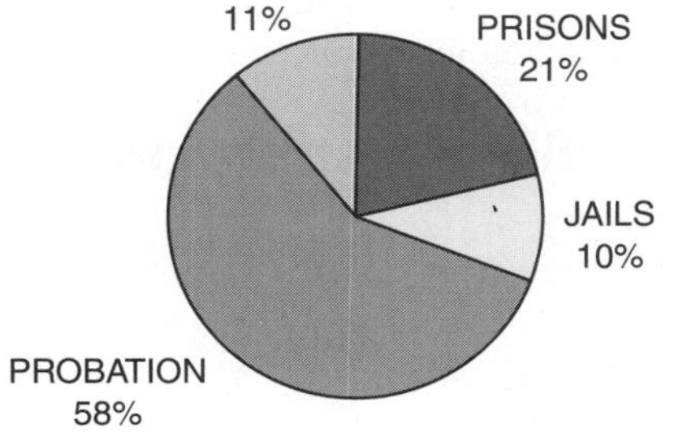

Figure 10-1

Percent distribution of adults under four main forms of correctional supervision in the U.S.

served time for homicide had the lowest re-arrest rates, 2.5% and 1.2%, respectively. The low re-arrest for rapists may be due to sex offender treatment programs, statutes requiring registration of sex offenders, more intensive parole supervision, or the aging of the offender, because rapists typically receive longer prison terms than property offenders. The low re-arrest for homicide is not surprising; it has long been documented that offenders who kill generally do not kill again after release from prison (Clear & Cole, 2000).

Findings such as the above lead many observers to question whether incarceration is the best route to take in dealing with the problem of crime. In addition to the excessive use of incarceration, legal scholars and researchers in the social sciences raise concerns about disparities in lengths of sentences, conditions of confinement, prison violence, and the effectiveness of rehabilitation, among many other issues. In this chapter we will focus only on the psychological aspects of institutional confinement, particularly within a prison setting, although some reference will be made to short-term confinement in jails. The chapter begins with an overview of key concepts in corrections and a review of the work of correctional psychologists in institutional settings. Following that, we will be interested in the effect of incarceration on the inmate's psychological well being, focusing on such special topics as overcrowding, solitary confinement, and the special needs of offenders who are mentally disordered. We will also examine from a psychological perspective the goals of the correctional system, most particularly goals of rehabilitation and deterrence. The chapter ends with an overview of the legal rights of inmates, focusing particularly on those that are pertinent to psychological concepts.

Overview of Correctional Facilities

Prisons and Jails

Persons detained, accused, and convicted, when not allowed to remain in their own homes, are housed in three types of facilities: jails, prisons, and community-based facilities. **Jails** are operated by local governments to hold persons temporarily detained, held for lack of bail while awaiting trial or other court proceedings, or sentenced to confinement after having been convicted of a misdemeanor. On any given day, approximately half of the individuals held in jails are innocent; they have not been convicted of the crime of which they are accused. Approximately another half is serving short-term sentences for misdemeanor offenses. This varies widely by jurisdiction, though. In some facilities, up to 70% of the population comprises pre-trial detainees. Jails also may house a wide variety of individuals awaiting transfer, such as to prison, to a mental institution, to another state, to a juvenile facility, or to a military detention facility. Thus, they hold a collection of persons at various stages of criminal, civil, or military justice processing. Overall, slightly below one-third of those *incarcerated* are housed in jails ⊠ (see **Figure 10-1**). Jails have been called "the cruelest form of punishment" (Irwin, 1985), because they are often overcrowded, deteriorating, and limited in programming and treatment services.

Prisons, by contrast, are operated by states or by the federal government and hold persons convicted of felonies and serving sentences greater than a year. Inmates in prisons are more likely than inmates in jail to have access to programs, including recreation, substance abuse treatment, and a variety of rehabilitative programs. Compared with jails, prisons also are more likely to draw the attention of researchers. Prisons are classified partly by the level of security maintained over the inmates: maximum, medium, and minimum. In the 1990s, the U.S. prison system saw the introduction of a new version of the maximum security facility, the "super-max," which is an extremely high security facility intended to hold the most recalcitrant inmates. We will discuss special problems associated with these facilities later in the chapter.

Different custody levels are also found within as well as among prisons. An inmate may be kept in close custody in a medium security prison for disciplinary reasons, and an inmate in a maximum security prison may have attained "trustee" status, requiring minimal custody. Women inmates, who made up 6.6% of the prison population and 10% of the jail population in the year 2000 (Bureau of Justice

Statistics, 2002a) are less likely than men to be assigned to different prisons based on security level. Women, who are also less likely than men to need close supervision, nevertheless have a greater likelihood of being placed in an overly restrictive environment. This is because there are fewer facilities for women, in some states only one. Thus, when a state builds its one prison for women, it will err on the side of more rather than less security (Owen, 2000).

The lexicon of corrections has changed rapidly over the years, such that it is not always possible to tell from the name of an institution whether it is a jail or a prison. For example, "detention centers" is the term sometimes used to hold those awaiting trial. Prisons may be called "institutes," "correctional centers," "facilities," or "penitentiaries." In six states, a combined jail-prison system exists, meaning that persons accused of crime, convicted of misdemeanors, and convicted of felonies can be housed in the same facility. Within the facilities, however, the individuals may be kept in separate units.

Prisons and jails are often brutal, demeaning places that promote isolation, helplessness, and subservience through the use of overwhelming power and often through fear. This is especially true of maximum security facilities and most particularly of super-max facilities. Nonetheless, correctional professionals maintain that both jails and prisons also can be operated in a humane fashion and can achieve society's dual hope of protecting the public from crime and rehabilitating offenders.

Community-Based Facilities

Community-based facilities are operated by state or federal governments or by private organizations under governmental contract. (The private sector also operates some jails and prisons and receives inmates on a contractual basis.) Community-based facilities hold individuals for less than twenty-four hours of each day to allow them some opportunity to work, attend school, or participate in other community activities. The goal is to provide an alternative to jail or prison confinement, both because the nation's prisons and jails are overcrowded and because of a growing recognition that the majority of persons convicted of crimes neither need nor benefit from incarceration. The term "community-based corrections" also includes situations in which persons convicted of crime remain in their own homes. They may be on standard probation or parole, or also under house arrest, intensive supervision, electronic monitoring, or a combination of these. Probation and parole are by far the most common methods of supervising persons under correctional supervision; approximately three of every four persons under correctional supervision are on probation or parole.

This chapter will focus almost exclusively on institutional rather than community corrections, despite the fact that the latter affects and encompasses more clients. Additionally, the typical psychologist—though perhaps not the typical correctional psychologist—is far more likely to have contact with a person under correctional supervision in the community than with a person incarcerated. Nevertheless, incarceration presents intractable problems for both society and the profession of psychology. It has been the focus of a multitude of research studies as well as legal decisions. Compared with community corrections, incarceration represents to many citizens the failure of our society to afford equal opportunity and truly provide justice. A necessary but overused evil, it deserves all of the attention it can get.

Goals of Corrections

Traditionally, four fundamental rationales were in operation when offenders were sentenced: incapacitation, retribution, rehabilitation, and deterrence (Clear & Cole, 2000). Over the past decade, a fifth rationale, restoration—embodied in calls for "restorative justice"—has been added. **Restorative justice** refers to the need to "make whole" the community that has suffered from the offender's crime, while also reintegrating that offender into the community when appropriate (Braithwaite, 1985; Karmen, 2001). "It is guided by values that emphasize healing and social well-being of those affected by crime" (Presser & Van Voorhis, 2002, p. 162). The implementation of restorative justice envisions a need for systemic social change (Braithwaite, 1999).

Programs emphasizing restorative justice are quite new, varied, and are resistive to traditional methods of evaluation (Braithwaite, 1999; Clear & Karp, 1999; Presser & Van Voorhis, 2002). Examples are programs that mediate between victims and offenders and the family conferencing models that are sometimes used with juvenile offenders. Thus far, restorative justice has been applied more in the community corrections context, in programs directed toward probationers and to a lesser extent parolees. Although we do not discount its value or its potential appeal, it has not been widely embraced in prisons and jails, which are of primary concern in this chapter. Focusing on imprisonment, we will examine each of the four *traditional* rationales from a psychological perspective. It is important to realize, though, that these four goals can be reached in community-based settings as well as through incarceration. In fact, for some offenders, they are met far more easily when the offenders are *not* incarcerated.

Incapacitation

Incapacitation, which has the effect of protecting society from the individual, is the most straightforward justification for punishment, particularly for confinement. If an offender is dangerous to society, it is obvious that, while incarcerated, he or she is unable to harm society. Incarceration does eliminate further infractions of the criminal code by the individual unless he or she still can operate behind prison walls through cohorts on the outside. Additionally, prisoners may display violent behavior toward other prisoners or staff, such as assault, rape, or murder, and also may commit property offenses. Despite these possibilities, incapacitation is often touted as the most effective method of containing crime.

The problem is, of course, that it is neither possible nor desirable to incapacitate all persons convicted of crime. It is impossible because the resources are simply not available. It is undesirable, because not all crimes require the harsh punitive response that incarceration entails. This has led to calls for **selective incapacitation**, which refers to the lengthy imprisonment of those offenders who are believed to pose the greatest threat to society. Selective incapacitation is typically achieved through the use of the popular "three strikes you're out" statutes that flooded state legislatures in the 1990s. These statutes typically require lifetime imprisonment upon conviction of a third violent or serious felony. By 1997, 25 states and the federal government had variants of such laws (Austin & Irwin, 2001).

These laws have been widely criticized, not only because they contribute to prison overcrowding, but also because they sometimes result in life sentences for persons whose crimes were neither violent nor excessive with respect to property loss. In 2003, the U.S. Supreme Court upheld California's "three-strikes law" in two companion cases (*Ewing v. California* and *Lockyer v. Andrade*). The offender in the *Ewing* case had four prior burglary and robbery convictions and was convicted of another felony, stealing golf clubs from a sporting goods store. The offender in *Andrade* stole children's videos worth $153.

Attempts to identify, prosecute, and incarcerate "career criminals" are other variants of selective incapacitation. Incapacitating the career criminal is similar to the three-strikes approach. Ideally, however, the career criminal has been clearly identified as a high rate offender, typically one who began offending early in his life. Critics of both career criminal approaches and three-strikes laws argue that they cast a wide net over many offenders and for a wide range of offenses, not all of which warrant a life-time of imprisonment. Doris MacKenzie (2000, p. 464), in a thoughtful review of what works in corrections, notes "there is evidence that locking up offenders who are not at the end of their criminal careers is effective in reducing crimes in the community." She adds, however, that the difficulty is "in identifying who these high-rate offenders are and the diminishing return of invested dollars with the increased incarceration rates."

Selective incapacitation is problematic, both from psychological and philosophical perspectives. It raises the same questions about dangerousness as we have encountered throughout the text. Though psychologists have been making considerable headway in their development of risk assessment instruments, the concept of "dangerousness" continues to be vague. In the context of selective incapacitation, its implementation is highly imprecise, particularly under three strikes laws, where clinical factors are not even taken under consideration. Typically, these laws focus on specific target offenses that range from murder and rape to home invasion and any drug offense punishable by more than five years, depending on the state (Austin & Irwin, 2001).

Those who object to sentencing decisions made on the basis of presumed dangerousness consider selective incapacitation philosophically unjust, because offenders are not being punished for what they did as much as for what they might do. "(T)he concept of dangerousness for sentencing purposes is an equivocal principle that leads to gross injustice" (Morris, 1974, p. 63). It is also believed to have contributed to the rising incarceration rates and consequent overcrowding of jails and prisons.

Retribution

Retribution, the second rationale for sentencing, embodies the principle that a wrongful act must be "repaid" by a punishment that is as severe as the wrongful act. Therefore, the offender should receive what he or she rightfully deserves ("just deserts"). In its purest form, retribution requires a punishment that is carefully calibrated to the seriousness of the offense—no more, no less. The retributive philosophy, therefore, is incompatible with the concept of selective incapacitation, because selective incapacitation enhances the length of a sentence.

Twenty-five years ago, when the effectiveness of rehabilitation was being seriously questioned, the just-deserts model received the endorsement of a Task Force on the Role of Psychology in the Criminal Justice System (American Psychological Association, 1978). That APA-commissioned group concluded that the retribution model was the most conducive to the ethical use of psychologists in corrections. Noting that a just-deserts approach was not without its conceptual difficulties, the task force decided that it was more acceptable than the rehabilitative approach, because of the demonstrated ineffectiveness of the treatment methods tried during the 1970s. Rehabilitation was closely aligned with the concept of the indeterminate sentence, in which an offender is given a sentence range (say, four to eight years). The offender could be released at some point within that range if he or she had been "rehabilitated." According to the APA task force:

> While it [just-deserts approach] will not ameliorate the horrendous human degradation that is part of many prisons—and nothing an offender has done could "deserve" the physical and sexual violence rampant in American "correctional" institutions—it has the important virtue of placing an upper limit on the power of the state to expose persons to such conditions. . . .
>
> Even in the unlikely event that substantial improvements in the prediction of criminal behavior were documented, there would still be reason to question the ethical appropriateness of extending an offender's confinement beyond the limits of what he or she morally "deserves" in order to achieve a utilitarian gain in public safety [American Psychological Association, 1978, pp. 1109–1110].

Were the task force to meet again today, it may have second thoughts about its endorsement of the just-deserts model, particularly when many psychologists are intent on "reaffirming rehabilitation" (see, generally, Cullen & Applegate, 1998). If it were truly possible to allocate the just sentence for each criminal offense, just deserts would have considerable appeal. However, sentences for specific crimes are first set by legislatures, then allocated to individual offenders by judges or juries. In the rehabilitation or indeterminate model, legislatures give judges a range from which to choose. In the retribution model, associated with determinate sentencing, the legislative body carefully circumscribes the appropriate sentence, leaving little discretion to judges. We have learned that when elected representatives control the sentencing scheme, they set unusually harsh sentences, often more than the offenders really deserve. The move to determinate sentencing in the federal government and in some states has contributed to the overcrowding of prisons.

The third and fourth rationales of sentencing are of major concern here since one may involve psychotherapy and presumed psychological change, and one centers on the effects of punishment—threatened or applied—on behavior. The rationales of deterrence and rehabilitation, therefore, merit our careful scrutiny.

Deterrence

Any discussion of the precise meaning of deterrence as a rationale for punishment leads to a jungle of heavy conceptual foliage. Andenaes (1968) suggested dividing deterrence into two categories, general and specific. **General deterrence** refers to the threat of punishment or, more broadly, the threat of the force of law. One of the goals of corrections, therefore, is to "threaten" the general public with sanctions for violation of the law. Presumably, the anticipation of unpleasant consequences for specified behavior will discourage or deter us from engaging in that behavior. Many people are prevented from cheating on their income tax returns by the threat of social embarrassment or even imprisonment. In fact, the Internal Revenue Service is probably the government agency that utilizes general deterrence to its fullest impact, using the threat of an audit to discourage people from exaggerating their income or not reporting large portions. Interestingly, research in criminal justice indicates that large percentages of citizens do, nevertheless, under-report their income, so the threat may not be a very effective one. According to Green (1997), self-report studies of various forms of tax evasion reveal that anywhere from 8 to 25% of respondents admit to this form of offending. **Specific** (or special) **deterrence** is a term reserved for the actual experience of punishment, which presumably will deter the punished individual from engaging in future transgressions. In evaluating the effectiveness of special deterrence, we ask, do certain forms of punishment reduce or suppress certain behaviors?

Criminal justice researchers and policy makers have adopted the approach suggested by Andenaes. Additionally, the vast majority of deterrence research has been conducted by criminologists who have not focused their attention on psychological principles. For example, the typical deterrence study does one of the following: (1) compares crime statistics before and after a tough law (e.g., mandatory sentencing) has gone into effect; (2) asks respondents whether they have been discouraged from committing crime as a result of a new approach, such as a police crackdown; or (3) introduces a deterrent effect, either in the laboratory or in cooperation with police or courts. Criminal justice literature in this area is replete with illustrations of this research.

One way of determining the effectiveness of general deterrence is to study the behavior of large aggregates of people after statutes or policies have been changed. Statutory changes might include the abolition (or establishment) of capital punishment, or the adoption of mandatory penalties, like a one year sentence added to the usual sentence if a crime is committed with a gun. Legal policy changes might include increased active detection of and arrests for certain offenses, such as roadblocks to apprehend drunken drivers or mandatory arrests in domestic violence situations.

The threat of punishment has an effect on certain sectors of the population and for certain crimes, but the question remains: how much of an effect, and to what sectors? Interestingly, threats of informal punishment from one's community and circle of family and friends may have more of a deterrent effect than punishment from the state. Research also indicates that white collar offenders are more likely to be deterred by the threat of punishment than other categories of offenders. Most critically, however, persons who commit crime, particularly violent crime, rarely stop to calculate the risk of being caught—a mental exercise that would have to be done in order for general deterrence to be at work. And, if they do stop to calculate, they perceive that the benefits outweigh the risks. It is for this reason that some criminal justice professionals advocate taking specific steps that raise the stake for the offender, such as tougher sentences, police crackdowns, and other messages that crime will not be tolerated. Again, however, the offender has to stop and make the calculation, and this is not typically done. Consider the high percentages of crimes that are committed under the influence of alcohol or illegal drugs, for example.

Supporters of the death penalty often make the argument that it will deter people from committing heinous crimes. Empirical research on this question began with Theodore Sellin (1959) who found no support for a deterrent effect. Since that time, a large majority of the research also has not found any evidence for the general deterrent effect of execution (Bandura, 1986; Berkowitz, 1993; Decker & Kohfeld, 1990). There have been some notable exceptions (e.g., Ehrlich, 1975, 1977; Layson, 1985; Yunker, 1976), but due to methodological shortcomings they have not been convincing. In sum, there is very little empirical evidence that the death penalty deters people from committing murder (Bohm, 1999).

One explanation for the ineffectiveness of capital punishment to deter is that the arousal level is usually extremely high in times of violence. In fact, social psychologists have consistently found that extremely high arousal disengages us from our normal and logical ways of thinking. Thus, it is unlikely that a highly aroused offender is thinking about the negative consequences of the behavior at the time. In addition, they may also realize that there is no guarantee that they will get caught, much let get the death penalty (Berkowitz, 1993).

There is some evidence (e.g., Bailey, 1998; Bowers & Pierce, 1980) that executions may actually increase the murder rate rather than reduce it. This phenomenon is called the **brutalization effect**. Executions legitimize violent behavior in others and devalue human life. "When society executes offenders, it conveys a dual message condemning murder but also morally sanctioning violence by modeling the very abhorrent behavior it wishes to discourage in others" (Bandura, 1986, p. 333). Through modeling, a killing that is morally justified heightens human cruelty.

In summary, the research literature does not support the concept of general deterrence as having a powerful influence on illegal behavior except under very restricted conditions, and rarely are these conditions met by the criminal justice system. Neither the symbolism of vicarious punishment nor the presumed fear generated by the threat of punishment have any significant impact on most future offending.

Specific deterrence does not fare much better. Studies in this area focus on the effect of a variety of criminal justice sanctions on the individual offenders. One deterrent strategy is **shock probation**, which place offenders in jail for a short period of time before allowing them on probation. Another is the highly publicized "*Scared Straight*" approach, which attempts to frighten young offenders by exposing them to the harshness of jail and prison environments. Neither approach has been found effective (MacKenzie, 2000). MacKenzie notes that a wide range of **intermediate sanctions**, such as intensive supervision programs, urine testing, boot camps, and home confinement, also have not been demonstrated to be effective when control of the offender was the priority. On the other hand, intermediate sanctions that offer treatment along with control show more promising research results. Thus, a specific deterrent strategy combined with treatment may make sense for some offenders.

Rehabilitation

In its broadest sense, rehabilitation refers to any intervention that seeks "to reduce criminal propensities by changing the attitudes, cognitive patterns, social relationships and/or resources of offenders" (Cullen & Applegate, 1998, p. xiv). In this text, we are most concerned about the form of rehabilitation that focuses on psychological interventions intended to bring about change in behavior patterns. Other forms of rehabilitation, such as education or job training, may be just as effective, or even more so, but they are not considered here. As noted by many other writers, the debate about the effectiveness of rehabilitation became particularly heated when R. M. Martinson (1974), after an extensive review of the literature evaluating rehabilitation programs, questioned their overall effectiveness. Martinson, who reviewed 234 of the most methodologically sound studies assessing both psychological and nonpsychological methods of rehabilitation, concluded that, "With few and isolated exceptions, the rehabilitative efforts that have been reported so far have had no appreciable effect on recidivism" (p. 25). His literature review, published in the journal *Public Interest*, has become one of "the most frequently quoted and least frequently read in the criminal justice rehabilitation literature" (Gendreau & Ross, 1987, p. 349). Martinson was widely interpreted to have concluded that nothing worked, although, as Farabee (2002a, p. 189–190) has noted, the phrase "was a contrivance of the popular press and never actually appeared in his article." Moreover, in later articles, Martinson (1979; Martinson & Wilks, 1977) attempted to clarify his views, asserting he had not condemned rehabilitation overall, and that there were, indeed, many studies that demonstrate successful rehabilitation. Nevertheless, during the 1970s and 1980s disenchantment with rehabilitation was widespread. By contrast, in the 1990s and to the present, a number of prominent scholars and researchers are engaged in attempts to reaffirm rehabilitation and have not given up on the possibility of effecting significant change in the lives of offenders. MacKenzie (2000, p. 464) is representative of this group when she comments, "There is now substantial evidence that rehabilitation programs work. . . . A body of research supports the conclusion that some treatment programs work with at least some offenders in some situations."

A distinction can be made between "rehabilitation" and "treatment," although the two are obviously integrally related. Psychologists working in correctional settings are typically more involved in providing treatment, particularly for sex offenders, offenders with mental disorders, or stable offenders in crisis situations. Nonetheless, they also may be involved in programs that seek to change cognitions and behaviors of offenders who are mentally stable but not in acute crisis (see **Box 10-1**). Programs for substance abusers or domestic abusers fall into this category. Finally, another category of services seeks to help the offenders cope with the issues that arise primarily *because* the offender is incarcerated. An example might be a program for imprisoned mothers who need to cope with concerns about their

BOX 10-1
Cognitive Self-Change

Following is a description of a treatment program similar to many that are offered in correctional facilities for both adults and juveniles.

In 1988, the State of Vermont began a pilot treatment program for incarcerated male offenders based on cognitive theory. Specifically, the program relied heavily on Yochelson and Samenow's (1976, 1977) model of criminogenic "thinking errors." Initially designed as a group treatment program for violent offenders, the Cognitive Self-Change Program (CSC) was expanded to include both violent and nonviolent offenders.

Offenders in the program learn to recognize their cognitive distortions and how these might relate to their criminal behavior. Among male violent offenders, for example, a common distortion is that physical aggression is a sign of "manhood" and is an appropriate way of solving problems. Non-violent, property offenders may believe that no one was harmed by their actions, or that the victim of their crime deserved the victimization. Once offenders have developed insight into their thinking, they are taught strategies for avoiding future lapses (Henning & Frueh, 1996).

Offenders in the program meet with treatment staff three to five times per week in group sessions. Primary treatment staff are case workers and correctional officers specifically trained for this purpose, but mental health counselors and graduate students in clinical psychology are also involved. Ongoing workshops and supervision are offered by the program's director.

During the session, one offender presents a "thinking report" to the group. He reports on a previous instance of antisocial behavior and lists the thoughts and feelings he had in association with the event. The group then helps the offender identify the cognitive distortions, sometimes through role play exercises. All participants keep a daily journal, have homework assignments, and meet with treatment staff on an ongoing basis.

Preliminary evaluation results indicated that the program was successful at reducing recidivism once offenders had been released to the community. The researchers (Henning & Frueh, 1996) were careful to note the limitations of the study (no random assignment to treatment, reliance on recidivism as a sole outcome measure, homogeneity of the sample). As they correctly noted, though, these are limitations that are not unusual for correctional research. Methodological strengths of the study included a large sample, the inclusion of treatment dropouts in the analysis, and an attempt to control for pre-existing differences between the treatment group and the control group.

children. All of the foregoing might fall under the rubric "rehabilitation."

Without a doubt, even after Martinson's critique, evaluations of rehabilitation programs within correctional facility have produced discouraging results. Many realities of life behind bars militate against successful treatment outcomes. Additionally, however, the quality of the studies themselves must be taken into consideration.

Coercion First, institutional treatment often operates on the principle that psychological change can be coerced. Traditional forms of psychological treatment have been successful only when subjects were willing and motivated to participate. This basic principle applies regardless of whether the person is living in the community or within the walls of an institution that has overwhelming power over the lives of its inmates. Thus, while inmates have a right to refuse rehabilitation and treatment programs, their refusal can create far more problems than their grudging acceptance. For example, refusal may mean transfer to another facility, delay in being released, or a restriction on privileges.

In recent years, however, some researchers have begun to question the conventional wisdom that coercion and treatment cannot coexist (see generally, Farabee, 2002b, special issue). The critical variable appears to be, not the fact that the individual is incarcerated, but rather the individual's willingness to participate or perceived need for treatment. Additionally, some studies indicate that even a recalcitrant inmate can eventually benefit from treatment programs (e.g., Burdon & Gallagher, 2002; Prendergast, Farabee, Cartier, & Henkin, 2002).

Environment Another stumbling block to rehabilitation is the unusual nature of the prison environment itself. The physical surroundings of most prisons simply are not conducive to effective treatment. The list of negative features ranges from overcrowding, violence, and victimization by both other prisoners and staff to isolation from families and feelings of a lack of control over one's life. Acknowledgement of this problem led to the establishment of milieu therapy or "therapeutic communities" in corrections in the late 1950s and 1960s. These were specialized living quarters where inmates, on a voluntary basis, would be housed separately from the rest of the prison population. They would be involved in decision-making, group therapy, and operating their own community within the broader prison setting. Follow-up research indicated that inmates who had participated in these special programs did not have significantly better recidivism rates than inmates who had not, however (Gendreau & Ross, 1984). Nevertheless, supporters of the therapeutic community concept note that prison life was made more tolerable and that both staff and inmates benefitted from a safer, more humane environment while they were incarcerated. The therapeutic community concept remains alive in some correctional facilities, particularly with offenders with substance abuse problems (Wexler, Falkin, & Lipton, 1990). Research has documented the effectiveness of these programs when they are intensive, behavior-based, and focused on targeting an offender's drug use (Lurigio, 2000; MacKenzie, 2000). However, since the mid-1980s, many prison-based therapeutic communities have been discontinued due to budget constraints, overcrowding, and other systemic problems (Lurigio, 2000).

The integrity of treatment is often compromised by the reality of the prison environment, something which therapeutic communities tried to overcome. In the typical prison, it is not unusual for inmates to "miss" appointments with clinicians, for a wide variety of reasons. Even when inmates themselves want to attend, they may be prevented from doing so for security reasons. A cell block may be locked down for a day, for example, while prison officials conduct cell searches, investigate a disturbance, or even conduct medical tests. The crippling effect of overcrowding in the 1980s overshadowed a host of other problems which demanded the attention of correctional institutions, including how to respond to the AIDS crisis, the increasing numbers of offenders with mental disorders, special problems of women inmates, and budgetary constraints, to name a few. Under these conditions, rehabilitation and treatment often took, and continue to take, a secondary role in many of the nation's prison systems.

Integrity of the Research The dismal outcomes reported in the evaluation literature are also to some extent due to the quality of the research.

Some time ago, Quay (1977) reported that the program evaluations in corrections left much to be desired. He pointed out that it is impossible to evaluate properly the effectiveness of treatment in the correctional environment unless the researcher carefully delineates the type of treatment and assures that the therapists administering it are using the same methods. Many studies neglected to include these preliminary steps. More recently, MacKenzie (2000) addressed similar concerns. She notes that, even though an extensive body of research literature on effectiveness is available, the evaluations vary widely in scientific merit. "Some evaluations are descriptive and cannot be used to judge effectiveness; similarly, other evaluations are of such poor scientific quality they should not be used for decision making" (MacKenzie, 2000, p. 469).

Treatment evaluation studies often struggle with the criteria to be used to determine effectiveness. Many researchers favor a recidivism index as the most sensitive measure of effectiveness. However, they fail to agree upon whether it is more useful to measure the proportion of pre- to postincarceration arrests or simply the incidence of postincarceration arrest and conviction. Furthermore, even when the criterion of recidivism is agreed upon, the time limit is an important consideration. A rehabilitation program followed by a year of "successful" post-release behavior is far less impressive than one followed by five years of such behavior.

Nevertheless, champions of rehabilitation as a meritorious goal of imprisonment have not given in, and many report positive outcomes (e.g., Andrews & Bonta, 1998; Cullen & Applegate, 1998; Gendreau, Little, & Goggin, 1996; Lipsey, 1992). Interestingly, Farabee (2002a) has recently taken to task critics of Martinson who have responded to the "nothing works" mentality by dramatizing the effectiveness of programs. "It is understandable that evaluators advocate expanding programs or interventions that, in their experience, have demonstrated value in reducing recidivism. But wholesale advocacy of rehabilitation (e.g., 'treatment works'), without specifying in what form, for whom, and under what circumstances, is an inappropriate role for evaluators and erodes our credibility" (Farabee, 2002a, p. 192). He suggests that the field is still too replete with "perfunctory programs, enabled by protreatment evaluation, [that] not only fail to adequately serve their clients, but . . . drain tax revenue and chip away at society's cautious belief that our drug addicts, mentally ill, and criminally involved can change" (p. 192).

The task ahead is to hone the many programs competing for funds and carefully select those that have the most promise. Some time ago Gendreau and Ross (1984) summarized features held in common by programs that have shown positive results. They included programs based on social learning theory, where inmates are expected to take responsibility for their actions, and where decision-making and social skills are developed. This cognitive-behavioral approach continues to have the most promise in a variety of treatment contexts. Pearson, Lipton, Cleland, and Yee (2002) performed a meta-analysis on the 69 primary research studies on the effectiveness of behavioral and cognitive behavioral treatment and found it significantly associated with lower recidivism rates. The effect was mainly due to the cognitive behavioral rather than behavior modification interventions, however. That is, such aspects as problem solving, interpersonal skills training, role playing, and negotiation skills training—all associated with a cognitive behavioral approach—were linked with effectiveness. Token economies, contingency management, and behavioral contracts—all associated with behavior modification—had little effect. MacKenzie (2000) agrees that the effectiveness of cognitive-behavioral therapy in reducing recidivism has been demonstrated. She cautions, though, that the research is typically conducted by those who developed the programs. "We do not know if their close oversight of the implementation and delivery of the program is an important aspect of the findings. Future studies will be particularly important to see if these results generalize to other settings with different researchers" (MacKenzie, 2000, p. 465).

In sum, under the present working conditions that exist in the prison setting, effective rehabilitation will have limited success if the outcome is measured in traditional recidivism terms. It should come as no surprise that the track record of psychological change for confined offenders has been less than impressive. Nevertheless, attempts to bring about change cannot be abandoned, and there is clear indication that some programs work with some offenders, as Martinson (1974) acknowledged. Furthermore, apart from the focus on rehabilitation and recidivism, it is essential that psychologists and other clinicians continue to meet the needs of the substantial portion of offenders that is experiencing severe psychological crisis (Toch & Adams, 2002).

Another factor to consider is that offenders return to a society that is too often not ready to accept them. They are confronted with many of the same survival problems they encountered before their convictions, and often return to the same social situations, where crime may be a way of life. Despite efforts by correctional authorities to re-integrate former offenders into the community by such means as parole supervision and gradual release, the resources available are severely taxed.

We turn now to a closer look at the work done by psychologists and other mental health practitioners working in correctional settings. After an overview of recent surveys and a discussion of professional standards, we will focus on assessment and treatment tasks, which are of course tied closely to the goal of rehabilitation.

Correctional Psychologists

Correctional psychologists are sometimes distinguished from psychologists working in correctional facilities. The correctional psychologist typically has "specific academic and/or program training in correctional philosophy, systems, offender management, forensic report writing, treatment aimed at reducing recidivism, and outcome research" (Althouse, 2000, p. 436). Many—if not most—psychologists working in corrections do not have this specific background. Nevertheless, they clearly offer valuable services to corrections. For our purposes, therefore, we use the terms interchangeably.

As noted in ◀ Chapter 1, correctional psychologists find no shortage of tasks to perform within and in consultation with correctional facilities. In a nationwide survey, Bartol, Griffin, and Clark (1993) found that the psychological services most commonly provided by psychologists working full-time in corrections are counseling or treatment (14.1%) and psychological assessment (12.9%). A similar finding was reported by Clingempeel, Mulvey and Reppucci (1980) during the 1970s. More recently, Boothby and Clements (2000) conducted a more extensive survey of 830 psychologists working in state and federal prisons across the United States. Fifty-nine percent held a doctorate. All who worked in federal prisons held this degree, while state prisons employed master's and doctoral level psychologists about equally. An overwhelming majority of the psychologists (92%) identified themselves as Caucasian, and 62% were male and 38% female. Boothby and Clements noted that the demographic breakdown was similar to that of psychologists working in other settings, with the exception of the gender differences. In most other settings, women outnumber men or the distribution is about equal.

Like the earlier surveys, the Boothby and Clements study reported breakdowns of the tasks performed by the psychologists. Interestingly, respondents also were asked how they would *prefer* to spend their time. With reference to "actual" tasks, psychologists reported the largest percentage of their work time (30%) spent at administrative tasks. Direct treatment accounted for 26% of their time, and assessment 18%. Crisis intervention, consultation, and staff training all accounted for less than 10% of their time, while research accounted for approximately 2%. When asked for their "ideal" distribution of tasks, psychologists wished for more time to provide treatment, staff training, consultation, and research, but particularly treatment. Not surprisingly, they wished for less time on administrative tasks. Interestingly, they would ideally allocate slightly less time to both assessment and crisis intervention than they actually had to provide.

Psychologists working in correctional facilities are guided by a series of recently updated standards developed by the American Association for Correctional Psychology (2000). These standards provide the minimum acceptable levels for psychological services offered to offenders, whether they are adults or juveniles, held in local, state, or federal facilities, as well as in the community. They cover a wide range of principles as well as services, including licensure, staffing requirements, confidentiality issues, duty to warn, professional development, informed consent, segregation, and a host of other topics relating to this work.

Psychological Assessment in Corrections

At a *minimum*, assessment is warranted at four points in an inmate's career: (1) at the entry level, when he or she enters the correctional system; (2) when decisions are to be made concerning the offender's exit into the community; (3) at times of psychological crisis; and (4) in death penalty cases, when competency to be executed is raised. Reassessments should be done on a periodic basis, however, and in progressive prison systems they are. "Behavioral changes in inmates, which occur as time is served, demand constant reassessment and reassignment" (Palmer & Palmer, 1999, p. 307).

Initial Inmate Classification

As a matter of institutional or system-wide policy, correctional facilities require entry-level assessments so that inmates can be "psychologically processed" and assigned to a particular facility or unit. In jails, especially for pre-trial detainees, the classification process may be very cursory. It will revolve primarily around deciding how much custody is needed and whether the inmate is a suicide risk. In prisons, classification becomes more complex. In many states, an offender is first sent to a classification or reception center, which may or may not be within the facility to which the offender is eventually sent. States with large prison systems (e.g., Texas, New York, California, and Florida) have centralized processing centers. The new inmate may spend several days or even many weeks in this assessment center, separated from the inmates already in-system, until assigned to an institution based on security needs as well as to specific programs. Although the classification process addresses both security and treatment needs, inmates do not have a legal right to participate in or to be offered specific programs. Nor can they challenge their placement or transfer to a higher security prison in most states.

Generally, courts have upheld the classification decisions of prison officials unless they are demonstrated to be arbitrary, abusive, capricious, or discriminatory on racial or religious grounds. Additionally, if inmates are assigned a special status that would limit substantially their eligibility for parole, work release, or furlough programs, some due process protections are afforded them, such as a right to appear before a neutral decision maker (Palmer & Palmer, 1999). In rehabilitation-oriented prison systems, the reception unit—as classification centers are often called—includes psychologists, psychiatrists, social workers, or other professionals who administer tests, interview the offender, review records, and offer programming and treatment recommendations. In many prisons, classification committees are referred to as "adjustment committees," presumably because they are intended to help the inmate adjust to the prison environment. The committee might recommend, for example, that an inmate be offered substance abuse treatment and that contacts with her children be facilitated.

The chief concern of many correctional systems, however, is to use the classification for management purposes. Classification for custody, rather than classification for treatment, becomes the dominant goal. Therefore, estimates of dangerousness and potential escape risks become very important. Clear and Cole (2000, p. 321) note that "classification committees often revert to stereotypes rather than diagnostic criteria in assigning inmates. Common stereotypes include members of racial or ethnic gangs, predators who demand everything from sex to cigarettes, weak victim types, and informers seeking protection . . . " Furthermore, classification decisions are often based on the institution's needs more than those of the offender. Thus, although an offender might benefit from learning computer skills, she might be assigned to housekeeping duties because the facility has a great need for inmates performing institutional maintenance.

Robert Johnson (1996) thinks that even a smoothly-operating classification system and careful placement in the optimal custody level and programs are not enough to insure an inmate's adjustment. "Even the most accommodating prison environment can be a source of stress, particularly at the outset when the disjuncture between free world and prison world is apt to be great and, for some persons, traumatic. For most prisoners, the initial stress of entering the prison produces social withdrawal and retreat within an emotional shell" (1996, p. 263).

The psychologist involved in the classification process, then, must live with the fact that prison officials may or may not follow the recommendations of the adjustment committees. Even if high-quality and conscientious assessments are provided, the recommendations may not be followed because the reports do not link up adequately with ongoing or available programs. In some cases, administrators do not know how to apply the results or know what they want from classification programs, because they have not clarified their own goals or the goals of the institution (Bartollas, 1981).

Parole Decision Making

Psychological assessments for exit decisions are most likely to occur in indeterminate sentencing states, where parole boards exercise discretion as to whether to release prisoners to serve the rest of their sentence in the community. In the federal system, and in approximately ten states, such decisions—based on whether rehabilitation has been achieved—are no longer made. The *U.S. Sentencing Reform Act of 1984* abolished the procedure of routinely releasing inmates in Federal prison to parole. Instead, the federal system has adopted determinate sentencing, wherein judges use strict guidelines to impose prison sentences that are served in full, except for sentence reduction for good behavior. The goal is to have 80–85% of the sentence served in prison. Even here, though, a system of "supervised release" is available, whereby offenders return to the community but are kept under supervision of federal probation officers (Wilson, 1989).

Assessments for exit decisions are usually prepared at the request of state parole boards (Brodsky, 1980). They often ask specific questions about the value of continued imprisonment, the extent to which the inmate will be a risk to the community, and the probability of recidivism. As we have seen in previous chapters, psychology has made substantial progress in developing risk assessment instruments over the past 20 years (e.g., Monahan, Steadman, Silver, et al., 2001; Steadman et al., 1998). Psychologists who consult with parole boards in this enterprise typically meet with the inmate, review his or her prison files, and administer psychological tests. As we saw from the Boothby and Clements survey, however, it is not altogether clear that risk assessment *instruments* are widely used. Nevertheless, instruments recommended for this purpose include the PCL-R, the VRAG, and the HCR-20 (Heilbrun, Marczyk, & Dematteo, 2002), all of which were discussed in ◀ Chapter 2. We should note, also, that psychologists are not routinely consulted in making parole release decisions. They are most likely to be consulted when the prisoner has a history of mental disturbance and corrections officials are concerned about future dangerousness. It is common, in these situations, for the psychologist to recommend community monitoring and treatment services for offenders who may be deemed at moderate risk of re-offending.

Crisis Intervention

A third area requiring the assessment skills of correctional psychologists is crisis intervention. Suicide attempts, emotional agitation, psychotic behaviors, and refusal to eat or to participate in programs may precipitate a request for psychological assessment and consultation. In extreme situations—such as a suicide attempt or severe hallucinations—the inmate will be removed from the general population and placed in a "safe cell" for observation. As will be noted later in the chapter, such cells can be stripped down and very stark, but courts have allowed these conditions for limited time periods and with the understanding that treatment is offered. Alternately, the inmate may be kept in such a cell while awaiting transfer to a treatment facility. Prison officials are interested in obtaining from the psychologist both immediate solutions to the crisis and long-range solutions that will help avoid a similar problem in the future.

Although assessment is a critical component of crisis intervention, it is typically followed by some treatment services. There is strong indication that crisis intervention may be needed even more in jails than in prisons. Although jail detentions are short term, arrest and subsequent incarceration is clearly a traumatic event for many detainees. In a confusing, noisy, often crowded and unclean environment, detainees may experience "entry shock" (Gibbs, 1992). Significantly, suicide is the leading cause of death in jails. Ironically, however, jails are much less likely than prisons to have well-developed mental health services available to inmates (Steadman & Veysey, 1997).

Competency to be Executed

A fourth area demanding the assessment skills of correctional psychologists revolves around the death penalty. Inmates on death row may have special needs for services, and their psychological adjustment needs continual monitoring, since they are at risk of suffering significant psychological deterioration as their execution date nears (Johnson, 1996). It has long been a principle at common law that offenders must be "competent" before they are executed (Melton et al., 1997). In 1986, the U.S. Supreme Court in a Florida case—*Ford v. Wainwright*—extended this common law principle to a Constitutional principle. In this context, a person is "incompetent" if he or she is unaware of the punishment that is about to be imposed and why he or she has to suffer it (Bohm, 1999). Because this is an extremely controversial area, and because psychologists and other clinicians are not of one mind as to whether they should conduct evaluations of competency to be executed, we give special attention to the topic.

Like other death penalty states, Florida had a procedure for determining an offender's competency to be executed. Florida's statute placed the decision in the hands of the governor, who relied on clinical reports. The death-sentenced inmate was neither permitted to challenge the clinical reports nor to be heard. In striking down Florida's procedure, the Court held that it was a violation of the Constitution to execute an incompetent inmate, but it did not specify which procedures or which standard would satisfy the law. "(T)he Court did not explicitly establish a right to counsel at competency proceedings, nor did it require that the prisoner have a formal opportunity to cross-examine opposing experts or be provided funds for an independent expert" (Melton et al., 1997, p. 182). Thus, while executing an incompetent offender offended humanity, had no retributive value, and violated the dignity of both the prisoner and the law, the Court gave little direction on how this could be avoided. The prohibition against executing an incompetent had been recognized long before the Court gave it constitutional status. Nevertheless, the Court's decision in *Ford v. Wainwright* re-opened philosophical debate on the critical role of mental health professionals with respect to offenders sentenced to die (e.g., Bonnie, 1990; Brodsky, 1999; Ewing, 1987; Mossman, 1987; Radelet & Barnard, 1986).

Many unanswered questions remained after the Court's decision, including what standard should be applied in deciding whether the offender was indeed competent, who should conduct the evaluation, whether the examiner's testimony was needed at a subsequent hearing, and what are the appropriate consent requirements (Mossman, 1987). Not surprisingly, there is little consistency among states (Heilbrun, 1987) and very little research on how evaluations of competency to be executed are being conducted. Both the American Psychological Association and the American Psychiatric Association, however, say that the ultimate decision as to whether the offender is competent to be executed should be made by the court, and that adversarial expert witnesses are essential in this context. In other words, the psychologist or psychiatrist conducting the evaluation should neither be the sole examiner nor the decision maker.

Ethical Considerations Clinicians conducting evaluations of an offender's competency to be executed face many ethical dilemmas, aptly summarized by Mossman (1987). First, evaluating an offender's competency to be executed appears to conflict with the basic ethical principles to avoid harm (called the **principle of nonmalificence**), relieve suffering, and preserve life. Second, the issue of informed consent to be evaluated is clouded in this area, because an offender who truly understood the purpose of the evaluation probably would not allow it to occur. Third, by participating in the death penalty process, the psychologist is inappropriately improving the image of the death penalty, a social policy which remains extremely controversial.

Mossman and others (e.g., Bonnie, 1990; Melton et al., 1997), nevertheless believe that mental health experts should be involved in this process unless their repugnance toward the death penalty would make it difficult, if not impossible, to conduct an objective evaluation. They maintain that the arguments against participation can be satisfactorily addressed.

The psychologist can help relieve the suffering of the death row inmate and help him or her prepare for impending death. This in itself is consistent with the principle of nonmalificence. Bonnie (1990) notes that a significant proportion of death sentences are eventually set aside. By being involved in the process, the clinician has the opportunity to monitor the inmate's mental health needs and offer suggestions to prison officials. Conversely, the clinician that refuses to participate forgoes the opportunity to make a difference in the prisoner's life. Those who support a clinician's involvement in this process also point out that psychologists consult in numerous other situations where consent is a cloudy issue, including assessments of competency to stand trial and criminal responsibility. Finally, although the death penalty is a controversial social policy, so too are other areas in which clinician's provide service, including imprisonment itself, detention of juveniles, and involuntary civil commitment.

In the final analysis, it is left to individual psychologists to decide for themselves whether to participate as examiners of a person's competency to be executed. This still may be objectionable, however, because individual biases might affect the outcome of the evaluation. In a questionnaire mailed to 335 forensic psychiatrists and psychologists (with an impressive 74% response rate), Deitchman, Kennedy and Beckham (1992) discovered significant attitudinal differences between those who were willing to conduct evaluations and those who were not. Clinicians who were philosophically opposed to the death penalty and were least likely to attribute responsibility to individuals rather than to environmental factors were also least likely to participate in evaluations. Deitchman and her colleagues believe that this could suggest bias in the outcome of the evaluation. Even so, there was considerable overlap. For example, a large number of willing examiners did not favor capital punishment and a large number of unwilling examiners did favor it.

Death Penalty Assessment Although most of the literature deals with the ethical implications of involvement in the death penalty process, mental health practitioners are beginning to publish articles on the evaluation process itself. Heilbrun (1987), for example, discusses a variety of issues to be considered when evaluating death row prisoners, ranging from the selection of appropriate examiners to the production of reports clearly outlining clinical data that are pertinent to the relevant legal criteria. Small and Otto (1991) have addressed the issue of how competency for execution evaluations should be conducted. Recognizing that these evaluations will be scrutinized by courts, they highlight the importance of informing the prisoner of the purpose of the evaluation, describing its procedure, and explaining who will get the results and the interpretation of the findings. Additionally, they recommend videotaping the assessment to document that the above steps have been taken.

Small and Otto maintain that *traditional* psychological tests and procedures may not be helpful at the assessment stage, though they would be at the treatment stage, when the clinician is providing services to help the convicted person adjust to impending death. "Central to the evaluation is the clinical interview," (Small & Otto, 1991, p. 154) which should be an effort to determine whether the prisoner understands that he or she was convicted and is about to be executed. In some states, they note, the ability to assist one's attorney remains a critical criterion for competency to be executed, because an attorney presumably is continuing the appeals process. In other words, if a person is so disordered that he cannot help an attorney, competency to be executed is questionable.

For some clinicians, the assessment of an inmate's competency to be executed is an extensive, time-consuming process, reflecting the gravity of the outcome. Heilbrun, Marczyk, and Dematteo (2002) highlight the importance of attributing the clinician's sources of information in the report ultimately provided. They say this is especially important in this type of evaluation because of the likelihood that the clinician will not be providing oral testimony to explain his or her findings. Discrepancies in the observations of different family members or other third parties are common, thus source attribution is critical.

Forensic psychologist Mark Cunningham provided a model report published by Heilbrun et al. (2002, p. 96). In his evaluation, Cunningham used the following techniques: (1) clinical and forensic interview of the prisoner; (2) psychological testing, including the MMPI-2 and the PAI; (3) interview of a corrections officer on the death row unit; (4) cell observation; (5) a second interview with the prisoner; and (6) seven telephone interviews with friends, relatives, the prisoner's ex-wife, and his spiritual advisor. The phone interviews ranged in length from 70 minutes to 12 minutes. The clinician also reviewed numerous legal, health, military, and prison records, as well as journal entries and letters in support of clemency.

Treatment of Death Row Inmates One final issue related to the death penalty evaluation refers to treatment. If a prisoner is found incompetent to be executed, how should clinicians proceed? In this situation, providing treatment would seem to assure that the prisoner eventually is put to death, an outcome that violates the personal ethical principles of many clinicians. Some, like Bonnie (1990) oppose participation in treatment unless the prisoner specifically wants the treatment, in which case the clinician is ethically obliged to provide it. Melton et al. (1997) note that another solution is to commute to a life sentence the death sentences of those found not competent to be executed. They acknowledge, however, that this would encourage attempts on the part of death row inmates to feign incompetence and would thus complicate the assessment process even more.

In sum, the principle that offenders may not be put to death unless they are "competent" has presented ethical dilemmas for the clinical professions as a whole. Although many psychologists and other clinicians have been able to justify their participation in the process, many others are ambivalent, and some are adamantly opposed. As a social policy, the death penalty will likely be a reality for many years to come. It is now an option in 36 states as well as the federal system, and public opinion surveys continue to find most citizens in favor (Bohm, 1999). This suggests that, unless the courts intervene, a significant number of offenders will continue to receive the ultimate penalty. Their need for psychological services will not likely be abated.

The recent Court decision prohibiting the execution of the mentally retarded (*Atkins v. Virginia*, 2002) presents different concerns. The Court defined, as mentally retarded, an individual with an IQ below 70 and an inability to function independently in matters of daily living. Corrections officials anticipate a sizeable number of requests from death row inmates for intelligence testing. Although psychologists are likely to be involved in these assessments, the case for retardation is more clearcut and is unlikely to pose the ethical dilemmas involving the mentally disordered. A mental disorder can be stabilized with medication, as we noted above; mental retardation, however, cannot be "cured," so psychologists are not likely to be drawn into the seemingly intractable position of assessing an inmate, finding an IQ below 70, and then trying to raise the intelligence score.

As can be seen from the foregoing, the assessment tasks of psychologists working in corrections are multiple and varied. Recall that in the Boothby and Clements (2000) study, psychologists reported that assessment took up 18% of their time. The study did not distinguish among the specific contexts for making assessments (e.g., entry-level classification, exit, crisis intervention, or other points during an offender's prison stay). The psychologists also reported that their typical assessment is an assessment of personality characteristics (42%), followed by intellectual assessment (19%). Risk and symptom assessments were relatively rare, at 13% and 12% respectively. Neuropsychological assessments (5%) and behavioral analyses (3%) were even rarer. The most widely used psychological instrument was the MMPI–2, a test typically given during the initial classification process. Psychologists in the survey reported using other personality assessment instruments, including the Millon Clinical Multiaxial Inventory (MCMI), the Rorschach, projective drawings, and the Personality Assessment Inventory (PAI). Boothby and Clements found very little use of risk assessment instruments among the small number of psychologists (13%) who reported conducting risk assessments. "It seems that many correctional psychologists rely on instruments such as the MMPI regardless of the referral question" (Boothby & Clements, 2000, p. 724.)

Recall also that the Boothby and Clements study found that very little time—less than 2% overall—was spent on the research endeavor. Edwin Megargee (1995) has lamented this shortcoming in correctional settings, particularly as it relates to research on assessment. Acknowledging the many problems encountered by psychologists working in correctional institutions as well as the many demands on their time, Megargee nevertheless pleads with psychologists not to forego this critical task. The revised standards of the American Association for Correctional Psychologists (AACP, 2000), while recognizing the difficulty in setting aside time to conduct research, nevertheless encourage psychologists to do so. Particularly critical are studies that hope to improve institutional or program effectiveness.

Treatment and Rehabilitation in Correctional Facilities

A dominant task of the psychologist in the correctional system is to provide psychological treatment, a term that encompasses a wide spectrum of strategies, techniques, and goals. As noted earlier, "treatment" and "rehabilitation" are distinct concepts, yet they are integrally related. **Psychological treatment** (or **psychotherapy**) implies that the individual suffers from a cognitive deficiency or adjustment problem that can be addressed and hopefully corrected by professional intervention. By contrast, cognitive deficiency is not a prerequisite for **rehabilitation**, which is the umbrella term for a variety of interventions that "seek to reduce criminal propensities by changing the attitudes, cognitive patterns, social relationships, and/or resources of offenders" (Cullen & Applegate, 1998, p. xiv). A stable offender may benefit from programs that increase his or her level of education, teach job or communication skills, or help the offender learn alternatives to violent behavior. All of these fall under the rubric "rehabilitation" but are not likely to require "treatment."

There is considerable overlap between the two concepts, however, to the point where it may not be wise to separate them, and many commentators do not. Many offenders are in need of both treatment and rehabilitation. Furthermore, at least some of the approximately 75% of offenders who are not considered to need mental health services will at some point need them, even if only during a crisis period. The stable offender who learns of the death of her child is a good example. Nevertheless, it is important to recognize the distinction between the two terms, primarily because the courts have distinguished them. Thus, offenders have a Constitutional right to treatment for their mental disorders, but they do not have a Constitutional right to rehabilitation. Put another way, if an offender is psychotic, he has a right to be treated for that serious mental disorder, under the assumption that psychosis is an illness. The same offender, however, does not have a right, under the Constitution, to be offered a slot in a job training program. It is left to correctional officials to decide whether to offer the latter.

Correctional psychologists are in the business of both treating and rehabilitating, although we are most likely to think of them as offering treatment in the form of various therapies directed at changing the behavior or the cognitions of the offender. Recall that Boothby and Clements (2000) reported that direct treatment took up approximately 26% of psychologists' time, second only to administrative tasks. Among the most common treatments used within correctional institutions are person-centered therapy, cognitive therapy, behavior therapy, group and milieu therapy, transactional analysis, reality therapy, and responsibility therapy (Kratcoski, 1989; Lester, Braswell, & Van Voorhis, 1992). It should be noted that psychologists are just one of several professional groups providing this therapy. Psychiatrists, social workers, and mental health counselors also may be involved. The Boothby and Clements (2000) survey of 830 correctional psychologists indicated that 60% of the treatment they provided was in an individual format. The balance was divided approximately between psycho-educational groups (18%) and process groups (15%). The researchers note that this focus on individual treatment amounts to a problematical allocation of resources, given the increasing number of inmates needing mental health services and the high psychologist to inmate ratio estimated in their study (1:750). Thus, they urged correctional psychologists to explore ways of expanding their services through group methods.

With respect to a treatment *model* (or a treatment approach), an overwhelming majority of respondents (88%) used a cognitive model, while 69% had a behavioral orientation and 40% a rational-emotive approach. "Though we did not specifically pose an 'eclectic' option, most endorsed one or more secondary theoretical orientations, suggesting an eclectic approach to psychotherapy" (Boothby & Clements, 2000, p. 721). The researchers also note that it is encouraging that so many psychologists are using a cognitive/behavioral approach, since this approach has garnered the most positive evaluation results (as we noted earlier in the chapter).

As noted above, the study did not poll psychiatrists, clinical social workers, or clinicians working in jail settings. Thus, treatment with psychoactive drugs—also a common approach—does not emerge as an option. The method of treatment used depends largely on the professional training and orientation of the clinician. Psychiatrists, for example, are more likely to favor psychoactive drugs as part of a treatment regimen, although recent studies suggest that this approach is increasingly being supplemented with individual therapy (Heilbrun & Griffin, 1999). Social workers are more likely to use group treatment approaches, in which inmates talk about their concerns, experiences, and anxieties while the clinician generally directs and controls the topic flow. The Boothby and Clements study indicates—rather surprisingly—that group therapy may not be the norm among psychologists in correctional facilities, but it is still widely used by other clinical professionals.

Morgan, Winterowd, and Ferrell (1999) have also called for a greater use of group psychotherapy, noting that it has several advantages over individual therapy. It is, of course, more practical, given the limited treatment staff and high prison population. Additionally, group therapy provides inmates with opportunities for socialization, group decision making, developing altruism, and developing functional peer relationships that individual treatment typically does not provide. In a survey yielding 162 respondents representing 79 state correctional facilities for male inmates, Morgan et al. found that 72% provided group therapy to inmates. (It should be noted that the survey included a range of professional groups, including clinical and counseling psychologists, social workers, psychiatrists, and counselors.) In contrast to Boothby and Clements' study, the present survey found that about equal amounts of time were spent at group and individual therapy. The therapists also reported that, on average, 20% of the male inmate population received some group therapy. Only 16% of the participants reported that their departments were conducting *research* on group therapy. This finding is consistent with other studies that uncover very little opportunity for research on the effectiveness of therapeutic intervention in correctional settings. Additionally, 20% of the survey respondents indicated that no supervision was offered to professionals who facilitated group therapy sessions. As Morgan et al. note, doctoral-level psychologists, by virtue of their extensive clinical and research training, are in a good position both to offer supervision to other professionals facilitating group therapy and to conduct research on the efficacy of such therapy.

Review of Model Treatment Approaches

Heilbrun and Griffin (1999) reviewed model treatment approaches in forensic hospitals and community-based settings in the United States, Canada, and the Netherlands. The forensic hospitals accepted a range of patients, including persons found not guilty by reason of insanity, incompetent to stand trial, severely mentally ill inmates transferred from prisons or jails, and mentally disordered sex offenders. A very wide variety of treatment approaches were used in both hospital and community programs. These included traditional clinical services, both group and individual, and contemporary approaches like time management and social skills training. In addition to describing the programs in their respective settings, Heilbrun and Griffin reviewed evaluation research when it was available. They concluded that there was no single ideal forensic program, but that it was important to use "the full range of treatment modalities that have been developed during the past decade. . . . By employing treatments such as recently developed psychotropic medications, psychosocial rehabilitation, skill-based psychoeducational interventions designed to improve relevant areas of deficits, and relapse prevention, it is likely that treatment response in a forensic program will be enhanced" (Heilbrun & Griffin, 1999, p. 270).

Heilbrun and Griffin then offered two sets of principles based on their review of forensic treatment: ten established principles and seven emerging principles. Among their established principles were the following: a) the need to address clinical symptomatology and functional deficits; b) the importance of communication among professionals in the mental health and criminal justice systems; and c) the need to differentiate between short term goals for some patients—like IST defendants and emergency transfers from prisons—and long term goals for others—like NGRI acquittees who might be returned to the community.

The emerging principles identified by Heilbrun and Griffin were more intriguing, in that they suggest greater challenges for mental health practitioners. For example, Heilbrun and Griffin point to the need to hire qualified mental health staff in jails and prisons and the need for outcome studies that use clinical and behavioral outcomes rather than just rearrest and rehospitalization. They posit that "(t)he epidemiology of forensic populations is weak" (p. 267), and that contemporary forms of treatment should be expanded. "The use of psychosocial rehabilitation, relapse prevention, and multimodal treatment addressing anger and impulse control are examples of treaments that have been developed and used successfully with nonforensic populations" (p. 268). Heilbrun and Griffin also recommend a greater use of review boards or other administrative mechanisms to make decisions about privileges (such as community visits) and release. To some extent, this shields the treatment provider from having to make these decisions. They find that, where operating, such review boards have increased the accuracy and the uniformity of release decisions, although this has been demonstrated anecdotally but not yet empirically.

Sex Offender Treatment

The number of sex offenders under correctional supervision has reached alarming proportions. By the end of the 1990s, approximately 296,100 individuals convicted of rape or sexual assault were in this category, with about 40% of them in jails or prisons (Bureau of Justice Statistics, 2001). Observers have noted, however, that these figures represent the offense for which an offender was convicted and sentenced; an undetermined number of additional inmates also have offended sexually in the past, but are not incarcerated for sex offenses (Burdon & Gallagher, 2002). Additionally, some prison inmates are clinical sex offenders but not legal sex offenders. That is, they have a clinically diagnosable paraphilic disorder that may or may not have resulted in a conviction (Burdon & Gallagher, 2002). **Paraphilia** is a relatively new term for a variety of sexual deviations, where sexual arousal cannot occur without the presence of unusual imagination or behaviors ◙ (see **Box 13-4**).

Psychologists and other clinicians have responded to the above figures by continuing to search for effective strategies to prevent future crime among sex offenders who, as a group, are highly resistant to changing their deviant behavior patterns (Bartol, 1991a, 2002). After an extensive review of the research and clinical literature on the subject, Furby, Weinroth, and Blackshaw (1989, p. 27) were forced to conclude, "There is as yet no evidence that clinical treatment reduces rates of sex reoffenses in general and no appropriate data for assessing whether it may be differentially effective for different types of offenders." The Furby et al. review included all variants of therapeutic approaches.

Despite this pessimistic appraisal, other reviews have been more favorable. Recent meta-analyses of the sex offender treatment literature have indicated that, on the whole, sex offenders are better treated than untreated (e.g., Gallagher et al., 1999). Additionally, some approaches have shown more promise than others. Cognitive-behavioral approaches, in particular, have received more favorable reviews (Laws, 1995). The cognitive-behavior approach contends that maladaptive sexual behaviors are learned according to the same principles as normal sexual behaviors are learned and are largely the result of attitudes and beliefs. Cognitive-behavior therapy, compared to traditional verbal, insight-oriented therapy, has demonstrated short-term effectiveness in eliminating exhibitionism and fetishism (Kilmann et al., 1982), some forms of pedophilia (Marshall & Barbaree, 1988), and sexual violence and aggression (Gallagher et al., 1999; Hall, 1995; Polizzi, MacKenzie, & Hickman, 1999; Quinsey & Marshall, 1983). Cognitive-behavioral treatment currently offers the most effective method in the temporary cessation of deviant sexual behavior in motivated individuals.

It should be noted that medical treatments, such as chemical and surgical castration, have also received favorable research reviews (Burdon & Gallagher,

2002). Chemical castration requires that the offender continue to take needed drugs that eliminate sexual arousal, and it is not considered a desirable approach unless combined with other treatments, such as cognitive-behavioral programs. Surgical castration, as Burdon and Gallagher note, is irreversible and currently not available in the American criminal justice system.

The key words relative to the success of cognitive behavioral treatment are temporary cessation and motivated individual. There is now widespread agreement among researchers and clinicians that sex offenders cannot be "cured." The problem of cognitive-behavior—and all therapies for that matter—is not in getting the motivated offender to stop the deviant sexual patterns, but in preventing relapse across time and situations. It is analogous to dieting. Although most dieting regimens are effective in getting the motivated individual to lose weight initially, the real problem is the eventual relapse into old eating patterns. Thus, a treatment approach demonstrating much promise in the treatment of sex offenders is called Relapse Prevention (RP). "RP is a self-control program designed to teach individuals who are trying to change their behavior how to anticipate and cope with the problem of relapse" (George & Marlatt, 1989, p. 2). The program emphasizes self-management; clients are considered responsible for the solution of the problem.

Sex offender treatment programs exist in virtually every state and in the Federal prison system, but the number of inmates who actually receive treatment is unknown (Burdon & Gallagher, 2002). One study in the mid 1990s uncovered 90 prison-based programs (Freeman-Longo, Bird, Stevenson, & Fiske, 1994), which represented a 139% increase in programs over a decade. The typical program is based on the cognitive-behavioral model, but traditional psychotherapy and behavior modification techniques are still used in some prisons. Neither of these approaches has received favorable evaluation reviews. A critical component of many sex offender treatment programs, the need for the offender to self-disclose past offending, was the subject of a recent Supreme Court decision, *McKune v. Lile* (2002) ◙ (see **Box 10-2**).

In sum, sex offender treatment in correctional facilities, specifically prison, is alive and well, and it represents a significant portion of the work performed by correctional psychologists, but it varies widely in approach and in its degree of success. Treatment programs are less likely to be available to jail inmates because of the short-term nature of jail confinement. However, inmates who are subsequently released to the community may be referred, as probationers, to community treatment programs. The Freeman-Longo et al. study mentioned above (1994) identified 620 such programs across the United States.

Confidentiality Much of the research and commentary on psychological treatment in correctional settings makes reference to the critical issue of confidentiality (e.g., Brodsky, 1980; Mobley, 1999; Morgan et al., 1999). In working with inmate populations, confidentiality cannot be guaranteed when the security of the institution is at stake, the inmate presents a threat of suicide, or a third party is in danger. Examples of limits of confidentiality include "knowledge of escape plans, intentions to commit a crime in prison, introduction of illegal items (e.g., contraband) into prison, in addition to suicidal or homicidal ideation and intention, court subpoenas, and reports of child or elder abuse or neglect" (Morgan et al., p. 602). Psychologists and other treatment providers are advised to inform inmates of these limitations on confidentiality prior to the provision of assessment and treatment services. Because—as a result of these limits—the inmate often perceives the treatment provider as a representative of the administration, the work of psychologists in correctional facilities becomes especially challenging (Milan, Chin, & Nguyen, 1999). Some psychologists have even charged that the work of psychologists in corrections is essentially "window-dressing," and that no meaningful treatment can be provided under the current system, which places clinical work under the auspices of departments of corrections. "(W)e strongly believe that the long-term resolution of psychologists' role conflicts can best be achieved by placing the locus of control for mental health services under health or mental health departments" (Weinberger & Sreenivasan, 1994, p. 166).

Despite the above discussion of assessment and treatment, it is extremely important to realize that the lack of adequate mental health care in jails and

BOX 10-2
McKune v. Lile

Lile was an inmate in a Kansas prison, convicted of rape and related crimes. Prior to his scheduled release, he was ordered to participate in a Sexual Abuse Treatment Program (SATP). To participate, inmates had to sign a form admitting responsibility for their crimes and fill out a sexual history form, detailing all prior sexual activities, including any for which they had not been charged. There was no guarantee that the information would not be used to prosecute the individual in future criminal proceedings, although there was no evidence that this had ever been done. Lile was told that he faced the risk of being transferred to a potentially more dangerous prison if he refused to participate. Additionally, a number of privileges would be curtailed, including certain work opportunities, canteen access, and some visitation privileges.

Lile argued that his Fifth Amendment right not to incriminate himself was violated by the requirement that he reveal past sexual activities. He said the prison essentially compelled him to incriminate himself by virtue of the punishment inflicted by his refusal to participate. Lower courts agreed. The Tenth Circuit Court of Appeals noted that the state's goal of rehabilitating sex offenders could be reached without violating their rights. For example, the state could treat the inmate's admissions as privileged information or could grant immunity from prosecution.

In a 5–4 decision, however, the U.S. Supreme Court did not see the curtailment of privileges as significantly punitive, to the point of compelling Lile to incriminate himself. The majority of Justices considered the curtailment an incentive for inmates to participate in the treatment. The four Justices in the minority saw "threats" rather than "incentives," and noted that such threats were unacceptably punitive. The threatened transfer, for example, represented a significant, adverse change from the condition Lile had earned as a result of his good behavior in prison. In essence, the dissenting Justices said, Lile was ordered to incriminate himself, was not provided with any immunity when he did so, and was then punished for refusing to incriminate himself. The state's refusal to give leeway to the inmate placed him in a game he could not possibly win, without a guarantee that he would not be prosecuted.

The dissenting Justices did not question the appropriateness of the SATP program. "Mental health professionals seem to agree that accepting responsibility for past sexual misconduct is often essential to successful treament, and that treatment programs can reduce the risk of recidivism by sex offenders." Like the lower federal court, the dissenters noted that the program's laudable goals could still be achieved if the state were willing to grant use immunity for incriminating statements made by the inmate. Alternately, the state could make participating in the program totally voluntary, with no loss of privileges from refusal to participate.

prisons across the U.S. is widely acknowledged by commentators and courts alike (Cohen, 2003; Heilbrun & Griffin, 1999; Morris, Steadman, & Veysey, 1997). Although specialized treatment exists for forensic populations, a great number of mentally disordered individuals continue to languish in jails and prisons with little if any psychological intervention provided. It has been estimated that 16% of all prison inmates and 10% of jail detainees and inmates are in need of treatment for mental disorder (Bureau of Justice Statistics, 2001a). The needs of jail inmates are often more acute, because they are more likely to be in crisis situations. Studies also indicate that the need among female inmates is even greater than among males (Clear & Cole, 2000). This estimate is somewhat confounded by the fact that women, compared with men, are probably more likely to self-disclose their need for mental health services. The adequacy of medical services, including both physical and mental health, is a frequent point of litigation in class action suits brought by incarcerated individuals. In some jurisdictions, services are provided to fewer than 25% of the inmates requiring them (*Feliciano v. Gonzalez*, 1998). We will return to this issue at the end of the chapter, as we discuss legal rights of inmates.

Psychological Effects of Imprisonment

By its very nature, imprisonment is a stressful situation for both inmates and those who supervise them. Once the initial shock of being incarcerated has dissipated, however, most inmates seem to adapt and adjust to prison life. Nonetheless, as noted earlier in the chapter, a significant number of inmates in both prisons and jails do experience emotional disturbances that result in needs for crisis treatment and/or transfer to hospital settings. For the time being, however, we discuss the effects of incarceration on the general prison population.

The Stanford Prison Experiment

A classic study in social psychology conducted in the 1970s first brought attention to the possibility that imprisonment, itself, was psychologically damaging because of the control exercised over inmates. Haney, Banks, Jaffe, and Zimbardo (1973) conducted an experiment to try to understand what it means psychologically to be a prisoner or a guard. (Today, the preferred term is "corrections officer.") The researchers created their own "prison" in the basement of the Stanford University Psychology Department. Small rooms were arranged to simulate six-by-nine-foot cells, a small "yard" was provided, and the researchers even added a solitary confinement "hole" (actually a closet). The "prison," according to the researchers, had all the physical and psychological markings of an actual security institution: bars, prison drab, identification numbers, uniformed guards, and other features which not only closely approximated a prison environment but also encouraged deindividuation, a process by which persons lose their sense of identity.

The participants in the mock prison were young male largely middle-class, white students who responded to a newspaper ad for volunteers for a psychological experiment. The experiment required two roles: "guard" and prisoner. Guards were allowed to develop their own formal rules for maintaining law, order, and respect, and they were relatively free to improvise new rules during their eight-hour, three-person shifts. They were uniformed and carried various symbols of power: a nightstick, keys to cells, whistles, and handcuffs. Prisoners wore uniforms with stripes and caps. They had been unexpectedly picked up at their homes and subjected to a variety of humiliating procedures (frisking, "delousing") before being placed in their cells. They were required to obtain permission from the guards to do even routine things, like writing letters or smoking cigarettes. Prisoners were referred to only by number, their toilet visits were supervised, and they were lined up three times a day for a count. In addition, they were required to do pushups, clean toilets, and memorize sixteen rules and recite them on demand.

The events that occurred in the prison were observed and recorded on videotape, and the guards and prisoners were interviewed at various points throughout the project. Although the study was intended to continue for two weeks, it had to be terminated within six days because the behavior of the college men degenerated rapidly. Zimbardo (1973, p. 163) wrote:

> In less than a week the experience of imprisonment undid (temporarily) a lifetime of learning; human values were suspended, self-concepts were challenged and the ugliest, most base, pathological side of human nature surfaced. We were horrified because we saw some boys (guards) treat others as if they were despicable animals, taking pleasure in cruelty, while other boys (prisoners) became servile, dehumanized robots who thought only of escape, of their own individual survival and of their mounting hatred for the guards.

The Stanford Prison Experiment does reveal vividly the power and pervasiveness of situations over individual behavior. It demonstrates what confinement, monitored and controlled by persons who have been given awesome power over the behavior of those confined, can do to the psychological functioning of both prisoners and those who supervise them. Critics of the experiment contend that the subjects might have been merely playing roles they thought they should be playing. Therefore, while situational properties may have had considerable impact on behavior, expectancies were also involved. On the other hand, we can assume that expectancies also play a part in the behavior of the participants in the real prison system.

The most frequent critique of the study, however, is that it lacked external validity and its findings cannot be generalized to "real" prisoners and corrections officers (Monahan & Walker, 1990). Despite having the trappings of high security, Zimbardo's basement facility did not truly approximate a prison setting. Robert Johnson (1996) notes that the volunteers used in the experiment were implicitly encouraged to act out *stereotypical* conceptions of corrections officer and inmate roles, including the brutal "guard" and the passive, controlled inmate. As Johnson (1996, pp. 200–201) notes, "In the real prison world, inmate adjustment is quite diverse and, in most cases, oriented to action and denial rather than to passivity and depression." In the Stanford experiment, volunteers who acted as guards received no training, in contrast to the training actually received by corrections officers. A number of other details simply did not ring true: for example, some "guards" wore mirrored sunglasses and carried long nightsticks. Corrections officers in many prisons today carry no weapons, with the exception of batons that are not an essential part of the uniform. The uniforms worn by the inmates in Zimbardo and Haney's study were reminiscent of uniforms worn in the early 20th century penitentiary, complete with humiliating stocking caps and sacklike coveralls.

As Johnson and others have pointed out (e.g., Toch & Adams, 2002) the stereotypical picture of the brutal, power-hungry, illiterate "guard" is highly entrenched both in social science literature and in the public mind via entertainment media. Consider, for example, such contemporary films as *The Green Mile* (released 1999, Warner Bros.) and *Monsters Ball* (released 2001, Lions Gate Films). When a compassionate corrections officer is depicted in the media, he or she is seen as the exceptional case. In reality, although the victimization of prisoners by guards is documented, the deviant officer is the exception rather than the rule. Even in the Stanford experiment, which encouraged psychological abuse, only one-third of the guards abused their power. Obviously, abuse by even a *small* percentage is unacceptable, however.

Writing about the Stanford Prison Experiment 25 years later, Haney and Zimbardo (1998) continued to maintain that the study was groundbreaking in its contribution to the social psychology literature and clearly has relevance to prisons today. "Our study represented an experimental demonstration of the extraordinary power of *institutional* environments to influence those who passed through them. . . . Our 'institution' rapidly developed sufficient power to bend and twist human behavior in ways that confounded expert predictions and violated the expectations of those who created and participated in it" (Haney & Zimbardo, 1998, p. 710). They continue that, contrary to what they had hoped, prisons today have become even more coercive than they were at the time of the original experiment. "For the first time in the 200-year-history of imprisonment in the United States, there appear to be no limits on the amount of prison pain the public is willing to inflict in the name of crime control" (p. 712). Haney and Zimbardo write about disproportionate increases in the incarceration of drug offenders, disproportionate incarceration of racial groups, particularly Black men, and the rise of the supermax prison (to be discussed below)—all indicators of harsh, punitive social policies. They argue that the results of their experiment are even more chilling in the face of this increasing punitiveness. Thus, while critics of the experiment have raised questions about its external validity, Haney and Zimbardo remain convinced that the important message that they offered must be heeded. They make it a point to add individual components to the situational factors they first identified, however. "Pathology that is *inherent in the structure of the prison situation* (italics added) is likely given a boost by the pathology that some prisoners and guards (sic) bring with them into the institutions themselves. Thus, although ours was clearly a study of the power of situational characteristics, we certainly acknowledge the value of interactional models of social and institutional behavior" (Haney & Zimbardo, 1998, p. 719).

Research on Prison Adjustment

Doubtlessly, and as demonstrated by many case studies and anecdotal evidence, imprisonment can be brutal, demeaning, and generally psychologically devastating for many individuals (Zamble & Porporino, 1988; Bartollas, 1981; Toch & Adams, 1989a, 1989b, 2002), and part of this is a reflection of the inevitable imbalance of power between inmates and officers. Like Haney and Zimbardo, numerous researchers and other scholars have expressed concerns about the nation's excessive punitiveness and the coercive nature of correctional facilities. Unfortunately, we are unlikely to see this situation change dramatically in the years ahead, and psychologists and other professionals must continue to cope with the realities of working in these environments.

Prison and Jail Suicide The fact that incarceration is stressful to many individuals may be reflected in the suicide rates. According to one estimate (Hayes, 1995) the suicide rate among prisoners in the 10-year period up to the mid-1990s was 20.6 deaths per 100,000, which was 50% greater than the rate in the general population. The jail suicide rate is even higher, with researchers estimating it at least five times higher than the prison rate (Cohen, 1998; Steadman et al., 1989). It is well recognized in corrections that the suicide rate in jails is higher than that in prisons (Clear & Cole, 2000). Suicide is usually committed by young, unmarried white males during the early stages of confinement, and the usual method is hanging. Other inmates try to mutilate themselves with razor blades, fragments of metal, glass, or wire, or even eating utensils.

Psychologist Hans Toch has written extensively about the "mosaic of despair" that overwhelms some inmates and leads them to injure themselves or take their own lives (e.g., Toch, 1992; Toch & Adams, 2002). He writes about the "crises of self-doubt, hopelessness, fear, or abandonment" as well as psychotic crises that create delusions or panic. "At best, self-directed violence mirrors helplessness, and involves coping problems with no perceived solutions." Toch and Adams note that crises vary with the type of population, reflecting age, cultural, and gender differences. Young, white, and Latin inmates are the most likely groups to face acute psychological crises. Married inmates feel more vulnerable in jail, while single inmates suffer more in prisons. Women are most likely to have problems with loneliness, while Latin inmates are distressed if they face the abandonment of relatives. They emphasize, though, that response to the jail or prison environment is very individualistic, which suggests that correctional officials must be carefully attuned to the risks of suicide among particular inmates.

Despite the disturbing rates of suicide among incarcerated populations, considerable research indicates that most inmates are remarkably adaptive to their prison environments (e.g., Toch & Adams, 1989a, 1989b; Zamble & Proporino, 1988). Zamble and Proporino (1988) studied the coping strategies and adjustment of inmates in several Canadian penitentiaries. They found that emotional disruption and adjustment were clearly problems for most inmates during the early segments of their sentences. The deleterious reactions were a result of the dramatic disruption in customary behavior created by the many restrictions, deprivations, and constraints inherent in prison life. However, these initial reactions soon dissipated for most inmates, and, as the inmates became accustomed to prison routine, no lasting emotional problems were discernible.

Toch and Adams (1989a) reported a similar pattern of adjustment in their research on American prisoners. These researchers found that emotional distress was highest among inmates during the early stages of their sentences. Furthermore, these same inmates were the most troublesome and disruptive toward prison rules and regulations. Gradually, however, most inmates become "prisonized." **Prisonization** was first defined by Clemmer (1940, p. 299) as "the process by which a new inmate absorbs the customs of prison society and learns to adapt to the environment." A similar process, jailing, occurs in the jail environment. Some researchers have suggested that the inmate loses interest in the outside world, views the prison as home, loses the ability to make independent decisions, and, in general, defines him or herself totally within the institutional context (MacKenzie & Goodstein, 1985). Adjustment to prison life is highly idiosyncratic, however, and we cannot assume that these features are characteristic of all or even a high proportion of inmates.

The Toch-Adams data also supported the frequent observation that age is a strong correlate of prison violations, with the younger inmates being much more prone to engage in prison misconduct than older inmates. In fact, Richard McCorkle (1992) reports that younger inmates assume a more aggressive, violent stance toward all individuals within the prison walls compared to their older counterparts, and thus are more likely the targets of more violent victimization. Older inmates, on the other hand, assume more passive, avoidance techniques in adapting to the expectations of the prison environment.

Gender Differences Most of the research dealing with prison adjustment has been done on male inmates. Part of the explanation for this neglect has traditionally been that female inmates make up only 3 to 4% of those incarcerated in state and federal prisons. In recent years, women's rates of incarceration have increased faster than those of men, although no scholars predict that they will ever "catch up." Presently, women make up 6.6% of all state and federal prison inmates and approximately 10% of all jail inmates and detainees (Bureau of Justice Statistics, 2001a). Although increasing research attention is now being given to women inmates, they still remain forgotten offenders compared with males.

Scholars agree that problems faced by female prisoners are similar to but also distinct from the problems faced by male prisoners. For example, due to the small numbers of women in prison, there are far fewer correctional facilities available, thus severely restricting opportunities to be near their families or to have occupational, educational, or social activities while incarcerated. More importantly, their relationships with their children are often severely hampered, resulting in a more severe deprivation than typically found for the male parent (MacKenzie et al., 1989). This parent-child deprivation is especially severe for long-term women inmates, who may lose their major source of identity when they lose their parental role (Weisheit & Mahan, 1988). Weisheit and Mahan (1988) note that women inmates have on average two children and often are the head of their household. Moreover, they are likely to be poor, poorly educated, and be members of a racial or ethnic minority. Female inmates are also more likely than male inmates to have experienced sexual abuse as a child and physical abuse as an adult (Austin & Irwin, 2001; Owen, 2000).

Some observers have estimated that over 60% of the female prison population requires mental health services and that a vast majority of women offenders have a need for substance abuse services (e.g., Owen, 2000). As Owen (2000, p. 196) observes, "(c)losely related to mental health problems is the need to recognize the impact of the physical, sexual, and emotional abuse experienced by women offenders."

Doris Layton MacKenzie and her colleagues (1989) studied the characteristics, adjustment, and coping of women serving three types of prison sentences in Louisiana's only prison for adult women. These researchers found that those inmates serving short sentences were more likely to be members of pseudo-families than those inmates serving longer sentences. Play families are organized voluntarily by mutual agreement among inmates, and may or may not include homosexual relationships. Family members are given titles, such as mother, child, uncle, aunt, father, or sister. These families seem to provide a coping and protective structure for women inmates new to the prison environment. Women serving long-term sentences were less likely to belong to play families but also reported more situational problems such as boredom, missing luxuries, and lack of opportunities. The researchers concluded that these situational problems were not due to an inability to cope as much as a realistic appraisal of the limitations of the prison environment for opportunities, as well as its social restrictions.

Much of the literature on the psychological effects of prison life neglects the important variable of offense conviction. In most correctional facilities, there exists a social hierarchy determined by individual criminal histories and types of crimes committed. For example, prisoners often despise fellow inmates who were convicted of certain sexual crimes, such as child rape or molestation. These offenders not only are placed at the bottom of the prisoner hierarchy, but they are also harassed to the point where they must seek protection from other inmates. Material acquisition offenses (e.g., robbery and burglary) are high status offenses, particularly if they were performed ingeniously. Therefore, the nature of one's offense can either add to one's confinement woes or make them lighter. Additionally, social support systems appear as important in prisons as they do in the free world. Both male and female inmates, therefore, form and join groups that provide them protection from aggressors and emotional support in coping with the stress of incarceration. Male inmates are more likely to form groups, including gangs, divided along racial or ethnic lines, while female inmates are more likely to form family-like groups (Clear & Cole, 2000).

Conclusions Some researchers (e.g., Zamble & Porporino, 1988) maintain that prison inmates on the whole do not suffer permanent psychological harm from their incarceration. Zamble (1992, p. 410) summarizes: "We included a wide variety of measures of behavior, cognitions, and emotional experience, and examined these changes over a $1\frac{1}{2}$-year period in prison. These measures failed to show a generalized pattern of emotional damage from imprisonment, and, except for a reduction in dysphoria and a loss of apparent motivation for change, psychological functioning was remarkably stable over time in prison." On the other hand, they could not conclude that there were positive psychological effects of imprisonment either. "Our data show very little positive behavioral change in prison, just as earlier we could see little evidence for generalized negative effects" (p. 151). However, when the researchers expanded the period of time to seven years, they were able to conclude "When we follow a group of men over time, we find much more evidence of improvement than of deterioration" (Zamble, 1992, p. 421).

Zamble and his associates found that changes in adaptation particularly occurred in the areas of socialization. That is, the majority of the long-term inmates withdrew from the prison social networks, and spent much of their discretionary time in their cells, or with one or two close friends. Long-termers seem to be living within a world of their own, physically inside the prison, but cognitively outside. "They avoided the entanglements that result from involvement with other inmates, and they began to monitor, analyze, and control their own behavior better" (Zamble, 1992, p. 422).

Toch and Adams also assert that prison experiences can provide positive effects for some inmates, particularly the younger inmates under 25. "Young inmates, who are presumably more rambunctious and less mature than older inmates, appear to derive some benefit from this forced environment. . . it is encouraging to find that prison inmates who are initially most resistant to restrictions on their personal liberty demonstrate increasing levels of conformity over time" (pp. 19–20). Precisely why these effects happen remains largely a mystery, although Toch and Adams (1989a) suggest that the maturation process facilitated by humane prison environments plays a critical role. The researchers contend that inmate behavior is likely to improve when inmates learn the association between behavior and its positive or negative consequences within the institution, and when they have psychological support, the opportunity to participate in conventional activities, to form attachment bonds, and to build relationships.

The above changes in behavior relate to adaptation to prison environments that are humane and supply inmates with a modicum of activities and privileges. To some critics, the "humane prison" may be an oxymoron, but it is clear that there are wide variations in how prisons are operated. Even when inmates adapt and adjust reasonably well to a prison environment, however, their model behavior does not necessarily generalize to behavior in the community, once released. In fact, the discouraging recidivism statistics cited at the beginning of this chapter suggest that, for a large proportion of inmates, the prison experience does not serve as a deterrent to criminal activity. As some psychologists have pointed out, however, recidivism is not the best outcome measure for gauging the effectiveness of *psychological* interventions with inmates (Heilbrun & Griffin, 1999).

In summary, a vast majority of inmates do not exhibit long-standing psychological impairment or problems as a direct result of incarceration. A number of scholars and researchers suggest, though, that current conditions in the nation's prisons and jails are likely to affect this optimistic assessment. Specifically, they argue that we are facing mental health problems of crisis proportions (e.g., Cohen, 2000; Haney & Zimbardo, 1998; Steadman & Veysey, 1997). Of particular concern are the prison and jail conditions associated with crowding and isolation.

Psychological Effects of Crowding

The issue of crowding is becoming increasingly important as correctional institutions are forced to house far more inmates than they were designed to hold. What Haney and Zimbardo (1998, p. 712) call "the runaway punishment train, driven by political steam and fueled by media-induced fear of crime," resulted in the highest rate of incarceration in the nation's history at the end of the 20th century. During the 1980s, state and federal prison population in the U.S. increased by 76%, with the federal prison system growing at a faster rate than the state prison systems (Pelissier, 1991). By the end of 2000, state prisons were operating between full capacity and 15% above capacity, and federal prisons were operating at 31% above capacity (Bureau of Justice Statistics, 2001a). Although we will refer primarily to prison crowding in this section, the reader should be aware that jails have also faced a population crisis. The number of detainees and inmates held in jails more than doubled between 1983 and 1993 (Clear & Cole, 2000).

Not only does such crowding reduce the personal physical and psychological space available, but it also means that the already marginally adequate work and activity programs are offered to fewer inmates or for shorter time periods, thereby increasing inmate confinement and time spent with nothing to do. Crowding brings increases in noise "pollution," and it reduces the opportunity for inmates to remove themselves from constant view and surveillance. Although inmates do not have a right to privacy in their cells, the double-celling that may be necessitated by overcrowding intrudes on what little personal space they have. The problem of crowding is particularly relevant in the dormitory arrangements now common in many prisons, where as many as sixty prisoners may be housed in one large room, spending twenty or more hours together. In some institutions, makeshift accommodations are created in mess halls and gymnasiums.

Crowding can be measured physically or psychologically. Psychologically, crowding is a subjective condition that is based on a person's perception of discomfort as the number of people in his immediate environment increases. Crowding can also be defined objectively as the number of square feet per inmate, a measurement referred to as physical density. In addition, three major categories of dependent variables are used as indices of the effects of crowding: (1) physiological, (2) psychological, and (3) behavioral. Physiological reactions to stress most often include blood pressure. Behavior measures include the number of infractions of prison rules or other forms of misconduct. Psychological measures encompass self-reports of anxiety, depression, hostility, feelings of helplessness, and other indicators of emotional discomfort.

Early and still relevant research suggests that prison and jail overcrowding is associated with higher incidences of physical illness, socially disruptive behavior, and emotional distress (Bukstel & Kilmann, 1980; Cox, Paulus, & McCain, 1984; Ruback & Innes, 1988). Some researchers have further suggested that disruptive behavior and violence in correctional facilities increases directly as the available living space decreases (Megargee, 1976; Nacci, Prather, & Teitelbaum, 1977; Gaes & McGuire, 1984). This relationship seems to be particularly strong for juvenile institutions (Megargee, 1976), and for women prison inmates (Ruback & Carr, 1984).

The available evidence implies that crowding generates stress, which further instigates behavior of trying to cope with it by any available means. Carl Clements (1979) observes that in a New Mexico state penitentiary of 2,000 inmates, 300 were fortunate enough to "earn" solitary confinement for twenty-three hours per day, foregoing programs and many other "privileges." Clements found that these single cells were a sought-after premium, despite the fact that inmates confined to them would be the subjects of disciplinary reports sent to parole boards.

In a 15-year study on prison crowding, Paulus (1988) discovered that increasing the number of residents in correctional facilities significantly increased the negative psychological (tension, anxiety, depression) and physical reactions (e.g., headaches, high blood pressure, cardiovascular problems) in inmates. The critical factor appeared to be the number of residents sharing a particular space rather than simply the footage of space available. For example, providing at least some privacy and limiting the visual and physical contact of other inmates, such as providing cubicles instead of open dormitories, reduces the negative impact of living there.

Paulus also ascertained that socioeconomic level, education level, and prior prison or jail confinements were related to inmate reactions to crowded conditions. That is, the higher the socioeconomic and education level, the more difficult the adjustment to and the lower the tolerance for crowded conditions. One explanation for the socioeconomic-education finding is that many members of lower socioeconomic status are accustomed to living under crowded conditions. Therefore, they are more tolerant of invasions of privacy and other factors involved in crowded environments. Other research, however, has indicated that "advantaged" inmates—those of higher educational and economic levels—actually adjust better overall to being imprisoned than do disadvantaged inmates (e.g., Adams, 1992; DeRosia, 1995). It appears that advantaged inmates are able to benefit from a number of personal and outside resources not available to others.

In the Paulus research, prior confinement in a correctional facility interfered with adjustment to crowded conditions. Specifically, inmates who had some history of prior incarceration exhibited more problems in adjustment than those without prior time. Paulus suggests that individuals with extensive prison histories probably spent at least part of their sentence in single cells or under less crowded conditions and thus were not accustomed to the present-day crowded conditions. Paulus did not find significant gender differences, race or ethnic differences in how individuals react to variations in social density in correctional institutions.

Overcrowding also taxes the correctional staff to the point where it is safest for all if inmates are kept in cells and dormitories as much as possible, except for meal calls. There are fewer constructive jobs for inmates, little exercise, and less access to therapeutic programs, all of which generates inactivity and boredom and, consequently, stress. The forced idleness also engenders a lowering of self-esteem and feelings of incompetence, hardly conducive to any form of rehabilitation or self-improvement.

In summary, the available research does indicate that prison crowding is associated with negative psychological and health reactions for a substantial number of inmates, even though some are able to tolerate these conditions. The U.S. Supreme Court, however, has rejected the argument that overcrowding per se is cruel and unusual punishment in violation of the Eighth Amendment (*Rhodes v. Chapman*, 1981). In the *Rhodes* case, overcrowding was created by the double-celling of inmates into cells measuring 63 square feet. The Court noted that it was not the overcrowding per se, but rather the "totality of the conditions" that should be looked at to determine whether overcrowding represented cruel and unusual punishment. The maximum-security facility in which inmates were housed was less than ten years old and had gymnasiums, schoolrooms, workshops, a recreation field, a garden, and visiting areas, among other amenities. Inmates had ample opportunity to be out of their cells for a substantial portion of the day, and there was a variety of programming options available to them. Thus, despite the double-celling that occurred in the facility, the Court decided that the overall conditions did not reach the status of a Constitutional violation. Nevertheless, three concurring Justices indicated that, although the facility in question did not deprive inmates of the Constitutional rights, overcrowding in other facilities might indeed be cruel and unusual punishment. The present decision, they noted, "should not be construed as a retreat from careful judicial scrutiny of prison conditions" (452 U.S. at 353). Justice Marshall, the lone dissenter, referred to the extensive literature and indicated that each inmate should have sufficient space "to avoid serious mental, emotional, and physical deterioration" (452 U.S. at 371).

Some scholars (e.g., Gaes, 1985) have argued that the direct causal link between crowding and negative effects has yet to be convincingly established. Part of the problem created by overcrowding may be the result of bad management, either in a particular prison or the entire prison system. Administrative changes can be made to reduce the negative effects of high social density. For example, Pelissier (1991) studied the effects of a rapid doubling (in less than 6 months) of the inmate population at a federal correctional facility. Random samples of both staff and prisoners were interviewed before and after the dramatic population expansion. Results showed no overall increase in the rate of rule infractions or illness complaints. Pelissier attributed the findings to the preparedness of the prison staff and administration for the increase. Correctional personnel made certain that prison programs and services were not adversely affected by the rapid growth. In other words, effective management seemed to neutralize any major negative effects of crowding for a majority of both the inmates and the prison staff.

Psychological Effects of Isolation

Inmates may be physically isolated from each other for many different reasons and under a wide variety of conditions. Isolation, solitary confinement, segregation, restrictive housing, and special housing are broad terms used to cover this separation of inmates from the general population. More specifically, *disciplinary segregation* (or punitive isolation) is imposed as punishment for violation of prison rules and regulations. It is limited in time and is typically accompanied by a loss of good time credits. *Administrative segregation* refers to a variety of situations resulting from decisions by corrections officials. They may decide to "lock down" or "keeplock" inmates in their cells for security purposes, while they are investigating an incident in the facility. They may also lock inmates in cells when there is a shortage of staff. (For example, inmates may be locked down while a large number of corrections officers are taking a promotional exam.) Inmates also may be locked down when the population is undergoing medical testing, as for tuberculosis. Under these conditions, the segregation is temporary and, as noted, is in the inmate's regular residential unit. However, administrative segregation also refers to the placement of an inmate into a high-security unit because he or she is considered a threat to prison security, staff, and to the general population. In that case, the segregation may last for years. Inmates assigned to "super-max" or "ultra-max" facilities, to be discussed in more detail below, are in administrative segregation. Another form of isolation is **protective custody**, by which the inmate is separated to protect him or her from possible harm. If the threat of harm comes from the inmate him or herself—for example, the inmate is a suicide risk—the isolation is considered observational in nature and is temporary, until the inmate can be stabilized or transferred to a treatment facility. When the threat of harm comes from other inmates—e.g., in the case of an inmate believed to be vulnerable to sexual assault or a former law enforcement officer—the isolation is longer in duration. Protective custody is not considered a punitive form of isolation; nevertheless, these inmates may have little or no opportunity to participate in prison programs or earn good time credits toward early release.

One little-known illustration of the isolation of inmates occurred in the federal prison system, in Lexington Penitentiary. Three women inmates were kept in an underground, high-security unit for nearly two years. The inmates maintained that they were political prisoners, punished not for their behavior in prison but for their political beliefs. The story of the underground unit is told in the award-winning documentary by Nina Rosenbaum, "Through the Wire." The women were under constant observation by correctional officers, including male officers while they were showering, and all walls and ceilings in the unit were painted a stark white. No natural light came into the environment, and they slept with a light constantly on. The women maintain that they were not only being punished for their beliefs, but were also being subjected to an experiment in sensory deprivation. The Federal Bureau of Prisons shut down the underground unit after the inmates brought court action challenging the conditions of their confinement.

Isolating inmates is not a typical procedure, however. The vast majority of inmates in correctional facilities are housed with the general population. In 1997, for example, the total segregated population comprised only 6.9% of all inmates (Austin & Irwin, 2001). For this small percentage, however, many concerns have been raised, relating both to physical conditions and the psychological effect on inmates. Courts have determined that a minimum quality of care is Constitutionally guaranteed to inmates in all categories of isolation. This care includes adequate food and drink, ventilation, opportunity to exercise, and generally hygienic conditions. When reviewing conditions in isolation, courts also typically take into consideration the amount of time an inmate spends there. Thus a short-term confinement in a stripped-down cell or "safe cell" for the purposes of calming down an inmate in psychological crisis or while awaiting transfer to a treatment facility is acceptable. A lengthy period of confinement in the same cell without treatment is not.

Nevertheless, courts have allowed the segregation of non-mentally disturbed inmates for very long periods of time. In the case of disciplinary or punitive segregation, which may involve not only isolation but also a loss of good time credits, the U.S. Supreme Court gave inmates charged with serious misconduct certain due process guarantees (*Wolff v. McDonnell*, 1974). These included the right to written notice of the charges at least 24 hours in advance; a hearing before an impartial tribunal (but not an outside hearing body); and a written statement of the evidence relied on and the reasons for the disciplinary action taken. In addition, inmates were given a conditional right to call witnesses or present evidence if doing so would not be unduly hazardous to institutional security. No Constitutional right to an attorney was given, but illiterate inmates or those facing complex charges could get assistance from others, including competent inmates or staff. In a later case, *Sandin v. Conner* (1995), the Court ruled that not all disciplinary segregation required the type of hearings provided for in *Wolff v. McDonnell*. Only if the deprivation the inmate faced was "significant and atypical" would a *Wolff*-type hearing be required. In that case, 30 days of disciplinary segregation without a hearing was not considered significant or atypical. Cohen (2000) notes that lower courts continue to struggle with the meaning of that phrase, and that disciplinary segregation of a year without a hearing has even been allowed. "One thing is clear: not very much that is punitive is also an atypical or significant hardship" (pp. 3–25).

Super-Max Facilities In recent years, the form of segregation known as the "super-max" has gained more scrutiny from the public as well as from courts. The super-max (sometimes called "ultra-max") is a high-security unit intended for recalcitrant inmates. Corrections officials maintain that inmates are not typically assigned to these units unless they have created security problems in the general population or are considered serious threats to do so (Riveland, 1999). Inmates who assault staff or other inmates and who do not benefit from ordinary disciplinary segregation are routed to the super-max unit. Today, approximately 41 states have such facilities, holding approximately 100,000 inmates (Cohen, 2000). The state of California has taken the lead, having built four such prisons with a total capacity of 12,000 (Austin & Irwin, 2001). Although the facilities vary in design and operation, their common features include extremely high security, isolation of inmates from each other and correctional officers, and the locking down of the inmate for virtually the whole day, with the exception of time allowed in an exercise yard or area. Cell doors are typically made of stainless steel with slots allowing the delivery of food trays. Alternately, they may be constructed wholly or in part of heavy duty plexiglass that prevents the inmate from throwing anything at security staff.

The threat of harm to inmates and staff continues to be a serious problem in corrections. In 1990, 76 prison homicides were reported in state and federal facilities, and there were close to 10,000 inmate-on-inmate assaults that required medical attention that same year (McCorkle, 1992; Camp & Camp, 1991). In 1998, 79 homicides were reported (Austin & Irwin, 2001). Clear and Cole (2000, p. 258) note that "each year about 150 prisoners commit suicide, about 90 perish in deaths 'caused by another,' and 400 die of unknown causes that were apparently not natural, self-inflicted, accidental, or homicide." They add that there are about 25,000 assaults by other inmates. Sexual assaults add even more incidents; by some estimates, 290,000 males behind bars are sexually assaulted each year (Clear & Cole, 2000). The level of violence in women's prisons is significantly lower, but women inmates are more subject to being sexually assaulted by corrections officers or other staff.

Victims of sexual assault—female and male—frequently resort to self-imposed solitary, spending most of their time in their cells and away from areas in the compound where they may be attacked again (McCorkle, 1992). Many inmates fearful of any physical attack request protective custody, preferring to be locked up 24 hours per day rather than risk attack. Those inmates who do venture into areas of the institution often carry crude weapons constructed from raw materials gathered from their cells or work stations (McCorkle, 1992). For all of the above reasons, the super-max facility is an appealing concept to those who see this high-security approach as a legitimate way of controlling violence. In reality, however, super-max facilities house more than the predatory inmates.

Critics (e.g., Austin & Irwin, 2001; Haney & Zimbardo, 1998) maintain that super-max facilities are a quick fix to the violence within prisons and create far more problems than they solve. Super-max prisons not only are expensive to build, but also may play havoc with inmate adjustment. From a psychological perspective, conditions of isolation for long periods of time are psychologically damaging to inmates. Critics also argue that the super-max units are overused; that prison officials punish inmates who belong to groups considered subversive, or who are predicted to be dangerous, but without their having demonstrated violent behavior. Classification committees, for example, regularly accept the observations of staff, including those of questionable validity (Austin & Irwin, 2001). Most reprehensibly, these facilities are being used for inmates who are mentally disordered. Such inmates are often disruptive, aggressive, and resistant to rules, thereby making them "good" candidates for the super-max facility. However, isolation only aggravates their mental disorder, critics maintain. Additionally, critics are concerned that inmates are released directly to the community from such facilities.

A recent government-sponsored survey of super-max facilities nationwide highlights the legitimacy of a number of the above concerns (Riveland, 1999). Interestingly, there was no common definition or operation among the facilities identified in over 30 states. Some jurisdictions held in "super-max" inmates who needed protective custody, not disciplinary segregation. Some placed mentally ill inmates in their super-max, believing the level of control was necessary because of the paucity of mental health resources available in the system. Minimum lengths of stay varied widely, as did the reported need for supermax beds (ranging from 0% to 20% of the total capacity). Riveland's report ended with a number of recommendations for states, including recommendations that they initiate research on the effects of these facilities on both inmates and staff. He also suggested that professional standards be developed specific to these "extended control" facilities.

A super-max facility in California, The Security Housing Unit (SHU) at Pelican Bay prison was the subject of a class action suit (*Madrid v. Gomez*, 1995). Pelican Bay gained national notoriety when television's "60 Minutes" visited the facility and spoke with some of the inmates and corrections officials involved in the pending suit. In one particularly appalling sequence, an inmate revealed the skin grafts he had received as a result of being forcefully placed in a scalding bath. In another, a clearly mentally disordered inmate described his fears and hallucinations as a result of being locked in his high-tech cell for close to 23 hours a day. Interestingly, two thirds of the inmates are double celled, essentially being forced to spend 23 hours of their day with one other human being. A prison official told the reporter that Pelican Bay was a "success story," that the incidents of violence in the general population had decreased significantly, and that officers and inmates felt safer as a result of having the super-max facility available. As sobering as the television coverage was, it was the court case that outlined in great detail the wide variety of abuses that were endemic to the facility. We will cover this case again later in the chapter.

Conclusions about Isolation The psychological effects of isolation are of major concern. Enlightened prison officials, clinicians, legal scholars, and human rights advocates agree that conditions of sensory and social deprivation are inappropriate for persons with serious mental disorders. However, there is less agreement on the issue of whether a stable individual is harmed psychologically by being placed in isolation (Benjamin & Lux, 1977). Psychiatrist Stuart Grassian (1983), who testified in the Pelican Bay case, argues forcefully that solitary confinement in itself produces a strong likelihood that even a stable person will develop chronic mental illness and that an already mentally ill individual will deteriorate even further.

Much of what we know about the psychological effects of isolation has come from research using college-student or community volunteers, who submit to social isolation for varying periods of time, usually in cells similar to those used in correctional settings. Generally, the methodology has been sound, and relevant but very tentative conclusions can be drawn (Bukstel & Kilmann, 1980). The ecological validity of this research remains questionable, however, primarily because conditions used in the research rarely simulate those in prison settings. Furthermore, as noted above, there is a wide range of conditions under which inmates are isolated. In one prison, inmates may be able to see and even communicate with others similarly isolated. In another, the cells may be covered with plexiglass, allowing them to see but not throw things. In still another, a small, barred opening in the cell door may be their only way of seeing out.

It comes as no surprise, also, that the research with volunteers has found that individuals respond differently to solitude; some are glad to be away from the noise and activity of everyday living, while others demonstrate behavioral indicators of stress and frustration. Solitary confinement of a week or less does not appear to produce significant changes in motor behavior or perceptual or cognitive functioning (Walters, Callagan & Newman, 1963; Weinberg, 1967). Additional data suggest that, for most persons, solitary confinement does not generate more stress than would be expected in normal prison life (Ecclestone et al., 1974; Gendreau et al., 1972). These data are based on situations in which the primary focus was on social isolation for brief periods of time, and not on sensory deprivation or the deprivation of necessities of life. The introduction of additional deprivations, like cutting off food supplies or any sounds, is known to produce substantial changes in a number of psychological functions (Zubek, 1969). In the prison context, food supplies would not be cut off but they might be limited. Additionally, conditions in isolation may be "eerily silent," the term used by the reporter covering the Pelican Bay story.

The very few studies examining the effects of involuntary solitary confinement in correctional facilities have found that there do not seem to be any deleterious effects on inmates over the short haul (less than seven days) (Suedfeld, Ramirez, Deaton, & Baker-Brown, 1982), but there might be for those inmates placed in solitary confinement for up to a year (Grassian, 1983). Taken as a whole, the research does not show long-lasting deleterious effects, and the negative effects that are reported may heavily depend upon how the inmate is treated while in solitary. "When inmates are dealt with capriciously by management or individual custodial officers, psychological stress can be created even in the most humane of prison environments" (Bonta & Gendreau, 1990, p. 361).

Legal Rights of Inmates

Inmates do not lose their Constitutional rights at the prison gate. This principle has been established in a wide range of Supreme Court decisions involving procedures, practices, and conditions of confinement. Although we have referred to some of these decisions throughout this and earlier chapters, we will summarize here the key doctrines that are most relevant to psychologists consulting with prison systems or offering services to inmates. Readers are referred to the excellent treatises of Cohen (1998, 2000, 2003) and Palmer and Palmer (1999) for comprehensive coverage of correctional law.

When the Supreme Court interprets the Constitution to guarantee certain rights to citizens, those rights are the *minimum* that must be provided. State constitutions and statutes may provide additional protections to inmates within the custody of their state systems, and many do. For example, in some states inmates are allowed to cast ballots in general elections. Some states have liberal visitation privileges, whereas others limit visits to one or two days a month. The amount of "good time" credit earned by an inmate also varies widely from state to state. The Constitutional rights and limitations, as interpreted by the Supreme Court, are of course the law and of the land and will be the focus of our discussion here.

Although inmates do not have a right to rehabilitation, they do have a right to adequate medical care, as stated by the Court in *Estelle v. Gamble* (1976). Although the case involved care for physical ailments, it has widely been interpreted to include psychological or psychiatric assistance for mental disorder. To deprive the inmate of medical care violates the Eighth Amendment ban on cruel and unusual punishment. The standard for what is adequate medical care is troubling, however. In *Estelle v. Gamble*, the Court indicated that "deliberate indifference to the needs of inmates" violates the Constitution. In a later case, *Farmer v. Brennan* (1999), however, the Court retreated from the breadth of this standard. A prison official may not be found liable for denying an inmate humane conditions of confinement, the Justices said, "unless the official knows of and disregards an excessive risk to inmate health or safety. The Court added that if an official *should have known* of a substantial risk, but did not, the official's failure to alleviate the risk did not constitute cruel and unusual punishment. Farmer was a pre-operative transsexual who was raped soon after his transfer to a federal penitentiary that had a violent environment and a history of sexual assaults. Following the court decision, he had the extremely difficult task of proving that officials knew of the dangers he faced and nonetheless disregarded those dangers by placing him in the general population (Cohen, 2000).

Inmates cannot be forced to participate in treatment programs, although as we saw in *McKune v. Lile* (2002), incentives very much resembling punishment—though not defined as punishment by corrections officials—may be given for failure to participate if the state has a strong interest in achieving rehabilitation. Lile was a convicted rapist within two years of serving his sentence and being released, so the state had a strong interest in enrolling him in a sex offender treatment program that required him to disclose his history of offending, without guaranteeing that the information would be privileged. Likewise, though inmates have a right to refuse medication, the Court has allowed prison officials to give an inmate psychoactive drugs against his will, if it is determined in an administrative hearing that such medication is necessary to control the inmate's disruptive behavior (*Washington v. Harper*, 1990).

Despite the negative psychological effects of overcrowding, the Supreme Court has rejected the premise that overcrowding, in and of itself, violates the Constitution's ban on cruel and unusual punishment (*Rhodes v. Chapman*, 1981). The Court also refused to give inmates a Constitutional right to privacy that prohibited prison officials from searching their cells without warning and out of their presence (*Hudson v. Palmer*, 1984). Lower federal courts, however, have given inmates a right to privacy with respect to opposite sex corrections officers. For example, when male inmates are showering or toileting, they have a right not to be observed by female officers, and vice versa. Similar prohibitions have been placed against body cavity searches, an unfortunate reality of prison life.

Jail detainees, who have not been convicted, have been given very little protection by the U.S. Supreme Court. In *Bell v. Wolfish* (1979), the leading case, the Supreme Court allowed a range of policies and procedures designed to preserve institutional security. Thus, detainees were unsuccessful in their attempt to prevent jail officials from opening packages and other mail, conducting body cavity searches, and holding them in crowded conditions affording virtually no privacy. Although the detainees regarded the conditions as punitive, the Court ruled that jail officials did not intend them to be punitive. Rather, they were necessary for maintaining the security of the facility.

A number of court cases, including U.S. Supreme Court cases, have addressed special situations encountered by mentally disordered inmates in the nation's prisons. As noted earlier in the chapter, inmates facing the death penalty may not be executed if they are "incompetent," which is generally defined as being too mentally disordered to appreciate what is happening to them or why it is occurring (*Ford v. Wainwright*, 1986). It is now unconstitutional to execute the mentally retarded as well (*Atkins v. Virginia*, 2002). Mentally disordered inmates have a right to treatment under the disease model recognized in *Estelle v. Gamble* (1976). Mentally disordered inmates facing a transfer to a mental health facility are entitled to a hearing to challenge that transfer (*Vitek v. Jones*, 1980), though as we noted in ◀ Chapter 5, such transfers are rarely challenged (Cohen, 2000).

Interestingly, the increasing numbers of mentally disordered offenders in the nation's jails and prisons have led to an unfortunate reality. Mentally stable inmates have feared for their own safety and, in some cases, have been physically assaulted by disruptive mentally ill inmates. This has led to suits by non-mentally ill detainees and offenders who do not want to be housed with their disordered counterparts. Thus far, the suits have been restricted to the lower courts. One court, writing in support of stable inmates, referred to the "pandemonium and bedlam the mentally stable inmates must suffer because they are intermingled with the mentally ill inmates who either cannot or do not control their behavior. One particular portion of cellhouse 220 was so bad that it was commonly known as 'the bug range'" (*Goff v. Harper*, 1999). In the *Goff* case, the court made it very clear that correctional facilities must attend to the rights of the non-mentally disordered when they assign inmates to housing units. Cohen (2000) raises an important consideration, however. "One hopes that the emphasis on problems caused by inmates with mental illness does not further demonize this group. That is, the kind of disruption imposed on the complaining inmates should be per se intolerable. With the mentally ill, and especially during periods of medication noncompliance, some inmates may have no control over their hallucinations, their talking or crying at night, and their screaming [however]" (Cohen, 2000, p. S11–5).

The segregation of mentally disordered inmates also can create legal problems. Courts have allowed severely disturbed inmates to be placed in stripped down observation cells—sometimes referred to as "safe cells"—for their own protection. They may be kept under extremely stark conditions while awaiting transfer to a treatment facility or until they can be stabilized with appropriate medication, but there are limitations on this type of confinement. A suit against the New York Department of Corrections (*Perri v. Coughlin*, 1999), is illustrative. Perri was an extremely disruptive, severely disordered inmate in the New York State prison system that was held in an observational cell on three separate occasions, for a total of 108 days. The cell contained only a sink and toilet, and a brightly glaring light was on 24 hours a day. He had no clothes or blankets and had to sleep naked on the floor. The observational unit provided no opportunity for exercise, recreation, or group therapy. Essentially, there was no programming. Numerous other deprivations are outlined in the suit, which Perri eventually won. Lengthy confinement, coupled with failure to offer treatment, apparently led to the court's decision holding the Department of Corrections liable for damages (Cohen, 2000).

The Supreme Court has yet to hear a case involving conditions of confinement in "super-max" facilities, but lower courts have weighed in on this issue, as was discussed earlier in the chapter. In a major class action suit brought by inmates at California's Pelican Bay facility (*Madrid v. Gomez*, 1995), the federal district court issued a lengthy opinion outlining numerous findings of fact relating to the use of force, physical and mental health care, and a variety of other conditions facing inmates of the facility. The court found Constitutional violations in a pattern of excessive force, the provision of medical and mental health care, and in the maintaining of mentally ill inmates in the secure housing unit (SHU). Nevertheless, the court did not find a Constitutional violation in the SHU for *stable* inmates. "Conditions in the SHU may well hover on the edge of what is humanly tolerable for those with normal resilience, particularly when endured for extended periods of time. They do not, however, violate exacting Eighth Amendment standards, except for the specific population subgroups identified in this opinion." The special populations referred to were those who were already mentally ill and those who were at unreasonably high risk of suffering serious mental illness as a result of the conditions. In similar fashion, the confinement of mentally ill inmates in an administrative segregation unit of the Texas prison system were declared in violation of the Constitution (*Ruiz v. Johnson*, 1999).

Many inmate Constitutional rights were recognized by the Supreme Court in the 1960s and 1970s, before a more conservative judiciary took the bench. Since 1980, inmates tend to have won fewer cases at the Supreme Court level, although there have still been notable victories. In *Pennsylvania v. Yeskey* (1999), the Supreme Court ruled unanimously that inmates in state prisons were covered by the *Americans With Disabilities Act* (ADA). Thus, prisons must make reasonable accommodations for inmates. The law, which has been in effect since 1996, protects disabled individuals from discrimination in a wide range of settings. Since the law's passage, numerous lawsuits have been brought and courts have struggled with defining the disability intended by Congress as well as determining when employers in particular had violated the law.

In recent years, the U.S. Supreme Court has issued a number of decisions limiting the range of the ADA, however. In rejecting the claim of an employee who alleged discrimination because she had carpal tunnel syndrome, the Court ruled that the disability must be of the sort that prevents or severely restricts activities that are of central importance to most people's lives (*Toyota v. Williams*, 2002). The Court also said, in the same year, that a company may refuse to hire a person with a disability for a job that could exacerbate the problem (*Chevron v. Echazabal*, 2002). In a close decision (5-4), the Court ruled that an employer does not have to bypass its seniority system to offer a job to a disabled employee with less seniority (*U.S. Airways v. Barnett*, 2002). In a significant decision especially relevant to our discussion, the Court ruled unanimously that punitive damages were inappropriate when individuals sued the government under the ADA or the closely related Rehabilitation Act of 1973 and won (*Barnes v. Gorman*, 2002). Gorman, a paraplegic, sued Kansas City after its police officers transported him in a van which did not have proper accommodations for his disability. Gorman, who had been arrested after an altercation in a bar, suffered a bladder infection and lower-back pain and spasms, leaving him unable to work. A jury awarded Gorman $1 million in compensatory damages and $1.2 million in punitive damages. In striking down the punitive damages, the Court said that allowing such damages could be disastrous for state and local governments. The decision has obvious implications for suits against correctional authorities. Still, inmates, like other plaintiffs, might still be able to collect damages for the harms they *actually* suffered.

Also in recent years, Congress has notably restricted inmate suits with the passage of the *Prison Litigation Reform Act* (PLRA), signed into law in 1996. The law reflected Congressional concerns with an influx of inmate claims in the federal courts, which by the mid 1990s had absorbed more than 15% of the federal caseload (Palmer & Palmer, 1999). Although correctional observers recognize that many inmate suits are frivolous, corrections law also documents the many meritorious claims that have reached the courts. "The emphasis and purpose of the new legislation was to limit the ability of prisoners to complain about their conditions of confinement and to limit the jurisdiction of the federal courts to issue orders relieving conditions of confinement that allegedly violated the constitutional rights of prisoners" (Palmer & Palmer, 1999, p. 338). The Act places many restraints on inmate litigation, discourages the filing of *in pauperis* petitions, limits the remedies available to inmates, and cuts funds for special masters, who are typically lawyers assigned by the courts to monitor court-ordered changes. A key and very controversial provision of the PLRA is its requirement that all administrative remedies be exhausted before federal courts may consider inmate suits brought with respect to prison conditions. In a recent interpretation of that section of the law, the U.S. Supreme Court in *Porter et al. v. Nussle* (2002) made it clear that this restriction applies to all inmate condition suits, even those based on very individualized incidents alleging the use of excessive force.

Nussle, an inmate in a Connecticut prison, filed suit in federal court, charging that Porter and other correction officers had singled him out for a severe beating, in violation of the Eighth Amendment's prohibition of cruel and unusual punishment. (Corrections officials, like law enforcement officers, may use reasonable force under certain conditions. For example, force is not considered excessive if used in self-defense, defense of third persons, to enforce prison rules and regulations when necessary, to prevent escape, or to prevent a crime (Palmer & Palmer, 1999). Beatings must not be inflicted as punishment, however.) Nussle alleged that officers struck him with their hands, kneed him in the back, pulled his hair, and told him they would kill him if he reported the beating.

Although the Connecticut Department of Correction, like all state systems, had a grievance process in place, Nussle bypassed this process and went directly to federal district court, which dismissed his complaint because he had not exhausted the administrative remedies available to him. The Second Circuit Court of Appeals reversed, however, noting that the PLRA did not require exhaustion in inmate claims of assault or excessive force. Officer brutality, the

Appeals Court indicated, was far different from the frivolous suits Congress hoped to discourage with the passage of the PLRA. The U.S. Supreme Court noted that other federal appeals courts had ruled quite differently from the 2nd Circuit in similar cases, and therefore accepted the case to resolve the conflict.

According to the Court, all inmate suits, including those alleging excessive force, must exhaust inmate grievance or other administrative procedures before the initiation of a federal case. In a unanimous opinion delivered by Justice Ruth Bader Ginsburg, the Court noted that Congress intended that corrections officials be given time and opportunity to address complaints internally and to improve prison conditions. Such a requirement would also filter out some frivolous claims. Furthermore, an administrative record would help clarify the contours of the case if it eventually reached the federal court. Critics of the decision agree with the 2nd Circuit, however, that officer brutality and excessive force are special circumstances that should not be left to in-house investigation. The surprisingly unanimous decision by the Court may signal its desire to leave the running of prisons to prison officials in all but the most egregious of cases affecting the total inmate population as a whole. As Palmer and Palmer (1999, p. 339) conclude, "Congress, in effect, mandated a return to 'hard time' for prisoners." With this latest decision, the Supreme Court seems to have given its blessing. And, as another scholar has stated, "Today the federal courts have been relegated to remote outposts to be contacted only in the case of extreme emergencies. Even after contact is made, so to speak, the desired help likely will not be there" (Cohen, 2003, p. S20-6).

Summary and Conclusions

The late John Conrad, an expert in corrections, wrote (1982, p. 328) that the prison will exist for the foreseeable future and will inevitably be an authoritarian community. "Intelligently managed, it can be a benevolent despotism at best; stupidly managed, it will belie our national claim to magnanimity, becoming either a dangerous anarchy or the worse of tyrannies." An intelligently managed prison, Conrad argued, was safe and secure for both inmates and staff, industrious, lawful, and hopeful. As we have suggested throughout this chapter, many observers of prisons and jails today might argue that we have made little progress in achieving Conrad's standards of intelligent management. The blame lies, not solely or even primarily with correctional administrators, but rather with contemporary social policies that promote punitive responses without regard to the predictable outcomes.

Psychologists working in institutional corrections can play a significant role in helping to achieve safety and security, but most importantly in providing hope. We have focused in this chapter on their two main, broad functions, to assess and to treat. Through their involvement in the classification process, psychologists can recommend programs which will best match offenders to their needs. These might include substance abuse treatment programs, development of reading and writing skills, decision making, anger control, meaningful job training, contact with families, or sex offender treatment. Unfortunately, due to numerous factors ranging from budgetary constraints to staff resistance, recommended programs may not be available. Psychologists also can be alert to signs of impending serious mental disorder and recommend preventive measures. In their treatment role, they may offer individual or group therapy to inmates on a voluntary basis, with a minimum goal of helping them to cope with the realities of prison life. Ideally, however, treatment also should result in permanent change that will be reflected in pro-social behavior once an inmate has been released.

Most offenders adjust to their confinement and manage to survive, with the earliest and latest stages appearing to be critical periods. Special adjustment problems face certain categories of offenders, including those in solitary confinement and the mentally disordered. Jail detainees and inmates need at least as much psychological attention as prison inmates; as noted in the chapter, the suicide rate in jails is significantly higher than that in prisons. Gender and cultural differences also may affect how one copes with the pains of imprisonment. Adjustment to prison is extremely individualistic, however, and it cannot be assumed that an individual belonging to a vulnerable group will have trouble coping, nor that a normally stable offender will not be in need of crisis services. Although we have not discussed them here, other categories of offenders such as elderly inmates and those with AIDS or other physically debilitating illnesses also need special attention. Overcrowding, which was the number one problem for correctional institutions in the 1980s, continues to be vexing, to say the least; it has had a significant, negative psychological effect on prison inmates, as the research in that area demonstrates.

The goals or rationales of sentencing were examined from a psychological perspective. Incapacitation, as we noted, has little justification if it is based on predictions of dangerousness, as selective incapacitation tends to be. Retribution, which seems to be a noble goal, is seldom truly achieved. Furthermore, retributive sentencing, which is most usually harsh, has contributed to the overcrowding problem and has not reduced disparity in sentencing. There is some indication that general deterrence works for some offenders and crimes. However, much more research in this area is needed before we can say with confidence that there is psychological support for this rationale. With respect to crimes that carry the death penalty, however, general deterrence is not supported. In fact, there is some evidence that capital punishment has a brutalizing effect on society. If recidivism statistics are any indication, the specific deterrent effect of incarceration is not impressive.

Psychology has directed a good deal of attention toward the merits of rehabilitation in the prison setting, and again the research is not heartening. Martinson's (1974) conclusions, although overstated, still apply to many rehabilitative programs offered by prisons, particularly when rehabilitation is measured with the recidivism yardstick. Nevertheless, some psychological approaches, particularly those based on bringing about cognitive-behavioral change, show promise. As with all therapeutic measures, psychological rehabilitation in the prison setting is most likely to occur if the offenders are motivated to obtain the treatment and if the "system" does not place obstacles in its way.

The chapter ended with an overview of those legal rights of inmates that are most closely related to psychology. Although the Supreme Court, lower federal courts, and state courts have supported many inmate claims, they also have allowed practices and procedures that, to many observers, seem incompatible with a humane approach to incarceration. Decisions that allow overcrowded conditions of confinement, deny inmates a right to appeal their transfer to other prisons, or place obstacles in the way of inmates attempting to document cruel and unusual treatment with reference to their health needs are but a few examples. With the passage of the PLRA, Congress also has put inmates on notice that their access to the federal courts has been limited.

In the light of ever-present challenges facing prison administrators, and in light of troubling conditions in many of the nation's prisons and jails, society must recognize that it cannot continue to incarcerate its offenders at unprecedented rates. The wisest policy approaches to pursue include broad, society based crime prevention programs, the decriminalization of some offenses, and the development of suitable community-based alternatives to incarceration.

Key Terms

Brutalization effect
Community-based facilities
General deterrence
Incapacitation
Intermediate sanctions
Paraphilia
Principle of nonmalificence
Prison
Prisonization
Protective custody
Psychological treatment
Psychotherapy
Rehabilitation
Restorative justice
Retribution
"Scared Straight"
Selective incapacitation
Shock probation
Specific deterrence

Questions for Review

1. What are the main differences between prisons and jails?
2. Identify and explain briefly the four traditional goals of corrections.
3. Discuss Martinson's 1974 study and its effect on attitudes toward rehabilitation.
4. Identify features of prison environments that present challenges to the successful psychological treatment of inmates.

5. At a minimum, at which points in an inmate's incarceration should psychological assessment occur?
6. What legal and ethical issues are involved when psychologists conduct evaluations of an inmate's competency to be executed? What guidelines have been provided to psychologists conducting such evaluations?
7. Distinguish between the terms psychological treatment and rehabilitation. What do the two have in common?
8. List and define briefly the most common forms of treatment offered by psychologists in correctional facilities.
9. Describe the Stanford Prison Experiment and its results, and discuss the criticisms that have been directed at it.
10. Discuss findings from research on (a) prison and jail suicide; (b) gender differences in prison adjustment; and (c) overall adaptation of inmates to prison.
11. Which features of the prison environment are most psychologically damaging to vulnerable inmates?
12. What are super-max or ultra-max facilities, and what is controversial about them from a psychological perspective?

CHAPTER 11

Psychology and Family Law

Family law includes some of the most wrenching and contentious issues facing society, issues relating to marriage, divorce, child custody, children's rights, medical decisions, the end of life, and a wide range of matters influencing the welfare of children. It covers statutes, court decisions, and provisions that relate to family relationships, rights, duties, and finances. The subset of family law that encompasses children's issues—e.g., child dependency, neglect, abuse, and child custody—is usually referred to as "child welfare law" (Brooks, 1999). A further distinction can be made between child welfare law and juvenile law, with the latter focusing on children and adolescents who have violated or are at serious risk of violating the law. ▶ [Because juvenile law has expanded dramatically and raises a host of separate legal questions, we will be dealing with it in a separate chapter, Chapter 12.]

Still another topic closely related to family law but not generally considered under its rubric is education law, which comprises rights and responsibilities of students, particularly in public elementary and secondary schools. Wandering into the area of education law would take us well beyond the bounds of this book, despite the fact that education law clearly encompasses psychological issues. For example, topics revolving around educational testing, sexual harassment, sex education, special education, freedom of expression, privacy, and corporal punishment are the "stuff" of education law.

Without doubt, psychologists as researchers and as practitioners have much to offer family law, and their contributions have increased and expanded steadily over the past quarter century. The primary purpose of this chapter is to offer a necessarily brief overview of the knowledge obtained as a result of that research and practice. A second goal is to provide basic information about concepts and procedures associated with family law, including child welfare law but excluding, for the time being, juvenile law.

It should be recognized, however, that a substantial number of psychologists are uncomfortable about delving into an arena that intrudes into family life, especially when the law is partner in this process. This reluctance is particularly evident in the divorce context when child custody decision making is involved. It is one thing to provide psychological evaluations, counseling, and treatment directly to members of a family; it is quite another to provide information and testimony to courts that may then be used against the wishes of one or both parents. Some clinicians also prefer not to participate in matters relating to the termination of parental rights or the competence of adolescents to make decisions. Others are hesitant to be involved in end of life issues such as the right to die, where family members may be pitted against one another or even against the wishes of a terminally ill individual.

The law itself has historically been reluctant to invade the sanctity of family life. We have seen this particularly in the domestic violence context, where courts historically allowed husbands to beat their wives and parents to discipline their children with minimal oversight. Punitive, legal responses to domestic violence—a willingness to place a criminal assault label on it, for example—are less than 50 years old in many jurisdictions. Moreover, there continues to be resistance to the prosecution of domestic violence cases in some states, particularly when adults are victims (Caringella-MacDonald, 1997; Crowell & Burgess, 1996).

Psychologists and other clinicians, as well as legal practitioners, also debate among themselves the merits of adversary versus conciliatory approaches to family problems. The paradigms of **therapeutic jurisprudence** and **preventive law** have zealously invaded the family law arena (e.g., Brooks, 1999; Winick, Wexler, & Dauer, 1999). Therapeutic jurisprudence, as we have noted in previous chapters, advocates the use of law as a therapeutic agent and has been discussed in a wide range of contexts (see, generally, Wexler, 1999; Wexler & Winick, 1991). Preventive law is a recently-identified approach in law that tries—through a variety of mediational and conciliatory techniques—to minimize the risk of litigation and ensure that people's rights and responsibilities are respected and recognized (Brooks, 1999; Schneider, 1999). An active and vocal group of scholars have called for reforms in the family law context that would benefit the family system as a whole and would serve society better than the current adversarial and divisive approaches. Tesler (1999a, 1999b), for example, calls for a "collaborative law" paradigm in response to the harms of family law litigation and the limitations of some forms of family mediation. By contrast, Bryan (1999) considers collaborative law a quick fix that does not serve the best interests of women and dependent children. We will return to these arguments later in the chapter, in our discussion of divorce, mediation, and related topics.

It should be emphasized at the outset that the very definition of "family" is undergoing both social and legal change. Although family in most jurisdictions still is limited to relationships by blood or marriage, legal decisions in a variety of contexts indicate a willingness to recognize alternative relationships. For example, domestic partnerships between individuals who can not otherwise legally marry may qualify as family, with consequent rights and responsibilities. The State of Vermont has led the nation in passing landmark legislation recognizing legal civil unions between gays and lesbians. Under the new law, gay and lesbian partners who formalize their union are entitled to the same legal rights as those who marry under the state's marriage statutes. Similar laws are under consideration in other states, and the issue itself is presently before the Massachusetts Supreme Judicial Court, the court of last resort in that state. Also, in some states, court decisions have supported the rights of adolescents to define their own family preference or to become emancipated.

Family systems theory, as championed by those who argue for a preventive law approach, depends upon the mutual interaction and shared responsibility within a family group. It seeks to identify common interests and arrive at decisions that will most ideally promote them. As Brooks (1999) notes, this does not mean that the family will necessarily stay together as a unit. "Family systems analysis sets up a framework and a process of thinking; it does not preference a specific outcome" (Brooks, 1999, p. 961). Brooks also notes that the family system is defined by bonds of intimacy and may include extended family members as well as other individuals who have no biological connections to one another.

The chapter begins with a focus on the dissolution of the traditional family group and its effects on dependent children. When courts are asked to decide on the custody of dependent children, this can be a difficult and heart-wrenching task. Judges often turn to psychologists and other mental health practitioners for assistance.

Divorce and Child Custody

Divorce rates have remained steady in recent years, with approximately 50% of first marriages ending in divorce within 15 years (U.S. Bureau of the Census, 2002). It is estimated that over 40% of all children will experience the divorce of their parents during their childhood and adolescence (Krauss & Sales, 2000), and that between 50 and 60% of children born in the 1990s will live, at some point, in single-parent families (Hetherington, Bridges, & Insabella, 1998). There is considerable agreement that, on average, children from divorced and remarried families have more problems in adjustment than do those in non-divorced, two-parent families, but there is less agreement on the size of these effects (Hetherington et al., 1998). It is widely believed, and supported by empirical research, that divorce itself is likely to have negative effects on children (Krauss & Sales, 2000), at least in the short term. Long term effects are less clearcut. About 75% of divorced mothers and 80% of divorced fathers remarry; the divorce rate for remarriages, however, is even higher than for first marriages (Hetherington et al., 1998). Therefore, children are at risk not only to suffer the emotional upheaval of family discord and custody associated with the initial divorce, but many also experience a series of marital transitions and household breakups in subsequent divorces.

In a divorce, four major areas of potential dispute must be settled: (1) property division; (2) spousal support; and, if there are children, (3) child support; and (4) custody and visitation. The psychological research in the area has been almost exclusively on issues surrounding custody and visitation, an area we shall focus on in this chapter.

Since mental health professionals are frequently involved when courts decide child custody, this is an important topic to cover. Nevertheless, we should keep in mind that a relatively small proportion of these custody decisions is made by the courts. Large scale studies have revealed that courts make the ultimate decision in only 6 to 20% of custody cases, the remaining being resolved by joint agreement between the divorcing parents, with or without the help of out-of-court dispute resolution or mediation (Melton et al., 1997).

The decision as to who will have custody over a minor child may arise in several contexts, not just divorce (Hess & Brinson, 1999). First, parents or other relatives of the child may be involved in a custody dispute following not only a divorce but also the death of one or both parents. Second, a state agency may be seeking to assume temporary or permanent custody over the children of parents who are allegedly neglectful or abusive. Third, and more rarely, in a variety of situations surrogate parents, unwed fathers, domestic partners, or friends may seek to gain custody. The great majority of the research in this area has focused on the determination of custody in divorce situations.

Custodial Arrangements

In most states there are four basic custodial arrangements: sole custody, divided custody, joint custody, and split custody. These four arrangements are based on two fundamental categories of parental decision making authority: legal and physical. **Legal parental authority** refers to decision making concerning the child's long-term welfare, education, medical care, religious upbringing, and other issues significantly affecting the child's life. **Physical authority** involves decisions affecting only the child's daily activities, such as deciding whether the child can stay overnight at a friend's house, attend a party, or have access to the parent's car. In some situations, however, the dividing line between legal and physical authority is blurred, as when a 15-year-old wants to work 20 hours a week to earn extra spending money. It could be argued that, although this seems to relate to the child's day to day life, the decision may have long-term implications if school work suffers as a result. The type of authority—legal or physical—exercised over the child will vary according to the custodial arrangement.

The most common arrangement is **sole custody**, where one parent has both legal and physical authority and the other parent does not, although the noncustodial parent usually retains visitation rights. In most sole custody decisions (85 to 90%), the mother becomes the custodial parent and the father the noncustodial parent (Glick, 1988; Hetherington et al., 1998). Another arrangement is **divided custody**, where each parent is afforded legal and physical decision making powers, but on an alternating basis. That is, the parental decision making authority shifts (usually on a six month basis), depending on which parent the child is living with as well as the location of the child's school district. If the parents live close to each other within the child's district, the "shift" may be as often as every five days or weekly. At the time the child is with one parent, that parent makes both the legal and physical decisions for the child. **Joint custody** is where both parents share legal authority but the children live predominantly with one parent, who will have the physical authority to make the day-to-day decisions. Deciding upon physical authority, however, is often troublesome in joint custody arrangements and can result in conflict and disagreement between the parents. One resolution of this problem is an arrangement called **limited joint custody** where both parents share legal authority but one parent is given exclusive physical authority and the other parent is awarded liberal visitation rights. **Split custody** is a custodial arrangement where the legal and physical authority of one or more children is awarded to one parent, and the legal and physical authority of the remaining children to the other. Normally, each parent is given reciprocal visitation rights. Although there may be variants of any of the above arrangements, one of the four is generally observed.

Child Custody Evaluations

In those cases in which courts must decide who will be given custody of a minor child, they often turn to mental health examiners for assistance. Psychologists appear to be the most frequently used examiners (Mason & Quirk, 1997). Child custody evaluations are extremely difficult and challenging to perform, however, and numerous commentators have remarked that they are emotionally charged and pose many ethical dilemmas. They are among the most dangerous and risky endeavors for psychologists, because of the high levels of stress, threat of litigation, risk of licensing board complaints, and the risk of personal harm (Kirkland & Kirkland, 2001). Furthermore, child custody evaluations require not only knowledge of the legal system, but also "expertise in child development and psychopathology, adult adjustment and psychopathology, family systems, and special custody issues arising from allegations of substance abuse, domestic violence, physical abuse, sexual abuse, or any combination of these" (Bow & Quinnell, 2001, p. 261).

The reliance on experts in this area can be attributed to a variety of factors, including high divorce rates and the heavy workload of family court judges. However, research also documents that the very process of assessment often leads to a settlement of the custody dispute between parents, without need for further court intervention (Radovanovic et al., 1994). Lawyers have indicated that assessment is a desirable alternative to litigation, although they have also preferred mediation with its greater likelihood of solving family problems (Lee, Beauregard, & Hunsley, 1998). There are contrary views on this matter, though, as we will see later in the chapter. Both the legal and the scientific community have typically expressed the view that judges alone, without input from other professionals, are the least desirable decision makers when it comes to determining custody. Additionally, the doctrines traditionally used by courts in making custody decisions no longer necessarily apply. For example, throughout most of the twentieth century courts applied the **tender years doctrine**, which held that fostering the mother-child relationship, particularly before age seven, was critical to the child's development; thus the mother was presumed to be deserving of custody unless it was demonstrated that she was unfit.

The tender years doctrine was articulated as follows by an Illinois Appellate Court in 1899, in *People v. Hickey*. "In awarding care and custody of children of divorced persons, an infant of tender years will generally be left with the mother, where no objection is shown to exist as to her, even if the father be without blame, *because of the father's inability to bestow on it that tender care which nature requires, and which it is the peculiar province of the mother to supply*; and this rule will apply with much force in case of female children of a more advanced age" (Einhorn, 1986, p. 128).

The tender years doctrine has virtually been abolished or abandoned in most states, largely on the basis of three challenges (Santilli & Roberts, 1990). *First*, it has been argued that the tender years doctrine is a violation of the equal protection provided under the Fourteenth Amendment (Radcliff, 1977). *Second*, the doctrine is also in violation of equal rights amendments found in many state constitutions. *Third*, it makes a number of psychological assumptions about parenting that may or may not be valid.

Today, we know that mothers and fathers are equally capable of nurturing their children (Lamb, 1996). Nevertheless, feminist scholars raise the critical point that, in reality, the female parent has usually been the primary caretaker of the child, is most likely to want custody, and has a greater pre-divorce investment in the child (Fineman, 1988). Failure to recognize this reality places the female parent at a disadvantage when other standards are applied.

A standard with similar deficiencies to the tender years doctrine is the "psychological parent" rule, which was proposed by psychoanalytically-oriented psychologists (Goldstein, Freud, & Solnit, 1979) who believed that a child's primary need was a seemingly omnipotent, omnipresent attachment figure (Melton et al., 1997). This standard thus attempts to identify the parent to whom the child is most attached. It also suggests that this parent should have the sole custody of the child and be empowered to make all legal and medical decisions. Furthermore, the standard would allow the psychological parent to regulate all contact with the "nonpsychological parent," including the frequency of visitation. In essence, contact with the noncustodial parent could be minimized. In the event that both parents were equally attached to the child, they would draw straws for custody. As Krauss and Sales (2000) have noted, the empirical research has expressly contradicted the theory on which the psychological parent rule is based. The assumption that one parent is psychologically unfit to care for the child is unwarranted. Furthermore, attempts to measure "attachment" create methodological as well as ethical problems. Although the psychological parent standard is not applied in many courts today, "it is still a factor in some court decisions and an element of the child custody assessments performed by many psychologists (Krauss & Sales, 2000, p. 847).

The **best interests of the child** standard (BICS) has become the predominant one used in most courts when rendering custody decisions. According to this standard, the parents' legal rights should be secondary to what is best for the child, though how to arrive at that determination remains extremely problematic. As we will explain shortly, some commentators have proposed a more realistic, **least detrimental alternative** standard. The best interests of the child standard was recommended in the *Uniform Marriage and Divorce Act*, developed by the National Conference of Commissioners on Uniform State Laws and endorsed by the American Bar Association (Lowery, 1984). However, the best interest standard has been criticized as being overly vague and leaving too much discretion to the judge (Fineman, 1988; Schneider, 1991; Scott, 1992). Presumably, factors to be taken into consideration under BICS may include primary caretaking, moral fitness, emotional attachment, the child's wishes, and who can better provide for the child's physical needs, among many others. Consequently, there is no universal agreement over what actually constitutes the best interest of the child. One well-regarded approach, the Michigan Best Interests of the Child statutory criteria, provides a list of specific factors to consider in child custody cases. Evaluators do not necessarily agree on the respective weights to give to the factors, however. Moreover, different courts attach more importance to some than others (Gould, 1998; Mason & Quirk, 1997). Finally, as Bow and Quinnell (2001) discovered, a term such as "moral fitness" is elusive and can refer to a wide variety of behaviors.

In sum, numerous factors are taken into account today in awarding custody, including the wishes of the children themselves. In a case where custody is contested, therefore, either court appointed neutral experts or examiners hired by the parties are used. Although counselors, social workers, and psychiatrists are sometimes involved in these custody evaluations, members of the legal profession seem to prefer psychologists (LaFortune & Carpenter, 1996).

A wide variety of problems with custody evaluations have been identified, however. They include lack of specific training, questions about the validity of the evaluation methods, lack of neutrality, and quality of the reports submitted to the courts. Custody evaluations are also associated with ethical problems and with complaints to state licensing boards (Bow & Quinnell, 2001; Fineman, 1988; Kirkland & Kirkland, 2001; LaFortune & Carpenter, 1998). Kirkland and Kirkland (2001) report that approximately 10% of all new cases of ethics violations compiled by the American Psychological Association involve custody evaluation complaints. In an effort to bring some direction to the process of custody evaluations, the APA has adopted *Guidelines for Child Custody Evaluations* (1994). The 16 guidelines focus on the purpose of the evaluation, the expertise needed by the examiner, and standards relating to the examination process itself ◙ (see **Box 11-1** for a summary of these guidelines).

Surveys of Custody Evaluation Practices. The custody evaluation process itself has come under the research microscope, and this has often led to conclusions that are critical of existing practices. Some commentators (e.g., Melton et al., 1997; Roseby, 1995) have protested the use of classic IQ and personality tests, arguing that they are irrelevant to the legal issues that must be resolved by the courts. Keilin and Bloom (1986) found that interviews and observations were the primary methods used in making child custody recommendations, resulting in opinions that have been criticized as having no scientific basis. In

BOX 11-1
Guidelines for Child Custody Evaluations in Divorce Proceedings*

Note: The Guidelines, according to the American Psychological Association, are not meant to be exhaustive or mandatory. They are divided into three broad areas, as outlined below in boldface. Each specific guideline is accompanied by annotated text. The material below that is not in boldface illustrates, but does not quote directly, some of the text annotations.

I. Orienting Guidelines

1. The primary purpose of the evaluation is to assess the best psychological interests of the child.
2. The child's interests and well-being are paramount.
3. The focus of the evaluation is on parenting capacity, the psychological and developmental needs of the child, and the resulting fit.

   The values of the parents relevant to parenting are considered. Psychopathology of parents may be relevant, but it is not the primary focus.

II. General Guidelines

4. The role of the psychologist is that of a professional expert who strives to maintain an objective, impartial stance.

   The psychologist should be impartial, regardless of whether retained by the court or by one of the parties. The psychologist should not act as an advocating attorney.

5. The psychologist gains specialized competence.

   This guideline encourages the psychologist to be familiar with the laws of the state, to seek additional training and supervision as needed, and to use current knowledge of the profession. Competence in performing psychological assessments of children, adults, and families is necessary but not sufficient.

6. The psychologist is aware of personal and societal biases and engages in nondiscriminatory practice.
7. The psychologist avoids multiple relationships.

   It is recommended that psychologists generally avoid conducting an evaluation in a case in which they have served in a therapeutic role. Therapeutic

a replication, Ackerman and Ackerman (1997) surveyed 201 psychologists and learned that the average amount of time spent on testing had more than doubled, to 5.2 hours. Most recently, examiners are beginning to use a variety of instruments specifically designed to assess the parent-child relationship or to evaluate parenting competencies. (See Heinze & Grisso, 1996, for a review of these instruments.) Podrygula (1997) has urged psychologists to rely on such instruments as the Parent-Child Relationship Inventory (PCRI), Parenting Stress Index (PSI), Bricklin Perceptual Scales (BPS), Perception of Relationship Test (PORT), and a variety of custody batteries, such as ASPECT and ACCESS. Krauss and Sales (2000), however, suggest that these instruments are not grounded in research and that they are more likely to reflect what the instrument designer believes is a measure of good parenting. In a similar vein, Otto and Heilbrun (2002), commenting on the current state of forensic psychology, warn against premature use of instruments, including some mentioned above, that have been published with limited research data and prior to any formal peer review. As mentioned earlier in the book, Otto and Heilbrun have remarked that attorneys and judges are becoming increasingly sophisticated and knowledgeable about the science of assessment. A 2002 court decision involving parental rights from the Texas Court of Appeals is illustrative. The court faulted the trial court for its blind reliance on expert testimony describing the results of a psychological test (the Abel Assessment) and reversed a jury's termination of

BOX 11-1
Continued

contact following an evaluation should be undertaken with caution.

III. Procedural Guidelines

8. The scope of the evaluation is determined by the evaluator, based on the nature of the referral question.
9. The psychologist obtains informed consent from all adult participants and, as appropriate, informs child participants.
10. The psychologist informs participants about the limits of confidentiality and the disclosure of information.
11. The psychologist uses multiple methods of data gathering.

    Psychologists are encouraged to make use of the clinical interview, observation, and/or psychological assessments. It is also recommended that they obtain relevant reports, such as from schools or child care providers, and contact third parties. When information from third parties is significant and may form the basis for a conclusion, such information should be corroborated and documented wherever possible.

12. The psychologist neither overinterprets nor inappropriately interprets clinical or assessment data.
13. The psychologist does not give an opinion regarding the psychological functioning of any individual who has not been personally evaluated.
14. Recommendations, if any, are based on what is in the best psychological interests of the child.

    The Guidelines do not take a position on the "ultimate issue" question, noting that there is no consensus. However, psychologists should be aware of the arguments on both sides of this issue and should guard against relying on their own biases if they choose to render an opinion.

15. The psychologist clarifies financial arrangements.
16. The psychologist maintains written records.

    All data are recorded with an eye toward possible review by other psychologists or the court.

parental rights (Harris, 2002). The judge in the trial court had failed to press the expert on the technique or methodology from which he derived his opinions.

LaFortune and Carpenter (1998) surveyed 165 mental health professionals in five states whose work includes child custody evaluations. Their 196-item questionnaire sought information on demographics, experience and training, attitudes toward legal professionals and the legal process, methods of conducting evaluations, time spent, and fees. The researchers also hoped to measure the extent to which the evaluators adopted the *APA Custody Evaluation Guidelines*.

They learned that the examiners were primarily therapists rather than researchers or assessors. Custody evaluations were a modest part of their work, conducting on average eight such evaluations per year. In light of the critical importance of custody evaluations and the need to have them performed by persons with specialized competence, Kirk Heilbrun (1995) argues that no less than 25% of an assessor's clinical work should be devoted to these assessments.

The examiners in LaFortune and Carpenter's sample of respondents did not lack general training in assessment. For example, 87% had had a graduate course on assessment of families and children. However, less than one-third (29.7%) were involved in research. In fact, respondents considered performing research relatively unimportant. Furthermore, they were not highly concerned about perceptions that their assessment methods lacked validity.

The examiners were moderately to strongly dissatisfied with the legal system, particularly with the adversarial nature of custody proceedings. They strongly preferred being appointed by the courts as neutral examiners rather than being employed by one party. Interestingly, a sizeable portion of respondents (47.3%) felt they should advocate for one party or the other, and 53.4% felt they should help attorneys for one or the other side. As LaFortune and Carpenter note, this raises ethical questions, since the *APA Custody Guidelines* advocate neutrality on the part of the examiner.

In a broader study, Quinnell and Bow (2001) reviewed surveys obtained from 198 psychologists nationwide (38 states) who performed custody evaluations. They were particularly interested in learning the extent to which evaluators relied upon psychological tests, and if so, on which tests. They also wanted to determine the extent to which the current practices employed by the psychologists were congruent with the *APA Guidelines*. Both psychological testing of the child and psychological testing of the parent ranked behind clinical interviews and observations. However, approximately 90% of the adults and 60% of the parents were tested. The use of IQ tests appears to be declining from earlier studies, although a small subgroup continued to administer them to every adult (17%) and every child (14%). The objective personality test used the most extensively was the MMPI–2, used by 94% of the psychologists for adults and 43% for adolescents. Psychologists also used the Rorschach Ink Blot Test (44% with adults; 23% with children and adolescents). The projective test used the most frequently with children and adolescents was Family Drawing or Kinetic Family Drawing (45%).

The most dramatic change uncovered was the increased use of parent rating scales and parenting inventories, the second generation of testing instruments reviewed by Heinze and Grisso (1996). Summarizing their research, Bow and Quinnell noted that they had identified five discernible trends in psychological testing: (1) Psychological testing is moderately important, less than clinical interviews; (2) Objective tests are used widely with adults; projective tests used with children; (3) Children are being tested less frequently than in the past; (4) IQ tests are being used less frequently; and (5) Parent inventories are being used more. (Parent inventories are questionnaires that probe such things as the attitudes and child rearing practices of parents.)

The average cost of the evaluations, based on a family of two parents and two children, was $3,335, a figure that limits their affordability for many families. However, the cost does not seem excessive when the comprehensive nature of the evaluation is considered. Quinnell and Bow learned that the average number of hours devoted to the process was 24.5, with a range of 5-90 hours. The average time frame from beginning to end was 9.27 weeks.

The results of the study indicated that psychologists responding to the surveys used multiple methods of data collection, as recommended by the *Guidelines*, and also had developed specialized experience through workshops and seminars. Virtually all respondents (94%) routinely made explicit recommendations to the courts about the ultimate issue of custody/visitation. The respondents were also asked to rank order the three most important criteria from the attributes of the Michigan Best Interests Scale, considered a model approach to making custody decisions (Gould, 1998). The capacity and disposition to provide love, affection, and guidance was at the top, followed by a willingness to encourage a continuing relationship with the other parent. The presence and impact of family violence was a third crucial criterion. Factors such as the permanence of the family unit, school records, and moral fitness of the parents were the least crucial.

Ethical Considerations Bow and Quinnell concluded that psychologists seem to be doing a better job conducting custody evaluations than previous studies had indicated. Increases in legal awareness, professionalism, and training have resulted in improved performance of evaluators. They find, though, that certain ethical dilemmas remain unresolved. For example, some of the evaluators handled attorney requests for raw test data by either refusing to provide them or by sending the data directly to lawyers without question. *Ethical Principles* of the APA (APA, 1992) indicate that raw data should be released only to qualified individuals and only when legally permitted. Most of the respondents did forward requested raw data to another licensed psychologist chosen or approved by the attorney requesting the data, however, which is in keeping with the principles. Another ethical dilemma involved payment, with the vast majority of respondents requiring full payment before releasing their reports. As mentioned earlier, the high costs of these evaluations suggests that they will be unavailable to many families who might be able to benefit from them.

Conducting custody evaluations, whether for the courts or for private parties, is an area fraught with ethical and legal pitfalls. In the Bow and Quinnell (2001) survey, 35% of the respondents had had at least one complaint filed against them before professional conduct boards. Ten percent reported malpractice suits. Although these complaints and suits may have been dismissed, as respondents noted in marginal comments, they are still a source of stress and financial strain to the practitioner as well as to the parties involved in the custody proceeding. It is in the clinician's best interest, therefore, in addition to the best interest of the child, to obtain specialized training, be aware of developments in the law, and follow guidelines adopted by her or his profession.

Psychologists have much knowledge to offer on the psychosocial development and adjustment of children, adult adjustment, and a variety of issues that may be relevant to making a custody decision (Bow & Quinnell, 2001). Not everyone agrees that this knowledge is *directly* relevant for determining standards and guidelines for legal custody following a separation, divorce, or remarriage, however (Krauss & Sales, 2000; Melton et al., 1997). There is disagreement over whether psychologists should be involved in these assessments at all, and most particularly whether they should offer opinions on the "ultimate issue" of which parent should obtain custody (O'Donohue & Bradley, 1999; Weisz, 1999). Recall that Bow and Quinnell's (2001) study revealed that almost all of the psychologists in their sample did, indeed, provide a recommendation.

Krauss and Sales (2000) maintain that psychological knowledge cannot tell what custody arrangements are effective, but rather can tell which are *unlikely* to be effective. For example, if there is high hostility between parents, a shared custody arrangement is unlikely to be effective. Krauss and Sales urge the adoption of a **least detrimental alternative** (LDA) standard, which better reflects both what is actually done and what both the legal and psychological world is capable of achieving. In reality, "judges determine child custody on the basis of a negative standard—which custodial arrangement will do the least harm to the child rather than which custodial arrangement will be in the child's best interest" (p. 873).

Krauss and Sales also note that psychological instruments tend to be pathology-focused, measuring deficits more than strengths. Additionally, a rich store of research has identified child, parental, family process, and legal characteristics that affect a child's adjustment to divorce. This is the knowledge that should be most useful to the courts. Even with these data, though, Krauss and Sales urge psychologists to refrain from making specific custodial recommendations for specific children, or generalizing from the group data to what is appropriate for a particular child. We turn now to a review of some of this research.

Psychological Effects of Divorce and Custody Arrangements

The psychological effects of divorce and custody arrangements may be looked at both separately and in concert. Divorce and custody represent two discernible sequences in the life of the child, and much of the research literature in this area focuses on one or the other. Other research, however, focuses on their joint effect.

A caveat is in order before proceeding. Although there exists a rich store of studies on the effects of divorce and custody arrangements, the methodological rigor of many studies has been seriously questioned (Bricklin & Elliot, 1995; Melton et al., 1997; Krauss & Sales, 2000; Rohman et al., 1990). Krauss & Sales (2000) classify these methodological problems into three distinct categories: operational definition problems, internal validity problems, and external validity problems. Particularly salient in the first category is inability of researchers to develop a uniform construct for the BICS (an inability not limited to researchers).

Psychological Effects of Divorce The most heavily cited empirical studies on the effects of divorce are the Virginia Longitudinal Study of Divorce conducted by E. Mavis Hetherington, M. Cox, and R. Cox (1979) and the Wallerstein ongoing studies of 60 divorced families in Northern California (e.g. Wallerstein & Kelly, 1980). The Virginia project was a quasi-experimental study of 72 white, middle-class four- and five-year-old children and their divorced parents. The researchers learned that marital discord and divorce often results in an increase in behavioral problems, and that the nature of these problems is largely dependent on the age of the child (Hetherington, 1979). Later research began to suggest that young children experienced greater short-term harmful effects to both divorce and custody arrangements, while older children experienced more long-term effects (Rohman et al., 1990; Sales et al., 1992).

Early research (e.g., Hetherington, 1979) also indicated that behavioral problems are generally more pervasive and longer lasting for boys than girls. Emotional disturbances and social adjustment problems in girls largely disappeared within two years after the divorce. Moreover, the period of adjustment for children seems to be longer when a parent remarries, especially for older children (Hetherington et al., 1979). In fact, the bulk of the research evidence suggests that divorce is harder on adolescents than on very young children. Later research began to suggest that girls were more likely than boys to internalize problems associated with the divorce. Reviews of research that incorporate recent studies, however, indicate that there is now no clearcut evidence that gender has a significant effect on post-divorce adjustment (Krauss & Sales, 2000).

The Wallerstein project (Wallerstein & Kelly, 1980; Wallerstein, 1989) is an extensive clinical investigation of 131 children and their parents from 60 predominately white, middle-class families. Wallerstein found that children's initial responses to divorce depended on, among other things, the individual differences in the children's perception of the divorce, developmental factors, and their adaptive capacities. Each age group reacted differently to the divorce, ranging from anger to regression.

James Bray (1990, 1991), in his work on the effects of divorce, also emphasizes that children's reactions to parental separation, divorce, and remarriage differ significantly as a function of age. Bray posits that these events are *not* necessarily worse for children of certain ages; only that children of various ages have different reactions and, in some case, different behavior disorders. He notes that there is yet no direct evidence on the effects of custodial or visitation arrangements for infants (birth to six months), although research on the effects of daycare on infants may provide helpful information for making custody decisions. The daycare research suggests that very young children can adapt to short and regular separations from custodial parents. During the pre-school ages (three to five years), children may experience separation anxiety (fear of leaving parent) if their parents also become particularly tense and upset about the parent-child separation. As Bray notes, children are generally highly susceptible to the feelings of parents at this age and react, sometimes strongly, to any conflict between parents. During the school age and pre-adolescent period, children have developed clear preferences for one or both parents and are very sensitive to subtle pressures and loyalty conflicts between parents (Bray, 1991). Further, Bray finds that children at this age are usually not able to fully understand divorce or to separate themselves psychologically from parental influence. However, during adolescence, children are usually able to understand the divorce process and tend not to be overly influenced by parental wishes or reactions. Recall, though, that other research indicates that divorce is particularly hard on adolescents.

In their review of the literature, Amato and Keith (1991) conclude that children of divorce have lower levels of well-being than do children who experience parental death. This finding, Amato and Keith note, suggests that there must be something else operating in divorced family dynamics than simple parental loss. Amato and Keith also found that children living with a step-parent exhibited significantly more problems than did children living with both biological parents.

As described previously, divorce often leads to a decline in the standard of living, particularly in mother-headed families. However, the research shows that the economic effect of divorce shows only a modest association with the emotional well-being of the children. Many studies do not control for socioeconomic status, however, so we must interpret this with caution (Bryan, 1999). On the other hand, the conflict between the parents before and after the divorce is a severe stressor for children. The negative effect of family conflict on the emotional well-being of children is commonly reported in the literature. In fact, the evidence suggests that children of divorced families appear to have a higher level of well-being than do children of high-conflict *intact* families. Post-divorce conflict between parents is also associated with low level of well-being among children (Bryan, 1999).

Interestingly, research is mixed with respect to the effect of a custodial parent's emotional adjustment. Some studies suggest that children are negatively impacted if the custodial parent is emotionally unstable, such as by having personality disorders, being anxious, or depressed (e.g., Johnston, 1995), while others suggest that other factors are more important than the parent's emotional state (Bricklin & Elliot, 1995). Krauss & Sales (2000) note that, considering the fact that methodologically sound studies have reached conflicting conclusions, emotional adjustment of the parent should be considered but should not play a primary role in determining custody.

Warm parent-child relationships and parenting skills, however, are consistently empirically supported as a critical factor in positive adjustment. Maccoby et al. (1993) found that a number of such skills were linked to good outcomes for children of divorce. For example, adequate monitoring, consistent expectations, joint decision making when appropriate between the custodial parent and the child, and an organized household all contributed to positive adjustment.

The quality of the relationship between the divorcing couple also has been demonstrated to affect the child's adjustment. If the parents are hostile to one another, this is likely to have a negative impact on the child's adjustment (Maccoby et al., 1993; Johnston, 1995; Bricklin & Elliot, 1995; Kelly, 1993). On the other hand, there is also evidence that the effect of the hostility between parents can be tempered if the child does not perceive him or herself in the middle of the conflict (Bricklin & Elliot, 1995; Johnston, 1995; Kelly, 1993).

Bryan (1999, p. 1005), reviewing much of the available literature documenting negative effects of divorce, is careful to add a cautionary note. "Some of the negative research findings on divorced children come from populations of children in therapy. Moreover, many early studies do not compare the findings on divorced children to findings on children from intact families." She adds that other studies do not control for socioeconomic status, noting that downward financial mobility may account for negative effects. "Moreover, researchers consistently find that children adapt better in a well-functioning single-parent family than in a conflict-ridden two-parent family" (Bryan, 1999, p. 1005).

Interestingly, some research on the *long term effects* of divorce suggest that a majority of children adjust well to divorce (Grych & Fincham, 1992). Children seem to be more competent, resilient, and adaptive than adults assume. In fact, many parents have more difficulty adjusting to divorce than the children. But there is clear evidence that, at least over the *short term*, many children do have difficulty adjusting. According to Grych and Fincham (1992), most of the child behavioral problems reported in divorced families are *externalizing problems* (going against the social environment). That is, aggression and conduct problems are more prevalent in children from divorced families than children from intact families (Camara & Resnick, 1988). This seems especially the case for boys. The literature also reports a number of *internalizing problems* (such as depression, anxiety, and social withdrawal) in children who have experienced divorce, particularly during the first two years after the divorce (Grych & Fincham, 1992). Whether the psychological reactions and behavioral problems demonstrated by children of divorced parents are directly due to the divorce or other factors is unclear. Some research, for example, reports that child behavioral problems, assumed to be caused by divorce, may have existed long before the divorce proceedings began, while the family was still intact (Block, Block, & Gjerde, 1986). Unfortunately, we cannot know the extent to which parental discord might have affected the child's problems.

In summary, while we must be very careful in applying group data to individual adaptation, a few conclusions can be drawn from the divorce adjustment research. First, high hostility or conflict between parents is detrimental to children, both in intact families and during and after divorce. This is attenuated somewhat if the child does not perceive him or herself as being at the root of the conflict.

Second, warm parent-child relationships and parenting skills in at least one parent—and preferably both—are predictive of positive adjustment to divorce. Third, though research on gender and age differences in adjustment has produced mixed results, adolescents seem to be particularly negatively affected by divorce. Finally, the well documented decline in standard of living for mothers and children does not appear to affect the *emotional* well being of the children, but more research in this area is clearly needed.

Psychological Effects of Custody Arrangements Research on the effects of custody arrangements is as mixed and inconclusive as research on the effects of divorce itself, but like that research some tentative conclusions can be drawn. Most of the attention has been directed at exploring the merits of joint custody. Additionally, some of this research has compared children in joint and sole custody situations.

Two early reviews of the research on joint custody (Clingempeel & Reppucci, 1982; Scott & Derdeyn, 1984) concluded that few conclusions could be drawn about its effect on the development of children. In their review, Clingempeel and Reppucci (1982, p. 124) asserted: "The available studies (on joint custody) are egregiously inadequate, and for the most part the debates have been nourished solely by opposing ideologies" (parenthesis added).

Margaret Crosbie-Burnett (1991) examined the effects of joint custody and sole custody arrangements on white adolescents living in remarried families. Seventy-eight families living in a small midwestern city volunteered for the project. The Revised Children's Manifest Anxiety Scale and Stepfamily Adjustment Scale administered in each family's home were used as the measures of adjustment. The results supported the hypothesis that adolescents of joint custody arrangements are better adjusted that those of sole custody arrangements. Some significant gender differences also emerged. The adolescent girls seemed to benefit more from joint custody than the boys, but the reasons for this difference remain unclear.

Likewise, some research (e.g., Buchanan, Maccoby, & Dornsbusch, 1991; Johnston, 1995; Maccoby et al., 1993) has indicated that girls adjust better when placed with a sole maternal parent or in a joint custody arrangement than when placed with a sole paternal parent. No similar finding has yet been reported for boys.

Some early research on joint custody suggested that it was stressful and magnified the problems children already experience as a result of the divorce. However, parental hostility was usually considered the variable that contributed significantly to the "failure" of joint custody; if parents were not hostile toward one another, joint custody would work (Buchanan et al., 1991; Johnston, 1995; Maccoby et al., 1993). Meta-analyses produced somewhat more favorable reviews of joint custody. Bauserman (1997), performing a meta-analysis of 21 studies, concluded that children in joint residential custody scored better on a wide range of adjustment variables than children in sole maternal custody. More recently, Bauserman (2002) extended his meta-analysis to 33 studies published between 1982 and 1999. He concluded that children in joint custody arrangements had fewer behavior and emotional problems, higher self-esteem, better family relations and better school performance than children in sole custody arrangements. Nevertheless, Bauserman does not support joint custody in all situations. He notes that if one parent is abusive or neglectful or has a serious mental or physical health problem, joint custody is not recommended.

A recent study by Gunnoe and Braver (2001), attempts to put these seemingly contradictory findings into perspective and suggests that we should be very cautious in drawing conclusions about the respective benefits of sole and joint custody. The researchers compared families in which mothers had sole custody with families in which the parents shared *legal* custody but the children resided with the mother. (The families were derived from a data set of the Study of Separating Families (SSF), an NICHD-funded longitudinal study of 340 families (Braver, Wolchik, & Sandler, 1985). Two years after the divorce, both children and fathers benefited by the joint custody, as indicated by more frequent father-child visitation and fewer child adjustment problems. Mothers were more dissatisfied by the arrangement, however. More rapid re-partnering of mothers was associated with joint legal custody, a fact that can create new adjustment problems for the children. Interestingly, the researchers found that pre-decree parental conflict did not affect the findings, nor did the custody arrangement affect post-divorce conflict.

Furthermore, although some evidence suggests that, in most instances, joint custody arrangements appear to be psychologically more healthy for the children involved than sole custody (Bauserman, 2002; Kelly, 1988; Maccoby et al., 1993), at least two warnings are in order. First, the available research also indicates that the overall effects of joint custody may be only *slightly* more positive than other forms of custody arrangements (Grych & Finchman, 1992). Second, joint custody may be contraindicated when certain family process variables, such as hostility between the parents, are present (Buchanan et al., 1991; Johnston, 1995; Maccoby et al., 1993).

Researchers also have begun to examine the effects of mediated custodial arrangements as opposed to those litigated in the courts (Dillion & Emery, 1996; Emery et al., 1994; Kitzmann & Emery, 1993; Pearson & Thoennes, 1989). There is very little evidence that a mediated custodial arrangement results in a significantly better adjustment for the child than one imposed by the court. Mediation as it applies to divorce in general will be discussed shortly.

In summary, conclusions concerning the psychological effects of divorce or custodial arrangements are difficult to make because much of the research is (1) inconclusive; (2) of limited generalizability; and (3) flawed by serious methodological problems (Grych & Fincham, 1992; Barber & Eccles, 1992; Krauss & Sales, 2000). Very few longitudinal studies have been conducted, making it nearly impossible to untangle preexisting differences in values, behavior patterns, and personality from differences that are directly a result of divorce (Block, Block, & Gjerde, 1986). Long-term studies create their own problems however, as Bricklin (1995) and Krauss and Sales (2000) have pointed out in their respective reviews of methodological problems. They are expensive and time consuming, and, more importantly from a validity perspective, they have high drop out rates. We cannot assume that the participants who remain with the study are representative of the original sample.

Although the research on the psychological effects of custodial arrangements on children remains inconclusive, there are trends in the data. What little evidence we have suggests that a child's adjustment to various arrangements depends on many factors, including the age and gender of the child, the length of time the process takes place, family economic resources, parental conflict before and after the divorce, and the personality differences of the child (Barber & Eccles, 1992). There is some evidence that joint custody may be slightly better for the child from a psychological perspective, but these effects may be due more to the quality of the post-divorce relationship between the parents than to the arrangement itself. Additionally, the literature is very clear that for the great majority of women and children, standard of living declines after a divorce, which obviously affects the "success" of a sole custody arrangement. It seems quite clear that joint custody is a questionable arrangement when there is high hostility between parents; furthermore, it appears that sole custody provided to the male parent has a greater negative effect on girls than joint custody or sole custody to the female parent. Even so, caution is urged. After an extensive review of the literature in this area, Krauss & Sales (2000, pp. 858–859) concluded as follows: "(E)mpirical research does not support the superiority of one custodial arrangement, presumptive custody standard, or legal procedure to solve custody disputes. The assumptions underlying the tender years doctrine, the psychological parent rule, the joint custody presumption, and the mandatory mediation presumption have received little (if any) empirical support from the existing psychological research."

Divorce Mediation

Divorce mediation is a process of trying to resolve divorce disputes with the help of a professional mediator. A primary objective of the process is to reduce the adversarial relations between the divorcing parties. Proponents of mediation maintain that adversarial maneuvering by the parties often prolongs court involvement and affects minor children in a negative way. Adversary proceedings, particularly relative to custody determinations, often further strain already fragile relationships between the divorcing parents.

"In divorce mediation, the marital partners meet together with an impartial third party in order to identify, discuss, and ultimately resolve their disputes" (Emery & Wyer, 1987a, p. 472). The goal is not *reconciliation* but negotiation of a *fair agreement* between the parties. Traditionally, divorce settlements have been reached either through often-bruising litigation or out-of-court negotiations between the parties' lawyers. Divorce mediation differs from these traditional strategies in three fundamental ways: (1) The communication takes place with a single professional mediator; (2) the mediation is based on an assumption of cooperation; and (3) the parties make their own decisions (Emery & Wyer, 1987a). The third feature also distinguishes mediation from arbitration because mediators have no authority to impose decisions on the parties. They act as neutral agents who provide opinions and guidance in the search for a settlement. Professional mediators, who are members of the Family Mediation Association, must have a minimum of 40 hours' training. They are frequently trained psychologists or social workers but may also be attorneys.

Robert Emery and Melissa Wyer identify two major reasons why divorce mediation became so popular, beginning in the mid to late 1960s. One is the enactment of "no fault" divorce laws by all 50 states, a development that renders mediation a reasonable alternative to adversary proceedings. The second involves changes in the guidelines for awarding custody. "The rapid increase in no-fault divorce and elimination of the tender-years presumption leave the judiciary with no strong guidelines for making custody determinations as the best-interests standard is a vague directive open to many alternative interpretations" (Emery & Wyer, 1987a, p. 473). The best solution in many instances, therefore, rests with divorce mediation where a voluntary settlement and custody arrangement can be reached. As we noted earlier, however, there is no evidence that a mediated custody arrangement is significantly better for the adjustment of the child than a voluntary or court-imposed arrangement (Dillion & Emery, 1996).

Nevertheless, early research in this area uncovered a variety of positive effects. Mediation kept a significant number of families out of court, and custody agreements reached through this process took half the time of in-court litigation (Emery et al., 1994; Emery & Wyer, 1987a). Between one-half and three-quarters of couples who went through mediation were believed to reach mutually satisfactory agreements. Mediation seemed to lead to greater compliance with child support and to greater cooperation between parents (Pearson & Thoennes, 1989). Available data also suggested that court mediators worked primarily with divorcing partners who had attempted but failed to reach a settlement out of court (Emery & Wyer, 1987a). Joint custody was the most common mediation agreement. Mediation also appeared to reduce substantially the amount of re-litigation (going back to court) on custody arrangements later on.

Not all research was positive, however. Kelly (1996) remarked that the mediation movement encompassed such a vast array of strategies that results of evaluations could not be generalized. Divorce mediation may or may not involve attorneys, mediators work alone or in teams, sessions vary in length and location, and there is wide variance in the degree of training provided to mediators. Other scholars (e.g., Rifkin, 1989; Bryan, 1999) have expressed grave concerns about power imbalances between the spouses, particularly when there are dependent children and the woman has little or no independent income.

And while some data suggest that divorcing parties are generally more satisfied with mediation than with adversary procedures (Emery & Wyer, 1987a; Kelly, 1996), when couples have children, there may be some differences in satisfaction between mothers and fathers (Emery & Wyer, 1987a; Emery, Matthews, & Wyer, 1994). Men report considerably greater satisfaction with the mediation process than women. Specifically, men are positive about its impact on them personally as well as their relationships with their former spouses. Women, on the other hand, may be positive about its effect on children, but they also feel that they personally won less and lost more than did women who had gone through litigation (Dillion & Emery, 1996). Women who experienced mediation also report more depression than women who went through litigation for custody determination (Emery, Matthews, & Wyer, 1994).

One explanation for these negative effects could be the residual effects of the long-standing tender years presumption, which had traditionally favored awarding custody to the mother. Thus, within that legal tradition, mediation may be seen as a loss for mothers and gain for fathers. Several writers have argued that culturally-developed power imbalances between men and women are more apt to be at fault (e.g., Bryan, 1999; Emery & Wyer, 1987a; Grych & Fincham, 1992; Rifkin, 1989). Numerous scholars have commented that the interests of women and children are not addressed sufficiently in mediation (Rifkin, 1989; Bryan, 1999). Men have been traditionally employed in occupations that require negotiation, bargaining, financial, and management skills. Thus, many women may be at a strong disadvantage in mediation. Furthermore, women often have less power in the marital relationship. Therefore, although the mediation process assumes the parties are on equal footing, this is often not the case. Rifkin (1989) adds that mediators themselves may not be well trained to understand the dynamics of such unequal circumstances. When gender imbalances cannot be recognized and accounted for, mediation should not be undertaken.

In a review of the divorce mediation research, Beck and Sales (2000) have concluded that the earlier enthusiasm for divorce mediation might well have been premature. They identify a wide range of methodological problems, including inadequate sample sizes, lack of control groups, and nonrandom assignment, among many deficiencies. Inconsistent findings also exist across studies. For example, gender differences in satisfaction with the mediation process are not that apparent; many studies document dissatisfaction among men as well as women, but for different reasons. Beck and Sales also note that the time and cost saving aspects of mediation is not universally demonstrated.

Despite the above concerns, there appears to be continued support among legal professionals for the mediation approach, particularly when children are involved (Lee, Beauregard, & Hunsley, 1998). Mediation presents a way to avoid the acerbic courtroom battle that devastates the family. Rather than do away with it, mediation should be "fixed." Some scholars suggest alternate paradigms. Tesler (1999a), for example, champions "collaborative law," which she argues is superior to the traditional mediation approach. Although mediation can work for some couples, she cites several weaknesses, including many of those discussed above. Collaborative law, by contrast, has both lawyers committed to finding a solution that will be satisfactory to both sides. Both parties agree to continue to work toward this outcome; should one party threaten litigation, both attorneys are obliged to withdraw from the case. Consultants and experts are retained jointly, so that there is no pitting of one expert against another. Critics of the collaborative approach (e.g., Bryan, 1999) argue that it has many of the same shortcomings of both traditional lawyer representation and mediation. "(W)e cannot reasonably expect to 'fix' a complex social problem with a simple procedure. If our children truly represent our future, we must enact reforms that comprehensively address the significant social problems that divorce implicates" (Bryan, 1999, p. 1017).

Domestic Violence

During the 1970s and 1980s, family violence came to the forefront of public attention, and research in that area has proliferated. Although the phenomenon originally focused on parental assault of children and spousal abuse, it has since expanded to encompass sibling violence, abuse of elderly parents by their adult children, and violence between cohabiting but unmarried partners, including same-sex partners. Essentially, family violence refers to any assault, battery, sexual assault, sexual battery, or any criminal offenses resulting in personal injury or death of one family or household member by another who is residing in the same single-dwelling unit (Wallace & Seymour, 2001). Furthermore, family violence "is an ongoing, debilitating experience of physical , psychological, and/or sexual abuse in the home, associated with increased isolation from the outside world and limited personal freedom and accessibility to resources" (Wallace & Seymour, 2001, p. 4).

Note that the definition encompasses individuals residing together who might not traditionally been considered "family," which is why many researchers prefer the term *domestic violence*. Thus, non-married couples with or without children, adults caring for unrelated children or elderly persons, and long-term room-mates would all come under the rubric. Still another category of violence not covered in the above term, however, is violence between intimate partners who are not living together or between former intimate partners. Although there is research in all of the above areas, we will concentrate on child abuse and intimate partner violence, specifically on violence against women.

Child Abuse and Neglect (Maltreatment)

The modern era of child abuse research began in 1962 when a Denver pediatrician (C. Henry Kempe) and four of his medical colleagues published a paper entitled "The Battered Child Syndrome" in the Journal of the American Medical Association. The article documented evidence of repeated multiple bone fractures of children suspected of being physically abused. The paper certainly was not the only precipitating factor in prompting interest and research in child abuse. During the 1960s, an influential child welfare movement, intent on drawing public and political attention to the plight of abused and neglected children, was also a strong factor. Nevertheless, it was not until the last quarter of the 20th century that society began to realize that child abuse is a serious matter, worthy of state scrutiny. Even in 1970, national polls reported that only 10% of the general population considered child abuse a serious problem. In 1983, however, over 90% of the population considered it a serious problem (Wolfe, 1985).

Many researchers have noted that incidences of child abuse and neglect have increased in recent years (U.S. Advisory Board on Child Abuse and Neglect, 1995). Wang and Daro (1998) cited a 41% increase in reports to child protective services over the ten year period 1988 to 1997. The reports were substantiated for one-third of the children involved, specifically 1,054,000 children. According to experts, the dramatic increase in child abuse cases is not necessarily due to any explosion in maltreatment of children. Rather, it probably reflects a combination of better recording procedures and more awareness on the part of social agencies, the public, and medical professionals, leading to increased reporting. In fact, all states now have statutes that require various professionals, such as physicians, other health care workers, and teachers, to report suspected child abuse to social service and sometimes law enforcement officials.

As noted at the beginning of the chapter, state legislatures and courts have traditionally claimed that family relationships require or deserve special immunity from the law and have given parents broad authority in the rearing of their children. Included in this traditional perspective is the contention that parents have the right to discipline children as they see fit, even if it involves "reasonable" physical punishment. The **doctrine of family privacy** was at the heart of the legal and legislative debate about acceptable governmental intervention into family life. According to that doctrine, what went on within the intact family unit is of concern only to the family itself, as long as there was no serious threat to any member or members of the family. Thus, "(The) taking of life, parental incest, and the imminent threat to the life or health of a minor child all trigger the law's willingness to penetrate the privacy of family life because the family privacy considerations are outweighed by other important public goals" (Zimring, 1989, pp. 552–553). Otherwise, the privacy of the family had been traditionally held to be sacred.

This view was energetically challenged by various interest groups attempting not only to acquaint the public with the problems of family violence, child neglect, and abuse but also to activate lawmakers toward more stringent and social sanctions. By the end of the 20th century, some headway had been made. In 1974 Congress passed the original *Child Abuse Prevention and Treatment Act (CAPTA)*, which was both rewritten and amended at several points, with the most recent amendment occurring in 1996. The Act sets up a national Office on Child Abuse and Neglect and a national clearinghouse for information relating to child abuse, and it earmarks funds for research, evaluation, and the establishment of model abuse prevention programs. The amended Act also provides grant money to states to set up community-based programs providing support to families on a wide range of issues. One goal of this section was to coordinate services among the plethora of existing agencies that provide services to families, including agencies dealing with respite care, child care, job readiness, self-sufficiency, child and family development, housing, and education.

Despite these modern reforms, family privacy continues to play a substantial role in the development and enactment of family law (Zimring, 1989). Thus, the physical discipline of children is usually not for legal review unless if represents a gross threat to the child. Interestingly, the manner in which each parent disciplines the child can become an issue in divorce cases where custody is contested. "[The] spanking parent may, for example, be immune from tort liability [or criminal prosecution], yet the same inappropriate physical discipline may deprive him or her of the custody of a child after divorce" (Zimring, 1989, p. 554). Privacy of the family dissipates when the family dissolves.

With the passage of the *Child Abuse Prevention and Treatment Act*, however, Congress apparently hoped to put states on notice that the well-being of children is a paramount consideration. Community programs that provide support to families—including educating parents about disciplinary practices—will be well regarded and rewarded with federal government funding. Child advocates are often concerned, however, that even well-intentioned initiatives will ultimately not be carried out. In the wake of the September 11 terrorist attacks and the war against Iraq, for example, the federal budget has been dramatically altered. It remains to be seen whether funds allocated for prevention and support programs will actually be made available.

Incidence of Child Maltreatment

In reviewing statistics on child victimization, it is important to note distinctions in terms. In keeping with the definitions found in the *Child Abuse Prevention and Treatment Act*, we will use "**maltreatment**" as a generic term to cover four major types of abuse and neglect. They are **physical abuse, child neglect, sexual abuse**, and **emotional abuse** ◙ (see **Box 11-2** for definitions). In 2000, an estimated 879,000 children were victims of maltreatment nationwide (National Child Abuse and Neglect Data System, 2002). Of this total, almost two-thirds (63%) suffered neglect (including medical neglect); 19% were physically abused; 10% were sexually abused; and 8% were emotionally abused. Over one-quarter of the children were victims of more than one type of maltreatment. The rate of child victims per 1,000 children has been steadily decreasing, from 15.3 victims per 1,000 children in the population in 1993 to 12.2 per 1,000 children in 2000. Victimization rates decline as age of the child increases. Child fatalities due to maltreatment, however, appear to be on the increase, with approximately 1,200 children dying of abuse or neglect in the year 2000.

Until recently, information such as the above was provided primarily from child welfare sources. Child abuse is a crime, however, and some of it does come to the attention of police. It is well documented, though, that only a fraction of all crime is known to police. Victimization surveys, for example, tell us that less than 50% of crime, overall, is reported. Certain victimizations, such as rape and burglary, have very low reporting rates. Even when crimes against children are *reported* to police and tabulated in the FBI's *Uniform Crime Report* (UCR) ▶ [a system of measuring crime that will be discussed in Chapter 13], it is difficult to disentangle reported crimes against children from crimes against adults. *Arrest* data include a category called crimes against children, but they offer few details about offenses. With a new type of recording system, the National Incidence-Based Recording System (NIBRS), information about this problem from law enforcement officials is becoming more readily available.

Finkelhor and Ormrod (2001) provide information on an analysis of NIBRS data from 12 states for 1997. They were able to conclude that about one-fifth of all violent crimes against juveniles (ages 0–17) were perpetrated by parents or caretakers. Most of these crimes (73%) were physical rather than sexual assaults. Male offenders were responsible for three-quarters of the child abuse incidents reported to police (and 92% of the sexual assaults). Not surprisingly, when the researchers compared this police data with child welfare records, they found that only a small fraction of the abuse investigated and substantiated by child welfare authorities made it into police statistics.

Boys and girls were almost equally victimized, with the exception of sexual assault cases, where victims were overwhelmingly girls (80% vs. 20%).

BOX 11-2
Definitions and Categories of Child Maltreatment

Child Abuse and Neglect (as defined in *Child Abuse Prevention and Treatment Act (CAPTA))*
At a minimum, any recent act or failure to act on the part of a parent or caretaker, which results in death, serious physical or emotional harm, sexual abuse or exploitation, or an act or failure to act which presents an imminent risk of serious harm.

Sexual Abuse (as defined by *CAPTA*)
The employment, use, persuasion, inducement, enticement, or coercion of any child to engage in, or assist any other person to engage in, any sexually explicit conduct or simulation of such conduct for the purpose of producing a visual depiction of such conduct; or

The rape—and in cases of caretaker or inter-familial relationships, statutory rape—molestation, prostitution, or other form of sexual exploitation of children, or incest with children.

Emotional Abuse (as defined by U.S. Department of Health and Human Services (HHS))
Includes acts or omissions by parents or other caretakers that have caused, or could cause, serious behavioral, cognitive, emotional, or mental disorders. In some cases of emotional abuse, the acts of parents or other caregivers alone, without any harm evident in the child's behavior or condition, are sufficient to warrant child protective services intervention (e.g., extreme or bizarre forms of punishment, such as confinement of a child in a dark closet).

Physical Abuse (U.S. Department of HHS)
Characterized by the infliction of physical injury as a result of punching, beating, kicking, biting, burning, shaking or otherwise harming a child. The parent or caretaker may not have intended to hurt the child; rather, the injury may have resulted from over-discipline or physical punishment.

Child Neglect (U.S. Department of HHS)
Characterized by a failure to provide for the child's basic needs. Neglect can be physical, educational, or emotional.

There were gender differences in victimization according to age, however. For example, as juvenile males got older, their likelihood of physical victimization decreased compared with girls. Similarly, girls' likelihood of being sexually victimized increased as they got older.

Legal Process in Child Abuse

By 1967, child abuse reporting laws were in effect in all 50 states. Criminal penalties for willful failure to report suspected cases have been established in 45 states (Finlayson & Koocher, 1991). These laws require specified professionals who are likely to come in contact with children (e.g., pediatricians, social workers, nurses, teachers, psychologists, family counselors, psychiatrists) to report suspected abuse and neglect to child protective agencies (Zellman, 1990). However, exactly what behaviors or indicators prompt a professional to report a suspected case of child abuse is not at all clear. Moreover, there is some evidence that female professionals are more likely to report child sexual abuse than male professionals (Attias & Goodwin, 1985; Finlayson & Koocher, 1991), but the reasons for this have not been explored.

Child abuse cases may be litigated through a confusing array of legal proceedings: criminal prosecution, dependency proceedings, child custody and visitation litigation, proceedings to terminate parental rights, civil proceedings initiated by victims for monetary damages, and even civil litigation against child welfare agencies (Sagatun, 1991). Most commonly, however, two basic forms of legal intervention occur in child abuse or neglect cases: (1) criminal prosecution against the offender; or (2) child protection intervention and civil action in juvenile or family court (Bulkley, 1988). Either one or both interventions may take place. It should be mentioned that many victims of child abuse (sexual or otherwise) refuse to testify against their abusers not only because they fear the abuser, but also because they fear being moved away from the only home they know.

Bulkley (1988) notes that sexual abuse of a child by an adult typically results in criminal prosecution, whereas parental physical abuse or neglect usually results in child protection intervention, unless the child is permanently or severely injured or dies. In recent years, however, victims of child sexual abuse—which took place many years previously—are filing more civil lawsuits seeking money damages against individuals, or institutions, such as schools, day-care centers, and churches (Bulkley, 1988). In 2002, the U.S. was stunned by reports of sexual abuse by Catholic priests, along with awareness that the Catholic Church had often hidden the abuse by transferring priests to other parishes or reaching confidential financial settlements with victims. In a related development, the U.S. Supreme Court heard arguments in 2003 in a case in which a state had retroactively nullified the statute of limitations in a child molestation case. In other words, it allowed prosecutors to file charges after legal deadlines had passed (*Stogner v. California*). American society has seen a discernible shift away from a therapeutic approach and toward a more punitive approach to abusive adults, including parents. During the 1980s legislatures have enacted harsher penalties for child abuse of all kinds and increased the emphasis on criminal prosecution (Myers, 1985–86). One of the consequences of this legislative action is the demand for testimony from children, particularly in sex abuse cases. Because this is such a critical topic and has elicited considerable research attention, we will highlight it here.

Child Testimony in Sexual Abuse Cases

No national statistics are available on the number of child sexual-abuse victims who are required to testify in criminal prosecutions. Prosecutors report, however, that children in the U.S. are more likely to testify in sexual-abuse cases than in any other kind of criminal case (Goodman et al., 1992). A long line of social science research has established that children, particularly young children, experience anxiety about testifying, and that this anxiety hampers the accuracy of their testimony (Goodman, Levine, Melton, & Ogden, 1991). As we noted in ◀ Chapter 9, the U.S. Supreme Court has recognized this stress, ruling in 1990 (*Maryland v. Craig*) that the closed-circuit testimony of a child witness in a sexual assault case did not deprive the defendant of his Sixth Amendment right to confront witnesses against him. Today, the majority of states authorize judges to permit the closed-circuit testimony of children on a case-by-case basis. Even so, judges are very reluctant to do so.

Prosecutors generally prefer to present live victims and witnesses to juries (Goodman et al., 1992), and defense attorneys prefer to question them in open court. The presumption, then, is that attorneys generally will not support closed-circuit televised (CCTV) testimony unless it is absolutely necessary. CCTV also raises a number of questions. For example, are jurors more or less likely to convict if a child testifies in that manner? Is the child more or less likely to be accurate? Does the age of the child influence the accuracy of such testimony?

Gail Goodman and her colleagues (Goodman et al., 1998) staged an elaborate experiment in an attempt to answer these and other questions. The effect of CCTV on both children's testimony and on jurors' decision making was examined. Children aged five and six and eight and nine participated in play sessions with an unfamiliar male confederate. During these play sessions, which were videotaped and also viewed by parents through a one-way mirror, the confederate instructed the children to place stickers either on their clothing (the not guilty condition) or on exposed bare skin (the guilty condition). Thus, some "defendants" committed the "crime" of encouraging children to place stickers on their bare skin.

Mock trials in actual courtrooms were held, with "testimony" being provided either via closed-circuit television or in open courtroom. Mock jurors, made up of community recruits, completed individual ratings of the child witness and the defendant, then also deliberated in groups to reach verdicts.

Briefly, the experiment produced results supportive of closed-circuit televised testimony. Younger children in particular made fewer errors of omission and were less suggestible to questioning in the closed-circuit condition than in the open court condition. In the open court condition, the younger children made more omission errors than the older children, and also made more errors than younger children who were testifying via CCTV.

The trial condition did not significantly affect jurors' ratings of guilt. Moreover, demographic variables of jurors (e.g., whether they were parents) did not predict their ratings of either the children or the trial. Jurors as a group did not view closed circuit trials as more or less fair to the defendant. There were gender differences, however. Women jurors did view closed circuit trials as less fair to the defendant and less fair overall. However, they also viewed *regular* trials as less fair than closed circuit trials to *children*. Male jurors were slightly more sympathetic to the defense and more likely to think the children misunderstood the defendant's actions and were suggestible. Both men and women viewed younger children as less believable than the older children, regardless of the open versus closed condition. Moreover, jurors were unable to discern accuracy in testimony better in either the closed circuit or the regular trials.

Goodman and her colleagues conclude that closed circuit testimony of child witnesses is not unfair to defendants. Jurors neither give excessive weight to such testimony, nor do they discount it. Furthermore, allowing young children to testify via closed-circuit television has benefits. Not only does it reduce anxiety and fear generated by the courtroom environment and confrontation with the defendant, but it also leads to more accurate testimony.

Despite continuing efforts to provide alternatives to testifying in open court, a word of warning is needed, however. It would be unfortunate if results of experiments such as those of Goodman led to a presumption that children should not testify in open court. Furthermore, efforts to provide alternatives do not necessarily increase accuracy, as Goodman has noted elsewhere (Goodman et al., 1999). As the U.S. Supreme Court noted in *Maryland v. Craig*, and as most statutes allowing CCTV testimony specify, this decision should be made on a case by case basis, in consideration of the facts alleged and the age of the child. Furthermore, attorneys are not absolved of their role in enabling more reliable testimony, in both open and closed-circuit situations. As Goodman et al. (1999) have noted, the way in which lawyers ask questions may be a primary culprit in reducing the accuracy of children's testimony. "Unfortunately, it is not a rare occurrence for children to be asked questions in 'legalese,' that is, complex questions with convoluted sentence formations, such as double negatives and dual-part questions" (Goodman et al., 1999, p. 251). The task of formulating developmentally-appropriate questions, therefore, remains a responsibility of the legal profession.

Clinical Evaluations of Children in Maltreatment Situations

Mental health professionals are often asked to conduct evaluations of abused and/or neglected children. These evaluations may be requested by caseworkers, the courts, attorneys, or by other members of the family. Budd et al. (2002, p. 3) summarize the questions that are often asked of clinicians. "(C)linicians may be asked to assess the child's developmental or emotional functioning and needs, the effects of maltreatment on the child, the risk of harm should the child be reunited with his or her parents, the impact of separation from the biological family on the child's functioning, or the advantages and disadvantages of potential visitation or placement options." Note that some of the above reflect concerns similar to those raised in custody determinations. Children who have been abused or neglected, however, have presumably experienced more trauma than children in a non-abusive but disintegrating family.

◼ **Box 11-3** highlights a controversial topic related to the evaluation of children who may have been subjected to sexual abuse. Anatomically-detailed dolls (AD dolls) are used by physicians, in law enforcement, and in psychological practice to help young children communicate when their language skills or emotional concerns preclude direct verbal responses (APA, 1991; Koocher, Goodman, White, et al., 1995). They are also used as props

BOX 11-3
Anatomically Detailed Dolls

A wide variety of both medical and mental health professionals make use of anatomically detailed dolls in their work with children. Physicians use them to explain medical procedures to children, and therapists use them to facilitate communication. Some children who have difficulty verbalizing their fears or their experiences are better able to do this with the use of dolls that approximate the human form. Adult dolls have breasts (if female), genitalia, and pubic hair, while child dolls have the nonmature features of children. Depending on the manufacturer, AD dolls may have a variety of facial expressions and moving parts.

The dolls are particularly controversial when used in cases of alleged child sexual abuse. Critics maintain that the dolls heighten the suggestibility of young children and may even stimulate sexual fantasies, thereby throwing into question the validity of the child's reports. Early research indicated that the dolls do not generally produce false reports of abuse in children who have not been abused (Goodman & Aman, 1990). However, as noted in the text, more recent studies have uncovered inaccuracy (e.g., Bruck, Ceci, Francoeur, & Renick, 1995), and there is growing concern about using these dolls, especially with children under four or five.

Even supporters of using the dolls urge caution in their use. Boat and Everson (1988) provided a variety of suggestions, including the following:

- Use commercially manufactured dolls which have been carefully tested and are less likely to be flawed.
- In their initial presentation, the dolls should be fully clothed.
- Match dolls to the race of the child; if the suspected perpetrator is of a different race, the child should be allowed to choose dolls.
- Interview the child in a comfortable room with a one-way mirror to avoid needlessly subjecting the child to multiple interviews with other individuals.
- If law enforcement officers are in the vicinity, they should be wearing civilian clothes and not have weapons in sight.
- Interview the child alone, unless the child cannot separate from the caretaker or needs an interpreter.
- Plan on two or three interviews, each lasting about thirty minutes.
- Siblings should always be interviewed separately.

It is important to keep in mind, though, that the sexual abuse investigation process itself can be a traumatic event for children, arousing fears of harm and separation from family members. When evidence of abuse is strong, many children need to hear assurances that the incident was not their fault. Nevertheless, the examiner must avoid making promises that she or he may not be able to keep, such as promises that the abuse will never happen again (Boat & Everson, 1988).

The controversy over the appropriate use of AD dolls is continuing. At this point, using the dolls with young children in sex abuse investigation appears questionable. Regardless of the age of the child, however, these dolls are not a failsafe method for obtaining information and should be used only by trained examiners.

when older children have difficulty expressing themselves verbally on sexual topics (APA, 1991). The practice of using them to evaluate whether a child has been sexually abused is highly questionable, however. Critics (e.g., Ceci & Bruck, 1993; Bruck, Ceci, & Francoeur, 2000; Gardner, 1991) maintain that AD dolls heighten the child's suggestibility and may stimulate sexual and other fantasies. They note, as well, that improperly trained interviewers or clinicians who are unfamiliar with appropriate validity standards may place unwarranted emphasis on the information gained from children through the use of these dolls (Koocher, Goodman, White et al., 1995).

After a comprehensive review of the research and controversy surrounding AD dolls, Koocher et al. (1995) concluded that they can be a useful communication tool, when used by trained, professional interviewers. However, they added the following caveats:

- They should not be considered psychological tests with predictive or postdictive validity per se.
- Caution is urged with children aged four and under, especially when leading and misleading questions about "being touched" are used.
- Valid doll-centered assessment techniques may not exist; this may not be the best available practical solution to the problem of investigating child abuse.
- Training in the use of AD dolls should include recognition of normative differences between children of different racial groups and socioeconomic strata.

A more critical perspective is offered by Bruck, Ceci, and Francoeur (2000) who conclude that AD dolls should not be used at all with children below the age of five. Previous research by Bruck and her colleagues (Bruck, Ceci, Francoeur, & Renick, 1995) had indicated that three-year-old children had great difficulty providing accurate reports about whether they had been touched on genitals or buttocks during routine medical examinations. Errors of both omission and commission were common, regardless of whether AD dolls were used. The doll condition increased the error rate, however, because the children falsely indicated that the pediatrician conducting the examination inserted a finger or an instrument into their anal or genital cavity. In their later, more extensive study, Bruck, Ceci, and Francoeur (2000) examined the responses of both three-year-olds and four-year-olds. Although the older group was more accurate in describing how the doctor had used certain props (e.g., stethoscope, earscope, stickers), the age groups did not differ in the accuracy of their reports about genital and buttock touching. Even the oldest children were quite inaccurate in providing information about bodily touching. The researchers hypothesized that errors were made both because their memory of the event was poor and they were sensitive to the demands of the interviewing situation. A technique so highly fraught with error, they concluded, should be reconsidered when used with such young children.

Statistics on the numbers of abuse evaluations conducted annually are not available. Additionally, the examination process itself has received little research attention. One exception is the research by Karen Budd and her colleagues (2001, 2002), who have studied both the assessment of children and the assessment of parents in child protection cases as part of a multidisciplinary project initiated by the Circuit Court of Cook County, Illinois. The goal of the project is to understand and improve the way clinical information is used in legal decision making concerning children and families (Budd et al., 2002).

Budd and her colleagues studied 207 mental health assessment reports on child abuse or neglect cases. A total of 280 children were assessed. The researchers sought to obtain a wide range of information, including information about assessors and the children assessed and about the methods of conducting the evaluations. Their research provides a wealth of data about the process of conducting evaluations in child abuse cases.

Psychologists were the most common evaluators, and psychological evaluations comprised the majority (65%) of the assessments. Other identified evaluations were developmental, bonding/parenting, and evaluations conducted by a Parent Assessment Team (PAT). The latter represented the lengthiest process, averaging nearly five sessions and including both home and clinic visits. There were interesting differences in the types of measures used in the various types of evaluations. For example, and perhaps not surprisingly, the psychological evaluations used a wide variety of measures, including projective personality tests in over 90% of the cases. Psychological evaluations typically did not include either parent-child observation or child observation alone. Each of these observations occurred in one or more of the other types of evaluations, however.

Almost all reports included recommendations, with the three most common being recommendations for therapy or counseling, educational services, or a recommendation on case disposition. Again, researchers found different patterns of recommendations depending upon the type of evaluation conducted.

In considering the implications of their findings, Budd et al. (2002) expressed concerns in a variety of areas pertaining to forensic psychology. They noted that evaluations often fell short of the multi-source, multi-session approach advocated by the APA (APA Committee on Professional Practice and Standards, 1998). They noted also an absence of an ecological focus, or information about a child's relationships with parents or other children, behavior in school, or physical home environment. Indeed, examiners typically did not observe the child interacting with parents. The reports also were more likely to focus on the child's weaknesses than strengths. Again contrary to recommended practice, relatively few reports described the purpose of the referral or the problems leading to the referral. (Researchers noted that examiners told them they often did not receive this information, and therefore conducted a generic evaluation.)

Recognizing that their data had limitations, including its focus on one urban court, Budd et al. nevertheless note that their findings add to the developing literature on the process of conducting evaluations. The findings also are not inconsistent with literature on assessment in other contexts (e.g., Ackerman & Ackerman, 1997; Bow & Quinnell, 2001). Recall, also, that others have convincingly proclaimed a need for better assessment practices (Nicholson & Norwood, 2000; Otto & Heilbrun, 2002).

Intimate Partner Violence

The last quarter of the 20th century saw increasingly greater attention given to the troubling issue of violence against intimate partners. It should be noted that this broad term covers spousal abuse (wife and husband), as well as abuse of intimate partners who are not married, whether or not they share a domicile. In the early 1970s, the Women's Movement was highly influential in bringing attention to violence against women and girls, and shortly thereafter was instrumental in social and legal attention to marital rape. The Women's Movement fought for and achieved legislation to increase or establish penalties for abuse of women and girls, to strengthen civil remedies, and to make it easier for victims to file criminal charges against their assailants, including their husbands (Pleck, 1989). However, despite these formal changes, the legal system was slow and resistant to recognizing violence against women as a serious or widespread problem (Mahoney, 1991). There seems to be a strong and long-standing tendency in society (and in the courtroom) to blame women for their abuse and to deny or trivialize the violence involved (Mahoney, 1991; Caringella-MacDonald, 1997). In 1994, Congress passed the *Violence Against Women Act* (VAWA), a law which indicated a willingness to tackle this problem on a national level. Among many other provisions, the law presumably makes it easier for women to obtain protective orders against abusers and also easier to enforce them across state lines. Additionally, persons who cross state lines to harass or physically abuse are subject to federal penalties. Nevertheless, state laws place a variety of restrictions on obtaining protective orders, and advocates for women often consider them illusory protections. Gist et al. (2001) found that 28% of women requesting a protective order did not qualify, primarily because they did not have a cohabiting relationship with their abuser.

Whereas early research was almost exclusively devoted to domestic violence and the victimization of women by men in that context, contemporary research has extended the inquiry to couples who are not necessarily living together, to same-sex couples, and to violence by women against men. Nonetheless, it is consistently documented that the greatest incidence of intimate partner violence is perpetrated by men against women (Cardarelli, 1997; Gist et al., 2001). Women are eight times more likely than men to be assaulted by an intimate partner, and the great majority of victims (85%) are women (Greenfield, et al., 1998). Stalking, another form of victimization

▶ [that will be discussed in Chapter 13], often goes hand in hand with intimate partner violence. The *National Violence Against Women Survey* (Tjaden & Thoennes, 1998) indicated that 81% of the women who reported being stalked were also physically assaulted by the same person. The research is also clear that women are far more likely than men to be killed by their abusers. For example, women comprise three out of every four victims killed by intimates. One-third of all murdered women are killed by an intimate partner (Meuer, Seymour, & Wallace, 2001). This compares to 6% of all murdered men (Greenfield et al., 1998).

Studies estimating the prevalence of such abuse differ significantly in their figures. The most conservative estimates suggest that women are physically abused in 12% of all marriages. Some scholars project that as many as 50% or more of all women will be battering victims at some point in their lives (Mahoney, 1991). Overall, in 1998, women were the victims of intimate partner violence five times more often than men (Meuer, Seymour, & Wallace, 2001). Steinmetz (1977) estimated that 3.3 million wives and .25 million husbands out of a total population of 47 million married couples were subjected to *severe* beatings by their spouses. In one of the early national surveys on this issue conducted in 1975 at the Family Research Laboratory at the University of New Hampshire, 28% of the married persons interviewed said they had experienced marital violence at some point in the marriage (Straus, Gelles, & Steinmetz, 1980). Sixteen percent reported some kind of physical violence between spouses during the year of the survey. In another nationwide survey conducted in 1985 (Straus & Gelles, 1986), the incidence of spouse physical abuse actually decreased 27% from the 1975 figure. These data contrast sharply with claims of an epidemic of abuse during the 1970s and 1980s. Regardless of this apparent reduction, which may be attributed to a variety of factors ranging from more empowerment of women to more fear in reporting, violence against women remains a very serious issue.

The 1985 data of the Family Research Laboratory did reveal the very significant fact that abuse often does not begin *during* marriage, but rather before it. In another research study, over one-third of women about to be married reported having been the victims of physical violence from their *fiancés* (O'Leary & Curley, 1986). A substantial number of battered women continue to live with their assailants (Strube, 1988). Unfortunately, women are often reluctant to seek aid for their abuse and often do so only when it becomes life threatening. "Why doesn't she leave?" is the question continually asked, and it tends to be asked much more often than, "Why doesn't he stop?" For a variety of reasons, including lack of community support, fear of retaliation, and hope that things will improve, women who are battered may perceive themselves unable to leave a battering relationship (Sullivan, 1997). Additionally, although the Violence Against Women Act seemingly facilitated the obtaining of protective orders, as noted earlier such orders are often considered an illusory protection at best; furthermore, many women in abusive situations do not qualify for the protective orders (Gist et al., 2001).

Psychological Profiles of Abusers

Despite several attempts to develop psychological categories for the wife or child abuser (e.g., Megargee, 1982), there does not seem to be any evidence for "typical" psychological profiles for either "wife batterers" or child abusers. The search for typical *demographic* variables of abusers has been equally unsuccessful (Weis, 1989; Hotaling & Straus, 1989). Wife and child abuse appear to cut across all socioeconomic, occupational, regional, religious, racial, and ethnic lines. Alcohol and other drug abuse do seem to play an exacerbating role, but it is a mistake to call them *causes* of the violence. Abusive men with severe alcohol or drug problems are apt to abuse their wives both when drunk and when sober. However, abusive men who drink heavily are violent more frequently, and they inflict more serious injuries on their wives and children than do abusive men who do not have a history of alcohol or drug problems (Frieze & Browne, 1989). Abusive men generally use alcohol or other drugs as an excusing agent that allows them to escape some culpability for their antisocial or violent actions as well as to avoid the full impact of legal sanctions. It should be noted, however, that marijuana and other illegal drugs have not been shown to be connected to violent behavior, whether in the domestic context or any other.

Once the abuse has occurred, it tends to be repeated (Frieze & Browne, 1989). Over time, wife abuse, if not skillfully sanctioned, may also become more severe and more frequent. Recall the discussion of the cycle of violence identified by Lenore Walker (1989). Being violently victimized by a spouse over an extended period of time may result in emotional reactions and psychological scars decidedly different than those seen in victims of violent crime perpetrated by strangers.

There have been very few systematic studies on the effectiveness of particular strategies for reducing child or spouse abuse. One of the more influential investigations examining the effectiveness of police intervention into spouse abuse was the Minnesota Domestic Violence Experiment (Sherman & Berk, 1984). The police officers participating in the experiment were instructed to handle marital discord in one of three ways: arrest, separating the parties, or advising (or mediating) the parties. Follow-up of the effectiveness of each of these approaches over a six-month period suggested that arrest was the most effective strategy for reducing domestic assaults. However, the study had serious design problems that undermine both its external and internal validity. In addition, there is now evidence that the impact of an arrest wears off over a relatively short period of time (eight to twelve months), and the number and severity of the assaults return to their original level (Elliott, 1989). Moreover, arrest strategies have different effects for different offenders (Sherman & Smith, 1992). This is not to suggest that arrest is never a good strategy. Rather, it seems that arrest followed by effective intervention, informal community sanctions, and continued community support for the victim or victims are essential (Pate & Hamilton, 1992). Though progress has been made in this area, some categories of victims tend to be overlooked in many communities. Sullivan (1997), discussing the value of shelters for battered women, notes that these shelters need to reach out more to younger women, older women, women of color, working-class women, and lesbians.

Additionally, initiating a motivation to change in an abuser is a formidable task. It requires establishing a series of events where the psychological and material costs for the abuse outweigh its psychological benefits. Usually, abusers have had a life-long learning experience within their subculture in developing belief systems about the power men should have over family members. They also probably have had considerable reinforcement for their aggressive actions. Thus, it will not be easy to break this behavioral cycle. Legal sanctions should have an effect, but often the abuser realizes that these sanctions are weak.

Serious, concentrated efforts by the legal system to put some bite into these sanctions may be effective over the long haul. One arrest, fine, or lecture is unlikely to have much effect. It is more likely that a string of aversive and costly events, such as strong legal sanctions combined with social sanctions from the community (public disclosure, frequent visits by a social welfare agency) and emotional sanctions from the victim (reporting abuse regularly to the authorities, leaving the home, separating, initiating divorce proceedings) will wear the abuser down to a point where a change in the abuse cycle becomes necessary. Fundamentally, however, a change in the cycle of violence requires a society-wide attack on the social conditions that promote it. The domestic violence courts highlighted in ◀ Chapter 3 ◘ (see **Box 3-1**) are a step in the right direction.

Additionally, as Cardarelli (1997) notes, a comprehensive, integrated model to understand intimate violence is sorely needed. The concept of family has changed dramatically over the last quarter century, and research has not often kept up with these changing definitions. Cardarelli (1997, p. 180) comments, "There have been few attempts at developing integrated theoretical models capable of incorporating the patterns of abuse and violence that take place within the varied intimate partnerships . . . " He adds that intimate violence is only one form of violence along a continuum of interpersonal violence. Additionally, there is a continuum within intimate violence, "(from dating to courtship to engagement to cohabitation to marriage and including ex-spouses)" (1997, p. 180). Various strategies of abuse and survival occur along the continuum, and the response of the law may vary along the continuum as well. Researchers need to give more attention to documenting and exploring these differences, in order for treatment providers and society in general to respond more effectively.

The Concept of Consent by Minors

One topic in family law that has received increasing attention from researchers involves the competence of adolescents to make decisions in their best interests. The question of competence is raised in a wide variety of contexts, ranging from body piercing to waiving Constitutional rights. In this chapter, we will focus on the hotly-debated issue of abortion. In ▶ Chapter 12 the competence of adolescents to participate in court proceedings and to waive a variety of Constitutional rights will be discussed.

In the eyes of the law, adults are presumed competent to make decisions in their own interest until proved otherwise in a court of law; children, by contrast, are presumed incompetent (Koocher, 1987). In most states, 18 is the chronological age that signals adulthood; in some states, the age is 16 or 17. Additionally, many states have an "emancipated minor" provision in their laws, allowing courts to recognize some children, on a case by case basis, as independent and eligible for adult status.

Despite the presumption of incompetence, there are several circumstances under which children may be heard on their own behalf or may be treated as adults (Koocher, 1987). For example, a juvenile offender charged with a serious crime, such as murder or rape, may be tried as an adult in all states, although age limits and procedures vary widely. Many jurisdictions grant minors the right to seek medical treatment on their own authority under certain circumstances (Koocher, 1987). This is especially the case if treatment of the illness is deemed in the public interest. For example, if a minor has a sexually-transmittable disease, it is in the best interest of both the child and society that this be treated, even without parental consent if necessary.

Nevertheless, there is considerable ambivalence expressed by researchers, courts, legal scholars, and practitioners on this issue. Statutes in most states require the notification and consent of parents and guardians before any medical procedures can be undertaken. Furthermore, although there is some evidence that adolescents by the age of 15 can make health care and other decisions that demonstrate autonomous reasoning (Ambuel & Rappaport, 1992; Melton, 1983; Hart, 1991), researchers caution that the evidence is tentative (Scott, 2000). Whether and how youthful capacities for reasoning and understanding are employed may be quite variable, and "adolescent performance is not necessarily like that of adults in various contexts" (Scott, 2000, p. 303). Similarly, Hart (1991, p. 56) commented that knowledge concerning the precise age at which children can make responsible judgments about their health and welfare is " . . . not sufficient enough to provide clear or convincing direction to a society ambivalent about children's self-determination rights" (Hart, 1991, p. 56). In short, "(A) comprehensive and empirically validated design for the progressive development of the self-determination capacities of children does not exist" (Hart, 1991, p. 56).

U.S. Supreme Court and the Abortion Issue

Nowhere is ambivalence about adolescent decision making more apparent than with respect to the controversial topic of abortion. As noted above, this is one of the most hotly debated issues in family law. In 1973, the U.S. Supreme Court held in *Roe v. Wade* that the "Constitutional right of privacy founded in the Fourteenth Amendment is broad enough to encompass a woman's decision whether or not to terminate her pregnancy" (p. 706). Since that time the Supreme Court has made decisions on at least eight different cases involving a *minor's right* to an abortion (Pliner & Yates, 1992). In general, the Court has held " . . . that while a minor female, like an adult female, does have the right to an abortion, the minor's right is more restricted" (Pliner & Yates, 1992, p. 204). Further "(T)he basis for the restrictions that have been imposed lies in the law's presumption that minors are immature and, therefore, not competent to give informed consent to undergo a medical procedure, such as an abortion" (Pliner & Yates, 1992, p. 204).

Two Supreme Court cases on this issue are instructive. In *Hodgson v. Minnesota* (1990), the Court considered a state law that required girls under 18 years of age to notify both of their parents *and* wait at least 48 hours after that notification has been made before having an abortion. A deeply divided Court upheld the waiting period but considered the "two-parent rule" too burdensome. Notification of at least one parent would be sufficient to address parental interest in the girl's welfare as well as any concerns that her immaturity, inexperience, and lack of judgment may impair her ability to exercise her rights wisely. However, since the state statute also had a judicial bypass provision, by which a girl could avoid parental notification by convincing a judge that she was sufficiently mature or that notification would not be in her best interests, the statute was not struck down.

In *Planned Parenthood v. Casey* (1992), the Court reviewed another state statute, this one including a variety of requirements for both women and minors seeking abortions. In the section relevant only to minors, the law mandated the informed consent of one parent, but provided for a judicial bypass procedure. As it had in *Hodgson v. Minnesota*, the Court found this parental notification Constitutional. With respect to adult women, the law required that they be provided with certain information about abortion at least 24 hours prior to obtaining one; married women must sign statements indicating that they had notified their husbands of their intent to seek abortions. The Court upheld the first provision but struck down the second, noting that the liberty and privacy interests of married women outweighed the spouse's interest in the welfare of the fetus. The Court in *Casey* also reaffirmed the central holding of *Roe v. Wade* in each of its three parts: (1) that women have a right to choose abortion before fetal viability without undue interference from the State; (2) that states may restrict abortion after viability, as long as they make exceptions for pregnancies endangering a woman's life or health; and (3) that states have a legitimate interest from the outset of the pregnancy in protecting the health of the woman and the life of the fetus that may become a child.

About 12% of all legal abortions in the U.S. are obtained by minors (Russo, Horn, & Schwartz, 1992). Most minors seeking abortions do not have dependent children and are white, enrolled in school, unmarried, and with no prior abortions (Russo, et al., 1992). On the other hand, more than 13% of these pregnant minors have had prior abortions, 9% already are mothers, and about 17% of the mothers already have two or more children. Moreover, this group of young mothers was generally economically disadvantaged and high in ethnic minority representation (nearly 80%). Abortion plays an important role in delaying transition to parenthood for minors (Russo, et al., 1992). Although reasons for seeking an abortion are multiple and complex, more than 75% of unmarried minors seeking abortion feel they are not mature enough to raise a child (Russo, et al., 1992; Torres & Forrest, 1988).

States vary widely in their approach to the abortion issue as it relates to both women and girls. Some, like Minnesota and Pennsylvania, have narrowed access to abortion by requiring parental notification and/or consent for minors, imposing waiting periods for all abortion seekers, and placing limitations on information that family planning clinics can provide about abortion. Although the basic right to an abortion has been left intact, courts have allowed these restrictions. Additionally, although the U.S. Supreme Court has opened the way for vigorous prosecution of abortion opponents who engage in illegal activity (*N.O.W. v. Scheidler*, 1994), the Court also has given protesters considerable leeway in demonstrating outside of women's health centers. In *Schenck v. Pro Choice Network of New York* (1997), the Court upheld "fixed buffer zones" to protect women from being approached by abortion opponents. However, it ruled that "floating buffer zones"—which essentially protected the woman while she walked to her car, as an example—violated the First Amendment rights of the protesters.

Parental Notification Issues

The parental notification rules applying to minors are particularly noteworthy from a psychological perspective. Although the statutes generally provide for a judicial over-ride in the cases of mature minors, precisely what "mature" means remains open to debate and interpretation. The overall effects of such restrictions have yet to be evaluated. However, based on empirical work on child-parent relationships, these mandated restrictions are very unlikely to have notable positive effects on most minors. Indeed, the Interdivisional Committee on Adolescent Abortion (1987) of the American Psychological Association has identified three ways in which parental notification requirements may actually promote negative effects on pregnant adolescents.

First, research has shown that confidentiality is an important factor for adolescents in their decisions as to whether to seek services from family planning clinics. If clinics are required to notify parents, pregnant adolescents—particularly the younger ones—are likely to delay professional help until late into their pregnancy. This procrastination increases the psychological and physical risks of both abortion and bearing a fetus to term. The longer the delay, the more likely would inducing labor be involved, and the greater the risk for adverse medical and psychological effects (Russo, 1992). Fortunately, more than 90% of all abortions are performed during the first trimester, and fewer than 1% take place after 20 weeks of pregnancy (Russo, 1992). Typically, abortions are performed in the third trimester only when the woman or girl's life is in danger.

Second, there is little evidence that parent-child communication will improve simply because some agency notifies the parents about the pregnancy. Third, the Committee asserted that " . . . it is . . . clear that there are circumstances in which parental consultation is likely to result in neither more reasoned decision making nor diminished risk of psychological harm" (Interdivisional Committee, 1987, p. 74). In fact, for most adolescents who resist informing their parents, the forced communication promotes more psychological stress. In some cases, it threatens the physical wellbeing of the adolescent.

In summary, although research on adolescent decision making is complex and somewhat equivocal (Grisso & Schwartz, 2000), there is ample evidence to suggest that many adolescents can make informed decisions and choices about their medical needs. Additionally, women's health centers provide guidance to adolescents, as well as to adult women, along with a wide variety of information about preventing pregnancy, sexually transmitted diseases, health during pregnancy, and child care and development. Rather than creating obstacles, states should ensure that caring adults are made available to those adolescents whose decision making may be questionable.

Hastened Death

Among the many legal controversies facing the U.S. at the end of the 20th century was that revolving around the right of a competent individual to receive help in ending his or her own life when faced with a terminal, irreversible, or chronic illness. Leading up to this controversy were U.S. Supreme Court decisions that acknowledged a Constitutional, but conditional, right to refuse artificial, life-sustaining treatment. In the case *In the Matter of Karen Quinlan* (1976), the Court allowed the parents of a patient who was in a persistent vegetative state to substitute their judgment for hers and take her off life-support. Nearly 15 years later, in *Cruzan v. Director* (1990), the Court re-affirmed the right to refuse treatment. However, the Court also said that, in the case of an incompetent individual, states could require by clear and convincing evidence that refusing treatment would be in keeping with the person's wishes. Each of these decisions encouraged state legislatures to enact legislation authorizing the use of living wills and health care advance directive instruments (Winick, 1998). Thus, when individuals have made clear, preferably in writing, the type of care they would and would not accept were they to become mentally incompetent, treatment providers are presumably bound to respect their wishes. Nevertheless, it has been suggested that as many as 25% of advance directive instruments are ignored (Winick, 1998).

There are three major forms of "hastening death," but not all are universally affirmed (see generally, Benjamin, Werth, & Gostin, 2000). First, medical practitioners may withdraw life-sustaining treatment, such as hydration or nutrition. This was the form addressed in the *Quinlan* and *Cruzan* cases. Second, aggressive palliative care may be provided; this refers to hastening death by giving drugs that are known to pose a high risk that the patient will not tolerate them. Third, death may be hastened intentionally and directly through terminal sedation. The latter two forms are particularly controversial because they typically require a physician's prescription of the needed drug.

Many lower courts have affirmed the right of individuals to hasten their own deaths, particularly by way of refusing treatment. Nevertheless, virtually every court decision in this area also makes careful note of the government's interest in preserving life (Cantor, 1989). Moreover, in 1997, in two separate cases the U.S. Supreme Court refused to establish a Constitutional right to physician-assisted suicide, by ruling that a state's prohibition against assisting, causing, or aiding a suicide did not violate the Constitution (*Vacco v. Quill*, 1997; *Washington v. Glucksberg*, 1997). To date only one state, Oregon, specifically allows terminally ill patients to request life-ending medication from their physicians and physicians to prescribe it. We will discuss Oregon's law shortly.

Those who support hastened death argue that this has long been a common decision between physicians and their patients. Some studies suggest that as many as one half of patients ask their physicians for medication or lethal injections to hasten death as the end of their lives approaches and that approximately 10% of physicians polled have participated (Benjamin, 2000). Interestingly, the percentages may fluctuate according to the type of disease; in one survey, for example, 60% of physicians treating persons with AIDS hastened their deaths on the patient's first request, while only 3% of these consulted with another physician (Slome, Mitchell, Charlebois, Benevedes, & Abrams, 1997). Supporters of allowing patients to hasten their own deaths maintain that giving patients such control over their own lives recognizes individual dignity, privacy, and autonomy. Public sentiment also appears to favor a right to die, as illustrated by the advance directive legislation that appears in some form in all states. Additionally, federal law requires that all hospitals receiving federal funds advise patients of advance directives, living wills, and durable powers of attorney (Finkel, Hurabiell, & Hughes, 1993).

Those in opposition or hesitant to endorse the practice wholeheartedly argue that many decisions to hasten death are not properly supervised, too often represent an abuse of the authority of physicians, and place patients in the position of being coerced to end their lives. With regard to the above-mentioned survey involving AIDS patients, for example, Benjamin (2000, p. 266) asks, "Could these patients have reached their decisions free of coercion and undue influence? Were their physicians not affected by their patient's vulnerability?" Opponents also maintain that the government's strong interest in preserving life is diminished by right to die legislation and practice. Moreover, they note that physicians are discouraged from treating pain aggressively or continuing in their search for curing the individual, even the individual with a poor prognosis. Finally, while polls indicate that most adults favor advance directives, fewer than one-third have actually executed them, leading observers to wonder whether public sentiment is truly in favor of such legislation.

Oregon's Death with Dignity Law

Even a competent individual may have opposition when he chooses to actively hasten death, such as through drugs, however. Although the law in most states allows the withdrawal of life support as well as palliative care, only Oregon allows a direct request for medication to end one's life. Oregon's *Death With Dignity Act* enables mentally competent adults with less than six months to live to ask their physicians for medication that will hasten death. Under the law, two physicians—the attending physician and a consulting physician—must review and approve of the request. The patient must be fully informed about the progress of the disease and the probabilities of life expectancy, and a variety of other safeguards are in place both to prevent a rash decision and to maximize the quality of end of life care. An evaluation by a psychiatrist or psychologist is required only if either or both physicians suspect that the patient may have impaired judgement due to a mental disorder, such as clinical depression.

Oregon's law, passed in 1995, went into effect in 1997. It has been watched closely, including by the federal government. In early November 2001, Attorney General John Ashcroft directed the Drug Enforcement Agency (DEA) to investigate and prosecute doctors in Oregon who prescribed life-ending medication to their patients. Although state law makes this legal, the action, according to Ashcroft, violates federal law, specifically the Controlled Substances Act. A federal judge almost immediately enjoined Ashcroft's order. However, in a related development, the U.S. Supreme Court has ruled in a medical marijuana case that there is no medical necessity exception to the Controlled Substances Act (*U.S. v. Oakland Cannabis Buyers' Cooperative et al.*, 2001). These decisions have made many lawmakers reluctant to support proposed legislation that would conflict with federal law.

Some research indicates that Oregon's *Death with Dignity Act* has been implemented effectively and has actually led to a better standard of care for terminally ill patients (Batavia, 2000; Lee & Werth,

2000). White and Callahan (2000), however, challenge these findings, suggesting that the confidentiality of medical records and other factors simply do not allow for a valid appraisal. "No statutory requirement exists for doctors or lay people to report abuses, nor are there strong incentives to do so (and physicians are notoriously reluctant to blow the whistle on each other)" (White & Callahan, 2000, p. 331). They fear the law will lead to abuse of the most vulnerable patients. Similarly, Orentlicher (2000) cautions that the research to date is preliminary and that a controlled, carefully designed study is needed before concluding that the law is accomplishing what it was intended to accomplish.

Competency Evaluations of Hastened Death Decisions

The hastened death controversy has numerous facets and will likely be the subject of extensive research for years to come. For our purposes, we focus on the issue of the patient's competency to make the decision to hasten his or her death, which is where psychologists and other mental health practitioners are most likely to be involved. In most jurisdictions, clear indication of a desire to avoid being kept alive on life-support systems—in the form of a living will or advance directives—will lead a court to abide by the individual's wishes, even when challenged by the family. A *sudden* request, however, may raise judicial eyebrows. Opponents of hastened death under these circumstances argue that patients with terminal illnesses lack the capacity to make competent judgements. Thus, psychologists and other clinicians may be asked to assess competency for making this critically important decision.

As in other competency areas (e.g., competency to stand trial, competency to waive Miranda rights), clinicians have been provided with guidelines for assessing the mental capacity to hasten one's death (e.g., Werth, Benjamin, & Farrenkopf, 2000). Interestingly, the MacArthur network's competency to consent to treatment instrument (MacCAT-T) has been suggested as an appropriate tool for use in end of life decision making. Recall that this instrument, discussed in ◀ Chapters 2 and 5, is designed to measure an individual's ability to refuse or accept treatment. As a general legal principle, individuals have the right to refuse treatment unless they are adjudicated incompetent to do so (Perry, 2000). Thus, the determination of a person's competency is a critical inquiry for courts when the person refuses treatment.

Werth, Benjamin, and Farrenkopf (2000) suggest that the MacCAT–T might be one of a number of measures useful to evaluating clinicians in this context. Additionally, they note that clinical interviews with the individual requesting assisted death as well as collateral interviews with the person's loved ones and with treating professionals are all warranted. The guidelines they propose include: (1) a review of the individual's previous and current medical and psychological records; (2) use of appropriate objective assessment instruments (e.g., the MacCAT-T, the Beck Depression Inventory, Schedule of Attitudes Toward Hastened Death); and (3) a clinical interview, including a number of components such as the ability to give informed consent, understanding of medical status, and assessment of the presence of mood disorders. Werth, Benjamin, and Farrenkopf (2000, p. 271) conclude their lengthy, suggested guidelines by noting that "the evaluator should not allow the assisted death to proceed until he or she is convinced that the person is not experiencing impaired judgment." Robert Burt (2000), responding to the guidelines, refers to them as "misguided," and argues that they tap subtle and complex psychological issues that could not practically be determined in the short time span envisioned by the legislation. According to Burt, it would be highly unlikely that anyone would be found competent if the guidelines were adopted; alternately, they would receive only token compliance.

The involvement of psychologists in hastened death decisions is too recent and too undefined to draw broad conclusions at this point. Nevertheless, the philosophical and ethical issues this raises are becoming widely debated in the psychological and legal literature (e.g., Winick, 1998; Benjamin, Werth, & Gostin, 2000) and will likely continue to be a controversial area for many years to come. Policy decisions should be informed by empirical research, however, and this is sorely lacking. Rosenfeld (2000) notes that, while interest in assisted suicide grows, "demand for empirically based answers to the various policy questions and clinical quagmires has increased. Unfortunately, answers are lacking for many of the critical questions that fuel the assisted suicide debate" (p. 559). In his excellent summary article, Rosenfeld (2000) identifies a wide range of methodological concerns and areas in which more research is needed. These include physician attitudes and practices; adequate measures of depression and psychological distress in patients; better measures of demographic variables, including race, religion, and acculturation or ethnic identity; and distinctions among medical conditions, to name but a few untapped research possibilities.

Summary and Conclusions

The broad field of family law has developed rapidly over the last decade, perhaps more than any other area involving an interface between law and psychology. Psychologists are becoming increasingly involved—in research and practice—in divorce and custody proceedings, domestic violence, and child sexual abuse cases. They are also more involved in the psychological aspects of abortion, particularly the mental and emotional competence of adolescents who must make decisions regarding the termination of an unwanted pregnancy. Most recently, the competency of terminally ill medical patients to decide to hasten their deaths by requesting life-ending drugs has been the subject of vigorous debate. As we discussed in the chapter, we are now beginning to see guidelines for conducting those critical competency evaluations.

Although we have covered highlights of what may seem to be disparate topics, three themes dominate the chapter. First, more recognition is being given to the rights and needs of children. This has encouraged a reevaluation of the doctrine of *parens patriae*, where the best interest of the child was presumed but often not achieved. Thus, questions of a child's competence to make autonomous decisions and interests of the child in a custody decision occur frequently in the literature. Second, there is increasing recognition of domestic violence, the "dark side" of families. The rights and needs of victims of abuse, including sexual abuse, are finding their way into both research and practice. Third, the role of the psychologist in the family law context is not a comfortable one for many practitioners. While mental health professionals have traditionally provided treatment to families in crisis, they are now increasingly being asked to participate in decision making that may pit family members against one another. This is particularly a problem in the child custody arena, where research on "who makes the better parent" or which is the preferred custodial arrangement is quite equivocal. Furthermore, instruments often used to measure parenting skills or the best interest of the child have not been validated. As we noted in the chapter, some factors, such as age or conflict or hostility between parents, tend to be predictive of poor adjustment to divorce and custody arrangements. Nevertheless, researchers urge extreme caution in making generalizations, because children and adolescents vary widely in individual adjustment to divorce.

Domestic violence, a phenomenon which began to come to public attention in the 1970s, challenges the resolve of the legal system as well as mental health practitioners. The legal system is still divided on the best policy approach to take to this highly troubling issue. Cases of child or intimate partner abuse, for example, when not ignored, are often handled by family or juvenile courts, rather than treated as criminal offenses. Intimate partners also may be referred to mediation, which has been called "a paradox for women" (Rifkin, 1989), both in the divorce and domestic abuse context. While mediation was widely endorsed as a way of resolving family conflicts in both domestic violence and divorce/custody situations in the early 1990s, enthusiasm had tapered somewhat by the turn of the century. As we saw in this chapter, both legal and mental health professionals working in the field of family law are guarded about this approach, although they recognize that mediation, if done properly, has many advantages compared to the traditional antagonistic and adversarial legal suit. Proponents of therapeutic jurisprudence and preventive law have also been very active, arguing that these approaches are particularly conducive to dealing with family issues.

Many of the topics raised in this chapter have only begun to be explored by researchers. Additionally, legal principles are still evolving. This is particularly true of issues surrounding the decision making ability of adolescents and hastened death.

Key Terms

Best interests of the child	Maltreatment
Child neglect	Physical abuse
Divided custody	Physical authority
Doctrine of family privacy	Preventative law
Emotional abuse	Sexual abuse
Joint custody	Sole custody
Least detrimental alternative	Split custody
Legal parental authority	Tender years doctrine
Limited joint custody	Therapeutic Jurisprudence

Questions for Review

1. What are the four basic custodial arrangements in divorce situations?
2. Identify and distinguish among the doctrines used by courts in making custody decisions.
3. Why are child custody evaluations considered among the most difficult and stressful for forensic psychologists?
4. Identify 5–8 key features of the APA Custody Evaluation Guidelines.
5. What discernible trends in testing were identified by Bow and Quinnell in their research on custody evaluations?
6. What conclusions have been drawn from research on the psychological effects on children of (a) divorce and (b) custody arrangements?
7. Identify the positive and negative effects of divorce mediation.
8. Distinguish between the two forms of legal intervention that may occur in child abuse and neglect cases.
9. Summarize the effect of closed-circuit testimony on (a) accuracy of the testimony and (b) juror ratings of guilt.
10. State the controversy involving the use of AD dolls in child sexual abuse cases.
11. Have researchers been successful at identifying the profile of a typical spouse or child abuser? Explain your answer.
12. Give examples of the equivocal findings of research on adolescent decision making.
13. What are the key features of Oregon's Death With Dignity Law?
14. List the ways in which forensic psychologists may be involved in hastened death situations.

CHAPTER 12

Juvenile Delinquency and Justice

The previous chapter covered many matters relating to children and adolescents, including issues relating to divorce and custody and problems associated with child abuse. In this chapter, we focus on juveniles who have violated the law or who are at serious risk of doing so. Not surprisingly, there are many misconceptions about these juveniles, often fueled by media accounts of sensational crimes, such as the school shootings of the 1990s. Recent statistics indicate that juvenile crime is decreasing, however, although it is still high compared to juvenile crime 20 years ago. Juveniles do get arrested disproportionately to adults, but part of this is due to their tendency to commit crime in groups. Additionally, the typical juvenile is more likely to be a victim of crime than an offender. This is not to diminish the significance of juvenile offending, which is a persistent, challenging problem in society. Furthermore, some scholars predict that juvenile crime will increase in the first decade of the 21st century, with the concomitant expected increase in the population of individuals in the criminogenic age group.

One classic longitudinal study of delinquency—by the sociologist Marvin Wolfgang and his colleagues (Wolfgang, Figlio, & Sellin, 1972)—found that a small proportion of juveniles is responsible for the largest proportion of serious juvenile offending. Specifically, about 6% of juveniles are chronic recidivists, responsible for over half of all juvenile crime and closer to three-fourths of serious juvenile crime. This chronic 6% comprises about 20% of the delinquent sample. The original Wolfgang et al. research involved a cohort of 9,945 boys born in 1945. In later studies, researchers studied both boys and girls born in 1958 (Wolfgang, 1983) and also followed up a subset of the 1945 cohort until age 30 (Wolfgang, Thornberry, & Figlio, 1987). Donna Hamparian and her colleagues (1978, 1982) conducted similar longitudinal research and reached similar conclusions. In essence, it has been consistently shown in the research that a very small percentage of juveniles are responsible for most juvenile offending. Furthermore, approximately one-fourth of the juveniles who do offend continue to be chronic offenders. That chronic group, however, has a high likelihood of becoming persistent offenders into adulthood (Wolfgang, Thornberry, & Figlio, 1987). The challenge to the juvenile justice system is to identify those juveniles who will not desist, or grow out of crime, and to provide them with effective alternatives to criminal behavior.

Juvenile Crime

Juveniles can commit two types of law violations. The first, and most common, are the **status offenses** that only they can commit by virtue of the fact that they are young. Depending upon the state, these may include running away, truancy, possession or use of alcohol, possession or use of tobacco, and the very broadly defined "incorrigibility." The second type of violation is the criminal offense—the act that violates the criminal law regardless of the age of the perpetrator. Until the 1970s, status offenses were routinely considered "delinquency." Today, in most states status offenses still exist and may land the youth in juvenile court, but the disposition will be different. A chronic 14-year-old truant, for example, is more likely to be adjudicated a "child in need of supervision" than a juvenile delinquent. If the chronic truant also commits burglaries, however, he is likely to be adjudicated delinquent; in some states, he would bypass juvenile proceedings completely and be dealt with in criminal court.

For over a century, juveniles and adults charged with crimes have been processed in different courts. Juveniles have been considered more in need of protection, less accountable for their actions, and more amenable to rehabilitation. Furthermore, much juvenile offending has been considered a "rite of passage" through adolescence, and something that, with time, would cease (Bernard, 1992). Research on juvenile crime did indeed support this desistance phenomenon (Whitehead & Lab, 1999). Rising crime rates in the 1980s, however, together with dire predictions that we faced an increase of juvenile "superpredators," tested public patience with the supposedly gentler approach with juveniles. The super-predator myth was debunked in the late 1990s, with evidence of a 9% decline in the violent juvenile arrest rate and a 31% drop in the juvenile homicide rate (Howell, 1998). Nonetheless, members of the public and policy makers alike are often not aware of such statistics.

At just over 100 years old, the juvenile court system is considered by many to be floundering, if not in major crisis. During the second half of the 20th century, liberals and conservatives alike became disenchanted with the broken promises of the separate system and the seeming futility of trying to rehabilitate. A punitive orientation was accompanied by calls to get tougher on juveniles. In the 1990s, specifically between 1992 and 1997, 47 states made their laws more punitive as they applied to juveniles (Snyder & Sickmund, 1999). A major shift in this direction was the increasing numbers of juveniles whose cases were heard in criminal courts. At the same time, scholars associated with a "rights orientation" expressed concerns that juveniles were deprived of due process protections in juvenile courts and documented disparities in treatment based on race, gender, and socioeconomic class (e.g., Feld, 1999; MacDonald & Chesney-Lind, 2001).

This chapter begins with a brief history of juvenile justice in the United States, including a review of the landmark Supreme Court decisions and legislation that put into place a variety of legal protections for juveniles. After a discussion of delinquency and some of the psychological factors that relate to it, we then review steps in the processing of juveniles that are most likely to involve consultation with psychologists and other clinicians. Critical questions pertaining to the competency of juveniles to waive their rights, to participate in proceedings, and to consent to treatment will also be addressed. The chapter concludes with an overview of juvenile rehabilitation, focusing on contemporary programs that have achieved success or that raise questions about effectiveness. It should be noted that additional discussion of juvenile offending can be found in ▶ Chapter 13, on criminal behavior.

History of Juvenile Justice

Juvenile justice was officially launched in the United States on the last day of the 1899 session of the Illinois legislature when that body passed the ***Juvenile Court Act***. The Act created a juvenile court in Illinois and gave it jurisdiction over delinquent, dependent, or neglected children. Although other states had adopted various procedures and regulations to deal with youth, the Illinois *Juvenile Court Act* represented the first *comprehensive* attempt at codification. The Act did *not* create a new or separate court system in Illinois but established a special division within the existing system. The first entirely separate juvenile court was established in Indiana in 1903.

The Illinois *Juvenile Court Act* did four things directly relevant to juvenile justice: (1) refined the definition of juvenile delinquency (a term which included status offending); (2) removed the jurisdiction of juvenile cases from the adult criminal court; (3) authorized the placement of juveniles in separate facilities away from adult offenders; and (4) provided for a system of probation, allowing the state to supervise the child outside a facility or institution.

The Illinois law quickly became the model for juvenile justice throughout the country. By 1911, 22 states had adopted similar measures, and by 1925, all but two states (Maine and Wyoming) had established juvenile courts (Tappan, 1949). The first juvenile court within the Federal Court system was created in 1906 in the District of Columbia, with jurisdiction over delinquent, dependent, incorrigible, and truant children. By 1938, the Federal system had developed a national model for juvenile court under federal jurisdiction. Today, the lower federal courts deal primarily with juveniles tried as adults on serious federal charges. The *Comprehensive Crime Control Act* passed by Congress in 1984 encourages federal prosecutors to leave the prosecution of juveniles to the states. In situations where the federal courts hold sole jurisdiction, such as in the District of Columbia and native American reservations, this is not possible.

Early Juvenile Courts

From the beginnings of the juvenile court, it was argued or implied that children below a certain age have different Constitutional rights than adults. These differences were justified because children, it was assumed, do not have the emotional or mental maturity to make important decisions for themselves and exercise those rights. Thus the doctrine of ***parens patriae***, discussed in ◀ Chapter 5 as it relates to civil commitment, was a critical component in the philosophy of the juvenile court. *Parens patriae* gives the state authority to intercede in the child's life, even over the objections of parents or guardians, with the presumption that such intervention is in the child's best interest. Thus, juvenile courts were allowed wide discretion in decision making during their first 50 years (Grisso, Tomkins, & Casey, 1988).

Children also were assumed to be more "rehabilitatable" than adults. Therefore, the early juvenile courts were encouraged to operate in a paternalistic manner, obtain extensive background information, and encourage children to "open up" and confess their illegal behavior. Judges, often at the recommendation of mental health representatives and social workers, had widespread authority to order children to institutions or to be removed from their homes and placed in foster homes, even when their transgressions were minor. There is ample documentation of the abuses associated with institutions for juveniles in the 20th century (Bernard, 1992; Rothman, 1980; Platt, 1969). Although lawyers were allowed in juvenile courts, they were not considered a necessity. In fact, they were more likely to be considered a hindrance to the rehabilitative process. Judges also had the power to remove the "hopeless" juvenile from the jurisdiction of the juvenile court and transfer the case to criminal court.

Due Process and Statutory Changes

The 1960s and 1970s brought major legal changes to juvenile justice. The rights-oriented Supreme Court led by Chief Justice Earl Warren in the 1960s found the juvenile court process highly flawed, and it required a number of changes, as we will see below. Additionally, in 1974, Congress stepped in and passed landmark legislation, the *Juvenile Justice and Delinquency Prevention Act* (JJDPA), which established federal oversight of juvenile justice and provided funding for grants, research, and treatment programs. Included in that law were provisions intended to remove status offenders from secure institutions and all juveniles from adult jails. Numerous lower court decisions across the United States also have affected the way juveniles are processed and cared for in the juvenile system. Interestingly, the U.S. Supreme Court has not ruled on conditions of confinement once juveniles are institutionalized. Lower courts, however, have protected institutionalized juveniles from cruel and unusual punishment (e.g., *Morales v. Turman*, 1974; *Nelson v. Heyne*, 1974) and some have declared that they have a right to treatment (e.g., *Morales v. Turman*, 1974). As a result of many court decisions and statutes, detained youth also have "a right to protection from violent inmates, abusive staff, unsanitary living quarters, excessive isolation, and unreasonable restraints. They must also receive adequate medical and mental health care, education (including special education for youth with disabilities), access to legal counsel, and access to family communication, recreation, exercise, and other programs" (Puritz & Scali, 1998, p. xi).

In the 1990s, advocates for children brought many legal challenges to conditions in detention and treatment facilities nationwide. Laws passed by Congress during the last quarter of the 20th century enabled some of this litigation, although the laws have been underutilized (Puritz & Scali, 1998). One such law, for example, is the *Civil Rights of Institutionalized Persons Act* (CRIPA), passed in 1980. It allows the Department of Justice (DOJ) to pursue legal action when there is systemic violation of the rights of youth held in juvenile detention and correctional facilities. Puritz and Scali (1998) noted that in the first 17 years of CRIPA's existence, the DOJ investigated 73 juvenile institutions; 17 of the investigations were closed because no systemic violation was found or the facility shut down. For the remainder of the facilities, investigation was either ongoing or the DOJ was monitoring them to assure compliance with the terms of a consent decree. Puritz and Scali describe conditions in 20 facilities in Puerto Rico, where juveniles committed and attempted suicide without staff intervention or treatment. Rats and other vermin produced widespread infections, and juveniles were forced to drink water from their toilet bowls because of defective plumbing. In similar matter, the international human rights group Amnesty International (AI), has produced a damning report on conditions and policies within juvenile justice institutions in the United States and the juvenile justice system in general (1998).

Another federal law affording juveniles an opportunity to challenge their conditions of confinement is the *Individuals with Disabilities Education Act* (IDEA) passed in 1975. This law guarantees that persons with disabilities will have education and related services individually designed to meet their special needs. Disabilities covered include mental retardation, deafness, hearing impairment, speech or language impairment, visual impairment, serious emotional disturbance, orthopedic impairment, other health impairment, blindness, specific learning disability, autism, traumatic brain injury, or multiple disabilities (Puritz & Scali, 1998). Puritz and Scali provide a list of 25 class action suits filed under the IDEA since 1975, with 15 of the 25 filed in the 1990s. "(T)he cases emanated from many different regions of the United States, clearly illustrating that the inadequacy of special education services in juvenile correctional facilities is a nationwide concern" (Puritz & Scali, 1998). It is important to note, also, that all but five of these suits also challenged the general conditions of the facility, as well as the special education problem. The suits were about evenly distributed between detention facilities and training schools.

For the most part, legal protections for juveniles have been outlined by Congress on the federal level and state courts and legislatures. The United States Supreme Court has heard relatively few cases dealing with juvenile justice. Nonetheless, its decisions in this area have significantly affected the juvenile justice process at several stages. We turn now to a discussion of these landmark decisions.

Supreme Court and Juvenile Justice

The first landmark U.S. Supreme Court decision dealing directly with a juvenile offender was *Kent v. U.S.* (1966). Although the Court had heard other juvenile cases, *Kent* was distinguished because of its wide reach. Morris Kent, Jr. was a 16-year-old charged with housebreaking, robbery, and rape while on probation under the jurisdiction of the District of Columbia Juvenile Court. When arrested, the teenager admitted committing the offenses and was placed in a receiving home for children. The juvenile court transferred his case to adult criminal court over the strong objections of his lawyer, who argued that Kent had rehabilitative potential that should be developed in a juvenile home. The lawyer also requested that he be allowed to review Kent's social service records, a request the juvenile court denied. In criminal court, Kent was found not guilty by reason of insanity of the rape charge but guilty of housebreaking and robbery. He was sentenced to 30 to 90 years and transferred to St. Elizabeth's Hospital for the mentally ill in Washington, DC. Kent appealed the original decision to transfer him to criminal court.

In reviewing Kent's appeal, the U.S. Supreme Court first recognized that there was no Constitutional requirement for a separate juvenile court system. Where there is a separate court system, however, the juvenile court may not waive jurisdiction and transfer the juvenile to criminal court without a hearing and accompanying safeguards. "There is no place in our legal system for reaching a verdict of such serious consequences without a hearing, without effective assistance of counsel, and without the statement of the reasons" (383 U.S. at 554). The Court also ruled that Kent's lawyer should have been given access to the boy's social service records.

The opinion, written by Justice Abe Fortas, strongly criticized the operations of the juvenile court and the unchecked discretionary power it wielded over the lives of juveniles. It noted that the child received the worst of both worlds, getting neither the due process protections given to adults nor the solicitous attention seemingly promised by the juvenile system. The *Kent* case sent the signal that the Supreme Court would change radically the procedures through which juveniles would be processed. The transfer decision today remains one of the most significant phases of the juvenile justice process, with increasingly more juvenile cases being heard in adult courts. As we will see later in the chapter, psychologists and other mental health professionals are often called upon to advise judges about the wisdom of such a transfer. Furthermore, ongoing research efforts are providing information about the effects of these waivers to criminal courts.

A year after *Kent*, in *In re Gault* (1967), the Court extended broad procedural safeguards to juveniles in delinquency proceedings, drastically changing the procedures under which juvenile courts were operating. Gerald Gault was a 15-year-old Arizona boy accused of making an obscene phone call to a neighbor. The Supreme Court, in reviewing the facts of the case, called his comments "of the irritatingly offensive, adolescent sex variety." Shortly after the call, which was reported to police by the neighbor, the boy was taken into police custody without his parents' knowledge and placed in a children's detention home. When Gault's mother arrived home from work, she asked her older son to find Gerald's whereabouts. Upon learning that he was confined in detention, they went to see him and were abruptly told that a hearing was scheduled for the following afternoon. His mother, Gerald, and his older brother, along with two probation officers, appeared before the juvenile court judge in chambers. The father was working out of town and could not attend.

What transpired in the judge's chambers was not recorded, and a disagreement about exactly what was said resulted. A week later another hearing was held. Gerald was not represented by counsel. The next door neighbor never appeared to testify against him and be submitted to cross-examination. Gerald was pronounced a "delinquent" and was committed to the State Industrial School where he faced a maximum six-year confinement, until he reached the age of 21. Making lewd or obscene phone calls qualified as a misdemeanor in the state of Arizona at that time. Had Gerald been an adult, his maximum penalty would have been $50 or two months in jail.

The Supreme Court used the *Gault* case as an opportunity to criticize extensively the juvenile court process. In the lengthy majority opinion, Justice Fortas wrote that the court was run like a "kangaroo court" and that "(N)either the Fourteenth Amendment nor the Bill of Rights is for adults alone" (at 13). Justice Fortas reviewed the history of the juvenile court, and concluded that juveniles were receiving the worst of possible worlds, neither due process nor effective treatment. The Court held that juveniles appearing before a juvenile court in a delinquency proceeding have the following Constitutional rights:

1. to have adequate written notice of the charges against them in order to afford them a reasonable opportunity to prepare a defense;
2. to have the assistance of counsel, and if indigent, to have counsel be appointed;
3. to be able to invoke the privilege against self-incrimination; and
4. to be able to confront and cross–examine witnesses.

The *Gault* decision was both heralded as a just and sensible decision that was long overdue and condemned as a decision which would gut the juvenile system. Opponents feared that the due process guarantees were not in the best interests of delinquent youths, whose best hope for change was to be taken under the paternalistic wing of the juvenile court. Those who supported the decision, however, pointed to the widespread, documented abuses that had been allowed to develop both in the courts and in the institutions that were intended to care for juveniles.

Interestingly, although the *Gault* decision clearly changed procedures in the juvenile courts, its impact is still questionable. Although states have complied with the Court's mandate to offer Constitutional protections, these Constitutional rights are often waived. Barry Feld (1992, p. 80), who has conducted extensive research on the issue, notes that "juveniles in most states never see a lawyer, waive their right to counsel without consulting with or appreciating the consequences of relinquishing counsel, and confront the power of the state alone and unaided." More recent data suggest that the use of attorneys by juveniles is increasing, however. In a 15-state study, it was learned that use of lawyers ranged from 65% to 97% of juvenile cases, depending upon the jurisdiction (U.S. General Accounting Office, 1995). When juveniles *do* waive their rights, it can be problematic, however. Many observers have questioned whether juveniles are even competent enough to do this (see, generally, Grisso & Schwartz, 2000). As will be discussed shortly, this has led to a call for the development of forensic assessment instruments specifically geared toward addressing this competence to waive rights.

In the 1970s, the Supreme Court decided several other landmark cases relating to juveniles. Some extended juvenile rights, while others were more cautious. In *In re Winship* (1970) the Court held that, before juveniles can be adjudicated "delinquent," there must be proof beyond reasonable doubt of every fact necessary to constitute the offense with which they have been charged. Until *Winship*, juvenile courts routinely adjudicated youths delinquent on the basis of less stringent standards, such as a preponderance of the evidence or clear and convincing evidence. In *Breed v. Jones* (1975) the Court applied the Constitutional ban on double jeopardy to delinquency proceedings. That is, a child could not be tried in a criminal court after receiving a disposition in the juvenile court.

In *McKeiver v. Pennsylvania* (1971), however, the Court ruled that juveniles did not have a Constitutional right to a jury trial. Noting that it did not wish to make juvenile proceedings identical to those in criminal courts, the Court indicated it wished to retain an element of informality and recognize the juvenile court's emphasis on treatment, rather than punishment. Nothing prevents a state from allowing trial by jury in juvenile proceedings, however, and this is now allowed in some states on a case by case basis. It should be noted, also, that juveniles tried in *criminal* courts have the same Constitutional rights to a jury trial as adults. Recall that criminal defendants have a right to a jury trial if they face a sentence of at least six months' incarceration (*Baldwin v. New York*, 1970).

Other Supreme Court decisions relating to juveniles reflect a similar *parens patriae* orientation. In *Schall v. Martin* (1984), for example, the Court ruled in a 6–3 decision that juveniles may be held in preventive detention if there is a serious risk that they will commit any crime before their next court appearance. The detention facility holding Gregory Martin and other juveniles who joined in this class action suit was crowded and deteriorating, and juveniles remained there for an average of 17 days. Adults charged with similar offenses would be given the opportunity to post bail; bail would be denied only if the adult was a threat to society, a dangerousness that would have to be demonstrated in a judicial hearing. In the case of juveniles, the Court ruled that protecting the juveniles from their own propensity to commit more crime was sufficient reason to hold them.

In a Fourth Amendment search and seizure case, *New Jersey v. T.L.O.* (1985), the Court allowed public school officials to search the possessions of students (in this case, a student's purse) without a warrant or probable cause to believe a crime had been committed. T.L.O. was found smoking in the school lavatory. School officials then searched her purse and found marijuana, a pipe, money, names of students, and other material that implicated her in marijuana dealing. The student was charged in juvenile court. The Supreme Court ruled that public school officials needed only "reasonable grounds" to believe that a student was in violation of school rules or in violation of the law in order to conduct a search. The Court emphasized that it was loosening the Fourth Amendment restriction on searches in this case in order to maintain an environment in which learning can take place. It should be noted that the case is limited to public schools because public school officials are representatives of the government and thus are governed by Constitutional requirements. Furthermore, it is because public high school students are not adults that the Court allowed a less restrictive standard. The case does not extend to public college and university settings, where students have achieved adulthood. In those situations, lower courts have ruled that agents of government need probable cause to conduct a search without consent (del Carmen, Parker, & Reddington, 1998).

In the above cases, we have seen the Supreme Court attempting to strike a balance between affording juveniles Constitutional protections similar to those of adults and protecting juveniles "for their own good"—even if it means restricting their freedoms. A few more cases will be integrated into the chapter, as they relate to topics on which we will focus. ◉ **Box 12-1** provides a summary of key Supreme Court cases relevant to juveniles.

Juvenile Delinquency

Juvenile delinquency is an imprecise social and legal label for a wide range of law- and norm-violating behavior. Legally, the term refers to behavior against the criminal code committed by an individual who has not reached adulthood. Immediately, a problem arises as to what is meant by "adulthood." Although the legal definition has traditionally been restricted to persons under age 18, the age varies by state. In some states, when persons reach the age of 17 they are no longer considered "juveniles," though they may be handled as "youthful offenders" by the criminal courts. In a small minority of states, the cut off age is 16.

Developmental Theory

A variety of theories have been proposed to explain juvenile delinquency. Over the past three decades, the psychological study of delinquency has shifted away from accepting personality traits as major determinants of delinquency toward a more interactive cognitive and developmental focus (Bartol, 2002). There is good evidence that the serious, persistent delinquency we are most concerned about begins in early childhood with aggressive, belligerent behaviors that often result in rejection by peers and some adults (Hartup, 1983; Coie, Underwood, & Lochman, 1991).

As a group, highly aggressive, troublesome children demonstrate social and interpersonal skills that are below average for their age (Bartol, 2002). They perform below average in school achievement tasks, have low vocabulary, and poor verbal reasoning, all of which have been found to correlate significantly with later delinquency (Farrington, 1979, 1987). Other predictors of later repetitive offending are habitual stealing in elementary school, lying, truancy, and running away (Loeber & Dishion, 1983).

From a psychological viewpoint, perhaps the most useful observations of delinquency have been made by Terrie Moffitt and her colleagues (1993a, 1993b). Moffit views delinquency as proceeding along at least two developmental paths. On one path, a child develops a life long trajectory of delinquency and antisocial behavior at a very early age. Moffitt (1993a, p. 679) writes: "Across the life course, these individuals exhibit changing manifestations of antisocial behavior: biting and hitting at age four, shoplifting and truancy at age ten, selling drugs and stealing cars at age 16, robbery and rape at age twenty-two, and fraud and child abuse at age thirty." These individuals, whom Moffitt calls "**life-course-persistent**" (**LCP**) offenders, continue their antisocial behavior across a wide variety of situations and do not restrict their offending to any one type of offense. Probably more troubling, LCP offenders generally commit many aggressive and violent crimes over their lifetimes.

Moffit discovered that many of these LCP offenders exhibit neurological problems during their childhoods, such as difficult temperaments as infants, attention deficit disorders or attention deficit/hyperactive disorders (ADHD) as children, and learning problems during their later school years. As children, LCPs miss opportunities to acquire and practice pro-social and interpersonal skills at each critical stage of development. This is partly because they are rejected and avoided by their childhood peers (they are often not pleasant to be with), and partly because their parents or caretakers become frustrated with their behavior and give up on them (Coie, Belding, & Underwood, 1988; Coie, Dodge, & Kupersmith, 1990). In addition, such factors as disadvantaged home environments, inadequate schools, and violent neighborhoods are likely to exacerbate the ongoing and developing antisocial behavior patterns.

The great majority of delinquents are not LCPs, however. They are individuals who begin offending during their early adolescent years and then stop offending as they approach adulthood (around age eighteen). Moffitt labels these offenders "**adolescent-limited**" (**AL**). Unlike the LCP offender, their developmental histories do not reflect the very early and persistent antisocial and behavioral problems. However, the frequency of the offending—and in some cases the violence level—of some AL offenders during the *teen years* may be as high as that of the LCP offender. In effect, the *teenage* offending patterns of the AL and the LCP may be highly similar in some cases (Moffitt et al., 1996). In this sense, a professional mental health worker or criminologist could not easily identify whether the child is an LCP or AL based on juvenile arrest records, self-reports,

BOX 12-1
The Supreme Court and Juveniles

***Kent v. U.S.* (1966)**
Brief facts: Kent, charged with housebreaking and rape, was transferred to criminal court by a juvenile court judge without a hearing.
Holding: Prior to a judicial waiver, juveniles have a right to an adversary hearing and the assistance of a lawyer to challenge the waiver. The Court also gave guidelines for judges to use in deciding whether to transfer the case.

***In re Gault* (1967)**
Brief facts: Gault, a 15-year-old charged with making an obscene phone call to a neighbor, was adjudicated delinquent in what the Court termed were "Kangaroo court proceedings." He faced incarceration in a training school until the age of 21.
Holding: In delinquency hearings, where incarceration is a possibility, juveniles have the following due process guarantees: right to written notice of charges, privilege against self-incrimination, right to a lawyer, and right to confront and cross-examine witnesses against them.

***In re Winship* (1970)**
Brief facts: A juvenile was adjudicated delinquent in juvenile court based on preponderance of the evidence that he had committed the offense.
Holding: The burden of proof in delinquency hearings is proof beyond a reasonable doubt.

***McKeiver v. Pa.* (1971)**
Brief facts: A 16-year-old charged with felonies in juvenile court requested a jury.
Holding: Juveniles in juvenile court have no Sixth Amendment right to a trial by jury. (States are free to provide juries if they wish, however.)

***Breed v. Jones* (1975)**
Brief facts: A juvenile was adjudicated delinquent in juvenile court. He was then sent to criminal court, where he was convicted.
Holding: Juveniles have a Fifth Amendment protection against double jeopardy. It was a violation of his Constitutional rights to adjudicate him in juvenile court and try him in adult court for the same offense.

***Fare v. Michael C.* (1979)**
Brief facts: A juvenile being interrogated by police asked to see his probation officer. Police informed him of his right to a lawyer, but denied the request to see the probation officer. He then waived his right to a lawyer.
Holding: Juveniles do have a Fifth Amendment right to see a lawyer before custodial interrogation. However, a probation officer is not a lawyer substitute; juveniles have no "special" *Miranda* rights.

***Schall v. Martin* (1984)**
Brief facts: Juveniles in a detention center challenged their detention, arguing that adults

or the information provided by parents or caretakers alone. On the other hand, one clue might be available from children's records or accounts: if the child had serious behavioral problems dating back to preschool years, he or she would be more likely to be LCP.

The AL delinquent is most likely, during the teen years, to engage in offenses that symbolize adult privilege and/or demonstrate autonomy from parental control. For example, they commit drug and alcohol offenses, thefts, and "status" offenses, such as running away or truancy. Although AL delinquents are likely to engage in crimes that are profitable and rewarding in the sense that they symbolize adult privileges or autonomy, they also have the willingness to abandon these actions when noncriminal actions become more rewarding and socially acceptable. For example, the onset of young adulthood brings on opportunities not attainable during the teen years, such as leaving high school for college, obtaining a full-time job, and entering a

BOX 12-1
Continued

charged with similar offenses would be eligible for pre-trial release.
Holding: Juveniles may be kept in preventive detention if there is a serious risk they will commit any crime. They are being protected from themselves. It is in their best interest (*parens patriae* rationale).

Eddings v. Oklahoma **(1982)**
Brief facts: A 16-year-old was sentenced to death, but the Court did not take some mitigating factors into account. He challenged the death sentence both on the basis of his age and the refusal to consider mitigating factors.
Holding: The Court did not reach the issue of age, except to say that it was a mitigating factor that should be taken into account. Other mitigating factors, such as a childhood marred by abuse, should also have been considered.

New Jersey v. T.L.O. **(1985)**
Brief facts: A public-high-school student caught smoking had her purse searched by a school official. When evidence of drug activity was found, school officials called police, who then took her into custody. She was referred to juvenile court.
Holding: School officials had sufficient reason to search her purse. This was not an unreasonable search and seizure in violation of the Fourth Amendment.

Thompson v. Oklahoma **(1988)**
Brief facts: 15-year-old tried for murder in criminal court was convicted and sentenced to death.
Holding: When a state does not specify a minimum age, the death penalty may not be imposed on a juvenile who was 15 years old at the time of his crime. (Case is widely believed to outrightly reject the death penalty for 15-year-olds.)

Stanford v. Kentucky **(1989)**
Brief facts: 16-year-old (and a 17-year-old in a companion case) argued that the death penalty was unconstitutional if applied to juveniles.
Holding: The death penalty is not unconstitutional when applied to juveniles who were 16 or 17 at the time of their crime. (Note: In 2002, the Supreme Court refused to revisit this issue of minimum age.)

Chicago v. Morales **(1999)**
Brief facts: Chicago had a "gang control" ordinance that allowed police to order gang members and friends who were loitering "with no apparent purpose" to move on. If they refused, they were arrested.
Holding: The ordinance, as written, violates the Fourteenth Amendment. Concurring Justices saw a First Amendment violation as well. Language in the decision seemed to invite Chicago to re-write its ordinance in such a way that would pass Constitutional muster.

relationship with a pro-social person. Most AL delinquents soon realize that they have something to lose if they continue offending into adulthood.

A critical difference between ALs and LCPs is that the ALs are significantly more likely to have learned social and interpersonal skills, and how to get along with others. They normally acquire a satisfactory repertoire of skills that enable them to get ahead academically, socially, and occupationally. The LCPs, on the other hand, have had substantially less opportunity to acquire these skills because of the social rejection from others they have received during their formative years. Therefore, the developmental histories and personal dispositions of the AL youth allow them the option of exploring new life pathways, an opportunity often denied the LCP youth.

Interestingly, more recent research has found that a simple dual developmental path may not adequately capture all the variations in criminal careers (Donnellan, Ge, & Wenk, 2000). Using data from three studies of crime and delinquency conducted in London, Philadelphia, and Racine, Wisconsin, some researchers (D'Unger, Land, McCall, & Nagin, 1998; Nagin, Farrington, & Moffitt, 1995; Nagin & Land, 1993) have identified *four* developmental paths that perhaps reflect more comprehensively the reality of offending patterns. The four are: (1) the adolescent-limited; (2) the life-course persistent (also called "high-level chronic offenders"); (3) the low-level chronic offenders (LLCs); and (4) a non-offending pattern (NCs). The ALs followed Moffitt's hypothesized offending pattern, beginning in their early teens, peaking at around age 16, and then showing a steady decline during their late teens and early adulthood (Nagin, Farrington, & Moffitt, 1995). The LPCs on the other hand, exhibited a rise in offending through early adolescence, reached a plateau by mid-teens, and remained at the same offending level well past age 18. The LCPs demonstrated their usual pattern of beginning antisocial behavior early and at a high level throughout their lifetimes. Finally, research by White, Bates, and Buyske (2001) suggests that it might be meaningful to introduce a fifth category, characterized by youths who engaged in relatively little delinquency in early adolescence but for whom delinquency increased from late adolescence into adulthood. As should be evident from the above, research on the developmental trajectories of juvenile offending is still very much a work in progress.

The developmental histories of LCPs are often punctuated with neurological problems, such as attention deficit disorder. It should be immediately emphasized that persons who have been diagnosed with an attention deficit disorder (ADD) or attention deficit hyperactivity disorder (ADHD) are not necessarily chronic offenders. On the other hand, chronic juvenile offenders frequently are diagnosed as ADHD at some point during their early school years.

Attention Deficit Hyperactivity Disorder (ADHD)

Attention deficit hyperactivity disorder (ADHD) ◀ (see ▲ **Table 4-1**) is characterized by three major symptoms: (1) inattention (does not seem to listen, or is easily distracted); (2) impulsivity (acts before thinking, shifts quickly from one activity to another); and (3) excessive motor activity (cannot sit still, fidgets, runs about, is talkative and noisy). The American Psychiatric Association (1994) in its DSM–IV recognizes three subtypes of ADHD: inattentive, hyperactive, and combined, depending on which of the three symptoms predominate. The DSM-IV also prefers to focus only on two major symptoms: inattention and impulsivity/hyperactivity (combining these two). For clarity, we will continue to use the three–symptom perspective in this section.

The terms "attention deficit hyperactivity disorder" and "ADHD" are relatively new. Descriptions of the syndrome, however, can be found in the medical literature at least since the 1900s (Lynam, 1996). In the 1940s and 1950s, the disorder was labeled "minimal brain damage syndrome" or "minimal brain disorder" (MBD). In the 1960s it was called "hyperkinetic reaction of childhood" or more commonly "hyperactivity." In the 1970s and 1980s, the disorder was referred to as an "attention disorder" or AD. And in 1987, the term "attention deficit hyperactivity disorder" was ushered in by the American Psychiatric Association (1987). Now the term "hyperactivity—impulsivity—attention disorder" (HIA) is often used. For our purposes here, however, we will use the still popular and umbrella term ADHD.

ADHD symptoms arise relatively early in childhood, typically before the age of 7 and usually remain throughout a person's lifetime (Barkley, 1997; Nigg, 2001). ADHD is the leading psychological diagnosis for American and Canadian children, occurring in approximately 3 to 7% of the childhood population, with boys being overrepresented by a ratio of about three to one (Barkley, 1997; Centers for Disease Control and Prevention, 2002). Educators report that ADHD children have difficulty staying on task, remaining cognitively organized, sustaining academic achievement in the school setting, and maintaining control over their behavior. But the disorder extends to many behavioral problems. For example, Barkley (1997, p. 65) provides the following list of problems: "Over development, ADHD is associated with greater risks for low academic achievement, poor school performance, retention in grade, school suspensions and expulsions, poor peer and family relations, anxiety and depression, aggression, conduct problems and delinquency, early substance experimentation and abuse, driving accidents and speeding violations, as well as difficulties in adult social relationships, marriage and employment."

ADHD is a puzzling problem, the cause of which is largely unknown. Some scientists and medical practitioners maintain that ADHD children are born with a biological predisposition toward hyperactivity; others argue that some children are exposed to environmental factors that damage the nervous system. Rolf Loeber (1990), for example, found that exposure to toxic substances during the preschool years, such as lead paint or toxic waste, often damages children's neurological development and leads to symptoms of ADHD. Other researchers contend that cognitive deficits that prevent adequate control of behavior and motivation may be the principal component (Barkley, 1997). Although the causes of ADHD are probably multiple and extremely difficult to specifically identify in most children, neuropsychological factors are gaining acceptance by experts in the field (Nigg, Hinshaw, Carte, & Treuting, 1998).

One thing about ADHD appears quite clear, however. ADHD is not so much a disorder of activity as it is a disorder of interpersonal relationships. Even those individuals who are not hyperactive or aggressive still have problems in their social interactions. They seem to chronically lack friendship and intimacy (Henker & Whalen, 1989). Educators report that the overriding feature of ADHD children is their tendency to annoy and irritate other children around them, leading to social rejection by their peers. In addition, the most common problem associated with ADHD is not emotional or psychological disorder, such as serious depression, but delinquency and drug abuse. Terrie Moffitt (Moffitt & Silva, 1988; Moffitt, 1993b) reports that a very large proportion of ADHD children report delinquent behaviors in early adolescence. She also found that children between the ages of five and seven who exhibit the characteristics of both ADHD and antisocial behavior not only have special difficulty with social relationships but also, if untreated, have a high probability of consistent serious delinquency into adolescence and beyond (Moffitt, 1990). The data suggest that youth with both ADHD symptoms and antisocial behavior are at very high risk for developing the most lengthy and serious criminal careers (Moffitt, 1990). David Farrington (1991) discovered that violent offenders often have a history of hyperactivity, impulsivity, and attention problems.

Habitual antisocial behaviors in children and adolescents may lead to a diagnosis of **conduct disorder** ◀ (see ▲ **Table 4-1**). Stealing, setting fires, skipping school, destroying property, fighting, being cruel to animals and people, and frequently telling lies are all examples of such antisocial behaviors. The diagnosis conduct disorder is usually confined to childhood or adolescence. It is to be distinguished from the clinical term **antisocial personality disorder** ◀ (see ▲ **Table 4-1**), a diagnostic category designated primarily for adults who displayed conduct disorders during their childhood or adolescence and continue serious offending into adulthood. The research evidence so far strongly supports the observation that ADHD in children and adolescents has a frequent connection with conduct disorder (Nigg, 2001; Nigg, et al., 1998) as well as psychopathic behavior (Frick, Barry, & Bodin, 2000; Lynam, 1996). [We will include a discussion of juvenile psychopathy in ▶ Chapter 13.]

Special Topic: School Violence

The topic of school violence took on a chilling urgency in the late 1990s, when a rash of school shootings made headlines. Communities across the United States that had previously had a low profile—West Paducah, Kentucky; Jonesboro, Arkansas; Pearl, Mississippi; Springfield, Oregon—suddenly became notorious. The most infamous case was the mass murder of twelve students and one teacher at Columbine High School in Littleton, Colorado, in April 1999. The two teenage boys who did the shooting (Dylan Klebold and Eric Harris) committed suicide during the incident. An additional 20 students were injured. To the public and the news media, the shooters appeared to be two "ordinary boys" from "normal" middle-class families living in an affluent suburb of Denver. Although there had been a number of school shootings prior to Columbine (there had been at least ten school shootings between 1996 and 1999), the Columbine shooting prompted considerable concern and outrage nationwide. In addition, the media and some experts rashly made gross generalization about the out-of-control school violence problem, advocating or demanding quick and extensive solutions.

Mary Ellen O'Tool (2000) lists the usual wrong or unverified impressions of school violence promoted by the news media. For example, the media have asserted that school violence is an epidemic, or implied that all school shooters are alike, or that any unusual or aberrant interest or hobbies are hallmarks of the student destined to become violent. Despite the heavy media attention directed at school violence in recent years, however, there is very little evidence that it is a widespread problem or any different in incidence than previous years. O'Tool, after extensive study, concludes—while admitting school violence is always terrifying—that "Overall, the level of violence in American schools is falling, not rising" (p. 33).

The most recent National Crime Victimization Survey (NCVS) data on school violence confirm O'Tool's observations as do supplementary data collected by the Bureau of Justice Statistics (BJS). According to a BJS report (Kaufman et al., 2001), national indicators affirm that the levels of crime in school have continued to decline, that acts that promote fear and detract from learning are decreasing, and that students feel more safe in school than they did several years ago. Lawrence (1998, p. 29) asserts that "There is no strong evidence that serious crime in schools is an extensive problem or that the problem has increased significantly; serious physical injuries or financial loss are rare in schools, although minor victimizations and verbal threats do occur regularly." Furthermore, Lawrence notes that, with the exception of some urban schools in high crime areas, students and teachers are safer in most schools than they are in other parts of the community.

Nevertheless, about 2.5 million students between the ages of 12 through 18 were victims of school crime in 2000. Approximately 186,000 of these students were victims of serious crimes in school (rape, sexual assault, robbery, and aggravated assault). In an effort to maximize the safety of students and teachers, many governmental and private funds have been made available to schools to develop a plethora of programs designed to guard school premises and/or to resolve conflicts among students. In some communities, police officers are assigned to patrol schools and school grounds. During the 1990s and early 2000, teen courts and peer mediation centers were established, sometimes on school premises, to educate youth about the justice system, engage them in solving their own problems, and hold each other accountable for unacceptable behavior.

The Juvenile Justice Process

In many ways the juvenile justice process parallels the adult criminal justice progress, as it was described in ◀ Chapter 3. Recall that in that chapter we reviewed the steps of the criminal process, including the role of psychologists at each stage. In the juvenile context, the terminology is somewhat different and, in some situations, the legal rights are not identical.

Early Processing

Although juveniles, like adults, may be arrested if police believe there is probable cause to believe they committed or are in process of committing a crime, in some jurisdictions the preferred term is "taken into custody." In fact, under the laws of all states, juveniles may be taken into custody for reasons other than committing a crime. Thus, in a typical statute, a juvenile may be taken into custody not only in "arrest" situations, but also (a) pursuant to an order of the juvenile court (as when the juvenile is a truant); (b) if the juvenile is in danger from his or her surroundings; or (c) if police have either suspicion or probable cause to believe he or she is a runaway. Immediately, we see a distinction between the deprivation of freedom permitted in the juvenile context and that permitted in the adult context.

In a recent case, *Chicago v. Morales* (1999), the Supreme Court placed restrictions on the power of police officers to take into custody juveniles who refused to "move on" when ordered to by police. The City of Chicago had an ordinance designed to attack its juvenile gang problem. Officers were allowed to approach known gang members who were gathered for the apparent purpose of planning illegal activity. Police could then order them to disburse, and if they refused to do this, to take them into custody pursuant to the laws of arrest. Note that the ordinance did not require a finding of *probable cause* to believe the individuals were engaged in crime, which is the legal standard needed for an arrest. The Supreme Court ruled that the ordinance violated the 14th Amendment's due process guarantee, and some Justices also saw it as a 1st Amendment violation. While recognizing Chicago's interest in preventing illegal activity on the part of gang members, the Court said that simply "being a gang member" was not sufficient to incur law enforcement activity of this sort.

Once arrested (or otherwise taken into custody), juveniles typically must be taken to juvenile court or to their parents or guardians. In arrest situations, most jurisdictions do not allow custodial interrogation by police without the presence of a parent or a guardian, but as we will see, it is not unusual for parents and guardians to allow this questioning, even without the presence of an attorney. If the juvenile is taken to court, an intake officer will then make a decision to detain the juvenile or to release him to parents or guardians. A detention order will result in either secure or non-secure detention, the latter typically achieved in a group home or shelter. It is important to note that the bail issue does not typically arise in the juvenile context, although some states are experimenting with offering bail to juveniles. Bail may not be denied to adults unless there is evidence of dangerousness (*U.S. v. Salerno*, 1987); in the juvenile context, in keeping with the doctrine of *parens patriae*, preventive detention is allowed to protect the juvenile from his or her own continuing illegal activity (*Schall v. Martin*, 1984). Statistics indicate that only a small minority of juveniles (10–20%) are subjected to secure detention (Puritz & Scali, 1998). Nevertheless, the conditions in detention facilities and the over-representation of minority groups have raised numerous concerns about the use of detention in the juvenile justice system (Leiber, 2002; Whitehead & Lab, 1999).

At this early stage of processing, many juveniles are diverted from the juvenile justice system, either formally or informally. For example, police may have questioned the juvenile and decided not to turn her over for juvenile court processing. Intake officers may make a similar decision, deciding to give the juvenile another chance or to refer him to a community diversion program. In diversion programs, first-time offenders typically admit their guilt and then agree to participate in programs and/or make restitution to victims or to the community (Whitehead & Lab, 1999). Because of the increasing seriousness of the juvenile drug problem, many jurisdictions have also established drug courts specifically for juvenile offenders. Like the adult drug courts discussed in ◀ Chapter 3, these treatment-oriented courts are a good alternative to prosecution and possible incarceration for juveniles whose crimes can be attributed to substance abuse.

Delinquency Petitions

If the juvenile's case is not diverted, the process continues with the filing of a petition of delinquency. This is the juvenile equivalent of the adult charging process through a complaint, information, or indictment. The delinquency petition, prepared by the prosecutor upon notification by the intake officer, outlines the allegations against the juvenile. At this point, the juvenile's case may be waived to criminal court via several possible routes, which we will discuss later in the chapter. A case that remains in juvenile court will then go to a delinquency hearing. This is an adversarial proceeding that is typically closed to the public. If there is a possibility that the juvenile might be institutionalized (a possibility that exists in virtually all delinquency cases), the juvenile has the right to written notice of charges, to be represented by an attorney, to call and cross-examine witnesses, and to be free from self-incrimination (*In re Gault*, 1967). Juveniles do not have a Constitutional right to a trial by jury in juvenile court (*McKeiver v. Pennsylvania*, 1971). If the judge, as finder of fact, finds the juvenile guilty beyond a reasonable doubts of the facts alleged in the petition, the juvenile is adjudicated a delinquent (whereas an adult would be "convicted"). There follows a disposition hearing, which is the equivalent of sentencing in the adult context.

Disposition

The juvenile justice system provides a vast array of dispositional options, including both community and institutionally-based sanctions. The most common disposition is juvenile probation, which is typically ordered in about 60% of the cases that receive some sanction (Black, 2001). Juvenile probation, which has been called "the workhorse of the juvenile justice system" (Torbet, et al., 1996), is accompanied by a range of supervisory and treatment approaches directed at rehabilitating the juvenile and protecting the community from future offending. About 25% of delinquency cases reaching juvenile courts result in residential placement (Black, 2001). As we proceed through the chapter, we will be describing and reviewing research on some of the programs used by the juvenile justice system in both institutional and community settings. There, the distinctions between the AL and LCP delinquents discussed earlier in the chapter will be reintroduced. At present, however, we will focus on critical topics relating to psychological involvement at various stages of the juvenile justice process.

Competency to Waive Constitutional Rights

A major issue in juvenile justice deals with the ability of juveniles to waive their Constitutional rights. Like the adult suspect and defendant, the juvenile encounters several stages at which a waiver of rights can occur. For example, a juvenile might waive the right to a lawyer before custodial interrogation by police, or may waive the right to legal representation during a delinquency hearing. Researchers have learned that many juveniles are not represented by lawyers during their delinquency proceedings (Feld, 1992, 2000), a fact suggesting that they have waived that right. An alternate, but less likely explanation is that they were not informed of the right.

Miranda v. Arizona (1966) established the Constitutional requirement that persons accused of crimes must be informed of their rights to an attorney and to avoid self-incrimination prior to being subjected to custodial interrogation by law enforcement officers. Upon indication by the person in custody that he or she wishes an attorney, interrogation must stop. Information gained after the *Miranda* warning is given is admissible as evidence only if the person has given a knowing, intelligent, and clearly voluntary waiver of these rights. This central aspect of the *Miranda* requirement—*knowing, intelligent and voluntary*—is a critical issue for both psychology and law. Where juveniles are concerned, this is particularly problematic. At what age can the average juvenile meet these standards? And, even if the average juvenile can meet these standards, is *this* juvenile capable of making this decision? Can even the average adult understand and competently exercise his or her rights within the *Miranda* context? Similar questions are raised about the issue of waiving the right to a lawyer during delinquency proceedings (*in re Gault*, 1967).

The U.S. Supreme Court case *Fare v. Michael C.* (1979) involved a juvenile's waiver of his right to a lawyer during custodial interrogation. Michael C. was a 16-year-old charged with rape and robbery. At the police station, he was told he had a right to see a lawyer, but he apparently interpreted this *Miranda* warning as a police ruse. "How do I know you guys won't pull no police officer in and tell me he's an attorney" (p. 711)? Described as immature, distraught, and poorly educated, Michael C. repeatedly asked to see his probation officer instead of an attorney. He was told his probation officer would be contacted after he answered police questions. Asked again if he wished an attorney, he said he did not.

The Supreme Court considered the question of whether his request to speak to his probation officer before police interrogation was equivalent to a wish to speak with an attorney. The Court (by a 5–4 vote) confirmed that juveniles, like adults, had a Constitutional right to a lawyer before custodial interrogation, but rejected the argument that the boy's request to see his probation officer should have been granted before questioning continued. The majority held that a probation officer is in no position to represent the interests of a juvenile, as intended by *Miranda*, because the probation officer has an obligation to represent the state, not the juvenile.

However the Court expressed concern, as to whether juveniles really have the capacity to understand the warnings given to them, the nature of their Constitutional rights, or the consequences of waiving them. Thus, *Fare* warned judges to consider the circumstances (or the social context) of the interrogation as well as characteristics of the juvenile, such as age, education, background, and intelligence in deciding whether a waiver was valid. Relevant circumstances, for example, might be the length of detention prior to the interrogation, the emotional state of the parents, or the officer's style of questioning (although police are given considerable leeway in this area). Relevant characteristics of the juvenile would include past experience with the juvenile justice system, as well as the demographic variables mentioned above.

The Supreme Court, in the *Fare* case, did not give juveniles a Constitutional right to see anyone other than a lawyer prior to custodial interrogation. Many state legislatures as well as state courts, however, have given juveniles a right to see their parents or guardians. In fact, in some jurisdictions, police officers are forbidden to question juvenile suspects who are in custody without the presence of their parents, guardians, lawyers, or another interested adult. The "in-custody" requirement is crucial; police officers often question juveniles in a wide range of informal situations, without being obliged to contact the adults who are responsible for them. Even when parents or guardians are present, and even when they are well intended, however, we cannot assume that they will act in the juvenile's best interest (Grisso, 1981; Grisso & Ring, 1979). One study found that 70–80% of the parents offered no advice to their children on the issue of speaking with police (Grisso, 1981). As Grisso (1998, p. 44) comments, "At the time of their children's arrests, many parents themselves are anxious, fearful, or confused during the police encounter. Others are angry at the youth and contribute to the coercive pressure of the interrogation."

Barry Feld (2000) has been a vocal critic of the juvenile court process. Feld, who has advocated the abolition of the juvenile court and the establishment of a "youth discount" system in criminal courts (Feld, 1997), argues cogently that juveniles are not provided with the due process protections they deserve in the juvenile courts seemingly established in their best interests. Noting that juveniles routinely waive the right to counsel, both at custodial interrogation and in delinquency and pre-delinquency proceedings, Feld compliments the few states that require counsel or that bar any out-of-home placement for unrepresented youth (Feld, 2000). Even represented youth, however, may not be well served. Feld discusses the institutional pressures on defense lawyers to cooperate by providing less-than-zealous advocacy to their clients.

Role of Psychologists

The final decision as to whether to waive rights is left to the juvenile. Questions about the validity of the waiver will arise later in the juvenile process, when the psychologist or other mental health professional is brought in to assess, in hindsight, the juvenile's competency to waive. Typically, at this point the juvenile has confessed to a crime, and the defense lawyer is seeking to have the confession excluded because the waiver of the right against self-incrimination was not a voluntary, knowing, and intelligent waiver. It is a rare situation whereby a psychologist would be consulted *before* the juvenile waives the right and provides police with a confession.

There is good empirical evidence suggesting that many juveniles cannot understand Constitutional rights (Grisso & Schwartz, 2000). Psychologists or other clinicians who consult with the courts on this issue must be knowledgeable, not only about the law and the research in this area, but also about adolescent development and decision making (Grisso, 1998; Heilbrun, Marczyk, & DeMatteo, 2002). Grisso (1998, p. 55) also adds that they must "attend to questions of psychosocial maturity, mental disorder, and emotional disturbance." Early research by Grisso (1981) examined the ability of juveniles to understand the *Miranda* warnings and to comprehend their function and significance within the context of interrogation and subsequent court proceedings. The Grisso research found that most juveniles age 14 and younger do not really understand the meaning of the *Miranda* warnings nor their implications. Therefore, it is highly questionable whether they can meaningfully waive their rights to an attorney during questioning or interrogation, or even waive their rights to remain silent. Furthermore, juveniles between the ages of 15 and 16 with below average intelligence also are unable to comprehend the meaning of the *Miranda* in a manner that meets the knowing, intelligent standard set forth in the *Miranda* ruling.

On the other hand, 15 and 16 year juveniles of at least average intelligence did as well in their understanding of *Miranda* as the adults—who, as a group, did not do particularly well either. Grisso discovered that at least one-quarter of the adult groups failed to meet the absolute standard for adequately understanding *Miranda* and its implications. Surprisingly, many juveniles *and* adults were convinced that refusal to talk about one's illegal involvements when questioned by a judge would amount to perjury. Many also believed that the right to remain silent can be given or taken away by the judge at his or her discretion. Grisso (1981) concluded, " (U)sing adults as the standard, then, our results indicate that juveniles' competence to waive their rights to silence and counsel is seriously diminished by their inferior understanding of the function and significance of those rights" (p. 128). The one exception to this conclusion was for the juvenile with a great deal of experience with court processes (those referred for felony charges three or more times in the past). Even so, not all youths with prior police and court experience were sophisticated about the law or legal procedures.

Because the law gives little guidance to judges in how to assess the ability of juveniles to waive their rights, juvenile courts often turn to information provided by mental health professionals, especially in the evaluations they submit to the court (Grisso, Tomkins, & Casey, 1988; Hecker & Steinberg, 2002). However, the laws also do not provide guidance on what kinds of information clinicians are supposed to present to the court. Grisso (1998) has been at the forefront of offering suggestions in this endeavor and has developed a forensic assessment instrument specifically for the purpose. He recommends that psychologists and other clinicians thoroughly understand the request, be it from the defense attorney or the court, before undertaking the evaluation. Upon accepting the assignment, the clinician then obtains available records and reports (school, mental health, delinquency). Interviews with the parents or other adults as well as with the youth are also a routine part of the process. Grisso also recommends three standardized measures that may be helpful: (1) the Comprehension of *Miranda* Rights (CMR) and its offshoots, Comprehension of *Miranda* Rights-Recognition (CMR–R), Comprehension of *Miranda* Vocabulary (CMV), and Function of Rights in Interrogation (FRI); (2) standardized tests of cognitive abilities; and (3) personality tests. The *Miranda* Comprehension tests were initially developed and administered to 431 male youths in juvenile detention centers and treatment programs, as well as 203 male adults in half-way houses following their prison terms (Grisso, 1981). Although these were in the first-generation of forensic assessment instruments, they remain the only *Miranda* comprehension FAIs available to clinicians today.

Adjudicative Competence

An issue that is beginning to receive considerable attention among forensic psychologists is that of a juvenile's adjudicative competence, the equivalent of competency to stand trial in the adult context (e.g., Grisso, 1998; Heilbrun, Marczyk, & DeMatteo, 2002; McKee & Shea, 1999; Oberlander et al., 2001). Essentially, **adjudicative competence** is the ability to participate in a wide variety of juvenile court proceedings. As Oberlander et al. (2001) note, juvenile proceedings can involve a range of pre-trial strategies and decisions. For example, juveniles often must decide whether to admit guilt to an offense or to require the state to undertake delinquency proceedings. In jurisdictions where lawyers are not automatically assigned, they must decide whether to accept the assistance of an attorney. They may be given a choice between a diversionary program (where they typically must admit guilt) and delinquency proceedings (where they formally plead guilty or their guilt must be established by the prosecutor beyond a reasonable doubt). When a judicial waiver to criminal court is a possibility, the juvenile must decide whether to challenge such a waiver. Considering the range of possible decisions a juvenile must make, the question of his or her competence to make these decisions is of paramount importance.

Competency to stand trial becomes an important issue for those juveniles whose cases have been transferred to criminal court. Are juveniles significantly less competent than adults to understand legal proceedings, assist their attorney, and make decisions which are in their best interest? Questions of competency to stand trial have traditionally revolved around a defendant's mental illness or mental retardation. However, many commentators argue that—in the case of juveniles—cognitive and emotional development should also be a factor.

Age and Developmental Considerations

Thomas Grisso (1997, 1998) has provided excellent reviews of the research in this area. Grisso notes that many studies address *adolescent* cognitive development and decision-making skills, but far more research focusing on *delinquents* and the particular situations facing them is needed. Thus far, it seems clear that children age 13 and below are at a significantly greater risk than adults for not being able to play the role of defendant. Children aged 14–16, on the other hand, vary considerably. Some seem to have developed legally relevant cognitive abilities, while others are significantly developmentally delayed. As Grisso and others (see, generally, Grisso & Schwartz, 2000) have noted, for this age group, age alone is a poor indicator of their competence to stand trial. Some research suggests, for example, that 14-year-olds are no different than adults in their ability to make decisions and conceptualize their rights (Melton, 1987). However, when subsets of delinquents are studied, they see their rights as what one is "allowed" to do rather than as entitlements. Delinquents also are more skeptical than non-delinquents about the benefits of legal counsel. Grisso notes that research on the developmental abilities of adolescents as a group should not be generalized to the developmental abilities of delinquents, whose life experiences often have placed them at a cognitive disadvantage. Delinquents also are *more likely* than adolescents as a group to have learning disabilities, low intellectual functioning, and emotional disturbances, all of which place them at risk of not being competent to stand trial in criminal courts. We must be careful *not* to stereotype delinquents, though, because many are *not* learning disabled, of low intelligence, or emotionally disturbed.

Another issue rarely addressed relates to the chronological age of juveniles entering the juvenile justice system. Approximately 9% of all juvenile arrests involve children 12 and under (Office of Juvenile Justice and Delinquency Prevention, 2000). Police questioning of children this young obviously raises concerns. Juvenile courts also are increasingly faced with a younger population, including children as young as seven. Thus far, in discussing competence to waive *Miranda* and adjudicative competence, we have focused upon juveniles who are adolescents. From a developmental psychology perspective, much research suggests that a line of demarcation must be drawn between children who have reached this stage and those who have not.

Until recently, the competency question was rarely raised in the juvenile justice system. Juvenile courts have traditionally operated according to a *parens patriae* philosophy and have been assumed to be protective, acting in the best interest of the children who appeared before them. With increasing due process protections provided to juveniles, however, the issue of their competency to stand trial began to be raised. Furthermore, the increasing punitiveness of many juvenile courts, including the possibility of transfer to criminal courts, has made adjudicative competency an important consideration. The U.S. Supreme Court has not addressed whether the pre-delinquency hearing stages in juvenile court are subject to the *Dusky* standard of competency discussed in ◀ Chapter 4. However, statutes or case law in approximately half the states as well as in federal jurisdictions do support some form of inquiry into the adjudicative competence of juveniles (Grisso, 1998; Heilbrun, Hawk, & Tate, 1996; McKee & Shea, 1999). When juvenile cases are heard in criminal courts, it is clear that the *Dusky* standard applies, although it has sometimes been altered (Oberlander et al., 2001). The present discussion of adjudicative competency should be taken to apply to that context, as well.

The MacArthur Project and the Role of Psychologists

Once again, the MacArthur Foundation Research Network provides some help in understanding this important topic. In 1999, researchers began to gather data for a multi-site Juvenile Competence Study. Goals included comparing adjudicative competency in juveniles and in adults as well as identifying the specific abilities on which the two groups differed. Researchers also wished to identify what youths were at greatest risk for incompetence due to developmental immaturity, as well as explore the role of mental disorder in adjudicative incompetence.

The above research project also seeks to advise psychologists and other clinicians on identifying those youths who are seriously deficient in adjudicative competency. This is a critical issue, because up to this point standards relating to the juvenile competence inquiry vary widely (Oberlander et al., 2001). For example, in some states immaturity is considered to be a legitimate basis for a finding of incompetence. Other states do not recognize immaturity, but do recognize mental disease or defect as legitimate bases. Some states also have altered the first prong of the *Dusky* standard, requiring a factual but not a rational understanding of the legal proceedings (Oberlander et al., 2001).

In support of some adjustment of the standard, Barnum (2000) discusses several factors that distinguish the juvenile competency question from the adult competency question. He notes, for example, that many delinquency proceedings are rehabilitative in orientation; thus, it is important to establish the extent to which the juvenile understands this goal. Additionally, juvenile procedures vary widely in their degree of formality. They may be informal, in private, with only the major participants present, or they may be "as procedurally elaborate as a major criminal trial" (Barnum, 2000, p. 195). The context in which the juvenile will be expected to make decisions must be considered within the competency evaluation process. Barnum also notes that the juvenile's relationship with parents or guardians is an important component in the assessment process, since the law assumes that children are not autonomous and that parents will act on the child's behalf.

The extent to which juveniles can effectively communicate with their lawyers, the second prong of the *Dusky* standard, also merits some consideration. Again, Barnum (2000) provides useful suggestions to the clinician conducting the evaluation. He recommends that both the lawyer and the juvenile should be interviewed. Lawyers may perceive their clients as having a higher degree of understanding than they actually have; alternately, they may overestimate the degree of cognitive or emotional deficit. Furthermore, a lawyer with limited experience with children, particularly children with developmental difficulties, may find it problematic to communicate effectively with his or her client. Thus the inability to assist counsel on one's behalf may reflect a shortcoming of the lawyer, rather than the juvenile.

The competency assessment instruments discussed in ◀ Chapters 2 and 4 are used by some psychologists to assess adjudicative competence in juveniles, even though these instruments were not developed or standardized for juvenile populations. Thus, forensic examiners seem even more reluctant to use these instruments with juveniles than with adults. As Barnum (2000, p. 211) states, "(T)o rely on the simple transfer from adult settings of such instruments for gathering the basic required information about a youth's understanding and collaboration risks missing areas of strength and weakness that may be relevant to the youth's participation in the juvenile case." However, there have been some recent attempts to modify existing screening instruments to evaluate competency in adolescents (Cooper, 1997).

In recent years, commentators have begun to call for more research specifically focusing upon juvenile competency (e.g., Heilbrun, Hawk, & Tate, 1996; Oberlander, et al., 2001). Hence, the research report from the MacArthur Network is eagerly awaited. Powerful arguments can be made that age, particularly below a certain point (e.g., pre-adolescence), should be a heavily weighed criterion in making a competency determination, but clearly other criteria are at least as relevant. Heilbrun et al. (1996) have described the complex case of a 10-year-old charged with grand larceny who had a juvenile court record, a diagnosis of Attentive Deficit/Hyperactivity Disorder (ADHD), a learning disability, and a full scale IQ of 95, among other things. Heilbrun et al. then bemoaned the absence of behavioral science research on juvenile competence to rely upon, though they noted that research on juvenile decision making or ability to waive rights (viz., Grisso, 1981; Steinberg & Cauffman, 1996, for reviews) was clearly relevant to their tasks. Nevertheless, they call for development of assessment instruments and methods specifically sensitive to the developmental maturity of juveniles.

Ethical Considerations

Clinicians offering services to the juvenile justice system are also concerned about issues revolving around privacy, privilege, confidentiality, and consent to treatment—which were discussed in ◀ Chapters 4 and 5. In the juvenile context, the principles are not identical. Defense attorneys or parents may wish to be present during evaluations, for example, and in some states they have a right to be there (Grisso, 1998). Juveniles do not possess the same right as adults to refuse treatment, nor are they asked to consent to treatment, even when treatment involves medication. In justifying limitations on rights of juveniles and allowing adults to act in their best interests, the Supreme Court has noted that "children are always in some form of custody" (*Parham v. J.R.*, 1979; *Schall v. Martin*, 1984). Psychologists working in juvenile settings need to be aware of these differences and to adapt their practices to the legal requirements and the needs of juvenile offenders.

Juveniles Found Incompetent

Although research on pre-adjudication competence in juveniles is sparse, some studies have begun to identify what type of juvenile is most likely to be recommended by clinicians as incompetent or ruled incompetent by a court. Thus far, and not surprisingly, chronological age appears as a crucial factor. An early study (Savitsky & Karras, 1984) compared both incarcerated and non-incarcerated juveniles to non-incarcerated adults on scores on the Competency Screening Test (Lipsitt, Lelos, & McGarry, 1971). Chronological age had a significant effect on CST scores, with scores improving as age increased. Cowden & McKee (1995) studied 144 juveniles between the ages of 9 and 16 who had been assessed by multi-disciplinary assessment teams for trial competence. Age again emerged as a significant determinant of the teams' judgments; additionally, diagnosis was a critical component. Almost three-fourths (72.4%) of the juveniles with no diagnosis were judged competent. Another critical factor was the juvenile's history of remedial education, with fewer than half (46.1%) of the juveniles with that background being judged competent. Variables that did not influence competency judgements were sex, race, seriousness and number of charges, mental health history, and history of previous contacts with the courts.

A third study that also found age a significant variable, also found that *arrest* history did influence *court* findings, however. McKee and Shea (1999) studied a sample of 112 juvenile defendants in family court, who had been subjected to court-ordered competency evaluations. Although 61% had been considered by case psychiatrists to have at least one deficit that might lead to a court finding of incompetence, only 14% were actually found IST. McKee and Shea compared the demographic, historical, clinical, and offense characteristics of the two groups (competent and incompetent defendants). Only age, intelligence level, and history of juvenile arrest differentiated them.

Conclusions

In sum, adjudicative competency has become an important issue in juvenile justice. It will be interesting to see how juveniles will be treated as presumably more of them are ruled incompetent. Thus far, we have very little research and primarily anecdotal accounts of the relatively rare incompetence findings. Recall that adults found IST are either treated for restoration of competency or their cases are dismissed. In the case of juveniles, a third option is possible. In a less formal proceeding than a delinquency hearing, the juvenile may be adjudicated a *child* or *juvenile in need of supervision*. Although such an adjudication limits the dispositions available to the juvenile judge, considerable control over the juvenile's life is still possible. For example, the judge cannot send the juvenile to a secure institution for treatment or protection of the community, but can commit the juvenile to the care of social service agencies. A range of options—including community treatment, group homes, camps, and other non-secure facilities—then become available. It should also be noted that parents may be persuaded to place their children in private treatment facilities. The juvenile who lacks adjudicative competence also may be diverted to other community programs or placed on informal probation. In fact, it is far more likely that such approaches will be taken than that attempts will be made to restore the juvenile to competency. Essentially, "restoration" is inappropriate in many juvenile cases; because of the juvenile's level of development and maturity, he or she had not yet achieved competence in the first place.

Transferring Juveniles to Criminal Courts

The cases of most juveniles charged with violating the law are heard in juvenile or family court, which is guided by a rehabilitative rather than punitive philosophy. In the 1980s and 1990s, however, increasingly more of these cases were heard in criminal courts, in part reflecting society's retributive orientation, particularly toward juveniles who are violent (Grisso, 1996). Despite the fact that juvenile violence has shown signs of abating, transfers to criminal court have not lessened—in fact, the trend is to transfer more juvenile cases to criminal court (Heilbrun et al., 1997; Snyder, Sickmund, & Poe-Yamagata, 2000). Furthermore, juveniles are being transferred for a wide variety of offenses, not just violent ones. In 1993, for example, offenses against persons accounted for 42% of judicially waived cases, property offenses accounted for 38%, drug offenses 10% and public order offenses 9% (Snyder, Sickmund, & Poe-Yamagata, 1996). Nonetheless, transfer is typically reserved for the most serious cases and the most serious juvenile offenders. In a comprehensive, four-state study of juvenile transfers in the 1990s, Snyder, Sickmund, & Poe-Yamagata (2000) found that weapon use, victim injury, age of the offender, and nature of the court history were important variables in the transfer decision making. Thus, if a juvenile charged with a public order offense is transferred to criminal court, the juvenile probably is close to the age where he would no longer be under the jurisdiction of the juvenile court or has a history of more serious offending.

Waiver Options

There are three primary ways by which juvenile cases can be heard in criminal courts. Until recently, the most common was the *judicial waiver*, which was at issue in *Kent v. U.S.*. Here, a juvenile court judge makes the transfer decision after a hearing in which factors such as those suggested by the Court in the *Kent* case, and discussed earlier in the chapter, are considered. These judicial waiver hearings, sometimes called bindover or certification hearings, may involve testimony and/or reports from clinicians that have conducted evaluations of the juveniles. This is particularly likely when the juvenile's lawyer challenges the transfer. Research indicates, however, that judges typically support the prosecutor's request for the transfer (Snyder, Sickmund, & Poe-Yamagata, 2000).

Judicial waiver no longer is the dominant form of waiver, however. "Legislative exclusion and prosecutorial waiver have overtaken judicial waiver as the primary vehicles by which transfers are made. Indeed, if current trends continue, judicial waiver may become obsolete" (Bishop, 2000, p. 124.) Under **legislative waiver**, also called waiver by statute, statutory exclusion or automatic waiver, juveniles of specified ages, charged with specified crimes, are "automatically" sent to criminal court. For example, in most states the case of a 15-year-old charged with murder will be heard in criminal court. Technically, no "transfer" process occurs, but in effect the case has been shifted from juvenile to adult jurisdiction. When legislative waivers are in effect, judges may have the discretion to transfer the case back to juvenile court (called reverse waivers), but they generally do not do this. A third type of waiver is the **prosecutorial waiver**, or direct file, whereby prosecutors are given the choice of filing the case in juvenile or adult court. This is a form of concurrent jurisdiction, where two different courts would have the authority to hear a case. States giving prosecutors the discretion to file in either court generally limit that discretion to older juveniles and those charged with serious offenses (although these are not universally applied criteria). Again, judges generally abide by the prosecutor's decision. A fourth but rarer form of waiver is the **demand waiver**, whereby a defense lawyer will ask that a juvenile's case be transferred to criminal court.

The transfer of a juvenile from juvenile to criminal court has major implications. Juveniles tried in criminal court have the same Constitutional rights as adults, including the right to a trial by jury, which they do not have in juvenile court (*McKeiver v. Pennsylvania*, 1971). They also are eligible for pretrial release. However, juveniles tried in criminal court lose their protections against publicity and are subject to the same punishments as adults, including life sentences and capital punishment. (There is, however, an age limitation on the latter. Specifically, the U.S. Supreme Court has ruled it unconstitutional to execute an individual who was younger than 16 at the time of the crime (*Thompson v. Oklahoma*, 1988).) Juveniles transferred to criminal court also face the risk of imprisonment, whereas in juvenile court community-based sanctions are more likely to be imposed. Institutionalization nevertheless remains a real possibility after a juvenile court hearing. As noted earlier, about a quarter of the cases reaching delinquency proceedings result in residential placement (Black, 2001). Juveniles tried in criminal courts and sent to prison are more likely than adults to need protection, are more disruptive, and less likely to earn good-time credits or even qualify for job-training and other rehabilitative programs (McShane & Williams, 1989). Furthermore, transferred juveniles are placed in the general prison population in 40 states and most often receive no special programs or services (Reddington & Sapp, 1997).

In the past, considerable research indicated that juveniles transferred to criminal court received less harsh sentences than adults for the same crimes (Champion, 1989). They also seemed to get less severe sanctions than juveniles treated in the juvenile system (Bortner, 1996; Houghtalin & May, 1991). More recent research distinguishes property and violent offending, however. Juveniles transferred for serious offenses get about the same as adults for the same offenses (Grisso, 1996). Chronic property offenders in criminal court seem to get less severe sentences than their counterparts in juvenile court, but youths convicted of violent offenses in criminal court get more severe sentences than their counterparts in juvenile court (Podkopacz & Feld, 1995). In an empirical study of judicial waiver in Minnesota, Podkopacz and Feld (1995) also found that criminal courts incarcerated youth at much higher rates than juvenile courts, even when the severity of the offense was controlled. Recent research also suggests that transferred youth are more likely to recidivate than youths whose cases were heard in juvenile courts (Bishop, 2000; Snyder, Sickmund, & Poe-Yamagata, 2000).

Each of the three primary types of waivers has its critics. Prosecutorial waivers have been criticized because of the inordinate discretion given to prosecutors who rarely are equipped to make decisions about individual differences among juveniles (Bishop et al., 1989; Ewing, 1990; Grisso, 1998). Furthermore, because prosecutors often lack clear standards and guidelines and can easily bypass judicial oversight in these decisions, they are in a position "to alter fundamentally the juvenile justice system" (Bishop et al., 1989). In one study involving prosecutorial decision making (Singer, 1996) the number of parents in the household emerged as a significant factor in whether the prosecutor referred a juvenile case to the grand jury for indictment.

Automatic waivers are also questionable. These waivers do not take into consideration individual treatment needs or the varied developmental levels of juveniles (Ewing, 1990; Grisso, 1996, 1998). Automatic waivers also leave juveniles who are convicted as first-time offenders with criminal records. Because most juveniles "grow out of" property offending and many grow out of violent offending, critics of these waivers argue that juveniles are labeled unnecessarily. It should be noted, though, that in many states judges have the power to make "reverse transfers," even if a juvenile appears in criminal court as a result of a prosecutorial waiver or an automatic waiver (or waiver by statute) (Grisso, 1998).

Nevertheless, despite the procedural protection established in *Kent v. U.S.* judicial waivers are often arbitrary and discriminatory (Champion, 1989, Hamparian et al., 1982, Feld, 1992). The three factors most predictive of transfer are the age of the juvenile, the nature of the crime, and the juvenile's past record (Snyder & Sickmund, 1999). However, some studies indicate that geography (Feld, 1988; Poulos & Orchowski, 1994), race, gender, and ethnicity (Federle & Chesney-Lind, 1992), individual differences among judges (Podkopacz & Feld, 1995), and the recommendations of probation officers and psychologists (Podkopacz & Feld, 1995) significantly affect the judicial transfer decision. In a study of courts in 34 states, Grisso et al. (1988) found that judges are most likely to transfer to criminal courts juveniles who are unwilling to accept treatment, are self-reliant similar to adults, and have a prior record reflecting serious offending. Later studies indicate that the youths most likely to be transferred are older, charged with serious offenses and/or having a prior history of juvenile offending (Snyder, Sickmund, & Poe-Yamagata, 2000).

Additionally, judges also tend to concur with the prosecutor. In their review of the lessons learned from four major transfer studies, Snyder, Sickmund, and Poe-Yamagata (2000) noted that juvenile court judges supported the prosecutor's request for transfer in approximately four out of five cases.

Role of Psychologists

Despite deference to prosecutors, there is evidence that judges also rely heavily on the recommendations of psychologists in making the transfer decision, when psychologists have been involved (Podkopacz & Feld, 1995). Thus, in cases where the juvenile challenges the transfer to criminal courts, the clinical assessments, reports, and testimony may carry significant weight.

In recent years, psychologists have received more guidance in conducting transfer evaluations for the juvenile courts, just as they have in conducting competency and sanity evaluations (e.g., Barnum, 2000; Grisso, 1998; Heilbrun, Marczyk, & DeMatteo, 2002; Kruh & Brodsky, 1997; Salekin, Rogers, & Ustad, 2001). Kruh and Brodsky (1997) recommend that any maturity assessment provided to the court for deciding whether to transfer a juvenile should also include an assessment of the juvenile's mental state at the time of the offense (MSO) and competency to stand trial. Some evaluators prefer not to discuss the crime during these transfer evaluations, and a minority of statutes specifically forbid this (Grisso, 1998). If the crime is discussed, the examiner must carefully warn the juvenile about self-incrimination (Barnum, 1987). Grisso (1998) believes that not discussing the crime renders the evaluation of limited use.

Psychologists familiar with this area are generally in agreement that the traditional methods of psychological assessment are of little use to courts, because they do not address the criteria that are relevant to the transfer issue. Heilbrun, Marczyk, and DeMatteo (2002, p. 209) recommend that the relevant legal behaviors and capacities be the following: "the threat to public safety or any individual posed by the child, the adequacy and duration of dispositional alternatives, whether the child is amenable to treatment or rehabilitation, mental capacity, maturity, criminal sophistication, and any other relevant factors." Others have compressed these legal behaviors into three psychological constructs: (1) amenability to treatment in the juvenile system; (2) risk of dangerousness; and (3) the juvenile's own sophistication-maturity (Ewing, 1990; Melton et al., 1997; Salekin, Rogers, & Ustad, 2001).

According to Salekin et al. (2001), these "fuzzy concepts" need more careful delineation before they can be of use to the courts. Based on research with practicing psychologists, these three constructs can be consolidated into general themes or behavioral clusters. For example, behaviors associated with "dangerousness" include extreme unprovoked violence, aggressive or antisocial personality, lack of remorse/guilt and empathy, and a leadership role in the crime. Behaviors associated with "sophistication/maturity" include being capable of planning and premeditating crime, understanding behavioral norms, being savvy about criminal activity, and being able to identify alternative actions to commit crime. "Amenability to treatment" would include such things as motivation for change, remorse, expectation that treatment would be of benefit, knowledge of right from wrong, and, interestingly, family stability and support.

The forensic clinicians in Salekin et al.'s study indicated that the youths who had been transferred were rated low on amenability to treatment and moderately high on dangerousness. Interestingly, they were moderately low in emotional and intellectual maturity (maturity/sophistication construct). Salekin et al. suggest that either forensic psychologists or the judges who make the transfer decision considered dangerousness and amenability to treatment more important. The researchers discovered that the sophistication/maturity construct is a complex one that interacts with both dangerousness and amenability to treatment, and they urge clinicians to be cautious in assessing it. On the one hand, a youth's maturity could indicate that he or she is amenable to treatment and consequently more likely to benefit from remaining in the rehabilitation-oriented juvenile system. On the other, maturity/sophistication could suggest a greater accountability for the crime because the juvenile was more likely to have acted in a planned, deliberate fashion and to have understood the consequences of violating the law.

We should note that psychologists are not of one voice on the issue of risk assessment, particularly as it applies to juveniles. Assessing risk is of course an important component in arriving at a transfer decision. While some argue that it is a clinical responsibility to offer such assessments (e.g., Grisso, 1998), others believe that psychologists have a strong ethical responsibility to emphasize the limited validity of such predictions (e.g., Ewing, 1990). Also, disparity in approaches to assessing risk persists, which leads to inconsistency in recommendations (Kruh & Brodsky, 1997).

Mental health practitioners who are called upon to conduct transfer evaluations obviously have a very critical role to play in proceedings that are rapidly becoming commonplace. Although clinicians are receiving more direction as to how these transfer evaluations should be conducted, "systematic and empirical studies of the transfer evaluation and its individual components are almost nonexistent . . . Research-based guidelines, standardized procedures, and psychometrically sound assessment measures are essential to understanding how well transfer evaluations serve juveniles and courts" (Kruh & Brodsky, 1997, p. 162).

Juvenile Rehabilitation

In the typical juvenile situation, the justice system intervenes in the juvenile's life *before* he or she has been adjudicated a delinquent. There exists a plethora of programs intended to divert juveniles from the juvenile court, as well as a separate group of programs intended to offer services on an informal basis. Rather than being referred to a prosecutor, who would file a delinquency petition, for example, juveniles may be placed on "informal probation" by juvenile court intake workers. If a delinquency petition is filed and the youth is subsequently found delinquent, efforts are made to provide supervision and services within the community whenever possible. Juvenile justice professionals recognize that juvenile offending often goes hand in hand with adolescence, and that most juveniles grow out of crime. For this great majority of juveniles, the task of the juvenile justice system becomes one of helping them get through adolescence (Bernard, 1992). The wide variety of programs available for this purpose (e.g., court diversion, mentoring, teen courts, street programs) are amply described elsewhere (e.g., Bartol & Bartol, 1998; Chesney-Lind & Shelden, 1998; Roberts, 1998). The juvenile justice system is also replete with programs geared to the goal of changing the attitudes and character of juveniles whose law violating behavior is considered more serious. These range from highly structured programs, where every moment of the day is accounted for, to community based group or individual therapy programs. Decision making programs, youth wilderness programs, boot camps, anger management, sex offender treatment programs, probation camps, intensive supervision—all illustrate the diversity of approaches. Shortly we will discuss research on the effectiveness of some of these approaches. Before that, however, we turn to the role played by psychologists who are asked to help juveniles courts determine whether a given juvenile can be rehabilitated.

Amenability for Rehabilitation

Juvenile courts often call upon psychologists and other mental health professionals to assess the extent to which a particular juvenile will be amenable to rehabilitation. Grisso (1998) summarizes the three main situations under which such an assessment might be warranted. First, amenability to rehabilitation is at issue in the *waiver decisions* discussed earlier in the chapter. Recall that the guidelines outlined by the U.S. Supreme Court in *Kent v. U.S.* included a consideration of whether the youth could be rehabilitated in the juvenile system. Second, once a juvenile has been adjudicated delinquent, the court must decide on a ***disposition***, which is the equivalent of a sentence in the adult context. Because juvenile court judges have a wide range of options at their disposal, disposition evaluations "provide courts with information to determine the types of services and degree of security that are needed for a particular youth" (Grisso, 1998, p. 161). Hecker and Steinberg (2002) examined records of 172 adolescent offenders who had been referred for such evaluations and found that judges relied heavily on the recommendations of the clinicians, even when the reports were not of professionally high quality. Finally, clinicians may be called upon to perform *progress and outcome evaluations*. This would occur when a court is considering extending the commitment of a juvenile, moving her to a more or less restrictive setting, or to a different type of setting altogether.

Grisso (1998) offers detailed advice to psychologists performing each of the rehabilitation evaluations described above. He notes that matching the needs of the individual youth with the resources that are reasonably available within the juvenile justice system is a critical factor. Obviously, clinicians should be thoroughly familiar with the array of services offered in a given jurisdiction. In some cases, the ideal program for a youth might be out of reach, although the evaluating clinician should not refrain from suggesting it nevertheless. Juvenile courts have been known to expend considerable financial resources to provide a treatment program for a juvenile offender. In one state, for example, a 14-year-old boy who apparently had a history of emotional and physical abuse, and who was described as very immature and withdrawn, suffocated his 11-year-old cousin during a sexual assault. Because of his age and the nature of the crime, his case came under the jurisdiction of the criminal court (legislative waiver), although he asked to be transferred to the juvenile court. Clinicians evaluated him and testified to his amenability to rehabilitation if provided with intensive treatment. Although the judge ruled against the transfer, and the state's Supreme Court supported that decision, the juvenile was provided with services. He pleaded guilty in criminal court, and the state sent him to an out-of-state intensive treatment facility, where he obtained treatment that would have been unavailable in his home state. One could argue that the clinical evaluations, together with zealous representation by the boy's defense attorney, kept him from the adult prison system, where age-appropriate treatment would be far less likely to be provided.

Grisso recommends a structure for conducting rehabilitation evaluations as well as the specific assessment tools that might be of help to the clinician. These include, but are not limited to, the Quay typology for classifying delinquent youths (Quay, 1964, 1966, 1987); the Revised Behavior Problem Checklist (Quay & Peterson, 1987); and the various Child Behavior Checklists developed by Achenbach (Achenbach, 1991a, 1991b, 1991c). Grisso also recommends a variety of structured interview methods for assessing psychopathology in adolescents (Grisso, 1998, p. 177 for review). As for the PCL–R (Hare, 1991) discussed in ◀ Chapter 2, Grisso suggests that the jury is still out. "At this writing . . . there has not been sufficient research to determine the validity of the use of the PCL–R (or the formal concept of psychopathy) with adolescents" (Grisso, 1998, p. 175). More recently, however, a youth version of the PCL has been developed and tested (PCL:YV) and is showing promising results (Forth, Kossen, & Hare, in press). As Grisso notes, youth identified with psychopathic characteristics would have poor prognosis for success in most rehabilitation programs. Emerging research does bear this out (Forth, Kossen, & Hare, in press).

Grisso (1998) also notes that clinicians can only describe to the court the likelihood that the youth will change, given the recommended interventions and the youth's particular circumstances. This is particularly crucial in waiver evaluations, where amenability to rehabilitation may be the key factor weighed by the decision maker. Statements about the likelihood of rehabilitation also must be made very carefully in other contexts as well, however. A pessimistic report, Grisso notes, may become a self-fulfilling prophecy if rehabilitation staff become discouraged. "Reservations about the prospects for change, therefore, should always be coupled with suggestions to staff that might increase the prospects" (Grisso, 1998, p. 192).

The amenability to rehabilitation evaluation, when conducted early in the juvenile process, raises important questions regarding the rights of juveniles. Recall that the U.S. Supreme Court has ruled that information obtained during a pre-trial competency evaluation cannot be used at the guilt-determination or disposition stages (*Estelle v. Smith*, 1981). Essentially, persons being evaluated have a Fifth Amendment right not to incriminate themselves. It is assumed that juveniles have the same privilege, when competency evaluations are involved. Amenability to rehabilitation evaluations are far more wide ranging, however. At least two lower courts have seemingly arrived at differing conclusions. In *U.S. v. A.R.* (1994), the Third Circuit Court of Appeals ruled that amenability evaluations to aid in making a transfer decision did not require Fifth Amendment protections, nor were they a critical stage requiring the assistance of a lawyer under the Sixth Amendment. The 17-year-old juvenile in this case argued that he had not been warned of a right to remain silent nor provided with a lawyer during the evaluation. In a New Mexico case, however, the court ruled very differently (*Christopher P. v. New Mexico*, 1991). Here, the juvenile was ordered to submit to an amenability evaluation and, over the objections of the boy's lawyer, to discuss with the psychologist the alleged delinquent acts. Furthermore, the court allowed the prosecutor to view the evaluation from a one-way mirror, along with the defense attorney. The record indicated that the psychologist relied on the boy's statements about the crime in recommending that he was not amenable to rehabilitation. The court granted the prosecutor's motion to transfer the juvenile's case to criminal court. The Appeals Court reversed the decision, noting that the judge had violated the juvenile's Fifth Amendment privilege against self-incrimination both by commanding him to discuss the facts of the crime and by allowing the prosecutor to view the evaluation process. The critical stage, to this court, was the transfer proceeding, however, not the evaluation itself. Nevertheless, the ancillary proceeding that was the evaluation came under the umbrella of protection afforded to the juvenile, because "information obtained therein could have substantial influence over the court in determining appropriate jurisdiction" (del Carmen, Parker, & Reddington, 1998, p. 123).

While the two above cases appear to be conflicting, the scope of the amenability evaluation helps to distinguish them. In the New Mexico case, the Court noted, "We do not suggest the [Fifth Amendment] privilege excludes a court-ordered evaluation properly limited in scope" (cited in del Carmen, et al., 1998, p. 122). Had the judge not ordered the juvenile to discuss the facts of the alleged delinquent act, and had the psychologist not relied on the juvenile's account to recommend a transfer, the amenability evaluation would likely have been acceptable to the court. The lesson for the psychological examiner, therefore, is to limit the amenability evaluation conducted to help the court make a transfer decision to facts relating to the juvenile's development, background, and available resources, and to steer clear of facts directly relating to the presenting offense.

Prevention and Treatment of Juvenile Offending

Programs aimed at the prevention and treatment of juvenile delinquency run into the thousands, but the great majority of them have not been formally evaluated. Many that have been evaluated have not been demonstrated to be highly effective at reducing delinquency. Particularly ineffective have been programs that try to change serious delinquency, especially in LCP offenders (Borduin et al., 1995; Moffitt, 1993a). Evaluations of residential treatment programs, which are also the most expensive, have yielded discouraging results (Lipsey & Wilson, 1998). In the juvenile justice system, though, institutionalization is usually viewed as a last resort and usually only when less restrictive community alternatives have been attempted. Thus, when psychologists are asked to conduct amenability for rehabilitation evaluations, they are typically asked to indicate whether an alternative to institutionalization would be effective. The preferred approach in juvenile justice today is a system of graduated sanctions designed to fit both the offense and the individual offender (Howell, 1998).

Serious, violent offending, is of course of major concern. Approximately 10–14% of juveniles who are not diverted from court are believed to be serious violent offenders (Howell, 1998). They are probably also life-course persistent offenders. These juveniles, as discussed earlier in the chapter, require a different form of intervention. If they are kept in the juvenile justice system, as opposed to being transferred to criminal courts, they are most often institutionalized and exposed to a range of treatment strategies. The most effective of these programs seem to be those that provide interpersonal skills training, cognitive-behavior treatment, or teaching family homes (Bilchik, 1998). (A **teaching family home** is a living arrangement that seeks to simulate as closely as possible a "family" situation within a community, complete with adult parent figures.) It is important to note, however, that—in an analysis of

200 juvenile programs—Lipsey and Wilson (1998) found that programs for serious offenders were most effective when administered by mental health professionals rather than correctional personnel. Serious, violent delinquents also may be kept in the community and monitored closely, while offered counseling or other treatment approaches. "The most effective programs for non-institutionalized offenders involve interpersonal skills training, behavioral contracting, or individual counseling" (Bilchik, 1998, p. 6).

The "get tough" approach illustrated by the trend to deal with juveniles in criminal court is partly based on the assumption that programs to prevent juvenile crime or rehabilitate offenders have not been effective. Rehabilitation programs within an institutional setting, or secure custody, have been especially questionable. Proponents of getting tough often suggest that treating juveniles as adults will give them the message that crime doesn't pay. To them, transferring juveniles to the adult system, "scaring" them with prison tours, or placing them through rigorous "boot camps"—all common deterrence strategies—make sense. Research on deterrence suggests, however, that such programs are ineffective at reducing recidivism among juveniles (MacKenzie, 2000; Lipsey, 1992; Lipsey & Wilson, 1998). Punishment has been found to be especially ineffective with juveniles (Gendreau, 1996).

In a thoughtful review of juvenile treatment, Woolard, Fondacaro and Slobogin (2001) acknowledge that considerable research does point to positive outcomes in a variety of treatment settings (e.g., Lipsey, 1992; Mulvey, Arthur, & Reppucci, 1993). However, they maintain that "the individual and contextual characteristics that make anyone treatable remain unidentified" (Woolard et al., 2001, p. 15.) Furthermore, because it is consistently demonstrated that the vast majority of juveniles desist from juvenile offending as they move into adulthood, the positive outcomes found in the empirical literature may be a result of natural desistance rather than the treatment itself.

Crime Prevention Models

In discussing the response to crime, including juvenile crime, scholars and researchers often examine the topic from a public health model (Bartol, 2002; Lab, 1997). This model divides prevention into three sometimes overlapping categories, primary prevention, secondary prevention, and tertiary prevention. **Primary prevention** includes strategies designed to prevent behavior before it emerges or before a pattern begins to occur. With reference to juveniles, programs would be established early in the developmental sequence of the child, preferably before ages seven or eight (Bartol, 2002). They are often associated with school systems and cover large groups of children. Project Headstart (Zigler, 1994), is a good example of such a strategy. Another is mentoring, generally known as "Big Brother" or "Big Sister" programs. Research on mentoring has been extremely supportive of its effectiveness (OJJDP, 2000; Sherman et al., 1998). For some children, mentoring also can be considered a secondary prevention program.

Secondary prevention programs are intended for children who show some early signs of aggressive, antisocial, or law-violating behavior, but have not yet been formally adjudicated delinquent (Bartol, 2002). The basic assumption here is that early intervention, once signs of behavioral problems occur, will prevent more serious criminal activity later on. Examples of secondary prevention are a wide variety of programs associated with juvenile diversion. Diversion is a process that steers juveniles—usually first-time, non-serious offenders—away from formal court proceedings. It typically places them in programs with the goal of preventing future offending. Diversion is extremely difficult to evaluate because the programs vary so widely. However, some of the individual programs have obtained impressive research results (Bartol, 2002). These include teen courts (or youth or peer courts) and some gang-intervention programs.

Tertiary prevention strategies are those that focus on offenders who are already heavily involved in criminal activity. In the juvenile context, they would be applied to juveniles who have been adjudicated delinquent and placed in a treatment setting, either within an institution or in the community. Because psychologists are most likely to be involved in tertiary prevention than primary or secondary prevention, we will focus on this category.

Institutional Programming

Juveniles who end up in residential facilities tend to be those who have either committed the most serious offenses or who have been the most intractable, having "failed" in a variety of community-based programs. They are often LCPs who began their antisocial careers early, sometimes very early. This is particularly true of secure institutions, which are the equivalent of the adult prison.

Courts have split over whether juveniles have a right to treatment (in the non-medical sense) when they are institutionalized after an adjudication of delinquency. As a result, scholars reviewing these court decisions have reached different conclusions. Cohen (2003)—while suggesting that there should be such a right—maintains that it has not been so ordered. He emphasizes, though, that there *is* a right to treatment for serious mental disorder. Others have relied on the 1974 case *Morales v. Turman* and the due process protections of *In re Gault* (1967) as affirming a broad right to treatment (Fagan, 1999). Cohen, however, notes that the Court in the *Gault* case only declared that due process "need not impede a program of treatment or rehabilitation" (Cohen, 2003, p. 20–7). This is not the same as guaranteeing a right to treatment.

Regardless of one's position on this issue, there is no guarantee that any treatment that is provided will be state of the art or effective. Moreover, while states have a duty to protect the juveniles in their care, the victimization of vulnerable juveniles within some institutions is well documented. Indeed, many observers would agree with Barry Feld (1992, p. 75) that "The juvenile court's rhetorical commitment to rehabilitation has been contradicted since its inception by the reality of custodial institutions."

Nonetheless, some positive results have been obtained with rehabilitation in an institutional setting. The critical factors appear to be the size of the institution, high staff-juvenile ratio, and the careful selection of juveniles matched to available programs. Even so, we cannot assume that rehabilitation of even a majority of youths will be accomplished. There are numerous, carefully conducted studies that report discouraging results for a wide variety of rehabilitative approaches. For example, Gelber (1988) reports on a two-year intensive treatment program with hard-core juvenile offenders in Miami. Highly trained staff were available to the juveniles on a round-the-clock basis, and the program was supplemented by efforts to meet the social needs of the juveniles' families. Most of the youths were released, reverted to criminal conduct, and eventually were incarcerated in adult prisons. A closely watched evaluation of an innovative treatment center for serious male juveniles in Paint Creek, Ohio (Greenwood & Turner, 1993) provided similarly discouraging results.

Meta-analytic reviews of treatment programs have produced variable conclusions, although the conclusions tend to be more favorable than those based on conventional reviews of the literature (Lipsey, 1992; Lipsey & Wilson, 1998). Nevertheless, after conducting his own meta-analytic review in an effort to throw some light on the "checkered history of research reviews in delinquency treatment" (p. 126), Lipsey was pessimistic. "While not so close as to justify the 'nothing works' rhetoric of the 1970s, convincing positive effects would be difficult to discern in any sample from this literature" (Lipsey, 1992/1997, p. 126). Even so, he adds, the wide variability of effects found in the numerous studies of delinquency treatment helps explain why meta-analytic reviews have come, quite honestly, to different conclusions.

A major focus of many treatment programs—both institutional and community—is the problem of substance abuse, which is believed to contribute significantly not only to past offenses but also to subsequent delinquent activity. Scores of studies document the devastating effect of alcohol and other drug abuse on juveniles (Crowe, 1998; Snyder & Sickmund, 1999; Weeks, Moser, & Langevin, 1999). Virtually every juvenile justice system in the United States provides some form of substance abuse treatment, in private, public, or outpatient settings. Evaluations of these treatment programs, not surprisingly, have found varying degrees of success. The most effective programs have incorporated principles of effective intervention outlined above, such as targeting high-risk offenders with high needs and using cognitive-behavioral approaches to achieving change (Cullen & Gendreau, 2000; Farabee et al., 1999). Lately, variables relating to the *delivery of services* have begun to emerge in the literature as important factors relating to outcome

(Broome, Simpson, & Joe, 1999; Mears & Kelly, 2002). Process variables include, for example, the quality and method of delivery of the treatment and the youth's own attitude and performance in the program. Mears and Kelly (2002) evaluated a five-site drug treatment program for youthful offenders in Texas. Overall, more than half the youths were rearrested within two years of their release. However, significant differences were found among the five sites. The more successful sites were characterized by one or more of the following variables: low staff turnover (both caseworker and correctional officer staff); a long reputation for commitment to the central importance of rehabilitation; and/or better funding, resources, and high energy associated with a new program. Mears and Kelly call for more attention to these service delivery variables in evaluation research. "Without such assessments, the likely possibility arises that programs that are or can be effective instead will be assumed to be ineffective" (p. 111).

Numerous researchers and practitioners have observed that to be effective, programs must be matched with offenders on risks, needs, and offender characteristics (e.g., Andrews, Zinger, et al., 1990; Gendreau and Ross, 1984; Leverant et al., 1999). Offender characteristics cover a broad range of attributes. For example, feminist criminologists began to note in the 1980s that gender-specific programming is crucial, since the needs of girls and boys are obviously not identical. Chesney-Lind and Shelden (1998), have reviewed and commented upon a wide range of programs available for girls in trouble ◙ (see **Box 12-2**). The Office of Juvenile Justice and Delinquency Prevention (OJJDP, 2000) has supported initiatives in this direction.

In the 1990s, researchers noted that race and ethnicity are important characteristics and argued that culturally specific programming is sorely needed in the juvenile justice system. Therefore, we are beginning to see evaluations of programs acknowledging the cultural identity of African American, Latino, and Asian–American youth (Eron, Gentry, & Schlegel, 1994; Goddard, 1993; King et al., 2001; Morris, 1993; Wooldredge et al., 1994). Youths participating in these culturally sensitive programs have performed better on measures of juvenile recidivism and self-efficacy than their counterparts in generic, non-culturally sensitive programs (King et al., 2001). Proponents do not suggest that ethnocentric programming alone makes the difference; other principles for facilitating positive change also must be applied. King et al. (2001, p. 570) call such programs a syringe rather than a cure. "Syringes do not heal people by themselves; however, syringes are indispensable tools for delivering medicine." From the research thus far, it appears that both gender and culturally specific programming should be considered indispensable components of the juvenile justice system.

Some advocates for youth argue that treating children fairly, rather than emphasizing traditional rehabilitation, is more in their best interest (e.g., Feld, 1998; Krisberg et al., 1995). Particularly when rehabilitation involves institutional confinement, the conditions within institutions and the lack of effective treatment do not serve juveniles well. Barry Feld (1998), for example, maintains that rehabilitation oriented practices impose indeterminate and non proportional dispositions on juveniles that fly in the face of justice. Once "sentenced," juveniles are at the mercy of treatment providers who will not recommend release until progress has been made. On the other hand, over half the states are now adopting tougher sentencing strategies for juveniles, particularly juveniles found to have committed serious offenses. Determinate sentences, for example, hold juveniles accountable for their crimes and typically mandate minimum incarceration periods (Torbet et al., 1996). As critics have noted, these statutes tend to be excessively punitive in orientation. While the old style indeterminate schemes provide too much discretion to treatment providers, the new generation determinate schemes contribute to overcrowding of facilities and increase institutional populations.

Community Based Programs

As noted earlier, when clinicians are asked to assess amenability to rehabilitation in delinquents and to suggest treatment options, they are typically advised to recommend the least restrictive alternative available (e.g., Grisso, 1998; Heilbrun, Marczyk, & DeMatteo, 2002). If possible, and provided that community safety is protected, juveniles should be assigned to programs or individual therapy within

BOX 12-2
Programs for Girls

In the 1990s, the Office of Juvenile Justice and Delinquency Prevention (OJJDP) announced that it would encourage and fund research specifically designed to address the needs of girls in the juvenile justice system. To this, many advocates for girls said, "It's about time." Services, programs, shelters, and other resources are sorely needed. Below are brief descriptions of innovative approaches to dealing with girls who are at risk or have been adjudicated delinquent.

Friendly PEERsuasion—Nationwide
Sponsored by Girls, Inc., the program tries to help young women avoid substance abuse by providing accurate information, resistance skills, and offering alternative activities to reduce stress.

Harriet Tubman Residential Center—Auburn, New York
The program works with delinquent girls to focus on self-management, relationship building, empowerment and self-direction, and future orientation. The program is specifically designed to recognize differences in development and needs between girls and boys.

P.A.C.E. Center for Girls—Jacksonville, Florida
This is a non-residential community program that provides services to at-risk girls between the ages of 12–18. Life management skills, counseling, self-esteem building, and community service are among its emphases.

Children of the Night—Los Angeles, California
This is a private program staffed primarily by volunteers. It reaches out to young prostitutes, who are very often girls who have run away from abusive homes. The program operates a 24-hour hot line and offers a walk-in center providing medical aid, clothing, crisis intervention, and a variety of referral services. Volunteer psychologists, psychiatrists, and social workers offer professional counseling.

Marycrest Euphrasia Center, Independence, Ohio
This is a residential center for female offenders who are mothers, ranging in age from 13–21. They are allowed to have their children live with them in the program. The Center provides health services, counseling, family therapy, education, parenting skills training, and substance abuse therapy, as needed. Job readiness training is also offered.

Source: Chesney-Lind & Shelden, 1998.

the community. Statutes and case law in most states also support depriving juveniles of their liberty only after less restrictive alternatives have been considered and rejected. Thus, despite the continued interest in a punitive orientation to juveniles, there exist a wide range of non-secure facilities (such as group homes), wilderness camps, ranches, day reporting centers, and other community options, including counseling and mentoring. Youths assigned to these facilities and programs are typically on juvenile probation, under the supervision of probation agencies and subject to court oversight. In some cases, however, community options are used before juveniles have been adjudicated delinquent, when they are considered "at risk," or have committed minor offenses that do not merit a prosecutor's filing of a delinquency petition. In these cases, a secondary prevention strategy would be taken. The youth may be placed on "informal probation" or may be referred to diversion or to counseling. It should be noted that psychologists or other mental health professionals are rarely involved in this early screening. Decisions are typically made by juvenile court intake workers, who may be probation officers, case workers, or other social service professionals. Very little research is available on the intake process nationwide, despite the wide discretion available to intake workers. The U.S. Supreme Court has not heard a juvenile intake case, but lower courts have ruled that juveniles do not have a right to counsel at intake (*In re Frank H.*, 1972). However, statements made to intake officers are not admissible during a subsequent proceeding to determine guilt, including both delinquency hearings and criminal trials (*In re Wayne H.*, 1979).

Juvenile probation, in contrast to "informal probation," occurs after a finding of delinquency and is the most common sanction used by the juvenile courts. The fact that a youth is on probation tells us nothing about the treatment he or she is receiving, however. Like adults on probation, juveniles are given conditions they must meet to the satisfaction of the court and/or the probation agency. These conditions may or may not involve participation in programs or the delivery of treatment services, such as substance abuse or sex offender therapy. Juveniles also can be placed on intermediate sanctions, which are sometimes referred to as "probation plus." Youths on intermediate sanctions are considered at higher risk of re-offending and having greater needs

BOX 12-3
MST—Intensive Community Treatment

Can juvenile offenders—even serious juvenile offenders—be successfully treated and rehabilitated within the community, while still living in their own homes? Yes, says psychologist Scott Henggeler, who with his colleagues pioneered Multi-Systemic Therapy (MST). MST is a treatment approach that targets multiple determinants of serious behavior and emotional problems in children and adolescents, including those who have been adjudicated delinquent. A main goal of MST is to avoid out-of-home placement. Thus, MST falls under a "family preservation" model of treatment.

Therapists meet intensively with juveniles and family members over a limited period of time: 3–5 months. Meetings are in the child's natural setting: the home, the school, a recreational center, or another setting where the family feels comfortable. Teams of two to four therapists are available to the family around the clock, seven days a week. The treatment team identifies both the risk factors and resilience factors in the child's social systems (individual, family, peer, school, and neighborhood/community). The staff then intervenes as needed and helps the child and family make use of resources for future coping. For example, a risk factor associated with the family may be lack of monitoring of the adolescent's activities. On the other hand, a resilience factor may be a genuine attachment to parents. Treatment staff might then recommend greater monitoring and also identify organized activities within the community in which the adolescent could participate. Referral to a mentoring program—where the youth could obtain a Big Brother or Big Sister—might also be appropriate.

MST programs have been implemented in over 40 sites across the United States and Canada. A wide variety of evaluation research supports its use as an approach that is both treatment effective and cost effective for juvenile offenders as well as other child and adolescent populations (see Edwards et al., 2001 for a review). MST Services has the exclusive licensing agreement with the Medical University of South Carolina to disseminate MST technology and intellectual property (Edwards et al., 2001). Henggeler and his colleagues support the program's dissemination to other sites. However, they appear concerned that the integrity of the program will suffer if it is not applied properly. Thus, pre-site evaluation, orientation training for MST staff, and continuing monitoring and supervision of the program at distant sites has been put in place.

than are typical juveniles. Examples of intermediate sanctions include electronic monitoring, intensive supervision programs, and house arrest.

The criminal justice and juvenile justice literature is replete with evaluations of many of these community programs (e.g., Lab, 1997; OJJDP, 2000). Particularly noteworthy in recent years are evaluations of boot camps, which are now being used in both residential and community settings for a wide variety of juveniles (MacKenzie, Gover, Armstrong, & Mitchell, 2001). There is very little support for positive, long-lasting positive change in juveniles who participate in those programs, however (Chesney-Lind & Sheldon, 1998; MacKenzie et al., 2000; Gover et al., 2000; Trulson, Triplett, & Snell, 2001). Researchers have noted that, though they may have short-term benefits in the sense of instilling respect, discipline, and self-worth in participants, there is very little evidence that these effects are long lasting. Boot camps rarely integrate components of effective therapy.

One closely watched community based approach relates more directly to the forensic professional. It is a strategy with serious juvenile offenders that is based on a **family preservation model**. According to this model, juveniles should, if at all possible, remain in the community with their families, and the juvenile system should provide services, including tangible support, in order to allow this to happen. Family preservation programs are widely used in social services when children are involved in status offending and are at risk of removal from their homes. They are premised on the belief that the most effective way of helping children and adolescents is to keep the family unit together. Psychologist Scott Henggeler, however, has pioneered a family preservation program for *serious delinquents*, utilizing **multi-systemic therapy** (MST). This is a therapeutic program that combines intensive individual counseling with family, school, and community support (Henggeler & Borduin, 1990; Henggeler, Melton, & Smith, 1992; Scherer et al., 1994; Henggeler, 1996). The program has been used with youths from a variety of cultural and ethnic backgrounds (Brown, Borduin, & Henggeler, 2001). Research on MST and similar family preservation approaches has been encouraging, leading to conclusions that even serious delinquents can benefit from intensive, multi-faceted treatment in the community (Borduin et al., 1995; Burns, et al., 2000; Henggeler, 2001 ◙ See **Box 12-3**).

In sum, researchers and policy makers continue to search for effective programs for use with juvenile offenders, particularly those who commit violent crimes or engage in serious, repetitive non-violent offenses. We have noted elsewhere (Bartol, 2002, p. 54) that "The programs that have demonstrated long-term success have used multi-faceted approaches focusing on treating children through their broad social environment, and with particular sensitivity to the family's cultural background and heritage." In addition to the family, the other social systems in which the child or adolescent is imbedded—the school, the community, and the peer group, for example—need to be taken into account.

Summary and Conclusions

Just 100 years after the establishment of the first juvenile courts, the juvenile justice system is seen by some as being at a stage of crisis. Statutes in many states have been modified to demand more accountability and a more punitive approach to juvenile crime. Nevertheless, although some scholars and policy makers call for the abolition of the juvenile court—or at least a drastic change in its operations—most maintain that a separate system is still needed. Juveniles as a group are thought to be more amenable to rehabilitation or treatment, less accountable for their offenses because of their cognitive immaturity, and less likely to be deterred by punitive approaches. Although the validity of these assumptions is questioned (e.g., Woolard, Fondacaro, & Slobogin, 2001), juvenile justice professionals typically hold them and continue to search for programs that will improve the lives of juveniles and decrease their probability of re-offending.

This rehabilitative approach, however, is being increasingly accompanied—if not replaced—in many jurisdictions by a model that recognizes rights of juveniles while demanding accountability for their illegal behavior. We reviewed in the chapter the landmark decisions of the U.S. Supreme Court that set into motion a trend toward protecting Constitutional rights in a variety of legal proceedings, including custodial interrogation, waiver hearings, detention, and delinquency proceedings. Although the U.S. Supreme Court has not spoken on other juvenile issues, lower courts and state supreme courts have issued rulings relating to intake, right to treatment, clinical evaluations, and conditions of confinement, among many others.

In recent years, much attention has been brought to the developmental capacities of children and adolescents, specifically as they relate to the legal matters discussed in this chapter. The issue of adjudicative competence—whether juveniles are competent to participate in delinquency hearings and other juvenile proceedings—is of major concern. The shift away from a strict *parens patriae* orientation and toward more accountability for juveniles has made adjudicative competence a critical issue. Similar questions are being raised about the competence of juveniles to waive their rights, which occurs very frequently in the juvenile justice context. The great majority of juveniles speak to police in custodial interrogation situations without a lawyer present; most are not represented by counsel in delinquency proceedings, although this varies greatly by jurisdiction. Finally, we question whether juveniles have the competence to consent to various treatment options, or whether indeed they should be given a voice in this matter. Thus far, researchers have found wide variability in the extent to which juveniles understand the consequences of such important decisions as waiving their Constitutional rights. While a juvenile's chronological age is a highly relevant factor, developmental maturity and the presence of mental disorder are also critical. In many jurisdictions, these abilities are not assessed until the juvenile's case has progressed to the delinquency hearing or the judicial waiver stage. We noted in the chapter that the MacArthur Research Network is also actively involved in researching these competency issues.

Psychologists and other clinicians are increasingly involved in conducting amenability evaluations for the juvenile courts. Such evaluations require an assessment of whether the juvenile is a good candidate for rehabilitation, and if so, what specific approaches might be attempted. Many programs are available for use with juveniles, but the efficacy of these programs is widely debated. Not surprisingly, program evaluations have produced varying results. Meta-analyses that try to disentangle the various factors associated with treatment outcomes have produced slightly more favorable reviews than the traditional evaluation research. Nevertheless, even meta-analyses have been somewhat pessimistic. Successful programs—defined as those less likely to result in further offending and most likely to produce positive change—are cognitively based, focused on intensive work with serious offenders, and carefully geared to the needs of the juvenile in question. "One size fits all" approaches, including deterrence strategies and approaches designed to "toughen" juveniles, have not received favorable reviews.

Psychologists also may be involved in providing treatment for juveniles, either in community or institutional setting. Ethical guidelines caution against offering treatment services to individuals who are assessed for competence or criminal responsibility. Thus, Grisso (1998) urges clinicians to refrain from performing evaluations of youths they are treating or have treated in the past. In many communities, this conflict of interest is difficult to avoid, since clinicians knowledgeable about youths are highly likely to have offered services to them in the future. Again in small communities, clinicians tend not to restrict their practices to assessments alone. It is highly likely, then, that a clinician will be called upon to provide treatment services to a juvenile whom he or she has assessed.

Despite pessimistic reviews of the state of juvenile rehabilitation, the juvenile justice system persists in trying to identify programs that will make a positive difference in the lives of juveniles who commit crime (Howell, 1998). Reviews of treatment programs indicate that the majority of successful rehabilitation programs, for both juveniles and adults, are community based (Gendreau & Ross, 1984). Indeed, the goal in the juvenile justice system is to avoid institutionalization if at all possible. Unfortunately, some juveniles clearly need to be removed from the community and treated in more secure environments. It has become apparent, however, that institutionalization has been overused, particularly for vulnerable populations. Nevertheless, institutionalization is needed for some youths, and gains have been made in providing effective treatment for juveniles, even within institutional settings.

There is, in the words of some authors, reason to hope (Eron, Gentry, & Schlegel, 1994). Increasingly, the juvenile justice system is making distinctions among prevention approaches (primary, secondary, and tertiary) and identifying effective programs within each of these approaches. It is now widely recognized that a system of graduated sanctions is appropriate for meeting the needs of a wide variety of juvenile offenders. Additionally, researchers are making progress in identifying those juveniles who simply need help getting through adolescence—such as the adolescent limited offenders—and those who need more serious intervention services—the life-course persistent offenders. Unfortunately, the latter are particularly resistant to effective treatment approaches. While a number of effective treatment programs are emerging in the literature, at each level of prevention, more programs and services that focus on the needs of special populations—e.g., girls, racial and ethnic minorities, and the mentally disordered—are desperately needed.

In a different direction, advocates for the legal rights of juveniles are persistent, resulting in better legal representation being afforded in many jurisdictions. We still have a long way to go in this respect, however, because as we have seen juveniles often are not represented by lawyers and are waiving their Constitutional rights with little understanding of the implications. Furthermore, the disproportionate institutional confinement of racial and ethnic minorities is an issue requiring continual attention.

Key Terms

Adjudicative competence
Adolescent limited offenders
Antisocial personality disorder
Conduct disorder
Demand waiver
Disposition
Judicial Waiver
Juvenile Court Act
Legislative waiver
Life-course-persistent offenders
Multi-systemic therapy
Parens patriae
Primary prevention
Prosecutorial waiver
Secondary prevention
Status offenses
Teaching family home
Tertiary prevention

Questions for Review

1. How did the due process changes of the 1960s and 1970s modify the operations of juvenile courts and other juvenile institutions?
2. What did the U.S. Supreme Court decide (holding) in each of the following juvenile justice cases: *Kent v. U.S., In re Gault, In re Winship, McKeiver v. Pennsylvania, Schall v. Martin*?
3. Summarize the main features of the adolescent limited offender and the life-course-persistent offender, as identified and studied by Moffitt.
4. Although ADHD is frequently associated with a diagnosis of conduct disorder, the two are not synonymous. Explain the difference between the two terms.
5. What are the roles of (a) police and (b) intake workers during early stages of juvenile processing?
6. Summarize the research findings on juveniles' comprehension of *Miranda* warnings and their accompanying rights.
7. What is meant by "adjudicative competence" as it relates to juveniles? What role can psychologists play in determining this competence?
8. Identify the three primary ways in which juvenile cases can be heard in criminal courts, and describe the role of psychologists when waiver decisions are made.
9. What is an "amenability for rehabilitation" evaluation? Provide a list of recommendations for clinicians conducting these evaluations.
10. Comment on each of the following rehabilitative approaches: institutional treatment; drug treatment; ethnocentric programs; boot camps; multi-systemic therapy.

CHAPTER 13

The Psychology of Criminal Behavior

Criminology, the multidisciplinary study of crime, can be psychological, sociological, biological, political, psychiatric, or economic in emphasis. To a large extent, however, criminology has been dominated over the years by three disciplines: sociology, psychology, and psychiatry. **Sociological criminology** traditionally has emphasized the effects of variables like age, race, gender, social group, interpersonal relationships, and social class on crime. This approach allows us to conclude, for example, that young males from the low socioeconomic class are disproportionately more likely to be both the perpetrators and the victims of violence. The sociological approach also probes the situational factors most conducive to criminal action, such as the time, place, and circumstances surrounding crime or the kinds of weapons used. Homicides, for instance, often occur after considerable alcohol has been ingested by either the offender or the victim; the weapon most often used is a firearm; and in most cases, the offender and victim have known one another, frequently as relatives or friends. In addition to providing information about correlates of crime, however, the sociological perspective encourages us to explore underlying social conditions which may precipitate criminal activity, such as inequities in educational and employment opportunity or differential treatment by agents of the criminal justice system.

Psychological criminology, which is emphasized in this text, is the science of the behavior and mental processes of individuals who commit crimes. Of special concern are those who commit serious and/or repetitive crimes. While sociological criminology focuses on group variables and society in general, psychological criminology concentrates on individual antisocial behavior—how it is acquired, evoked, maintained, and modified. Both environmental and personality influences on antisocial behavior are considered, along with the mental processes that mediate the behavior. In this context, personality refers to all of the traits and the biological and cognitive features of the human being that psychology has identified as important in the mediation and control of behavior. Beginning in the early 1990s, psychological criminology shifted noticeably to cognitive aspects, and more recently, is beginning to give considerable attention to neurophysiological factors.

Psychological criminology is often confused with **psychiatric criminology**, which dominated the individual perspective of the study of crime at the turn of the 20th century and continues to enjoy strong support today. The confusion between the two approaches is understandable because sharp demarcations between psychology and psychiatry are often difficult to make. It is perhaps more meaningful to distinguish psychiatric and psychological criminology on the basis of their primary perspectives of human nature and their approaches to the study of human behavior.

Broadly, psychiatric criminology is involved in the research of antisocial behavior and in clinical practice as it pertains to the assessment, treatment, and prevention of that behavior. At this point, we should make the distinction between psychiatric criminology and forensic psychiatry. Forensic psychiatry is ". . . a subspeciality of psychiatry in which scientific and clinical expertise is applied to legal issues in legal contexts embracing civil, criminal, correctional, or legislative matters . . ." (Rosner, 1989, p. 323). Thus, psychiatric criminology is concerned with the study of criminal behavior, whereas forensic psychiatry is more practical or more applied.

The discipline may be divided into two perspectives, traditional and contemporary. Much of the *traditional* literature in psychiatric criminology follows the Freudian, psychoanalytic, or psychodynamic perspectives, and views human nature as innately antisocial. In some circles of traditional psychiatric criminology, overt behavior is believed to represent symbolic distortions of underlying unconscious structures that make up the personality (e.g., Sadoff, 1975; MacDonald, 1976; Abrahamsen, 1960). According to this view, criminal behavior is believed to spring from unconscious urges and conflicts that are basically animalistic, unruly, and antisocial in nature. According to this perspective, society is the mechanism that holds innate, biological, animalistic urges in check. Without an organized society with rules and laws, humans would aggress, steal, and even kill at will.

Contemporary psychiatric criminology views human nature differently. Contemporary psychiatric criminology is much more diverse, increasingly research based, and is considerably less steeped in the belief that criminals are acting out their uncontrolled animalistic, unconscious, or biological urges.

Psychiatric criminology has developed largely on the basis of clinical experience, observation, and anecdotal data. It places heavy emphasis on clinical material as a reliable source for systematically understanding the universal dynamics of human nature. While the psychiatric perspective uses clinical data (procedural evidence) for the development of criminal theories, the psychological viewpoint relies heavily on empirical investigations (validating evidence). The price paid for the reliance on validating evidence is that it becomes extremely difficult to offer all-encompassing theories of criminality or empirically sound proposals for the reduction of antisocial behavior. Science requires patience and a high tolerance for conflicting, contradictory data that are highly susceptible to multiple interpretations. Scientific knowledge is gained slowly and often cannot provide glib answers and easy solutions, even when answers are demanded by political, economic, and social forces. We will now take a more focused look at psychological criminology.

Psychological Criminology

As defined earlier, psychological criminology is the *science* of determining how criminal behavior is acquired, evoked, maintained, and modified. It assumes that various criminal behaviors are acquired by daily living experiences, in accordance with the principles of learning, and are perceived, coded, processed, and stored in memory in a unique fashion for each individual. Criminal behaviors depend on how each individual perceives and interprets a situation and upon what he or she expects to gain by acting in a certain way. An analysis of a given criminal behavior requires inquiry into the perpetrator's learning history and expectancies and into how these interact with the situation and the social environment.

Psychological criminology concentrates on the individual as a subject of study, but it emphasizes the cognitive and social context of behavior as well. Mainstream psychology, since the turn of the century, has seen humans as neutral creatures malleable to the culture and social environment surrounding them. The traditional psychologies, such as behaviorism and trait theory, believe genetics and biological predispositions do place certain restrictions on human behavior (and perhaps play other significant roles), but the major force in influencing human behavior has been considered the social environment.

Contemporary psychological criminology stresses that three factors are critical to explaining criminal behavior: (1) the reciprocal interaction between the individual and the social environment; (2) the enormous power of arousal (e.g., anger, fear, anxiety, sexual excitement); and (3) the cognitive processes of the individual (each person's version of the world).

Reciprocal interaction refers to the continual process of the person, through behavior and beliefs, influencing the social environment, and the environment in turn influencing the person. For example, while parents affect the development of the child, the child also influences the development and growth of the parents, including their own relationship, relationships with friends, and even their level of job satisfaction. Even the newborn elicits a certain type of parental behavior, as the parent elicits certain behaviors in the newborn. A fussy, irritable baby may try the patience of most parents, and a parent ill-equipped to deal with such an infant may treat the baby harshly or may fail to provide emotional comfort. Eventually, this reciprocal cycle is apt to result in serious problems between the child and parent. Continuation of the parental rejection over subsequent developmental stages may eventually promote antisocial behavior.

Another illustration of the importance of reciprocal interaction is the case of the former offender who has served his time, but whom society persists in regarding as a criminal. Despite his efforts to secure gainful employment, he is shunned by the community but accepted by a peer group which is involved in various criminal activities. It is not a simple task for the former offender to reach out to law-abiding individuals in the hope that, eventually, someone will reciprocate in kind. This example demonstrates that reciprocal interaction does not simply occur at one level of social exchange, such as one person to another, but occurs at different levels, such as a person's interactions with the community, the town government, the school system, the workplace, the peer group, and the family unit. These "systems" influence a person's behavior, beliefs, and emotions which, in turn, influence the systems in a reciprocal fashion. The importance of this reciprocal interaction between the individual and the various systems within the person's environment will be covered in more detail later in the chapter.

Physiological arousal, the second aspect critical to explaining criminal behavior, is often prominent when humans engage in violence and destruction. The widely-respected psychologist Donald Hebb (1955, p. 249) once noted that arousal "is an energizer, but not a guide, an engine but not a steering gear." Very high levels of arousal interfere with cognitive processes that mediate our judgment, common sense, and consideration of our internal codes of conduct. People often do things under high arousal that they wish they had not done. When very angry, for instance, a person may say cruel words, kick the dog, or knock over the entertainment center in rage. Highly aroused people in the midst of an escalating quarrel may reach for a handgun, a scenario that sometimes ends with the shooting death of a family member. Arousal is the irrational demon of human conduct. It disengages us from our normal way of behaving and from our internal (cognitive) standards and beliefs. One cardinal rule followed by law enforcement officers in domestic disturbances, for example, is to utilize strategies that quickly reduce the escalating arousal of the individuals involved. Otherwise, arousal may promote unpredictability, impulsiveness, and danger.

There is little evidence that human beings are simply driven by animal instincts, genetic programming, chromosomal anomalies, hormonal imbalances, or primitive biological urges from their evolutionary past. Rather, the contemporary contention is that **cognitive processes** can override the biology of human nature. Humans are thinking, active agents with dreams, goals, and unique (sometimes bizarre) versions of the world. Repetitively violent and chronically antisocial individuals may be those who are essentially trapped in an isolated, socially closed-off, and self-constructed cognitive system that relies on simple, straightforward aggressive solutions to survive (Bartol, 1991a). Physical aggression is, after all, a very straight-forward, simplistic solution to problems compared to the more complicated processes of discussion, negotiation, and compromise. Mass murderers and serial murderers, for example, appear to be those who have fallen out of mainstream society, in part because they see the world differently than the rest of society. The isolation further propels their already deviant cognitive system to become more narrow and restrictive, enabling them to make decisions to kill other human beings.

Neuropsychological and Genetic Influences on Criminal Behavior

It should be emphasized that not all psychologists who study crime are strictly in the cognitive or psychosocial camp. Some believe that genetic and neuropsychological factors play prominent roles in some type of crime, especially violence. It is clear that human aggression is multidetermined and, in some cases, neuropsychological influences may help explain the behavior. For example, Diana Fishbein (2000) outlines three major kinds of human aggression: (1) defensive; (2) premeditated (e.g., predatory); and (3) impulsive (e.g., non-premeditated). Defensive aggression, she explains, is generally seen within the normal, acceptable range of human behavior. Premeditated aggression is planned and thought out. Impulsive aggressive behaviors, however, are likely to be associated with different factors.

> Research into their etiologic determinants has focused on various sociologic, psychologic, biochemical, and genetic factors. Whereas environmental influences on these behaviors are substantial and widely documented, biological susceptibility is also significant but not as well delineated (Fishbein, 2000, pp. 140–141).

Terrie Moffitt (1993a) reports that many serious violent juvenile offenders exhibited minor neuropsychological problems during their childhood, such as difficult temperaments as infants, attention deficit disorders or hyperactivity as children (ADHD), and learning disorders in school. She finds, for example, that ADHD features may alienate some children from peers and teachers, a behavioral pattern that places these children at a disadvantage for developing academic and social skills. These academic and interpersonal deficiencies may result in a person following a life-long career of crime and violence.

Adrian Raine (1993), a leading expert on biological/neurological determinants of behavior and author of the frequently-cited book The *Psychopathology of Crime*, divides the contemporary research on the biology of crime into six, somewhat overlapping, areas: (1) evolution; (2) genetics; (3) biochemistry; (4) neuropsychology; (5) brain imaging; and (6) psychophysiology. We cannot discuss each of these topics at this point, but we will discuss the criminal psychopath in some detail later in the chapter. Research in that area has identified some intriguing possibilities of neuropsychological factors that interfere with normal cognitive functioning (Hare, 1996). Raine's division does underscore the enormous complexity involved in the study of biological and neurological determinants of behavior. Each area he delineates has been surrounded with considerable controversy and debate about the magnitude of its influence on human behavior and crime. For example, in the area of behavioral genetics, Robert Wachbroit (2001, p. 25) writes: "The promise of behavioral genetics—especially the prospects of discerning a relationship between genes and violent behavior—is surely one of the most contentious issues in genetics, if not in all of biology."

Some of the controversy centers on the aspect of criminal responsibility. Some opponents to biological, neuropsychological, or genetic research on criminal behavior, for instance, fear that violent individuals will not be held accountable for their offenses and will avoid appropriate punishment for their actions. Others fear that such biological approaches will take attention away from the more social determinants of criminal behavior. Still others are concerned that specific groups—particularly the poor and racial and ethnic minorities—will be targeted for biological intervention.

While there is some evidence that biological and genetic elements play a role in the crime equation, the overwhelming evidence indicates that psychosocial factors play substantially greater roles. A "difficult" temperament due to neuropsychological and genetic influences when combined with other risk factors—such as poor parenting, poor health care, an inadequate educational system, impoverished living conditions, a delinquent peer group—may *predispose* a child to a developmental trajectory of delinquency and violence. Research on temperament not only recognizes the bi-directional, reciprocal influences between the child and parents, however. It is also beginning to explore other influences as well, such as the self-selection of social environments by the participants themselves. In the final analysis, the manner in which the child is treated by the social environment—not the temperament itself—is more likely to emerge as the dominant factor. As noted by David Wasserman (2001, p. 322), a leading expert on the relationship between genetic research, public policy, and crime, "Any genetic contribution to violent or antisocial behavior, or to a violent or antisocial character, is likely to be indirect and contingent, mediated by an array of developmental and social variables."

Defining Crime

Crime is commonly defined as "an intentional act in violation of the criminal law committed without defense or excuse, and penalized by the state as a felony or misdemeanor" (Tappan, 1947, p. 100). Crime also can be an omission or a failure to act, as in failure to pay income taxes or failure to come to the aid of persons in distress, if the law obliges one to do so. Criminal behavior, therefore, refers to the broad span of behavior which violates the criminal code. If we abided strictly by Tappan's definition, we could refer to most of the U.S. population as, in some sense, "criminal." Have you, the reader, never engaged in some action that could be regarded as criminal according to the above definition? Have you ever committed a behavior that could justifiably be considered a misdemeanor or felony and carry with it a possible jail or prison sentence? Illegal drug use, willfully damaging property, shoplifting, stealing from one's employer, and punching another individual all qualify. Driving while intoxicated is another example of behavior in violation of criminal codes.

In a dated but relevant self-report survey of criminal conduct (Wallerstein & Wyle, 1947), approximately 1,700 adults were asked to indicate on a list of 49 criminal offenses which, if any, they had committed. The list excluded traffic violations but included both felonies and misdemeanors. Fully 91% of the respondents admitted they had committed one or more offenses for which they might have received jail or prison sentences. More recent data indicate that, among teenagers (ages 13 to 18), more than 50% admit to theft, 35% admit to assault, 45% admit to property destruction, and 60% admit to participating in more than one type of antisocial behavior (Lynam, 1996).

Therefore, unless we plan to include a conservative 75% of the population in our criminal sample, we should give our definition more specific limits. Other proposed definitions may be just as troublesome, however. For example, for research purposes a "criminal" is typically defined as one who has been both arrested and convicted, though technically one does not become a criminal until one has been convicted. We know, though, that less than one-half of all crime is reported to police, and that police clear or solve less than 20% of the crime that is reported. Thus, there are many individuals who are "really" criminals but who will never be arrested or convicted.

Restricting ourselves to convicted persons to help us define crime is also troublesome because of the discriminatory practices associated with the criminal justice system. A person's background, social status, age, sex, race or ethnicity, and even the choice of lawyer may affect the criminal justice process as much as the circumstances surrounding the crime itself (Austin & Irwin, 2001; Walker, Spohn, & DeLone, 2000). Accepting this legal definition, therefore, means that our definition of criminal behavior would be contaminated with the biases and discriminatory practices inherent in the system.

Finally, there is a host of behavior that is technically not criminal, but still illegal. It is the violation of administrative law that carries civil penalties, including fines or an order to cease and desist a certain activity. Examples of such behavior are an employer's failure to abide by government-established safety regulations and a corporation's violation of rules of the Federal Trade Commission or other government regulatory agencies. Sociologist Edwin Sutherland (1949), in his classic book *White Collar Crime*, argued that such behavior should be regarded as criminal in our society because of its widespread harmful effect. Although many criminologists today agree, there continues to be a double standard in favor of corporations, whose law-breaking activities are not usually regarded as criminal (Mokhiber, 1988). With the corporate scandals of the early 21st century, we may come to see more criminalization of corporate wrongdoings, but the law is still quite protective of corporations compared with individuals. It is also more likely to enforce and prosecute visible street crimes compared with white-collar offenses.

Defining criminal behavior, therefore, is no easy task. Precise operational definitions often fail to include all possible violations or relevant behavior. Even by conservative estimates, 36 to 40 million Americans—16 to 18% of the total U.S. population—have arrest records for non-traffic offenses (U.S.

Department of Justice, 1988). Since almost all the available data on crime are based on arrest or conviction records, victimization, and self-report data, the chapter's research content will be directed at these populations. The theoretical discussion, however, is expanded to include criminal behavior broadly defined, or any behavior that violates prevailing codes of conduct and for which criminal or civil penalties may be imposed, whether or not the perpetrator has been identified.

Crime Statistics

Official Statistics

Official crime statistics kept by law enforcement agencies, such as those found in the Federal Bureau of Investigation's *Uniform Crime Reports* (UCR) and its modification, the National Incident Based Reporting System (NIBRS) are the basis of most public information about crime. The UCR is an annual document containing crimes known to police and arrest information. These data are received on a voluntary basis from nearly 17,000 local and state law enforcement agencies throughout the United States. The UCR is available on the FBI Web Site www.fbi.gov. Because many crimes are not reported, however, the official law enforcement reports underestimate the total actual crimes committed—a total known as the **dark figure**.

The UCR, compiled since 1930, is the most-cited source of U.S. crime statistics. It allows comparison of national data broken down by age, gender, and race of the alleged offender as well as the offense. The more recently developed FBI *Supplementary Homicide Report* contains data on victim and offender demographics, the offender-victim relationship, the weapon used, and the circumstances surrounding the homicide. Other supplementary reports include data on campus crimes, hate crimes, and law enforcement officers killed in the line of duty.

In the UCR, crimes are divided into index crimes and non-index crimes, with the former chosen to serve as an "indicator" of the crime problem in the United States. Although the index crimes are sometimes regarded as the more serious, this is misleading. Felony offenses are also included in the non-index group. The index crimes are murder and non-negligent manslaughter, forcible rape, robbery, aggravated assault, burglary, larceny-theft, motor vehicle theft, and arson. Definitions of each can be found in ◙ **Box 13-1**. Non-index crimes are a wide ranger of offenses, which include embezzlement, fraud, vandalism, carrying illegal weapons, offenses against the family and children, certain sex offenses, a variety of drug offending behaviors, and buying, receiving, and possessing stolen property. Only arrest data are included for these non-index crimes. Definitions of some of the more common non-index crimes can be found in ◙ **Box 13-1**.

It must be emphasized that the FBI reports a **crime rate** only on index crimes. The crime rate is the number of crimes known to police per 100,000 people. Thus, in 2001, the violent crime rate was 504.4 crimes per 100,000 people. Because crime rate is provided only for index crimes, the nation's violent crime rate relates to four offenses: murder, aggravated assault, rape, and robbery. Violent crimes that would come under the non-index crimes list (e.g., simple assault and sex crimes against children that would not qualify as rape) are not included in the FBI's violent crime rate.

It should be obvious from this brief discussion that UCR data are not without problems. The compilation center relies on the accuracy and compliance of local and state agencies to report crime statistics, and these reports are strongly influenced by the social, economic, and political climate at the time they are reported. For example, drug offenses may be the focus of law enforcement at one period of time, while terrorism will be the focus at another time. If terrorism is the focus, police may not give priority to drug arrests and the public may not report larcenies or burglaries. The UCR also does not include federal crimes. In addition, it utilizes a "hierarchy" rule, where only the most serious crime in a series of crimes occurring at one time will be counted. For example, if a person breaks into your home (burglary), takes a valuable coin collection (larceny), kills your brother (homicide), and steals your car (auto theft), only the homicide gets counted. (The NIBRS—to be discussed shortly—requires that each of these be counted.) Also, the UCR provides very little data on victims or offenders, including the victim-offender relationship. An

BOX 13-1
Definitions of Crimes in the UCR

Index Crimes	
Murder and Nonnegligent Manslaughter	The willful (nonnegligent) killing of one human being by another.
Forcible Rape	The carnal knowledge of a female forcibly and against her will. Included are assaults and attempts to commit rape by force or threat of force. Statutory rape (without force) and other sex offenses are excluded.
Robbery	The taking or attempting to take anything of value from the care, custody, or control of a person or persons by force or threat of force or violence and/or by putting the victim in fear.
Aggravated Assault	An unlawful attack by one person upon another for the purpose of inflicting severe or aggravated bodily injury. This type of assault is usually accompanied by the use of a weapon or by means likely to produce death or great bodily harm. Attempts to inflict injury are included.
Burglary	The unlawful entry of a structure to commit a felony or theft. There are three classifications: forcible entry, unlawful entry where no force is used, and attempted forcible entry.
Larceny-Theft	The unlawful taking, carrying, leading, or riding away of property from the possession or constructive possession of another. It includes crimes such as shoplifting, pocket-picking, purse-snatching, thefts from motor vehicles, thefts of motor vehicle parts and accessories, and bicycle thefts.
Motor Vehicle Theft	The theft or attempted theft of a motor vehicle, including the stealing of automobiles, trucks, buses, motorcycles, motorscooters, and snowmobiles.
Arson	Any willful or malicious burning or attempt to burn, with or without intent to defraud, a dwelling house, public building, motor vehicle or aircraft, or personal property of another.

Common Nonindex Crimes	
Other Assaults (Simple)	Assaults and attempted assaults where no weapon is used and that do not result in serious or aggravated injury to victim.
Forgery and Counterfeiting	Making, altering, uttering, or possessing, with intent to defraud, anything false in the semblance of that which is true.
Fraud	Fraudulent conversion and obtaining money or property by false pretenses.
Embezzlement	Misappropriation or misapplication of money or property entrusted to one's care, custody, or control.
Stolen Property	Buying, Receiving, Possessing: Buying, receiving, and possessing stolen property, including attempts.
Offenses against the Family and Children	Nonsupport, neglect, desertion, or abuse of family and children.
Drug Abuse Violations	State and/or local offenses relating to the unlawful possession, sale, use, growing, and manufacturing of drugs.
Sex Offenses (Except Forcible Rape, Prostitution, and Commercialized Vice)	Statutory rape and offenses against chastity, common decency, and morals.
Gambling	Promoting, permitting, or engaging in illegal gambling.
Vandalism	Willful or malicious destruction, injury, disfigurement, or defacement of any public or private property, real or personal, without consent of the owner or persons having custody or control.

Source: Adapted from FBI (1997). *Uniform Crime Reports, 1996* (Washington, DC: U.S. Department of Justice).

BOX 13-2
The UCR and September 11

"Like every other organization and individual in the United States, the FBI has struggled to comprehend the events of September 11, 2001." Thus begins a special report released to the public in 2002 as a supplement to the UCR. The report notes that the current UCR is limited in its ability to report offenses committed at the World Trade Center, the airways above Pennsylvania, and the Pentagon. Different perspectives view the events as an act of war, a local crime, an international conspiracy, or a classic act of terrorism.

The FBI treated the crimes of 9/11 as homicides, even though they may not meet the UCR's traditional definition of a criminal homicide. However, the crimes are not included in the UCR report for 2001, because the murder count was so high that it would skew all types of data analysis for that year as well as years to come. According to the reports available to the FBI, there were 3,047 victims, roughly 75.6% males and 24.3% female. (See accompanying **Table 13-1** for gender and race breakdowns of the victims.)

Data are also provided for age of the victims at each of the three locations. Nine victims were under the age of 18. Five of these were under the age of 5, and all of these were at the World Trade Center. The four remaining juveniles were at the Pentagon. Of the victims, 71 were law enforcement officers killed in the line of duty. Because UCR data does not report occupation—with the exception of law enforcement officers killed—we do not know how many victims were firefighters or members of other occupational groups who helped at the scene.

The FBI provided data on the 19 offenders directly involved. All were white males, four under the age of 22. Twelve of the offenders were aged 20 to 24, and the remaining 7 were aged 25 to 34.

Like UCR data as a whole, data for this special report were provided by law enforcement agencies. The FBI cautioned readers not to confuse the age, gender, and race statistics with being able to identify individuals through fingerprints, dental records, or DNA. "It may be months or years before some victims of this tragedy will be positively identified," the report notes.

Source: FBI, *Crime in the United States, 2001, Special Report.*

exception is the UCR's *Supplementary Homicide Report*. Another major shortcoming of the UCR is its emphasis on street crime to the neglect of the equally serious corporate and professional crimes. (see ◙ **Box 13-2** for a discussion of the UCR and the events of September 11, 2001.)

During the late 1970s, the law enforcement community called for the expanded use of the UCR and more detailed information on crime in place of the straightforward statistics offered in the traditional UCR. In response to these concerns, the UCR reporting system was evaluated under federal contracts by ABT Associates of Cambridge, Massachusetts, which made a number of far reaching recommendations for improvement. These recommendations formed the basis of the *National Incident-Based Reporting System* (NIBRS) under the support of the *Uniform Federal Crime Reporting Act* passed by the U.S. Congress in 1988. In this act, Congress required all federal law enforcement agencies, including those agencies within the Department of Defense, to collect and report more complete data to the FBI on two categories of offenses: Group A, which includes twenty-two serious offense categories, such as arson, assault, homicide, fraud, embezzlement, larceny-theft, and sex offenses; and Group B, which includes eleven less serious offenses, such as passing bad checks, driving

TABLE 13-1

Murder Victims of 9/11/2001 Terrorist Attacks by Race, Sex, and Location

		Sex		
Race	**Total**	**Male**	**Female**	**Unknown**
All Locations				
Total	**3,047**	**2,303**	**739**	**5**
White	2,435	1,908	527	0
Black	286	170	116	0
Other	187	127	60	0
Unknown	139	98	36	5
World Trade Center				
Total	**2,823**	**2,175**	**648**	**0**
White	2,279	1,811	468	0
Black	234	148	86	0
Other	184	124	60	0
Unknown	126	92	34	0
Pentagon				
Total	**184**	**108**	**71**	**5**
White	120	79	41	0
Black	49	21	28	0
Other	2	2	0	0
Unknown	13	6	2	5
Somerset County, Pennsylvania				
Total	**40**	**20**	**20**	**0**
White	36	18	18	0
Black	3	1	2	0
Other	1	1	0	0
Unknown	0	0	0	0

under the influence of alcohol, engaging in disorderly conduct, drunkenness, nonviolent family offenses, and liquor law violations.

Concurrently, state law enforcement agencies were asked to phase in this same reporting system, which it was hoped would ultimately replace the UCR. Thus, while the UCR currently tabulates the incidents and arrests for index crimes and counts arrests for non-index crimes, the NIBRS focuses more on detailed incident data on forty-six offenses in twenty-two offense categories listed in Group A. Only arrest data are reported for the eleven Group B offenses. Presumably, the added information from Group A data will become an indispensable tool for law enforcement agencies and researchers because it will provide detailed data about when and where specific types of crime take place, what forms they take, and the characteristics of their victims and perpetrators. Since reporting agencies are expected to submit a brief account of each incident, the NIBRS data includes the number of offenders, the number of victims, and/or multiple attributes (i.e., weapons, property loss, drugs, alcohol, and so forth) for each crime. To date, data from this system are still in their infancy in terms of nationally representative information, and many agencies have been slow in linking into the system. Nevertheless, researchers are beginning to gather and interpret NIBRS data.

◀ [We saw an example of this in Chapter 11, when we discussed Finkelhor and Ormrod's (2001) analysis of violent crimes against children.] The NIBRS has the promise of being the first explicitly computer-based and standardized reporting system in U.S. law enforcement, providing a rich source of data for researchers and policy makers.

Self-Report Surveys

Individuals are sometimes asked to report the number and extent of their own criminal offending, typically under the promise of anonymity. Although some persons may inflate or deflate personal reports of their own criminal activity, the data provided in these self-report measures can be helpful in our understanding of the crime picture. A good example of an extensive, well regarded self-report study is *Monitoring the Future*, a nationwide drug survey of 50,000 high school students in 420 public and private schools. It is an ongoing project conducted by the Institute for Social Research at the University of Michigan. Since 1991, the survey has included not only high school seniors but eighth and tenth graders as well.

Often, self-report measures are supplemented by some confirming support measure. For example, in 1999 the *Arrestees Drug Abuse Monitoring Program* (ADAM) collected data from more than 30,000 adult males and 10,000 adult females located in about three dozen geographical locations across the country. In their data collection procedures, the ADAM utilized both urinalysis and self-report data to identify the level of recent drug use by the arrestees. The urinalysis provided a validity check on the openness of the arrestees in providing information about their drug use.

Self-report studies are typically not government-sponsored, however, although private researchers often obtain government grants to conduct them. It is believed that people are far more likely to admit their criminal activity to a private researcher than to a government agent. However, the surveys are usually administered to "captive audiences," like high school students or prison inmates. Occasionally, a self-report survey will be administered to a sample of the general population. In an early survey, Charles Tittle (1980), for example, polled close to 2,000 persons in three different states and found that slightly more than 10% of them admitted to cheating on their income taxes. Although self-report surveys help to document the prevalence of offending among youth and adults, they do not provide as valid a measure of criminal activity as do the victimization statistics to be discussed below.

Victimization Surveys

Victimization surveys shed further light on crime. Based on representative sampling of households, these surveys provide information about the victim's experiences with crimes. They are typically asked to provide information both about crimes they reported to the police and those they did not—and if not, why. From victims, then, we learn details of the criminal events, the circumstances under which they occurred, and the effect of the crimes on the victim.

One of the more ambitious projects is the *National Crime Victimization Survey* (NCVS) which is sponsored by the Department of Justice and conducted by the Bureau of Census. The NCVS reports the results of contacts with a large national sample of households (approximately 49,000) representing 101,000 persons over the age of twelve. A member of the household is first asked whether anyone experienced crime during the previous six months. If the answer is yes, the victim—if 12 or over—is interviewed more extensively. The NCVS is currently designed to measure the extent to which households and individuals are victims of offenses comparable to six of the eight index crimes (all but murder and arson). However, the NCVS asks about both simple and aggravated assault, whereas only aggravated assault is an index crime. Furthermore, the NCVS asks about varieties of sexual assault, not just forcible rape.

The NCVS originated in 1973 (it was then called the National Crime Survey—NCS) and was extensively revised in 1992, when its name was changed. The redesign of the survey included a more sensitive and more comprehensive approach to asking victims about sexual assault. As a result, the estimate of the number of rapes increased 157% the first year of the re-design (Kindermann & Lynch, 1997). Earlier, in the mid-1980s, the survey had added questions about the offender, such as whether he or she was high on illegal drugs or alcohol at the time of the crime. Additionally, the survey began to ask victims what they were doing at the time (e.g., going to work, shopping) (Karmen, 2001). The recent revisions of the NCVS also ask victims how law enforcement officers responded if they did report the crime. A victimization rate, expressed by the number of victimizations per 1,000 potential victims, is obtained and reported to the public. The NCVS also includes periodic supplementary victimization surveys, including surveys of commercial establishments and surveys of school and workplace victimization.

The NCVS is most useful in estimating crimes against victims who understand what happened to them, how it happened, and are willing to report what they know to the persons conducting the surveys. Many people do not know they have been victimized, however. This is particularly the case with white-collar crimes. Patients are generally not aware that a physician files false Medicare claims on their behalf, for example, even though they receive periodic reports of the claims. Some people may not even be aware that their homes have been burglarized. Also, the NCVS does not tap certain sectors of the population, such as people in homeless shelters. Like other forms of obtaining crime data, the victimization survey is far from perfect. However, it is an extremely useful supplement to the UCR and to self-report surveys. Some criminologists, as a matter of fact, consider victimization surveys the most valid instruments available for measuring the extent of crime in our society.

In addition to the NCVS, statistics are available from victimization surveys conducted by private researchers, including some sponsored by the government. Chief among these is the *Violence Against Women Survey*, which was mentioned briefly in ◀ Chapter 11 (Tjaden & Thoennes, 1998). The survey polled 8,000 women and 8,000 men in the mid 1990s. Researchers have found a far greater prevalence of violence against women when analyzing the results of that survey compared with the results of the NCVS. One reason for the striking discrepancies is that the VAW survey asked about lifetime victimization (have you ever been assaulted?) as opposed to the NCVS's approach of asking about victimization over the past six months. Additionally, the VAW survey includes information about stalking and other threatening behaviors in its definition of violence.

The data collected through the NCVS are extensive. For illustration, we will consider the highlights of a recent report, especially those characteristics relating to violent personal crimes. The intention here is not to present definitive statistics, but rather to give the reader an idea of the type of information derived from the NCVS. The interested reader is encouraged to examine the original source for additional information. Like the UCR, the NCVS is available on line, www.ojp.usdoj.gov/bjs/.

Demographics of Crime Victims

According to the NCVS, the personal crimes of violence are highest against males, the young (ages 16–19), African-Americans, Latinos and Hispanics, the divorced or separated, the poor, and the unemployed. African-Americans are more likely to be victims of household burglary or motor vehicle theft, but not household larceny. The poor are the most likely victims of burglary, but the least likely victims of household larceny or motor vehicle theft.

Overall, males are far more likely to be victims of personal robbery (8.7 per 1,000) and assault (37.5) than females (4.0 and 16.9, respectively). With regard to personal larceny (e.g., purse snatching, pocket picking) males also are more likely to be victimized (107.9 versus 87.5 per 1,000).

According to the NCVS, about five women in every 1,000 are raped. This statistic is extremely questionable, as are the assault statistics. A woman who was raped may be no more willing to report this to an interviewer than to police. As noted above, other self-report surveys (e.g., Tjaden & Thoennes, 1998), suggest that the incidence of rape is far higher than this. We will return to this issue shortly, as we discuss some of the research specifically associated with this particular crime.

NCVS data suggest that the most likely woman to be raped is one who was separated or divorced (2.8 per 1,000), followed by victims who never were married (1.7), those married (0.3), and those widowed (0.6). The age group most frequently raped is between 16–19 (5.3); the least frequently raped group is between 50–64 (0.1). Of the three violent personal crimes, rape is most likely to have happened inside victims' homes. Furthermore, approximately as many rapes occur inside or near victims' residences as in outdoor areas away from their dwellings.

For personal crimes of violence and personal crimes of theft, the NCVS indicates that the age bracket 12–14 has the highest victimization rate, and the elderly (ages 65 and over) are the lowest. Actually, persons under age 25 have a violent crime victimization rate three times higher than that for persons aged 25 and older, and the rate difference between these two age groups for crimes of theft is approximately 2 to 1. These characteristics are especially representative of young males.

Minorities (African-Americans and Latino/Hispanics) report the highest victimization rate when it comes to violent crime. This has been a consistent finding in the sociological literature, especially as it pertains to African-Americans. For example, in his classic investigation of 588 homicides in Philadelphia between the years 1948 and 1952, Marvin Wolfgang (1958, 1961) found that about 73% of the offenders and 75% of the victims were African-American. In almost all the reported cases (about 94%), violence was intraracial, not inter-racial.

Stranger-to-stranger offenses comprised 63% of all personal crimes of violence, ranging from 59% for assaults to 75% for personal robberies. In terms of victimization rates, 21.4 per 1,000 victimizations were a result of stranger-to-stranger contact, compared to 12.6 per 1,000 victimizations being a result of contact with acquaintances, friends, or relatives. In addition, approximately one-half of all personal robberies were carried out by two or more offenders. Also, multiple offenders were more likely to engage in more serious assaults (aggravated assault) than in the less serious simple assaults.

The NCVS found that the extent to which a crime was reported to the police depended on the type or seriousness of victimization, and there was a good deal of consistency in the reasons given by victims for not notifying the police. Altogether, only 30% of all personal crimes were reported, compared to 38% for household crimes. This implies that about two out of every three crimes go unreported. The highest report rate was associated with motor vehicle theft (88.6%), while the lowest was associated with household larcenies where the loss amounted to less than $50 (14.4%).

Although serious crimes tended to be reported, slightly more than half of the rapes had been reported (58.4%), while two-thirds of the robberies with injury were reported. Only about a quarter of the personal larcenies were reported, varying, of course, with the amount stolen.

The two most common reasons victims gave for not reporting crimes were: (1) nothing could have been done; and (2) the offense was not important enough to warrant police attention. Inconvenience and fear of reprisal were rarely mentioned as reasons. It is important to note that both rape and assault victims were more likely than robbery victims to view their victimizations as a private or personal matter. This was especially true when the offender was an acquaintance, friend, or relative.

The above review of statistics has hopefully provided readers with a basic understanding of attempts by the government and by researchers to measure crime. In the following sections, we will discuss concepts and research in psychological criminology that relate to the explanation of criminal behavior. We will begin with one of the most heavily researched topics in recent years, the criminal psychopath.

The Psychopath

One of the most intriguing observations in criminal behavior is the phenomenon of psychopaths, the clinical or diagnostic group of individuals who demonstrate certain behavioral, cognitive, and neuropsychological characteristics that are not usually found in the general population. While it is always wise to be cautious in cataloging humans into neat diagnostic packages, the clinical entity called the psychopath does have some validity as a distinguishing behavioral pattern.

Psychopaths, as a general category, should not be confused with sociopaths or antisocial personality disorders (APD). The term "sociopath" is most often used by sociologists and criminologists to refer to a person who is repetitively in conflict with the law, with apparently limited capacity to learn from past experiences. Sociopathy was also used in 1952 by the American Psychiatric Association to describe a wide variety of behaviors, such as sexual deviations, alcoholism, and dissocial/antisocial reactions (Gacono, 2000). The term is rapidly coming into disuse, however. The label "antisocial personality disorder" is most often used by mental health clinicians to refer to an *adult* person who displays serious habitual misbehavior or deviant behavior, especially when the behavioral pattern involves direct and harmful actions against others. Mental health professionals reserve the term "conduct disorder" (frequently abbreviated CD) to refer to similar behavioral patterns demonstrated by *children*. ▲ [see **Table 4-1** for review of these categories].

The term "psychopath" refers to an individual who exhibits a discernible pattern that differs from the general population in its level of sensitivity, empathy, compassion, and guilt. The typical, true psychopath (also called a *primary* psychopath) may or may not engage in criminal activity, but he or she does demonstrate callous and unemotional feelings toward others and a lack of concern for societal rules and regulations.

The characteristic behaviors of the psychopath were most ably described by Hervey Cleckley (1976) in his classic *The Mask of Sanity*. Two disarming features include glib and superficial charm and grandiose sense of self-worth, both of which are especially apparent during initial contacts. Psychopaths seem to be friendly, sociable, outgoing, likeable, and alert. They often appear well-educated, knowledgeable, and interested in a wide variety of things. However, they possess a variety of less appealing features. Typical behaviors include extreme selfishness (often referred to as egocentricity) and inability to love or give affection to others. Psychopaths demonstrate a lack of empathy, guilt and remorse, and are highly deceitful and manipulative. They exhibit a discernible lack of enduring attachments to people, values, or goals. They are often unable to learn from past mistakes and become vulgar, domineering, loud, and boisterous under the influence of alcohol. The cardinal trait of psychopaths appears to be an unusually high need for stimulation and tendency to become bored easily. Most of their behavior seems to be a result of attempts to satisfy their insatiable requirement for excitement and stimulus input.

Although some psychopaths may be involved in socially deviant behaviors, they generally do not exhibit behaviors that would qualify as clinical descriptors of neurosis or psychosis. Under even the most stressful conditions, psychopaths are likely to remain cool and calm, demonstrating few of the typical indicators of anxiety. They appear emotionally flat, with few mood swings, and display few signs of a genuine sense of humor. Collectively, these features are described by clinicians as "shallow" emotions. However, psychopaths are not completely free of psychological disorders. There is a significant relationship between alcohol and drug abuse/dependence disorders, and, of course, they are frequently diagnosed as having antisocial personality disorders (Hare, Hart, & Harpur, 1991).

In many ways, psychopaths are unreliable, impulsive, irresponsible, and unpredictable, regardless of the importance of the occasion or the consequences of their actions. This pattern is cyclical, however. For extended periods, the psychopath may appear responsible and may have outstanding achievements. For a while, the psychopath seems to be your best friend. Then, without warning, the psychopath will do something that jeopardizes his status. For example, the psychopath may open a window and scream obscenities at the crowd below a third floor executive suite, go on a drunken spree, steal a car, or impulsively drive off into the sunset. Because of this cyclic pattern, psychopaths rarely pursue consistent, successful criminal careers. Rather, they are more likely to participate in capers or hastily planned crimes for immediate satisfaction. According to Hare (1998a, p. 196), psychopaths can also participate successfully in the political process, and can emerge as leaders or patriots "who wrap themselves in a flag of convenience and enrich themselves by callously exploiting ethnic, cultural, or racial tensions and grievances."

It is assumed that many criminal behaviors, as well as other behavioral problems, are rooted in the home, usually in homes with conflict, inadequate discipline, poor family models, or inadequate parenting. Psychopathy is no exception. Marshall and Cooke (1999), for instance, found that psychopaths are more likely to have experienced family problems, such as parental antipathy, indifference, abuse, and neglect. Forth and Mailloux (2000, p. 39) concluded from their literature review that "... psychopathy is associated with a range of adverse factors: physical abuse, sexual abuse, parental criminality, parental alcoholism, childhood separation, maternal psychopathetic traits, and poor parental strategies (inadequate parental supervision, inconsistent discipline)."

Hare (1998a) states that the biological and environmental factors that are responsible for the development of psychopathy are not well understood. However, psychopathy is likely to be a product of a complex interaction between social forces and neuropsychological factors. These neuropsychological factors are widely recognized. For example, psychopaths seem to have an under-aroused nervous system, whereby they do not get the full impact of their environment, a finding that may account for their difficulty in learning the rules and expectations of society (Hare & Schalling, 1978; Raine, 1993). Research has also shown that psychopaths fail to appreciate the emotional significance of an event or experience and seem unable or unwilling to process or use the emotional sincerity of language (Hare, 1998a). As described by Johns and Quay (1962), the typical psychopath seems to know the words but not the music. Similarly, Grant (1977) posits that the psychopath knows only the book meaning of words, not the living meaning. Despite this shortcoming, psychopaths tend to be very skillful in psychologically and socially manipulating others. "Intense eye contact, distracting body language, charm, and a knowledge of the listener's vulnerabilities are all part of the psychopath's armamentarium for dominating, controlling, and manipulating others" (Hare, 1998a, p. 204).

It is important that we underscore the predisposition factor. Whether a person who is neurophysiologically predisposed ultimately engages in criminal behavior depends on the person's learning history, cognitive expectancies, and the situation at hand. Theoretically, if the person has learned to meet needs for excitement and stimulation in ways that run counter to society's rules, and if socialization (conditioning) has done little to generate anxiety when codes are violated, then antisocial behavior is likely to result.

Although psychopaths *as a group* do not pursue consistent criminal careers, those that *do* have continual contact with the criminal justice system because of frequent offending are referred to as **criminal psychopaths**. Although their criminal behavior runs the gamut of petty theft and fraud to murder, criminal psychopaths are especially vicious and violent, and their motivations for the violence are sometimes difficult to identify. Hare (1996) reports that nearly half of the law enforcement officers who die in the line of duty are killed by individuals who closely match the personality profile of the criminal psychopath. Hare et al. (1991, p. 395) describe the violence committed by criminal psychopaths as callous and cold-blooded "without the affective coloring that accompanied the violence of nonpsychopaths." Criminal psychopaths frequently engage in violence as a form of revenge or retribution, or during a bout of heavy drinking. The sex crimes and serial murders committed by criminal psychopaths tend to be more violent, brutal, unemotional, and sadistic than those committed by other sex offenders or murderers (Hare, Clark, Grann, & Thornton, 2000). It also appears that psychopathic rapists are more likely than other rapists to be motivated by anger, vindictiveness, sadism, and opportunism (Hart & Dempster, 1997).

The Psychopathy Checklist (PCL)

Currently, the best measuring instruments for adult criminal psychopathy are the 20-item Psychopathy Checklist-Revised (PCL–R) (Hare, 1991), shorter 12-item form called the *Psychopathy Checklist: Screening Version* (PCL:SV), and the *P-Scan: Research Version*. All three measures are conceptually similar and require considerable training to administer professionally. Although the checklists include many of the same psychopathic behaviors described earlier, all three focus on the affective (emotional), interpersonal, behavioral, and social deviance of *criminal* psychopathy. The P-scan is a quick screening instrument that requires less training and serves as a very rough screen for possible psychopathic features. The P-Scan still needs much more research before it can be used as a valid measure in actual practice.

The PCL–R has been the most heavily researched and used in recent years and will be the center of discussion in this section. It is estimated that the PCL–R is used in about 60,000 to 80,000 evaluations each year (Otto & Heilbrun, 2002). So far, the research has strongly supported the reliability and validity of the PCL–R for distinguishing criminal psychopaths from criminal nonpsychopaths (Hare, 1996, 1998b; Hare, Forth, & Strachan, 1992). Cutoff scores of 30 on the PCL–R have been found to be useful diagnostic indicators of psychopathy, although some clinicians have used scores ranging from 25 to 33 (Simourd & Hoge, 2000). Usually, a score of 20 or less suggests a behavioral pattern that qualifies as a "nonpsychopath." It is important to note that the PCL–R is a dimensional measure of psychopathy rather than a categorical measure where a person is classified either a psychopath or a nonpsychopath. In other words, the more psychopathic features a person displays, the more likely that person qualifies for psychopathy. The PCL–R provides researcher and mental health professionals with a common measurement in the assessment of psychopathy that facilitates international and cross-cultural communication concerning theory, research, and clinical practice (Hare et al., 2000). In addition to studies in the United States and Canada, the PCL–R has prompted research in the United Kingdom, Sweden, Denmark, Norway, Belgium, Spain, Portugal, and many other countries. Research data so far suggest that its predictive validity is strongest for North American, white males.

The items of the PCL–R are especially powerful at identifying two important factors or behavioral clusters of psychopathy. These factors were identified through a statistical method called factor analysis. One factor reflects the interpersonal and emotional components common in the psychopath and consists of items measuring selfishness, callousness, and lack of guilt. The second factor is most closely associated with a deviant lifestyle, as characterized by poor planning, impulsiveness, an excessive need for stimulation, a tendency to become bored easily, and a lack of realistic goals (Hare, 1991; Hart, Hare, & Forth, 1993). Research indicates that the interpersonal and emotional factor may be a stronger indicator of psychopathy than the lifestyle factor (Cooke, Michie, Hart, & Hare, 1999). In other words, the lack of empathy may be a more pronounced feature of the psychopath than social deviance driven by needs for stimulation. More recent research (Cooke & Michie, 2001; Frick, Bodin, & Barry, 2000; Kosson et al., 2002) suggests that there may be *three* behavioral dimensions or factors at the core of psychopathy rather than just two. The third factor reflects an arrogant and deceitful interpersonal style toward life. It is demonstrated by an approach toward others described as superficially charming, glib, and dishonest, and a grandiose sense of self-worth that is highly unrealistic.

The leading expert on psychopathy, Robert Hare, estimates that about 1% of the general population and 15 to 25% of incarcerated offenders meet the PCL–R criteria for psychopathy (Hare et al., 1992; Hare, 1996). Other research, however, has yielded smaller percentages. Simourd and Hoge (2000), for example, found that 11% of their sample of high-risk offenders qualified as psychopaths. "This finding was unexpected given the high-risk nature of the present sample, in which all participants were serving a current sentence for violent offending, more than half had a previous conviction for violence, and almost all had extensive criminal careers" (Simourd & Hoge, 2000, p. 267–268).

In prison, those offenders who meet the PCL–R criteria exhibit violent and aggressive behaviors—including verbal abuse, threats, intimidations—at a much higher rate that other inmate populations (Hare, Hart, & Harpur, 1991; Serin, 1991). Psychopaths appear to be especially well represented among convicted rapists, with reports as high as 35 to 43% among serial rapists or rapists who killed their victims (Hare, 1996). Moreover, psychopathic inmates commit a much greater variety of offenses than nonpsychopathic inmates (Kosson, Smith, & Newman, 1990). Female criminal psychopaths, although rare, are believed to follow similar patterns (Hare et al., 1992). The percentages reported above do not include female inmates, however.

Research by Hare and his colleagues also indicates that criminal psychopaths begin their antisocial activities early in their lives, as least by age 15 or 16 (Hare, 1991). Criminal psychopaths continue to offend and cause social and emotional distress to others throughout their lifetimes. As a group, they seem to continue to commit both violent and nonviolent crimes, even after age 60 (Harris, Rice & Cormier, 1991). However, there is also some evidence that criminal psychopaths reduce their violent offending as they get older, especially as they approach 40, although their nonviolent offending continues to remain high throughout their lifetimes (Hare, et al., 1992). The reasons for this intriguing pattern remain unknown.

The Psychopathy Screening Device (PSD; Frick, O'Brien, Wooton, & McBurnett, 1994) and the Childhood Psychopathy Scale (CPS; Lynam, 1997) are two of the very few instruments to date that have been developed specifically to assess psychopathy in childhood, and the Psychopathy Checklist: Youth Version (PCL:SV; Forth & Mailloux, 2000) is one of the very few instruments for measuring psychopathy in adolescence.

Juvenile Psychopathy

One of the limitations of the research on psychopathy is that a very large segment of it has concentrated on adults (Frick et al., 2000). During the past five years, though, research on juvenile (adolescent and child) psychopathology has increased substantially. The emerging attention directed at juveniles has engendered considerable debate, however. One debate centers on whether the features of adult psychopathy even exist in juveniles. One of the major problems in identifying juvenile psychopaths is that disorder may be very difficult to measure reliably because of the transient and constantly changing developmental patterns that are so characteristic of childhood and adolescence. Consequently, psychopathic symptoms in childhood may look very different from those exhibited in adulthood (Hart, Watt, & Vincent, 2002). That is, some of the behavioral patterns of children and adolescents may be similar to adult psychopaths for a variety of reasons but may not really be signs of psychopathy. For example, children in an abusive home often demonstrate an abnormally restrictive range of emotions which are similar to the emotional characteristics of psychopathy. Actually, they are a child's way of coping with a very stressful home environment (Seagrave & Grisso, 2002).

A second debate focuses on the belief that, even if psychopathy can be identified in juveniles, there may be serious long-term social, ethical, and emotional consequences accompanying the label "psychopath" for the child. This label carries a wide assortment of negative connotations and social stigma, such as poor prognosis for treatment, a predicted high rate of violent offending and recidivism, and the intrinsic and biological basis of the disorder. The fear is that once a child is "tagged" or labeled a "psychopath," others will begin to see him as such and treat him accordingly. Under these conditions, the reactions of others become the primary source of the individual's sense of self, and the child becomes the very thing he is described as being.

A third debate contends that any psychopathic assessments of youth must achieve an exceptionally high level of accuracy before they can be judiciously employed in the criminal and juvenile justice systems (Seagrave & Grisso, 2002). Any misstep in assessment procedures by the clinician—even minor ones—may have grave consequences fo the juvenile, vis-à-vis the courts in disposition or sentencing, treatment strategies, and aftercare or parole.

Gender Differences in Psychopathy

Similar to the research on juvenile psychopathy, very little research has been conducted so far on the female psychopath. Some preliminary statistics on gender differences for psychopaths have been gathered, but not much information is available. It is generally believed that there are significantly more male psychopaths than female psychopaths. For example, Salekin, Rogers, and Sewell (1997) report that the number of female psychopaths in a jail setting was 15%, compared to the 25 to 30% rate estimated for men. In another study, Salekin, Rogers, Ustad and Sewell (1998) found that 12.9% of female inmates met the criteria for psychopathy. Vitale, Smith, Brinkley and Newman (2002) found that only 9% of their 528 incarcerated women (from a combination of minimum, medium, and maximum security facilities) could be classified as psychopathic.

There is some evidence that female psychopaths are less violent than male psychopaths (Mulder, Wells, Joyce, & Bushnell, 1994) and may recidivate less often than their male counterparts (Salekin et al., 1998). Additional research has found evidence for at least two broad categories of female psychopaths. One category appears to be characterized by lack of empathy or guilt, interpersonal deception, sensation seeking, and a strong proneness to boredom. The second category appears to be characterized by early behavioral problems, promiscuous sexual behavior, and adult antisocial (but not violent) behavior.

Psychosocial Factors of Criminal Behavior

In their efforts to explain criminal behavior, psychologists tend to focus on principles associated with learning or conditioning. As we saw with reference to the psychopath, learning can be problematic for some individuals. Behavior that enables us to obtain rewards or avoid punishing circumstances is likely to be repeated when similar conditions reoccur. This illustrates **instrumental learning**. The rewards may be physical (e.g., money, material goods), psychological (e.g., feelings of control over one's life), or social (e.g., improved status). Even behaviors that are considered antisocial or criminal may bring rewards that are worth the psychological risks and costs. This is similar to early criminological thought—specifically the classical school in criminology—that saw offenders as weighing the costs and benefits of committing crime. If the costs (or risks) outweighed the benefits, the rational individual would not commit crime. The classical school in criminology was philosophical in its orientation, however, and it did not apply principles of psychology to its theories.

In psychological parlance, rewards are termed reinforcements. The acquisition of physical, psychological or social rewards as a consequence of behavior is called positive reinforcement. The successful avoidance of negative or aversive events as a result of behavior is called negative reinforcement. Avoiding a painfully boring meeting by malingering provides negative reinforcement and is likely to be repeated if the ploy is successful.

Instrumental learning, the concept we have been referring to, is a process which, to many psychologists, offers the most easily grasped explanation of criminality. People who commit crimes are seeking to gain or avoid something. A person may wish to terminate the pain caused by an abusive spouse (negative reinforcement) or may yearn for the yacht that can be obtained by embezzling company profits. The reinforcements may seem fairly straightforward, but they also can be deceptively complex. Some antisocial behavior may be directed at gaining the social approval of a significant subgroup, such as a youth gang, or the psychological feeling of personal control over one's plight, and it may be independent of the obvious material gain promised by the successful completion of the crime. The behavior also may be intended to gain reward in more than one area. Consider the crime of perjury, as when a law enforcement officer lies under oath to see a defendant convicted. Although there are no material gains evident, the solidarity of the law enforcement subgroup, the likely incarceration of the offender, and the officer's feeling of personal control over the outcome of the case are reinforcement enough.

If the eventual reinforcement makes the investment worthwhile, the behavior is likely to be repeated. Therefore, criminal behavior will continue to be practiced if it is materially, socially, or psychologically lucrative. But this is only part of the story, because criminal behavior can also occur as a result of observational learning, or more broadly, cognitive-social learning.

Cognitive-Social Learning Theory

Julian Rotter (1954, 1966, 1972) is a major contributor to cognitive social learning theory because of his emphasis on the cognitive, mediating aspects of human learning. Cognition refers to structures and processes within the brain that make up mental activity, including thinking, planning, deciding, wishing, organizing, reconciling, and mental transformation. Cognitive psychology, the study of the above processes, is the dominant force in psychology today.

Cognitive psychology emphasizes the internal or "mind" representations of the external world. Generally, it sees behavior as a function of the subjective world transformed and represented by the person's mind. That is, people behave in accordance with their subjective thoughts and interpretations about the world rather than in reaction to how the outside world objectively or "really" is.

The traditional learning theories of classical conditioning and instrumental learning fail to take into careful consideration what goes on between the time the organism perceives a stimulus and responds or reacts to that stimulus. Cognitive-social learning posits that this classical view is too simple and too general to allow complete understanding of human behavior.

Expectations Rotter stresses the importance of the individual's cognitive expectations about the consequences of behavior and the rewards that will be gained from the behavior. In other words, before responding to a given set of circumstances, an individual evaluates: "What has happened to me before in this situation, and what will I gain if I do this?" This self-questioning process may occur very rapidly or may take place with much deliberation. According to Rotter, the probability of a specific behavior occurring depends upon the individual's expectancies regarding the outcomes of the behavior and the subjectively perceived gain that will result. Therefore, behavior is a function of the person's relevant expectancies, acquired from past experiences, and the perceived importance of the rewards gained by the behavior. Over the long haul of daily living, the person will develop generalized expectancies which tend to be stable and consistent across relatively similar circumstances (Mischel, 1976).

Modeling With reference to criminal action, we can posit that the individual expects or anticipates the action to be effective in the acquisition of status, power, affection, material goods, or generally positive living conditions. The specific behavior chosen (and its concomitant expectancies) need not have been directly reinforced previously, however. An individual may obtain the cognitive imagery of a particular behavior simply by observing another person perform the action. This is known as observational learning or modeling (Bandura, 1973; 1986). Consider, for example, the use of a gun. Although many individuals have never directly fired a gun, almost everyone knows how to do so. Although there are technical aspects of the firearm, like the safety catch and loading mechanisms, the overall general behavioral pattern is familiar to most: point the barrel and pull the trigger. How do we learn this behavioral pattern? By observing others using firearms.

Albert Bandura (1973) postulates that much of our behavior is acquired initially by watching others, who are known as models. The more significant and meaningful these models are to us, the greater the likelihood that the observed behavior will be imitated. Models may be parents, teachers, siblings, friends, peers, and even symbolic figures like television or film characters or the protagonist in a favorite novel.

The observed behavior may be copied immediately or at a future time deemed most appropriate by the observer. Once tried, its continuance depends substantially upon its consequences. If the new behavior delivers gain or reinforcement, it will probably be used again. If not, it is likely to drop out of our behavioral repertoire. Therefore, although initial cognitive representation may be gained through observation, its maintenance usually depends upon the nature of its rewards.

Although we have outlined cognitive-social learning theory in relatively simple terms, it would be a mistake to assume that the observer simply mimics the behavior of the model. The observer also notes if, how, and when the model is rewarded, disregarded, or punished. Adults in particular also evaluate the consequences in relation to their own position and capacities. Hence, the observer assesses self-evaluative components as well as external outcomes. "People do not indiscriminately absorb the influences that impinge upon them" (Bandura, 1974, p. 862). They evaluate and consider, and once they have decided to behave a certain way, they expect something.

Most criminal behavior is intended to gain something that is subjectively useful or meaningful to the acting person. In this sense, criminal behavior may be perceived as subjectively adaptive rather than simply deviant or emotionally sick. It may be antisocial or deviant in reference to society's rules and values, but for that particular person, at that particular time, in the particular psychological state, the conduct is perceived as the best choice possible.

Thus far, we have discussed neurophysiological predispositions to classical conditioning, instrumental learning, and cognitive-social learning as psychological factors that help explain crime. The reader may be wondering at this point, "Which is the culprit?" Criminal behavior appears to be due to a varying *composite* of all of these factors. People who engage in crime, however defined, do so for a variety of subjective reasons stemming from their learning history, their neurophysiological predispositions, and their cognitive styles and competencies. Therefore, antisocial or criminal behavior can best be regarded as subjectively adaptive—even if socially deviant—behavior. The development of criminal behavior is also a result of an ongoing interaction between the person and the social environment, a process called reciprocal determinism.

Reciprocal Determinism Thus far, however, we have also emphasized the individual and neglected the situation. Cognitive-social learning theory tries to accommodate both personal (or dispositional) and situational factors. It analyzes behavior in relation to reciprocal interaction, which we discussed briefly early in the chapter, but also in relation to determinism (Bandura, 1974, 1977). "Determinism" in this context signifies "the production of effects by events, rather than in the doctrinal sense that actions are completely determined by a prior sequence of causes independent of the individual" (Bandura, 1978, p. 345). Reciprocal determinism refers to the hypothesis that behavior is influenced by the environment, but also that the environment is partly of a person's own making. By their own actions people create their social milieu; the social milieu, in turn, affects their actions. Therefore, from a cognitive-social learning perspective, criminal behavior is a result of a continuous reciprocal interplay between behavioral, cognitive, and environmental influences.

Reciprocal interaction needs further elaboration before the reader can obtain a clear understanding of the interaction between person and environment. According to Bandura (1978), "interaction" has been used in three fundamentally different ways: unidirectional, partially bidirectional, and reciprocal interaction.

In unidirectional interaction, the person and the situation are conceptualized as independent entities that combine to produce behavior. The person finds himself or herself faced with a set of circumstances, remembers previous, similar circumstances, and responds accordingly. Therefore, neither the person nor the situation affects one another.

In the partially bidirectional conception, the person and the situation are considered interdependent causes of behavior. The person's behavior influences the situation, and the situation in turn influences the behavior in reciprocal fashion.

What is missing from both of the above interpretations is cognition, an element which Bandura's third type of interaction—reciprocal determinism, takes into account. In psychological functioning, cognitions influence both behavior and the situation, and these, in turn, influence cognitions.

Deindividuation

The above discussion makes it clear that any complete understanding of criminal behavior from a psychological perspective requires an analysis of the reciprocal interaction which occurs. A vivid illustration can be found in the literature on deindividuation, a process whereby a group can activate behaviors, including antisocial and brutal ones, in individuals not normally so inclined (Festinger, Pepitone, & Newcomb, 1952). Crowd violence, looting, vandalism, gang rapes, and crowd panic are all examples of this phenomenon.

Deindividuation is dependent upon an interplay between each individual's perceptions of himself or herself (cognitions), his or her behavior (individual behavior), and the actions of the crowd (situation). The process usually follows a sequence. First, the presence of many other persons prompts one to begin to feel part of a group, or at least personally diffused into the group, so that one cannot be singled out or easily identified. During this phase, the behavior of others influences a person's cognitions and self-awareness, and the person's behavior in turn begins to influence the actions of others in the group, in a reciprocal fashion. During the second phase, the behavior of the group is imitated, usually cautiously and tentatively. In news footage of crowd violence, for example, we often observe individuals who are surveying the illegal activity around them (e.g., brick throwing), seemingly hesitant about joining in.

Once begun, the antisocial or violent behavior is found rewarding and pleasurable, bringing physiological arousal into play. The behavior is providing the cognitive component of the triad with feedback, and the cognitive component in turn interacts with the behavioral component, "urging it on." Meanwhile, of course, the person is still receiving and providing behavior and cognitive cues (attitudes and values about the behavior) from and to the crowd.

In the third and final deindividuation phase, the behavior of the individuals and the collective crowd reaches a crescendo of violence, brutality, and destruction. All three components are involved in reciprocal interaction. Once the group action has reached this stage, very little can be done to terminate it until there is a change in the state of the group (e.g., people become fatigued or injured), a change in the state of victims (e.g., they lose consciousness or die), or a change in the weapons used (e.g., bullets rather than bricks), including measures to dispel the crowd. Because the crowd has reached the final stage of deindividuation, and because individuals are melded into the group, appeals to reason are unlikely to be effective.

Escalation Escalation is another psychological process which illustrates triadic reciprocal determinism. Here, one offended or humiliated person resorts to salvaging self esteem by "going one better" and insulting his or her humiliator. Thus, two people become caught up in an escalating conflict, and exchanges of barbs will continue until one person decides to stop or must stop. Verbal insults become pushes, pushes become punches, and ultimately, lethal weapons may be used. However, during each step of the escalation, each individual is continually appraising the conflict, the other person's behavior, the situation, his or her own behavior, the antecedents, and the consequences. In the beginning of the scenario, neither party may have wished for the final outcome. The nature of the conflict, the context, and the cognitive appraisals of the actors at each progressive step determined the ultimate action. Many homicides and aggravated assaults follow this escalating pattern.

Prediction of Criminal Behavior

Since person-situation reciprocity indicates that the factors involved in crime are dynamic, ever-changing, and complex, can we make predictions about the likelihood of anyone engaging in criminal behavior? Can we even talk about criminal "personalities" with any degree of confidence? Cognitive-social learning theory certainly casts doubt on the validity of the long-standing search for the personality of the murderer, the person engaged in securities fraud, or the child abuser. However, examining a particular individual's response pattern under certain conditions gives us some predictive power. Past behavior is perhaps one of the best predictors of future behavior we have available. A repeat offender who has engaged in a string of burglaries is predictable to some degree. But any predictive equation will have to examine the individual's competencies, expectancies, and other relevant behavioral patterns, as well as the specific conditions which activate the behavior or burglary. Even after careful study, the predictive equation will likely result in only a rough estimation of behavioral occurrence within a certain time frame.

The concepts of cross-situational and temporal consistency should also help in any analysis of criminal behavior. As the reader will recall from material in ◀ Chapter 2, cross-situational consistency refers to the degree to which behaviors or traits generalize from one situation to another dissimilar situation. Temporal consistency refers to the degree to which behaviors are consistent over time, in similar situations. Research has found that individuals in general reflect greater temporal consistency than cross-situational consistency. Therefore, criminal behavior that has been reinforced in a particular context is more apt to recur in a similar context than across a wide variety of situations. Thus, a person who has engaged in a lifetime of burglary is more likely to burglarize again if surrounded by familiar situations. On the other hand, if his or her environment has changed substantially (e.g., long-time partner in crime has died; person is now living in Lubec, Maine, instead of Boston, Massachusetts), it is less likely that the criminal activity will continue.

Psychologists have often remarked that their discipline helps them to predict some of the people some of the time (Bem & Allen, 1974). Actually, we can be more optimistic and say that we should be able to predict most people's behavior much of the time if we apply the principles covered in this chapter. It is also important to take note of a "discovery" brought to light by several psychologists (Kenrick & Stringfield, 1980; Mischel, 1973, 1976). A valuable resource in helping psychologists improve their predictive power is the information people provide about themselves. The best clues to understanding people are the traits and behaviors they say they have, and people are surprisingly willing to reveal such information. Rather than dismiss such reports because they are self-serving, psychologists are listening more carefully and applying these comments to their evaluations. A person who admits he is often hostile, loses his temper, and feels like physically abusing others, and who has a history of assault convictions, would probably merit careful monitoring. On the other hand, without these self-reported behaviors, the predictive power is less convincing.

In sum, full appreciation of criminal behavior requires analysis of the triadic reciprocal system, the situation, and the "personality" (defined here as expectancies, learning history, competencies, subjective values, cognitive structures, and the self-regulatory systems and plans). We make no pretense that this is a simple task. It is often more appealing to advance dogmatic, simplified generalizations that are more manageable cognitively than to tackle the immense problem of understanding, predicting and changing criminal behavior. We will return to the topic of prediction of human behavior in ▶ Chapter 14 when we discuss criminal profiling.

At this point, we shift our discussion to specific crimes. Of necessity, we must focus on a select number of crimes, and we have chosen to focus on three quite distinct categories, all of which lend themselves well to psychological interpretations. Crimes of intimidation, crimes of violence (sexual and non-sexual), and arson will be highlighted.

Crimes of Intimidation

Stalking

Stalking is defined as "a course of conduct directed at a specific person that involves repeated physical or visual proximity, nonconsensual communication, or verbal, written, or implied threats sufficient to cause fear in a reasonable person" (Tjaden, 1997, p. 2). Systematic information on stalking in the United States is limited, despite the attention it receives from the media and legislatures. The best estimates of stalking at this time are that 8% of women and 2% of men have been stalked at some point in their lives (Tjaden, 1997). In most cases, the stalking lasts less than one year, but some people are stalked for five years or more.

Most of the previous research has concentrated on the stalking of famous personalities, entertainment icons, or politicians, collectively called "celebrity stalking." However, a substantial increase in the stalking of "noncelebrities" over the past decade has generated numerous media accounts of stalking and the passage of antistalking laws in all 50 states and the District of Columbia, Guam, and the Virgin Islands (Tjaden & Thoennes, 1998). The first anti-stalking law was passed in California in 1990. The impetus for this legislation was not the stalking and eventual homicide of television star Rebecca Schaeffer as commonly believed, but rather several cases involving brutal domestic violence (Lemon, 1994). A California municipal court judge initiated the development and passage of the anti-stalking law following his frustration over existing laws that failed to protect four Orange County women who were killed in different incidents despite the issuance of restraining orders against their assailants.

Although legal definitions of stalking vary from state to state, most states define stalking in their statutes as the willful, malicious, and repeated following and harassing of another person. State stalking laws generally consider the type of repeated behavior that is prohibited, whether a threat is required as part of stalking, the reaction of the victim to the stalking, and the intent of the stalker (Office of Victims of Crime, 2002). In most states, stalking is a misdemeanor, except under certain circumstances, such as stalking in violation of a protective order, stalking while armed, or repeat stalking. Some statutes include such activities as lying-in-wait, surveillance, nonconsensual communication, telephone harassment, and vandalism (Tjaden & Thoennes, 1998). Most states require at least two or more incidents before enforcement can be initiated. In 1996, Congress enacted the *Interstate Anti-Stalking Punishment and Prevention Act* to prohibit stalkers from traveling across state lines in pursuit of their victims. The Act was passed to improve the anti-stalking provisions of the *Violent Crime Control and Law Enforcement Act of 1994*. Recall also that the *Violence Against Women Act* has provisions that make it easier for women to obtain protective orders against abusers.

In an attempt to learn more about the nature of stalking among the general population, the Center for Policy Research conducted a comprehensive survey of 8,000 women and 8,000 men eighteen years of age or older (Tjaden & Thoennes, 1998). The survey discovered that 87% of the time the stalker is male, and 80% of time the victim is female. The survey also clearly pointed out that, in most stalking incidents, the victims know their stalker, often well. About half of the female victims are stalked by current or former marital or co-habiting partners, and a majority of these women (about 80%) had been physically assaulted by that partner, either during the relationship, during the stalking episode, or during both. In about one-third of the cases, stalkers vandalized the victim's property, and about 10% of the time the stalker killed or threatened to kill the victim's pets. In nearly half the cases, the stalker made serious overt threats to the victim. The survey dispelled the myth that most stalkers are psychotic or delusional. Only 7% of the victims perceived their stalkers as "crazy" or chronic abusers of drugs or alcohol. According to the survey, the motives for stalking are most often to control, intimidate, or frighten their victims, regardless of whether the victims are male or female.

J. Reid Meloy (1998) posits that stalkers rarely inflict serious physical injury to their victims, threaten with weapons, or use weapons. However, the story may be quite different in situations involving stalking by intimate partners. Mary Brewster (2002) conducted an in-depth semi-structured interview with 187 female victims of stalking by former intimate partners. She discovered that nearly two-thirds of the women had been physically abused during their prior relationship with the victim. After removing themselves from the relationship, the victims described being subjected to a variety of disturbing behaviors, including phone calls (90%), watching (79%), and following (68%). Approximately three-quarters of the women said their stalkers had made threats of violence against them, and nearly half reported actual physical assaults during the stalking.

In the Tjaden-Thoennes survey, half of the stalking victims reported the incident to the police, and one-quarter of the female victims obtained a restraining order. About 70% of the time, however, the restraining order was violated by the stalker. And in those cases where the restraining order was violated, about 25% of the victims pursued prosecution of the offender. The prosecution strategy appears successful, with most cases resulting in conviction of the stalker and well over half receiving some jail or prison time.

Most cases challenging the constitutionality of stalking laws focus on one of two questions: whether the statute is unconstitutionally overbroad or whether it is unconstitutionally vague. A statute is unconstitutionally overbroad when it inadvertently criminalizes legitimate behavior. It is vague when it "either forbids or requires the doing of an act in terms so vague that men of common intelligence must necessarily guess at its meaning and differ as to its application (*Connally v. General Construction Company*, 1926, p. 391). For example, the Kansas Supreme Court ruled that that state's stalking statute was unconstitutionally vague because it used the terms "alarms," "annoys," and "harasses" without defining them or using an objective standard to measure the prohibited conduct (*State v. Bryan*, 1996). The state legislature then went to work to amend the statute, and the state Supreme Court found the revised law constitutional largely because it now included an objective standard and clearly defined key terms (*State v. Rucker*, 1999).

The psychological damage to the victims of stalking is usually substantial and incalculable. In a survey involving 145 stalked victims (120 females, 25 males), Doris Hall reports that the experience of being stalked results in major life changes. "Many move or quit jobs, some change their names, others have gone underground, leaving friends and family in order to escape the terror (Hall, 1998, p. 134). Some victims change their physical appearance or wear a wide assortment of disguises. Others become excessively or "pathologically" suspicious of the motives of all others, often leading to lonely and socially isolated lives. Many victims constantly worry that their stalker will find them again, starting the entire experience all over again.

Hate or Bias Crimes

During the last decade of the 20th century, considerable public attention was drawn to the problem of hate crimes in the United States. Hate crimes—also called bias crimes—are those that are motivated by hatred of a victim based on the victim's actual or perceived status. The statuses that are of particular concern are those that reflect discrimination or prejudice in society, such as race and ethnicity, religion, sexual orientation, or gender. High-profile, shocking incidents of hate crimes across the U.S. during the 1980s and 1990s prompted legislation directed at examining this problem more closely and punishing those who committed such offenses. It should be mentioned that when hate crime legislation was first proposed, it attracted considerable criticism. Critics charged that hate or bias crime statutes violated equal protection, mental privacy, or freedom of expression (Delgado, 2002). However, as it became apparent that legislation was necessary to stem the frequency of crime motivated by bias, the criticism subsided, although it has not completely disappeared.

In 1989, the U.S. Congress mandated that the Department of Justice gather data on "hate" or bias crimes. Known as the *Hate Crime Statistics Act*, it requires data collection of violent attacks, intimidation, arson, or property damage that are directed at a person or group of persons because of race, religion, sexual orientation, or ethnicity. Note that gender is not included in this list. In 1994, the *Violent Crime Control and Law Enforcement Act* amended the Hate Crime Statistics Act to add disabilities—both physical and mental—to the hate crime category. In that same year, Congress also passed a bill that provides for longer sentences for those convicted of hate crimes, called the *Hate Crimes Sentencing Enhancement Act*. In 1996, due to a dramatic increase in the torching of places of worship (especially African-American places located in Southeastern U.S.), the *Church Arson Prevention Act* was signed into law. More recently, the *Hate Crimes Prevention Act of 1999* prohibits persons from interfering with an individual's federal right, such as voting or employment, by violence or threat of violence due to his or her race, color, religion, or national original. Thus, at this writing, the federal law is directed at punishing specifically those crimes motivated by hatred of a victim because of the victim's perceived race, religion, sexual orientation, ethnicity or national origin, or disability.

In addition to the hate crime legislation of the federal government, over 40 states and the District of Columbia have hate crime statutes (Wessler & Moss, 2001). Almost all jurisdictions that have hate crime laws cover bias based on race, religion, ethnicity, and national origin, but significantly fewer states have statutes that cover bias based on gender, disability, and sexual orientation. Some states also include age and veteran status in their statutes. Virtually all states, in addition to the federal government, provide for an enhancement of penalties once a person has been convicted of a bias or hate crime. The U.S. Supreme Court has upheld the constitutionality of a hate crime statute that called for an enhanced sentence (*Wisconsin v. Mitchell*, 1993), but it struck down a hate crime statute that punished protected freedom of expression (*R.A. v. City of St. Paul*, 1992). In the St. Paul case, the Court ruled that a juvenile who burned a cross on a black family's lawn was entitled to First Amendment protection. In a more recent case, *Apprendi v. New Jersey*, the court ruled that a judge could not enhance a sentence using new information that had not been made available to jurors deciding the case ◙ (see **Box 13-3**).

The federal government collects hate crime data for eleven traditional offenses that are divided into two major classifications, crimes against persons and crimes against property. Crimes against persons include murder and non-negligent manslaughter, forcible rape, aggravated assault, simple assault, and intimidation. Crimes against property include robbery, burglary, larceny-theft, motor vehicle theft, arson, and destruction/damage/vandalism of property. Nearly two out of every three hate crimes in 2001 were crimes against persons, with intimidation being the most frequent at 55.9% (Federal Bureau of Investigation, 2002). Recent data suggest that a majority of hate crimes are motivated by racial bias (44.9%), followed by ethnic/national origin bias (21.6%), religious bias (14.3%), sexual orientation bias (14.3%), and disability bias (0.3%). Sixty-four percent of the hate crime victims were individuals, while the remaining victims were businesses, religious institutions, or other institutions and organizations. Destruction, damage, or vandalism was reported in 83.7% of hate crimes against property.

The psychology of hate crime and the trauma it brings to victims have become increasingly important areas for social scientists over the past decade (Bingham et al., 2002). Hate crime and violence appear to have their roots in an individual's learned prejudice against particular social groups. This learned prejudice, combined with fear, can escalate

BOX 13-3
The Supreme Court and Hate Crimes

Following are facts and holdings from three hate crime cases that made it to the highest court in the land.

R.A. v. City of St. Paul

R.A., a juvenile, placed a burning cross on the lawn of an African-American family. He was prosecuted under a city ordinance that made it a misdemeanor to place a variety of symbols, including burning crosses, on private property. He was adjudicated delinquent as a result of his action, and courts in Minnesota upheld the delinquency finding. The U.S. Supreme Court, however, reversed, stating that the ordinance violated the Constitution. R.A., the Court said, was exercising his 1st Amendment freedom of expression and could not be punished for doing that. However, he could have been charged with criminal trespass, a charge the prosecutor did not file.

Wisconsin v. Mitchell

After watching the movie, "Mississippi Burning," which included a scene of white men beating a black boy, a group of black boys chased and severely assaulted a white youth. They were prosecuted and convicted under Wisconsin's bias crime statute, which allowed an enhanced penalty for a person convicted of a crime motivated by prejudice. The state lost its case before the Wisconsin Supreme Court, which believed the statute would not survive considering the U.S. Supreme Court's ruling in the R.A. case. However, the U.S. Supreme Court upheld the statute. Mitchell, the Court said, was punished for an action that was clearly a crime (assault), not for an action that was Constitutionally protected.

Apprendi v. New Jersey

Apprendi fired several shots into the home of an African-American family who had moved into an all-white neighborhood. He initially told police he had done this because he did not want black families moving in, but then retracted the statement. He pled guilty to possession of a firearm for an unlawful purpose and unlawful possession of an antipersonnel bomb. At his sentencing hearing, a judge reviewed the facts of the case and imposed an enhanced sentence under the state's hate crime law. The statute allowed an additional 10 to 20 years beyond the maximum sentence if a judge found by a preponderance of evidence that a defendant intended to intimidate a victim because of race, color, gender, handicap, religion, sexual orientation, or ethnicity.

Apprendi was given a 12-year sentence, but the Supreme Court overturned it. Any facts—other than prior conviction—that enhance a sentence beyond the statutory maximum, the Court said, must be submitted to a jury and must be found beyond a reasonable doubt. The *Apprendi* decision was a surprise to many observers and is expected to affect sentencing practices in many states as well as the federal government.

into violence when a member of the prejudicial group believes his or her lifestyle is under attack. When hate crimes are committed by groups, deindividuation may be a significant factor. Bias crimes often have long-term psychological and social repercussions that are extremely destructive to both the victims and their families (Seymour, Hook, & Grimes, 2001). Black Americans still view racial discrimination and bias crimes to be dominant forces in their lives, despite the belief by white Americans that black Americans are faring about as well or better than the average white person and that there has been substantial reduction in bias crimes directed at blacks (Dovidio et al., 2002). Contemporary racism is more subtle than the "old-fashioned" racism that was blatant and aversive, but it is still insidious. Furthermore, black Americans continue to have a profound distrust for police and the criminal justice system (Cole, 1999), and about a third are overtly distrustful of whites in general (Dovidio et al., 2002). It should be noted that over 50% of those offenses motivated by bias because of ethnicity/national origin have been directed at Hispanics or Latinos. Since the tragic destruction of the World Trade Center on September 11, 2001, hate or bias crimes against persons perceived as having Middle Eastern origins are also likely to show a substantial increase in the coming years.

Most of social science research examining the psychological causes and effects of bias crime in recent years has shifted to investigating the ramifications of sexual orientation bias. Research consistently reveals that over 90% of gay men and lesbians report some form of victimization over their lifetime. Nearly half say they have been threatened with physical violence, and one-fifth report being punched, kicked, or beaten because of their sexual orientation (Bernat, Calhoun, Adams, & Zeichner, 2001). Most of the aggressors are young men in their late teens or early twenties, who mainly attack persons whom they perceive to be gay men. Hate and violence toward homosexuals has most often been attributed to homophobia, but consistent definitions of that term are difficult to find (Bernat et al., 2001). Most definitions include any negative attitude, belief, reaction, or action against homosexuality. The psychological effects of bias crimes based on sexual orientation may be more substantial than the effects from other non-bias crimes. For example, Herek, Gillis, and Cogan (1999) report, on the basis of their survey, that hate-crime victimization was associated with greater psychological distress for both gay men and lesbians, compared to victims of equally violent but non-bias crimes. Overall, victims of bias crimes due to sexual orientation manifested more symptoms of depression, anger, anxiety, and post-traumatic stress than the non-bias crime victims.

Violent Crimes: Sex Offenses

As we noted in ◀ Chapter 10, statistics on the number of sex offenders under correctional supervision are sobering. Recent data indicate that there are approximately 234,000 sex offenders under the care, custody, or control of correctional agencies on any given day in the United States (Chaiken, 1998). In recent years, several brutally violent attacks were perpetrated by several convicted-but-released sex offenders on young, vulnerable victims. These incidents had an enormous influence on prompting state and federal legislation to prevent future incidents by known sex offenders. A considerable amount of legislation during the late 1990s was developed from the comprehensive *Violent Crime Control and Law Enforcement Act of 1994*. The Act has formed the basis for the U.S. Department of Justice's strategy for dealing with violent offenders, most particularly violent sex offenders.

During the mid-1990s, the U.S. Congress enacted three statutes that collectively require states to strengthen the procedures they use to keep tabs on sex offenders. The statutes are: (1) The *Jacob Wetterling Crimes Against Children and Sexually Violent Offender Registration Act* (enacted in 1994); (2) the federal version of *Megan's Law* (enacted in 1996); and (3) the *Pam Lychner Sexual Offender Tracking and Identification Act* (also enacted in 1996). All three statutes require states to establish registration programs so that local law enforcement and community officials will know the whereabouts of sex offenders released into their jurisdiction, and enforce notification programs so that the public can be warned about sex offenders living in the community (Chaiken, 1998).

The *Jacob Wetterling Act* encourages states—through financial incentives—to require convicted child molesters and sexually violent offenders to notify law enforcement officials of their whereabouts for ten years following release from prison, parole, or community supervision. The required notification time may be extended if the offender has been adjudicated as a "sexually violent predator." The Act defines a "sexually violent predator" as a person who has been convicted of a sexually violent offense *and* who suffers from a mental abnormality or personally disorder that renders the person likely to engage in predatory sexually violent offenses. "Mentally abnormality" refers to condition involving a disposition to commit criminal sexual acts of such a degree as to make the person a menace to others. On the other hand, "personality disorder" is not defined by the Act.

The Act was named in honor of eleven-year old Jacob Wetterling of St. Joseph, Minnesota, who was abducted at gunpoint by a masked man on October 22, 1989, as he, his brother, and a friend rode their bikes near the Wetterlings' home. Neither Jacob nor the abductor was ever found. Since the kidnapping, Jacob's mother, Patty Wetterling, has been very active in the campaign to protect children from sexual exploitation and abduction.

The second statute, known as *Megan's Law*, requires states to release registration information to the public when it is necessary for public safety, a requirement often referred to as "mandatory community notification." While the *Wetterling Act* does not require that communities be notified of the release of sex offenders, *Megan's Law* mandates that local communities be notified. More specifically, the *Law*, signed on May 17, 1996 by President Clinton, allows the states discretion to establish criteria for disclosure, but requires them to make private and personal information on registered sex offenders available to the public.

Megan's Law was named after seven-year-old Megan Kanka of Hamilton Square, New Jersey, who in 1994 was assaulted, raped, and murdered by a twice-convicted sex offender living across the street. The offender, Jesse Timmendequas, lured the child into his house to see a puppy, then raped and strangled her with a belt. He then dumped her body in a park. In 1999, the New Jersey Supreme Court affirmed the conviction and death sentence of Timmendequas by a 4–3 vote. The Court rejected the defense position that the 1997 trial was tainted by prejudicial pre-trial publicity.

The *Lychner Act* amended the *Violent Crime Control and Law Enforcement Act of 1994* to require the FBI to establish the national offender database and to handle sex offender registration and notification in states unable to maintain "minimally sufficient" programs on their own. Basically, the *Lychner Act* established more stringent registration requirements for sex offenders living within the community. Under the Act, offenders considered most dangerous to public safety will be required to register wherever they go, for life. The *Lychner Act* was named in honor of a Houston real estate agent named Pam Lychner. In 1990, a twice-convicted felon brutally assaulted Lychner while she was showing a house to a prospective buyer in the Houston area. Her life was saved when her husband arrived on the scene and interrupted the attack. The attacker received a sentence of 20 years, but was released on parole after two years. He then proceeded to sue Lychner for ruining his life, an action that angered and consequently prompted Lychner to become extremely active in pushing for tougher laws against crime. Tragically, Pam Lychner and her two young daughters were later killed on their way to France in the explosion of TWA Flight 800 off the coast of Long Island, New York, in July, 1996.

Registration of sex offenders and notification to the public are extremely controversial issues. While most states have followed Congress's lead and have enacted similar legislation, these state laws differ widely and not all courts have upheld them. New Jersey's own *Megan's Law* had to be modified to allow individuals a hearing to challenge the placement of their names on the registry, for example. Many of these laws do not require an individual determination that the person is likely to re-offend. As we will note shortly, though, the U.S. Supreme Court has ruled that a state does *not* have to document the offender's *current* dangerousness. There have also been anecdotal reports of serious harassment of sex offenders who have served their sentences and are not troubling the community. Opponents of the laws—particularly the community notification provisions—also argue that they create a false sense of security in the community. The individual who has not yet been detected—and thus does not appear on these registries—is in many instances more of a danger than the individual who has served a sentence and is trying to start a new life. In 2003, the U.S. Supreme Court ruled in two cases involving aspects of sex offender registration and notification laws in two states, Alaska (*Smith et al. v. Doe et al.*, 2003) and Connecticut (*Connecticut Department of Public Safety v. Doe*, 2003). Alaska's law is particularly draconian, requiring—among other things—that persons convicted of aggravated sex offenses or of two or more sex offenses (even if nonaggravated) register for life. They are also required to provide quarterly verification of their information. Persons convicted of one nonaggravated sex crime are required to register for 15 years. Both states include provisions for posting names on the Internet. The offenders in the Alaska case argued that the statute, which was not in effect when they were convicted, could not be applied retroactively. The offenders in the Connecticut case argued that the statute did not grant them a right to hearing to establish that they were currently dangerous. In both cases, the offenders lost their cases, suggesting that states will continue to have wide leeway in constructing and enforcing their registration and notification laws.

Another federal law, the *Violence Against Women Act* (VAWA) passed by Congress in 1994 and discussed in ◀ Chapter 11, also addresses sex offending. This law initiated the first major federal effort to address violence against women, and early on, it was primarily directed at combating domestic violence, stalking, and sexual assault (Reno, 1999a). The Act increased penalties for sex offenders and domestic abusers, such as doubling the maximum term of imprisonment for repeat sex offenders and authorizing severe federal sentences for abusers who travel interstate with the intent to injure, harass, or intimidate a domestic partner or violate a protection order. One provision of the Act, which allowed women to sue their aggressors for damages in federal courts, was, however, later struck down by the U.S. Supreme Court (*U.S. v. Morrison*, 2000).

Sexual Assault: Definition and Prevalence

Definitions of sexual assault vary widely from state to state. In a majority of states the term sexual assault has replaced rape in the criminal statutes. Additionally, it is an offense which can be perpetrated against males as well as females. The term rape is still widely used in the literature, however, as well as in the UCR and a variety of other measures of crime. According to the U.S. Department of Justice, rape is "unlawful sexual intercourse . . . by force or without legal or factual consent" (U.S. Department of Justice, 1988, p. 2). The National Crime Victimization Survey (NCVS) defines rape much more comprehensively and adds categories of sexual assault that do not meet the definition of rape. According to the standard used by the survey, rape is forced sexual intercourse including psychological coercion as well as physical force. Forced sexual intercourse means vaginal, anal, or oral penetration by the offender(s). This category also includes incidents where the penetration is from a foreign object such as a bottle.

The *FBI Uniform Crime Reports* distinguishes forcible rape from statutory rape and rape by fraud. It does not recognize rape when males are the victims. According to the UCR, forcible rape is "the carnal knowledge of a female, forcibly and against her will" and includes rape by force, assault to rape, and attempted rape. **Forcible rape** is to be contrasted with **statutory rape**, where the age of the victim is the crucial distinction, regardless of whether she gives her consent to engage in sexual intercourse. The age limit appears to be an arbitrary legal cutoff considered to be the age at which the person has the cognitive and emotional maturity to give her meaningful consent and understand the consequences. Although age limits vary from state to state, most cutoff points are age sixteen or eighteen. Therefore, if it can be determined to the satisfaction of the court that an adult male has engaged in sexual relations with a female who was under the legal age at the time, he can be convicted of statutory rape. **Rape by fraud** refers to the act of having sexual relations with a consenting adult female under fraudulent conditions, such as when a physician or psychotherapist has sexual intercourse with a patient under the guise of "effective treatment." The legal scope of forcible rape has traditionally been confined to imposed sexual contact or assault of adolescent and adult females who are not related to the offender. However, today rape is been expanded to include sexual assault of a wife by her husband.

Still, many people (including some victims themselves) do not define sexual attacks as rape unless the assailant is a stranger. Thus, if a woman is sexually assaulted by a husband, boyfriend, or a "date," she is unlikely to report the incident. Some criminal justice officials and some members of the general public consider marital or date rape unimportant because they believe they are less psychologically traumatic to the victim, and are more difficult to prove. Prosecutors, for example, admit they are reluctant to prosecute marital or date rape cases because of concerns that it is difficult to convince juries that husbands or boyfriends could be sexual assailants (Kilpatrick et al., 1988). However, available data suggest that over 40% of the total rapes that occur may be committed by husbands or male friends (Kilpatrick, et al., 1988).

Prevalence and Incidence of Rape

Based on available data, the United States has the highest rape rate in the world. During the past decade, official (based on the *FBI Uniform Crime Reports*) incidents of reported rape hover between 65 to 75 for every 100,000 women. In 2001, there were 62.2 forcible rapes per 100,000 females in the nation (Federal Bureau of Investigation, 2002). These figures probably greatly underestimate the actual incidence, however, because data suggest that only 55% of rape victims report the assault in the U.S., and only 38% of the victims report the incident in Canada (Roberts & Gebotys, 1992).

Individual victimization studies provide an even more disconcerting picture. As we noted above, even these figures are in question, of course, because of reluctance even to report that one did not report a rape. Russell (1983) interviewed 930 women living in the San Francisco Bay area, and found that 19% said that they had been the victim of at least one completed extramarital rape. Another 13% said they had been the victim of at least one attempted extramarital rape. Only 8% of all victims of completed or attempted rape reported the incident to the police. Koss and her colleagues (Koss, Gidycz, & Wisniewski, 1987) discovered that 28% of the college women surveyed in a national study involving 32 U.S. colleges and universities had been victims of rape or attempted rape. More surprising, however, was the fact that virtually none of the incidents were reported to the police and therefore were not included in the official crime statistics. Based on her data, Koss estimates the victimization rate for women to be 3,800 per 100,000, a rate drastically different from the official rates of 65 to 75 per 100,000. According to the NCVS, persons 12 and older experienced an average annual 140,990 completed rapes, 109,230 attempted rapes, and 152,690 completed and attempted sexual assaults (Rennison, 2002).

Additional victimization data suggest that there is approximately a one in five chance a woman will be raped at some time during her lifetime (Furby, Weinrott, & Blackshaw, 1989). If attempted rapes were included in the statistics, the odds approach three to one. A startling number of women are sexually victimized while on a date. Approximately 22% of women surveyed said they had been subjected to a coercive sexual encounter (e.g., fondling, oral sex, or intercourse) by a date at some point in their lives (Yegidis, 1986; Dull & Giacopassi, 1987).

Psychological Consequences The rape victim is frequently twice victimized—by the sexual assailant and by exposure to the judicial process (Borgida, 1980). Rape cases require thorough investigation and attention to detail, which demand keen recall and the description of intimate, stressful sexual events. Victims are also required to undergo a medical examination to establish physical evidence of penetration and use of physical force.

If the victim is able to withstand these stressful conditions, which are often exacerbated by negative reactions from parents, husband, and friends, and sometimes by threats from the assailant, the next step requires the preparation and successful prosecution of the case in court. Ninety-two percent of the prosecutors surveyed by the Law Enforcement Assistance Administration (LEAA) (1977) asserted that the credibility of the victim was one of the most important elements in convincing juries to convict for forcible rape. Therefore, the defense traditionally concentrated upon the victim's prior sexual history to destroy credibility and to portray her as a women with loose morals. The procedure of derogating the victim by using her sexual history came under attack in the 1970s, and within 15 years all states had revised their rape laws in an effort to limit this tactic (Marsh, 1988). Most states have enacted rape shield reform statutes which restrict, to varying degrees, the admissibility of the victim's sexual history into the courtroom (Borgida, 1980).

In addition to impeaching the victim's credibility via sexual history, some defense attorneys invoked corroboration rules, which required evidence other than the victim's testimony before a person could be charged with rape. Many states have relaxed the type of evidence required to corroborate the victim's testimony, while others have abolished the requirement altogether.

A third practice peculiar to rape law was the judge's cautionary instructions to the jury, which stressed that a rape charge could be easily levied by a woman and was often difficult to prove. Therefore, the jury was told that the victim's testimony should be viewed with caution.

All three of the above practices center on the credibility of the victim and some still exist in varying degrees in different jurisdictions. In addition, and closely aligned to victim credibility, the defendant often used a defense of consent, maintaining that the sexual contact between the two individuals was consensual. Consent is a defense that is typically used in marital rape, acquaintance rape, or date rape cases.

There are three major concerns involved in any revision of forcible rape law: (1) the legal definition of rape; (2) rules of evidence, especially concerning the admissibility of sexual history and corroboration that the crime occurred; and (3) a penalty structure (Marsh, 1988; Loh, 1980). Comprehensive reforms of the rape law deal with all three aspects; while limited reforms generally focus on rules evidence, especially admissibility of sexual history (Marsh, 1988). Moreover, the new provisions in forcible rape legislation show a notable shift in the definition of the crime. Specifically, rape law reforms shift the cause of the crime from the victim to the offender, and redefines rape as a violation of a personal right (a woman's right to choose to engage in sexual activity) rather than an infringement of a property right (Marsh, 1988).

Very few studies have examined the effects of rape law reform on the judicial process. Jeanne Marsh (1988), in her review of the extant research, finds that comprehensive reforms in the states of Michigan and Washington have increased the number of convictions for rape. Criminal justice officials in these two states report that two particular aspects of these comprehensive reform statutes have had the greatest influence on improved conviction rates: (1) better definitions of rape; and (2) clarified evidentiary requirements, such as restrictions on past sexual history evidence and changed standards in resistance or consent requirements. However, although these comprehensive reforms did alter formal evidentiary requirements and did increase the conviction rates for rape, they did not alter the factors considered by police and prosecutors when assessing convictability. Law Enforcement officials and prosecutors continued to use their old traditional ways of determining whether an arrest should be made and whether they should proceed with the prosecution. Similar findings are reported in Canada by Roberts and Gebotys (1992) on the judicial effects of nationwide, comprehensive rape reform legislation passed in 1983.

Psychological Correlates of Rapists

Several attempts have been made to classify rapists into groups. Such classification systems, either based on personality traits or behavioral patterns of individuals, are called typologies, and they have been moderately successful in their ability to add to our understanding of criminal behavior. A group of researchers at the Massachusetts Treatment Center (MTC) (Cohen, Seghorn & Calmas, 1969; Cohen et al., 1971; Knight & Prentky, 1987; Prentky & Knight, 1986) have developed a useful typology based on the behavioral patterns of convicted rapists, including the appearance of aggressive and sexual patterns in the sexual assaults. The MTC research group has identified four major categories of rapist based on the offender's primary motivation: (1) the pervasively angry rapist; (2) the non-sadistic rapist; (3) the sexually motivated rapist; and (4) the impulsive-opportunistic rapist. The researchers have also identified nine subtypes that accompany the four categories (Knight, Warren, Reboussin, & Soley, 1998). The nine subtypes are differentiated on the basis of six variables that have been consistently reported by clinicians and researchers to play an important role in the behavioral, emotional, and thought patterns of a wide array of rapists. The typology is called the Massachusetts Treatment Center, Rapist, Version 3, and is abbreviated MTC:R3. For our purposes, however, we will briefly describe only the four major categories of rapist outlined in the MTC:R3, not the nine subtypes.

The **pervasively angry rapists,** also called displaced anger or anger retaliation type in other classifications systems, demonstrate a predominance of violent and aggressive behaviors with a minimum or total absence of sexual feeling in their attacks. It appears that these men use the act of rape to harm, humiliate, and degrade women. The victims are brutally assaulted and subjected to sadistic acts such as biting, cutting, or tearing of breasts, genitals, or other parts of the body. In most instances, the victims are complete strangers and only serve as the best available objects for the rapists' aggression. The assaults are not usually sexually arousing for the assailants, who often have to masturbate to become tumescent. From the information gained about these rapists' behavior during the assaults, it appears that physical resistance only makes them more violent.

Although many of these rapists are married, their relationships with women are often characterized by periodic irritation and violence, and they probably qualify as wife abusers. These men generally perceive women as demanding, hostile, and unfaithful. They sometimes select their victim because they perceive something in her behavior or appearance which communicates assertiveness, independence, and professional activity. The attacks typically follow some incident which has made them angry about women and their behavior.

Thus, this rapist is labeled the displaced aggressive rapist because the victim of the assault and sexual arousal does not play any direct role in generating the violent attack. His major focus is aggression and anger toward women in general.

His occupational history is usually stable and often reveals some level of success. More often than not, his occupation is a "masculine" one, such as truck driver, carpenter, mechanic, or plumber. According to Knight and Prentky (1987), an offender must demonstrate the following characteristics during the attack to be classified displaced aggressive type:

1. The presence of high degree of nonsexualized aggression or rage expressed either through verbal and/or physical assault that clearly exceeds what is necessary to gain compliance of the victim;
2. Clear evidence, in verbalization or behavior, of the intent to demean, degrade, or humiliate the victim;
3. No evidence that the aggressive behavior is eroticized or that sexual pleasure is derived from the injurious acts; and
4. The injurious acts are not focused on parts of the body that have sexual significance.

Non-sadistic rapists assault, or attempt to assault, because of an intense sexual arousal prompted by specific stimuli in the environment. Although rape is, by definition, clearly a violent act, supplemental aggression is not a significant feature in this form of, attack. Rather, the fundamental motivation is the desire to prove sexual prowess and adequacy. Behaviorally, these men tend to be unusually passive, withdrawn, and lacking in social skills. They live in a world of fantasy, oriented around themes of how victims will yield eagerly under attack, submit to pleasurable intercourse, and find their skill and performance so outstanding that the victims will plead for a return engagement. These rapists fantasize that they will at last be able to prove their masculinity and sexual competence.

Acquaintances often describe these men as quiet, shy, submissive, and lonely. Although they are dependable workers, their poor social skills and resulting low self esteem prevent them from succeeding at occupational advancement. Because their sexual attacks are an effort to compensate for overwhelming feelings of inadequacy, these offenders are called compensatory rapists.

The victim of such a rapist is most often a stranger, but the rapist has probably watched and followed her for some time. Certain stimuli about her have drawn his attention and excited him. For instance, he may be attracted to wealthy college women who normally would pay him little attention. If the victim physically resists this offender he is likely to flee the scene. During the attack, there are few additional indicators of violence. Moreover, this sexually excited passive assailant will often ejaculate spontaneously, even upon mere physical contact with the victim. Generally, he confines his illegal activity to sexual assault and is not involved in other forms of antisocial behavior.

The **sexually motivated rapist** exhibits both sexual and aggressive elements in his assault. Victim pain is a prerequisite for sexual excitement. He believes women enjoy being abused, forcefully raped, aggressively dominated, and controlled by men. Therefore, this type of rapist interprets the victim's resistance and struggle as a game, and the more the victim resists, the more excited and aggressive he becomes. As a result, there is often a direct relationship between physical and verbal resistance by the victim and the amount of injury she sustains.

These offenders are frequently married, but show little commitment to marriage. Their backgrounds often are replete with antisocial behavior beginning during adolescence or before and ranging from truancy to rape-murder. They have often been severe behavior problems in school, and throughout their lifetimes they have displayed poor behavior control and a low frustration tolerance. On occasion, this type of rapist engages in sexual sadism much like the pervasively angry rapist; in its extreme, the woman is viciously violated and murdered. In order to qualify as a sexual aggressive rapist, the offender must demonstrate:

1. A level of aggression or violence that clearly exceeds what is necessary to force compliance of the victim; and
2. the explicit, unambiguous evidence that aggression is sexually exciting and arousing to him.

The **impulsive-opportunistic rapist** engages in sexual assault simply because the opportunity to rape presents itself. The rape usually occurs within the context of some other antisocial act, such as a robbery or burglary, and a victim happens to be available. The opportunistic rapist is not perceived to be "person-oriented" and sees the victim only as a sexual object. He seems to have little interest in trying to arouse the victim and little concern for the victim's fear or discomfort. To be classified into this group the offender must show:

1. Callous indifference to the welfare and comfort of the victim; and
2. clear evidence of impulsivity and lack of self-control.

Although human beings rarely fit neatly into typologies, the MTC typology is useful in understanding sexual assault. It takes into consideration behavioral patterns, rather than simply personality traits, as well as the context within which the behavior patterns occur. Furthermore, the typologies are helpful in understanding why some sex offenders respond better to sex offender treatment than others, ◄ [a topic discussed in Chapter 10]. In sum, the MTC:R3 categories represent an interactionist approach more than a trait or situationism approach, and they provide a good beginning framework for theory development.

Etiology or Explanations for Sexual Assault

Sexual socialization and social learning both play very critical roles in the development of those who choose to sexually assault. Sexual behavior and attitudes toward women are acquired through the day-to-day contacts with peers, others, and media. Koss and Dinero (1988) found that sexually aggressive men express greater hostility toward women, frequently use alcohol, frequently view violent and degrading pornography, and were closely connected to peer groups that reinforce highly sexualized and dominating views of women. These same men were more likely to believe that force and coercion are legitimate ways to gain compliance in sexual relationships. Koss and Dinero conclude: "In short, the results provided support for the developmental sequence for sexual aggression in which early experiences and psychological characteristics establish conditions for sexual violence" (p. 144).

Research by Abel and his associates (1977, 1978) found that rapists become equally sexually aroused to audiotaped portrayals of both rape and consenting sexual acts. The researchers found that convicted rapists became highly sexually excited by rape depictions in which the victim experienced terror and pain rather than sexual pleasure. Nonsexually aggressive men, on the other hand, demonstrated sexual excitement to sexual pleasure depictions but not to assaultive depictions. And some convicted rapists became sexually aroused by even nonsexual assaults of women.

Research reveals that a majority of sexually aggressive men subscribe to attitudes and ideology that encourage men to be dominant, controlling, and powerful, whereas women are expected to be submissive, permissive, and compliant. Such an orientation seems to have a particularly strong disinhibitory effect on sexually aggressive men, encouraging them to interpret the ambiguous behavior of females as come-ons, to believe that women are not really offended by coercive sexual behaviors, and to perceive rape victims as desiring and deriving gratification from being sexually assaulted (Lipton, McDonel, & McFall, 1987). Some sexually aggressive men believe that women must be kept in their place—even if it means humiliating them—and the best way to achieve this world order is to assault them physically and sexually.

More disturbing is the evidence that male beliefs and fantasies about pleasurable aspects of denigrating women may be more widespread than commonly realized. For example, in a survey conducted by Malamuth (1981), 35% of male college students on several campuses felt there was some likelihood that they would sexually assault a female if they could be sure of getting away with it. In another study, 60% of a group of 352 male undergraduates indicated that they might rape or force a female to perform sexual acts against her will if given the opportunity (Briere, Malamuth, & Centi, 1981).

This section of the chapter has described one type of criminal behavior, outlining statistical, sociological, and psychological data available on both the victim and the offender. A solid, testable theory of criminal behavior will require careful analysis and integration of each sector partially described here. Theoretical integration of statistical data or frequencies requires a keen understanding of the limitations and pitfalls that accompany tabulation. Criminal behavior theory building also requires careful consideration of the knowledge available from several disciplines, especially those of sociology and psychology.

Pedophilia

Pedophilia, commonly known as "child molestation" or child sexual abuse, is defined by the DSM–IV (1994, p. 528) as a condition in which, "over a period of at least 6 months, recurrent, intense sexually arousing fantasies, sexual urges, or behaviors involving sexual activity with a prepubescent child or child (generally age 13 years or younger) occur." The DSM–IV further specifies that some pedophiles are sexually attracted only to children (the exclusive type); whereas others are sexually attracted to both children and adults (nonexclusive type). The term is derived from the Greek words "pais" meaning child and "philein" meaning love. If the child victim is the offender's relative, the pedophilia is called incest. Some clinicians approach pedophilia by arguing that pedophilia and child molestation should mean two different things, with the former limited to fantasies

of sexual attraction to children, while the latter refers to the act itself. In this section, however, we will continue to use the term pedophilia as advocated by the DSM–IV. Pedophilia is also often categorized by mental health workers under the umbrella term "paraphilia," from the Latin word "parere" meaning to bring forth. The essential features of paraphilia "are recurrent sexual arousing fantasies, sexual urges, or behaviors generally involving (1) non-human objects, (2) the suffering or humiliation of oneself or one's partner, or (3) children or other nonconsenting persons, that occur over a period of at least 6 months" (DSM–IV, 1994, p. 522). A list of paraphilias is provided in ◉ **Box 13-4.**

Few crimes are considered as despicable as the sexual abuse of children, and yet so little is understood about the causes, incidence, and reoffense risk of pedophilia (Prentky, Knight, & Lee, 1997b). Data on pedophilia are difficult to obtain, since there is no central or national objective recording system for tabulating sexual offenses against children. The evidence is that the offenses are grossly underreported. Also, offenders may be arrested and prosecuted under a variety of statutes and for a variety of offenses, including child rape, aggravated assault, sodomy, incest, indecent exposure, or lewd and lascivious behavior. Although the UCR lists sex offenses, it does not differentiate pedophilia from the mixture of other possible sexual offenses. However, several self-report surveys indicate that from a quarter to a third of all females and a tenth or more of all males in the United States were sexually molested during childhood (Finkelhor & Lewis, 1988; McBride, 1996; Peters, Wyatt, & Finkelhor, 1986).

The offender, or pedophile, is almost always male, but the victim may be of either gender. Heterosexual pedophilia—male adult with female child—appears to be the more common type, with available data suggesting that three-quarters of pedophiles choose female victims exclusively (Lanyon, 1986; Langevin, 1983). Homosexual pedophilia—adult male with male child—appears to be substantially less frequent, occurring in about 20 to 23% of the reported cases. A small minority of pedophiles prefer children of both genders. The behavior of most pedophiles is usually limited to caressing the child's body, fondling the child's genitals, and/or inducing the child to manipulate

BOX 13-4
The Paraphilias

The paraphilias are a variety of sexual behaviors that will result in a diagnosis of sexual dysfunction if:

(1) they involve nonhuman objects, the suffering or humiliation of oneself or one's partner, or children or other non-consenting persons, *and* occur over a period of at least six months; AND
(2) they cause clinically significant distress or impairment in social, occupational, or other important areas of functioning.

The paraphilias as listed in the DSM–IV include the following:

- Exhibitionism (exposure of genitals)
- Fetishism (use of nonliving objects)
- Frotteurism (touching and rubbing against a nonconsenting person)
- Pedophilia (focus on prepubescent children)
- Sexual masochism (receiving humiliation or suffering)
- Sexual sadism (inflicting humiliation or suffering)
- Transvestic fetishism (cross-dressing)
- Voyeurism (observing sexual activity)
- Paraphilia not otherwise specified (less frequently encountered illustrations)

Note that many of the above behaviors qualify as crimes, regardless of whether they qualify as sexual dysfunction in the clinical sense. Depending upon the nature of the conduct, they may be sexual assault, aggravated sexual assault, lewd and lascivious behavior, rape, exhibitionism, sexual offense against children, or a range of other sex-related offenses as defined in criminal statutes.

his or her genitals. Penetration is apparently involved in only a small minority of the total number of offenses.

The offender and the victim often know one another, often very well, and they are frequently related (incest). Many victims are simply looking for affection, wanting to be only hugged or cuddled, or to have human contact. The offender frequently misinterprets this behavior as a form of "seduction" and misgauges the amount of power he has over the child. Very often, the child may participate in the molestation primarily because he or she is too frightened to protest. Research indicates that pedophiles, on average, tend to have positive feelings toward their victims, generally perceiving them as willing participants, and frequently victimize children living in their immediate households (Miner, Day, & Nafpaktitis, 1989). In many cases, the sexual behavior between the offender and the same child has gone on for a sustained period of time.

Research offers strong support for the assumption that sexual abuse in childhood (both violent and nonviolent) produces long-term psychological problems (Briere, 1988). Reports of severe depression, guilt, strong feelings of inferiority or inadequacy, substance abuse, suicidality, anxiety, sleep problems, and fears and phobias are common. Children may feel responsible for the abuse because no obvious force or threat was used by the adult, and only after the victims become adults to they realize they were powerless to protect themselves.

Offender Characteristics Prentky, Knight and Lee (1997b) conclude from their extensive research investigations of sex offenders that classification and diagnosis of pedophiles are complicated by a high degree of variability among individuals in their sexual preferences, personal characteristics, life experiences, criminal histories, and explanations for offending. Essentially, there is no single "profile" that accurately portrays all pedophiles. Consequently, any attempt at classification or general description of pedophiles is fraught with numerous exceptions. Only very broad and rough summaries will be presented in this section.

Although there is considerable age variability, the average age of convicted pedophiles ranges between 36 and 40. Prentky et al. (1997b) assert that the more an offender's sexual preference is limited to children, the less socially competent he is likely to be. Socially competence in this context is reflected by the strength and range of social and sexual relationships he has with adults. Many studies (e.g., Marshall, Barbaree & Fernandez, 1995; Marshall & Mazzucco, 1995; Prentky et al., 1997b) have continually documented the observation that pedophiles are inadequate socially, lack interpersonal skills, are under-assertive, and have poor self-esteem.

Perhaps because of the extremely negative attitudes the public has toward child sexual abuse, pedophiles rarely take full responsibility for their actions. Many claim that they went blank, were too intoxicated to know what they were doing, could not help themselves, or did not know what came over them. Overall, they demonstrate a strong preference for attributing their behavior to external forces or motivating factors largely outside their personal control.

Similar to their development of the MTC:R3 for rapist typing, the Massachusetts Treatment Center (MTC) (Cohen, Seghorn, & Calmas, 1969; Knight, 1988; Knight & Prentky, 1990; Knight, Rosenberg, & Schneidier, 1985) has developed one of the most useful typologies or empirically based classifications systems for pedophiles yet constructed. Called the MTC:CM3 (Child Molesters, Revision 3) the system underscores the importance of viewing pedophilia as characterized by multiple behavioral patterns and intentions. Although the system is quite complex, we will describe only four core behavioral patterns: (1) the fixated type; (2) the regressed type; (3) the exploitative type; and (4) the aggressive or sadistic type.

The **fixated** (or **immature**) **pedophile** displays a long-standing preference for children as both sexual and social companions. He has never been able to form a mature relationship with adult peers, male or female, and he is described by people who know him as socially immature, passive, timid, and dependent. He feels most comfortable with children. The fixated pedophile is rarely married, and has a history of steady employment, although the type of work is often below his ability and intellectual capacity. Sexual contact with the child occurs after they become fully acquainted through a number of social encounters. He rarely is aggressive or uses physical force, or engages in genital intercourse. The primary desire is generally to touch, fondle, or caress the child. However, the fixated pedophile is the most difficult to treat and is most likely to recidivate because he is not disturbed or troubled about his exclusive preference for children.

The **regressed pedophile**, on the other hand, had a fairly normal adolescence and good peer relationships and sexual experiences, but later developed feelings of sexual inadequacy and self-doubt. These feelings of inadequacy were further exacerbated by failures in the their occupational, social, or sexual lives. The regressed child offender's background repeatedly includes alcohol abuse, divorce, and a poor employment history. Each pedophilial act is usually precipitated by a significant disappointment to the offender's sexual adequacy, either by female or male peers. Unlike the fixated pedophile, the regressed pedophile prefers victims who are strangers and who live outside his neighborhood or area. The victims are nearly always female, and he seeks genital sex with the victim. Unlike the fixated pedophile, this offender often feels remorseful and is willing to change.

The **exploitative pedophile** seeks children to satisfy his sexual needs. He exploits the child's vulnerability any way he can, and attempts various strategies and ploys to get the child to comply. This pedophile does not care about the emotional or physical well-being of the victim, and only sees the child strictly as a sexual object. This offender usually has a long history of criminal and antisocial behavior. His relationships with peers are unpredictable, difficult, and stormy. He is unpleasant to be around, uncomfortable to work with, and generally moody and irritable. His very poor and abrasive interpersonal skills may be the principle reason he selects children as victims (Knight, Rosenberg, & Schneider, 1985). This individual is very difficult to treat.

The **aggressive** (or **sadistic**) **pedophile** is drawn to children for both sexual and aggressive purposes. This pedophile is apt to have a long history of antisocial behavior and poor adjustment to his environments. Most aggressive pedophiles prefer male children. Since the primary motive is to obtain stimulation without consideration for the victim, this offender often assaults the child viciously and sadistically. The more harm and pain inflicted, the more this individual becomes excited. Aggressive pedophiles are most often responsible for child abductions by strangers and murders. They are very difficult to treat, and fortunately are also very rare. A well-known example of this offender would be John Wayne Gacy Jr., who sadistically murdered thirty-three teenage boys and young men and buried their bodies in the cellar of his suburban Chicago home.

The MTC typology has been updated in recent years based on further research on sex offenders, and is referred to as the MTC:CM3 (referring to the Massachusetts Treatment Center: Child Molester, Version 3). The researchers have discovered that the original classification system is slightly more complicated then originally supposed and consequently have added some further subcategories to the four main categories (see Knight, Carter & Prentky, 1989, for further information).

Psychological Effects of Child Sexual Abuse

The overwhelming evidence from both clinical and empirical studies is that most victims of sexual abuse are negatively affected by their experience (Haugaard & Reppucci, 1988). However, the long-term effects of child sexual abuse are unclear and appear to differ significantly from individual to individual. Although some victims apparently suffer no negative long-term consequences, studies with adults confirm the long-term effects of sexual abuse mentioned in the clinical literature for a majority of the victims (Browne & Finkelhor, 1986). For example, adults who were sexually victimized as children are more likely to manifest depression, self-destructive behavior, anxiety, feelings of isolation and stigma, poor self-esteem, and substance abuse. A history of childhood sexual abuse is also associated with greater risk for mental health and adjustment problems in adulthood. Many children also seem to suffer the immediate effects of abuse; one-fifth to two-fifths of sexually abused children who are seen in mental health clinics manifest some type of psychological disturbance (Tufts' New England Medical Center, 1984).

Studies also indicate that sexual abuse by fathers or stepfathers has a more negative impact than abuse by perpetrators outside the home (Browne & Finkelhor, 1986). Moreover, presence of force or physical coercion seems to result in more trauma for the victim (Browne & Finkelhor, 1986). Not surprisingly, experiences involving intercourse or attempted intercourse and genital contact by mouth seem to be more troubling than acts involving touching of unclothed breasts or genitals. Penetration is especially traumatic for the victim.

It must be emphasized that studies reporting these findings are often plagued by sample, design, and measurement problems that could undermine the validity of their findings. For example, results are often based on either adults seeking treatment or children whose molestation has been reported (Browne & Finkelhor, 1986). These samples are very self-selected, because only the more seriously troubled victims may seek counsel. Some of the studies suggesting long-term trauma associated with child sexual abuse are actually reports of the prevalence of trauma among specialized populations, such as prostitutes or psychiatric patients. This is by no means to diminish the seriousness of child sexual abuse. It is merely to emphasize that research in the area must be improved, such as by obtaining random samples from the general population.

The **child sexual abuse syndrome** (CSAS) or **child sexual abuse accommodation syndrome** (CSAAS) originally proposed by Summit (1983) has received considerable attention in the literature. The syndrome is reserved for a cluster of behaviors that occur in children who have been victims of sexual abuse by a family member or by a trusted adult. According to Summit, children do not necessarily have an innate sense that sexual activity with an adult is wrong. However, if the sexual activity continues, the adults usually must pressure or make threats toward the child to prevent others from knowing about the activity. Often, the abuser presents these threats and pressures in such a way that the child is led to believe something terrible will happen (perhaps to a family member) if this "private" knowledge becomes known. Hence, the child is placed in the position of being responsible for the welfare of the family. The child also feels helpless to stop the activity. Thus, the child must "accommodate" these secrets into his or her daily living pattern.

The behavioral indicators of CSAS may be seen in all ages (Koszuth, 1991). The child may become overly compliant and unable to make decisions. The child may also present a façade of mature behavior because she or he is now called on to take more responsibility for the safety and care of the family. According to Koszuth (1991), the list of behavioral indicators of sexual abuse also include persistent and inappropriate sexual play (including sexual aggressiveness) with peers or toys, detailed and age-inappropriate understanding of sexual behavior, arriving early at school and leaving late combined with few absences, extraordinary fear of adult males, running away from home, poor peer relationships or inability to make friends, depression, expression of suicidal feelings, and sleep disturbances. It is also usual for the child to delay reporting or talking about the sexual abuse, and some refuse to talk about it at all.

Since the gathering of physical or medical evidence is extremely difficult, CSAS is sometimes used by the courts to supplement a victim's testimony. Several courts have allowed the evidence to be admitted (e.g., *Keri v. State*, 1986; *People v. Gray*, 1986; *People v. Luna*, 1988; *People v. Payan*, 1985), but others have not (e.g., *Johnson v. State*, 1987; *Lantrip v. Commonwealth*, 1986; *People v. Bowker*, 1988; *People v. Roscoe*, 1985; *State v. Haseltine*, 1984). (See Sagatun, 1991, for more detail on these cases.) Sagatun (1991) posits that CSAS has been admitted in criminal cases primarily as rebuttal to the notion that the child's behavior does not reflect sexual abuse. On the other hand, courts are more likely to reject expert opinion that utilizes the CSAS as evidence that sexual abuse *did* occur.

However, there is still question whether the child sexual abuse syndrome actually exists. Haugaard & Reppucci (1988, pp. 177–178), for example, wrote: "The principal flaw with the notion of a specific syndrome is that no evidence indicates that it can discriminate between sexually abused children and those who have experienced other trauma. Because the task of a court is to make such discrimination, this flaw is fatal." According to Haugaard and Reppucci, a syndrome must have **discriminant ability**. This means that a group of behaviors must occur regularly in a group of children who have certain experiences, and they must not occur in children who have not had that experience. Many of the behaviors listed by Summit may occur in any child who has experienced other types of trauma beside sexual abuse, although the behaviors usually do not demonstrate precocious sexual awareness. "As a result, one cannot reliably say that a child exhibiting a certain combination of behaviors has been sexually abused rather than, for instance, physically abused, neglected, or brought up by psychotic or antisocial parents" (Haugaard & Reppucci, 1988, p. 178). Similar questions have been raised about other "syndromes," including those that are considered forms of Post-Traumatic Stress Disorder (PTSD) ◄ [discussed in Chapters 8 and 9.]

Violent Crimes: Criminal Homicide

The least typical violent crime is the crime in which the victim dies. Aggravated assaults, sexual assaults, simple assaults, and robberies all have far more victims than criminal homicide, which is causing the death of another person without legal justification or excuse. The two major levels of criminal homicide are usually identified in the law as murder and manslaughter. Murder is reserved for the "unlawful killing of one human by another with malice aforethought, either expressed or implied" (Black, 1990, p. 1019). Manslaughter refers to an *unintended* killing that results from *unjustifiable* conduct that places others at risk (Morawetz, 2002). The person who aimlessly fires a loaded weapon, even if he does not "intend" to kill anyone, is still responsible for their deaths if victims happen to be in his path. Manslaughter also includes an *intended* killing "for which there is mitigation, acts that are provoked by the victim, or that result from temporary and understandable circumstances that compromise the actor's normal responsibility" (Morawetz, 2002, p. 398). For example, a father who comes upon an accident scene, discovers that his daughter has been killed, and chokes to death the inebriated driver of the car that hit her, would likely be charged with manslaughter, not murder. Most states have additional gradations in their homicide statutes, depending on the level of seriousness. First degree murder, for instance, may be considered a capital offense, punishable by death or life in prison. The *Uniform Crime Reports* include both murder and "non-negligent" manslaughter under the term "criminal homicide" for reporting purposes. In this section, we will focus upon the rarest among the already rare group of criminal homicide, which are also the ones that elicit the most public attention and fear of crime.

Multiple Murders

One of the more incomprehensible homicides is the random killing of groups of people, either in one episode, or individually over a period of time. Although multiple murderers are still rare occurrences compared to the total homicide rate, the more extreme and atypical cases are extensively covered by the news media, often catching the attention of large sectors of the general public. In an effort to make crime news more entertaining and appealing to consumers, the news media overrepresent multiple murders because they are dramatic, tragic, and rare in occurrence (Duwe, 2000).

Surprisingly, in spite of the extensive media coverage, a vast majority of the research on multiple homicide has been conducted only within the past 20 to 25 years. Researchers have all but ignored multiple murders because they have been regarded as merely special cases of homicide, "explainable by the same criminological theories applied to single-victim incidents, and therefore not deserving of special treatment" (Fox & Levin, 1998, p. 409). Unfortunately, a considerable portion of the contemporary research on multiple murder suffers from selection bias because it is far too often based on relatively small samples of the *best-known* incidents (Duwe, 2000). Duwe (2000, p. 370) writes: "The narrow focus on widely publicized cases stems from the fact that these studies have relied mainly on national media coverage as a source of data." Relying on high-profile to the exclusion of more common, less-publicized cases is likely to misrepresent the representative data on multiple murder. In addition, Fox and Levin (1998) report that most of the scholarly research on multiple killings has been anecdotal and heavily descriptive in nature. Consequently, until further research is conducted, the following material on the characteristics of multiple murder is presented tentatively and cautiously.

Definitions of Multiple Homicide

Multiple murder or homicide is often classified by researchers and police investigators on the basis of the number of victims, circumstance, and the time interval between the killings. **Serial murder** usually refers to incidents in which an individual (or individuals) separately kills a number of individuals (usually a minimum of three) over time. The time period—sometimes referred to as the "cooling-off" period—may be days or weeks, but is more likely months or years. **Spree murder** normally refers to the killing of three or more individuals without a cooling-off period, usually at two or three different locations. Usually, the offender is a fugitive from another crime, such as robbery. A convenient store robber who kills some individuals at the store, and kills a number of others during a county-wide chase would be an example of a spree murderer. **Mass murder** involves the killing of three or more persons at a single location with no cooling-off period between the killings. The FBI identifies two types of mass murder: classic and family. An example of a classic mass murder is when an individual barricades himself inside a public building, such as a fast-food restaurant, randomly killing the patrons and any other persons he has contact with. Two catastrophic examples of mass murder in modern history are Timothy McVeigh's 1995 bombing of the Federal Building in Oklahoma City in which 168 people were killed, and the terrorist attacks on September 11, 2001, in which 3047 people were killed ◙ (**Box 13-2**). A family mass murder is when at least three family members are killed by another family member or relative. If a stranger kills members of a family in one incident, however, we do not refer to this as a family mass murder.

Incidence of Multiple Homicide

While the multiple murders receive considerable media attention because of their drama and sensationalism, they are, as mentioned above, statistically rare occurrences. The frequent media onslaught of violence and multiple murder on the nightly news eventually develops the impression that these incidents are much more frequent than they actually are. When the news media show graphic and dramatic accounts of violence, the normal cognitive reaction of people watching is to store the vivid details and then have them ready at the "top of their mind" for future references. However, the drawback of this process is the public's tendency to conclude that violence and multiple murders are dramatically increasing, when in reality they are not. This phenomenon is called the **availability heuristic**. For example, mass and serial murders seem to be on the increase in the United States because accounts in the media are readily available. However, a careful review of the data, simply does not lend support to this perspective.

Certainly multiple killings *appear* to be on the increase due to the media coverage of high-profile cases. However, there is no evidence that low-profile, regional multiple killings—which are actually more typical of multiple killings—are on the increase. The reported increases in serial murder may be due to the dramatic improvement in communication and computer networks among law enforcement agencies and the new media. Prior to 1970, information exchange between the agencies was difficult and primitive by today's standards. Therefore, serial murderers who moved from one geographic location to another (as serial killers commonly do) probably went undetected.

Nationwide data on the incidence of multiple murders are very difficult to find. Most of it comes from the analysis of newspaper articles across the country. For example, between 1977 and October 1992, the FBI Academy conducted a computer search of the wire services through the Nexis system on a monthly basis using the terms "mass murder" and "serial murder." During that time interval, the computer search discovered that 201 mass murderers were responsible for the deaths of 975 victims and attempted murder of 339 victims. In addition, the search found that 111 spree murderers killed 463 persons, and attempted to kill 145 others. The 357 serial murderers killed 1,826 victims, attempted to kill 279 and are suspected in the deaths of an additional 1,343. Most of these multiple murderers have been identified, convicted, and incarcerated. Grant Duwe (2000) analyzed newspaper, network television news, and newsweekly magazine coverage of mass killings that took place between 1976 and 1996. He found a total of 30,027 articles from 117 newspapers that reported on 495 mass killings that took place during the 21-year period. We have no idea how many offenders were responsible for these crimes, however.

High-profile crimes have traditionally been the catalyst for the identification of social problems (Duwe, 2000), such as missing children (Best, 1990), serial murder (Jenkins, 1988, 1993, 1994), drug violence (Chermak, 1997), stalking (Lowney & Best, 1995), and money laundering (Nichols, 1997). High-profile crimes have also been the provocateurs for changes in social policy and legislation. Kelleher (1997), for example, believes that Patrick Sherrill's killing of 14 people at an Edmond, Oklahoma, post office in 1986 prompted congressional hearings on the issue of violence in the U.S. Postal Service. Subsequent high-profile postal killings were instrumental in increased governmental involvement in such agencies as the National Institute of Occupational Safety and Health, the Centers for Disease Control and Prevention, and the Occupational Safety and Health Administration (Duwe, 2000; Kelleher, 1997).

Mass Murder

Surprisingly little research has been directed at mass murder, especially in comparison to the attention given to serial murder. Perhaps this is because mass murder, while tragic and troubling, is not as intriguing or mysterious as serial murder. Furthermore, mass murder happens quickly and unpredictably without warning, and then it's over. It is often clear who the offender is, although the motives are often unclear.

A common assumption about mass murder is that suicide is a primary motive of the offender. In other words, they plan to die at the crime scene, either at their own hand or by police gunfire. However, Grant Duwe (2000), from his sample of 495 mass killings over a 21-year period, found that only 21% of mass murderers committed suicide, while another 2% attempted suicide, and 3% were fatally shot by the police.

The motives of mass murderers are highly variable. "The motivations for mass murder can range from revenge to hatred, from loyalty to greed; and the victims can be selected individually, as members of a particular category or group, or on a random basis" (Fox & Levin, 1998, p. 430). Mass murderers are described as frustrated, angry people who feel helpless about their lives. They are usually between the ages of 35 and 45, and they are generally convinced there is little chance that things will get better for them. Their personal lives have been a failure by their standards and they have often suffered some tragic or serious loss, such as loss of meaningful employment or rejection by a spouse or partner. George Hennard, for example, the 35-year old who drove his pickup into the plate glass window of Luby's Cafeteria in Killeen, Texas, and proceeded to shoot to death 22 patrons, had lost his cherished job as a merchant marine.

Mass murderers are often socially isolated and withdrawn people who lack a strong social network of friends. Their isolation is probably due to an active dislike of people compounded by their own inadequate social and interpersonal skills. Attacking several or many others at one time provides these lonely, angry people a chance to get even, to dominate others, to take control, and to gain recognition.

Mass murderers often take a very active interest in guns. About two-thirds of the mass killings (both classic and family) involved the use of guns, usually semiautomatic firearms with high magazine capacities (Duwe, 2000). In other words, they used guns that make it easier to shoot lots of people quickly.

The data reported by Duwe (2000) do not bear out reports claiming that most mass murders take place at the workplace or in public locations. For example workplace massacres are quite rare, accounting for only 4% of the incidents, and only 27% of the incidents involved offenders who killed their victims in a public place. The remainder took place within a residential setting, often involving family members or acquaintances. Consequentially, a majority of mass murders are family mass murders.

Serial Murder

Serial murder generally receives the most amount of media attention, and it most often creates a high amount of fear and anxiety in the public, particularly in locations where the killings have taken place. Serial murder also presents an enormous challenge for law enforcement and requires a considerable amount of investigative time and energy. In the fall of 2002, the nation's attention was riveted to media coverage of the Washington area sniper case and the apparent communication made to the snipers by the police chief who led the investigation. ◙ (see ◀ **Box 8-1**).

It should be realized that the social science research on serial homicides is in its infancy. In one of the most extensive investigations of serial murder, Hickey (1997) examined 337 cases of serial murder that occurred in the United States from 1800 to 1995. The victims are most often strangers (Hickey, 1997), whereas in single-victim murders the victim is often an acquaintance, friend or family member. Gender differences are also reported for serial killers. According to Fox and Levin (1998), male serial killers most often prey on strangers whom they select on the basis of some sexual fantasy involving capture and control. Female serial killers, on the other hand, generally kill victims with whom they have a relationship, such as nursing home patients.

The percentage of serial killers who are black (20%) is roughly the same as their representation in the general population (Fox & Levin, 1998). "Serial murder, like murder generally, tends to be intraracial: serial killings of black victims, especially those who are impoverished and marginalized politically, are less likely to be connected, prioritized for investigation, and subsequently solved" (Fox & Levin, 1998, p. 414).

In most instances, serial killers do not use firearms to kill their victims, although there are, of course, exceptions. Again, the serial snipers who terrorized the mid-Atlantic states during October 2002 are notable examples. Hickey (1997) reports that only 19% of male and 8% of female serial killers murdered their victims with a firearm, although many used a firearm to intimidate and control their victims.

Similar to mass murderers, the motives of serial killers are variable. Apparently, many seek the dominance and control over their victims that each murder provides (Hickey, 1997). Certainly, some seek the widespread publicity and historical infamy the killings offer, especially if the murders are done skillfully to maximize the public's fear and anxiety.

By generating fear within a community, the offender is able to manipulate and dominate the lives of thousands of area residents. For the sexually-motivated serial killer, he is able to fulfill his frequent fantasies. Through his "trial runs" of serial homicides, "the killer strives to make his real-life experiences as perfect as his fantasy" (Fox & Levin, 1998, p. 417). Fox and Levin (1998, p. 417) elaborate further by pointing out, "Not only is his behavior driven by fantasy, but the fantasy itself is altered and reinforced through the offenses that he has committed. As a result, the killer's crime can increase in severity as he constantly updates his fantasy in a never-ending spiral of image and action."

According to the limited data that is available to researchers, the victims of serial killers tend to be white, female, and very young or very old (Fox & Levin, 1998). These victim characteristics seem to be especially representative of sexually motivated killers. Often, the victims tend to be the most vulnerable, such as prostitutes, drug users, hitchhikers, children, and runaways. Once again, the serial snipings did not meet many of the above criteria. While it is important to gather data and identify common factors in serial (or mass) murderers, we must be careful not to assume the data support a particular profile.

Workplace Violence

Workplace violence is a complex phenomenon, encompassing a wide assortment of threatening and injurious behaviors that occur within one's place of employment. The most recent statistics indicate that, in any given year, there are 1.5 million simple assaults, 396,000 aggravated assaults, 51,000 rapes and sexual assaults, 84, 000 robberies, and 1,000 homicides (Gregorie & Wallace, 2001). Police officers are victims of the highest rate of workplace violence, followed by correctional officers, taxi drivers, private security guards, and bartenders. Workplace violence refers not only to the more physically violent incidents, but also to the more subtle forms of violence, such as coercion, intimidation, threats, and harassment. In fact, although the media focuses on the more serious violence, the incidents that actually occur most frequently in the workplace are *threats* of violence (Budd, Arvey, & Lawless, 1996). It is estimated that approximately 7% of those in the workforce are threatened every year, amounting to over six million workers in the United States (Barling, Rogers, & Kelloway, 2000). Workers who report being physically assaulted in the workplace per year average around 2.5%, or approximately two million U.S. workers. ◙ (See Box 13-5 for more information on workplace violence.)

Physical workplace violence has been classified into four major types on the basis of the assailant's relationship to the workplace (California Occupational Safety and Health Administration, 1995; Gregorie, 2000; LeBlanc & Kelloway, 2002). In the first type, the assailant does not have a legitimate relationship to the workplace or to the victim. He or she usually enters the workplace to commit a criminal action, such as a robbery or theft. Robbery is the principal motive for most workplace homicide, accounting for 85% of the workplace deaths (Gregorie & Wallace, 2000). Fast-food and convenience store employees are most susceptible. The second type of assailant is the recipient of some service provided by the workplace or victim, and may either be a current or former client, patient, or customer. Most often, this individual is unhappy with the product or service he or she received from the agency or company. The third type has an employment-related involvement with the workplace, either as a current former employee, supervisor or manager. Often, this assailant is referred to as a "disgruntled employee" who enters the workplace to punish or get back at some individual, or the agency or company in general. The disgruntled employees account for a large portion of the remaining homicides, approximating 10% (Gregorie & Wallace, 2001). The fourth type has an indirect involvement with the workplace because of a relationship with an employee, such as a current or former spouse or partner. Often, this situation concerns domestic violence or spousal/partner abuse.

There have been very few systematic studies that have examined the predictors or causes of workplace violence. Most of the work to date has focused on either: (1) describing the assailant of co-worker violence, or (2) identifying the job characteristics that increase the risk for violence (LeBlanc & Kelloway, 2002). Considerably more research needs to be done on identifying the causes and implementing

BOX 13-5
Going Postal?

After several incidents of violence in the workplace involving U.S. Postal Service workers were publicized in the late 1980s and early 1990s, the term "going postal" became part of the national lexicon. There was a perception that postal service employees were at great risk of violent victimization at the hands of their fellow employees. In reality, the Center for Disease Control (CDC) estimated that the risk was 2.5 times lower than that of all workers nationwide.

According to a special report from the NCVS (Duhart, 2001), the occupations with the highest rates of violent victimization in the workplace were police officers, corrections officers, and taxi cab drivers (each with over 100 victimizations per 1,000 workers). These figures, however, do *not* include homicide, to be discussed below. Other high rates of victimization (between 50 and 100 per 1,000 workers) were given to private security officers, bartenders, professional and custodial mental health workers, special education teachers, gas station attendants, junior high school teachers, and convenience store workers.

Significant in the data is the revelation that 88.2% of the victims were uninjured. Slightly over 10% of all victims suffered minor injuries, such as bruises, black eyes, cuts, and bruises. How would victims of violent crime be uninjured? The answer lies in the definition of a violent crime. Robberies and attempted simple assaults were included in the data. A robbery is a violent crime, even when no injuries occur. An attempt is a crime that is not completed. Although both of these crimes engender fear in a victim, they do not necessarily involve injury.

The NCVS does not collect data on homicide, thus Duhart (2001) obtained homicide data from the U.S. Department of Labor. According to these statistics, workplace homicide decreased 39% over the six-year period 1993–1999. In 1999, there were 651 work-related homicides. In the six-year period, an overwhelming number of homicides (84%) were committed by offenders who were strangers to the victim, typically during a robbery or attempted robbery. Coworkers or former coworkers committed 7% of the homicides. Personal acquaintances committed approximately 1% of the workplace homicides, and more than 80% of all workplace homicides were committed with a firearm.

preventive measures in the workplace. In recent years, workplace violence litigation has dramatically increased (Kaufer & Mattman, 2002). The legal action and civil lawsuits at this point in time concentrate on four major areas: (1) negligent hiring (failure to screen employees properly); (2) negligent retention (failure to terminate unsuitable and threatening employees); (3) negligent supervision (failure to monitor performance); and (4) inadequate security (Kaufer & Mattman, 2002). Consequently, legal and regulatory obligations for employers to provide safe and secure work environments are bound to increase, and mandatory prevention and training programs are likely to be commonplace across all private and public organizations in the near future.

Arson

Arson is defined as "any willful or malicious burning or attempt to burn, with or without intent to defraud, a dwelling, house, public building, motor vehicle, or personality property of another" (Federal Bureau of Investigation, 2000, p. 54). Arson was added to the FBI *Uniform Crime Reports* list of index crimes in 1978, signifying its seriousness and its frequency. It is the number one cause of all fires, representing 25% of the nation's fire problem, and it annually kills approximately five hundred to eight hundred Americans, injures thousands more, and causes billions of dollars in damage each year (U.S. Fire Administration, 1997, 2002). The fire death risk of senior citizens over age 70 and children under age five is double the risk of the average population. Children under the age of ten accounted for nearly 20% of all fire deaths in any given year (U.S. Fire Administration, 2000a). And, according to the National Fire Incident Reporting System, firefighters are three times more likely to be injured or killed while responding to arson compared to non-arson fires (U.S. Fire Administration, 2002).

Arson is difficult to spot because the evidence is often destroyed in the fire, especially if torched by a professional arsonist. The annual clearance rate for arson is estimated to average only about 16% (Federal Bureau of Investigation, 2001). Even with evidence that a fire was set, the motive is often difficult to establish. Most of the known arsonists are young males. In fact, the offense of arson has a higher percentage of juvenile involvement than any other index crime. Of all arson offenses cleared in 2001, 45.2% involved only juvenile offenders (below age 18) (Federal Bureau of Investigation, 2002), mostly between the ages of 10 and 14 (U.S. Fire Administration, 2000b). Recent studies report that between 75 and 85% of all known firesetting is done by males, with an increasing number of females (ages 13 to 17) beginning to engage in the activity (Stadolnik, 2000).

Adult Repetitive Firesetters

Similar to multiple murderers, repetitive or serious arsonists can be organized into three, somewhat overlapping categories: serial, spree, and mass. A **serial arsonist** is one who sets three or more fires at different times. The time interval between the firesetting may be days, weeks, or even years. A **spree arsonists** set fires at three or more separate locations, usually with no emotional cooling-off period between them. The **mass arsonist** sets three or more fires at the same location within a brief period of time. For example, serial arsonists may set fires to synagogues across the country over a two year period, whereas a spree arsonist may set fires to different synagogues within a city during the same day. A mass arsonist may continually set fires at the same synagogue over a two or three day period.

One of the more consistent findings on adult repetitive arsonists is that they, as a group, experience and perceive little control over their personal lives. Many adult arsonists began firesetting as children. Generally, they tend to be unassertive, have limited or marginal interpersonal skills for dealing with others, be underemployed or unemployed, and have a propensity to fall into depression or feelings of helplessness easily (Murphy & Clare, 1996). Often, adult firesetters are from a socially disadvantaged segment of the population (Jackson, Glass, & Hope, 1987), and were brought up in highly disruptive family environments (Fritzon, 2000). Overall, the most consistent picture of adult repetitive arsonists is one of interpersonal inadequacy, educational failure, social passivity, and social isolation.

Although repetitive firesetting is motivated by a diverse range of reasons, repetitive firesetting is the arsonist's attempts to take control of his or her life, gain some social recognition or attention, or get back at some person or group. For example, the firesetting episodes appear to be prompted by events that exacerbate the arsonist's feelings of low self-esteem and inadequacy. In addition, many arsonists remain at the scene of the fire, often even sound the alarm and fight the fire, increasing their adequacy and a sense of control in their lives. In some cases, they engage in courageous attempts to save lives. Jackson et al. (1987) find that most acts of repetitive firesetting progress from small fires to larger fires, and the firesetters become increasingly involved in fighting the fire.

Arsonists with limited mental ability are often passive individuals who have poor verbal skills. They also have trouble interacting with others and use firesetting as a communicative device in response to conflict and stress (Day & Berney, 2001).

Juvenile Firesetters

Fascination and experimentation with fire are common features of normal child development. Match play is especially common. Kafrey (1980) points out that curiosity about fire appears to be nearly universal in children between the ages of five and seven, and that this curiosity begins as early as three in many children. Ellen Garry (1997) divides juvenile firesetters into three groups based on chronological age. The first group involves children under age seven who set fires accidentally or from curiosity. Firesetting usually declines after this age, probably because of frequent admonishments of its dangers by parents and other adults. The second group Garry identifies ranges in age from eight to 12. Although a few from this group continue to set fires because of curiosity or experimentation, many set fires due to underlying psychosocial conflicts or emotional problems. Many children in this group tend to have poor relationships with their parents and are also often the victims of physical and emotional abuse (Jackson, Glass, & Hope, 1987). The third group, noted by Garry, ranges in age from 13 to 18, and these firesetters tend to have a long history of undetected fireplay and firesetting behavior. These adolescent firesetters are usually plagued by emotional problems or are prone to engage in antisocial behavior. Adolescents in this firesetting group tend to be more mischievous, energetic, adventurous, and impulsive than their peers. Persistent juvenile firesetters are more likely to demonstrate symptoms of ADHD during their childhood (Forehand et al., 1991), and many are diagnosed as "conduct problems" by mental health professionals. Not surprisingly, most persistent juvenile firesetters are males, averaging 80% of the juvenile total.

The frequent observation that juvenile firesetters are considered conduct problems, impulsive, hyperactive, and more physically and verbally aggressive than their peers appears to be in sharp contrast to the behavior of repetitive adult firesetters. These behavioral patterns puts them at risk for being disliked and excluded, thereby missing opportunities for learning social and interpersonal skills. The lack of these skills, of course, can lead to social isolation, inadequacy, and low self-esteem. Significant research finds that ill-tempered and socially inept children sometimes grow up to have considerable personal, marital, social and financial failure throughout their lifetimes, a pattern very similar to the pattern demonstrated by repetitive adult firesetters (Caspi, Elder, & Bem, 1987). In addition, both the frequent juvenile firesetters and the repetitive adult arsonists often have a continual battle with their social environments, as demonstrated by their frequent contacts with the criminal justice system. Therefore, firesetting may be only one of a large collection of maladaptive behaviors they display.

Summary and Conclusions

The position taken in this chapter is that criminal behavior defies easy explanations or pat solutions. Crime cannot be explained solely by external factors like poverty, the corporate environment, racism, unemployment, or the quality of the educational system. Nor can crime be explained solely by internal factors like psychological deficiencies in the superego, emotional maturity, mental balance, or criminal personalities. From a psychological perspective, criminal behavior must be perceived as unique behavior which is a result of each individual's conditioning, instrumental learning, and cognitive-social learning processes in reciprocal relation to the situation. Each crime must be seen as subjectively adaptive for each individual, for a particular set of circumstances. Understanding criminal behavior, therefore, will require at the very least an individualized appraisal of how the antisocial individual perceives his or her predicament. Assessment, theories, and empirical study which fail to take into consideration the cognitive, subjective value of the acts for the individual are destined to provide fragmentary, "outside" perspectives. To neglect the individual's social situation—family, peers, school, work, community, and society—is equally unwarranted. Moreover, the reciprocal nature of crime renders predictions of dangerousness and future criminal behavior exceedingly difficult and prone to inaccuracy.

The chapter samples various topics that fall within the rubric of psychological criminology, the *science* of the behavioral and mental processes of the criminal offender. Psychological criminology is primarily concerned with how criminal behavior is acquired, evoked, maintained, and modified. The discipline also examines and evaluates prevention, intervention, and treatment strategies that have been tried in reducing and treating criminal behavior.

While it is always wise to be cautious in cataloging humans into neat diagnostic packages, extensive research in recent years has revealed that term "psychopath" does have considerable validity as a distinguishing behavioral pattern. The term "psychopath" refers to an individual who exhibits a discernible pattern that differs from the general population in its level of sensitivity, empathy, compassion, and guilt. The typical, true psychopath (also called a *primary* psychopath) may or may not engage in antisocial or criminal behavior, although he does demonstrate callous and unemotional feelings toward others and a lack of concern for societal rules and regulations.

Psychopaths who have continual contact with the criminal justice system because of frequent offending are referred to as *criminal psychopaths*. Although their criminal behavior runs the gamut of petty theft and fraud to murder, criminal psychopaths are especially vicious and violent, and their motivations for the violence are sometimes difficult to identify. Robert Hare (1996), one of the world's leading experts on psychopathy, reports that nearly half of the law enforcement officers who died in the line of duty were killed by individuals who closely matched the personality profile of the criminal psychopath.

Currently, the best measuring instruments for adult criminal psychopathy are the Psychopathy Checklist series developed by Robert Hare and his associates. The PCL–R is by far the most extensively researched of all of the instruments designed to measure psychopaths. Overall, the research has strongly supported the reliability and validity of the PCL–R for distinguishing criminal psychopaths from criminal nonpsychopaths and the general public.

We directed our attention to a number of crimes that lend themselves well to psychological commentary. In doing so, we recognize the omission of numerous other crimes that are often more common and may be equally harmful, although in different ways. Crimes of intimidation, such as stalking and hate crimes, have received considerable attention in recent years. The psychological damage done to victims of these crimes can be substantial and life-long. Some of the more serious crimes of violence, such as sexual offenses and homicide, were described in some detail. Recent sex offender legislation, strongly advocated by the public due to the heinous acts of several sexual predators, was covered. This legislation is extremely controversial, however, and courts are in the process of striking a balance between community safety and the rights of former offenders. The chapter also outlined several typologies of rapists and pedophiles that have been developed during the past 30 years, with the Massachusetts Treatment Center research teams leading the way. The psychological effects of child sexual abuse can be devastating for children, and researchers have been exploring various ways to identify and treat the long-term effects of the abuse.

Some aspects of homicide were explored, with particular attention directed at the more unusual homicides—mass, spree, and serial murders. We also discussed workplace violence, which accounts for approximately 1,000 deaths a year according to recent data. Additionally it includes robberies, rapes and other sexual assaults, aggravated assaults, and more than a million simple assaults. The chapter ended with a discussion of arson, an area that has received substantial research attention from behavioral scientists over the past 20 years.

From this book's perspective, the most effective approach toward the reduction and partial control of criminal behavior is to first understand it. This understanding can emerge not only from continued psychological research activity directed at the learning, maintenance, and extinction processes of criminal behavior, but also at theoretical development, which ultimately could translate into realistic policies and procedures to be adopted by the criminal justice system. Therefore, in the spirit of the psychology and law relationship, it behooves the science of psychology to pursue empirical investigations that may help lead to the formulation of legal policies that insure the safety of the members of society, without massive curtailment of freedom.

Key Terms

Aggressive pedophile
Availability heuristic
Child sexual abuse accommodation syndrome
Cognitive processes
Crime rate
Criminal psychopaths
Dark figure
Discriminant ability
Exploitative pedophile
Fixated pedophile
Immature pedophile
Impulsive-opportunistic rapist
Instrumental learning

Mass arsonist
Mass murder
Non-sadistic rapist
Pervasively angry rapist
Psychiatric criminology
Psychological criminology
Reciprocal interaction
Regressed pedophile
Sadistic pedophile
Serial arsonist
Serial murder
Sexually motivated rapist
Sociological criminology
Spree arsonist
Spree murder

Questions for Review

1. Distinguish among sociological, psychological, and psychiatric criminology.
2. According to psychological criminology, what three factors are critical to explaining criminal behavior? Briefly describe each.
3. What are the two primary sources of crime and victimization data in the United States? Briefly discuss the type of information found in each.
4. What are self-report surveys?
5. Define the term "psychopath," and identify the instruments used to measure it.
6. Provide illustrations of how each of the following psychological concepts might help explain criminal behavior: (a) instrumental learning; (b) expectations; (c) modeling; (d) reciprocal determinism; (e) deindividuation; (f) escalation.
7. Distinguish between cross-situational and temporal consistency. Is either one more important in understanding criminal behavior? Explain your answer.
8. Using stalking or hate crimes to illustrate, discuss the actual and potential contributions of psychology to the study of crimes of intimidation.
9. Summarize (a) the psychological correlates of rapists and (b) the psychological consequences of rape.
10. Describe each of the four core behavioral patterns of pedophiles.
11. What is the child sexual abuse accommodation syndrome? Describe its behavioral indicators and state the controversy over its existence.
12. Identify and define briefly the three different forms of multiple homicide.
13. Summarize what has been learned thus far from research on workplace violence. Provide a list of questions that still need to be addressed.
14. List the categories and behavioral characteristics of both adult and juvenile firesetters.

CHAPTER 14

The Psychology of Law Enforcement

Law enforcement is the broad term used to cover the work of police officers at four levels of government: federal, state, county, and local (or municipal). There are approximately 18,000 law enforcement agencies in the United States. As these agencies have become more professional, law enforcement officers and administrators better educated, and the public has demanded more accountability, the role of psychological services to law enforcement has become more critical and prevalent. Additionally, research psychologists have delved into areas directly related to law enforcement work, such as screening of candidates, fitness–for–duty evaluations (FFDEs), promotional assessments, hostage team negotiations, deadly force incidents, crisis intervention techniques, stress management, and special unit evaluations. Special unit evaluations include the selection and training of officers assigned to special weapons and tactical teams (SWATs), tactical response teams (TRTs), and hostage negotiation teams (HNTs). Police psychologists are also increasingly requested to do investigative type activities, such as criminal profiling, psychological autopsies, hand-writing analysis, and eyewitness (or earwitness) hypnosis.

This chapter will examine some of the law enforcement areas in which both research and practicing police psychologists have been the most active. We begin by exploring the empirical evidence for the "police personality," addressing the question, "Does law enforcement work attract people with distinguishable behavioral patterns or specific personalities?" Next, we turn to the issue of women in law enforcement work. Their contributions to law enforcement and the particular social and psychological stressors they encounter will be discussed. Then, we shift our attention to psychological evaluations of law enforcement, including cognitive assessment, interviewing, and personality assessment. This topic will be followed by law enforcement discretionary behavior and how "occupational socialization" may influence this behavior. The next topic will be criminal profiling. Although this activity is very infrequent for most forensic psychologists, the topic receives an inordinate amount of attention from the media, and consequently a careful appraisal of its usefulness and validity is in order. Finally, we will focus on the many dimensions of stress and its relationship to law enforcement, including fitness-for-duty evaluations. Stress has an important influence on the attention, memory, and decision making not only of first-line participants in the criminal justice system—the law enforcers—but also on the participants at all levels of the criminal justice process. Neither witnesses, plaintiffs, defendants, judges, nor lawyers are immune to its effects.

The Police Personality

The public's perception of law enforcement officers ranges over a broad spectrum of images. Some people associate them with the rigid, dogmatic institutions that perpetuate social injustices and benefit the financially, politically, and socially powerful. Others feel that the police are unappreciated, caring individuals trying to protect the community from the onslaughts of crime. Some scholars have promoted the image of the typical law enforcement officer as an authoritarian, cynical, politically conservative, socially and psychologically insensitive person. By contrast, some of the entertainment media have been instrumental in encouraging images of free-wheeling, unorthodox cops who, in the face of political and organizational pressures, unrelentingly pursue criminals to the end, even if it means losing their jobs. Some of the entertainment media also have not shied away from depictions of officers who violate the civil rights of citizens or are otherwise engaged in corrupt activities (e.g., the film *Training Day*, released 2001, Warner Brothers). On the other hand, the entertainment media also have presented realistic and more favorable portrayals of police work, such as the popular NBC show, *Law and Order*. Often, though, novice officers and police academy recruits model the more flamboyant media characters, but they soon learn through the socialization process that this image is unrealistic.

What, then, is the "police personality?" Is there such a thing? Does law enforcement attract certain types of people? The search for the "police personality" has not been promising. It is clear that law enforcement draws a wide spectrum of personalities, most of which do a commendable job of policing across a wide range of tasks and responsibilities. Consequently, further attempts to discover a particular type of *fixed* personality best suited for law enforcement are unlikely to be productive. The "personality" changes with the job. That is, it is more likely that inexperienced police officers learn or change their "occupational personalities" through their interactions with other police officers, especially those they respect and wish to model. Jerome Skolnick (1973) referred to this ongoing development as the "working personality" of police officers. These shared experiences shape their attitudes, values and beliefs of the occupation, a process generally called "occupational socialization."

The Police Socialization Process

Socialization is a process whereby people learn to conform to their culture's norms, values and roles (McNamara, 1999). In occupational or organizational socialization, individuals learn the attitudes, values, and beliefs of that particular occupational group. John Van Maanen (1974, p. 81) writes: "Organizational socialization . . . provides . . . the new member with a set of rules, perspectives, prescriptions, techniques, and/or tools necessary for him to continue as a participant in the organization." When it comes to the occupational socialization of police officers, Van Maanen (1974, p. 215) concludes, "the police culture can be viewed as molding the attitudes—with numbing regularity—of virtually all who enter." Despite this assertion, we must be careful not to assume that all members of any group adapt to environments in the same way. While the stages discussed below are helpful in understanding the socialization process in law enforcement, individual responses will vary.

Usually, the new officer will undergo a probationary period (usually one year), during which he or she will be evaluated frequently by supervisory personnel. Implicit in the evaluation process is feedback on the progress the officer is making in becoming socialized to the departmental attitudes, roles, and "tricks of the trade." Although training and the probationary period have an enormous impact on the socialization of the officer, it is likely that socialization is an ongoing process, perhaps changing during different stages of an officer's career.

In his influential work on police organizations, Van Maanen (1973, 1974, 1975) identified four discernible stages new police officers go through early in their careers: (1) entry; (2) introduction; (3) encounter; and (4) metamorphosis. The *entry* phase refers to the reasons individuals desire to become police officers in the first place. He found that people generally do not go into law enforcement for the pay, status, or security, but rather because they have close friends or family members who have been or are police officers themselves. In addition, the support they receive from this social network of friends and family helps them through the long and arduous selection procedures (sometimes taking a year or more). This process is called "anticipatory socialization." It is expected that the numerous hurdles that must be passed assure that those who join the occupation will have strong positive attitudes concerning their new job.

The second phase, *introduction*, refers to the initial training the recruit receives, which traditionally has been based on a para-military model. After selection, police recruits begin the socialization process at the police academy, where they not only learn the skills and techniques needed to become an effective police officer, but hear the "war stories" from the more experienced officers about how to handle situations they are likely to encounter on the street. Acceptable and unacceptable behaviors are communicated to the recruit in these stories, as well as the police worldview (McNamara, 1999). Some researchers have described the process as the beginnings of an "identity transformation" (Ainsworth, 1995; Fielding, 1988). But before the academy can effect an identity transformation, it needs to tear away some of the recruit's existing attitudes and beliefs. "The newcomer—surrounded by 30 to 40 contemporaries—is introduced to the often arbitrary discipline of the organization" (Van Maanen, 1975, p. 221). The degrading nature of the recruit's role during academy training serves to detach the newcomers from their old attitudes, and begins to bring them around to attitudes of fellow officers. Paradoxically, those recruits who enter the academy highly motivated and committed to making the world a better place quickly learn that these traits are not necessarily beneficial or rewarded by seasoned police instructors. Traits like loyalty to fellow officers or respect for the chain of command—critical components of the para-military model—are more likely to be rewarded.

The *encounter* phase refers to being on the street after graduation from the academy. Here, newcomers learn what attitudes and behaviors are appropriate and expected of the police officers within that *particular* department or agency. Most often, this early exposure is supervised and monitored by a mentor or field training officer. Often, "street" performance at the agency does not match academy rankings, indicating that the criteria on which academy instructors evaluate and rate the police recruits do not correspond to the criteria used by the field supervisors of that agency.

In his research, Van Maanen (1975) also found that those recruits who were least motivated to work hard tended to be ranked as the better police officers by supervisors and seasoned officers. "Those officers who persist in approaching their job from what police like to call a "gung-ho" perspective are distrusted and eyed cautiously by field supervisors" (Van Maanen, 1975, p. 222). In addition, those newcomers who expressed more commitment, loyalty, and in-group solidarity to the department were evaluated as better officers by supervisors.

The fourth stage, *metamorphosis*, is when the attitudes, beliefs, values and behaviors of the rookie begin to approximate those of their more experienced colleagues. For most recruits, this stage begins to set in after about six months on the job. This perspective emphasizes to the newcomer "to lay low, hang loose and don't expect too much" (Van Maanen, 1975, p. 225). Proactive policing is to be avoided because there is the risk that one may have to use force that can be adjudged excessive (Toch, 1996). To be accepted, new officers begin to recognize that there is little they can do in the world, and they often develop a cynical, tough outer shell to ward off the demands of the work. During this phase, "the newcomer is rigorously assessed as to his motivation, trustworthiness, ability, and loyalty" (Van Maanen, 1975, p. 226). Those rookies whose attitudes and actions conflict with the normal work approach in the agency or precinct are perceived as a threat to the intimate cooperation necessary among members of the team.

In sum, according to McNamara (1999, p. 9), "the police personality emerges as a result of the very nature of police work and of the socialization process which most police officers experience." Police officers generally prefer to associate with their "own kind" and develop values and interests that correspond closely to those exhibited by their "in-group." "Police work places a high premium on social support from other police officers, whose lives may literally depend on each other in dangerous situations and whose work-related stress may only be completely comprehensible to other officers who have experienced the complexities of the job" (Morris, 1996, p. 226). Through personal experience and socialization, " . . . many, perhaps most, police officers become part of a closely knit subculture that is protective and supportive of its members while sharing similar attitudes, values, understanding, and views of the world" (McNamara, 1999, p. 9).

The police model described by Van Maanen is the traditional model of policing, where the police culture is inward looking, socially isolated, and expressing the working personality characteristics described by Skolnick (1973). The traditional model of policing also includes skepticism and cynicism among the police, the development of a code of secrecy to fend off external control and oversight, and often a general distrust for the public at large (Greene, 2000). As outlined by Van Maanen (1975), minimizing contact with the public and staying out of trouble are hallmarks of traditional policing.

Many police departments today are embracing a different model, community policing. In contrast to the traditional model, this new approach emphasizes contact with the public and encourages communities to be participants in shaping police objectives and interventions as well as evaluating them (Greene, 2000). "Common core elements of community policing programs include a redefinition of the police role to increase crime prevention activities, greater reciprocity in police and community relations, area decentralization of police services and command, and some form of civilianization" (Greene, 2000, p. 312). It is believed—although not documented—that community policing is less likely to produce the public distrust and the cynicism referred to above. Because police cynicism is a frequently encountered topic in police literature—we saw it above in the discussion of Van Maanen's work—we now turn to it for more elaboration.

Police Cynicism

Police cynicism was first identified by Niederhoffer (1967) in his study of New York City police officers. While the existence of the collection of *fixed* traits suitable for law enforcement has not been supported, the learned *individual* trait of cynicism in law enforcement has received support. Niederhoffer (1967) argued that urban officers go through stages of anomie and cynicism during their careers. "Anomie" was a term developed by the French sociologist Emile Durkheim and later refined by the American sociologist Robert Merton (1957). Although Durkheim and Merton viewed anomie or normlessness as a characteristic of society, Niederhoffer saw it as a feature of individuals who are alienated from their society. Anomie—as it was experienced by the officers in Niederhoffer's study—included a loss of faith in people, a feeling of alienation from society at large, and a turning toward the police organization as the principal hope for social salvation. He saw cynicism as a way of adapting to these frustrating feelings brought on by anomie. In police officers, **cynicism** is characterized as " . . . diffuse feelings of hate and envy, impotent hostility, and the sour grapes pattern" (Niederhoffer, 1967, p. 99). Impotent hostility springs from personal feelings of inability to express hostility against society; a police officer must remain calm, even when spat on. The sour grapes behavior pattern refers to the feelings of police officers that their desired but unattainable goals are really not all that important or valuable. For instance, college-educated patrol officers may find that their expectations of promotion do not become fulfilled, and they may try to convince themselves that promotion really does not mean all that much to them. On the other hand, non-college-educated officers may rationalize that higher education is not necessary.

Niederhoffer contended that cynicism was discernible at all levels and in all fields of law enforcement. He postulated two kinds of police cynicism. One was directed toward society; the other toward the police organization itself. The first is characteristic of police at all levels, running from the patrol officers to the police chief. It is the attitude that most people would commit crimes if they knew they could get away with it. Cynicism toward the police organization is most often found in the patrol officer and is much less likely to affect the ranking officer. Niederhoffer explained that cynicism toward the organization was less likely in the ranking officer because he or she hoped to transform and eventually control the system. This hope usually keeps organizational cynicism at bay—at least for a while. The patrol officer, on the other hand, develops a greater degree of frustration with the criminal justice process. The daily encounters of front-line officers with crime and victimization are more likely to promote frustrations about the ineffectiveness of the "system."

According to Niederhoffer, police cynicism—of either type—passes through four distinct stages of development. The first stage, which he called *pseudo-cynicism*, is most recognizable among recruits at the police academy. Although they express cynical attitudes to mimic their police models at the academy, they can barely conceal the idealism and commitment they actually feel. *Romantic cynicism*, the second stage, is reached during the first five years of the police career. Although Niederhoffer did not define the precise behavior, it appears that the most idealistic, young members of the force are the most disillusioned by the reality of police work and hence most vulnerable to this type of cynicism. The third stage, *aggressive cynicism*, gradually builds until it becomes most prevalent during the tenth year of service. According to Niederhoffer, it corresponds to a resentment which is best expressed by the catch phrase, "I hate civilians," and it results in a diffuse resentment and hostility toward society and the department. The fourth stage, *resigned cynicism*, occurs during the last few years of a police career. It is demonstrated by acceptance of the job situation and capacity to come to terms with the flaws of the criminal justice system. This final stage is viewed by Niederhoffer as the successful culmination of a career marked by much dissatisfaction and conflict.

Niederhoffer observed that, for the first few years of a police career, cynicism increases in proportion to the length of service. It then tends to level off sometime during the fifth and tenth years of service. He believed cynicism was learned as part of a socialization process typical of the police occupation, a process estimated to take about five years. This differs from Von Maanen's view, because Von Maanen believed that the final stage of socialization set in after about six months on the job.

Reiser (1973) hypothesized a process similar to Neiderhoffer's, which he called the **John Wayne Syndrome**, after the popular hero of movie "westerns" of the 1950s and early 60s. According to Reiser, the John Wayne Syndrome begins early in the career of a law enforcement officer and lasts for three to four years. This behavior pattern is characterized by coldness toward others and emotional withdrawal, authoritarian attitudes, cynicism, overseriousness, and a black-or-white, inflexible approach to daily problem solving.

Violanti (1983) identified law enforcement career stages that have a close similarity to Niederhoffer's. Violanti outlined four distinct stages: (1) the alarm stage (0–5 years); (2) the disenchantment stage (6–13 years); (3) the personalization stage (14–20 years); and (4) the introspective stage (20 years and over). In the alarm stage, the new officer experiences "reality shock," which is realization that law enforcement work is different than what is learned at the academy. After about five years, disenchantment sets in and continues until midcareer (12–14 years). During this stage, bitter disappointment develops when mid-career officers realize that pressures and demands of law enforcement work far outweigh their ability to respond effectively. At the end of mid-career (14–20 years), Violanti believes officers go through a personalization stage, where they focus more on their personal goals before retirement and pay less attention to the goals of the law enforcement agency. This stage represents a kind of "mid-age crisis" for officers, at which point they evaluate whether they are where they want to be professionally. Finally, at around 20 years of service, an introspective stage emerges. The officer "looks back on earlier years as the good old days" and becomes secure and settled in the job. It is at the introspective stage that dissatisfaction and boredom sets in, and performance correspondingly drops. According to Violanti, this pattern is one of the reasons why officers normally retire after 20 years of service.

Niederhoffer's theory and the 20-item questionnaire of police cynicism he developed has generated more research than any other theory of police attitude and career changes. Much of the research has examined the cynicism scale's reliability and validity, but the research has not found the scale particularly promising so far (Lefkowitz, 1975; Anson, Mann, & Sherman, 1986; Langworthy, 1987). One thing does appear clear: The scale is multidimensional and measures a number of things besides cynicism (Regoli, Crank, & Rivera, 1990). The lack of research support for the scale's reliability and validity, however, does not mean that Niederhoffer's theory of cynicism is unsupported. Rather, it may mean the scale is seriously flawed but that the theory itself remains untested.

Other Representative Research

Several other researchers have searched for clues to a police personality, with equally discouraging results. A study by C. Abraham Fenster, Carl F. Wiedemann, and Bernard Locke (1977) is representative of much of this research. Over 700 male subjects were divided into four groups, depending on whether they had law enforcement experience or a college background. All were comparable in age (with an average age in the late 20s). A variety of group mental and personality tests were administered to all subjects, and comparisons were made between the scores of the four groups. However, as in most studies on the police personality, little theoretical rationale was offered as to why these particular tests were selected, nor was validity information described. Several of the tests used have notoriously questionable validity and weak theoretical bases for their construction, important points to consider in assessing the research.

Results showed that law enforcement officers demonstrated significantly lower neuroticism scores (reactivity to stressful events) than the non-police groups. In addition, law enforcement officers obtained lower authoritarian scores and slightly higher intelligence scores. The authors concluded that this law enforcement sample "may represent a superior sub-sample of the general population" (p. 104) and that the law enforcement groups were better adjusted psychologically than the non-law enforcement groups. Overall, however, there was little evidence of specific personality traits associated with law enforcement.

A study by Carol Mills and Wayne Bohannon (1980) illustrated a trend toward better research design and a more vigorous attempt to link test scores with theory. The Mills-Bohannon project tried to identify those personality characteristics associated with supervisory ratings on leadership and overall suitability for law enforcement work. Further, the study was designed to test two predictive models of law enforcement effectiveness and leadership (viz., Hogan, 1971; Gough, 1969).

The measuring instrument used to delineate personality characteristics was the empirically constructed California Psychological Inventory (CPI). Forty-nine male Maryland state police officers with one year's experience served as subjects. Each subject was rated by two supervisors on a 7-point scale for leadership and "overall suitability for police work." There was a good amount of interjudge reliability (.78) between the two supervisory ratings for each subject.

The results showed that the Hogan model of police effectiveness was significantly better able to predict leadership than Gough's model. Hogan's model uses the four CPI personality variables of social presence, self-acceptance, achievement via independence, and intellectual efficiency to predict law enforcement performance. "Social presence" refers to the personality trait of being poised and self-confident in personal and social interaction. "Self-acceptance" refers to a tendency to feel competent, combined with a capacity for independent thinking and action. "Achievement via independence" denotes motivation to achieve in settings where autonomy and independence are encouraged. "Intellectual efficiency" refers to the ability to think clearly and planfully.

The results of the Mills-Bohannon study suggest that the personality requirements for successful law enforcement leadership are the above described four traits in combination, although caution is advised when generalizing to other law enforcement agencies in other states and other countries (ecological validity). Also, the vagueness of the personality traits is troublesome, because it renders them susceptible to multiple interpretations. For example, what precisely does "the ability to think clearly and planfully" mean, and in what context?

There is evidence to suggest that law enforcement officers in general tend to be conservative, conventional, and concerned with maintaining the status quo (Lefkowitz, 1975). Hence, at least one component of the authoritarian personality is supported in the research literature. This conventional outlook appears to be fostered by para-military regulations and rules of conduct expected by some law enforcement agencies. Beyond this conservative aspect, the "average" law enforcement officer seems to display personality characteristics similar to those of the "average" population—normal and free of pathology.

It should not be surprising that the research on the police personality continues to be equivocal and inconsistent. Individual behavior (personality) and situational context intermingle. The search for consistent behaviors must consider what kind of consistency (temporal or cross-situational) is being measured, and in what context. The fact that some researchers report law enforcement officers to be authoritarian or cynical while others do not underscores this interaction. Some law enforcement agencies, through peer pressures, expect their officers to assume an authoritarian role, while others do not. Some agencies look for applicants who already "fit the mold," while others anticipate that the young officers will acquire appropriate roles through peer pressure or occupational experience. It is entirely possible that law enforcement behavior is shaped more by the agency-appropriate roles the officer is expected to assume than by the officer's own personality variables. In other words, the **occupational socialization** process may override individual differences or personality styles. Furthermore, individuals regarded ineffective by one police department are often seen as effective in another (Bartol, 1991b, 1996). It seems that law enforcement agencies have "personalities" roughly similar to individual personalities, and that these "organizational personalities" may play a critical role in predictions of job success and failure. In this sense, the psychological characteristics of law enforcement officers as measured by personality inventories may be irrelevant to success in law enforcement.

In conclusion, it does not appear productive to search for any entity called the "universal police personality" that characterizes, even in part, the person who becomes a law enforcement officer. It may be more appropriate to limit one's research conclusions to the specific law enforcement agency in which the subjects are employed. Research findings on the "personality" of law enforcement officers may reveal more about the characteristics and expectations of the law enforcement agency than about the officers therein.

Women in Law Enforcement

Women remain a small minority in law enforcement nationwide. The most recent statistics from the UCR (2002) indicate that they comprise 11.2% of all law enforcement officers. This is consistent with an estimate from the National Center for Women and Policing (2000), which indicates that women comprise less than 15% of sworn police officers. The larger the department, the higher the proportion of women police officers (Cole & Smith, 2001). For example, approximately 20% of the sworn officers on the Detroit police force are women (Cole & Smith, 2001).

Researchers also have found that women are making progress in acquiring promotions and administrative position, although they encounter continuing resistance from supervisors (Martin, 1980, 1992). Less than 4% of supervisory positions are held by female officers, though again the percentages are higher in larger departments (Meloy, 2000).

The first full-time, sworn woman officer in the United States was Alice Stebbins Wells, who was appointed policewoman in Los Angeles in 1910 (Buwalda, 1945; Higgins, 1961). Although her duties were primarily to supervise young women and girls in places of public recreation, such as dance halls, theaters, and skating rinks, she was the first to be called a policewoman by an organized police department. Other women were in law enforcement in this country long before 1910 but they were appointed as "matrons," restricted to taking care of detained women and girls.

Wells' appointment received widespread national recognition and drew front page stories, often critical and accompanied by negative caricatures. However, Wells utilized her unique position to become a prime mover in the policewomen's movement, and helped form the International Association of Policewomen in 1915 (More, 1992). Today the organization is known as the International Association of Women Police (IAWP).

Other departments were slow to accept women in law enforcement. When they did, they were generally restricted to desk jobs, working as clerks, secretaries, and dispatchers. They worked with juvenile cases or supervised women detainees. They were also charged with identifying community "moral hazards" and presenting them to community leaders and civic groups for action (Buwalda, 1945). Patrol work and investigation were left to men. Law enforcement administrators did not believe women had the physical strength or stamina, or the psychological temperament to exert forceful authority over adults.

It took 20 more years before women gained law enforcement positions at the state level. In May, 1930, Lotta Caldwell and Mary Ramsey were enlisted into the Massachusetts State Police, the first women to gain entry into a state police or highway patrol agency (Higgins, 1961). The 1930 U.S. census listed 1,534 women employed in law enforcement, and by 1940 this number had increased slightly to 1,775 (More, 1992). In 1960, the number had increased to 5,617, a figure which still represented only 2.3% of the total officers nationally (Martin, 1980). The situation dramatically changed in the 1970s, however, with the enactment of the *Equal Employment Opportunity Act of 1972*, which protected women and minorities from discrimination in hiring by state and local governments. (The *Civil Rights Act of 1964* already applied to federal hiring.) Between 1971 and 1978, the proportion of women entering law enforcement more than doubled (2% to 4.2%), and between 1978 and 1986, the proportion more than doubled again (4.2% to 8.8%) (Martin, 1992).

Much of the contemporary research (beginning in the 1970s) on women in law enforcement has concentrated on comparing job performance of men and women to determine if women can physically and psychologically handle the rigors of law enforcement work, particularly patrol assignments. This research has consistently found that women can do law enforcement work at least as effectively as men in large metropolitan departments (Pendergrass & Ostrove, 1984; Feinman, 1986; Balkin, 1988) and small-town departments (Bartol, Bergen, Volckens, & Knoras, 1992). Despite the growing research that continually finds women can do law enforcement work, women officers still face many obstacles and stressors. Interestingly, one of the greatest barriers to accepting women into law enforcement does not come from the public but from male officers, particularly male supervisors (Wexler & Logan, 1983; Bartol et al. 1992).

Researchers have studied how women adapt and adjust to the barriers and gender discrimination found in male dominated police culture. Some writers (e.g., More, 1992; Berg & Budnick, 1986) have asserted that female officers go through a period of stages, running from the honeymoon stage, to the ambivalent stage, to the transition stage. However, as noted earlier in the chapter before our discussion of socialization and cynicism, it is an oversimplification to assume that all members of any group go through a series of stages and adapt to environments the same way. Another approach is to try to identify the various ways women use to adapt to law enforcement work.

Judie Gaffin Wexler (1985) identified four role styles adopted by women in law enforcement: (1) neutral-impersonal; (2) feminine; (3) semi-masculine; and (4) mixed. The largest number of women officers in her sample adopted the neutral-impersonal style, where a business-like attitude toward their male colleagues was apparent. Women who followed this style wanted to be treated with respect as full and equal members of the work group, and they shunned special treatment from colleagues or administrators. Wexler found, however, that the women in this group believed some aspects of law enforcement work had to be approached differently than the traditional approach used by their male counterparts. For example, they believed that force was often not necessary in accomplishing certain goals, such as making arrests. Wexler also discovered that women who adopted the neutral-impersonal style typically did not do much socializing with their male colleagues, and half of them described their relationships with the male officers as distant and tenuous.

The semi-masculine style was defined by Wexler as a tendency to be professional and to do the job well, all the while believing that they would not be totally accepted as equals in this male-dominated profession. The women adopting this style did expect to be treated as individuals, however. In contrast to the neutral-impersonal officers, the semi-masculine officers believed that they could be accepted as individuals by socializing with the male officers, by joking with them, going out after work for drinks, and cheering for, or participating in, departmental sports teams.

Women who adopted what Wexler called the feminine style put more emphasis on the fact that they were women in the physical sense. "Being attractive at work was important to them" (Wexler, 1985, p. 752). Interactions with male officers often carried a sexual undertone, where they used their femininity to gain acceptance. Women in this group accepted or desired special treatment from colleagues or supervisors, and also accepted male protectiveness on the job. Wexler observed that women who followed this style were really not accepted in the informal work group and they were not taken seriously enough by the male officers for information to be shared with them.

The mixed style is characterized by utilization of all three styles, with no particular style dominating. These officers wanted to get respect by hard work and interpersonal distance, but they often resorted to a combination of conscientious hard work, flirting, and teasing to reach their goals. They also wanted to be treated as equals and refused special treatment.

While Wexler's research is interesting, there are some problems with her approach. Her choice of the term "feminine" to refer to women who appear to use their sexuality on the job is unfortunate. As we will see shortly, other researchers have identified "feminine" characteristics in law enforcement that transcend this physical emphasis. Additionally, Wexler's styles apply more to behavior with male colleagues than to work in the field, although approach to their job is considered to some extent. Finally, it is likely that effective police officers—male or female—use a variety of styles, depending on the situation. Some preliminary data indicate that women do, in fact, use multiple styles or strategies (Bartol & Urzillo, 1993), and it is likely that men do so as well.

Alissa Worden (1993) found very few differences between male and females officers in their *attitudes* toward policing. She writes: "Overall, female as well as male police officers were predictably ambivalent about restrictions on their autonomy and the definition of their role, only mildly positive about their public clientele, complimentary of their colleagues, and unenthusiastic about working conditions and supervisors" (Worden, 1993, p. 229). She attributes (cautiously) much of this gender similarity in policing to occupation socialization, a process which seems to wash out many of the major differences in gender roles.

Anne Morris (1996) has extended the study of gender differences to encompass minority issues. Like women as a group, minority officers as a group are also minorities within their departments. They also may encounter resistance from fellow officers and from the public. Interestingly, Morris found that women and minorities in the NYPD received considerable social support from their police colleagues and reported generally positive professional and social interactions while on the job. The one major gender difference she identified was that women officers were far less likely than men to socialize informally off the job with other police officers. They counted fewer fellow officers among their close, personal friends.

Some research does suggest that the style of law enforcement utilized by women as a group may be more effective than styles employed by men as a group. For example, many law enforcement administrators and a large segment of the public believe that female officers are better able than male officers to defuse a potentially dangerous or violent situation (Balkin, 1988; Bell, 1982; Weisheit & Mahan, 1988). A study by Johnson (1991) underscores observations that women have a "gentling effect" when dealing with the public. Johnson focused on gender differences in job strain. Specifically, she looked at "internal burnout," characterized by feelings of being emotionally depleted on the job, and "external burnout," characterized by feelings of being emotionally hardened by the job and lacking compassion for citizens. While there were no significant gender differences in self-described internal burnout, men showed a greater tendency to report feelings of external burnout. Johnson concluded that the relatively low external burnout rate of women officers was perhaps a result of their less-aggressive and more gentle policing style. Johnson found in her interviews that women officers spoke about the compassion they brought to the job, as well as their strong preference for dealing with the public verbally and psychologically rather than physically. Interestingly, Worden (1993) found that women police officers seem to be guided more by altruistic and social motives than men, who tended to be more motivated by the financial rewards of the occupation.

These research discoveries, along with consistent findings that women are perfectly capable of meeting the physical and emotional demands of law enforcement work, suggest that the future for women in law enforcement should be bright. It is important, however, that the quality of their work not be measured by a male yardstick but rather be judged on its own merit (see Tavis, 1992). It is equally important that we recognize both male and female officers should be encouraged to develop qualities associated with success in law enforcement work.

Jennifer Hunt (2000) has called for studies of women and policing that adopt a more qualitative methodology. Specifically, she suggests that interviews and field observations are sorely needed to detect changes that have occurred in policing as a result of women being hired. "(B)ecause studies of police in the 1980s and 1990s have relied on survey research rather than intensive fieldwork and unstructured interviews, researchers have focused on surface norms and behaviors. They have failed to probe possible changes in the police subculture's hidden understandings, latent values, and behaviors through which police define their occupation and distinguish themselves from outsiders. Whether the presence of increasing numbers of women officers has changed the informal policing subculture thus remains a largely unexamined issue for future research," she asserts (Hunt, 2000, p. 174).

Psychological Assessment in Law Enforcement

A massive amount of research on the validity and legal aspects of psychological assessment and testing has focused on the selection of law enforcement officers. This scrutiny was prompted by six different Presidential Commissions on Law Enforcement and Crime during the 1960s, all of which emphasized the value of properly selected law enforcement officers. Implicit in these recommendations was the pressing need for reliable and valid instruments that would evaluate the intellectual capacity, emotional stability, and personality characteristics of law enforcement personnel. Keep in mind, however, especially in the testing context, that it is important to distinguish between screening-in and screening-out procedures for police officer selection. *Screening-in* procedures are intended to identify those attributes that distinguish one candidate over another as being a potentially more effective officer. Implicit in this approach is the ability to rank order applicants, allowing agencies to select the top candidates from a pool who passed the initial screening procedures. This approach assumes that there are traits, habits, reactions, and attitudes that distinguish an outstanding law enforcement officer from a satisfactory one. There is virtually no evidence to date that psychologists can reach this goal in any satisfactory, valid manner.

Screening-out procedures, on the other hand, try to eliminate those applicants who demonstrate significant signs of psychopathology or emotional instability, or who lack the basic ability or mental acuity to perform the job in a safe and responsible manner. Screening-out procedures are the procedures most commonly applied by police psychologists when screening police candidates.

In 1967, the Task Force on the Police (President's Commission on Law Enforcement and the Administration of Justice) underscored the lack of adequate screening in most law enforcement agencies. Six years later, the National Advisory Commission on Criminal Justice Standards and Goals recommended that every law enforcement agency "employ a formal process for the selection of qualified police applicants. This process should include a written test of mental ability or aptitude, an oral interview, a physical examination, a psychological examination, and an in-depth background investigation" (Spielberger, 1979, p. xi).

Law enforcement selection was traditionally based upon minimum (or maximum) standards of age, health, height, vision, hearing, physical fitness, weight, agility, and appearance. Whether these specifications related to actual job performance was generally unknown; the relationship was unexamined, but it was assumed that these specifications were important for doing the job effectively. With the introduction of the *Civil Rights Act of 1964* and federal guidelines such as those of the Equal Employment Opportunity Commission (EEOC), it became clear that many of these earlier criteria would need to be more carefully scrutinized. Departments were prompted to re-examine their existing practices, to develop new ones, or to drop existing criteria of questionable validity. If they did not abide by the guidelines, they were leaving themselves open to EEOC compliance measures or to civil suits by aggrieved parties.

Selecting capable law enforcement officers is a demanding responsibility for law enforcement administrators. The presence of even a few undesirable officers is potentially damaging to both the agency itself and the population the agency serves. For example, one officer's overzealous behavior and poor judgment can result in psychological, social, and financial costs within the department and the community. From a financial standpoint, every new officer who is terminated because of misconduct, incompetence, or dissatisfaction costs each law enforcement agency thousands of dollars in training and equipment. It is crucial, therefore, that carefully designed and valid screening devices be available, at least to screen out potentially problematic candidates.

Psychological devices used without adequate validation, however, very likely will literally have their day in court, forced to demonstrate their worth when lawsuits are filed by victims or by disgruntled law enforcement candidates claiming they were screened out of law enforcement work unjustifiably. To avoid costly litigation and embarrassment to the agency, law enforcement agencies must avoid using haphazard screening procedures and must support efforts to validate the methods they are using.

Recent research on law enforcement selection indicates agencies are using four broad measures or procedures in the selection process:

1. Psychological tests, including measures of intelligence, aptitude, attitudes, interest, and personality;
2. Situational tests, in which job behaviors are simulated or a candidate's behavior is observed in "test" situations, as in polygraph examinations;
3. Background and physical data, including education, performance on physical ability tests, indications of substance abuse, and prior criminal involvement; and
4. The interview, which includes oral boards and possibly clinical data gathered by a psychologist or psychiatrist.

In the following sections, we will discuss the three measures which are directly related to the practice of police psychology: psychological testing, situational tests, and the interview.

Psychological Testing in Law Enforcement

Over the past three decades, various psychological tests and inventories have been tried in the law enforcement selection process. In the late 1970s, law enforcement agencies began to shift away from broad, largely invalidated "intelligence" and "aptitude" tests and projective personality instruments. These were replaced with objective personality measures, usually of a paper-and-pencil variety given to law enforcement candidates in a group setting. Several major surveys illustrate the shift.

In a survey of assessment techniques used in metropolitan police departments (Narrol & Levitt, 1963), 85% of the departments reported using objective tests specifically intended to assess aptitude for law enforcement work. However, the testing programs were described only vaguely, and the departments appeared to be using them as a symbolic gesture to appease the community and meet newly-introduced governmental standards rather than as empirically conceived instruments of valid selection. Most of the tests were little more than unstandardized cognitive ability tests of questionable design or validity. Concurrent or predictive validity—the measures of how the tests actually related to performance—were unknown or not even examined by most departments. Only 22% of the departments reported using "personality measures" in their selection process, and only one department reported doing any original research to determine the validity of the tests it used.

Nearly ten years later, Murphy (1972) surveyed 258 local law enforcement agencies employing at least 100 officers and 49 state police forces. While his data indicated no significant shift in the percentage of departments using psychological exams, he found a substantial shift away from questionable aptitude, intelligence, or projective tests. Instead, departments were adopting more standardized and somewhat more valid psychological measures of personality and emotional status. About 44% of the local police departments used "psychological examinations" to screen police candidates, but only 13% of the state law enforcement agencies used them. Although this percentage is considerably lower than that found in the Narrol and Levitt survey (85%), it is important to note that Murphy's questionnaire was worded differently. It specified "psychological tests," whereas Narrol and Levitt had asked to be informed of any type of examination.

Most of the tests reported in the Murphy study were objective, paper-and-pencil personality measures. The MMPI was by far the most common personality test used, with 48.75% of the agencies using it alone or in combination with other tests. Murphy also learned that 41.25% of the agencies used a "psychiatric interview" in the screening procedure.

In a later nationwide survey, Delprino and Bahn (1988) reported that 52% of the municipal and state police departments responding indicated they used psychological screening on police applicants. More recently, Cochrane, Tett, and VandeCreek (in press), in another nationwide survey, found that 91% of the municipal police departments use psychological tests in their selection procedures, a dramatic increase from the Delprino and Bahn survey more than a decade earlier. Although the departments used a wide variety of selection tools, Cochrane et al. discovered that the most frequently used instruments were the MMPI–2 (71.6%), the California Psychological Inventory (CPI) (24.5%), the 16PF (18.7%), and the Inwald Personality Inventory (IPI) (11.6%).

Although many different assessment techniques are currently used in the screening, selection, and promotion of law enforcement officers, it is usually not known whether any of these testing procedures are valid predictors of effective on-the-job law enforcement performance (criterion-related validity) (Spielberger, 1979). This is a sobering fact because any selection procedure should ultimately be validated. Empirical investigations evaluating relationships between initial selection standards (predictors) and the actual job performance of law enforcement officers should be undertaken, supported by attempts at determining construct validity.

Using psychological tests as predictors of effective law enforcement performance is problematic, partly due to the diversity and complexity of behaviors required of law enforcement officers. Their duties range from preventing and detecting crime to investigating accidents, intervening in disputes, handling domestic disturbances, dealing with juveniles, and responding to a wide range of requests from the public. The smaller the department, the more varied the responsibilities of individual officers. It is not unusual to find a local, small-town law enforcement officer offering first-aid tips to an elementary school class and on the same day dealing with a violent domestic altercation or trying to calm a mentally-disordered individual. Because specialization is a luxury very small departments cannot afford, it is very difficult to establish objective performance criteria upon which to base predictions. Some officers may perform very competently on some tasks while failing at others. The officer who relates exceptionally well to adolescents may perform less adequately in crisis situations involving very young children.

To tap the heterogeneity of law enforcement activities, screening devices must contain a number of predictors based upon a multitude of behaviors, and few are able to do this. In addition, because law enforcement work differs substantially from one jurisdiction to another, a test may be adequate for a given department but may not suffice elsewhere. Rural or small town law enforcement requires different behaviors and talents from metropolitan or urban law enforcement work. Also, many states have sheriff's departments which often offer very different services from those of municipal or state law enforcement agencies.

Another obstacle to validating psychological tests is determining what precisely constitutes successful performance. Interjudge agreement about performance ratings is often difficult to obtain, even within one department. What one supervisor considers superior performance in the field may be only average performance to another supervisor. Predictors of success, therefore, are elusive.

The wide scope of law enforcement, together with the urgent need for more vigorous and sophisticated methods of study, warn us that we should expect few solid conclusions in the research literature as to what are adequate predictors of success or failure in law enforcement work. As expected, the literature is littered with inconclusive or mixed results. This does not mean that reliable and valid psychological assessment is beyond reach. It may mean, though, that a successful testing program may have to be tailor-made to the needs of a particular agency.

Cognitive Assessment One of the first U.S. studies on law enforcement selection was conducted in 1917 by psychologist Louis M. Terman, who gave an abbreviated form of his Stanford-Binet Intelligence Scale to 30 male applicants for police and firefighter positions in San Jose, California. He found that a large majority of the candidates were functioning near the dull normal range of intelligence; only three candidates obtained a cognitive ability score over 100, the score considered average for the general population. Terman concluded that police and firefighting positions attracted individuals of exceptionally low intelligence. He recommended that all candidates who scored below 80 be eliminated automatically from further job consideration. He also urged police administrators to keep the cognitive ability scores and compare them with later job performance, but apparently this was never done. As a result of Terman's project, an IQ score of 80 was established as an arbitrary score to indicate ability to perform police responsibilities.

Professionalism in law enforcement and an increase in the rewards of law enforcement work over the years have attracted significantly more intellectually capable law enforcement officers. In later studies, law enforcement officers obtained at least average intelligence scores (Matarazzo et al., 1964; Gordon, 1969). In a review of the literature, Poland (1978, p. 376) notes that "if police agencies can attract applicants with some college education, they have an applicant pool of above average intelligence." As encouraging as it may be to know that law enforcement personnel are not substandard intellectually, this tells us little about the relationship between intelligence level and actual job performance. Is high intelligence a predictor of superb or even satisfactory functioning as a law enforcement officer?

In general, intelligence and ability tests have been useful predictors of police academy performance, but less reliable for predicting how well an officer actually performs in the field (Spielberger, Ward, & Spaulding, 1979; Henderson, 1979). Studies using general cognitive ability tests like the Army General Classification Test, the Wonderlic, and the California Test of Mental Maturity, typically report correlations between test scores and academy grades in the .35 to .70 range, with the most frequent correlations clustering around .50 (e.g., Dubois & Watson, 1950; Hess, 1973; Mills, McDevitt, & Tonkin, 1966; Mullineaux, 1955). However, there are few parallel correlations between intelligence measure and field performance, or between academy and field performance. McKinney (1973) reported that a tailor-made written examination used in Phoenix, Arizona, to select officers had value in predicting on-the-street job performance, but had much better predictive power when applied to police academy performance.

Personality Assessment Fortunately, law enforcement selection procedures have now shifted from using poorly defined examinations of intelligence and vague assessments of personality dynamics to using more objective measures of personality that are able to provide criterion-related validation data. The most widely used objective personality inventory in the selection of law enforcement is the Minnesota Multiphasic Personality Inventory (MMPI) (and the revised MMPI–2), used as part of required entrance requirements in many federal, state, and local law enforcement agencies (Beutler et al., 1985; Inwald & Kenny, 1989; Shaw, 1986). Although we discussed the MMPI in ◀ Chapter 2, we will apply it specifically to the law enforcement context here.

Most MMPI research in law enforcement has been of the concurrent validation variety, where the personality characteristics of already employed law enforcement officers are assessed and used to establish predictors of good performance. Typically, the inventory is administered to officers representing varying degrees of success in law enforcement work, with "success" determined by supervisor ratings. For instance, if a high percentage of officers evaluated by supervisors as "successful" respond differently to questions on a subscale of the MMPI than a group of "unsuccessful" officers, that scale can be considered a good predictor of on-the-job performance. Research that examines individuals already on a law enforcement force has a critical limitation, however, because it ignores the characteristics of officers who were hired but dropped out because of hurdles along the way. Thus, significant segments of the population are missed. One of the reasons for using any screening device is to discover the potential drop-outs or failures as soon as possible.

Predictive validation is a more useful and vigorous research procedure than concurrent-related validation, but it is rarely implemented because of the time it requires and the percentage of the law enforcement budget it consumes. Predictive validation demands longitudinal study to decide how well initial assessments and standards predict a candidate's success or failure as a law enforcement officer. In this method, the MMPI is administered to candidates and, several years hence, the researcher determines which of the candidates "succeeded" in law enforcement.

Both concurrent validation and predictive validation studies of the MMPI used in selection are confusing and ambiguous in their hypotheses, designs, results, and conclusions. Clear, cogent, or unequivocal conclusions and recommendations are rarely found in the existing literature. Some researchers have reported good, even exceptional results, while others have found little in the way of encouraging data. However, it should be emphasized that there is much to be gained through testing programs founded on well-designed and well-executed research. Valid psychological measures hold great promise for the efficiency and accuracy of personnel selection.

The Los Angeles Police Department reported one of the earliest attempts to use the MMPI as a law enforcement selection tool (Rankin, 1957). The triggering event for this innovation was an incident in which law enforcement officers allegedly used unnecessary force and brutality toward suspects in their custody. After the incident, the LAPD instituted a candidate-screening program to answer public criticism and hopefully prevent similar occurrences. The program included the MMPI, the Rorschach, and a psychological interview. Unfortunately, procedural and statistical details about the program, as reported by Rankin (1957), were not sufficient to permit generalizations to other departments. Rankin said he rejected a substantial number of potentially "unsuitable" law enforcement officers on the basis of psychological test results. He posited that 11% of the 2,000 applicants screened over a six-year period were rejected for "psychiatric reasons." Rankin only assumed, however, that vaguely defined psychiatric problems would lead to unsatisfactory performance on the job. Later research on the MMPI attempted to demonstrate this association, with little success.

Over the years, some studies have reported a weak or nonexistent relationship between MMPI scores and job performance (Gottesman, 1975; Henderson, 1979; Kent & Eisenberg, 1972; Spielberger, Spaulding, & Ward, 1978). Others have reported moderate relationships between some performance standards and one or more of the MMPI subscales (Azen, Snibble, & Montgomery, 1973; Blum, 1964; Colarelli & Siegel, 1964; Hooke & Kraus, 1971; Marsh, 1962; Matarazzo, Allen, Saslow, & Weins, 1964; Nowicki, 1966; Rankin, 1957).

George Hargrave and Deirdre Hiatt (Hargrave & Hiatt, 1987; Hiatt & Hargrave, 1988b) tried to identify a relationship between MMPI scores and various measures of performance. In one study (Hiatt & Hargrave, 1988a), the MMPI profiles of officers who had been involved in serious disciplinary actions were compared with a matched group of officers who had not been involved in such actions. Several subscales were identified as decent predictors of disciplinary actions. Furthermore, the problem officer was twice as likely to have a T–score above 70 on at least one of the MMPI subscales.

A few predictive validation studies also have been done. Beutler et al. (1985) followed officers from three different agencies (a community college security department, a large university security department, and a large urban police department) over a two-year period. The researchers reported that suspensions were strongly related to certain score elevations on the MMPI, but they did not specify which scales. In another project (Beutler, Nussbaum, & Meredith, 1988), 11 officers were followed over a four-year period to see if their MMPI profiles changed significantly as a result of their experience in the field. They concluded that they had, but again did not specify the changes. Hiatt and Hargrave (1988b) followed 55 urban officers over a three-period and discovered that the unsatisfactory group had higher mean scores on 11 of the 13 MMPI scales, although only two were statistically significant.

In a longitudinal study spanning 13 years, Bartol (1991b) followed 600 police officers over their careers to see who would be rated unsuccessful in small-town law enforcement. Officers who "failed" were most often described by their supervisors as immature and inappropriate. They were frequently reprimanded for such behaviors as excessive and inappropriate use of authority in dealing with the public. They had frequent accidents with police vehicles, demonstrated inappropriate use of firearms and other equipment, and showed little commitment to police work. Supervisors said they had serious concerns as to whether these officers could be counted on or trusted in times of crisis or emergency situations. A combination of three MMPI scales emerged as a powerful predictor of eventual failure in three-quarters of the officers. The combination, called the "immaturity index," may generalize to other police departments and help identify those officers who do not succeed in law enforcement.

Although the immaturity index needs further research attention, the study demonstrates that the MMPI and the MMPI–2 might be valuable tools in the screening and selection of law enforcement officers if we focus on establishing predictive validity.

Now that the MMPI–2 has been purged of the offensive questions that appeared on the earlier version, the test should continue to be a useful aid in the screening and selection of law enforcement officers, and perhaps candidates for other positions as well. The test samples over 500 self-report behaviors, is the prototype of personality testing, and has stimulated nearly 4,000 research articles examining its strengths and weaknesses. According to Maloney and Ward (1976, p. 342), "Problems, critics, and rivals notwithstanding, the MMPI will probably continue to be a dominant force in the field. This is primarily due to the vast wealth of accumulated data and 'wisdom' that it possesses."

The California Psychological Inventory The California Psychological Inventory (CPI) was empirically developed from the MMPI and is similar in that personality dimensions are scored and plotted to produce a personality profile. However, where the MMPI is keyed to detect psychopathology, the CPI describes normal personality patterns. Constructed between 1956 and 1960, the CPI consists of fifteen scales that measure such personality dimensions as achievement, dominance, responsibility, and sociability. Three validity scales measure test-taking attitudes. The test has 480 items that require a true or false answer. The item content is less distasteful to the respondent and has not evoked charges of invasion of privacy that were seen with reference to the original MMPI.

However, the CPI has not been extensively used in the screening and promotion of law enforcement, partly because the instrument has received mixed reviews (Sherman, 1979). Three main criticisms are associated with the test. First, it has so many scales that it provides too much data for a clinician to integrate effectively. Second, there are no suggested standards for interpreting CPI profiles and response patterns. Finally, several of the scales are repetitive, measuring similar personality characteristics.

Some researchers, though, have reported good success with the CPI (e.g., Spielberger, Spaulding, & Ward, 1978) and have suggested it should be considered for use in screening programs. Hogan (1971) examined the personality characteristics of three classes of police cadets and state police officers with one year's experience. Staff and supervisory ratings served as the criterion measures. Hogan cross-validated the concurrent "prediction" of the supervisory job-performance ratings with scores on the CPI and found that the CPI scales which related to intelligence, self-confidence, and sociability discriminated highly-rated officers from those less highly rated. Nevertheless, although the CPI may hold promise as a screening tool, there are too few supportive studies to recommend its widespread use.

The Interview

Most, if not the great majority, of law enforcement agencies use "oral boards" as part of the screening process. In the oral board, the candidate meets with a small number of interviewers (2–5) who ask questions. The questions often revolve around hypothetical scenarios. A candidate might be asked, for example, what he would do if he discovered that the driver of the car he just stopped for speeding was the son of the mayor of the city. Interviews, whether person-to-person or of an oral board nature, have not been found to be particularly valid devices for discriminating or predicting which candidates will become successful police officers (Stotland & Berberich, 1979; McDonough & Monahan, 1975; Landy, 1976). In fact, contrary to what would be expected in light of its widespread use, the interview is not a particularly helpful tool for making screening decisions, even outside law enforcement (Fisher, Epstein, & Harris, 1967; McKinney, 1973). Interviews probably test the potential compatibility of an employer and a prospective employee rather than subsequent job performance itself. Indeed, some researchers have suggested that, if it is to be used to screen police candidates, the interview should be considered a rapport builder and an educating medium for the candidate, rather than an evaluating device (McDonough & Monahan, 1975). Moreover, reliability between oral interviewers (the degree to which the interviewers agree with one another about an applicant's ability to succeed) is also poor (Stotland & Berberich, 1979). Despite these facts, oral examinations or interviews continue to be among the most commonly used police candidate selection methods. They are not, however, the *only* method of selection. In fact, the typical hiring process includes not only the oral board, but also the psychological evaluation, aptitude tests, a polygraph examination, and the background check. Thus, despite the lack of validity associated with interviews, there is some comfort in knowing that they are not used exclusively.

Recent research also emphasizes the need to consider differences in interviewers when assessing the validity of the interviewing process (Miner, 1992). Some interviewers seem to be better at predicting than others, and a few appear to have a very good record of identifying successful employees (Dreher, Ash, & Hancock, 1988). Furthermore, structured interviews can also enhance prediction if used properly. A structured interview is one in which questions are standardized and the responses are recorded in a systematic manner (Miner, 1992). The interviewer asks questions that have been shown to predict job performance and records the answers according to a standardized checklist. Structured interview procedures have been found to be twice as valid as unstructured interviews (Miner, 1992; Wiesner & Cronshaw, 1988; Wright, Lichtenfels, & Pursell, 1989). Thus, recent findings indicate that a carefully trained interviewer, following a valid structured interview format, may add to the predictive accuracy of screening and selection in law enforcement.

Conclusion

In the early 1970s two writers concluded that with few exceptions the quality of research pertaining to police selection was poor and of limited use (Kent & Eisenberg, 1972). The same conclusion, again with some exceptions, can be offered 30 years later. Predictive (as opposed to concurrent) and construct validation for police selection are desperately needed. Research examining officers already on the police force must be evaluated cautiously, for such concurrent studies ignore the potential and characteristics of applicants who dropped out because of the hurdles along the way. A theory to explain why given behaviors are predictive of good performance while others are predictive of unsatisfactory performance is also desirable.

It is clear that no one procedure or variable, by itself, is powerful enough to predict on-the-job performance. This includes the most commonly used instrument, the MMPI (now MMPI–2), although it has more support in the empirical literature than any other single test. Furthermore, the task of predicting successful police performance or even identifying some factors associated with it is complicated because police duties are multidimensional and highly variable from one agency to another. As a result, agencies often become discouraged and eschew predictive validation methodology, shifting to job-related validation. This last trend was noted by Kent and Eisenberg (1972) and continues today.

In selecting screening devices, police administrators should look for testing instruments that are able to predict the probabilities of success in law enforcement prior to entry. It is probably unrealistic to expect administrators to evaluate construct validity also, but the psychologist involved in the screening process should certainly be aware of it. The administrator should also be aware of probabilities—the number of "hits" an instrument is expected to make compared to "misses." The hits come into two categories: those that allow rejection of poor candidates (screening out) and those that allow the retention of good ones (screening in). Likewise, misses also come in two categories: (1) those that missed identifying poor candidates and (2) those that rejected potentially good candidates. When cost considerations are important, it is more critical that an instrument be able to identify as many poor candidates as possible, while still not rejecting a large number of potentially good candidates. There is no fast rule about which cut-off score to use in selection. This is an administrative decision that hinges upon the social, psychological, and material costs the agency is willing to risk.

Police Discretion

"Discretion involves the ability to act on the basis of personal judgment, uncontrolled by prearticulated rules of law" (Nimmer, 1977, p. 257). It is the central ingredient in the day-to-day activities of the law enforcement officer, who deals directly and frequently with the public. Because of their enormous discretionary powers, there is considerable variability among law enforcement officers in how they apply the law (Reiss, 1992). Moreover, these discretionary decisions are generally not seen by the public, but only by the law enforcement officers and the accused (Reiss, 1992).

Participants in the criminal justice process consider discretion both indispensable and impossible to eliminate. It is a reality at all levels of the system (Cole, 1992). The maxim "Squeeze out discretion here and it will emerge there" (Wilkins, 1979, p. 46) is widely accepted. "In practice, police officers encounter a variety of complex situations and must exercise their discretion to make decisions and rapid judgments based on their experience of what they consider appropriate rather than what is required by the logic of rules" (Bell, 2002, p. 15).

The discretionary behavior of law enforcement officers depends on a number of factors, including the ambiguity in the statutes and ordinances that police are charged with enforcing (Bell, 2002). This lack of precise clarity in many laws allows considerable discretionary powers by the police. Under these conditions, police use their discretions to achieve what they believe to be the "spirit of the law." The discretionary powers are also affected by the nature of the offense at issue. Generally speaking, the more serious the act the less latitude there is for discretionary action by the law enforcement officer (Gallagher, 1979). Although the official limits of an officer's actions appear to be strictly delineated, there is wide discretion in minor matters. Thus, the police have considerable discretion in handling such matters as moving traffic violations, *minor* juvenile offenses and family disturbances, exhibitionism, and drunkenness, but very little in handling homicides, aggravated assaults, rapes, or robberies.

Discretion is also influenced by community concerns. If the community places great pressure on law enforcement to eliminate prostitution in a given area of the city, or to keep intoxicated persons off the streets, the scope of discretionary behavior is somewhat narrowed. Other limiting factors are the officer's frame of mind at the time he or she investigates the offense and the perpetrator's reaction to the officer (Gallagher, 1979). If the officer has encountered recent personal difficulties, he or she may be less generous in handling minor violations. If the offender is hostile to the officer, an escalation effect may occur, where each challenging remark or action is met with increased action by the other party. In the juvenile context, for example, research has shown that officers are more likely to take into custody juveniles who either challenge their authority or are overly (and suspiciously) deferential (Whitehead & Lab, 1999).

Along with the factors already mentioned, law enforcement discretion is influenced by the feedback the officer receives from the legal system itself. That is, how will peers, supervisory personnel, the prosecuting attorney, the judge, and other agents of the system react to the discretionary behavior? As Saks and Miller (1979, p. 74) have noted, "It is the behavior of other actors in the system that regulates the behavior of any given actor, not the written law."

The prosecuting attorney's strategy in handling a case is often dictated by the anticipated behavior of the judge and defense. Judges make decisions that often serve as messages to the police and prosecutors about how to handle future cases. Prosecuting attorneys also give messages to the police about what will "go" in court and what is a legitimate case. Among these messages is one that excessive zeal in arresting and charging perpetrators of minor offenses will overload the system. Such behavior may also generate public outcry that police should "Catch the criminals and stop harassing the citizens." When traffic court dockets are full, an officer may issue a stern warning rather than a citation to appear in court. In some cases the capacity of the jails and prisons affects decisions made by first-line participants. An officer who knows the local jail is overcrowded may hesitate to arrest a belligerent reveler and detain him overnight.

An officer usually learns how to use discretion by modeling the more experienced officers within the agency. Heavy peer pressure about the "right way" to do things and handle incidents appears to be continually exerted, and excessive deviance from the norm is usually not tolerated. Unfortunately, the norm in some departments or among some working groups of officers may be legally inappropriate. The officer who uses discretion in an atypical way may be inviting occupational and social sanction from colleagues, occupational termination, or even prosecution. Alternately, his or her actions may be neutralized by the actions of others, like a supervisor or the prosecuting attorney.

Behavior that stays within the limits of the law enforcement officer's legally and departmentally defined role will be interpreted by outside observers as legitimate discretion (Saks & Miller, 1979), while behavior that exceeds these limits will be considered deviant. Therefore, discretion is partly based on the judgment of the individual, but also partly (perhaps even largely) based on the department's code of expected conduct. Experienced officers show the rookies strategies to use in handling incidents, and the rookies model the veterans. In many instances, the "war stories" of the veteran cop offset the training and strategies presented by the police academy; in most instances, instructors who are also well seasoned officers are given greater credibility than instructors who have not been "on-the-street." It is occupational socialization, therefore, which probably has the most influence on the development of discretion in police officers.

Police Discretion with the Mentally Disordered

One area that has received considerable research attention is police handling of incidents involving mentally-disordered individuals. As noted by Linda Teplin (2000, p. 9), "Police involvement with mentally ill persons is grounded in two common law principles: (1) The power and responsibility of the police to protect the safety and welfare of the public, and (2) *parens patriae*, which dictates protection for disabled citizens such as mentally ill persons." Recall that *parens patriae* (Latin for "parent of the country") is the legal doctrine which establishes the right of the government to take care of those individuals who cannot or will not take care of themselves. Although this legal doctrine legitimizes the police officer's power to intervene, it does not dictate the officer's response in any given situation. In short, the police officer must exercise considerable discretion in choosing the most appropriate action for dealing with persons who are emotionally disturbed. Unfortunately, there are not always clear, step-by-step departmental procedures or systematic training for how to deal with mentally disordered or irrational persons.

Officers who encounter a mentally disordered person creating a disturbance generally have three basic choices: (1) transport the person to a psychiatric facility; (2) arrest the person; or (3) resolve the matter on the spot (Teplin, 2000). In practice, these choices are limited. Transporting an irrational person is fraught with bureaucratic obstacles and the legal challenges of obtaining commitment or treatment (Teplin, 2000). In addition, not all psychiatric facilities will accept mentally-disordered persons considered dangerous to others, or those who have substance abuse problems. Arrest is often the only option available to the officer in situations where individuals do not appear to be disturbed enough to be accepted by a psychiatric facility, even on an emergency basis, but where the deviance is sufficient enough not to be ignored. This option is especially preferred in conditions where the person is unknown by the police, in contrast to the "neighborhood characters" whose idiosyncrasies are well known. However, the arrest approach is criticized by many mental health professionals who contend that arresting the mental disordered is essentially criminalizing mentally-disordered behavior. Teplin (2000) believes there is *some* validity to this contention. However, she points out that many mental health hospitals or psychiatric facilities do not accept many of the mentally disordered brought in by the police (usually because of drastic budget reductions), and the police are left in many cases with only the arrest option. "Consequently, jails and prisons may have become the long-term repository for people with mental disorders" (Teplin, 2000, p. 12). Recall that we discussed this issue in some detail in ◀ Chapter 10 and also referred in ◀ Chapter 3 to the creation of mental health courts, specifically intended to meet the needs of mentally-disordered defendants. The research on this issue finds that police try to avoid arrest or hospitalization whenever possible. Teplin (2000) found police tried to resolve the problem on the spot 72% of the time. This included defusing a crisis situation on their own or referring the individual to community services. They made an arrest 16% of the time and initiated emergency hospitalization 12% of the time.

Teplin recommends that police agencies provide their officers with adequate training in recognizing and handling mentally disordered citizens. In addition, police officers must have a clear set of procedures on how to handle such persons.

Police Use of Force

A little after midnight on March 3, 1991, Rodney Glen King was driving his Hyundai with two friends at a very high speed down a Los Angeles freeway, after drinking about 40 ounces of beer and watching a basketball game at a friend's home in suburban Los Angeles. A husband and wife team of the California Highway Patrol spotted the Hyundai and sped after him for nearly eight miles with flashing lights, sometimes at speeds of 117 miles/hour. King ignored the flashing lights, sped off an exit, and ran a red light, nearly causing an accident. King finally came to a stop near the entrance to Hansen Dam Park.

Almost immediately, the vehicle was surrounded by three Los Angeles police cars as a police helicopter hovered overhead. The police ordered the occupants out of the car, and they were told to lie face down. King's two companions complied, but King remained in the car. One of the police officers shouted at King to get out, which he reluctantly did. Still, the police perceived King as largely uncooperative in following the commands shouted to him by the officers. He was beaten into submission by three LAPD officers, while a police sergeant directed from nearby. King was hit with approximately 56 baton strokes, kicked in the head and body six times, and shot with a Taser electronic stun gun. Twenty-three other law enforcement officers were also present during the beating.

The commotion woke up a citizen who was sleeping in his apartment. He immediately began to videotape the incident from his apartment balcony, and the video was obtained by Los Angeles television station KTLA. Within days, the videotape depicting the three LAPD police officers brutally attacking Rodney King while other officers stood by was repeatedly shown by television stations around the world.

This incident raised nationwide concern about police abuse of citizens. In mid-March, a Los Angeles grand jury—after viewing the videotape and listening to testimony from King and others—returned indictments against the three officers and the sergeant who presumably directed the attack. They were charged in state court with assault with a deadly weapon. Attorneys for the four officers then requested the upcoming trial to be moved out of Los Angeles County. The trial judge denied the motion, but the California Court of Appeals unanimously overturned the judge's decision and granted the change of venue. The trial was moved to suburban Simi Valley, a conservative and largely white community. The resulting trial jury was white and politically conservative. King was black. After summation by attorneys, the jury debated the officers' fate for seven days. On April 29, 1992, the jury acquitted all four officers of assault with a deadly weapon. Almost immediately after the verdict, the five-day Los Angeles riot of 1992 erupted, resulting in death, widespread destruction and injury. Fifty-four people (mostly Latinos and Asians) were killed, 2,383 were injured (including 60 firefighters), and property damage was estimated to be between 700 million and one billion dollars. During the riot, over 13,000 people were arrested. There were also violent protests in several other cities across the country after the verdict.

The officers were subsequently tried again on federal criminal charges. Although many people believed this was an example of double jeopardy, it was not. In the state case, the officers were charged with assault; in the federal case, a different charge—depriving a citizen of his Constitutional rights during an arrest—was brought. Sergeant Stacey Koon and Officer Laurence Powell were convicted in April 1993 and sentenced to 30 months' imprisonment. Prior to the King incident, Powell, who was a training officer, had been the subject of several excessive force complaints and at least one civil lawsuit which cost the city $70,000 in a settlement after he broke a man's elbow with baton strikes.

We have discussed the King case in detail here because of its wide impact on law enforcement practices. The repeated showings of the videotape documenting the beating of King created a nationwide concern about excessive force by law enforcement. The Department of Justice called for research that would identify the nature, extent, and strategies for controlling the use of force by the nation's law enforcement personnel (Scrivner, 1994). It should be emphasized that the Department of Justice was not concerned about the use of reasonable, justifiable force, but rather at preventing the force that can be considered excessive.

Among other data gathering efforts, the National Institute of Justice (NIJ) (Adams et al., 1999) has released a report summarizing what is known about police use of force. The report, which included a review of literature from a wide range of social science as well as government sources, found that:

- Police use force infrequently.
- Police use of force typically occurs at the lower end of the force spectrum, involving grabbing, pushing or shoving.
- Use of force typically occurs when police are trying to make an arrest and the suspect is resisting.

Both the entertainment media and the news media highlight instances where force is used, leading to the public perception that this is typical procedure among police. The research does not support this perception, however. In 1996 the U.S. Census Bureau interviewed a national randomly-selected sample of 6,421 persons age 12 or older (Greenfeld, Langan, & Smith, 1997). Interviewers determined that 1,308 persons out of the total had face-to-face contact with the police during that year. Of those 1,308 persons, only 14 (less than 1%) said they were hit, pushed, choked, threatened with a flashlight, restrained by a police dog, threatened with or actually sprayed with chemical or pepper spray, threatened with a gun, or that they experienced some other form of force. Unfortunately, the small number of persons who were the subject of police force prevents a reliable comparison of police use of force experienced by black, white, or Latino respondents. These data do suggest, however, that the use of police force is a relatively rare phenomenon. Additional data from citizen complaint reports, use-of-force reports, and observational methods consistently indicate that only a small percentage of police-public interactions involve the use of force (Adams et al., 1999). As mentioned above, available data also indicate that most uses of force are at the lower end of the force spectrum, mostly grabbing. This finding is not a surprise, considering that police officers are trained to use force progressively along a continuum and the usual departmental policy requires that officers use the least amount of force necessary to accomplish their goals.

When the level of force exceeds the level considered justifiable under the circumstances, it is called excessive force, and it should not be tolerated. Excessive force is a deviant behavior either demonstrated by an individual officer or reflective of a pattern of practice within an entire department, precinct, or unit. A number of researchers have studied the use of force among officers, but few focus on excessive force. Bayley and Garofalo (1989) studied 36 particular instances of use of force (not excessive force) among police in New York City. They found that age, gender, and ethnicity of both the officers and the suspects were unrelated to these incidents.

In the National Institute of Justice study referred to above, psychologist Ellen Scrivner (1994) describes the role of police psychologists in the prevention and identification of individual police officers at risk for use of excessive force. She also discusses factors that contribute to police use of excessive force in performing their duties. Scrivner identifies five different officer profiles that are prone to excessive force complaints or charges. They are:

- Officers with personality disorders such as lack of empathy for others, and antisocial, narcissistic, and abusive tendencies.
- Officers with previous job-related experiences, such as involvement in justifiable police shootings.
- Officers who experienced early career stage problems having to do with their impressionability, impulsiveness, low tolerance for frustration, and general need for strong supervision.
- Officers who had a dominant, heavy-handed patrol style that is particularly sensitive to challenge and provocation.
- Officers who had personal problems such as separation, divorce, or perceived loss of status that caused extreme anxiety and destabilized job functioning.

Unfortunately, the Scrivner study focused only on the psychological profile of police officers, and very little discussion was directed at the properties of entire police organizations that may implicitly promote or condone excessive force within its ranks. That is, the organization may have an aggressive police policy that encourages confrontational tactics that increase the probability of violence from either the citizen or the officer. As Adams et al. (1999, p. 11) posit: "A major gap in our knowledge about excessive force by police concerns characteristics of police agencies that facilitate or impede this conduct." They add, "Many formal aspects of the organization—such as hiring criteria, recruit training, in-service programs, supervision of field officers, disciplinary mechanisms, operations of internal affairs, specialized units dealing with ethics and integrity, labor unions, and civilian oversight mechanisms—plausibly are related to the levels of officer misconduct" (p. 11). Clearly, the influence of the organization or agency on the behavior of its officers is a major factor that has yet to be studied in any systematic fashion. It is possible that each law enforcement agency can be placed on a continuum signifying the degree of aggressive policing it advocates in the community, especially in areas that have high crime rates. Moreover, violence-prone officers working within those organizations may represent the greater proportion of officers who use excessive force.

Fortunately, research data consistently indicate that a small minority of police officers generates a significant proportion of the citizen complaints of excessive force. An "early warning system," used by an increasing number of departments, can help identify problem officers early and intervene through counseling or training to correct problem behaviors (Walker, Alpert, & Kenney, 2001). **Early warning systems** are data-based management tools, usually consisting of three basic phases: (1) selection; (2) intervention; and (3) post-intervention monitoring. The criteria by which officers are selected vary from agency to agency, but usually include some threshold combination of citizen complaints, civil litigation, firearms-discharge or use-of-force reports, high-speed pursuits, and resisting-arrest incidents (Walker et al., 2001). Some early research on the effectiveness of early warning systems suggest that they are effective, especially if used in combination with department-wide attempts to raise standards of performance and improve the quality of police services.

Profiling: The Psychological Sketch

An infrequent but important task for the police psychologist is **profiling**, a task that requires sketching the significant psychological features of a person or persons who likely committed a crime. In some instances, the profile summarizes the psychological features of persons who *may* commit a crime, such as profiling passengers who may hijack a plane. After the terrorist attacks of September 11, 2001, and with the heightened threat of more terrorism, psychologists and behavioral scientists were asked to develop profiles that would help security personnel identify potential terrorists from the passenger lists (Armstrong & Pereia, 2001). However, profiling is not the major task of a vast majority of police psychologists, despite its popularity in the media. Moreover, some psychologists question this technique. In a nationwide survey of police psychologists, 70% did not feel comfortable profiling and seriously questioned its validity and usefulness (Bartol, 1996). Still, the topic is an important one for the police psychologist. We will cover criminal profiling, psychological autopsies, geographical profiling, and racial profiling in this section.

Criminal Profiling

Criminal profiling is the process of identifying personality traits, behavioral tendencies, geographical location, and demographic or biographical descriptors of an offender (or offenders) based on characteristics of a particular type of crime. In a sense, criminal profiling is a form of prediction. Based on a myriad of crime scene data and patterns, the profiler tries to "predict" who the offender or offenders might be, and where and how the next crime will occur. It should be emphasized, however, that profiling—even in its most sophisticated form—rarely can point directly to *the* person who committed the crime. Instead, the process helps develop a reasonable set of hypotheses for determining who *may* have been responsible for the crime. If done correctly, a profile will provide some statistical probabilities of the demographic, geographic, and psychological features of the offender. More importantly, it should eliminate large sectors of the population from further investigation. To a very large extent, the profiling process is dictated by a data base collected on previous offenders who have committed similar offenses.

Criminal profiling has been called many things, including offender profiling, psychological profiling, criminal personality profiling, or more technically "criminal investigative analysis," "crime scene analysis, or crime scene investigation." The last three terms are very broad, however, including a wide variety of investigative techniques that are not all psychological in orientation. Psychological profiling was used by the Office of Strategic Services (OSS) during World War II (Ault & Reese, 1980), but the technique pre-dated that era. Profiling has long been used in some capacity. Even the fictional detective Sherlock Holmes, first created by Sir Arthur Conan Doyle in 1887 in the story *A Study of Scarlet*, employed profiling in his always masterful search for the offender. Profiling has gained popularity in law enforcement circles since first used by the Federal Bureau of Investigation in 1971 (Pinizzotto & Finkel, 1990). In more recent years, profiling has fascinated the public as a result of films like *Silence of the Lambs* (Orion Pictures, 1990) and TV series like *CSI: Crime Scene Investigation, CSI: MIAMI*, or *Profiler* in the United States and *Cracker* in the UK. Despite this fascination and interest in these exciting portrayals of the search for the elusive criminal, the job opportunities in the field of criminal profiling are *extremely* limited, particularly with respect to psychological profiling. Many students express a strong desire to become profilers, but the actual need in law enforcement or public safety is minimal. Students interested in seeking a career in "criminal profiling" are likely to be very disappointed and discouraged. On the other hand, careers in the broader area of crime scene investigation are more realistic (once a person has gained considerable education and/or considerable experience in law enforcement).

Outside of sociological data describing the "average" offender within certain crime categories, scientific and systematic study on the reliability and validity of profiling is generally lacking and often very limited in practical usefulness. Contrary to popular belief, profiling is not restricted to serial murder or serial sexual assaults, but has considerable *potential* value when applied successfully to property crimes, including arson, burglary, shoplifting, robbery, and "white collar" crime (Canter & Allison, 1999, 2000). However, because of the limited research base available, its effectiveness in these areas has not yet been demonstrated.

To date experienced profilers assert that profiling is most successful when the offender demonstrates some form of psychopathology at the crime scene, such as sadistic torture, evisceration, post mortem slashings and cuttings, and other mutilations (Pinizzotto, 1984). Profiling appears to be particularly useful in sexual offenses, such as serial rape and serial sexual homicides (Pinizzotto & Finkel, 1990). This is because we have a more extensive research base on sexual offending than we do on other crimes. The Behavioral Science Unit of the FBI receives numerous requests for profiles from various law enforcement agencies, primarily for cases involving homicide (65%), rape (35%), or kidnapping (8%) (Pinizzotto, 1984). For example, in a homicide case the information gathered includes: (1) color photos of crime scene; (2) the nature of the neighborhood (economic and social data); (3) the medical examiner's report; (4) a map of victim's travels prior to the death; (5) complete investigative report of the incident; and (6) complete background of victim, including habits and life style.

Computer-based models of offender profiles based on extensive statistical data collected on similar offenses hold considerable promise. However, professional profilers often claim—like experienced clinicians—that accurate profiling must rely heavily on common sense, logic, intuition, and experience (Pinizzotto, 1984). It is " . . . an art developed through experience" (McCann, 1992, p. 479). However, profiling based on anything but a strong data base is likely to be plagued by many of the same biases, cognitive distortions, and inaccuracies so characteristic of clinical judgment in predictions of dangerousness. To date, there is very little research data on the utility, reliability, and validity of criminal profiling. Much needs to be done in this area before even tentative conclusions can be advanced.

BOX 14-1
Profilers Off Base on D.C. Snipers

"While alleged sniper John Allen Muhammad repeatedly confounded police attempts to catch him during three weeks of random murders, he also defied many criminal profilers' efforts to describe him" (Anderson, 2002, p. A4). Known as the D.C. serial sniper, Muhammad went on a three-week rampage of randomly shooting 13 persons in the Maryland, Virginia, and Washington, D.C. area, killing 10 and seriously wounding three others. A former Army sergeant and marksman, the 41-year-old did not fit the profile of notorious serial murderers in their physical, social, and behavioral characteristics, nor did his alleged partner in crime, 17-year-old John Malvo.

Profilers from across the country, many of them self-proclaimed experts, continually stated in media interviews that the sniper was very likely a white male, in his 30s, who worked alone, and perhaps had some weapons training in his background. He was likely employed but below his abilities, was from the immediate area because he could escape police detection so easily, and had a primary motivation to control and frighten the region to make up for his feelings of insignificance and inadequacy in his life. Nearly every one of these predictions was wrong. The suspect was an unemployed black man, working with a teenage boy, drifting across the country, apparently indiscriminately killing people and making frequent efforts to communicate with law enforcement through ransom notes and phone calls, while demanding 10 million dollars. The demand for money was especially baffling to a vast majority of "profilers" (Anderson, 2002).

Franklin Zimring, a law professor and criminologist at the University of California at Berkeley, had this to say about the many experts who came forth with their favorite theories on serial murder. "To the extent that people were self-announced experts on serial killers, there will be a brief interlude of humility before the spins are put on the facts in the case and the amendments are put on the theories . . . And then they'll emerge as able to explain everything again" (Anderson, 2002, p. A4).

During the serial sniper incidents in Maryland, Washington, DC, and Virginia over a three-week period in October, 2002, television news stations had profilers on the air who made predictions about the snipers that—in the end—were demonstrated to be blatantly wrong and misguided. ■ (see **Box 14-1**). Although some carefully tempered their comments, others were quite dogmatic in their assertions. This may have done a disservice to those profilers who are empirically based and more cautious in their assertions. The terrorist attacks on September 11, as well as suicide bombings in the Middle East, also have defied typical psychological profiles. Until that time, a typical hijacker or suicide bomber was believed to be a young, uneducated male loner, with few family ties. The September 11 hijackers were male, but they had ties, were older than predicted, and several were well educated. Likewise, in the Middle East, educated individuals—including women—have joined the ranks of suicide bombers.

The Psychological Autopsy

More recently, a similar attempt at reconstructing the personality profile and cognitive features (especially intentions) of *deceased* individuals has gained some popularity. This postmortem psychological analysis is called **reconstructive psychological evaluation** (RPE), **equivocal death analysis** (EDA) (Poythress, Otto, Darkes, & Starr, 1993), or, more commonly, **psychological autopsy** (Brent, 1989; Ebert, 1987; Selkin, 1987). The psychological autopsy was originally devised to assist certifying officials to clarify deaths that were initially ambiguous, uncertain or equivocal as to the mode of death (Shneidman, 1994). Today, the psychological autopsy is undertaken in an effort to make a reasonable determination of what was in the mind of the deceased person leading up to and at the time of death—often deaths that are or appear to be suicides. "It does this by looking at lifestyle, behavioral history, as well as the characterogical elements that contribute to that history: the degree of ambivalence, the clarity of cognitive functioning, the amount of organization or obsession, the state of turmoil or agitation, and the amount of psychic pain" (Shneidman, 1994, p. 76). The procedure consists largely of conducting interviews with family members and people who knew the decedent, the examination of personal documents (suicide notes, diaries, and letters), and other materials, such as the autopsy by the medical examiner, other medical reports, and police reports.

In the legal contexts, the psychological autopsy is frequently done to determine the reasons for the suicide and ultimately to establish some legal culpability by other persons or organizations. For example, in a civil suit for damages, the plaintiff (e.g., the victim's spouse) may wish to establish that the suicide was directly caused by some company policy or procedure.

Psychological autopsies differ from criminal profiling in two important ways: (1) the profile is constructed on a dead person; and (2) the identity of the person is already known. However, as noted in ◀ Chapter 1 ◙ (**Box 1-4**), the reliability and validity of the RPE and its variants (psychological autopsies) have yet to be demonstrated. Norman Poythress et al. (1993, p. 12) warn that " . . . persons who conduct reconstructive psychological evaluations should not assert categorical conclusions about the precise mental state or actions suspected of the actor at the time of his or her demise. The conclusions and inferences drawn in psychological reconstructions are, at best, informed speculations or theoretical formulations and should be labeled as such." Ault, Hazelwood, & Reboussin (1994, p. 73) agree, concluding that a psychological autopsy is an investigative technique that is ultimately "a professional opinion based on years of law enforcement experience with indirect assessment and violent death." Selkin (1994) points out that clear, definitive procedures for carrying out psychological autopsies have never been established, and investigators have a long way to go before standardized methods for conducting the psychological autopsy are established.

Geographical Profiling and Mental Mapping

One of the more interesting features of offending patterns is that they often occur or cluster within certain geographical areas, such as a specific area of a city. There are two major ways these crime patterns may be analyzed: geographical profiling and geographical mapping. **Geographical profiling** is concerned with analyzing the spatial movements of a *single* serial offender, whereas **geographical mapping** is concerned with analyzing the spatial patterns of crimes committed by numerous offenders over a period of time. In other words, geographical profiling takes an idiographic approach, whereas geographical mapping takes a nomothetic approach.

Geographic mapping of crime has had nearly 160 years of development and maturation (Dent, 2000). Geographical mapping of crime and delinquency were conducted in Europe at least as early as the first half of the 19th century. These early studies reported on crime distributions city by city or province by province, but they did not focus on areas and regions within a city. In the United States, Sophonisba Breckenridge and Edith Abbott of the Chicago School of Civics and Philanthropy published in 1912 a report illustrating the geographic distribution of juvenile delinquency within the city of Chicago (Bartol & Bartol, 1989). Breckenridge and Abbott used all the cases which came to the attention of the juvenile court of Cook County between the years 1899 and 1909 as their index of delinquency. They then constructed a map pinpointing the homes of the children and illustrating the fact that a disproportionately large number of the juvenile offenders were from impoverished areas of the city where housing was inadequate. Ernest Burgess and Robert Park, and later Clifford Shaw and Henry McKay adopted a similar methodology and launched what became known as the ecological approach to crime. With the advent of more sophisticated and thorough data collection and increasingly powerful computers and software, crime mapping continues to add valuable information about crime patterns. However, our focus on this section will be on geographical profiling.

In 1995, D. Kim Rossmo wrote a doctoral dissertation at Simon Frasier University's School of Criminology on a method of geographical profiling that has become an intriguing tool for serial offender identification. Rossmo, who became Detective Inspector in charge of the Vancouver Police Department's Geographic Profiling Section, developed a computer program, labeled "Criminal Geographic Targeting" or CGT, which is designed to analyze the spatial characteristics of an offender's crimes. The program is used to produce a topographic map that assigns probabilities to different areas for the location of the offender's residence or base of operations. The CGT takes into account known movement patterns, possible comfort zones, and hypothesized hunting patterns of a specific offender. According to Rossmo, the term "hunting patterns" may be divided into four descriptors: (1) hunter; (2) poacher; (3) troller; and (4) trapper. As noted by Rossmo, some offenders are geographically stable (stay in a certain region) and some are transient (travel around a lot). "Hunters are those criminals who specifically set out from their residence to look for victims, searching through the areas in their awareness space that they believe contain suitable targets" (Rossmo, 1997, p. 167). The crimes of the hunter are usually near the offender's place of residence or neighborhood, and, consequently, are geographically stable. Poachers, on the other hand, tend to be more transient, usually traveling some distance from their home area in search of their victims. Trollers refer to those offenders who are not specifically searching for victims but rather randomly encounter them during the course of some other routine activity. A trapper creates a situation to draw a victim to him. This strategy may be accomplished through entertaining suitors, placing want-ads, taking in boarders, or by assuming positions or occupations where potential victims come to them. Rossmo recommends that geographical profiling be combined with psychological profiling for maximum effectiveness in developing probabilities for offender identification. Furthermore, he warns that geographical profiling is essentially an investigative tool that does not necessarily solve crimes, but should help in the surveillance or monitoring of specific locations.

The value of geographical profiling lies on the assumption that *some* serial offenders commit crimes within the geographical area they know and feel comfortable in, sometimes near their own residence. All of us develop mental or cognitive maps of our familiar surroundings and residence, and offenders certainly do the same. Mental maps shape how we find our way around the environment, how we find our way home or the grocery store and help us make decisions about what we do and where. "Cognitive mapping is an abstraction that includes all cognitive abilities of a person that allow them to collect, organize, store, recall, and manipulate information about their spatial environments" (Turnbull, Hendrix, & Dent, 2000, p. 184). An important distinction is that *cognitive mapping* is a process undertaken by all individuals, whereas a *cognitive map* is a product constructed by professional profilers and police investigators. A cognitive map, based on the known spatial movements of the offender, is usually constructed so that surveillance in the identified areas will lead to the detection and arrest of the offender. Professor David Canter from the University of Liverpool's Centre for Investigative Psychology has pioneered much of the new research in to this emerging field.

Racial Profiling

During the late 1990s, racial profiling became a serious and very troubling issue in the United States. **Racial profiling** is defined as "police-initiated action that relies on the race, ethnicity, or national origin rather than the behavior of an individual as being, or having been, engaged in criminal activity" (Ramirez, McDevitt, & Farrell, 2000, p. 3). In other words, while police can use race or ethnicity to determine whether a person matches a specific description of a particular suspect, they may not use these characteristics in deciding whom to stop. Racial profiling became so well-known to the communities of color that they began to label the phenomenon "driving while black" or "driving while brown" (commonly abbreviated DWB), as a play on the legally recognized term DWI (driving while intoxicated). A Gallup Poll released in 1999 revealed that 72% of black men between the ages of 18 and 34 believed that they had been stopped by law enforcement while driving because of their race, compared to 6% of the white males from the same age bracket. For instance, young black men describe frequently being stopped for minor traffic violations, such as under-inflated tires, failure to signal properly before switching lanes, vehicle equipment failure (i.e., a plate light), or "speeding" less than 10 miles above the posted speed limit. During these stops, police officers have frequently asked to inspect the vehicle further, clearly with unveiled intentions of looking for drugs or other contraband, such as weapons. Critics of such "consent searches" maintain that—while legal—they are too often a form of police harassment. Many if not most drivers are too intimidated to refuse consent. Stops for such minor violations are relatively infrequent for young white males. Another common complaint is that police often stop people of color traveling through predominately white neighborhoods because the officers believe that they are "up to no good" and are probably engaging in criminal activity, such as burglary. Other forms of traveling—by bus, train, or plane—are also subject to racial profiling, particularly since the events of 9/11. (**Box 14-2** illustrates an everyday occurrence of racial profiling.)

One of the first cases involving the empirical evidence of racial profiling was *Wilkins v. Maryland State Police* (cited in Harris, 1999). The case was a class-action lawsuit against the Maryland State Police on behalf of Robert L. Wilkins and other African-Americans alleging discrimination. Wilkins was an African-American attorney who was stopped, detained, and searched by the MSP for no apparent reason. A survey, sponsored by the American Civil Liberties Union (ACLU) in that case, found that about 75% of the 5,354 speeders stopped by the Maryland State Police were white, and 17.5% were African American. However, 73% of those motorists searched were black, while only 20% of white motorists were searched.

The "war on drugs" during the 1970s and 1980s was the major impetus for developing the drug "courier profile." In 1985 when the war on drugs was at its prime, the Florida Department of Highway Safety and Motor Vehicles issued guidelines for law enforcement on identifying drug couriers. The guidelines encouraged officers to be suspicious of rental cars, drivers who are scrupulously obeying traffic laws, drivers wearing lots of gold jewelry,

BOX 14-2
Drinking Coffee While Black

A daily newspaper included in its "letters to the editor" in 2002 a letter from a reader expressing grave concerns about an incident in her community. According to the woman, an acquaintance of hers had stopped at a convenience store for coffee on his way to work. It was early in the morning, before 6 a.m. Because he was running a bit early, he chose to sit in his car in the store's parking lot, drinking his coffee and smoking a cigarette.

The clerk called police because the man—an African American who had lived in the area for two years—"looked suspicious." Police arrived and immediately asked him, "Where's your weapon?" They then proceeded to search the car to the extent that was legally allowed. No weapons were found. Police asked him where he was going, and on being told he was going to work, they asked him to produce the keys to his workplace, which he did.

The letter writer expressed dismay that this incident had occurred. "I have lived in this area all of my life and . . . I believe, as Abe Lincoln said, all men are created equal. . . . I know we are all scared these days, but is there a need for extremism? I think the police would be very busy if they questioned everyone who sits in their cars drinking their coffee and smoking a cigarette, don't you?"

drivers whose status does not "fit" the motor vehicle, and drivers who represent ethnic groups associated with the drug trade. The unsubstantiated conclusion of the various law enforcement agencies was that African Americans and Latinos were the principle participants in the drug trade business. In 1986, a racially biased drug courier profile was introduced by the Drug Enforcement Administration (DEA) to various law enforcement agencies across the nation. The profile was used extensively in their training methods for officers in "Operation Pipeline" (Harris, 1999). In 1999, a survey conducted by the San Diego California Police Department discovered that Latino and African-American drivers were far more likely to be stopped and searched than other drivers (Dvorak, 2000). Several surveys in New Jersey and New York reported similar results (Ramirez et al., 2000).

The drug-courier profile is also applied in airports, bus terminals, and train stations as well as the nation's highways. David Cole (1999, p. 47), in a hard-hitting indictment of racism in the criminal justice system, maintains that the drug courier profile "is a scattershot hodgepodge of traits and characteristics so expansive that it potentially justifies stopping anybody and everybody." Cole notes that federal law enforcement agents have asserted all of the following as traits indicating someone fit the profile: arrived late at night, arrived early in the morning, arrived in the afternoon; wore expensive clothes and gold jewelry, dressed casually; walked quickly through the airport, walked slowly, walked aimlessly. Cole includes many other examples in a list of seemingly all-inclusive traits.

International surveys indicate that racial profiling is not restricted to the United States. A 1998 study conducted by the British government's Home Office examined the racial and ethnic demographics of the stop-and-search patterns of police agencies in England and Wales. The study found that blacks were seven-and-one-half times more likely to be stopped and searched, and four times more likely to be arrested than whites (Ramirez et al., 2000). According to the 1999 UK census data, Britain is 93% white and 7% racial and ethnic minorities.

In summary, empirical research and survey data confirm the existence of racial profiling as a troubling social problem. Numerous states and the federal government have been prompted to gather data on police stops to determine the extent of the problem and where it is occurring. Some state courts are beginning to rule in favor of plaintiffs who allege they were subjected to selective enforcement on the basis of race or ethnicity. While African-Americans and Hispanics have been considered primary victims of racial profiling in the past, following September 11th and the 2003 war against Iraq the racial and ethnic and religious profiling of Arabs, Muslims, and South Asians may also become serious problems.

An issue closely related to racial profiling is that of selective prosecution of defendants in criminal court. In the 1990s, it became quite clear that a vast number of drug defendants prosecuted in federal courts are black Americans. Furthermore, blacks and other minorities were more likely to be prosecuted for possession and distribution of crack cocaine, while Caucasians were more likely to incur powdered cocaine charges. Penalties for crack are significantly higher (sometimes as high as 200% higher) than for powdered cocaine. According to a special report to Congress prepared by the United States Sentencing Commission (1995), it is undisputed that the brunt of elevated federal penalties falls heavily on blacks. Interestingly, 65% of persons who have used crack are white; yet in 1993 whites represented only 4% of the federal offenders convicted of trafficking in crack (U.S. Sentencing Commission Report, 1995). While some black defendants have attempted to make the argument that they were unfairly targeted for prosecution, the U.S. Supreme Court has made it very difficult for them to support this claim in federal courts ◙ (see **Box 14-3** for a discussion of *U.S. v. Armstrong* (1996)).

Psychological Stress in Law Enforcement

For several decades law enforcement work was believed to rank among the top of all occupations in the amount and variety of stress it promotes. But stress—and its accompanying arousal—is not only germane to law enforcement; it is also pertinent if we seek to evaluate eyewitness testimony and victim accounts of traumatic incidences. Also, any empirical study of criminal behavior requires major attention to stress and physiological arousal.

BOX 14-3
Selective Prosecution? *U.S. v. Armstrong*

Armstrong and his fellow respondents were indicted in U.S. District Court for the Central District of California on charges relating to the possession with intent to distribute crack cocaine, along with federal firearms offenses. Armstrong, who is black, maintained that he and the other respondents were singled out for prosecution because of their race. They sought access to government documents which, they maintained, would prove that prosecutors failed to prosecute similarly situated white individuals. In other words, suspected white cocaine users and dealers did not call forth the same prosecutorial zeal as the suspected black users and dealers did.

At the district court level, Armstrong submitted a variety of affidavits. In one, a paralegal stated that, in every one of the relevant drug cases closed by the federal public defender's office in 1991, the defendant was black. Another affidavit was submitted by a drug counselor, who stated that there were equal numbers of Caucasian and minority illegal drug users. Even evidence filed by the government indicated that black defendants were highly disproportionately represented in federal crack cocaine violations. The District Court granted the discovery motion, allowing the defendants to review the prosecutor's files. When the government refused to comply with the order, the court dismissed the case.

The government appealed the dismissal and lost its case before the Ninth Circuit Court of Appeals. According to that court, to support a claim of selective prosecution, "A defendant is not required to demonstrate that the government has failed to prosecute others who are similarly situated." The U.S. Supreme Court, however, disagreed. The Court ruled both that it *was* necessary to demonstrate that *and* that defendants were not entitled to prosecutor's files before they had provided some evidence to support their claim.

The Armstrong case revolves around technical issues relating to rules of procedure in the federal criminal courts that are not discussed here. The Court's final word, however, makes it very difficult for defendants to support a claim of selective prosecution in the federal courts.

David Cole (1999, p. 159) puts it very succinctly. "Criminal defendants making selective prosecution claims face a classic catch-22. To establish selective prosecution, a defendant must prove that the prosecutor singled him out for prosecution because of his race, and did not prosecute others engaged in the same conduct." The evidence of this, Cole notes, is in the prosecutor's keeping. Yet the defendant has no right to see the prosecutor's files until he can show some evidence of selective prosecution. "Thus, a defendant must provide evidence of selective prosecution before he gets any access to the documents and other evidence necessary to establish the claim. In the vast majority of cases, this is an insurmountable hurdle" (Cole, 1999, p. 159).

Although the focus will be on the stress faced by law enforcement officers, the principles outlined could be applied to all other actors in the legal system.

Definition

"Stress" was first used as an engineering term referring to any external force directed at a physical object (Lazarus, 1966). It was introduced into the life sciences in 1936 by endocrinologist Hans Selye (Appley & Trumbull, 1967), who became one of the world's leading researchers of biological stress. Selye directed most of his attention to effects of biological stress on the physiological and biochemical functions of the living organism. He defined stress as "the nonspecific response of the body to any demand" (Selye, 1976, p. 15). Thus, the bodily reaction is presumed to be generalized, with the whole body system as a unit engaged in reducing or eliminating "agents" which cause stress. The agents, which Selye called stressors, may be external to the organism (exogenous) or within the organism (endogenous), and they may develop from a virus, physical injury, or disease-causing agent.

For our purposes here, we will suggest that psychological stress occurs when a stimulus initiates a response which does not lead to greater perceived or actual control over the stimulus. The behavioral pattern of the person involved is relatively unique, but it typically involves sympathetic activity in the autonomic nervous system and a restriction in the range of cues which are used to guide behavior. In other words, stress as a response involves physiological arousal and a reduction in the ability to use environmental guides (Easterbrook, 1959). To keep the discussion short, we will focus attention briefly on the input-output factors and skip the behavioral strategies for coping, unless they relate directly to law enforcement.

The input elements are the stressors or the stimuli which a person considers stressful—the stimuli or events which are evaluated as threatening, frustrating, or conflicting. The output element is the person's reaction or response. In psychology, the most common response is called anxiety, a term often used interchangeably with stress reaction. Anxiety is an unpleasant emotional state marked by worry, fear, anger, apprehension, and muscular tension, and manifested in behavior. Thus, the anxious person may stammer or display other speech disturbances, may chain-smoke, display irritability, avoid a situation, or assume any number of other behavioral postures, all of which may be responses to stressors.

Occupational Stressors in Law Enforcement

Since the mid-1970s, considerable research interest has been directed at stress among males in metropolitan or urban law enforcement, often with the implicit assumption that law enforcement work is the most stressful of all occupations (Malloy & Mays, 1984). However, persons in many occupations may argue that they face more physical danger than law enforcement officers. Construction workers, miners, stunt pilots, firefighters, and demolition workers are all exposed to potential death and physical injury. Paramedics and other medical personnel, though less likely to be exposed to physical harm, contend that theirs is as stressful as any occupation. However, it is likely that few occupations encounter the variety of stressors (e.g., physical, psychological, social) as consistently as law enforcement work. The nature of the police officer's job is characterized by frequent encounters with danger, violence, and human misery, all of which are especially conducive to stress-related problems.

A number of studies have compared police work with other occupations on measures of health and social problems, such as disease, suicide, and divorce. Malloy and Mays (1984) carefully analyzed several studies often cited as good illustrations of the high personal costs of law enforcement. They concluded that these studies failed to demonstrate that police work is any more stressful than a number of other occupations. Terry (1985) has also observed that the issue of stress among law enforcement officers may be overstated. Furthermore, it is not clear to what extent the stressors listed by law enforcement officers affect their job performance. The literature in industrial/organizational psychology, however, clearly suggests that stress and job performance are inversely related; that is, the higher the stress, the lower the satisfactory job performance. For example, Miner (1992, p. 156) writes: "Performance—whether measured by supervisor ratings, organizational perceptions of effectiveness, or job performance on job-related examinations—has repeatedly been found to decrease with increasing levels of stress." To date, however, the police stress literature is lacking in assessments of the impact of stress on performance (Sewell, Ellison, & Hurrell, 1988; Malloy & Mays, 1984).

There are, however, some educated guesses about the nature of the relationships among law enforcement experience, stress, and job performance. These hunches may be placed into three major categories based on the relationship between job experience and job stress: (1) the positive linear hunch; (2) the curvilinear hunch; and (3) the negative linear hunch. Niederhoffer's research (1967) illustrates the positive linear hunch. He supposes that as law enforcement experience increases, self-reports of stress should correspondingly increase, provided the individual remains a patrol officer (as opposed to being promoted to administrator). According to Niederhoffer, therefore, we can expect job performance to decrease with experience. John Violanti (1983) represents the curvilinear hunch. He hypothesizes a curvilinear relationship between stress and experience, with stress increasing during the first 14 years of experience, decreasing after 14 to 20 years of experience (the personalization stage), and increasing again prior to retirement (after 20 to 25 years of experience). Following Violanti's position, we would predict an inverted U-shaped function, with job performance low and stress high in an officer's early years, performance at its best in the middle years when stress is low, and performance declining when stress increases toward the end of the officer's career. The negative linear hunch is represented by Ezra Stotland (Stotland, 1986, 1991; Stotland, Pendleton, & Schwartz, 1989), who predicts that as job experiences increases, job stress will decrease. Correspondingly, we would expect job performance to increase with experience.

Unfortunately, research examining these three relationships is sparse. Bartol (1991b) has reported on preliminary data on 869 small town officers followed over a 13-year period. The data suggest that job performance—as evaluated by supervisors—improves with experience, while both self-reported and supervisory-reported stress decreases. This tentative finding provides support for the negative linear hunch. On the other hand, Patterson (1992), using data from nearly 4,500 police, correctional, and probation/parole officers, found some curvilinearity for law enforcement and probation\parole officers, but not for correctional officers. When only first line officers were considered (in contrast to ranking officers), a linear pattern did emerge, with stress increasing as experience increased. This pattern suggests a positive linear hunch. It is obvious that much research needs to be conducted before we can disentangle these complex relationships.

Types of Police Stress

A common strategy employed in the police stress literature is to divide the stressors identified by urban or metropolitan police officers into four major categories: (1) organizational, (2) external, (3) task-related, and (4) personal (Kroes, Hurrell, & Margolis, 1974; Wexler & Logan, 1983). **Organizational stressors** generally refer to the policies and practices of the police department itself. They include poor pay, excessive paperwork, insufficient training, inadequate equipment, weekend duty, shift work, limited promotional opportunities, poor supervision and administrative support, and poor relationships with supervisors or colleagues. Several surveys have reported shift work as a major occupational stressor (Eisenberg, 1975; Hilton, 1973; Kroes, 1976; Margolis, 1973). Shift work not only interferes with sleep and eating habits, but also with family life. Moreover, irregular hours often preclude social get-togethers and family activities, a job characteristic that socially isolates the law enforcement officer even more. Also, the organizational structure of large police departments often promotes office politics, lack of effective consultation, nonparticipation in decision making, and restrictions on behavior (Cooper & Marshall, 1976).

Task-related stressors refer to the nature of police work, such as inactivity and boredom, situations requiring the use of force, responsibility of protecting others, the use of discretion, the fear that accompanies danger to oneself and colleagues, dealing with violent or aggressive individuals, making critical decisions, frequent exposure to death, continual exposure to people in pain or distress, and constant need to keep one's emotions under close control.

External stressors include frustration with the courts, the prosecutor's office, the criminal process, the correctional system, the media, and public attitudes. For example, for every 100 felony arrests, 43 are typically dimissed or not prosecuted (Witkin, 1990). Moreover, many law enforcement officers feel court appearances are excessively time consuming, and they are often frustrated over judicial procedures, inefficiency, and court decisions. It has also been suggested that one of the predominant stressors confronting law enforcement officers is alienation (Niederhoffer, 1967). Jirak (1975) found that alienation due to perceived lack of support from political groups, the press, courts, and the public was a dominant stressor for New York City law enforcement. He also found that feelings of alienation usually increased throughout an officer's career, reaching a peak about the 15th year of service, at which point they decreased, apparently due to anticipated retirement. This trend was also reported by Lotz and Regoli (1977). Law enforcement-community relations are presumed to be important contributing factors to feelings of alienation (Skolnick, 1973). In a survey study by Chappell and Meyer (1975), only 2% of U.S. police officers polled believed the public held them in high esteem. Related to this is the often reported role conflict between what law enforcement officers think they should be doing (e.g., crime detection and arrest) and what the public believes they should be doing (e.g., protecting citizens, settling family disputes, chasing unleashed dogs) (Wilson, 1968). It would be expected that officers in departments moving toward the community policing approach discussed earlier in the chapter would exhibit less stress than officers in more traditional departments. To our knowledge, research has not yet explored this possible connection.

Personal stressors involve marital relationships, health problems, addictions, peer group pressures, feelings of helplessness and depression, and lack of achievement. In a survey conducted by Kroes, Hurrell, and Margolis, (1974), 79 of the 81 married police officers interviewed felt that the nature of their work had an adverse effect on their home life. More specifically, the officers thought that police work gave a negative public image to their family, that their spouses worried regularly about their safety, that they took the tremendous pressures of the job home, that their job made them less able to plan social events, and that the job inhibited nonpolice friendships. A survey of 100 police spouses—all women—(Rafky, 1974) revealed that nearly one-fourth were dissatisfied with their husbands' careers and that particular aspects of the job resulted in frequent family arguments.

Although criminal justice literature frequently mentions exceedingly high divorce rates and general marital unhappiness among law enforcement officers, documentation is very difficult to obtain. One extensive study by the National Institute of Occupational Safety and Health (NIOSH), however, does reveal some evidence that the divorce rate is high for law enforcement officers and that marital problems are a chief reason for leaving the force. The NIOSH study (cited by Blackmore, 1978) polled 2,300 officers in 29 departments around the United States and found that 22% of the law enforcement officers in the sample had been divorced at least once (compared to a national divorce rate of 13.8% among urban white males (1970 census)). The NIOSH study also revealed a 26% divorce rate for officers married before joining the force, compared to an 11% rate for those who married after joining. Officers also reported that marital problems are the prime cause of resigning from the force before retirement.

Hageman (1978) found evidence that as length of service increases, marital unhappiness and discontent also increase. Because no comparison was made with marriages in the general population, it is not clear whether the increasing disenchantment was directly due to length of service. However, the study did report that the increasing "emotional detachment" of the officer was one of the primary factors in marital conflict.

Kroes et al. (1974), using semi-structured interviews, found that perceived sources of stress for Cincinnati male police officers were largely organizational in nature. Task-related stressors did not emerge as a major source of stress, contrary to what is commonly supposed (e.g., Somodevilla, 1978). In one of the few studies examining stress in smaller departments, Crank and Caldero (1991) investigated self-reported stress in eight medium-sized Illinois municipal police departments ranging in size from 40 to 100 sworn full-time officers. The researchers passed out a questionnaire to officers present at roll-call for all shifts. Their study focused on one item in the questionnaire requesting officers to write a statement "about what you think is your greatest source of stress, and why" (p. 341). Only six of the 162 officers were identified as women, precluding a meaningful comparison by gender. More than two-thirds (68.3%) of the respondents perceived the organization as their principal source of stress, reflected particularly in problems with superior officers (usually their immediate supervisors). The second most frequent stress source identified was task-related (16.2%), followed by the court system, an external source (7.2%). Level of stress intensity was not measured.

Stressors of Small-Town Law Enforcement

Whether the stresses faced by small-town police officers (communities with a population of less than

50,000 and away from an urban sprawl) are similar to metropolitan or urban police remains an unanswered question. Informal discussions with rural officers in Maine (Sandy & Devine, 1978) suggested that there may be four stressors unique to small-town or rural patrol. Three are task-related: security, working conditions, and inactivity. The fourth, social, is external. Security stress factors center around the extreme sense of isolation experienced by officers confronting incidents in the field, including domestic disturbances. Rural and small-town officers usually work alone, without readily available backup. Moreover, contributing to perceived lack of security is the belief that a majority of homes in rural areas contain a collection of firearms purchased either for protection, hunting, or both. Stressful working conditions include the small salary and marginal benefits, and inadequate equipment and resources. Finally, inactivity and boredom can be significant stressors. Sitting alone in a cruiser at night while a small, isolated town closes down can be stressful. Social stressors in the rural context refer to the lack of anonymity experienced by officers, both on and off patrol. Like those of other residents of a small community, the habits and behaviors of law enforcement officers are open to public scrutiny. Moreover, the rural officer may be reminded "who's paying your salary." Officers frequently refer to this phenomenon as the "fishbowl effect." Also, according to Sandy and Devine (1978), a majority of small-town and rural officers have been born and raised within the community. Enforcing the law against people they have known all of their lives often produces dilemmas that may be highly stressful.

Gender Differences

Women entering the male-dominated occupation of law enforcement may face an array of stressors not usually experienced by men (Yarmey, 1990), including sexual harassment, negative attitudes of male officers and supervisors, working as the sole female officer, and lack of role models. Wexler and Logan (1983) interviewed 25 women patrol officers in a large metropolitan police department in Northern California. They found that the officers mentioned organizational stressors and stressors associated with being women in male-dominated departments most often during interviews. Inadequate training, rumors about them within the department, and lack of promotional opportunities were the organizational stressors mentioned most frequently. Negative attitudes of the male officers, lack of role models, and group blame (one poorly–performing woman officer prompts men officers and the general public to generalize to all women officers) were the second group of stressors mentioned repeatedly. These findings prompted Wexler and Logan to add a fifth category of stressors called "female-related stressors" to those previously identified in the literature. The Wexler and Logan study did not include a control group of male officers and did not measure the intensity of the perceived stress.

Another study examining the stress experienced by female officers was conducted by Pendergrass and Ostrove (1984). They conducted a department-wide survey of police employees (sworn officers, police technicians, and civilians) on perceptions of stress in police work and its health consequences. The study focused on both self-reported physiological consequences and psychological/behavioral consequences of stress. However, the researchers, because of the "high disparate group numbers," did not statistically analyze the data, but simply listed mean scores. Therefore, it is difficult to determine whether there were actual gender differences in the officers as a result of stress.

While sources of stress are often reported in the police literature, stressor intensity is often ignored. Officers are asked to say what stresses them, but not to indicate the level of stress they experience. Therefore, it is seldom clear whether their lists represent common complaints of people performing a difficult job, or whether their lists represent serious threats to health, social adjustment, job performance, longevity, or mortality (thoughts or attempts at suicide). Post-shift interaction among officers often resonate with complaints about the absurdities of the day with the courts, supervisors, the public, and the media. We can surmise that generalized complaints reach the status of serious stressors, however, when officer performance is adversely affected.

Malloy and Mays (1984) assert that longitudinal studies are necessary if the research on police stress is to progress to a more sophisticated level. They suggest that there may be an as yet unidentifiable personality feature that might forecast stress problems at the time of entry into police work. Malloy and Mays urge researchers to adopt the Davidson and Neale (1982) model, termed the Diathesis-Stress paradigm. Diathesis refers to a personality or constitutional predisposition that, under certain environmental conditions, is most susceptible to stress-related problems.

A study conducted by Bartol and his colleagues (1992) examined the stressors and problems faced by officers in small-town municipal law enforcement. The study examined: (1) whether female and male officers in the same department experience the same stressors; (2) how stressors affect performance; and (3) whether there are identifiable predictors of susceptibility to police-related stress. Performance was measured by supervisory evaluations of 11 behaviors believed to be critical for adequate performance in small-town or rural law enforcement. Stress was measured both by observations of supervisors and the self-report of the officers themselves. Predisposition susceptibility to stress (diathesis variables) was measured by MMPI scores obtained at the time of initial screening, prior to any law enforcement experience.

The results revealed that external stressors emerged as the category that small-town police officers, both men and women, found the most stressful, followed closely by organizational stressors. Based on written comments of the officers, the "liberal" attitude of the courts, dealing with the prosecutors who are "always playing let's make a deal," and "constantly being in the public eye" (the fishbowl effect) were among the leading specific external stressors. Specific organizational stressors included the constant politics within the department, lack of recognition for good work, inadequate retirement plans, insufficient personnel to do the job effectively, and colleagues not carrying their fair share of the load. The perceived stress caused by the job itself (task-related) was significantly less than external or organizational stress, a finding also reported by Crank and Caldero (1991) for medium-size police departments in Illinois.

Interestingly, the Bartol study found that women and men experienced the same stressors, to a large extent. The one exception was for task-related stress, with female officers finding more stress in this area than male officers. Nevertheless, this higher level stress reported by female officers did not translate into poor performance. This finding suggests that women may be more sensitive and empathetic in their policing than their male counterparts. Women indicated they are strongly affected by the tragedy, pain, and death they encounter in police work. In fact, five female officers noted that frequently encountering abused and sometimes dead children was one of the most stressful aspects of the job. A similar finding was reported in the Wexler and Logan (1983) study. Female officers also reported more stress than their male counterparts as a result of the sense of responsibility they have for the lives and safety of the public as well as for the safety of their police colleagues.

Little is known, also, about how male police administrators view female officers (Weisheit & Mahan, 1988). In small-town law enforcement, this is a critical variable because the chain-of-command is direct and uncomplicated. We also know very little about how small-town policewomen view their supervisors.

Police administrators report their own unique occupational stressors. Being "the person-in-the-middle" in the organizational structure is apparently a major problem (Kroes, Hurrell & Margolis, 1974). The administrator is responsible for his or her own actions and for the conduct and efficiency of subordinates. The responsibility is both to the community and to upper police echelons.

In light of the above data, it is not surprising that police departments are increasingly hiring full-time police psychologists or psychological, counseling, or psychiatric consultants who are available not only to consult on cases but also to offer their services to individual officers. Delprino and Bahn (1988) reported that 53% of police agencies studied used counseling services for job-related stress. About one-third of these agencies also hired psychologists to provide relevant workshops and seminars. In addition, many family support groups are appearing throughout the country, frequently at the instigation of police spouses who band together to discuss and solve common problems (Brandreth, 1978).

Environmental Stressors

With the exception of extreme and sudden life-threatening situations, it is reasonable to assume that no stimulus is a stressor to all individuals exposed to it (Appley & Trumbull, 1967). Whether stress develops depends greatly on how the person perceives and appraises the stimulus, in combination with other personality variables. Therefore, the above occupational conditions are not invariably stressors for all law enforcement personnel. Also, the same individual may enter into a stress condition in response to one presumably stressful situation and not to another. Accordingly, a great variety of different environmental conditions are capable of producing stress.

For example, Stotland (1991) makes a connection between workload and stress. He divides law enforcement careers into two categories, depending on the amount of fast-moving action they experience on a daily basis. Those officers who are exposed daily to shootings, crime, drugs, and violent incidents are called high workload officers. Contrary to what might be expected, these individuals maintain a steady level of job performance (neither going up or down to any great extent) and remain largely unaffected by police department politics or elevations. Low workload officers are exposed to much less violent and high-paced incidents, but may experience more stress. They serve the community by engaging in more ordinary tasks, such as we would find in small, low-crime communities. However, such concerns as their appearance and courtesy with the public is important both to them and the department, and their performance is highly influenced by supervisory evaluations. Therefore, they strive to increase their performance throughout much of their careers. High workload officers, on the other hand, are more concerned with "doing their thing" and striving toward doing a good job in their own eyes rather in the eyes of the supervisor sitting behind the desk.

When Adaptation Fails

In this section, we will consider some of the more common maladaptive patterns especially related to law enforcement personnel. The reader should be forewarned that law enforcement is one of the most difficult professions about which to gather information regarding failures to adapt. Unfortunately, most of the data are based on anecdotal or incomplete clinical or agency information. This procedural information is valuable, but it should be balanced with validation evidence in the form of experimental studies, which are to this point lacking.

Alcoholism

It has been reported by various sources, but not confirmed, that approximately 20 to 25% of law enforcement officers have a serious alcohol abuse problem (Hurrell & Kroes, 1975; Somodevilla, 1978). Furthermore, alcohol abuse appears to be more common in the older, more experienced law enforcement officers, over age 40, with 15 to 20 years of service (Unikovic & Brown, 1978). Although some police departments would concur with these statistics, many others would deny them. Some preliminary data reported by Pendergrass and Ostrove (1984) suggests that law enforcement officers may be heavier consumers of alcohol than the general population. The drinking problems appear to get worse during retirement (Violanti, 1992).

We have little evidence of the extent of substance abuse other than alcohol, however. In light of recent concerns relating to law enforcement officers and the temptations placed in their paths by drug traffickers, abuse of illegal substances would not be surprising. However, much work needs to be done before conclusions can be advanced in either this or the alcohol abuse issue.

Burnout

Burnout is a common phenomenon within the helping professions as well as those which both help and control, such as law enforcement, the judiciary, and juvenile and adult corrections. Burnout was first identified and defined in this way by Herbert Freudenberger (1974): " . . . to fail, wear out, or become exhausted by making excessive demands on energy, strength, or resources" (p. 159). Burned-out individuals feel emotionally drained or exhausted, depressed, and exhibit irritability and negative, cynical attitudes toward people they work with. They feel unhappy about themselves and are dissatisfied with their accomplishments on the job. Eventually, burnout may lead to increased tardiness, absenteeism, and a reduction in job performance. The scale most commonly employed to measure burnout is the Human Service Inventory (formerly the Maslach Burnout Inventory) (Maslach & Jackson, 1981).

Burnout appears to develop through three stages. In the first, emotional exhaustion, the individual has little energy or verve left for the job. The second stage, depersonalization, is characterized by a cynical, insensitive attitude toward others. Burned-out professors become cynical and negative toward students; burned-out social workers become distrustful and insensitive toward clients; burned-out nurses feel unappreciated by physicians, patients, supervisors, and the organization; and burned-out law enforcement officers become cynical and noncaring toward the public. The third phase is marked by feelings of low personal accomplishment, where the individual begins to feel that rewards and achievement no longer accompany the job. Because the person no longer thinks that what he or she does really makes a difference in the scheme of things, the person stops trying.

Post-shooting Traumatic Reactions

This syndrome (PSTR) represents a collection of psychological reactions that occurs after a law enforcement officer shoots someone in the line of duty. The pattern is especially apparent when the victim dies. Although the victim may be someone who was suspected of a crime and was about to be arrested, this is not necessarily the case. In a highly-publicized shooting in New York in 1999, police shot a Haitian immigrant, Amidou D'Allou, whom they sought to question because he fit the description of a criminal suspect. D'Allou—who had little knowledge of the English language—apparently reached for his wallet to remove his "green card"—proof of being in the country legally. Police believed he was reaching for a gun and shot him 41 times. The incident was highly publicized across the country.

Such tragic events do not occur only in large, urban areas. Police in a small, northeast community were called to a church, where a man was said to be brandishing a knife and talking incoherently to the assembled congregation. Upon entering the church, officers approached the individual, asked him to drop the knife, and soon after shot him to death. Officers indicated that the man posed a serious threat because the knife he held was a deadly weapon. The incident was investigated by the state attorney general's office and the officers were cleared of wrongdoing, but it had a devastating effect on the town and its confidence in its police force. While many residents supported the police and saw the shooting as tragic but necessary, others believed the police acted precipitously and unjustifiably.

Fortunately, most law enforcement officers complete their career without ever firing a weapon in the line of duty. Still, in the U.S., about 3,600 individuals are shot at annually by law enforcement officers (More, 1992). Of that total, 600 are killed, 1,200 are wounded, and 1,800 are shot at but missed (More, 1992). Although a widely recognized phenomenon, PSTR has not been subjected to well-executed empirical research. As Zeling (1986, p. 410) writes, "The study of post shooting trauma is illustrative of a concept in police psychology that is widely accepted yet has little empirical support."

Solomon and Horn (1986) conducted a self-report survey of 86 law enforcement officers who had been involved in a shooting and found some common psychological effects both during and after the shooting incident. One of the strongest psychological phenomena that occurred during the incident was perceptual distortion, divided into three categories. Eighty-three percent of the officers experienced time distortion during the shooting. Most of them said that time seemed to slow down to a point where everything was happening in slow motion. One officer remembered thinking, "How come I'm moving so slowly?" On the other hand, a minority of officers thought everything speeded up during the event. Fifty-six percent of the officers reported visual distortions, and 63% experienced auditory distortions. The most frequent visual distortion was "tunnel vision," where the officer became so focused on one object that everything else at the scene went unnoticed. This phenomenon is frequently experienced by victims of a terrifying event as well. Some officers reported seeing everything more intensely and in greater detail than normal. Common auditory distortions included not hearing sounds (such as the shots fired), or hearing them less or more intensely.

Following the incident, officers experienced a number of reactions. The five most common were a heightened sense of danger, anger, sleep difficulties, isolation/withdrawal, and flashbacks. Officers who were shot or observed other officers get shot often lost their sense of invincibility and began to perceive their job as more dangerous than they originally thought. Anger at the victim of the shooting, at the department, at colleagues, or at society in general for having to shoot someone was the second most frequent reaction. Officers had difficulty both falling asleep and staying asleep because of thoughts of the episode. Many of the officers also needed to withdraw for a while to get their thoughts together and to work through what happened. The fifth common reaction was the reoccurrence of thoughts of the scene intruding into the officer's daily life.

Solomon and Horn found that reactions varied widely in intensity. About 37% of the officers described their reactions as mild, 35% as moderate, and 28% as severe. The intensity of these reactions are similar to those reported by Stratton, Parker and Snabbe (1984). The researchers (Solomon & Horn, 1986; Stratton et al., 1984) also agree that the intensity of the reaction depends partly on the perceived "fairness" of the shooting incident. "Being outnumbered, having a limited field of fire due to bystanders, going against a shotgun when armed with a revolver, and having to shoot someone who points an unloaded weapon (unknown to the officers), are examples of factors affecting the 'fairness' of the situation" (Solomon & Horn, 1986, p. 390).

Other clinicians have reported a variety of symptoms or reactions to PSTR but their observations are based on cases they encounter during their work as police psychologists. Systematic research with carefully designed methodology is badly needed in this area.

Suicide

The ultimate behavioral manifestation of depression is suicide. Although other factors can lead to suicide (e.g., terminal illness, killing oneself for a cause), the bulk of suicide in the general population appears to be precipitated by feelings of hopelessness and helplessness (Bedrosian & Beck, 1979). Statistics in this area are misleading, because it is often difficult to tell whether a person's death was suicidal or accidental. For example, car accidents and drownings are sometimes suspected to be self-induced, but the theory is impossible to prove. There are probably many suicide attempts that are thwarted by relatives or friends and that go unreported. About 30,000 official suicidal deaths are reported per year in the U.S. (about 12.8 out of every 100,000 inhabitants) (Durand & Barlow, 2000). Because of the likely under-reporting, however, the actual number is believed to be between 50,000 and 100,000 (Comer, 1992; Rosenhan & Seligman, 1984). It is also estimated that about 600,000 persons in the U.S. and more than 2 million people throughout the world attempt to kill themselves each year, a phenomenon known as parasuicide (Comer, 1992). When successful suicide rates are examined, the following facts emerge:

- The male rate is four to five times greater than the female (Durand & Barlow, 2000; McIntosh, 1991). However, women make about three times as many suicide attempts as men.
- Men commonly kill themselves by violent and lethal means, especially with firearms (Durand & Barlow, 2000). Women most commonly use less violent options, such as drug overdoses (Gallagher-Thompson & Osgood, 1997).
- The suicide rate for whites in the U.S. is twice as high as that of African-American or Latino groups (Comer, 1992; Durand & Barlow, 2000).
- The suicide rate for adolescent males and young adult men (ages 18 to 24) in the United States is now the highest in the world (Durand & Barlow, 2000).

When we narrow the statistics to police suicide we find that data are extremely difficult to obtain. To date, fewer than a dozen published studies are available. Kroes (1976) suggested that many departments fail to report police suicides because of the stigma (the blot on the police image). Survivors do not report them because of possible loss of insurance benefits. There are frequent assertions in the literature that the actual rate is two to six times higher than the rate for other occupations (Stratton, 1978; Blackmore, 1978; Somodevilla, 1978), and some perceive the suicide rates of police officers to be an "epidemic in blue" (Violanti, 1996). However, careful analysis of the data suggest otherwise. Michael Aamodt and Nicole Stalnaker (2001) conclude from their analysis of nationwide data that the suicide rate among police officers is not only different from the general population, but may actually be substantially lower (by 26%). Aamodt and Stalnaker point out that the incident reports usually compare police suicide rates to the rates of the general population. However, if researchers and analysts would compare the police suicide rate to the rates found in the segment of the population that is comparable to police officer gender, age, and race, they would find that the police suicide incidence is significantly lower.

Reasons for police suicide appear to be multiple, including depression, relationship difficulties, internal investigations, financial difficulties, and easy access to weapons (Herndon, 2001). The overwhelming reason for police suicide appears to be marital or intimate partner relationship difficulties, followed by legal problems and internal investigations (Aamodt & Stalnaker, 2001).

If suicide rates for law enforcement personnel are indeed lower than found in the general population, this may be due to a number of factors, such as a more sophisticated screening procedure and rigorous evaluation at times of hiring, increased use of stress-awareness training, greater use of psychological or psychiatric consultants in police departments, and better police training, enabling officers to feel more competent at their jobs. On the other hand, data that show lower suicide rates among officers may be due to the resistance of departments and families to report the death as a suicide. In any event, considerably more systematic research into the overall incidence and reasons for police suicide are needed.

Special Issues

Suicide by Cop

In the 1990s, researchers became aware of another type of suicide associated with law enforcement, one in which the suicide victim literally "used" the police officer to achieve his own death. **Suicide by cop**, generally abbreviated SbC, refers to "incidents in which individuals, bent on self-destruction, engage in life-threatening and criminal behavior to force the police to kill them" (Geberth, 1993, p. 105). Thomas Monahan (2001, p. 638) defines the phenomenon similarly, "SbC occurs when an individual bent on self-destruction opts to provoke a deadly force reaction from a law enforcement officer rather than commit suicide by his or her own hand." The terms "victim-precipitated homicide" and "victim-assisted homicide" are also used in the research literature. In its classic sense, however, "victim-precipitated homicide" refers to situations in which the person who was killed took the first step toward violence, without intending to be killed. Thus, the aggressor who ends up being killed because his intended victim acted in self-defense is the classic "victim" of victim-precipitated homicide, a term coined by the sociologist Marvin Wolfgang (1958).

According to some experts, approximately 10% of all police deadly force incidents are a result of SbC situations (Homant & Kennedy, 2001; Lord, 2000; Scoville, 1998). Some data suggest it may be even higher, approximating 25% (Oyster, 2001). Although the diagnosis is usually not known by the police, many of the SbC victims have a history of mental disorders, usually schizophrenia or depression (Lord, 2000). A considerable amount of research needs to be done in this area, however, before firm conclusions can be advanced. A large number of SbC victims are also under the influence of either alcohol or hard drugs, such as cocaine, at the time of incident. A majority possessed either a gun (73.4%) or knife (21.9%) at the time of the incident (Lord, 2000). In most instances, the SbC subjects, by statements or actions, clearly indicate their intentions to die at the hands of the police. For example, SbC subjects refuse to drop the weapon (because to do so would cause an immediate de-escalation of the incident and interrupt the suicide process) and then often approach the officer in a threatening manner (Lindsay, 2001). Even so, we cannot assume that the individual is asking to be killed. On the other hand, some victims will directly, verbally express a desire to be killed by the police (Van Zandt, 1993). Not surprisingly, SbC victims with guns were more likely to be fatally shot by officers (93.3%) than those with knives (Lord, 2000). Most SbC subjects have no criminal record, but those who do most often have a record of domestic violence or drug-related offenses. Those subjects who did not reside in the area long and are unknown by the police are more likely to be successful in their attempt to have the police kill them than long-term residents whom the police know (Lord, 2000).

The psychological reactions of the officers who do fatally shoot SbC individuals are multiple, but many experience disbelief. For several weeks after the incident, most officers report sleep disturbances, chronic replaying of the incident, and second-guessing of their actions (Prial, 2001). Many officers relive the experience in their mind in excruciating, vivid detail (Prial, 2001). Some officers express anger at the victim for using them as an instrument of death, some referring to the victim as acting cowardly and irresponsibly. Interestingly, Elizabeth Prial (2001, p. 675, Attachment A) included in her article a letter from a SbC victim. The letter was addressed: "To the Officer that shot me!" and read:

> Officer,
> It was a plan. I'm sorry to get you involved. I just needed to die. Please send my letters and break the news slowly to my family and let them know I had to do this. And that I love them very much. I'm sorry for getting you involved. Please remember that this was all my doing, You had no way of knowing.

Fitness-for-Duty Evaluations

Police officers who witness an especially disturbing event, such as deaths of children or catastrophes involving fellow officers may exhibit intense emotional or psychological reactions. In some cases, evaluations are needed to determine whether the officer has the mental and psychological stability to continue as an effective officer on the street, at least for the foreseeable future. Some departments require evaluations as standard procedure after a shooting incident or at any time the officer demonstrates problematic behavior. Frequent complaints from the public, including complaints of excessive force, will often initiate an evaluation. The assessment is called a **fitness-for-duty evaluation** (FFDE), and it is highly recommended that it be done by a qualified mental health professional, usually a licensed psychologist.

It is usually recommended that psychologists conducting the FFDE employ a variety of methods in their assessments, including psychological tests and a standard clinical interview that assesses mental status as well as obtaining background information. The evaluations must be done with the informed consent of the officer, of course, but the examiner is under no obligation to explain the results to the officer. On the other hand, "the agency is not entitled to any more psychological information regarding an employee than is necessary to document the presence or absence of job-related personality traits, characteristics, disorders, propensities, or conditions that would interfere with the performance of essential job functions" (International Association of Chiefs of Police, 2002). Knowing exactly how information from an FFDE may be used is critical. In one case, a psychologist exercised his "duty to warn" when an officer threatened superiors during an FFDE. The officer was demoted, subsequently sued the psychologist, and won (Cohen, 2003).

Hostage Taking Incidents

The hostage taker holds victims against their will and uses them to obtain material gain or personal advantage. Typically, the offender threatens to take the lives of victims if certain demands are not met within a specified time period. Included in the broad hostage-taking category are abductions and kidnappings, vehicle abductions (including aircraft or other forms of public transportation), and some acts of terrorism. The incidence of hostage taking across the country is currently unknown, and nationwide systematic research is badly needed.

Most police experts classify hostage takers into four very broad categories: (1) the political activists or terrorist; (2) prisoners; (3) individuals who have committed a crime; and (4) the mentally disordered (Fuselier, 1988; Fuselier & Noesner, 1990). Political terrorists, who primarily take hostages to gain as much publicity as possible for their cause are the most difficult with whom to deal. Their demands often go beyond the authority of the local police departments and usually require the involvement of federal officials (Fuselier, 1988). According to Fuselier (1988, p. 176), political terrorists take hostages for four basic reasons: "(a) to show the public that the government cannot protect its own citizens; (b) to virtually guarantee immediate coverage and publicity for their cause; (c) to support their hope that after repeated incidents the government will overreact and place excessive restrictions on its citizens; and (d) often to demand the release of members of their group who have been incarcerated."

Prisoners usually take hostages to protest conditions within the correctional facility, and the hostages are usually correctional personnel. The hostage taker who committed a crime is usually trapped while committing the crime, such as robbery or domestic violence, and is trying to negotiate some form of escape.

The mentally disordered person takes hostages for a variety of reasons, but primarily to establish his or her sense of control over a life situation. Research suggests that over 50% of all hostage taking incidents are perpetrated by mentally disordered individuals (Borum & Strenz, 1993).

Police negotiators are trained in a number of strategies for dealing with hostage takers or barricaded individuals. A barricade situations is one in which an individual has fortified or barricaded himself or herself in a building or residence, and threatens violence, either to self or others, or both. What precisely makes a good negotiator, such as the personality traits and emotional demeanor required, remains unknown. Just about every large police department, however, does have a negotiation team, and they tend to be well trained in the strategies and tactics to be employed in handling a hostage-taking incident. The procedures are largely the same for all hostage-taking conditions. First, the person should be denied the excitement, stimulation, publicity, or personal gain he or she hopes to obtain. This requires that a potentially chaotic situation be handled as calmly as possible, with minimum media attention. The reduction of stress and arousal of the offender is a critical requirement; otherwise things become unpredictable and dangerous for all involved. Experienced negotiators believe that conversation distracts the offender from violence and generally calms the situation, especially if the negotiator maintains a calm and steady demeanor. Second, offenders must be allowed to feel that they are in some control of the situation. Helplessness and powerlessness may have prompted the hostage situation in the first place. If the captors do not feel they have attained any control, they make take steps to prove the opposite, such as shooting one of the hostages. Third, in hostage or barricade situations, time is usually a very strong ally for the police. Once the early stages of a crisis have passed and some stability and calm have been achieved, the passage of time plays a positive role. Time has several effects. After the high-arousal state, the body winds down and eventually the offender begins to feel tired, sluggish, and depressed. Under these conditions, the event takes on aversive properties for the hostage taker, and the offender is likely to begin to wish the situation were over.

Training manuals usually recommend consultation with a clinical or police psychologist during a hostage situation, particularly if the hostage taker appears to be mentally disordered or extremely distressed (Fuselier, 1988). However, most psychologists are unaware or unfamiliar with the process and approaches to be used. Fuselier (1988, p. 175) recommends that "If psychologists are going to participate in the negotiation process in addition to providing postincident treatment to victims, then it would be prudent for those psychologists to familiarize themselves with the body of knowledge in that area."

Summary and Conclusions

This chapter provided an overview of police psychology. Police psychology is the research and application of psychological principles and clinical skills to law enforcement and public safety. Although it is a commonly held assumption that law enforcement officers are conservative, rigid, dogmatic, or insensitive, the existence of a "police personality" characterizing individuals who go into law enforcement work has yet to be supported. Police officers as a group exhibit personality characteristics not unlike those of the general population. There is evidence that many officers display one component of the authoritarian personality—namely, conservatism—but it is unclear whether this feature is developed on the job or whether law enforcement work attracts individuals with a conventional, cautious approach to the world. The police socialization process, discussed early in the chapter, is widely believed to be the factor that has the primary influence on law enforcement officers.

With increases in the number of women in law enforcement, researchers have been examining both what they contribute and how they adapt to a traditionally male occupation. It is clear that women can do law enforcement work. Psychological research also suggests that they adopt different styles of policing. An even more promising area of research is the discovery that many women bring to the job characteristics that are desirable in all law enforcement officers, male or female. Furthermore, because many of the obstacles to women's advancement in law enforcement relate to attitudes of male officers, it would be helpful to apply attitude-change research to address this problem.

We examined the investigative methods and types of profiling (e.g., criminal, geographical, racial) used to identify certain or suspected offenders. Criminal profiling refers to the process of identifying personality traits, behavioral tendencies, geographical location, and demographic or biographical descriptors of an offender based on characteristics of the crime. Criminal profiling also has been called psychological profiling and criminal personality profiling. It is a technique that falls under the broader term "criminal investigative analysis" or "crime scene analysis."

The ultimate goal of criminal profiling is to provide a rough behavioral composite of a suspect which will aid law enforcement in reducing the pool of possible suspects to a manageable number. It is by no means a precise science, despite entertainment and news media claims to the contrary. To a very large extent, the profiling process is dictated by the quality of the research data that has been collected on previous offenders who have committed similar crimes. It should be emphasized that criminal profiling is *not* restricted to the violent crimes of serial murder or serial sexual offending, but also can be extended to property crimes, including arson, burglary, shoplifting, fraud, and robbery.

In a sense, criminal profiling is a form of prediction. Based on a myriad of crime scene data and patterns, the profiler tries to "predict" who the offender or offenders might be, and where and how the next crime will occur. It should be emphasized, however, that profiling—even in its most sophisticated form—rarely can point directly to *the* person who committed the crime. Instead, the process helps develop a reasonable set of hypotheses for determining who may have done the crime. If completed correctly, a profile will provide some statistical probabilities of the demographic, geographic, and psychological features of the offender. More importantly, it should eliminate large sectors of the population from further investigation.

The value of geographical profiling lies in the assumption that *some* serial offenders commit crimes within the geographical area they know and feel comfortable in, sometimes near their own residence. All of us develop mental or cognitive maps of our familiar surroundings and residence, and offenders certainly do the same. Mental maps shape how we find our way around the environment, how we find our way home or the grocery store, and help us make decisions about what we do and where.

Police officers are the first-line participants in the criminal justice process. As such, they often determine which cases will encounter the courts and the correctional system. Their ability to exercise discretion effectively becomes an important aspect of their work. We saw in this chapter that discretion, especially with respect to minor offenses, is both encouraged and shaped within the law enforcement network. This occupational socialization, which teaches each officer the acceptable way to exercise judgment, is one of the implicit realities within criminal justice. Discretion is also affected by the wishes of the public and the acts of other participants in the system, like the various attorneys, the judge, supervisors, and even the victim and alleged perpetrator of a crime.

We discussed examples of what can occur when a police officer fails to adapt satisfactorily to stress.

Alcoholism, suicide, depression, and other maladaptive behaviors were examined. It is important to note that, although law enforcement officers are often assumed to exhibit these failures to adapt, there are not enough data to support this assumption. Although it is difficult to obtain information about police alcoholism, illegal substance abuse, depression, and suicide, we have no reason to believe that these stress reactions are any more prevalent in law enforcement than they are in other occupations and the general public.

The chapter ended with special issues in the psychology of law enforcement, such as post-shooting trauma reactions, suicide by cop, fitness-for-duty evaluations, and hostage-taking incidents. Although each of these is unlikely to occupy the police psychologist to a great extent, each does represent a crisis situation in the life of some law enforcement officers. They are occasions when the law enforcement officer may be the most vulnerable to psychological breakdown and consequently the most in need of professional services.

Key Terms

Cynicism	Organizational stressors
Early warning systems	Personal stressors
Equivocal death analysis	Profiling
External stressors	Psychological autopsy
Fitness-for-duty evaluation	Racial profiling
Geographical mapping	Reconstructive psychological evaluation
Geographical profiling	Suicide by cop
John Wayne syndrome	Task-related stressors
Occupational socialization	

Questions for Review

1. Describe the police socialization process, as described by Van Maanen.
2. Identify Niederhoffer's stages of development of cynicism.
3. Is there a police personality? Explain your answer.
4. Summarize the research on gender differences in policing, focusing on such themes as motivation, style, ability, stress, and effect on police subculture.
5. What four broad measures or procedures are used in the police selection process? Of the four, which three are most directly related to the practice of police psychology?
6. Comment on the relative merits of the MMPI–2 and the CPI as personality measures for use in law enforcement.
7. According to research by Scrivner, what five officer profiles are prone to excessive force complaints?
8. Identify and define briefly four different forms of profiling.
9. Identify the four major categories of police stress, and provide illustrations of each.
10. What role might a police psychologist play in the following situations: suicide by cop, fitness for duty evaluations, and hostage-taking scenarios?

Glossary

A priori method. Method for eliminating doubt about one's world through logic and systematic reason.

Abuse, child. Intentional, nonaccidental injury, harm, or sexual assault inflicted on a child.

Acquisition. (Also called the **encoding** or **input stage**). The point at which perception registers in the various areas of the cortex and is initially stored.

Actuarial method. A prediction method that employs statistics to identify certain parameters about the person's background and behavior that are related to the behavior being predicted.

Actuarial prediction. Based on how *groups* of individuals with similar characteristics have acted in the past.

Adjudicative competence. Refers to the ability of an adolescent to understand and participate in a wide variety of juvenile court proceedings.

Administrative law. Law created and enforced by representatives of the numerous administrative agencies of national, state, or local governments.

Admonitions. Warnings or instructions given by a trial judge in an effort to prevent jurors from misusing potentially prejudicial information.

Adolescent limited (AL) offender. A term proposed by Terrie Moffitt to represent an individual who demonstrates delinquent or antisocial behavior during his or her teen years and then usually stops offending during his or her early adult years.

Adversarial model. A process adopted by the American judicial system as the most effective way to arrive at the truth in legal disputes or controversies. It involves two sides each presenting its case before a neutral decision maker (judge or jury).

Aggravating circumstances. Circumstances surrounding a crime that heighten its seriousness for purposes of sentencing. In death penalty case, must be weighed before imposing or recommending death.

Aggressive pedophile. An adult drawn to children for both sexual and aggressive (violent) purposes. Also known as **sadistic pedophile**.

All-suspect lineup. A lineup condition where there are no distractors or foils who are known to be innocent. All members in the lineup observed by the witness are potential suspects.

Amicus curiae. (Latin for "friend of the court"). An *amicus curiae* brief is a document submitted to an appellate court by an outside party to call attention to evidence or legal rules that might otherwise escape the court's attention.

Amnesia. Complete or partial memory loss of an incident, series of incidents, or some segment of life's experiences.

Analogue field study. Refers to a study where the volunteers are genuinely concerned about the outcome of their performance.

Anamnestic prediction. Prediction based on how a *particular* person acted in the past in similar situations.

Anterograde amnesia. Memory loss largely confined to the acquisition and retention of new material.

Antisocial personality disorder (APD). A disorder characterized by a history of continuous behavior in which the rights of others are violated.

Appellate courts. Higher level courts that hears appeals from trial court decisions on points of law.

Archival method. A method of data collection where the researcher relies on previously recorded events, such as court documents or case records.

Arraignment. The criminal court proceeding during which defendants are formally charged with an offense and asked to enter a plea.

Authoritarianism. The term used to describe an ideology or an attitude system holding that one should unquestionably accept authority from recognized powerful people and institutions.

Availability heuristic. The cognitive shortcuts that people use to make inferences about their world. It is the information that is most readily available to us mentally, and is usually based extensively on the most recent material we gain from the news or entertainment media.

Backfire effect. The backfire effect occurs when jurors pay greater attention to information after it has been ruled inadmissible than if the judge had said nothing at all about the evidence and allowed jurors to consider it. For example, the backfire effect often occurs when jurors are instructed to ignore inadmissible evidence which indicates the defendant had a prior criminal record, and then they turn around and use the information in their decision making.

Base rate. Refers to the frequency or probability of an occurrence. In testing, base rate refers to the proportion of persons expected to succeed on a criterion if selected without a test.

Bench trial. A trial in which the judge, rather than a jury, is the factfinder.

Bench trial verdict. A verdict rendered only by a judge.

Best interests of the child. The legal doctrine that the parents' legal rights should be secondary to what is best for the child.

Brawner Rule. A standard for evaluating the insanity defense which recognizes that there must be a condition which *substantially* (a) affects mental or emotional processes or (b) impairs behavioral controls.

Brutalization effect. The observation that executions may actually increase violence in the general population rather than reduce it.

Case law or **"judge-made" law.** Law based on judicial precedent rather than legislative enactments or statutes.

Caveat paragraph of the ALI Rule. The section of the rule excludes abnormality manifested only by repeated criminal or anti-social conduct. This provision was intended to disallow the insanity defense for psychopaths.

Certiorari. Certification by the U.S. Supreme Court that it will hear a case. When petitioners request appellate review, they are said to request *Cert.* The Court then grants or denies *Cert.* See also ***writ of certiorari***.

Challenge for cause. Exercised whenever it can be demonstrated that a would be juror does not satisfy the statutory requirements for jury duty or is predisposed to favor one side.

Charging instructions. Instructions given by the judge to the jury explaining the jury's role, describing the relevant procedural and substantive law, and providing suggestions on how to organize deliberations and evaluate evidence.

Child sexual abuse syndrome (CSAS). (Or the **child sexual abuse accommodation syndrome**). Originally proposed by Summit (1983), it is a term reserved for a cluster of behaviors that occur in children who have been victims of sexual abuse by a family member or an adult with whom the child has a trusting relationship.

Chronic organic amnesia. Refers to a wide range of neurological damage due to physical head trauma (such as a car accident), disease (Alzheimers), or organic dysfunction (such as the result of a stroke).

Civil law. That part of the law concerned with non-criminal matters pertaining to the rights and duties of citizens.

Clinical or **experience prediction.** Prediction of human behavior based on experience dealing with past patients or situations.

Clinical psychologist. Usually a doctorate level psychologist trained and specializing in the study, diagnosis and treatment of mental and psychological disorders.

Cognitive behavioral viewpoint. A perspective of hypnosis which maintains that a hypnotized person is not in a special state of consciousness. Rather, hypnosis is a product of certain attitudes, motivations, and expectancies toward the "hypnotic state."

Cognitive processes. The internal processes that enable humans to imagine, to gain knowledge, to reason, and to evaluate. Each person has his or her own cognitive version of the world.

Cognitive psychology. The study of the internal or "mind" representations of the external world.

Commitment bias. A phenomenon that once people commit to a certain viewpoint or identification of a face, they are less likely to change their minds.

Common law. The law that emerged from judicial decisions rather than legislative enactments. The principles of this type of law are often determined by the social needs of the community.

Commonsense justice. What ordinary people (usually a jury) think is just and fair.

Communication modality. The medium through which the child's testimony is presented to the jury.

Community-based facilities. Facilities that hold individuals for less than twenty-four hours of each day to allow them limited opportunity to work, attend school, or participate in other community activities.

Compensatory offenders. A classification of rapists that categorizes those men who rape, or attempt to rape, because of an intense sexual arousal prompted by specific stimuli in the environment.

Competency to stand trial. Refers to the legal question of whether an individual has the capacity, at the time of the trial preparation and the trial itself, to understand the charges and legal proceedings, and to be able to help his or her attorney in the preparation of a defense.

Composition bias. Refers to prejudicial use of foils in a lineup to contaminate the identification of a suspect.

Concurrent jurisdiction. Situation where two or more courts may have the authority to hear a case. For example, a particular law violation may have the potential of involving both federal and state courts.

Concurrent validity. In psychological testing, validity measured by comparing one test with another, already established one.

Conduct disorder. A diagnostic label used to identify children who demonstrate habitual misbehavior.

Confounding variable. An extraneous variable that interferes with or clouds the research findings.

Consent defense. An affirmative defense to a criminal charge, where the defendant contends that the activity was consensual (e.g., rape cases).

Constitutional law. Law based on the U.S. Constitution and the constitutions of individual states. It provides the guidelines for the organization of national, state, and local government, and places limits on the exercise of government power (e.g., through a Bill of Rights).

Construct validity. Answers the question "to what extent does the test or experiment measure a theory or theoretical construct?"

Content validity. Involves the systematic examination of the test content to determine whether it covers a representative sample of the behavior domain to be measured.

Control (Experimental). Refers to the systematic attempts by the researcher to account for all potentially influential variables on the relationship being investigated.

Control-of-question test (CQT). The most preferred procedure by professional polygraphers in cases requiring specific incident investigation, such as criminal acts. The technique uses a variety of questioning techniques based on three types of questions: (1) irrelevant or neutral questions; (2) relevant questions; and (3) control questions.

Convenience function. The practice of warehousing in a mental institution or similar facility of one or more family members considered bothersome.

Correctional psychologists. Psychologists who work within or in consultation with jails, prisons, and community corrections.

Correlation coefficient. A mathematical index of the relationship between two variables.

Corroboration rules. A legal standard that requires evidence other than the victim's testimony before a person can be charged and/or convicted of rape.

Crime rate. Refers to the number of crimes known to police per 100,000 people within a certain geographical region.

Criminal law. Law concerned with crime and its punishments; may be substantive or procedural.

Criminal psychopaths. Refers to those psychopaths who have continual contact with the criminal justice system because of frequent offending.

Criminal profiling. (Also called **psychological profiling** or **criminal personality profiling**). Refers to the process of identifying personality traits, behavioral tendencies, and demographic variables of an offender based on characteristics of the crime.

Criminal responsibility. The extent a person is held personally responsible for a criminal act they committed. Requires proof of the concurrence of a criminal act and a guilty mind.

Criminalization thesis. The suspicion that the mentally disordered are charged with minor criminal acts in order that they may receive needed mental health services.

Crisis intervention. The intervention of mental health practitioners into emergency or crisis situations, such as suicide attempts, emotional agitation, psychotic behaviors, and refusal to eat or to participate in programs.

Criterion-related validity. Validity based on the power of a measure to predict an individual's performance in specified activities.

Criterion variable. Any variable that is predicted or potentially predictable by a predictor variable.

Cross-situational (or **trans-situational**) **consistency.** The extent a person's behavior remains the same across different or similar situations.

Cue utilization theory. The hypothesis that highly anxious or tense individuals will not scan their environments as broadly as less anxious individuals.

Curative instructions. Judicial instructions to the jury that are presumed to correct or "cure" potential errors in the trial process.

Cured-error doctrine. Judicial assumption that warnings to disregard are effective, or at least partially effective, on the thinking process and prejudice of the jury.

Cynicism. The observation that law enforcement officers with increasing experience begin to have diffuse feelings of hate and envy, impotent hostility, and the sour grapes pattern toward the public and colleagues.

Dark figure. The number of crimes that go unreported in official crime data reports.

Death qualified jurors. Jurors who are not so against the death penalty that they are believed able to render a guilty verdict and recommend a sentence of death.

Decision rule. The proportion of the total number of jurors required to reach a verdict.

Defendant. The person or party against whom a lawsuit or prosecution is brought.

Deindividuation. Process where people feel they cannot be identified, are aroused, and are inclined to commit actions, including antisocial, bizarre, or brutal ones, not usually committed under normal conditions.

Deinstitutionalization. Refers to having individuals supervised, cared for and/or treated outside the confines of traditional large institutions.

Demand waiver. A situation whereby a defense lawyer will ask that a juvenile's case be transferred to criminal court.

Dependent variable. The variable that is measured to see how it is changed by manipulations in the independent variable.

Deposition. Proceedings during which potential witnesses, including expert witnesses, are questioned by attorneys for the opposing side, under oath and in the presence of a court reporter, although typically away from the courtroom.

Depot drugs. Drugs which are injected under the skin and released slowly into the bloodstream over time.

Differential experience hypothesis. The argument that the frequency of meaningful and positive contacts one has with other races or ethnic groups engenders perceptual skill in accurate facial discrimination.

Diminished capacity or **diminished responsibility.** (Also known as partial insanity). The lack of capacity to achieve a state of mind requisite for the commission of crime. This consideration allows the judge to reduce the punishment or severity of the offense, even though the impairment does not qualify as insanity under the prevailing test.

Discovery process. An important component of the pretrial process in both criminal and civil cases. It is the legal requirement that each side must make available information at its disposal to the other side in the preparation of its case. A prosecutor in a criminal case, for example, is obliged to make known exculpatory evidence to the defense.

Discriminant ability. Refers to the requirement that a group of behaviors must occur regularly in a group of children who have certain experiences, and they must not occur in children who have not had that experienced.

Dismissed without prejudice. Persons found IST with little likelihood of being restored to competency often have their cases dismissed without prejudice, which gives the prosecutor the option of reinstituting charges in the event that the person does regain competency.

Displaced aggressive rapist. (Also called **displaced anger** or **anger retaliation rapist**). Rapists that demonstrate a predominance of violent and aggressive behaviors with a minimum or total absence of sexual feeling in their attacks.

Disposition. In criminal law, the sentence a defendant or juvenile offender receives.

Dissociative identity disorder. Another diagnostic term for multiple personality disorder.

Divided custody. Court decision where each parent is afforded legal and physical decisionmaking powers, but on an alternating basis.

Doctrine of family privacy. The doctrine that what goes on within the intact family unit is of concern only to the family itself, as long as there is no serious threat to any member or members of the family.

Domestic violence. Violent behavior among residents of a household.

Dual-purpose evaluation. A simultaneous evaluation of both the defendant's competency to stand trial and mental state at the time of the offense.

Durham Rule. (Also known as the **product rule**). A legal standard of insanity where the accused is not held criminally responsible if his or her unlawful act was the product of a mental disease or mental defect.

Duty to warn/protect. In some jurisdictions, the legal duty of a mental health practitioner to warn or to protect a third party from dangerous actions based on a patient's credible threat.

Dynamic risk factors. Aspects of a person's developmental history that change over time, such as attitudes, opinions, beliefs, and knowledge.

Dynamite charge. (Also known as the shotgun instruction, the third degree instruction, the nitroglycerin charge or the hammer instruction). Refers to situations where judges confronted with the possibility of a hung jury instruct the jury to try to arrive at a verdict.

Early warning systems. Refers to data-based management tools that are designed to identify problem police officers early and intervene through counseling or training to correct those problem behaviors.

Ecological validity. The degree of practical or useful application of a theory or idea to the "real world."

Emergency detention. Temporary confinement intended to protect individuals from imminent serious harm to themselves or to prevent injury to others.

Entry-level assessments. Psychological assessments in correctional facilities conducted at the time an inmate enters the facility.

Equivocal death analysis (EDA). The FBI's term for reconstructive psychological investigation.

Escalation. A process whereby each party in a conflict increases the magnitude or intensity of a response in reaction to the increased response received from the other party.

Estimator variables. Refers to the basic nature and processes of human perception and memory involved in eyewitness or earwitness evidence.

Evidence-driven deliberation style. A jury deliberation style where the jurors decide to delay the vote until after considerable discussion focusing on evaluations of the evidence in the case.

Exclusionary Rule. The doctrine that evidence obtained illegally—in violation of Constitutional rights—is subject to being excluded from a criminal trial.

Exit decisions. Most likely to occur in indeterminate sentencing states, where parole boards exercise discretion as to whether to release prisoners to serve the rest of their sentence in the community.

Expectancy-violation model. The theory that any nonverbal behavior that violates the norm will raise suspicions that the person is lying.

Experimental method. A research method that requires careful control and measurement of the phenomena being studied.

Experimental or **treatment groups.** In a controlled experiment, the group that is subjected to a change in the independent variable.

Exploitative pedophile. An adult who seeks children almost exclusively for sexual gratification.

Ex post facto clause. That part of the U.S. Constitution which prohibits the punishment of individuals if the law under which they are punished was not in effect at the time they committed their crime.

External stressors. Stressors experienced by law enforcement officers that are outside their daily tasks. They include frustration with the courts, the prosecutor's office, the criminal process, the correctional system, the media, and public attitudes.

External validity. (Also called **ecological validity**). Refers to the degree of generalizability research findings have to other populations and other situations.

Externalizing problems. Behavior patterns that go against other people and, more generally, the social environment.

Face validity. Refers not to what the test actually measures, but to what it superficially *appears* to measure.

False negative. A prediction that someone will not do something, but they do.

False positive. A prediction that someone will do something, and they do not.

Family preservation model. A model of service delivery that attempts to keep the original family unit together as much as possible.

Fitness-for-duty evaluations (FFDE). Psychological evaluations requested by law enforcement agencies after a shooting incident or at any time the officer demonstrates problematic behavior.

Fixated pedophile. A male who demonstrates a long-standing, exclusive preference for children as both sexual and social companions. Also called an **immature pedophile**.

Forcible rape. In the OCR, the carnal knowledge of a female, forcibly and against her will. The term includes rape by force, assault to rape, and attempted rape.

Forensic neuropsychology. The psychological assessment of brain injury and nervous system functioning for the legal system.

Forensic psychiatrist. Medical doctor (MD) with advanced clinical training who specializes in assessment and treatment of legally relevant behavioral disorders.

Forensic psychologist. Psychologists who work or consult with the legal system; particularly applied to work with courts.

Forensic psychology. The acquisition and application of psychological knowledge to the legal system.

Friendly parent rule. A situation where sole custody is granted to the parent most likely to facilitate the noncustodial parent's involvement with the children.

Functional retrograde amnesia. Refers to memory loss due to severe psychological or emotional trauma, such as being the victim of a violent crime.

Functional size. The number of lineup members who resemble the suspect in physically relevant features.

Fundamental attribution error. A tendency to underestimate the importance of situational determinants and to overestimate the importance of personality or dispositional determinants.

General deterrence. Deterrence concerned with the overall symbolic impact punishment has on the population as a whole.

General jurisdiction. Refers to those trial courts that have broad authority to deal with a wide range of issues.

General pre-trial publicity. Information that is prominently in the news but is directly *unrelated* to the particular case being tried.

Geographical mapping. Concerned with analyzing the spatial patterns of crimes committed by numerous offenders over a period of time.

Geographical profiling. Concerned with analyzing the spatial movements of a *single* serial offender.

Grand jury. A body of people (usually 23 in number) that is directed by the prosecutor to weigh evidence and decide whether there is enough to charge a person with a criminal offense.

Grave disability statutes. In the civil commitment context, laws that allow the commitment of individuals who are gravely disabled and unable to care for themselves.

Guilty but mentally ill (GBMI). An option intended to be an alternative to, not a substitute for, the verdict NGRI.

It allows jurors a "middle-ground" verdict in the case of allegedly insane defendants.

Guilty-knowledge test (GKT). A method of polygraphy requiring knowledge about a crime or incident not known by the public.

Guardian ad litem. A broad legal term referring to an individual officially appointed by the court to represent the interests of minors or incapacitated persons in court proceedings.

***Habeas corpus* petition.** A procedure for obtaining a judicial determination of the legality of an individual's custody or confinement.

Hindsight bias. Biased judgments of past events after the outcome is known.

Hypnotic age regression. A hypnotic process where the hypnotized individual is asked to relive an experience from childhood.

Hypnotic hypermnesia. The enhancement or revival of memory through hypnosis.

Hypnotic trance theory. The perspective that hypnosis represents a special state of consciousness that promotes a high level of responsiveness to suggestions and changes in bodily feelings.

Hypothesis. A speculative explanation of behavior.

Idiographic approach. A focus on the individual rather than the group. Emphasizes the intensive study of one individual.

Impulsive or **exploitative rapist.** Engages in sexual assault simply because the opportunity to rape is available.

Incapacitation. Sentencing perspective which emphasizes crime prevention and societal protection through isolating the offender from society.

Independent variable. The measure whose effect is being studied, and, in most scientific investigations, is manipulated by the experimenter in a controlled fashion.

Index crimes. The more serious crimes as defined in the FBI's Uniform Crime Reports.

Indictment. A grand jury's formal written statement of the reasons why an individual should be charged with an offense.

Individual cognitive ability tests. Designed to be administered to one examinee at a time by a highly trained examiner.

Injunctions. Court orders directing someone to do something or refrain from some activity.

***In pauperis* petition.** A request from an individual unable to afford legal representation that an appeal court hear his or her case.

Insanity. A judicial determination involving the degree or quantity of mental disorder that relieves one of the criminal responsibility for his or her actions.

Insanity Defense Reform Act of 1984. A statute passed by Congress that is designed to make it more difficult for defendants using the insanity defense in the federal courts to be acquitted.

Interference theory. According to this theory, forgetting is caused by both interference from material learned previously (called by cognitive psychologists "proactive interference") and interference from material learned afterward ("retroactive interference").

Inter-judge reliability. The degree to which a test produces the same results when scored or interpreted by different clinicians or examiners.

Intermediate sanctions. Variety of sanctions that fall somewhere between prison and probation, such as intensive supervision programs, boot camps, home confinement, and electronic monitoring.

Internal consistency. The extent to which different parts of a psychological test yield the same results.

Internal validity. Deals with the level of confidence we can place in the results obtained in a particular study due to its methodology and design.

Internalizing problems. Childhood problems that are a result of internal processes, such as depression, anxiety, and social withdrawal.

Irrationality. The judicial determination of the extent a person is or was in control of his or her *mental processes*.

Irresistible impulse test. A standard of the Brawner Rule that recognizes that, in some instances, an impulse or desire is uncontrollable.

IST. Acronym for the judicial determination of Incompetency to Stand Trial.

Iterative Classification Tree (ICT). A method that uses a yes/no flow chart to provide mental health professionals with a technique for estimating the probability of violence of individuals with behavioral or mental disorders.

Jail. Operated by local governments to hold persons temporarily detained, awaiting trial, or sentenced to confinement after having been convicted of a misdemeanor.

John Wayne syndrome. Normally begins early in the career of a law enforcement officer and lasts for three to four years. A behavior pattern characterized by coldness toward others and emotional withdrawal, authoritarian attitudes, cynicism, overseriousness, and a black-or-white, inflexible approach to daily problem solving.

Joined trial. When multiple defendants or multiple offenses are combined into a single trial.

Joint custody. An arrangement where both parents share legal authority but the children live with one parent, who will have the authority to make the day-to-day decisions.

Judicial waiver. The decision by a judge to transfer a juvenile case to criminal court. Must be preceded by a waiver hearing.

Jurisdiction. Refers to the authority given to a particular court in resolving a dispute. Jurisdiction is best understood as the geographic area, subject matter, or persons over which a court can exercise authority.

Jury nullification. The power of a criminal trial jury to disregard the evidence or judicial instructions and find a defendant not guilty because they believe the law is wrong, nonsensical, or misapplied to a particular case.

Just world hypothesis. A belief that one gets what one deserves and deserves what one gets.

Juvenile Court Act. Passed by the Illinois legislature in 1899, the Act created a juvenile court in Illinois and gave that court jurisdiction over delinquent, dependent, or neglected children.

Least detrimental alternative. Refers to the observation that judges determine child custody on the basis of a negative standard. Namely, which custodial arrangement will do the least harm to the child rather than which custodial arrangement will be in the child's best interest.

Legal parental authority. Refers to the decisionmaking authority regarding the child's long-term welfare, education, medical care, religious upbringing, and other issues significantly affecting the child's life.

Legal system. An umbrella term meant to encompass the courts, both civil and criminal, law enforcement agencies, corrections, and a wide array of administrative agencies.

Legislative waiver. Also called waiver by statute. Refers to the statutory exclusion or automatic waiver of juveniles of specified ages, charged with specified crimes, to criminal court. For example, in most states the case of a 15-year-old charged with murder will be heard in criminal court rather than juvenile court.

Leniency bias. A tendency for juries to be more lenient than judges in rendering verdicts.

Less restrictive alternative. A standard that requires decisionmakers to consider living arrangements that offer the least confinement or restriction of an inmate or patient, and still provides protection of society and the individual.

Life course persistent (LCP) offender. A term proposed by Terrie Moffitt to represent offenders who demonstrate a life-long pattern of antisocial behavior and who are resistant to treatment and rehabilitation.

Limited amnesia. A pathological inability to remember a specific episode, or small number of episodes, from the recent past.

Limited joint custody. An arrangement where both parents share legal authority but one parent is given exclusive physical authority and the other parent is awarded liberal visitation rights.

Limited jurisdiction. Refers to entry-level courts which usually cannot conduct felony trials, although judges in those courts can hold preliminary hearings, issue search warrants, and conduct a variety of pre-trial proceedings.

Limiting instructions. Judicial instructions that warn jurors not to use evidence to evaluate or decide on a certain issue, although the evidence may be used for another issue.

Long-term confinement. Confinement in a mental institution for years, often without opportunity to be released.

Mass arsonist. A person who sets three or more fires in quick succession at the same location without a cooling-off period.

Mass murder. Murder of three or more persons at a single location with no cooling-off period between the murders.

Match-to-description strategy. Where the selection of distracters in a lineup is based on the witness's description of the perpetrator.

Match-to-suspect strategy. Refers to when there is an attempt to match a suspect in every conceivable variable and beyond the description provided by the eyewitness.

Meta-analysis. A statistical technique for combining the results of separate studies into an overall evaluation of the magnitude or consistency of effect of their common independent variable.

Method of authority. A method for eliminating doubt and gaining knowledge that relies on the information provided by experts in the field.

Method of tenacity. A method for eliminating doubt that relies heavily on stereotypes and prejudices.

Minimum credibility standard. Assumes that any child testimony (or adult testimony) can be rejected if it can be established that he or she lacks the necessary powers of observation, recordation, recollection, and recount so as to be untrustworthy.

Misinformation effect. The phenomenon that when people see an event and are later exposed to new and misleading information about it, their recollections often become distorted.

Mitigating circumstances. Conditions which, while not completely exonerating the person charged, at least reduce the penalty connected to the offense. An example would be a childhood marred by extensive physical or sexual abuse.

M'Naghten Rule. An insanity standard that is based on the conclusion that if a defendant has a defect of reason, or a disease of the mind, as not to know the nature and quality of his or her actions—or did not realize what they were doing was wrong—then they cannot be held criminally responsible.

Mock juries. Experimental or simulated juries used by researchers to study the structure and dynamics of actual juries. Also used for "artificial" or training juries with which lawyers or prospective lawyers practice.

Moderate reform exclusionary rules. State statutes that permit a partial limitation on the admissibility of sexual history.

Moderating variable. A factor that influences the strength and direction of the relationship between two other variables.

Multiple personality amnesia. Memory deficits specifically observed in individuals with MPD.

Multiple personality disorder (MPD)—also called Dissociative Identity Disorder (DID)—A mental disorder characterized by the existence within an individual of two or more distinct personalities, each of which may be dominant at any given time.

Multi-systemic therapy (MST). A treatment approach for serious juvenile offenders that focuses on the family while being responsive to the many other contexts surrounding the family, such as the community, the neighborhood, and the school.

National Crime Victimization Survey (NCVS). A government survey that involves contacts with a large national sample of households to learn the extent of criminal victimization.

Neglect. Lack of essential care, such as food, clothing, shelter, medical attention, education, or supervision as a result of the behavior of a caretaker.

Nominal size. The actual number of members within the lineup, which theoretically may include some very dissimilar foils.

Nomothetic approach. A research approach that concentrates on general principles, relationships, and patterns that transcend the single individual.

Nonhypnotic hypermnesia. Enhancement or recovery of memory through non-hypnotic methods, such as free association, fantasy, recall techniques.

Normative distribution. Also called norms, refers to distribution of scores of a representative sample of the population for which that test is designed. The sample is called a standardization or normative group.

Objective test. Basically, a test is objective to the extent that scorers can apply a scoring key and agree about the result.

Observational learning or **modeling.** The hypothesis that individuals may learn a particular behavior simply by observing another person perform the action.

Occupational socialization. Refers to the effect of an organization or agency on one's working behavior, drastically reducing the effects of personality on that behavior.

Optimality hypothesis. Refers to the theory that the more optimal the conditions, the stronger the positive relationship between eyewitness accuracy and confidence.

Orders of nonhospitalization. Outpatient commitment orders where a person is ordered to take part in some form of treatment, such as drugs and counseling, both delivered at a local mental health center.

Organizational stressors. Law enforcement stressors confined to the policies and practices of the police department itself. They include poor pay, excessive paperwork, insufficient training, inadequate equipment, weekend duty, shift work, limited promotional opportunities, poor supervision and administrative support, and poor relationships with supervisors or colleagues.

Own race bias (ORB). The finding that people are better able to discriminate among faces of their own race or ethnic group in comparison to the faces of other races or ethnic group.

Paraphilia. A relatively new term for a variety of sexual deviations, where sexual arousal cannot occur without the presence of unusual imagination or behaviors.

Parens patriae. (Literally, "parent of the country") is the doctrine in law which establishes the right of the state to substitute its presumably benevolent decisionmaking for that of individuals who are said to be unable or unwilling to make their own decisions.

Pattern jury instructions. A standard or uniform jury instruction that can be applied across *different* jurisdictions.

Perceived coercion. In involuntary commitment research, an individual's perception that he or she is being forcibly institutionalized, or treated.

Perception. A process where sensory inputs (what one sees, hears, smells, touches, tastes) are transformed and organized into a meaningful experience for the individual.

Perceptual adaptation or **contrast effects.** When stereotypes are violated, there is a tendency for human beings to perceive the individual as *more* dissimilar to the stereotype than he or she really is.

Peremptory challenge. A rule that allows a lawyer to request the removal of a prospective juror without giving reason.

Petit jury. Also called trial jury. The jury that decides facts of a case and renders a verdict.

Physical authority. A judicial determination that allows a parent decisions affecting only the child's daily activities, such as deciding whether the child can stay overnight at a friend's house, attend a party, or have access to the parent's car.

Plaintiff. The person or party who initially brings a legal suit.

Police bias. Bias either in the use of police officers as foils in a lineup or in the questioning techniques used by the police investigator.

Police power. The obligation and responsibility of the state to protect the public from harm to persons or to property. It encompasses the state's power to make laws and regulations for the protection of public health, safety, welfare, and morals.

Police psychologists. Psychologists specializing in working with law enforcement.

Polling the jury. A practice whereby jurors are asked individually by the judge, after the verdict is read in the courtroom, whether they assented, and still assent, to the verdict.

Positive law. Sometimes referred to as "the law on the books," it is the law found in constitutions, statutes, case decisions, and the rules of administrative agencies.

Postidentification-feedback effect. Refers to the increase in eyewitnesses' confidence in their identification of a suspect after they have been told they identified a person other witnesses have also identified.

Predecisional distortion. Material that does not fit into one's thinking is rejected, and material that fits is accepted.

Predictive validity. The degree to which a test predicts a person's subsequent performance on the dimensions and tasks the test is supposed or designed to measure.

Predictor variable. A term analogous to the term "independent variable" in experimental research. In psychology, a predictor variable generally refers to some measurable factor (an antecedent) that aids in forecasting an outcome or a behavior.

Preliminary hearing. A pre-trial hearing to determine whether there is probable cause to hold the accused for the grand jury or, if no grand jury, to continue with prosecution.

Preliminary instructions. Instructions given at the beginning of the trial, before opening arguments. The judge instructs the jury about the respective roles of judge and jury during the course of the trial. For example, judge will routinely warn non-sequestered jurors in high-profile cases not to expose themselves to media accounts of the case and not to discuss the case with others or among themselves until it is time for deliberation.

Pre-sentence investigation (PSI). Refers to an investigation of a crime, the offender, and the impact on the victim, conducted for the court before sentencing, usually done by the probation department.

Pre-sentence report. A document submitted to the judge that is intended to provide helpful sentencing information.

Preventive detention. Holding a defendant in custody pending trial in the belief that he or she is likely to commit further criminal acts or flee the jurisdiction.

Primary prevention. An intervention program designed to prevent antisocial behavior or behavioral disorders *before* any signs of the behavior emerges.

Principle of nonmalificence. The ethical requirement and understanding among the medical profession that its members do no harm. Evaluations of competency to be executed are believed by some to violate this principle.

Prisonization. The observation that inmates adopt and internalize the prisoner subculture within any particular institution.

Prisons. Correctional facilities operated by state and federal governments to hold persons convicted of felonies and sentenced, generally to terms of more than one year.

Procedural default doctrine. The rule that if an objection is not placed on the record during the trial, a person has lost the right to appeal to a higher court on the basis of that particular issue. In some jurisdictions, there is an additional requirement that the appellant must have also requested a remedy.

Procedural evidence. Clinical information and hunches that clinicians suspect to be correct based on their personal observations, assessments, and interpretations.

Procedural instructions. Those instructions that enlighten jurors about the various rules that apply across a wide variety of cases. For example, the judge explains the roles of judge and jury during the course of the trial or informs jurors whether their decision must be unanimous.

Procedural justice. The doctrine that all court hearings should have the appearance of fairness, providing individuals with dignity, a voice, and engendering trust in the system.

Procedural law. Law that outlines the rules for the administration, enforcement, and interpretation of substantive law in the mediation of disputes.

Process method. A research method that directly investigates the type and amount of treatment delivered to the patients. Patient records are examined to determine how often the patients were seen, by whom, and for what purposes.

Profiling. The process of identifying personality traits, behavioral tendencies, and demographic variables of an offender based on known characteristics of the crime.

Projective tests. Psychological tests designed under the assumption that personality attributes are best revealed when a person responds to ambiguous stimuli.

Prosecutorial waiver or **direct file.** Refers to situations whereby prosecutors are given the choice of filing the case of a juvenile in juvenile or adult court.

Protective custody or **protective seclusion.** Isolation or confinement in a special area for the primary purpose of protecting inmates from possible harm from themselves or other inmates.

Psychiatric criminology (also called **forensic psychiatry**). The field of psychiatry, working within the legal system and represented by the Freudian, psychoanalytic, or psychodynamic perspectives, that *traditionally* views human nature as *innately* antisocial.

Psychoactive drugs. Drugs that exert their primary effect on the brain, thus altering mood or behavior.

Psychological assessment. Refers to *all* the techniques used to measure and evaluate an individual's past, present, or future psychological status. It usually includes interviews, observations, and various measuring procedures which may or may not include psychological tests and inventories.

Psychological autopsy. See **reconstructive psychological evaluation**.

Psychological criminology. The science of the behavior and mental processes of antisocial individuals.

Psychological testing. The use of psychological measuring devices, which are but one component of the assessment process.

Psychological tests. Measuring devices that include measures of intelligence, aptitude, attitudes, interests, and personality.

Psychological theory. An explanation that systematically connects many different behaviors.

Psychological treatment or **psychotherapy.** A series of systematic verbal and emotional interactions involving primarily talk, between a person who is trained to aid in reducing psychological problems and an individual suffering from them.

QUEST (Qualification by Example Selection Test). A questionnaire approach suggested for use with potential death penalty jurors.

Quorum juries. Those which do not require a unanimous vote to convict.

Racial profiling. Refers to police-initiated action that relies primarily on the race, ethnicity, or national origin of a person rather than the suspected criminal actions of that individual.

Rape by fraud. The act of having sexual relations with a supposedly consenting adult under fraudulent conditions, such as when a physician or psychotherapist has sexual intercourse with a patient under the guise of "effective treatment."

Rape shield reform statutes. Statutes which restrict, to varying degrees, the admissibility of the victim's sexual history into the courtroom.

Reactance. A motive to protect or restore one's sense of freedom. For example, telling jurors to disregard or to segment the evidence is likely to highlight the material in their minds even more, and consequently they are apt to do just the opposite.

Reality monitoring. In the context of child victimizations, this refers to the child's ability to distinguish *actual* from imagined events.

Reciprocal determinism. The perspective that cognitions influence both behavior and the situation, and these, in turn, influence cognitions.

Reciprocal interaction. Refers to the continual process of the person, through behavior and beliefs, influencing the social environment, and the environment in turn influencing the person.

Reconstructive memory. The position that believes memory is a reconstructive, integrative process, developing with the flow of new experiences and thoughts.

Reconstructive psychological evaluation (RPE) or **equivocal death analysis.** A technique designed to develop a psychological image of what a dead person was like (his or her personality, habits, intentions, dreams, motivations, life-style) when alive.

Regressed pedophile. A male who had fairly normal relationships with adults but later reverted to children for sexual intimacy and social companionship because of feelings of inadequacy.

Rehabilitation. Any attempt intended to bring about change in behavior patterns.

Reinforcement. Anything that increases responding.

Relapse prevention (RP). A self-control program designed to teach individuals who are trying to change their behavior how to anticipate and cope with temptations to revert to earlier behavior.

Relative judgment error. A process in which the eyewitness chooses the lineup member who most resembles the culprit relative to the other members of the lineup.

Relevant-irrelevant test. A polygraph technique developed in 1917 by the lawyer-psychologist, William M. Marston, primarily for criminal investigation.

Reliability. The consistency of measurement. A test is reliable if it yields the same results over and over again.

Replicability. The requirement that the descriptions of the variables studied and the procedures used to study them be precise and objective enough so that any researcher can do the experiment again.

Repressed memory. Refers to the psychological process of unconsciously keeping something out of awareness for extended periods of time because of the unpleasant emotions associated with it.

Restorative justice. Refers to the need to "make whole" the community that has suffered from the offender's crime, while also reintegrating that offender into the community when appropriate.

Retention. (Also called the storage stage). The second stage of memory when information becomes "resident in the memory."

Retribution. The principle that a wrongful act must be "repaid" by a punishment that is as severe (although not identical) as the wrongful act. Also referred to as "just deserts."

Retrograde amnesia. Memory loss involving past or old material.

Right-from-wrong test. Another term for the M'Naghten standard of insanity.

Risk assessment. Prediction of dangerousness based on psychological assessment.

Scientific jury selection. Refers to the use of behavioral and social scientists by lawyers to find the type of juror who would be most sympathetic to their side.

Secondary prevention. An intervention program designed for individuals who demonstrate early signs or indications of behavior problems or antisocial behavior.

Secondary variables. Extraneous variables that may influence the results of an experiment, like intelligence, time of day, gender, age, or even room temperature.

Selective incapacitation. The imprisonment for longer terms of offenders who are believed to pose the greatest threat to society.

Self-defense. The right to use physical force against an imminent threat of grave bodily harm from another individual.

Self-report method. A method of research that expects people to report various aspects about themselves. Used as a measure of crime and delinquency.

Self-serving bias. A tendency to attribute positive things that happen to us to our ability and personality, and to attribute negative things to something outside ourselves or events beyond our control.

Sequential jury selection method. A rule that requires lawyers to exercise their challenges without knowing the characteristics of the next juror to be interviewed.

Sequential lineup. A lineup condition where the eyewitness is presented with one lineup member at a time in sequence.

Serial arsonist. A firesetter who sets three or more fires at different times.

Serial murder. Incidents in which an individual (or individuals) kill a number of individuals (usually a minimum of three) over time.

Sexual aggressive rapist. This rapist exhibits both sexual and aggressive elements in his assault. Victim pain is a prerequisite for sexual excitement. He believes women enjoy being abused, forcefully raped, aggressively dominated, and controlled by men.

Shock probation. A strategy which place offenders in jail for a short period of time before allowing them on probation.

Show-up. An identification procedure in which police present a single suspect to the eyewitness to see if the eyewitness will identify that person as the perpetrator.

Similarity-to-suspect strategy. An attempt to create lineups where all members of a lineup look very much alike.

Simulation research. Research conducted in a laboratory that is designed to mimic as closely as possible the "real world." Often used in jury research.

Single-suspect lineup. A lineup condition where there is one suspect and the other lineup members are known innocents serving as distractors, foils, or fillers.

Situational tests. Assessment techniques where an applicant's behavior is observed under simulated conditions, such as that of a job situation.

Sociological criminology. A study of crime that emphasizes the effects on crime of variables such as age, race, gender, social group, interpersonal relationships, social class, and power differentials in society.

Sociopath. A person who is *repetitively* in conflict with the law, with apparently limited capacity to learn from past experiences.

Sole custody. A judicial ruling where one parent receives both legal and physical custody of the child, although the noncustodial parent usually retains visitation rights.

Specialized courts. Courts that focus or specialize on particular points of law, such as bankruptcy courts or patent courts, or on particular cases, such as mental health and domestic violence courts.

Special or **specific deterrence.** Deterrence based on the actual experience of punishment, which presumably will deter the punished individual from engaging in future transgressions.

Spillover effect. A situation where knowledge that a defendant has several charges pending, psychologically "spills" onto the evidence presented on any single charge.

Split custody. A custodial arrangement where the legal and physical authority of one or more children is awarded to one parent, and the legal and physical authority of the remaining children to the other.

Spree arsonist. A person who sets fires at three or more locations with no emotional cooling-off period between them.

Spree murder. The killing of three or more individuals without any cooling-off period, usually at two or more locations.

Solitary confinement. In corrections, refers to complete social isolation of persons for specified or unspecified periods of time, usually for disciplinary reasons, with minimum basic necessities of life being provided.

Standard error of measurement (SEM). (Also called the standard error of a score.) A mathematical index of how much variation we can expect in a test score each time a person takes that same test.

Standardization or **normative group.** A representative sample of the population for which a test is designed.

Stare decisis. (Latin, "to stand by past decision"). A doctrine that encourages courts to be slow and cautious about interfering with principles announced in former decisions. The doctrine of precedence in law.

State-dependent learning or **memory.** Refers to the observation that the things we learn in one state—be it happiness, sadness or intoxication—are sometimes easier to recall when we are again in the same state.

Static risk factors. Aspects of a person's developmental history that do not change, such as biological parents, gender, birth order, and ethnic background.

Status offenses. Offenses by juveniles that would not be offenses if committed by adults, such as running away from home, violating curfew, being "incorrigible," or truant.

Statutory rape. Rape where the age of the female is the crucial distinction, regardless of whether she gives her consent to engage in sexual intercourse.

Statutory law. Written rules drafted and approved by a federal, state, or local law-making body.

Story model. The theory that jurors construct in their minds a story of how events—testified to at the trial—took place, even before hearing all the evidence.

Strict liability offenses. Unlawful acts whose elements do not contain the need for criminal intent or *mens rea.*

Struck jury method. A rule whereby the judge decides all challenges for cause before the parties claim any peremptories.

Structural analysis. A research method that focuses on the structure of the institution and uses criteria such as staff-patient ratios and per capita expenditure to determine the adequacy of treatment.

Substantive law. Law that defines the rights and responsibilities of members of a given society as well as the prohibitions of socially sanctioned behavior.

Substantive law instructions. Instructions given during or at the end of the trial process on aspects of the law as applied to a particular case. For example, if a defendant is charged with embezzlement, the judge instructs the jury on the elements of that crime and on what must be proved by the prosecution beyond a reasonable doubt.

Suicide by cop. Generally abbreviated **SbC**, refers to incidents in which individuals, bent on self-destruction, engage in life-threatening and criminal behavior to force the police to kill them.

Survey research. Involves obtaining information about people by asking them well-prepared questions, usually in written form.

Syndrome. A collection of thoughts, feelings, and behaviors that are believed to be held in common by individuals.

System variables. Refer to those variables that can be controlled by people in the criminal justice system when gathering information from eyewitnesses. For example, the number of people in the lineup and how closely they resemble the suspect are things the police can control.

Task-related stressors. Stressors related to the nature of police work itself.

Teaching family home. Refers to a living arrangement that seeks to simulate as closely as possible a "family" situation within a community, complete with adult parent figures.

Temporal consistency. The degree of consistency of any given behavior over time.

Tender years doctrine. A legal assumption, derived from the traditional belief, that the mother is the parent ideally and inherently suited to care for children of a "tender age."

Tertiary prevention. Intervention strategy designed to reduce or eliminate behavior problems or antisocial behavior that has become fully developed in juveniles or adults.

Test-retest reliability. A measure of whether the same test yields the same results when administered to the same person at two different times.

Theory. A set of interrelated constructs (concepts), definitions, and propositions that present a systematic view of phenomena by specifying relations among variables, with the purpose of explaining and predicting the phenomena.

Therapeutic jurisprudence. A position by Wexler and Winick that attempts to reconcile the goals and principles of due process and therapeutic intervention.

Trial court. Judicial body with primarily original jurisdiction in civil and criminal cases.

Trivial persuasion. Available evidence suggests that witnesses whose testimony is replete with detail, even if it is not directly relevant to the case may play a powerful role in encouraging jurors to believe the testimony.

True negative. Predicting something will not happen, and it does not.

True positives. Predicting something will happen, and it does.

Type I error. Made when an innocent person is convicted.

Type II error. Made when a guilty person is released.

Typology. In psychology, a classification system, either based on personality traits or behavioral patterns of individuals.

Ultimate issue. The final legal question that must be decided by a court (for example, whether a person is competent or which parent should be awarded custody).

Unconscious transference. Occurs when a person seen in one situation is confused with or recalled as a person seen in another situation.

Validating evidence. Evidence or knowledge gained through careful, controlled research.

Validity. The psychological standard that a test should measure what it claims to be measuring.

Venire. The pool of prospective jurors drawn from an eligible population presumed to be representative of a local geographical area.

Verdict-driven deliberation style. Refers to a jury deliberation style where the ultimate goal is to reach a verdict as soon as possible

Viable minorities. In the jury context, defined as at least two members not in agreement with the majority.

Victimization rate. Expressed as the ratio of the number of victimizations over the number of potential victims.

Voir dire. A process that allows the judge and attorneys to question the prospective jurors and possibly disqualify them from jury duty.

Volitional prong. Relating to the insanity defense, acceptance of the possibility that a defendant could not control his or her behavior to conform to the requirements of the law.

Waiver or **bindover hearings.** Adversary court proceeding during which evidence is heard as to whether a juvenile case should be transferred to criminal court from juvenile court. A reverse waiver hearing considers whether the case should be transferred from criminal to juvenile court.

Weapon focus. The concentration of some victims' or witnesses' attention on a threatening weapon, paying less attention to other details and events of a crime, resulting in poor recall of some important aspects of a crime.

Writ of certiorari. Issued from an appellate court for the purpose of obtaining from a lower court the record of its proceedings in a particular case.

Yerkes-Dodson Law. First proposed in 1908, it refers to the observation that moderate levels of arousal produce optimal performance on a variety of tasks.

Cases Cited

Addington v. Texas, 99 S.Ct. 1804 (1979).
Ake v. Oklahoma, 470 U.S. 68 (1985).
Alabama v. Shelton, _____ U.S. _____ (2002).
Albermarle v. Moody, 95 S.Ct. 2362 (1975).
Apodaca, Cooper, and Madden v. Oregon, 406 U.S. 404 (1972).
Apprendi v. New Jersey, 120 S.Ct. 2348 (2000).
Argersinger v. Hamlin, 407 U.S. 25 (1972).
Arizona v. Fulminante, 499 U.S. 279 (1991).
Ashcraft v. Tennessee, 322 U.S. 143 (1944).
Atkins v. Virginia, _____ U.S. _____ (2002).
Baldwin v. New York, 399 U.S. 66 (1970).
Ballew v. Georgia, 435 U.S. 223 (1978).
Barefoot v. Estelle, 463 U.S. 880 (1983).
Barker v. Wingo, 407 U.S. 514 (1972).
Barnes v. Gorman, _____ U.S. _____ (2002).
Batson v. Kentucky, 476 U.S. 79 (1986).
Bell v. Wolfish, 441 U.S. 520 (1979).
Berkemer v. McCarty, 468 U.S. 420 (1984).
Borawick v. Shay, 68 F.3d 597 (2nd Cir. (Conn.)) 1995, cert. denied, 116 S.Ct. 1869, 134 L.Ed. 2d 966 (1996).
Boy Scouts of America v. Dale, _____ U.S. _____ (2000).
Breed v. *Jones*, 421 U.S. 519 (1975).
Brewer v. Williams, 430 U.S. 386 (1977).
Brown v. Board of Education of Topeka, 347 U.S. 483 (1954).
Brown v. Mississippi, 297 U.S. 278 (1936).
Buck v. Bell, 274 U.S. 200 (1927).
Burch v. Louisiana, 441 U.S. 130 (1979).
Bush v. Gore, _____ U.S. _____ (2000).
Carter v. U.S., 252 F.2d 608 (D.C. Cir. 1957).
Chandler v. Florida, 101 S.Ct. 802 (1981).
Chevron v. Echazabal, _____ U.S. _____ (2002).
Chicago v. Morales, _____ U.S. _____ (1999).
Christopher P. v. New Mexico, 816 P.2d 485 (N.M. 1991).
Colgrove v. Battin, 413 U.S. 149 (1973).
Commonwealth v. Lykus, 327 N.E.2d. 671 (Mass. Sup. Jud. Ct. 1975).
Commonwealth v. Roddy, 184 Pa.274, 39 A.211 (1898).
Connally v. General Construction Company, 269 U.S. 385 (1926).
Connecticut Department of Public Safety v. Doe, _____ U.S. _____ (2003).
Cooper v. Oklahoma, 116 S. Ct. 1373 (1996).
Coy v. Iowa, 108 S.Ct. 2798 (1988).
Cruzan v. Director, Missouri Department of Health, 497 U.S. 261 (1990).
Currie v. U.S., 836 F.2d 209 (4th Cir. 1987).
Daubert v. Merrell Dow Pharmaceuticals, Inc., 509 U.S. 579 (1993).
Davis v. U.S., 114 S.Ct. 2350 (1994).
Dickerson v. U.S., 530 U.S. 428 (2000).
Drope v. Missouri, 420 U.S. 162 (1975).
Duckworth v. Eagan, 109 S.Ct. 2875 (1989).
Durham v. U.S., 214 F.2d 862 (D.C. Cir. 1954).
Dusky v. U.S., 362 U.S. 402 (1960).
Eddings v. Oklahoma, 455 U.S. 104 (1982).
Escobedo v. Illinois, 378 U.S. 478 (1964).
Estate of Davis v. Yong-Oh Lhim, 422 N.W.2d 688 (Michigan Supreme Court, 1987).
Estelle v. Gamble, 429 U.S. 97 (1976).
Estelle v. Smith, 451 U.S. 454 (1981).
Estes v. Texas, 381 U.S. 532 (1965).
Ewing v. California, _____ U.S. _____ (2003).
Fare v. Michael C., 442 U.S. 707 (1979).
Farmer v. Brennan, 511 U.S. 725 (1999).
Feliciano v. Gonzales, 13 F.Supp.2d 151 (D.P.R. 1998).
Ford v. Wainwright, 477 U.S. 399 (1986).
Foucha v. Louisiana, 504 U.S. 71 (1992).
Frye v. United States. 54 app. D.C. 46, 47 293 F. 1013, 1014 (1923).
Furman v. Georgia, 408 U.S. 238 (1972).
General Elec. Co. v. Joiner, 522 U.S. 136 (1997).
Georgia v. McCollum, 505 U.S. 42 (1992).
Gideon v. Wainwright, 372 U.S. 335 (1963).
Gilbert v. California, 388 U.S. 263 (1967).
Godinez v. Moran, 113 S.Ct. 2680 (1993).
Goff v. Harper, 59 F.Supp. 2d 910 (S.D. Iowa 1999).
Gregg v. Georgia, 428 U.S. 153 (1976).
Griggs v. Duke Power Co., 401 U.S. 424 (1971).
Harding v. State, 5 Md. App. 230, 246 A.2d 302 (1968), *cert. denied, Harding v. Maryland*, 395 U.S. 949, 89 S.Ct. 2030, 23 L.Ed2d 468 (1969).
Harris v. Forklift Systems, Inc., (1993).
Harris v. New York, 401 U.S. 222 (1971).
Hedlund v. Superior Court of Orange County, 669 P.2d 41 (Cal. Sup. Crt 1983).
Hobson v. Hansen, 269 F. Supp. 401 (D.C. Cir. 1967).
Hodgson v. Minnesota, 497 U.S. 417 (1990).
Hudson v. Palmer, 468 U.S. 517 (1984).
Huntoon v. TCI Cablevision of Colorado, 969 P.2d 681 (1998).
In re Frank H., 337 N.Y.S.2d 118 (1972).
In re Gault, 387 U.S. 1 (1967).
In re Oakes, Monthly Law Reporter (Mass.) 1845, 8, 122–129.
In re Quinlan, 70 N.J. 10, 355 A.2d. 647, *cert. denied sub nom.* (1976).
In re Wayne H., 596 P2d 1 (Cal. 1979).
In re Winship, 397 U.S. 358 (1970).
Irvin v. Dowd, 366 U.S. 717 (1961).
Jackson v. Indiana, 406 U.S. 715 (1972).
Jaffe v. Redmond, 116 S.Ct. 1923 (1996).
J.E.B. v. Alabama ex rel T.B. (1994).
Jenkins v. U.S., 307 F.2d 637 (D.C. Cir. 1962 *en banc*).
Johnson v. Louisiana, 406 U.S. 356 (1972).
Johnson v. State, 292 Ark. 632, 732 S.W.2d 817 (1987).
Jones v. U.S., 463 U.S. 354 (1983).
Kansas v. Crane, _____ U.S. _____ (2002).
Kansas v. Hendricks, 117 S.Ct. 2072 L.Ed.2d (1997).
Kent v. U.S., 383 U.S. 541 (1966).
Keri v. State, 179 Ga. App. 664, 347 S.E.2d 236 (1986).

Kirby v. Illinois, 406 U.S. 682 (1972).
Kumho Tire Co., Ltd. v. Carmichael, 119 S. Ct. 1167 (1999).
Lake v. Cameron, 364 F.2d 657 (1966).
Landers v. Chrysler Corporation, 963 SW.2d 275 (1997).
Lantrip v. Commonwealth, 713 S.W.2d 816 (Ky. 1986).
Larry P. v. Riles, 343 F. Supp. 1306 (N.D. Cal. 1972) (order granting preliminary injunction), *aff'd,* 502 F.2d 963 (9th Cir. 1974), 495 F. Supp. 926 (N.D. Cal. 1979) (decision on the merits) *aff'd* (9th Cir. Jan 23, 1984).
Lessard v. Schmidt, 349 F. Supp. 1078 (E.D. Wisc. 1972), *vac and remanded on other grounds*, 94 S.Ct. 713 (1974), *reinstated* 413 F. Supp. 1318 (E.D. Wisc. 1976).
Lockhart v. McCree, 476 U.S. 162 (1986).
Lockyer v. Andrade, _____ U.S. _____ (2003).
Lowenfield v. Phelps, 108 S.Ct. 546 (1988).
McClesky v. Kemp, 481 U.S. 279 (1987).
McKeiver v. Pennsylvania, 403 U.S. 538 (1971).
McKune v. Lile, _____ U.S. _____ (2002).
M'Naghten, 10 Clark & Fin.200, 210, 8 Eng.Rep. 718 (1843).
Madrid v. Gomez, 889 F.Supp. 1149 (N.D. Cal. 1995).
Maryland v. Craig, 497 U.S. 836 (1990).
Medina v. California, 505 U.S. 437 (1992).
Menendez v. State of California, 194 Cal. Rptr. 805 (S.Ct. Cal 1992).
Merriken v. Cressman, 364 F. Supp. 913 (E.D. Pa. 1973).
Michigan v. Tucker, 417 U.S. 433 (1974).
Miranda v. Arizona, 384 U.S. 436 (1966).
Missouri v. Hutching, 927 S.W. 2d 41 (1996).
Montana v. Cowan, 861 P.2d 884 (1994M+).
Morales v. Turman, 383 F. Supp. 53 (E.D. Tex. 1974).
Nartional Kidney Patients Assoc. v. Sullivan, 506 U.S. 1049 (1993).
NBC subsidiary (KNBC-TV), Inc. v. Superior Court, 86 Cal Rptr. 2d 778, 980 p.2d 337 (Cal. 1999).
Nebraska Press Assoc. v. Stuart, 427 U.S. 539 (1976).
Neil v. Biggers, 409 U.S. 188 (1972).
Nelson v. Heyne, 491 F.2d 352 (7th Cir. 1974).
New Jersey v. T.L.O., 469 U.S. 325 (1985).
New York v. Quarles, 467 U.S. 649 (1984).
N.O.W. v. Scheidler, 510 U.S. 249 (1994).
O'Connor v. Donaldson, 422 U.S. 563 (1975).
Ohio v. Akron Center, 497 U.S. 502 (1990)
Olmstead v. L.C., 527 U.S. 581 (1999).
Parham v. J.R., 442 U.S. 584 (1979).
PASE v. Hannon, 506 F. Supp. 831 (N.D. Ill. 1980).
Pate v. Robinson, 383 U.S. 375 (1966).
Peck v. Counseling Center of Addison County, 146 Vt. 61 (1985).
Pennsylvania v. Yeskey, 119 S.Ct. 2139 (1999).
Pennsylvania Association of Retarded Citizens (PARC) v. Pennsylvania, 334 F.Supp. 1257 (E.D. PA, 1972).
Pennsylvania v. Muniz, 496 U.S. 582 (1990).
Penry v. Lynaugh, 492 U.S. 302 (1989).
People v. Bowker, 202 Cal. App.3d, 231 Cal. Rptr. 886 (1988).
People v. Brock, 143 A.D.2d 678 N.Y.S.2d 903 (1988).
People v. Buckey, N. A–750900 (Los Angeles SUP. CT. 1990).
People v. Gray, 187 Cal. App.3d, 231 Cal. Rptr. 658 (1986).
People v. Hickey, 86 Ill. App. 20 (1899).
People v. Luna, 204 Cal. App.3d 776, 250 Cal. Rptr. 878 (1988).
People v. McQuillan, 392 Mich. 511, 221 N.W.2d 596 (1974).
People v. Payan, 173 Cal. App.3d 27, 220 Cal. Rptr. 126 (1985).
People v. Rosco, 168 Cal. App.3d 1093, 215 Cal. Rptr. 45 (1985).
Perri v. Coughlin, WL 395374 (N.D.N.Y. 1999).
Perry v. Louisiana, 111 S.Ct. 449 (1990).
Planned Parenthood of Southeastern Pennsylvania v. Casey, 505 U.S. 833 (1992).
Porter et al. v. Nussle, _____ U.S. _____ (2002).
Press-Enterprise v. Superior Court of California, 464 U.S. 501 (1984).
Price-Waterhouse v. Hopkins, 490 U.S. 228 (1989).
Purkett v. Elem, 63 L.W. 3807 (1995).
R. A. v. City of St. Paul, 112 S.Ct. 2538 (1992).
Regina v. Oxford, 175 Eng. Rep. 941 (1840).
Rennie v. Klein, 720 F.2d 266 (3d Cir. 1983).
Rhode Island v. Innis, 446 U.S. 291 (1980).
Rhodes v. Chapman, 452 U.S. 337 (1981).
Richmond Newspapers, Inc. v. Virginia, 448 U.S. 555 (1980).
Riggins v. Nevada, 504 U.S. 127 (1992).
Ring v. Arizona, _____ U.S. _____ (2002).
Rock v. Arkansas, 483 U.S. 44 (1986).
Roe v. Wade, 410 U.S. 113 (1973).
Rogers v. Okin, 634 F.2d 650 (1st Cir. 1980).
Romer, Governor of Colorado et al. v. Evans et al., 517 U.S. 620 (1996).
Rouse v. Cameron, 373 F.2d 541 (D.C. Cir. 1966).
Ruiz v. Johnson, 37 F. Supp. 2d 855 (S.D. Tex. 1999).
Sandin v. Conner, 115 S.Ct. 2293 (1995).
Schall v. Martin, 467 U.S. 253 (1984).
Sell v. U.S., _____ U.S. _____ (2003).
Shannon v. U.S., 114 S.Ct. 2419 (1994).
Schenck v. Pro Choice Network, 519 U.S. 357 (1997).
Sheppard v. Maxwell, 384 U.S. 333 (1966).
Simmons v. U.S., 390 U.S. 377 (1968).
Smith et al. v. Doe et al., _____ U.S. _____ (2003).
Soroka v. Dayton Hudson Corporation, 235 Cal. App. 3d 654 (1991).
Spano v. New York, 360 U.S. 315 (1959).
Stanford v. Kentucky, 492 U.S. 361 (1989).
State v. Andretta, 269 A.2d 644 (N.J. 1972).
State v. Bryan, 259 Kansas 143, 910 P.2d 212 (1996).
State v. Haseltine, 120 Wis.2d 92, 352 N.W.2d 673 (1984).
State ex rel Hawks v. Lazaro, 202 S.E.2d 109 (W.Va. 1974).
State v. Lannegan, 192 Ore. 691, 696, 236 P.2d 438, 441 (1951).
State v. Michaels, 625 A.2d. 498 (N.J. Super. 1993).
State v. Milligan, No. 77-CR-11–2908 (Franklin Co., Ohio) (Dec 4, 1978).
State v. Rodrigues, 679 P.2d 615 (Hawaii, 1984).
State v. Rucker, 1999 Kan. Lexus 410 (1999).
State v. Thomas, 66 Ohio St. 2d 518, 423 N.E. 2d 137 (1981).
Stogner v. California, _____ U.S. _____ (2003).

Stovall v. Denno, 388 U.S. 293 (1967).
Swain v. Alabama, 380 U.S. 202 (1965).
Tarasoff v. Regents of the Univ. of Cal., 529 P.2d 553 (Cal. 1974), *vac., reheard en banc,& aff'd* 131 Cal. Rptr. 14, 551 P.2d 334 (1976).
Thompson v. Oklahoma, 487 U.S. 815 (1988).
Toyota v. Williams, _____ U.S. _____ (2002).
Tran Van Khiem v. U.S., 51 Cr.L. 1061 (D. C. Cir. 1992).
U.S. v. A. R., 38 F,3d 699 (3rd Cir. 1994).
U.S. v. Armstrong, 517 U.S. 456 (1996).
U.S. v. Baller, 519 F.2d 463 (4th Cir. 1975).
U.S. v. Brandon, 158 F.3d 947 (6th Cir. 1998).
U.S. v. Brawner, 471 F.2d 969 (D.C. Cir. 1972).
U.S. v. Charters, 863 F.2d 302 (4th Cir. 1988).
U.S. v. Cordoba, 104 F.3d 225 (9th cir. 1999).
U.S. v. Dougherty, 473 F.2d 11 13 (D.C. Cir. 1972).
U.S. ex rel Gonzalez v. Zelker, 477 F.2d 797 (2d. cir. 1973).
U.S. v. Franks, 511 F.2d 25 (6th Cir. 1975).
U.S. v. Gipson, 24 M.J. 246 (C.M.A. 1987).
U. S. v. Manduiano, 425 U.S. 564 (1975).
U.S. v. Morgan, 193 F.3d 252 (4th Cir. 1999).
U.S. v. Morrison et al., 169 F.3d 820 (2000).
U.S. v. Oakland Cannabis Buyers' Cooperative et al. _____ U.S. _____ (2001).
U.S. v. Piccinonna, 885 F.2d 1529 (11th Cir. 1988).
U.S. v. Sahhar, 917 F. 2d 1207 (1990).
U.S. v. Salerno, 481 U.S. 739 (1987).
U.S. v. Sanchez, 118 F.3d 192 (4th cir. 1997).
U.S. v. Scheffer, 523 U.S. 303 (1998).
U.S. v. Wade, 388 U.S. 218 (1967).
U.S. v. Weston, 134 F. Supp. 2d 115 (D.D.C. 2001).
US Airways v. Barnett, _____ U.S. _____ (2002).
Vacco v. Quill, 521 U.S. 793 (1997).
Vitek v. Jones, 445 U.S. 480 (1980).
Wainwright v. Witt, 105 S.Ct. 844 (1985).
Ward's Cove Packing Co., Inc. et al. v. Atonia, 490 U.S. 642 (1989).
Washington v. Glucksberg, 117 S.Ct. 2258 (1997).
Washington v. Harper, 494 U.S. 210 (1990).
Wilkins v. Maryland State Police, Civil Action No. CEB-93-483 (D. Md. 1993).
Williams v. Florida, 399 U.S. 78 (1970).
Williamson v. Liptzin, 539 S.E.2d 313 (N.C. Ct. App. 2000).
Witherspoon v. Illinois, 391 U.S. 510 (1968).
Wisconsin v. Mitchell, 113 S.Ct. 2194 (1993).
Wolff v. McDonnell, 418 U.S. 539 (1974).
Wyatt v. Stickney, 325 F. Supp. 781 (S.D. Ala. 1971)., *enfrc in* 334 F. Supp. 1341 (S.D. Ala. 1971).
Zinermon v. Burch, 110 S.Ct. 975 (1990).

References

Aamodt, M., & Stalnaker, N. (2001). Police officer suicide: Frequency and officer profiles, In D. C. Sheehan & J. I. Warren (Eds.), *Suicide and law enforcement*. Washington, DC: FBI Academy.

Abadinsky, H. (1995). *Law and justice* (2nd ed). Nelson-Hall Publishers.

Abbott, W. F., & Batt, J. (1999). *A handbook of jury research*. Philadelphia, PA: American Law Institute/American Bar Association.

Abel, G. G., Barlow, D. H., Blanchard, E. B., & Gould, D. (1977). The components of rapists' sexual arousal. *Archives of General Psychiatry, 34*, 895–903.

Abel, G. G., Becker, J. V., Blanchard, E. B., & Djenderedjian, A. (1978). Differentiating sexual aggressives with penile measures. *Criminal Justice and Behavior, 5*, 313–332.

Abisch, J. B. (1995). Mediational lawyering in the civil commitment context: A therapeutic jurisprudence solution to the counsel role dilemma. *Psychology, Public Policy, and Law, 1*, 120–141.

Abney, D. (1986). Mutt and Jeff meet the Constitution: The propriety of good guy/bad guy interrogation. *Criminal Law Bulletin, 22*, 118–130.

Abraham, H. J. (1998). *The judicial process* (7th ed.). New York: Oxford University Press.

Abrahamsen, D. (1960). *The psychology of crime*. New York: Columbia University Press.

Abrams, S. (1989). *The complete polygraph handbook*. Lexington, MA: Lexington Books.

Achenback, T. (1991a). *Manual for the Child Behavior Checklist and 1991 profile*. Burlington, VT: University of Vermont, Department of Psychiatry.

Achenback, T. (1991b). *Manual for the teacher's report and 1991 profile*. Burlington, VT: University of Vermont, Department of Psychiatry.

Achenback, T. (1991c). *Manual for the youth self-report and 1991 profile*. Burlington, VT: University of Vermont, Department of Psychiatry.

Acker, J. R. (1990). Social science in Supreme Court criminal cases and briefs: The actual and potential contribution of social scientists as amici curiae. *Law and Human Behavior, 14*, 25–43.

Acker, J. R. (1991). Social science in Supreme Court death penalty cases: Citation practices and their implications. *Justice Quarterly, 8*, 421–446.

Acker, J. R., Bohm, R. M., & Lanier, C. S. (1998). Eds., *America's experiment with capital punishment: Reflections on the past, present and future of the ultimate penal sanction*. Durham, NC: Carolina Academic Press.

Acker, J. R., & Irving, R. (1998). *Basic legal research for criminal justice and the social sciences*. Gathersburg, MD: Aspen Publishers, Inc.

Ackerman, M. J., & Ackerman, M. C. (1997). Custody evaluation practices: A survey of experienced professionals (revisited). *Professional Psychology: Research and Practice, 28*, 137–145.

Ackerman, M. J., & Schoendorf, K. (1992). *ASPECT: Ackerman-Schoendorf Scales for Custody Evaluation*. Los Angeles, CA: Western Psychological Services.

Adams, K. (1992). Adjusting to prison life. In M. Tonry (Ed.), *Crime and justice: A review of the research* (Vol 16). Chicago: University of Chicago Press.

Adams, K., Alpert, G. P., Dunham, R. G., Garner, J. H., Greenfield, L.A., Henriquez, M. A., Langan, P. A., Maxwell, C. D., & Smith, S. K. (1999, October). *Use of force by police: Overview of national and local data series: Research report.* Washington, DC: National Institute of Justice and Bureau of Justice Statistics.

Ainsworth, P. B. (1995). *Psychology and policing in a changing world*. Chichester, UK: Wiley.

Alschuler, A. W. (1979). Plea bargaining and its history. *Law & Society Review, 13*, 211–245.

Althouse, R. (2000). AACP standards: A historical overview (1978–1980). *Criminal Justice and Behavior, 27*, 430–432.

Amato, P., & Keith, P. (1991). Parental divorce and the well-being of children: A meta-analysis. *Psychological Bulletin, 110*, 26–46.

Ambuel, B., & Rappaport, J. (1992). Developmental trends in adolescents' psychological and legal competence to consent to abortion. *Law and Human Behavior, 69*, 129–154.

American Association for Correctional Psychology. (2000). Standards for psychology services in jails, prisons, correctional facilities, and agencies. *Criminal Justice and Behavior, 27*, 433–493.

American Educational Research Association, American Psychological Association, and National Council in Measurement in Education. (1999). *Standards for educational and psychological testing*. (3rd ed.). Washington, DC: American Educational Research Association.

American Psychiatric Association. (1987). *Diagnostic and statistical manual of mental disorders*. (3rd ed.). Washington, DC: Author.

American Psychiatric Association. (1994). *Diagnostic and statistical manual of mental disorders*. (4th ed.). Washington, DC: Author.

American Psychiatric Association. (2000). *Diagnostic and statistical manual of mental disorders* (revised). Washington, DC: Author.

American Psychiatric Association Task Force. (1992). *The use of psychiatric diagnosis in the legal process*. Washington, DC: American Psychiatric Association.

American Psychological Association (APA). (1991). Minutes of the Council of Representatives. *American Psychologist, 46*, 722.

American Psychological Association (APA). (1994). Guidelines for child custody evaluations in divorce proceedings. *American Psychologist, 49*, 677–680.

American Psychological Association Working Group on Investigation of Memories of Childhood Abuse. (1998). Final conclusions. *Psychology, Public Policy, and Law, 4*, 933–940.

Anastasi, A. (1988). *Psychological testing* (4th ed.). New York: Macmillan.

Andenaes, J. (1968). Does punishment deter crime? *The Criminal Law Quarterly, 11*, 76–93.

Andenaes, J. (1990). The Scandinavian countries. In J. R. Spencer, G. Nicholson, R. Flin, & R. Bull (Eds.), *Children's evidence in legal proceedings: An international perspective* University of Cambridge, UK: Faculty of Law.

Anderson, L. (2002, October 27). Sniper suspects didn't fit profile, baffled experts. *The Sunday Times Argus*, A4.

Andrews, D. A., & Bonta, J. (1998). *The psychology of criminal conduct* (2nd ed). Cincinnati, OH: Anderson.

Andrews, D. A., Bonta, J., & Hoge, R. D. (1990). Classification for effective rehabilitation: Rediscovering psychology. *Criminal Justice and Behavior, 17*, 19–52.

Andrews, D. A., Zinger, I., Hoge, R., Bonta, J., Gendreau, P., & Cullen F. T. (1990). Does correctional treatment work? A clinically relevant and psychologically informed meta-analysis. *Criminology, 28*, 369–404.

Anson, R. H., Mann, J. D., & Sherman, D. (1986). Niederhoffer's cynicism scale: Reliability and beyond. *Journal of Criminal Justice, 14*, 295–305.

Appelbaum, P. S. (1992). Civil commitment from a systems perspective. *Law and Human Behavior, 16*, 61–74.

Appelbaum, P. S., & Grisso, T. (1988). Assessing patients' capacities to consent to treatment. *New England Journal of Medicine, 319*, 1635–1638.

Appelbaum, P. S., & Grisso, T. (1995). The MacArthur treatment competence study: I. Mental illness and competence to consent to treatment. *Law and Human Behavior, 19*, 105–126.

Appelbaum, P. S., & Grisso, T. (2001). *MacArthur Competence Assessment Tool for Clinical Research.* Sarasota, FL: Professional Resource Press.

Appelbaum, P. S., Jick, R. Z., Grisso, T., Givelbar, D., Silver, E., & Steadman, H. J. (1993). Use of posttraumatice stress. *Psychiatry, 150*, 229–234.

Appley, M. H., & Trumbull, R. (1967). *Psychological stress.* New York: Appleton-Century-Crofts.

Armstrong, D., & Pereira, J. (2001, October 23). Nation's airlines adopt aggressive measures for passenger profiling. *Wall Street Journal*, 1, A12.

Arrestees Drug Abuse Monitoring Program. (2000, June). *1999 annual report on drug use among adult and juvenile arrestees.* Washington, DC: National Institute of Justice.

Arther, R. O.. (1965). *The scientific investigator.* Springfield, IL: C. C. Thomas.

Arvanites, T. M. (1988). The impact of state mental hospital deinstitutionalization on commitments for incompetency to stand trial, *Criminology, 26*, 307–320.

Asch, S. E. (1951). Effects of group pressure upon the modification and distortion of judgment. In H. Guetzkow (Ed.), *Groups, leadership, and men.* Pittsburgh, PA: Carnegie Press.

Asch, S. E. (1952). *Social psychology*. Englewood Cliffs, NJ: Prentice-Hall.

Asch, S. E. (1955). Opinions and social pressure. *Scientific American, 193* (5), 31–35.

Asch, S. E. (1956). Studies of independence and conformity: A minority of one against unanimous majority. *Psychological Monographs, 70* (Whole No. 416).

Attias, R., & Goodwin, J. (1985). Knowledge and management strategies in incest cases: A survey of physicians, psychologists, and family counselors. *Child Abuse and Neglect, 9*, 527–533.

Aubrey, A. S., & Caputo, R. R. (1980). *Criminal interrogation* (3rd ed.). Springfield, IL: C. C. Thomas.

Ault, R. L., Hazelwood, R. R., & Reboussin, R. (1994). Epistemological status of equivocal death analysis. *American Psychologist, 49*, 72–73.

Ault, R., & Reese, J. T. (1980). A psychological assessment of criminal profiling. *F.B.I. Law Enforcement Bulletin, 49*, 22–25.

Austin, J., & Irwin, J. (2001). *It's about time: America's imprisonment binge* (3rd ed.). Belmont, CA: Wadsworth/Thomson Learning.

Ayd, F. J. (1975). The depot fluephenazines: A reappraisal after 10 years' clinical experience. *American Journal of Psychiatry, 132*, 491–500.

Azen, S., Snibbe, H., & Montgomery, H. K. (1973). A longitudinal predictive study of success and performance of law enforcement officers. *Journal of Applied Psychology, 57*, 190–192.

Bachrach, A. J. (1979). Speech and its potential for stress monitoring. In C. E. C. Lundgren (Ed.), *Proceedings, workshop on monitoring vital signs in the diver.* Bethesda, MD: Undersea Medical Society and Office of Naval Research.

Bailey, W. C. (1998). Deterrence, brutalization, and the death penalty: Another examination of Oklahoma's return to capital punishment. *Criminology, 36*, 711–733.

Bailis, D., Darley, J., Waxman, T., & Robinson, P. (1995). Community standards of criminal liability and the insanity defense. *Law and Human Behavior, 19*, 425–446.

Balch, R. W, Griffiths, L. T, Hall, E. O., & Winfree, L. T. (1976). The socialization of jurors: The voir dire as a rite of passage. *Journal of Criminal Justice, 4*, 271–283.

Baldus, D. C., Pulaski, C., & Woodworth, G. (1983). Comparative review of death sentences: An empirical study of the Georgia experience. *Journal of Criminal Law and Criminology, 74*, 661–753.

Baldus, D. C., & Woodworth, G. (1998). Racial discrimination and the death penalty: An empirical and legal overview. In J. R. Acker, R. M. Bohm, and C. S. Lanier (Eds.), *America's experiment with capital punishment: Reflections on the past, present and future of the ultimate penal sanction*. Durham, NC: Carolina Academic Press.

Bales, R. F., & Borgatta, E. F. (1955). Size of group as a factor in the interaction profile. In A. P. Hare, E. F. Borgatta & R. F. Bales (Eds.), *Small groups*. New York: Knopf.

Balkin, J. (1988). Why policemen don't like policewomen. *Journal of Police Science and Administration, 16*, 29–37.

Bandewehr, L. J., & Novotny, R. (1976). Juror authoritarianism and trial judge partiality: An experiment in jury decision making. *Journal of Experimental Study in Politics, 5*, 28–33.

Bandura, A. (1973). *Aggression: A social learning analysis*. Englewood Cliffs, NJ: Prentice-Hall.

Bandura, A. (1974). Behavior theory and the models of man. *American Psychologist, 29*, 859–869.

Bandura, A. (1977). *Social learning theory*. Englewood Cliffs, NJ: Prentice Hall.

Bandura, A. (1978). The self system in reciprocal determinism. *American Psychologist, 33*, 344–358.

Bandura, A. (1986). *Social foundations of thought and action: A social cognitive theory*. Englewood Cliffs, NJ: Prentice-Hall.

Barber, B. L., & Eccles, J. S. (1992). Long term influence values, behaviors, and aspirations. *Psychological Bulletin, 111*, 108–126.

Barber, T. X., Spanos, N. R, & Chaves, J. F. (1974). *Hypnosis, imagination, and human potentialities*. New York: Pergamon Press.

Barkley, R. A. (1997). Behavioral inhibition, sustained attention, and executive functions: Constructing a unifying theory of ADHD. *Psychological Bulletin, 121*, 65–94.

Barland, G. H. (1988). The polygraph use in the USA and elsewhere. In A. Gale (Ed.), *The polygraph test: Lies, truth and science*. London: Sage.

Barland, G. H., & Raskin, D. C. (1973). Detection of deception. In W. F. Prokasy & D. C. Raskin (Eds.), *Electrodermal activity in psychological research*. New York: Academic Press.

Barling, J., Rogers, A. G., & Kelloway, E. K. (2000). Behind closed doors: In-home workers' experience of sexual harassment and workplace violence. *Journal of Occupational Health Psychology, 6*, 255–269.

Barnett, A. (1985). Some distribution patterns for the Georgia death sentence. *University of California, Davis Law Review, 18*, 1327–1374.

Barnum, R. (1987). Clinical evaluation of juvenile delinquents facing transfer to adult court. *Journal of the American Academy of Child and Adolescent Psychiatry, 26*, 922–925.

Barnum, R. (2000). Clinical and forensic evaluation of competence to stand trial in juvenile defendants. In T. Grisso, & R. G. Schwartz (Eds.), *Youth on trial*. Chicago: University of Chicago Press.

Baron, R. A., & Byrne, D. (1981). *Social psychology: Understanding human interaction* (3rd ed.). Boston: Allyn & Bacon.

Baron, R. A., & Byrne, D. (2000). *Social psychology*. Boston: Allyn & Bacon.

Barrett, G. V., & Morris, S. B. (1993). The American Psychological Association's amicus curiae brief in *Price Waterhouse v. Hopkins*: The values of science versus the values of the law. *Law and Human Behavior, 17*, 201–215.

Bartol, C. R. (1991a). *Criminal behavior: A psychosocial approach* (3rd ed.). Englewood Cliffs, NJ: Prentice-Hall.

Bartol, C. R. (1991b). Predictive validation of the MMPI for small-town police officers who fail. *Professional Psychology: Research and Practice, 22*, 127–132.

Bartol, C. R. (1996). Police psychology: Then, now, and beyond. *Criminal Justice and Behavior, 23*, 70–89.

Bartol, C. R. (2002). *Criminal behavior: A psychological approach* (6th ed.). Saddle River, NJ: Prentice Hall.

Bartol, C. R., & Bartol, A. M. (1989). *Juvenile delinquency: A systems approach*. Englewood Cliffs, NJ: Prentice-Hall.

Bartol, C. R., & Bartol, A. M. (1998). *Delinquency and justice: A psychosocial approach*. Saddle River, NJ: Prentice Hall.

Bartol, C. R., Bergen, G. T., Volckens, J. S., & Knoras, K. M. (1992). Women in small-town policing: Job performance and stress. *Criminal Justice and Behavior, 19*, 240–259.

Bartol, C. R., Griffin, R., & Clark, M. (1993). *Nationwide survey of American correctional psychologists*. (unpublished manuscript).

Bartol, C. R. & Urzillo, B. (1993). *Women in small-town law enforcement*. (unpublished manuscript).

Bartollas, C. (1981). *Introduction to corrections*. New York: Harper & Row.

Batavia, A. I. (2000). So far so good: Observations on the first year of Oregon's Death with Dignity Act. *Psychology, Public Policy, and Law, 6*, 291–304.

Bauchner, J. E., Brandt, D. R., & Miller, G. R. (1977). The truth/deception attribution: Effects of varying levels of information availability. In B. D. Ruben (Ed.), *Communication Yearbook 1*. New Brunswick, NJ: International Communication Association.

Bauserman, R. (1997, October). *Child adjustment in joint custody versus sole custody arrangements: A meta-analytic review*. Paper presented at the 11th Annual Conference of the Children's Rights Council, Arlington, Virginia.

Bauserman, R. (2002). Child adjustment in joint-custody versus sole-custody arrangements: A meta-analytic review. *Journal of Family Psychology, 16*, 38–53.

Bayley, D. H., & Garofalo, J. (1989). The management of violence by police patrol officers. *Criminology, 27*, 1–27.

Beck, C. J. A., & Sales, B. D. (2000). A critical reappraisal of divorce mediation research and policy. *Psychology, Public Policy, and Law, 6*, 989–1056.

Bedrosian, R. C., & Beck, A. J. (1979). Cognitive aspects of suicidal behavior. *Suicide and Life-Threatening Behavior, 9*, 87–96.

Begley, S. (2002, October 25). Eyewitnesses to crime are often blinded by shock, adrenaline. *Wall Street Journal*, p. B1.

Belcher, J. R. (1989). On becoming homeless: A study of chronically mentally ill persons. *Journal of Community Psychology, 17*, 173–185.

Belenko, S. (1998). *Research on drug courts: A critical review*. New York: National Center on Addiction and Substance Abuse.

Bell, B. E., & Loftus, E. F. (1988). Degree of detail of eyewitness and mock juror judgments. *Journal of Applied Social Psychology, 18*, 1171–1192.

Bell, B. E., & Loftus, E. F. (1989). Trivial persuasion in the courtroom: The power of (a few) minor details. *Journal of Personality and Social Psychology, 56*, 669–679.

Bell, D. J. (1982). Policewomen: Myths and reality. *Journal of Police Science and Administration, 10*, 112–120.

Bell, J. (2002). *Policing hatred*. New York: New York University Press.

Bell, S. T., Kuriloff, P. J., & Lottes, I. (1994). Understanding attributions of blame in stranger rape and date rape situations. *Journal of Applied Psychology, 24*, 1719–1734.

Bem, D. J. (1967). Self-perceptions: An alternative interpretation of cognitive dissonance phenomenon. *Psychological Review, 74*, 183–200.

Bem, D. J. (1972). Self-perception theory. In L. Berkowitz (Ed.), *Advances in experimental social psychology* (Vol. 6). New York: Academic Press.

Bem, D. J., & Allen, A. (1974). On predicting some of the people some of the time: The search for cross situational consistencies in behavior. *Psychological Review, 81*, 506–520.

Benesh, S. C., & Howell, S. E. (2001). Confidence in the courts: A comparison of users and non-users. *Behavioral Sciences and the Law, 19*, 199–214.

Benjamin, G. A. H. (2000). A continued debate about hastened death. *Psychology, Public Policy, and Law, 6*, 261–267.

Benjamin, G. A. H., Werth, J. L., & Gostin, L. O. (2000). (Eds.). Special theme: Hastened death. *Psychology, Public Policy, and Law, 6*, 261–267.

Benjamin, L. T. (2001). American psychology's struggles with its curriculum: Should a thousand flowers bloom? *American Psychologist, 56*, 735–742.

Benjamin, T. B., & Lux, K. (1977). Solitary confinement as psychological punishment. *California Western Law Review, 13*, 265–296.

Ben-Shakhar, G. (2002). A critical review of the control questions test (CQT). In M. Kleiner (Ed.), *Handbook of polygraph testing*. San Diego, CA: Academic Press.

Ben-Shakhar, G., Bar-Hillel, M., & Lieblich, I. (1986). Trial by polygraph: Scientific and juridical issues in lie detection. *Behavioral Sciences and the Law, 4*, 459–479.

Ben-Shakhar, G., & Dolev, K. (1996). Psychophysiological detection through the guilty knowledge technique: The effects of mental countermeasures. *Journal of Applied Psychology, 81*, 273–281.

Ben-Shakhar, G., & Elaad, E. (2002). The guilty knowledge test (GKT) as an application of psychophysiology: Future prospects and obstacles. The comparison questions test. In M. Kleiner (Ed.), *Handbook of polygraph testing*. San Diego, CA: Academic Press.

Ben-Shakhar, G., & Furedy, J. J. (1990). *Theories and applications in the detection of deception: A psychophysiological and international perspective*. New York: Springer-Verlag.

Berg, B. L., & Budnick, K. L. (1986). Defeminization of women in law enforcement: A new twist in the traditional police personality. *Journal of Police Science and Administration, 10*, 180–185.

Berg, K. S., & Vidmar, N. (1975). Authoritarianism and recall of evidence about criminal behavior. *Journal of Research in Personality, 9*, 147–157.

Berkowitz, L. (1993). *Aggression: Its causes, consequences, and control*. New York: McGraw-Hill.

Bermant, G. (1977). *Conduct of the voir dire examination: Practices and opinions of federal district judges*. Washington, DC: Federal Judicial Center.

Bermant, G., & Shapard, J. (1981). The voir dire examination, juror challenges, and adversary advocacy. In B. D. Sales (Ed.), *Perspectives in law and psychology* (Vol. 2), *The trial process*. New York: Plenum.

Bernard, T. (1992). *The cycle of juvenile justice*. New York: Oxford University Press.

Bernat, J. A., Calhoun, K. S., Adams, H. E., & Zeichner, A. (2001). Homophobia and physical aggression toward homosexual and heterosexual individuals. *Journal of Abnormal Psychology, 110*, 179–187.

Bersh, P. J. (1969). A validation of polygraph examiner judgments. *Journal of Applied Psychology, 53*, 399–403.

Bersoff, D. N. (1979). Regarding psychologists testily: Legal regulations of psychological assessment in the public school. *Maryland Law Review, 39*, 27–120.

Bersoff, D. N. (1981). Testing and the law. *American Psychologist, 36*, 1047–1056.

Bersoff, D. N. & Ogden, D. W. (1991). APA Amicus Curiae briefs: Furthering lesbian and gay male civil rights. *American Psychologist, 46*, 950–956.

Best, J. (1990). *Threatened children*. Chicago: University of Chicago Press.

Beutler, L. E., Nussbaum, P. D., & Meredith, K. E. (1988). Changing personality patterns of police officers. *Professional Psychology: Research and Practice, 19*, 303–307.

Beutler, L. E., Storm, A., Kirksih, P., Scogini, F., & Gaines, J. A. (1985). Parameters in the prediction of police officer performance. *Professional Psychology: Research and Practice, 16*, 324–335.

Bezanson, R. P. (1975). Involuntary treatment of the mentally ill in Iowa: The 1975 legislation. *Iowa Law Review, 61*, 261–396.

Bilchik, S. (1998). Serious and violent juvenile offenders. *Juvenile Justice Bulletin,* Office of Juvenile Justice and Delinquency Prevention, 1–8.

Bingham, R. P., Porché-Burke, L., James, S., Sue, D. W., & Vasquez, M. J. T. (2002). Introduction: A report on the National Multicultural Conference and Summit II. *Cultural Diversity and Ethnic Minority Psychology, 8*, 75–87.

Bishop, D. M. (2000). Juvenile offenders in the adult criminal justice system. In M. Tonry (Ed.), *Crime and justice: A review of research* (Vol. 27). Chicago: University of Chicago Press.

Bishop, D. M., Frazier, C. E., & Henretta, J. C. (1989). Prosecutorial waiver: Case study of a questionable reform. *Crime & Delinquency, 35*, 179–198.

Black, H. C. (1990). *Black's law dictionary*. St. Paul, MN: West Publishing.

Black, M. C. (2001). *Juvenile delinquency probation caseload, 1989–1998. Fact sheet*. Washington, DC: Office of Juvenile Justice and Delinquency Prevention.

Blackmore, J. (1978, July). Are police allowed to have problems of their own? *Police Magazine*, 47–55.

Blanck, P. D. (1985). The appearance of justice: Judges' verbal and nonverbal behavior in criminal jury trials. *Stanford Law Review, 38*, 89–164.

Blanck, P. D., & Berven, H. M. (1999). Evidence of disability after *Daubert*. *Psychology, Public Policy, and Law, 5*, 16–40.

Blinkhorn, S. (1988). Lie detection as a psychometric procedure. In A. Gale (Ed.), *The polygraph test: Lies, truth and science*. London: Sage.

Block, J. H., Block, J., & Gjerde, P. F. (1986). The personality of children prior to divorce: A prospective study. *Child Development, 57*, 827–840.

Blum, R. H. (1964). *Police selection*. Springfield, IL: C. C. Thomas.

Blunk, R., & Sales, B. D. (1977). Persuasion during the voir dire. In B. D. Sales (Ed.), *Psychology in the legal process*. New York: Spectrum.

Boat, B. W., & Everson, M. D. (1988). Use of anatomical dolls among professionals in sexual abuse evaluations. *Child Abuse and Neglect, 12*, 171–179.

Boccaccini, M. T., & Brodsky, S. L. (1999). Diagnostic test usage by forensic psychologists in emotional injury cases. *Professional Psychology: Research and Practice, 30*, 253–259.

Boehm, V. (1968). Mr. prejudice, Miss sympathy, and the authoritarian personality: An application of psychological measuring techniques to the problems of jury bias. *Wisconsin Law Review, 12*, 734–750.

Boehnert, C. E. (1989). Characteristics of successful and unsuccessful insanity pleas. *Law and Human Behavior, 13*, 31–39.

Boer, D. P., Hart, S. D., Kropp, R. P., & Webster, D. C. (1997). *Manual for the Sexual Violence Risk-20: Professional guidelines for assessing risk of sexual violence*. Vancouver, British Columbia: British Columbia Institute on Family Violence.

Bohm, R. M. (1991). *The death penalty in America: Current research*. Cincinnati, OH: Anderson.

Bohm, R. M. (1999). *Deathquest: An introduction to the theory and practice of capital punishment in the United States*. Cincinnati, OH: Anderson.

Bolocofsky, D. N. (1989). Use and abuse of mental health experts in child custody determinations. *Behavioral Sciences and the Law, 7*, 197–213.

Bond, C. F., Omar, A., Pitre, V., Lashley, B. R., Skaggs, L. M., & Kirk, C. T. (1992). Fishy-looking liars: Deception judgment from expectancy violation. *Journal of Personality and Social Psychology, 63*, 969–977.

Bonnie, R. J. (1990). Dilemmas in and administering the death penalty: Conscientious abstentions, professional ethics, and the needs of the legal system. *Law and Human Behavior, 14*, 67–90.

Bonnie, R. J. (1992). The competence of criminal defendants: A theoretical reformulation. *Behavioral Sciences and the Law, 10*, 291–316.

Bonnie, R. J., & Grisso, T. (2000). Adjudicative competence and youthful offenders. In T. Grisso & R. G. Schwartz (Eds.), *Youth on trial*. Chicago: University of Chicago Press.

Bonnie, R. J., & Monahan, J. (Eds.). (1997). *Mental disorder, work disability, and the law*. Chicago: University of Chicago Press.

Bonowitz, J. C., & Bonowitz, J. S. (1981). Diversion of the mentally ill into the criminal justice system: The police intervention perspective. *American Journal of Psychiatry, 138*, 973–976.

Bonta, J., & Gendreau, P. (1990). Reexamining the cruel and unusual punishment of prison life. *Law and Human Behavior, 14*, 347–372.

Bonta, J., Law, M., & Hanson, K. (1998). The prediction of criminal and violent recidivism among mentally disordered offenders: A meta-analysis. *Psychological Bulletin*, 3, 123–142.

Boothby, J. L., & Clements, C. B. (2000). A national survey of correctional psychologists. *Criminal Justice and Behavior, 27*, 716–732.

Borduin, C. M., Mann, B. J., Cone, L. T., Henggeler, S. W., Fucci, B. R., Blaske, D. M., et al. (1995). Multisystemic treatment of serious juvenile offenders: Long-term prevention of criminality and violence. *Journal of Consulting and Clinical Psychology, 63*, 569–578.

Borgida, E. (1980). Evidentiary reform of rape laws: A Psycholegal approach. In P. D. Lipsitt & B. D. Sales (Eds.), *New directions in psycholegal research*. New York: Van Nostrand Reinhold.

Borgida, E., DeBono, K. G., & Buckman, L. A. (1990). Cameras in the courtroom: The effects of media coverage on witness testimony and juror perceptions. *Law and Human Behavior, 14*, 489–510.

Borgida, E., & Park, R. (1988). The entrapment defenses: Juror comprehension and decision making. *Law and Human Behavior, 12*, 19–31.

Bornstein, B. H. (1999). The ecological validity of jury simulations: Is the jury still out? *Law and Human Behavior, 23*, 75–91.

Bornstein, B. H., Whisenhunt, B. L., Nemeth, R. J., & Dunaway, D. L. (2002). Pretrial publicity and civil cases: A two-way street? *Law and Human Behavior, 26*, 3–17.

Bortner, M. A. (1996). Traditional rhetoric, organizational realities: Remand of juveniles to adult court. *Crime & Delinquency, 32*, 53–73.

Borum, R. (1996). Improving the clinical practice of violence risk assessment: Technology, guidelines, and training. *American Psychologist, 51*, 945–956.

Borum, R., Deane, M. W., Steadman, H. J., & Morrissey, J. (1998). Police perspective on responding to mentally ill people in crisis: Perceptions of program effectiveness. *Behavioral Sciences and the Law, 16*, 393–405.

Borum, R., Fein, R., Vosekuil, B., & Berglund, J. (1999). Threat assessment: Defining an approach for evaluating risk of targeted violence. *Behavioral Sciences and the Law, 17*, 323–337.

Borum, R., & Fulero, S. M. (1999). Empirical research on the insanity defense and attempted reforms: Evidence toward informed policy. *Law and Human Behavior, 23*, 375–394.

Borum, R., & Grisso, T. (1995). Psychological test use in criminal forensic evaluations. *Professional Psychology: Research and Practice, 26*, 465–473.

Borum, R., & Otto, R. (2000). Advances in forensic assessment and treatment. *Law and Human Behavior, 24*, 1–7.

Borum, R., & Reddy, M. (2001). Assessing violence risk in *Tarasoff* situations: A fact-based model of inquiry. *Behavioral Sciences and the Law, 19,* 375–385.

Borum, R., & Strentz, T. (1993, April). The borderline personality: Negotiation strategies. *FBI Law Enforcement Bulletin,* 6–10.

Borum, R., Swanson, J., Swartz, M., & Hiday, V. (1997). Substance abuse, violent behavior, and police encounters among people with severe mental disorders. *Journal of Contemporary Criminal Justice, 13,* 236–249.

Bothwell, R. K., Deffenbacher, K. A., & Brigham, J. C. (1987). Correlation of eyewitness accuracy and confidence: The optimality hypothesis revisited. *Journal of Applied Psychology, 72,* 691–695.

Bottoms, B. L., Goodman, G. S., Schwartz-Kenney, B. M., & Thomas, S. N. (2002). Understanding children's use of secrecy in the context of eyewitness reports. *Law and Human Behavior, 26,* 285–313.

Bourgeois, M. J., Horowitz, I. A., & ForsterLee, L. (1993). The effects of technicality and access to trial transcripts on verdicts and information processing in a civil trial. *Personality and Social Psychology Bulletin, 19,* 220–227.

Bow, J. N., & Quinnell, F. A. (2001). Psychologists' current practices and procedures in child custody evaluations five years after American Psychological Association Guidelines. *Professional Psychology: Research and Practice, 32,* 261–268.

Bower, G. H. (1981). Mood and memory. *American Psychologist, 36,* 129–148.

Bowers, K. (1973). Situationalism in psychology: An analysis and a critique. *Psychological Review, 80,* 307–336.

Bowers, W. J. (1995). The Capital Jury Project: Rationale, design, and preview of early findings. *Indiana Law Review, 70,* 1043–1068.

Bowers, W. J., & Pierce, G. L. (1980). Deterrence or brutalization: What is the effect of executions? *Crime & Delinquency, 26,* 453–484.

Bradley, M. T., & Ainsworth, D. (1984). Alcohol and the psychophysiological detection of deception. *Psychophysiology, 21,* 63–71.

Braithwaite, J. (1985). *To punish or persuade: Enforcement of coal mine safety.* Albany, NY: SUNY Press.

Braithwaite, J. (1999). Restorative justice: Assessing optimistic and pessimistic accounts. In M. Tonry (Ed.), *Crime and justice: A review of research* (Vol. 25). Chicago: University of Chicago Press.

Brandreth, D. (1978). Stress and the policeman's wife. *Police Stress, 1,* 41–42.

Braver, S. L., Wolchik, S. A., & Sandler, I. N. (1985). *Noncustodial parents: Parents without children.* Grant proposal submitted to the National Institute of Child Health and Human Development (HD19383).

Bray, J. H. (1990). Impact of divorce on the family. In R. E. Rakel (Ed.), *Textbook of family practice* (4th ed.). Philadelphia: W. B. Saunders.

Bray, J. H. (1991). Psychosocial factors affecting custodial and visitation arrangements. *Behavioral Sciences and the Law, 9,* 419–437.

Bray, R. M., & Kerr, N. L. (1979). Use of simulation method in the study of jury behavior: Some methodological considerations. *Law and Human Behavior, 3,* 107–120.

Bray, R. M., & Noble, A. M. (1978). Authoritarianism and decisions of mock juries: Evidence of jury bias and group polarization. *Journal of Personality and Social Psychology, 36,* 1424–1430.

Bray, R. M., Struckman-Johnson, C., Osborne, M.D., McFarlane, J. B., & Scott, J. (1978). The effects of defendant status on the decisions of students and community juries. *Social Psychology, 41,* 256–260.

Brehm, J. W. (1966). *A theory of psychological reactance.* New York: Academic Press.

Brent, D. A. (1989). The psychological autopsy: Methodological issues for the study of adolescent suicide. *Suicide and Life-Threating Behavior, 19,* 43–57.

Brewster, M. P. (2002). Domestic violence theories, research, and practice. In A. R. Roberts (Ed.), *Handbook of domestic violence intervention strategies.* Oxford, UK: Oxford University Press.

Bricklin, B. (1984). *Bricklin Perceptual Scales.* Furlong, PA: Village Publishing.

Bricklin, B. (1994). *Perception of Relationships Test Manual.* Furlong, PA: Village Publishing.

Bricklin, B. (1995). *The child custody evaluation handbook: Research-based solutions and applications.* New York: Bruner/Mazel.

Bricklin, B., & Elliot, G. (1995). Postdivorce issues and relevant research. In B. Bricklin (Ed.), *The child custody evaluation handbook: Research-based solutions and applications* (pp. 27–67). New York: Bruner/Mazel.

Briere, J. (1988). The long-term clinical correlates of childhood sexual victimization. In R. A. Prentky & V. L. Quinsey (Eds.), *Human sexual aggression: Current perspectives.* New York: New York Academy of Sciences.

Briere, J., Malamuth, N., & Ceniti, J. (1981). *Self-assessed rape proclivity: Attitudinal and sexual correlates.* Paper presented at APA Meeting, Los Angeles.

Brigham, J. C. (1980). Perspectives on the impact of lineup composition, race, and witness confidence on identification accuracy. *Law and Human Behavior, 4,* 315–321.

Brigham, J. C., & Cairns, D. L. (1988). The effect of mugshot inspections on eyewitness identification accuracy. *Journal of Applied Social Psychology, 18,* 1394–1410.

Brimacombe, C. A. E., Quinton, N., Nance, N., & Garrioch, L. (1997). Is age irrelevant? Perceptions of young and old adult eyewitnesses. *Law and Human Behavior, 21,* 619–634.

Brodsky, S. L. (1977). The mental health professional on the witness stand: A survival guide. In B. D. Sales (Ed.), *Psychology in the legal process.* New York: Spectrum Publications.

Brodsky, S. L. (1980). Ethical issues for psychologists in corrections. In J. Monahan (Ed.), *Who is the client? The ethics of psychological intervention in the criminal justice system.* Washington, DC: American Psychological Association.

Brodsky, S. L. (1991). *Testifying in court: Guidelines and maxims for the expert witness.* Washington, DC: American Psychological Association.

Brodsky, S. L. (1999). *The expert witness: More maxims and guidelines for testifying in court.* Washington, DC: American Psychological Assocation.

Brodzinsky, D. M. (1993). On the use and misuse of psychological testing in child custody evaluations. *Professional Psychology: Research and Practice, 24*, 213–219.

Brooks, A. (1987). The right to refuse antipsychotic medications: Law and policy. *Rutgers Law Review, 39*, 121–179.

Brooks, A. D. (1974). *Law, psychiatry and the mental health system.* Boston: Little, Brown.

Brooks, R. R. W., & Jeon-Slaughter, H. (2001). Race, income, and perceptions of the U.S. court system. *Behavioral Sciences and the Law, 19*, 249–264.

Brooks, S. L. (1999). Therapeutic jurisprudence and preventive law in child welfare proceedings: A family systems approach. *Psychology, Public Policy, and Law, 5*, 951–965.

Broome, K. M., Simpson, D. D., & Joe, G. W. (1999). Patient and program attributes related to treatment process indicators in DATOS. *Drug and Alcohol Dependence, 57*, 127–135.

Brown, D., Scheflin, A. W., & Whitfield, C. L. (1999). Recovered memories: The current weight of the evidence in science and in the courts. *Journal of Psychiatry and Law, 27*, 5–15.

Brown, D., Scheflin, A. W., & Hammond, D. C. (1998). *Memory, trauma treatment, and the law*. New York: Norton.

Brown, E., Deffenbacher, K., & Sturgill, W. (1977). Memory for faces and the circumstances of encounter. *Journal of Applied Psychology, 62*, 311–318.

Brown, J., Gilliard, D., Snell, T., Stephan, J., & Wilson, D. (1996). *Correctional populations in the United States, 1994* (NCJ-160091). Washington, DC: National Institute of Justice.

Brown, T. L., Borduin, C. M., & Henggeler, S. W. (2001). Treating juvenile offenders in community settings. In J. B. Ashford, B. D. Sales, & W. H. Reid (Eds.), *Treating adult and juvenile offenders with special needs*. Washington, DC: American Psychological Association.

Browne, A., & Finkelhor, D. (1986). Impact of child sexual abuse: A review of the research. *Psychological Bulletin, 99*, 66–77.

Bruck, M., Ceci, S. J., & Francoeur, E. (2000). Children's use of anatomically detailed dolls to report genital touching in a medical examination. *Journal of Experimental Psychology: Applied, 6*, 74–83.

Bruck, M., Ceci, S. J., Francoeur, E., & Renick, A. (1995). Anatomically detailed dolls do not facilitate preschoolers' reports of a pediatric examination involving genital touching. *Journal of Experimental Psychology: Applied, 1*, 95–109.

Bryan, P. E. (1999). "Collaborative divorce": Meaningful reform or another quick fix? *Psychology, Public Policy, and Law, 5*, 1001–1017.

Buchanan, C., Maccoby, E., & Dornbusch, S. (1991). Caught between parents: Adolescents' experience in divorced homes. *Child Development, 62*, 1008–1029.

Buckhout, R. (1974). Eyewitness testimony. *Scientific American, 321*, 23–31.

Buckhout, R. (1977). Eyewitness identification and psychology in the courtroom. *Criminal Defense, 4*, 5–10.

Budd, J. W., Arvey, R. D., & Lawless, P. (1996). Correlates and consequences of workplace violence. *Journal of Occupational Health Psychology, 1*, 197–210.

Budd, K. S., Felix, E. D., Poindexter, L. M., Naik-Polan, A. T., & Sloss, C. F. (2002). Clinical assessment of children in child protection cases: An empirical analysis. *Professional Psychology: Research and Practice, 33*, 3–12.

Budd, K. S., Poindexter, L. M., Felix, E. D., & Naik-Polan, A. T. (2001). Clinical assessment of parents in child protection cases: An empirical analysis. *Law and Human Behavior, 25*, 93–108.

Bukstel, L. H., & Kilmann, P. R. (1980). Psychological effects of imprisonment on confined individuals. *Psychological Bulletin, 88*, 469–493.

Bulkley, J. (1988). Legal proceedings, reforms, and emerging issues in child sexual abuse cases. *Behavioral Sciences and the Law, 6*, 153–180.

Bulkley, J. A. (1989). The impact of new child witness research on sexual abuse prosecutions. In S. J. Ceci, D. F. Ross, & M. P. Toglia (Eds.), *Perspectives on children's testimony.* New York: Springer-Verlag.

Bull, R. H. (1988). What is the lie-detection test? In A. Gale (Ed.), *The polygraph test: Lies, truth and science*. Newbury Park, CA: Sage.

Bumby, K. M. (1993). Reviewing the guilty but mentally ill alternative: A case of the blind "pleading" the blind. *Journal of Psychiatry and Law, 21*, 191–220.

Burdon, W. M., & Gallagher, C. A. (2002). Coercion and sex offenders: Controlling sex-offending behavior through incapacitation and treatment. *Criminal Justice and Behavior*, 29, 87–109.

Bureau of Justice Statistics (2001). *Prisoners in 2000.* Washington, DC: U.S. Department of Justice, Bureau of Justice Statistics.

Bureau of Justice Statistics. (2002a*). Prisoners in 2001.* Washington, DC: U.S. Department of Justice, Bureau of Justice Statistics.

Bureau of Justice Statistics. (2002b). *Recidivism of prisoners released in 1994.* Washington, DC: U.S. Department of Justice, Bureau of Justice Statistics.

Burgess, C. A., & Kirsch, I. (1999). Expectancy information as a moderator of the effects of hypnosis on memory. *Contemporary Hypnosis, 16*, 22–31.

Burns, B. J., Schoenwald, S. K., Burchard, J. D., Faw, L., & Santos, A. B. (2000). Comprehensive community-based interventions for youth with severe emotional disorders: Multisystemic therapy and the wraparound process. *Journal of Child and Family Studies, 9*, 283–314.

Burt, R. A. (2000). Misguided guidelines. *Psychology, Public Policy, and Law, 6*, 382–387.

Butler, M., Retzlaff, P., & Vanderploeg, R. (1991). Neuropsychological test usage. *Professional Psychology: Research and Practice, 22*, 510–512.

Buwalda, I. W. (1945). The policewoman—yesterday, today and tomorrow. *Journal of Social Hygiene, 31*, 290–293.

Byrne, C.(1994). *Drug data summary.* Rockville, MD: Drugs and Crime Data Center and Clearinghouse.

Byrne, D. (1971). *The attraction paradigm.* New York: Academic Press.

Byrne, D. (1974). *An introduction to personality* (2nd ed.). Englewood Cliffs, NJ: Prentice Hall.

Byrne, D., & Nelson, D. (1965). Attraction as a linear function of proportion of positive reinforcement. *Journal of Personality and Social Psychology, 1*, 659–663.

California Occupational Safety and Health Administration. (1995). *Guidelines for workplace security*. Sacramento, CA: Author.

Callahan, L. A., Steadman, H. J., McGreevy, M. A., Robbins, P. C. (1991). The volume and characteristics of insanity defense pleas: An eight-state study. *Bulletin of Psychiatry and the Law, 19*, 331–338.

Camara, K. A., & Resnick, G. (1988). Interparental conflict and cooperation: Factors moderating children's post-divorce adjustment. In E. M. Hetherington & J. Aratesh (Eds.), *Impact of divorce, singleparenting, and stepparenting on children*. Hillsdale, NJ: Erlbaum.

Camara, W. J., & Merenda, P. F. (2000). Using personality tests in pre-employment screening. *Psychology, Public Policy, and Law, 6*, 1164–1186.

Camara, W. J., Nathan, J. S., & Puente, A. E. (2000). Psychological test usage: Implications in professional psychology. *Professional Psychology: Research and Practice, 31*, 141–151.

Camp, G. M., & Camp, C. G. (1991). *Corrections yearbook*. South Salem, NY: Criminal Justice Institute.

Canter, D. (1994). *Criminal shadows: Inside the mind of a serial killer*. London: HarperCollins.

Canter, D., & Alison, L. (Eds.) (1999). *Profiling in policy and practice*. Aldershot, UK: Ashgate.

Canter, D., & Alison, L. (Eds.) (2000). *Profiling property crimes*. Aldershot, UK: Ashgate.

Cantor, N. L. (1989). The permanently unconscious patient, nonfeeding and euthanasia. *American Journal of Law and Medicine, 15*, 381–437.

Cardarelli, A. P. (Ed.) (1997). *Violence between intimate partners*. Boston: Allyn & Bacon.

Caringella-MacDonald, S. (1997). Women victimized by private violence: A long way to justice. In A. P. Cardarelli (Ed.), *Violence between intimate partners*. Boston: Allyn & Bacon.

Carlson, K. A., & Russo, J. E. (2001). Biased interpretation of evidence by mock jurors. *Journal of Experimental Psychology: Applied, 7*, 91–103.

Carmody, D. C., & Washington, L. M. (2001). *Journal of Interpersonal Violence, 16*, 424–437.

Carroll, D. (1988). How accurate is polygraph lie detection? In A. Gale (Ed.), *The polygraph test: Lies, truth and science* Newbury Park, CA: Sage.

Carroll, J. S., Kerr, N. L., Alfini, J. J., Weaver, F. M., MacCoun, R. J., & Feldman, V. (1986). Free press and fair trial: The role of behavioral research. *Law and Human Behavior, 10*, 187–201.

Cascardi, M., Poythress, N. G., & Hall, A. (2000). Procedural justice in the context of civil commitment: An analogue study. *Behavioral Sciences and the Law, 18*, 731–740.

Casey, P., & Rothman, D. B. (2000). Therapeutic jurisprudence in the courts. *Behavioral Sciences and the Law, 18*, 445–457.

Casper, J. D., Benedict, K., & Perry, J. L. (1989). Juror decision making, attitudes, and the hindsight bias. *Law and Human Behavior, 13*, 291–310.

Caspi, A., Edler, G. H., & Bem, D. J. (1987). Moving against the world: Life course patterns of explosive children. *Developmental Psychology, 23*, 308–313.

Cavior, N., & Howard, L. R. (1973). Facial attractiveness and juvenile delinquency among black offenders and white offenders. *Journal of Abnormal Child Psychology, 1*, 202–213.

Ceci, S. J., & Bruck, M. (1993). Suggestibility of the child witness: A historical review and synthesis. *Psychological Bulletin, 113*, 403–439.

Ceci, S. J., Ross, D. F., & Toglia, M. P. (1987). Age differences in suggestibility: Narrowing the uncertainties. In S. J. Ceci, M. P. Toglia, & D. F. Ross (Eds.), *Children's eyewitness memory*. New York: Springer-Verlag.

Centers for Disease Control and Prevention. (2002, May 21). *Attention deficit disorder and learning disability: United States, 1997–1998.* Hyattsville, MD: U.S. Department of Health and Human Services.

Chaiken, J. M. (1998, April). Forward. *National Conference on Sex Offenders*. Sacramento, CA: SEARCH Group.

Champion, D. J. (1989). Teenage felons and waiver hearings: Some recent trends, 1980–1988. *Crime & Delinquency, 35*, 577–585.

Chance, J. E., & Goldstein, A. G. (1976). Recognition of faces and verbal labels. *Bulletin of the Psychonomic Society, 7*, 384–386.

Chance, J. E., Goldstein, A. G., & McBride, L. (1975). Differential experience and recognition memory for faces. *Journal of Social Psychology, 97*, 243–253.

Chappell, D., & Meyer, J. C. (1975). Cross-cultural differences in police attitudes: An exploration in comparative research. *Australian and New Zealand Journal of Criminology, 8*, 5–13.

Charrow, R. P., & Charrow, V. R. (1979). Making legal language understandable: A psycholinguistic study of jury instructions. *Columbia Law Review, 79*, 1306–1374.

Chermak, S. M. (1997). The presentation of drugs in the news media: The news sources involved in the construction of social problems. *Justice Quarterly, 14*, 687–719.

Chesney-Lind, M., & Shelden, R. G. (1998). *Girls, delinquency, and juvenile justice* (2nd ed.). Belmont, CA: West/Wadsworth.

Chiroro, P., & Valentine, T. (1995). An investigation of the contact hypothesis of the own-race bias in face recognition. *Quarterly Journal of Experimental Psychology, 48A*, 979–894.

Christianson, S. (1992). Emotional stress and eyewitness memory: A critical review. *Psychological Bulletin, 112*, 284–309.

Cirincione, C., & Jacobs, C. (1999). Identifying insanity acquittals: Is it any easier? *Law and Human Behavior, 23*, 487–497.

Cirincione, C., Steadman, H., & McGreevy, M. (1995). Rates of insanity acquittals and the factors associated with successful insanity pleas. *Bulletin of the American Academy of Psychiatry and Law, 23*, 399–409.

Clear, T. R., & Cole, G. F. (2000). *American corrections* (5th ed.). Belmont, CA: West/Wadsworth.

Clear, T. R., & Karp, D. R. (1999). *The community justice ideal: Preventing crime and achieving justice*. Boulder, CO: Westview.

Cleckley, H. (1976). *The mask of sanity* (5th ed.). St. Louis: Mosby.

Clements, C. B. (1979). Crowded prisons: A review of psychological and environmental effects. *Law and Human Behavior, 3*, 217–225.

Clemmer, D. (1940). *The prison community*. Boston: Christopher.

Clifford, B. R., & Hollin, C. R. (1981). Effects of the type of incident and the number of perpetrators on eyewitness memory. *Journal of Applied Psychology, 66*, 365–370.

Clifford, B. R., & Scott, J. (1978). Individual and situational factors in eyewitness testimony. *Journal of Applied Psychology, 63*, 352–359.

Clingempeel, W. G., & Reppucci, N. D. (1982). Joint custody after divorce: Major issues and goals for research. *Psychological Bulletin, 91*, 102–127.

Clingempeel, W. G., Mulvey, E., & Reppucci, N. D. (1980). A national study of ethical dilemmas of psychologists in the criminal justice system. In J. Monahan (Ed.), *Who is the client? The ethics of psychological intervention in the criminal justice system*. Washington, DC: American Psychological Association.

Clore, G. L., & Byrne, D. (1974). A reinforcement-affect model of attraction. In T. L. Huston (Ed.), *Foundations of interpersonal attraction*. New York: Academic Press.

Cochrane, R. E., Grisso, T., & Frederick, R. I. (2001). The relationship between criminal charges, diagnoses, and psycholegal opinions among federal defendants. *Behavioral Sciences and the Law, 19*, 565–582.

Cochrane, R. E., Tett, R. P., VandeCreek, L. (in press). Psychological testing and the selection of police officers: A national survey. *Criminal Justice and Behavior*.

Cocozza, J., & Steadman, H. (1976). The failure of psychiatric prediction of dangerousness: Clear and convincing evidence. *Rutgers Law Review, 29*, 1084–1101.

Cogan, N. H. (1970). Juvenile law before and after the entrance of "parens patriae." *South Carolina Law Review, 22*, 147–181.

Cohen, F. (1998). *The mentally disordered inmate and the law*. Kingston, NJ: Civic Research Institute.

Cohen, F. (2000). *The mentally disordered inmate and the law (2000–2001 supplement)*. Kinsgton, NJ: Civic Research Institute.

Cohen, F. (2003). *The mentally disordered inmate and the law (2003 supplement)*. Kingston, NJ: Civic Research Institute.

Cohen, F. (1966). The function of the attorney and the commitment of the mentally ill. *Texas Law Review, 44*, 424–459.

Cohen, M. E., & Carr, W. J. (1975). Facial recognition and the von Restorff effect. *Bulletin of the Psychonomic Society, 6*, 383–384.

Cohen, M. L., Garafalo, R., Boucher, R., & Seghorn, T. (1971). The psychology of rapists. *Seminars in Psychiatry, 3*, 307–327.

Cohen, M. L., Seghorn, T., & Calmas, W. (1969). Sociometric study of the sex offender. *Journal of Abnormal Psychology, 74*, 249–255.

Cohen, R. L., & Harnick, M. A. (1980). The susceptibility of child witnesses to suggestions: An empirical study. *Law and Human Behavior, 4*, 201–210.

Coie, J. D., Belding, M., & Underwood, M. (1988). Aggression and peer rejection in childhood. In B. Lahey & A. Kazdin (Eds.), *Advances in clinical child psychology* (Vol. 2). New York: Plenum.

Coie, J. D., Dodge, K., & Kupersmith, J. (1990). Peer group behavior and social status. In S. R. Asher & J. D. Coie (Eds.), *Peer rejection in childhood*. Cambridge, UK: Cambridge University Press.

Coie, J. D., Underwood, M., & Lochman, J. E. (1991). Programmatic intervention with aggressive children in the school setting. In D. J. Pepler & K. H. Rubin (Eds.), *The development and treatment of childhood aggression*. Hillsdale, NJ: Erlbaum.

Colarelli, J. J., & Siegel, M. (1964). A method of police personnel selection. *Journal of Criminal Law, Criminology and Police Sciences, 55*, 287–289.

Cole, D. (1999). *No equal justice*. New York: The New Press.

Cole, G. F. (1992). *The American System of Criminal Justice* (6th ed.). Pacific Grove, CA: Brooks/Cole.

Cole, G. F., & Smith, C. E. (2001). *The American system of criminal justice* (9th ed.). Belmont, CA: Wadsworth/Thomson Learning.

Coleman, B. L., Stevens, M. J., & Reeder, G. D. (2001) What makes recovered-memory testimony compelling to jurors? *Law and Human Behavior, 25*, 317–338.

Comer, R. J. (1992). *Abnormal psychology*. New York: Freeman.

Comment. (1972). Police power in Illinois: The regulation of private conduct. *University of Illinois Law Forum*.

Committee on Ethical Guidelines for Forensic Psychologists. (1991). Specialty guidelines for forensic psychologists. *Law and Human Behavior, 15*, 655–665.

Conley, J. M. (2000). Epilogue: A legal and cultural commentary on the psychology of jury instructions. *Psychology, Public Policy, and Law, 6*, 822–831.

Conrad, J. (1982). What do the underserving deserve? In R. Johnson & H. Toch (Eds.), *The pains of imprisonment*. Prospect Heights, IL: Waveland.

Consigli, J. E. (2002). Post-conviction sex offender testing and the American Polygraph Association. In M. Kleiner (Ed.), *Handbook of polygraph testing*. San Diego, CA: Academic Press.

Constantini, E., & King, J. (1980/81). The partial juror: Correlates and causes of prejudgment. *Law and Society Review, 15*, 9–40.

Cooke, D. J., & Michie, C. (2001). Refining the construct psychopathy: Toward a hierarchical model. *Psychological Assessment, 13*, 171–188.

Cooke, D. J., Michie, C., Hart, S. D., & Hare, R. D. (1999). Evaluation of the screening version of the Hare Psychology Checklist—Revised (PCL:SV): An item response theory analysis. *Psychological Assessment, 11*, 3–13.

Cooper, C. L., & Marshall, J. (1976). Occupational sources of stress: A review of the literature relating to coronary heart disease and mental ill health. *Journal of Occupational Psychology, 49*, 11–28.

Cooper, D. K. (1997). Juveniles' understanding of trial-related information: Are they competent defendants? *Behavioral Sciences and the Law, 15*, 167–180.

Cooper, J., & Neuhaus, I. M. (2000). The "hired gun" effect: Assessing the effect of pay, frequency of testifying, and credentials on the perception of expert testimony. *Law and Human Behavior, 24*, 149–171.

Cooper, R. P., & Werner, P. D. (1990). Predicting violence in newly admitted inmates: A lens model analysis of staff decisions. *Criminal Justice and Behavior, 17*, 431–447.

Cornfeld, R. S. (1993). Help stamp out junk science: A practical approach. *For the Defense, 35*, 27–29.

Costanzo, M., & Costanzo, S. (1992). Jury decision making in the capital penalty phase: Legal assumptions, empirical findings, and a research agenda. *Law and Human Behavior, 16*, 185–201.

Cowan, C. L., Thompson, W. C., & Ellsworth, P. C. (1984). The effects of death qualification on jurors' predisposition to convict and on the quality of the deliberation. *Law and Human Behavior, 8*, 53–79.

Cowden, V. L., & McKee, G. R. (1995). Competency to stand trial in juvenile delinquency proceedings: Cognitive maturity and the attorney-client relationship. *University of Louisville Journal of Family Law, 33*, 629–660.

Cox, M., & Tanford, S. (1989). An alternative method of capital jury selection. *Law and Human Behavior, 13*, 167–183.

Cox, V. C., Paulus, P. B., & McCain, G. (1984). Prison crowding research: The relevance for prison housing standards and general approach regarding crowding phenomena. *American Psychologist, 39*, 1148–1160.

Crank, J. P., & Caldero, M. (1991). The production of occupational stress in medium-sized police agencies: A survey of line officers in eight municipal departments. *Journal of Criminal Justice, 19*, 339–349.

Crosbie-Burnett, M. (1991). Impact of joint versus sole custody and quality of co-parental relationship on adjustment of adolescents in remarried families. *Behavioral Sciences and the Law, 9*, 439–449.

Cross, J. F., Cross, J., & Daly, J. (1971). Sex, race, age and beauty as factors in recognition of faces. *Perception and Psychophysics, 10*, 393–396.

Crowe, A. H. (1998). *Drug identification and testing in the juvenile justice system*. Washington, DC: Office of Juvenile Justice and Delinquency Prevention.

Crowell, M. A., & Burgess, A. W. (Eds.). (1996). *Understanding violence against women*. Washington, DC: National Academy Press.

Cruise, K. R., & Rogers, R. (1998). An analysis of competency to stand trial: An integration of case law and clinical knowledge. *Behavioral Sciences and the Law, 16*, 35–50.

Cullen, F. T., & Applegate, B. K. (Eds.). (1998). *Offender rehabilitation: Effective correctional intervention*. Dartmouth, UK: Ashgate.

Cullen, F. T., & Gendreau, P. (2000). Assessing correctional rehabilitation: Policy, practice, and prospects. In J. Horney (Ed.), *Criminal justice 2000: Vol. 3. Policies, processes, and decisions of the criminal justice system*. Washington, DC: National Institute of Justice.

Cunningham, M. D., & Reidy, T. J. (1998). Integrating base rate data in violence risk assessments at capital sentencing. *Behavioral Sciences and the Law, 16*, 71–96.

Cunningham, M. D., & Reidy, T. J. (1999). Don't confuse me with the facts: Common errors in violence risk assessment at capital sentencing. *Criminal Justice and Behavior, 26*, 20–43.

Cunningham, M. D., & Reidy, T. J. (2001). A matter of life or death: Special considerations and heightened practice standards in capital sentencing evaluations. *Behavioral Sciences and the Law, 19*, 473–490.

Cutler, B. L., Moran, G. P., & Narby, D. J. (1992). Jury selection in insanity defense cases. *Journal of Research in Personality, 26*, 165–182.

Cutler, B. L., Penrod, S. D., & Martens, T. K. (1987). Improving the reliability of eyewitness identification: Putting content with context. *Journal of Applied Psychology, 72*, 629–637.

Dahlstrom, W. C. (1972). Whither the MMPI? In J. N. Butcher (Ed.), *Objective personality assessment*. New York; Academic Press.

Dalbert, C. & Yamauchi, A. (1994). Belief in a just world and attitudes toward immigrants and foreign workers: A cultural comparison between Hawaii and Germany. *Journal of Applied Social Psychology, 24*, 1612–1626.

Daly, K., & Tonry, M. (1997). Gender, race, and sentencing. In M. Tonry (Ed.), *Crime and justice: A review of the research* (Vol. 22). Chicago: University of Chicago Press.

Daniels, C. W. (2002). Legal aspects of polygraph admissibility in the United States. In M. Kleiner (Ed.), *Handbook of polygraph testing*. San Diego, CA: Academic Press.

Dann, B. M. (1993). Learning lessons and speaking rights: Creating educated and democratic juries. *Indiana Law Journal, 68*, 1229–1279.

Darley, J. M., & Latane, B. (1968). Bystander intervention in emergencies: Diffusion of responsibility. *Journal of Personality and Social Psychology, 8*, 377–383.

Davidson, G. C., & Neale, J. M. (1982). *Abnormal psychology: An experimental clinical approach*. New York: Wiley.

Davies, G. (1999). The impact of television on the presentation and reception of children's testimony. *International Journal of Law and Psychiatry, 22*, 241–256.

Davies, G., & Noon, E. (1991). An evaluation of the live link for child witnesses. London: Home Office.

Davies, G., van der Willik, P., & Morrison, L. J. (2000). Facial composite production: A comparison of mechanical and computer-driven systems. *Journal of Applied Psychology, 85*, 119–124.

Davis, G., Ellis, H., & Shepherd, J. (1978). Face recognition accuracy as a function of mode of representation. *Journal of Applied Psychology, 63*, 180–187.

Davis, J. H., Bray, R. M., & Holt, R. W. (1977). The empirical study of decision processes in juries: A critical review. In J. L. Tapp & F. J. Levine (Eds.), *Law, justice, and the indi-*

vidual in society: Psychological and legal issues. New York: Holt, Rinehart & Winston.

Davis, J. H., Kerr, N. L., Atkin, R. S., Holt, R., & Meek, D. (1975). The decision processes of 6- and 12-person mock juries assigned unanimous and two-thirds majority rules. *Journal of Personality and Social Psychology, 32*, 1–14.

Davis, J. M. (1976). Overview: Maintenance therapy in psychiatry: II. Affective disorders. *American Journal of Psychiatry, 133*, 1–13.

Davis, M. F. (1998). Dogmatism and belief formation: Output interference in the processing of supporting and contradictory cognitions. *Journal of Personality and Social Psychology, 75*, 456–466.

Dawes, R. M. (1989). Experience and validity of clinical judgment: The illusory correlation. *Behavioral Sciences and the Law, 7*, 455–467.

Dawes, R. M., Faust, D., & Meehl, P. E. (1989). Clinical vs. actuarial judgment. *Science, 243*, 1668–1674.

Day, K., & Berney, T. (2001). Treatment and care for offenders with mental retardation. In J. B. Ashford, B. D. Sales, & W. H. Reid (Eds.), *Treating adult and juvenile offenders with special needs*. Washington, DC: American Psychological Association.

Decker, J. F. (1996). The Sixth Amendment right to shoot oneself in the foot: An assessment of the guarantee of self-representation 20 years after *Faretta*. *Seton Hall Constitutional Law Journal, 6*, 483–507.

Decker, S. H., & Kohfeld, C. W. (1990). The deterrent effect of capital punishment in the five most active execution states: A times series analysis. *Criminal Justice Review, 15*, 173–191.

Deffenbacher, K. A. (1980). Eyewitness accuracy and confidence. Can we infer anything about their relationship? *Law and Human Behavior, 4*, 243–260.

del Carmen, R. V., Parker, M., & Reddington, F. P. (1998). *Briefs of leading cases in juvenile justice*. Cincinnati, OH: Anderson.

de la Garza, R. O., & DeSipio, L. (2001). A satisfied clientele seeking more diverse services: Latinos and the courts. *Behavioral Sciences and the Law, 19*, 237–248.

Deland, F. H., & Borenstein, N. M. (1990). Medicine court II: Rivers in practice. *American Journal of Psychiatry, 147*, 38–43.

Delprino, R. P. & Bahn, C. (1988). National survey of the extent and nature of psychological services in police departments. *Professional Psychology: Research and Practice, 19*, 421–425.

Dennis, D., & Monahan, J. (Eds.). (1996). *Coercion and aggressive community treatment: A new frontier in mental health law*. New York: Plenum.

Dent, B. D. (2000). Brief history of crime mapping. In L. S. Turnbull, E. H. Hendrix, & B. D. Dent (Eds.), *Atlas of crime: Mapping the criminal landscape*. Phoenix, AZ: Oryx Press.

DePaulo, B. M., & Pfeifer, R. L. (1986). On-the-job experience and skill at detecting deception. *Journal of Applied Social Psychology, 16*, 249–267.

DeRosia, V. R. (1995). *Living inside prison walls: Adjustment behavior*. Westport, CT: Praeger.

Dershowitz, A. M. (1974). The origins of preventive confinement in Anglo-American law. Part 2, The American experience. *University of Cincinnati Law Review, 43*, 781–846.

Deutsch, A. (1949). *The mentally ill in America*. New York: Columbia University Press.

Devine, D. J., Clayton, L. D., Dunford, B. B., Seying, R., & Pryce, J. (2001). Jury decision making: 45 years of empirical research on deliberating groups. *Psychology, Public Policy, and Law, 7*, 622–727.

Dexter, H. D., Cutler, B. L., & Moran, G. (1992). A test of voir dire as a remedy for the prejudicial effect of pretrial publicity. *Journal of Applied Social Psychology, 22*, 819–832.

Diamond, S. S. (1993). Instructing on death: Psychologists, juries, and judges. *American Psychologist, 48*, 423–434.

Diamond, S. S. (1997). Illuminations and shadows from jury simulations. *Law and Human Behavior, 21*, 561–571.

Diamond, S. S., & Levi, J. N. (1996). Improving decisions on death by revising and testing jury instructions. *Judicature, 79*, 224–232.

Dickey, W. (1980). Incompetency and the nondangerous mentally ill client. *Criminal Law Bulletin, 16*, 25–40.

Dillion, P., & Emery, R. (1996). Divorce mediation and resolution of child custody disputes: Long-term effects. *American Journal of Orthopsychiatry, 66*, 131–140.

Dilworth, D. C. (1997, August). Federal judges can remove jurors who refused to convict. *Trial, 33*, 17–20.

Dion, K. K. (1972). Physical attractiveness and evaluations of children's transgressions. *Journal of Personality and Social Psychology, 24*, 207–213.

Dion, K. K., Berscheid, E., & Walster, E. (1972). What is beautiful is good. *Journal of Personality and Social Psychology, 24*, 285–290.

Ditton, P. M. (1999). *Mental health and treatment of inmates and probationers*. Washington, DC: U.S. Department of Justice, Bureau of Justice Statistics.

Dodrill, C. B., & Warner, M. H. (1988). Further studies of the Wonderlic Personnel Test as a brief measure of intelligence. *Journal of Consulting and Clinical Psychology, 56*, 145–147.

Doerr, H. O., & Carlin, A. S. (Eds.). (1991). *Forensic neuropsychology: Legal and scientific bases*. New York: Guilford Press.

Dohm, T. E., & Iacono, W. G. (1993). *Design and pilot of a polygraph field validation study* (Technical Report No. 227). Minneapolis, MN: Personnel Decisions Research Institute.

Donnellan, M. B., Ge, X., & Wenk, E. (2000). Cognitive abilities in adolescent-limited and life-course-persistent criminal offenders. *Journal of Abnormal Psychology, 109*, 396–402.

Doob, A. N., & Kirshenbaum, H. M. (1973). Bias in police lineups—Partial remembering. *Journal of Police Science and Administration, 1*, 287–293.

Douglas, K., Ogloff, J., Nicholls, T., & Grant, I. (1999). Assessing risk for violence among psychiatric patients: The HCR-20 Violence Risk Assessment Scheme and the Psychopathy Checklist: Screening version. *Journal of Consulting and Clinical Psychology, 67*, 917–930.

Dovidio, J. F., Gaertner, S. L., Kawakami, K., & Hodson, G. (2002). Why can't we just get along? Interpersonal biases and interracial distrust. *Cultural Diversity and Ethnic Minority Psychology, 8*, 88–102.

Dowdle, M., Gillen, H., & Miller, A. (1974). Integration and attribution theories as predictors of sentencing by a simulated jury. *Personality and Social Psychology Bulletin, 1*, 270–272.

Dreher, G. G., Ash, R. A., Hancock, P. (1988). The role of the traditional research design in underestimating the validity of the employment interview. *Personnel Psychology, 41*, 315–327.

Drug Use Forecasting. (1995). *Annual Report*. Washington, DC: National Institute of Justice.

Dubois, P. H., & Watson, R. I. (1950). The selection of patrolmen. *Journal of Applied Psychology, 34*, 90–95.

Duhart, D. T. (2001). *Violence in the workplace. 1993–1999. Special report*. Washington, DC: U.S. Department of Justice, Bureau of Justice Statistics.

Dull, R. T., & Giacopassi, D. J. (1987). Demographic correlates of sexual and dating attitudes: A study of date rape. *Criminal Justice and Behavior, 14*, 175–193.

Dunford, F. W., Huizinga, D., & Elliott, D. S. (1990). The role of arrest in domestic assault: The Omaha police experiment. *Criminology, 28*, 183–206.

D'Unger, A. V., Land, K. C., McCall, P. L., & Nagin, D. S. (1998). How many latent classes of delinquent/criminal careers? Results from mixed Poisson regression analysis. *American Journal of Sociology, 103*, 1593–1630.

Dunning, D. (1989). Research on children's eyewitness testimony: Perspectives on its past and future. In S. J. Ceci, D. F. Ross & M. P. Toglia (Eds.), *Perspectives on children's testimony*. New York: Springer-Verlag.

Durand, V. M., & Barlow, D. H. (2000). *Abnormal psychology* (2nd ed.). Belmont, CA: Wadsworth/Thomson Learning.

Durham, M. L., & La Fond, J. Q. (1990). A search for the missing premise of involuntary therapeutic commitment: Effective treatment of the mentally ill. In D. B. Wexler (Ed.), *Therapeutic jurisprudence*. Durham, NC: Carolina Academic Press.

Duwe, G. (2000). Body-count journalism: The presentation of mass murder in the news media. *Homicide Studies, 4*, 364–399.

Dvorak, J. A. (2000, December 21). Kansas launches racial profiling study. *The Kansas City Star*, 1, 11.

Dwyer, J., Neufeld, P., & Scheck, B. (2000). *Actual innocence: Five days to execution and other dispatches from the wrongly convicted*. New York: Doubleday.

Dysart, J. E., Lindsay, R. C. L., Hammond, R., & Dupuis, P. (2001). Mug shot exposure prior to lineup identification: Interference, transference, and commitment effects. *Journal of Applied Psychology, 86*, 1280–1284.

Easterbrook, J. A. (1959). The effect of emotion on cue utilization and the organization of behavior. *Psychological Review, 66*, 181–201.

Ebert, B. W. (1987). Guide to conducting a psychological autopsy. *Professional Psychology: Research and Practice, 18*, 52–56.

Ecclestone, J. E. J., Gendreau, P., & Knox, C. (1974). Solitary confinement of prisoners: An assessment of its effects on inmates personal constructs and cortical activity. *Canadian Journal of Behavioral Science, 6*, 178–191.

Edens, J. F., Hart, S. D., Johnson, D. W., Johnson, J. K., & Olver, M. E. (2000). Use of the Personality Assessment Inventory to assess psychopathy in offender populations. *Psychological Assessment, 12*, 132–139.

Edwards, D. L., Schoenwald, S. K., Henggeler, S. W., Strother, K. B. (2001). A multi-level perspective on the implementation of multisystemic therapy (MST): Attempting dissemination with fidelity. In G. A. Bernfeld, D. P. Farrington, & A. W. Leschied (Eds.), *Offender rehabilitation in practice*. New York: Wiley.

Efran, M. C. (1974). The effect of physical appearance on the judgment of guilt, interpersonal attraction, and severity of recommended punishment in a simulated jury task. *Journal of Research in Personality, 8*, 5–54.

Ehrlich, I. (1975). The deterrent effect of capital punishment: A question of life and death. *American Economic Review, 65*, 397–379.

Ehrlich, I. (1977). Capital punishment and deterrence: Some further thoughts and additional evidence. *Journal of Political Economy, 85*, 741–788.

Einhorn, J. (1986). Child custody in historical perspective: A study of changing social perceptions of divorce and child custody in Anglo-American law. *Behavioral Sciences and the Law, 4*, 119–135.

Eisenberg, T. (1975). Labor-management relations and psychological stress: View from the bottom. *The Police Chief, 42*, 54–58.

Ekman, P. (1985). *Telling lies: Clues to deceit in the marketplace, politics, and marriage*. New York: Norton.

Ekman, P. & Friesen, W. (1969). Nonverbal leakage and clues to deception. *Psychiatry, 32*, 88–106.

Ekman, P, & Friesen, W. (1974). Detecting deception from the body and face. *Journal of Personality and Social Psychology, 29*, 288–298.

Ekman, P., Friesen, W. V., & Scherer, K. R. (1976). Body movement and voice pitch in deceptive interaction. *Semiotica, 16*, 23–27.

Ekman, P., & O'Sullivan, M. (1991). Who can catch a liar? *American Psychologist, 46*, 913–920.

Ekman, P., O'Sullivan, M., Friesen, W. V., & Scherer, K. (1991). *Journal of Nonverbal Behavior, 15*, 125–135.

Elaad, E. (1990). Detection of guilty knowledge in real-life criminal investigations. *Journal of Applied Psychology, 75*, 521–529.

Elaad, E., Ginton, A., & Jungman, N. (1992). Detection measures in real-life criminal guilty knowledge tests. *Journal of Applied Psychology, 5*, 757–767.

Elliot, E. S., Wills, E. J., & Goldstein, A. G. (1973). The effects of discrimination training on the recognition of white and oriental faces. *Bulletin of the Psychonomic Society, 2*, 71–73.

Elliott, D. S. (1989). Criminal justice procedures in family violence crimes. In L. Ohlin & M. Tonry (Eds.), *Family violence* (Vol. 11.). Chicago: University of Chicago Press.

Elliott, R. (1987). *Litigating intelligence: IQ tests, special education, and social science in the courtroom*. Dover, MA: Auburn House.

Elliott, R., & Robinson, R. J. (1991). Death penalty attitudes and the tendency to convict or acquit: Some data. *Law and Human Behavior, 15*, 389–404.

Ellis, H. D., Deregowski, J. B., & Shepherd, J. W. (1975). Descriptions of white and black faces by white and black subjects. *International Journal of Psychology, 10,* 119–123.

Ellison, K. W., & Buckhout, R. (1981). *Psychology and criminal justice.* New York: Harper & Row.

Ellsworth, P. C., Butkaty, R. M., Cowan, C. L., & Thomspon, W. C. (1984). The death qualified jury and the defense of insanity. *Law and Human Behavior, 8,* 81–93.

Ellsworth, P. C., & Reifman, A. (2000). Juror comprehension and public policy: Perceived problems and proposed solutions. *Psychology, Public Policy, and Law, 6,* 788–821.

Elwork, A. (1992). Psycholegal treatment and intervention: The next challenge. *Law and Human Behavior, 16,* 175–183.

Elwork, A., Alfini, J. J., & Sales, B. D. (1987). Toward understandable jury instructions. In L. S. Wrightsman, S. M. Kassin, & C. E. Willis (Eds.), *In the jury box: Controversies in the courtroom.* Newbury Park, CA: Sage.

Elwork, A., Sales, B. D., & Alfini, J. J. (1977). Juridic decisions: In ignorance of the law or in light of it? *Law and Human Behavior, 1,* 163–189.

Elwork, A., Sales, B. D., & Alfini, J. J. (1982). *Making jury instructions understandable.* Indianapolis, IN: Miche/Bobbs-Merrill.

Emery, R. E., & Wyer, M. M. (1987a). Divorce mediation. *American Psychologist, 42,* 472–480.

Emery, R. E., & Wyer, M. M. (1987b). Child custody mediation and litigation: An experimental evaluation of the experience of parents. *Journal of Consulting and Clinical Psychology, 2,* 179–186.

Emery, R., Mathews, S., & Kitzmann, R. (1994). Child custody mediation and litigation: Parents' satisfaction 1 year after settlement. *Journal of Consulting and Clinical Psychology, 62,* 124–129.

Ennis, B. J., & Litwack, T. J. (1974). Psychiatry and the presumption of expertise: Flipping coins in the courtroom. *California Law Review, 62,* 693–752.

Ensminger, J. J., & Liguori, T. D. (1990). The therapeutic significance of the civil commitment hearing: An unexplored potential. In D. B. Wexler (Ed.), *Therapeutic jurisprudence.* Durham, NC: Carolina Academic Press.

Eron, L. D., Gentry, J. H., & Schlegel, P. (Eds.). (1994). *Reason to hope: A psychosocial perspective on violence and youth.* Washington, DC: American Psychological Association.

Esses, V. M., & Webster, C. D. (1988). Physical attractiveness, dangerousness, and the Canadian Criminal Code. *Journal of Applied Social Psychology, 18,* 1017–1031.

Everington, C. T. (1990). The competence assessment for standing trial for defendants with mental retardation (CAST-MR): A validation study. *Criminal Justice and Behavior, 17,* 147–168.

Ewing, C. P. (1987). *Battered women who kill: Psychological self defense as legal justification.* Lexington, MA: Heath.

Ewing, C. P. (1990). Juveniles or adults? Forensic assessment of juveniles considered for trial in criminal court. *Forensic Reports, 3,* 3–13.

Executive Summary. (2001, February). *The MacArthur coercion study.* Available: www.macarthur.Virginia.edu/coercion.html.

Fagan, J. (1999). Punishment or treatment for adolescent offenders: Therapeutic integrity and the paradoxical effects of punishment. *Quinnipiac Law Review,* 502–516.

Farabee, D. (2002a). Reexamining Martinson's critique: A cautionary note for evaluators. *Crime & Delinquency, 48,* 189–192.

Farabee, D. (2002b). Foreword to special issue: Making people change. *Criminal Justice and Behavior, 29,* 3–4.

Farabee, D., Prendergast, M., Cartier, J., Wexler, H., Knight, K., & Anglin, M. D. (1999). Barriers to implementing effective correctional drug treatment programs. *The Prison Journal, 79,* 150–162.

Farabee, D., Shen, H., & Sanchez, S. (2002). Perceived coercion and treatment need among mentally ill parolees. *Criminal Justice and Behavior, 29,* 76–86.

Farkas, B. M., DeLeon, P. H., & Newman, R. (1997). Sanity examiner certification: An evolving national agenda. *Professional Psychology: Research and Practice, 28,* 73–76.

Farrington, D. P. (1979). Environmental stress, delinquent behavior, and conviction. In I. G. Sarason & C. D. Spielberger (Eds.), *Stress and anxiety* (Vol. 6). Washington, DC: Hemisphere.

Farrington, D. P. (1987). Predicting individual crime rates. In D. M. Gottfredson & M. Tonry (Eds.), *Prediction and classification* (Vol. 10). Chicago: University of Chicago Press.

Farrington, D. P. (1991). Childhood aggression and adult violence: Early precursors and later life outcomes. In D. J. Pepler & K. H. Rubin (Eds.), *The development and treatment of childhood aggression.* Hillsdale, NJ: Erlbaum.

Farwell, L. A., & Donchin, E. (1991). The truth will come out: Interrogative polygraphy ("lie detection") with event-related brain potentials. *Psychophysiology, 28,* 531–547.

Farwell, L. A., & Smith, S. S. (2001). Using brain MERMER testing to detect knowledge despite efforts to conceal. *Journal of Forensic Sciences, 46,* 1–9.

Faust, D., & Ziskin, J. (1988). The expert witness in psychology and psychiatry. *Science, 241,* 31–35.

Feder, B. J. (2001, October 9). Truth and justice, by the blip of a brainwave. *New York Times,* A6.

Federal Bureau of Investigation. (2000). *Uniform crime reports—1999.* Washington, DC: U.S. Department of Justice.

Federal Bureau of Investigation. (2001). *Uniform crime reports—2000.* Washington, DC: U.S. Department of Justice.

Federal Bureau of Investigation. (2002). *Uniform crime reports—2001.* Washington, DC: U.S. Department of Justice.

Federal Judicial Center. (1987). *Jury instructions.* Washington, DC: Author.

Federle, K. H., & Chesney-Lind, M. (1992). Special issues in juvenile justice: Gender, race and ethnicity. In I. M. Schwartz (Ed.), *Juvenile justice and public policy: Toward a national agenda.* New York: Maxwell-MacMillan International.

Feinman, C. (1986). *Women in the criminal justice system* (2nd ed.). New York: Praeger.

Feinman, S., & Entwisle, D. R. (1976). Children's ability to recognize other children's faces. *Child Development, 47,* 506–510.

Feld, B. C. (1988). *In re Gault* revisited: A cross-state comparison of the right to counsel in juvenile court. *Crime & Delinquency, 34,* 393–424.

Feld, B. C. (1992). Criminalizing the juvenile court: A research agenda for the 1990s. In I. M. Schwartz (Ed.), *Juvenile justice and public policy*. New York: Praeger.

Feld, B. C. (1997). Abolish the juvenile court: Youthfulness, criminal responsibility, and sentencing policy. *Journal of Criminal Law and Criminology*, *88*, 68–136.

Feld, B. C. (1998). Juvenile and criminal justice systems' responses to youth violence. In M. Tonry, & M. H. Moore (Eds.), *Youth violence: Crime and justice: A review of research* (Vol. 24). Chicago: University of Chicago Press.

Feld, B. C. (1999). *Bad kids: Race and the transformation of the juvenile court.* New York: Oxford University Press.

Feld, B. (2000). Juveniles' waiver of legal rights: Confessions, *Miranda*, and the right to counsel. In T. Grisso & R. G. Schwartz (Eds.), *Youth on trial*. Chicago: University of Chicago Press.

Felthous, A. R. (2001). Introduction to this issue: The clinician's duty to warn or protect. *Behavioral Sciences and the Law*, *19*, 321–324.

Felthous, A. R., & Kachigian, C. (2001). To warn and to control: Two distinct legal obligations or variations of a single duty to protect? *Behavioral Sciences and the Law*, *19*, 355–373.

Fenster, C. A., Wiedemann, C. F., & Locke, B. (1977). Police personality: Social science folklore and psychological measurement. In B. D. Sales (Ed.), *Psychology in the legal process*. New York: Spectrum.

Festinger, L., Pepitone, A., & Newcomb, T. (1952). Some consequences of deindividuation in a group. *Journal of Abnormal and Social Psychology*, *47*, 382–389.

Fielding, N. (1988). Socialisation of recruits into the police role. In P. Southgate (Ed.), *New directions in police training*. London: HMSO.

Fineman, M. (1988). Dominant discourse, professional language, and legal change in child custody decision-making. *Harvard Law Review*, *101*, 727–774.

Finkel, N. J. (1988). *Insanity on trial*. New York: Plenum.

Finkel, N. J. (1991). The insanity defense: A comparison of verdict schemas. *Law and Human Behavior*, *15*, 533–555.

Finkel, N. J. (1995). *Commonsense justice: Jurors' notions of the law*. Cambridge, MA: Harvard University Press.

Finkel, N. J. (2000). Commonsense justice and jury instructions: Instructive and reciprocating connections. *Psychology, Public Policy, and Law*, *6*, 591–628.

Finkel, N. J., Hurabiell, B. A., & Huges, B. A. (1993). Competency, and other contructs, in right to die cases. *Behavioral Sciences and the Law*, *11*, 135–140.

Finkel, N., Shaw, R., Bercaw, S., & Kock, J. (1985). Insanity defenses: From the jurors' perspective. *Law and Psychology Review*, *9*, 77–92.

Finkelhor, D., & Lewis, I. A. (1988). An epidemiologic approach to the study of child molestation. In R. A. Prentky & V. I. Quinsey (Eds.), *Human sexual aggression: Current perspectives*. New York: New York Academy of Sciences.

Finkelhor, D., & Ormrod, R. (2001). Child abuse reported to the police. *Juvenile Justice Bulletin*. Washington, DC: U.S. Department of Justice, Office of Juvenile Justice and Delinquency Prevention.

Finlayson. L. M., & Koocher, G. P. (1991). Professional judgment and child abuse reporting in sexual abuse cases. *Professional Psychology: Research and Practice*, *22*, 464–472.

Finn, M. A., & Stalans, L. J. (2002). Police handling of the mentally ill in domestic violence situations. *Criminal Justice and Behavior*, *29*, 278–307

Fishbein, D. (2000). Neuropsychological function, drug use, and violence: A conceptual framework. *Criminal Justice and Behavior*, *27*, 139–159.

Fisher, J., Epstein, L., & Harris, M. (1967). Validity of the psychiatric interview: Predicting the effectiveness of the first Peace Corps volunteers in Ghana. *Archives of General Psychiatry*, *17*, 744–750.

Fiske, S. T., Bersoff, D. N., Borgida, E., Deaux, K., & Heilman, M. E. (1993). Accuracy and objectivity on behalf of the APA. *American Psychologist*, *48*, 55–56.

Fitzgerald, R. E., & Ellsworth, P. C. (1984). Due process vs. crime control: Death qualification and jury attitudes. *Law and Human Behavior*, *8*, 31–51.

Flanagan, T. J., & Maguire, K. (Eds.). (1991). *Sourcebook of criminal justice statistics*. Washington, DC: USGPO.

Flanagan, T., & Longmire, D. (Eds.). (1996). *Americans view crime and justice: A national public opinion survey*. Thousand Oaks, CA: Sage.

Foley, M. A., & Johnson, M. K. (1985). Confusion between memories for performed and imagined actions. *Child Development*, *56*, 1145–1155.

Fong, G. T., Lurigio, A. J., Stalans, L. J. (1990). Improving probation decisions through statistical training. *Criminal Justice and Behavior*, *17*, 370–388.

Forehand, R., Wierson, M., Frame, C. L., Kemptom, T., & Armistead, L. (1991). Juvenile firesetting: A unique syndrome or an advanced level of antisocial behavior? *Behavioral Research and Therapy*, *29*, 125–128.

Forsterlee, L., Horowitz, I. A., & Bourgeous, M. J. (1993). Juror competence in civil trials: Effects of preinstruction and evidence technicality. *Journal of Applied Psychology*, *78*, 14–21.

Forth, A. E., & Mailloux, D. L. (2000). Psychopathy in youth: What do we know? In C. B. Gacono (Ed.), *The clinical and forensic assessment of psychopathy*. Mahwah, NJ: Erlbaum.

Forth, A. E., Kosson, D. S., & Hare, R. D. (in press). *Hare Psychopathy Checklist: Youth Version*. Toronto: Multi-Health Systems.

Fox, J. A., & Levin, J. (1998). Multiple homicide: Patterns of serial and mass murder. In M. Tonry (Ed.), *Crime and justice: A review of research* (Vol. 23). Chicago: University of Chicago Press.

Fox, S. G., & Walters, H. A. (1986). The impact of general versus specific expert testimony and eyewitness confidence upon mock juror judgment. *Law and Human Behavior*, *10*, 215–228.

Frank, J. (1949). *Courts on trial: Myth and reality in American justice*. Princeton, NJ: Princeton University Press.

Frank, M. G., & Ekman, P. (1997). The ability to detect deceit generalizes across different types of high-stake lies. *Journal of Personality and Social Psychology*, *72*, 1429–1439.

Frazier, P. A., & Borgida, E. (1992). Rape trauma syndrome: A review of case law and psychological research. *Law and Human Behavior, 16*, 293–311.

Frederick, R. I. (2000). Mixed group validation: A method to address the limitations of criterion group validation in research on malingering detection. *Behavioral Science and the Law, 18*, 693–718.

Frederick, R. I., & Denny, R. L. (1998). Minding your Ps and Qs when conducting forced-choice recognition tests. *The Clinical Neuropsychology, 12*, 193–205.

Freeman, W. & Watts, J. W. (1942). *Psychosurgery*. Springfield, IL: C. C. Thomas.

Freeman-Longo, R. E., Bird, S., Stevenson, W. F., & Fiske, J. A. (1994). *Nationwide survey of treatment programs and models*. Brandon, VT: Safer Society Press.

Frehsee, D. (1990). Children's evidence within the German legal system. In J. R. Spencer, G. Nicholson, R. Flin, & R. Bull (Eds.), *Children's evidence in legal proceedings: An international perspective*. Cambridge, UK: Cambridge University, Faculty of Law.

Freudenberger, H. (1974). Staff burnout. *Journal of Social Issues, 30*, 159–163.

Frick, P. J., Barry, C. T., & Bodin, S. D. (2000). Applying the concept of psychopathy to children: Implications for the assessment of antisocial youth. In C. B. Gacono (Ed.), *The clinical and forensic assessment of psychopathy*. Mahwah, NJ: Erlbaum.

Frick, P. J., Bodin, S. D., & Barry, C. T. (2000). Psychopathic traits and conduct problems in community and clinic-referred samples of children: Further development of the psychopathy screening device. *Psychological Assessment, 12*, 382–393.

Frick, P. J., O'Brien, B. S., Wooton, J. M., & McBurnett, K. (1994). Psychopathy and conduct problems in children. *Journal of Abnormal Psychology, 103*, 700–707.

Fried, C. S., & Reppucci, N. D. (2001). Criminal decision making: The development of adolescent judgment, criminal responsibility, and culpability. *Law and Human Behavior, 25*, 45–61.

Friend, R. M., & Vinson, M. (1974). Leaning over backwards: Jurors' responses to defendants' attractiveness. *Journal of Communication, 24*, 124–129.

Frieze, I. H., & Browne, A. (1989). Violence in marriage. In L. Ohlin & M. Tonry (Eds.), *Family violence* (Vol. 11). Chicago: University of Chicago Press.

Fritzon, K. (2000). The contribution of psychological research to arson investigation. In D. Canter & L. Arson (Eds.), *Profiling property crimes*. Dartmouth, UK: Ashgate.

Fulero, S. M. (1987). The role of behavioral research in the free press/fair trial controversy. *Law and Human Behavior, 11*, 259–264.

Fulero, S. M. (2002). Afterword: The past, present, and future of applied pretrial publicity research. *Law and Human Behavior, 26*, 127–133.

Fulero, S., & Finkel, N. (1991). Barring ultimate issue testimony: An "insane" rule? *Law and Human Behavior, 15*, 496–507.

Furby, L., Weinroth, M. R., & Blackshaw, L. (1989). Sex offender recidivism: A review. *Psychological Bulletin, 105*, 3–30.

Furnham, A. (1993). Just world beliefs in twelve societies. *Journal of Social Psychology, 133*, 317–329.

Fuselier, G. D. (1988). Hostage negotiation consultant: Emerging role for the clinical psychologist. *Professional Psychology: Research and Practice, 19*, 175–179.

Fuselier, G. D., & Noesner, G. W. (1990, July) Confronting the terrorist hostage taker. *FBI Law Enforcement Bulletin*, 9–12.

Gacono, C. B. (2000). Suggestions for the implementation and use of the Psychopathy Check-Lists in forensic and clinical practice. In C. B. Gacono (Ed.), *The clinical and forensic assessment of psychopathy: A practitioner's guide*. Mahwah, NJ: Erlbaum.

Gaes, G. G. (1985). The effects of overcrowding in prison. In M. Tonry & N. Morris (Eds.), *Crime and justice: An annual review of research* (Vol. 6). Chicago: University of Chicago Press.

Gaes, G. G., & McGuire, W. J. (1984). Prison violence: The contribution of crowding versus other determinates of prison assault rates. *Journal of Research in Crime & Delinquency, 22*, 41–65.

Gallagher, C. A., Wilson, D., Hirschfield, P., Coggeshall, M. B., & MacKenzie, D. (1999). A quantitative review of the effects of sex offender treatment and sexual reoffending. *Corrections Management Quarterly, 3*, 19–29.

Gallagher, T. (1979). Discretion in police enforcement. In L. E. Abt & I. R. Stuart (Eds.), *Social psychology and discretionary law*. New York: Van Nostrand Reinhold.

Gallagher-Thompson, D., & Osgood, N. J. (1997). Suicide later in life. *Behavior Therapy, 28*, 23–41.

Garb, H. N. (1989). Clinical judgment, clinical training, and professional experience. *Psychological Bulletin, 105*, 387–396.

Gardner, W., Hoge, S. K., Bennett, N., Roth, L. H., Lidz, C. W., Monahan, J., & Mulvey, E. P. (1993). Two scales for measuring patients' perceptions for coercion during mental hospital admission. *Behavioral Sciences and the Law, 11*, 307–321.

Gardner, R. (1991). *Sex abuse hysteria: Salem witch trials revisited*. Cresskill, NJ: Creative Therapeutics.

Garry, E. M. (1997, January). *Juvenile firesetting and arson*. Washington, DC: Office of Juvenile Delinquency and Prevention.

Gearing, M. L. (1979). The MMPI as a primary differentiator and predictor of behavior in prison: A methodological critique and review of the recent literature. *Psychological Bulletin, 86*, 929–963.

Geberth, V. J. (1993, July). Suicide-by-cop: Inviting death from the hands of a police officer. *Law and Order*, 105–106.

Geimer, W. S., & Amsterdam, J. (1988). Why jurors vote life or death: Operative factors in ten Florida death penalty cases. *Journal of Criminal Law, 15*, 1–54.

Gendreau, P. (1996). The principles of effective interventions with offenders. In A. T. Harland (Ed.), *Choosing correctional options that work*. Thousand Oaks, CA: Sage.

Gendreau, P., Freedman, N. Wilde, G. T. S., & Scott, G. D. (1972). Changes in EEG alpha frequency and evoked response latency during solitary confinement. *Journal of Abnormal Psychology, 79*, 54–59.

Gendreau, P., Little, T., & Goggin, C. (1996). A meta-analysis of the predictors of adult offender recidivism: What works! *Criminology, 34*, 575–607.

Gendreau, P., & Ross, R. R. (1984). Correctional treatment: Some recommendations for effective intervention. *Juvenile and Family Court Journal, 34*, 31–39.

Gendreau, P., & Ross, R. R. (1987). Revivification of rehabilitation: Evidence from the 1980s. *Justice Quarterly, 4*, 349–407.

Gendreau, P., & Ross, R. R. (1991). Correctional treatment: Some recommendations for effective intervention. In K. C. Haas & G. O. Alpert (Eds.), *The dilemmas of corrections*. Prospect Heights, IL: Waveland Press.

George, W. H., & Marlatt, G. A. (1989). Introduction. In D. R. Laws (Ed.), *Relapse prevention with sex offenders*. New York: Guilford Press.

Gerbasi, K. D., Zuckerman, M., & Reis, H. (1977). Justice needs a new blindfold: A review of mock jury research. *Psychological Bulletin, 84*, 323–345.

Gibbs, J. J. (1992). Jailing and stress. In H. Toch (Ed.), *Mosaic of despair: Human breakdown in prison*. Washington, DC: American Psychological Association.

Gilbert, C., & Bakan, P. (1973). Visual asymmetry in perception of faces. *Neuropsychologia, 11*, 355–362.

Gist, J. H., McFarlane, J., Malecha, A., Fredland, N., Schultz, P., & Wilson, P. (2001). Women in danger: Intimate partner violence experienced by women who qualify and do not qualify for a protective order. *Behavioral Sciences and the Law, 19*, 637–647.

Glass, L. S. (1991). The legal base in forensic neuropsychology. In Doerr & Carlin (Eds.), *Forensic neuropsychology: Legal and scientific bases*. New York: Guilford Press.

Glick, P. C. (1988). The role of divorce in the changing family structure: Trends and variations. In S. A. Wolchik & P. Karoly (Eds.), *Children of divorce: Empirical perspective on adjustment*. New York: Gardner Press.

Goddard, L. L. (Ed.). (1993). *An African-centered model of prevention for African-American youth at high risk*. Rockville, MD: U.S. Department of Health and Human Services.

Going, M., & Read, J. D. (1974). Effects of uniqueness, sex of subject, and sex of photograph on facial recognition. *Perceptual and Motor Skills, 39*, 109–110.

Goldberg, L. R. (1968). Simple models or simple processes? Some research on clinical judgments. *American Psychologist, 23*, 483–496.

Goldberg, L. R. (1970). Man vs. model of man: A rationale, plus some evidence for a method of improving on clinical inferences. *Psychological Bulletin, 73*, 422–432.

Goldberg, L. R., & Werts, C. E. (1966). The reliability of clinician's judgments: A multitrait-multimethod approach. *Journal of Consulting Psychology, 30*, 199–206.

Golden, M. (1964). Some effects of combining psychological tests on clinical inferences. *Journal of Consulting Psychology, 28*, 440–446.

Golding, S. L. (1992). The adjudication of criminal responsibility: A review of theory and research. In D. Kagehiro & W. Laufer (Eds.), *Handbook of psychology and law*. New York: Springer-Verlag.

Golding, S. L. (1993). *Interdisciplinary Fitness Interview-Revised: A training manual*. State of Utah Division of Mental Health.

Golding, S. L., & Roesch, R. (1987) The assessment of criminal responsibility: A historical approach to a current controversy. In I. B. Weiner & A. K. Hess (Eds.), *Handbook of forensic psychology*. New York: Wiley.

Golding, S. L., Roesch, R., & Schreiber, J. (1984). Assessment and conceptualization of competency to stand trial: Preliminary data on the Interdisciplinary Fitness Interview. *Law and Human Behavior, 8*, 321–334.

Golding, S. L., Skeem, J. L., Roesch, R., & Zapf, P. A. (1999). The assessment of criminal responsibility: Current controversies. In I. B. Weiner & A. K. Hess (Eds.), *Handbook of forensic psychology*. New York: Wiley.

Goldkamp, J. S., & Irons-Guynn, C. (2000). *Emerging judicial strategies for the mentally ill in the criminal caseload: Mental health courts in Fort Lauderdale, Seattle, San Bernardino, and Anchorage*. Washington, DC: U.S. Department of Justice, Office of Justice Programs, Bureau of Justice Assistance.

Goldkamp, J. S., & Weiland, D. (1993). *Assessing the impact of Dade County's felony drug court*. Washington, DC: National Institute of Justice.

Goldstein, A. G. (1977). The fallibility of the eyewitness: Psychological evidence. In B. D. Sales (Ed.), *Psychology in the legal process*. New York: Spectrum Publications.

Goldstein, A. G., & Chance, J. E. (1964). Recognition of children's faces. *Child Development, 35*, 129–136.

Goldstein, A. G., & Chance, J. E. (1970). Visual recognition memory for complex configurations. *Perception and Psychophysics, 9*, 237–241.

Goldstein, A. G., & Chance, J. E. (1976). Measuring psychological similarity of faces. *Bulletin of Psychonomic Society, 7*, 407–408.

Goldstein, A. G., & Chance, J. E. (1978). Judging face similarity in own and other races. *Journal of Psychology, 98*, 185–193.

Goldstein, A. G., & Chance, J. E. (1979). Do "foreign" faces really look alike? *Bulletin of the Psychonomic Society, 13*, 111–113.

Goldstein, J., Freud, A., & Solnit, A. (1979). *Beyond the best interest of the child*. New York: Macmillan.

Goodman, G. S., & Aman, C. (1990). Children's use of anatomically detailed dolls to recount an event. *Child Development, 61*, 1859–1871.

Goodman, G. S., & Hahn, A. (1987). Evaluating eyewitness testimony. In I. B. Weiner & A. K. Hess (Eds.), *Handbook of forensic psychology*. New York: Wiley.

Goodman, G. S., & Reed, R. S. (1986). Age differences in eyewitness testimony. *Law and Human Behavior, 10*, 317–332.

Goodman, G. S., Aman, C., & Hirschman, J. (1987). Child sexual and physical abuse: Children's testimony. In S. J. Ceci, M. P. Toglia, & D. F. Ross (Eds.), *Children's eyewitness memory*. New York: Springer-Verlag.

Goodman, G. S., Bottoms, B. L., Hersocvici, B. B., & Shaver, P. (1989). In S. J. Ceci, D. F. Ross, & M. P. Toglia (Eds.), *Perspectives on the child witness*. New York: Springer-Verlag.

Goodman, G. S., Golding, J. M., Helgeson, V., Haith, M., & Michelli, J. (1987). When a child takes the stand: Jurors' perception of children's eyewitness testimony. *Law and Human Behavior, 11*, 27–40.

Goodman, G. S., Hepps, D., Reed, R. S. (1986). The child victim's testimony. In A. Haralambie (Ed.), *New issues for child advocates*. Phoenix, AZ: Arizona Associates of Council for Children.

Goodman, G. S., Levine, M., Melton, G. B., & Ogden, D. (1991). *Craig v. Maryland*: Amicus brief to the U.S. Supreme Court on behalf of the American Psychological Association. *Law and Human Behavior, 15*, 13–30.

Goodman, G. S., Pyle-Taub, E., Jones, D. P. H., England, P., Port, L. P., Rudy, L., & Prado, L. (1992). Emotional effects of criminal court testimony on child sexual assault victims. *Monographs of the Society for Research in Child Development, 57* (Serial No. 229).

Goodman, G. S., Redlich, E. D., Qin, J., Ghetti, S., Tyda, K. S., Schaaf, J. M., & Hahn, A. (1999). Evaluating eyewitness testimony in adults and children. In I. B. Weiner & A. K. Hess (Eds.), *Handbook of forensic psychology*. New York: Wiley.

Goodman, G. S., Tobey, A. E., Batterman-Faunce, J. M., Orcutt, H., Thomas, S., Shapiro, C., & Sachsenmaier, T. (1998). Face-to-face confrontation: Effects of closed-circuit technology on children's eyewitness testimony and jurors' decisions. *Law and Human Behavior, 22*, 165–203.

Goodman-Delahunty, J. (1997). Forensic psychological expertise in the wake of *Daubert*. *Law and Human Behavior, 21*, 121–140.

Gordon, C. C. (1969). *Perspectives on law enforcement. I. Characteristics of police applicants*. Princeton, NJ: Educational Testing Service.

Gordon, N. J., & Fleisher, W. L. (2002). *Effective interviewing and interrogation techniques*. San Diego, CA: Academic Press.

Gordon, R., & Peek, L. (1989). *The Custody Quotient Research Manual*. Dallas, TX: Wilmington Institute.

Gorenstein, G. W. & Ellsworth, P. C. (1980). Effect of choosing an incorrect photograph on a later identification by an eyewitness. *Journal of Applied Psychology, 65*, 616–622.

Gothard, S., Rogers, R., & Sewell, K. W. (1995). Feigning incompetency to stand trial: An investigation of the Georgia Court Competency Test. *Law and Human Behavior, 4*, 363–373.

Gottesman, J. (1975). *The utility of the MMPI in assessing the personality patterns of urban police applicants*. Hoboken, NJ: Stevens Institute of Technology.

Gottfredson, M. R., & Gottfredson, D. M. (1988). *Decision-making in criminal justice: Toward the rational exercise of discretion* (2nd ed.). New York: Plenum.

Gough, H. G. (1969). A leadership index on the California Psychological Inventory. *Journal of Counseling Psychology, 16*, 283–289.

Gould, J. W. (1998). *Conducting scientifically crafted child custody evaluations*. Thousand Oaks, CA: Sage.

Gover, A. R., MacKenzie, D. L., & Styve, G. J. (2000). Boot camps and traditional correctional facilities for juveniles: A comparison of the participants, daily activities, and environments. *Journal of Criminal Justice, 28*, 53–68.

Grant, V. (1977). *The menacing stranger*. New York: Dover.

Grassian, S. (1983). Psychopathological effects of solitary confinement. *American Journal of Psychiatry, 140*, 1450–1454.

Green, G. S. (1997). *Occupational crime* (2nd ed.). Chicago: Nelson-Hall Publishers.

Greene, E. (1990). Media effects on jurors. *Law and Human Behavior, 14*, 439–450.

Greene, E., & Bornstein, B. (2000). Precious little guidance: Jury instructions on damage awards. *Psychology, Public Policy, and Law, 6*, 743–768.

Greene, E., & Loftus, E. F. (1985). When crimes are joined at trial. *Law and Human Behavior, 9*, 193–207.

Greene, J. R. (2000). Community policing in America: Changing the nature, structure, and function of the police. *Policies, Processes, and Decisions of the Criminal Justice System, 3*, 299–370.

Greenfeld, L. A., Langan, P. A., & Smith, S. K. (1997, November). *Police use of force: Collection of national data*. Washington, DC: U.S. Department of Justice, Bureau of Justice Statistics.

Greenfield, L. A., Rand, M. R., Craven, D., Klaus, P. A., Perkins, C. A., Ringel, C., Wrachol, F., Maston, C., & Fox, J. A. (1998). *Violence by intimates: Analysis of data on crimes by current and former spouses, boyfriends, and girlfriends*. Washington, DC: U.S. Department of Justice.

Greenwood, P. W., & Turner, S. (1993). Evaluation of the Paint Creek Youth Center: A residential program for serious delinquents. *Criminology, 31*, 263–279.

Greer, A., O'Regan, M., & Traverso, A. (1996). Therapeutic jurisprudence and patients' perceptions of procedural due process of civil commitment hearings. In D. Wexler & B. Winick, (Eds.), *Law in a therapeutic key: Developments in therapeutic jurisprudence*. Durham, NC: Carolina Academic Press.

Gregorie, T. (2000). Workplace violence. In G. Coleman, M. Gaboury, M. Murray, & A. Seymour (Eds.), *1999 National Victim Assistance Academy*. Washington, DC: U.S. Department of Justice.

Gregorie, T., & Wallace, H. (2000). Workplace violence: Supplement. In A. Seymour, M. Murray, J. Sigmon, M. Hook, C. Edmonds, M. Gaboury, & G. Coleman (Eds.), *2000 National Victim Assistance Academy*. Washington, DC: U.S. Department of Justice.

Gregorie, T., & Wallace, H. (2001). Workplace violence. In A. Seymour, M. Murray, J. Sigmon, M. Hook, C. Edmonds, M. Gaboury, & G. Coleman (Eds.), *2001 National Victim Assistance Acad*emy *textbook*. Washington, DC: U.S. Department of Justice.

Gretton, H. M., McBride, M., Hare, R. D., O'Shaughnessy, R., & Kumka, G. (2001). Psychopathy and recidivism in adolescent sex offenders. *Criminal Justice and Behavior, 28*, 427–449.

Griffitt, W., & Jackson, T. (1973). Simulated jury decisions: The influence of jury-defendant attitude similarity-dissimilarity. *Social Behavior and Personality, 1*, 1–7.

Grisso, T. (1981). *Juveniles' waiver of rights: Legal and psychological competence*. New York: Plenum.

Grisso, T. (1986). *Evaluating competencies: Forensic assessments and instruments*. New York: Plenum

Grisso, T. (1988). *Competency to stand trial evaluations: A manual for practice*. Sarasota, FL: Professional Resource Exchange.

Grisso, T. (1996). Society's retributive response to juvenile violence: A developmental perspective. *Law and Human Behavior, 20*, 229–247.

Grisso, T. (1997). The competence of adolescents as trial defendants. *Psychology, Public Policy, and Law, 3*, 32–48.

Grisso, T. (1998). *Forensic evaluation of juveniles*. Sarasota, FL: Professional Resource Press.

Grisso, T., & Appelbaum, P. S. (1998a). *MacArthur Competence Assessment Tool for Treatment (MacCAT-T)*. Sarasota, FL: Professional Resource Press.

Grisso, T., & Appelbaum, P. (1998b). *Assessing competence to consent to treatment: A guide for physicians and other health professionals*. New York: Oxford University Press.

Grisso, T., & Appelbaum, P. S. (1991). Mentally ill and non-mentally-ill patients' abilities to understand informed consent disclosures for medication: Preliminary data. *Law and Human Behavior, 15*, 377–388.

Grisso, T., & Appelbaum, P. S. (1992). It is unethical to offer predictions of future violence. *Law and Human Behavior, 16*, 621–633.

Grisso, T., & Appelbaum, P. S. (1995). The MacArthur Treatment Competence Study: III. Abilities of patients to consent to psychiatric and medical treatment. *Law and Human Behavior, 19*, 149–174.

Grisso, T., Appelbaum, P., Mulvey, E., & Fletcher, K. (1995). The MacArthur Treatment Competence Study II: Measures of abilities related to competence to consent to treatment. *Law and Human Behavior, 19*, 127–148.

Grisso, T., & Ring, M. (1979). Parents' attidudes toward juveniles' rights in interrogation. *Criminal Justice and Behavior, 6*, 221–226.

Grisso, T., & Saks, M. J. (1991). Psychology's influence on constitutional interpretation. *Law and Human Behavior, 15*, 205–211.

Grisso, T., & Schwartz, R. G. (Eds.). (2000). *Youth on trial*. Chicago: University of Chicago Press.

Grisso, T., Tomkins, A., & Casey, P. (1988). Psychosocial concepts in juvenile law. *Law and Human Behavior, 12*, 403–437.

Grove, W. M., & Barden, R. C. (1999). Protecting the integrity of the legal system. *Psychology, Public Policy, and Law, 5*, 224–242.

Grove, W. M., & Meehl, P. E. (1996). Comparative efficiency of informal (subjective, impressionistic) and formal (mechanical, algorithmic) prediction procedures: The clinical-statistical controversy. *Psychology, Public Policy, and Law, 2*, 293–323.

Groves, P., & Schlesinger, K. (1979). *Introduction to biological psychology*. Dubuque, IA: Wm. C. Brown.

Grych, J. H., & Fincham, F. D. (1992). Interventions for children of divorce: Toward a greater integration of research and action. *Psychological Bulletin, 111*, 434–454.

Gudjonsson, G. H. (1984). A new scale of interrogative suggestibility. *Personality and Individual Differences, 5*, 303–314.

Gudjonsson, G. H. (1988). How to defeat the polygraph tests. In A. Gale (Ed.), *The polygraph test: Lies, truth and science*. London: Sage.

Gudjonsson, G. H. (1992). *The psychology of interrogations, confessions and testimony*. London: Wiley.

Guilmette, T. J., & Faust, D. (1987, October). *A survey of U.S. clinical neuropsychologists*. Presentation at the Annual Convention of the National Academy of Neuropsychologists, Chicago, IL.

Guinther, J. (1988). *The jury in America*. New York: Roscoe Pound Foundation.

Gunnoe, M. L., & Braver, S. L. (2001). The effects of joint legal custody on mothers, fathers, and children controlling for factors that predispose a sole maternal versus joint legal award. *Law and Human Behavior, 25*, 25–43.

Gutheil, T. G. (2001). Moral justification for Tarasoff-type warnings and breach of confidentiality: A clinician's perspective. *Behavioral Sciences and the Law, 19*, 345–353.

Gutheil, T., & Appelbaum, P. (2000). *Clinical handbook of psychiatry and the law* (3rd ed.). Baltimore, MD: Williams & Wilkins.

Haber, R. N., & Haber, L. (2000). Experiencing, remembering, and reporting events. *Psychology, Public Policy, and Law, 6*, 1057–1097.

Hafemeister, T. L., Ogloff, R. R. P., & Small, M. A. (1990). Training and careers in law and psychology: The perspective of dual degree programs. *Behavioral Sciences and the Law, 8*, 263–283.

Hafer, C. L. (2000). Do innocent victims threaten the belief in a just world? Evidence form a modified stroop task. *Journal of Personality and Social Psychology, 79*, 165–173.

Hageman, M. J. C. (1978). Occupational stress and marital relationships. *Journal of Police Science and Administration, 6*, 402–409.

Hall, D. M. (1998). The victim of stalking. In J. R. Meloy (Ed.), *The psychology of stalking: Clinical and forensic perspectives*. San Diego, CA: Academic Press.

Hall, G. C. N. (1995). Sexual offender recidivism revisited: A meta-analysis of recent treatment studies. *Journal of Consulting and Clinical Psychology, 63*, 802–809.

Halleck, S. (1980). *Law in the practice of psychiatry*. Washington, DC: National Institute of Mental Health.

Hamparian, D. M., Estep, L. K., Muntean, S. M., Priestino, R. R., Swisher, R. G., Wallace, P. L., & White, J. L. (1982). *Youth in adult courts: Between two worlds*. Washington, DC: USGPO.

Hamparian, D. M., Schuster, R., Dinitz, S., & Conrad, J. D. (1978). *The violent few*. Lexington, MA: Lexington Books.

Haney, C. (1980). Psychology and legal change: On the limits of a factual jurisprudence. *Law and Human Behavior, 4*, 147–200.

Haney, C. (1984). Examining death qualification: Further analysis of the process effect. *Law and Human Behavior, 8*, 133–151.

Haney, C., Banks, W, Jaffe, D., & Zimbardo, P. (1973). Interpersonal dynamics in a simulated prison. *International Journal of Criminology, 1*, 69–97.

Haney, C., & Lynch, M. (1994). Comprehending life and death matters. *Law and Human Behavior, 18*, 411–436.

Haney, C., & Zimbardo, P. (1998). The past and future of U.S. prison policy: Twenty-five years after the Stanford prison experiment. *American Psychologist, 53*, 709–727.

Hans, V. P. (1990). Law and the media: An overview and introduction. *Law and Human Behavior, 14*, 399–408.

Hanson, R. K., & Harris, A. J. R. (2000). Where should we intervene? Dynamic predictors of sexual offense recidivism. *Criminal Justice and Behavior, 27*, 6–35.

Hare, R. D. (1985). Comparison of procedures for the assessment of psychopathy. *Journal of Consulting and Clinical Psychology, 53*, 7–16.

Hare, R. D. (1991). The Hare Psychopathy Checklist—Revised. Toronto: Multi-Health Systems.

Hare, R. D. (1996). Psychopathy: A clinical construct whose time has come. *Criminal Justice and Behavior, 23*, 25–54.

Hare, R. D. (1998a). Psychopaths and their nature: Implications for the mental health and criminal justice systems. In T. Millon, E. Simonsen, M. Birket-Smith, & R. D. Davis (Eds.), *Psychopathy: Antisocial, criminal, and violent behavior*. New York: Guilford Press.

Hare, R. D. (1998b). The Hare PCL-R: Some issues concerning its use and misuse. *Legal and Criminal Psychology, 3*, 99–119.

Hare, R. D., Clark, D., Grann, M., & Thornton, D. (2000). Psychopathy and the predictive validity of the PCL-R: An international perspective. *Behavioral Sciences and the Law, 18*, 623–645.

Hare, R. D., Forth, A. E., & Strachan, K. E. (1992). Psychopathy and crime across the life span. In R. D. Peters, R. J. McMahan, & V. L. Quinsey (Eds.), *Aggression and violence throughout the life span*. Newbury Park, CA: Sage.

Hare, R. D., Hart, S. D., & Harpur, T. J. (1991). Psychopathy and the DSM-IV criteria for antisocial personality disorder. *Journal of Abnormal Psychology, 100*, 391–398.

Hare, R. D., McPherson, L. M., & Forth, A. E. (1988). Male psychopaths and their criminal careers. *Journal of Consulting and Clinical Psychology, 56*, 710–714.

Hare, R. D., & Schelling, D. (Eds.). (1978). *Psychopathic behaviour: Approaches to research*. Chichester, UK: Wiley.

Hargrave, G. E., & Hiatt, D. (1987). Law enforcement selection with the interview, MMPI, and CPI. *Journal of Police Science and Administration, 15*, 110–117.

Harmon, L. D. (1973, November). The recognition of faces. *Scientific American*, pp. 71–82.

Harris, A. (2002, January). Unsupported expert testimony inadmissible. *National Law Journal*, p. 14.

Harris, D. A. (1999, June). *Driving while black: Racial profiling on our nation's highways*. New York: American Civil Liberties Union.

Harris, G. T., & Rice, M. E. (1994). *Mentally disordered offenders: What research says about effective service*. Penetanguishene, Ontario: Mental Health Centre Research Reports.

Harris, G. T., Rice, M. E., & Cormier, C. A. (1991). Psychopathy and violent recidivism. *Law and Human Behavior, 15*, 625–637.

Harris, G. T., Rice, M. E., & Quinsey, V. L. (1993). Violent recidivism of mentally disordered offenders: The development of a statistical prediction instrument. *Criminal Justice and Behavior, 20*, 315–335.

Harris, P., Brown, E., Marriott, C., Whittall, S., & Harmer, S. (1991). Monsters, ghosts, and witches: Testing the limits of the fantasy-reality distinctions in young children. *British Journal of Developmental Psychology, 9*, 105–123.

Hart, S. D. (1998). The role of psychopathy in assessing risk for violence: Conceptual and methodological issues. *Legal and Criminological Psychology, 3*, 121–137.

Hart, S .D., Cox, D., & Hare, R. D. (1995). *The Hare Psychopathy Checklist: Screening Version*. Toronto: Multi-Health System.

Hart, S. D., Hare, R. D., & Forth, A. E. (1993). Psychopathy as a risk marker for violence: Development and validation of a screening version of the Revised Psychopathy Checklist. In J. Monahan & H. Steadman (Eds.), *Violence and mental disorder: Development in risk assessment*. Chicago: University of Chicago Press.

Hart, S. D., & Dempster, R. J. (1997). Impulsivity and psychopathy. In C. D. Webster & M. A. Jackson (Eds.), *Impulsivity: Theory, assessment and treatment*. New York: Guilford.

Hart, S. D., Kropp, P. R., & Hare, R. D. (1988). Psychopathy and conditional release from prison. *Journal of Consulting and Clinical Psychology, 56*, 227–232.

Hart, S. D., Watt, K. A., & Vincent, G. M. (2002). Commentary on Seagrave and Grisso: Impressions of the state of the art. *Law and Human Behavior, 26*, 241–245.

Hart, S. D., Webster, C. D., & Menzies, R. J. (1993). A note on portraying the accuracy of violence predictions. *Law and Human Behavior, 17*, 695–700.

Hart, S. W. (1991). From property to person status: Historical perspective on children's rights. *American Psychologist, 46*, 53–59.

Hartman, D. E. (1995). *Neuropsychological toxicology* (2nd ed.). New York: Plenum.

Harvard Law Review. (1985). The testimony of child victims in sex abuse prosecutions: Two legislative innovations. *Harvard Law Review, 98*, 806–827.

Hasselbrack, A. M. (2001). Opting in to mental health courts. *Corrections Compendium, Sample Issue*, 4–5.

Hastie, R., Penrod, S. D., & Pennington, N. (1983). *Inside the jury*. Cambridge, MA: Harvard University Press.

Hastie, R., Schkade, D., & Payne, J. (1998). A study of juror and jury judgments in civil cases: Deciding liability for punitive damages. *Law and Human Behavior, 22*, 287–314.

Hastroudi, S., Parker, E. S., DeLisi, L. E., Wyatt, R. J., & Mutter, S. A. (1984). Intact retention in acute alcohol amnesia. *Journal of Experimental Psychology: Learning, Memory, and Cognition, 10*, 156–163.

Haugaard, J. J., & Reppucci, N. D. (1988). *The sexual abuse of children*. San Francisco: Jossey-Bass.

Hawkins, K. A., Faraone, S. V., Pepple, J. R., Seidman, L. J., & Tsuang, M. T. (1990). WAIS-R validation of the Wonderlic Personnel Test as a brief intelligence measure in a psychiatric sample. *Psychological Assessment: A Journal of Consulting and Clinical Psychology, 2*, 198–201.

Hawkins, S. A., & Hastie, R. (1990). Hindsight: Biased judgments of past events after the outcomes are known. *Psychological Bulletin, 107*, 311–327.

Hayes, L. M. (1995). *Prison suicide: An overview and guide to prevention*. Boulder, CO: National Institute of Corrections.

Hebb, D. O. (1955). Drives and the C.N.S. (Conceptual Nervous System). *Psychological Review, 62*, 243–254.

Hecker, T., & Steinberg, L. (2002). Psychological evaluation at juvenile court disposition. *Professional Psychology: Research and Practice, 33*, 300–306.

Heilbrun, K. S. (1987). The assessment of competency for execution: An overview. *Behavioral Sciences and the Law, 5*, 383–396.

Heilbrun, K. S. (1992). The role of psychological testing in forensic assessment. *Law and Human Behavior, 16*, 257–272.

Heilbrun, K. (1995). Child custody evaluation: Critically assessing mental health experts and psychological tests. *Family Law Quarterly, 29*, 63–78.

Heilbrun, K. (2001). *Principles of forensic mental health assessment.* New York: Kluwer Academic/Plenum.

Heilbrun, K., & Griffin, P. (1999). Forensic treatment: A review of programs and research. In R. Roesch, S. D. Hart, & J. R. P. Ogloff (Eds.), *Psychology and law: The state of the discipline.* New York: Kluwer Academic/Plenum Publishers.

Heilbrun, K., Hawk, G., Tate, D. C. (1996). Juvenile competence to stand trial: Research issues in practice. *Law and Human Behavior, 20*, 573–578.

Heilbrun, K., Leheny, C., Thomas, L., & Huneycutt, D. (1997). A national survey of U.S. states on juvenile transfer: Implications for policy and practice. *Behavioral Science and the Law, 15*, 125–149.

Heilbrun, K., Marczyk, G. R., & DeMatteo, D. (2002). *Forensic mental health assessment: A casebook.* New York: Oxford University Press.

Heilbrun, K., Rogers, R., & Otto, R. K. (2000). Forensic assessment: Current status and future directions. In J. R. P. Ogloff (Ed.), *Psychology and law: Reviewing the discipline.* New York: Kluwer/Plenum.

Heinze, M. C., & Grisso, T. (1996). Review of instruments assesing parenting competencies used in child custody evaluations. *Behavioral Science and the Law, 14*, 293–313.

Hemphill, J. F., Hare, R. D., & Wong, S. (1998). Psychopathy and recidivism: A review. *Legal and Criminal Psychology, 3*, 139–170.

Henderson, N. D. (1979). Criterion-related validity of personality and aptitude scales. In C. D. Spielberger (Ed.), *Police selection and evaluation: Issues and techniques.* Washington, DC: Hemisphere Publishing.

Henggeler, S. W. (1996). Treatment of violent juvenile offenders —we have the knowledge. *Journal of Family Psychology, 10*, 137–141.

Henggeler, S. W. (2001). Multisystemic therapy. *Residential Treatment for Children and Youth, 18*, 75–85.

Henggeler, S. W., & Borduin, C. M. (1990). *Family therapy and beyond: A multisystemic approach to treating the behavior problems of children and adolescents.* Pacific Grove, CA: Brooks/Cole.

Henggeler, S. W., Melton, G. B., & Smith, L. A. (1992). Family preservation using multisystemic therapy—an effective alternative to incarcerating serious juvenile offenders. *Journal of Consulting and Clinical Psychology, 60*, 953–961.

Henker, B., & Whalen, C. K. (1989). Hyperactivity and attention deficits. *American Psychologist, 44*, 216–224.

Henning, K. R., & Frueh, B. C. (1996). Cognitive-behavioral treatment of incarcerated offenders: An evaluation of the Vermont Department of Corrections' Cognitive Self-Change Program. *Criminal Justice and Behavior, 23*, 523–541.

Herek, G. M., Gillis, J. R., & Cogan, J. C. (1999). Psychological sequelae of hate-crime victimization among lesbian, gay, and bisexual adults. *Journal of Consulting and Clinical Psychology, 67*, 945–951.

Herndon, J. S. (2001). Law enforcement suicide: Psychological autopsies and psychometric traces. In D. C. Sheehan & J. I. Warren (Eds.), *Suicide and law enforcement.* Washington, DC: U.S. Department of Justice, Federal Bureau of Investigation.

Hess, A. K. (1999). Serving as an expert witness. In A. K. Hess & I. B. Weiner (Eds.), *The handbook of forensic psychology* (2nd ed.). New York: Wiley.

Hess, J. E. (1997). *Interviewing and interrogation for law enforcement.* Cincinnati, OH: Anderson.

Hess, J. H., & Thomas, H. E. (1963). Incompetency to stand trial: Procedures, results and problems. *American Journal of Psychiatry, 119*, 713–720.

Hess, K. D., & Brinson, P. (1999). Mediating domestic law issues. In A. K. Hess, & I. B. Weiner (Eds.), *The handbook of forensic psychology* (2nd ed.). New York: Wiley.

Hess, L. R. (1973). Police entry tests and their predictability of score in police academy and subsequent job performance. *Dissertation Abstracts International*, 33-B, 5552.

Hetherington, E. M. (1979). Divorce: A child's perspective. *American Psychologist, 34*, 851–858.

Hetherington, E. M., Bridges, M., & Insabella, G. M. (1998). What matters? What does not? Five perspectives on the association between marital transitions and children's adjustment. *American Psychologist, 53*, 167–184.

Hetherington, E. M., Cox, M., & Cox, R. (1979). Family interaction and the social, emotional, and cognitive development of children following divorce. In V. Vaughn & T. Brazelton (Eds.), *The family: Setting priorities.* New York: Science & Medicine.

Heuer, L., & Penrod, S. D. (1988). Increasing jurors' participation in trials: A field experiment with jury note taking and question asking. *Law and Human Behavior, 12*, 409–430.

Heuer, L., & Penrod, S. D. (1989). Instructing jurors: A field experiment with written and preliminary instructions. *Law and Human Behavior, 13*, 231–261.

Heuer, L., & Penrod, S. D. (1994). Juror note taking and question asking during trial: A national field experiment. *Law and Human Behavior, 18*, 121–150.

Hiatt, D., & Hargrave, G. E. (1988a). MMPI profiles of problem peace officers. *Journal of Personality Assessment, 52*, 722–731.

Hiatt, D., & Hargrave, G. E. (1988b). Predicting job performance problems with psychological screening. *Journal of Police Science and Administration, 16*, 122–125.

Hickey, E. W. (1997). *Serial murderers and their victims.* Belmont, CA: Wadsworth.

Hiday, V. A. (1977). Reformed commitment procedures: An empirical study in the courtroom. *Law and Society Review, 11,* 651–666.

Hiday, V. A. (1988). Civil commitment: A review of empirical research. *Behavioral Sciences and the Law, 6,* 15–44.

Hiday, V. A. (1990). Dangerousness of civil commitment candidates. *Law and Human Behavior, 14,* 551–567.

Hiday, V. A., & Scheid-Cook, T. L. (1987). The North Carolina experience with outpatient commitment: A critical appraisal. *International Journal of Law and Psychiatry, 10,* 215–232.

Hiday, V. A., & Scheid-Cook, T. L. (1989). A follow-up of chronic patients committed to outpatient treatment. *Hospital and Community Psychiatry, 40,* 52–58.

Higgins, L. L. (1961). *Policewoman's manual.* Springfield, IL: C.C. Thomas.

Hilgard, E. R. (1965). *Hypnotic susceptibility.* New York: Harcourt Brace Jovanovich.

Hill, C., Rogers, R., & Bickford, M. (1996). Predicting aggressive and socially disruptive behavior in a maximum security forensic psychiatric hospital. *Journal of Forensic Sciences, 51,* 56–59.

Hilton, J. (1973). Psychology and police work. In J. C. Anderson & P. J. Stead (Eds.), *The police we deserve.* London: Wolfe Publishers.

Hogan, R. (1971). Personality characteristics of highly rated policemen. *Personnel Psychology, 24,* 679–686.

Hoge, S. K., Appelbaum, P. S., Lawlor, T., Beck, J. C., Litman, R., Greer, A., Gutheil, T. G., & Kaplan, E. (1990). A prospective, multi-center study of patients' refusal of antipsychotic medication. *Archives of General Psychiatry, 47,* 949–956.

Hoge, S. K., Bonnie, R. G., Poythress, N., Monahan, J., Eisenberg, M., & Feucht-Haviar, T. (1997). The MacArthur Adjucative Competence Study: Development and validation of a research instrument. *Law and Human Behavior, 21,* 141–179.

Hoge, S. K., Bonnie. R. J., Poythress, N., & Monahan, J. (1997). *The MacArthur Competence Assessment Tool—Criminal Adjudication (MacCAT-CA).* Lutz, FL: Psychological Assessment Resources.

Hoge, S., Lidz, C., Eisenberg, M., Gardner, W., Monahan, J., Mulvey, E., Roth, L., & Bennett, N. (1997). Perceptions of coercion in the admission of voluntary and involuntary psychiatric patients. *International Journal of Law and Psychiatry, 20,* 167–181.

Hoge, S., Lidz, C., Mulvey, E., Roth, L., Bennett, N., Siminoff, L., Arnold, R., & Monahan, J. (1993). Patient, family, and staff perceptions of coercion in mental hospital admission: An exploratory study. *Behavioral Sciences and the Law, 20,* 281–293.

Hollien, H. (1980). Vocal indicators of psychological stress. In F. Wright, C. Bahn, & R. W. Rieber (Eds.), *Forensic psychology and psychiatry. Annals of the New York Academy of Sciences* (Vol. 347). New York: Academy of Sciences.

Homant, R. J., & Kennedy, D. B. (1987). Subjective factors in clinicians' judgments of insanity: Comparison of a hypothetical case and an actual case. *Professional Psychology: Research and Practice, 5,* 439–446.

Homant, R. J., & Kennedy, D. B. (1998). Psychological aspects of crime scene profiling: Validity research. *Criminal Justice and Behavior, 25,* 319–343.

Homant, R. J., & Kennedy, D. B. (2001). A typology of suicide of police incidents. In D. C. Sheehan & J. T. Warren (Eds.), *Suicide and law enforcement.* Washington, DC: U.S. Department of Justice, FBI Behavioral Science Unit.

Honts, C. R. (1987). Interpreting research on polygraph countermeasures. *Journal of Police Science and Administration, 15,* 204–209.

Honts, C. R., & Amato, S. L. (2002). Countermeasures. In M. Kleiner (Ed.), *Handbook of polygraph testing.* San Diego, CA: Academic Press.

Honts, C. R., Devitt, M. K., Winbush, M., & Kircher, J. C. (1996). Mental and physical countermeasures reduce the accuracy of the concealed knowledge test. *Psychophysiology, 33,* 84–92.

Honts, C. R., Hodes, R. L., & Raskin, D. C. (1985). Effects of physical countermeasures on the physiological detection of deception. *Journal of Applied Psychology, 70,* 177–187.

Honts, C. R., & Perry, M. V. (1992). Polygraph admissibility: Changes and challenges. *Law and Human Behavior, 16,* 357–379.

Honts, C. R., Raskin, D. C., & Kircher, J. C. (1987). Effects of physical countermeasures and their electromyographic detection during polygraph tests for deception. *Journal of Psychophysiology, 1,* 241–247.

Hooke, J. F., Krauss, H. H. (1971). Personality characteristics of successful police sergeant candidates. *Journal of Criminal Law, Criminology and Police Science, 62,* 104–106.

Horowitz, I. A., Bordens, K. S., & Feldman, M. S. (1980). A comparison of verdicts obtained in severed and joined criminal trials. *Journal of Applied Social Psychology, 10,* 444–456.

Horowitz, I. A., & Forsterlee, L. (2001). The effects of note-taking and trial transcript access on mock jury decisions in a complex civil trial. *Law and Human Behavior, 25,* 373–391.

Horowitz, I. A., & Kirkpatrick, L. C. (1996). A concept in search of a definition: The effects of reasonable doubt instructions on certainty of guilt standards and jury verdicts. *Law and Human Behavior, 20,* 655–670.

Horvath, F. S. (1977). The effect of selected variables on interpretation of polygraph records. *Journal of Applied Psychology, 62,* 127–136.

Hotaling, G. T., & Straus, M. A. (1989). Intrafamily violence, and crime and violence outside the family. In L. Ohlin & M. Tonry (Eds.), *Family violence* (Vol. 11). Chicago: University of Chicago Press.

Houghtalin, M., & May, G. L. (1991). Criminal dispositions of New Mexico juveniles transferred to adult court. *Crime & Delinquency, 37,* 393–407.

Howell, J. C. (1998). A new approach to juvenile crime. *Corrections Compendium, 23,* 1–4, 24–25.

Howells, T. H. (1938). A study of ability to recognize faces. *Journal of Abnormal and Social Psychology, 33,* 124–127.

Huber, P. W. (1991). *Galileo's revenge: Junk science in the courtroom.* New York: Basic Books.

Hunsley, J., Lee, C. M., & Aubry, T. (1999). Who uses psychological services in Canada? *Canadian Psychology, 40*, 232–240.

Hunt, J. C. (2000). Police subculture and gender. In Rafter, N. H. (Ed.), *Encyclopedia of women and crime*. Phoenix: Oryx Press.

Hurrell, J. J., & Kroes, W. H. (1975). Stress awareness. In W. H. Kroes & J. J. Hurrell (Eds.), *Job stress and the police officer: Identifying stress reduction techniques*. Washington, DC: USGPO.

Iacono, W. G., Cerri, A. M., Patrick, C. J., & Fleming, J. A. E. (1992). Use of antianxiety drugs: Countermeasures in the detection of guilty knowledge. *Journal of Applied Psychology, 77*, 60–64.

Iacono, W. G., & Lykken, D. (1997). The validity of the lie detector: Two surveys of scientific opinion. *Journal of Applied Psychology, 82*, 426–433.

Iacono, W. G., & Patrick, C. J. (1987). What psychologists should know about lie detection. In I. B. Weiner & A. K. Hess (Eds.), *Handbook of forensic psychology*. New York: Wiley.

Iacono, W. G., & Patrick, C. J. (1999). Polygraph ("lie detector") testing: The state of the art. In A. K. Hess & I. B. Weiner (Eds.), *The handbook of forensic psychology* (2nd ed.). New York: Wiley.

Ichheiser, G. (1943). Misinterpretation of personality in everyday life and the psychologist's frame of reference. *Character and Personality, 12*, 145–160.

Inbau, F. E., & Reid, J. E. (1967). *Criminal interrogation and confessions*. Baltimore: Williams & Wilkins.

Inbau, F. E., Reid, J. E., & Buckley, J. P. (1986). *Criminal interrogation and confessions* (3rd ed.). Baltimore: Williams & Wilkins.

Interdivisional Committee on Adolescent Abortion. (1987). Adolescent abortion. *American Psychologist, 42*, 73–78.

International Association of Chiefs of Police (IACP) (2002). *Fitness for duty evaluation guidelines*. Alexandria, VA: Author.

Inwald, R., & Kenny, D. J. (1989). Psychological testing of police candidates. In D. J. Kenny (Ed.), *Police and policing: Contemporary issues*. New York: Praeger.

Irwin, J. (1985). *The jail*. Berkeley, CA: University of California Press.

Irwin, J., & Austin, J. (2001). *It's about time: America's imprisonment binge*, (3rd ed.). Belmont, CA: Wadsworth/Thomson Learning.

Izzett, R., & Fishman, L. (1976). Defendant sentences as a function of attractiveness and justification for actions. *Journal of Social Psychology, 100*, 285–290.

Izzett, R., & Leginski, W. (1974). Group discussion and the influence of defendant characteristics in a simulated jury setting. *Journal of Social Psychology, 93*, 271–279.

Jackson, H. F., Glass, C., & Hope, S. (1987). A functional analysis of recidivistic arson. *British Journal of Clinical Psychology, 26*, 175–185.

James, F., Jr. (1965). *Civil procedure*. Boston: Little, Brown.

James, R. (1959). Status and competence of jurors. *American Journal of Sociology, 64*, 563–570.

Janus, E. S., & Meehl, P. E. (1997). Assessing the legal standard for predictions of dangerousness in sex offender commitment proceedings. *Psychology, Public Policy, and Law, 3*, 33–64.

Jenkins, N., & Dambrot, J. (1987). The attribution of date rape: Observer's attitude and sexual experiences and the dating situation. *Journal of Applied Social Psychology, 17*, 875–895.

Jenkins, P. (1988). Serial murder in England 1940–1985. *Journal of Criminal Justice, 16*, 1–15.

Jenkins, P. (1993). Chance or choice: The selection of serial murder victims. In A. V. Wilson (Ed.), *Homicide: The victim/offender connection*. Cincinnati, OH: Anderson.

Jenkins, P. (1994). *Using murder: The social construction of serial homicide*. New York: Aldine de Gruyter.

Jirak, M. (1975). Alienation among members of the New York City Police Department of Staten Island. *Journal of Police Science and Administration, 3*, 149–161.

Johns, J. H., & Quay, H. C. (1962). The effect of social reward on verbal conditioning in psychopathic military offenders. *Journal of Consulting Psychology, 26*, 287–296.

Johnson, C., & Haney, C. (1994). Felony voir dire: An exploratory study of its content and effect. *Law and Human Behavior, 18*, 487–506.

Johnson, C., & Scott, B. (1976). *Eyewitness testimony and suspect identification as a function of arousal, sex of witness, and scheduling of interrogation*. Paper presented at meeting of the American Psychological Association, Washington, DC.

Johnson, H., & Steiner, I. (1967). Some effects of discrepancy level on relationships between authoritarianism and conformity. *Journal of Social Psychology, 9*, 179–183.

Johnson, J. D., Whitestone, E., Jackson, L. A., & Gatto, L. (1995). Justice is still not color blind: Differential racial effects of exposure to admissible evidence. *Personality and Social Psychology Bulletin, 21*, 893–898.

Johnson, L. B. (1991). Job strain among police officers: Gender comparisons. *Police Studies, 14*, 12–16.

Johnson, R. (1996). *Hard time: Understanding and reforming the prison* (2nd ed). Belmont, CA: Wadsworth.

Johnston, J. R. (1995). Research update: Children's adjustment in sole custody compared to joint custody families and principles for custody decision making. *Family and Conciliation Courts Review, 33*, 415–425.

Jones, C. & Aronson, E. (1973). Attribution of fault to a rape victim as a function of respectability of the victim. *Journal of Personality and Social Psychology, 2*, 415–419.

Jones, R. A. (1977). *Self-fulfilling prophecies: Social psychological, and physiological effects of expectancies*. Hillsdale, NJ: Erlbaum.

Judson, C. J., Pandell, J. J., Owens, J. B., McIntosh, J. L., & Matschullat, D. L. (1969). A study of the California penalty jury in first degree murder cases. *Stanford Law Review, 21*, 1296–1497.

Julien, R. M. (1992). *A primer of drug action* (6th ed.). New York: W. H. Freeman.

Jurow, G. L. (1971). New data on the effect of a "death-qualified" jury on the guilt determination process. *Harvard Law Review, 84*, 567–611.

Kahneman, D., & Tversky, A. (1973). On the psychology of prediction. *Psychological Review, 80*, 237–251.

Kafrey, D. (1980). Playing with matches: Children and fire. In D. Canter (Ed.), *Fires and human behaviour*. Chichester, UK: Wiley.

Kairys, D., Schulman, J., & Harring, S. (1975). *The jury system: New methods for reducing prejudice*. Philadelphia: National Jury Project and National Lawyers Guild.

Kalven, H. Jr., & Zeisel, H. (1966). *The American jury*. Boston: Little, Brown.

Kaplan, M. F. (1977). Discussion polarization effects in a modified jury decision paradigm: Informational influences. *Sociometry, 40*, 262–271.

Kaplan, M. F., & Kemmerick, G. D. (1974). Juror judgments as information integration: Combining evidential and nonevidential information. *Journal of Personality and Social Psychology, 30*, 493–499.

Kaplan, M. F., & Miller, L. E. (1978). Reducing the effects of juror bias. *Journal of Personality and Social Psychology, 36*, 1443–1455.

Kaplan, S. (1985, July). Death, so say you all. *Psychology Today*, 48–53.

Karlin, R. A., & Orne, M. T. (1997). Hypnosis and the iatrogenic creation of memory: On the need for a *per se* exclusion of testimony based on hypnotically influenced recall. *Cultic Studies Journal, 14*, 172–206.

Karmen, A. (2001). *Crime victims* (4th ed). Belmont, CA: Wadsworth/Thomson Learning.

Kasl, Q. V, & Mahl, G. F. (1965). The relationship of disturbances and hesitations in spontaneous speech to anxiety. *Journal of Personality and Social Psychology, 1*, 425–433.

Kassin, S. M. (1997). The psychology of confession evidence. *American Psychologist, 52*, 221–233.

Kassin, S. M., Ellsworth, P. C., & Smith, V. L. (1989). The "general acceptance" of psychological research on eyewitness testimony: A survey of the experts. *American Psychologist, 44*, 1089–1098.

Kassin, S. M., & Fong, C. T. (1999). "I'm innocent!": Effects of training on judgment of truth and deception in the interrogation room. *Law and Human Behavior, 23*, 499–516.

Kassin, S. M., & Garfield, D. A. (1991). Blood and guts: General and trial-specific effects of videotaped crime scenes on mock jurors. *Journal of Applied Social Psychology, 21*, 1459–1472.

Kassin, S. M., & Kiechel, K. L. (1996). The social psychology of false confessions: Compliance, internalization, and confabulation. *Psychological Science, 7*, 125–128.

Kassin, S. M., & McNall, K. (1991). Police interrogations and confessions: Communicating promises and threats by pragmatic implication. *Law and Human Behavior, 15*, 233–251.

Kassin, S. M., Smith, V. L., & Tulloch, W. F. (1990). The dynamic charge: Effects on the perceptions and deliberation behavior of mock jurors. *Law and Human Behavior, 14*, 537–550.

Kassin, S. M., Tubb, V. A., Hosch, H. M., & Memon, A. (2001). On the "general acceptance" of eyewitness testimony research. *American Psychologist, 56*, 405–416.

Kassin, S. M., & Wrightsman, L. S. (1979). On the requirements of proof: The timing of judicial instruction and mock juror verdicts. *Journal of Personality and Social Psychology, 37*, 1877–1887.

Kassin, S. M., & Wrightsman, L. S. (1985). Confession evidence. In S. M. Kassin & L. S. Wrightsman (Eds.), *The psychology of evidence and trial procedure*. Beverly Hills, CA: Sage.

Katz, L. S., & Reid, J. F. (1977). Expert testimony on the fallibility of eyewitness identification. *Criminal Justice Journal, 1*, 177–206.

Kaufer, S., & Mattman, J. W. (2002). *Workplace violence: An employer's guide*. Palm Springs, CA: Workplace Violence Research Institute.

Kaufman, P., Chen, X., Choy, S. P., Peter, K., Ruddy, S. A., Miller, A. K., Fleury, J. .K., Chandler, K. A., Planty, M. G., & Rand, M. R. (2001). *Indicators of school crime and safety*. Washington, DC: U.S. Department of Education and Justice.

Kebbell, M. R., & Wagstaff, G. G. (1998). Hypnotic interviewing: The best way to interview eyewitnesses. *Behavioral Sciences and the Law, 16*, 115–129.

Keeler, E. (1984). *Lie detector man*. Boston, MA: Telshare Publishing.

Keilin, W. G., & Bloom, L. J. (1986). Child custody evaluation practices: A survey of experienced professionals. *Professional Psychology: Research and Practice, 17*, 338–346.

Kelleher, M. D. (1997). Profiling the lethal employee: Case studies of violence in the workplace. Westport, CT: Praeger.

Kelly, J. (1993). Current research on children's post-divorce adjustment: No simple answers. *Family and Conciliation Courts Review, 31*, 29–49.

Kelly, J. B. (1996). A decade of divorce mediation research: Some answers and questions. *Family and Conciliation Courts Review, 34*, 373–385.

Kelman, H. (1958). Compliance, identification, and internalization. *Journal of Conflict Resolution, 2*, 51–60.

Kelman, H. C., & Hamilton, V. L. (1989). *Crimes of obedience*. New Haven, CT: Yale University Press.

Kempe, C. H., Silverman, F. N., Steele, B. B., Droegemueller, W., & Silver, H. K. (1962). The battered-child syndrome. *Journal of the American Medical Association, 181*, 17–24.

Kendall, P. C., & Hammen, C. (1995). *Abnormal psychology*. Boston: Houghton Mifflin.

Kennedy, T. D., & Haggard, R. C. (1992). The discrediting effect in eyewitness testimony. *Journal of Applied Social Psychology, 22*, 70–82.

Kenrick, D. T., & Stringfield, D. O. (1980). Personality traits and the eye of the beholder: Crossing some traditional philosophical boundaries in the search for consistency in all of the people. *Psychological Review, 87*, 88–104.

Kent, D. A., & Eisenberg, T. (1972). The selection and promotion of police officers: A selected review of recent literature. *The Police Chief, 39*, 20–29.

Kerlinger, F. N. (1973). *Foundations of behavioral research* (2nd ed.). New York: Holt, Rinehart & Winston.

Kerr, N. L., Nerenz, D., & Herrick, D. (1979). Role playing and the study of jury behavior. *Sociological Methods and Research, 7*, 337–355.

Kilmann, P. R., Sabalis, R. F., Gearing, M. L., Bukstel, L. H., & Scovern, A. W. (1982). The treatment of sexual paraphilias: A review of the outcome research. *Journal of Sex Research, 18*, 193–252.

Kilpatrick, D. G., Best, C. L., Saunders, B. E., & Veronen, L. J. (1988). Rape in marriage and in dating relationships: How bad is it for mental health? In R. A. Prentky & V. L. Quinsey (Eds.), *Human sexual aggression: Current perspectives*. New York: New York Academy of Sciences.

Kinderman, C., & Lynch, J. (1997). *Effects of the redesign on victimization estimates*. Washington, DC: U.S. Department of Justice.

King, W. R., Holmes, S. T., Henderson, M. L., & Latessa, E. J. (2001). The community corrections partnership: Examining the long-term effects of youth participation in an Afrocentric Diversion Program. *Crime & Delinquency, 47*, 558–572.

Kircher, J. C., & Raskin, D.C. (2002). Computer methods for the psychophysiological detection of deception. In M. Kleiner (Ed.), *Handbook of polygraph testing*. San Diego, CA: Academic Press.

Kirkland, K., & Kirkland, K. (2001). Frequency of child custody evaluations complaints and related disciplinary action: A survey of the association of state and provincial psychology boards. *Professional Psychology: Research and Practice, 32*, 171–174.

Kirscht, J. P., & Dillehay, R. C. (1967). *Dimensions of authoritarianism: A review of research and theory*. Lexington: University of Kentucky Press.

Kittrie, N. N. (1971). *The right to be different: Deviance and enforced therapy*. Baltimore, MD: Johns Hopkins University Press.

Kitzmann, R., & Emery, R. (1993). Procedural justice and parent's satisfaction in a field study of child custody dispute resolution. *Law and Human Behavior, 17*, 553–567.

Klatzky, R. L. (1975). *Human memory: Structures and processes*. San Francisco: W. H. Freeman.

Kleiner, M. (2002). Physiological detection of deception in psychological perspectives: A theoretical proposal. In M. Kleiner (Ed.), *Handbook of polygraph testing*. San Diego, CA: Academic Press.

Knapp, M. L. (1978). *Nonverbal communication in human interaction* (2nd ed.). New York: Holt, Rinehart & Winston.

Knapp, M. L., Hart, R. P., & Dennis, H. S. (1974). An exploration of deception as a communication construct. *Human Communication Research, 1*, 15–29.

Knapp, S., & VandeCreek, L. (1997). *Jaffee v. Redmond*: The Supreme Court recognizes a psychotherapist-patient privilege in federal courts. *Professional Psychology: Research and Practice, 28*, 567–572.

Knight, R. A. (1988). A taxonomic analysis of child molesters. In R. A. Prentky & V. L. Quinsey (Eds.), *Human sexual aggression: Current perspectives*. New York: New York Academy of Science.

Knight, R. A., Carter, D. L., & Prentky, R. A. (1989). A system for the classification of child molesters: Reliability and application. *Journal of Interpersonal Violence, 4*, 3–23.

Knight, R. A., & Prentky, R. A. (1987). The development antecedents and adult adaptations of rapist subtypes. *Criminal Justice and Behavior, 14*, 403–426.

Knight, R. A., & Prentky, R. A. (1990). Classifying sexual offenders: The development and corroboration of taxonomic models. In W. L. Marshall, D. R. Laws, & E. E. Barbaree (Eds.), *The handbook of sexual assault: Issues, theories, and treatment of the offender*. New York: Plenum.

Knight, R. A., Rosenberg, R., & Schneider, B. A. (1985). Classification of sexual offenders: Perspectives, methods, and validation. In A. W. Burgess (Ed.), *Rape and sexual assault*. New York: Garland.

Knight, R. A., Warren, J. I., Reboussin, R., & Soley, B. J. (1998). Predicting rapist type from crime-scene variables. *Criminal Justice and Behavior, 25*, 30–45.

Koehn, C. E., & Fisher, R. P. (1997). Constructing facial composites with the Mac-A-Mug Pro system. *Psychology, Crime & Law, 3*, 209–218.

Kohnken, G. (1987). Training police officers to detect deceptive eyewitness statements: Does it work? *Social Behaviour, 2*, 1–17.

Koocher, G. P. (1987). Children under law: The paradigm of consent. In G. B. Melton (Ed.), *Reforming the law: Impact of child development research*. New York: Guilford Press.

Koocher, G. P., Goodman, G. S., White, C. S., Friedrich, W. N., Sivan, A. B., & Reynolds, C. R. (1995). Psychological science and the use of anatomically detailed dolls in child sexual-abuse assessments. *Psychological Bulletin, 118*, 199–222.

Koss, M. P., & Dinero, T. E. (1988). Predictors of sexual aggression among a national sample of male college students. In R. A. Prentky & V. L. Quinsey (Eds.), *Human sexual aggression: Current perspectives*. New York: New York Academy of Sciences.

Koss, M. P., Gidycz, C. A., & Wisniewski, N. (1987). The scope of rape: Incidence and prevalence of sexual aggression and victimization in a national sample of higher education students. *Journal of Consulting and Clinical Psychology, 55*, 162–170.

Kosson, D. S., Cyterski, T. D., Steverwald, B. L., Neuman, C. S., Walker-Matthes, S. (2002). The reliability and validity of the Psychopathy Checklist Youth Version (PCL:YV) in nonincarcerated adolescent males. *Psychological Assessment, 14*, 97–109.

Kosson, D. S., Smith, S. S., & Newman, J. P. (1990). Evaluating the construct validity of psychopathy on Black and White male inmates: Three preliminary studies. *Journal of Abnormal Psychology, 99*, 250–259.

Koszuth, A. M. (1991). Sexually abused child syndrome: *Res Ipsa Loquitur* and shifting the burden of proof. *Law and Psychology Review, 15*, 277–297.

Kovera, M. B., Penrod, S. D., Pappas, C., & Thill, D. L. (1997). Identification of computer-generated facial composites. *Journal of Applied Psychology, 82*, 235–246.

Kramer, G. P., Kerr, N. L., & Carroll, J. S. (1990). Pretrial publicity, judicial remedies, and jury bias. *Law and Human Behavior, 14*, 409–438.

Kramer, G., & Koening, D. (1990). Do jurors understand criminal jury instructions? Analyzing the results of the Michigan juror comprehension project. *University of Michigan Journal of Law Reform, 23*, 401–437.

Kramer, T. H., Buckhout, R., & Eugenio, P. (1990). Weapon focus, arousal, and eyewitness memory: Attention must be paid. *Law and Human Behavior, 14*, 167–184.

Krapohl, D. J. (2002). The polygraph in personnel selection. In M. Kleiner (Ed.), *Handbook of polygraph testing*. San Diego, CA: Academic Press.

Kratcoski, P. C. (1989). *Correctional counseling and treatment* (2nd ed.). Propsect Heights, IL: Waveland Press.

Krauss, D. A., & Sales, B. D. (2000). Legal standards, expertise, and experts in the resolution of contested child custody cases. *Psychology, Public Policy, and Law, 6*, 843–879.

Krauss, D. A., & Sales, B. D. (2001). The effects of clinical and scientific expert testimony on juror decision making in capital sentencing. *Psychology, Public Policy, and Law, 7*, 267–310.

Kraut, R. E., & Poe, D. (1980). On the line: The deception judgments of customs inspectors and laymen. *Journal of Personality and Social Psychology, 39*, 784–798.

Krisberg, B., Currie, E., Onek, D., & Wiebush, R. G. (1995). Graduated sanctions for serious, violent, and chronic juvenile offenders. In J. C. Howell, B. Krisberg, J. D. Hawkins, & J. J. Wilson (Eds.), *A sourcebook: Serious, violent, and chronic juvenile offenders*. Thousand Oaks, CA: Sage.

Kritzer, H., & Voelker, J. (1998). Familiarity breeds respect: How Wisconsin citizens view their courts. *Judicature, 82*, 58–64.

Kroes, W. H. (1976). *Society's victim—the policeman: An analysis of job stress in policing*. Springfield, IL: C. C. Thomas.

Kroes, W. H., Hurrell, Jr., & Margolis, B. (1974). Job stress in police administrators. *Journal of Police Science and Administration, 2*, 381–387.

Kropp, P. R., Hart, S. D., Webster, C. W., & Eaves, D. (1995). *Manual for the spousal assault risk assessment guide* (2nd ed.). Vancouver: British Columbia Institute on Family Violence.

Kruh, I. P., & Brodsky, S. L. (1997). Clinical evaluations for transfer of juveniles to criminal court: Current practices and future research. *Behavioral Sciences and the Law, 15*, 151–165.

Kubis, J. (1973). *Comparison of voice analysis and polygraph as lie detection procedures*. Aberdeen Proving Ground, MD: U.S. Army Land Warfare Laboratory.

Kubis, J. F. (1950). Experimental and statistical factors in the diagnosis of consciously suppressed affective experience. *Journal of Clinical Psychology, 6*, 12–16.

Kugler, S. (2002, October 27). Co-owner of seized vehicle is held in Michigan. *Boston Sunday Globe*, P. A32.

Kuhn, T. S. (1970). *The structure of scientific revolutions* (2nd ed.). Chicago: University of Chicago Press.

Kulka, R. A., & Kessler, J. B. (1978). Is justice really blind?—The influence of litigant physical attractiveness on juridical judgment. *Journal of Applied Social Psychology, 8*, 366–381.

Kulka, R. A., Schlenger, W. E., Fairbank, J. A., Jordan, B. K., Hough, R. L., Marmar, C. R., & Weiss, D. S. (1991). Assessment of post-traumatic stress disorder in the community: Prospects and pitfalls from recent studies of Vietnam veterans. *Psychological Assessment: A Journal of Consulting and Clinical Psychology, 4*, 547–560.

Lab, S. P. (1997). *Crime prevention: Approaches, practices and evaluations* (3rd ed.). Cincinnati, OH: Anderson.

Laboratory of Community Psychiatry. (1974). *Competency to stand trial and mental illness*. DHEW Publication No. ADM 74–103. Rockville, MD: Department of Health, Education, & Welfare.

LaFortune, K. A., & Carpenter, B. N. (1996). *Attorneys' perceptions of the usefulness of extrajudicial procedures and mental health evaluations in domestic court*. Paper presented at the biennial meeting of the American Psychology-Law Society, Hilton Head, South Carolina.

LaFortune, K. A., & Carpenter, B. N. (1998). Custody evaluations: A survey of mental health professionals. *Behavioral Sciences and the Law, 16*, 207–224.

Lamb, M. E. (Ed.). (1996). *The role of the father in child development* (3rd ed.). New York: Wiley.

Landsman, S. (1999). The civil jury in America. *Law and Contemporary Problems, 62*, 285–306.

Landy, D., & Aronson, E. (1969). The influence of the character of the criminal and his victim on the decisions of simulated jurors. *Journal of Experimental Social Psychology, 5*, 141–152.

Landy, F. J. (1976). The validity of the interview in police officer selection. *Journal of Applied Psychology, 61*, 193–198.

Langevin, R. (1983). *Sexual strands*. Hillsdale, NJ: Erlbaum.

Långström, N., & Grann, M. (2000). Risk for criminal recidivism among young sex offenders. *Journal of Interpersonal Violence, 15*, 855–871.

Langworthy, R. H. (1987). Police cynicism: What we know from the Niederhoffer scale. *Journal of Criminal Justice, 15*, 17–35.

Lanyon, R. I. (1986). Theory and treatment in child molestation. *Journal of Consulting and Clinical Psychology, 54*, 176–182.

Laughery, K. R., Alexander, J. E., & Lane, A. B. (1971). Recognition of human faces: Effects of target exposure time, target position, pose position, and type of photograph. *Journal of Applied Psychology, 55*, 477–483.

Laughery, K. R., Durval, G. C., & Fowler, R. H. (1977). *Factors affecting facial recognition* (Rep. No. UHMUG-3). Houston: University of Houston, Mug File Project.

Laughery, K. R., & Fowler, R. H. (1978). *Analysis of procedures for generating facial images*. Paper presented at the annual meeting of the American Psychological Association, Toronto.

Laughery, K. R., Fessler, P. K., Lenorovit, D. R., & Yoblick, D. A. (1974). Time delay and similarity effects in facial recognition. *Journal of Applied Psychology, 59*, 490–496.

Laurence, J. R., & Perry, C. (1983). Hypnotically created memory among highly hypnotizable subjects. *Science, 222*, 523–524.

Laurent, J., Swerdlik, M., & Rayburn, M. (1992). Review of validity research on the Stanford-Binet Intelligence Scale (4th ed.). *Psychological Assessment, 4*, 102–112.

Lavrakas, P. J., Burl, J. R., & Mayzner, M. S. (1976). A perspective on the recognition of other-race faces. *Perception and Psychophysics, 20*, 475–481.

Law Enforcement Assistance Administration. (1977). *Forcible rape: A national survey of the response by prosecutors*. Washington, DC: USGPO.

Lawrence, R. (1998). *School crime and juvenile justice*. New York: Oxford University Press.

Laws, D. R. (1995). Central elements in relapse prevention procedures and sex offenders. *Psychology, Crime, and Law, 2*, 41–53.

Layson, S. (1985). Homicide and deterrence: A reexamination of the United States time series evidence. *Southern Economic Journal, 52*, 68–89.

Lazarus, R. S. (1966). *Psychological stress and the coping process*. New York: McGraw-Hill.

Leary, M. R. (1991). *Introduction to behavioral research methods*. Belmont, CA: Wadsworth.

LeBlanc, M. M., & Kelloway, E. K. (2002). Predictors and outcomes of workplace violence and aggression. *Journal of Applied Psychology, 87*, 444–453.

Leblanc-Allman, R. J. (1998). Guilty but mentally ill: A poor prognosis. *South Carolina Law Review, 49*, 1095–1144.

Lee, B. C., & Werth, J. L. (2000). The first year of the Oregon Death With Dignity Act: Responses to the commentators. *Psychology, Public Policy, and Law, 6*, 342–347.

Lee, C. M., Beauregard, C. P. M., & Hunsley, J. (1998). Lawyers' opinions regarding child custody mediation and assessment services: Implications for psychological practice. *Professional Psychology: Research and Practice, 29*, 115–120.

Leestma, J. E. (1991). Neuropathology and pathophysiology of trauma and toxicity. In H. O. Doerr & A. S. Carlin (Eds.), *Forensic neuropsychology: Legal and scientific bases*. New York: Guilford Press.

Lefkowitz, J. (1975). Psychological attributes of policemen: A review of research and opinion. *Journal of Social Issues, 31*, 3–26.

Leiber, M. J. (2002). Disproportionate minority confinement (DMC) of youth: An analysis of state and federal efforts to address the issue. *Crime & Delinquency, 48*, 3–45.

Leifer, R. (1964). The psychiatrist and tests of criminal responsibility. *American Psychologist, 19*, 825–830.

Leippe, M. R. (1980). Effects of integrative memorial and cognitive processes on the correspondence of eyewitness accuracy and confidence. *Law and Human Behavior, 4*, 261–274.

Leippe, M. R., Brigham, J. C., Cousins, C., & Romanczyk, A. (1989). The opinions and practices of criminal attorneys regarding child witnesses: A survey. In S. J. Ceci, D. F. Ross, & M. P. Toglia (Eds.), *Perspectives on children's testimony*. New York: Springer-Verlag.

Leippe, M. R., Manion, A. P., & Romanczyk, A. (1992). Eyewitness persuasion: How and how well fact finder judge the accuracy of adults' and children's memory reports. *Journal of Personality and Social Psychology, 63*, 181–197.

Leippe, M. R., & Romanczyk, A. (1987). Children on the witness stand: A communication/persuasion analysis of jurors' reactions to child witness. In S. J. Ceci, M. P. Toglia, & D. F. Ross (Eds.), *Children's eyewitness memory*. New York: Springer-Verlag.

Leippe, M. R., & Romanczyk, A. (1989). Reactions to child (versus adult) eyewitnesses: The influence of jurors' preconceptions and witness behavior. *Law and Human Behavior, 13*, 103–132.

Leippe, M. R., Wells, G. L., & Ostrom, T. M. (1978). Crime seriousness as a determinant of accuracy in eyewitness identification. *Journal of Applied Psychology, 63*, 345–351.

Lemon, N. K. D. (1994, December). *Domestic violence & stalking: A comment on the Model Anti-Stalking Code proposed by the National Institute of Justice*. Duluth, MN: Battered Women's Justice Project.

Leo, R. A. (1996). Miranda's revenge: Police interrogation as a confidence game. *Law & Society Review, 30*, 259–288.

Leonard, M. (2002, October 27). Sniper suspect defies profile. *The Boston Sunday Globe*, pp. A1, A32.

Lerner, M. J. (1970). The desire for justice and reactions to victims. In J. Macaulay & L. Berkowitz (Eds.), *Altruism and helping behavior*. New York: Academic Press.

Lerner, M. J. (1977). The justice motive: Some hypotheses as to its origins and forms. *Journal of Personality, 45*, 1–52.

Lerner, M. J. (1980). *The belief in a just world: A fundamental delusion*. New York: Plenum.

Lerner, M. J., & Simmons, C. H. (1966). Observer's reaction to the "innocent victim": Compassion or rejection? *Journal of Personality and Social Psychology, 4*, 203–210.

Lester, D., Braswell, M., & Van Voorhis, P. (1992). *Correctional counseling* (2nd ed.). Cincinnati, OH: Anderson.

Leverant, S., Cullen, F. T., Fulton, B., & Wozniak, J. F. (1999). Reconsidering restorative justice: The corruption of benevolence revisited? *Crime & Delinquency, 45*, 3–27.

Levi, J. (1990). The study of language in the judicial process. In J. Levi & A. G. Walker (Eds.), *Language in the judicial process*. New York: Plenum.

Levine, J. P. (2002). Jury: Right to jury trial. In K. L. Hall (Ed.), *The Oxford companion to American law*. New York: Oxford University Press.

Li, J. C., Dunning, D., & Malpass, R. S. (1998, March). *Cross-racial identification among European-American: Basketball fandom and the contact hypothesis*. Paper presented at the biennial meeting of the American-Law Society, Redondo Beach, CA.

Lickey, M. E., & Gordon, B. (1991). *Medicine and mental illness*. New York: W. H. Freeman.

Lidz, C. W., Hoge, S., Gardner, W., Bennett, N., Monahan, J., Mulvey, J., Mulvey, E., & Roth, L. (1995). Perceived coercion in mental hospital admission: Pressures and process. *Archives of General Psychiatry, 52*, 1034–1039.

Lidz, C. W., Mulvey, E. P., Appelbaum, P. S., & Cleveland, S. (1989). Commitment: The consistency of clinicians and the use of legal standards. *American Journal of Psychiatry, 146*, 176–181.

Lidz, C. W., Mulvey, E. P., & Gardner, W. (1993). The accuracy of predictions of violence to others. *Journal of the American Medical Association, 269*, 1007–1011.

Lieberman, J. D., & Arndt, J. (2000). Understanding the limits of limiting instructions: Social psychological explanations for the failures of instructions to disregard pretrial publicity and other inadmissible evidence. *Psychology, Public Policy, and Law, 6*, 677–711.

Lieberman, J. D., & Sales, B. D. (1997). What social science teaches us about the jury instruction process. *Psychology, Public Policy, and Law, 3*, 589–644.

Lieberman, J. D., & Sales, B. D. (2000). Jury instructions: Past, present, and future. *Psychology, Public Policy, and Law, 6*, 587–590.

Liggett, J. (1974). *The human face*. London: Constable.

Lilienfeld, S. O., & Loftus, E. (1998). Repressed memories and World War II: Some cautionary notes. *Professional Psychology: Research and Practice, 29*, 471–478.

Lilienfeld, S. O., Wood, J. M., & Garb, H. N. (2001). The scientific status of projective techniques. *Psychological Science in the Public Interest, 20*, 27–66.

Lindsay, M. S. (2001). Identifying the dynamics of suicide by cop. In D. C. Sheehan & J. T. Warren (Eds.), *Suicide and law enforcement*. Washington, DC: U.S. Department of Justice, FBI Behavioral Science Unit.

Lindsay, R. C. L., Wells, C. L., & Rumpel, C. M. (1981). Can people detect eyewitness identification within and across situations? *Journal of Applied Psychology, 66*, 79–89.

Lipsey, M. W. (1992). Juvenile delinquency treatment: A meta-analytic inquiry into the variability of effects. In T. D. Cook, H. Cooper, D. S. Cordray, H. Hartman, L. V. Hedges, R. J. Light, T. A. Louis, & F. Mosteller (Eds.), *Meta-analysis for explanation: A casebook*. New York: Russell Sage.

Lipsey, M. W., & Wilson, D. B. (1998). Effective intervention for serious juvenile offenders: A synthesis of research. In R. Loeber & D. P. Farrington (Eds.), *Serious and violent juvenile offenders: Risk factors and successful interventions*. Thousand Oaks, CA: Sage.

Lipsitt, P., Lelos, D., & McGarry, A. L. (1971). Competency to Stand Trial: A screening instrument. *American Journal of Psychiatry, 128*, 105–109.

Lipton, D. N., McDonel, E. C., & McFall, R. M. (1987). Heterosocial perception in rapist. *Journal of Consulting and Clinical Psychology, 55*, 17–21.

Littlepage, G., & Pineault, T. (1978). Verbal, facial, and paralinguistic cues to the detection of truth and lying. *Personality and Social Psychology Bulletin, 4*, 461–464.

Litwack, T. R. (2001). Actuarial versus clinical assessments of dangerousness. *Psychology, Public Policy, and Law, 7*, 409–443.

Litwack, T. R., & Schlesinger, L. B. (1987). Assessing and predicting violence: Research, law, and application. In I. B. Weiner & A. K. Hess (Eds.), *Handbook of forensic psychology*, New York: Wiley.

Litwack, T. R., & Schlesinger, L. B. (1999). Dangerousness risk assessments: Research, legal, and clinical considerations. In A. K. Hess & I. B. Weiner (Eds.), *Handbook of forensic psychology* (2nd ed.). New York: Wiley

Lloyd-Bostock, S. (1989). *Law in practice: Application of psychology to legal decision making and legal skills*. Chicago: Lyceum.

Loeber, R. (1990). Development and risk factors of juvenile antisocial behavior and delinquency. *Clinical Psychology Review, 10*, 1–41.

Loeber, R., & Dishion, T. (1983). Early predictors of male delinquency: A review. *Psychological Bulletin, 94*, 68–99.

Loftus, E. F. (1975). Leading questions and the eyewitness report. *Cognitive Psychology, 7*, 560–572.

Loftus, E. F (1977). Shifting human color memory. *Memory and Cognition, 5*, 696–699.

Loftus, E. F. (1979). *Eyewitness testimony*. Cambridge, MA: Harvard University Press.

Loftus, E. F. (1986). Ten years in the life of an expert witness. *Law and Human Behavior, 10*, 241–263.

Loftus, E. F. (1991). Made in memory: Distortions in recollections from misleading information. In G. H. Bower (Ed.), *The psychology of learning and motivation: Advances in research and theory* (Vol. 27). London: Academic Press.

Loftus, E. F., & Ketcham, K. (1991). *Witness for the defense: The accused, the eyewitness, and the expert who puts memory on trial.* New York: St. Martin's Press.

Loftus, E. F., & Ketcham, K. (1996). *The myth of repressed memory: False memories and allegations of sexual abuse*. New York: St. Martin's Griffin.

Loftus, E. F., Loftus, G. R., & Messo, J. (1987). Some facts about "weapon focus." *Law and Human Behavior, 11*, 55–62.

Loftus, E. F., Miller, D. G., & Burns, H. J. (1978). Semantic integration of verbal information into a visual memory. *Journal of Experimental Psychology: Human Learning and Memory, 4*, 19–31.

Loftus, G. R. (1972). Eye fixations and recognition memory. *Cognitive Psychology, 3*, 525–557.

Loftus, G. R., & Loftus, E. F. (1976). Human memory: The processing of information. Hillsdale, NJ: Erlbaum.

Loh, W. D. (1979). Psychology and law: A coming of age. *Contemporary Psychology, 24*, 164–166.

Loh, W. D. (1980). The impact of common law and reform rape statutes on prosecution: An empirical study. *Washington Law Review, 55*, 543–652.

Lord, V. B. (2000). Law enforcement-assisted suicide. *Criminal Justice and Behavior, 27*, 401–419.

Lott, A. J., & Lott, B. E. (1974). The role of reward in the formation of positive interpersonal attitudes. In T. Huston (Ed.), *Foundations of interpersonal attraction*. New York: Academic Press.

Lotz, R., & Regoli, R. M. (1977). Police cynicism and professionalism. *Human Relations, 30*, 176–186.

Lowery, C. R. (1984). The wisdom of Solomon: Criteria for child custody from the legal and clinical points of view. *Law and Human Behavior, 8*, 371–380.

Lowney, K. S., & Best, J. (1995). Talking changes and lovers: Changing media typification of a new crime problem. In J. Best (Ed.), *Images of issues: Typifying contemporary problems.* New York: Aldine de Gruyter.

Luginbuhl, J. (1992). Comprehension of judges' instructions in the penalty phase of a capital trial. *Law and Human Behavior, 16*, 203–218.

Luginbuhl, J., & Middendorf, K. (1988). Death penalty beliefs and jurors' responses to aggravating and mitigating circumstances in capital trials. *Law and Human Behavior, 12*, 263–281.

Lurigio, A. J. (2000). Drug treatment availability and effectiveness: Studies of the general and criminal justice populations. *Criminal Justice and Behavior, 27*, 495–528.

Lurigio, A. J., & Carroll, J. S. (1985). Probation officers' schemata of offenders: Content, development, and impact on treatment decisions. *Journal of Personality and Social Psychology, 48*, 1112–1126.

Luus, C. A. E., & Wells, G. (1991). Eyewitness identification and the selection of distracters for lineups. *Law and Human Behavior, 15*, 43–57.

Luus, C. A. E., Wells, G. L., & Turtle, J. W. (1995). Child eyewitness: Seeing is believing. *Journal of Applied Psychology, 80*, 317–326.

Lykken, D. T. (1974). Psychology and the lie detector industry. *American Psychologist, 29*, 725–739.

Lykken, D. T. (1988). The case against polygraph testing. In A. Gale (Ed.), *The polygraph test: Lies, truth and science*. London: Sage.

Lykken, D. T. (1998). *A tremor in the blood: Uses and abuses of the lie detector* (2nd ed.). New York: Plenum.

Lynam, D. R. (1996). Early identification of chronic offenders: Who is the fledging psychopath? *Psychological Bulletin, 120*, 209–234.

Lynam, D. R. (1997). Pursuing the psychopath: Capturing the fledging psychopath in a nomological net. *Journal of Abnormal Psychology, 10*, 425–438.

Lynch, M., & Haney, C. (2000). Discrimination and instructional comprehension: Guided discretion, racial bias, and the death penalty. *Law and Human Behavior, 24*, 337–358.

Lynn, S. J., Lock, T. G., Myers, B., & Payne, D. (1997). Recalling the unrecallable: Should hypnosis be used to recover memories in psychotherapy? *Current Directions in Psychological Science, 6*, 79–83.

Maass, A., & Kohnken, G. (1989). Eyewitness identification: Simulating the "weapon effect." *Law and Human Behavior, 13*, 397–408.

Maccoby, E., Buchanan, C., Mnookin, R., & Dornsbusch, S. (1993). Postdivorce roles of mother and father in the lives of their children. *Journal of Family Psychology, 1*, 24–38.

MacCoun, R. J., & Kerr, N. L. (1988). Asymmetric influences in mock jury deliberation: Jurors' bias for leniency. *Journal of Personality and Social Psychology, 54*, 21–33.

MacDonald, J. M. (1976). *Psychiatry and the criminal* (3rd ed.). Springfield, IL: C. C. Thomas.

MacDonald, J. M., & Chesney-Lind, M. (2001). Gender bias and juvenile justice revisited: A multiyear analysis. *Crime & Delinquency, 47*, 173–195.

Macdonald, J. W., & Michaud, D. L. (1987). *The confession: Interrogation and criminal profiles for police officers.* Denver, CO: Apache.

MacKay, Lord of Clashfern. (1990). Introduction. In J. R. Spencer, G. Nicholson, R. Flin, & R. Bull (Eds.), *Children's evidence in legal proceedings: An international perspective.* University of Cambridge, UK: Faculty of Law.

MacKenzie, D. L. (2000). Evidence-based corrections: Identifying what works. *Crime & Delinquency, 46*, 457–471.

MacKenzie, D. L., & Goodstein, L. (1985). Long-term incarceration impacts and characteristics of long-term offenders: An empirical analysis. *Criminal Justice and Behavior, 12*, 395–414.

MacKenzie, D. L., Gover, A. R., Armstrong, G. S., & Mitchell, O. (2000). *A national study comparing the environments of boot camps with traditional facilities for juvenile offenders.* Washington: U.S. Department of Justice, Office of Justice Programs, National Institute of Justice.

MacKenzie, D. L., Robinson, J. W., & Campbell, C. S. (1989). Long-term incarceration of female offenders: Prison adjustment and coping. *Criminal Justice and Behavior, 16*, 223–238.

MacLaren, V. V. (2001). A quantitative review of the guilty knowledge test. *Journal of Applied Psychology, 86*, 674–683.

MacLaughlin, G. H. (1953). The lie detector as an aid in arson and criminal investigation. *Journal of Criminal Law and Criminology, 43*, 693–694.

MacLin, O. H., MacLin, M. K., & Malpass, R. S. (2001). Race, arousal, attention, exposure, and delay: An examination of factors moderating face recognition. *Psychology, Public Policy, and Law, 7*, 134–152.

MacLin, O. H., & Malpass, R. S. (2001). Racial categorization of faces: The ambiguous race face effect. *Psychology, Public Policy, and Law, 7*, 98–118.

MacNitt, R. D. (1942). In defense of the electrodermal response and cardiac amplitude as measures of deception. *Journal of Criminal Law and Criminology, 33*, 266–275.

Mahoney, M. R. (1991). Legal images of battered women: Redefining the use of separation. *Michigan Law Review, 90*, 1–94.

Malamuth, N. M. (1981). Rape proclivity among males. *Journal of Social Issues, 37*, 138–157.

Malloy, T. E., & Mays, G. L. (1984). The police stress hypothesis: A critical evaluation. *Criminal Justice and Behavior, 11*, 197–223.

Maloney, M. P, & Ward, M. P. (1976). *Psychological assessment: A conceptual approach.* New York: Oxford University Press.

Malpass, R. S., & Kravitz, J. (1969). Recognition for faces of own- and other-race faces. *Journal of Personality and Social Psychology, 13*, 330–334.

Malpass, R. S., Lavigueur, H., & Weldon, D. E. (1973). Verbal and visual training in face recognition. *Perception and Psychophysics, 14*, 285–292.

Margolis, B. L. (1973). Stress is a work hazard too. *Industrial Medicine, Occupational Health and Surgery, 42*, 20–23.

Marin, B. V., Holmes, D. L., Guth, M., & Kovac, P. (1979). The potential of children as eyewitnesses: A comparison of children and adults on eyewitness tasks. *Law and Human Behavior, 3*, 295–306.

Mark, V. H., & Ervin, F. R. (1970). *Violence and the brain.* Hagerstown, MD: Harper & Row.

Marquart, J. W., & Sorensen, J. R. (1988). Institutional and post release behavior of Furman-commuted inmates in Texas. *Criminology, 26*, 677–693.

Marquart, J. W., & Sorensen, J. R. (1989). A national study of the Furman-commuted inmates: Assessing the threat to society from capital offenders. *Loyola of Louisiana Law Review, 23*, 5–28.

Marsh, J. C. (1988). What we have learned about legislative remedies for rape? In R. A. Prentky & V. L. Quinsey (Eds.), *Human sexual aggression: Current perspectives.* New York: New York Academy of Sciences.

Marsh, S. H. (1962). Validating the selection of deputy sheriffs. *Public Personnel Review, 23*, 41–44.

Marshall, J. (1966). *Law and psychology in conflict.* New York: Bobbs-Merrill.

Marshall, J. (1968). *Intention in law and society.* New York: Minerva Press.

Marshall, J. (1972). Trial, testimony and truth. In S. S. Nagel (Ed.), *The rights of the accused* (Vol. 1). Beverly Hills, CA: Sage.

Marshall, L. A., & Cooke, D. J. (1999). The childhood experiences of psychopaths: A retrospective study of familial and societal factors. *Journal of Personality Disorders, 13*, 211–225.

Marshall, W. L. (1999). Diagnosing and treating sexual offenders. In A. K. Hess & I. Weiner (Eds.), *Handbook of forensic psychology* (2nd ed.), New York: Wiley.

Marshall, W. L., & Barbaree, H. E. (1988). An outpatient treatment program for child molesters. In R. A. Prentky and V. L. Quinsey (Eds.), *Human sexual aggression: Current perspectives*. New York: New York Academy of Sciences.

Marshall, W. L., Barbaree, H. E., & Fernandez, M. (1995). Some aspects of social competence in sexual offenders. *Sexual Abuse: A Journal of Research and Treatment, 7*, 113–127.

Marshall, W. L., & Mazzucco, A. (1995). Self-esteem and parental attachments in child molesters. *Journal of Research and Treatment, 7*, 279–285.

Martell, D. A. (1991). Homeless mentally disorder offenders and violent crime. *Law and Human Behavior, 15*, 333–347.

Martell, D. A. (1992). Forensic neuropsychology and the criminal law. *Law and Human Behavior, 16*, 313–336.

Martin, S. E. (1980). *Breaking and entering: Policewomen on patrol*. Berkeley, CA: University of California Press.

Martin, S. E. (1989). Women on the move? A report on the status of women in policing. *Women and Criminal Justice, 1*, 21–40.

Martin, S. E. (1992). The effectiveness of affirmative action: The case of women in policing. *Justice Quarterly, 8*, 489–504.

Martinson, R. M. (1974). What works—questions and answers about prison reform. *Public Interest, 35*, 22–54.

Martinson, R. M. (1979). New findings, new views: A note of caution regarding sentencing reform. *Hofstra Law Review, 7*, 242–258.

Martinson, R. M., & Wilks, J. (1977). Save parole supervision. *Federal Probation, 41*, 23–27.

Maslach, C., & Jackson, S. E. (1981). The measurement of experienced burnout. *Journal of Occupational Behaviour, 2*, 99–113.

Mason, M. A., & Quirk, A. (1997). Are mothers losing custody? Read my lips: Trends in judicial decision-making in custody disputes—1920, 1960, 1990, and 1995. *Family Law Quarterly, 31*, 215–236.

Matarazzo, J. D. (1990). Psychological assessment versus psychological testing. *American Psychologist, 45*, 999–1017.

Matarazzo, J. D., Allen, B. V, Saslow, G., &Wiens, A. (1964). Characteristics of successful policemen and firemen applicants. *Journal of Applied Psychology, 48*, 123–133.

McAllister, S. R. (1998). Sex offenders and mental illness: A lesson in federalism and the separation of powers. *Psychology, Public Policy, and Law, 4*, 268–296.

McBride, K. (1996). *Policing in Central and Eastern Europe: Comparing firsthand knowledge with experience in the west*. Slovenia: College of Police and Security Studies.

McCann, J. T. (1992). Criminal personality profiling in the investigation of violent crime: Recent advances and future directions. *Behavioral Sciences and the Law, 10*, 475–481.

McCann, J. T. (1998a). Broadening the typology of false confessions. *American Psychologist, 53*, 319–320.

McCann, J. T. (1998b). A conceptual framework for identifying various types of confessions. *Behavioral Sciences and the Law, 16*, 441–453.

McCann, T., & Sheehan, P. W. (1988). Hypnotically induced pseudomemories—Sampling their conditions among hypnotizable subjects. *Journal of Personality and Social Psychology, 54*, 339–346.

McClintock, C. G., & Hunt, R. C. (1975). Nonverbal indicators of affect and deception in an interview setting. *Journal of Applied Social Psychology, 5*, 54–67.

McCloskey, M., Egeth, H., & McKenna, J. (1986). The experimental psychologist in court: The ethics of expert testimony. *Law and Human Behavior, 10*, 1–13.

McConkey, K. M., & Sheehan, P. W. (1995). *Hypnosis, memory, and behavior in criminal investigation*. New York: Guilford Press.

McCorkle, R. C. (1992). Personal precautions to violence in prison. *Criminal Justice and Behavior, 19*, 160–173.

McDonough, L. B., & Monahan, J. (1975). The quality control of community caretakers: A study of mental health screening in a sheriff's department. *Community Mental Health Journal, 11*, 33–44.

McGarry, A. L. (1971). The fate of psychiatric offenders returned for trial. *American Journal of Psychiatry, 127*, 1181–1184.

McGinley, H., & Pasewark, R. A. (1989). National survey of the frequency and success of the insanity plea and alternate pleas. *Journal of Psychiatry and Law, 17*, 205–221.

McIntosh, J. L. (1991). Epidemiology of suicide in the U.S. In A. A. Leenaars (Ed.), *Life span perspectives of suicide*. New York: Plenum.

McKee, G. R., & Shea, S. J. (1999). Competency to stand trial in family court: Characteristics of competent and incompetent juveniles. *Journal of the American Academy of Psychiatry and Law, 27*, 65–73.

McKinney, T. S. (1973). *The criterion-related validity of entry level police officer selection procedures*. Phoenix, AZ: City of Phoenix Personnel Department.

McNamara, R. P. (1999). The socialization of the police. In D. J. Kenney & R. R. McNamara (Eds.), *Police and policing: Contemporary issues*. Westport, CT: Praeger.

McPherson, S. B. (1996). *Psychological aspects of mitigation in capital cases*. Unpublished manuscript, cited in Cunningham and Reidy, 1998.

McShane, M., & Williams, F. P. (1989). The prison adjustment of juvenile offenders. *Crime & Delinquency, 35*, 254–269.

Mears, D. P., & Kelly, W. R. (2002). Linking process and outcomes in evaluating a statewide drug treatment program for youthful offenders. *Crime & Delinquency, 48*, 99–113.

Meehl, P. E. (1954). *Clinical versus statistical prediction*. Minneapolis, MN: University of Minnesota Press.

Meehl, P. E. (1957). Some ruminations on the validation of clinical procedures. *Canadian Journal of Psychology, 13*, 102–128.

Meehl, P. E. (1965). Seer over sign: The first good example. *Journal of Experimental Research in Personality, 1*, 27–32.

Meehl, P. E. (1971). Law and the fireside inductions: Some reflections of a clinical psychologist. *Journal of Social Issues, 27*, 65–100.

Meesig, R., & Horvath, F. (1995). *Polygraph, 24*, 57–136.

Megargee, E. I. (1976). Population density and disruptive behavior in a prison setting. In A. K. Cohen, F. G. Cole, & R. G. Bailey (Eds.), *Prison violence*. Lexington, MA: Lexington Books.

Megargee, E. I. (1982). Psychological determinants and correlates of criminal violence. In M. E. Wolfgang & N. A. Wiender (Eds.), *Criminal violence*. Beverly Hills, CA: Sage.

Megargee, E. I. (1995). Assessment research in correctional settings: Methodological issues and practical problems. *Psychological Assessment, 7*, 359–366.

Mehrabian, A. (1971). Nonverbal betrayal of feeling. *Journal of Experimental Research in Personality, 5*, 64–73.

Mehrabian, A., & Williams, M. (1969). Nonverbal concomitants of perceived and intended persuasiveness. *Journal of Personality and Social Psychology, 13*, 37–58.

Meissner, C. A., & Brigham, J. C. (2001). Thirty years of investigating the own-race bias in memory for faces: A meta-analytic review. *Psychology, Public Policy, and Law, 7*, 3–35.

Meloy, J. R. (1998). The psychology of stalking. In J. R. Meloy (Ed.), *The psychology of stalking: Clinical and forensic perspectives.* San Diego, CA: Academic Press.

Meloy, M. (2000). Police organizations. In N. H. Rafter (Ed.), *Encyclopedia of women and crime*. Phoenix, AZ: Oryx Press.

Melton, G. B. (1983). Toward "personhood" for adolescents: Autonomy and privacy as values in public policy. *American Psychologist, 38*, 99–103.

Melton, G. B. (1987). Bringing psychology to the legal system: Opportunities, obstacles, and efficacy. *American Psychologist, 42*, 488–495.

Melton, G. B. (1992). The law is a good thing (psychology is, too): Human rights in psychological jurisprudence. *Law and Human Behavior, 16*, 381–398.

Melton, G. B., Petrila, J., Poythress, N. G., & Slobogin, C. (1987). *Psychological evaluations for the courts*. New York: Guilford Press.

Melton, G. B., Petrila, J., Poythress, N. G., & Slobogin, C. (1997). *Psychological evaluations for the courts: A handbook for mental health professionals and lawyers* (2nd ed.). New York: Guilford Press.

Melton, G. B., Weithorn, L., & Slobogin, C. (1985). *Community mental health center and the courts: An evaluation of community based forensic services*. Lincoln, NE: University of Nebraska Press.

Melton, G. B., & Wilcox, B. L. (2001). Children's law: Toward a new realism. *Law and Human Behavior, 25*, 3–12.

Memon, A., Dionne, R., Short, L., Maralani, S., MacKinnon, D., & Geiselman, R. E. (1988). Psychological factors in the use of photospreads. *Journal of Police Science and Administration, 16*, 62–69.

Memon, A., & Vartoukian, R. (1996). The effects of repeated questioning on young children's eyewitness testimony. *British Journal of Psychology, 87*, 393–403.

Menzies, R. J. (1989). *Survival of the sanest: Order and disorder in a pre-trial psychiatric clinic*. Toronto: University of Toronto Press.

Menzies, R. J., Webster, C. D., Roesch, R., Jensen, F., & Eaves, D. (1984). The Fitness Interview Test: A semi-structured instrument for assessing competency to stand trial. *Medicine and Law, 3*, 151–162.

Menzies, R., Webster, C. D., McMain, S., Staley, S., & Scaglione, R. (1994). The dimensions of dangerousness revisited: Asessing forensic predictions about violence. *Law and Human Behavior, 18*, 1–28.

Merckelbach, H., Muris, P., Wessel, I., & Van Koppen, P. J. (1998). The Gudjonsson Suggestibility Scale (GSS): Further data on its reliability, validity, and metacognition correlates. *Social Behavior and Personality, 26*, 203–210.

Merton, R. K. (1957). *Social theory and social structure* (Revised ed.). New York: The Free Press.

Meuer, T., Seymour, A., & Wallace, H. (2001). Domestic violence. In A. Seymour (Ed.), *2001 National Victim Assistance Academy textbook*. Washington, DC: U.S. Department of Justice.

Middendorf, K., & Luiginbuhl, J. (1981). *Personality and the death penalty*. Paper presented at the Annual Meeting of the Southeastern Psychological Association, Atlanta, GA.

Miethe, T. D., Lu, H., & Reese, E. (2000). Reintegrative shaming and recidivism risks in drug court: Explanations for some unexpected findings. *Crime & Delinquency, 46*, 522–541.

Milan, M. A., Chin, C. E., & Nguyen, Q. X. (1999). Practicing psychology in correctional settings: Assessment, treatment, and substance abuse programs. In Hess, A. K., & Weiner, I. B.. (Eds.), *Handbook of forensic psychology* (2nd ed.). New York: Wiley.

Miller, G. R., Bauchner, J. E., Hocking, J. E., Fontes, N. E., Kaminski, E. P., & Brandt, D. R. (1981). ". . . and nothing but the truth." How well can observers detect deceptive testimony? In B. D. Sales (Ed.), *Perspectives in law and psychology* (Vol. 2). *The trial process*. New York: Plenum.

Mills, R. B., McDevitt, R. J., & Tonkin, S. (1966). Situational tests in metropolitan police recruit selection. *Journal of Criminal Law, Criminology, and Police Science, 57*, 99–104.

Millon, T. (1994). *MCMI-III: Manual*. Minneapolis, MN: National Computer Systems.

Mills, C. J., & Bohannon, W. E. (1980). Personality characteristics of effective state police officers. *Journal of Applied Psychology, 65*, 680–684.

Miner, J. B. (1992). *Industrial-organizational psychology*. New York: McGraw-Hill.

Miner, M. H., Day, D. M., & Nafpaktitis, M. K. (1989). Assessment of coping skills: Development of situational competency test. In D. R. Laws (Ed.), *Relapse prevention with sex offenders*. New York: Guilford.

Miron, M. S. (1980). Issues of psychological evidence: Discussion. In F. Wright, C. Bahn, & R. W. Rieber (Eds.), *Forensic psychology and psychiatry*. Annals of the New York Academy of Sciences (Vol. 347). New York: New York Academy of Sciences.

Mischel, W. (1968). *Personality and assessment.* New York: Wiley.

Mischel, W. (1973). Toward a cognitive social learning reconceptualization of personality. *Psychological Review, 80,* 252–283.

Mischel, W. (1976). *Introduction to personality* (2nd ed.). New York: Holt, Rinehart & Winston.

Mischel, W. (1979). On the interface of cognition and personality: Beyond the person-situation debate. *American Psychologist, 34,* 740–754.

Mischel, W. (1981). *Introduction to personality* (3rd ed.). New York: Holt, Rinehard & Winston.

Mischel, W., & Mischel, H. N. (1977). *Essentials of psychology.* New York: Random House.

Mitchell, D. C. (2002). The pre-test interview: A preliminary framework. In M. Kleiner (Ed.), *Handbook of polygraph testing.* San Diego, CA: Academic Press.

Mitchell, H. E., & Byrne, D. (1973). The defendant's dilemma: Effects of jurors' attitudes and authoritarianism on judicial decisions. *Journal of Personality and Social Psychology, 25,* 123–129.

Mobley, M. J. (1999). Psychotherapy with criminal offenders. In A. K. Hess & I. B. Weiner (Eds.), *Handbook of forensic psychology* (2nd ed.). New York: Wiley.

Moffitt, T. E. (1990). Juvenile delinquency and attention deficit disorder: Boys' developmental trajectories from age 13 to age 15. *Child Development, 61,* 893–910.

Moffitt, T. E. (1993a). Adolescence-limited and life-course-persistent antisocial behavior: A developmental taxonomy. *Psychological Review, 100,* 674–701.

Moffitt, T. E. (1993b). The neuropsychology of conduct disorder. *Development and Psychopathology, 5,* 135–151.

Moffitt, T. E., Caspi, A., Dickson, N., Silva, P., & Stranton, W. (1996). Childhood-onset versus adolescent-onset antisocial conduct problems in males: Natural history from ages 3 to 18. *Development and Psychopathology, 8,* 399–424.

Moffitt, T. E., & Silva, P. A. (1988). Self-reported delinquency, neuropsychological deficit, and history of attention deficit disorder. *Journal of Abnormal Child Psychology, 16,* 553–569.

Mokhiber, R. (1988). *Corporate crime and violence.* San Francisco: Sierra Club Books.

Monahan, J. (1996). Violence prediction: The past twenty years and the next twenty years. *Criminal Justice and Behavior, 23,* 107–120.

Monahan, J., Ruggiero, M., & Friedlander, H. (1982). The Stone-Roth model of civil commitment and the California dangerousness standard: An operational comparison. *Archives of General Psychiatry, 39,* 1267–1271.

Monahan, J., & Shah, S. A. (1989). Dangerousness and commitment of the mentally disordered in the United States. *Schizophrenia Bulletin, 15,* 541–553.

Monahan, J., Steadman, H. J., Silver, E., Appelbaum, P. S., Robbins, P. C., Mulvey, E. P., Roth, L. H., Grisso, T., & Banks, S. (2001). *Rethinking risk assessment: The MacArthur Study of Mental Disorder and Violence.* New York: Oxford University Press.

Monahan, J., & Walker, L. (1988). Social science research in law: A new paradigm. *American Psychologist, 43,* 465–472.

Monahan, J., & Walker, L. (1990). *Social science and law: Cases and materials* (2nd ed.). Westbury, NY: The Foundation Press.

Monahan, J., & Wexler, D. B. (1978). A definite maybe: Proof and probability in civil commitment. *Law and Human Behavior, 2,* 37–42.

Monahan, T. F. (2001). Suicide by cop: Strategies for crisis negotiators and first responders. In D. C. Sheehan & J. T. Warren (Eds.), *Suicide and law enforcement.* Washington, DC: U.S. Department of Justice, FBI Behavioral Science Unit.

Monson, T. C., & Snyder, M. (1977). Actors, observers, and the attribution process: Toward a reconceptualization. *Journal of Experimental Social Psychology, 13,* 89–111.

Montada, L. & Lerner, M. J. (Eds.). (1998). *Responses to victimization and belief in a just world.* New York: Plenum.

Moran, G., & Comfort, J. (1986). Neither 'tentative' nor 'fragmentary': Verdict preference of impaneled felony jurors as function of attitudes toward capital punishment. *Journal of Applied Psychology, 71,* 146–155.

Moran, G., & Cutler, B. L. (1991). The prejudicial impact of pretrial publicity. *Journal of Applied Social Psychology, 21,* 345–367.

Morawertz, T. H. (2002). Homicide. In K. L. Hall (Ed.), *The Oxford companion to American law.* New York: Oxford University Press.

More, H. W. (1992). *Special topics in policing.* Cincinnati, OH: Anderson Publishing.

Morey, L. C. (1991). *The Personality Assessment Inventory: Professional manual.* Odessa, FL: Psychological Assessment Resources.

Morgan, R.D., Winterowd, C. L., & Ferrell, S. W. (1999). A national survey of group psychotherapy services in correctional facilities. *Professional Psychology: Research and Practice, 30,* 600–606.

Morris, A. (1996). Gender and ethnic differences in social constraints among a sample of New York City police officers. *Journal of Occupational Health Psychology, 1,* 224–235.

Morris, M. (1993). The complex nature of prevention in the African-American community: The problem of conceptualization. In L. L. Goddard (Ed.), *An African-centered model of prevention for African-American youth at high risk.* Rockville, MD: U.S. Department of Health and Human Services.

Morris, N. (1974). *The future of imprisonment.* Chicago: University of Chicago Press.

Morris, N., & Miller, M. (1985). Prediction of dangerousness. In M. Tonry & N. Morris (Eds.), *Crime and justice: An annual review of research.* Chicago: University of Chicago Press.

Morris, S. M., Steadman, H. J., & Veysey, B. M. (1997). Mental health services in United States jails: A survey of innovative practices. *Criminal Justice and Behavior, 24,* 3–19.

Morse, S. J. (1998). Fear of danger, flight from culpability. *Psychology, Public Policy, and Law, 4,* 250–267.

Mossman, D. (1987). Assessing and restoring competency to be executed: Should psychologists participate? *Behavioral Sciences and the Law, 5,* 397–409.

Mulder, R. T., Wells, J. E., Joyce, P. R., & Bushnell, J. A. (1994). Antisocial women. *Journal of Personality Disorders, 8*, 279–287.

Mullineaux, J. E. (1955). An evaluation of the predictors used to select patrolmen. *Public Personnel Review, 16*, 84–86.

Mulvey, E. P., Arthur, M. W., & Reppucci, N. D. (1993). The prevention and treatment of juvenile delinquency: A review of the research. *Clinical Psychology Review, 13*, 133–167.

Mumola, C. J. (1999). *Substance abuse and treatment, state and federal prisoners*. Washington, DC: Bureau of Justice Statistics.

Murphy, G. H., & Clare, C. H. (1996). Analysis of motivation in people with mild learning disabilities (mental handicap) who set fires. *Psychology, Crime, and Law, 2*, 153–164.

Murphy, J. J. (1972). Current practices in the use of psychological testing by police agencies. *The Journal of Criminal Law, Criminology and Police Science, 63*, 570–576.

Murray, K. (1995). *Live television link: An evaluation of its use by child witnesses in Scottish criminal trials*. Edinburgh, Scotland: Central Research Unit, The Scottish Office.

Myers, B., & Arena, M. P. (2001). Trial consultation: A new direction in applied psychology. *Professional Psychology: Research and Practice, 32*, 386–391.

Myers, D. G., & Kaplan, M. F. (1976). Group-induced polarization in simulated juries. *Personality and Social Psychology Bulletin, 2*, 63–66.

Myers, D. G., & Lamm, H. (1976). The group polarization phenomenon. *Psychological Bulletin, 83*, 602–627.

Myers, J. E. B. (1985–86). The legal response to child abuse: In the best interests of children? *Journal of Family Law, 24*, 149–244.

Nacci, P. L., Teitelbaum, H. E., & Prather, J. (1977). Population density and inmate misconduct rates in the federal prison system. *Federal Probation, 41*, 26–31.

Nagin, D. S., Farrington, D. P., & Moffitt, T. (1995). Life-course trajectories of different types of offenders. *Criminology, 33*, 111–139.

Nagin, D. S., & Land, K. C. (1993). Age, criminal careers, and population heterogeneity: Specification and estimation of a nonparametric mixed Poisson model. *Criminology, 31*, 163–189.

Narby, D. J., Cutler, B. L., & Moran, G. (1993). A meta-analysis of the association between authoritarianism on jurors' perceptions of defendant culpability. *Journal of Applied Psychology, 78*, 34–42.

Narrol, H. G., & Levitt, E. E. (1963). Formal assessment procedures in police selection. *Psychological Reports, 12*, 691–694.

National Center for State Courts (NCSC). (1978). *State courts: A blueprint for the future*. (Publication Number SC001). Williamsburg, VA: Author.

National Center for Women & Policing. (2000). *Equality denied: The status of women in policing*. Los Angeles, CA: Author.

National Child Abuse and Neglect Data System. (2002). *Summary of key findings from calendar year 2000*. Washington, DC: Children's Bureau.

National Commission on Correctional Health Care. (1999). *Correctional mental health care: Standard and guidelines for delivery services*. Chicago: Author.

Nemeth, C., & Sosis, R. M. (1973). A simulated jury: Characteristics of the defendant and the jurors. *Journal of Social Psychology, 90*, 221–229.

Neubauer, D. W. (2002). *America's courts and the criminal justice system*. Belmont, CA: Wadsworth/Thomson Learning.

Nichols, L. T. (1997). Social problems as landmark narrative: Bank of Boston, mass media, and "money laundering." *Social Problems, 44*, 324–341.

Nicholson, R. A. (1999). Forensic assessment. In R. Roesch, S. D. Hart, & J. R. P. Ogloff (Eds.), *Psychology and law: The state of the discipline*. New York: Kluwer Academic/Plenum.

Nicholson, R. A., & Kugler, K. E. (1991). Competent and incompetent criminal defendants: A quantitative review of comparative research. *Psychological Bulletin, 109*, 355–370.

Nicholson, R. A., & Norwood, S. (2000). The quality of forensic psychological assessments, reports, and testimony: Acknowledging the gap between promise and practice. *Law and Human Behavior, 24*, 9–44.

Niederhoffer, A. (1967). *Behind the shield: The police in urban society*. New York: Doubleday.

Niedermeier, K. E., Horowitz, I. A., & Kerr, N. L. (1999). Informing jurors of their nullification power: A route to a just verdict of judicial chaos? *Law and Human Behavior, 23*, 331–351.

Nietzel, M. T., McCarthy, D. M., & Kerr, M. J. (1999). Juries: The current state of the empirical literature. In R. Roesch, S. D. Hart, & J. R. P. Ogloff (Eds.), *Psychology and law: The state of the discipline*. New York: Kluwer Academic/Plenum.

Nigg, J. T. (2001). Is ADHD a disinhibitory disorder? *Psychological Bulletin, 127*, 571–598.

Nigg, J. T., Hinshaw, S. P., Carte, E. T., & Treuting, J. J. (1998). Neuropsychological correlates of childhood attention-deficit/hyperactivity disorder explainable by comorbid disruptive behavior or reading problems? *Journal of Abnormal Psychology, 107*, 468–480.

Nigro, G. N., Buckley, M. A., Hill, D. E., & Neslon, J. (1989). When juries "hear" children testify: The effects of eyewitness age and speech style on jurors' perceptions of testimony. In S. J. Ceci, D. F. Ross, & M. P. Toglia (Eds.), *Perspectives on children's testimony*. New York: Springer-Verlag.

Nimmer, R. T. (1977). The system impact of criminal justice. In J. L. Tapp & F. J. Levine (Eds.), *Law, justice, and the individual in society*. New York: Holt, Rinehart & Winston.

Nisbett, R. E., & Borgida, E. (1975). Attribution and the psychology of prediction. *Journal of Personality and Social Psychology, 32*, 932–943.

Nisbett, R. E., Borgida, E., Crandall, R., & Reed, H. (1976). Popular induction: Information is not necessarily informative. In J. S. Carroll & J. W. Payne (Eds.), *Cognition and social behavior*. Hillsdale, NJ: Erlbaum.

Nowicki, S. (1966). A study of the personality characteristics of successful policemen. *Police, 11*, 39–41.

Oberlander, L. B., & Goldstein, N. E. (2001). A review and update on the practice of evaluating Miranda comprehension. *Behavioral Sciences and the Law, 19*, 453–471.

Oberlander, L. B., Goldstein, N. E., & Ho, C. N. (2001). Preadolescent adjudicative competence: Methodological considerations and recommendations for standard practice standards. *Behavioral Sciences and the Law, 19*, 545–563.

O'Donohue, W., & Bradley, A. R. (1999). Conceptual and empirical issues in child custody evaluations. *Clinical Psychology: Science and Practice, 6*, 310–322.

Office of Juvenile Justice and Delinquency Prevention. (2000). *1999 Report to Congress: Title V incentive grants for local delinquency prevention programs.* Washington, DC: Author.

Office for Victims of Crime. (2002). *Strengthening antistalking statutes.* Washington, DC: U. S. Department of Justice.

Ogloff, J. R. P. (1991). A comparison of insanity defense standards on juror decision making. *Law and Human Behavior, 15*, 509–531.

Ogloff, J. R. P. (1999). Ethical and legal contours of forensic psychology. In R. Roesch, S. D. Hart, & J. R. P. Ogloff (Eds.), *Psychology and law: The state of the discipline.* New York: Kluwer Academic/Plenum.

Ogloff, J. R. P., & Cronshaw, S. F. (2001). Expert psychological testimony: Assisting or misleading the trier of fact? *Canadian Psychology, 42*, 87–91.

Ogloff, J. R. P., & Vidmar, N. (1994). The impact of pretrial publicity on jurors: A study to compare the relative effects of television and print media in a child sex abuse case. *Law and Human Behavior, 18*, 507–526.

O'Hara, C. E., & O'Hara, G. L. (1981). *Fundamentals of criminal investigation.* Springfield, IL: C. C. Thomas.

O'Leary, K. D., & Curley, A. D. (1986). Assertion and family violence: Correlates of spouse abuse. *Journal of Marital and Family Therapy, 12*, 281–289.

Olsen-Fulero, L., & Fulero, S. M. (1997). Commonsense rape judgments: An empathy-complexity theory of rape juror story making. *Psychology, Public Policy, and Law, 3*, 402–427.

Ondrovik, J., & Hamilton, D. (1991). Credibility of victims diagnosed as multiple personality: A case study. *American Journal of Forensic Psychology, 9*, 13–17.

Orcutt, H. K., Goodman, G. S., Tobey, A. E., Batterman-Faunce, J. M., & Thomas, S. (2001). Detecting deception in children's testimony: Factfinders' abilities to reach the truth in open court and closed-circuit trials. *Law and Human Behavior, 25*, 339–372.

Orentlicher, D. (2000). The implementation of Oregon's Death with Dignity Act: Reasurring, but more data are needed. *Psychology, Public Policy, and Law, 6*, 489–502.

Orne, M. T. (1970). Hypnosis, motivation and the ecological validity of the psychological experiment. In W. J. Arnold & M. M. Page (Eds.), *Nebraska symposium on motivation.* Lincoln, NE: University of Nebraska Press.

Orne, M. T., Dinges, D. F., & Orne, E. C. (1984). On the differential diagnosis of multiple personality in the forensic context. *The international Journal of Clinical and Experimental Hypnosis, 32*, 118–169.

Orne, M. T., Whitehouse, W. G., Dinges, D. F., & Orne, E. C. (1988). Reconstructing memory through hypnosis: Forensic and clinical implications. In H. M. Pettinati (Ed.), *Hypnosis and memory.* New York: Guilford Press.

Orne, M. T., Whitehouse, W. G., Orne, E. C., & Dinges, D. F. (1996). "Memories" of anomalous and traumatic autobiographical experiences: Validation and consolidation of fantasy through hypnosis. *Psychological Inquiry, 7*, 168–172.

Ornstein, P. A., Ceci, S. J., & Loftus, E. F. (1998). Comment on Alpert, Brown, and Courtois (1998): The science of memory and practice of psychotherapy. *Psychology, Public Policy, and Law, 4*, 996–1010.

Ostrom, B., & Kauder, N. (1999). *Examining the work of state courts.* Williamsburg, VA.: National Center for State Courts.

O'Tool, M. E. (2000). *The school shooter: A threat assessment perspective.* Quantico, VA: Criminal Incident Response Group, National Center for the Analysis of Violent Crime.

Otto, R. K., & Heilbrun, K. (2002). The practice of forensic psychology: A look toward the future in light of the past. *American Psychologist, 57*, 5–18.

Otto, R. K., Poythress, N. G., Nicholson, R. A., Edens, J. F., Monahan, J., Bonnie, R. J., Hoge, S. K., & Eisenberg, M. (1998). Psychometric properties of the MacArthur Competence Assessment tool-criminal adjudication. *Psychological Assessment, 10*, 435–443.

Owen, B. (2000). Prison security. In N. H. Rafter (Ed.), *Encyclopedia of women and crime.* Phoenix, AZ: The Oryx Press.

Oyster, C. K. (2001). Police reactions to suicide by cop. D. C. Sheehan & J. T. Warren (Eds.), *Suicide and law enforcement.* Washington, DC: U.S. Department of Justice, FBI Behavioral Science Unit.

Padawer-Singer, A. M., Singer, A. N., & Singer, R. L. J. (1974). Voir dire by two lawyers: An essential safeguard. *Judicature, 57*, 386–391.

Palmer, J. W., & Palmer, S. E. (1999). *Constitutional rights of prisoners* (6th ed.). Cincinnati, OH: Anderson.

Palmer, T. (1992). *The re-emergence of correctional intervention.* Newberry Park, CA: Sage.

Parry, C. D. H., Turkheimer, E., Hundley, P., & Creskoff, E. (1991). A comparison of respondents in commitment and recommitment hearings. *Law and Human Behavior, 15*, 315–324.

Partridge, A., & Bermant, G. (1978). *The quality of advocacy in the federal courts.* Washington, DC: Federal Judicial Center.

Pasewark, R., & McGinley, H. (1986). Insanity plea: National survey of frequency and success. *Journal of Psychiatry and Law, 13*, 101–108.

Pate, A. M. & Hamilton, E. E. (1992). Formal and informal deterrents to domestic violence: The Dade County spouse assault experiment. *American Sociological Review, 57*, 691–697.

Patrick, C. J., & Iacono, W. G. (1991). A comparison of field and laboratory polygraphs in the detection of deception. *Psychophysiology, 28*, 632–638.

Patterson, B. L. (1992). Job experience and perceived job stress among police, correctional, and probation/parole officers. *Criminal Justice and Behavior, 19*, 260–265.

Paull, D. (1993). *Fitness to stand trial.* Springfield, IL: C. C. Thomas.

Paulus, P. B. (1988). *Prison crowding: A psychological perspective.* New York: Springer-Verlag.

Pearson, F. S., & Lipton, D. S., Cleland, C. M., & Yee, D. S. (2002). The effects of behavior/cognitive-behavioral programs on recidivism. *Crime & Delinquency, 48*, 476–496.

Pearson, J., & Thoennes, N. (1989). Custody after divorce: Demographic and attitudinal patterns. *American Journal of Orthopsychiatry, 60*, 233–249.

Pelissier, B. (1991). The effects of a rapid increase in prison population. *Criminal Justice and Behavior, 18*, 427–447.

Pendergrass, V. E., & Ostrove, N. M. (1984). A survey of stress in women in policing. *Journal of Police Science and Administration, 12*, 303–309.

Pennington, N., & Hastie, R. (1986). Evidence evaluation in complex decision making. *Journal of Personality and Social Psychology, 51*, 242–258.

Pennington, N., & Hastie, R. (1992). Explaining the evidence: Tests of the story model for juror decision making. *Journal of Personality and Social Psychology, 62*, 189–206.

Penrod, S., & Cutler, B. L. (1987). Assessing the competence of juries. In I. B. Weiner & A. K. Hess (Eds.), *Handbook of forensic psychology*. New York: Wiley.

Penrod, S., & Cutler, B. L. (1995). Witness confidence and witness accuracy: Assessing their forensic relation. *Psychology, Public Policy, and Law, 1*, 817–845.

Peper, M. (1999). Neuropsychological toxicology: Selected fields of research and of application. *European Psychologist, 4*, 90–105.

Perlin, M. L. (1991). Power imbalances in therapeutic and forensic relationships. *Behavioral Science and the Law, 9*, 111–128.

Perlin, M. L. (1994). *The jurisprudence of the insanity defense*. Durham, NC: Carolina Academic Press.

Perlin, M. L. (1996). "Dignity was the first to leave": *Godinez v. Moran*, Colin Ferguson, and the trial of mentally disabled criminal defendants. *Behavioral Sciences and the Law, 14*, 61–81.

Perry, C. W., Laurence, J. R., D'eon, J., & Tallant, B. (1988). Hypnotic age regression techniques in the elicitation of memories: Applied uses and abuses. In H. M. Pettinati (Ed.), *Hypnosis and memory*. New York: Guilford Press.

Perry, S. J. (2000). Legal implications for failure to comply with advance directives: An examination of the incompetent individual's right to refuse life-sustaining medical treatment. *Behavioral Sciences and the Law, 20*, 253–269.

Petee, T. A., & Jarvis, J. (2000). Analyzing violent serial offending. *Homicide Studies, 4*, 211–218.

Peters, D. P. (1987). The impact of naturally occurring stress on children's memory. In S. J. Ceci, M. P. Toglia, & D. F. Ross (Eds.), *Children's eyewitness memory*. New York: Springer-Verlag.

Peters, S. D., Wyatt, G. E., & Finkelhor, D. (1986). Prevalence. In D. Finkelhor (Eds.), *Sourcebook on child sexual abuse*. Beverly Hills, CA: Sage.

Petrila, J. (1992). Redefining mental health law: Thoughts on a new agenda. *Law and Human Behavior, 16*, 89–106.

Pettinati, H. M. (1988). Hypnosis and memory: Integrative summary and future directions. In H. M. Pettinati (Ed.), *Hypnosis and memory*. New York: Guilford Press.

Pickel, K. L. (1995). Inducing jurors to disregard inadmissible evidence: A legal explanation does not help. *Law and Human Behavior, 19*, 407–424.

Pickel, K. L. (1999). The influence of context on the "weapon focus" effect. *Law and Human Behavior, 23*, 299–311.

Phillips, E. L. (1988). Length of psychotherapy and outcome: Observations stimulated by Howard, Kopta, and Orlinsky. *American Psychologist, 43*, 669–670.

Pinizzotto, A. J. (1984). Forensic psychology: Criminal personality profiling. *Journal of Police Science and Administration, 12*, 32–40.

Pinizzotto, A. J., & Finkel, N. J. (1990). Criminal personality profiling: An outcome and process study. *Law and Human Behavior, 14*, 215–234.

Piper, A. (1993). "Truth serum" and "recovered memories" of sexual abuse: A review of the evidence. *The Journal of Psychiatry and Law, 21*, 447–471.

Platt, A. (1969). *The child savers: The invention of delinquency*. Chicago: University of Chicago Press.

Platz, S. J., & Hosch, H. M. (1988). Cross-racial/ethnic eyewitness identification: A field study. *Journal of Applied Social Psychology, 18*, 972–984.

Pleck, E. (1989). Criminal approaches to family violence, 1640–1980. In L. Ohlin & M. Tonry (Eds), *Family violence*. Chicago: University of Chicago Press.

Pliner, A. J., & Yates, S. (1992). Psychological and legal issues in minors' rights to abortion. *Journal of Social Issues, 48*, 203–216.

Podkopacz, M. R., & Feld, B. C. (1995). Judicial waiver policy and practice: Persistence, seriousness, and race. *Law and inequality, 14*, 101–207.

Podlesny, J. A., & Raskin, D. C. (1977). Physiological measures and the detection of deception. *Psychological Bulletin, 84*, 782–799.

Podrygula, S. (1997). *Psychological tests used in child custody assessment: The current state of the art*. Workshop sponsored by the American Bar Association. Children, Divorce, and Custody: Lawyers and Psychologists Working Together. Los Angeles, CA.

Pokorny, L., Shull, R. D., & Nicholson, R. A. (1999). Dangerousness and disability as predictors of psychiatric patients' legal status. *Behavioral Sciences and the Law, 17*, 253–267.

Poland, J. M. (1978). Police selection methods and the prediction of police performance. *Journal of Police Science and Administration, 6*, 374–393.

Poletiek, F. H. (2002). How psychiatrists and judges assess the dangerousness of persons with mental illness: An 'expertise bias.' *Behavioral Sciences and the Law, 20*, 19–29.

Polizzi, D. M., MacKenzie, D. L., & Hickman, L. J. (1999). What works in adult sex offender treatment: A review of prison- and non-prison-based treatment programs. *International Journal of Offender Therapy and Comparative Criminology, 43*, 357–374.

Polvi, N. (1996). Assessing risk of suicide in correctional settings. In C. D. Webster & M. A. Jackson (Eds.), *Impulsivity: Theory, assessment, and treatment*. New York: Guilford.

Polvi, N., Jack, L., Lyon, D., Larid, P., & Ogloff, J. (1996). *Mock jurors' verdicts in a child sexual abuse case: The effects of pretrial publicity*. Paper presented at American Psychology-Law Society Conference, Hilton Head, SC.

Popper, K. (1962). *Conjectures and refutations: The growth of scientific knowledge*. New York: Basic Books.

Popper, K. (1968). *The logic of scientific discovery*. New York: Harper & Row.

Porter, S., Woodworth, M., & Birt, A. R. (2000). Truth, lies and videotape: An investigation of the ability of federal probation officers to detect deception. *Law and Human Behavior, 24*, 643–658.

Posner, R. (1985). *The federal courts: Crisis and reform*. Cambridge, MA: Harvard University Press.

Poulos, T. M., & Orchowsky, S. (1994). Serious juvenile offenders: Predicting the probability of transfer to criminal court. *Crime & Delinquency, 40*, 3–17.

Poythress, N. G. (1979). A proposal for training in forensic psychology. *American Psychologist, 34*, 612–621.

Poythress, N. G. (1992). Expert testimony on violence and dangerousness: Roles for mental health professionals. *Forensic Reports, 5*, 135–150.

Poythress, N. G., Nicholson, R., Otto, R. K., Edens, J. K., Bonnie, R. J., Monahan, J., & Hoge, S. K. (1999). *Manual for the MacArthur Competence Assessment Tool—Criminal Adjudication.* Odessa, FL: Psychological Assessment Resources.

Poythress, N. G., Otto, R. K., Darkes, J., & Starr, L. (1993). APA's expert panel in the Congressional review of the USS Iowa incident. *American Psychologist, 48*, 8–15.

Prager, I. G., Deckelbaum, G., & Cutler, B. L. (1989). Improving juror understanding for intervening causation instructions. *Forensic Reports, 3*, 187–193.

Prendergast, M. L., Farabee, D., Cartier, J., & Henkin, S. (2002). Involuntary treatment within a prison setting: Impact on psychosocial change during treatment. *Criminal Justice and Behavior, 29*, 5–26.

Prentky, R. A., & Knight, R. A. (1986). Impulsivity in the life style and criminal behavior of sexual offenders. *Criminal Justice and Behavior, 13*, 141–164.

Prentky, R. A., Knight, R. A., & Lee, A. F. S. (1997a). Risk factors associated with recidivism among extrafamilial child molesters. *Journal of Consulting and Clinical Psychology, 65*, 141–166.

Prentky, R. A., Knight, R. A., & Lee, A. F. S. (1997b, June). *Child sexual molestation: Research issues.* Washington, DC: National Institute of Justice.

Presser, L., & Van Voorhis, P. (2002). Values and evaluation: Assessing processes and outcomes of restorative justice programs. *Crime & Delinquency, 48*, 162–188.

Prial, E. (2001). Death at the hands of police: Suicide or homicide? In D. C. Sheehan & J. T. Warren (Eds.), *Suicide and law enforcement*. Washington, DC: U.S. Department of Justice, FBI Behavioral Science Unit.

Puritz, P., & Scali, M. A. (1998). *Beyond the walls: Improving conditions of confinement for youth in custody*. Washington, DC: Office of Juvenile Justice and Delinquency Prevention.

Quay, H. C. (1964). Dimensions of personality in delinquent boys as inferred from the factors analysis of case history data. *Child Development, 35*, 479–484.

Quay, H. C. (1966). Personality patterns in preadolescent delinquent boys. *Educational and Psychological Measurement, 16*, 99–110.

Quay, H. C. (1977). The three faces of evaluation. What can be expected to work. *Criminal Justice and Behavior, 4*, 341–354.

Quay, H. C. (1987). Intelligence. In H. C. Quay (Ed.), *Handbook of juvenile delinquency*. New York: Wiley.

Quay, H. C., & Peterson, D. (1987). *Manual for the Revised Behavior Problem Checklist*. Miami, FL: University of Miami.

Quinnell, F. A., & Bow, J. N. (2001). Psychological tests used in child custody evaluations. *Behavioral Sciences and the Law, 19*, 491–501.

Quinsey, V. L., Harris, G. T., Rice, M. E., & Cormier, C. A. (1998). *Violent offenders: Appraising and managing risk.* Washington, DC: American Psychological Association.

Quinsey, V. L., & Marshall, W. L. (1983). Procedures for reducing inappropriate sexual arousal: An evaluation review. In J. G. Greer & I. R. Stuart (Eds.), *The sexual aggressor*. New York: Van Nostrand Reinhold.

Quinsey, V. L., Rice, M. E., & Harris, G. T. (1995). Actuarial prediction of sexual recidivism. *Journal of Interpersonal Violence, 10*, 85–105.

Radcliff, D. H. (1977). Pennsylvania child custody: The tender years doctrine. *Dickenson Law Review, 81*, 775–792.

Radelet, M. L., & Bernard, G. W. (1986). Ethics and the psychiatric determination of competency to be executed. *Bulletin of the American Academy of Psychiatry and Law, 14*, 37–53.

Radovanovic, H., Bartha, C., Magnatta, M., Hodd, E., Sagar, A., & McDonough, H. (1994). A follow-up of families disputing child custody/access: Assessment, settlement, and family relationship outcomes. *Behavioral Sciences and the Law, 12*, 427–435.

Radwin, J. O. (1991). The Multiple Personality Disorder: Has this trendy alibi lost its way? *Law and Psychology Review, 15*, 351–373.

Rafky, D. M. (1974). My husband the cop. *Police Chief, 41*, 62–65.

Raine, A. (1993). *The psychopathology of crime: Criminal behavior as a clinical disorder*. San Diego, CA: Academic Press.

Ramirez, D., McDevitt, J., & Farrell, A. (2000). *A resource guide on racial profiling data collection systems: Promising practices and lessons learned*. Boston: Northeastern University Press.

Rankin, J. H. (1957). Psychiatric screening of police recruits. *Public Personnel Review, 20*, 191–196.

Raskin, D. C. (1988). Does science support polygraph testing? In A. Gale (Ed.), *The polygraph test: Lies, truth and science*. London: Sage.

Raskin, D. C., & Honts, C. R. (2002). The comparison questions test. In M. Kleiner (Ed.), *Handbook of polygraph testing*. San Diego, CA: Academic Press.

Raskin, D. C., Honts, C. R., & Kircher, J. C. (1997). The scientific status of research on polygraph techniques: The case for polygraph tests. In D. L. Furgman, D. Kaye, M. J. Saks, & J. Sanders (Eds). *Modern scientific evidence: The law and science of expert testimony*, St, Paul, MN: West.

Redding, R. E., & Reppucci, N. E. (1999). Effects of lawyers' socio-political attitudes on their judgments of social science in legal decision making. *Law and Human Behavior, 23*, 31–54.

Redding, R. E., Floyd, M. Y., & Hawk, G. L. (2001). What judges and lawyers think about the testimony of mental health experts: A survey of the courts and bar. *Behavioral Sciences and the Law, 19*, 583–594.

Reddington, F. P., & Sapp, A. D. (1997). Juveniles in adult prisons: Problems and prospects. *Journal of Crime and Justice, 20*, 138–152.

Regoli, B., Crank, J. P., & Rivera, G. F. (1990). The construction and implementation of an alternative measure of police cynicism. *Criminal Justice and Behavior, 17*, 395–409.

Reiman, J. (1995). *The rich get richer and the poor get prison* (4th ed.). Needham Heights, MA: Allyn & Bacon.

Reiser, M. (1973). *Practical psychology for police officers*. Springfield, IL: C. C. Thomas.

Reiss, A. J. (1992). Police organizations in the twentieth century. In M. Tonry & N. Morris (Eds.), *Modern policing*. Chicago: University of Chicago Press.

Rennison, C. M. (2002, August). *Rape and sexual assault: Reporting to police and medical attention, 1992–2000*. U.S. Dept of Justice, Bureau of Justice Statistics.

Reno, J. (1999a). *Statement of Janet Reno, Attorney General of the United States, before the committee on the judiciary, United States Senate concerning justice department oversight*, May 5, 1999.

Reno, J. (1999b). Message from the Attorney General. In Technical Working Group for Eyewitness Evidence, *Eyewitness Evidence: A guide for law enforcement*. Washington, DC: National Institute of Justice.

Rey, A. (1964). *L'examen clinique en psychologie* [The clinical examination in psychology]. Paris: Presses Universitaires de France.

Reynolds, E. D., & Sanders, M. S. (1973, April). *The effects of defendant attractiveness, age, and injury on severity of sentence given by simulated jurors*. Paper presented at the meeting of the Western Psychological Association, San Francisco.

Rice, M. E. (1997). Violent offender research and implications for the criminal justice system. *American Psychologist, 52*, 414–423.

Rice, M. E., & Harris, G. T. (1997). The treatment of mentally disordered offenders. *Psychology, Public Policy, and Law, 3*, 126–183.

Rifkin, J. (1989). Mediation in the justice system: A paradox for women. *Women and Criminal Justice, 1*, 41–54.

Riveland, C. (1999). *Supermax prisons: Overview and general considerations*. Washington, DC: U.S. Department of Justice, National Institute of Corrections.

Robbennolt, J. K., Penrod, S., & Heuer, L. (1999). Assessing and aiding civil juror competence. In A. K. Hess & I. B. Weiner (Eds.), *The handbook of forensic psychology* (2nd ed.). New York: Wiley.

Robbennolt, J. K., & Sobus, M. S. (1997). An integration of hindsight bias and counterfactual thinking: Decision making and drug courier profiles. *Law and Human Behavior, 21*, 539–560.

Roberts, A. R. (Ed.) (1998). *Juvenile justice: Policies, programs and services* (2nd ed.). Chicago: Nelson-Hall.

Roberts, J. V., & Gebobtys, R. J. (1992). Reforming rape laws: Effects of legislative change in Canada. *Law and Human Behavior, 16*, 555–573.

Robey, A. (1965). Criteria for competency to stand trial: A checklist for psychiatrists. *American Journal of Psychiatry, 122*, 616–622.

Robin, A., & MacDonald, D. (1975). *Lessons of leukotomy*. London: Henry Kimpton.

Robiner, W. N., & Crew, D. P. (2000). Rightsizing the workforce of psychologists in health care trends from licensing boards, training programs, and managed care. *Professional Psychology: Research and Practice. 31*, 245–263.

Robinson, P., & Darley, D. (1995). *Justice, liability and blame: Community views and the criminal law*. San Francisco: Westview Press.

Roesch, R. (1995). Creating change in the legal system: Contributions from community psychology. *Law and Human Behavior, 19*, 325–343.

Roesch, R., & Golding, S. (1980). *Competency to stand trial*. Urbana-Champaign, IL: University of Illinois Press.

Roesch, R., & Golding, S. (1987). Defining and assessing competency to stand trial. In I. B. Weiner & A. K. Hess, (Eds.), *Handbook of forensic psychology*. New York: Wiley.

Roesch, R., Zapf, P. A., Golding, S. L., & Skeem, J. L. (1999). Defining and assessing competency to stand trial. In A. K. Hess & I. B. Weiner (Eds.), *The handbook of forensic psychology* (2nd ed.). New York: Wiley.

Rogers, R. (1984). Rogers Criminal Responsbility Assessment Scales (R-CRAS) and Test Manual. Odessa, FL: Psychological Assessment Resources.

Rogers, R. (1997). *Clinical assessment of malingering and deception* (2nd ed.). New York: Guilford.

Rogers, R. (2001). Focused forensic interviews. In R. Rogers (Ed.), *Handbook of diagnostic and structured interviewing*. New York: Guilford.

Rogers, R., & Cavanaugh, J. L. (1981). Rogers criminal responsibility assessment scales. *Illinois Medical Journal, 160*, 164–169.

Rogers, R., Cavanaugh, J. L., Seman, W., & Harris, M. (1984). Legal outcome and clinical findings: A study of insanity evaluations. *Bulletin of the American Academy of Psychiatry and Law, 12*, 75–83.

Rogers, R., & Ewing, C. P. (1989). Ultimate issue proscriptions: A cosmetic fix and plea for empiricism. *Law and Human Behavior, 13*, 357–374.

Rogers, R., & Grandjean, N. (2000). *Competency measures and the Dusky standard: A conceptual mismatch?* Biennial convention of the American Psychology-Law Society, New Orleans.

Rogers, R., & Shuman, D. W. (1999). *Conducting insanity evaluations* (2nd ed.). New York: Guilford.

Rogers, R., & Sewell, K. W. (1999). The R–CRAS and insanity evaluations: A re-examination of construct validity. *Behavioral Sciences and the Law, 17*, 181–194.

Rogers, R., Gillis, J. R., Dickens, S. E., & Bagby, R. M. (1991). Standardized assessment of malingering: Validation of the Structured Interview of Reported Symptoms. *Psychological Assessment, 3*, 89–96.

Rogers, R., Grandjean, N, Tillbrook, C. E., Vitacco, M. J., & Sewell, K. W. (2001). Recent interview-based measures of competency to stand trial: A critical review augmented with research data. *Behavioral Sciences and the Law, 19*, 503–518.

Rohman, L., Sales, B., & Lou, M. (1990). The best interest standard in child custody decisions. In D. Weisstub (Ed.), *Law and mental health: International perspectives* (Vol. 5). New York: Pergamon.

Roper, R. (1980). Jury size and verdict consistency: "The line has to be drawn somewhere"? *Law and Society Review, 14*, 977–995.

Rose, V. G., & Ogloff, J. R. (2001). Evaluating the comprehensibility of jury instructions: A method and an example. *Law and Human Behavior, 25*, 409–431.

Roseby, V. (1995). Uses of psychological tests in a child-focused approach to child custody evaluations. *Family Law Quarterly, 29*, 97–110.

Rosenfeld, B. (2000). Methodological issues in assisted suicide and euthanasia research. *Psychology, Public Policy, and Law, 6*, 559–574.

Rosenfeld, B., & Ritchie, K. (1998). Competence to stand trial: Clinician reliability and the role of offense severity. *Journal of Forensic Science, 43*, 151–157.

Rosenfeld, H. M. (1966). Approval-seeking and approval-inducing functions of verbal and nonverbal responses in the dyad. *Journal of Personality and Social Psychology, 4*, 597–605.

Rosenhan, D. L., Eisner, S. L., & Robinson, R. J. (1994). Note-taking can aid juror recall. *Law and Human Behavior, 18*, 53–61.

Rosenhan, D. L., & Seligman, M. E. P. (1984). *Abnormal psychology*. New York: Norton.

Rosenzweig, M. R. (1992). Psychological science around the world. *American Psychologist, 47*, 718–722.

Rosner, R. (1989). Forensic psychiatry: A subspeciality. *Bulletin of the American Academy of Psychiatry and Law, 17*, 323–333.

Ross, D. F., Ceci, S. J., Dunning, D., & Toglia, M. P. (1994). Unconscious transference and mistaken identity: When a witness misidentifies a familiar but innocent person. *Journal of Applied Psychology, 79*, 918–930.

Ross, D. F., Dunning, D., Toglia, M. P., & Ceci, S. J. (1989). Age stereotypes, communication modality, and mock jurors' perceptions of the child witness. In S. J. Ceci, D. F. Ross, & M. P. Toglia (Eds.), *Perspectives on children's testimony.* New York: Springer-Verlag.

Ross, D. F., Dunning, D., Toglia, M. P., & Ceci, S. J. (1990). The child in the eyes of the jury: Assessing mock jurors' perceptions of the child witness. *Law and Human Behavior, 14*, 5–23.

Rossmo, D. K. (1997). Geographic profiling. In J. T. Jackson & D. A. Bekerain (Eds.), *Offender profiling: Theory, research and practice.* Chichester, UK: Wiley.

Rotgers, F., & Barrett, D. (1996). *Daubert v. Merrell Dow* and expert testimony by clinical psychologists: Implications and recommendations for practice. *Professional Psychology: Research and Practice, 27*, 467–474.

Rothman, D. J. (1971). *The discovery of the asylum: Social order and disorder in the new republic*. Boston: Little, Brown.

Rothman, D. J. (1980). *Conscience and convenience*. Boston: Little, Brown.

Rotter, J. B. (1954). *Social learning and clinical psychology*. Englewood Cliffs, NJ: Prentice-Hall.

Rotter, J. B. (1966). Generalized expectancies for internal versus external control of reinforcement. *Psychological Monographs, 80* (Whole No. 609).

Rotter, J. B. (1972). Beliefs, social attitudes and behavior: A social learning analysis. In J. B. Rotter, J. E. Chance, & E. J. Phares (Eds.), *Applications of social learning theory of personality*. New York: Holt, Rinehart & Winston.

Ruback, R. B., & Carr, T. S. (1984). Crowding in a woman's prison: Attitudinal and behavioral effects. *Journal of Applied Social Psychology, 14*, 57–68.

Ruback, R. B., & Innes, C. A. (1988). The relevance and irrelevance of psychological research: The example of prison crowding. *American Psychologist, 43*, 683–693.

Rubin, Z., & Peplau, A. (1973). Belief in a just world and reactions to another's lot: A study of participants in the national draft lottery. *Journal of Social Issues, 29*, 73–93.

Rubin, Z., & Peplau, A. (1975). Who believes in a just world? *Journal of Social Issues, 31*, 65–89.

Rubinsky, E. W., & Brandt, J. (1986). Amnesia and criminal law: A clinical overview. *Behavioral Sciences and the Law, 4*, 27–46.

Rumsey, M. G., & Castore, C. H. (1974). *The effect of group discussion on juror sentencing*. Paper Presented at the Annual Meeting of the Midwestern Psychological Association, Chicago.

Russell, D. E. H. (1983). The prevalence and incidence of forcible rape and attempted rape of females. *Victimology: An International Journal, 7*, 81–93.

Russo, N. F. (1992). Psychological aspects of unwanted pregnancy and its resolution. In J. D. Butler & D. F. Walbert (Eds.), *Abortion, medicine, and the law* (4th ed.). New York: Facts on File.

Russo, N. F., Horn, J. D., & Schwartz, R. (1992). U.S. abortion in context: Selected characteristics and motivations of women seeking abortions. *Journal of Social Issues, 48*, 183–202.

Ryan, H., & Taylor, M. (1988). Information usage and cue identification as a function of experience in police officers. *Journal of Police Science and Administration, 16*, 177–181.

Rychlak, J. F. (1968). *A philosophy of science for personality theory*. Boston: Houghton Mifflin.

Sadoff, R. L. (1975). *Forensic psychiatry*. Springfield, IL: C. C. Thomas.

Sadoff, R. L. (2001). Education and training in forensic psychiatry in the United States. *The Journal of Forensic Psychiatry, 12*, 263–267.

Sagatun, I. J. (1991). Expert witnesses in child abuse cases. *Behavioral Sciences and the Law, 9*, 201–215.

Saks, M. J. (1974). Ignorance of science is no excuse. *Trial, 10,* 18–24.

Saks, M. J. (1977). *Jury verdicts.* Lexington, MA: Lexington Books.

Saks, M. J. (1990). Expert witnesses, nonexpert witnesses and nonwitness experts. *Law and Human Behavior, 14,* 291–313.

Saks, M. J. (1993). Improving APA science translation amicus briefs. *Law and Human Behavior, 17,* 235–247.

Saks, M. J. (1997). What do jury experiments tell us about how juries (should) make decisions? *Southern California Interdisciplinary Law Journal, 6,* 1–53.

Saks, M. J., & Hastie, R. (1978). *Social psychology in court.* New York: Van Nostrand Reinhold.

Saks, M. J., & Marti, M. W. (1997). A meta-analysis of the effects of jury size. *Law and Human Behavior, 21,* 451–466.

Saks, M. J., & Miller, M. (1979). A systems approach to discretion in the legal process. In L. E. Abt & L. R. Stuart (Eds.), *Social psychology and discretionary law.* New York: Van Nostrand Reinhold.

Saks, M. J., & Ostrom, T. M. (1975). Jury size and consensus requirements: The laws of probability vs. the laws of the land. *Journal of Contemporary Law, 1,* 163–173.

Salekin, R. T., Rogers, R., & Sewell, K. W. (1997). Construct validity of psychopathy in a female offender sample: A multitrait-multimethod evaluation. *Journal of Abnormal Psychology, 106,* 576–585.

Salekin, R. T., Rogers, R., & Ustad, K. L. (2001). Juvenile waiver to adult criminal courts: Prototypes for dangerousness, sophistication-maturity, and amenability to treatment. *Psychology, Public Policy, and Law, 7,* 381–408.

Salekin, R. T., Rogers, R., Ustad, K. L., & Sewell, K. W. (1998). Psychopathy and recidivism among female inmates. *Law and Human Behavior, 22,* 109–128.

Sales, B., Manber, R., & Rohman, L. (1992). Social science research and child custody decision-making. *Applied and Preventive Psychology, 1,* 23–40.

Sanders, G. S., & Simmons, W. L. (1983). Use of hypnosis to enhance eyewitness accuracy: Does it work? *Journal of Applied Psychology, 68,* 70–77.

Sandy, J. P., & Devine, D. A. (1978, September). Four stress factors unique to rural patrol. *The Police Chief,* 42–44.

Sandys, M., & Dillehay, R. C. (1995). First ballot votes, predeliberation dispositions, and final verdicts in jury trial. *Law and Human Behavior, 19,* 175–195.

Santilli, L. E., & Roberts, M. C. (1990). Custody decisions in Alabama before and after the abolition of the tender years doctrine. *Law and Human Behavior, 14,* 123–136.

Sarason, I. C., & Stoops, R. (1978). Test anxiety and the passage of time. *Journal of Consulting and Clinical Psychology, 46,* 102–108.

Sauder, J. W. S. (2001). Experts in court: A view from the bench. *Canadian Psychology, 42,* 109–118.

Saulneier, K., & Perlman, D. (1981). The actor-observer bias is alive and well in prison: A sequel to Wells. *Personality and Social Psychology, 7,* 559–564.

Savitsky, J. C., & Karras, D. (1984). Competency to stand trial among adolescents. *Adolescence, 19,* 349–358.

Sawyer, J. (1966). Measurement and prediction, clinical and statistical. *Psychological Bulletin, 66,* 178–200.

Saywitz, K., Goodman, G., Nicholas, G., & Moan, S. (1991). Children's memory for genital exam: Implications for child sexual abuse. *Journal of Consulting and Clinical Psychology, 59,* 682–691.

Schacter, D. L. (1986). Amnesia and crime: How much do we really know? *American Psychologist, 41,* 286–295.

Scheflin, A. (1972). Jury nullification—The right to say no. *Southern California Law Review, 45,* 377–415.

Scheflin, A. W., Spiegel, H., & Spiegel, D. (1999). Forensic uses of hypnosis. In A. K. Hess & I. B. Weiner (Eds.), *The handbook of forensic psychology* (2nd ed.). New York: Wiley.

Scherer, D. G., Brondino, M. J., Henggeler, S. W., Melton, G. B., & Hanley, J. H. (1994). Multisystemic family preservation therapy: Preliminary findings from a study of rural and minority serious adolescent offenders. *Journal of Emotional and Behavioral Disorders, 2,* 98–206.

Schneider, A. K. (1999). The intersection of therapeutic jurisprudence, preventive law, and alternative dispute resolution. *Psychology, Public Policy, and Law, 5,* 1084–1102.

Schneider, C. (1991). Discretion, rules, and law: Child custody and the UMDA best interest standard. *Michigan Law Review, 89,* 215–246.

Schretlen, D. (1986). *Malingering: Use of psychological test battery to detect two kinds of simulation.* Ann Arbor, MI: University Microfilms International.

Schretlen, D., Wilkins, S. S., Van Gorp, W. G., & Bobholz, J. H. (1992). Cross-validation of a psychological test battery to detect faked insanity. *Psychological Assessment, 4,* 77–83.

Schuller, R. A., & Vidmar, N. (1992). Battered woman syndrome evidence in the courtroom: A review of the literature. *Law and Human Behavior, 16,* 272–292.

Schulman, J., Shaver, P., Colman, R., Emrich, B., & Christie, R. (1973, May). *Psychology Today,* 37–83.

Schwartz, H. I., Vingiano, W., & Perez, C. B. (1990). Autonomy and the right to refuse treatment: Patients' attitudes after involuntary medication. In D. B. Wexler (Ed.), *Therapeutic jurisprudence.* Durham, NC: Carolina Academic Press.

Schwitzgebel, R. K. (1977). Professional accountability in the treatment and release of dangerous persons. In B. D. Sales (Ed.), *Perspectives in law and Psychology* (Vol. 1): *The criminal justice system.* New York: Plenum.

Schwitzgebel, R. L., & Schwitzgebel, R. K. (1980). *Law and psychological practice.* New York: Wiley.

Scoboria, A., Mazzoni, G., Kirsch, I., & Milling, L. S. (2002). Immediate and persisting effects of misleading questions and hypnosis on memory reports. *Journal of Experimental Psychology: Applied, 8,* 26–32.

Scott, E. (1992). Pluralism, parental preference, and child custody. *California Law Review, 80,* 615–672.

Scott, E. S. (2000). Criminal responsibility in adolescence: Lessons from developmental psychology. In T. Grisso & R. Schwartz (Eds.), *Youth on trial.* Chicago: University of Chicago Press.

Scott, J., & Derdeyn, E. (1984). Rethinking joint custody. *Ohio State Law Journal, 45,* 455–498.

Scoville, D. (1998, November). Getting you to pull the trigger. *Police*, 36–44.

Scrivener, E.M. (1994). *The role of police psychology in controlling excessive force*. Washington, DC: National Institute of Justice.

Seagrave, D., & Grisso, T. (2002). Adolescent development and the measurement of juvenile delinquency. *Law and Human Behavior, 26*, 219–239.

Segal, S., Watson, M., Goldfinger, S., & Averbuck, D. (1988). Civil commitment in the psychiatric emergency room: II. Mental disorder indicators and three dangerousness criteria. *Archives of General Psychiatry, 45*, 753–758.

Selkin, J. (1987). *Psychological autopsy in the courtroom*. Denver, CO: Author.

Selkin, J. (1994). Psychological autopsy: Scientific psychohistory or clinical intuition? *American Psychologist, 49,* 74–75.

Sellin, T. (1959). *The death penalty*. Philadelphia, PA: The American Law Institute.

Seltzer, R., Venuti, M., & Lopes, G. (1991). Juror honesty during the *voir dire*. *Journal of Criminal Justice, 19*, 451–462.

Selye, H. (1976). *The stress of life* (2nd ed.). New York: McGraw-Hill.

Serin, R. C. (1991). Psychopathy and violence in criminals. *Journal of Interpersonal Violence, 6*, 423–431.

Serin, R. C., Peters, R. D., & Barbaree, H. E. (1990). Predictors of psychopathy and release outcome in a criminal population. *Psychological Assessment: A Journal of Consulting and Clinical Psychology, 2*, 419–422.

Sewell, J. D., Ellison, K. W., & Hurrell, J. J. (1988, October). Stress management in law enforcement: Where do we go from here? *Police Chief*, 94–99.

Seymour, A., Hook, M., & Grimes, C. (2001). Hate and bias crime. *National Victim Assistance Academy Textbook*. Washington, DC: U. S. Department of Justice, Office for Victims iof Crime.

Shaffer, D. R., & Wheatman, S. R. (2000). Does personality influence reactions to judicial instructions? Some preliminary findings and possible implications. *Psychology, Public Policy, and Law, 6,* 655–676.

Shapiro, D. L. (1999). Criminal responsibility evaluations: A manual for practice. Sarasota, FL: Professional Resource Press.

Shaw, J. H. (1986). Effectiveness of the MMPI in differentiating ideal from undesirable police officer applicants. In J. Reese & H. A. Goldstein (Eds.), *Psychological services for law enforcement*. Washington, DC: USGPO.

Sheehan, P. W. (1988). Confidence, memory and hypnosis. In H. M. Pettinati (Ed.), *Hypnosis and memory*. New York: Guilford.

Sheehan, P. W., & Tilden, J. (1983). Effects of suggestibility and hypnosis on accurate and distorted retrieval from memory. *Journal of Experimental Psychology: Learning, Memory, and Cognition, 9*, 283–293.

Sheehan, P. W., & Tilden, J. (1984). Real and simulated occurrences of memory distortion in hypnosis. *Journal of Abnormal Psychology, 93*, 47–57.

Shepherd, J. W. & Ellis, H. D. (1973). The effect of attractiveness on recognition memory for faces. *American Journal of Psychology, 86,* 627–633.

Sherman, L. W. (1992). Attacking crime: Policing and crime control. In M. Tonry & N. Morris (Eds.), *Modern policing*. Chicago: University of Chicago Press.

Sherman, L. W., & Berk, R. A. (1984). The specific deterrent effects of arrest for domestic assault. *American Sociological Review, 49*, 261–272.

Sherman, L. W., Gottfredson, D. C., MacKenzie, D. L., Eck, J., Reuter, P., & Bushway, S. D. (1998). *Preventing crime: What works, what doesn't, what's promising*. Washington, DC: U.S. Department of Justice.

Sherman, L.W., & Smith, D. (1992). Crime, punishment and stake in conformity: Legal and extralegal control of domestic violence. *American Sociological Review, 58*, 680–690.

Sherman, M. (1979). *Personality: Inquiry and application*. New York: Pergamon Press.

Shneidman, E. S. (1994). The psychological autopsy. *American Psychologist, 49*, 75–76.

Shoemaker, D. J., South, D. R., & Lowe, J. (1973). Facial stereotypes of deviants and judgments of guilt or innocence. *Social Forces, 51*, 427–433.

Shuman, D. W. & Sales, B. D. (1999). The impact of *Daubert* and its progeny on the admissibility of behavioral and social science evidence. *Psychology, Public Policy, and Law, 5*, 3–15.

Siegel, A. M., & Elwork, A. (1990). Treating incompetence to stand trial. *Law and Human Behavior, 14*, 57–65.

Sigall, H., & Ostrove, N. (1975). Beautiful but dangerous: Effects of offender attractiveness and nature of the crime on juridic judgment. *Journal of Personality and Social Psychology, 31*, 410–414.

Silver, E. (1995). Punishment or treatment? Comparing the lengths of confinement of successful and unsuccessful insanity defendants. *Law and Human Behavior, 19*, 375–388.

Silver, E., Cirincione, C., & Steadman, H. (1994). Demythologizing inaccurate perceptions of the insanity defense. *Law and Human Behavior, 18*, 63–70.

Simon, J. (1998). Managing the monstrous: Sex offenders and the new penology. *Psychology, Public Policy, and Law, 4*, 452–467.

Simon, R., & Aaronson, D. E. (1988). *The insanity defense*. New York: Praeger.

Simourd, D. J., & Hoge, R. D. (2000). Criminal psychopathy: A risk-and-need perspective, *Criminal Justice and Behavior, 27*, 256–272.

Singer, M. T., & Nievod, A. (1987). Consulting and testifying in court. In I. B. Weiner and A. K. Hess (Eds.), *Handbook of forensic psychology*. New York: Wiley.

Singer, S. I. (1996). *Recriminalizing delinquency: Violent juvenile crimes and juvenile justice reform.* New York: Cambridge University Press.

Skeem, J. L., Golding, S. L., Cohn, N. B., & Berge, G. (1998). Logic and reliability of evaluations of competency to stand trial. *Law and Human Behavior, 22*, 519–547.

Skeem, J. L., & Mulvey, E. P. (2001). Psychopathy and community violence among civil psychiatric patients: Results from the MacArthur Violence Risk Assessment Study. *Journal of Consulting and Clinical Psychology, 69*, 358–374.

Skolnick, J. (1973). A sketch of the policeman's working personality. In A. Niederhoffer & A. S. Blumberg (Eds.), *The ambivalent force*. San Francisco: Rinehart Press.

Slater, P. E. (1958). Contrasting correlates of group size. *Sociometry, 21*, 129–139.

Slobogin, C. (1985). The guilty but mentally ill verdict: An idea whose time should not have come. *George Washington Law Review, 53*, 494–580.

Slobogin, C. (1989). The "ultimate issue" issue. *Behavioral Sciences and the Law, 7*, 259–266.

Slobogin, C. (1999) The admissibility of behavioral science information in criminal trials: From primitivism to *Daubert* to voice. *Psychology, Public Policy, and Law, 5*, 100–119.

Slobogin, C. (2001). Informing juvenile justice policy: Directions for behavioral science research. *Law and Human Behavior, 25*, 13–24.

Slobogin, C., Melton, G. B., & Showalter, C. R. (1984). The feasibility of a brief evaluation of mental state at the time of offense. *Law and Human Behavior, 8*, 305–321.

Slome, L. R., Mitchell, T. F., Charlebois, E., Benevedes, J. M., & Abrams, D. I. (1997). Physician-assisted suicide and patients with human immunodeficiency virus disease. *New England Journal of Medicine, 336*, 417–420.

Slovenko, R. (1989). The multiple personality: A challenge to legal concepts. *The Journal of Psychiatry & Law*, Winter, 681–719.

Slovic, P., Monahan, J., & MacGregor, D. (2000). Violence risk assessment and risk communication: The effects of using actual cases, providing instruction, and employing probability versus frequency formats. *Law and Human Behavior, 24*, 271–296.

Small, M. H., & Otto, R. K. (1991). Evaluations of competency to be executed: Legal contours and implication for assessment. *Criminal Justice and Behavior, 18*, 146–158.

Smith, B., Penrod, S., Otto, A., & Park, R. (1996). Jurors' use of probabilistic evidence. *Law and Human Behavior, 20*, 49–82.

Smith, B. M. (1967). The polygraph. *Scientific American, 216*, 25–31.

Smith, V. L. (1991). Prototypes in the courtroom: Lay representations of legal concepts. *Journal of Personality and Social Psychology, 61*, 857–872.

Smith, V. L. (1993). When prior knowledge and law collide: Helping jurors use the law. *Law and Human Behavior, 17*, 507–536.

Smith, V. L., & Studebaker, C. A. (1996). What do you expect? The influence of people's prior knowledge of crime categories on fact finding. *Law and Human Behavior, 20*, 517–532.

Snyder, H. N., & Sickmund, M. (1999). *Juvenile offenders and victims: A national report*. Washington, DC: U.S. Department of Justice, Office of Juvenile Justice and Delinquency Prevention.

Snyder, H. N., Sickmund, M., & Poe-Yamagata, E. (1996). *Juvenile offenders and victims: 1996 update on violence*. Washington, DC: Office of Juvenile Justice and Delinquency Prevention.

Snyder, H. N., Sickmund, M., & Poe-Yamagata, E. (2000). *Juvenile transfers to criminal court in the 1990's: Lessons learned from four studies*. Washington, DC: U.S. Department of Justice, Office of Juvenile Justice and Delinquency Prevention.

Sobeloff, S. G. (1958). From M'Naghten to Durham and beyond. In R. W. Nice (Ed.), *Crime and insanity*. New York: Philosophical Library.

Solomon, M. R., & Schopler, J. (1978). The relationship of physical attractiveness and punitiveness: Is the linearity assumption out of line? *Personality and Social Psychology Bulletin, 4*, 483–486.

Solomon, R. M., & Horn, J. M. (1986). Post-shooting traumatic reactions: A pilot study. In J. T. Reese & H. A. Goldstein (Eds.), *Psychological services for law enforcement*. Washington, DC: USGPO.

Somodevilla, S. A. (1978). The role of psychologists in a police department. In W. Taylor & M. Braswell (Eds.), *Issues in police and criminal psychology*. Washington, DC: University Press of America.

Soskin, W. F. (1959). Influence of four types of data on diagnostic conceptualization in psychological testing. *Journal of Abnormal and Social Psychology, 58*, 69–78.

Spiegel, D., & Spiegel, H. (1987). Forensic uses of hypnosis. In I. B. Weiner & A. K. Hess (Eds.), *Handbook of forensic psychology*. New York: Wiley.

Spielberger, C. D. (Ed.). (1979). *Police selection and evaluation: Issues and techniques*. Washington, DC: Hemisphere Publishing.

Spielberger, C. D., Spaulding, H. C., & Ward, J. C. (1978). *Selecting effective law enforcement officers: The Florida police standards research project*. Tampa, FL: Human Resources Institute.

Spielberger, C. D., Ward, J. C., & Spaulding, H. C. (1979). A model for the selection of law enforcement officers. In C. D. Spielberger (Ed.), *Police selection and evaluation: Issues and techniques*. Washington, DC: Hemisphere Publishing.

Spitzer, R. L., & Fleiss, J. (1974). A re-analysis of the reliability of psychiatric diagnosis. *British Journal of Psychiatry, 125*, 341–347.

Spohn, C. (1999). Gender and sentencing of drug offenders. Is chivalry dead? *Criminal Justice Policy Review, 9*, 365–399.

Sporer, S. L. (2001). The cross-race effect: Beyond recognition of faces in the laboratory. *Psychology, Public Policy, and Law, 7*, 170–200.

Stadolnik, R. F. (2000). *Drawn to the flame: Assessment and treatment of juvenile firesetting behavior*. Sarasota, FL: Professional Resources Press.

Stalnaker, J. M., & Riddle, E. F. (1932). The effect of hypnosis on long-delayed recall. *Journal of General Psychology, 6*, 429–440.

Staub, E. (1978). *Positive social behavior and morality: Social and personal influences* (Vol. 1). New York: Academic Press.

Steadman, H. J. (1979). *Beating a rap?* Chicago: University of Chicago Press.

Steadman, H. J., Callahan, L. A., Robbins, P. C., & Morrissey, J. P. (1989). The maintenance of an insanity defense under

Montana's abolition. *American Journal of Psychiatry, 146*, 357–360.

Steadman, H. J., & Cocozza, J. J. (1974). *Careers of the criminally insane*. Lexington, MA: Lexington Books.

Steadman, H. J., Davidson, S., & Brown, C. (2001). Mental health courts: Their promise and unanswered questions. *Psychiatric Services, 54*, 457–458.

Steadman, H., Gounis, K., & Dennis, D. (2001). Assessing the New York City involuntary outpatient commitment pilot program. *Psychiatric Services, 52*, 330–336.

Steadman, H. J., McCarty, D. W., & Morrissey, J. P. (1989) *The mentally ill in jail: Planning for essential services*. NY: Guilford Press.

Steadman, H. J., McGreevy, M., Morrissey, J., Callahan, L., Robbins, P., & Cirincione, C. (1993). *Before and after Hinckley: Evaluating insanity defense reform*. New York: Guilford Press.

Steadman, H. J., Mulvey, E. P., Monahan, J., Robbins, P. C., Appelbaum, P. S., Grisso, T., Roth, L. H., & Silver, E. (1998). Violence by people discharged from acute psychiatric inpatient facilities and by others in the same neighborhoods. *Archives of General Psychiatry, 55*, 393–401.

Steadman, H. J., Silver, E., Monahan, J., Appelbaum, P., Robbins, P., Mulvey, E., Grisso, T., Roth, L., & Banks, S. (2000). A classification tree approach to the development of actuarial violence risk assessment tools. *Law and Human Behavior, 24*, 83–100.

Steadman, H. J., & Veysey, B. M. (1997). *Providing services for jail inmates with mental disorders*. Washington, DC: US. Department of Justice, National Institute of Justice.

Steblay, N. M. (1992). A meta-analytic review of the weapon focus effect. *Law and Human Behavior, 16*, 413–424.

Steblay, N. M., Besirevic, J., Fulero, S. M., & Jimenez-Lorente, B. (1999). The effects of pretrial publicity on juror verdicts: A meta-analytic review. *Law and Human Behavior, 23*, 219–235.

Steinberg, L., & Cauffman, E. (1996). Maturity of judgment in adolescence: Psychosocial factors in adolescent decision making. *Law and Human Behavior, 20*, 249–272.

Steinmetz, S. K. (1977). *The cycle of violence: Assaultive, aggressive, and abusive family interaction*. New York: Praeger.

Stephan, C., & Tully, J. C. (1977). The influence of physical attractiveness of a plaintiff on the decisions of simulated jurors. *Journal of Social Psychology, 101*, 149–150.

Stewart, J. (1991). *Den of thieves*. New York: Simon & Schuster.

Stewart, J. E. (1980). Defendant's attractiveness as a factor in the outcome of criminal trials: An observational study. *Journal of Applied Social Psychology, 10*, 348–361.

Stier, S. D., & Stoebe, K. J. (1979). Involuntary hospitalization of the mentally ill in Iowa: The failure of the 1975 legislation. *Iowa Law Review, 64*, 1284–1458.

Stone, A. (1975). *Mental health and law: A system in transition*. Washington, DC: USGPO.

Stoner, J. A. F. (1961). *A comparison of individual and group decisions involving risk*. Unpublished master's thesis, School of Industrial Management, MIT.

Stotland, E. (1986). Police stress and strain as influenced by police self-esteem, time on job, crime frequency and interpersonal relationships. In J. T. Reese & H. A. Goldstein (Eds.), *Psychological services for law enforcement*. Washington, DC: USGPO.

Stotland, E. (1991). The effects of police work and professional relationships on health. *Journal of Criminal Justice, 19*, 371–379.

Stotland, E., & Berberich, J. (1979). The psychology of the police. In H. Toch (Ed.), *Psychology of crime and criminal justice*. New York: Holt, Rinehart & Winston.

Stotland, E., Pendleton, M., & Schawartz, R. (1989). Police stress, time on the job, and strain. *Journal of Criminal Justice, 17*, 55–60.

Strand, S., Belfrage, H., Fransson, G., & Levander, S. (1999). Clinical and risk management factors in risk prediction of mentally disordered offenders—more important than historical data? *Legal and Criminological Psychology, 4*, 67–76.

Stratton, J. G. (1978). Police stress: An overview. *The Police Chief, 5*, 58–62.

Stratton, J. G., Parker, D., & Snabbe, J. (1984). Post-traumatic stress: Study of police officers involved in shooting. *Psychological Reports, 55*, 127–131.

Straus, M. A., & Gelles, R. J. (1986). Societal change and change in family violence from 1975 to 1985 as revealed by two national surveys. *Journal of Marriage and the Family, 48*, 465–479.

Straus, M. A., & Gelles, R. (1990). *Physical violence in American families*. New Brunswick, NJ: Transaction Press.

Straus, M. A., Gelles, R., & Steinmetz, S. K. (1980). *Behind closed doors: Violence in the American family*. New York: Doubleday.

Strieb, V. L. (1993). Death penalty for female offenders. In V. L. Streib (Ed.), *A capital punishment anthology*. Cincinnati, OH: Anderson.

Strier, F. (1999). Whither trial consulting? Issues and projections. *Law and Human Behavior, 23*, 93–115.

Strodtbeck, F. L., & Hook, L. H. (1961). The social dimensions of a twelve-man jury table. *Sociometry, 24*, 397–415.

Strodtbeck, F. L., James, R., & Hawkins, C. (1957). Social status in jury deliberation. *American Sociological Review, 22*, 713–719.

Strodtbeck, F. L., & Mann, R. (1956). Sex role differentiation in jury deliberations. *Sociometry, 29*, 3–11.

Strube, M. J. (1988). The decision to leave an abusive relationship: Empirical evidence and theoretical issues. *Psychological Bulletin, 104*, 236–250.

Stuckey, G. B., Roberson, C., & Wallace, H. (2001). *Procedures in the justice system* (6th ed.). Upper Saddle River, NJ: Prentice Hall.

Studebaker, C. A., & Penrod, S. D. (1997). Pretrial publicity: The media, the law and common sense. *Psychology, Public Policy and Law, 3*, 428–460.

Sue, S., Smith, R. E., & Caldwell, C. (1973). Effects of inadmissible evidence on the decisions of simulated jurors: A moral dilemma. *Journal of Applied Social Psychology, 3*, 345–353.

Suedfield, P., Ramirez, C., Deaton, J., & Baker-Brown, G. (1982). Reactions and attributes of prisoner in solitary confinement. *Criminal Justice and Behavior, 9*, 303–340.

Suggs, D., & Sales, B. D. (1978). The art and science of conducting the voir dire. *Professional Psychology*, *9*, 367–388.

Sullivan, C. M. (1997). Societal collusion and culpability in intimate male violence: The impact of community response toward women with abusive partners. In A. P. Cardarelli (Ed.), *Violence between intimate partners*. Boston: Allyn & Bacon.

Summers, G., & Feldman, N. S. (1984). Blaming the victim versus blaming the perpetrator: An attribtution analysis of spouse abuse. *Journal of Social and Clinical Psychiatry, 2*, 339–347.

Summit, R. C. (1983). The child sexual abuse accommodation syndrome. *Child Abuse and Neglect, 7*, 177–193.

Sundby, S. E. (1997). The jury as critic: An empirical look at how capital juries perceive expert and lay testimony. *Virginia Law Review, 83*, 1109–1188.

Sundby, S. E. (1998). The capital jury and absolution: The intersection of trial strategy, remorse, and the death penalty. *Cornell Law Review, 83*, 1557–1598.

Sutherland, E. H. (1949). *White collar crime*. New York: Holt, Rinehart & Winston.

Sutker, P. B., Uddo-Crane, M., & Allain, A. N. (1991). Clinical and research assessment of posttraumatic stress disorder: A conceptual overview. *Psychological Assessment: A Journal of Consulting and Clinical Psychology, 3*, 520–530.

Swanson, J. W., Borum, R., Swartz, M. S., & Hiday, V. A. (1999). Violent behavior preceding hospitalization among persons with severe mental illness. *Law and Human Behavior*, *23*, 185–204.

Swanson, J. W., Borum, R., Swartz, M. S., Hiday, V. A., Wagner, H. R., & Burns, B. J. (2001). Can involuntary outpatient commitment reduce arrests among persons with severe mental illness? *Criminal Justice and Behavior, 28*, 156–189.

Swartz, M. S., Swanson, J. W., & Hiday, V. A. (2001). Randomized controlled trial of outpatient commitment in North Carolina. *Psychiatric Services*, *52*, 325–329.

Swartz, M. S., Swanson, J., Wagner, H., Burns, B., Hiday, V., & Borum, R. (1999). Can involuntary outpatient commitment reduce hospital recidivism? Findings from a randomized trial with severely mentally ill individuals. *American Journal of Psychiatry, 156*, 1968–1975.

Swim, J., Borgida, E., & McCoy, K. (1993). Videotaped versus in-court witness testimony: Is protecting the child witness jeopardizing due process? *Journal of Applied Social Psychology*, *23*, 603–631.

Sydeman, S. J., Cascardi, M., Poythress, N. G., & Ritterband, L. M. (1997). Procedural justice in the context of civil commitment: A critique of Tyler's analysis. *Psychology*, *Public Policy, and Law*, *3*, 207–221.

Szasz, T. S. (1960). The myth of mental illness. *American Psychologist, 15*, 113–118.

Szasz, T. S. (1968). *Law, liberty and psychiatry*. New York: Collier Books.

Tanford, J. A. (1990). The law and psychology of jury instructions. *Nebraska Law Review, 69*, 71–111.

Tanford, J. A. (1991). Law reform by courts, legislatures, and commissions following empirical research on jury instructions. *Law & Society Review, 25*, 155–175.

Tanford, S., & Cox, M. (1987). Decision processes in civil cases: The impact of impeachment evidence on liability and credibility judgments. *Social Behavior, 2*, 165–182.

Tanford, S., & Cox, M. (1988). The effects of impeachment evidence and limiting instructions on individual and group decision making. *Law and Human Behavior, 12*, 477–497.

Tanford, S., & Penrod, S. (1982). Biases in trials involving defendants charged with multiple offenses. *Journal of Applied Social Psychology*, *12*, 453–480.

Tanford, S., & Penrod, S. (1984). Social inference processes in juror judgments of multiple-offense trials. *Journal of Personality and Social Psychology, 47*, 749–765.

Tappan, P. W. (1947). Who is the criminal? *American Sociological Review, 12*, 100–110.

Tappan, P. W. (1949). *Juvenile delinquency*. New York: McGraw-Hill.

Tavis, C. (1992). *The mismeasure of woman*. New York: Simon & Schuster.

Taylor, K. T. (1999). (Ed.), *Forensic art and illustration*. Boca Raton, FL: CRC Press.

Technical Working Group for Eyewitness Evidence. (1999). *Eyewitness evidence: A guide for law enforcement*. Washington, DC: U.S. Department of Justice, Officer of Justice Programs.

Teplin, L. A. (2000, July). Keeping the peace: Police discretion and mentally ill persons. *National Institute of Justice Journal*, 8–15.

Teplin, L. A., & Pruett, N. S. (1992). Police as streetcorner psychiatrist: Managing the mentally ill. *International Journal of Law and Psychiatry*, *15*, 139–156.

Terry, W. C. (1985). Police stress: The empirical evidence. In A. Blumberg & E. Niederhoffer (Eds.), *Ambivalent force* (2nd ed.). New York: Holt Rinehart & Winston.

Tesler, P. H. (1999a). Collaborative law: A new paradigm for divorce lawyers. *Psychology, Public Policy, and Law*, *5*, 967–1000.

Tesler, P. H. (1999b). The believing game, the doubting game, and collaborative law: A reply to Penelope Bryan. *Psychology, Public Policy, and Law*, *5*, 1018–1027.

Thompson, W. C., Cowan, C. L., Ellsworth, P. C., & Harrington, J. C. (1984). Death penalty attitudes and conviction proneness. *Law and Human Behavior, 8*, 95–113.

Tittle, C. (1980). *Sanctions and social deviance: The question of deterrence*. New York: Praeger.

Tjaden, P. (1997, November). The crime of stalking: How big is the problem? *NIJ Research Preview*. Washington, DC: U.S. Department of Justice.

Tjaden, P., & Thoennes, M. (1998). *Stalking in America: Findings from the National Violence Against Women Survey* (NCJ 169592). Washington, DC: U.S. Department of Justice.

Toch, H. (1992). (Ed.). *Mosiac of despair: Human breakdown in prisons*. Washington, DC: American Psychological Association.

Toch, H. (1996). The violence-prone police officer. In W. A. Geller & H. Toch (Eds.), *Police violence: Understanding and controlling police abuse of force*. New Haven, CT: Yale University Press.

Toch, H., & Adams, K. (1989a). *The disturbed offender*. New Haven, CT: Yale University Press.

Toch, H., & Adams, K. (1989b). *Coping: Maladaption in prisons*. New Brunswick, NJ: Transaction Publishers.

Toch, H., & Adams, K. (2002). *Acting out: Maladaptive behavior in confinement*. Washington, DC: American Psychological Association.

Tonry, M. (1987). Prediction and classification: Legal and ethical issues. In D. M. Gottfredson & M. Tonry (Eds.), *Prediction and classification*. Chicago: University of Chicago Press.

Tooley, V., Brigham, J. C., Maas, A., & Bothwell, R. K. (1987). Facial recognition: Weapon effect and attentional focus. *Journal of Applied Social Psychology, 17*, 845–859.

Torbet, P., Gable, R., Hust, H., Montgomery, I., Szymanski, L., & Thomas, D. (1996). *State responses to serious and violent juvenile crime: Research report.* Washington, DC: Office of Juvenile Justice and Delinquency Prevention, National Center for Juvenile Justice.

Torres, A., & Forrest, J. D. (1988). Why do women have abortions? *Family Planning Perspectives, 20*, 169–176.

Torrey, E., & Kaplan, R. (1995). A national survey of the use of outpatient commitment. *Psychiatric Services, 46*, 778–784.

Trovillo, P. V. (1939). A history in lie detection. *Journal of Criminal Law and Criminology, 29*, 848–881.

Truax, C. B., & Mitchell, K. M. (1971). Research on certain therapist interpersonal skills in relation to process and outcome. In A. E. Bergin & S. L. Garfield (Eds.), *Handbook of psychotherapy and behavior change*. New York: Wiley.

Trulson, C., Triplett, R., & Snell, C. (2001). Social control in a school setting: Evaluating a school-based boot camp. *Crime & Delinquency*, 47, 573–609.

Tucker, G. J., & Neppe, V. M. (1991). Neurological and neuropsychiatric assessment of brain injury. In H. O. Doerr & A. S. Carlin (Eds.), *Forensic neuropsychology: Legal and scientific bases*. New York: Guilford Press.

Tufts' New England Medical Center, Division of Child Psychiatry. (1984). *Sexually exploited children: Service and research project*. Final report for the Office of Juvenile Justice and Delinquency Prevention, Washington, DC: USGPO.

Tunnicliff, J. L., & Clark, S. E. (2000). Selecting foils for identification lineups: Matching suspects or descriptions? *Law and Human Behavior, 24*, 231–258.

Turkheimer, E., & Parry, C. D. H. (1992). Why the gap? Practice and policy in civil commitment hearings. *American Psychologist, 47*, 646–655.

Turnbull, L. S., Hendrix, E. H., & Dent, B. D. (2000). Mental mapping. In L. S. Turnbull, E. H. Hendrix, & B. D. Dent (Eds.), *Atlas of crime: Mapping the criminal landscape*. Phoenix, AZ: Oryx Press.

Tyler, T. R. (1990). *Why people obey the law*. New Haven, CT: Yale University Press.

Tyler, T. R. (1992). The psychological consequences of judicial procedures: Implications for civil commitment hearings. *SMU Law Review, 46*, 433–488.

Unikovic, C. M., & Brown, W. R. (1978, April). The drunken cop. *The Police Chief*, pp. 18–20.

U.S. Advisory Board on Child Abuse and Neglect. (1995). *A national shame: Fatal child abuse and neglect in the U.S.* (5th Rep.). Washington, DC: USGPO.

U.S. Bureau of Census. (2002). *2000 census of population and housing*. Washington, DC: USGPO.

U.S. Department of Justice. (1988). *Report to the nation on crime and justice: The data* (2nd ed.). Washington, DC: USGPO.

U.S. Fire Administration. (1997, August). *Arson in the United States*. Washington, DC: National Fire Data Center.

U.S. Fire Administration. (2000a, March 10). *Facts on fire*. Washington, DC: Federal Emergency Management Agency.

U.S. Fire Administration. (2000b). *Arson and juveniles: Responding to the violence*. Washington, DC: Federal Emergency Management Agency.

U.S. Fire Administration. (2002, May 3). *Arson in the United States*. Washington, DC: National Fire Data Center.

U.S. General Accounting Office. (1995). *Juvenile justice: Representation rates varied as did counsel's impact on court outcomes*. Washington, DC: Author.

U.S. Sentencing Commission (1995, February). *Special report to Congress: Cocaine and federal sentencing policy*. Washington, DC: Author.

Vago, S. (2000). *Law and society* (6th ed.). Upper Saddle River, NJ: Prentice Hall.

Valenstein, E. S. (1973). *Brain control*. New York: Wiley.

Vander Zander, J. W. (1977). *Social psychology*. New York: Random House.

Van Maanen, J. (1973). Observations on the making of policemen. *Human Organizations, 32*, 407–418.

Van Maanen, J. (1974). Working the street: A developmental view of police behavior. In J. Jacob (Ed.), *The potential for reform of criminal justice*. Beverly Hills, CA: Sage.

Van Maanen, J. (1975). Police socialization: A longitudinal examination of job attitudes in an urban police department. *Administrative Science Quarterly, 20*, 207–228.

Van Zandt, C.R. (1993, July). Suicide-by-cop. *The Police Chief, 15*, 24–30.

Vidmar, N. (1979). The other issues in jury simulation research: A commentary with particular reference to defendant character studies. *Law and Human Behavior, 3*, 95–106.

Vidmar, N. (2002). Case studies of pre- and midtrial prejudice in criminal and civil litigation. *Law and Human Behavior, 26*, 73–105.

Violanti, J. M. (1983). Stress patterns in police work: A longitudinal study. *Journal of Police Science and Administration, 11*, 211–216.

Violanti, J. M. (1992). *Police retirement: The impact of change*. Springfield, IL: C. C. Thomas.

Violanti, J. M. (1996). *Police suicide: Epidemic in blue*. Springfield, IL: C. C. Thomas.

Vitale, T. E., Smith, S. S., Brinkley, C. A., & Newman, J. P. (2002). The reliability and validity of the Psychopathy Checklist—Revised in a sample of female offenders. *Criminal Justice and Behavior, 29*, 202–231.

Vrij, A. (2000). *Detecting lies and deceit: The psychology of lying and the implications for professional practice.* Chichester, UK: Wiley.

Vrij, A., & Semin, G. R. (1996). Lie expert's beliefs about nonverbal indicators of deception. *Journal of Nonverbal Behaviour, 20*, 65–80.

Vrij, A. & Winkel, F. W. (1991). Cultural patterns in Dutch and Surinam nonverbal behaviour: An analysis of simulated police/citizen encounters. *Journal of Nonverbal Behaviour, 15*, 169–184.

Wachbroit, R. (2001). Understanding the genetics-of-violence controversy. In D. Wasserman & R. Wachbroit (Eds.), *Genetics and criminal behavior.* Cambridge, UK: Cambridge University Press.

Wagstaff, G. F. (1982). Hypnosis and recognition of a face. *Perceptual and Motor Skills, 55*, 816–818.

Waid, W. M., Orne, E. C., Cook, M. R., & Orne, M. T. (1981). Meprobamate reduces accuracy of physiological detection of deception. *Science, 212*, 71–73.

Walbert, D. F. (1971). The effect of jury size on the probability of conviction: An evaluation of *Williams v. Florida. Case Western Research Law Review, 22*, 529–554.

Walcott, D. M., Cerundolo, P., & Beck, J. C. (2001). Current analysis of the *Tarasoff* duty: An evolution towards the limitation of the duty to protect. *Behavioral Sciences and the Law, 19*, 325–343.

Walker, L. E. (1979). *The battered woman.* New York: Harper Colophon Books.

Walker, L. E. (1984). *The battered woman syndrome.* New York: Springer.

Walker, L. E. (1989) Psychology and violence against women. *American Psychologist, 44*, 695–702.

Walker, S., Alpert, G. P., & Kenney, D. J. (2001, July). *Early warning systems: Responding to the problem police officer.* Washington, DC: U.S. Department of Justice, National Institute of Justice.

Walker, S., Spohn, C., & DeLone, M. (2000). *The color of justice: Race, ethnicity, and crime in America* (2nd ed.). Belmont, CA: Wadsworth/Thomson Learning.

Wall, P. M. (1965). *Eyewitness identification in criminal cases.* Springfield, IL: C. C. Thomas.

Wallace, H., & Seymour, A. (2001). Domestic violence. In G. Coleman, M. Gaboury, M. Murray, & A. Seymour (Eds.), *1999 National Victim Assistance Academy.* Washington, DC: U.S. Department of Justice, Office of Victims Assistance.

Wallerstein, J. S. (1989, January 23). Children after divorce: Wounds that don't heal. *The New York Times Magazine*, pp. 19–21, 41–44.

Wallerstein, J. S., & Kelly, J. (1980). *Surviving the break-up: How children and parents cope with divorce.* NY: Basic Books.

Wallerstein, J. S., & Wyle, J. (1947). Our law-abiding law breakers, *Probation, 25*, 107–112.

Walters, R. H., Callagan, J. E., & Newman, A. F. (1963). Effects of solitary confinement on prisoners. *American Journal of Psychiatry, 119*, 771–773.

Wang, C., & Daro, D. (1998). *Current trends in child abuse prevention, reporting and fatalities: The 1997 fifty state survey.* Chicago: Prevent Child Abuse America.

Warren, C. (1977). Involuntary commitment for mentally disordered: The application of California's Lanterman-Petris-Short Act. *Law & Society Review, 11*, 629–649.

Warren, J. I., Fitch, W. L., Dietz, P. E., & Rosenfeld, B. D. (1991). Criminal offense, psychiatric diagnosis, and psycholegal opinion: An analysis of 894 pretrial referrals. *Bulletin of the American Academy of Psychiatry and Law, 19*, 63–69.

Warren, J. I., Rosenfeld, B., Fitch, W. L., & Hawk, G. (1997). Forensic mental health clinical evaluation: An analysis of interstate and intersystemic differences. *Law and Human Behavior, 21*, 377–390.

Wasserman, D. (2001). Genetic predisposition to violent and antisocial behavior: Responsibility, character, and identity. In D. Wasserman & R. Wachbroit (Eds.), *Genetics and criminal behavior.* Cambridge, UK: Cambridge University Press.

Webster, C. D., Douglas, K. S., Eaves, D., & Hart, S. D. (1997a). Assessing risk to violence to others. In C. D. Webster & M. A. Jackson (Eds.), *Impulsivity: Theory, assessment and treatment.* New York: Guilford.

Webster, C. D., Douglas, K. S., Eaves, D., & Hart, S. D. (1997b). *HCR-20: Assessing risk for violence, version 2.* Burnaby, British Columbia: Simon Fraser University.

Webster, C. D., Harris, G. T., Rice, M. E., Cormier, C., & Quinsey, V. L. (1994). *The violence prediction scheme: Assessing dangerousness in high-risk men.* Toronto: University of Toronto Press.

Weeks, J. R., Moser, A. E., & Langevin, C. M. (1999). Assessing substance-abusing offenders for treatment. In E. J. Latessa (Ed.), *Strategic solutions: The International Community Corrections Association examines substance abuse.* Lanham, MD: American Correctional Association.

Weinberg, M. M. (1967). Effects of partial sensory deprivation on involuntary subjects. *Dissertation Abstracts International, 28*, 2171B. (University Microfilms No. 67–14,558).

Weinberger, L. E., & Sreenivasan, S. (1994). Ethical and professional conflicts in correctional psychology. *Professional Psychology: Research and Practice, 25*, 161–167.

Weiner, I. B. (2001). Advancing the science of psychological assessment: The Rorschach Inkblot Method as exemplar. *Psychological Assessment, 13*, 423–432.

Weiner, I. B., Exner, J. E., Jr., & Sciara, A. (1996). Is the Rorschach welcome in the courtroom? *Journal of Personality Assessment, 67*, 422–424.

Weis, J. G. (1989). Family violence methodology and design. In L. Ohlin & M. Tonry (Eds.), *Family violence* (Vol. 11). Chicago: University of Chicago Press.

Weisheit, R., & Mahan, S. (1988). *Women, crime, and criminal justice.* Cincinnati, OH: Anderson.

Weissman, H. N. (1991). Child custody evaluations: Fair and unfair professional practices. *Behavioral Sciences and the Law, 9*, 469–476.

Weisz, V. G. (1999). Commentary on "conceptual and empirical issues in child custody evaluation." *Clinical Psychology: Science and Practice, 6*, 328–331.

Weiten, W., & Diamond, S. S. (1979). A critical review of the jury simulation paradigm: The case of defendant characteristics. *Law and Human Behavior, 3*, 71–94.

Weitzer, R., & Tuch, S. A. (1999). Race, class and perceptions of discrimination by the police. *Crime & Delinquency, 45,* 494–507.

Wells, G. L. (1978). Applied eyewitness testimony research: System variables and estimator variables. *Journal of Personality and Social Psychology, 36,* 1546–1557.

Wells, G. L. (1993). What do we know about eyewitness identification? *American Psychologist, 48,* 553–571.

Wells, G. L. (1995). Scientific study of witness memory: Implications for public and legal policy. *Psychology, Public Policy, and Law, 1,* 726–736.

Wells, G. L. (2001). Police lineups: Data, theory, and policy. *Psychology, Public Policy, and Law, 7,* 791–801.

Wells, G. L., & Bradfield, A. L. (1998). "Good, you identified the suspect": Feedback to eyewitnesses distorts their reports of the witnessing experience. *Journal of Applied Psychology, 83,* 360–376.

Wells, G. L., & Bradfield, A. L. (1999). Distortions in eyewitnesses' recollections: Can the postidentification-feedback effect be moderated? *Psychological Science, 1999, 10,* 138–144.

Wells, G. L., Leippe, M. R., & Ostrom, T. M. (1979). Guidelines for empirically assessing the fairness of a lineup. *Law and Human Behavior, 3,* 285–294.

Wells, G. L., Lindsay, R. C. L., & Ferguson, T. J. (1979). Accuracy, confidence, and juror perceptions in eyewitness identification. *Journal of Applied Psychology, 64,* 440–448.

Wells, G. L., Malpass, R. S., Lindsay, R. C. L., Fisher, R., Turtle, J. W., & Fulero, S. M. (2000). From the lab to the police station: A successful application of eyewitness research. *American Psychologist, 55,* 581–598.

Wells, G. L., & Olson, E. A. (2001). The other-race effect in eyewitness identification: What do we do about it? *Psychology, Public Policy, and Law, 7,* 230–246.

Wells, G. L., Small, M., Penrod, S., Malpass, R. S., Fulero, S. M., & Brimacombe, C. A. E. (1998). Eyewitness identification procedures: Recommendations for lineups and photospreads. *Law and Human Behavior, 22,* 603–647.

Wells, G. L., & Turtle, J. W. (1986). Eyewitness identification: The importance of lineup models. *Psychological Bulletin, 90,* 320–329.

Wells, G. L., Turtle, J. W., & Luus, C. A. E. (1989). The perceived credibility of child eyewitnesses: What happens when they use their own words? In S. J. Ceci, D. F. Ross, & M. P. Toglia (Eds.), *Perspectives on children's testimony.* New York: Springer-Verlag.

Werth, J. L., Benjamin, G. A. H., & Farrenkopf, T. (2000). Requests for physician-assisted death: Guidelines for assessing mental capacity and impaired judgment. *Psychology, Public Policy, and Law, 6,* 348–372.

Wessler, S., & Moss, M. (2001, October). *Hate crimes on campus: The problem and efforts to confront it.* Washington, DC: U.S. Department of Justice, Office of Justice Programs.

Wettstein, R. (Ed.). (1998). *Treatment of the mentally disordered offender.* New York: Guilford.

Wexler, D. B. (1981). *Mental health law: Major issues.* New York: Plenum.

Wexler, D. B. (1990a). Grave disability and family therapy: The therapeutic potential of civil libertarian commitment codes. In D. B. Wexler (Ed.), *Therapeutic jurisprudence.* Durham, NC: Carolina Academic Press.

Wexler, D. B. (1990b). An introduction to therapeutic jurisprudence. In D. B. Wexler (Ed.), *Therapeutic jurisprudence.* Durham, NC: Carolina Academic Press.

Wexler, D. B. (1992). Putting mental health into mental health law. *Law and Human Behavior, 16,* 27–38.

Wexler, D. B. (1999). Therapeutic jurisprudence and the culture of critique. *The Journal of Contemporary Legal Issues, 10,* 263–277.

Wexler, H. K., Falkin, G. P., & Lipton, D. S. (1990). Outcome evaluation of a prison therapeutic community for substance abuse treatment. *Criminal Justice and Behavior, 17,* 71–92.

Wexler, D. B., & Winick, B. J. (1991). *Essays in therapeutic jurisprudence.* Durham, NC: Carolina Academic Press.

Wexler, D. B., & Winick, B. J. (1996). *Law in a therapeutic key: Developments in therapeutic jurisprudence.* Durham, NC: Carolina Academic Press.

Wexler, J. G. (1985). Role styles of women police officers. *Sex Roles, 12,* 749–755.

Wexler, J. G., & Logan, D. D. (1983). Sources of stress among women police officers. *Journal of Police Science and Administration, 11,* 46–53.

Wheatman, S. R., & Shaffer, D. R. (2001). On finding for defendants who plead insanity: The crucial impact of dispositional instructions and opportunity to deliberate. *Law and Human Behavior, 25,* 167–183.

White, H. R., Bates, M. E., & Buyske, S. (2001). Adolescent-limited versus persistent delinquency: Extending Moffitt's hypothesis into adulthood. *Journal of Abnormal Psychology, 110,* 600–609.

White, M., & Callahan, D. (2000). Oregon's first year: The medicalization of control. *Psychology, Public Policy, and Law, 6,* 331–341.

Whitehead, J. T., & Lab, S. P. (1999). *Juvenile Justice* (3rd ed.). Cincinnati, OH: Anderson.

Whittemore, K. E., & Ogloff, J. R. (1995). Factors that influence jury decision making. *Law and Human Behavior, 19,* 283–303.

Wiener, R. L., Pritchard, C. C., & Weston, M. (1995). Comprehensibility of approved jury instructions in capital murder cases. *Journal of Applied Psychology, 80,* 455–467.

Wiesner, W. H., & Cronshaw, S. F. (1988). A meta-analytical investigation of the impact of interview format and degree of structure on the validity of the employment interview. *Journal of Occupational Psychology, 61,* 275–290.

Wiggins, J. S. (1973). *Personality and prediction: Principles of personality assessment.* Reading, MA: Addison-Wesley.

Wildman, R., Batcherlor, E., Thompson, L., Nelson, F., Moore, J., Patterson, M., & DeLaosa, M. (1980). *The Georgia Court Competency Test: An attempt to develop a rapid quantitative measure for fitness for trial.* Unpublished manuscript, Forensic Services Division, Central State Hospital, Milledgeville, GA.

Wiley, D. C. (2001). Black and white differences in the perception of justice. *Behavioral Sciences and the Law, 19,* 649–655.

Wilkins, L. T. (1979). Policy control, information, ethics, and discretion. In L. E. Abt & L. R. Stuart (Eds.), *Social psychology and discretionary law.* New York: Van Nostrand Reinhold.

Williams, C. (2002). *Outcome of the Commission on Education and Training Leading to Licensure in Psychology: Impact and implications for students and new psychologists*. Washington, DC: American Psychological Association. Available: *www.apa/apags/edtrain/comontrain.html.*

Williams, F. P., & McShane, M. D. (1991). Psychological testimony and the decisions of prospective death-qualified jurors. In R. M. Bohm (Ed.), *The death penalty in America: Current research*. Cincinnati, OH: Anderson.

Williams, G. (1963). *The proof of guilt* (3rd ed.). London: Stevens & Sons.

Williams, W., & Miller, K. (1981). The processing and disposition of incompetent mentally ill offenders. *Law and Human Behavior, 5*, 245–261.

Wilson, D. G. (1989). The impact of federal sentencing guidelines on community corrections and privatization. In D. Champion (Ed.), *The U.S. sentencing guidelines: Implications for criminal justice*. New York: Praeger.

Wilson, D. J. (2000). *Drug use, testing, and treatment in jails*. Washington, DC: Bureau of Justice Statistics.

Wilson, J. Q. (1968). *Varieties of police behavior: The management of law and order in eight communities*. Cambridge, MA: Harvard University Press.

Wingert, P. et al. (2002, November 4). Descent into evil. *Newsweek*, pp. 21–38.

Winick, B. J. (1991a). Competency to consent to treatment: The distinction between assent and objection. In D. B. Wexler (Ed.), *Therapeutic jurisprudence*. Durham, NC: Carolina Academic Press.

Winick, B. J. (1991b). Competency to consent to voluntary hospitalization: A therapeutic jurisprudence analysis of *Zinermon v. Burch*. In D. B. Wexler (Ed.), *Therapeutic jurisprudence*. Durham, NC: Carolina Academic Press.

Winick, B. J. (1995a). Restructuring incompetency to stand trial and plead guilty: A restated proposal and a response to Professor Bonnie. *Journal of Criminal Law and Criminology, 85*, 571–624.

Winick, B. J. (1995b). The side effects of incompetency labeling and the implications for mental health law. *Psychology, Public Policy, and Law, 1*, 6–42.

Winick, B. J. (1998). Foreword: Planning for the future through advance directive instruments. *Psychology, Public Policy, and Law, 4*, 579–609.

Winick, B. J., Wexler, D. B., & Dauer, E. A. (Eds). (1999). Therapeutic jurisprudence and preventive law: Transforming legal practice and education. Special Issue, *Psychology, Public Policy, and Law, 5*, 795–799.

Winick, C. (1979). The psychology of the courtroom. In H. Toch (Ed.), *Psychology of crime and criminal justice*. New York: Holt, Rinehart & Winston.

Wissler, R. L., & Saks, M. J. (1985). On the inefficacy of limiting instructions: When jurors use prior conviction evidence to decide on guilt. *Law and Human Behavior, 9*, 37–48.

Wohlmuth, P. C. (Ed.). (1990). Symposium: Alternative dispute resolution. *Journal of Contemporary Legal Issues*, Volume 3.

Wolf, S., & Montgomery, D. A. (1977). Effects of inadmissible evidence and level of judicial admonishment to disregard on the judgments of mock jurors. *Journal of Applied Social Psychology, 7*, 205–219

Wolfe, D. A. (1985). Child-abusive parents: An empirical review and analysis. *Psychological Bulletin, 97*, 462–482.

Wolfgang, M. E. (1958). *Patterns in criminal homicide*. Philadelphia, PA: University of Pennsylvania Press.

Wolfgang, M. E. (1961). A sociological analysis of criminal homicide. *Federal Probation, 25*, 48–55.

Wolfgang, M. E. (1983). Delinquency in two birth cohorts. *American Behavioral Scientist, 27*, 75–86.

Wolfgang, M. E., Figlio, R. M., & Sellin, T. (1972). *Delinquency in a birth cohort*. Chicago: University of Chicago Press.

Wolfgang, M. E., Thornberry, T., & Figlio, R. M.. (1987). *From boy to man, from delinquency to crime*. Chicago: University of Chicago Press.

Woodall, J. (1999). The nature of memory: Controversies about retrieved memories and the law of evidence. *Journal of Psychiatry and Law, 26*, 151–218.

Woolard, J. L., Fondacaro, M. R., & Slobogin, C. (2001). Informing juvenile justice policy: Directions for behavioral science research. *Law and Human Behavior, 25*, 13–24.

Woolard, J. L., & Reppucci, N. D. (2000). Researching juveniles' capacities as defendants. In T. Grisso & R. G. Schwartz (Eds.), *Youth on trial*. Chicago: University of Chicago Press.

Wooldredge, J., Hartman, J., Latessa, E., & Holmes, S. (1994). Effectiveness of culturally specific community treatment for African-American juvenile felons. *Crime & Delinquency, 40*, 589–598.

Worden, A. P. (1993). The attitudes of women and men in policing: Testing conventional and contemporary wisdom. *Criminology, 31*, 203–242.

Wortley, S., Hagan, J., & Macmillan, R. (1997). Just des(s)ert? The racial polarization of perceptions of criminal injustice. *Law & Society Review, 31*, 637–676.

Wright, P. M., Lichtenfels, P. A., & Pursell, E. D. (1989). The structured interview: Additional studies and a meta-analysis. *Journal of Occupational Psychology, 62*, 191–199.

Wrightsman, L. S. (1977). *Social psychology* (2nd ed). Monterey, CA: Brooks/Cole.

Yarmey, A. D. (1979). *The psychology of eyewitness testimony*. New York: The Free Press.

Yarmey, A. D. (1984). Age as a factor in eyewitness memory. In G. L. Wells & E. F. Loftus (Eds.), *Eyewitness testimony*. New York: Cambridge University Press.

Yarmey, A. D., & Kent, J. (1980). Eyewitness identification by elderly and young adults. *Law and Human Behavior, 4*, 359–371.

Yarmey, A. D. (1990). *Understanding police and police work: Psychosocial issues*. New York: New York University Press.

Yarmey, A. D., & Jones, H. P. T. (1983). Is the psychology of eyewitness identification a matter of common sense? In S. M. A. Lloyd-Bostock & B. R. Clifford (Eds.), *Evaluating witness evidence: Recent psychological research and new perspectives*. Chichester, UK: Wiley.

Yegidis, B. L. (1986). Date rape and other forced sexual encounters among college students. *Journal of Sex Education and Therapy, 12*, 51–54.

Yochelson, S., & Samenow, S. E. (1976). *The criminal personality* (Vol. 1). New York: Jason Aronson.

Yochelson, S., & Samenow, S. E. (1977). *The criminal personality* (Vol. 2). New York: Jason Aronson.

Yuille, J. C. (1980). A critical examination of the psychological and practical implications of eyewitness research. *Law and Human Behavior, 4*, 335–346.

Yuille, J. C. (1989). Expert evidence by psychologists: Sometimes problematic and often premature. *Behavioral Sciences and the Law, 7*, 181–196.

Yuille, J. C., & Tollestrup, P. A. (1990). Some effects of alcohol on eyewitness testimony. *Journal of Applied Psychology, 75*, 268–273.

Yunger, J. A. (1976). Is the death penalty a deterrent to homicide: Some time series evidence. *Journal of Behavioral Economics, 5*, 45–81.

Zamble, E. (1992). Behavior and adaptation in long-term prison inmates: Descriptive longitudinal results. *Criminal Justice and Behavior, 19*, 409–425.

Zamble, E., & Porporino, F. J. (1988). *Coping, behavior, and adaptation in prison inmates*. New York: Springer-Verlag.

Zamble, E., & Quinsey, V. L. (1997). *The criminal recidivism process*. Cambridge, UK: Cambridge University Press.

Zeisel, H. (1971). . . . And then there were none: The diminution of the federal jury. *University of Chicago Law Review, 38*, 710–724.

Zeisel, H. (1974). Twelve is just. *Trial, 10*, 13–15.

Zeisel, H., & Diamond, S. (1978). The effect of peremptory challenges on the jury and verdict. *Stanford Law Review, 30*, 491–531.

Zeling, M. (1986). Research needs in the study of post shooting trauma. In J. T. Reese & H. A. Goldstein (Eds.), *Psychological services for law enforcement*. Washington, DC: USGPO

Zellman, G. L. (1990). Child abuse reporting and failure to report among mandated reporters: Prevalence, incidence, and reasons. *Journal of Interpersonal Violence, 5*, 3–22.

Zigler, E. (1994). Reshaping early childhood interventions to be a more effective weapon against poverty. *American Journal of Community Psychology, 22*, 37–47.

Zilboorg, G. (1944). Legal aspects of psychiatry. In American Psychiatric Association (Ed.), *One hundred years of American psychiatry*. New York: Columbia University Press.

Zimbardo, P. G. (1973). The psychological power and pathology of imprisonment. In E. Aronson & R. Helmreich (Eds.), *Social psychology*. New York: Van Nostrand.

Zimring, F. E. (1989). Toward a jurisprudence of family violence. In L. Ohlin & M. Tonry (Eds.), *Family violence* (Vol. 11). Chicago: University of Chicago Press.

Ziskin, J., & Faust, D. (1994). *Coping with psychiatric and psychological testimony* (5th ed.). Marian Del Rey, CA: Law & Psychology Press.

Zubek, J. P. (Ed.). (1969). *Sensory deprivation: Fifteen years of research*. New York: Appleton-Century-Crofts.

Zuckerman, M., & Gerbasi, K. C. (1977). Belief in internal control or belief in a just world: The use and misuse of the I-E scale in prediction of attitudes and behavior. *Journal of Personality, 45*, 356–378.

Author Index

C

D

E

F

M

N

R

S

Y

Z

Subject Index